W9-CAR-417

THE COMPLETE
MANUAL OF
WOOD
WORKING

THE COMPLETE MANUAL OF WOODWORKING

ALBERT JACKSON, DAVID DAY
AND SIMON JENNINGS

ALFRED A. KNOPF NEW YORK 1999

THIS BOOK IS INTENDED FOR USE BY NON-PROFESSIONAL WOODWORKERS AND GREAT CARE HAS BEEN TAKEN TO RECOMMEND PROPER SAFETY PRECAUTIONS. IN THE UNITED STATES, PROFESSIONAL SAFETY STANDARDS ARE ISSUED BY THE OCCUPATIONAL SAFETY AND HEALTH ADMINISTRATION. EMPLOYEES SHOULD VERIFY THAT PROCEDURES AND EQUIPMENT DETAILED IN THIS PUBLICATION ARE ACCEPTABLE UNDER O.S.H.A. REGULATIONS BEFORE BEING USED BY EMPLOYEES.

TITLE PAGE & CHAPTER-OPENER PANELS MADE OF
SYCAMORE (OUTER BORDER) & BIRD'S-EYE MAPLE (CENTER PANEL)
TEXT SET IN 8½ ON 9PT TIMES NEW ROMAN
HEADLINES SET IN 28PT GOUDY HANDTOOLED
DISPLAY SETTING IN 48PT, 42PT & 12PT BEMBO ROMAN & ITALICS
CONCEIVED, EDITED & DESIGNED BY INKLINK

THE COMPLETE MANUAL OF WOODWORKING WAS CREATED BY INKLINK, LONDON, ENGLAND. THE TEXT WAS WRITTEN BY ALBERT JACKSON AND DAVID DAY, THE BOOK DESIGNED BY SIMON JENNINGS. ORIGINAL COLOR PHOTOGRAPHY BY NEIL WAVING. DRAWINGS BY ROBIN HARRIS, DAVID DAY AND ALBERT JACKSON. JOINT-MAKING EXAMPLES BY WILLIAM BROOKER. VENEER AND INLAY WORK BY DESMOND RYAN. WOODCARVING BY MARCUS CORNISH AND DAVID DAY.

BRITISH EDITION FIRST PUBLISHED BY
WILLIAM COLLINS SONS & CO. LTD UNDER THE TITLE
COLLINS COMPLETE WOODWORKER'S MANUAL.

THIS IS A BORZOI BOOK
PUBLISHED BY ALFRED A. KNOPF, INC.

PUBLISHED IN THE UNITED STATES BY ALFRED A. KNOPF, INC., NEW YORK
DISTRIBUTED BY RANDOM HOUSE, INC., NEW YORK

LIBRARY OF CONGRESS CATALOGING-IN-PUBLICATION DATA
JACKSON, A. (ALBERT)
THE COMPLETE MANUAL OF WOODWORKING
ALBERT JACKSON AND DAVID DAY—1ST ED.
P. CM
ISBN 0-394-56488-X
1. WOODWORK—HANDBOOKS, MANUALS ETC.
I. DAY, DAVID, 1944-
II. TITLE
TT180.J25 1989
684′.08—DC20
89-45263
CIP

MANUFACTURED IN THE UNITED STATES OF AMERICA
HARDCOVER EDITION PUBLISHED NOVEMBER 13, 1989
PUBLISHED NOVEMBER 30, 1996
REPRINTED ONCE
THIRD PRINTING, JANUARY 1999

INTRODUCTION

In our everyday lives we are all surrounded by wooden structures and wooden commodities. Our homes and workplaces are partially or even wholly constructed from wood; we frequently eat, sleep and work with wooden furniture and utensils; our children are raised with wooden playthings; and even as adults wood supplies our recreational needs in the form of sports equipment or game boards and pieces. In short, wood is so commonplace we invariably take it for granted. And yet once its special beauty has been revealed to anyone working it with blade or cutter, wood is anything but ordinary. Wood has lasting qualities like no other material – it is both warm and pleasing to the touch and its wealth of color and texture is a delight to the eye. Indeed, the nature of wood is such that it imparts a uniqueness to every single workpiece – something that cannot be said of even precious metals. Together with other concerned woodworkers around the world, we are acutely aware that certain woods are now a diminishing resource. Responsible action must be taken to preserve what remains of the world's rain forest and to replant native hardwood trees that are becoming rarer year by year. It is imperative that we take steps to protect and replace the sources of our precious raw material if future generations of woodworkers are to inherit the same privileges we enjoy today. We fully support those individuals and agencies dedicated to that end.

Albert Jackson David Day

CONTENTS

1 Chapter one
Wood The Raw Material

2 Chapter two
Designing in Wood

3 Chapter three
Hand Tools

4 Chapter four
Power Tools

5 Chapter five
Machine Tools

6 Chapter six
Home Workshops

CONTENTS

7 Chapter seven JOINERY

8 Chapter eight BENDING WOOD

9 Chapter nine VENEERING and MARQUETRY

10 Chapter ten WOOD CARVING

11 Chapter eleven FINISHING WOOD

12 Chapter twelve OTHER MATERIALS

13 Chapter thirteen SUPPLIES & FITTINGS

Reference section GLOSSARY & INDEX

INKLINK ARE ALSO GRATEFUL TO THE FOLLOWING INDIVIDUALS AND ORGANIZATIONS FOR THEIR CONTRIBUTIONS & ASSISTANCE:- FOR THE SUPPLY OF WOOD SAMPLES: C. F. ANDERSON & SON LTD., ANNANDALE TIMBER & MOULDING CO. PTY. LTD., THE ART VENEER CO. LTD., JOHN BODDY'S FINE WOOD & TOOL STORE LTD., EGGER LTD., FIDOR, GENERAL WOODWORKING SUPPLIES, HIGHLAND FOREST PRODUCTS PLC, E. JONES & SON, LIMEHOUSE TIMBER, RAVENSBOURNE COLLEGE OF DESIGN AND COMMUNICATION, SEABOARD INTERNATIONAL LTD., F. R. SHADBOLT & SONS LTD. HAND TOOLS: THE ART VENEER CO. LTD., JOHN BODDY'S FINE WOOD & TOOL STORE LTD., BURTON McCALL LTD., E. C. EMMERICH, GARRETT WADE CO. LTD., GEORGE HIGGINS LTD., RECORD MARPLES LTD., SKARSTEN MANUFACTURING CO. LTD., ALEC TIRANTI LTD., TOOLMAIL LTD. POWER TOOLS: THE BLACK & DECKER CORPORATION, BLACK & DECKER PROFESSIONAL PRODUCTS DIVISION, ROBERT BOSCH LTD., LEROY SOMER ELECTRIC MOTORS LTD., M & M DISTRIBUTORS LTD. MACHINE TOOLS: BLACK & DECKER PROFESSIONAL PRODUCTS DIVISION, CORONET LATHE AND TOOL CO., HEGNER LTD., RECORD MARPLES LTD., ROBERT SORBY LTD., STARTRITE MACHINE TOOL CO. LTD., TYME MACHINES LTD., WARREN MACHINE TOOLS LTD. BENCHES & ACCESSORIES: EMMERICH (BERLON) LTD. WOOD FINISHES: ENGLISH ABRASIVES & CHEMICALS LTD., GRACO LTD., RUSTINS LTD., JOHN MYLAND LTD. SUPPLIES & FITTINGS: EUROPEAN INDUSTRIAL SERVICES LTD., JOHN MYLAND LTD., WOODFIT LTD. ILLUSTRATION P. 10 MICHAEL WOODS. DRAWING EQUIPMENT P. 74 GELLIOT WHITMAN. ADDITIONAL REFERENCE SUPPLIED BY: ADVANCED MACHINERY IMPORTS LTD., AMERICAN PLYWOOD ASSOCIATION, AUSTRALIAN PARTICLEBOARD RESEARCH INSTITUTE INC., P & J DUST EXTRACTION LTD., BORDEN LTD., CIBA-GEIGY PLASTICS, CLICO TOOLING LTD., COUNCIL OF FOREST INDUSTRIES OF BRITISH COLUMBIA, DUNLOP ADHESIVES, EURO MODELS, EVODE LTD., FELDER WOODWORKING MACHINES, FINNISH PLYWOOD INTERNATIONAL, WALTER FISCHER, FURNITURE INDUSTRY RESEARCH ASSOCIATION, LOUISIANA-PACIFIC, LUNA TOOLS AND MACHINERY LTD., MICROFLAME LTD., THEODOR NAGEL (G.M.B.H. & CO.), IAN & BETTY NORBURY – THE WHITE KNIGHT GALLERY, PLYWOOD ASSOCIATION OF AUSTRALIA LTD., RYOBI LTD., TIMBER DEVELOPMENT ASSOCIATION (N.S.W.) LTD., TIMBER RESEARCH AND DEVELOPMENT ASSOCIATION, TIMBER TRADE FEDERATION, JOHN TIRANTI, U.S. FOREST PRODUCTS LABORATORY, VEREIN DEUTSCHER HOLZEINFUHRHÄUSER e.V., WOODWORKING MACHINES OF SWITZERLAND LTD., CARL ZEISS JENA LTD. SPECIAL CONSULTANTS: FREDERICK SPALDING – MACHINE TOOLS. LES REED – VENEERING & MARQUETRY. JOHN PERKINS – OTHER MATERIALS. JIM CUMMINS, U.S. CONSULTANT. INDEX COMPILED BY JILL FORD. PROOFREAD BY PHILIP HIND. DESIGNER-MAKERS: ASHLEY CARTWRIGHT PAGES 43BL; 45TR. CHRIS AUGER PAGE 44TR. DAVID COLWELL PAGE 49BR. DAVID FIELD PAGE 48TL, TR. DAVID PYE PAGE 45C. DEREK PEARCE PAGE 48B. DESMOND RYAN PAGES 44B; 45BL. GORDON RUSSELL PAGE 46TR. HUGH SCRIVEN PAGES 45TL; 47CR; 49TL, TR. HUW DAVIES PAGE 46CR. IAN NORBURY PAGES 275; 281TL. JANE CLEAL PAGE 42BL, BC. MATTHEW MORRIS PAGE 49CR. MIKE SCOTT PAGE 47B. NICHOLAS DYSON PAGES 47TL, TR; 49CL. PAUL PHILLIPS PAGE 49BL. RICHARD LA TROBE-BATEMAN PAGE 42BR. ROBERT WILLIAMS PAGES 41B; 46BR. ROD WALES PAGES 45BR; 46TL, BL. STEPHEN HOUNSLOW PAGE 47CL. STEWART LINFORD PAGE 41T. STUART GROVES PAGE 44TL. ALL PHOTOGRAPHS BY INKLINK EXCEPT: BLACK & DECKER PROFESSIONAL PRODUCTS DIVISION PAGES 133, 187. BUCKINGHAMSHIRE COLLEGE OF HIGHER EDUCATION PAGES 42BL, BC; 46TR; 49CR, BL. CARTWRIGHT DESIGNS PAGES 43BL; 45TR. DAVID FIELD PAGE 48TL, TR. GEORG OTT WERKZEUG- UND MASCHINENFABRIK GMBH & CO. PAGE 212BR. HUGH SCRIVEN PAGES 45TL; 47CR; 49TL, TR. KODAMA WOODWORK PAGE 46CR. NICHOLAS DYSON FURNITURE LTD. PAGES 47TL, TR; 49CL. PEARL DOT LTD. PAGES 41B; 46BR. RICHARD LA TROBE-BATEMAN PAGE 42BR. ROBERT BOSCH LTD: PAGE 149TR. ROD WALES PAGE 46TL. THEO BERGSTROM PAGE 41T. TRANNON FURNITURE PAGE 49BR. WARREN MACHINE TOOLS LTD. PAGES 186, 188, 190, 191. WOODWORKER MAGAZINE PAGE 44TR.

KEY TO PHOTOGRAPHIC CREDITS: L = LEFT, R = RIGHT, T = TOP, TL = TOP LEFT, TR = TOP RIGHT, C = CENTER, UC = UPPER CENTER, LC = LOWER CENTER, CL = CENTER LEFT, CR = CENTER RIGHT, B = BOTTOM, BL = BOTTOM LEFT, BR = BOTTOM RIGHT, BC = BOTTOM CENTER.

CHAPTER ONE

WOOD

The diversity of color and texture and the physical properties of stiffness or bendability and of strength in proportion to weight give each species of wood a character of its own, offering both a challenge and a source of inspiration to the creative woodworker. The antiquity of woodworking techniques is reflected in the design and construction of buildings and furniture over the centuries, yet despite its traditional links with the past, wood is also very much a modern material. It is being used at a greater rate today than ever before, and, thanks to modern manufacturing methods, new composite wood-based materials are constantly being developed, further expanding its versatility and range of applications. A selection

THE RAW MATERIAL

of softwoods and hardwoods from all over the world and manufactured materials in the form of veneers and man-made boards are illustrated on the following pages and their characteristics described.

HOW TREES GROW

Trees are undeniably a valuable source of wealth, but they are not valuable in the same way gold is. Although it could be argued that wood is as beautiful and desirable as any precious metal, the great value of trees lies in their being a renewable resource. Nor, historically, has any other material been so adaptable and of such immeasurable benefit to mankind as wood with its infinite variety of types and uses.

SEE ALSO

Converting wood	12
Softwoods	16-19
Hardwoods	20-29
Hand tools	75-114
Power tools	123-154
Machine tools	155-208

THE LIVING TREE

In order to appreciate the properties of wood and how it is worked and finished, it is worthwhile understanding something of the way trees grow.

Trees form an important division of the plant kingdom known as the Spermatophyta (seed-bearing plants). This division is subdivided into Gymnospermae and Angiospermae. Gymnosperms are needle-leaved coniferous trees commonly referred to as softwoods. Angiosperms are broad-leaved trees known as hardwoods and may be either deciduous or evergreen.

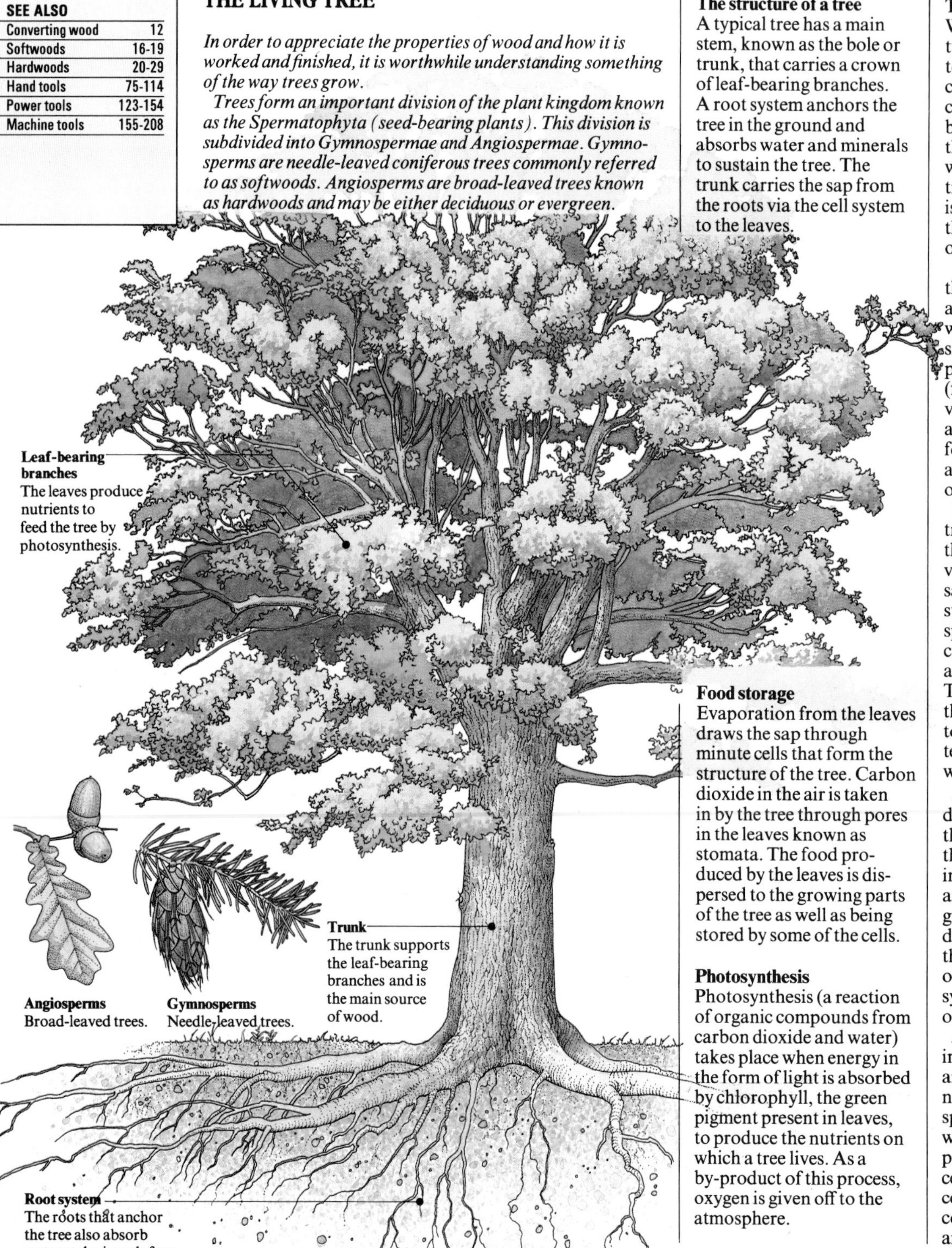

Leaf-bearing branches
The leaves produce nutrients to feed the tree by photosynthesis.

Trunk
The trunk supports the leaf-bearing branches and is the main source of wood.

Angiosperms
Broad-leaved trees.

Gymnosperms
Needle-leaved trees.

Root system
The roots that anchor the tree also absorb water and minerals from the ground.

The structure of a tree
A typical tree has a main stem, known as the bole or trunk, that carries a crown of leaf-bearing branches. A root system anchors the tree in the ground and absorbs water and minerals to sustain the tree. The trunk carries the sap from the roots via the cell system to the leaves.

Food storage
Evaporation from the leaves draws the sap through minute cells that form the structure of the tree. Carbon dioxide in the air is taken in by the tree through pores in the leaves known as stomata. The food produced by the leaves is dispersed to the growing parts of the tree as well as being stored by some of the cells.

Photosynthesis
Photosynthesis (a reaction of organic compounds from carbon dioxide and water) takes place when energy in the form of light is absorbed by chlorophyll, the green pigment present in leaves, to produce the nutrients on which a tree lives. As a by-product of this process, oxygen is given off to the atmosphere.

The structure of wood
Wood is a mass of cellulose tubular cells bonded together with an organic chemical called lignin. The cells vary in size and shape, but are generally long and thin and run longitudinally with the main axis of the tree's trunk or branches. It is this orientation of the cells that produces the direction of the grain.

Cells provide support for the tree, circulation of sap and food storage. Softwoods or conifers have a simple cell structure composed mainly of tracheid (fiber-like) cells that provide initial sap conduction and physical support. They form regular radiating rows and make up the main body of the tree.

Hardwoods or deciduous trees have fewer tracheids than softwoods and have vessels or pores that conduct sap and fibers that provide support. It is this cell specialization that enables cut wood to be identified as a softwood or hardwood. The size and distribution of the cells vary from species to species, producing fine-textured or coarse-textured wood.

A tree grows by an annual deposition of cells formed by the cambium layer. This is the thin layer of active living cells between the bark and the wood. During the growing period the cells subdivide to form new wood on the inner side and phloem or bast (tissue that conducts synthesized food to all parts of the plant) on the outside.

As the girth of the tree increases, the old bark splits and new bark is formed. The new wood cells develop into specialized cells to form sapwood. Sapwood is made up partly of living food-storage cells and partly of non-living cells that are capable of conducting sap up the tree and do not store food.

In addition to cells following the axis of the trunk, there are ray cells radiating from the center of the tree. These carry and store nutrients horizontally through the sapwood. Ray cells form flat vertical bands that are hardly visible in softwoods but plainly obvious in some hardwoods, such as oak, when they are quartersawn.

As the tree grows, a new ring of sapwood is built up around the previous year's growth. The oldest sapwood is now no longer used to conduct water, and gradual chemical changes convert it into heartwood to form the structural spine of the tree. In this way the heartwood increases in area, while the thickness of the sapwood remains relatively constant throughout the tree's life.

Sapwood and heartwood

Sapwood is light in color and is usually recognizable by its contrast with the darker heartwood. The color difference is not so marked on light-colored woods, particularly the softwoods. Sapwood is inferior to heartwood and is usually cut to waste by furnituremakers. It is not as resistant to fungal decay, and it is also prone to beetle attack because of the carbohydrates stored in some of the cells. The relatively thin-walled cells are porous and give up moisture quickly. As a result, sapwood shrinks more than the denser heartwood. However, its porosity allows stains and preservatives to be readily absorbed.

Since heartwood is the inner part of the maturing tree and is formed from old sapwood, it plays no active part in the growth of the tree. Hence the dead cells can become blocked with organic material, causing the cell walls to change color through the presence of chemical substances called extractives. The extractives are responsible for the rich colors found in many hardwoods. They also impart a measure of resistance to fungus and insect attack.

Earlywood and latewood

As with many plants, the way trees grow depends on climatic conditions. In a temperate climate there is generally rapid growth in the spring, less in summer and no new growth in winter.

Earlywood or springwood is, as the name implies, the part of the annual growth ring laid down in the early part of the growing season. Thin-walled tracheid cells in softwoods and open tube-like vessels in hardwoods form the bulk of the earlywood to facilitate the rapid conduction of sap. Earlywood can usually be recognized as the wider band of paler-colored wood in each annual growth ring.

Latewood or summerwood is the part of the annual ring that develops in the latter part of the growing season and produces thicker-walled cells, creating denser and usually darker wood that is less able to conduct sap but adds support to the tree.

This distinct banding corresponds to one season's growth, so reveals the age of the felled tree and the kind of climatic conditions in which it has grown. Wide annual rings indicate good growing conditions; narrow ones, poor or drought conditions.

The difference in texture between earlywood and latewood is important to the woodworker since it can render a wood more or less difficult to work. The lighter-weight earlywood is easier to cut than the denser latewood. This is not a particular problem for most hand and machine processes, provided the tools' cutting edges are sharp. However, the difference in hardness can show where latewood is left proud of earlywood after finishing with a sander. Generally, woods with even-textured growth rings are the easiest to work and finish.

The distribution of hardwood cells has a marked effect on the texture of the wood. "Ring-porous" hardwoods, such as oak or ash, have clearly defined rings of large vessels in the earlywood, and dense fibers and cell tissue in the latewood. These woods are more difficult to finish than "diffuse-porous" woods, such as beech, which have vessels and fibers distributed relatively evenly. Although woods like mahogany are often diffuse-porous, their larger cells can make them coarse-textured.

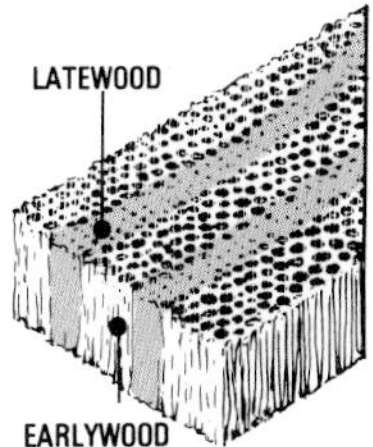

Earlywood and latewood

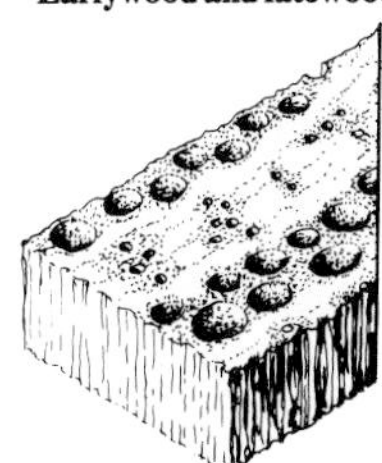
Ring-porous wood

Diffuse-porous wood

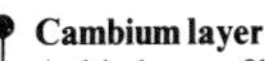

CONVERTING WOOD

It takes many years, hundreds in the case of some species, for a tree to grow to a commercially viable size. Yet with modern forestry methods, straight-growing trees, such as pine, can be cut down, topped and debarked in a matter of minutes. Since conifers are relatively fast-growing, with careful husbandry it is possible to control supply and demand of softwoods. It is a sad fact, however, that the forests of the world are being depleted – particularly of the slow-growing hardwoods, which are becoming increasingly scarce, though most specialist suppliers stock small pieces of exotic woods.

SEE ALSO

THE CONVERSION PROCESS

Most commercial wood is cut from the trunk of the tree. Some larger limbs may also be cut into logs, but branch material usually has asymmetric growth rings that produce unstable "reaction" wood, which warps and splits easily. Reaction wood is formed in limbs or trunks that do not grow upright. In softwoods the growth is mainly on the underside and produces "compression wood;" in hardwoods it forms on the upper side and is known as "tension wood."

Felled trees are cut into logs or butts and transported to local sawmills for conversion into roughsawn timber; the trimmings are usually made into paper products and manufactured boards. Exporters of wood may deal in whole or sawn logs, or both. But the producers of some exotic hardwoods, in Peninsular Malaysia, Indonesia, the Philippines and Brazil, for example, now trade in sawn wood only. This is in a quest to protect their trees from overcutting and also to provide employment for their people and an increase in revenue. Large top-quality logs with few knots command high prices and are usually converted into veneer.

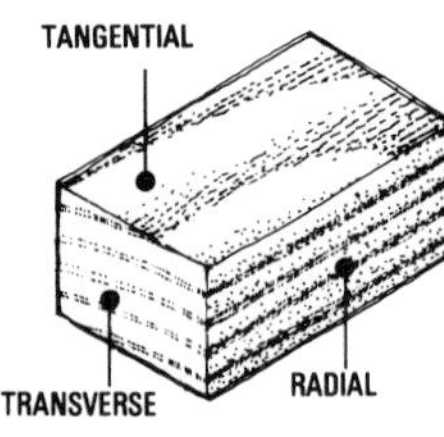

Planes of reference
The terms refer to the direction of the cut in relation to the growth rings.

Milling
Today most logs are converted into sawn wood by band-saw or circular-saw machines. Before the machine age, this task was achieved by hand, using the pit-saw technique. A large two-man saw was used, with one sawyer in a pit below the log and the other standing on top of it. Pushing and pulling the saw between them, they would gradually convert the log into boards or beams.

The main types of cut produced by modern methods are known as "plainsawn" and "quartersawn." Plainsawn boards are broadly those where the growth rings meet the face of the board at an angle of less than 45 degrees. Quartersawn is broadly defined as wood that has the growth rings at not less than 45 degrees to the face of the board.

Within both these categories other terms may be used. Plainsawn wood can be known as flatsawn, flat-grain or slashsawn; and quartersawn as riftsawn, comb-grain, edge-grain and vertical-grain.

In America, plainsawn boards are those where the growth rings meet the face at an angle of less than 30 degrees. Those where the rings meet at more than 30 degrees but at less than 60 degrees are known as riftsawn boards.

True quartersawn boards are cut radially with the annual rings perpendicular to the board's face, but in practice all boards with rings at an angle of not less than 60 degrees are classified as quartersawn.

Plainsawn boards are cut on a tangent to the annual growth rings and display a decorative and distinctive elliptical figure.

Riftsawn boards display a straight figure with some ray-cell patterning, and are sometimes referred to as comb-grain.

Quartersawing reveals a straight figure crossed with the ribbon-like or "flake" figure found in hardwoods such as oak.

Types of cut
1 Plainsawn
2 Riftsawn
3 Quartersawn

Converting a log
The stability and figure of the wood are determined by the plane of the saw in relation to the annual growth rings. The most economical method for converting a log is to cut it "through and through" **(1)**. This process makes parallel cuts through the length of the log and produces plainsawn, riftsawn and a small percentage of quartersawn boards. Plainsawn logs are cut partly through and through, and produce a mixture of plainsawn and riftsawn boards **(2)**.

Converting a log to produce quartersawn boards can be done in a number of ways. The ideal is to cut each board parallel with the rays, like the radiating spokes of a wheel, but this method is wasteful and not used commercially. The conventional method, albeit a compromise, is to cut the log into quarters and then cut each quadrant into boards **(3)**. Commercial quartersawing first cuts the log into thick slices, which are then converted into quartered boards **(4)**.

To select quartersawn wood, look at the end grain. Choose boards that have the growth rings at about 90 degrees to the surface. Not all suppliers will allow you to select random boards. In any case, expect selected boards to be more expensive.

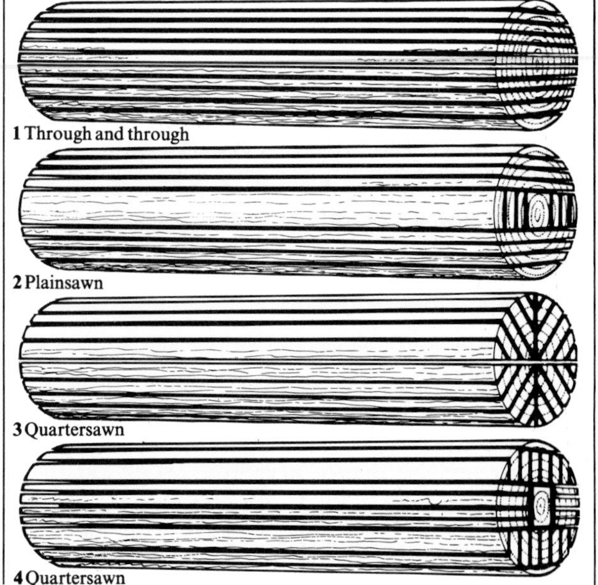

1 Through and through
2 Plainsawn
3 Quartersawn
4 Quartersawn

DRYING WOOD

Green wood newly cut from a log contains a very high percentage of moisture. The cell walls are saturated and free water is held by the cell cavities. Drying or "seasoning" wood is the process of removing the free water and much of the bound moisture from the cell walls. As the wood dries, free water is lost from the cell cavities until only the cell walls contain moisture. This is known as the fiber-saturation point and occurs at about 30 percent moisture content, depending on the species. It is when moisture starts to be lost from the cell walls that shrinkage begins. The loss of water will stop when it is in balance with the relative humidity of its surroundings. This is known as the equilibrium moisture content (EMC).

It is most important that the seasoning process be carried out properly, in order to prevent stresses from being created within the wood and to ensure that the EMC is at the appropriate level to avoid problems with swelling and shrinkage.

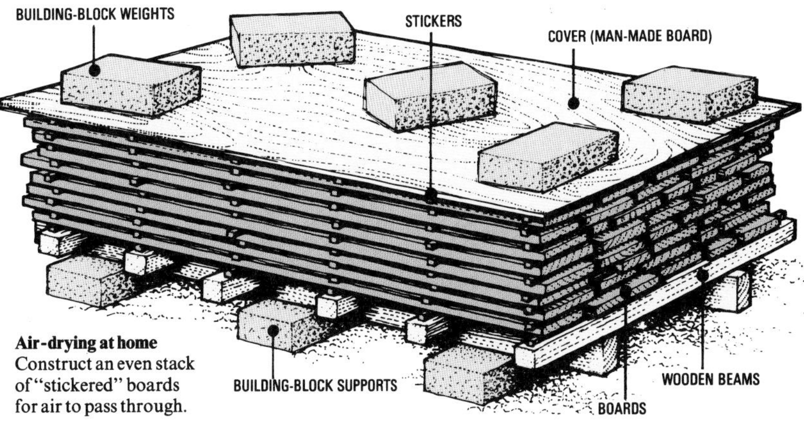

Air-drying at home
Construct an even stack of "stickered" boards for air to pass through.

Air-drying

Air-drying is the traditional method for seasoning wood. The boards are stacked evenly on spacer battens, or "stickers," which are 1in (25mm) square and are spaced 18in (450mm) apart. The stacks are usually built well away from the ground in a sheltered position and are protected from rain and direct sunlight. The natural airflow through the stack gradually dries the wood. As a rough guide, it takes about one year to dry every 1in (25mm) thickness for hardwoods and about half that time for softwoods.

This method is inexpensive but can only reduce the moisture content to about 14 to 16 percent, depending on the relative humidity. For interior use, the wood needs further drying in a kiln or may be left to dry naturally in the environment in which it is to be used.

Kiln-drying

Wood for interior use needs a moisture content of about 6 to 8 percent, or possibly lower, depending on the humidity of the location.

Kiln-drying is used commercially to reduce the moisture content of the wood below air-dry level, and takes only a matter of days. The boards are loaded onto dollies in stickered stacks and rolled into the kiln, where a carefully controlled mixture of hot air and steam is pumped through the piled wood and the humidity is gradually reduced to a specified moisture content according to the species of wood being dried.

Wood dried below air-dry level will try to take up atmospheric moisture if left exposed – so, where possible, keep kiln-dried wood in the environment in which it is to be used.

Checking moisture content

The moisture content of wood is given as a percentage of its oven-dry weight. This is calculated by comparing the original weight of a sample block (preferably taken from the center of the board rather than the end) with the weight of the sample after it has been fully dried in an oven. The dry weight is subtracted from the original weight to determine the weight loss, and the following equation is used to calculate the moisture-content percentage:

$$\frac{\text{Weight of water lost from sample}}{\text{Oven-dry weight of sample}} \times 100$$

Moisture meters with two-pin electrodes are a simple and convenient way to check the moisture content. The meter measures the resistance of the moist wood and gives an instant reading of the moisture-content percentage.

Insert the electrodes into the wood at various points along the board to check the average level, as not all parts of the board dry at the same rate.

Stability

When wood dries, it shrinks. The shape of the board can change or "move" as shrinkage takes place. In general, the shrinkage along the line of the annual rings amounts to approximately twice the shrinkage across them. Tangentially cut plainsawn boards therefore shrink more in their width. Quartersawn boards shrink only slightly in their width and very little in their thickness.

Shrinkage movement can also cause some distortion. The concentric growth rings of a tangentially cut plainsawn board run approximately edge to edge and differ in length. The longer outer rings shrink more than the inner rings, resulting in a tendency for the board to bend, or "cup," across its width. Square sections of wood are liable to become parallelograms, and round sections to become oval.

The growth rings of a quartered board run from face to face and, being virtually the same length, suffer little or no distortion. This stability, coupled with an even-wearing surface, makes quartered boards the preferred type for flooring and furnituremaking.

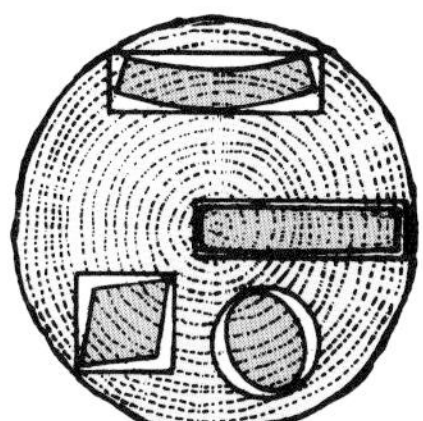

Shrinkage movement
Sections of wood will distort differently depending on orientation of the growth rings.

Commercial air-drying
Sawn boards, spaced apart with stickers, are placed on pallets and set in huge stacks at the mill (below).

SELECTING WOOD

Lumberyards usually stock spruce, fir and pine, the softwoods most commonly used for carpentry and joinery. These woods are generally sold as "dimension" or "dressed" lumber – that is, as sawn or surface-planed sections cut to standard sizes. One or more of the faces may be surfaced. Note that the planing process can remove at least $\frac{1}{8}$in (3mm) from each face of the wood, making the actual width and thickness less than the "sawn size" quoted by the wood supplier. The length, on the other hand, is always as quoted. Although the majority of hardwoods are generally sold as boards of random width and length, in some countries mahogany, teak, oak and ramin can be bought as dimension lumber. Dimension lumber is sold by the foot or in 300mm units. Check which system your supplier uses, as the metric unit is about $\frac{3}{16}$in (5mm) shorter than an imperial foot. Always allow extra on the length for waste.

SEE ALSO

Converting wood	12-13
Softwoods	16-19
Hardwoods	20-29
Veneers	32-33
Block plane	93
Knot sealer	284
Fillers	284

Grading

Softwoods are graded for evenness of grain and amount of allowable defects such as knots. The better-quality "appearance grades" and "nonstress grades" are probably of most interest to the general woodworker. Stress-graded softwoods are rated for structural use where strength is important. The term "clear wood" is often used for knot-free or defect-free wood, but this kind of wood is not usually available from suppliers unless specified.

The grading of hardwoods is determined by the area of defect-free wood. The greater the area, the higher the grade. The best grades are "firsts" and "firsts and seconds" (FAS).

Many specialist firms will supply wood by mail order, but whenever possible, select the wood yourself. When you go to buy wood, take a block plane with you so you can plane a small sample if the color and grain are obscured by dirt or by sawing.

WOOD DEFECTS

Unless wood is dried carefully, stresses can be introduced that mar it or make it difficult to work. Insufficient drying can lead to shrinkage of dimensioned parts, joints opening, and warping and splitting.

Before buying wood, check the surface for splits, knots and uneven grain. Look at the end section to identify the cut from the log and any distortion. Sight along the length to check for twisting or bowing.

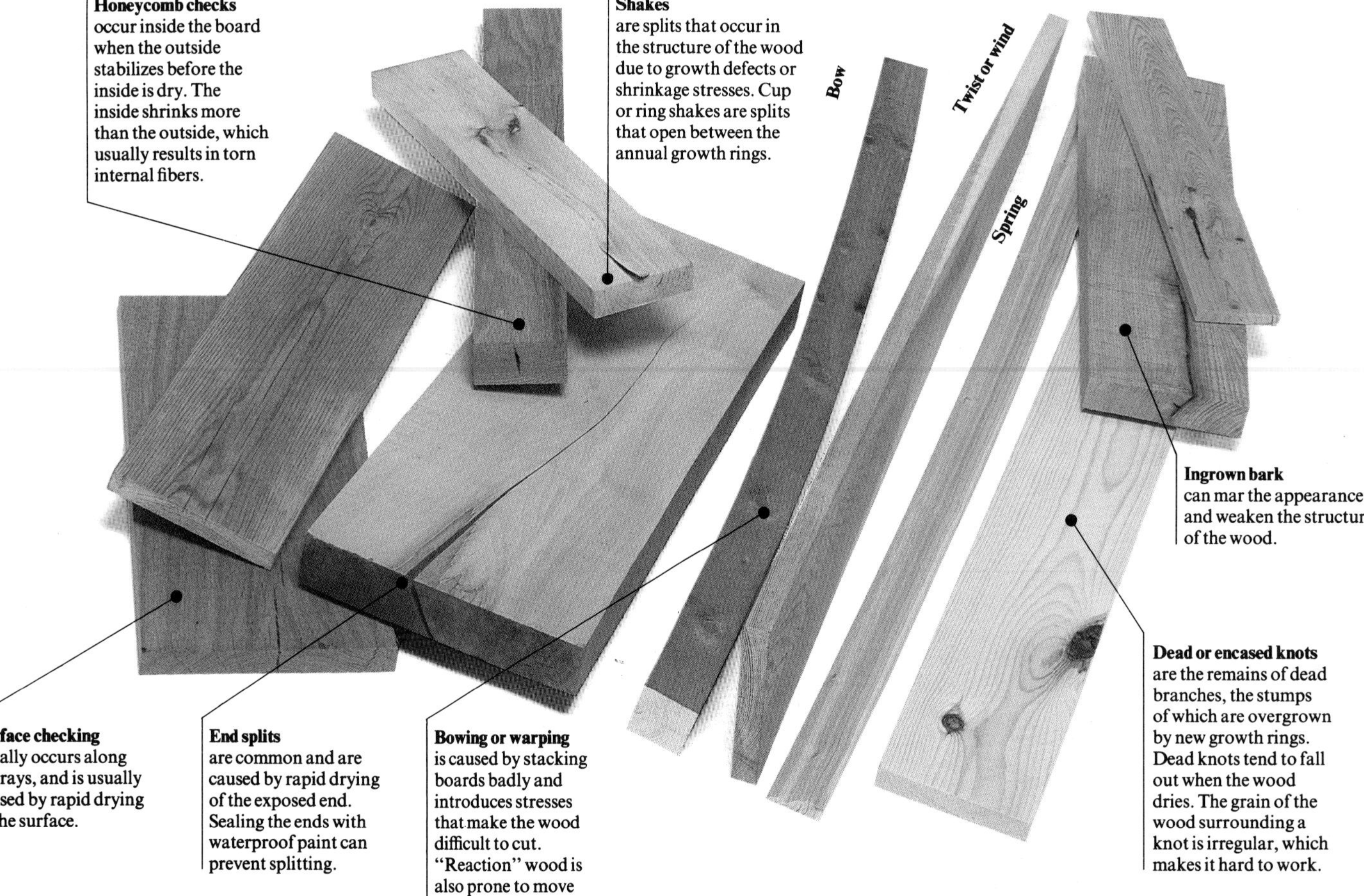

Honeycomb checks occur inside the board when the outside stabilizes before the inside is dry. The inside shrinks more than the outside, which usually results in torn internal fibers.

Shakes are splits that occur in the structure of the wood due to growth defects or shrinkage stresses. Cup or ring shakes are splits that open between the annual growth rings.

Ingrown bark can mar the appearance and weaken the structure of the wood.

Surface checking usually occurs along the rays, and is usually caused by rapid drying of the surface.

End splits are common and are caused by rapid drying of the exposed end. Sealing the ends with waterproof paint can prevent splitting.

Bowing or warping is caused by stacking boards badly and introduces stresses that make the wood difficult to cut. "Reaction" wood is also prone to move when dried or cut.

Dead or encased knots are the remains of dead branches, the stumps of which are overgrown by new growth rings. Dead knots tend to fall out when the wood dries. The grain of the wood surrounding a knot is irregular, which makes it hard to work.

THE PROPERTIES OF WOOD

Since wood is a product of nature, each piece is unique. Each section of wood taken from a tree, or even from the same board, will be different. It may have the same strength or color, but not the same grain pattern. It is this diversity of character, strength, color, workability and even scent that makes wood so appealing to woodworkers. Working wood is a learning process, and each piece of wood is a challenge to the worker's skills. Only by handling wood and experiencing the way it behaves can a full appreciation of its properties be gained. The natural characteristics of wood are briefly set out below, and different kinds of wood from all over the world are illustrated on the following pages.

NATURAL CHARACTERISTICS

The appearance of wood – the grain pattern, color and texture – is the prime consideration when choosing wood for a project. Its working or strength characteristics are usually a secondary consideration, but they are no less important and the wood must also be selected for fitness of purpose. If you are not familiar with a particular wood that appeals to you, discuss its properties with your supplier to make sure it will suit your requirements.

Selecting wood is a process of balancing appearance with strength, workability, pliability, weight, cost and availability. The appearance and characteristics of wood are determined by the nature of its cell structure.

Grain

The mass of the wood's cell structure constitutes the "grain" of the wood, which follows the main axis of the tree's trunk, and the nature of the grain is determined by the disposition and degree of orientation of these longitudinal cells.

Trees that grow straight and even produce "straight-grained" wood. "Cross-grained" wood is formed where the cells deviate from the main axis of the tree. Some trees twist as they grow and produce "spiral grain." In some instances the spiral growth veers from one angle to another, with each change taking place over a few growth rings; this results in "interlocked grain." "Wavy grain" and "curly grain" occur in trees that have an undulating cell structure; the former has short even waves, the latter is irregular.

Irregular-grained woods can be difficult to work and finish, as the cells constantly change direction, creating "wild grain."

Boards with random or undulating grain display various patterns according to the angle to the surface and light-reflectivity of the cell structure. These effects are exploited in the production of veneers.

The term grain is also used in referring to the way wood is cut or worked. Sawing "with the grain" refers to cuts made along the length of the wood, that is with the longitudinal cells.

Planing a surface "with the grain" follows the direction of the grain where the fibers are parallel or slope up and away from the direction of the cutting action. This results in a smooth, trouble-free cut.

Planing "against the grain" refers to cuts made where the fibers slope up and toward the direction of the planing action, producing a rough cut.

Sawing or planing "across the grain" refers to cuts made more or less perpendicular to the grain.

Figure

The term grain is commonly used to describe the appearance of wood, but what is really being referred to is a combination of natural growth features collectively known as the "figure."

The difference in growth between the earlywood and latewood, the density of the annual growth rings, the concentricity or eccentricity of the rings, the distribution of color, the effect of disease or physical damage and the method used to convert the wood into boards all contribute to the figure.

Most trees produce conically shaped trunks that when cut tangentially produce typical plainsawn boards displaying a U-shaped pattern where the layers of annual growth rings are exposed by the plane of the cut. When a log is cut radially or quartersawn, the annual rings are perpendicular to the plane of cut and the figure is less distinctive, showing a series of parallel lines. Some woods, however, have distinctive ray cells that are exposed by quartersawing and produce an attractive "ray-fleck" figure.

The form of the figure is not restricted to wood from straight trunks. The fork formed by a branch and the main stem of the tree produces "crotch" or "feather" figure much prized as veneer, as is burl wood, which is an abnormal growth caused by some injury. Stumpwood also yields interesting random-grain figure, which, like burl, can be used for turning work.

Texture

The term "texture" refers to the relative size of the wood's cells. Fine-textured woods have small closely spaced cells, while coarse-textured woods have relatively large cells. "Texture" is also used to describe the distribution of the cells in relation to the annual growth rings. Where the difference between earlywood and latewood is slight the wood is even-textured, whereas wood with marked contrast in the growth rings has an uneven texture.

A wood's texture affects not only how it cuts and planes, but also its appearance and character under a stain and final finish.

IDENTIFYING WOOD

Some common woods can be readily identified by their grain, color, texture and smell. However, unfamiliar woods can have even experts resorting to microscopic analysis of the cell structure.

The following pages show a selection of the world's commercial woods. Each wood is referred to by its standard name. Where appropriate, its commercial or local names are included.

The genus and species are given in italics. This "Latin" nomenclature is consistent worldwide, unlike commercial and local names, which can be misleading. The term "sp." or "spp." commonly means that a wood may be one of several within a genus, or "family," of trees.

The main source of supply is specified for each wood.

CONSERVATION

Unlike oil and minerals, trees are a renewable resource. However, unwise harvesting now threatens some species with extinction. The Convention on International Trade in Endangered Species of Wild Flora and Fauna, or CITES, has begun to classify certain trees for protection, in much the same way that the organization bans world trade in elephant ivory.

By agreement of participating nations, world trade in Rio Rosewood is now banned, and trees such as *Afromosia* and *Lignum Vitae* may soon be added to the list.

To join the effort to preserve the world's threatened timbers, some suppliers now sell only those imported woods that are certified as coming from managed plantations.

SOFTWOODS OF THE WORLD

The term softwood refers to the botanical grouping of the wood rather than its physical properties. Softwoods come from coniferous trees, which belong to the botanical group Gymnospermae (plants that bear exposed seeds). Most cone-bearing trees are evergreen and have narrow, needle-shaped leaves. The standing tree is commonly depicted as having a tall, pointed outline – but not all conifers are this shape. When converted into boards, a number of softwoods are readily identified by their relatively light color range, from pale yellow to reddish brown, and by the grain pattern created by the contrast in color and density between the earlywood and latewood in the annual growth rings.

SEE ALSO

How trees grow	10-11
Hardwoods	20-29
Man-made boards	34-38
Finishing wood	284-294

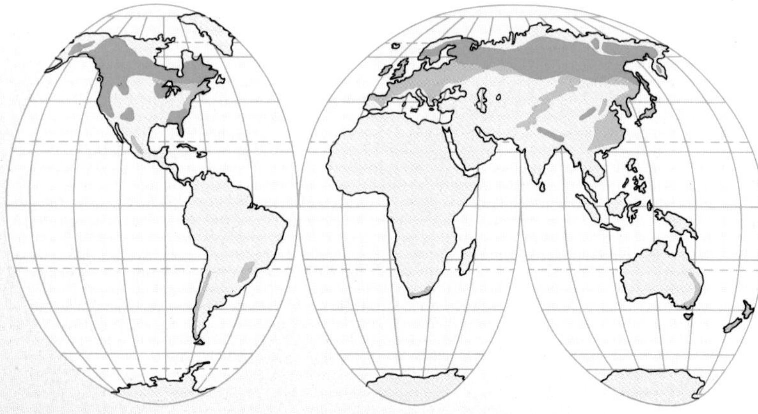

Distribution of softwoods
- Coniferous forest
- Coniferous and broad-leaved deciduous mixed forest

The scale of the map permits the areas of tree distribution to be shown in broad terms only.

The softwood regions of the world
The prime source of the world's supply of commercial softwoods is the Northern Hemisphere, which extends across the arctic and subarctic regions of Europe and North America down to the southeastern United States.

Conifers are relatively fast-growing, producing straight trunks that can be economically cultivated and harvested in man-made forests. They are cheaper than hardwoods and widely used for building construction and joinery and in the manufacture of fiberboard and paper.

Softwood boards
Whole boards of home-grown wood, complete with waney edge and bark, can be bought from local sawmills. The "waney edge" is the uncut edge of the board. Commercial boards are usually supplied debarked and square-edged. The larch example shows the bark, sapwood and mature heartwood. The sapwood is the light-colored wood, which is less resistant to fungal and insect attack than the heartwood.

Color changes
The color of wood can vary considerably, not only in the same species but also in the same tree. Most woods darken with exposure to light, though some lighten or even change color. Applied finishes, no matter how clear, tend to darken the color of the wood. The small square samples show the wood, actual size, before and after the application of a clear finish.

A simple test to see the effect of a clear finish on the color of a wood is to lick your finger and wet the surface of the wood.

CEDAR OF LEBANON
Cedrus libani
Other names: True cedar.
Sources: Middle East.
Characteristics: An aromatic wood, with light-brown heartwood. Clearly marked grain produced by contrasting earlywood and latewood. Can be knotty.
Workability: Good.
Average dried weight: 35lb/ft³ (560kg/m³).
Common uses: Interior and garden furniture, construction, joinery.
Finishing: Good.

CEDAR, WESTERN RED
Thuja plicata
Other names: Giant arbor vitae (USA); red cedar (Canada); British Columbia red cedar (UK).
Sources: Canada, USA, UK, New Zealand.
Characteristics: Relatively soft aromatic wood. Reddish brown in color, fading to silver-gray after long exposure to weathering.
Workability: Good.
Average dried weight: 23lb/ft³ (370kg/m³).
Common uses: Shingles, exterior boarding and siding, greenhouses and sheds.
Finishing: Good.

- **Color change**
  The small square samples show the actual grain size of each species and the effect when a clear finish is applied.

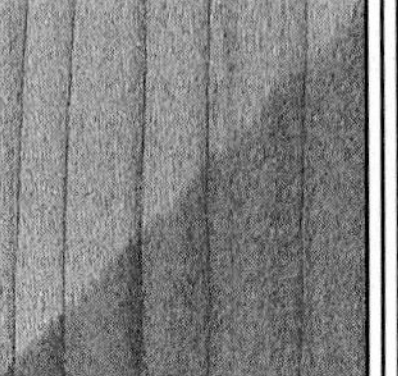

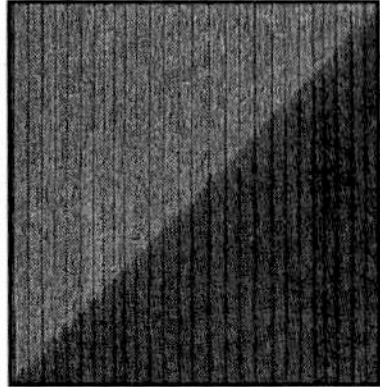

Cedar of Lebanon

Cedar, Western Red

CEDAR, YELLOW
Chamaecyparis nootkatensis
Other names: Alaska yellow cedar, Pacific Coast yellow cedar.
Sources: Pacific Coast of North America.
Characteristics: A pale-yellow even-textured wood, with fine straight grain. It is relatively light, stiff and stable when dry.
Workability: Good.
Average dried weight: 31lb/ft³ (500kg/m³).
Common uses: Furniture, boatbuilding, joinery, veneer.
Finishing: Good.

FIR, DOUGLAS
Pseudotsuga menziesii
Other names: British Columbian pine, Oregon pine.
Sources: Canada, Western USA, UK.
Characteristics: A straight-grained, reddish-brown wood, with pronounced grain. Obtainable in large knot-free sizes.
Workability: Good.
Average dried weight: 33lb/ft³ (530kg/m³).
Common uses: Plywood, joinery. Widely used in North America for building work.
Finishing: Fair.

FIR, SILVER
Abies alba
Other names: Whitewood, white fir.
Sources: Central and Southern Europe.
Characteristics: A pale-cream nonresinous and almost colorless wood, with straight grain and fine texture. Similar to and often marketed together with Norway spruce (*Picea abies*).
Workability: Good.
Average dried weight: 30lb/ft³ (480kg/m³).
Common uses: Joinery, construction, boxes, plywood, poles.
Finishing: Good.

HEMLOCK, WESTERN
Tsuga heterophylla
Other names: Pacific hemlock, British Columbia hemlock.
Sources: Canada, USA, UK.
Characteristics: A pale-brown semi-lustrous wood, with relatively distinct growth rings. It is even-textured, has straight grain and is nonresinous.
Workability: Good.
Average dried weight: 31lb/ft³ (500kg/m³).
Common uses: Construction work, joinery, plywood.
Finishing: Good.

KAURI, QUEENSLAND
Agathis spp.
Other names: North Queensland kauri, South Queensland kauri.
Sources: Australia.
Characteristics: A straight-grained wood, with fine even texture. Color varies from pale cream-brown to pinkish brown.
Workability: Good.
Average dried weight: 30lb/ft³ (480kg/m³).
Common uses: Joinery, furniture.
Finishing: Good.

LARCH
Larix spp.
Other names: Tamarack (USA).
Sources: Europe, Canada, USA.
Characteristics: Tougher than most conifers, it is a straight-grained wood of uniform texture. Pale to rich-red heartwood, light-colored sapwood. Larches shed their needles in winter.
Workability: Medium.
Average dried weight: 37lb/ft³ (590kg/m³).
Common uses: Joinery, construction, boat planking.
Finishing: Fair.

Cedar, Yellow **Fir, Douglas** **Fir, Silver** **Hemlock, Western** **Kauri, Queensland** **Larch**

PINE, HOOP
Araucaria cunninghamii
Other names: Queensland pine (though not a true pine).
Sources: Australia, Papua New Guinea.
Characteristics: A straight-grained fine-textured wood. Similar to Parana pine in appearance, it has wide light-brown sapwood with yellow-brown heartwood.
Workability: Good.
Average dried weight: 35lb/ft^3 (560kg/m^3).
Common uses: Joinery, furniture, turning, construction.
Finishing: Good.

PINE, PARANA
Araucaria angustifolia
Other names: Brazilian pine (USA).
Sources: Argentina, Brazil and Paraguay.
Characteristics: Even-textured straight-grained wood, with inconspicuous growth rings. Light-brown heartwood, with dark-brown core. Often has bright-red streaks.
Workability: Good.
Average dried weight: 33lb/ft^3 (530kg/m^3).
Common uses: Joinery, furniture, turning.
Finishing: Good.

PINE, PONDEROSA
Pinus ponderosa
Other names: Western yellow pine, Californian white pine (USA); British Columbia soft pine (Canada).
Sources: Western Canada and USA.
Characteristics: The wide pale-yellow sapwood is soft, nonresinous and even-textured. The heavier heartwood is deep yellow to reddish brown, and resinous.
Workability: Good/fair.
Average dried weight: 30lb/ft^3 (480kg/m^3).
Common uses: Pattern-making, doors, furniture (sapwood); joinery, construction (heartwood).
Finishing: Fair.

PINE, SUGAR
Pinus lambertiana
Other names: Californian sugar pine.
Sources: USA.
Characteristics: Moderately soft, with medium-coarse texture and even grain. It has white sapwood and pale to reddish-brown heartwood.
Workability: Good.
Average dried weight: 26lb/ft^3 (420kg/m^3).
Common uses: Joinery, light construction.
Finishing: Fair.

PINE, WESTERN WHITE
Pinus monticola
Other names: Idaho white pine.
Sources: Canada, USA.
Characteristics: A straight-grained even-textured wood. Pale yellow to reddish brown, with little variation in color between early-wood and latewood.
Workability: Good.
Average dried weight: 28lb/ft^3 (450kg/m^3).
Common uses: Joinery, construction, furniture, boatbuilding, plywood.
Finishing: Good.

PINE, WHITE
Pinus strobus
Other names: Eastern white pine (USA); Quebec pine, Weymouth pine, yellow pine (UK).
Sources: USA, Eastern Canada.
Characteristics: A soft pine with straight grain, fine even texture and inconspicuous annual growth rings. It is pale yellow to pale brown in color, with fine resin-duct marks.
Workability: Good.
Average dried weight: 26lb/ft^3 (420kg/m^3).
Common uses: Pattern-making, joinery, musical instruments, furniture, construction work.
Finishing: Good.

- **Color change**
The small square samples show the actual grain size of each species and the effect when a clear finish is applied.

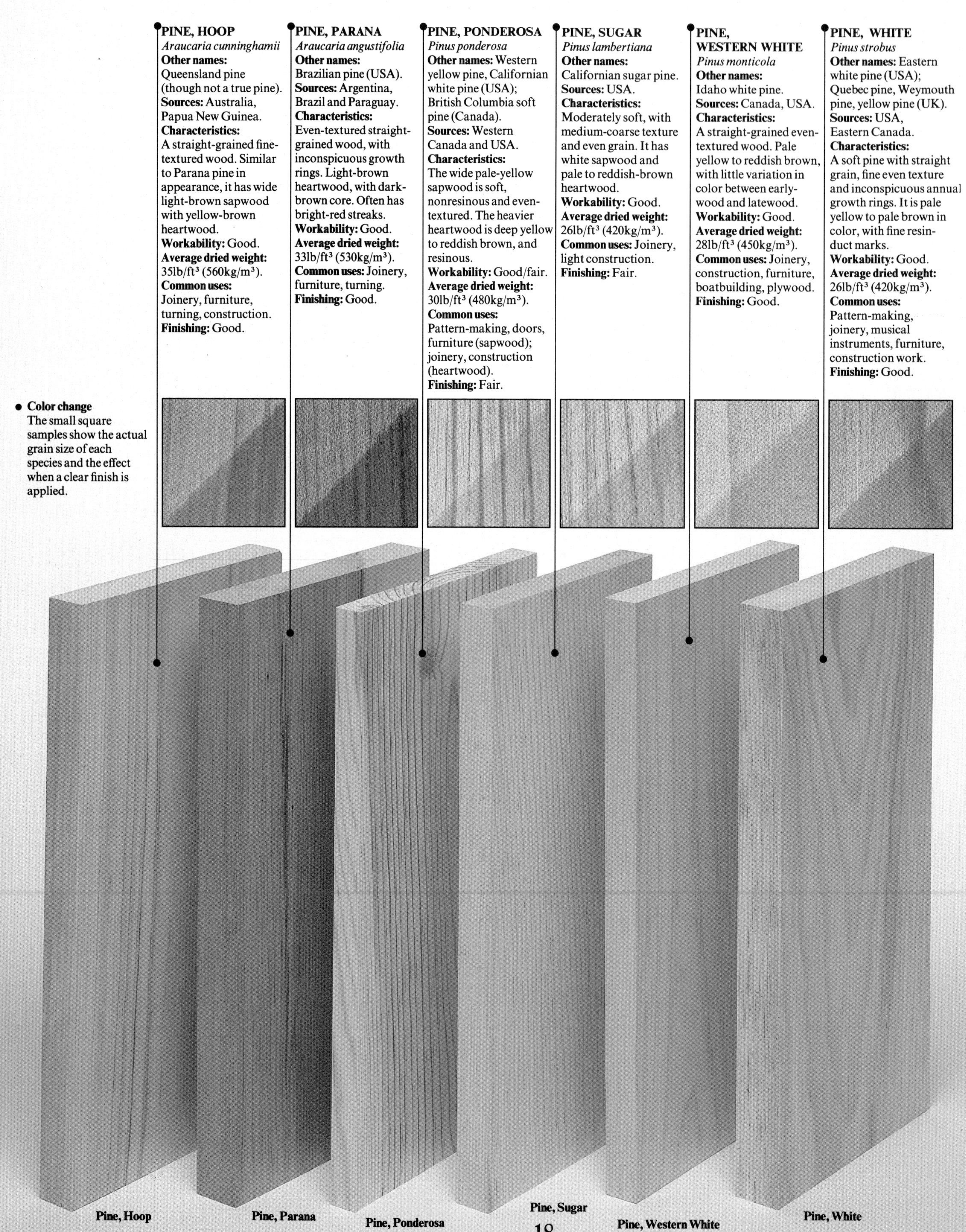

Pine, Hoop — Pine, Parana — Pine, Ponderosa — Pine, Sugar — Pine, Western White — Pine, White

RIMU
Dacrydium cupressinum
Other names: Red pine.
Sources: New Zealand.
Characteristics: A fine even-textured straight-grained wood. Heartwood is reddish brown, turning to lighter shades of brown through to the yellowish sapwood.
Workability: Good.
Average dried weight: 33lb/ft³ (530kg/m³).
Common uses: Furniture, joinery, plywood, veneers.
Finishing: Good.

REDWOOD, EUROPEAN
Pinus sylvestris
Other names: Scots pine, Scandinavian redwood, Russian redwood.
Sources: Europe, Northern Asia.
Characteristics: A light-colored resinous wood, with yellow-brown to reddish-brown heartwood and light white-yellow sapwood. Distinct figure, with light earlywood and reddish latewood.
Workability: Medium.
Average dried weight: 32lb/ft³ (510kg/m³).
Common uses: Furniture, joinery, construction work.
Finishing: Good.

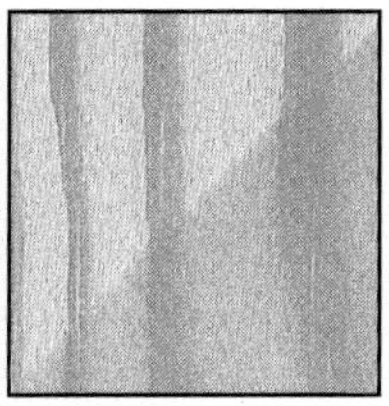

SEQUOIA
Sequoia sempervirens
Other names: Californian redwood.
Sources: USA.
Characteristics: A straight-grained reddish-brown wood, with marked contrast between earlywood and latewood. The texture can vary from fine and even to relatively coarse. It is nonresinous.
Workability: Fair.
Average dried weight: 26lb/ft³ (420kg/m³).
Common uses: Shingles, exterior siding, interior joinery, coffins, posts, plywood.
Finishing: Good.

SPRUCE, NORWAY
Picea abies
Other names: European whitewood, European spruce.
Sources: Europe.
Characteristics: A lustrous straight-grained even-textured wood, with almost white earlywood and pale yellow-brown latewood.
Workability: Good.
Average dried weight: 29lb/ft³ (470kg/m³).
Common uses: Construction, joinery, boxes, plywood, piano soundboards and violin bellies.
Finishing: Good.

SPRUCE, SITKA
Picea sitchensis
Other names: Silver spruce.
Sources: Canada, USA, UK.
Characteristics: A non-resinous creamy-white wood, with slightly pink heartwood. Usually straight-grained with even texture, depending on rate of growth.
Workability: Good.
Average dried weight: 28lb/ft³ (450kg/m³).
Common uses: Boatbuilding, interior joinery, construction, musical instruments, gliders, oars, racing sculls, plywood.
Finishing: Good.

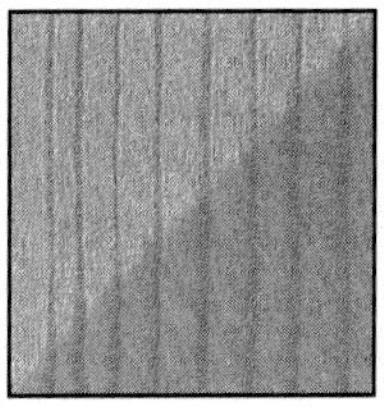

YEW
Taxus baccata
Other names: Common yew, European yew.
Sources: Europe, Asia Minor, North Africa, Burma and the Himalayas.
Characteristics: A tough, hard softwood. It has an orange-red heartwood, with distinct light-colored sapwood. The growth pattern makes the wood very decorative.
Workability: Difficult.
Average dried weight: 42lb/ft³ (670kg/m³).
Common uses: Furniture, turning, joinery.
Finishing: Good.

Rimu

Redwood, European

Sequoia

Spruce, Norway

Spruce, Sitka

Yew

HARDWOODS OF THE WORLD

The term hardwood (like softwood) refers to the botanical grouping of the wood rather than its physical properties. It is, however, a useful label since the majority of hardwoods are in fact harder than woods from the softwood group. The outstanding exception is balsa wood – which, although botanically a hardwood, is the softest wood in the two groups. Hardwoods come from broad-leaved trees, which belong to the botanical group Angiospermae (flowering plants). Angiosperms produce seed-bearing ovaries that develop after fertilization into fruits or nuts. This group is regarded as a higher evolutionary order than the older and more primitive coniferous Gymnosperms, which have a simpler cell structure. Most broad-leaved trees grown in temperate zones are deciduous and lose their leaves in winter – but not all, for some have developed into evergreens. Broad-leaved trees grown in tropical forests are mainly evergreen. Hardwoods are generally more durable than softwoods and offer a wider choice of color, texture and figure. They are also more expensive and many of them, particularly the highly prized exotic woods, are converted into veneer.

SEE ALSO

How trees grow	10-11
Softwoods	16-19
Veneers	30-33
Finishing wood	284-294

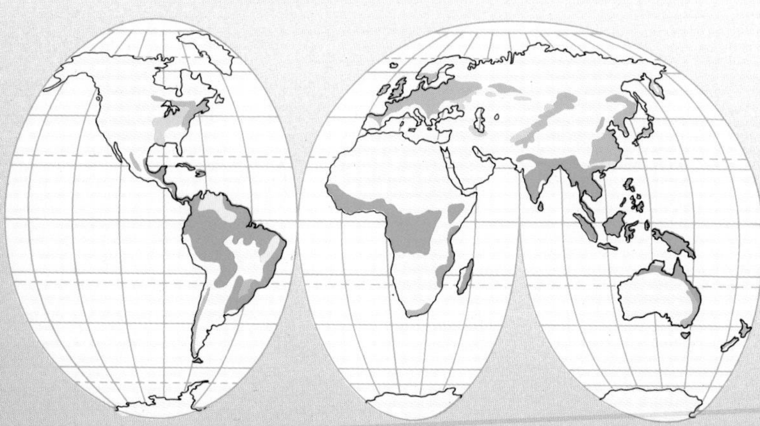

Distribution of hardwoods
- Broad-leaved evergreen forest
- Broad-leaved deciduous forest
- Broad-leaved evergreen and deciduous hardwood forest
- Broad-leaved deciduous and coniferous mixed forest

The scale of the map permits the areas of tree distribution to be shown in broad terms only.

Hardwood regions of the world
There are thousands of species of hardwood trees distributed throughout the world, hundreds of which are harvested for commercial use. Climate is the most important factor governing which species grows where. In general, deciduous broad-leaved trees are native to the temperate Northern Hemisphere and broad-leaved evergreens to the tropics and Southern Hemisphere.

Hardwoods grow relatively slowly, and, although programs for replanting help maintain the forests, the new trees are not always of such good quality as the older stock.

The map shows the distribution of broad-leaved evergreens and broad-leaved deciduous trees, evergreen and deciduous hardwoods, and broad-leaved and coniferous mixed forests.

Endangered species
The indiscriminate destruction of the world's rain forest is leading to a severe shortage of tropical hardwoods. To conserve valuable resources, use only those woods grown on plantations or managed forests. The species most at risk are marked with a felled-tree symbol.

Color change
The small square samples show the actual grain size of each species and the effect when a clear finish is applied.

AFROMOSIA
Pericopsis elata
Other names: Assemela (Ivory Coast, France); kokrodua (Ghana, Ivory Coast); ayin, egbi (Nigeria).
Sources: West Africa.
Characteristics: A durable wood, with straight to interlocked grain. The yellow-brown heartwood darkens to the color of teak, which it resembles, though it is finer textured and not as oily as teak.
Workability: Good.
Average dried weight: 44lb/ft³ (710kg/m³).
Common uses: Veneer, interior and exterior joinery, interior and exterior furniture, construction.
Finishing: Good.

ALDER, RED
Alnus rubra
Other names: Western alder, Oregon alder.
Sources: Pacific Coast of North America.
Characteristics: A soft relatively straight-grained even-textured wood, pale yellow to reddish brown in color.
Workability: Fair.
Average dried weight: 33lb/ft³ (530kg/m³).
Common uses: Furniture, turning, carving, plywood, veneer.
Finishing: Fair.

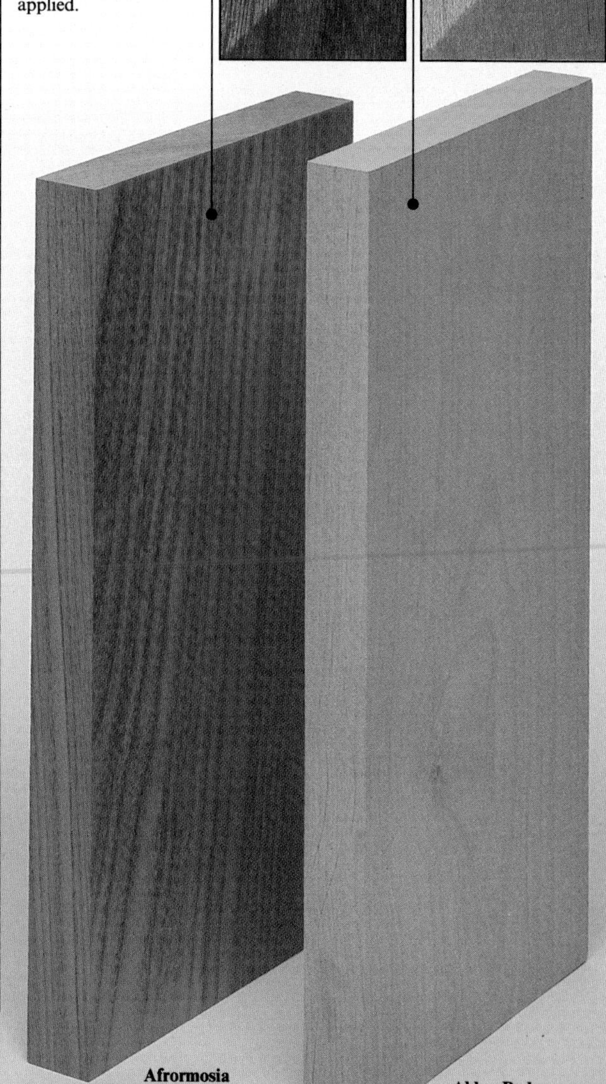

Afrormosia

Alder, Red

ASH, WHITE
Fraxinus americana
Other names: Canadian ash, American white ash (UK).
Sources: Canada and USA.
Characteristics: A coarse but generally straight-grained wood with almost white sapwood, and pale-brown heartwood similar to European ash.
Workability: Medium.
Average dried weight: 42lb/ft^3 (670kg/m^3).
Common uses: Baseball bats and tool handles, boatbuilding, joinery, bentwood furniture.
Finishing: Good.

ASH, EUROPEAN
Fraxinus excelsior
Other names: English, French, Polish ash, etc. (according to origin).
Sources: Europe.
Characteristics: A tough coarse-textured straight-grained wood, whitish to pale brown in color. Logs with dark stained heartwood are known as "olive ash."
Workability: Good.
Average dried weight: 44lb/ft^3 (710kg/m^3).
Common uses: Sports equipment and tool handles, bentwood furniture, cabinet-making, plywood, veneer.
Finishing: Good.

BALSA
Ochroma lagopus
Other names: Guano (Puerto Rico, Honduras); lanero (Cuba); polak (Belize, Nicaragua); topa (Peru); tami (Bolivia).
Sources: South America.
Characteristics: The softest and lightest commercial hardwood. An open straight-grained wood, with lustrous very pale beige to pinkish color.
Workability: Good.
Average dried weight: 10lb/ft^3 (160kg/m^3).
Common uses: Insulation, buoyancy aids, model-making, packaging.
Finishing: Fair.

BASSWOOD
Tilia americana
Other names: American lime.
Sources: Canada, USA.
Characteristics: A fine straight-grained even-textured wood. Creamy-white color, turning to pale brown on exposure.
Workability: Good.
Average dried weight: 26lb/ft^3 (420kg/m^3).
Common uses: Carving and turning, pattern-making, veneer, joinery.
Finishing: Good.

BEECH
Fagus grandifolia
Other names: American beech (UK).
Sources: Canada, USA.
Characteristics: Straight-grained wood, with fine even texture. Light brown to reddish brown in color, slightly coarser than European beech.
Workability: Medium.
Average dried weight: 46lb/ft^3 (740kg/m^3).
Common uses: Cabinetmaking, bentwood furniture, interior joinery, turning.
Finishing: Good.

BEECH, EUROPEAN
Fagus sylvatica
Other names: English, Danish, French beech, etc. (according to origin).
Sources: Europe.
Characteristics: Straight-grained wood, with fine even texture. Whitish brown, turning to yellowish brown on exposure. "Steamed beech" is reddish brown.
Workability: Medium.
Average dried weight: 45lb/ft^3 (720kg/m^3).
Common uses: Cabinetmaking, bentwood furniture, interior joinery, veneer, turning, plywood.
Finishing: Good.

Ash, White · **Ash, European** · **Balsa** · **Basswood** · **Beech** · **Beech, European**

Endangered species
The indiscriminate destruction of the world's rain forest is leading to a severe shortage of tropical hardwoods. To conserve valuable resources, use only those woods grown on plantations or managed forests. The species most at risk are marked with a felled-tree symbol.

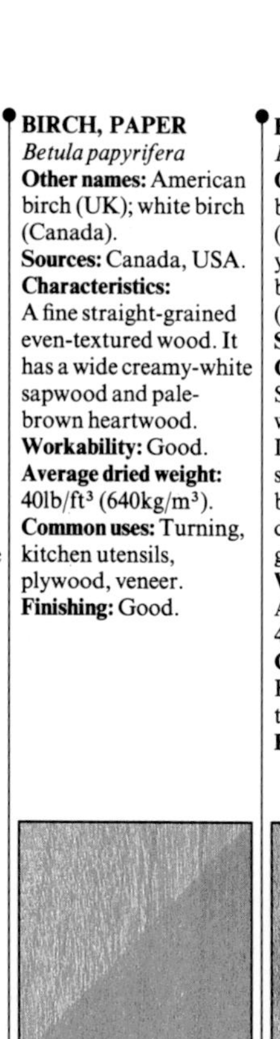

BIRCH, PAPER
Betula papyrifera
Other names: American birch (UK); white birch (Canada).
Sources: Canada, USA.
Characteristics: A fine straight-grained even-textured wood. It has a wide creamy-white sapwood and pale-brown heartwood.
Workability: Good.
Average dried weight: 40lb/ft³ (640kg/m³).
Common uses: Turning, kitchen utensils, plywood, veneer.
Finishing: Good.

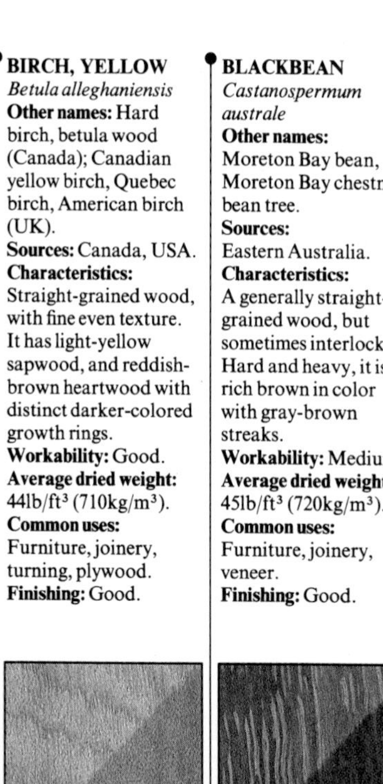

BIRCH, YELLOW
Betula alleghaniensis
Other names: Hard birch, betula wood (Canada); Canadian yellow birch, Quebec birch, American birch (UK).
Sources: Canada, USA.
Characteristics: Straight-grained wood, with fine even texture. It has light-yellow sapwood, and reddish-brown heartwood with distinct darker-colored growth rings.
Workability: Good.
Average dried weight: 44lb/ft³ (710kg/m³).
Common uses: Furniture, joinery, turning, plywood.
Finishing: Good.

BLACKBEAN
Castanospermum australe
Other names: Moreton Bay bean, Moreton Bay chestnut, bean tree.
Sources: Eastern Australia.
Characteristics: A generally straight-grained wood, but sometimes interlocked. Hard and heavy, it is rich brown in color with gray-brown streaks.
Workability: Medium.
Average dried weight: 45lb/ft³ (720kg/m³).
Common uses: Furniture, joinery, veneer.
Finishing: Good.

BLACKWOOD, AUSTRALIAN
Acacia melanoxylon
Other names: Black wattle.
Sources: Australia.
Characteristics: Generally straight-grained, but can be interlocked and wavy. A medium and even-textured wood, with lustrous golden-brown to dark-brown color.
Workability: Medium.
Average dried weight: 42lb/ft³ (670kg/m³).
Common uses: Furniture, interior joinery, turning, billiard tables, gunstocks and decorative veneer.
Finishing: Good.

BOXWOOD
Buxus sempervirens
Other names: European, Turkish, Iranian boxwood (according to origin).
Sources: Southern Europe, Asia Minor, Western Asia.
Characteristics: A fine even-textured wood. It is dense and heavy, can have straight to irregular grain and is light yellow in color.
Workability: Medium.
Average dried weight: 58lb/ft³ (930kg/m³).
Common uses: Carving, tool handles, turning, rulers, inlay, musical instruments.
Finishing: Good.

BRAZILWOOD
Guilandina echinata
Other names: Pernambuco wood, bahia wood, para wood.
Sources: Brazil.
Characteristics: Hard and heavy, with straight grain and fine even texture. Pale sapwood, contrasting with bright orange-red heartwood turning to red-brown. Striped figure.
Workability: Medium.
Average dried weight: 80lb/ft³ (1280kg/m³).
Common uses: Dye-wood, turning, violin bows, gunstocks, exterior joinery, veneer.
Finishing: Good.

- **Color change**
  The small square samples show the actual grain size of each species and the effect when a clear finish is applied.

Birch, Paper

Birch, Yellow

Blackbean

Blackwood, Australian

Boxwood

Brazilwood

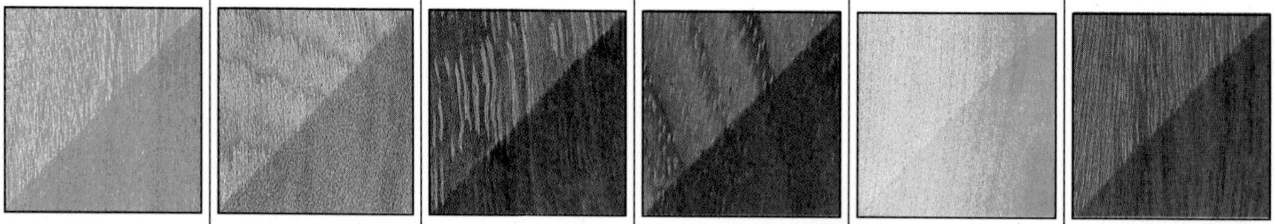

BUBINGA
Guibourtia demeusei
Other names: African rosewood; kevazingo (Gabon); essingang (Cameroons).
Sources: Cameroons, Gabon.
Characteristics: Moderately coarse even-textured wood. It can have straight or interlocked and irregular grain. Red-brown in color, with purple veining.
Workability: Good.
Average dried weight: 55lb/ft^3 (880kg/m^3).
Common uses: Furniture, veneer, wooden utensils.
Finishing: Good.

BUTTERNUT
Juglans cinerea
Other names: White walnut.
Sources: Canada, USA.
Characteristics: A straight-grained coarse-textured wood, with medium-brown heartwood.
Workability: Good.
Average dried weight: 28lb/ft^3 (450kg/m^3).
Common uses: Furniture, carving, interior joinery, veneer.
Finishing: Good.

CHERRY, BLACK
Prunus serotina
Other names: American cherry (UK).
Sources: Canada, USA.
Characteristics: A hard straight-grained wood, with fine texture. Heartwood is reddish brown to deep red, with brown flecks and some gum pockets.
Workability: Good.
Average dried weight: 36lb/ft^3 (580kg/m^3).
Common uses: Furniture, pattern-making, joinery, musical instruments, tobacco pipes.
Finishing: Good.

CHESTNUT
Castanea dentata
Other names: American chestnut (UK); wormy chestnut.
Sources: Canada, USA.
Characteristics: Coarse-textured, with wide growth rings. Similar to oak in appearance, but lacks broad rays. Because of blight, most lumber comes from standing dead trees. Insect attack causes "wormy chestnut."
Workability: Good.
Average dried weight: 30lb/ft^3 (480kg/m^3).
Common uses: Furniture, coffins, poles, stakes.
Finishing: Good.

CHESTNUT, EUROPEAN
Castanea sativa
Other names: Spanish chestnut, sweet chestnut.
Sources: Europe, Asia Minor.
Characteristics: Coarse-textured, with straight or spiralled grain. Color and texture similar to oak, but lacks oak ray figure. Reacts to ferrous metals.
Workability: Good.
Average dried weight: 35lb/ft^3 (560kg/m^3).
Common uses: Furniture, turning, coffins, poles, stakes.
Finishing: Good.

COCOBOLO
Dalbergia retusa
Other names: Granadillo (Mexico).
Sources: West Coast of Central America.
Characteristics: Hard, heavy, tough wood with irregular grain and medium texture. Attractive variegated color, from purple to yellow, with black markings turning to deep orange-red on exposure.
Workability: Good.
Average dried weight: 68lb/ft^3 (1100kg/m^3).
Common uses: Turning, knife handles, brush backs, veneer.
Finishing: Good.

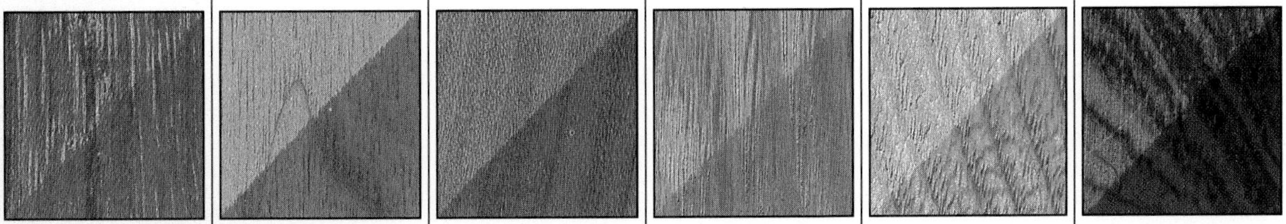

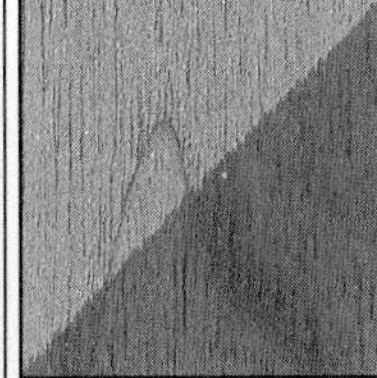

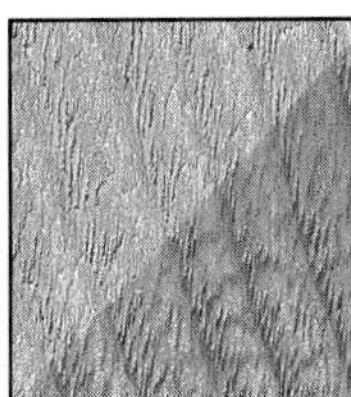

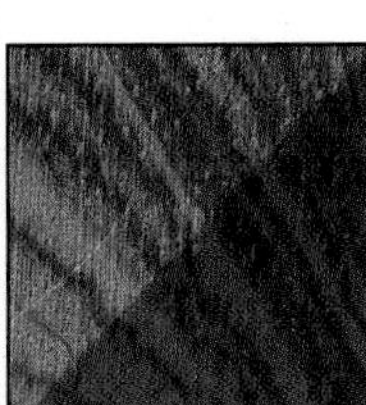

Bubinga

Butternut

Cherry, Black

Chestnut

Chestnut, European

Cocobolo

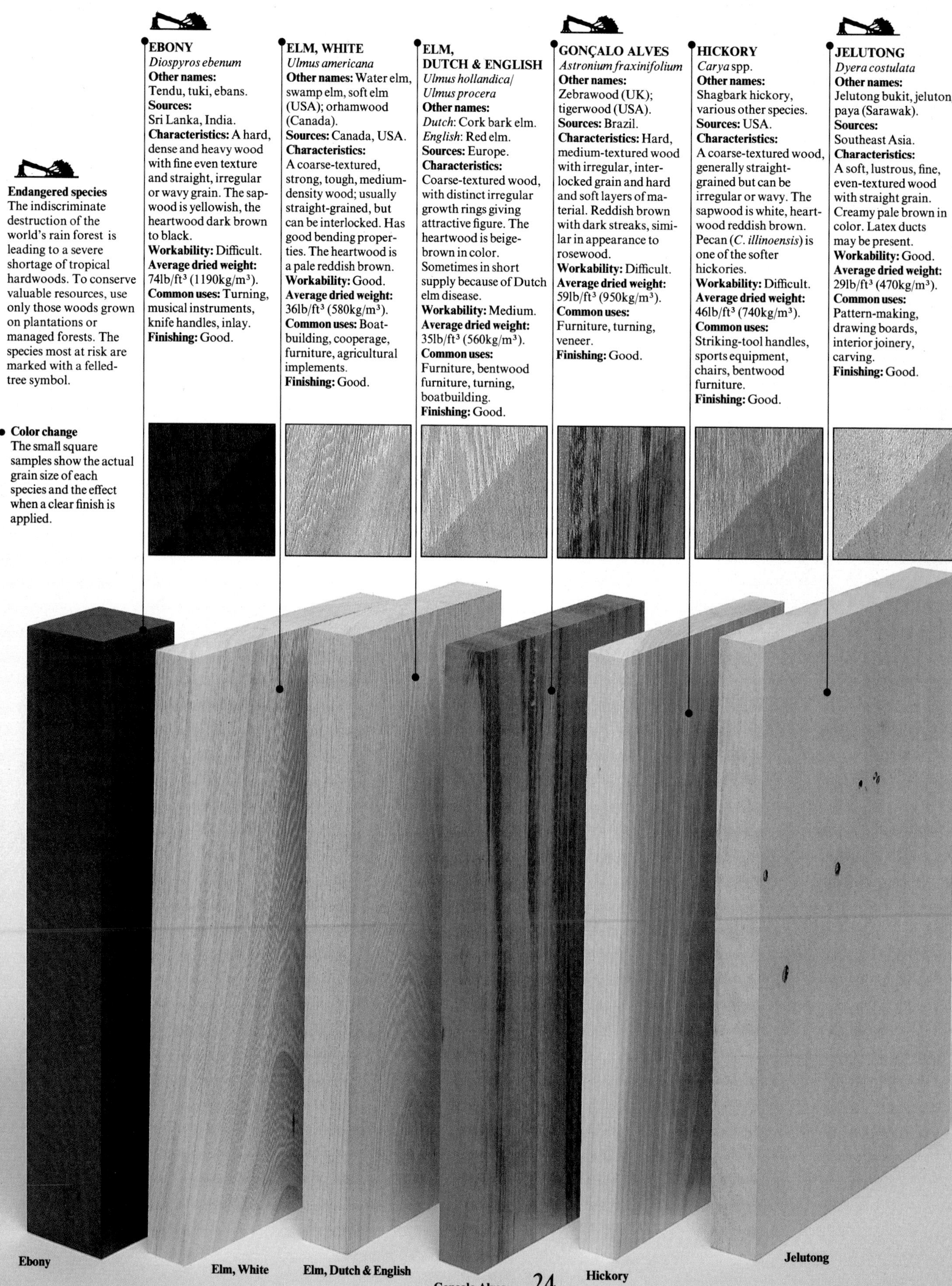

Endangered species
The indiscriminate destruction of the world's rain forest is leading to a severe shortage of tropical hardwoods. To conserve valuable resources, use only those woods grown on plantations or managed forests. The species most at risk are marked with a felled-tree symbol.

• **Color change**
The small square samples show the actual grain size of each species and the effect when a clear finish is applied.

EBONY
Diospyros ebenum
Other names: Tendu, tuki, ebans.
Sources: Sri Lanka, India.
Characteristics: A hard, dense and heavy wood with fine even texture and straight, irregular or wavy grain. The sapwood is yellowish, the heartwood dark brown to black.
Workability: Difficult.
Average dried weight: 74lb/ft³ (1190kg/m³).
Common uses: Turning, musical instruments, knife handles, inlay.
Finishing: Good.

ELM, WHITE
Ulmus americana
Other names: Water elm, swamp elm, soft elm (USA); orhamwood (Canada).
Sources: Canada, USA.
Characteristics: A coarse-textured, strong, tough, medium-density wood; usually straight-grained, but can be interlocked. Has good bending properties. The heartwood is a pale reddish brown.
Workability: Good.
Average dried weight: 36lb/ft³ (580kg/m³).
Common uses: Boatbuilding, cooperage, furniture, agricultural implements.
Finishing: Good.

ELM, DUTCH & ENGLISH
Ulmus hollandica/ Ulmus procera
Other names: *Dutch*: Cork bark elm. *English*: Red elm.
Sources: Europe.
Characteristics: Coarse-textured wood, with distinct irregular growth rings giving attractive figure. The heartwood is beige-brown in color. Sometimes in short supply because of Dutch elm disease.
Workability: Medium.
Average dried weight: 35lb/ft³ (560kg/m³).
Common uses: Furniture, bentwood furniture, turning, boatbuilding.
Finishing: Good.

GONÇALO ALVES
Astronium fraxinifolium
Other names: Zebrawood (UK); tigerwood (USA).
Sources: Brazil.
Characteristics: Hard, medium-textured wood with irregular, interlocked grain and hard and soft layers of material. Reddish brown with dark streaks, similar in appearance to rosewood.
Workability: Difficult.
Average dried weight: 59lb/ft³ (950kg/m³).
Common uses: Furniture, turning, veneer.
Finishing: Good.

HICKORY
Carya spp.
Other names: Shagbark hickory, various other species.
Sources: USA.
Characteristics: A coarse-textured wood, generally straight-grained but can be irregular or wavy. The sapwood is white, heartwood reddish brown. Pecan (*C. illinoensis*) is one of the softer hickories.
Workability: Difficult.
Average dried weight: 46lb/ft³ (740kg/m³).
Common uses: Striking-tool handles, sports equipment, chairs, bentwood furniture.
Finishing: Good.

JELUTONG
Dyera costulata
Other names: Jelutong bukit, jelutong paya (Sarawak).
Sources: Southeast Asia.
Characteristics: A soft, lustrous, fine, even-textured wood with straight grain. Creamy pale brown in color. Latex ducts may be present.
Workability: Good.
Average dried weight: 29lb/ft³ (470kg/m³).
Common uses: Pattern-making, drawing boards, interior joinery, carving.
Finishing: Good.

Ebony **Elm, White** **Elm, Dutch & English** **Gonçalo Alves** **Hickory** **Jelutong**

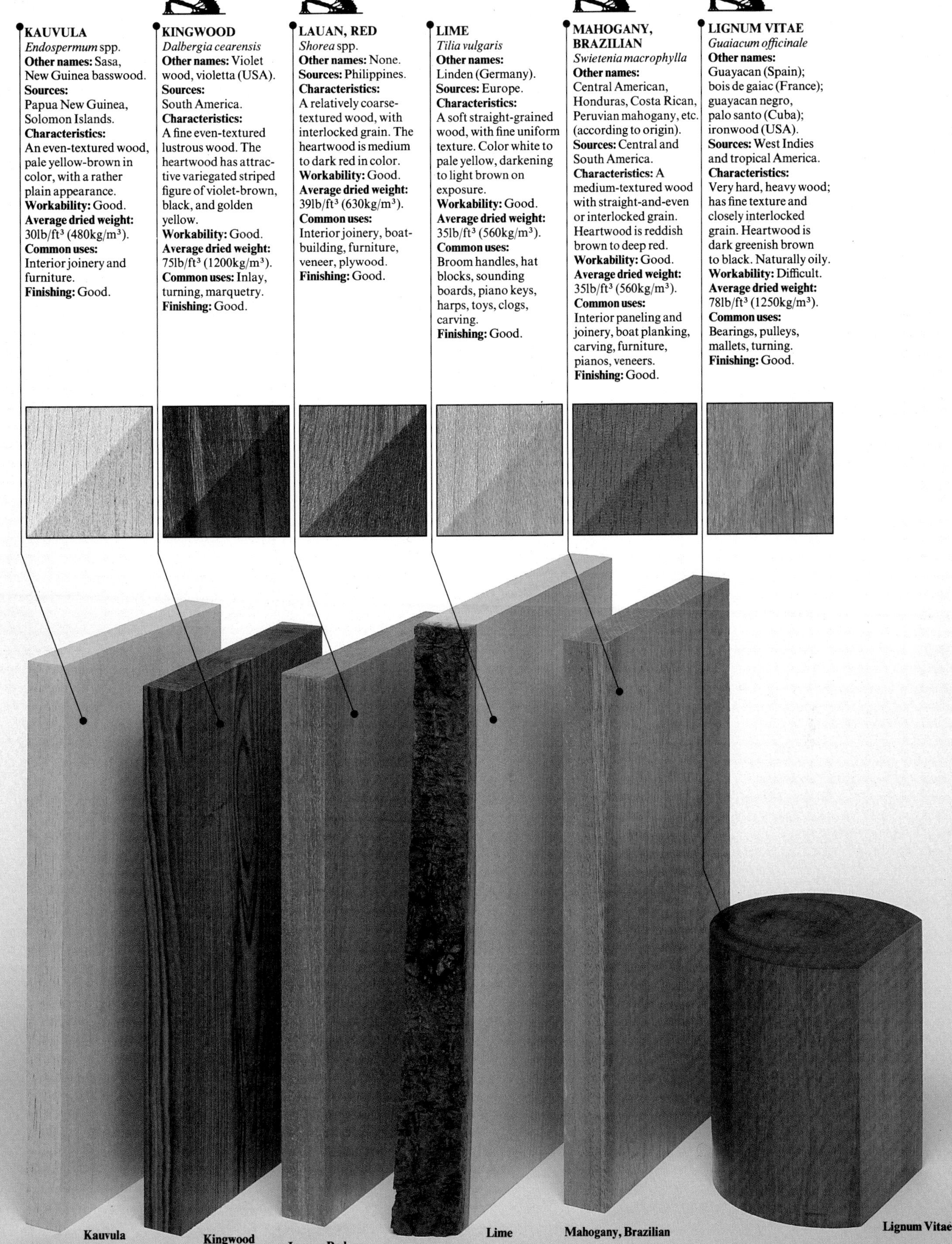

KAUVULA
Endospermum spp.
Other names: Sasa, New Guinea basswood.
Sources: Papua New Guinea, Solomon Islands.
Characteristics: An even-textured wood, pale yellow-brown in color, with a rather plain appearance.
Workability: Good.
Average dried weight: 30lb/ft^3 (480kg/m^3).
Common uses: Interior joinery and furniture.
Finishing: Good.

KINGWOOD
Dalbergia cearensis
Other names: Violet wood, violetta (USA).
Sources: South America.
Characteristics: A fine even-textured lustrous wood. The heartwood has attractive variegated striped figure of violet-brown, black, and golden yellow.
Workability: Good.
Average dried weight: 75lb/ft^3 (1200kg/m^3).
Common uses: Inlay, turning, marquetry.
Finishing: Good.

LAUAN, RED
Shorea spp.
Other names: None.
Sources: Philippines.
Characteristics: A relatively coarse-textured wood, with interlocked grain. The heartwood is medium to dark red in color.
Workability: Good.
Average dried weight: 39lb/ft^3 (630kg/m^3).
Common uses: Interior joinery, boatbuilding, furniture, veneer, plywood.
Finishing: Good.

LIME
Tilia vulgaris
Other names: Linden (Germany).
Sources: Europe.
Characteristics: A soft straight-grained wood, with fine uniform texture. Color white to pale yellow, darkening to light brown on exposure.
Workability: Good.
Average dried weight: 35lb/ft^3 (560kg/m^3).
Common uses: Broom handles, hat blocks, sounding boards, piano keys, harps, toys, clogs, carving.
Finishing: Good.

MAHOGANY, BRAZILIAN
Swietenia macrophylla
Other names: Central American, Honduras, Costa Rican, Peruvian mahogany, etc. (according to origin).
Sources: Central and South America.
Characteristics: A medium-textured wood with straight-and-even or interlocked grain. Heartwood is reddish brown to deep red.
Workability: Good.
Average dried weight: 35lb/ft^3 (560kg/m^3).
Common uses: Interior paneling and joinery, boat planking, carving, furniture, pianos, veneers.
Finishing: Good.

LIGNUM VITAE
Guaiacum officinale
Other names: Guayacan (Spain); bois de gaiac (France); guayacan negro, palo santo (Cuba); ironwood (USA).
Sources: West Indies and tropical America.
Characteristics: Very hard, heavy wood; has fine texture and closely interlocked grain. Heartwood is dark greenish brown to black. Naturally oily.
Workability: Difficult.
Average dried weight: 78lb/ft^3 (1250kg/m^3).
Common uses: Bearings, pulleys, mallets, turning.
Finishing: Good.

Endangered species
The indiscriminate destruction of the world's rain forest is leading to a severe shortage of tropical hardwoods. To conserve valuable resources, use only those woods grown on plantations or managed forests. The species most at risk are marked with a felled-tree symbol.

• **Color change**
The small square samples show the actual grain size of each species and the effect when a clear finish is applied.

MAPLE, HARD
Acer saccharum
Other names: Rock maple, sugar maple.
Sources: Canada, USA.
Characteristics: Hard, heavy, straight-grained wood with fine texture. White sapwood, with light reddish-brown heartwood. Sometimes with bird's-eye figure or curly figure.
Workability: Difficult.
Average dried weight: 46lb/ft^3 (740kg/m^3).
Common uses: Furniture, turning, musical instruments, butcher's blocks, flooring, veneer.
Finishing: Fair.

MAPLE, SOFT
Acer spp.
Other names: Red maple, silver maple, Oregon maple.
Sources: Canada, USA.
Characteristics: Straight-grained fine-textured wood, not as strong as hard maple. Light creamy-brown in color. Often with curly figure.
Workability: Medium.
Average dried weight: 39lb/ft^3 (630kg/m^3).
Common uses: Furniture, interior joinery, turning, veneer, musical instruments, flooring, plywood.
Finishing: Good.

OAK, RED
Quercus rubra
Other names: Northern red oak; American red oak (UK).
Sources: Canada, USA.
Characteristics: Straight-grained, with coarse texture and less attractive figure than white oak. Pinkish red in color.
Workability: Good.
Average dried weight: 49lb/ft^3 (790kg/m^3).
Common uses: Furniture, interior joinery, flooring, veneer.
Finishing: Good.

OAK, WHITE
Quercus alba
Other names: American white oak (UK).
Sources: USA, Canada.
Characteristics: Straight-grained, with medium-coarse to coarse texture. Similar in appearance to European oak, but more variable in color. Impervious to water.
Workability: Good.
Average dried weight: 48lb/ft^3 (770kg/m^3).
Common uses: Construction, flooring, furniture, interior joinery, plywood, veneer, barrels.
Finishing: Good.

OAK, JAPANESE
Quercus mongolica
Other names: Ohnara.
Sources: Japan.
Characteristics: Straight-grained and coarse-textured wood, milder than European and White oak. Light yellowish brown in color.
Workability: Good.
Average dried weight: 42lb/ft^3 (670kg/m^3).
Common uses: Furniture, paneling, flooring, boatbuilding, joinery, veneer.
Finishing: Good.

OAK, EUROPEAN
Quercus robur
Quercus petraea
Other names: English, French, Polish oak, etc. (according to origin).
Sources: Europe, Asia Minor, North Africa.
Characteristics: A coarse-textured and straight-grained wood, with distinct growth rings and broad rays when quartersawn. Pale brown in color.
Workability: Good.
Average dried weight: 45lb/ft^3 (720kg/m^3).
Common uses: Furniture, joinery, external woodwork, flooring, carving, boatbuilding.
Finishing: Good.

Maple, Hard **Maple, Soft** **Oak, Red** **Oak, White** **Oak, Japanese** **Oak, European**

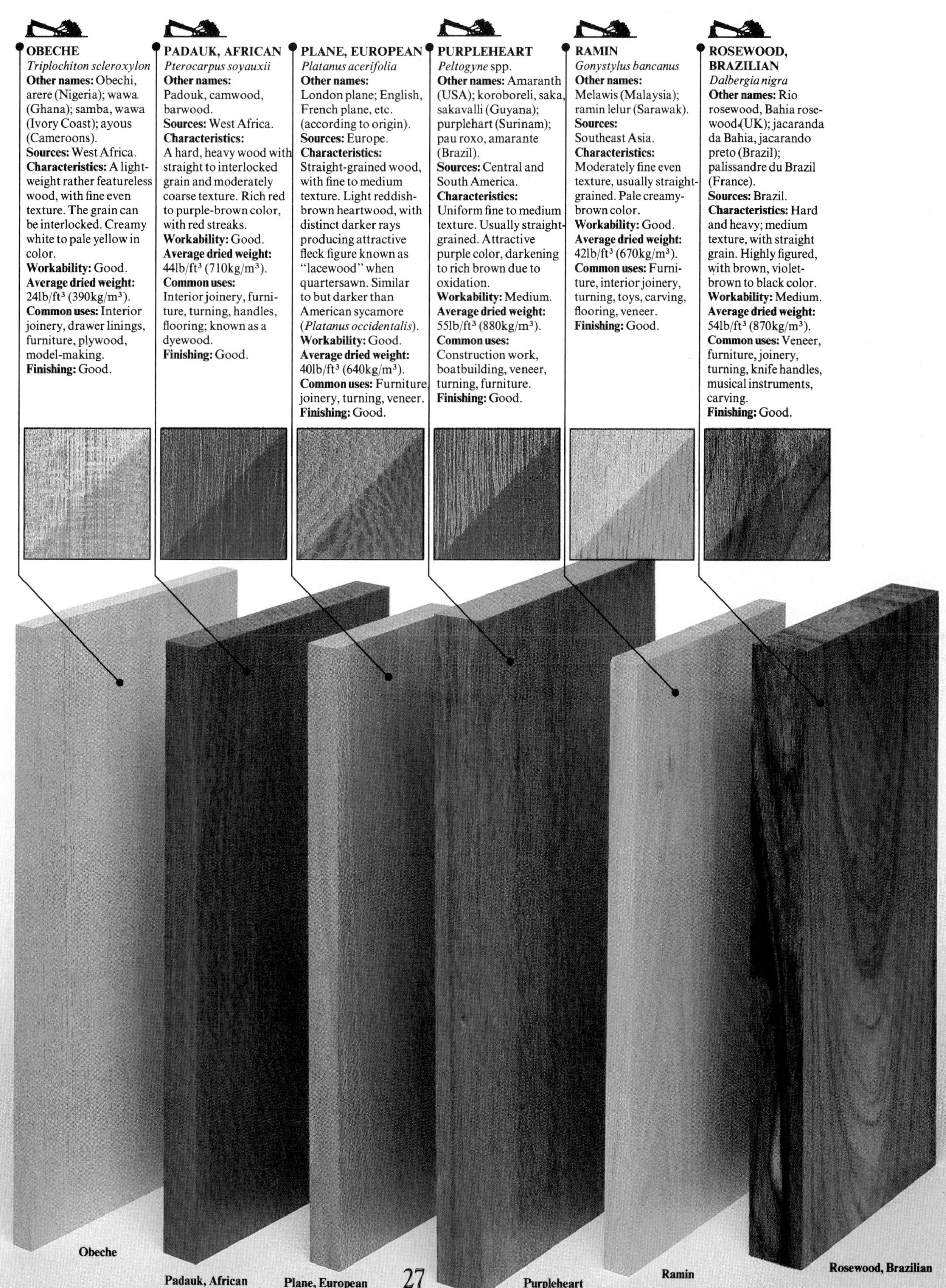

OBECHE
Triplochiton scleroxylon
Other names: Obechi, arere (Nigeria); wawa (Ghana); samba, wawa (Ivory Coast); ayous (Cameroons).
Sources: West Africa.
Characteristics: A lightweight rather featureless wood, with fine even texture. The grain can be interlocked. Creamy white to pale yellow in color.
Workability: Good.
Average dried weight: 24lb/ft³ (390kg/m³).
Common uses: Interior joinery, drawer linings, furniture, plywood, model-making.
Finishing: Good.

PADAUK, AFRICAN
Pterocarpus soyauxii
Other names: Padouk, camwood, barwood.
Sources: West Africa.
Characteristics: A hard, heavy wood with straight to interlocked grain and moderately coarse texture. Rich red to purple-brown color, with red streaks.
Workability: Good.
Average dried weight: 44lb/ft³ (710kg/m³).
Common uses: Interior joinery, furniture, turning, handles, flooring; known as a dyewood.
Finishing: Good.

PLANE, EUROPEAN
Platanus acerifolia
Other names: London plane; English, French plane, etc. (according to origin).
Sources: Europe.
Characteristics: Straight-grained wood, with fine to medium texture. Light reddish-brown heartwood, with distinct darker rays producing attractive fleck figure known as "lacewood" when quartersawn. Similar to but darker than American sycamore (*Platanus occidentalis*).
Workability: Good.
Average dried weight: 40lb/ft³ (640kg/m³).
Common uses: Furniture, joinery, turning, veneer.
Finishing: Good.

PURPLEHEART
Peltogyne spp.
Other names: Amaranth (USA); koroboreli, saka, sakavalli (Guyana); purplehart (Surinam); pau roxo, amarante (Brazil).
Sources: Central and South America.
Characteristics: Uniform fine to medium texture. Usually straight-grained. Attractive purple color, darkening to rich brown due to oxidation.
Workability: Medium.
Average dried weight: 55lb/ft³ (880kg/m³).
Common uses: Construction work, boatbuilding, veneer, turning, furniture.
Finishing: Good.

RAMIN
Gonystylus bancanus
Other names: Melawis (Malaysia); ramin lelur (Sarawak).
Sources: Southeast Asia.
Characteristics: Moderately fine even texture, usually straight-grained. Pale creamy-brown color.
Workability: Good.
Average dried weight: 42lb/ft³ (670kg/m³).
Common uses: Furniture, interior joinery, turning, toys, carving, flooring, veneer.
Finishing: Good.

ROSEWOOD, BRAZILIAN
Dalbergia nigra
Other names: Rio rosewood, Bahia rosewood (UK); jacaranda da Bahia, jacarando preto (Brazil); palissandre du Brazil (France).
Sources: Brazil.
Characteristics: Hard and heavy; medium texture, with straight grain. Highly figured, with brown, violet-brown to black color.
Workability: Medium.
Average dried weight: 54lb/ft³ (870kg/m³).
Common uses: Veneer, furniture, joinery, turning, knife handles, musical instruments, carving.
Finishing: Good.

Obeche

Padauk, African

Plane, European

Purpleheart

Ramin

Rosewood, Brazilian

Endangered species
The indiscriminate destruction of the world's rain forest is leading to a severe shortage of tropical hardwoods. To conserve valuable resources, use only those woods grown on plantations or managed forests. The species most at risk are marked with a felled-tree symbol.

● **Color change**
The small square samples show the actual grain size of each species and the effect when a clear finish is applied.

ROSEWOOD, INDIAN
Dalbergia latifolia
Other names:
East Indian rosewood; Bombay rosewood (UK); Bombay blackwood (India); palisander.
Sources: India.
Characteristics: Heavy, moderately coarse and uniform texture. Interlocked grain, producing narrow bands. Golden brown to purple-brown with streaks of dark purple or black.
Workability: Medium.
Average dried weight:
54lb/ft³ (870kg/m³).
Common uses:
Furniture, shop fittings, musical instruments, boatbuilding, veneer, turning, flooring.
Finishing: Good.

SATINWOOD
Chloroxylon swietenia
Other names:
East Indian satinwood.
Sources:
Central and Southern India, Sri Lanka.
Characteristics: Heavy lustrous wood, with fine even texture and interlocked grain producing striped figure. Golden brown with darker streaks.
Workability: Medium.
Average dried weight:
61lb/ft³ (990kg/m³).
Common uses:
Furniture, interior joinery, turning, veneer.
Finishing: Good.

SILKY OAK
Grevillea robusta
Other names:
Bull oak, Northern silky oak (Australia); Australian silky oak (UK).
Sources: Australia.
Characteristics: Coarse even-textured wood, usually straight-grained with large rays. Reddish-brown color similar to red oak, though not a true oak.
Workability: Good.
Average dried weight:
34lb/ft³ (550kg/m³).
Common uses:
Furniture, veneer, interior joinery.
Finishing: Good.

SYCAMORE
Platanus occidentalis
Other names:
American plane (UK); buttonwood (USA).
Sources: USA.
Characteristics: Fine even texture, usually with straight grain. Not to be confused with European sycamore, which we call sycamore maple. Botanically a plane tree, but lighter than European plane. Pale brown, with distinct darker rays producing lacewood when quartersawn.
Workability: Good.
Average dried weight:
35lb/ft³ (560kg/m³).
Common uses: Joinery, furniture, butcher's blocks, veneer.
Finishing: Good.

SYCAMORE, EUROPEAN
Acer pseudoplatanus
Other names:
Sycamore, sycamore plane, great maple (UK); sycamore maple (USA).
Sources:
Europe, Western Asia.
Characteristics: A maple, not a true sycamore (plane). Fine even texture. Straight-grained but may have fiddleback figure when quartersawn. White to yellowish-white color.
Workability: Good.
Average dried weight:
39lb/ft³ (630kg/m³).
Common uses:
Turning, furniture, kitchen utensils, flooring. Fiddleback wood is used for violin backs.
Finishing: Good.

TEAK
Tectona grandis
Other names: Kyun sagwan, teku, teka.
Sources: South and Southeast Asia, Africa, Caribbean.
Characteristics: Coarse uneven texture with oily feel. Straight or wavy-grained, according to origin. Burma teak is a uniform golden brown; others are darker and more marked.
Workability: Good.
Average dried weight:
41lb/ft³ (660kg/m³).
Common uses:
Interior and exterior joinery, boatbuilding, exterior and garden furniture, plywood, turning, veneer.
Finishing: Good.

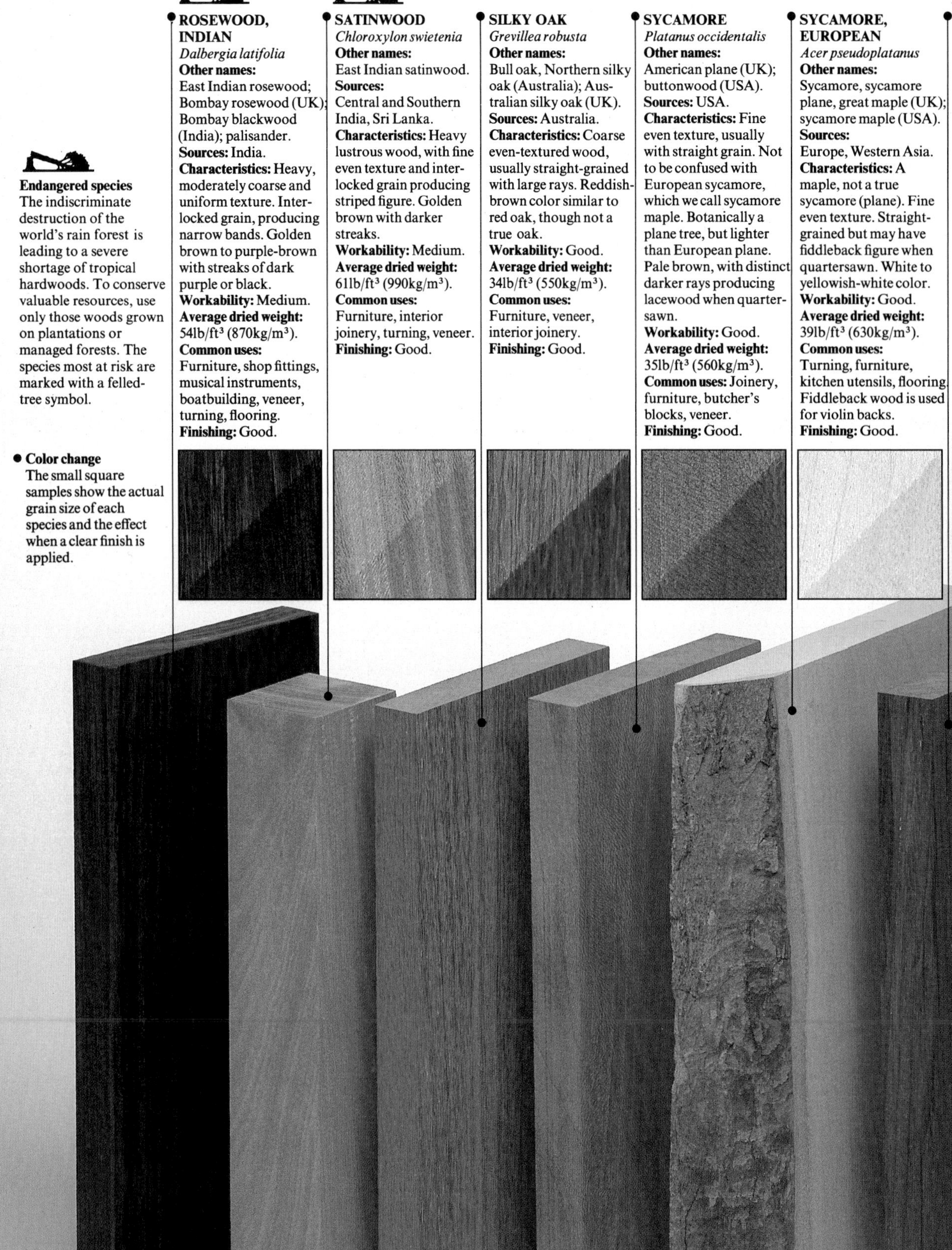

Rosewood, Indian — Satinwood — Silky Oak — Sycamore — Sycamore, European — Teak

TULIPWOOD
Dalbergia frutescens
Other names: Pinkwood (USA); bois de rose (France); pau rosa, jacaranda rosa, pau de fuso (Brazil).
Sources: Brazil.
Characteristics: Dense, hard wood with medium to fine texture; usually has irregular grain. Attractive pinkish-yellow color, with pink to violet-red stripes.
Workability: Difficult.
Average dried weight: 60lb/ft³ (960kg/m³).
Common uses: Turning, kitchen utensils, boxes, inlay, veneer.
Finishing: Good.

UTILE
Entandrophragma utile
Other names: Sipo (Ivory Coast); assie (Cameroons).
Sources: Africa.
Characteristics: A medium-textured wood; usually with interlocked grain, producing striped figure when quartersawn. Pinkish-brown color, turning to red-brown.
Workability: Good.
Average dried weight: 41lb/ft³ (660kg/m³).
Common uses: Furniture, interior and exterior joinery, boat-building, flooring, plywood, veneer.
Finishing: Good.

WALNUT, BLACK
Juglans nigra
Other names: Black American walnut, American walnut, Virginia walnut (UK); walnut (USA).
Sources: USA, Canada.
Characteristics: A tough wood, with rather coarse texture; usually straight-grained, but can be wavy. Rich dark brown to purplish black.
Workability: Good.
Average dried weight: 41lb/ft³ (660kg/m³).
Common uses: Furniture, gunstocks, interior joinery, musical instruments, turning, carving, plywood, veneer.
Finishing: Good.

WALNUT, EUROPEAN
Juglans regia
Other names: English, French, Italian walnut, etc. (according to origin).
Sources: Europe, Asia Minor, Southwest Asia.
Characteristics: Rather coarse texture, with straight to wavy grain. Gray-brown with darker streaks, though color and markings vary according to origin.
Workability: Good.
Average dried weight: 42lb/ft³ (670kg/m³).
Common uses: Furniture, interior joinery, gunstocks, turning, carving, veneer.
Finishing: Good.

WALNUT, QUEENSLAND
Endiandra palmerstonii
Other names: Australian walnut, walnut bean, Oriental wood.
Sources: Australia.
Characteristics: Similar to European walnut in appearance, but not a true walnut. Usually has interlocked and wavy grain. Wide color variation, from light to dark brown.
Workability: Difficult.
Average dried weight. 43lb/ft³ (690kg/m³).
Common uses: Furniture, interior joinery, shop fittings, flooring, veneer.
Finishing: Good.

YELLOW-POPLAR
Liriodendron tulipifera
Other names: Whitewood, tulip poplar (USA); tulip tree (UK and USA); canary whitewood (UK).
Sources: Eastern USA, Canada.
Characteristics: A moderately soft and lightweight wood, with straight grain and fine texture. White sapwood; pale olive-green to brown heartwood, with colored streaks.
Workability: Good.
Average dried weight: 31lb/ft³ (500kg/m³).
Common uses: Joinery, furniture, carving, light construction, interiors, boats, toys, plywood.
Finishing: Good.

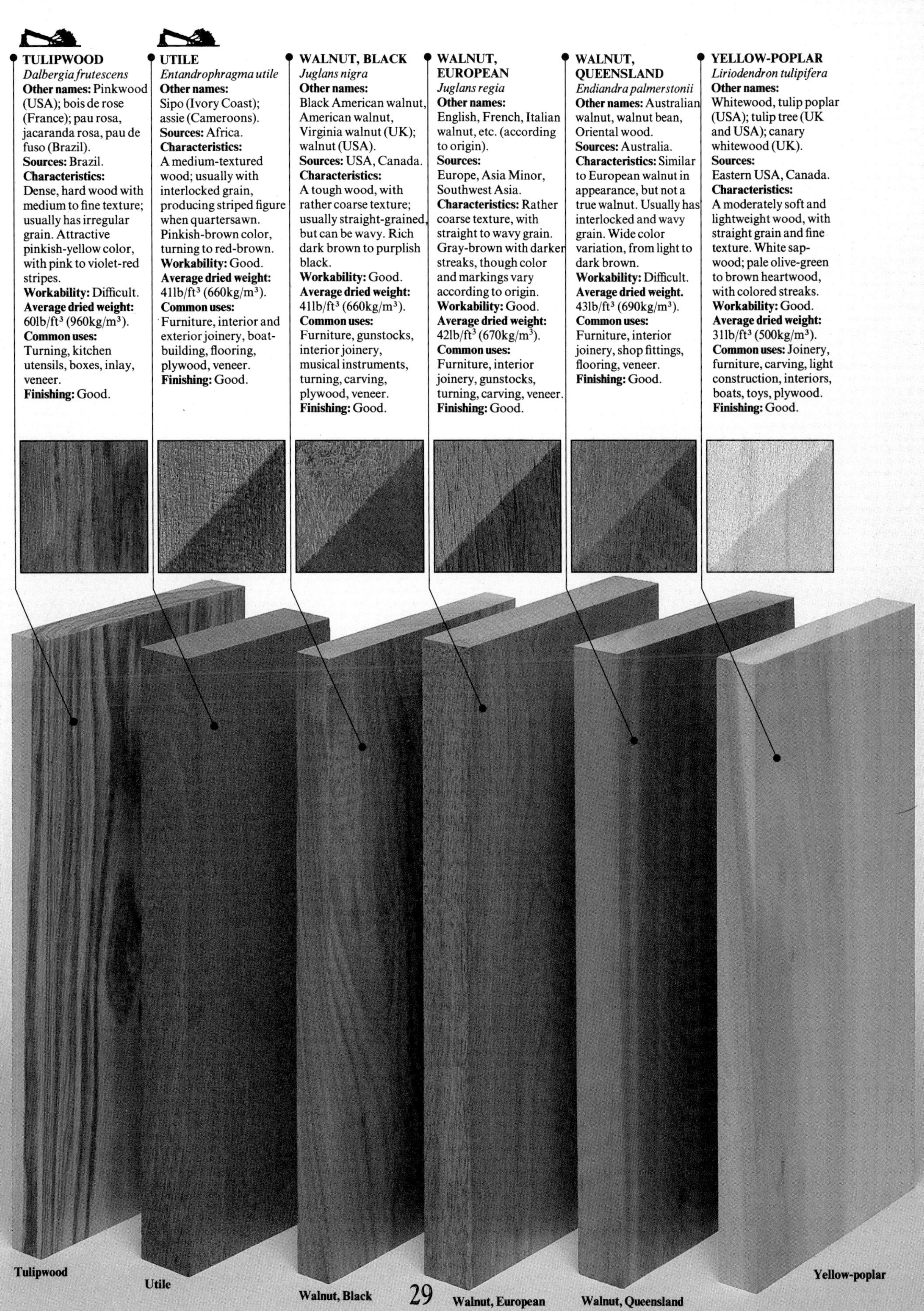

Tulipwood

Utile

Walnut, Black

Walnut, European

Walnut, Queensland

Yellow-poplar

VENEERS

Veneers are very thin sheets or "leaves" of wood that are cut from a log for constructional or decorative purposes. It is ironic that even though veneers of the rarest woods have been used in making some of the finest furniture ever produced, some people still regard veneering as inferior to solid wood. However, few would disagree that veneer, whether selected for its natural color and figure or worked into floral or formal patterns, brings a unique quality to furniture and woodwork. Today, with the widespread use of modern adhesives and stable man-made backing boards, veneered products are superior to solid wood in certain applications. With our natural resources of fine woods gradually disappearing, veneer enables us to use wood economically so we can continue to enjoy it.

SEE ALSO	
Man-made boards	34-38
Cabinet construction	40-49
Table saws	156-159
Band saws	172-177
Veneering	258-270

VENEER PRODUCTION

The manufacture of veneer requires specialized knowledge. The production starts with the log buyer, who must have the skill to interpret the quality of a log for conversion into commercially acceptable veneer. Using his judgement and experience, he has to assess the condition of the wood within the log solely on the basis of an external examination.

By looking at the end of the log, the buyer has to determine the quality of the wood, the potential figure of the veneer, the color, and the ratio of sapwood to heartwood. Other factors that will affect the value of the log must also be noted, including the presence and extent of any staining and any weaknesses or defects such as shakes, ingrown bark or excessive knots and resin ducts or pockets. Much of this information will be revealed by the first cut through the length of the log – but the buyer has, of course, to purchase the log before it is cut.

Once the log has been purchased and delivered to the sawmill, it is the expertise of the veneer cutter that counts, since it is the veneer cutter who has to decide the best way to convert the wood to yield the maximum number of high-quality veneers.

Grading

As decorative veneers are cut, they are taken from the slicer and stacked in sequence. The veneers then pass through a drying process before being graded. Most species are "clipped" on a guillotine to trim them into regular shapes and sizes. Others, such as yew or burl veneer, are left as they are cut from the log.

Veneers are priced according to their size and quality. They are checked for natural or milling defects, thickness, type of figure and color, for example, and graded accordingly. A particular log may yield veneers of various value. The better veneers are graded as "face quality" and have a greater value than the narrower or poorer "backing grade."

The veneers are kept in multiples of four for matching purposes and bound into "bundles" of 16, 24, 28 or 32 leaves. The bundles are restacked in consecutive order and the reassembled log is stored in a cool warehouse ready for sale.

CUTTING VENEER

Veneer logs are cut from the main stem of the tree between the root butt and the first branch. The bark is removed and the log checked for foreign matter such as nails.

Before the log is converted into veneer it is softened by immersion in hot water or by steaming. The whole log may be treated, or it may first be cut by a huge band saw into "flitches" to suit the veneer-cutting method. The duration of this conditioning is controlled according to the type and hardness of the wood and the thickness of the veneer to be cut. It may be a matter of days or weeks. Pale woods such as maple are not pretreated, as the process would discolor the veneer.

There are basically three methods for cutting veneer: saw cutting, rotary cutting and flat slicing.

Saw cutting

Until the early eighteenth century, when veneer-slicing machines were developed, all veneers were cut using first handsaws and then power saws. These veneers were relatively thick, some being about $\frac{1}{8}$in (3mm).

Sawn veneers, although wasteful of material, are still cut by huge circular saws, but only for special or difficult-to-work irregular-grained woods such as crotches or where it proves the most economical method. They are usually about $\frac{1}{32}$ to $\frac{1}{16}$in (1 to 1.5mm) thick.

You can use your workshop band saw or table saw to produce strips of veneer for laminating purposes, particularly if this proves to be more economical or will provide you with material better suited to your needs than the veneers that are commercially available.

Rotary cutting

Constructional veneers of softwood and some hardwoods are cut by the rotary peeling method. The whole log is set in a huge lathe that peels off a continuous sheet of veneer.

The log is rotated against a pressure bar and knife that run the full length of the machine. The knife is set just below the bar and forward of it by the thickness of the veneer. The setting of the bar and knife in relation to the log is critical, to prevent surface failures known as "checks." For each revolution of the log, the knife is automatically advanced by the thickness of the veneer.

Veneer produced in this way can be recognized by a distinctive watery-patterned figure where the continuous tangential cut has sliced through the growth rings.

Rotary cutting is a particularly efficient way to produce veneers suitable for the manufacture of man-made boards, as they can be cut to any width.

Although primarily used for the manufacture of constructional veneers, the method is also used to produce decorative veneers such as bird's-eye maple.

Off-center cutting

The rotary lathe can also be used to produce wide decorative veneers with sapwood on each edge in order to give a figure something like that of typical flat-sliced crown-cut veneer. This is done by offsetting the log in the lathe chucks to produce an eccentric cutting action.

A "stay-log" is a mounting positioned between the lathe centers to hold a full or half-round log. A veneer cut on a stay-log is cut at a shallower angle than one taken from an eccentrically mounted log but is not as wide. The figure is closer to that of flat-sliced crown-cut veneer.

Half-round logs can be mounted on a stay-log with the heartwood facing outward. This is known as "back cutting" and is used for cutting decoratively figured butts and crotches.

Flat slicing

Flat slicing produces decorative hardwood veneers. How the log is sliced depends on the natural characteristics of the wood. A log is first cut in two lengthwise and the grain assessed for figure. It may then be further cut into flitches, according to the type of figure required. It is the way the log is cut and mounted for slicing that determines the character of the figure. The width of flat-sliced veneer is limited by the size of the flitch.

A half or quartered log or flitch is mounted on a sliding frame that can move up and down. The pressure bar and knife are set horizontally in front of the wood, and a slice of veneer is removed with every downstroke of the frame. After each cut, the knife or flitch is advanced by the required thickness of the veneer.

A flat-sliced half-round log produces the crown-cut veneers commonly used in cabinet work. They have the same attractive figure as tangentially cut flatsawn boards.

Woods that display striking and attractive figure when radially cut are converted into quarter-cut or near quarter-cut flitches. These are mounted with the rays of the wood following the direction of the cut as closely as possible, to produce the maximum number of radially cut veneers.

Quartered flitches can also be mounted to produce tangentially cut flat-sliced veneer. These are narrower than crown-cut veneers cut from half-round logs but can display attractive figure.

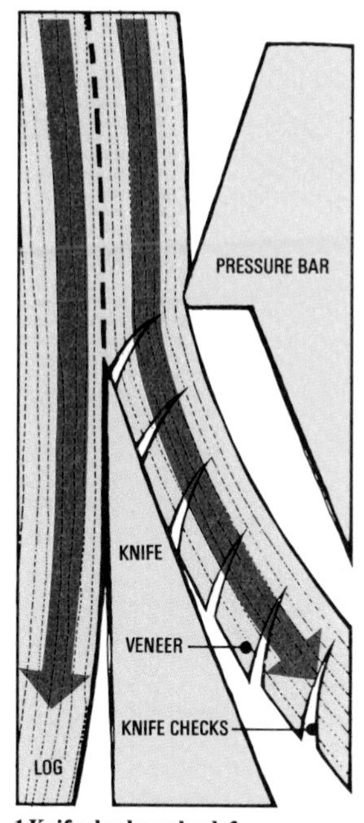

1 Knife checks on back face

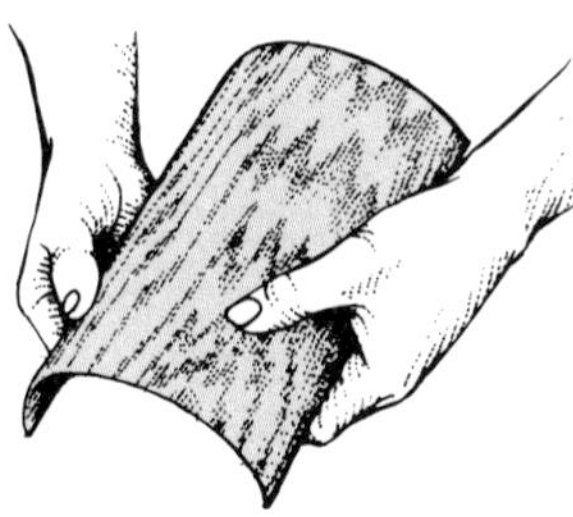

2 Bend the veneer as a test

KNIFE CHECKS

Veneer-slicing machines are like giant planes, with the veneer representing the shaving. In this case it is important that the "shaving" is produced to a fine tolerance and with a clean cut. The quality of the cut is controlled by the pressure bar and knife setting **(1)**.

Fine cracks known as "knife checks" can occur on the back face of the veneer, particularly when rotary-peeled. The back face of the veneer is called the "open" or "loose" face; and the other, the "closed" or "tight" face. You can identify the faces by flexing the veneer, which will bend to a greater degree when the open face is convex **(2)**.

Always try to lay veneer with the open face down, since the slightly coarser surface does not finish quite as well as the closed face. This is not always possible, however, because it is necessary to turn alternate veneers over when laying book-matched veneers.

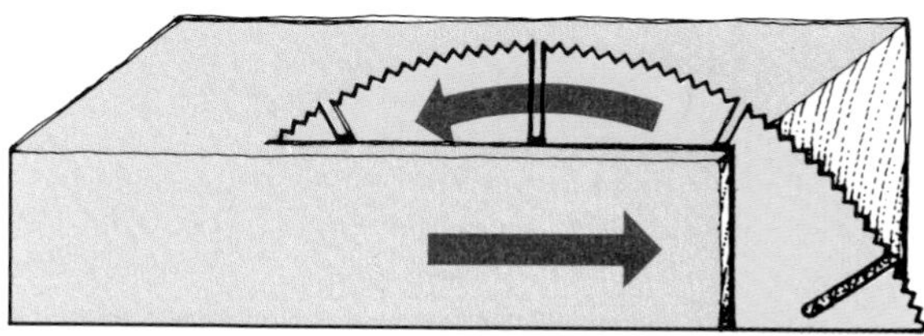

Saw cutting
This is not a common method today but is still used for some thick-cut veneers.

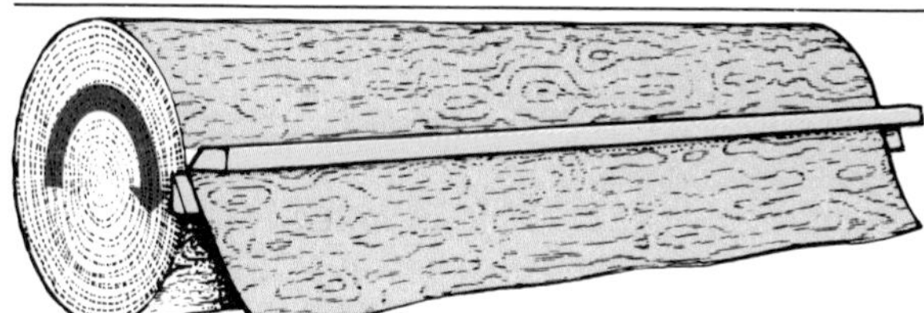

Rotary cutting
Widely used for constructional and some decorative veneers, such as bird's-eye maple.

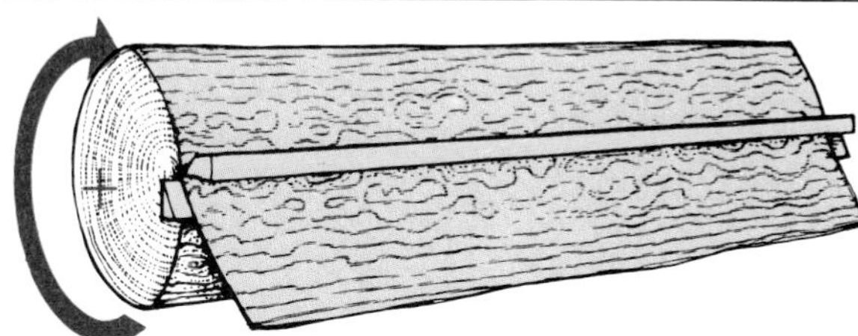

Off-center cutting
A rotary-cutting method that produces a figure similar to flat-sliced veneer.

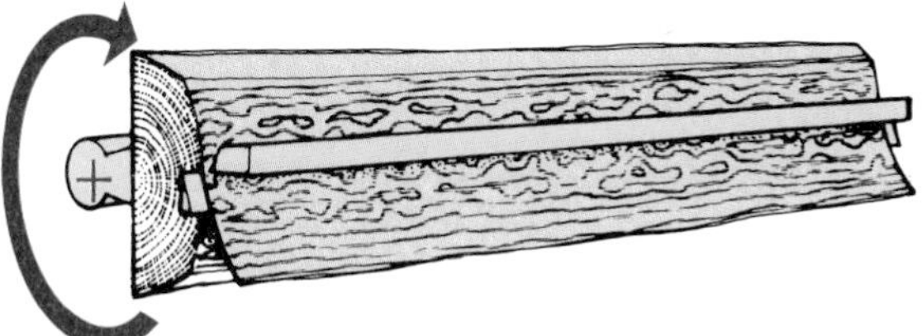

Half-round cutting
This is similar to off-center cutting, and also produces figure like flat-sliced veneer.

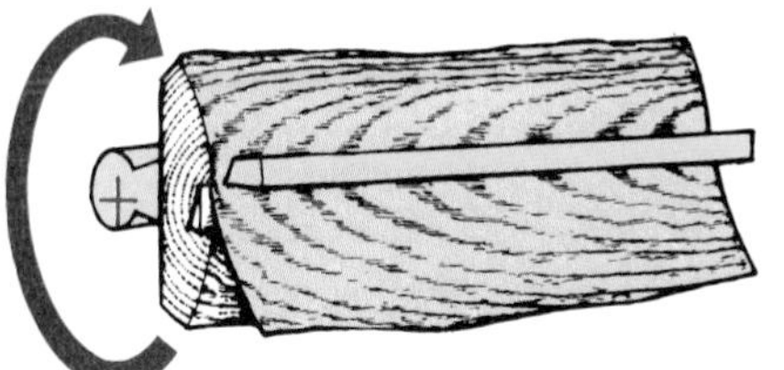

Back cutting
A rotary method used for cutting decorative butt and crotch veneers.

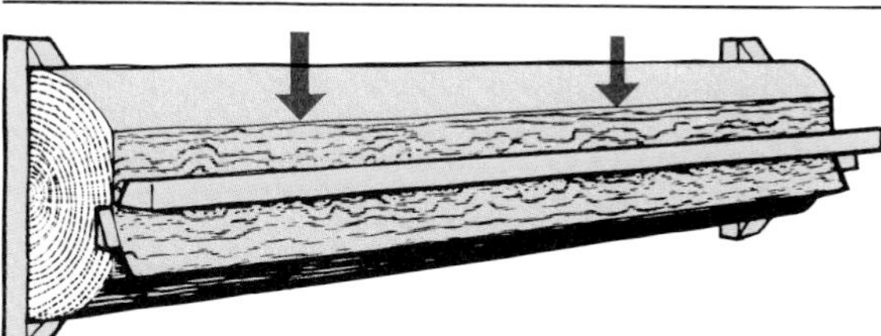

Flat slicing
A common method for producing traditional crown-cut veneers.

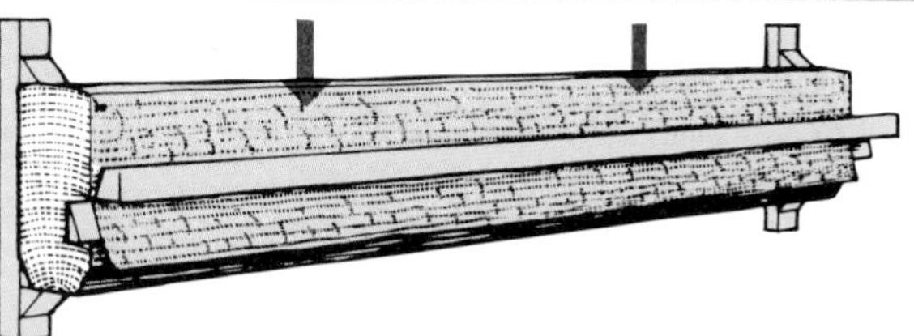

Quarter-cut slicing
Used to produce veneers displaying attractive quarter-cut figure.

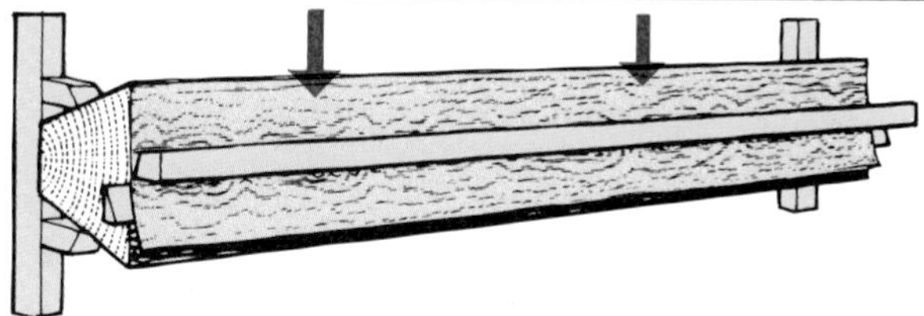

Flat-sliced quartered
Quartered logs are sometimes cut tangentially to make flat-sliced veneers.

TYPES OF VENEER

The veneer-manufacturing process makes a wide choice of hardwoods available, many of which are uneconomic or unsuitable for use in "solid" form. A tree can be converted into various types of decorative veneer. The figure depends not only on the natural features of the wood, such as color, grain and texture, but also on which part of the tree is used and how it is cut into veneer. Most veneer is cut from the main trunk, which gives the longest and usually the widest-figured veneers. The variety of types is obtained by slicing the log in different ways. The type description may refer to the method of cutting – as in "crown-cut walnut" – or to the part of the tree from which the veneer is cut, as in "burl" or "burr" veneer. Most sliced veneer is cut about $\frac{1}{42}$in (0.6mm) thick. Thicker veneer for furniture restoration is also produced in some woods.

SEE ALSO
Hardwoods 20-29
Veneering 258-270

BUYING VENEER

You can buy single leaves or full bundles of veneer from specialist suppliers and a few general woodworking firms, either by mail order or direct. Because it is important to keep the veneers in consecutive order for matching purposes, you will be supplied with veneer from the top of the stack. The supplier will not usually pull out selected leaves, as that would reduce the value of the veneer flitch.

Before buying veneer, calculate the area you need and make an allowance for waste. Err on the generous side – since each veneer is unique and if you have to order more you are unlikely to obtain a match. Full leaves are customarily priced by the square foot, and some suppliers will sell precut lengths at a set price per piece. Small pieces of contrasting veneers are available in assortments for marquetry.

Small orders of full veneers supplied through the mail are usually rolled for shipping. Small pieces of veneer, such as burls or curls, are generally packed flat – but they can also be sent with a package of rolled veneer, in which case they may be dampened to allow them to bend without breaking. Since veneers are fragile, open a rolled package carefully, so that it doesn't spring open and cause damage. End splits are not uncommon in veneer. Repair them promptly with gummed paper tape (particularly light-colored woods) to prevent dirt from entering.

If the veneer remains curled after unpacking, dampen it with steam, spray it, or pass it through a tray of water, then press it flat between sheets of chipboard. Change to fresh, dry boards every few days until the veneer is dry, or mildew may develop. Store veneers flat and protect them from dust and strong light, as wood is light-sensitive and can lighten or darken according to the species.

Burl or burr veneer
Burls or burrs are abnormal growths on the trunk of a tree. Burl veneers display an attractive pattern of tightly packed bud formations that appear as rings and dots. They are the most expensive type of veneer and are highly prized for furniture and small woodwork. Burl veneers are supplied in irregular shapes and various sizes, from 6 × 4in (150 × 100mm) to about 39in (1m) long by 18in (450mm) wide.

Butt veneer
Butt veneers are cut from the stump, or "butt," of certain trees. Highly figured veneers, caused by the distorted grain, occur by back cutting on a rotary lathe.

Colored veneer
Artificially colored veneers have been available for centuries. Light-colored woods, such as maple, are used. "Harewood" is chemically treated maple that turns silver-gray to dark-gray. Dyes are used to produce other colors, the veneer being pressure-treated for maximum penetration.

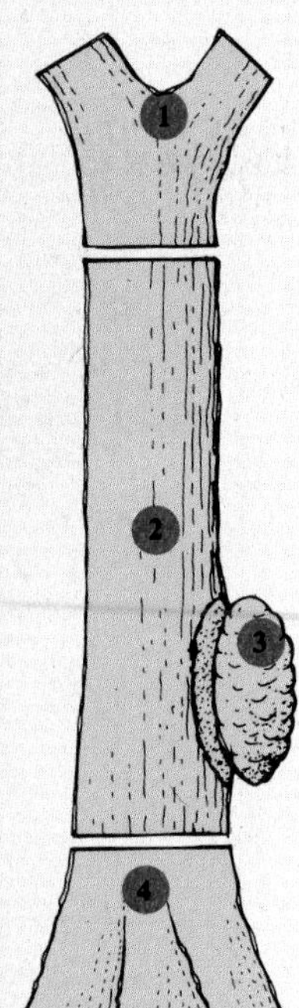

Parts of the tree used for veneers
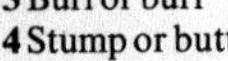
1 Crotch
2 Trunk
3 Burl or burr
4 Stump or butt

1
2
4

Examples of commercially available veneers
1 Thuya burl
2 Black walnut butt veneer
3 Chemically colored "harewood"
4 Dyed veneer
5 Crown-cut walnut
6 Curly-figured "fiddleback" veneer
7 Mahogany feather
8 Masur birch
9 Bird's-eye maple
10 Quilted willow
11 Quarter-cut "lacewood"
12 Quarter-cut "ray-fleck" oak
13 Stripe-figured zebrano
14 Ribbon-figured ayan

Crown-cut veneer
Tangentially cut flat-sliced veneer is known as "crown-cut." It displays an attractive figure of bold sweeping curves and ovals along the center of the leaf, with striped grain nearer the edges. Crown-cut veneer is produced in lengths of 8ft (2.4m) or more and in various widths, ranging from about 9in (225mm) to 2ft (600mm), depending on the species. It is used for furniture and wall paneling.

Curly-figured veneer
Wavy-grained woods produce veneers with bands of light and dark grain running across the width of the leaf. "Fiddleback" sycamore maple is a typical example. The wood gets its name from its use for violin backs.

Crotch veneer
This veneer is cut from the "crotch" or "fork" of a tree where the trunk divides. When the crotch is sliced perpendicularly to form two Ys, an attractive figure is revealed. The distorted diverging grain produces a lustrous upward-sweeping plume pattern known as "feather figure." It is available in sizes from 12 to 39in (300mm to 1m) long and 8 to 18in (200 to 450mm) wide.

Freak-figured veneer
Hardwood logs with irregular growth may be rotary-cut to produce veneer displaying various patterns. Bird's-eye maple and masur birch are examples. Irregular-grained woods can also produce veneer with "blistered figure" and "quilted figure."

Ray-figured veneer
Woods such as oak and sycamore have striking figure when quarter-cut. The distinct ray cells in oak produce "ray-fleck" or "splash" figure. Quarter-cut sycamore veneer is known as "lacewood."

Striped veneer
Quarter-cut veneers usually display a striped figure where the radial cut is taken across the width of the growth rings. A different kind of stripe, called "ribbon" veneer, occurs on woods that grow with interlocked reverse-spiral grain. The stripes of ribbon veneer appear to change from light to dark, depending on the angle they are viewed from.

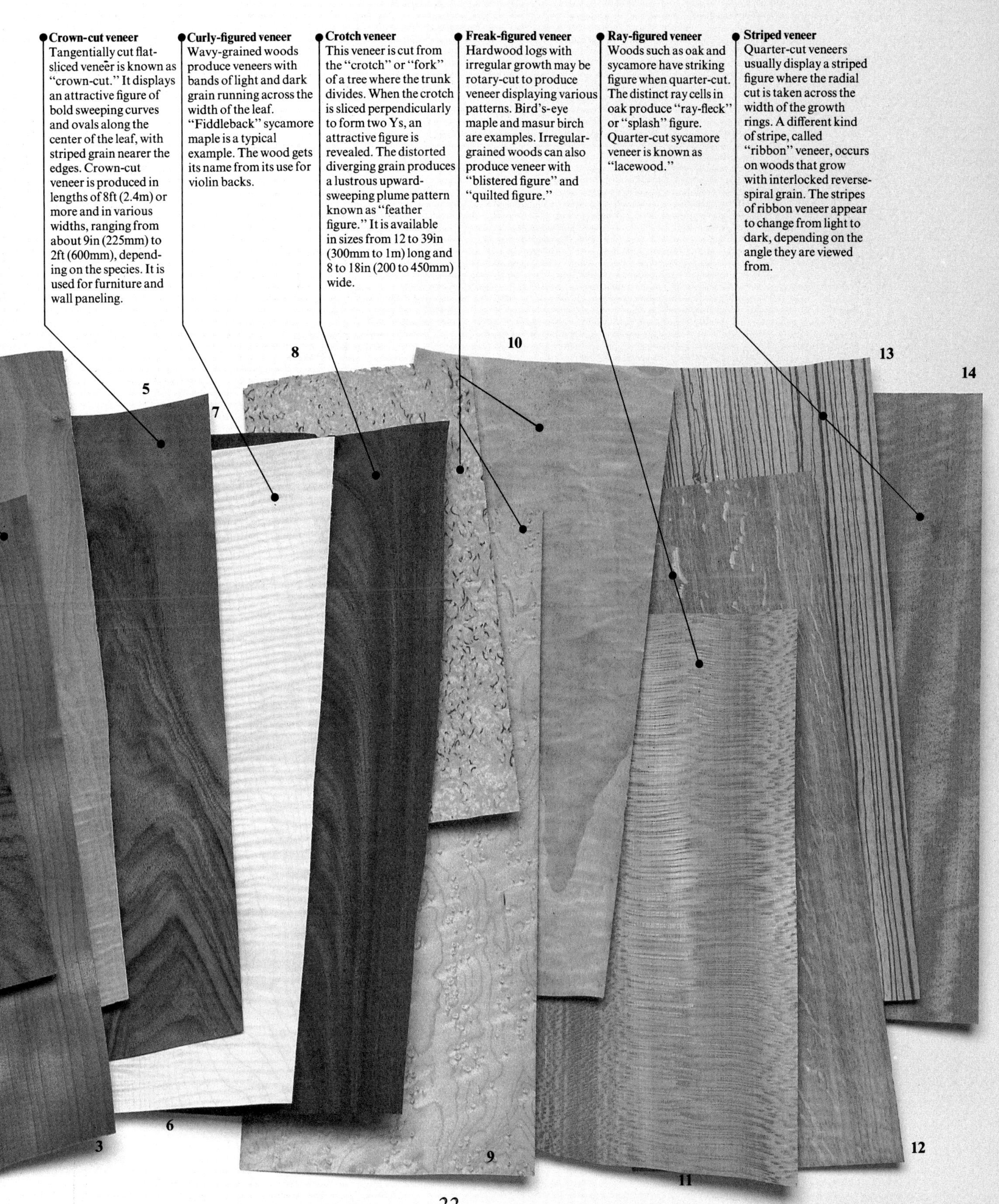

MAN-MADE BOARDS

Man-made boards are relatively new and have been taken up enthusiastically by industry and the home woodworker alike. Board manufacturers are constantly developing their products with a view to improving quality, economy of raw materials and ease of working. Consequently, there is a wide range of boards available today. These fall into roughly three categories: laminated boards, particleboards and fiberboards. As new products are introduced, some kinds of laminated boards, such as solid-core blockboard, may be replaced by cheaper particleboard and fiberboard types.

SEE ALSO

Softwoods	16-19
Hardwoods	20-29
Cabinet construction	63,65,70
Board joints	246-247
Working man-made boards	248

PLYWOOD

Plywood is a laminated material made from thin sheets of wood known as construction veneers, plies or laminates, that are bonded in layers to form a strong stable board. Laminating wood was a technique known to craftsmen in ancient times, but plywood is a relatively modern material first produced commercially around the mid-nineteenth century. Its panel size, stability and ease of working made it a useful material for interior joinery and carcase construction, but it was not until the development of waterproof adhesives in the 1930s that it found a place in the construction industry.

Plywood construction

A board of solid wood is relatively unstable and will shrink or swell to a greater degree across the fibers than it will along them. In so doing it is also likely to distort, depending on how it is cut from the tree. The tensile strength of wood is greatest following the direction of the fibers, but it will also readily split with the grain.

Plywood is constructed with the fibers or grain of alternate plies set at right angles to one another to counter movement of the wood. This produces a stable warp-resisting board that has no natural direction of cleavage. The greatest strength of a panel is usually parallel to the face grain.

Most plywood is made with an odd number of plies to give a balanced construction, three being the minimum. The number varies according to the thickness of the plies and the finished board. Whatever the number, the construction must be symmetrical about the center ply or the centerline of the panel thickness.

The surface veneers of a typical plywood board are known as "face plies." Where the quality of one of the outer plies is better than the other, the better ply is called "the face" and the other "the back." The grade of the face and back plies is usually specified by a letter code. The perpendicularly laid plies immediately beneath the face plies are known as "cross-bandings." The center ply (or plies) is known as "the core."

Sizes

Plywood is made in a wide range of sizes. The thickness of commercially available plywood generally ranges from $\frac{1}{8}$in (3mm) to $1\frac{3}{16}$in (30mm), in approximately $\frac{1}{8}$in (3mm) increments. Thinner "aircraft plywood" is available from specialist suppliers.

The typical width of a board is 4ft (1.22m), but 5ft (1.52m) boards are also available. The most common length is 8ft (2.44m), although boards up to 12ft (3.66m) are made. The dimensions are expressed in imperial or metric measurements depending on the source of manufacture or supply.

The grain of the face ply usually follows the longest dimension of the board, but not always. Grain may run parallel to the first dimension quoted by the manufacturer or supplier. Thus a 4 × 8ft (1.22 × 2.44m) board will have the grain running across the width. Ask if your supplier follows this system.

BONDING

The performance of plywood is determined not only by the quality of the plies but also by the type of adhesive used in its manufacture. Plywoods can be grouped according to usage.

Interior plywood

Plywoods of this grade should be used only for non-structural interior applications. They are generally produced with an appearance-grade face ply and a poorer quality for the back.

Interior plywoods are manufactured with urea-formaldehyde adhesive, which is light in color. Most boards are suitable for use in dry conditions, such as furniture or wall paneling. Modified adhesive employed in the manufacture of certain types of board affords them some degree of moisture resistance, enabling them to be used in areas of high humidity. Never use interior-grade plywood for exterior applications.

Exterior plywood

Exterior-grade plywoods can be used for fully or semi-exposed conditions (depending on the quality of the adhesive), where structural performance is not required.

Boards suitable for fully exposed conditions are bonded with dark-colored phenol-formaldehyde (phenolic) adhesive. This type produces "weather and boil proof" (WBP) plywood. WBP adhesives comply with an established standard and systematic tests, as well as their record in service over many years, have proved them to be highly resistant to weather, micro-organisms, cold and boiling water, steam and dry heat.

Exterior-grade plywoods are also produced using melamine urea-formaldehyde adhesive. This type of board is semi-durable under exposed conditions.

Exterior-grade plywood is a good material for kitchen cabinets and for applications around showers or bathrooms.

Marine plywood

Marine plywood is a high-quality face-graded structural plywood primarily produced for marine use. It is constructed from selected plies from a limited range of mahogany-type woods. Marine ply has no "voids," or gaps, and is bonded with a durable phenolic (WBP) adhesive. It can also be used for interior cabinets.

Structural plywood

Structural or engineering-grade plywood is manufactured for applications where strength and durability are the prime consideration. It is bonded with phenolic resin adhesive. An appearance-grade face ply of a lower quality is used, and the boards may not have been sanded. Many of these plywoods are "pressure treated" with chemical salts to retard rotting.

TYPES OF PLYWOOD

Different types of plywood are produced for such diverse applications as agricultural installations, aircraft and marine construction, structural building work, interior cabinets, toys and furniture. Performance and suitability of application depend on species of wood, type of bond and grade of veneer.

Plywood boards are manufactured in many parts of the world and the species of wood used varies according to place of origin. The face veneers and core may be made from different species or the boards may be constructed from the same species throughout.

Softwood boards are commonly made from Douglas fir or various species of pine; common hardwood types from light-colored temperate woods such as birch, beech and basswood. Tropical woods used for plywood construction include lauan, meranti and gaboon, all of which are red in color.

APPEARANCE GRADING

Plywood manufacturers use a coding system to grade the quality of the plies used in the manufacture of their boards.

A typical system uses the letters A, B, C, C-plugged and D. The A grade is the best quality, being smooth-cut with virtually no defects. The D grade is the poorest, having the maximim amount of permitted defects, such as knots, holes, splits and discoloration.

The letters quoted or stamped on the board refer to the appearance of the face plies only and do not indicate the structural performance of the board. An A-A grade plywood has two good faces, while a B-C board has poorer-grade outer plies (the better B grade being the face and the C grade the back). Decorative plywoods are faced with selected matched veneers, and are referred to by the face veneer.

Decorative plywood is faced with selected flat-sliced or quarter-cut matched veneers, usually of hardwoods such as afrormosia, beech, cherry or oak, and is mainly used for paneling. A balancing veneer of lesser quality is applied to the back of the board.

Three-ply board has the face veneers bonded to a single core veneer. Their thickness may be the same, or the core may be thicker to improve the balance of the construction. This type is sometimes called "balanced" or "solid-core" plywood. Thin three-ply boards are used for drawer bottoms and cabinet backs.

Drawer-side plywood is the exception to the cross-banding construction method. This type has the grain of all the plies running in the same direction. It is made of hardwood to a nominal thickness of ½in (12mm) and is used for drawer sides in place of solid wood.

Multi-ply has a core consisting of an odd number of plies. The thickness of each ply may be the same, or the cross-banded ones may be thicker. This helps give the board equal stiffness in its length and width. It is a good material for use in making veneered furniture.

Four-ply and six-ply Four-ply has two thick-cut plies bonded together, with their grain in the same direction and perpendicular to the face plies. This type is stiffer in one direction and is usually used for structural work. Six-ply (shown here) is similar to four-ply in construction but has the core parallel to the face, with cross-banded ply in between.

BLOCKBOARD AND LAMINBOARD

Blockboard is a form of plywood, being of laminated construction. It differs from conventional plywood in that the core is constructed from strips of solid wood cut approximately square in section and edge-butted, but not glued. The core is faced with one or two layers of ply on each side.

Laminboard is similar to blockboard but the core is constructed from narrow strips approximately $\frac{3}{16}$in (5mm) wide, which are usually edge-glued.

SEE ALSO

Cabinet construction	63,65,70
Home workshop	210-211
Veneering	258-270
Wood screws	304-305
Knock-down fittings	308

Laminboard
is superior to blockboard for veneer work, as the core is less likely to show through. It is also more expensive. Boards of three-ply and five-ply construction are produced. The plies of the five-ply type may either be perpendicular to the core or cross-banded.

Blockboard
is a stiff material suitable for furniture applications, particularly shelving and worktops. It makes a good substrate for veneer work, but the core strips can "telegraph" (i.e. show through). It is made in panel sizes similar to plywood, in thicknesses ranging from $\frac{1}{2}$in (12mm) to 1in (25mm). Thicker boards of three-ply are made up to $1\frac{3}{4}$in (44mm).

PARTICLEBOARDS

Wood-particleboards are made from small chips or flakes of wood bonded together under pressure. Various types are produced according to the shape and size of the particles, their distribution through the thickness of the board and the type of adhesive used to bind them together. Softwoods are generally used, although a proportion of hardwood material is sometimes included.

Types of board

Particleboards are stable and uniformly consistent materials. Those constructed with fine particles have featureless surfaces and are highly suitable as groundwork for veneer. A wide range of preveneered decorative boards using wood, paper foil or plastic laminates are available. Most particleboards are relatively brittle and have a lower tensile strength than plywood.

Chipboard

Most types of particleboard of interest to the woodworker are of interior quality, commonly known as chipboard. Chipboard, like other wood products, is adversely affected by excess moisture – the board swells in its thickness and does not recover when dried. However, moisture-resistant types suitable for flooring or wet conditions are made.

STORING AND USING BOARDS

Storing boards
To save space, store boards on edge. Make a rack to keep the edges clear of the floor and support the boards evenly at a slight angle. When storing thin boards, support the full area of each board with a thicker board underneath.

Using boards
Screws attached to the edges of man-made boards are not as strong and secure as those attached to the face.

Drill pilot holes in the edge of plywood to prevent splitting. The diameter of the screws used should not exceed 25 percent of the board's thickness.

Blockboard and laminboard will hold screws well in the side edges, but not in the end grain.

Screw holding in chipboard depends on the density of the board. It is usually relatively weak, but special chipboard screws hold better than standard wood screws. Always drill pilot holes, both for face screws and edge screws. Use special fastenings or inserts for improved holding.

Single-layer-chipboard is made from a mat of similar-sized particles evenly distributed throughout. It has a relatively coarse surface. This type is suitable for wood veneer or plastic laminate, although not for painting.

Three-layer chipboard has a core layer of coarse particles sandwiched between two outside layers of fine high-density particles. The outer layers contain a higher proportion of resin, which produces a smooth surface suitable for most finishes.

Graded-density chipboard has surfaces of very fine particles and a core of coarser particles. Unlike layered types, there is a gradual transition from the coarse particles to the fine surface.

Decorative chipboard is manufactured with a facing of selected wood veneer, plastic laminate or a thin melamine foil. The wood-veneered boards are sanded ready for polishing; the foil-faced and plastic-laminated boards need no finishing. Some plastic-laminated boards for worktops are made with finished profiled edges, while matching edging strips are available for lipping melamine-faced and wood-veneered boards.

Oriented-strand board is a three-layer material made from long strands of pine. The strands in each layer are laid in one direction, and each layer is perpendicular to the next in the same manner as plywood.

Flakeboard or waferboard uses large shavings of wood that are laid horizontally and overlap one another. These boards have greater tensile strength than standard chipboard.

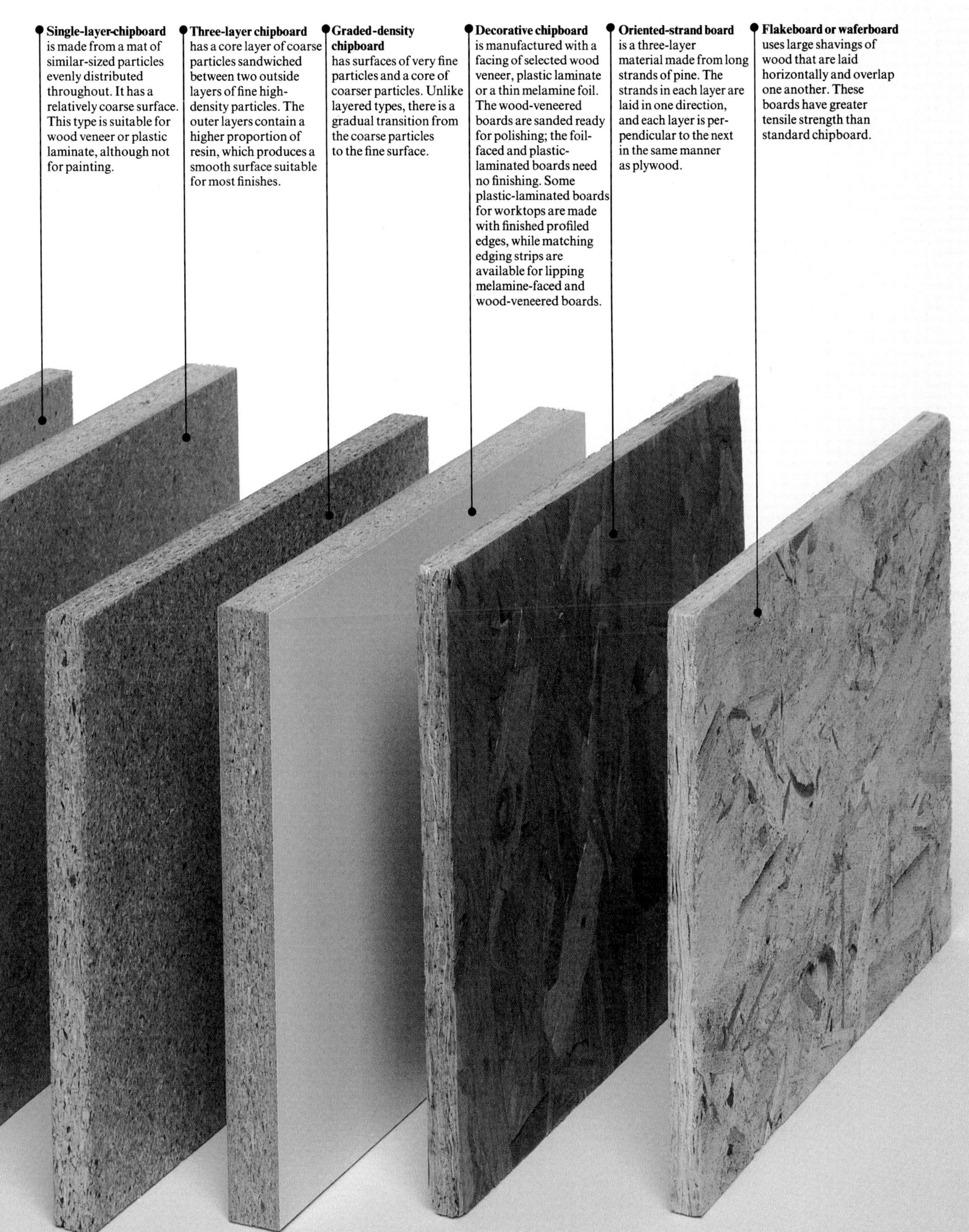

FIBERBOARDS

Fiberboards are made from wood that has been reduced to its basic fiber elements and reconstituted to make a stable homogeneous material. Boards of various density are produced, according to the pressure applied and the adhesive used in their manufacture.

SEE ALSO
Cabinet construction 63,65,70

Hardboards

Hardboard is a high-density fiberboard produced from wet fibers pressed at high pressure and temperature. The natural resins in the fibers are used to bond them together.

Tempered hardboard is a standard-density board that has been impregnated with resin and oil to produce a stronger material that is water- and abrasion-resistant.
Standard hardboard has only one smooth face. It is made in a wide range of thicknesses from $\frac{1}{16}$ to $\frac{1}{2}$in (1.5 to 12mm). A cheap material, it is commonly used for drawer bottoms and cabinet backs.
Duo-faced hardboard is similar to standard hardboard but has two smooth faces.
Decorative hardboard has a molded or lacquered surface.
Pegboard accepts removable hooks and fixtures.

Medium boards

Medium boards are made in a similar way to hardboard. They are produced in two grades. Low-density (LM) board, $\frac{1}{4}$ to $\frac{1}{2}$in (6 to 12mm) thick, is used for pinboard or wall paneling. High-density (HM) board is stronger and is used for interior paneling.

Medium-density fiberboard (MDF) is a fiberboard with two smooth faces manufactured by a dry process. The fibers are bonded together with a synthetic resin adhesive. It has a uniform structure and a fine texture that allows the edges and faces to be cleanly profile-machined.

This type of fiberboard can be worked like wood and can be used as a substitute for solid wood in some applications. It makes an excellent substrate for veneer and takes paint well. MDF boards are made in thicknesses of $\frac{1}{4}$ to $1\frac{1}{4}$in (6 to 32mm) and in a wide range of panel sizes.

Medium boards
1 High-density (HM) board
2 Low-density (LM) board
3 Medium-density fiberboard (MDF)
4 Oak-veneered MDF board

Hardboards
5 Standard hardboard
6 Tempered hardboard
7 Embossed hardboard
8 Decorative-faced hardboard
9 Pegboard

1 2 3 4

8 9

5 6 7

CHAPTER TWO

DESIGNING IN WOOD

Designing in three dimensions requires the ability to visualize how an object will eventually look before you actually make it. The design process is never easy, and if you are working with unfamiliar forms or materials, it becomes even more complex than usual. Indeed, you may find it is often necessary to construct a series of prototypes in order to evaluate every design decision and to make sure the object you are designing will function satisfactorily. However, even if you are a beginner, you can draw on the experience and expertise accumulated by generations of craftsmen-designers. This chapter looks at the various questions a designer needs to consider, including structure, safety and intended use, as well as aesthetic and decorative considerations. Also included are sketches illustrating the basic principles of chair, table and storage-unit construction, which you can use as a source of ideas and as a guide to the various practical aspects of furniture design, such as choice of joints and order of assembly.

THE DESIGN PROCESS

New forms or concepts are rarely dreamed up out of thin air. If you look back over the history of furniture design, for example, you will detect a gradually evolving pattern as woodworkers learned to deal with the inevitable movement of solid wood responding to humidity. You will see how techniques were modified as a result of changing technology, and how the appearance of furniture was influenced by contemporary taste. But the rate of change was slow. The majority of woodworkers were artisans, rather than designers in the modern sense. They would continue to make familiar objects, using the same tools, methods and materials as their fathers and grandfathers, knowing exactly what the results would be. Only the most fashionable workshops were producing innovative designs, for clients wealthy enough to pay what we today call development costs. These innovations had to be tried and tested before they became part of the average workman's repertoire. A modern-day woodworker could do a lot worse than follow this example while acquiring the basic skills of designing in wood. No one wants to stifle originality or discourage woodworkers from developing their creative talents, but it would be perverse to ignore that wealth of experience simply to avoid copying what's been done previously. Before attempting to break new ground, a designer should endeavor to understand how his or her chosen material behaves, appreciate how the finished item is to function and avoid visual gimmickry.

SEE ALSO

Designing a comfortable chair	50
Stick chairs	54
Designing a functional table	55
Designing storage	61
Strengthening shelves	62

FUNCTION

Much is talked about designing for function, but to understand what that means, one has to examine the concept from several angles. A solid block of wood can function as a stool, but a well-designed stool is something else. A bar stool supports a seated human being and so does a milking stool – yet they have completely different functions and, consequently, different dimensions. Should a stool be light enough to be portable – or should it, in a public building, be bolted to the ground to prevent it from being toppled, blocking a fire-escape route? Should a stool be adjustable in height? Should it fold for storage? Will it tip easily when someone shifts their weight? A designer has to pose questions of this nature to define how an object is to function, then provide a design solution based on real requirements, as opposed to preconceptions. Even then, the solution will almost certainly to some extent be a compromise. An elegant solution is one that comes close to answering all the questions – it will seldom, if ever, be perfect.

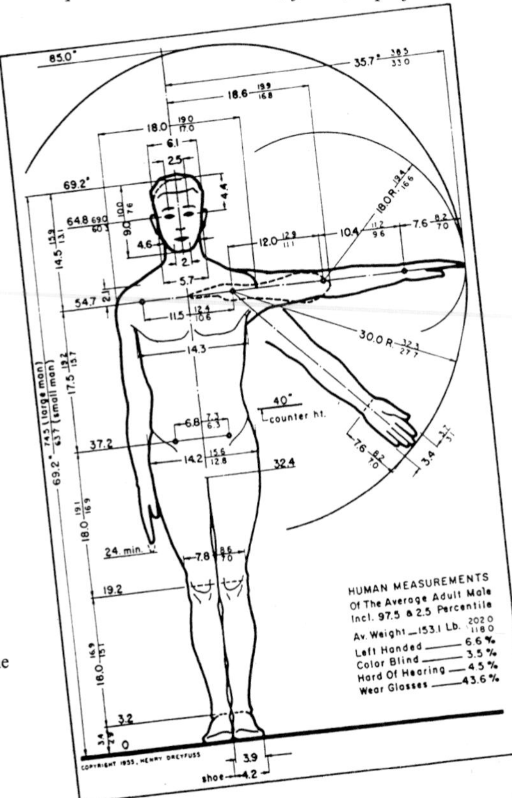

The average human
The American designer Henry Dreyfuss pioneered the study of anthropometrics. His book *Designing for People* provides us with detailed dimensions of the average male and female.

Designing for people
In order to be functional, most items of woodwork have to relate in some way to the human body. As a species, we differ widely in size, shape and weight – so when designing a chair for an individual, you need to take careful measurements of that person's anatomy before you can be sure the chair will be comfortable. However, anthropometry and ergonomics – the statistical sciences concerned with the comparative study of the human body and how it relates to its environment – provide designers with the optimum dimensions for furniture and work stations that suit people of average height and build. Most people are reasonably comfortable using furniture based on these dimensions, but if you are making something for a specific group of people, such as children or the elderly, you may have to create custom-built artifacts tailored to their needs. Specific anthropometric data is given where appropriate throughout this chapter.

Adaptability
Designing something to be adaptable increases its usefulness. Bunk beds that convert to two full-size beds – especially welcome in a family with growing children – are a good example of built-in adaptability. An ergonomic typist's chair is designed to be comfortable for people of any stature; and a draw-leaf table is an example of compactness coupled with flexibility. In a bookcase, adjustable shelves are more useful than fixed ones; and in a cupboard, simple drawers, sliding trays or baskets may give a greater degree of versatility than rigid compartments.

Structural requirements
Nothing functions well or lasts long unless it is properly constructed. A table that rocks when you are cutting your steak is annoying; a desk top that vibrates while you're typing is distracting; and a chair that suddenly collapses is positively dangerous, as well as being a nuisance.

A wooden structure can support considerable weight without noticeable distortion, provided it is designed to counteract the stresses and strains of normal use.

The leg frame of a traditional Windsor chair illustrates the principle perfectly. The four legs are plugged into the underside of a solid seat. Horizontal stretcher rails not only prevent the legs from bending under load, but also stop them from sliding apart. The angles at which the components meet are such that they reinforce one another against shifting forces, mainly because a straight pull is never exerted on any of the joints. And if the chair is tipped onto its splayed back legs, they are ideally placed to support the additional weight at that angle. The structure is, in fact, superbly suited to its intended purpose.

An overloaded shelf sags and may eventually break because of the combination of compression and tension. But if you cut off a 2in (50mm) strip, turn it through 90 degrees and glue it to the underside of the shelf, it will be able to support more weight without bending – by turning the strip on edge you have constructed an effective beam. The rails supporting a table top or chair seat perform a similar function.

The load on a beam is transferred to whatever is supporting it at each end – the legs of a table or chair, for example. The joints between the rails and legs must be capable of resisting shear forces (the downward pressure of the load being opposed by the rigid supports). Shear forces are increased considerably when sideways pressure is applied to a structure, exerting leverage on the joints. A strong dowel joint or the tongue of a mortise and tenon is able to cope with this leverage, especially if the rail is deep enough to provide decent shoulders for the joints and if glued corner blocks are used to reinforce the structure on the inside of the rails.

The joints of a cabinet or a box are especially vulnerable to sideways pressure, which causes the frame to "rack," forming a parallelogram. However, a rigid back panel, vertical pilasters or corner plates will prevent movement in the joints and create a rigid structure. A built-in plinth or shelf-support rails will achieve the same purpose, while metal-strip cross-bracing prevents racking by tying opposite diagonal corners together.

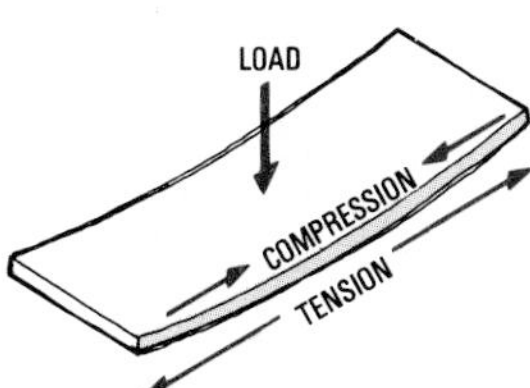

The effects of load on a shelf

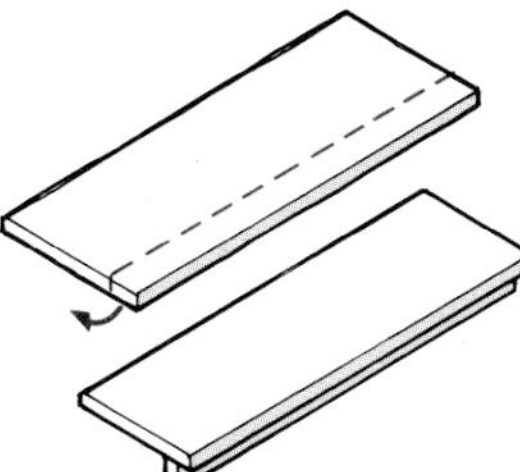
A strip on edge provides support

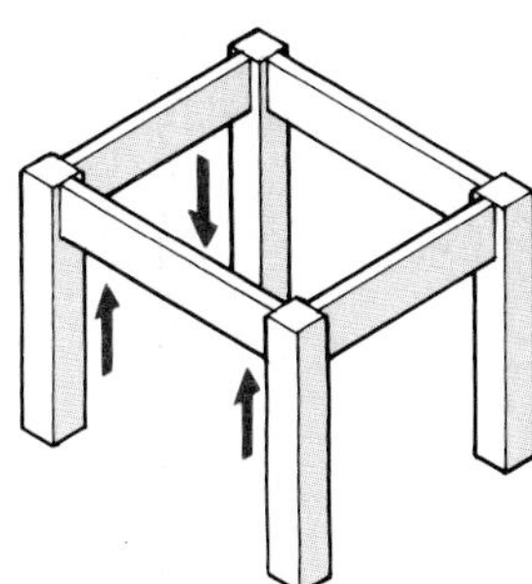
Legs oppose the load on a rail

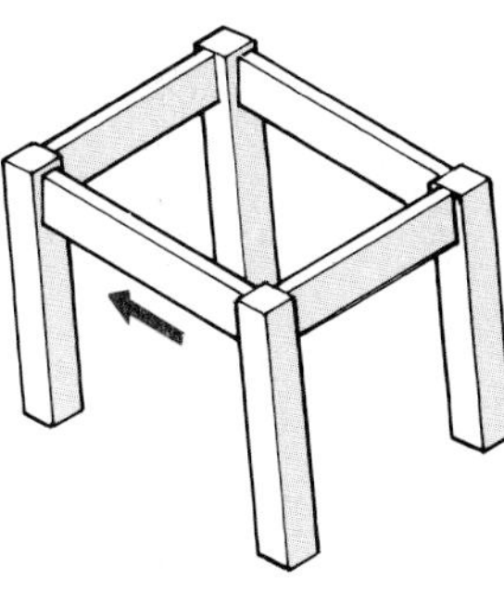
Sideways pressure exerts leverage on the joints

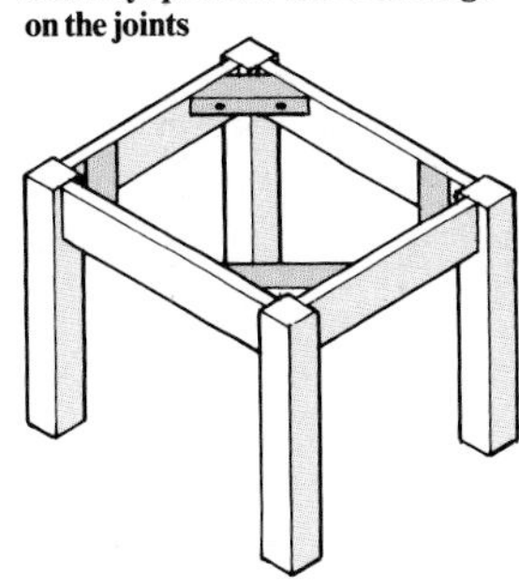
Strong joints and corner blocks hold the frame rigid

The traditional Windsor chair
The underframe components are ideally placed to counteract the stresses and strains imposed by normal use.

The near-perfect back rest
An ergonomic back rest is both beautiful and comfortable.

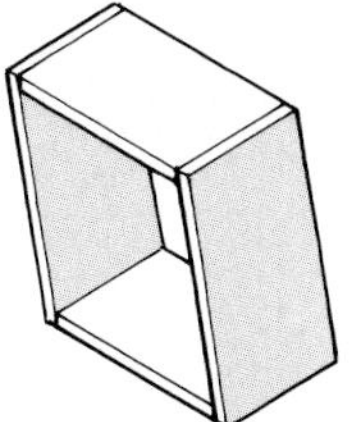
An unsupported box will collapse

Making a box rigid
To create a rigid structure, the joints of a box or cabinet must be reinforced using one of the following methods.

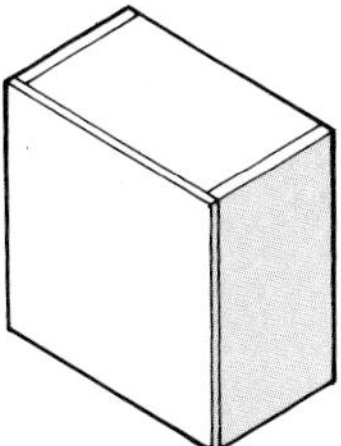
Rigid back panel

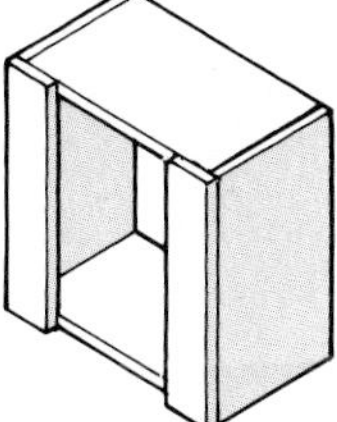
Vertical pilasters

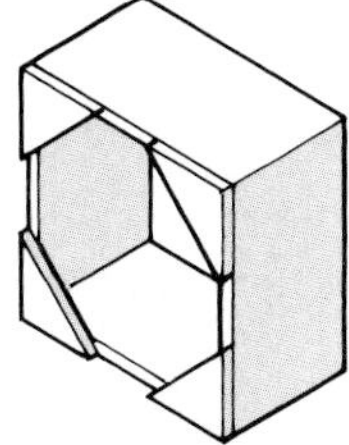
Corner plates

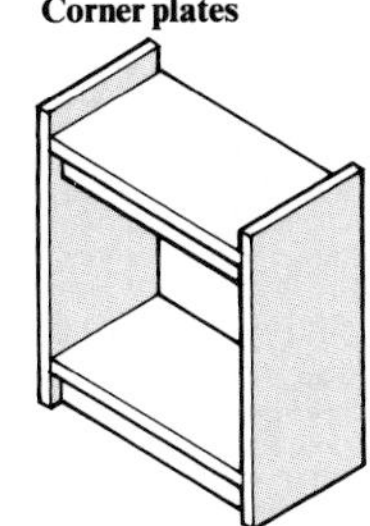
Plinth and shelf rails

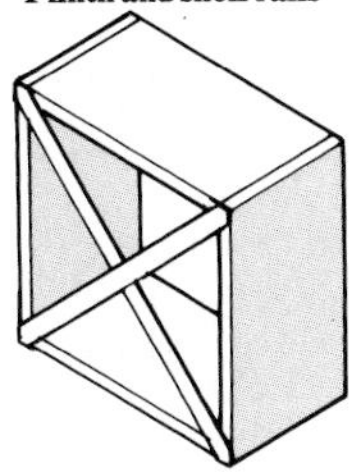
Cross-bracing

DESIGNING FOR SAFETY

If it is possible to misuse something, you can be sure someone will eventually do so. People often stand on the flimsiest of chairs or use the stretcher rails as a ladder to reach the top shelf of a bookcase, and tipping a chair onto its back legs after dinner is a common abuse. Even though a chair is not built for such purposes, you should take them into consideration as part of the design process and, if possible, modify your design to minimize the risk of an accident occurring.

SEE ALSO

Soft/hardwoods	10-29
Drying wood	13
Man-made boards	34-38
Attaching table tops	56
Frame-and-panel construction	66,70
Lopers	67
Fall-flap stays	67,310
Knobs and handles	310

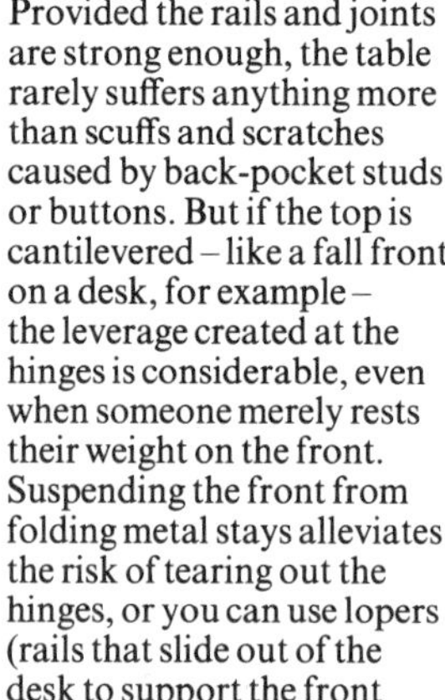

The effect of leverage
Levering a door against a drawer can pull it off its hinges.

The effects of leverage
People often sit on tables. Provided the rails and joints are strong enough, the table rarely suffers anything more than scuffs and scratches caused by back-pocket studs or buttons. But if the top is cantilevered – like a fall front on a desk, for example – the leverage created at the hinges is considerable, even when someone merely rests their weight on the front. Suspending the front from folding metal stays alleviates the risk of tearing out the hinges, or you can use lopers (rails that slide out of the desk to support the front from below). Both methods move the pivot point forward, away from the hinge line toward the outer edge of the front, thus decreasing the leverage.

If the door of a sideboard or kitchen unit is allowed to swing toward a tier of drawers next to it, it is only a matter of time before the corner of a drawer that has not been pushed home acts as a fulcrum to pull the door off its hinges. If you cannot alter the position of the door or drawers, use stays to stop the door from opening further than 90 degrees.

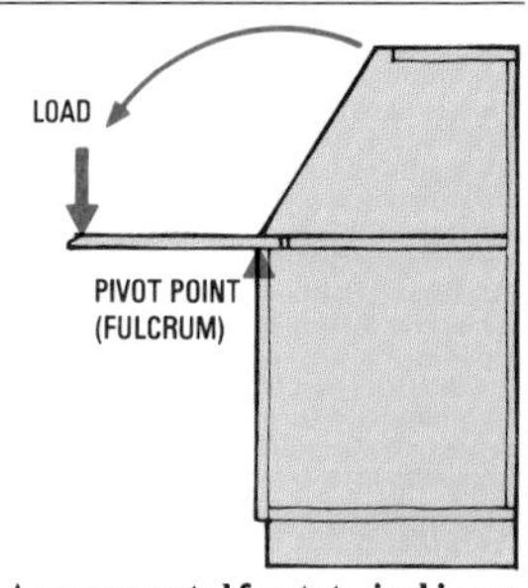

An unsupported front strains hinges

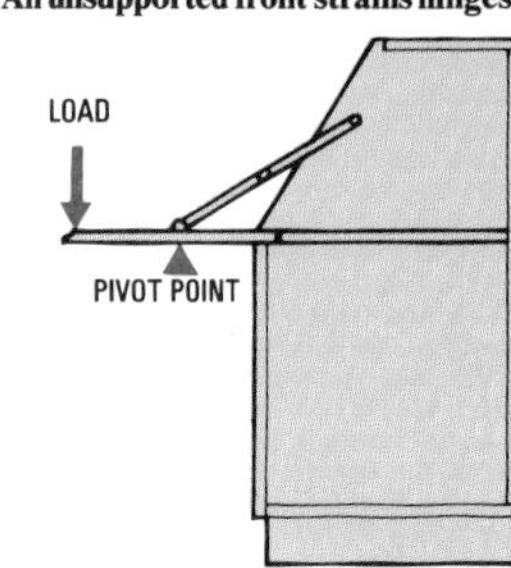

Folding stays decrease leverage

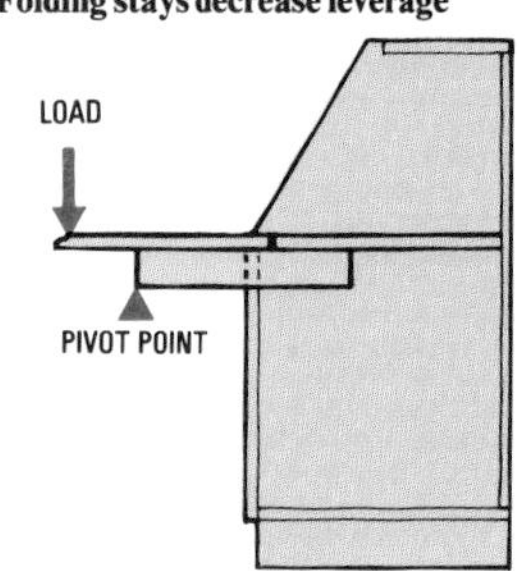

Lopers have a similar effect

Stability
A piece of furniture may be stable under normal circumstances, but ask yourself whether it can be easily toppled. A dining chair will be stable, provided its center of gravity remains within the area defined by the four points where the legs meet the floor **(1)** – but if leaning against the back rest moves the center of gravity outside that area **(2)**, the chair becomes unstable and will topple. For this reason, the back legs of a chair are often made to slope **(3)** so the chair will remain safely balanced even when tipped slightly backward **(4)**.

A chest of drawers can become dangerously unstable if all the drawers are open at the same time. However, a short cabinet with a wide base has a relatively low center of gravity and will maintain its equilibrium unless it is toppled deliberately. A taller cabinet may have to be screwed to the wall or floor. Similarly, large heavy doors that would cause a freestanding wardrobe to topple are usually made to slide, instead of being hinged.

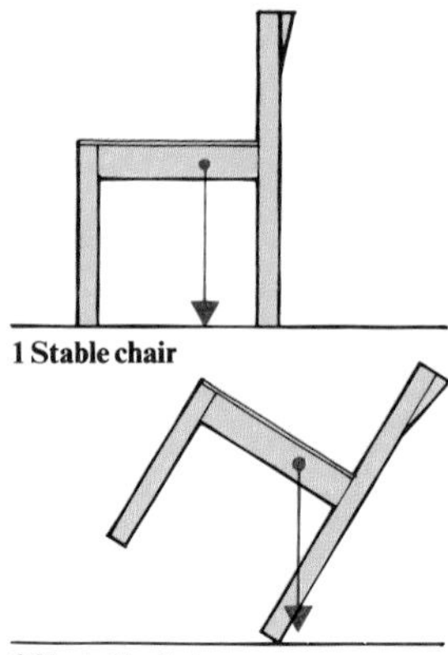

1 Stable chair

2 Unstable chair

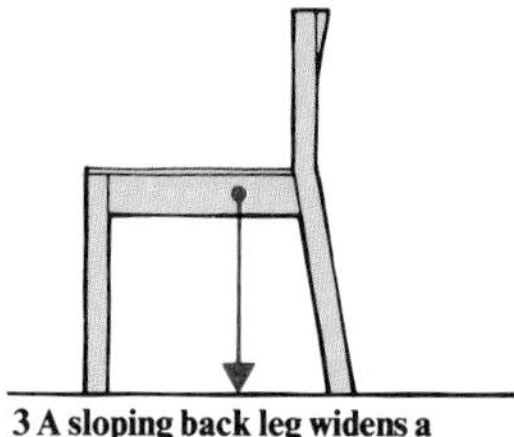

3 A sloping back leg widens a chair base

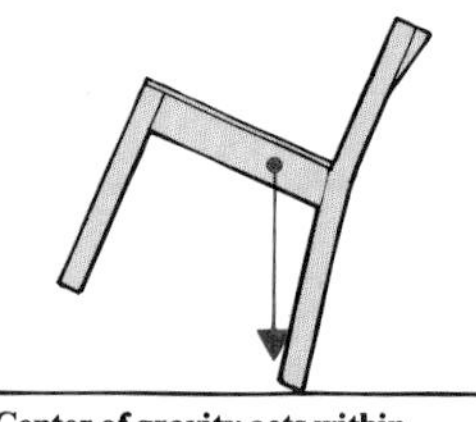

4 Center of gravity acts within base area

Oak bureau
Pull-out lopers housed in the underframe (below) support a leather-lined fall front (center).

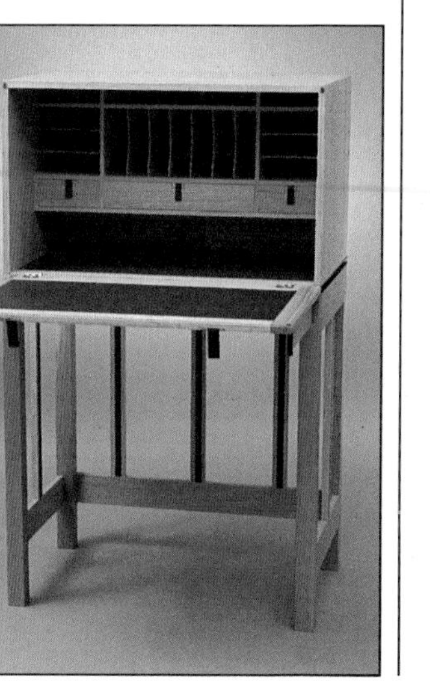

Splayed-leg chair
The wide base of this robust armchair prevents it from being toppled accidentally.

DESIGNING WITH WOOD IN MIND

Avoiding hazardous details

Even small details can cause serious injuries. Think twice about leaving sharp edges or corners, especially if they are at a level where children may fall against them. Glass table tops are especially dangerous in this respect. A round top is relatively safe, provided all the sharp edges are removed by polishing, but it is advisable to enclose a rectangular glass top within a rabbeted frame.

Sharp edges are even worse if they close with a scissor action. Trapping your fingers between a heavy inset lid and the side of a box is painful, to say the least; but the consequences of a similar accident with a folding chair collapsing under your weight can be far more serious.

A swiveling desk chair with arms constitutes a less obvious risk. There should be sufficient clearance for your knuckles between the underside of the desk top and the chair arms if you are to avoid an unpleasant surprise as you swivel the chair in order to stand up.

Sharp projecting handles can tear clothing, even though they may not cause actual physical harm, so choose smooth rounded knobs and handgrips or fit flush or drop handles.

Safe detailing
Integral drawer handles can be a safe yet striking feature.

In principle, most factors relating to function and safety are applicable no matter what material you are using, but when designing with wood in mind, you need to take into consideration the fact that wood continues to absorb and exude moisture according to the humidity of its immediate surroundings, regardless of when it was cut from the tree. If you take a 100-year-old chest of drawers from an unheated room and stand it next to a radiator, it will still dry out; and if you return it to its original environment, it will absorb moisture from the air. The problem for the woodworker is the dimensional changes that accompany these exchanges of moisture – wood shrinks as it loses water and expands when it absorbs it again. If this movement is restricted in any way, the wood will split or warp. Allowing for this movement to occur without detriment to the work is another aspect of the designer's job.

Allowing for movement

The differential movement that occurs within even a single piece of wood often causes problems.

Due to the grain structure of wood, a solid board will shrink or expand to a greater extent across its width than along its length (**1**). If you make a box from four pieces of similar wood, joining them at the corners so that all four pieces have their grain running in the same direction, they will move together by exactly the same amount and no damage or distortion will occur (**2**).

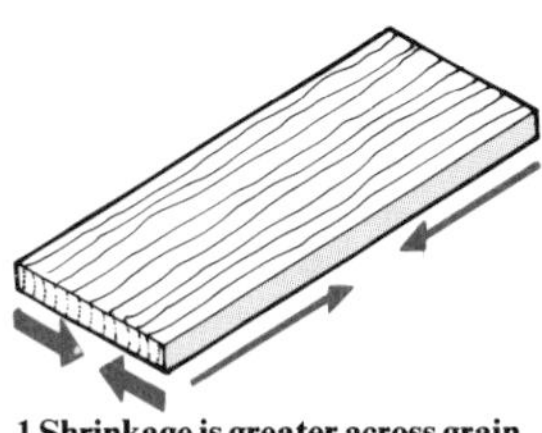

1 Shrinkage is greater across grain

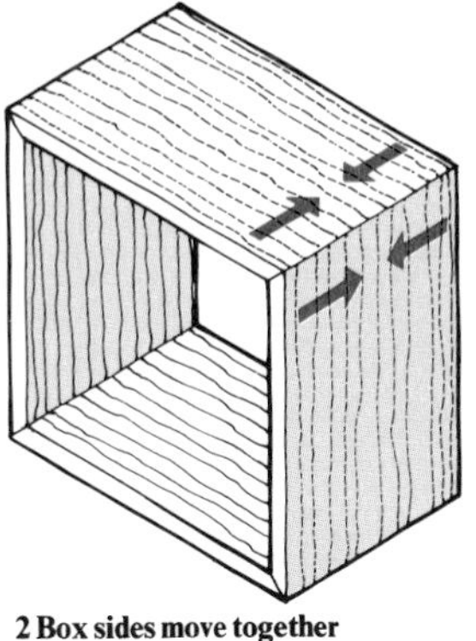

2 Box sides move together

If you attach other components rigidly with their grain running contrary to the wood grain of the box's sides, they restrict the natural movement across the box until the resulting stresses are relieved by splits opening along the grain (**3**). The solution is to devise a way of attaching the components with fastenings such as slotted screws that allow for an element of movement.

A common safeguard against movement in thin solid-wood panels is to locate them in grooves – they should never be glued in place. This is the principle employed in traditional frame-and-panel construction.

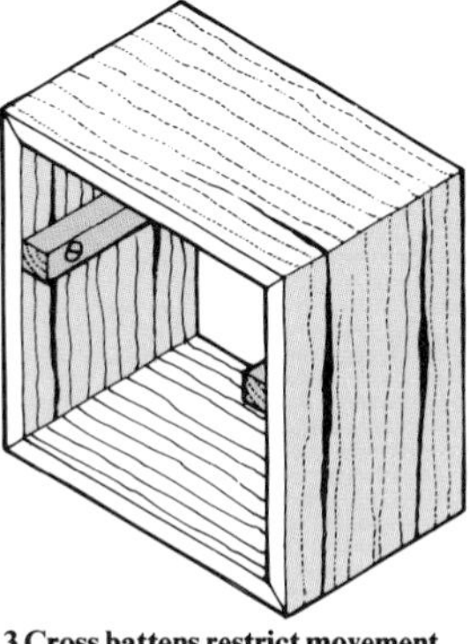

3 Cross battens restrict movement until splits relieve the stresses

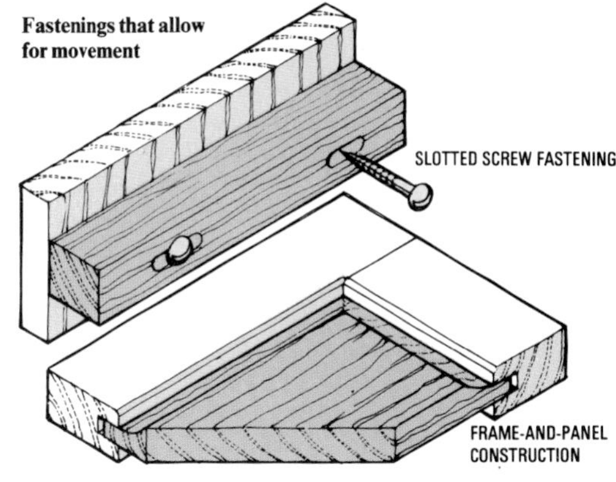

Fastenings that allow for movement

Disguising the effects of movement

An experienced designer uses some form of visual distraction whenever he or she anticipates that wood movement will affect the detailing of a workpiece. An inset drawer front may fit like a glove when it leaves the bench, but an unsightly gap can open up all around after only a few months. A narrow molding attached to or cut around the edges of the drawer front or surrounding frame is enough to disguise the gap (**1**).

Alternatively, you can make a feature of a gap from the outset, knowing that it is going to occur in any case. For example, the movement between the boards of tongue-and-groove paneling is imperceptible due to the strong linear pattern created deliberately by the open joints (**2**).

The edge of a table top planed flush with the underframe may look beautifully crisp at first, but the effect is spoiled as soon as the top shrinks (**3**). A rabbet cut in the top or rail creates a strong shadow-line so the movement is indiscernible (**4**). Alternatively, let the top overhang the rail (**5**) or mold and set back the edge from the face of the rail (**6**).

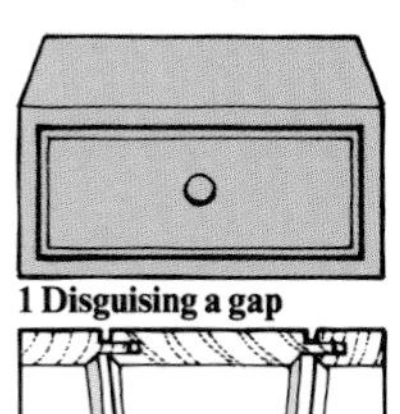

1 Disguising a gap

2 A deliberate feature

3 Shrinkage spoils the effect of a flush top

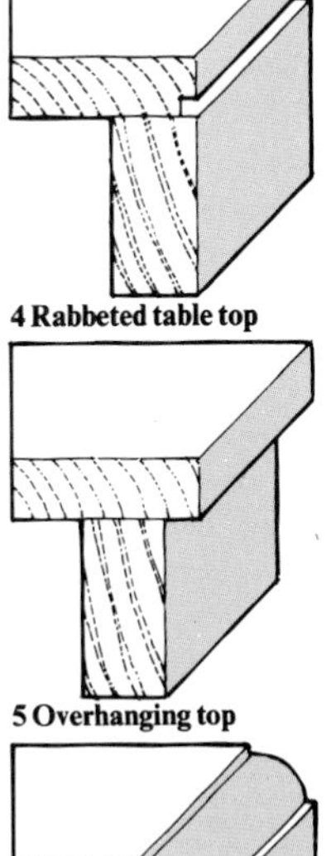

4 Rabbeted table top

5 Overhanging top

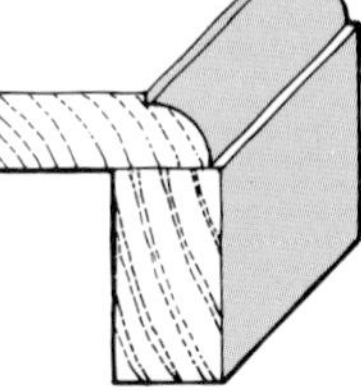

6 Set-back table top

Avoiding the problem

It is perfectly acceptable for a designer to select stable man-made boards for table tops or cabinet construction to avoid the problem of shrinkage that occurs in solid-wood panels.

DESIGNING FOR APPEARANCE

It might seem reasonable to suppose that the appearance of a piece you are designing should be largely determined by the selection of optimum dimensions and by those features or mechanical devices that combine to make the end product function as well as possible. Indeed, the overused maxim "Form follows function" is based on that premise. In reality, it is too simplistic a view. Designers go to great lengths in order to get something to look its best. They will tinker with its proportions, take time to select the piece of wood that will enhance its appearance and incorporate moldings, carvings, inlays or shaped components, all to increase its visual appeal. In short, the appearance of a piece of work is just as important as its pure function, but it is virtually impossible to be objective about the aesthetic merits of any design. The only solution is to develop your own sense of what is pleasing and what is most likely to be acceptable.

SEE ALSO

Soft/hardwoods	10-29
Veneers	30-33
Plywood	34-35
Finger joints	163,208
Inlays	265-266,297
Wood carving	272-282

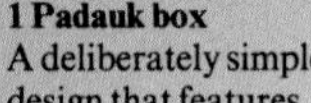

1 Padauk box
A deliberately simple design that features square-knuckle hinges cut from solid wood.

2 Hexagonal boxes
They are machined from solid Indian rosewood with burl-veneered lids.

3 Dominoes
African-blackwood dominoes inlaid with maple "spots."

4 One-piece box
A small decorative box cut from yew.

Antique-style Pembroke table
Copying genuine antiques is one way to ensure your work fits a period interior perfectly.

Traditional oak tool cabinet
A beautifully proportioned tool cabinet that seems almost too good for the workshop.

1

2

3

4

Suitability

How is it that we can appreciate the quality of a simple undecorated stick or Windsor chair yet find a fine carved Sheraton-style dining chair equally appealing? They could hardly be more different in appearance. One possible reason is the way we envisage them in totally different settings – in the rooms for which they were originally designed. Stick chairs would look ridiculous beside a highly polished table in an elegantly decorated dining room, while a Sheraton-style chair would look equally out of place in a country kitchen. Swap them around, and each fits naturally into its intended environment.

It is necessary to anticipate how and where an object is going to be used – then design it accordingly, selecting the appropriate woods, shapes, proportions and finish to achieve the desired result. Although some people have a talent for combining furniture and fittings of all styles and periods, it is certainly easier if you reflect the style and decor of the intended location. This doesn't mean you have to reproduce period furniture or fittings: If you use similar materials and detail, your design will at least be in harmony with its surroundings.

Veneered cabinet
A simple yet decorative cabinet for a modern interior. It is made from stained and painted maple.

Caned dining chair
Narrow edges to legs and seat rails add delicacy to a sturdy dining chair.

Carved wooden bowls
Cut and carved from solid cherry, rosewood and walnut, these bowls are decorated with precise fluting.

5

6

5 Nine men's morris
A game board made from burl-elm veneer inlaid with rosewood and brass. The pieces are turned from boxwood and cocobolo.

6 Pencil holder and bowl
Both items are made from thin birch plywood held with padauk buttons.

SIMPLICITY AND DECORATION

SEE ALSO

Soft/hardwoods	10-29
Veneers	30-33
Jointers/planers	180-185
Lathes	192-203
Joint making	216-248
Veneering	258-270
Wood carving	272-273
Finishing wood	284-294
Other materials	296-300

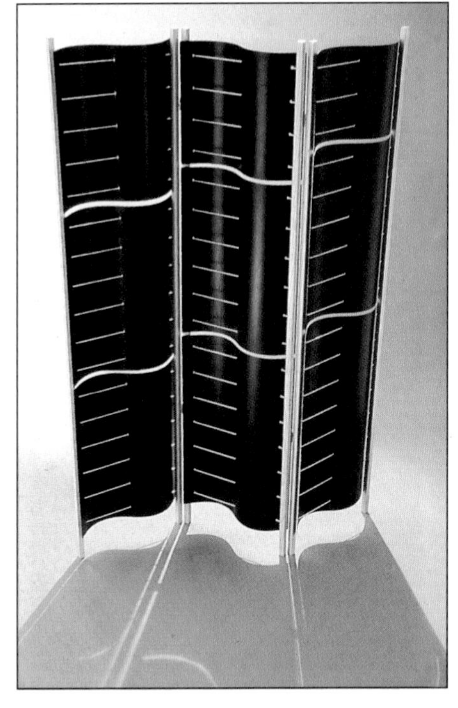

Folding screen
Constructed largely from bent-plywood panels, this folding screen is an attractive combination of black lacquer, ash and stainless steel.

London-plane cheval mirror
A stylish full-length pivoting mirror is surrounded by pigeon-hole storage compartments.

Aiming for simplicity

If there is no designated location for a piece you are making, it is best to aim for simplicity so it will look right in virtually any setting. But don't be misled into thinking this is an easy option. Professional designers spend years honing their skills in order to achieve the subtlety required to reduce a piece of work to its bare essentials and to arrive at precise proportions upon which the aesthetic qualities of the design will stand or fall. Moreover, making a simple workpiece requires craftsmanship of a high standard – since, when there is not the slightest embellishment to distract the eye, defects such as a less-than-perfect finish, imprecise joints or clumsy detailing may well become noticeable at a glance.

Including decoration

As previously described, moldings are often used to disguise the effects of shrinkage, and carving can be used to texture a surface that would otherwise have to be finished immaculately. This was a common ploy in the days when all woodwork was produced by hand; but now that machines are available to alleviate the chore of planing and sanding flat surfaces, designers tend to employ decoration purely for richness of effect. Exotic veneers, for example, are used exclusively for their decorative qualities, as are marquetry, parquetry and wood or metal inlays.

With imagination, you can exploit virtually any aspect of woodworking for visual impact. Indeed, skilled craftsmen sometimes design pieces specifically to focus attention on exquisitely made finger joints or decorative dovetails – deliberately creating features for fellow woodworkers to admire.

Decorative detailing
Padauk-veneer inserts interrupt the line of a laminated cherry lipping.

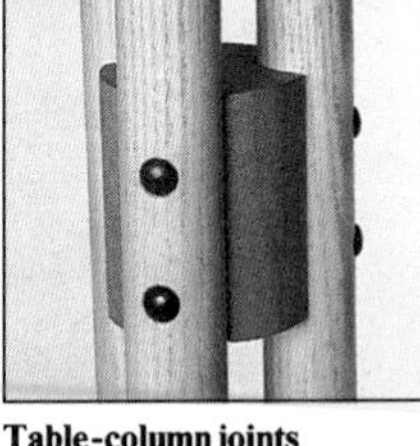

Table-column joints
Even simple joints can be enhanced by the careful selection of colored woods.

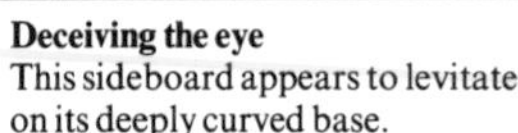

Deceiving the eye
This sideboard appears to levitate on its deeply curved base.

Refined simplicity
An ash tripod table that reflects the classic tradition for elegant drawing-room furniture.

The bare essentials
Stacked pivoting drawers and a rectangular top constitute a desk devoid of superfluous detail.

COLOR, TEXTURE AND ILLUSION

Color and texture

Selecting the right wood may be all that is needed to upgrade a mundane work-piece, but combining wood with other materials provides further opportunities to delight the eye. The cool, smooth texture of glass or marble can make a pleasing contrast to a rich grain pattern, and the gleam of polished brass fittings or inlay may add to the appeal of a dark-colored wood.

The choice of surface finish can transform the appearance of a piece significantly. Stains and clear finishes enhance any wood's depth of color, and then there is the difference between the reflective qualities of a matt finish and a gloss varnish. There are also endless possibilities for the application of pure color in the form of sprayed or brushed paint.

Creating optical illusions

If you are not satisfied with the exact proportions of a piece or want to make it appear lighter or heavier than it really is, you can use detailing to create the desired effect.

Adding a deep lipping to a shelf or the edge of a panel suggests solidity and mass without significantly increasing its weight. Conversely, applying a linear molding or inlay to a deep rail makes it look thinner.

You can lend elegance to a thick table top by cutting wide shallow bevels on the underside so that only a thin edge is visible all around. Tapering the legs of a table will make it look taller and lighter, and a deep curve cut in the underside of a plinth rail gives a lift to a heavy-looking sideboard or chest of drawers.

Even the texture and tone of the wood used for a piece can affect the way we perceive it. A large expanse of dark wood may dominate a room, whereas a paler tone is less obtrusive. A wild grain pattern can introduce a sense of vigor, while the striped nature of radial-cut veneer is more tranquil.

Richly decorated occasional table
Marquetry combines color and texture for a table top (right) on turned pear and wenge legs.

Decorative joint
This original laminated-oak leg joint is both strong and distinctive.

Eye-catching color
This freely painted table is an example of how color can be used to make a unique workpiece.

Turned bowl
Flaming the workpiece partway through the turning process accentuates the natural color and texture of an elm burl.

SEE ALSO

Soft/hardwoods	10-29
Veneers	30-33
Lathes	192-203
Laminated bending	254-256
Veneering	258-270
Wood carving	272-273
Glass	298-299

Freestanding cabinet
Derived from an original concept, this "tower" cabinet is accessible from two sides.

Duck-pond table
Dipping ducks support a glass table top that represents the surface of water.

DEVELOPING YOUR OWN STYLE

Developing a visual style that stamps their work with their own individuality is surely the ultimate goal of most craftsmen-designers. In order to be distinctive, your style does not have to be flamboyant or eccentric. For instance, you may draw your inspiration from a recognized historical style – not copying pieces faithfully in every detail, but using the essence of that style as a starting point or spring-board for your own ideas. On the other hand, it may be that a particular method of production holds a special fascination for you and has a strong influence on the forms and shapes you create. Designing for the woodturning lathe, for example, or using only curved components made from laminated veneers are both ways of channeling your thoughts and energies in a definite direction.

Perhaps the most difficult approach of all is deliberately setting out to break the rules. Challenging preconceived notions of what something is supposed to look like takes imagination and skill, as well as the courage to pull it off successfully. We take it for granted that storage units usually stand against a wall, but it is perfectly possible to make a freestanding unit with access from all sides. By convention, most tables have four legs, but a three-legged table would look arresting and, incidentally, be more stable on an uneven floor. And why take up valuable floor space with a bed when it may be possible to suspend it from the ceiling? Addressing such questions will not always elicit original answers. You may be drawn back to the accepted ways of making things again and again simply because they happen to work best – but just occasionally you may hit upon the germ of an idea that will lead to a truly original piece of work.

Nesting stools
Stained-ash stools that are designed to form an attractive group.

Laminated stools
A matching pair of stools with bowed side panels of laminated plywood bolted to solid cherry seats.

Veneered sideboard
A striking ash and rosewood cabinet with Art-Deco influences.

Walnut desk and chair
Made from solid walnut, this furniture is a comfortable blend of traditional and modern styles.

Chippendale-style chair
A carved mahogany dining chair.

Recliner and footstool
Flowing curves result from steam-bent components.

PRINCIPLES OF CHAIR CONSTRUCTION

The familiar upright dining chair has been with us for centuries in one form or another, and yet the basic design requirements remain unchanged. A chair must support the user in such a position that he or she can eat or work at a table comfortably and, if it has arms, sit down and get up without difficulty. It must be strong enough to bear the weight of the person yet light enough to be moved without effort. At first sight, it would appear to be a tall order but there are traditional "themes" to which every craftsman-designer returns to solve the problem. There are endless combinations, but the examples of chair construction that follow provide useful starting points from which to develop your own designs.

SEE ALSO

Inserting screws	119
Mortise & tenons	226-234
Dowel joints	236-237
Wood screws	304-305
Hinges	306-307

DESIGNING A COMFORTABLE CHAIR

To construct chairs that will be reasonably comfortable for the majority of the population, designers base their work on standard recommended dimensions, but to confirm the precise height, shape and angle of a chair's components, it may be necessary to make a mock-up of the critical elements or to test and modify certain details as the work progresses.

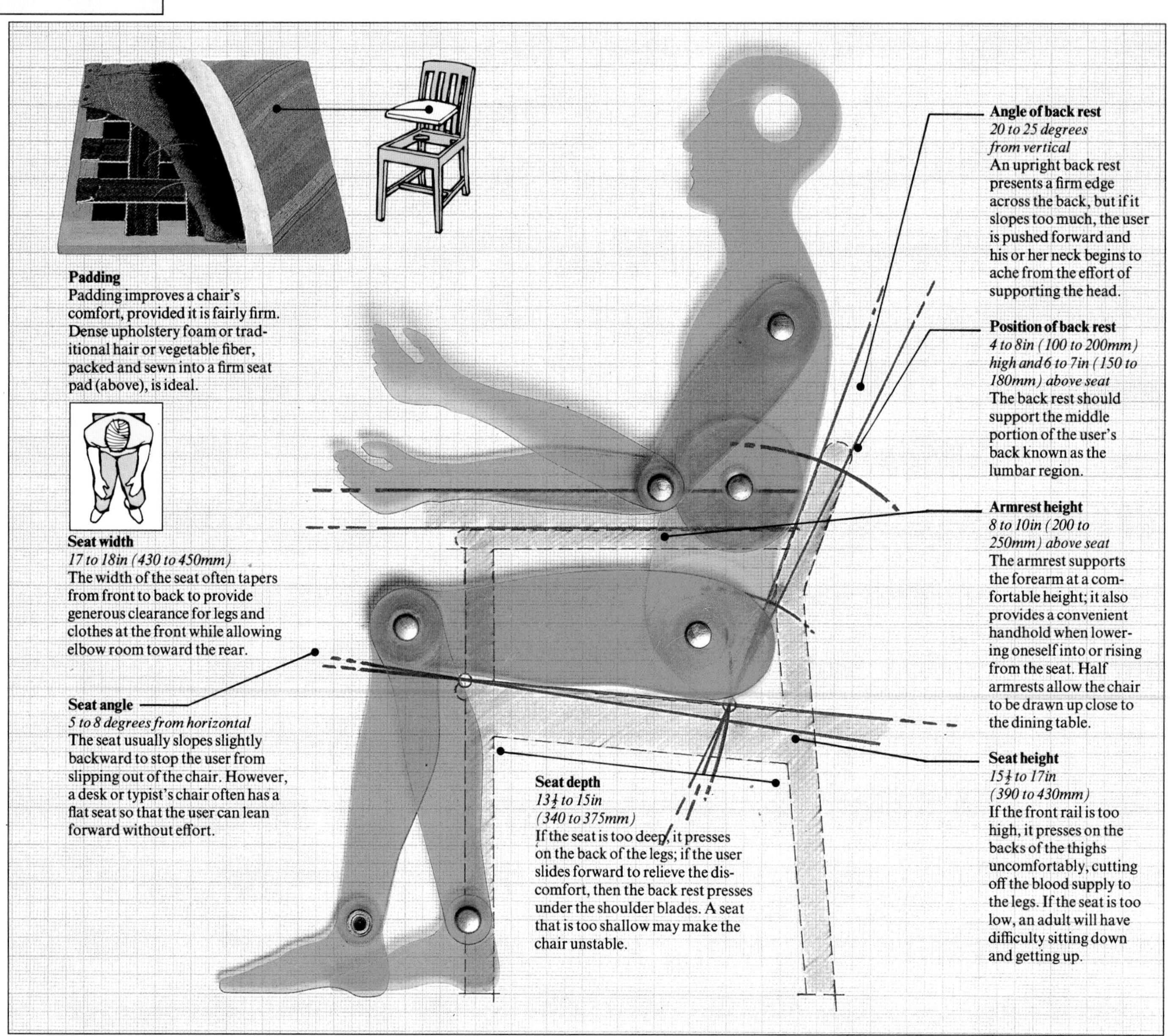

Padding
Padding improves a chair's comfort, provided it is fairly firm. Dense upholstery foam or traditional hair or vegetable fiber, packed and sewn into a firm seat pad (above), is ideal.

Seat width
17 to 18in (430 to 450mm)
The width of the seat often tapers from front to back to provide generous clearance for legs and clothes at the front while allowing elbow room toward the rear.

Seat angle
5 to 8 degrees from horizontal
The seat usually slopes slightly backward to stop the user from slipping out of the chair. However, a desk or typist's chair often has a flat seat so that the user can lean forward without effort.

Seat depth
13½ to 15in (340 to 375mm)
If the seat is too deep, it presses on the back of the legs; if the user slides forward to relieve the discomfort, then the back rest presses under the shoulder blades. A seat that is too shallow may make the chair unstable.

Angle of back rest
20 to 25 degrees from vertical
An upright back rest presents a firm edge across the back, but if it slopes too much, the user is pushed forward and his or her neck begins to ache from the effort of supporting the head.

Position of back rest
4 to 8in (100 to 200mm) high and 6 to 7in (150 to 180mm) above seat
The back rest should support the middle portion of the user's back known as the lumbar region.

Armrest height
8 to 10in (200 to 250mm) above seat
The armrest supports the forearm at a comfortable height; it also provides a convenient handhold when lowering oneself into or rising from the seat. Half armrests allow the chair to be drawn up close to the dining table.

Seat height
15½ to 17in (390 to 430mm)
If the front rail is too high, it presses on the backs of the thighs uncomfortably, cutting off the blood supply to the legs. If the seat is too low, an adult will have difficulty sitting down and getting up.

FRAME CHAIRS

The frame chair is the most versatile form of dining chair. The four rails of the seat frame are joined into a leg at each corner of the structure, while the back legs extend upward to form the main support of the back rest. The seat itself may be upholstered, caned, rush-covered or made from solid wood.

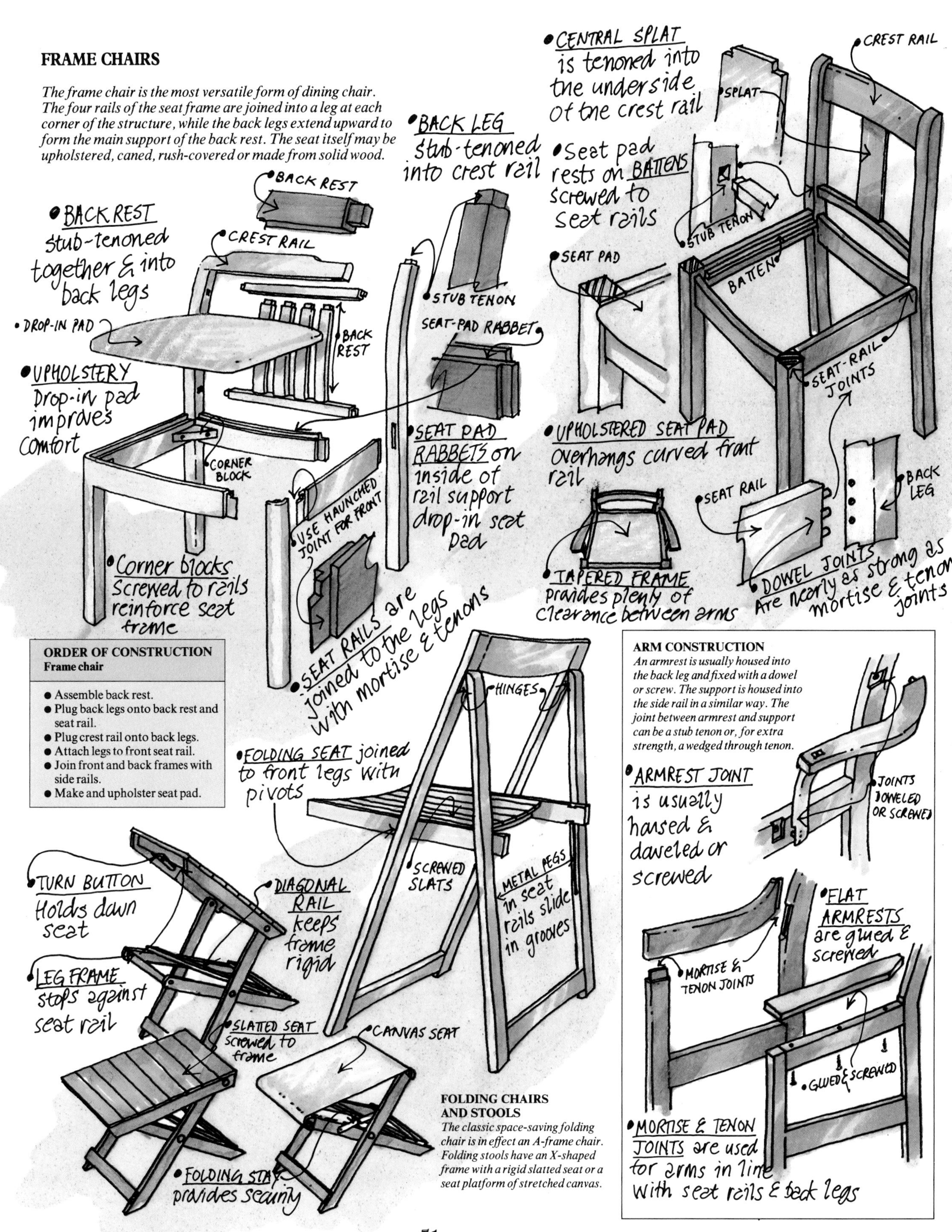

ORDER OF CONSTRUCTION
Frame chair

- Assemble back rest.
- Plug back legs onto back rest and seat rail.
- Plug crest rail onto back legs.
- Attach legs to front seat rail.
- Join front and back frames with side rails.
- Make and upholster seat pad.

ARM CONSTRUCTION

An armrest is usually housed into the back leg and fixed with a dowel or screw. The support is housed into the side rail in a similar way. The joint between armrest and support can be a stub tenon or, for extra strength, a wedged through tenon.

FOLDING CHAIRS AND STOOLS

The classic space-saving folding chair is in effect an A-frame chair. Folding stools have an X-shaped frame with a rigid slatted seat or a seat platform of stretched canvas.

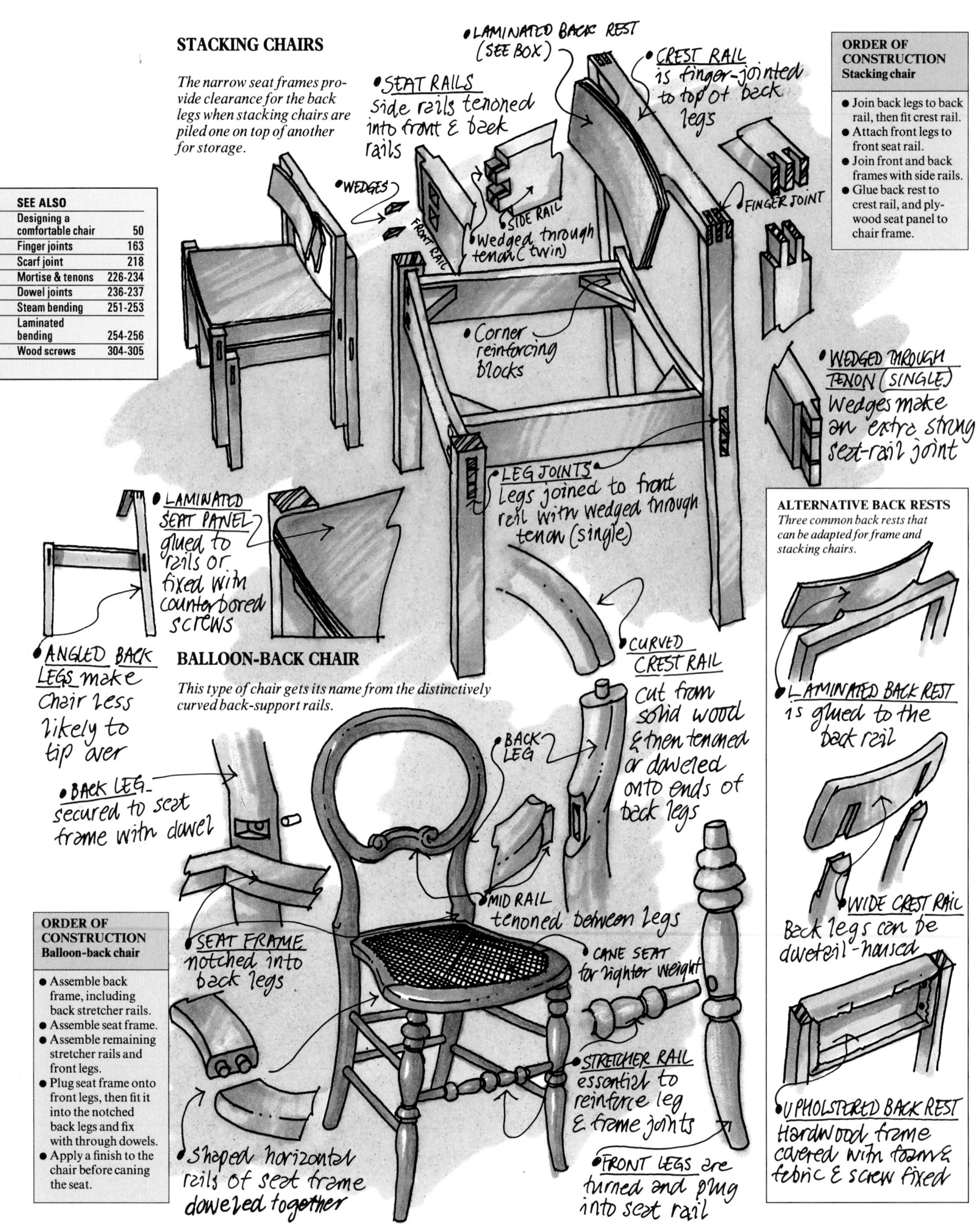

STACKING CHAIRS

The narrow seat frames provide clearance for the back legs when stacking chairs are piled one on top of another for storage.

SEE ALSO

Designing a comfortable chair	50
Finger joints	163
Scarf joint	218
Mortise & tenons	226-234
Dowel joints	236-237
Steam bending	251-253
Laminated bending	254-256
Wood screws	304-305

ORDER OF CONSTRUCTION
Stacking chair

- Join back legs to back rail, then fit crest rail.
- Attach front legs to front seat rail.
- Join front and back frames with side rails.
- Glue back rest to crest rail, and plywood seat panel to chair frame.

ALTERNATIVE BACK RESTS

Three common back rests that can be adapted for frame and stacking chairs.

BALLOON-BACK CHAIR

This type of chair gets its name from the distinctively curved back-support rails.

ORDER OF CONSTRUCTION
Balloon-back chair

- Assemble back frame, including back stretcher rails.
- Assemble seat frame.
- Assemble remaining stretcher rails and front legs.
- Plug seat frame onto front legs, then fit it into the notched back legs and fix with through dowels.
- Apply a finish to the chair before caning the seat.

BENTWOOD CHAIRS

Bentwood chairs are constructed by bolting and screwing together steam-bent components. This type of chair is extremely tough and resilient, provided the hardware is not allowed to work loose.

LAMINATED CHAIRS

Structurally weak short grain is avoided by making chair frames from thick laminated veneers. This type of structure is strong and resilient.

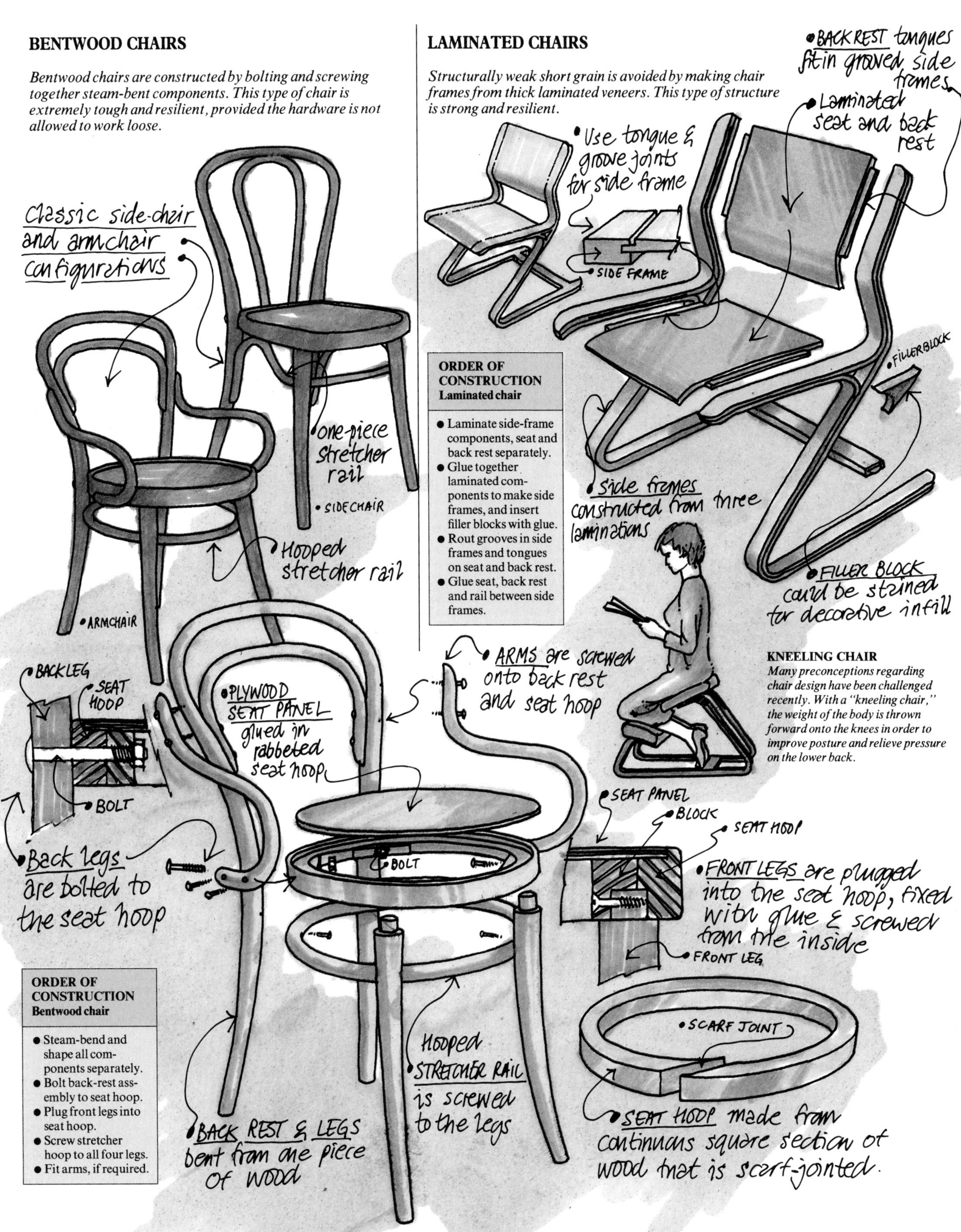

ORDER OF CONSTRUCTION
Laminated chair

- Laminate side-frame components, seat and back rest separately.
- Glue together laminated components to make side frames, and insert filler blocks with glue.
- Rout grooves in side frames and tongues on seat and back rest.
- Glue seat, back rest and rail between side frames.

KNEELING CHAIR

Many preconceptions regarding chair design have been challenged recently. With a "kneeling chair," the weight of the body is thrown forward onto the knees in order to improve posture and relieve pressure on the lower back.

ORDER OF CONSTRUCTION
Bentwood chair

- Steam-bend and shape all components separately.
- Bolt back-rest assembly to seat hoop.
- Plug front legs into seat hoop.
- Screw stretcher hoop to all four legs.
- Fit arms, if required.

STICK CHAIRS

The stick chair in its countless variations is a beautifully proportioned and functional piece of furniture that has evolved under the trained eye and experienced hands of craftsmen from all over Europe and America. Its strength and rigidity rely on the fact that the large number of components share the load in such a way that the forces applied to the structure do not attempt to pull it apart. Stick chairs have always been made from tough, dense native woods such as beech, oak, ash and elm, which can be softened with steam before being bent for the bow-back versions of the chair.

SEE ALSO

Designing a comfortable chair	50
Drawknives	109
Lathes	192-203
Wedged mortise and tenons	227
Adzes	274

ORDER OF CONSTRUCTION
Stick chair

- Assemble legs and stretcher rails.
- Lay seat board face down on a bench, then hammer legs into holes in the underside of the seat.
- Tap back spindles into seat board, then fit crest rail.
- Fit armrests and supports.

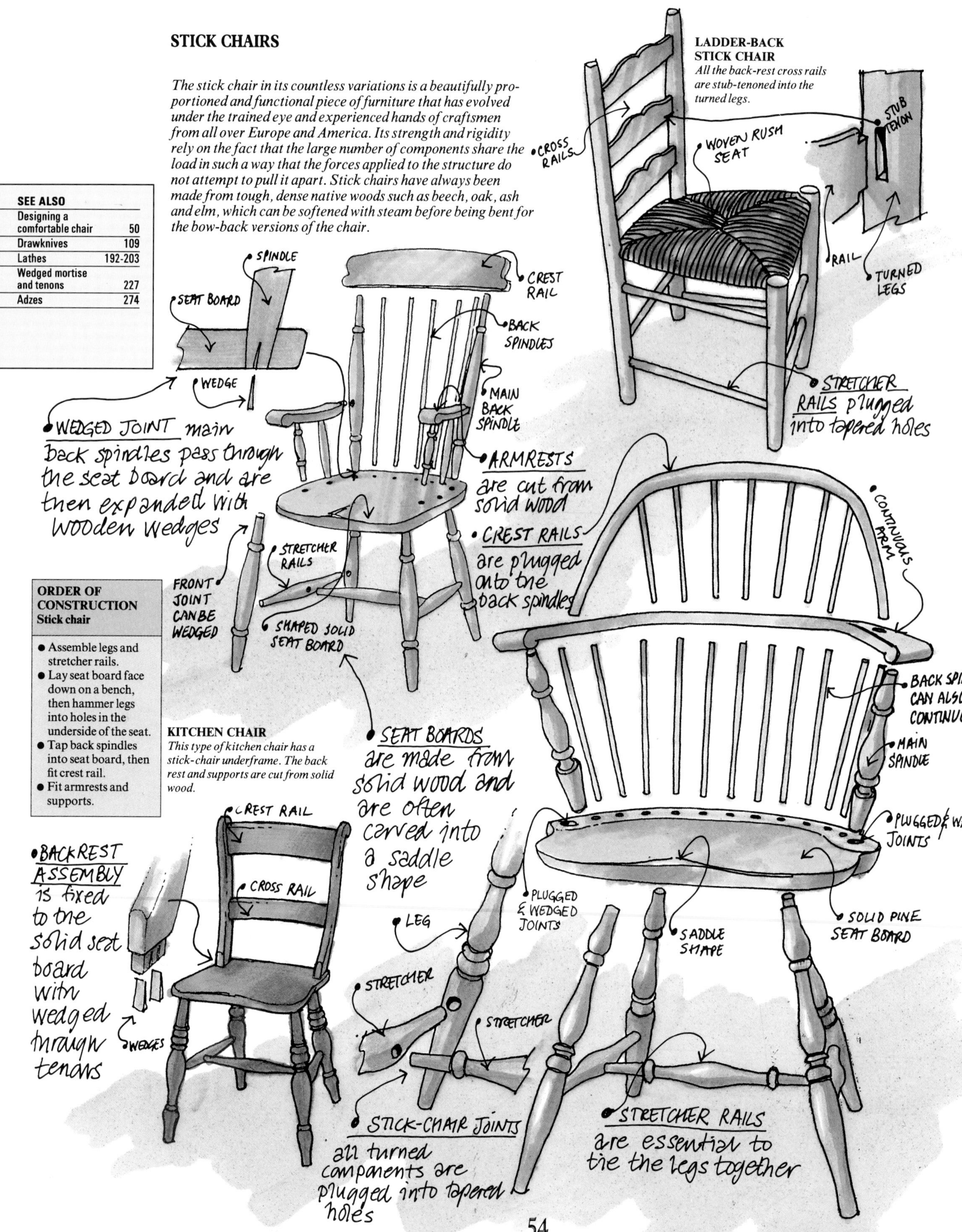

LADDER-BACK STICK CHAIR
All the back-rest cross rails are stub-tenoned into the turned legs.

KITCHEN CHAIR
This type of kitchen chair has a stick-chair underframe. The back rest and supports are cut from solid wood.

PRINCIPLES OF TABLE CONSTRUCTION

A table need be no more than a flat surface supported at a height that is convenient for dining, studying, typing or serving coffee, and yet designers have expended considerable creative energy on this seemingly simple category of furniture. They have experimented with table tops to see what is the best shape and size to accommodate the average dinner party; underframes range from straightforward structures designed to provide maximum leg room to exercises in functional sculpture; and perhaps most ingenuity has been invested in finding easy ways of increasing the size of compact tables when it is necessary to seat a large group of people. The examples that follow illustrate traditional methods and are applicable both to large and small tables. Basic folding and extending mechanisms are also described.

DESIGNING A FUNCTIONAL TABLE

Eating at a dining table can be either an enjoyable social occasion or a nightmare of cramped knees and colliding elbows, depending on the amount of room provided by the designer. Most people are able to write or draw comfortably at dining-table height, but before designing a table for someone to work at, find out whether he or she will be using a typewriter or a word processor, because at least part of the table top must be lowered to present a keyboard at the optimum level.

DINING TABLES

Moving a chair
2ft 4in (700mm)
A diner needs a space of this size in order to stand up from the table.

Dining-table height
2ft 4in (700mm)
This is a comfortable height for a dining table, though eating from a bowl with chopsticks is easier either at a table closer to the height of a kitchen worktop or sitting cross-legged at a low table little more than 1ft (300mm) from the ground.

Elbow room
2ft (600mm)
This is sufficient space for an adult to wield a knife and fork without obstructing his or her neighbor.

Leg room
2ft (600mm)
Allow at least this dimension between the table rail and the floor.

Knee clearance
10in (250mm)
This is the minimum distance from the edge of the top to a table leg in order to provide clearance for your knees when your chair is drawn up to the table.

Rectangular dining table
To seat six people comfortably, a rectangular dining table should be a minimum of 5ft × 3ft 3in (1.5 × 1m).

Circular dining table
A circular dining table of only 3ft 3in (1m) diameter will seat up to four persons. Increase the diameter to 4ft (1.2m) for six diners and to about 5ft (1.5m) to accommodate eight people.

WORKTABLES

Desk height
2ft 4in (700mm)
A desk should be the same height as a dining table.

Typing and word processing
2ft 2in (650mm)
A worktable should be 2in (50mm) lower than the average desk to accommodate typing or word processing.

Maximum reach
1ft 7in (475mm)
A seated person can reach a bookshelf at this height above a desk.

OCCASIONAL TABLES

1 to 2ft (300 to 600mm)
Occasional or coffee-table height varies a great deal. The lowest ones often look very stylish, but are a little too low for comfort.

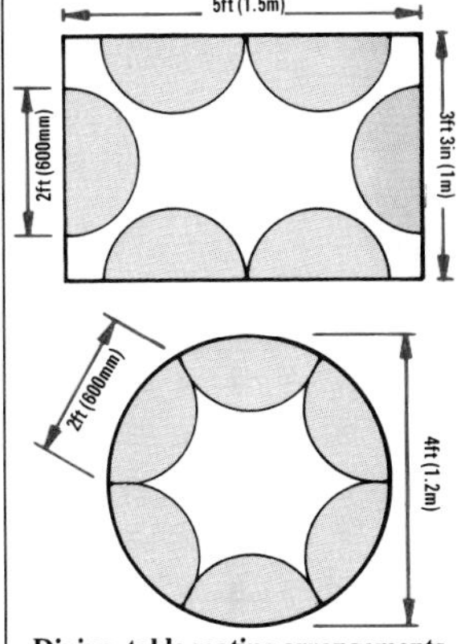

Dining-table seating arrangements

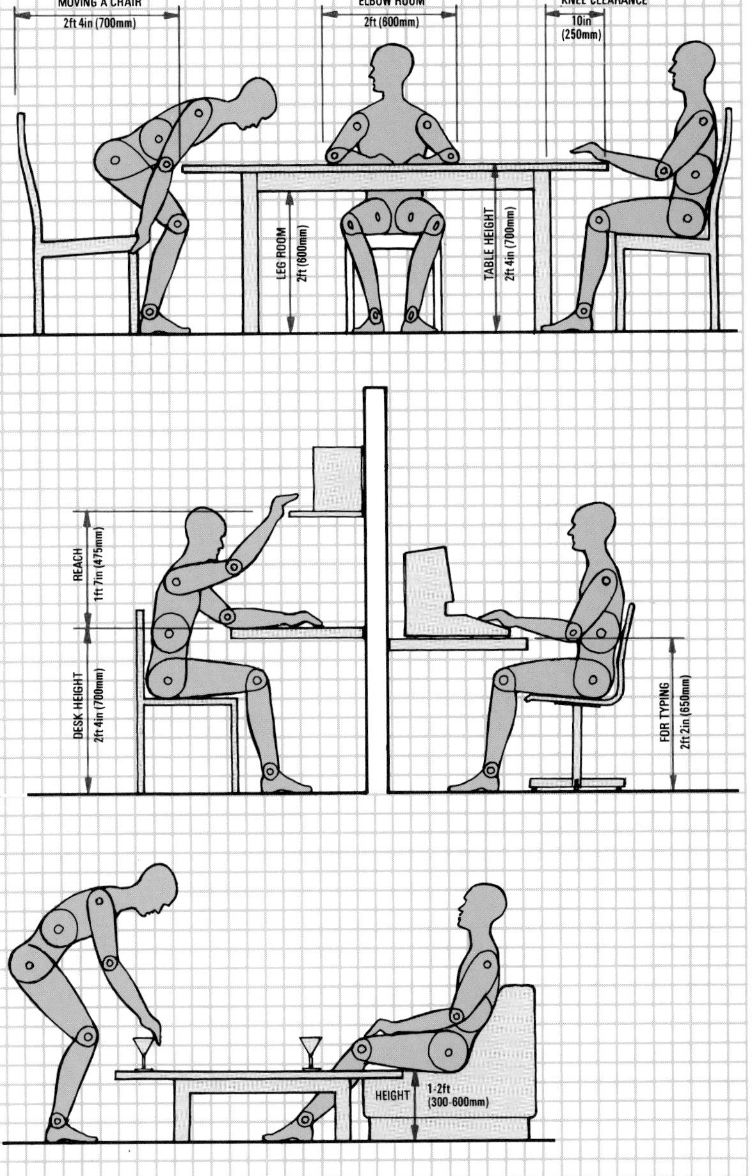

FRAME TABLES

A frame table has four legs, one at each corner. With strong mortise and tenon or dowel joints, the classic design can be adapted successfully for tables of practically any size. You can make the top from solid wood, but for stability, the larger ones are often constructed from lipped and veneered blockboard.

SEE ALSO

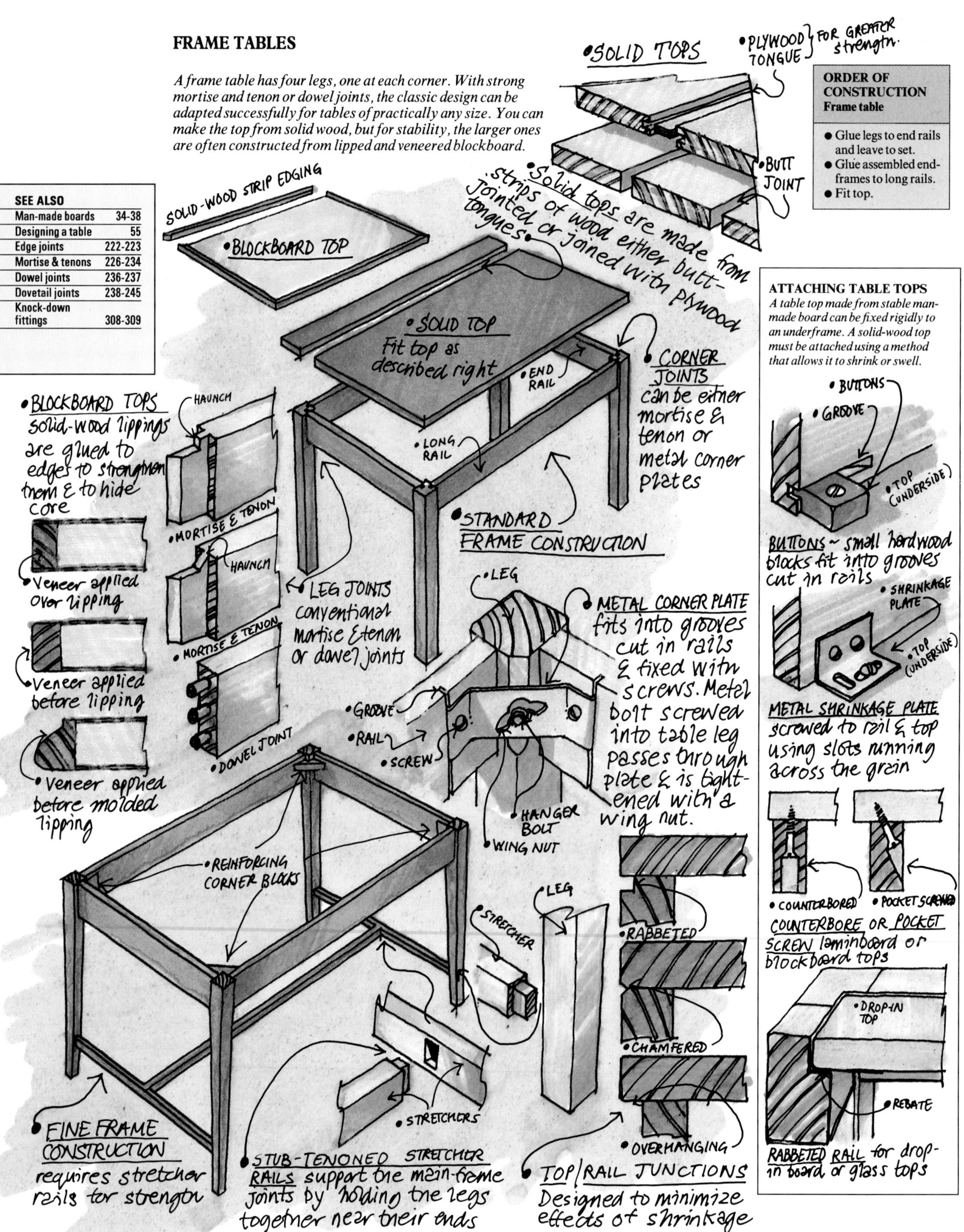

ORDER OF CONSTRUCTION
Frame table

- Glue legs to end rails and leave to set.
- Glue assembled end-frames to long rails.
- Fit top.

ATTACHING TABLE TOPS

A table top made from stable man-made board can be fixed rigidly to an underframe. A solid-wood top must be attached using a method that allows it to shrink or swell.

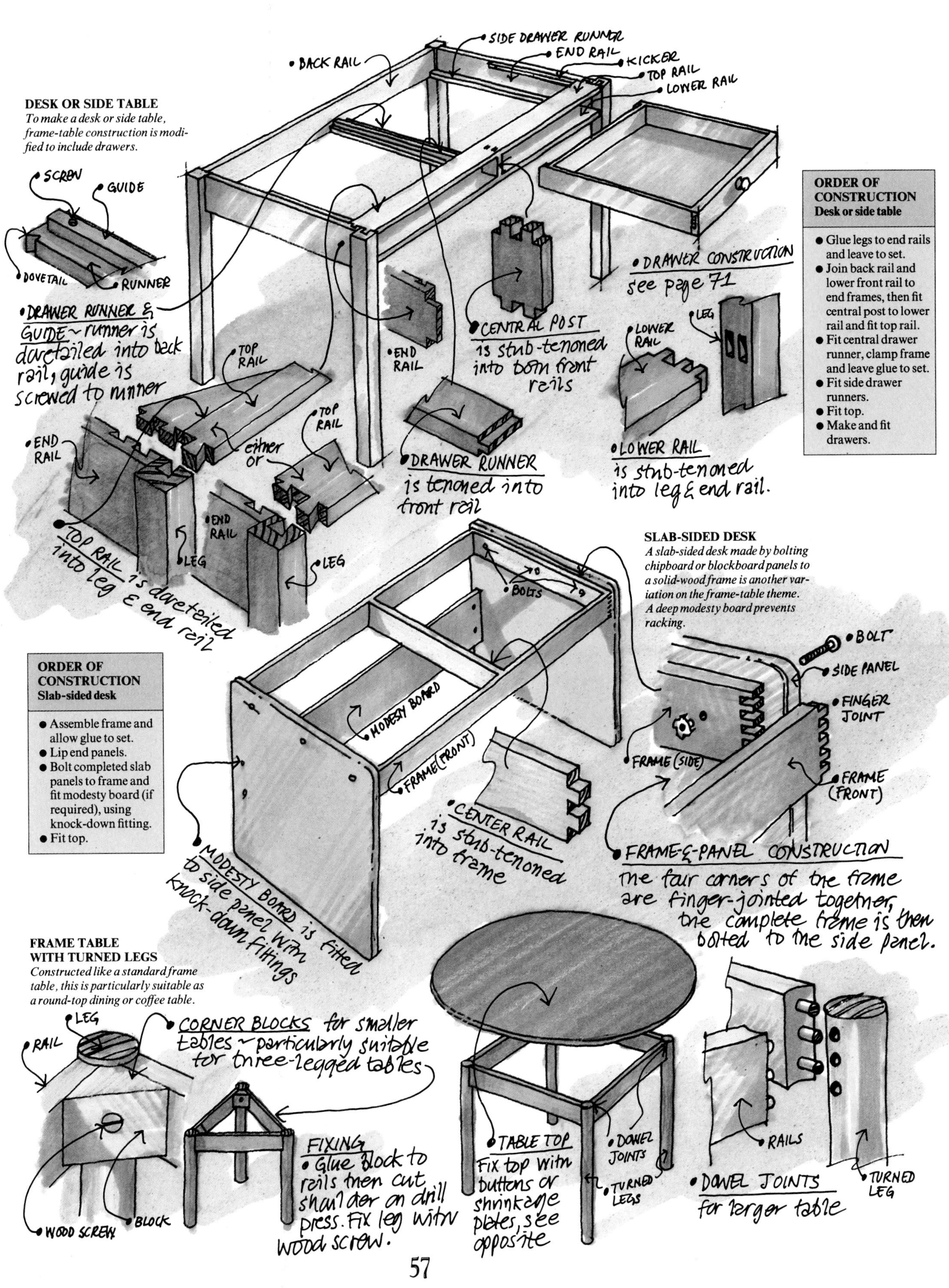

DESK OR SIDE TABLE
To make a desk or side table, frame-table construction is modified to include drawers.

ORDER OF CONSTRUCTION
Desk or side table

- Glue legs to end rails and leave to set.
- Join back rail and lower front rail to end frames, then fit central post to lower rail and fit top rail.
- Fit central drawer runner, clamp frame and leave glue to set.
- Fit side drawer runners.
- Fit top.
- Make and fit drawers.

SLAB-SIDED DESK
A slab-sided desk made by bolting chipboard or blockboard panels to a solid-wood frame is another variation on the frame-table theme. A deep modesty board prevents racking.

ORDER OF CONSTRUCTION
Slab-sided desk

- Assemble frame and allow glue to set.
- Lip end panels.
- Bolt completed slab panels to frame and fit modesty board (if required), using knock-down fitting.
- Fit top.

FRAME TABLE WITH TURNED LEGS
Constructed like a standard frame table, this is particularly suitable as a round-top dining or coffee table.

TRESTLE TABLE

This type of underframe is suitable for dining and coffee tables. It is usually made to "knock down" for transportation. Larger frames, especially, must be well made to prevent racking. Attach a solid top to the endframes, using shrinkage plates. A blockboard top can be attached with screws passed through the top rails of the endframes.

SEE ALSO

Designing a functional table	55
Lathes	192-203
Mortise & tenons	226-234
Dowel joints	236-237
Dovetail joints	238-245
Knuckle joints	307

ORDER OF CONSTRUCTION
Trestle table

- Assemble end frames and allow glue to set.
- Fit cross rail.
- Fit top.

DROP-LEAF TABLES

Deep flaps hinged to a fixed top are one way of providing a table top of variable size. When raised, the flaps are supported on pivoting legs or brackets.

ORDER OF CONSTRUCTION
Gate-leg table

- Assemble pivoting gates.
- Assemble both long side frames, fitting the gates between the rails at the same time. Allow glue to set.
- Join the long side frames with the shorter cross rails, fitting the upper drawer rail last.
- Fit drawer runners.
- Join flaps to central part of top.
- Fix central part of top to underframe.

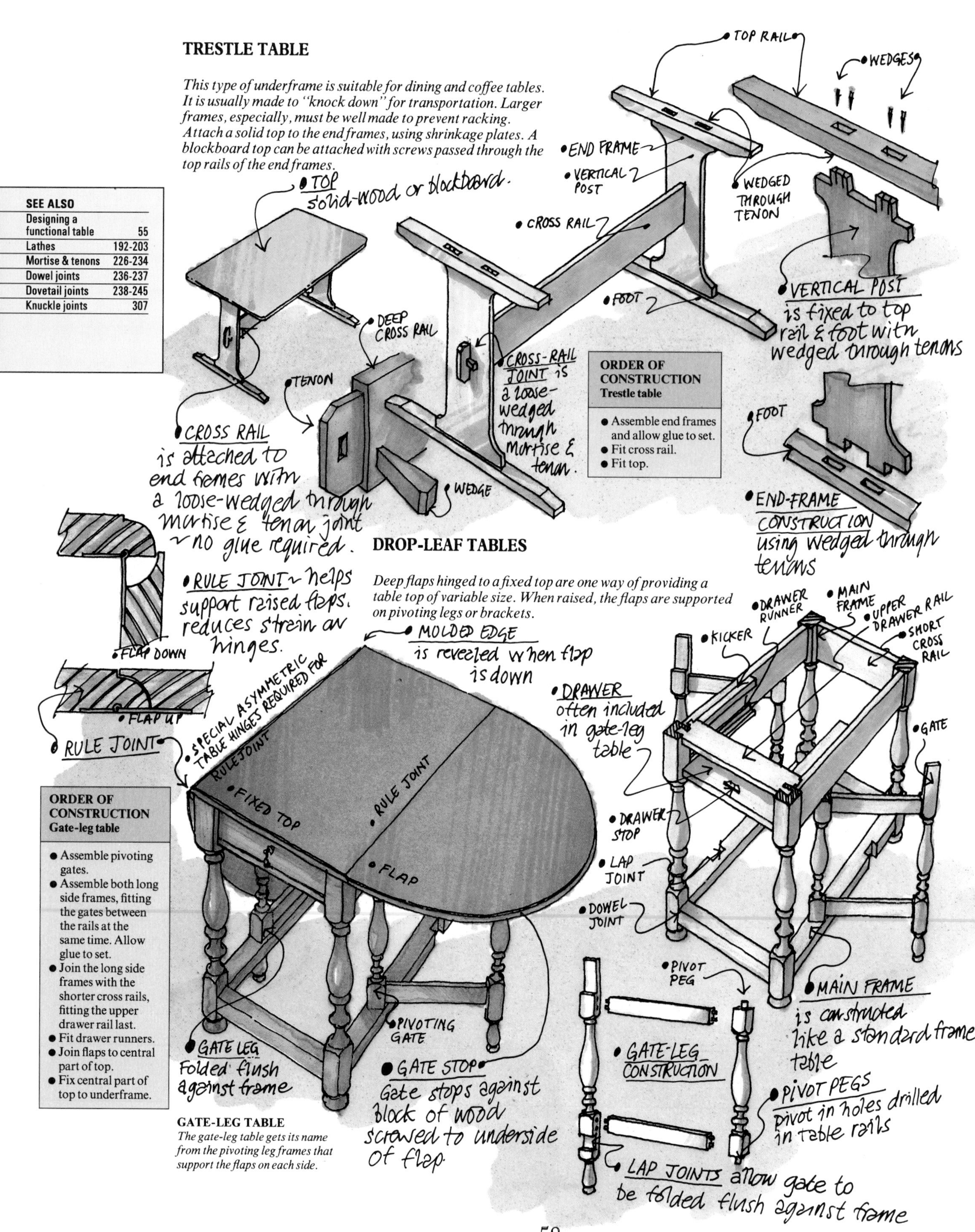

GATE-LEG TABLE
The gate-leg table gets its name from the pivoting leg frames that support the flaps on each side.

PEMBROKE TABLE

This is a small refined drop-leaf table. Its flaps are supported on hinged wooden brackets.

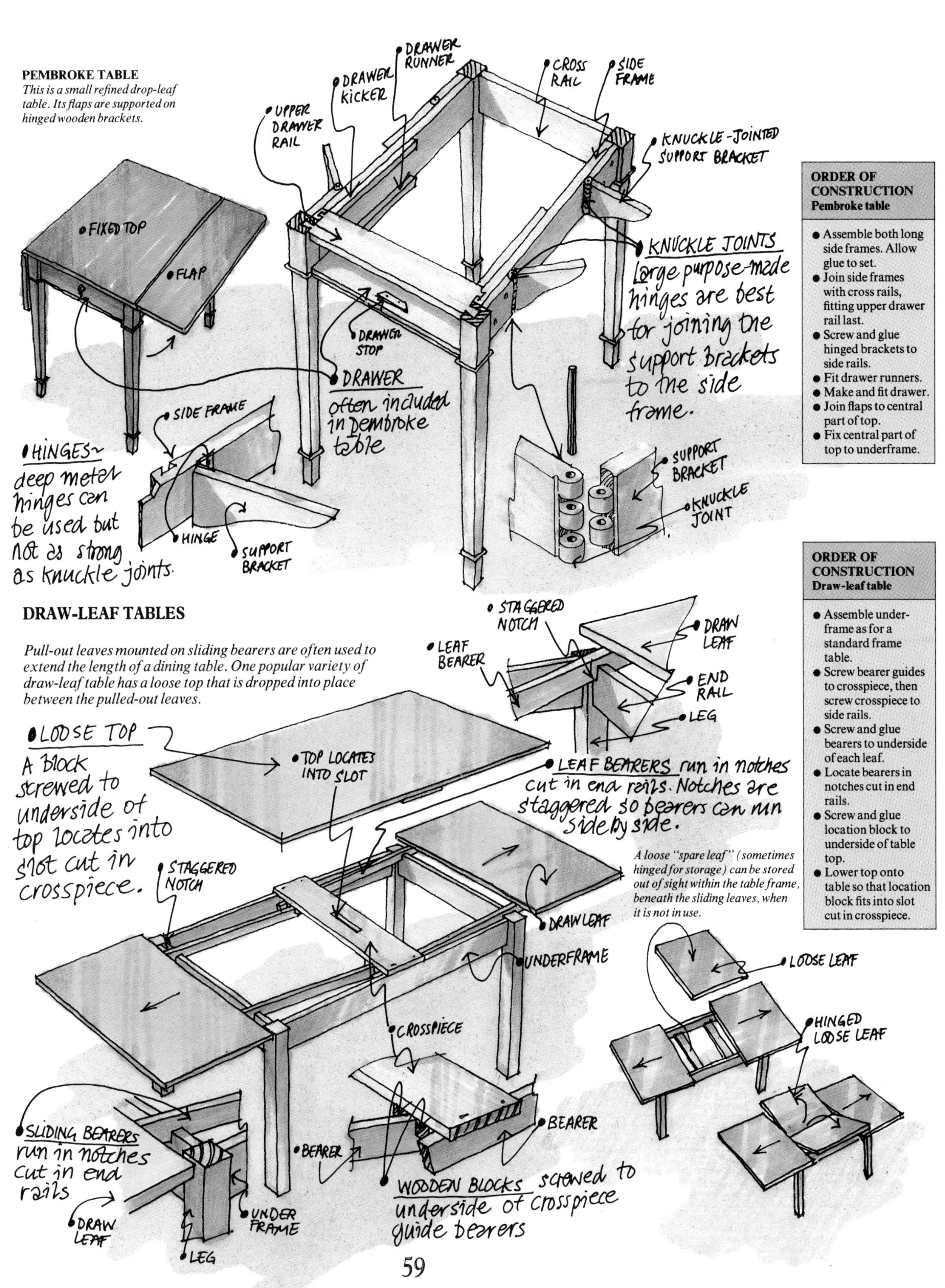

ORDER OF CONSTRUCTION
Pembroke table

- Assemble both long side frames. Allow glue to set.
- Join side frames with cross rails, fitting upper drawer rail last.
- Screw and glue hinged brackets to side rails.
- Fit drawer runners.
- Make and fit drawer.
- Join flaps to central part of top.
- Fix central part of top to underframe.

DRAW-LEAF TABLES

Pull-out leaves mounted on sliding bearers are often used to extend the length of a dining table. One popular variety of draw-leaf table has a loose top that is dropped into place between the pulled-out leaves.

A loose "spare leaf" (sometimes hinged for storage) can be stored out of sight within the table frame, beneath the sliding leaves, when it is not in use.

ORDER OF CONSTRUCTION
Draw-leaf table

- Assemble underframe as for a standard frame table.
- Screw bearer guides to crosspiece, then screw crosspiece to side rails.
- Screw and glue bearers to underside of each leaf.
- Locate bearers in notches cut in end rails.
- Screw and glue location block to underside of table top.
- Lower top onto table so that location block fits into slot cut in crosspiece.

FOLDING-TOP TABLES

One way to reduce the area of a table top when it is not in use is to split it down the middle and hinge it, so that one half can be folded over to lie on top of the other.

SIDE TABLE

A side table can be converted into a card table or small dining table by swiveling the two back legs on knuckle joints and opening the hinged top.

SEE ALSO

Topic	Pages
Designing a functional table	55
Dovetail housings	146,224
Mortise & tenons	226-234
Bridle joints	235
Hinges	306-307
Knuckle joints	307

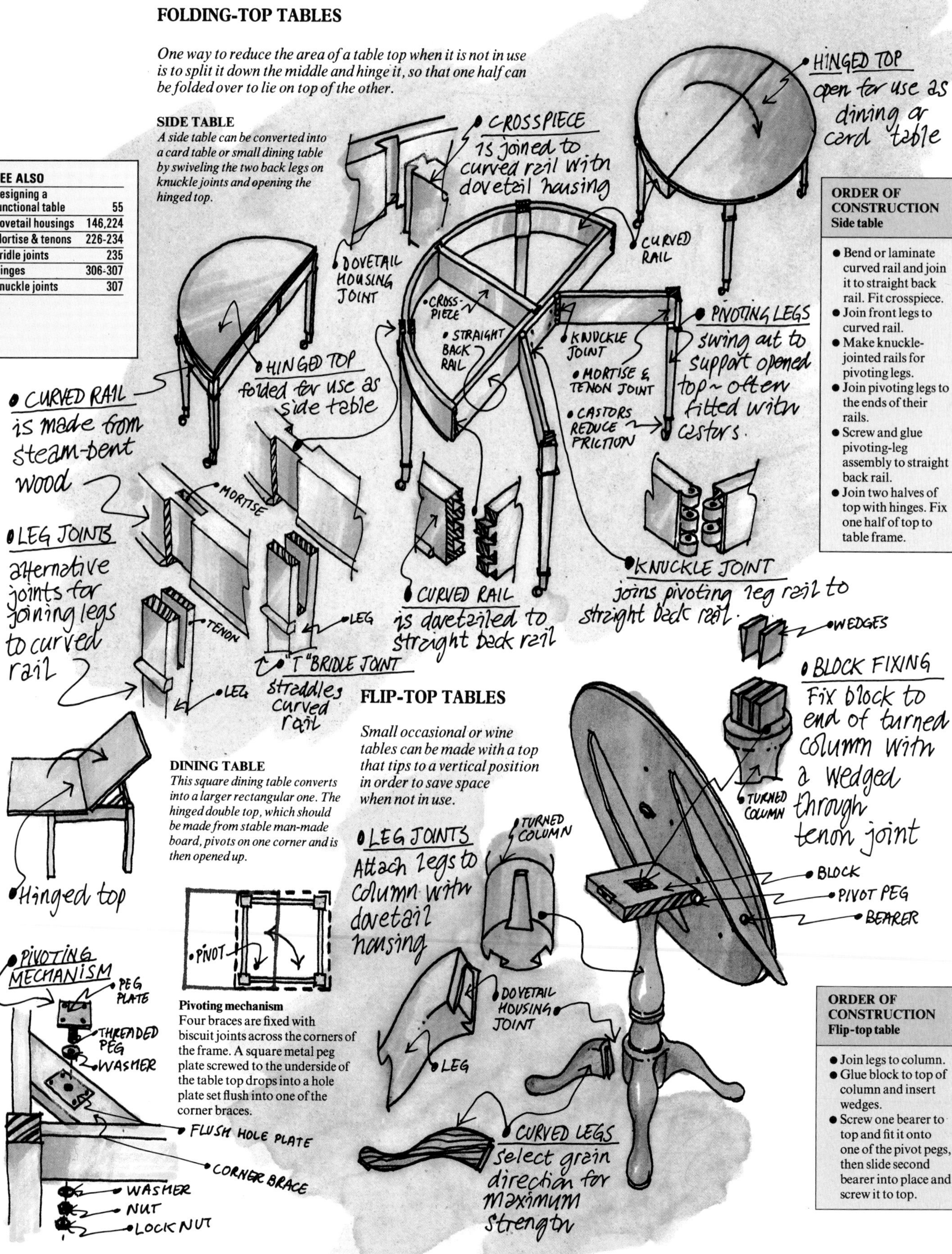

ORDER OF CONSTRUCTION
Side table

- Bend or laminate curved rail and join it to straight back rail. Fit crosspiece.
- Join front legs to curved rail.
- Make knuckle-jointed rails for pivoting legs.
- Join pivoting legs to the ends of their rails.
- Screw and glue pivoting-leg assembly to straight back rail.
- Join two halves of top with hinges. Fix one half of top to table frame.

DINING TABLE

This square dining table converts into a larger rectangular one. The hinged double top, which should be made from stable man-made board, pivots on one corner and is then opened up.

Pivoting mechanism
Four braces are fixed with biscuit joints across the corners of the frame. A square metal peg plate screwed to the underside of the table top drops into a hole plate set flush into one of the corner braces.

FLIP-TOP TABLES

Small occasional or wine tables can be made with a top that tips to a vertical position in order to save space when not in use.

ORDER OF CONSTRUCTION
Flip-top table

- Join legs to column.
- Glue block to top of column and insert wedges.
- Screw one bearer to top and fit it onto one of the pivot pegs, then slide second bearer into place and screw it to top.

STORAGE-UNIT CONSTRUCTION

As a rule, people are fairly tidy by nature and require an immense range of storage to keep their belongings hidden from view. Even collections of books, records or cassettes kept on open shelves need to be stored systematically so you can lay hands on a particular one without a prolonged search. Customarily, when we talk about the various kinds of furniture used for storage we refer to them by specific names – such as wardrobe, bureau, bookcase or dresser – that indicate their function and also their place in the home. Nowadays, many designers regard these traditional classifications as limiting and prefer to employ shelves, drawers and cupboards in whatever combination provides the most convenient and effective use of space – whether for kitchen, bedroom, office or elsewhere. In the following pages, some of the many ways of constructing cupboard, drawer and shelf units are illustrated and described, so you can use them, either individually or in combination, to design storage to meet your own needs.

DESIGNING ACCESSIBLE STORAGE

Plan storage systems using recommended dimensions that permit a person of average build to reach the top shelf or gain access to the back of a cupboard or drawer without stretching.

Maximum shelf height
6ft to 6ft 6in (1.8 to 2m)
An adult can reach a shelf this distance from the floor.

Eye-level shelf
5ft to 5ft 8in (1.5 to 1.7m)
Mount a shelf at this height for books, files, cassettes or other objects that you want to scan easily.

Maximum reach above worktop
3ft 6in (1.05m)
An adult can just reach a shelf at this height when leaning across a standard kitchen worktop.

Optimum reach above worktop
3ft (900mm)
Store frequently used objects at this height.

Lowest shelf above worktop
1ft 6in (450mm)
Shelves and cupboards mounted lower than this begin to obscure your view of the back of the worktop and obstruct the use of food mixers and blenders.

Standard worktop height
3ft (900mm)
A standing adult can work comfortably at a counter top fitted at this height.

Worktop depth
2ft (600mm)
Major electrical appliances (washing machines, dishwashers, etc.) are designed to fit beneath a worktop of this depth.

Wall-cabinet depth
1ft (300mm)
The optimum depth for a wall-hung cupboard mounted above a worktop.

Crouching at a cupboard
3ft 3in (1m)
Allow this space in front of a low cupboard.

Safe passing space
3ft (900mm)
Cramped kitchens and workshops cause accidents. Allow this width as a safe access corridor, plus an additional 1ft 6in (450mm) so there is room for someone standing at a worktop.

Access to drawers
4ft 2in (1.25m)
This amount of space is required for someone kneeling at an open drawer.

Hanging space
4ft 10in to 5ft 4in (1.45 to 1.6m)
Allow this space below a hanging rail to accommodate long coats and dresses.

2ft 10in (850mm)
Jackets and shirts will hang in this space.

2ft (600mm)
A storage unit of this depth will accommodate clothing hung on a rail.

Drawer size
1ft 5in to 1ft 8in (425 to 500mm)
Make drawers or trays this depth for folded shirts, sweaters and towels.

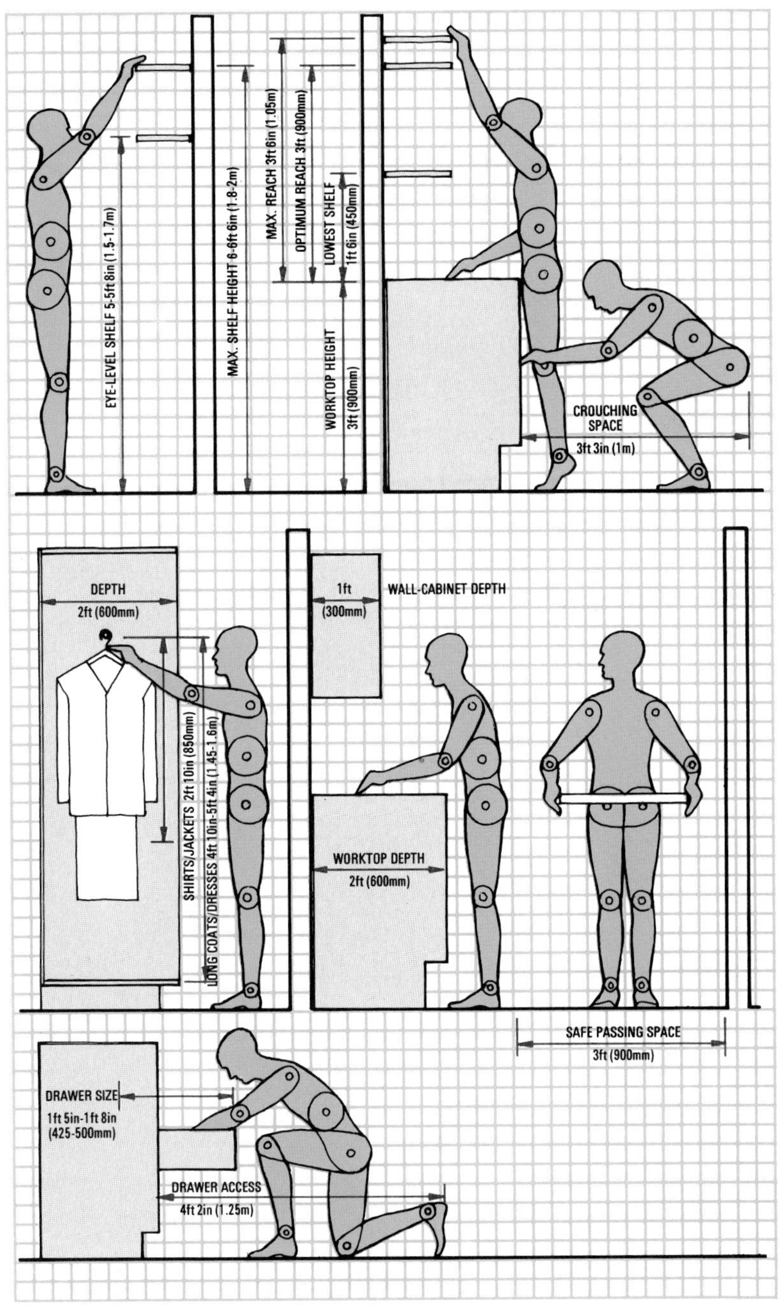

SHELF UNITS

Simple open shelf units constructed from solid wood or man-made boards are suitable for storing books or records and for displaying collections. Similar forms of construction are used when shelving is incorporated in more complex storage units.

SOLID-WOOD UNIT

Solid softwood and hardwood shelf units are stronger and more attractive than units constructed from man-made boards.

ORDER OF CONSTRUCTION
Solid-wood unit

- Fit fixed bottom shelf into dado in side panels.
- Tap dovetailed top into side panels, then square up and allow glue to set.
- Fix back in rabbet with fillets.
- Fit adjustable shelves.

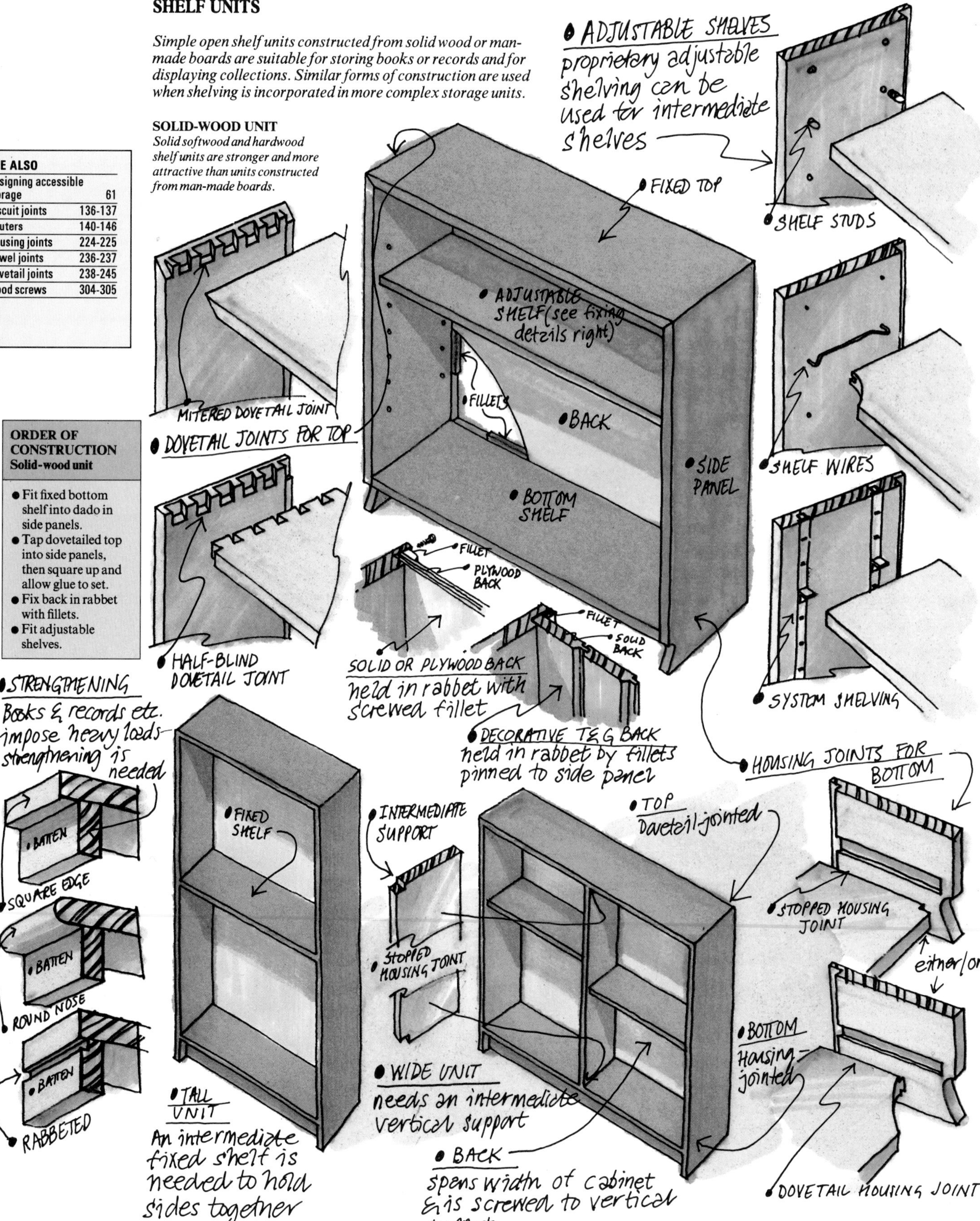

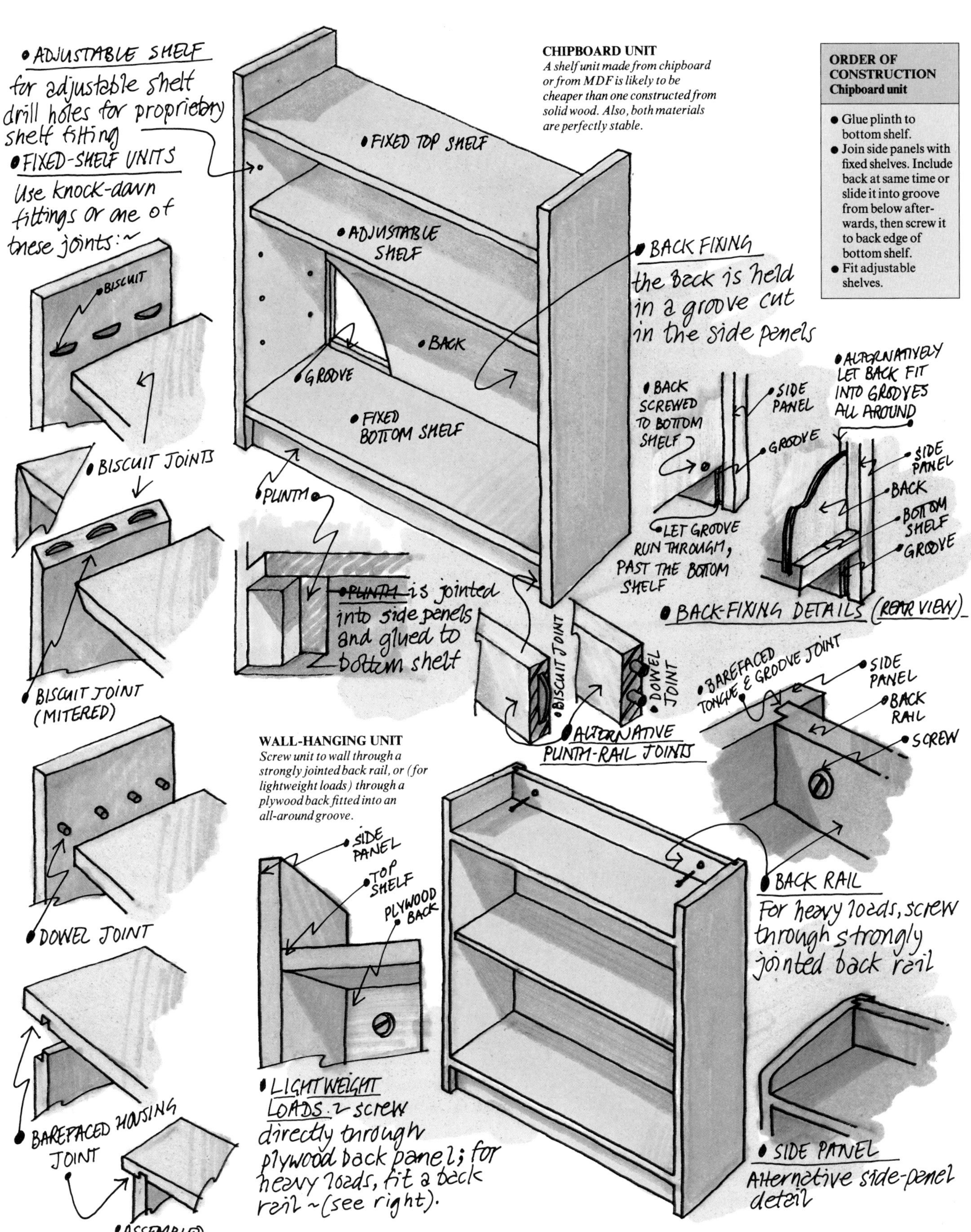

CHIPBOARD UNIT
A shelf unit made from chipboard or from MDF is likely to be cheaper than one constructed from solid wood. Also, both materials are perfectly stable.

ORDER OF CONSTRUCTION
Chipboard unit

- Glue plinth to bottom shelf.
- Join side panels with fixed shelves. Include back at same time or slide it into groove from below afterwards, then screw it to back edge of bottom shelf.
- Fit adjustable shelves.

WALL-HANGING UNIT
Screw unit to wall through a strongly jointed back rail, or (for lightweight loads) through a plywood back fitted into an all-around groove.

CUPBOARDS

Traditional or modern methods of construction can be utilized to make free-standing cupboards and, with modifications, used as a basis for designing and building kitchen storage units.

SEE ALSO

Door construction	66-67
Biscuit joints	136-137
Cutting moldings	142,144
Cutting miters/ bevels	160,167,169
Edge joints	222-223
Mortise & tenons	226-234
Dovetail joints	238-245

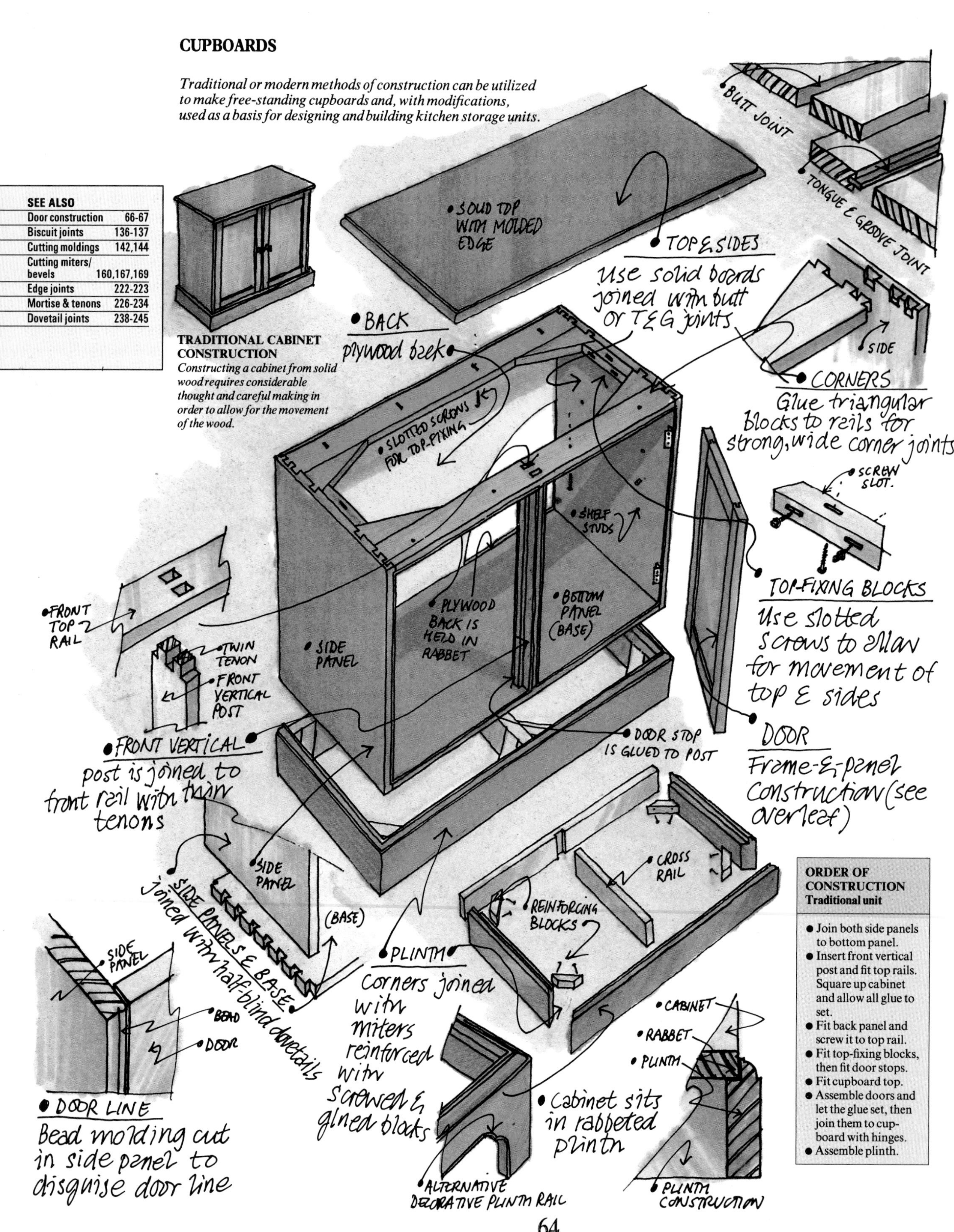

TRADITIONAL CABINET CONSTRUCTION
Constructing a cabinet from solid wood requires considerable thought and careful making in order to allow for the movement of the wood.

ORDER OF CONSTRUCTION
Traditional unit

- Join both side panels to bottom panel.
- Insert front vertical post and fit top rails. Square up cabinet and allow all glue to set.
- Fit back panel and screw it to top rail.
- Fit top-fixing blocks, then fit door stops.
- Fit cupboard top.
- Assemble doors and let the glue set, then join them to cupboard with hinges.
- Assemble plinth.

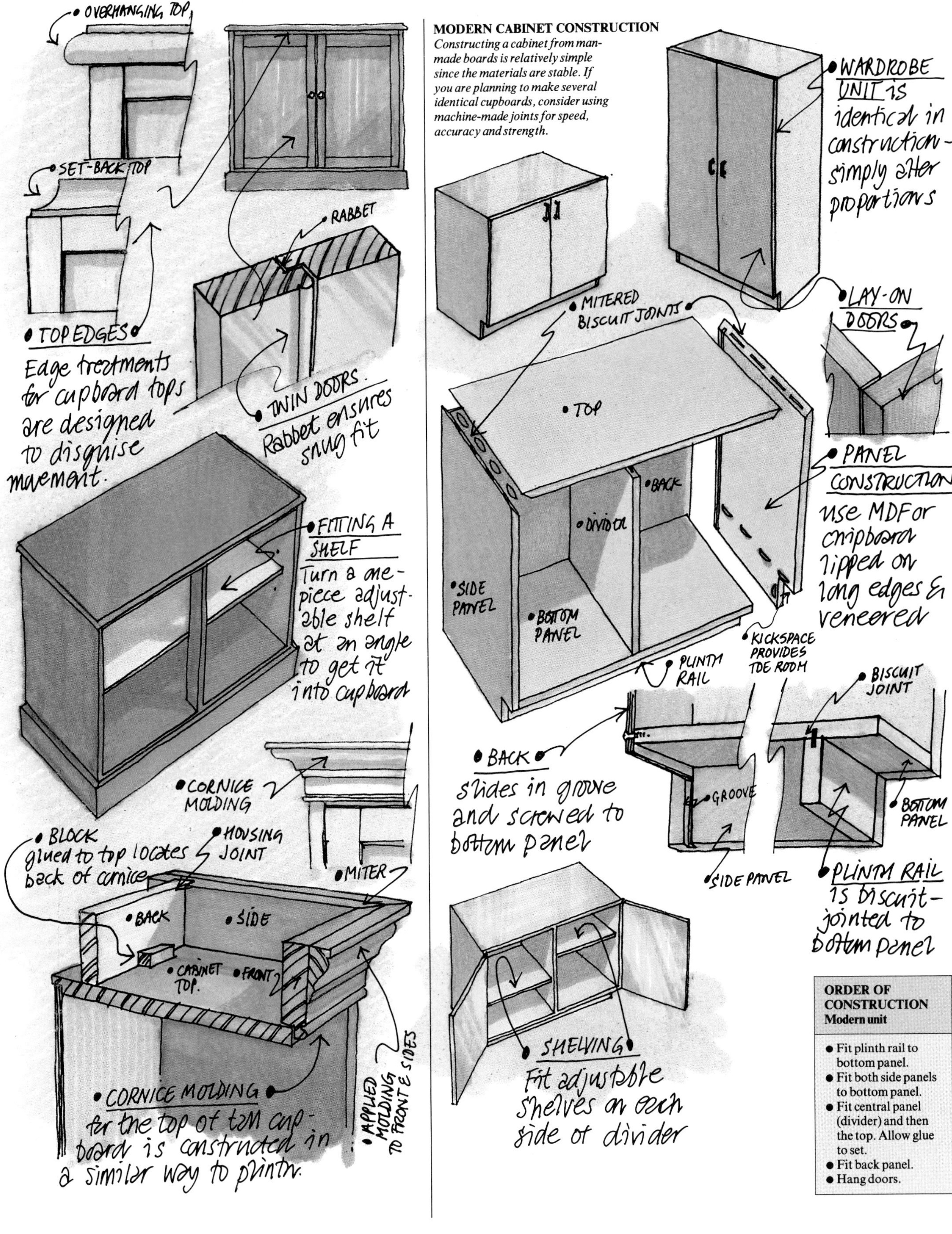

MODERN CABINET CONSTRUCTION

Constructing a cabinet from man-made boards is relatively simple since the materials are stable. If you are planning to make several identical cupboards, consider using machine-made joints for speed, accuracy and strength.

ORDER OF CONSTRUCTION
Modern unit

- Fit plinth rail to bottom panel.
- Fit both side panels to bottom panel.
- Fit central panel (divider) and then the top. Allow glue to set.
- Fit back panel.
- Hang doors.

CUPBOARD DOORS

All sorts of doors and flaps can be fitted to cupboards, storage units and other kinds of furniture. The most common forms of door construction are described and illustrated here.

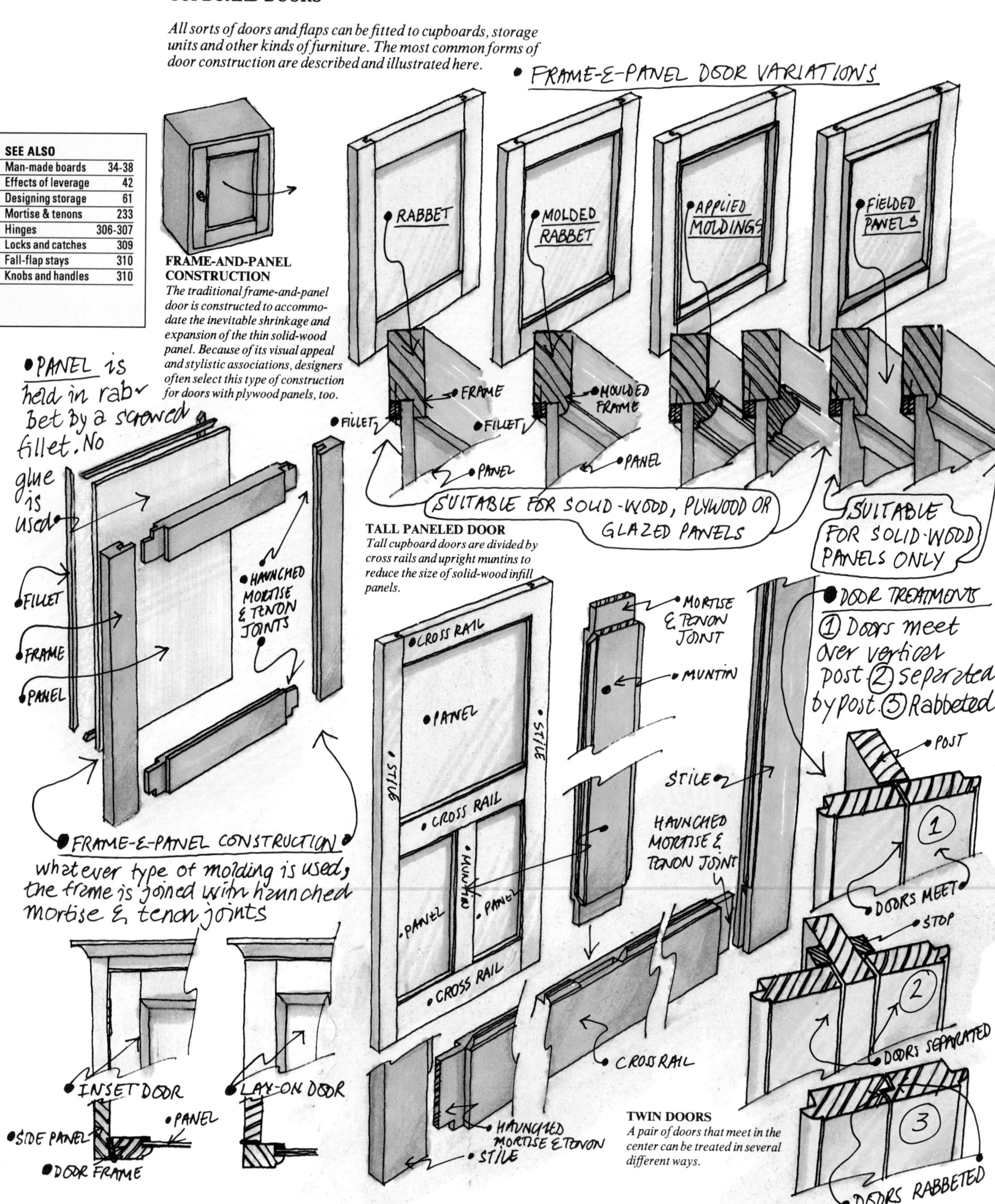

FRAME-AND-PANEL CONSTRUCTION
The traditional frame-and-panel door is constructed to accommodate the inevitable shrinkage and expansion of the thin solid-wood panel. Because of its visual appeal and stylistic associations, designers often select this type of construction for doors with plywood panels, too.

TALL PANELED DOOR
Tall cupboard doors are divided by cross rails and upright muntins to reduce the size of solid-wood infill panels.

TWIN DOORS
A pair of doors that meet in the center can be treated in several different ways.

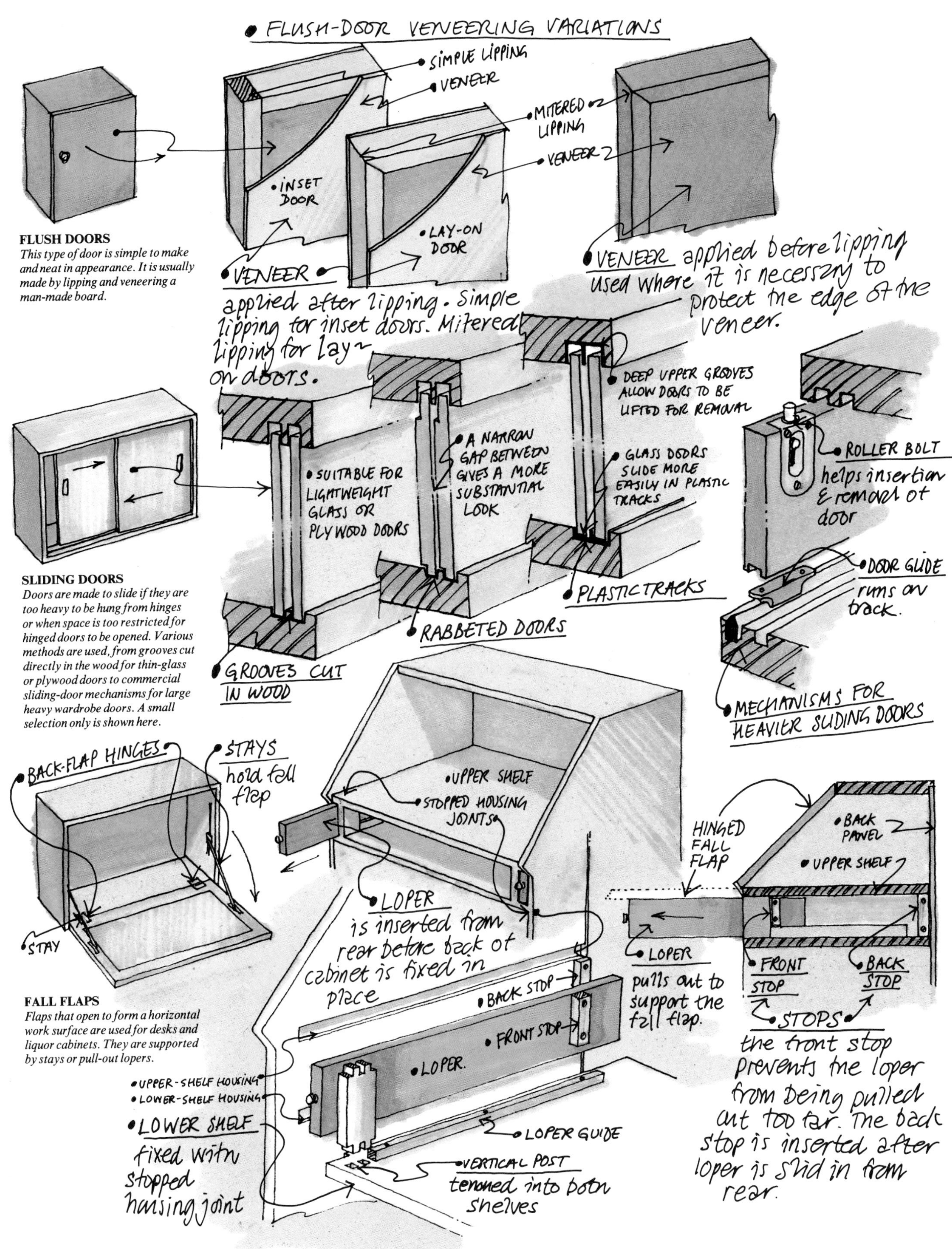

FLUSH DOORS
This type of door is simple to make and neat in appearance. It is usually made by lipping and veneering a man-made board.

SLIDING DOORS
Doors are made to slide if they are too heavy to be hung from hinges or when space is too restricted for hinged doors to be opened. Various methods are used, from grooves cut directly in the wood for thin-glass or plywood doors to commercial sliding-door mechanisms for large heavy wardrobe doors. A small selection only is shown here.

FALL FLAPS
Flaps that open to form a horizontal work surface are used for desks and liquor cabinets. They are supported by stays or pull-out lopers.

CUPBOARD DOORS

SEE ALSO

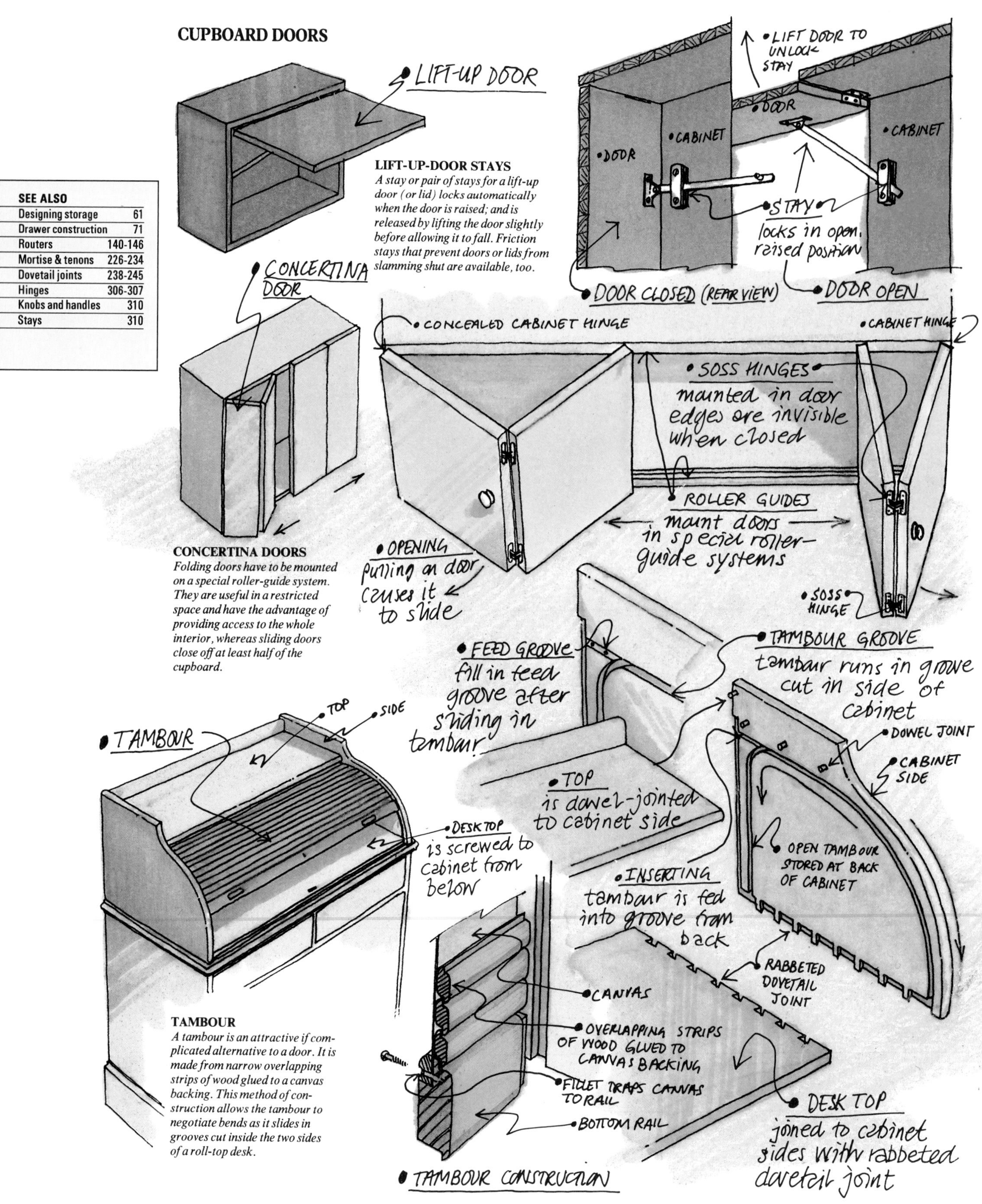

LIFT-UP-DOOR STAYS
A stay or pair of stays for a lift-up door (or lid) locks automatically when the door is raised; and is released by lifting the door slightly before allowing it to fall. Friction stays that prevent doors or lids from slamming shut are available, too.

CONCERTINA DOORS
Folding doors have to be mounted on a special roller-guide system. They are useful in a restricted space and have the advantage of providing access to the whole interior, whereas sliding doors close off at least half of the cupboard.

TAMBOUR
A tambour is an attractive if complicated alternative to a door. It is made from narrow overlapping strips of wood glued to a canvas backing. This method of construction allows the tambour to negotiate bends as it slides in grooves cut inside the two sides of a roll-top desk.

DRAWER UNITS

Constructing a drawer unit, especially one made from solid wood, is much more complicated than making a cupboard unit of similar size and construction. Also, greater accuracy is required in order to ensure that the drawers fit snugly and will continue to run smoothly.

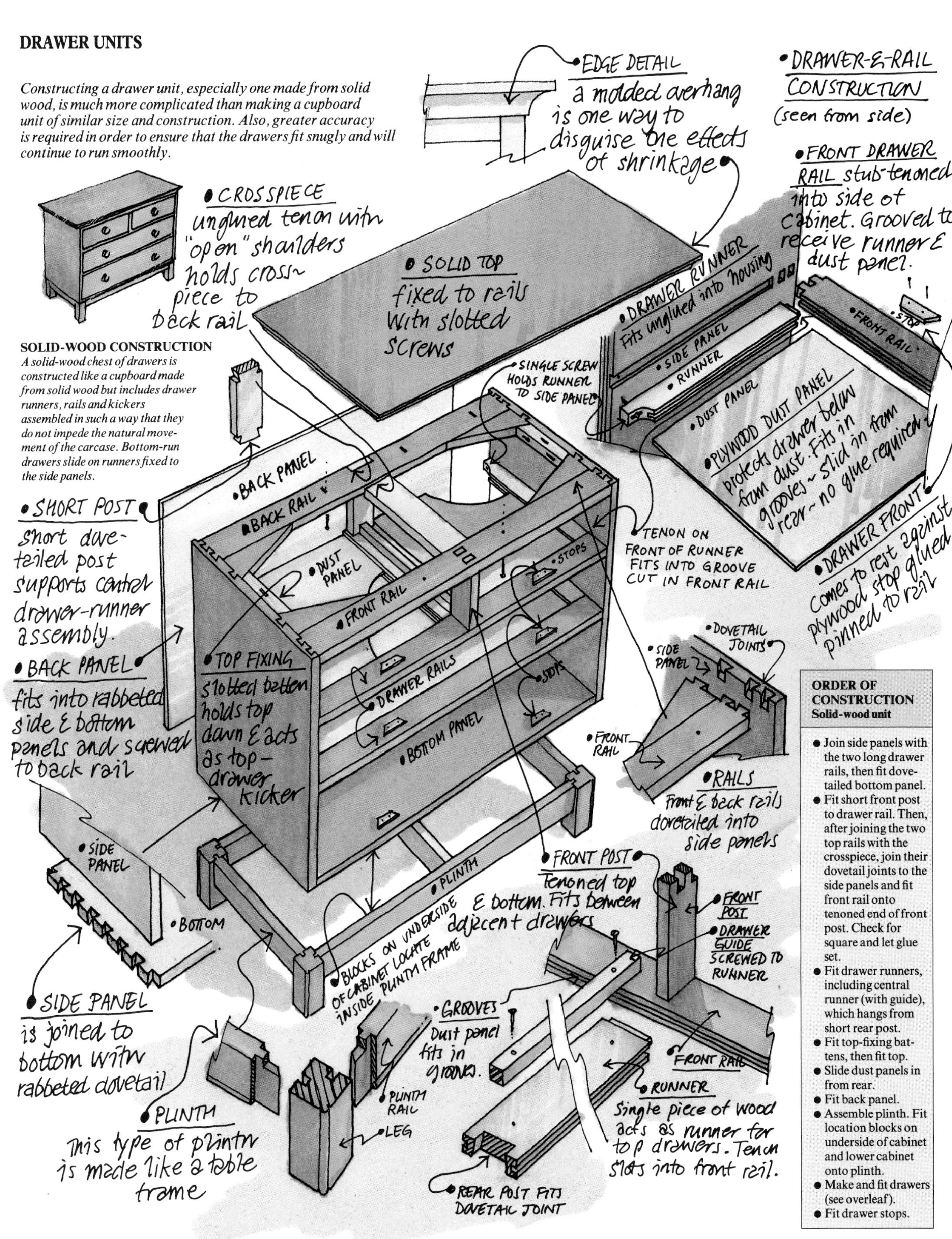

SOLID-WOOD CONSTRUCTION
A solid-wood chest of drawers is constructed like a cupboard made from solid wood but includes drawer runners, rails and kickers assembled in such a way that they do not impede the natural movement of the carcase. Bottom-run drawers slide on runners fixed to the side panels.

ORDER OF CONSTRUCTION
Solid-wood unit

- Join side panels with the two long drawer rails, then fit dovetailed bottom panel.
- Fit short front post to drawer rail. Then, after joining the two top rails with the crosspiece, join their dovetail joints to the side panels and fit front rail onto tenoned end of front post. Check for square and let glue set.
- Fit drawer runners, including central runner (with guide), which hangs from short rear post.
- Fit top-fixing battens, then fit top.
- Slide dust panels in from rear.
- Fit back panel.
- Assemble plinth. Fit location blocks on underside of cabinet and lower cabinet onto plinth.
- Make and fit drawers (see overleaf).
- Fit drawer stops.

DRAWER UNITS

FRAME-AND-PANEL CONSTRUCTION

Relatively lightweight cabinets can be made by using frame-and-panel construction with a solid top and a plywood back panel. This method of construction can be adapted to make a cupboard or drawer unit or a combination unit with cupboard and drawers.

SEE ALSO

Designing storage	61
Routers	140-146
Rabbet joints	218
Housing joints	224-225
Mortise & tenons	226-234
Dovetail joints	238-245
Knock-down fittings	308-309

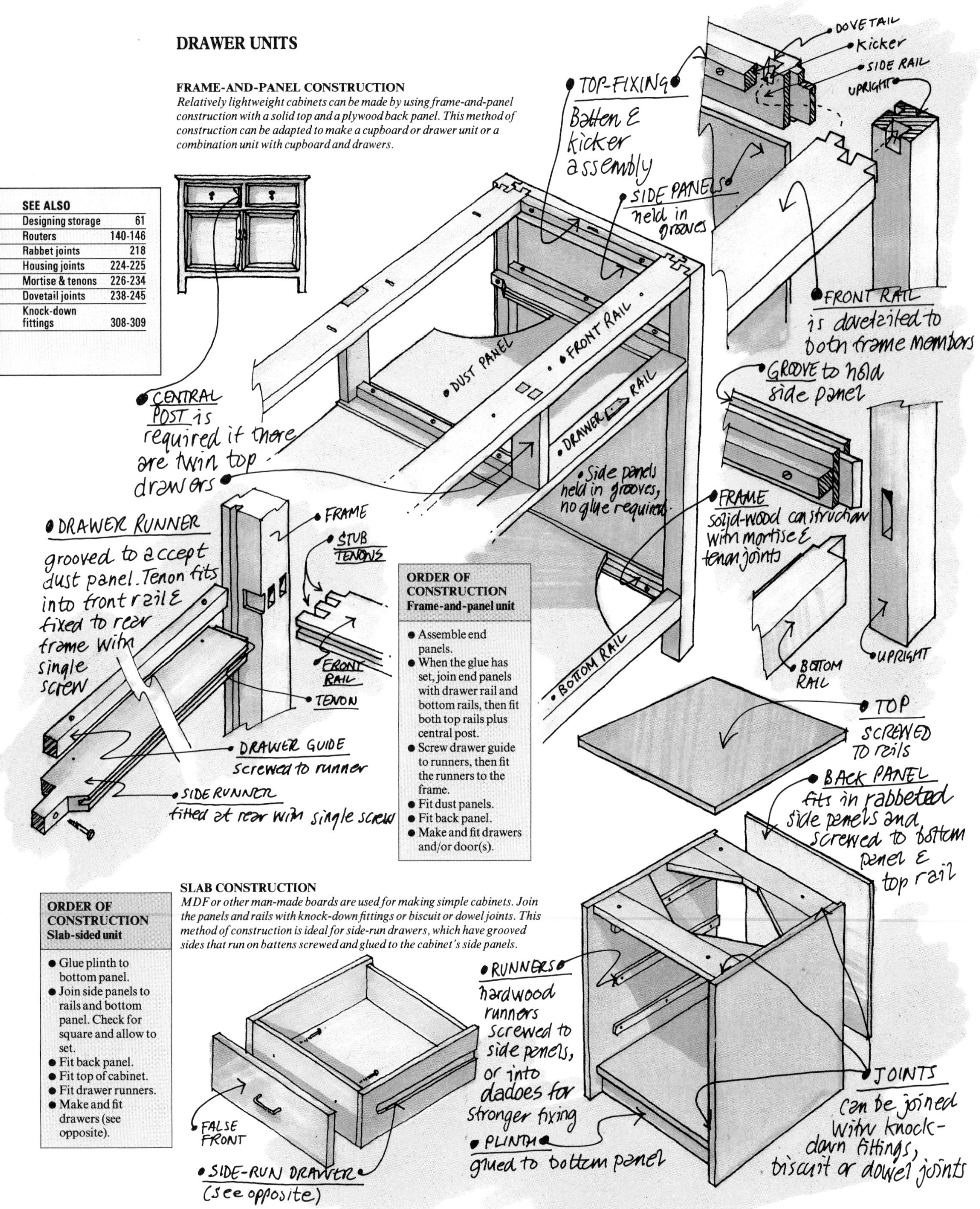

ORDER OF CONSTRUCTION
Frame-and-panel unit

- Assemble end panels.
- When the glue has set, join end panels with drawer rail and bottom rails, then fit both top rails plus central post.
- Screw drawer guide to runners, then fit the runners to the frame.
- Fit dust panels.
- Fit back panel.
- Make and fit drawers and/or door(s).

SLAB CONSTRUCTION

MDF or other man-made boards are used for making simple cabinets. Join the panels and rails with knock-down fittings or biscuit or dowel joints. This method of construction is ideal for side-run drawers, which have grooved sides that run on battens screwed and glued to the cabinet's side panels.

ORDER OF CONSTRUCTION
Slab-sided unit

- Glue plinth to bottom panel.
- Join side panels to rails and bottom panel. Check for square and allow to set.
- Fit back panel.
- Fit top of cabinet.
- Fit drawer runners.
- Make and fit drawers (see opposite).

DRAWERS

Drawers are designed to slide in and out of a cabinet in order to improve access to the interior. The drawer front protects the contents by filling the opening. Shallow widely spaced drawers or trays are often used as an alternative to shelves behind cupboard doors, especially in wardrobes or built-in storage units. Tray construction is usually very simple, often comprising no more than a finger-jointed box with a plywood bottom.

Bottom-run drawers
The bottom edges of the drawer's sides run on strips of hardwood fixed to the cabinet's side panels. The strips also act as "kickers," which prevent the drawer below from tipping when it is pulled out.

Side-run drawers
A stopped groove cut in each side of the drawer fits onto a hardwood batten screwed and glued to the cabinet. For a stronger fixing, cut a shallow dado in the sides of the cabinet for each runner.

Drawer slides
You can buy ready-made drawer-slide systems for screwing to the sides of heavier drawers. The drawer front must overlap at each side to cover the space needed for these fittings.

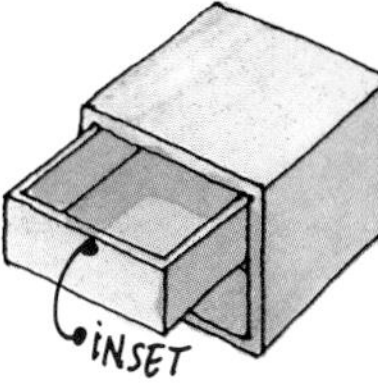

Inset drawers
Drawers of this type fit flush with the face of the cabinet. They need to fit snugly.

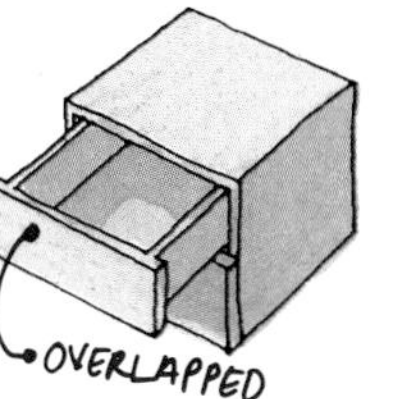

Overlapping drawers
Overlapping drawers are often made with a false front, which makes for much easier fitting.

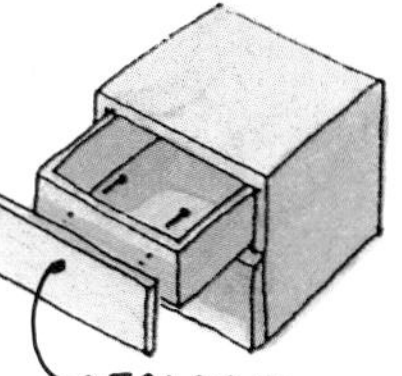

False front
Screwed to drawer.

TRADITIONAL BOTTOM-RUN DRAWER
A traditional bottom-run drawer has thin hardwood sides jointed with finely cut rabbet dovetails at the front and through dovetails at the back. The bottom panel is set in a groove at the front and has a grooved slip molding at each side.

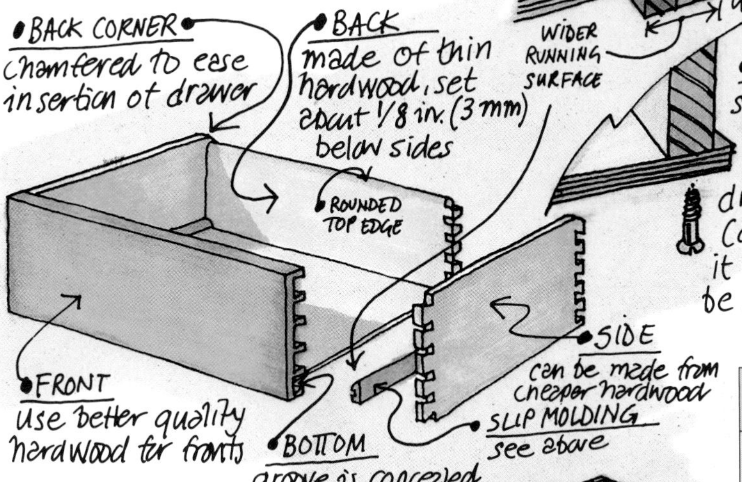

STIFFENING A WIDE DRAWER BOTTOM
A hardwood crosspiece known as a muntin is used to separate and support the two sections of a wide drawer bottom.

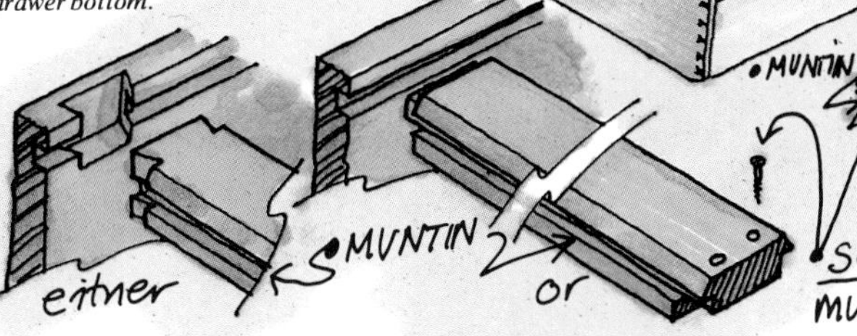

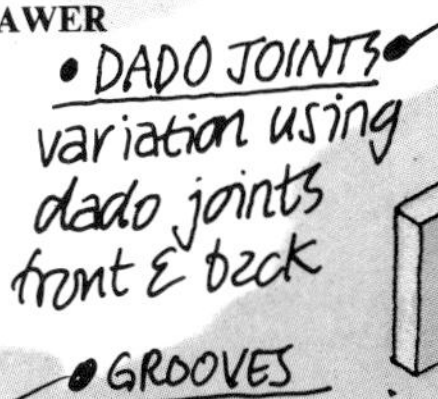

FITTING A DRAWER

First plane the drawer front to fit snugly in its opening. Make the other components to match the front, then assemble. If the finished drawer is a tight fit, look for shiny spots along the sides that indicate areas of friction. Skim them lightly with a plane, then lubricate all sliding surfaces by rubbing them with wax.

RABBETED-AND-HOUSED DRAWER
For cheaper-quality furniture, drawers can be made with simple rabbet joints at the front and dadoed housing joints at the back. The strength of the joints relies on the glue, but they can be reinforced with brads.

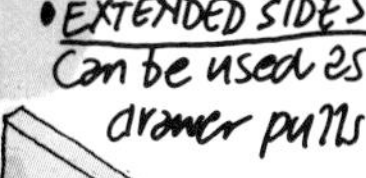

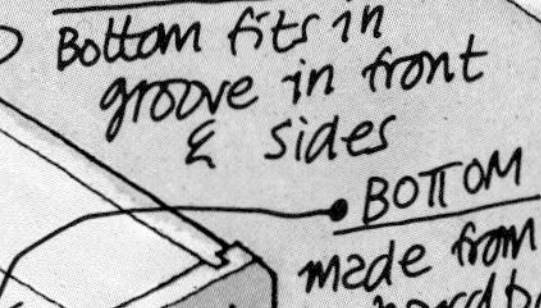

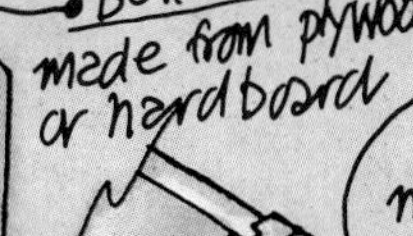

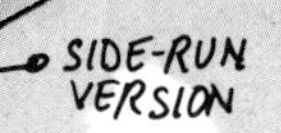

BUILT-IN STORAGE UNITS

Built-in units fitted from wall to wall are relatively cheap to make. An alternative method is to construct "modules" that are bolted side by side. Always make sure you can transport the units from your workshop and through doorways or up stairs. If necessary, assemble the components on site or construct sub-assemblies that can be joined with screws or bolts. If the units are to be painted, nails and screw-fixings can be disguised with filler.

SEE ALSO

Designing storage	61
Door construction	66-67
Miter joints	169,216-217
Mortise & tenons	229
Hinges	306-307
Knock-down fittings	308-309
Knobs and handles	310

ORDER OF CONSTRUCTION
Alcove unit

- Stand bottom panel in position, after gluing the plinth rails to it.
- Screw the rails and posts to the wall on each side of the cupboard.
- Screw the top to the rails directly, or screw a batten to each rail then screw the battens to the top.
- Scribe upright cover strips to the walls and fix them to the posts. Check that they are plumb, using a spirit level.
- Pin and glue molding along front edge of top.
- Assemble doors and attach with hinges to cover strips.
- Pin battens to underside of top to act as door stop.

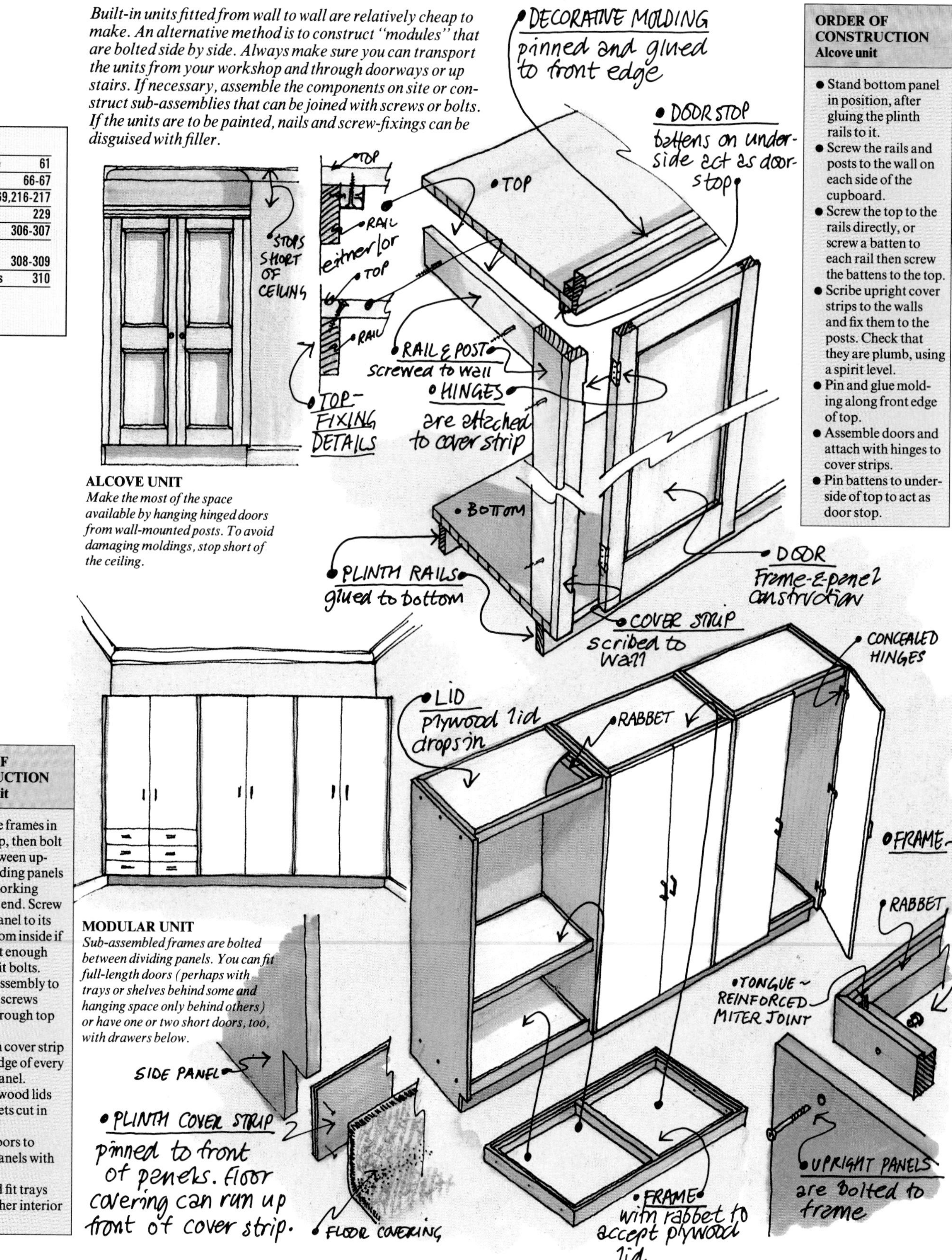

ALCOVE UNIT
Make the most of the space available by hanging hinged doors from wall-mounted posts. To avoid damaging moldings, stop short of the ceiling.

MODULAR UNIT
Sub-assembled frames are bolted between dividing panels. You can fit full-length doors (perhaps with trays or shelves behind some and hanging space only behind others) or have one or two short doors, too, with drawers below.

ORDER OF CONSTRUCTION
Modular unit

- Assemble frames in workshop, then bolt them between upright dividing panels on site, working from one end. Screw the last panel to its frames from inside if there isn't enough room to fit bolts. Anchor assembly to wall with screws passed through top frames.
- Pin plinth cover strip to front edge of every upright panel.
- Drop plywood lids into rabbets cut in frames.
- Attach doors to upright panels with hinges.
- Make and fit trays and/or other interior fittings.

FITTED-FRAME UNIT

Assemble the frame on site and screw it to the wall at each end, then scribe a filling strip to the ceiling. Use sliding doors across wide cupboard openings.

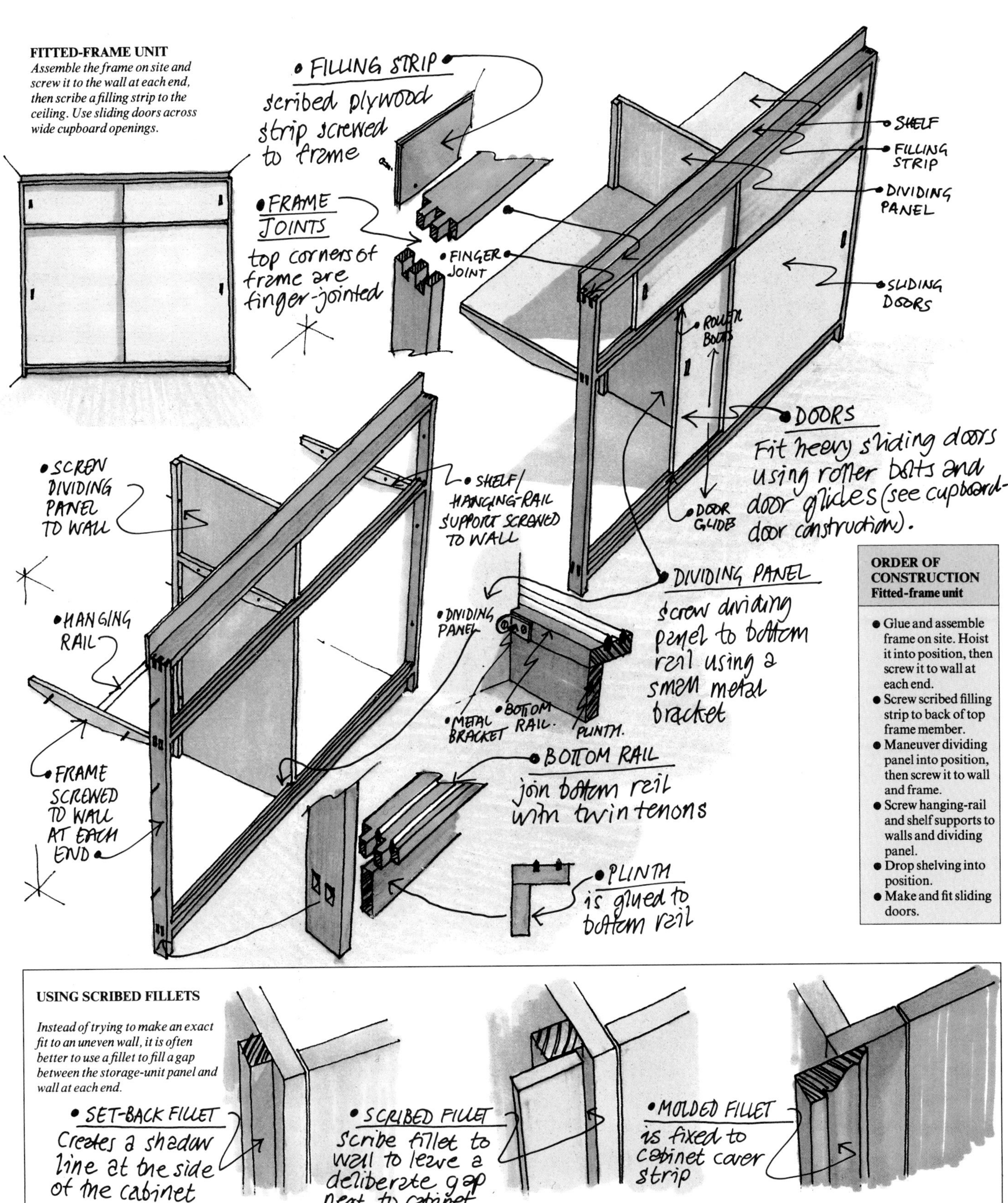

ORDER OF CONSTRUCTION
Fitted-frame unit

- Glue and assemble frame on site. Hoist it into position, then screw it to wall at each end.
- Screw scribed filling strip to back of top frame member.
- Maneuver dividing panel into position, then screw it to wall and frame.
- Screw hanging-rail and shelf supports to walls and dividing panel.
- Drop shelving into position.
- Make and fit sliding doors.

USING SCRIBED FILLETS

Instead of trying to make an exact fit to an uneven wall, it is often better to use a fillet to fill a gap between the storage-unit panel and wall at each end.

MAKING PLANS

An exceptionally gifted woodworker may be able to convert an idea into reality on the bench, but most people find it necessary to plan a design in detail on paper and perhaps try it out in three dimensions.

SEE ALSO

Tape measure	76
Glue gun	302

Sketch drawings
In order to conceive the shape and general construction of a new workpiece, a designer will normally put down his or her first thoughts on paper in the form of sketches. These are visual notes (similar to those shown on the preceding pages) used to explore the various possibilities until the designer arrives at a solution that appears to answer all the requirements. Unfortunately, it is all too easy to fool oneself with a sketch, either by underestimating the overall size of the piece or by exaggerating the section of a component. A prudent designer will make a measured scale drawing to check the proportions and constructional detail.

Scale drawings
A professional designer uses scale drawings to communicate information to the workshop or factory where an item is to be manufactured. It is convenient to use a similar system to work up your own sketch ideas. By convention, a designer normally adopts a scale of 1:4 ($\frac{1}{2}$in represents 2in) when using imperial measurements, and 1:5 (10mm represents 50mm) when using the metric system. You can use either system, but do not attempt to mix them. Smaller scales, typically 1:24 for imperial and 1:20 for metric, are more convenient when designing built-in furniture. Chairs and other relatively small workpieces are usually drawn full size.

Specific views of a workpiece are drawn side by side. They represent the front elevation (front view), side elevation (side view) and plan (top view); in addition, drawn sections (i.e. slices through the workpiece) show the internal structure. Areas that are unusually complex are often drawn full size to clarify their construction.

Professional draftsman's equipment is expensive, but you cannot make accurate drawings without a drawing board (any square-cut flat board will do), a T square for drawing horizontal lines and a large set square for the vertical ones. In addition, you will need a scale rule marked in increments representing all the common scale measurements and a protractor for measuring angles. Although not essential, it is worth investing in plastic guides known as French curves for drawing curved lines, a circle template for drawing small radii and a compass for larger circles. Make scale drawings on tracing paper (using a sharp, reasonably hard pencil) so you can overlay subsequent drawings as the design develops.

Front elevation

Side elevation

Plan

Section

Scale models
Having made a scale drawing, use it to construct a model of the workpiece out of balsawood and cardboard so you can see what your design looks like in three dimensions. Some designers like to make a fully detailed model using the actual materials specified for the full-size piece, but this is hardly ever necessary unless you want to impress a client.

Mock-ups
Making a full-size mock-up from workshop scraps and cheap materials can be extremely informative. It is the only way, for example, to make sure a chair is as comfortable or structurally sound as you imagine. Erecting a visual mock-up made from lightweight materials such as fiberboard or even corrugated cardboard is the ideal way to check the proportions of a large workpiece, especially if you can assemble it on site to see how it fits into its intended environment.

Cutting lists
Before ordering materials from a lumberyard, write a cutting list that specifies the length, width and thickness of every component in a workpiece. The list should also state the material from which each component is to be made and the quantity required. If possible, select stock that will allow the most straightforward cutting to size with the least waste.

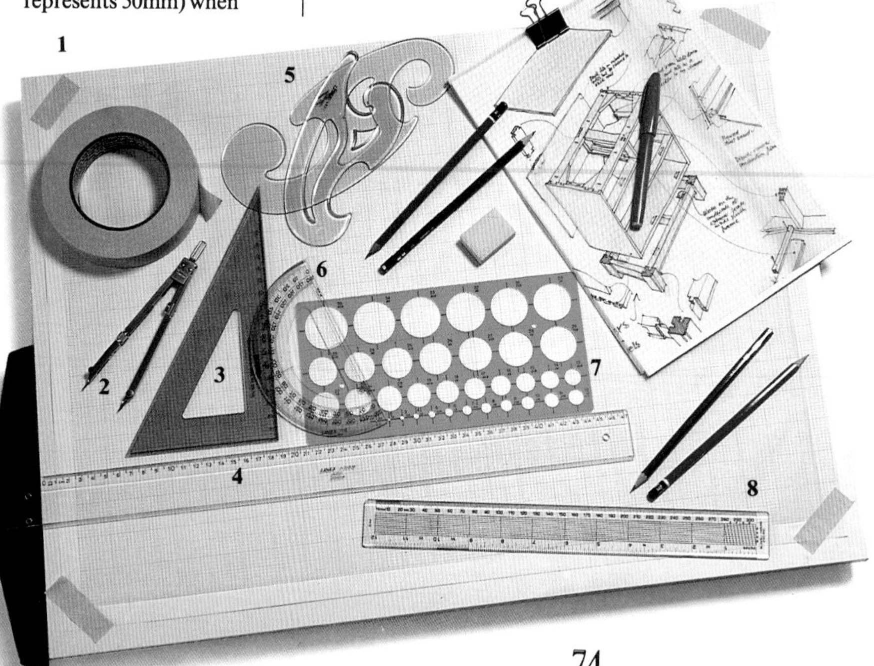

Drawing equipment
1 Drawing board
2 Compass
3 Set square
4 T square
5 French curves
6 Protractor
7 Circle template
8 Scale rule

SURVEYING A ROOM

Measure the room carefully and make notes of all the important features before you start to design built-in furniture.

- Use a long tape measure to take the main dimensions of the room, including the diagonals, in order to check whether it is square on plan. Don't assume the walls are perpendicular – take measurements at different heights where a good fit may be crucial.
- Measure the size and height of architectural features, such as ceiling cornices, baseboards, dadoes and picture rails.
- Measure windows and doors, and make a note or sketch of how they open.
- Note the position of fireplaces and radiators.
- Make a note of electrical outlets, switches and lighting fixtures that may have to be relocated to accommodate your design.

CHAPTER THREE

HAND TOOLS

At a time when more and more woodworkers are turning to machine tools for convenience or greater accuracy, someone coming fresh to woodwork might assume hand tools were merely relics left over from the leisurely days when craftsmen were paid for the quality of their products rather than for their labor. However, that simply isn't true. A competent woodworker can often finish a job by hand in the time it takes to set up a machine for the same purpose. Working by hand also gives a feel for materials that cannot be derived from operating a machine – the way different grains respond to the blade, for example, and how some woods are more forgiving while others show up the slightest error on the part of the woodworker. For these and other reasons, not least because of the pleasure of using them, a comprehensive set of hand tools will no doubt always figure among the equipment of even the most sophisticated workshop.

MEASURING & MARKING TOOLS

It is good woodworking practice always to mark one component from another whenever possible. The way one half of a dovetail joint is marked from the other is a perfect example. It is not only the most precise method, it also avoids the possibility of misreading a ruler or tape.

SEE ALSO

Wood defects	14
Miter joints	216-217
Marking dovetails	239, 243
Veneering tools	258-259

Four-fold rule
A traditional carpenter's folding rule is made from boxwood with brass hinges and protective end caps.

A well-made rule will stay rigid in its extended form until the hinges are folded deliberately. A 3ft (1m) rule, folding into four equal parts, is the most popular model. Whatever system of measurement you prefer, it makes sense to buy a rule with feet and inches marked on one side and metric dimensions on the other.

• Maintaining rulers
Treat rulers and other measuring and marking tools with respect or they will lose their accuracy. Never cut against a wooden or plastic ruler – use a metal one only. Metal rulers will rust in a damp atmosphere – wipe them with oil for long-term storage. If you fold and kink a retractable tape measure, it will not support itself when extended.

Steel ruler
A steel ruler is primarily a metalworker's tool, but you should have at least one 1ft (300mm) ruler for making very precise measurements. It is also useful as a short straightedge.

It is convenient if one side is marked as a center-finding ruler, calibrated with equal divisions from the center point toward each end of the ruler.

Straightedge
An unmarked strip of steel with one beveled edge, this tool is used to check the flatness of a surface and as a guide for cutting straight lines with a marking knife. Being thick and relatively heavy, a straightedge is especially useful for holding down veneers when trimming them to size. Straightedges range from 20in (500mm) to 78in (2m).

Retractable tape measure
A flexible steel tape measure, about 16ft (5m) long, is an essential tool for every workshop. Choose one that is calibrated with imperial and metric dimensions on opposite edges so you can readily convert one system to another.

The hook at the tip of the tape is loose on its rivets so that it can move fractionally to take internal and external measurements. This hook can become displaced if you allow the tape to snap back into its case. Buy a tape with a locking mechanism that prevents the tape from retracting accidentally.

Try square
A try square has a parallel-sided blade fixed at right angles to a wooden, cast-iron or plastic stock. It is used to check the accuracy of a 90-degree corner or for marking lines at right angles to an edge. If the tool is made with the top inside corner of the stock cut to 45 degrees, it can be used to mark out miter joints.

A square with a plastic or cast-iron stock will remain accurate because the materials are inert. A wooden stock can react to humidity and the rivets holding the blade can work loose if the tool is dropped. However, the square with a rosewood stock edged in brass remains a firm favorite with woodworkers because it is such a beautifully made tool.

A try square with a 1ft (300mm) long blade will prove to be the most useful.

Miter square
A miter square's blade passes through the stock at an angle of 45 degrees. It is used for marking out miter joints and for checking the accuracy of each half of the cut joint.

Sliding bevel
A sliding bevel functions like a miter square, but its blade can be adjusted to any angle and locked in place with a lever or screw.

Dovetail template
Use a special template to mark out dovetail joints. One blade is for tails in softwood with a slope of 1:6. The other has a ratio of 1:8 for hardwood tails.

Marking knife
Use a pencil for the preliminary marking of joints, but always use a marking knife to sever the wood fibers to ensure a clean edge when you saw to the line. The blade is beveled on one side only. Use the knife on the waste side of the line, running the flat face of the blade against a try square.

USING MEASURING AND MARKING TOOLS

Every woodworker requires several tools for the initial stages of measuring and marking wood. Use and store the tools with care. Rough or careless treatment can affect their accuracy.

Dividing a board equally
Mark a board into equal divisions using any ruler. To divide it by five, for example, align the tip of the ruler with one edge of the board and the fifth division with the other, then make a pencil mark against divisions one to four.

Dividing a board equally

Checking for winding
A badly warped board is obvious, but check for subtle "winding," as it is called, by holding a steel ruler across each end of the board. If the rulers look parallel, the board is flat.

Checking for winding

Checking for flatness
Place a straightedge on a surface you want to check for flatness. If you can see cracks of light beneath the edge or if it rocks on a bump, the surface is not flat. Turn the tool to various angles to check a wide surface.

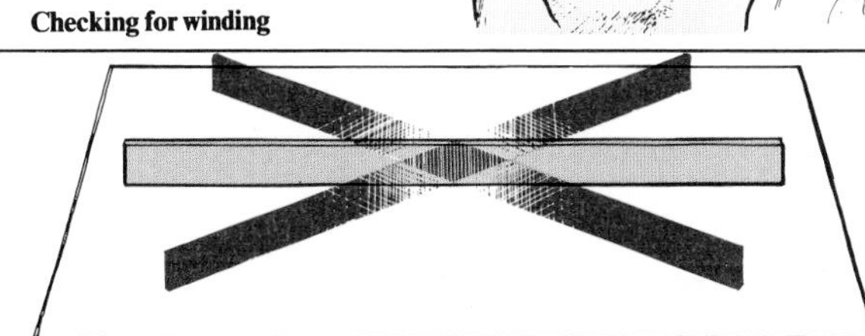

Checking for flatness on a wide surface

Taking internal and external measurements
When taking external measurements, hook the tape over one edge of the work and read the tape against the opposite edge (**1**). For internal measurements, read the tape where it enters the case, then add the length of the case itself to arrive at the true dimensions (**2**).

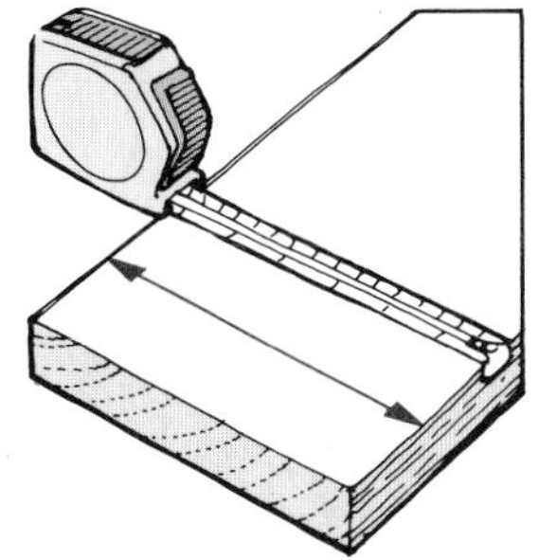

1 Taking external measurements

2 Taking internal measurements

Checking a try square
To check that a square is accurate, first use it to draw a line at right angles to a surface. Turn the blade over and align it with the marked line. The edge of the blade and the line should match exactly.

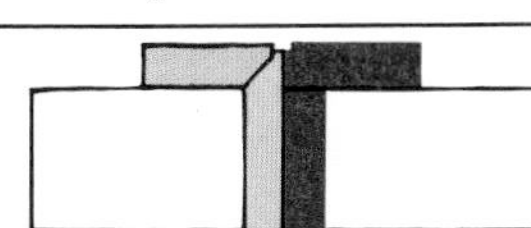

Checking a try square

Using a try square
Use a try square to make sure two parts of a joint meet at 90 degrees (**1**). To mark a right angle, hold the stock firmly against the work and draw a marking knife or pencil along the blade (**2**). To mark a miter, place the angled face of the stock against the work to mark a line at 45 degrees (**3**).

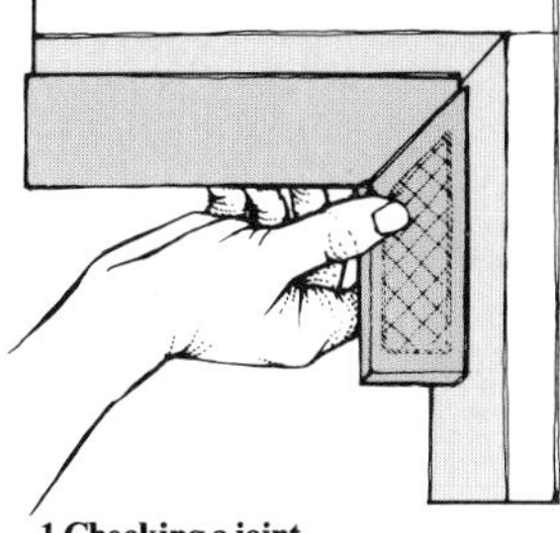

1 Checking a joint

2 Marking a right angle

3 Marking a miter

Checking a miter
Slide a miter square over the external corner of a mitered piece. The blade should be in contact across the entire width of the joint.

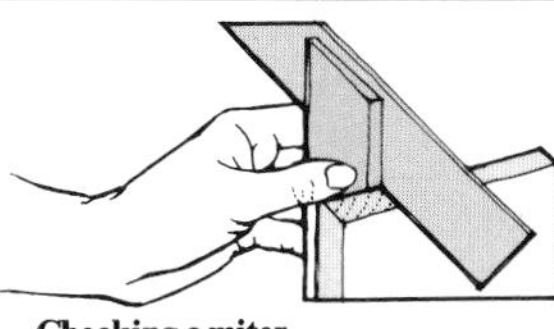

Checking a miter

MARKING & CUTTING GAUGES

SEE ALSO

● **Storing wooden gauges** The wooden stock of a gauge is such a close fit on the beam that it can jam if the wood swells. If your workshop is damp, keep the tool in a plastic bag.

Marking gauge
Mark a line parallel to a planed edge using a marking gauge. A sharp steel pin is fixed at one end of a hardwood beam. A fence, or "stock," slides on the beam and is locked the required distance from the pin with a thumbscrew. Brass strips are set flush with the working face of the stock to prevent wear. A standard beam is 8in (200mm) long, but you can get a 1ft (300mm) beam for marking wide boards.

Cutting gauge
A cutting gauge is similar in every respect to a marking gauge, but instead of a steel pin it has a small blade held in place with a brass wedge. It is designed for marking wood across the grain where the pin of a marking gauge would tear the surface of the wood. A rounded blade is standard, but this can be substituted with a pointed knife-like blade for cutting veneers.

Mortise gauge
A mortise gauge has two pins for scribing both sides of a mortise or tenon simultaneously. One pin is fixed, while the other is attached to a metal slide adjusted to fine tolerances by a thumbscrew at the end of the beam. Most mortise gauges are dual-purpose tools, having a single fixed pin on the opposite side of the beam like that on a standard marking gauge.

Curved-edge gauge
It is difficult to scribe a line parallel to a curved edge with the flat stock of an ordinary marking gauge. The special brass fence on a curved-edge gauge rests on two points to prevent the tool from rocking as it follows the edge of the work. It can also be used on straight edges.

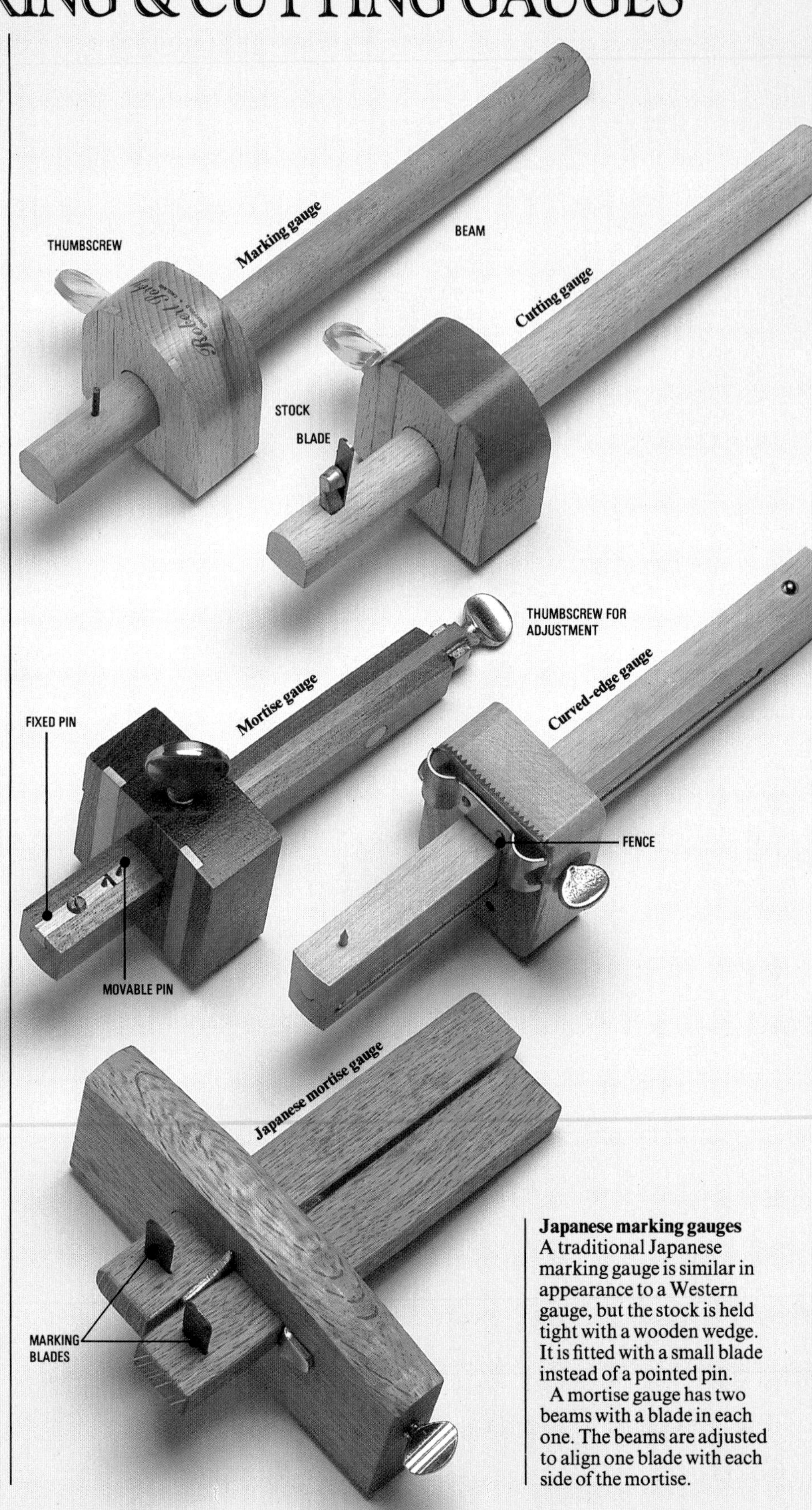

Japanese marking gauges
A traditional Japanese marking gauge is similar in appearance to a Western gauge, but the stock is held tight with a wooden wedge. It is fitted with a small blade instead of a pointed pin.

A mortise gauge has two beams with a blade in each one. The beams are adjusted to align one blade with each side of the mortise.

OTHER GAUGES

Profile gauge
A profile gauge has a row of metal pins or plastic blades that, when pressed against a molding, slide back to reproduce its shape exactly. A center spring holds the pins by friction.

Chalkline
It is not possible to gauge a straight line on a board with a waney edge, but you can use a length of string to mark a cut line. The easiest way is to use a chalkline. The string winds into a case containing colored chalk, which coats the string each time it is withdrawn. With an assistant, stretch the string taut along the intended cut line, then pluck it like a bowstring against the wood to deposit a chalked impression on its surface.

Profile gauge

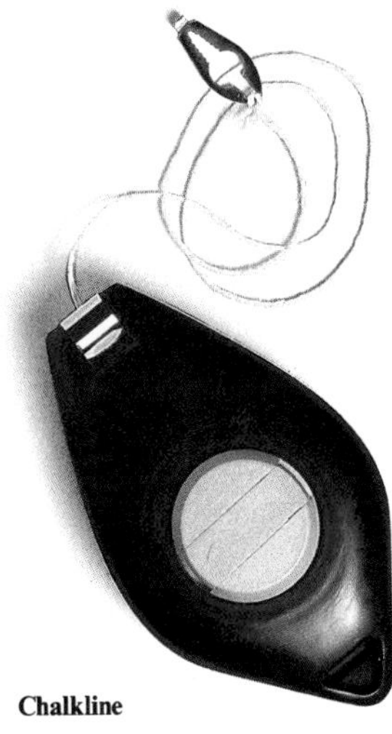
Chalkline

USING MARKING AND CUTTING GAUGES

When using marking and cutting gauges, the intention is to leave a clear but fine line on the work. Scoring a deep line can tear the wood, leading to inaccuracy.

Adjusting a marking gauge
Adjust the stock using a ruler **(1)** and lock it in place with its thumbscrew. Check the measurement and make fine adjustments by tapping the end of the beam on a bench to increase the distance between pin and stock **(2)**. Decrease it by tapping the tip of the beam **(3)**.

1 Set the stock using a ruler

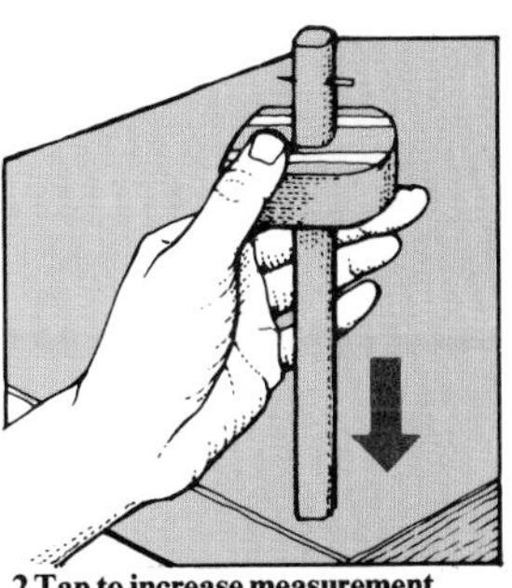
2 Tap to increase measurement

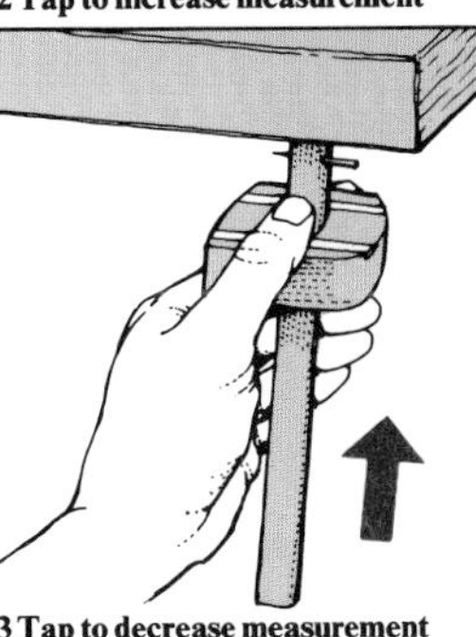
3 Tap to decrease measurement

Adjusting a mortise gauge
Set the pins to match the width of a mortise chisel, then adjust the stock to suit the thickness of the rail.

Set pins to match chisel

Scribing with a gauge
Press the stock of a gauge against the edge of the work, then push the tool away from you, allowing the pin to trail behind the beam with its point just marking the wood.

Finding a centerline
When marking out certain joints, it is essential to be able to find the exact center of a rail. Using a ruler is not an accurate method. Adjust a marking gauge as closely as possible to half the thickness of the rail, then check it by holding the stock against one side of the rail and making a single pinprick. Make a similar mark from the other side of the rail. If the two marks correspond exactly, the gauge is accurately set to the center of the rail. If they overshoot or fall short of the centerline, adjust the gauge until the marks coincide.

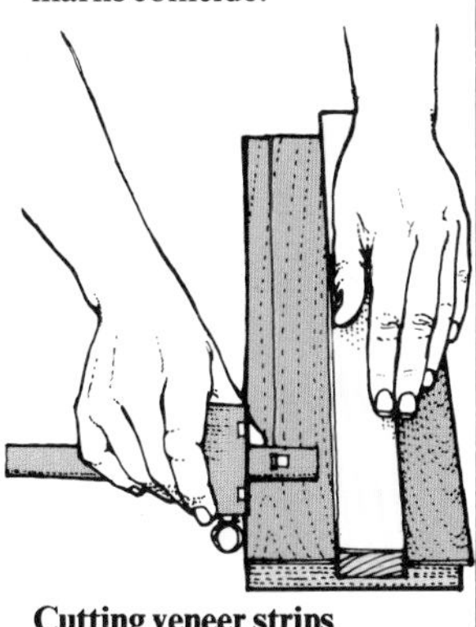

Cutting veneer strips
Align the planed edges of veneers with a straightedged board. Hold the veneers flat with a heavy batten and use a cutting gauge to slice off parallel-sided strips.

SQUARING UP WOOD

To plane a piece of wood flat and with adjacent surfaces at right angles to each other is known as "squaring up."

Method of squaring up
Select what appears to be the best face in terms of color, grain pattern and freedom from blemishes. Plane it flat and designate it "face side" with a penciled loop trailing off at one edge **(1)**. Plane this edge square to the face side, check it with a try square and mark it with an arrowhead pointing to the face-side loop **(2)**. This is now the "face edge."

All other measurements must be taken from either face side or face edge.

Set a marking gauge to the required thickness and mark a line on both edges from the face side **(3)**. Plane the unfinished side down to these lines **(4)**. Mark the width on both sides from the face edge **(5)**, then plane the wood to size **(6)**.

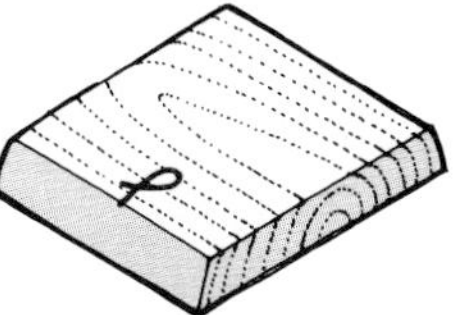
1 Mark face side

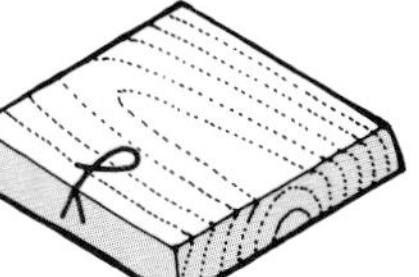
2 Mark face edge

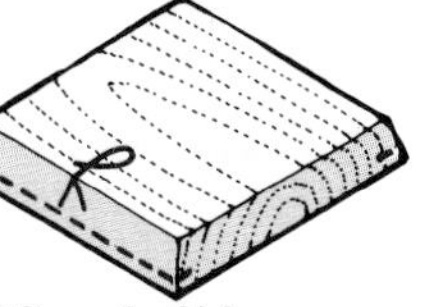
3 Gauge the thickness

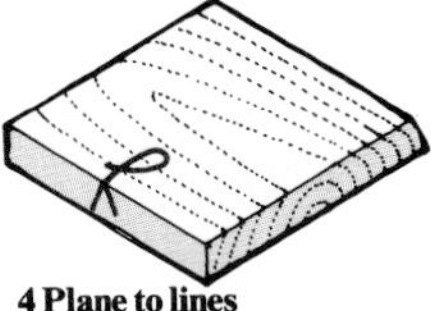
4 Plane to lines

5 Gauge the width

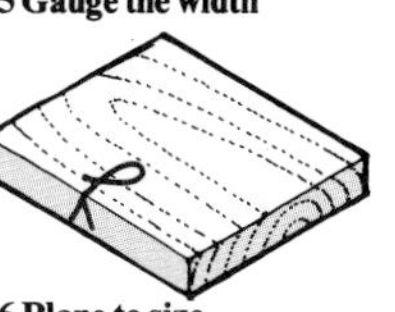
6 Plane to size

IMPROVISING A GAUGE

When absolute accuracy is not important, use the tip of your finger to guide a pencil point parallel to an edge **(1)**.

For a slightly wider measure, rest the pencil point against the end of a ruler held at right angles to the edge of the work. Use the finger holding the ruler like the stock of a marking gauge **(2)**.

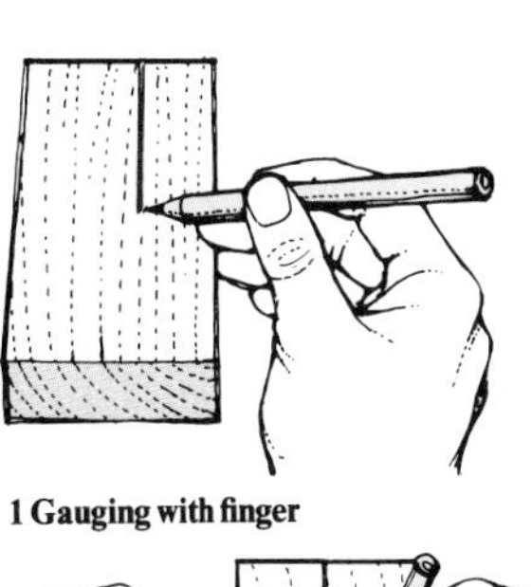
1 Gauging with finger

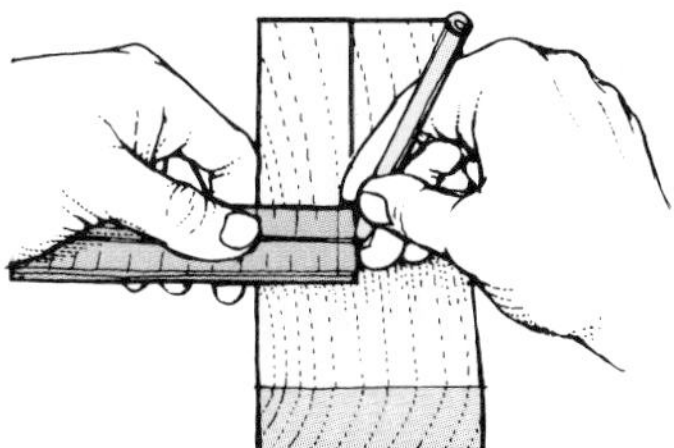
2 Gauging with ruler

HANDSAWS

All handsaws have long flexible blades, but because the blades are very deep they are capable of maintaining a straight cut. The best handsaw blades are taper-ground – that is reduced in thickness above the teeth to give a better clearance in the kerf. They are also skew-backed, with a slow "S" bend tapering sharply toward the toe to improve the balance of the tool. Blades are sometimes covered with polytetrafluoroethylene (PTFE) to reduce friction.

HOW A SAW WORKS

Woodworking saws have a very ancient pedigree stretching back more than 4,000 years. Through the centuries advances in technology have improved the quality of materials used in their production, and the ingenuity of successive generations of craftsmen has supplied us with a variety of solutions to the task of cutting wood – fast cutting, straight cutting, curved cutting, fine cutting and so on. Some saws are designed to cut on the push stroke, others on the pull stroke. Nevertheless, every saw cuts wood in basically the same way. A sawblade has a continuous row of pointed teeth along its cutting edge or edges. Each tooth acts like a miniature chisel or knife blade, cutting tiny shavings or slivers of wood that fall to the floor as sawdust.

SEE ALSO

Try square	76-77
Miter square	76-77
Caring for handsaws	82
Using handsaws	82
Replacing a tourniquet	85
Japanese saws	86
Sharpening saws	87

The set

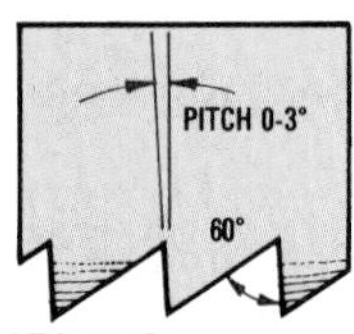

1 Rip teeth

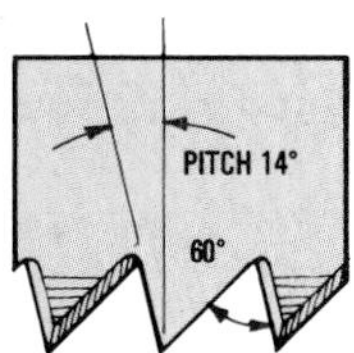

2 Crosscut teeth

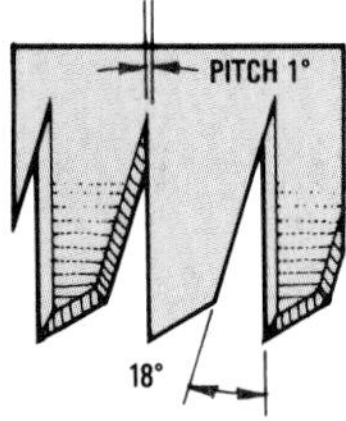

3 Japanese teeth

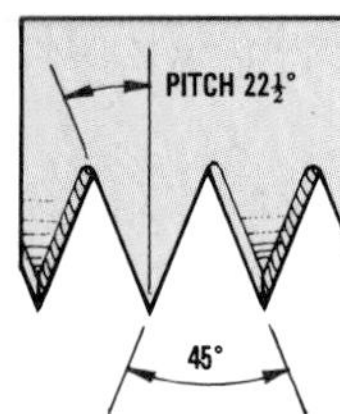

4 Dual-purpose teeth

The set of sawteeth
If the teeth were merely stacked one behind the other, the sawblade would jam in the cut after a few minutes' work. To solve the problem, all but the finest teeth are "set." Alternate teeth are bent to the right or left to cut a groove or "kerf" that is wider than the sawblade itself.

The shape of sawteeth
Sawteeth are shaped differently depending on the job they are required to do.
Rip teeth **(1)** are for cutting with the grain, such as sawing a plank to width. These are large teeth with upright leading edges. Each tooth is filed square to the face of the blade and its sharp tip slices wood like a chisel.
Crosscut teeth **(2)** are designed for sawing across the grain without tearing the wood fibers. This is necessary when cutting most joints or for sawing a plank to length. The leading edge of a crosscut tooth leans back slightly and is filed at an angle to form a sharp cutting edge and tip. Each tooth acts like a knife, scoring the wood on each side of the kerf, leaving the waste to fall out as it is cleared by the passage of the blade.
Japanese crosscut teeth **(3)** are similar in design, but they are tall and narrow with another bevel filed on the top of each one.
Dual-purpose teeth **(4)** are symmetrical and filed on both edges for cutting with and across the grain. They are also known as "fleam teeth."

The size of sawteeth
A saw designed for fine work – such as cutting a dovetail joint – will have small, finely set teeth. However, small teeth cut slowly. To be able to cut through wood quickly, especially resinous softwoods, a saw must have large teeth with deep "gullets" – the spaces between the teeth – which are capable of clearing large amounts of sawdust from the kerf.

Tooth size is measured by the number that fit into 1in (25mm) of sawblade. Despite metrication, saws are still specified in teeth per inch (TPI) – measured from the base of one tooth to the base of another. Alternatively, teeth are measured from point to point, in points per inch (PPI). There is always one more point per inch than teeth.

Occasionally a saw will be specified as having rising-pitch teeth – that is with progressively larger teeth toward the handle. The cut is started with the small teeth until the kerf is established, when the full length of the blade can be used.

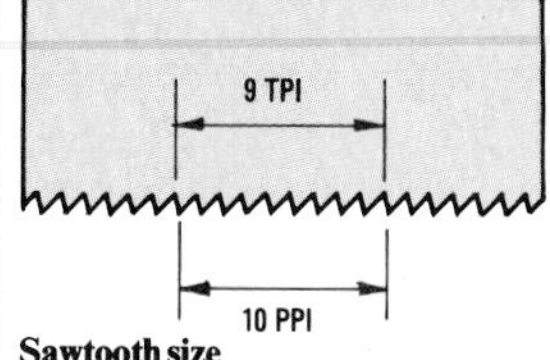

Sawtooth size

Hardened teeth
A lot of saws are made with electronically hardened teeth. They stay sharp longer than ordinary steel teeth, but they cannot be file-sharpened by hand.

A well-made handsaw

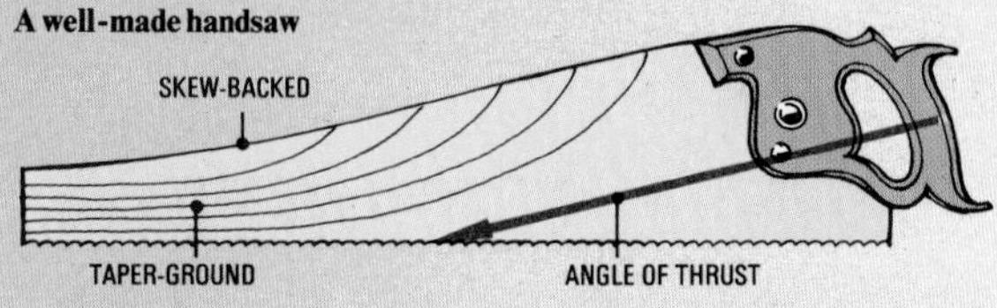

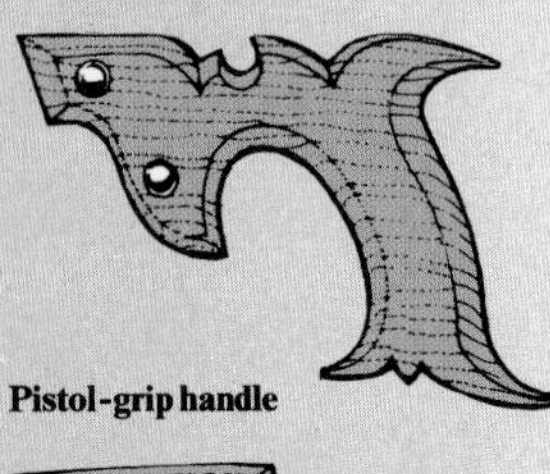

Pistol-grip handle

Closed wooden handle

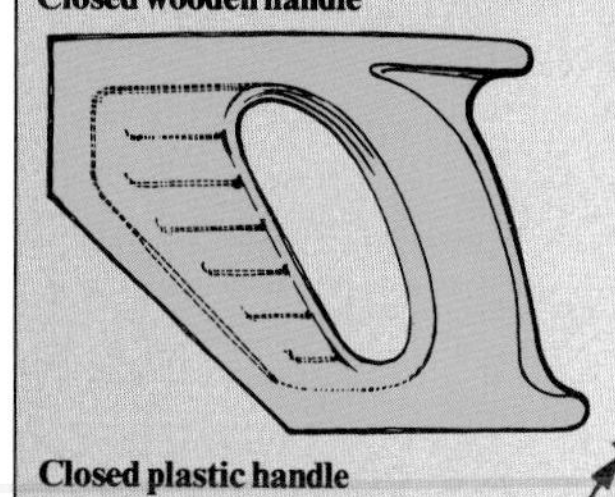

Closed plastic handle

HANDSAW HANDLES

The handles should be set low behind the blade for maximum thrust midway along the row of teeth. Although a few handsaws are still made with the old-fashioned pistol-grip handle, most are fitted with a stronger closed handgrip of wood or plastic. The traditional horned wooden handle is both functional and comfortable, but many manufacturers prefer the more economical plastic grips, which are often designed so the long straight back of the blade can be used as an extra-large try square.

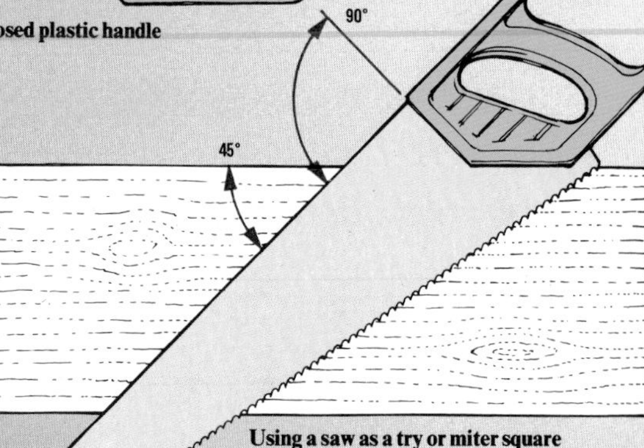

Using a saw as a try or miter square

Ripsaw
The ripsaw is the largest of the handsaws, with a blade length of 26in (650mm), having as few as 5 PPI. It is a specialized tool suitable only for cutting solid wood with the grain.

Crosscut saw
The crosscut saw is 24 to 26in (600 to 650mm) long, with 6 to 8 PPI. It is the ideal saw for cutting solid planks to length, but it is rather coarse for man-made boards. Some Western-style handsaws are made with fast-cutting Japanese-pattern crosscut teeth.

Panel saw
A panel saw has relatively fine crosscut teeth – 10 to 12 PPI – for cutting man-made boards, but it is also used as a general-purpose crosscut saw. Blade lengths vary from 20 to 22in (500 to 550mm).

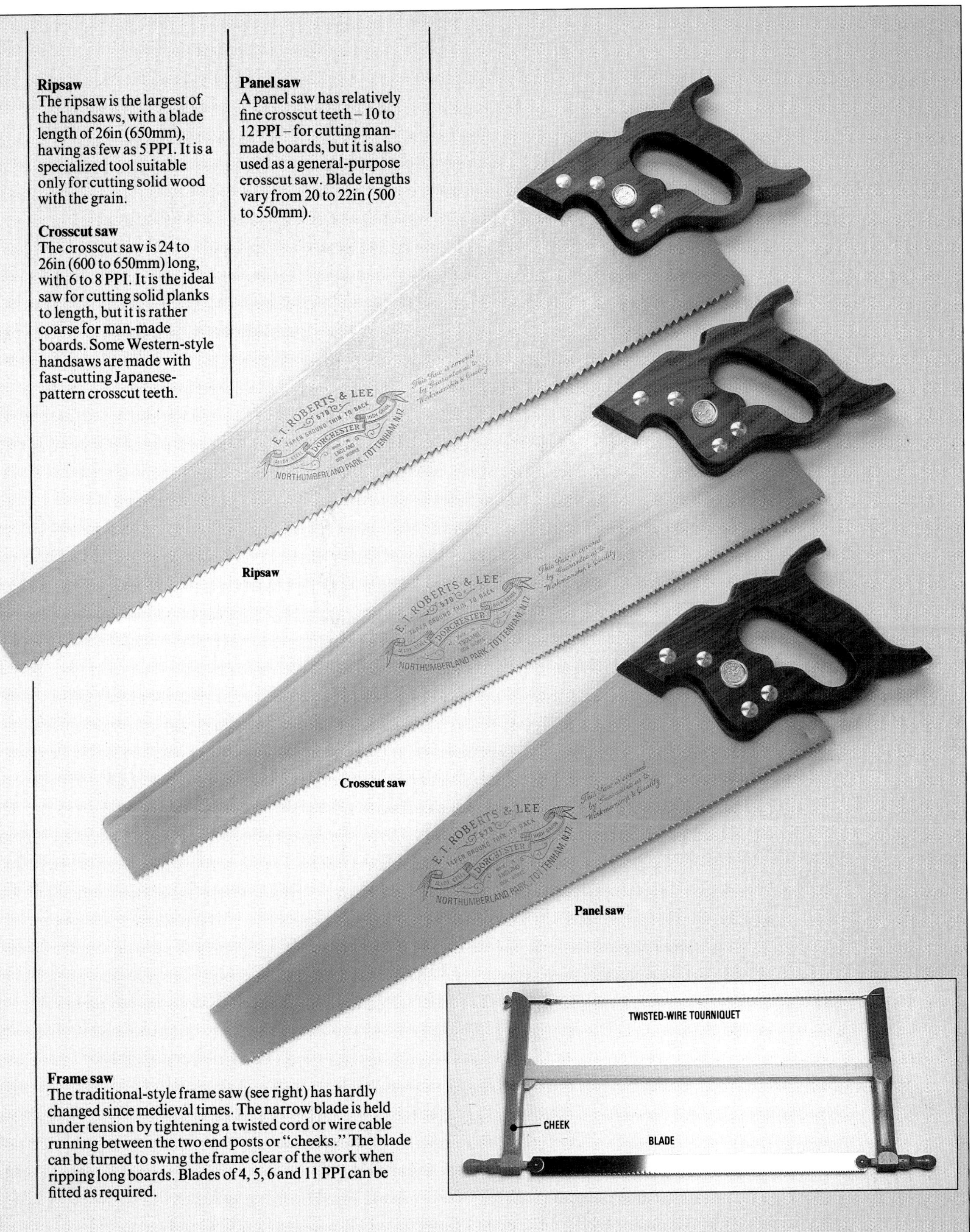

Ripsaw

Crosscut saw

Panel saw

Frame saw
The traditional-style frame saw (see right) has hardly changed since medieval times. The narrow blade is held under tension by tightening a twisted cord or wire cable running between the two end posts or "cheeks." The blade can be turned to swing the frame clear of the work when ripping long boards. Blades of 4, 5, 6 and 11 PPI can be fitted as required.

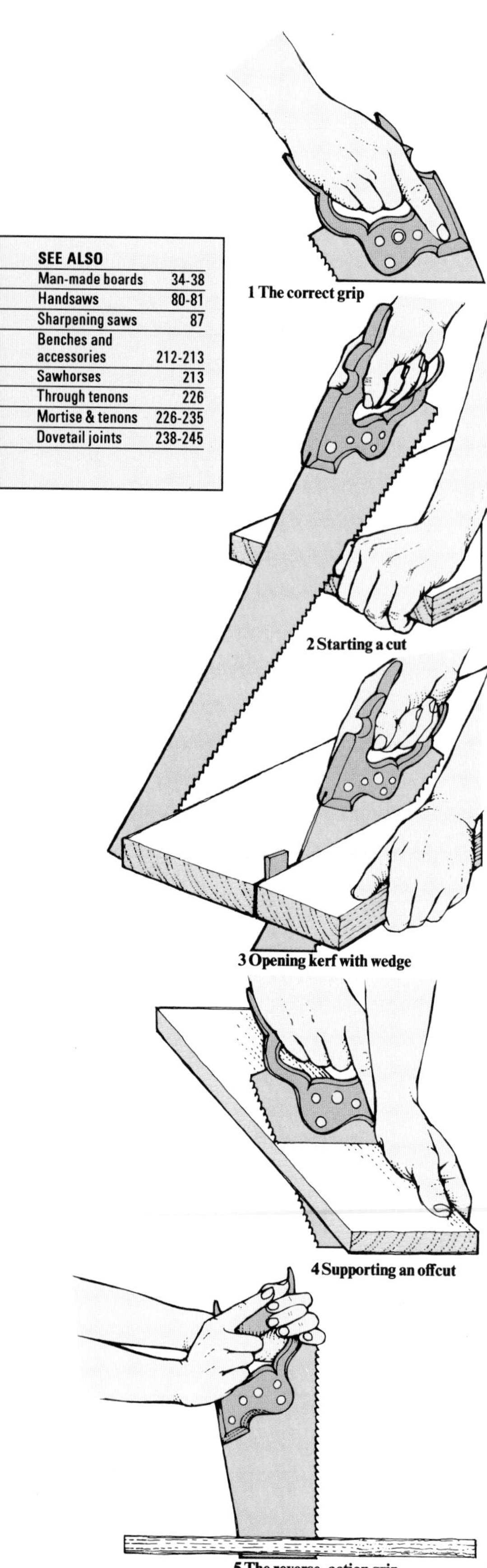

SEE ALSO

Man-made boards	34-38
Handsaws	80-81
Sharpening saws	87
Benches and accessories	212-213
Sawhorses	213
Through tenons	226
Mortise & tenons	226-235
Dovetail joints	238-245

1 The correct grip

2 Starting a cut

3 Opening kerf with wedge

4 Supporting an offcut

5 The reverse-action grip

USING AND CARING FOR HANDSAWS

Position the work so that you can saw at approximately 45 degrees to its surface and with the blade in line with your forearm.

Controlling a handsaw
Hold a handsaw with your forefinger extended toward the toe of the blade **(1)**. This will give you greater control over the blade and prevent the handgrip from twisting in your hand. To begin the cut, work just to the waste side of the marked line, guiding the blade with the thumb of your free hand **(2)** while making short backward strokes with the saw.

Once the kerf is established, use the full length of the blade with slow steady strokes. Fast erratic saw strokes are both tiring and inaccurate. If the saw begins to wander off line, twist the blade slightly to bring it back on course. If the kerf begins to close up and jam the blade, keep it open with a small wedge **(3)**. Rub the blade with wax for a smoother action.

Finishing the cut
As you finish sawing a plank to length, support the offcut with your free hand **(4)**. Work slowly and gently to sever the last few fibers without splitting the wood.

As you approach the end of a long plank or man-made board, either turn around and saw back toward the kerf you have just made or change your grip on the tool so that you can continue in the same direction but with the saw facing away from you **(5)**. You may have to position the work at bench height for this maneuver to avoid striking the floor with the toe of the saw.

Caring for handsaws
Slip a plastic guard over the sawteeth to protect them when the saw is not being used. For long-term storage, wipe an oily rag over the blade to keep it rust free. Remove rust spots with steel wool dipped in mineral spirits.

SUPPORTING THE WORK

Unless you support the work properly you cannot hope to saw efficiently or safely. Support planks of solid wood or man-made boards on 22in (550mm) high sawhorses. Thin sheet material will whip and bounce unless you support it from below on each side of the line with stiff planks. Hold down the work with your knee. If you are more comfortable sawing at bench height, clamp the work to the top with C-clamps or between bench stops.

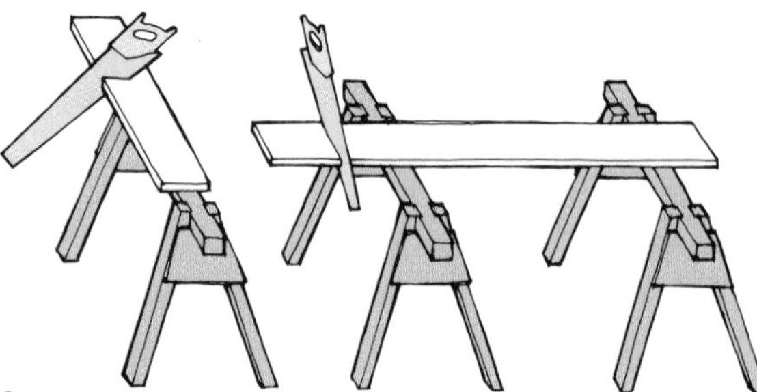

Crosscutting on sawhorses
You may be able to use a single sawhorse to cut short lengths, but support a long plank on two.

Ripping
As you ripsaw up to a sawhorse, move it to the far side of the blade and continue with the cut.

Supporting a thin board
Place planks beneath a thin man-made board.

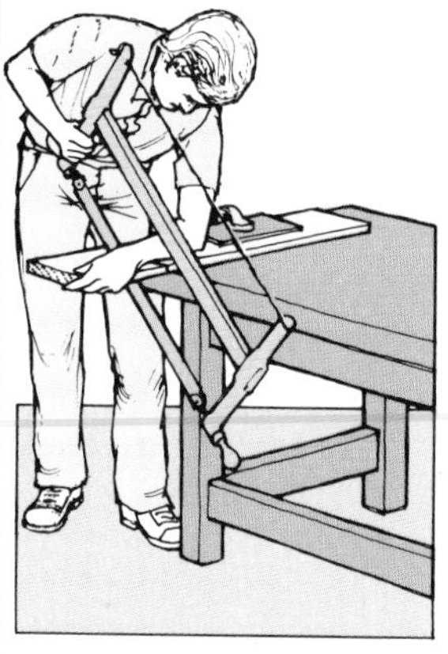

Crosscutting with a frame saw
To crosscut with a frame saw, set the blade just out of line with the frame so that you can see down the line of cut. Support the offcut as you finish sawing by passing your free hand through the frame and behind the blade.

Ripping with a frame saw
Clamp the work so that it overhangs the bench top. Set the blade at 90 degrees to the frame and use two hands to control the saw.

BACKSAWS

Backsaws, with their relatively thin blades and small finely set teeth, are the saws to use for precise work. The distinguishing feature of this family of saws is a heavy strip of brass or steel wrapped over the top edge of the blade. It keeps the blade straight and its weight makes for easy cutting without having to force the saw into the work.

Accessories
A bench hook is used for cross-cutting short lengths of wood with a backsaw. A miter box is a jig for cutting miters. The sawblade locates in slots in each side. A miter block is a cheaper version with one side.

Tenon saw
The tenon saw is the largest of the backsaws, having a 10 to 14in (250 to 350mm) blade with 13 to 15 PPI. It is a good general-purpose saw for cutting thick battens and large joints. It has a closed handle similar to those used for handsaws.

Dovetail saw
A dovetail saw is a smaller version of the tenon saw with an 8in (200mm) blade and 16 to 22 PPI. The finer teeth are not set in the accepted sense, relying on the burr produced by file-sharpening to provide sufficient blade clearance. The dovetail saw is traditionally made with a closed or an open pistol-grip handle. An alternative design of dovetail saw has a longer blade with a straight handle. Both patterns are for cutting fine joints in hardwood.

Offset dovetail saw
An offset dovetail saw is intended for flush-cutting through-tenons, dowels and so on. The reversible-handle version allows for right-hand or left-hand use.

Bead saw
The bead saw is a miniature backsaw with 26 PPI for cutting delicate work.

Blitz saw
The blitz saw is an extremely fine backsaw suitable for model-making. The teeth, at 33 PPI, are so small on the finest blitz-saw blades that they cannot be sharpened, so are replaceable.

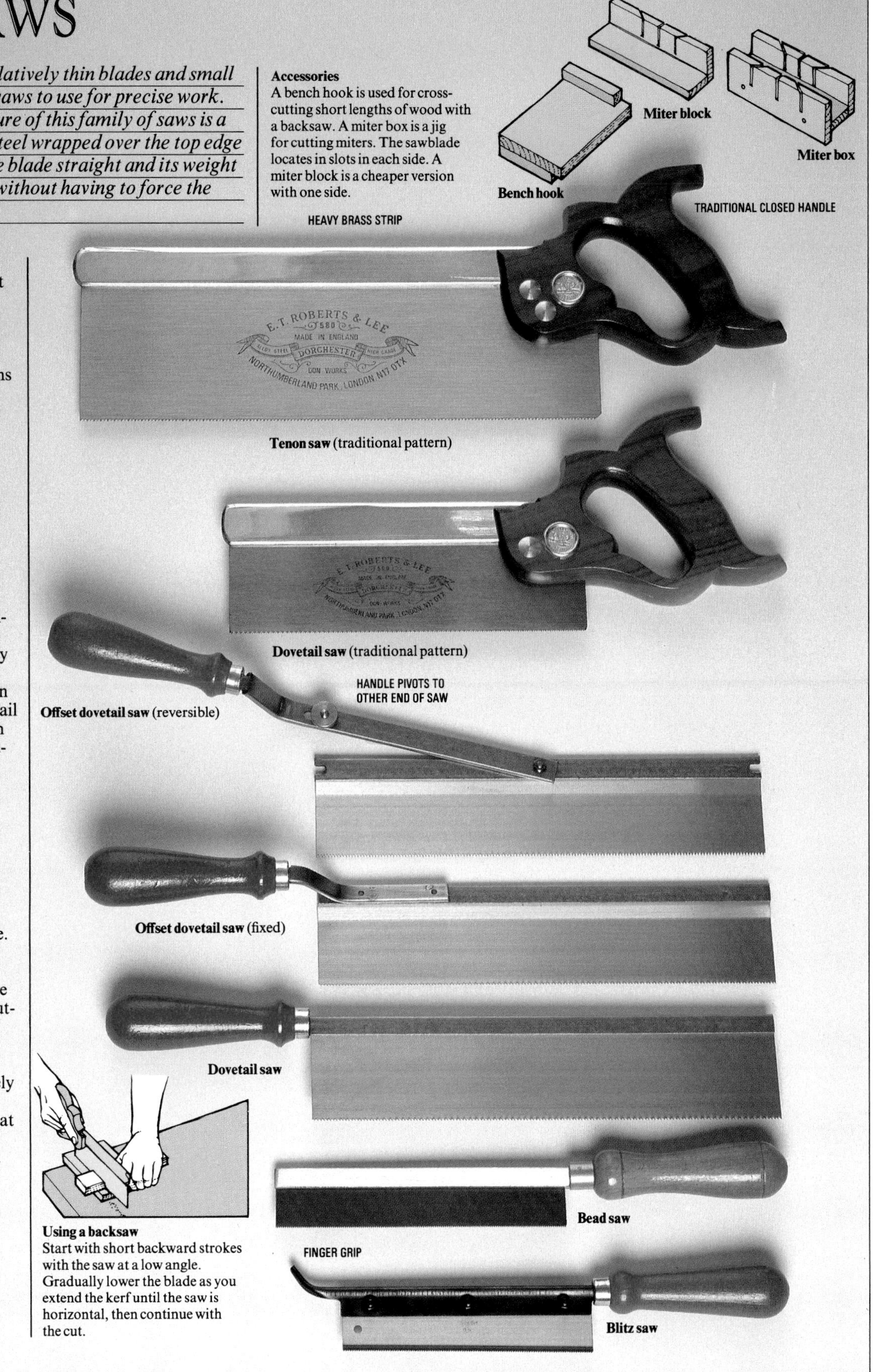

Tenon saw (traditional pattern)

Dovetail saw (traditional pattern)

Offset dovetail saw (reversible)

Offset dovetail saw (fixed)

Dovetail saw

Bead saw

Blitz saw

Using a backsaw
Start with short backward strokes with the saw at a low angle. Gradually lower the blade as you extend the kerf until the saw is horizontal, then continue with the cut.

CURVE-CUTTING SAWS

A family of special-purpose saws is available for cutting out curved components. The saws are graded in size to cope with work of all thicknesses, from thick hardwood planks to thin veneers.

SEE ALSO

Frame saw	81
Powered scroll saw	178-180
Piercing saw	296

Bowsaw
This small lightweight frame saw is fitted with narrow blades for making curved cuts. They are 8 to 12in (200 to 300mm) long with 9 to 17 PPI and are sturdy enough to saw quite thick sections of solid wood. Blades can be turned through 360 degrees to swing the frame out of the way.

Coping saw
A 6in (150mm) coping-saw blade is held under tension by the spring of the metal frame. It is for cutting curves in solid wood, and also in man-made boards. The blades, with 15 to 17 PPI, are too narrow to sharpen and are discarded when blunt or broken.

Scroll saw
A scroll saw, with its extra-deep bowed frame, is designed to make extremely tight curved cuts in thin man-made boards or veneers. With up to 32 PPI, the blades are very fragile.

Compass saw
It is not possible to use any of the bowed saws to make a cut in the middle of a large board. The narrow tapering blade of a compass saw is capable of making reasonably tight curves, but is also deep enough to keep on a straight course. The pistol-grip handle will take a variety of blades with 8 to 10 PPI.

A straight-handled version of the saw, known as a pad-saw or keyhole saw, is preferred by some woodworkers because it feels comfortable in the hand when sawing in any direction.

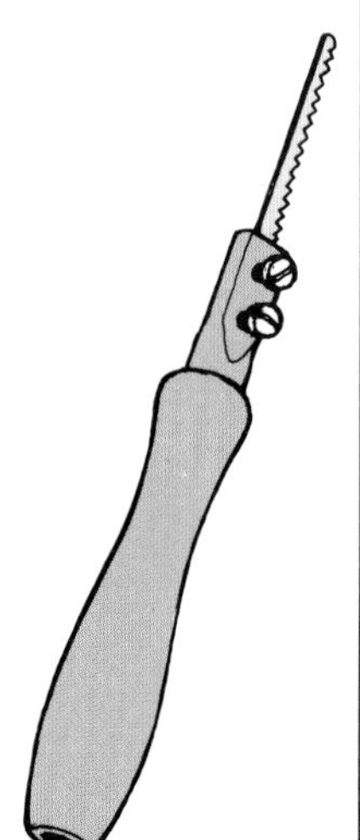

Padsaw
The retractable blade is clamped by screws in the ferrule.

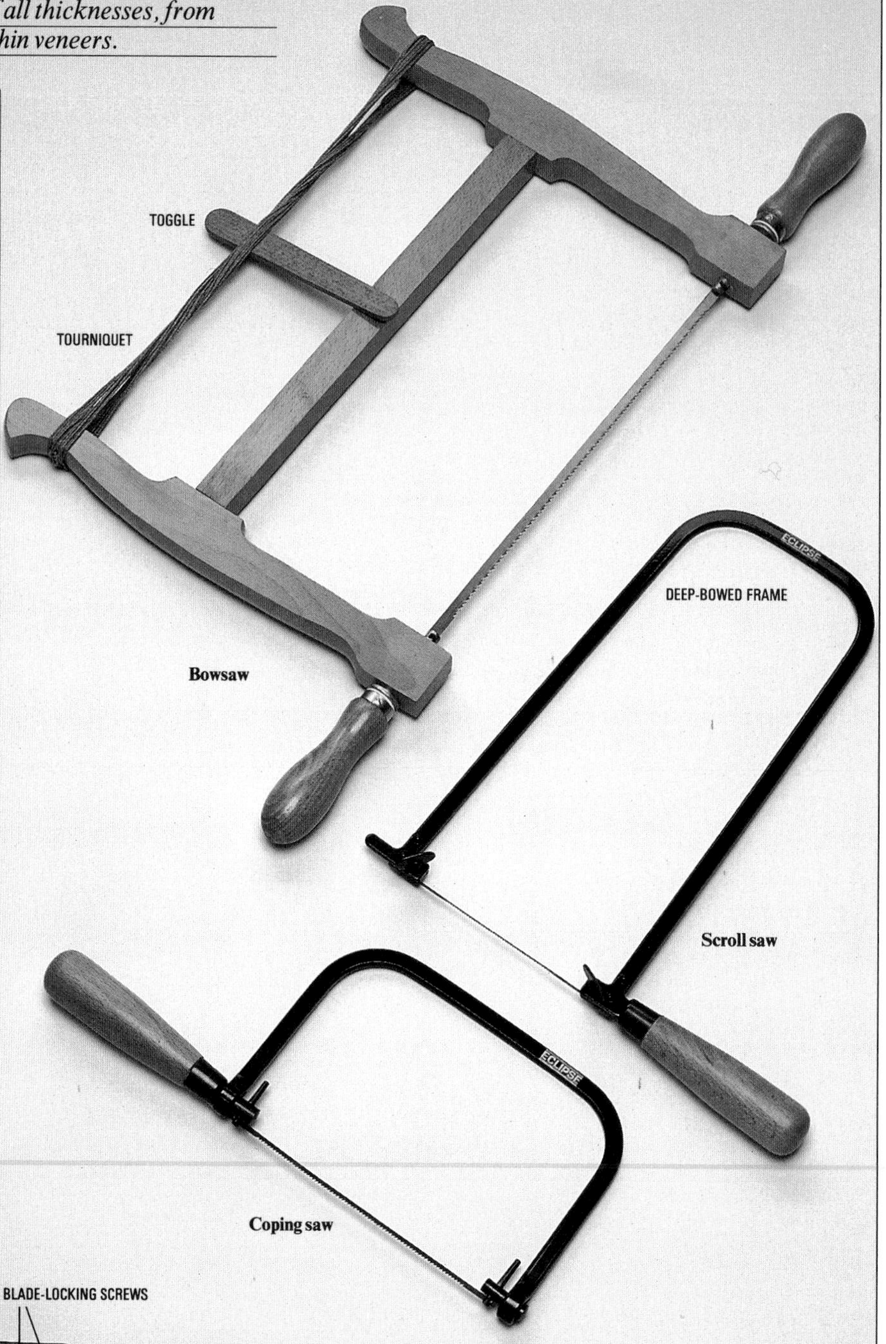

TOGGLE

TOURNIQUET

Bowsaw

DEEP-BOWED FRAME

Scroll saw

Coping saw

BLADE-LOCKING SCREWS

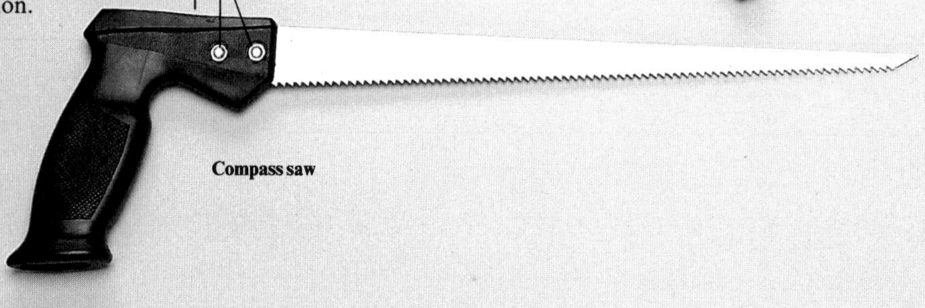

Compass saw

CHANGING CURVE-CUTTING SAWBLADES

Curve-cutting saws have relatively narrow blades that will eventually break or bend. Always have spare blades in stock.

Fitting a bowsaw blade
Loosen the cord tourniquet across the top of the saw, then locate the new blade, with the teeth facing away from you, in the slotted handle rods at each end **(1)**. Pass the pins through the holes in the rods and blade. Wind up the tourniquet to tighten the blade and place the toggle against the central stretcher rail. Turn the handle at each end of the saw **(2)** to straighten the blade.

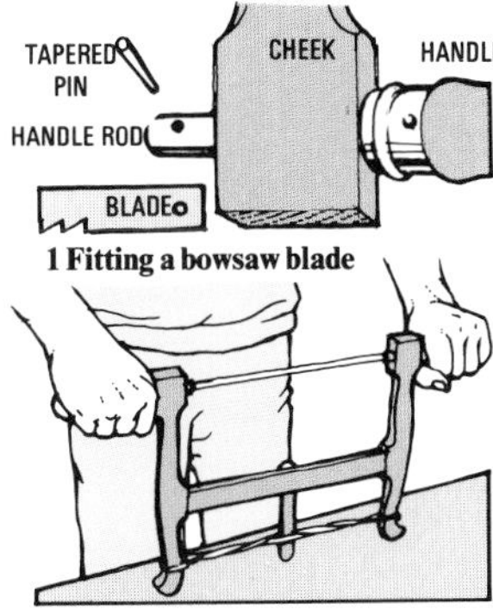

1 Fitting a bowsaw blade

2 Straightening the blade

Replacing a tourniquet
Replace a broken tourniquet with a length of new string. With the blade in position, lightly clamp the cheeks of the saw between bench stops. Tie the string to one cheek, then make a cord by winding it end-to-end about four times. Wind the loose end around the cord near one cheek and tie a knot through the strings **(1)**.
  Pass the wooden toggle through the center of the cord **(2)** and wind it up until the blade is tight.

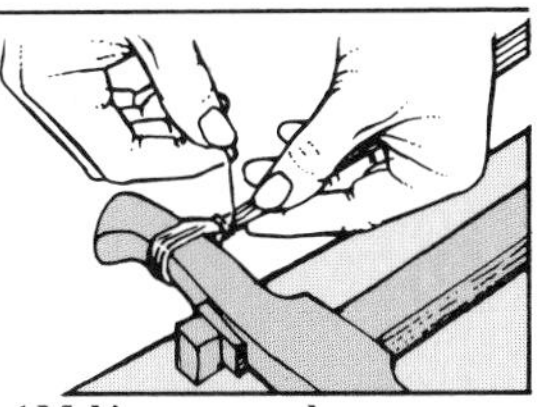
1 Making a new cord

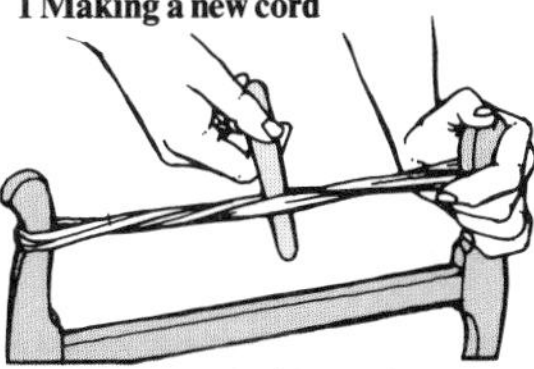
2 Wind up cord with toggle

Changing a coping-saw blade
A coping-saw blade fits into slots in large retaining pins at each end of the saw **(1)**. To fit a new blade, first turn the handle counterclockwise to reduce the gap between the retaining pins. Fit the blade at the toe of the saw with the teeth facing toward the handle, then flex the frame against the bench **(2)** to engage the other end of the blade. Holding its retaining pin, turn the handle to tighten the blade. Align the retaining pins by eye.

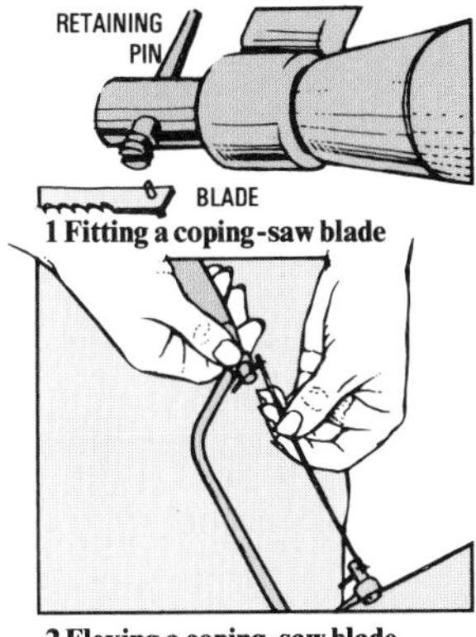

1 Fitting a coping-saw blade

2 Flexing a coping-saw blade

Fitting a scroll-saw blade
Each end is clamped by a thumbscrew. Compress the frame slightly as you fit the blade with the teeth facing the handle. A scroll saw cuts on the pull stroke.

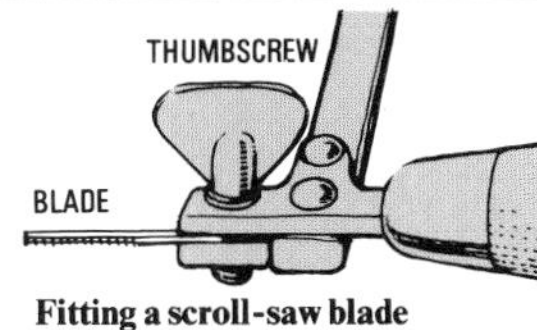

Fitting a scroll-saw blade

Fitting a compass-saw blade
To change a compass-saw blade, slacken the clamping screws and slide the slotted end of the blade into the handle. Then retighten.

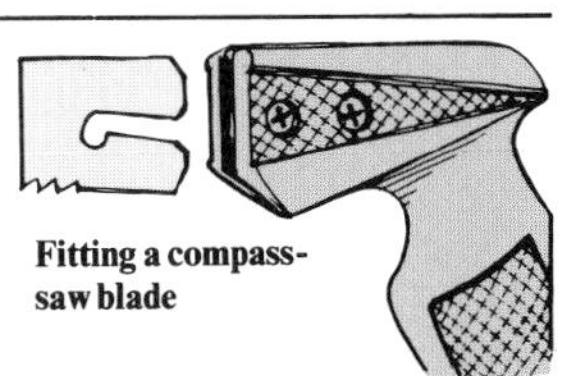
Fitting a compass-saw blade

USING CURVE-CUTTING SAWS

Except for the compass saw, which is used like a conventional handsaw, curve-cutting saws feel clumsy in the hands of an inexperienced woodworker. It is necessary to master specific techniques to compensate for the twisting force applied by their bowed frames.

Using a bowsaw
A bowsaw is unwieldy unless you use the proper two-handed grip to control the tool. Take hold of the handle with one hand, extending your index finger in line with the blade. Place your free hand alongside the other, with index and middle finger wrapped around the cheek on each side of the blade.

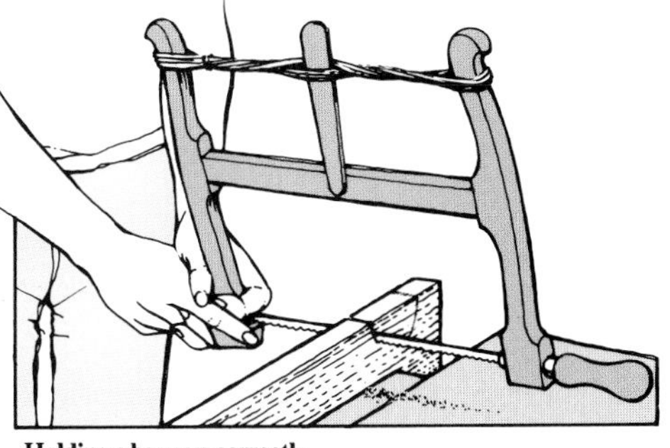
Holding a bowsaw correctly

Cutting with a coping saw
The narrow blade is difficult to keep on course. It is easier if you use a double-handed grip on the saw **(1)** or, alternatively, place the first joint of your extended index finger on the frame when using one hand. To make a closed cut some way from an edge, first drill a hole within the waste. Pass the blade through the hole and reconnect it to the saw frame **(2)**.

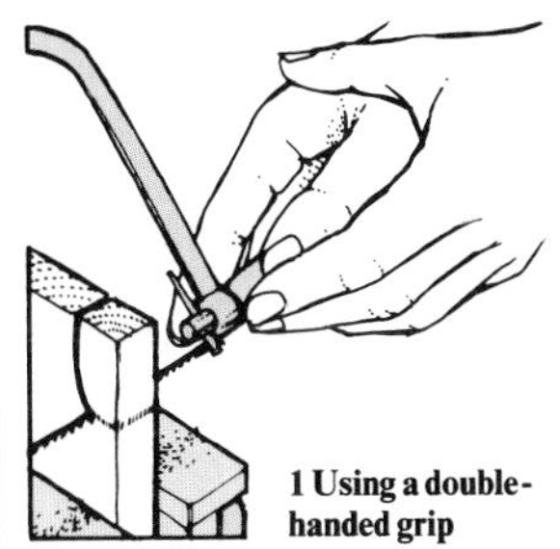
1 Using a double-handed grip

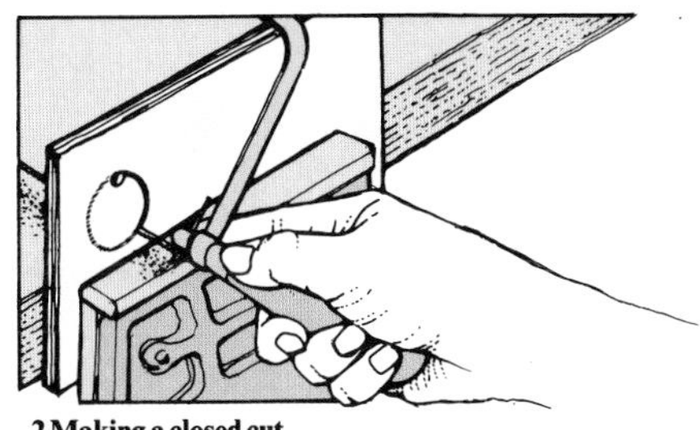
2 Making a closed cut

Using a scroll saw
Sit on a low stool when using a scroll saw and allow the work to overhang the edge of the bench top. The blade is so narrow it will make a tight curve without having to be swiveled in its frame.
  If the work is flexing and bouncing, cut a V-shaped notch in a block of wood or scrap plywood to support the work on each side of the blade. Clamp or screw the block to the bench.

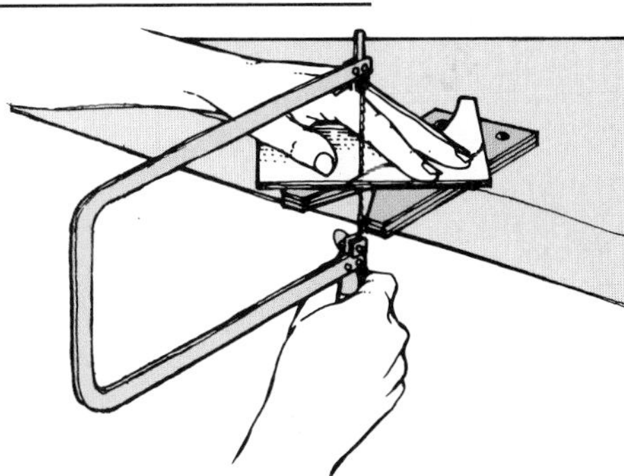
Using a scroll saw

Cutting with a compass saw
Drill a small hole in the waste to accept the tip of the saw. Work slowly and steadily to avoid buckling the narrow blade.

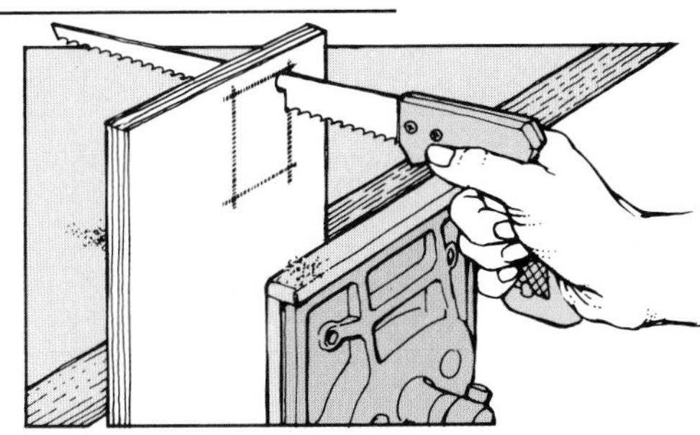
Using a compass saw

JAPANESE SAWS

Japanese saws cut on the pull stroke, so the blades can be made much thinner than their Western equivalents and the teeth are very finely set. As a result, they cut a narrow kerf with virtually no tearing of the grain. The best blades are taper-ground to reduce friction. Handles are bound with split bamboo.

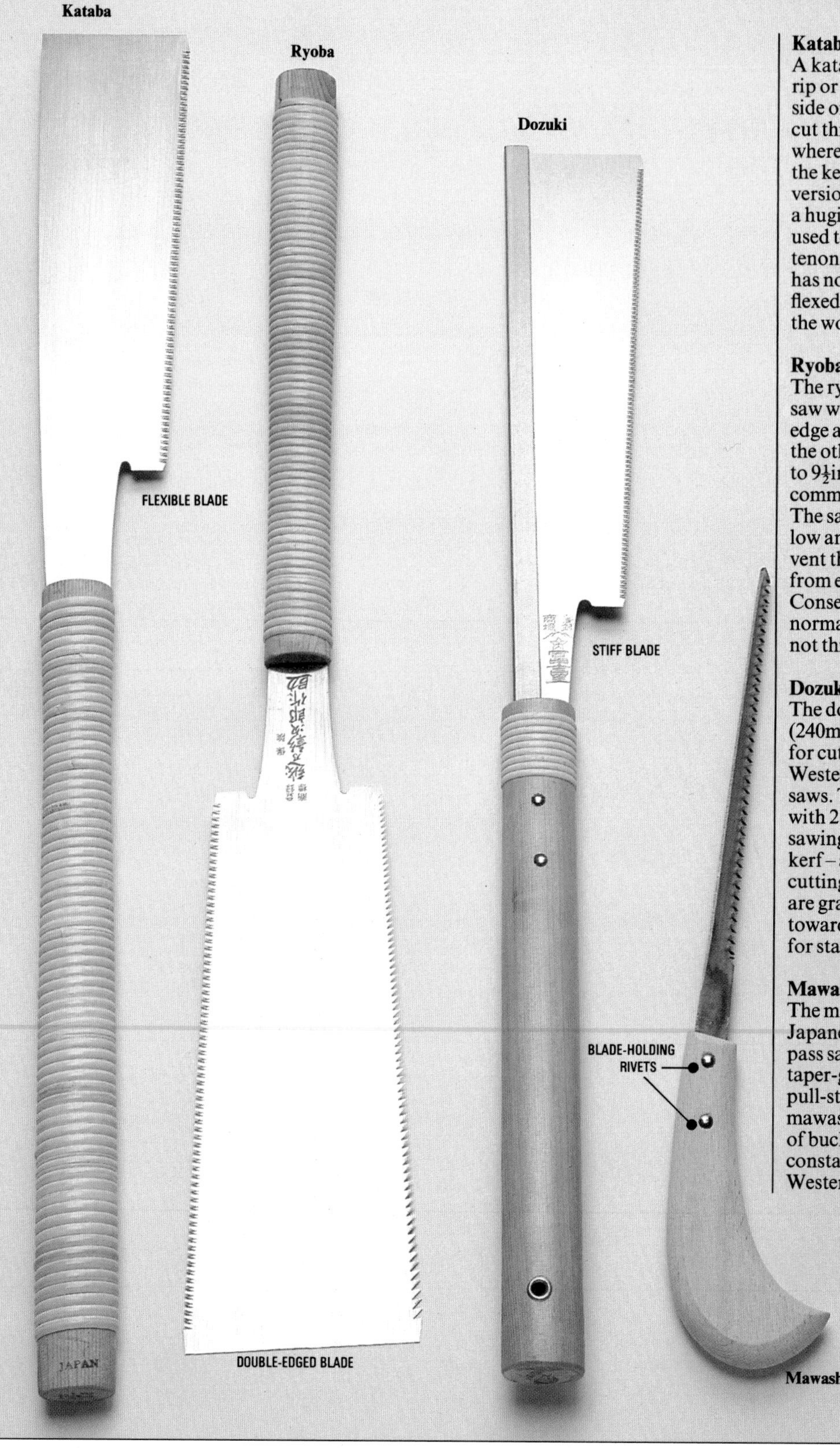

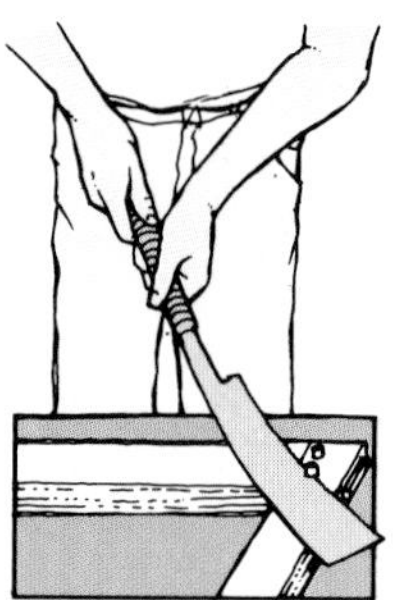

Using a hugihiki
Flex the blade against the work to cut a dowel flush with its surface.

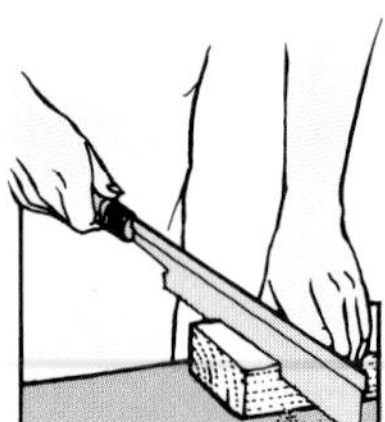

Cutting with a dozuki
Saw with the blade parallel to the bench. Some woodworkers like to saw a kerf on four sides before cutting through the work.

Kataba

FLEXIBLE BLADE

Ryoba

DOUBLE-EDGED BLADE

Dozuki

STIFF BLADE

BLADE-HOLDING RIVETS

Mawashibiki

Kataba
A kataba is made with either rip or crosscut teeth on one side only and can be used to cut thick sections of wood where a ryoba would bind in the kerf. An extra-flexible version of the saw, known as a hugihiki (dowel saw), is used to flush-cut through-tenons or dowel joints. It has no set on the teeth and is flexed against the surface of the work like a spatula.

Ryoba
The ryoba is a combination saw with rip teeth along one edge and crosscut teeth on the other. A blade of 8¼ to 9½in (210 to 240mm) is common, with 6 to 15 PPI. The saw must be used at a low angle to the work to prevent the upper row of teeth from entering the kerf. Consequently, a ryoba is normally used to cut boards, not thick beams of wood.

Dozuki
The dozuki is a 9½in (240mm) backsaw designed for cutting joints, like the Western tenon and dovetail saws. The dovetail version with 23 PPI is capable of sawing an especially narrow kerf – a real advantage when cutting fine joints. The teeth are graded with smaller ones toward the heel of the saw for starting the cut.

Mawashibiki
The mawashibiki is the Japanese keyhole or compass saw. Even with its thin taper-ground blade, the pull-stroke action of the mawashibiki reduces the risk of buckling the blade – a constant problem with the Western version of the saw.

SHARPENING SAWS

A saw needs to be sharpened as soon as it requires any real effort to drive it through the wood. Most woodworkers are happy to put the "edge" back on a saw, but might prefer to send it to a professional when it requires resetting. Resetting is necessary after four or five sharpenings or if you find the saw constantly runs off course due to uneven setting. Electronically hardened teeth cannot be sharpened by hand and fine disposable sawblades are always discarded when blunt.

SELECTING A SAW FILE

Saw	PPI	File length
Ripsaw	5 to 7	10in (250mm)
Crosscut saw	6 to 8	9in (230mm)
Panel saw	10 to 12	8in (200mm)
Tenon saw	13 to 15	7in (180mm)
Dovetail saw	16 to 22	6in (150mm)

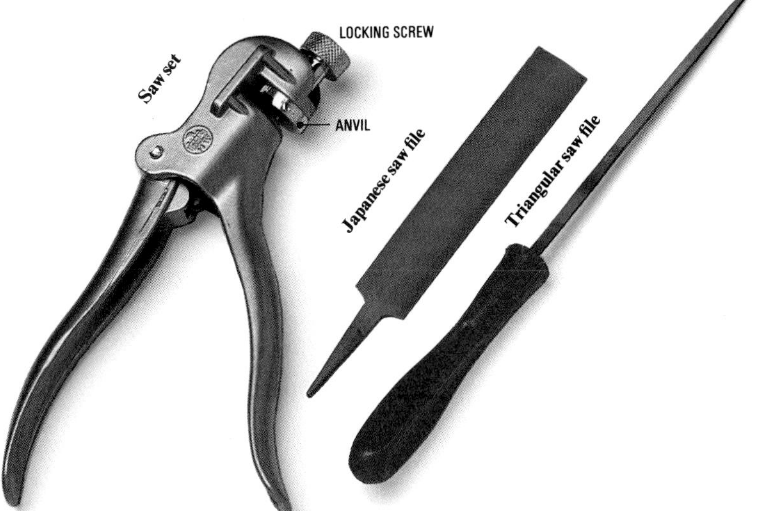

Saw files
The cutting edge of each sawtooth is maintained with a triangular file. Each side of the file should be about twice the height of the tooth. Use the chart as a rough guide to selecting a saw file.

Japanese saw files
Knife-edge files are available for sharpening Japanese saws. However, resetting and sharpening these saws is an exacting task best left to a professional.

Saw-file guide
A saw-file guide guarantees uniformity of angle and depth when sharpening tenon and handsaws.

Saw set
A saw set bends the top of sawteeth precisely to the required angle. Squeezing the handles together operates a plunger that presses the tooth against an angled anvil. The anvil is numerically graduated to correspond to tooth sizes up to 12 PPI. Saws with smaller teeth should be sent to a professional for resetting.

Saw clamp
A saw must be clamped firmly while being sharpened or it will vibrate noisily, throwing the file out of the gullet. Make an improvised clamp from two hardwood battens cut to match the length of the blade and shaped to fit around the handle. Clamp the saw between the battens in a bench vise. If necessary, attach a small C-clamp at one end.

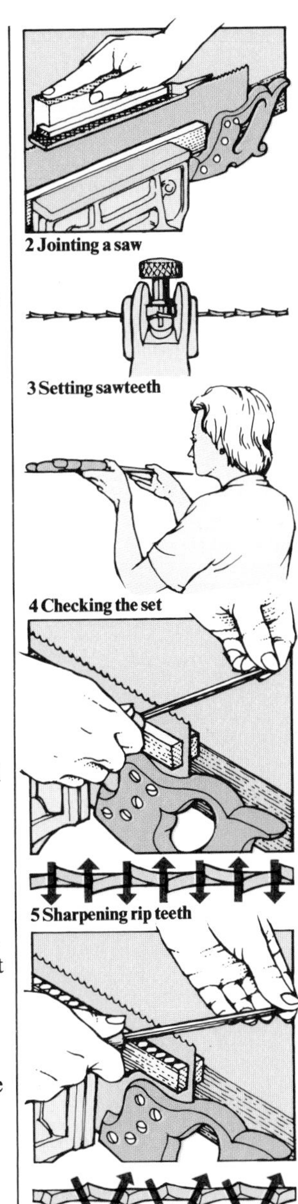
2 Jointing a saw
3 Setting sawteeth
4 Checking the set
5 Sharpening rip teeth
6 Sharpening crosscut teeth

Jointing a saw
Jointing a saw by filing the tips of the teeth level is absolutely necessary to bring all the teeth to the same height when the saw has been damaged or inexpertly filed. Additionally, a light jointing before sharpening puts a tiny bright point on every tooth that will prove to be an invaluable guide to even sharpening. Make a jointing jig by fitting a smooth file into a grooved block of hardwood **(1)**. Tapering the top of the groove will allow you to introduce a tightening wedge. Run the block against the face of the saw with the file resting on the toothed edge **(2)**. Two or three light passes should be enough to joint a saw in good condition ready for sharpening. If your saw requires heavy jointing before all the teeth show a bright point, send it to a professional who will reshape all the teeth before setting and sharpening.

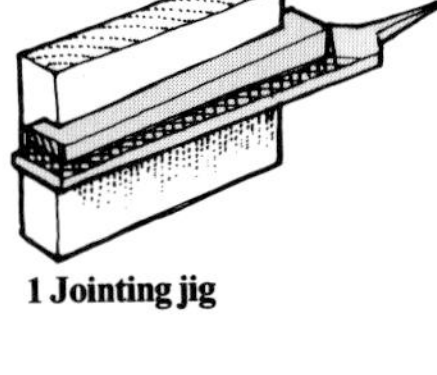
1 Jointing jig

Setting the teeth
Reset the teeth if your saw has been binding in the kerf or wandering off line. Adjust a saw set by undoing the locking screw, and turn the anvil to bring the required PPI number on its edge in line with the indicator on the tool. Retighten the locking screw. Working from one end of the saw, set every tooth that bends away from you **(3)**. Turn the saw around and set the other teeth. Hold the saw at eye level with the teeth facing away from you to see if you have skipped a tooth **(4)**.

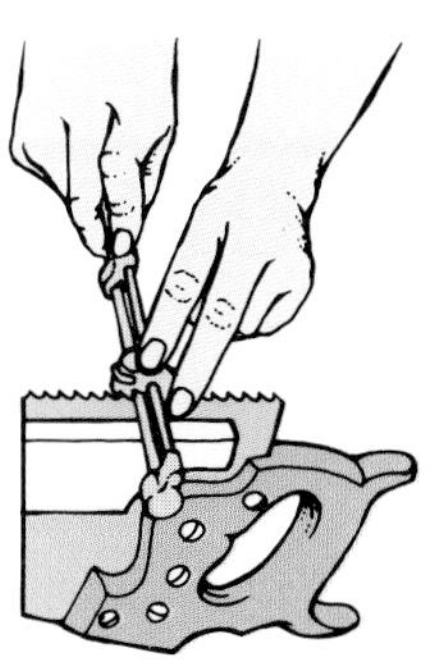
Saw-file guide
This jig fits onto the saw to guide the saw file at the required angle.

Sharpening with a file
Hold the saw in the vise with the clamping battens just below the teeth and with the handle to your right.

Steadying the file tip with your free hand, start at the toe of the saw by resting the file on the first tooth bent away from you and against the leading edge of the tooth next to it, which is bent toward you.

For a ripsaw, settle the file in the gullet, at right angles to the blade and perfectly horizontal. Make two or three strokes with the file, applying pressure on the forward pass only until about half the bright point on the tip of the tooth is removed. Moving toward the handle, file every other gullet. To sharpen the teeth bent the other way, turn the saw around and work from toe to heel again, filing the remaining gullets so that the bright points just disappear, leaving a sharp tip to each tooth **(5)**.

Sharpen a crosscut saw in the same way, but turn the file at an angle of about 65 degrees to the blade with the tip of the file toward the saw handle **(6)**. Parallel lines drawn at 65 degrees across the top of the clamping battens will help to keep the file at a constant angle.

BENCH PLANES

Bench planes are everyday "workhorses," used to smooth wooden surfaces while gradually reducing work to its finished dimensions. Wooden planes are lighter than their metal equivalents and skim smoothly across the work, but some of the more basic patterns are difficult to adjust when compared with a standard metal plane. Because they are mass-produced, metal planes are usually cheaper.

SEE ALSO

Using bench planes	91
Sharpening blades	102-107
Edge joints	222-223
Toothing plane	258-259

Scrub plane
A scrub plane is a specialized tool for quickly roughing wood to thickness. It is used diagonally across the grain in two directions before the wood is smoothed with a jack plane. The blade, with its convex cutting edge, is held in the body of the plane with a wooden wedge.

Wooden try plane

EXTRA-LONG SOLES FOR PLANING STRAIGHT EDGES AND FLAT SURFACES

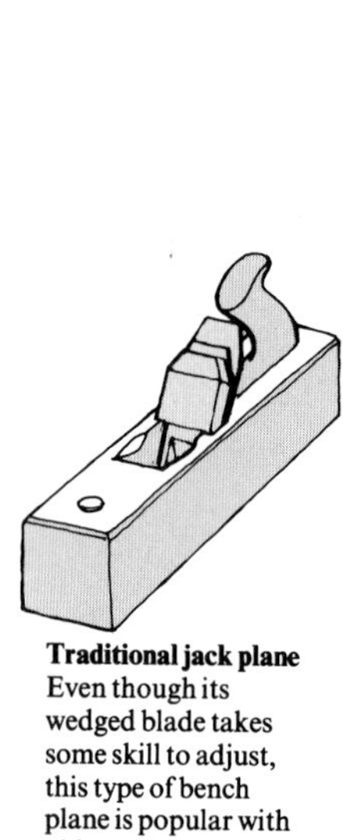

Traditional jack plane
Even though its wedged blade takes some skill to adjust, this type of bench plane is popular with old-tool enthusiasts. Brand-new models are still available from some suppliers.

BLADE-FIXING WEDGE

Scrub plane

Metal try plane

Scrub-plane blade

Try or jointer plane
A try or jointer plane has a sole up to 2ft (600mm) long that bridges undulations in the surface of the work. Consequently, it planes a perfectly straight edge where a shorter plane might follow the contours. A try plane is especially useful for making long butt joints between planks used to construct a wide panel.

Jack plane
The jack plane, between 14 and 15½in (350 and 387mm) long, is a general-purpose tool used to plane wood square and flat. Similar to other metal bench planes, a jack plane is made with a smooth sole or one that is corrugated to reduce friction when working on resinous woods.

Corrugated sole

Smoothing plane
A smoothing plane is used with a finely adjusted blade to skim the surface to put a final planed finish on the work. A modern wooden smoothing plane has a distinctive ergonomic handle at its toe. The best planes have self-lubricating lignum-vitae soles. Smoothing planes are up to 9in (225mm) long.

Metal jack plane

Wooden jack plane

Wooden smoothing plane

Metal smoothing plane

All-metal bench plane

1 Handle
2 Lateral-adjustment lever
3 Blade
4 Cap iron
5 Lever
6 Lever cap
7 Cap-iron locking screw
8 Knob
9 Mouth
10 Frog
11 Frog locking screws
12 Lever-cap screw
13 Depth-adjustment lever
14 Depth-adjustment nut
15 Frog adjusting screw
16 Sole

Adjustable wooden plane

1 Depth-adjustment screw
2 Cap-iron locking screws
3 Blade
4 Cap iron
5 Regulator
6 Regulator locking screw
7 Toe horn
8 Mouth-width adjustment screw
9 Crossbar
10 Tension screw
11 Coil spring
12 Tension-screw nut
13 Sole

THE CARE AND USE OF BENCH PLANES

Modern bench planes are precision-made tools, but as with all mass-produced items, a little judicious tinkering can make all the difference to their performance. In any case, all planes need to be serviced and adjusted from time to time to keep them functioning at their best.

Dismantling a metal plane
To remove the blade or cutting iron, first lift the lever on the lever cap and slide it from beneath its locking screw. Lift the blade with its cap iron out of the plane. Use a large screwdriver to loosen the cap-iron locking screw and slide the cap iron toward the cutting edge to pass the screw head through the hole in the blade, separating the two components.

Adjusting the frog
Removing the blade assembly exposes the frog. This is a wedge-shaped casting that incorporates both the blade-depth and the lateral-adjustment controls.

The frog itself slides backward or forward to regulate the size of the mouth – the opening in the plane sole through which the blade projects. For coarse planing, the mouth is opened to provide adequate clearance for thick shavings. When the blade is set to take a fine cut, the mouth is closed to encourage the thin shavings to break and curl against the cap iron.

To adjust the frog, release the two locking screws and turn the adjusting screw with a screwdriver. Tighten the locking screws.

Assembling and adjusting the plane
Having sharpened the blade, hold it bevel downward and lay the cap iron across it **(1)** to drop the screw head through the hole. Slide the cap iron away from the cutting edge and turn it to align with the blade **(2)**. Slide the cap iron to within $\frac{1}{16}$in (1.5mm) of the cutting edge **(3)** – or even closer for very fine shavings – and tighten the locking screw. Lower the blade assembly into the plane, cap iron up, fitting it over the lever-cap screw and onto the depth-adjustment lever. Replace the lever cap. Turn the depth-adjustment nut until the blade protrudes from the sole. Inspect the cutting edge from the toe of the plane while moving the lateral-adjustment lever to bring the edge parallel to the sole. Back off the depth adjustment to the required setting.

Dismantling a wooden plane
Back off the depth-adjustment screw by about $\frac{1}{2}$in (12mm) and loosen the tension-screw nut at the heel of the plane. Turn the crossbar at the front of the tension screw through 90 degrees so the blade assembly can be lifted out of the plane. Remove the two screws at the back of the blade to release the cap iron and regulator.

Assembling the plane
Having sharpened the blade, replace the cap iron and lower the assembly into the plane. Pass the tension-screw crossbar through the slot in the assembly and turn it to locate it in its seat in the cap iron. Slightly tighten the tension-screw nut and adjust the depth-adjustment screw until the blade protrudes. Use the regulator to make sure the cutting edge is parallel with the sole. Back off the depth-adjustment screw and finally tighten the tension-screw nut.

Set the mouth width by adjusting the screw behind the toe horn.

Replacing a cap iron

1 Lay cap iron across blade

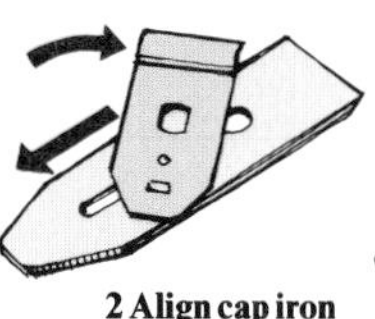

2 Align cap iron with blade

3 Slide cap iron up to cutting edge

TUNING A BENCH PLANE

More than likely your plane will function perfectly adequately direct from the supplier. However, if you are having problems achieving the desired results, check that there are none of the more obvious defects in its manufacture.

Warped sole
If you cannot get the plane to take a fine shaving, lay a straightedge across the sole to see if it is warped. You can flatten a metal sole on emery cloth held down to a sheet of glass with double-faced tape. This is a slow laborious process, however, and you might prefer to have the sole reground by a professional (or return the plane to the supplier).

Flattening a wooden plane on abrasive paper is easier. Withdraw the blade, hold the plane near its center and rub it back and forth across the abrasive. Check the sole regularly with the straightedge.

Blade chatter
A loose blade will vibrate and skid across the work. Tighten the lever-cap screw or tension-screw nut.

If the fault persists, make sure there are no foreign bodies trapped behind the blade and, in the case of a metal plane, under the frog.

Shavings jamming under the cap iron
Unless the cap iron beds down perfectly on the blade, shavings will jam under its leading edge.

If the blade is bent, lay it on a flat board and strike it firmly with a hammer.

Hone the meeting edge of the cap iron on an oilstone until it is flat.

General care of planes
Wooden soles will become "slick" with use and should not be treated in any way. Rubbing wax across a metal sole can help relieve a "sticky" plane. Retract the blades and store bench planes on their sides.

Using a metal bench plane

USING BENCH PLANES

The pattern of a tree's growth rings appears as dark lines or grain on the work. Clamp the work in a vise or lay it on the bench against bench stops so that these grain lines "lean" away from you. Planing with the grain in this way permits the blade to cut smoothly. Planing in the other direction, against the grain, tears the wood's fibers.

Handling and controlling a bench plane
Grasp the handle of a metal bench plane with your forefinger extended against the edge of the blade or frog. This will ensure control over the direction of the plane. Your free hand provides downward pressure on the plane, using the round knob on its toe.

To use a wooden smoothing plane, slip the crotch between thumb and forefinger around the shaped rest below the depth-adjustment screw. Grasp the body with fingers and thumb. Your free hand will fit naturally around the toe horn.

Stand beside the bench with your feet apart. Your rearward foot points toward the bench, the other is parallel to it. Keeping your feet firmly planted, move the upper part of your body to propel the plane.

As you start the stroke, put pressure on the toe of the plane, relieving it only as you finish the stroke to prevent rounding off at both ends of the work.

Holding the plane flat on the work but at a slight angle to the direction of travel produces a slicing action with the cutting edge that helps to shear through difficult grain.

Planing an edge square
To prevent the plane from rocking while planing a narrow edge, maintain downward pressure with your thumb and curl your fingers under the sole to act as a fence against the work. Use a similar grip to hold the plane at an angle when planing a chamfer along the edge.

Planing a surface flat
To plane a surface flat, choose a try or jack plane, depending on the length of the work.

Plane in the general direction of the grain but at an angle across the work in two directions. Check for flatness with a straightedge (a try plane tilted onto one long edge is ideal), then plane parallel to the work's edges using a finely set blade for a final finish.

If the work is very convex, remove the majority of waste with a scrub plane before taking up another plane.

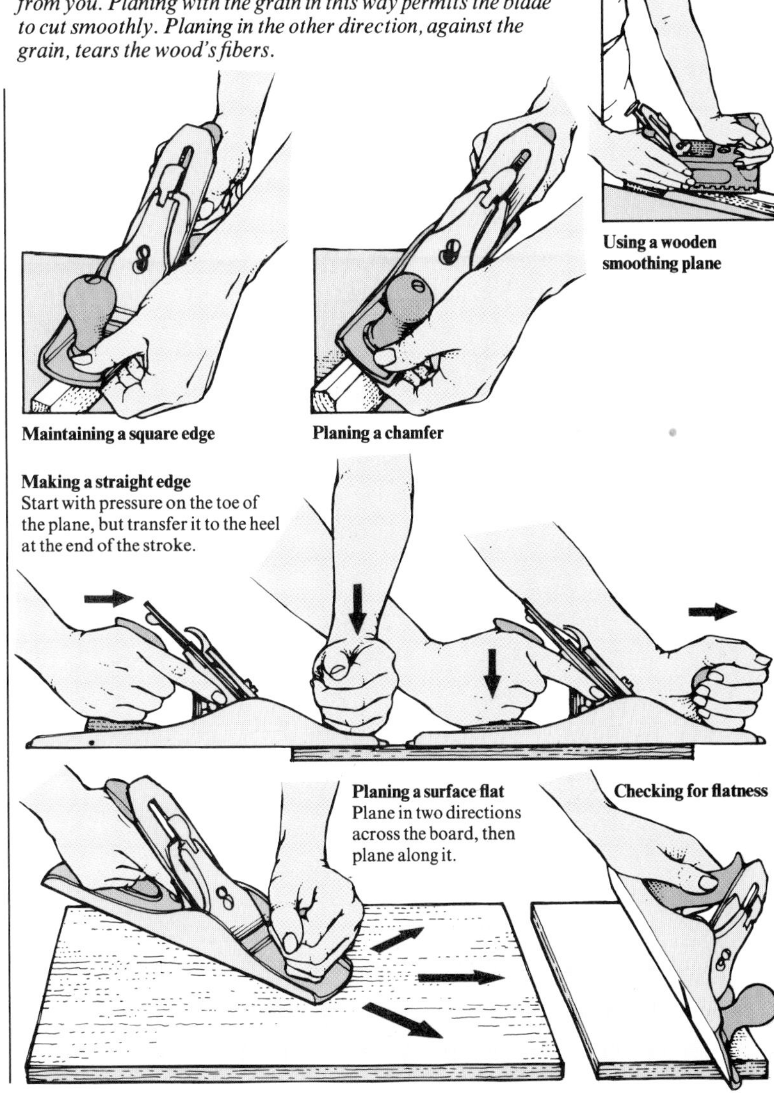
Using a wooden smoothing plane

Maintaining a square edge

Planing a chamfer

Making a straight edge
Start with pressure on the toe of the plane, but transfer it to the heel at the end of the stroke.

Planing a surface flat
Plane in two directions across the board, then plane along it.

Checking for flatness

RABBET PLANES

A rabbet is a rectangular-section recess along the edge of a piece of wood. It is often used to receive a square-edged panel at right angles to the rabbeted wood – as when a plywood back panel is fitted into a cabinet, for example. Special planes are required to cut rabbets.

SEE ALSO

Fitting cabinet backs	62-65,69-70
Sharpening blades	102-107
Shooting board	212-213
Edge joints	222-223
Mortise & tenons	226-235
Sanding end grain	285

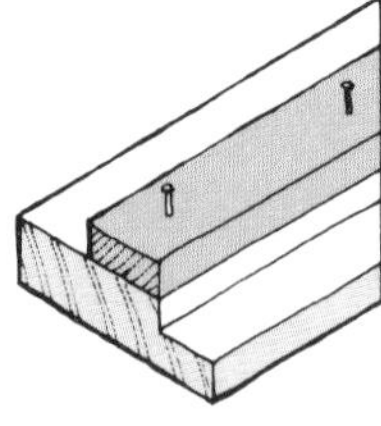

Using a fence
Pin or clamp a fence to the work when using a bench rabbet plane.

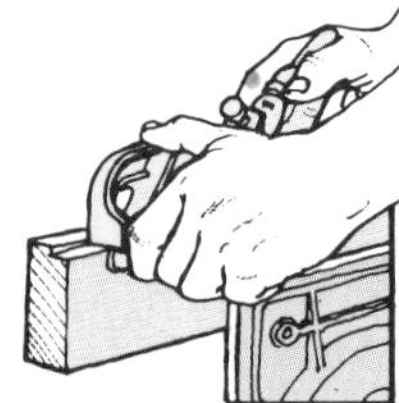

Using a rabbet and filister plane
Start at the far end of a workpiece and work gradually backward.

Bench rabbet plane
Large rabbets can be cut with a bench rabbet plane – a specialized version of the standard jack plane – with a blade extending across the entire width of the sole. It has no fence or depth stop and must be used against a straight batten nailed or clamped to the work until the rabbet itself is deep enough to guide the plane.

With the tool held firmly against the guide batten, plane down to a line marking the rabbet depth.

Rabbet and filister plane
This is a sophisticated rabbet plane with an adjustable guide fence and depth stop. The cutter can be mounted in two positions – one for normal use and one near the toe for planing to the end of a stopped rabbet. This type of plane is also fitted with a spur that scores ahead of the blade when rabbeting across the grain.

To cut a through rabbet, set the guides and start planing at the far end of the work with short strokes. Keeping the fence pressed against the work, move backward gradually lengthening the strokes. Plane the full length of the work until the depth stop prevents the plane from biting any further.

Bullnose plane
A short snub-nose version of the shoulder plane, this small lightweight plane is used to trim stopped rabbets or small joints. There are many versions of this plane in both wood and metal.

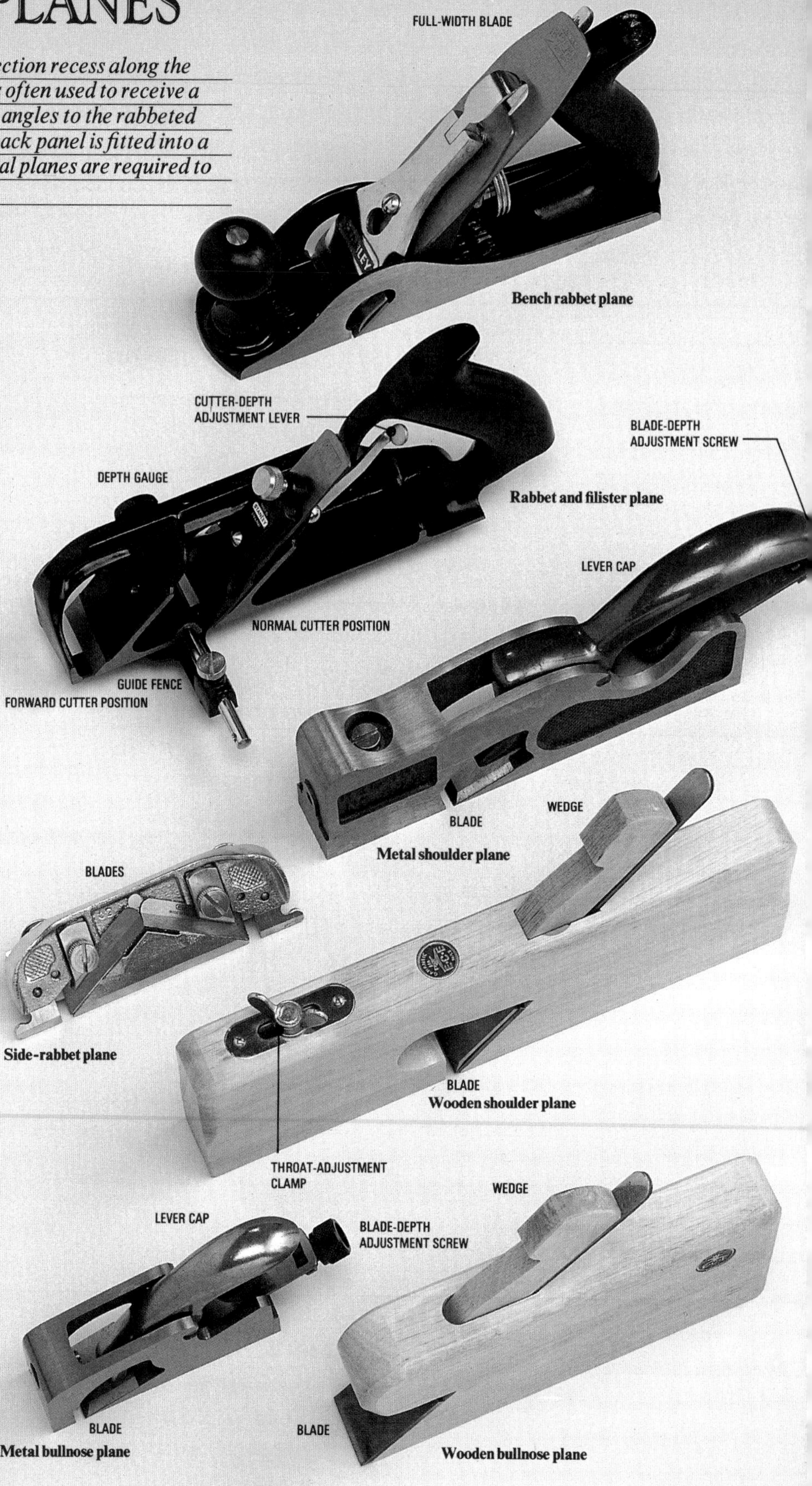

FULL-WIDTH BLADE
Bench rabbet plane

CUTTER-DEPTH ADJUSTMENT LEVER
DEPTH GAUGE
NORMAL CUTTER POSITION
GUIDE FENCE
FORWARD CUTTER POSITION
Rabbet and filister plane

BLADE-DEPTH ADJUSTMENT SCREW
LEVER CAP
BLADE
Metal shoulder plane

BLADES
Side-rabbet plane

WEDGE
BLADE
Wooden shoulder plane

THROAT-ADJUSTMENT CLAMP
LEVER CAP
BLADE-DEPTH ADJUSTMENT SCREW
BLADE
Metal bullnose plane

WEDGE
BLADE
Wooden bullnose plane

Shoulder plane
The shoulder plane has an accurately machined body with both sides perfectly square to the sole. It can be used like a bench rabbet plane, but is most useful as a means of trimming the square shoulders of large joints **(1)**. The blade is set at a low angle so it will shave end grain.

There are metal and wooden planes with one-piece bodies, while others have detachable front ends to convert them into small chisel planes to work into a square stopped rabbet.

Side-rabbet plane
This miniature plane is for shaving rabbets or easing the sides of narrow grooves **(2)**. It is used on edge, with the blade skimming the vertical wall. Having two opposing blades, the plane can be used to trim both sides of a groove from one direction – always working with the grain. Each nose is detachable for planing stopped grooves. The depth gauge riding on the top edge of the work helps to control the orientation of the blade.

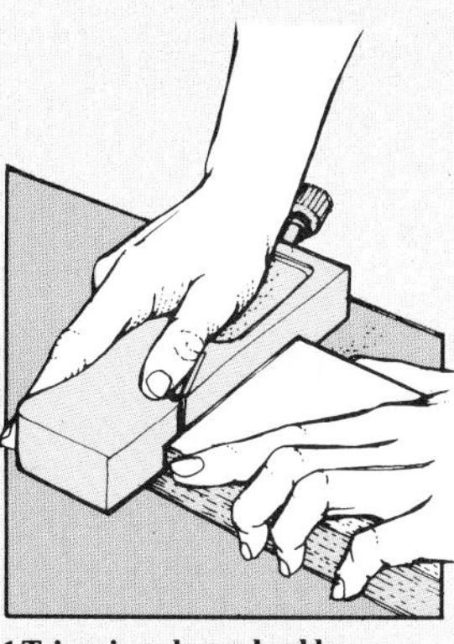

1 Trimming a large shoulder

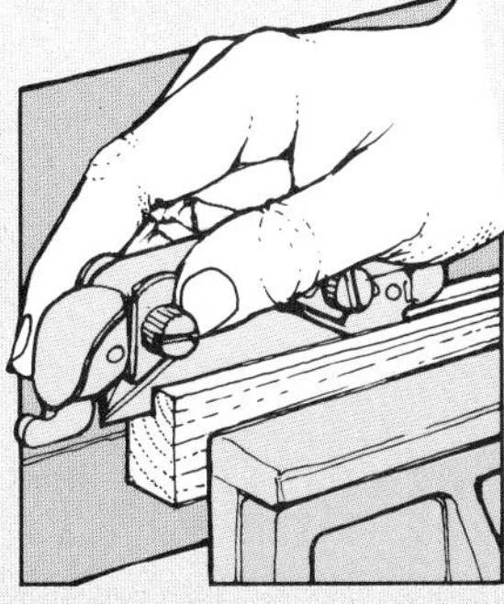

2 Easing a groove

BLOCK PLANES

The block plane is a lightweight general-purpose plane. It is used with one hand, but extra pressure can be exerted on the toe with the fingertips of your free hand.

Block-plane blades
The wooden version has a large depth-adjustment knob for precise setting.

On the more sophisticated metal version, the blade is set at an angle of 20 degrees specifically for trimming end grain. A low-angle plane is also available in which the blade is set at 12 degrees. Both planes have control over the depth and lateral movement of the blade, and an adjustable mouth. The blade is removed for sharpening by detaching the cast-metal lever cap, which is locked in place by a small lever. When replacing a block-plane blade, ensure it is fitted bevel up.

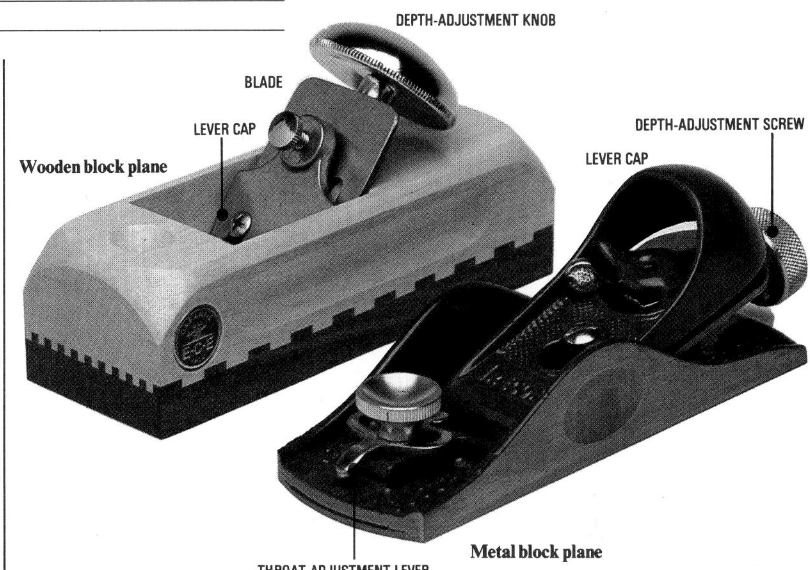

Wooden block plane

Metal block plane

PLANING END GRAIN

It is convenient to skim end grain with a lightweight block plane, but for a precise right angle or miter, use a bench plane on a shooting board.

Using a block plane
When trimming end grain with a block plane, make sure the blade is razor sharp and put plenty of pressure on the toe **(1)**. Plane from both ends toward the middle to avoid splitting wood from the edge of the work. Alternatively, plane a chamfer at one end down to the marked finished line **(2)** and plane toward that end only, or clamp a block of scrap wood against the work to support the edge **(3)**.

Using a shooting board
Trim end grain with a bench plane on a special jig called a shooting board. The work is held against a stop mounted across the top of the jig. The plane is run on its side and guided past the work by a wide rabbet. With the work just projecting from the stop, trim the end grain with a finely set sharp blade.

A shooting board with angled stops is used to trim miter joints.

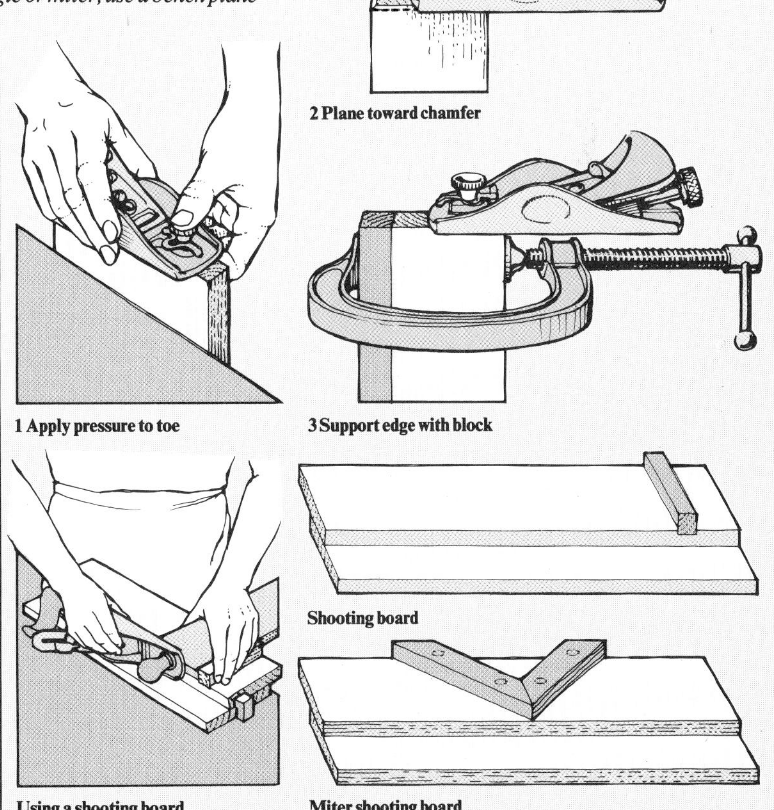

1 Apply pressure to toe

2 Plane toward chamfer

3 Support edge with block

Using a shooting board

Shooting board

Miter shooting board

JAPANESE PLANES

A traditional Japanese woodworking plane is very simply constructed, having a rectangular-section hardwood body, a blade and cap iron. A steel cross-pin keeps the cap iron pressed against the blade.

Almost legendary qualities are claimed for these planes. They cut on the pull stroke, with the work resting on a beam supported on a triangular sawhorse at one end, the other end butted against a wall.

SEE ALSO

Bench planes	88-89
Shoulder plane	92-93
Sharpening blades	102-107
Sharpening Japanese blades	105
Spokeshaves	108
Routers	140-141
Housing joints	224-225
Fitting a butt hinge	307

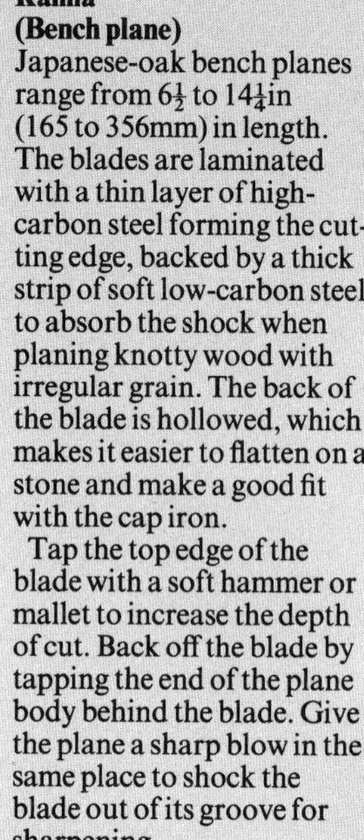

Kanna (Bench plane)
Japanese-oak bench planes range from $6\frac{1}{2}$ to $14\frac{1}{4}$in (165 to 356mm) in length. The blades are laminated with a thin layer of high-carbon steel forming the cutting edge, backed by a thick strip of soft low-carbon steel to absorb the shock when planing knotty wood with irregular grain. The back of the blade is hollowed, which makes it easier to flatten on a stone and make a good fit with the cap iron.

Tap the top edge of the blade with a soft hammer or mallet to increase the depth of cut. Back off the blade by tapping the end of the plane body behind the blade. Give the plane a sharp blow in the same place to shock the blade out of its groove for sharpening.

In order to reduce friction on the work, the larger bench planes have hollowed soles produced with a special scraper plane (Dai-nishi-kanna), leaving a point of contact at the toe, just in front of the mouth and at the back of the sole.

A hollowed sole
The sole of a kanna is hollowed to leave three points of contact with a workpiece.

Sakuri-kanna (Rabbet plane)
This wooden plane is used like a European shoulder plane. The blade, from $\frac{1}{2}$ to 1in (12 to 24mm) wide, is fitted into an oak body 11in (275mm) long.

BLADE
CAP IRON

Kanna (bench plane)

BLADE
CAP IRON

Sakuri-kanna (rabbet plane)

Kirimen-kanna (Chamfer plane)
This very specialized plane has screw-adjusted fences that open up to plane chamfers up to $\frac{3}{4}$in (20mm) wide. The small plane "body," with a skewed blade, slides sideways into the fences.

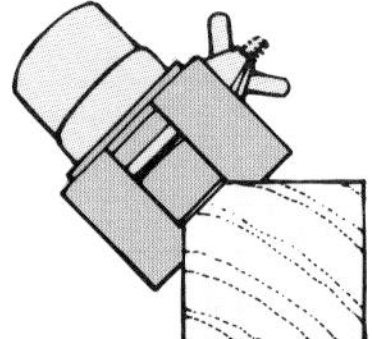

Using a Kirimen-kanna
This type of plane sits on the corner of the work.

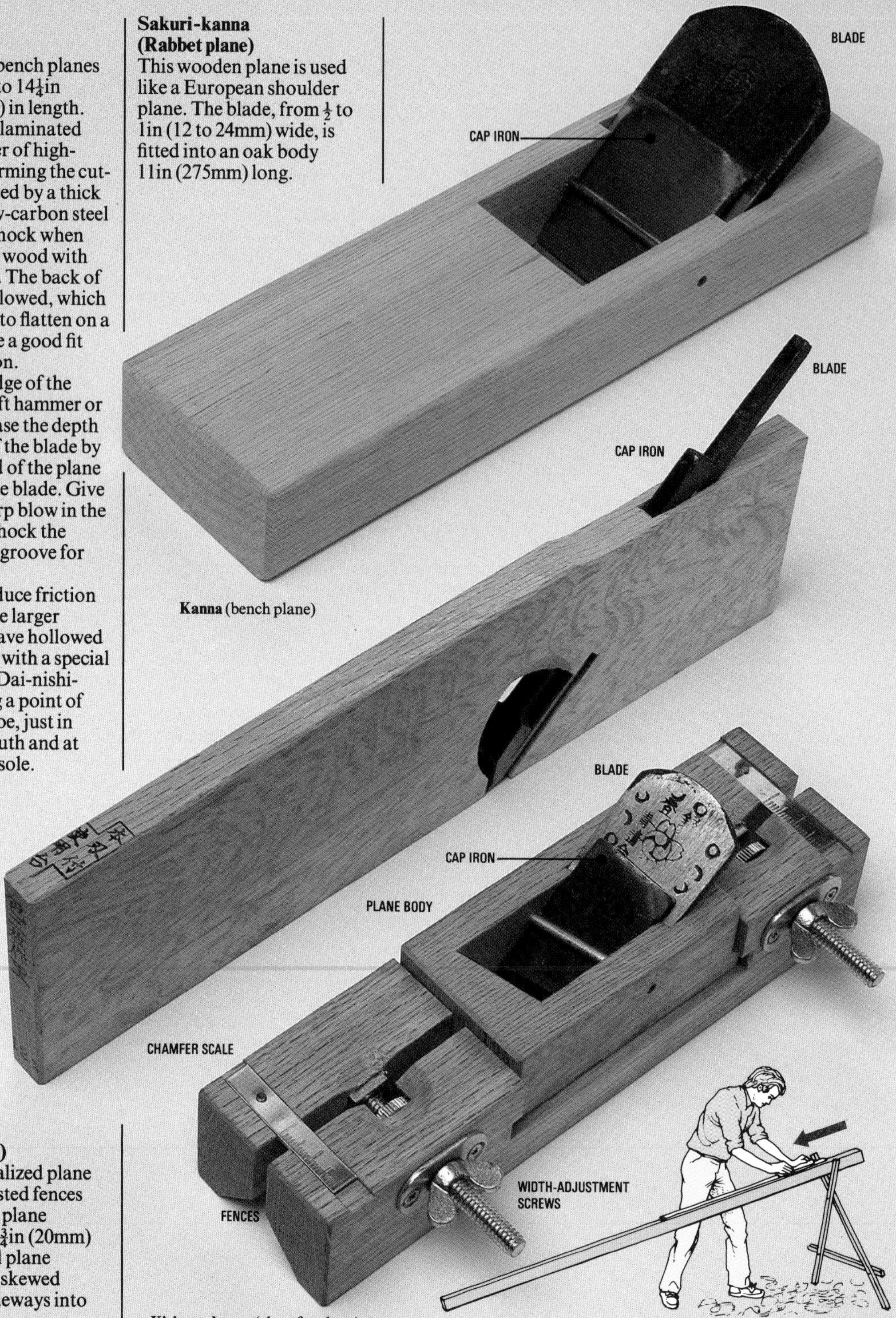

BLADE
CAP IRON
PLANE BODY
CHAMFER SCALE
FENCES
WIDTH-ADJUSTMENT SCREWS

Kirimen-kanna (chamfer plane)

Japanese planes cut on the pull stroke

SPECIALIZED PLANES

There are other ways to achieve the results obtained with specialized planes, but these tools enable the discerning woodworker to complete the job quickly and with a greater degree of accuracy.

Compass plane
A compass plane is fitted with a standard bench-plane blade, cap iron and lever cap, but the sole is made from a strip of flexible steel. It is adjusted by means of a large knurled nut to form a concave or convex curve.

The compass plane is especially useful for trimming gradual curves such as the edge of a round table where a spokeshave is likely to follow bumps and hollows.

Saw the wood roughly to shape and either set the sole of the plane to match the cut edge or draw the intended curve on a board as a guide to setting the sole exactly.

As you work, you must reposition the work periodically to be able to plane with the grain at all times.

BLADE

SOLE-ADJUSTMENT NUT

FLEXIBLE STEEL SOLE

Compass plane

BLADE

Wooden router plane

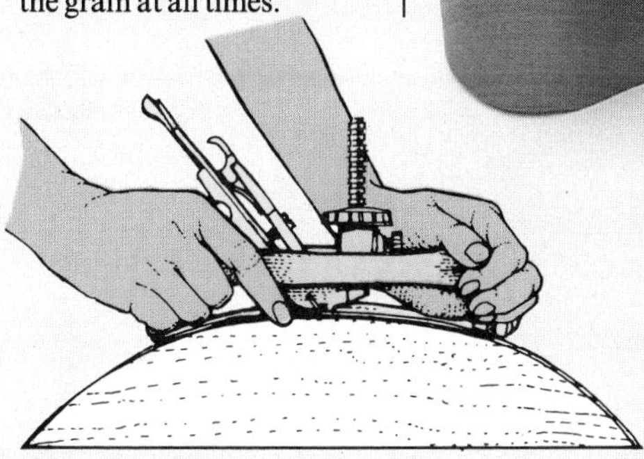

Using a compass plane

Router plane
The router plane, once the preferred tool for leveling the bottoms of dadoes, has been largely replaced by the electric router.

However, due to its relative cheapness and simplicity, it is still found in many workshops, especially for making small recesses for locks and hinges. A very basic wooden router plane may be shopmade or purchased, but the metal version is far more adaptable.

Special cutters are screw-adjustable to fine tolerances. Chisel-like cutters are used to level square-sided recesses and there is a pointed cutter for working the undercut sides of a dovetail housing or into tight corners. The plane will level a through-housing with a cutter mounted in the forward position of the cutter clamp. With a cutter mounted to the rear of the clamp, the plane is used in reverse to work up to the end of a stopped housing.

A small fence screwed to the sole guides a cutter at a set distance from a straight or curved edge. A depth gauge fitted with a small flat shoe closes the open throat at the front of the plane when the tool is used on a narrow edge where the bifurcated sole is ineffective.

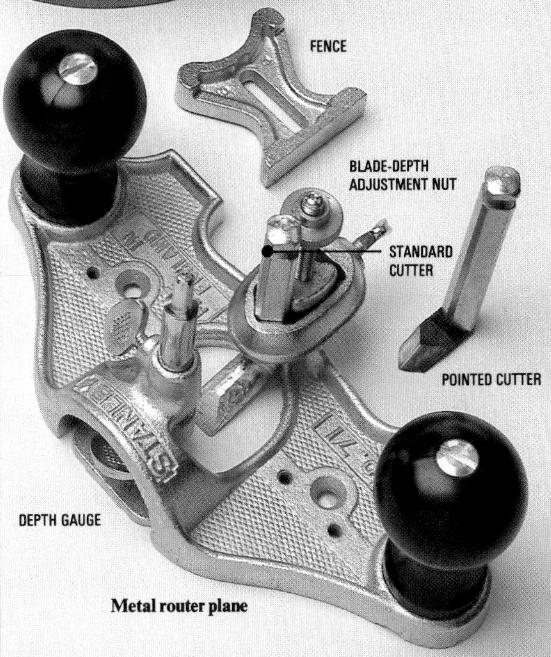

FENCE

BLADE-DEPTH ADJUSTMENT NUT

STANDARD CUTTER

POINTED CUTTER

DEPTH GAUGE

Metal router plane

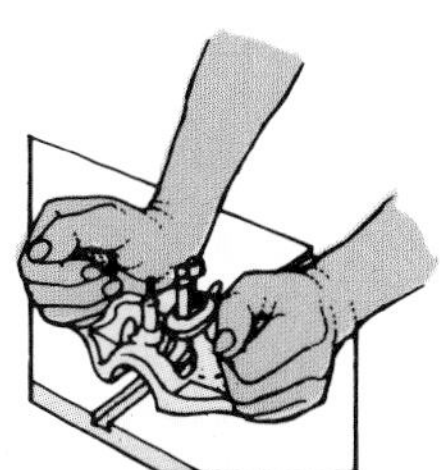

Cutting a dado
Saw down the line to the depth of the dado on both sides. Adjust the depth of the cutter little by little to remove the waste in stages down to the required depth.

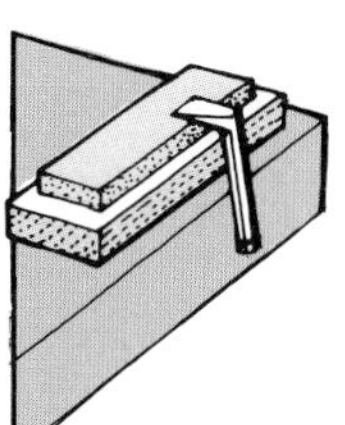

Sharpening cutters
Sharpen a router-plane cutter on an oilstone, like a chisel, but place the stone near the edge of a bench to provide clearance for the cutter shaft.

PLOW & COMBINATION PLANES

At the turn of the century the average woodworker would have had a tool chest half full of wooden molding planes, plow planes and matching tongue-and-groove planes – every one of them designed for a specific purpose with its specially shaped cutter. Not surprisingly, a single tool that would combine all these functions was bound to be a success, and despite competition from the electric router, the combination plane is still popular, as much as anything for its ingenuity.

SEE ALSO

Fitting cabinet backs	62-65,69-70
Frame-and-panel construction	66,70
Making drawers	71
Sharpening blades	102-107
Routers	140-146
Edge joints	222-223

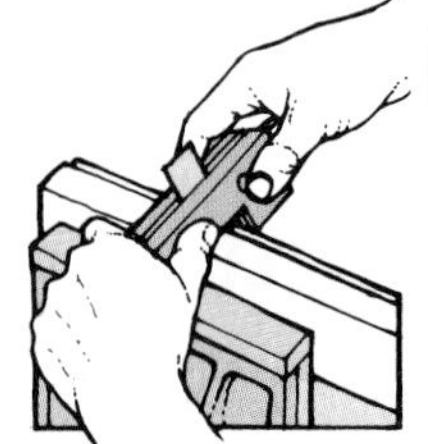

Using a scratch stock
Clamp the cutter between two identical pieces of plywood screwed together to form a simple stock with a built-in fence. Leaning the tool away from you, scrape the wood with the projecting part of the cutter until the stock comes to rest on the work.

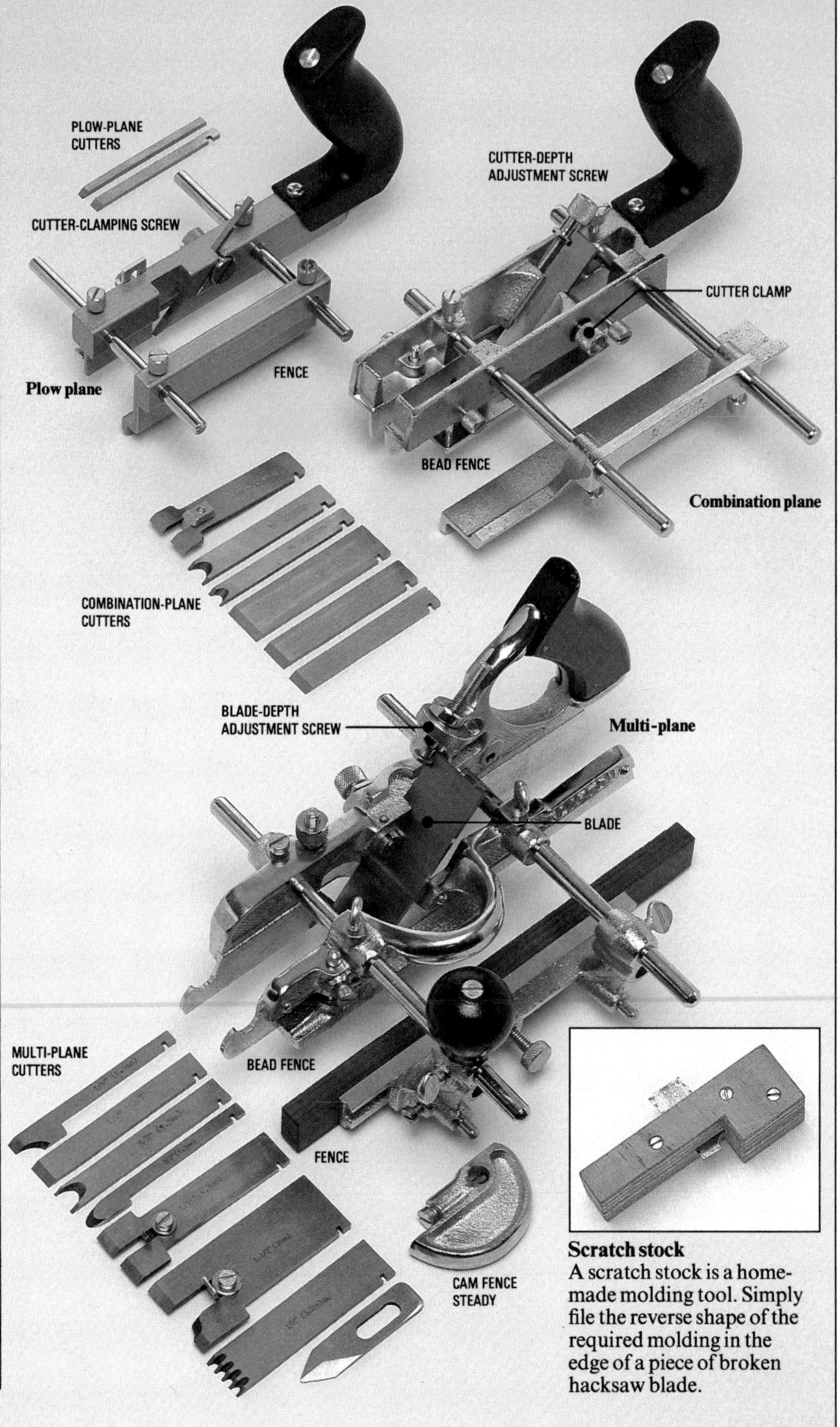

Plow plane
This is a specialized plane designed to cut grooves, though it can also be used to cut narrow rabbets. Square-edged cutters, from $\frac{1}{8}$ to $\frac{1}{2}$in (3 to 12mm) wide, are held in the plane by a sliding clamp, and adjusted up and down by a knurled screw. The plane is fitted with a fence and depth gauge. Wooden planes are still made for old-tool enthusiasts.

Combination plane
A combination plane is a plow plane with extra features to make tongue and groove joints, including the rounded beading often used to decorate the shoulder line and disguise shrinkage.

A special tonguing cutter with an adjustable depth stop is matched to one of the grooving cutters. Beading cutters range in width from $\frac{1}{8}$ to $\frac{1}{2}$in (3 to 12mm).

The cutter clamp extends to the toe of the plane as a complete sliding section to match the plane body. It carries an optional narrow fence for planing a bead on a tongued edge where the use of the standard fence would be impaired by the projecting tongue.

The plane body and sliding section each carries a knife-edge spur that slices the grain ahead when planing across the grain.

Multi-plane
A multi-plane is a combination plane with additional cutters. It will cut ovolo moldings, window-sash moldings, flutes and reeds. A slitting knife can be fitted in the plane to slice parallel strips of wood off the edge of a board.

PLOW-PLANE CUTTERS
CUTTER-CLAMPING SCREW
FENCE
Plow plane

CUTTER-DEPTH ADJUSTMENT SCREW
CUTTER CLAMP
BEAD FENCE
Combination plane

COMBINATION-PLANE CUTTERS

BLADE-DEPTH ADJUSTMENT SCREW
BLADE
Multi-plane
MULTI-PLANE CUTTERS
BEAD FENCE
FENCE
CAM FENCE STEADY

Scratch stock
A scratch stock is a home-made molding tool. Simply file the reverse shape of the required molding in the edge of a piece of broken hacksaw blade.

USING THE PLANES

Clamp the cutter in a plane and measure from it to set the fence and depth gauge. Settle the plane on the work at the far end, supporting the fence assembly with your left hand. Start with short strokes, gradually working backward until the plane is taking full-length shavings.

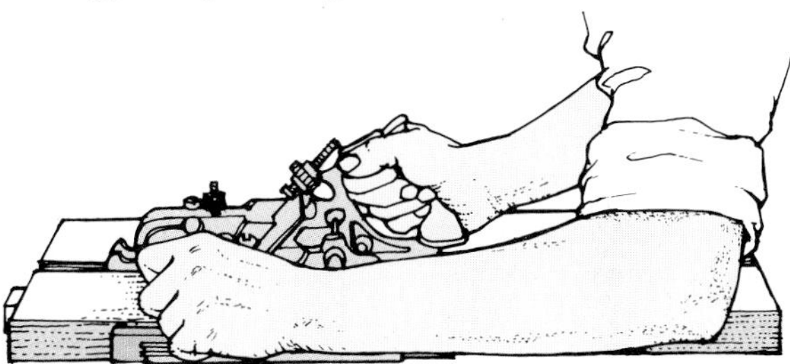

Support the fence assembly with your left hand

Cutting grooves
A groove is usually planed with the grain and often in the edge of a piece of wood. Any of the planes can be used. You can cut a groove across end grain, but to avoid splitting the edge at the end of the stroke, mark the work with a mortise gauge and chop out the waste at the far end with a saw and chisel before you use the plane.

Cutting a dado
A dado is a groove across the grain. Guide the body of a combination or multi-plane with a straight batten clamped to the work. Adjust spurs to score both sides of the dado.

Cutting a rabbet
To cut a rabbet, set up any of the planes to cut a groove, but adjust the fence to bring the cutter to the edge of the work. You can cut wider rabbets in stages by working back into the work one blade-width at a time.

Cutting a tongue and groove
Cut the tongue first with the special cutter clamped in a combination plane or multi-plane. Because the cutter has its own built-in depth stop, there is no need to attach one to the plane itself. Set the fence to center the tongue on the edge of the work. Match the grooving cutter to the planed tongue.

Cutting beads
To cut a bead along a tongued edge, fit the special narrow fence that automatically positions a beading cutter to plane the molding on the very edge of the work just above the tongue. A bead can be cut at a distance from a square edge using the standard fence.

Cutting an ovolo
Cut an ovolo like a rabbet. To mold all four edges of a solid-wood panel, plane across the grain at both ends first, then plane with the grain down both edges.

Cutting a window sash
Cut a window-sash molding on the edge of a board, planing first one half, then turning the work over to plane the other half. Finally, cut the molding from the board with the slitting knife.

Cutting a flute
Cut a flute like a bead, using the plane's depth gauge and standard fence.

Cutting reeds
A reed cutter produces a series of parallel beads at the same time. Set up the plane as for a bead or flute.

Sharpening cutters
Sharpen plane cutters on an oilstone, like chisels, but with a single grinding angle. These small cutters are easier to sharpen when clamped in a honing guide. Use a fine slipstone to sharpen the curved cutting edges.

Clamp cutter in a honing guide

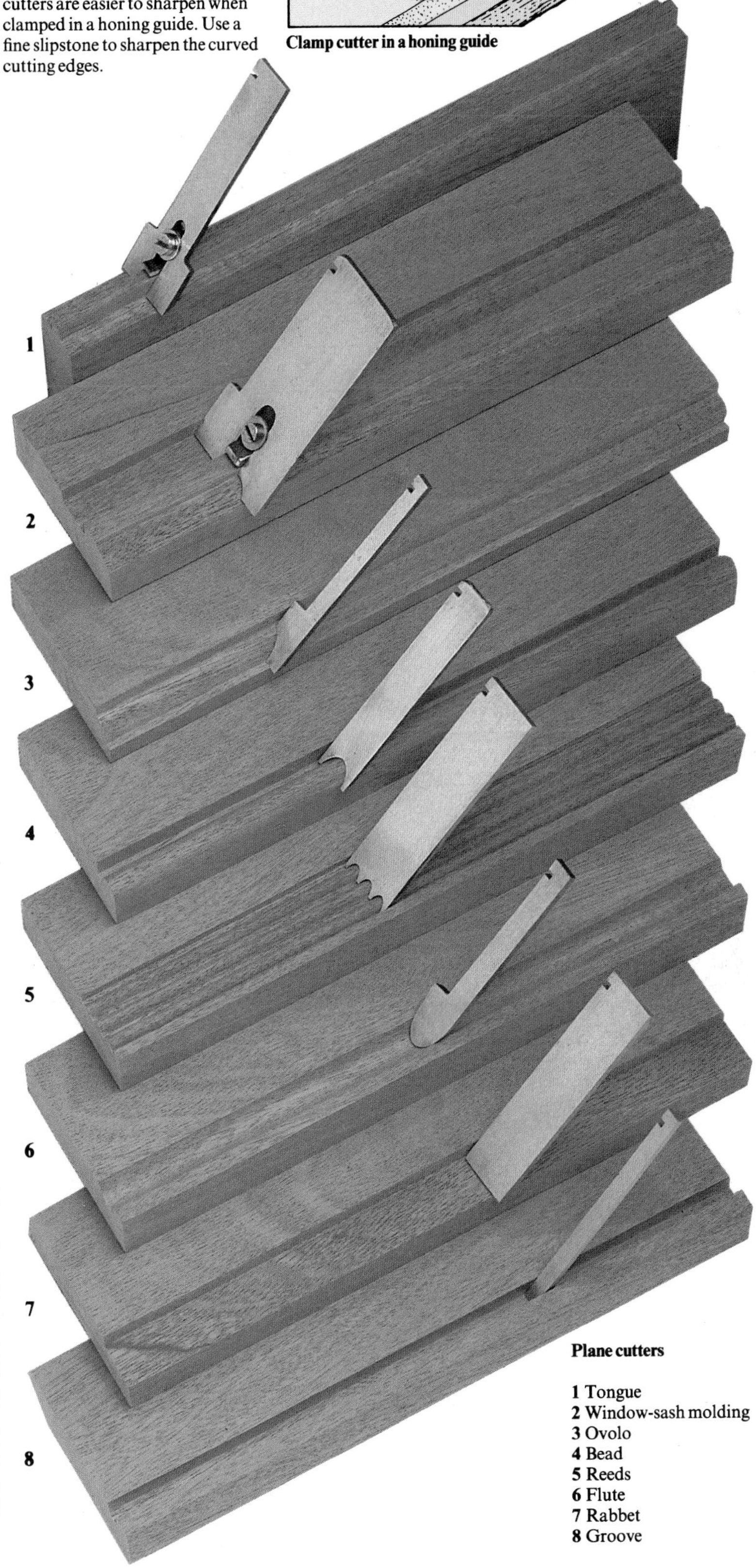

Plane cutters

1 Tongue
2 Window-sash molding
3 Ovolo
4 Bead
5 Reeds
6 Flute
7 Rabbet
8 Groove

CHISELS & GOUGES

Chisels and gouges rank with saws and planes as essential woodworking tools. They are primarily for removing waste wood from joints, although the lighter versions are also used to shape and trim workpieces. Strong stocky chisels and gouges are sometimes driven with a mallet when a lot of wood has to be removed, but most of the time the tools are used with hand pressure only.

SEE ALSO

Sharpening blades	102-107
Mallets	116
Home workshops	210-211
Housing joints	224-225
Dovetail joints	238-245

Firmer chisel

The firmer is the most basic general-purpose chisel. Its rectangular-section blade is strong enough to be driven through tough woods with a mallet. Firmer blades are made in regular increments from $\frac{1}{8}$ to $1\frac{1}{2}$in (3 to 38mm) in width, but a 2in (50mm) wide chisel is also available.

Bevel-edged chisel

The underside of the blade is flat like the firmer, but a shallow bevel is ground on the two long edges on the upper face. This makes a lightweight tool that should only be driven by hand, but it is ideal for chopping out the waste from dovetail joints. Bevel-edged chisels are made in the same range of sizes as firmers.

Paring chisel

A paring chisel is an extra long bevel-edged chisel for chopping the waste out of housing joints.

Cranked paring chisel

The cranked neck of this chisel enables a woodworker to keep the blade flat on the work even when paring in the center of a wide board.

Skew chisel

The end of the blade is skewed to an angle of 60 degrees to produce a slicing action at the cutting edge as the chisel is driven forward. This makes for smooth cutting, even through difficult grain, and the pointed tip is especially useful for cleaning out awkward corners. The range of blade widths is limited to $\frac{1}{2}$, $\frac{3}{4}$ and 1in (12, 18 and 25mm).

CHISEL SAFETY

Keep your chisels sharp. You have to apply more force to drive a dull chisel which can make it suddenly slip without warning.

Never pare toward your body, and keep both hands behind the cutting edge.

The long edges of new chisels can be sharp enough to cut your fingers while paring. Ease them with an oiled slipstone.

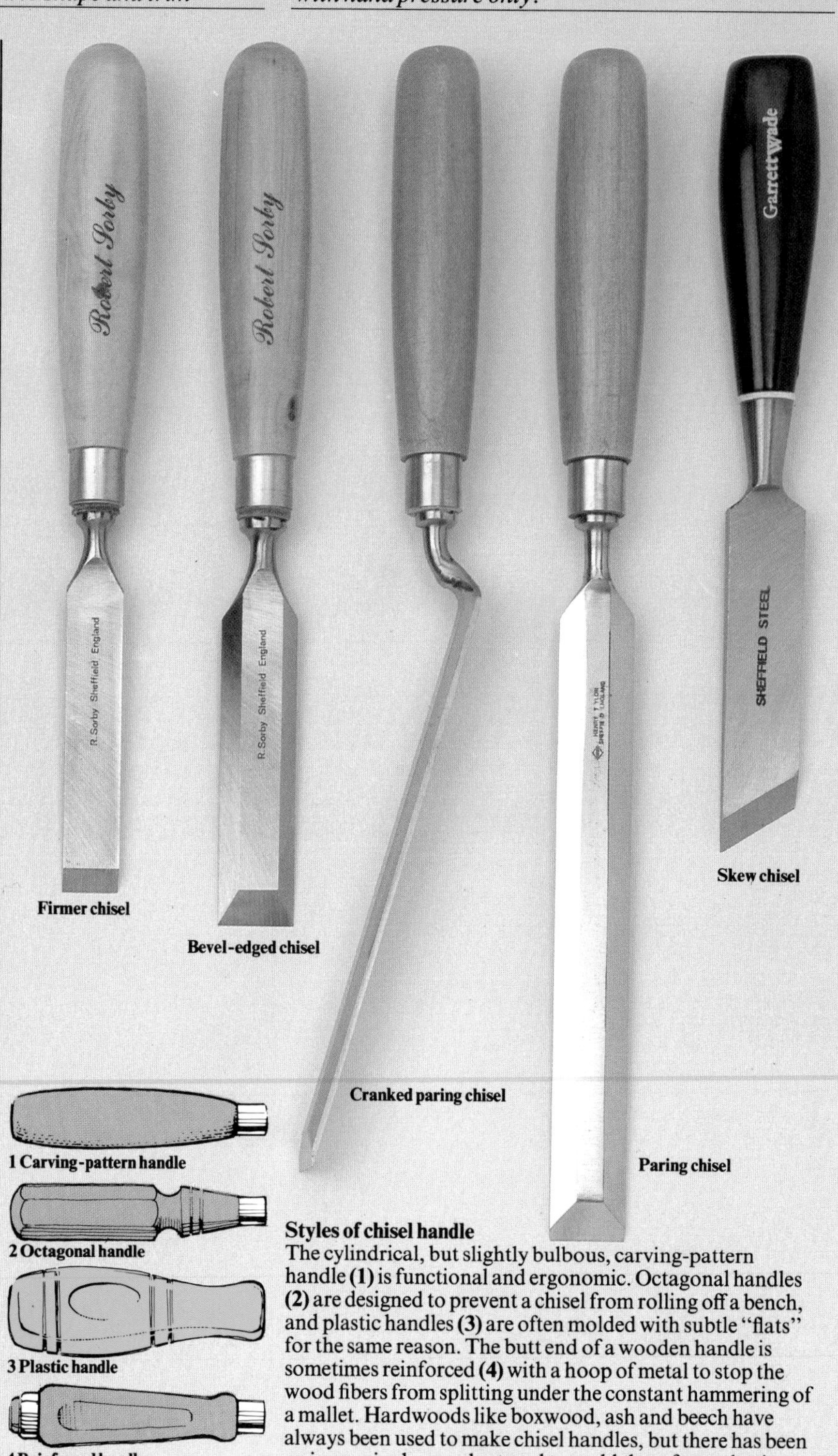

Firmer chisel

Bevel-edged chisel

Cranked paring chisel

Paring chisel

Skew chisel

1 Carving-pattern handle

2 Octagonal handle

3 Plastic handle

4 Reinforced handle

Chisel handles ▶
There has always been a wide variety of chisel handles, largely as a result of regional tradition. Plastic handles are so tough that they will withstand being driven with a metal hammer – a practice that would ruin a wooden handle.

Styles of chisel handle

The cylindrical, but slightly bulbous, carving-pattern handle **(1)** is functional and ergonomic. Octagonal handles **(2)** are designed to prevent a chisel from rolling off a bench, and plastic handles **(3)** are often molded with subtle "flats" for the same reason. The butt end of a wooden handle is sometimes reinforced **(4)** with a hoop of metal to stop the wood fibers from splitting under the constant hammering of a mallet. Hardwoods like boxwood, ash and beech have always been used to make chisel handles, but there has been an increasingly popular trend to mold them from plastics.

HOW CHISELS ARE MADE

Chisels vary in detail from type to type and from manufacturer to manufacturer, but they are essentially tools with stiff metal blades attached to roughly cylindrical straight handles. The joint between blade and handle distinguishes two families of chisels.

Blades
The average bench chisel has a blade 5 to 7in (125 to 175mm) long. Some woodworkers prefer the feel of the short heftier version, the butt chisel, with a blade length of 3 to 4in (75 to 100mm). Special-purpose chisels have blades up to 10in (250mm) long. The tip of a chisel blade is ground with a single bevel to form the cutting edge.

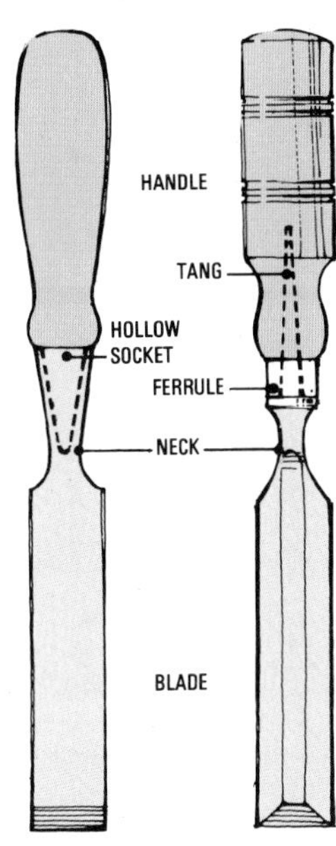

Strongly constructed chisels

Alternative designs
A chisel blade narrows noticeably at the "neck" just before the handle. At this point most blades are forged into a spike or "tang," which is driven into a wooden handle or molded into a plastic one. The junction between handle and blade is reinforced with a metal collar known as a ferrule.

Alternatively, the neck flares out again where it is formed into a hollow socket into which the handle fits.

STORING AND USING CHISELS

Storing chisels
It is bad practice to store your chisels loose in a tool chest. Keep them wrapped in a canvas roll with individual pockets for each chisel or store them in a tool rack behind your bench. You can buy a magnetic tool rack or make a rack from two strips of wood or plywood separated by short spacer blocks. Screw it to the wall and drop the chisel blades into the slots formed between the two strips. Some woodworkers prefer to fit plastic protectors over the tips of their chisels. These tight-fitting sleeves incorporate a ring for hanging the tools from pins or pegs driven into the workshop wall.

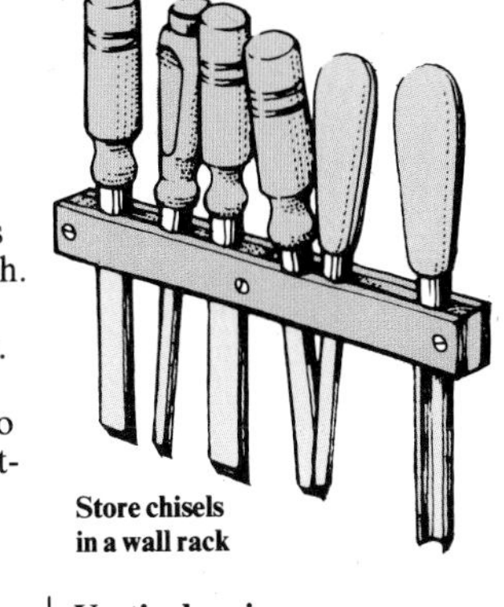

Store chisels in a wall rack

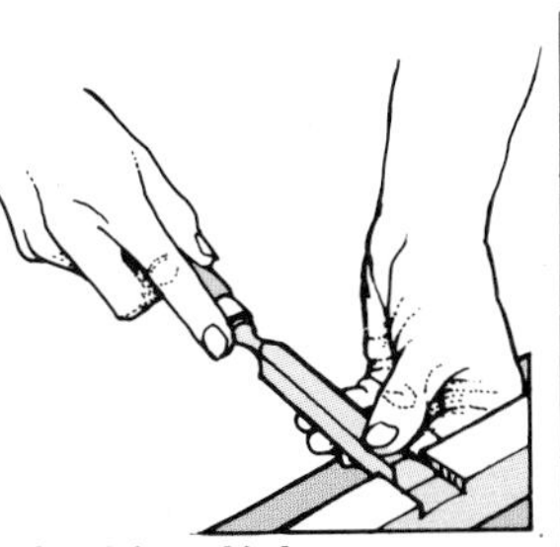

1 Steadying a chisel

Horizontal paring
When paring wood laid flat on a bench, hold the chisel handle with your index finger extended toward the blade. Keep your forearm in line with the chisel and tuck your elbow into your body. With your free hand, grip the blade behind the cutting edge between thumb and forefinger. This grip not only guides the tip of the tool, it also controls the force applied to the chisel by acting as a brake on the blade. Rest the other fingers of the same hand against the work to steady the tool **(1)**.

Stand in front of the bench with your forearm and chisel parallel to the floor. With your feet apart, use the weight of your body to move the chisel forward **(2)**. If you require extra force, strike the end of the handle with the heel of your hand **(3)**.

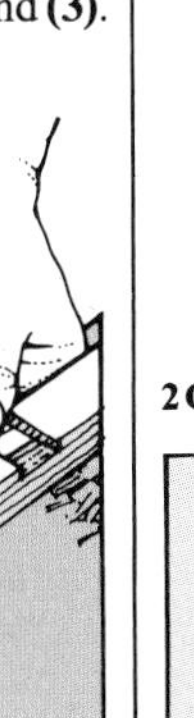
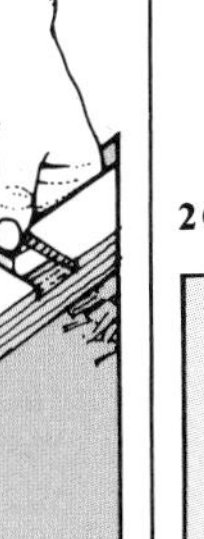

3 Exerting extra force

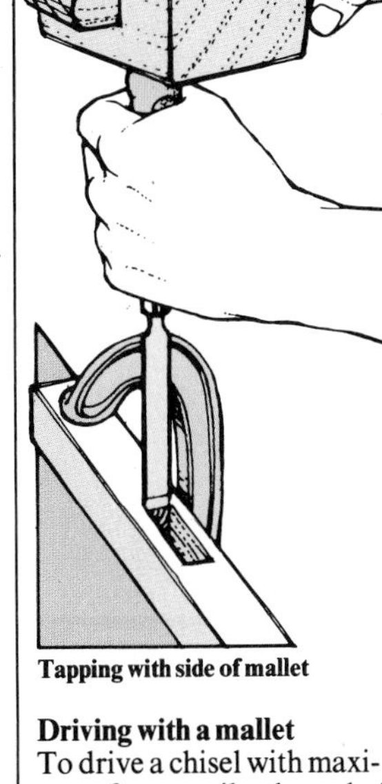

Tapping with side of mallet

Driving with a mallet
To drive a chisel with maximum force, strike the end of the handle squarely with the face of a mallet. There are, however, many situations where the weight of the mallet alone will exert enough force. For delicate work, grip the shaft just below the head and tap the chisel with the side of the mallet.

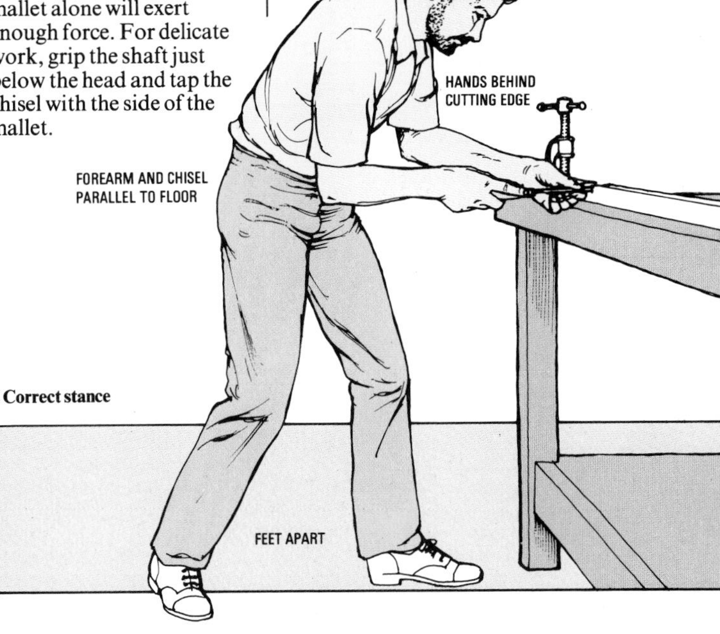

2 Correct stance

Vertical paring
Trim end grain toward the bench top with the chisel held vertically. Grip the handle with your thumb over the end and control the blade with thumb and forefinger. Use your shoulder, chest or chin to apply steady force to the chisel.

Vertical paring

MORTISE CHISELS

Cutting deep mortises requires a chisel that is designed for the job. Ordinary bench chisels are either too weak or will jam in the cut.

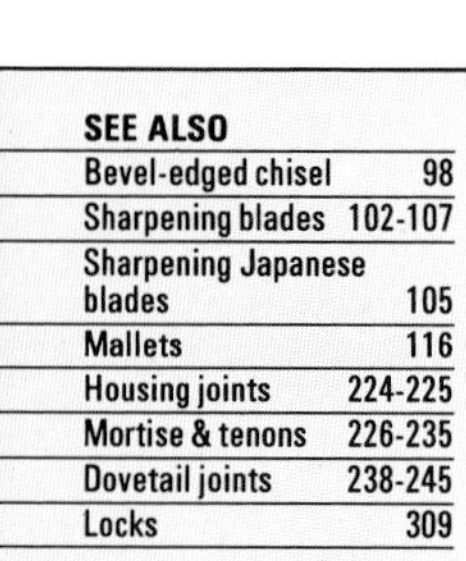

SEE ALSO

Bevel-edged chisel	98
Sharpening blades	102-107
Sharpening Japanese blades	105
Mallets	116
Housing joints	224-225
Mortise & tenons	226-235
Dovetail joints	238-245
Locks	309

A typical range of gouge profiles

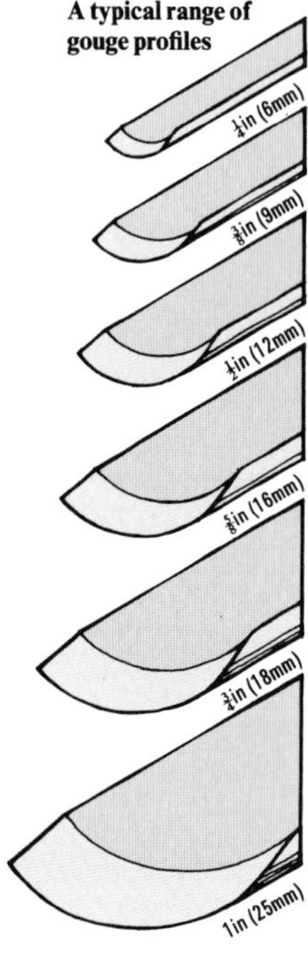

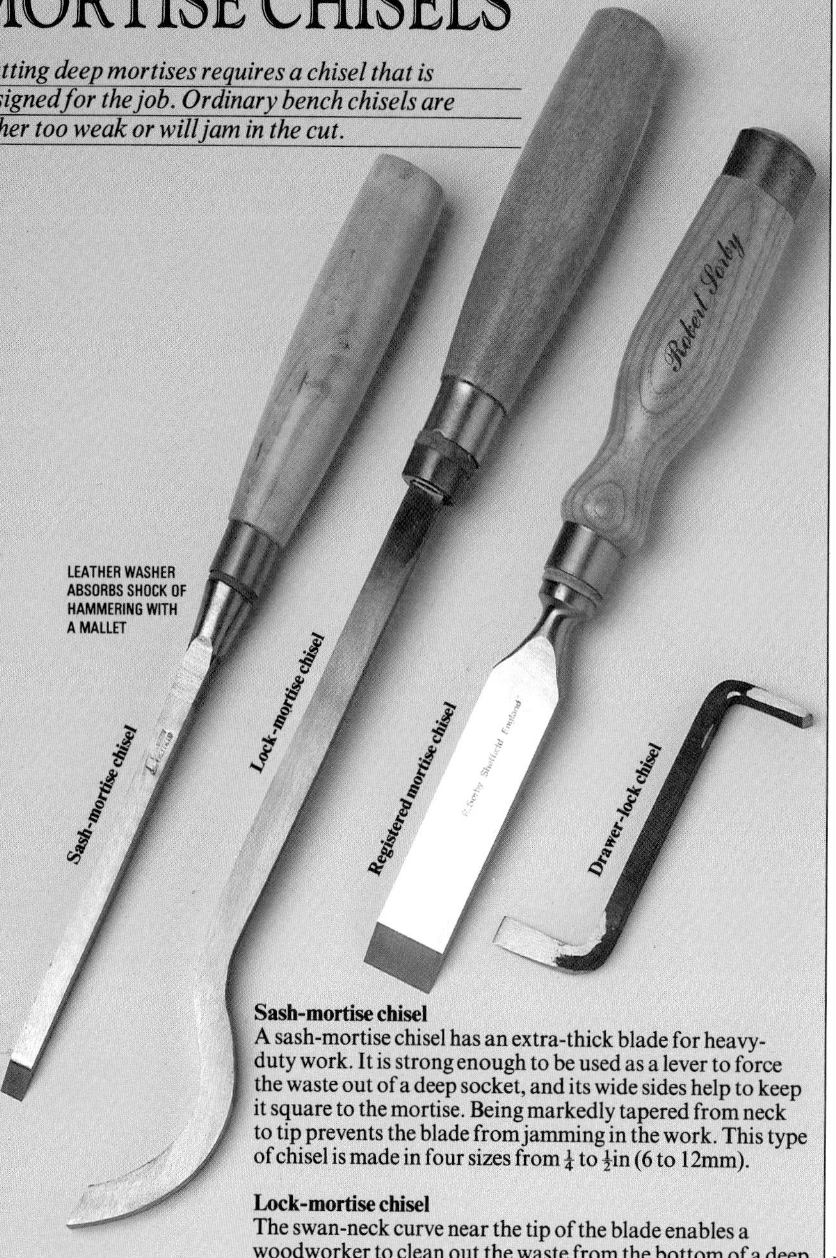

LEATHER WASHER ABSORBS SHOCK OF HAMMERING WITH A MALLET

Sash-mortise chisel

Lock-mortise chisel

Registered mortise chisel

Drawer-lock chisel

Sash-mortise chisel
A sash-mortise chisel has an extra-thick blade for heavy-duty work. It is strong enough to be used as a lever to force the waste out of a deep socket, and its wide sides help to keep it square to the mortise. Being markedly tapered from neck to tip prevents the blade from jamming in the work. This type of chisel is made in four sizes from $\frac{1}{4}$ to $\frac{1}{2}$in (6 to 12mm).

Lock-mortise chisel
The swan-neck curve near the tip of the blade enables a woodworker to clean out the waste from the bottom of a deep mortise. Having cut the mortise with a standard mortise chisel, choose a lock-mortise chisel of the same size or slightly smaller to finish the job.

Registered mortise chisel
Originally made for shipbuilders, the registered mortise chisel is available in widths up to 1$\frac{1}{2}$in (38mm) for constructing substantial framing. A leather washer between the handle and blade absorbs the shock of hammering with a mallet.

Drawer-lock chisel
This is an all-metal cranked chisel designed for cutting lock mortises and hinge housings in confined spaces where it would be impossible to wield an ordinary chisel. It has two cutting edges – one at right angles to the shaft, the other parallel to it. Holding the chisel on the work, strike the shaft with a hammer just behind the cutting edge.

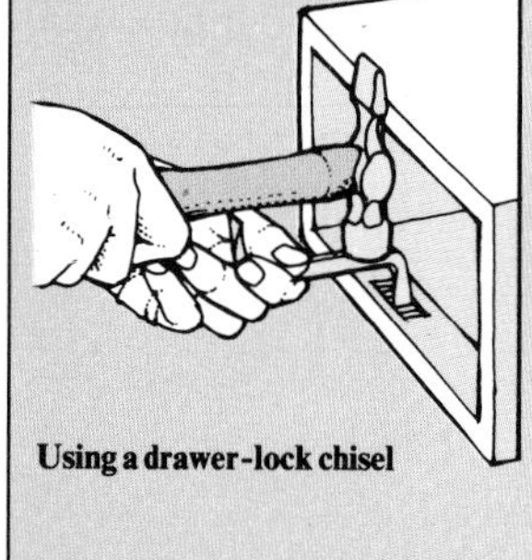

Using a drawer-lock chisel

FIRMER GOUGES

A gouge is a chisel with a blade curved in cross section. The tip is ground to a bevel on the outside (out-cannel) or on the inside (in-cannel).

An out-cannel gouge is used to scoop out hollows, while an in-cannel or scribing gouge is used for trimming curved shoulders such as those on the end of a chair rail joining a round leg. The average range of sizes for both types of gouge is $\frac{1}{4}$ to 1in (6 to 25mm).

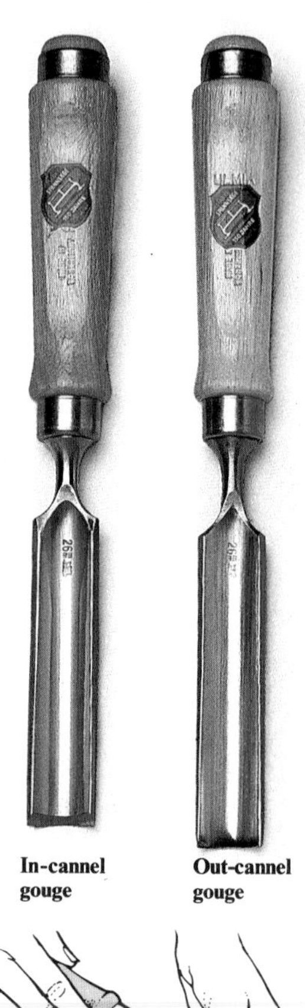

In-cannel gouge **Out-cannel gouge**

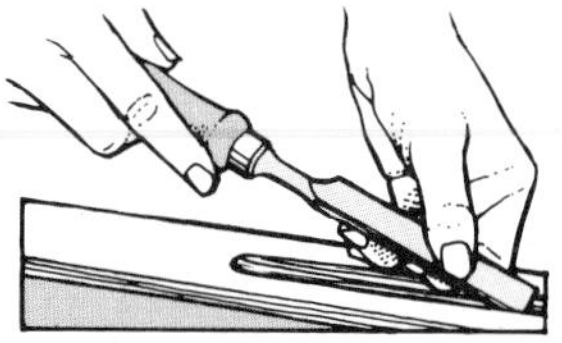

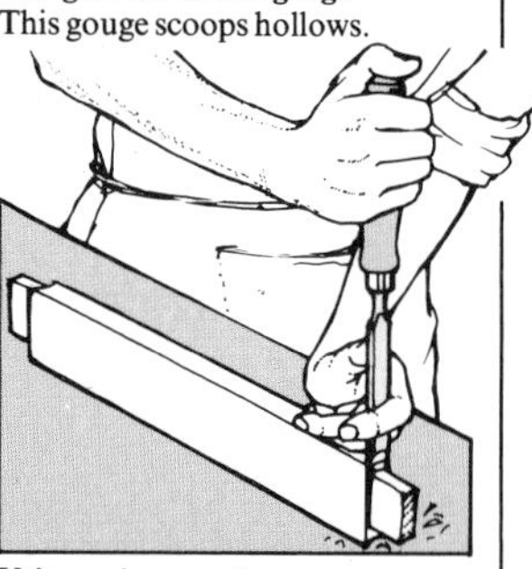

Using an out-cannel gouge
This gouge scoops hollows.

Using an in-cannel gouge
This gouge trims shoulders.

JAPANESE CHISELS

Japanese chisels are made with the same laminated-steel construction used for plane blades. It provides a hard hollow-ground back supported by a thick shock-absorbing strip of soft steel. Combining the tang and socket method of construction makes the strongest possible joint between blade and handle. All Japanese chisels have hardwood handles and most are fitted with a reinforcing hoop at the butt end.

Oiri-nomi
(Bevel-edged chisel)
The standard bench chisel is bevel-edged, but unlike its Western equivalent it is strong enough to be mallet-driven. Blade width varies from $\frac{1}{8}$ to $1\frac{5}{8}$in (3 to 42mm).

Shinogi-nomi
(Dovetail chisel)
The triangular cross-section blade is ideal for chopping out the waste from between the pins and tails of dovetail joints. Shinogi-nomis are $\frac{1}{8}$ to $\frac{1}{2}$in (3 to 12mm) wide.

Usu-nomi
(Paring chisel)
Japanese paring chisels are designed to be used with a two-handed grip. The blades, thinner than standard oiri-nomis, range from $\frac{1}{8}$ to $1\frac{5}{8}$in (3 to 42mm).

Kote-nomi
(Cranked paring chisel)
The cranked neck of this chisel allows a woodworker to clean up long rabbets and housings.

Mukomachi-nomi
(Mortise chisel)
The Japanese mortise chisel has a thick square-section blade capable of cutting deep sockets. It is available from $\frac{1}{4}$ to $\frac{3}{4}$in (6 to 18mm) wide.

Mori-nomi and Sokozarai-nomi
(Hooked mortise chisels)
These special-purpose tools are used with a mortise chisel to clean up the bottom and sides of a blind mortise. Both chisels are hooked for easy waste clearance.

Chokkatu-nomi
(Corner chisel)
This is a very specialized tool for cleaning up the corners of large mortises. Each half of the 90-degree cutting edge is $\frac{3}{8}$, $\frac{5}{8}$ or 1in (9, 16 or 25mm) wide.

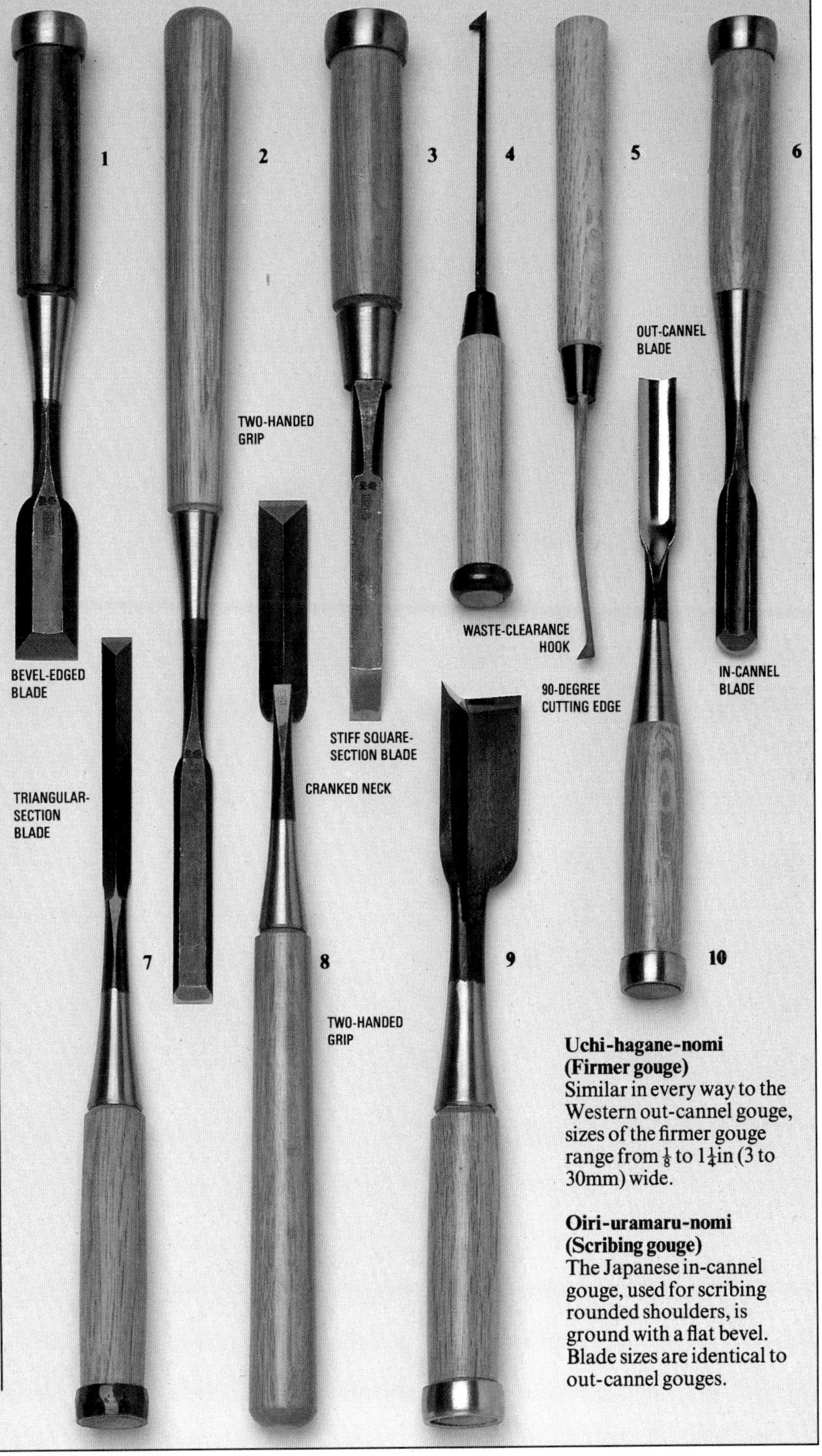

BEVEL-EDGED BLADE
TWO-HANDED GRIP
STIFF SQUARE-SECTION BLADE
WASTE-CLEARANCE HOOK
OUT-CANNEL BLADE
90-DEGREE CUTTING EDGE
IN-CANNEL BLADE
TRIANGULAR-SECTION BLADE
CRANKED NECK
TWO-HANDED GRIP

Uchi-hagane-nomi
(Firmer gouge)
Similar in every way to the Western out-cannel gouge, sizes of the firmer gouge range from $\frac{1}{8}$ to $1\frac{1}{4}$in (3 to 30mm) wide.

Oiri-uramaru-nomi
(Scribing gouge)
The Japanese in-cannel gouge, used for scribing rounded shoulders, is ground with a flat bevel. Blade sizes are identical to out-cannel gouges.

Japanese chisels

1 Oiri-nomi
2 Usu-nomi
3 Mukomachi-nomi
4 Mori-nomi
5 Sokozarai-nomi
6 Oiri-uramaru-nomi
7 Shinogi-nomi
8 Kote-nomi
9 Chokkatu-nomi
10 Uchi-hagane-nomi

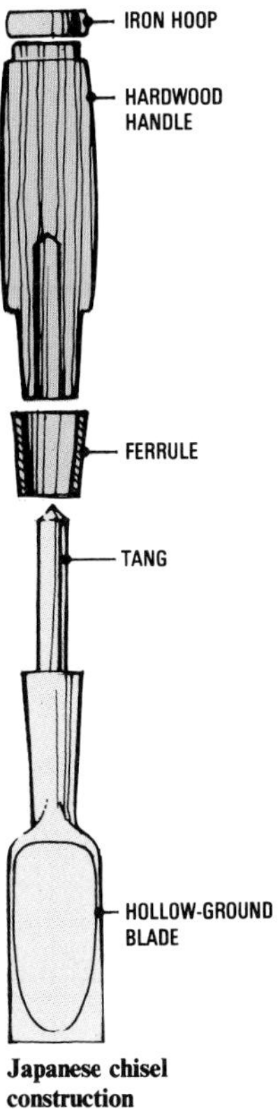

Japanese chisel construction

SHARPENING STONES

Maintaining a sharp edge on a tool is of paramount importance. Compared with a dull tool, a really sharp chisel or plane not only leaves a superior finish, but handles better without resistance and cuts with a clean crisp sound. With sharp tools woodwork is a pleasure – with dull tools it is a chore.

A plane iron or chisel comes ground to shape from the factory, but it cannot be described as sharp. Before it will perform satisfactorily the blade must be honed on a sharpening stone, and when performance drops below an acceptable level, be honed again.

Once a cutting edge is damaged by being chipped or misshapened by repeated honing, the original factory-made bevel must be reproduced by grinding the tool on a grinding wheel or coarse stone.

Woodworking tools are kept sharp by wearing away the metal to form a thin cutting edge on specially dressed blocks of abrasive stone. The best natural sharpening stones are expensive, but very acceptable results can be achieved on cheaper synthetic stones. Depending on the nature of the stone, it must be lubricated during the sharpening process with either water or oil. This prevents the steel from over-heating, and keeps the fine stone and metal debris in suspension to stop it from clogging the abrasive surface of the stone.

SEE ALSO

Planes	88-97
Chisels	98-101
Grinders	106-107
Drawknives	109
Carving chisels and gouges	272-273

Oilstones
Most woodworkers sharpen their edged tools on a rectangular block of stone lubricated with oil. Natural Arkansas stones are generally considered to be the finest oilstones available. The mottled-gray Soft Arkansas stones are coarse and will remove metal quickly for shaping edged tools. The white Hard Arkansas stones hone the tools to a sharp edge, but for an extra-fine edge use Black Hard Arkansas stones.

The equivalent synthetic oilstones, made from aluminum-oxide or silicon-carbide grit, are categorized as coarse, medium and fine.

Some woodworkers have a stone of each grade mounted on the bench so that they can move quickly from one to another. However, it is more economical to buy two stones of different grades glued back to back. These combination stones are usually a union of coarse/medium or medium/fine grades. You can also buy combinations of man-made and natural stones.

Carver's stones
Waterstones molded with shaped profiles to match the common carving tools are made in coarse, medium and fine grades.

- **Mounting benchstones** Ideally, mount your sharpening stones on a separate bench beside your workbench so they are always at hand. Storing a stone in its own box keeps the surface dust-free.

Diamond sharpening stones
Tough, durable sharpening "stones" are made with a grid-like pattern of diamond particles bonded in a plastic base. They are made in extra-coarse, coarse and fine grades. Diamond stones can be used to flatten worn waterstones and natural oilstones.

Diamond-spray sharpening
Spraying diamond particles onto a special ceramic tile produces a sharpening slurry for all edged tools. A spray can of 45-micron particles is for general sharpening. Fine (14-micron) and extra-fine (6-micron) particles are also available, but you need a separate tile for each grade.

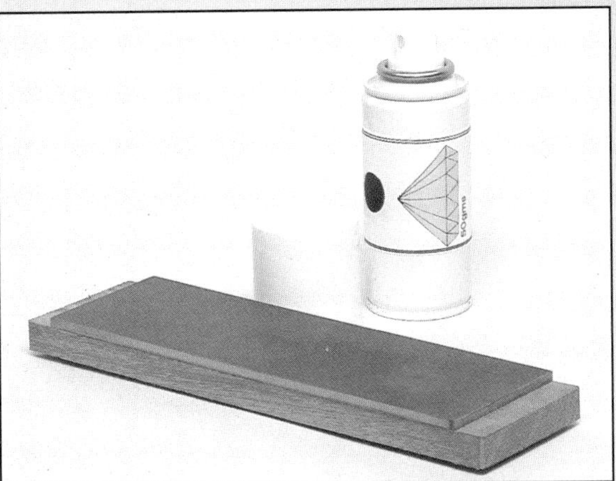
Diamond-spray kit

Slipstones and files
Small shaped stones are required for honing gouges and carving chisels. Natural and man-made waterstones and oilstones are made as slipstones and in the various grades. Teardrop-section and cone slips are the most useful, but there are specialized square-edged and knife-edged stones plus a range of shaped stone files with square, round and triangular sections.

Combination waterstone slips are made for honing drawknives, axes and garden tools.

Japanese waterstones
Japanese waterstones, both natural and synthetic, cut very quickly and are available in grades of fineness that go far beyond those for oilstones. They range from 800 grit at the coarse end, through 1000 grit as a medium/fine grade, to finishing grades of 4000, 6000 and 8000 grits. Natural waterstones are prohibitively expensive and only the most discerning craftsman would have natural stones in a range of grits. Most woodworkers are satisfied with man-made stones, but may have a slip of natural finishing stone. Combination stones are available in the usual pairings.

To improve the cutting action of a waterstone, build up a slurry on its wet surface prior to sharpening by rubbing it with a chalk-like Nagura stone. This is especially useful when honing on one of the hard extra-fine finishing stones.

Shaped slipstones

CARING FOR SHARPENING STONES

Keep your oilstones covered to prevent a build-up of dust on the surface. Eventually an oilstone will become clogged with oil and metal dust. As soon as it no longer cuts effectively, scrub the surface with paraffin and coarse burlap.

Soaking a waterstone
Before you use a waterstone it must be loaded with water by immersion. A coarse stone can take four or five minutes before it is saturated, but a hard fine stone will take somewhat less.

Store a waterstone in a specially fitted vinyl box to prevent the moisture from evaporating so that it is always ready for use. Alternatively, keep it immersed in a can of water. It is imperative to keep a waterstone from freezing or it will almost certainly crack.

Truing sharpening stones
Eventually all sharpening stones become hollow after repeated honing. Flatten an oilstone by grinding the surface on carborundum powder with water or oil on a sheet of glass. Resurface a waterstone by rubbing it on a piece of wet 200-grit silicon-carbide paper taped to a sheet of glass.

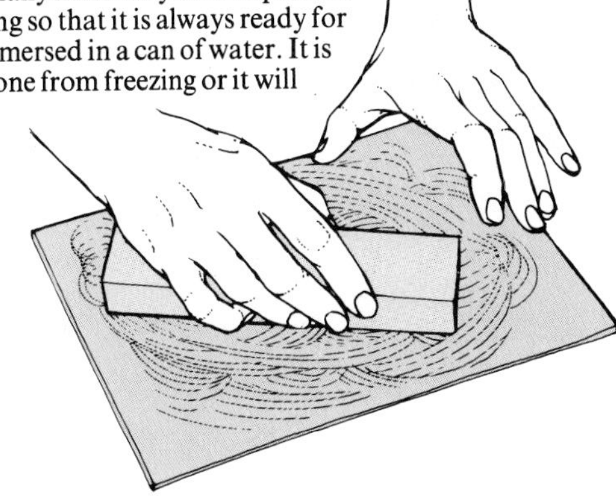
Flattening a sharpening stone

Sharpening-stone grades
Sharpening stones are graded in different ways. The various grading methods are listed below to compare one system with another. Every woodworker needs at least one medium and one fine stone.

GRADE	MAN-MADE OILSTONES	NATURAL OILSTONES	JAPANESE WATERSTONES
Extra-coarse			100 and 220 grits
Coarse	Coarse	Soft Arkansas	800 grit
Medium	Medium	Hard Arkansas	1000 grit
Fine	Fine	Black Hard Arkansas	1200 grit
Extra-fine			6000 and 8000 grits

Strops
Having honed your tools on a sharpening stone, use a strop to remove any remaining trace of the burr, leaving the cutting edge razor sharp. Make a simple strip of thick leather or buy a combination strop with one side covered in fine emery stone and the other three with coarse to fine leather. Lubricate all but the final leather surface with a fine stropping paste.

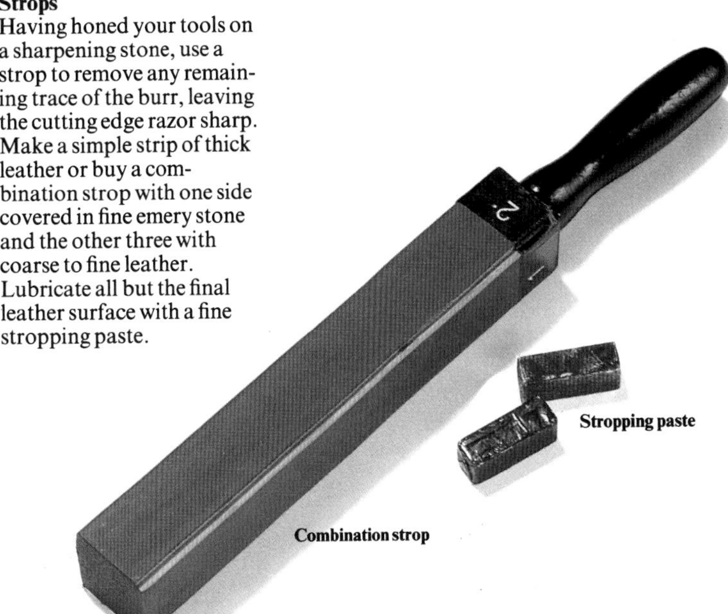
Stropping paste

Combination strop

SHARPENING CHISELS AND PLANES

The grinding process at the factory leaves a new plane iron or chisel with minute scratches on the back of the blade and across the cutting bevel. As a result, the actual cutting edge is serrated and incapable of very fine work. Both the back and bevel must be honed on medium and fine stones in order to remove the grinding marks and leave a perfectly sharp edge.

SEE ALSO

Planes	88-97
Japanese planes	94
Chisels and gouges	98-101
Japanese chisels and gouges	101
Sharpening stones	102-103
Carving chisels and gouges	272-273

Flattening the back of a new blade
Lubricate your stone and hold the blade flat on its surface, bevel up. Rub the blade along the stone, maintaining pressure with your fingertips to stop it from rocking. Repeat on a fine stone until the metal shines.

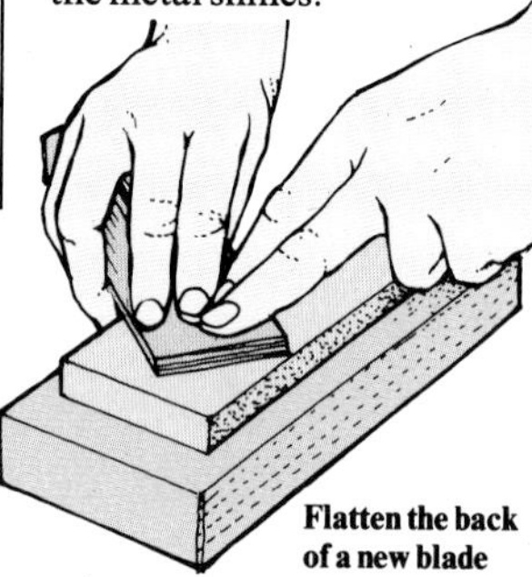

Flatten the back of a new blade

Sharpening the cutting edge
Bench-plane blades and chisels are ground with a bevel of about 25 degrees. Some woodworkers like to hone this bevel for cutting softwood, but the edge is too weak for hardwoods. A secondary bevel of 35 degrees is honed on the very edge of the blade to strengthen it. You will find this process makes for fast sharpening because you are removing very little metal.

Grasp the blade, beveled side down, in your right hand with index finger extended along one edge. Place the fingertips of your left hand on top of the blade, slipping your thumb beneath and across it **(1)**. Place the grinding bevel on a lubricated medium-grade stone and rock the blade until you can feel the bevel is flat on the surface. Rocking on the cutting edge, lift the blade slightly in order to hone the secondary bevel.

Keep your wrists rigid to maintain a constant angle and rub the blade up and down using the full length of the stone.

Turn a plane blade at an angle so that the whole cutting edge is in contact with the stone **(2)**. When honing a narrow chisel, move it from one side of the stone to the other to avoid wearing a hollow in the center **(3)**. Hone very narrow chisels on the edge of the stone.

Once you have honed a bevel about $\frac{1}{32}$in (1mm) wide, move on to a fine stone and hone the edge again. Honing raises a burr on the flat back of the blade. If you stroke your thumb over the edge you can feel it **(4)**. Remove the burr by honing the back flat on the stone, give the bevel a few light strokes, then hone the back once more. This process breaks off the burr, leaving a sharp edge.

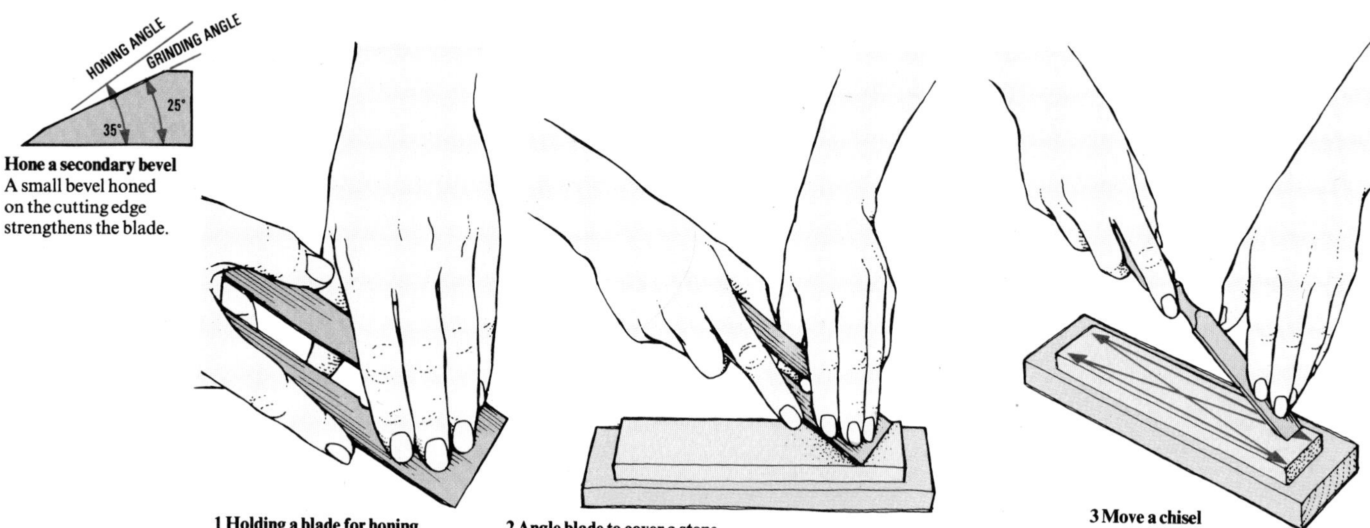

Hone a secondary bevel
A small bevel honed on the cutting edge strengthens the blade.

1 Holding a blade for honing

2 Angle blade to cover a stone

3 Move a chisel across a stone

USING A HONING GUIDE

Honing by hand is fast and efficient, but if you cannot master the technique, you can clamp plane blades and chisels in a device that will hold them at the required sharpening angle. There are many different styles of honing guides, but they all perform the same function.

Using a honing guide
Maintain pressure on the cutting edge to grind the bevel.

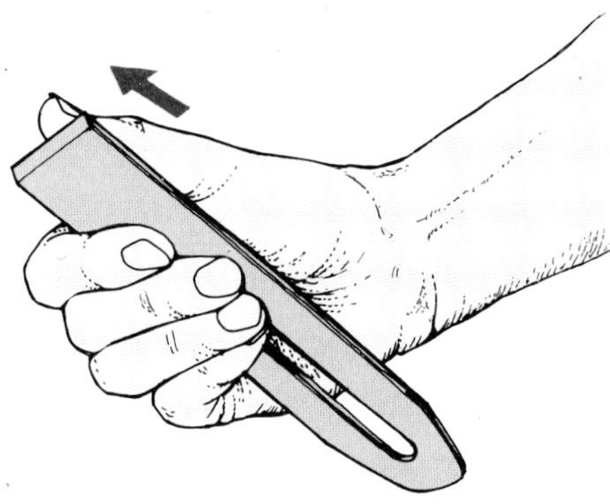

4 Feel burr with your thumb

SHARPENING GOUGES

To hone an out-cannel gouge turn your stone crossways and rub the tool from side to side along the stone in a figure-eight path to even out the wear **(1)**. Remove the burr raised on the inside of the gouge with a lubricated slipstone **(2)**.

Use a similar slipstone to hone a bevel on an in-cannel gouge **(3)**. Remove the burr by holding the tool flat on a benchstone and move it from side to side while rocking the blade **(4)**.

Carving gouges are sharpened in a similar way. Use knife-edge slipstones or stone files to hone the cutting edges of special carving chisels like the V-shaped parting tools and the squarish gouge-like macaronis and fluteronis.

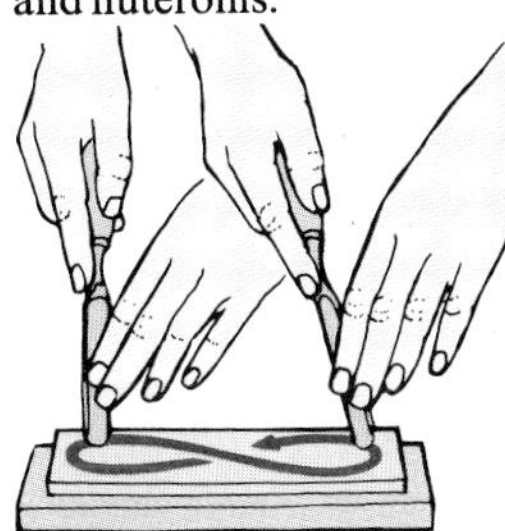

1 Honing an out-cannel gouge

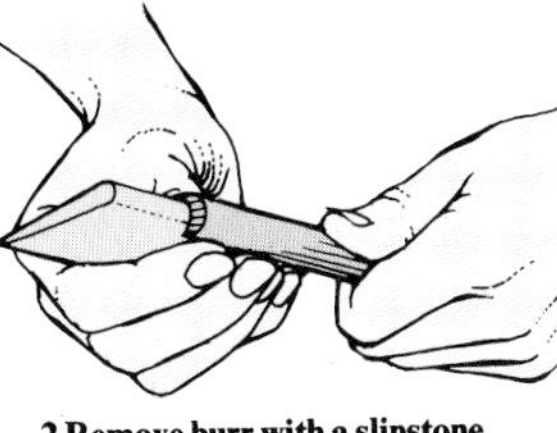

2 Remove burr with a slipstone

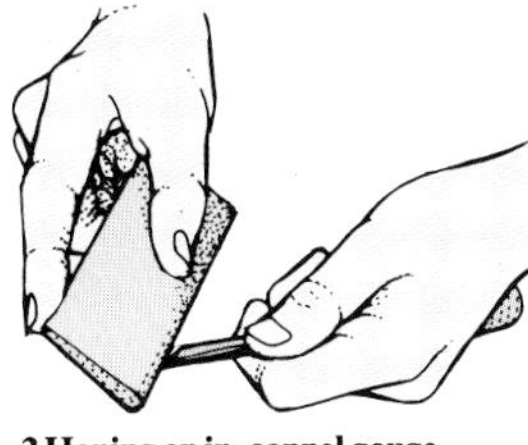

3 Honing an in-cannel gouge

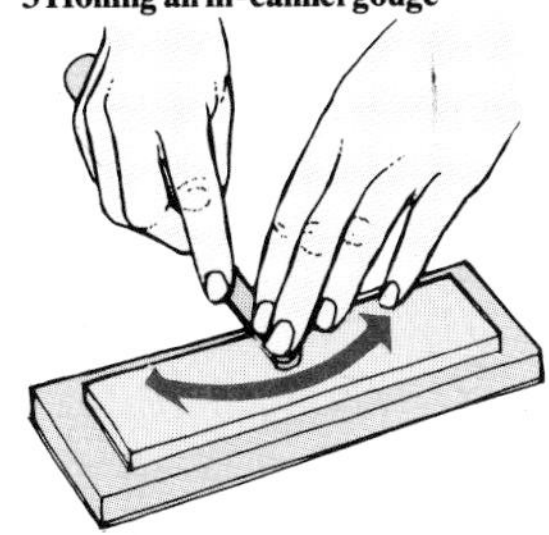

4 Remove burr on an oilstone

SHARPENING JAPANESE BLADES

Japanese planes and chisels are sharpened in a similar way to Western blades, but there are significant differences as a result of their peculiar construction. As each blade is laminated with a hard-steel cutting edge, there is no need to hone a secondary bevel to strengthen it.

The hollow grinding on the back of every blade creates a narrow border of metal that is easy to keep flat on a stone. Eventually, repeated honing of the bevel wears into this hollow so that the cutting edge is no longer continuous. Maintaining the narrow border can be achieved by flattening the back after every honing. However, this wears away the blade relatively quickly and is somewhat laborious when sharpening wide chisels and plane irons. Japanese craftsmen prefer to reshape the hollow periodically by hammering some metal into the narrow border behind the cutting edge.

Flattening a new blade
As with Western blades, the backs of new chisels and planes are flattened before the bevel is honed for the first time. Because the metal is so hard, this is done by grinding on a steel flattening plate, using a pinch of coarse carborundum or silicon-carbide powder mixed with a little water.

Hold the blade flat on the surface at right angles to the plate using a short length of softwood to apply pressure. When the narrow border surrounding the hollow is an even color and texture, repeat with finer powder.

Wipe the blade clean and move on to a medium sharpening stone to continue to flatten the back. Finish the job on a fine stone until the metal shines like a mirror.

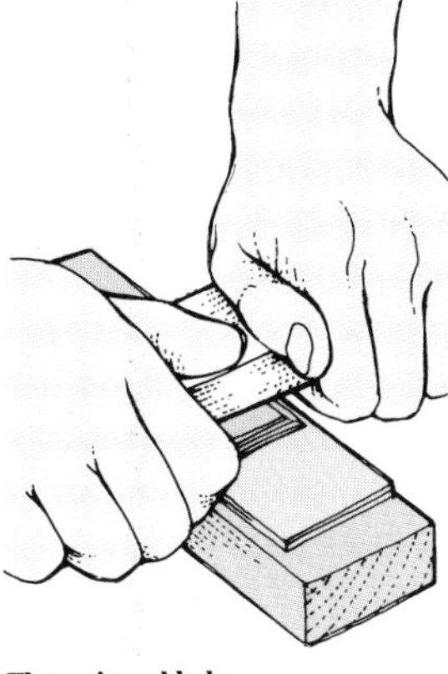

Flattening a blade
Grind the back of a blade, using a length of wood to apply pressure.

Sharpening the edge
Sharpen the cutting edges of Japanese blades like their Western equivalents, but hone the whole width of the bevel. Do not hone a secondary bevel on the cutting edge.

Maintaining the hollow back
Re-creating the leading edge of the hollow back is a skilled process. Traditionalists rest the back of the blade on the edge of a block of wood. A square hammer is used to tap the bevel, pushing metal out of the back to fill the hollow edge. Blows must be within the soft part of the bevel. The hard cutting edge is brittle and will chip if struck with the hammer.

Once the hollow is refilled, the back is flattened on a grinding plate as already described (see left).

Blade-hammering jig
Because the hammering process requires practice, a special jig is often used. A heavy metal bar, guided by a hollow tube, is dropped onto the beveled edge, which is backed up by a metal anvil. Alternatively, have your Japanese blades reshaped by a professional.

Reshaping a hollow back
One way is to tap the soft-metal bevel with a hammer.

Repeated honing wears into blade hollow

Hammering the soft-metal bevel reforms the edge

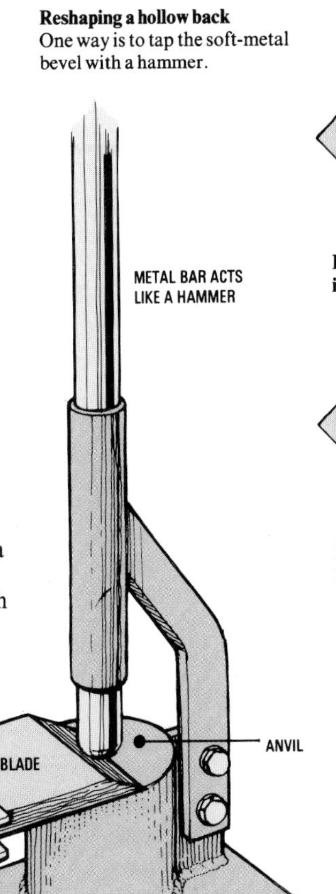

Blade-hammering jig
A jig provides an easier way to reshape a blade's hollow back.

GRINDERS

For centuries, chipped or worn blades have been reground on 100- to 200-grit coarse benchstones. Although this method is still perfectly adequate, many woodworkers prefer to repair the edges of chisels and plane irons on a high-speed bench grinder or a slow-speed motorized whetstone.

SEE ALSO

Planes	88-97
Chisels and gouges	98-101
Sharpening stones	102-103
Grinding drill bits	114
Grinding screwdrivers	119
Turning tools	194-196
Carving chisels and gouges	272-273

High-speed grinder
A standard bench grinder has a $\frac{1}{4}$ to $\frac{3}{4}$hp electric motor driving two aluminum-oxide grinding wheels at about 3000rpm. The majority of grinding wheels are between 5 and 8in (125 and 200mm) in diameter. The larger wheels are best for grinding blades because a small-diameter wheel produces an exaggerated hollow-ground bevel. Wheels are interchangeable, but most grinders are supplied with one coarse-grade and one fine-grade wheel.

All high-speed grinding wheels are guarded to prevent accidents and have transparent plastic spark deflectors to protect your eyes. An adjustable tool rest is mounted in front of each wheel.

Every grinder must be bolted securely to a bench before it is used.

High-speed grinders sharpen a blade quickly. With a range of grinding wheels, wire brushes and cloth buffing wheels, they can also shape, clean and polish all types of metalwork.

Rubberized abrasive wheels
Having ground a bevel on a blade, it is normally honed to a sharp edge on a benchstone. However, you can hone chisels, gouges and plane irons on a bench grinder using a neoprene-rubber wheel with silicon carbide embedded in it. The 4 to 6in (100 to 150mm) diameter wheels are resistant to oil and water and are available in coarse, medium and fine grades.

You grind a blade with the wheel turning toward you, but a rubberized abrasive wheel must be spinning away from you when honing or the blade will damage the relatively soft material. If you cannot reverse the direction on your bench grinder, you can trail the blade on the side of the wheel.

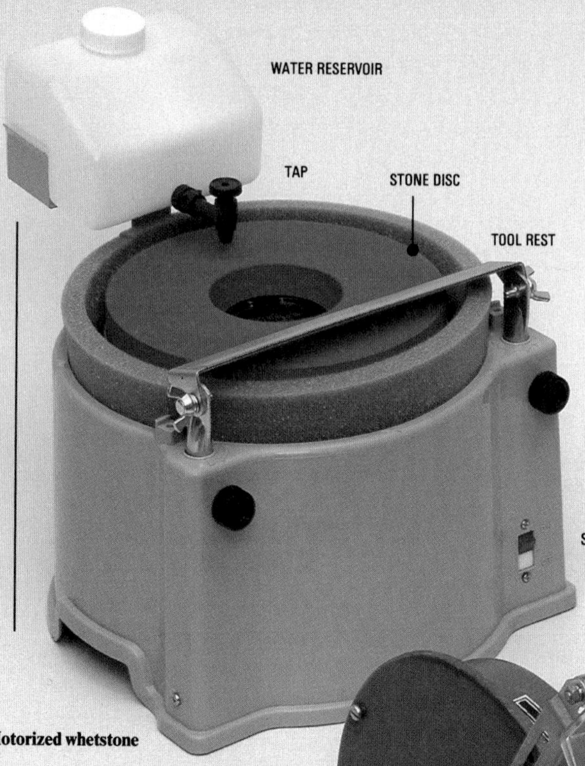

WATER RESERVOIR

TAP

STONE DISC

TOOL REST

SWITCH

Motorized whetstone

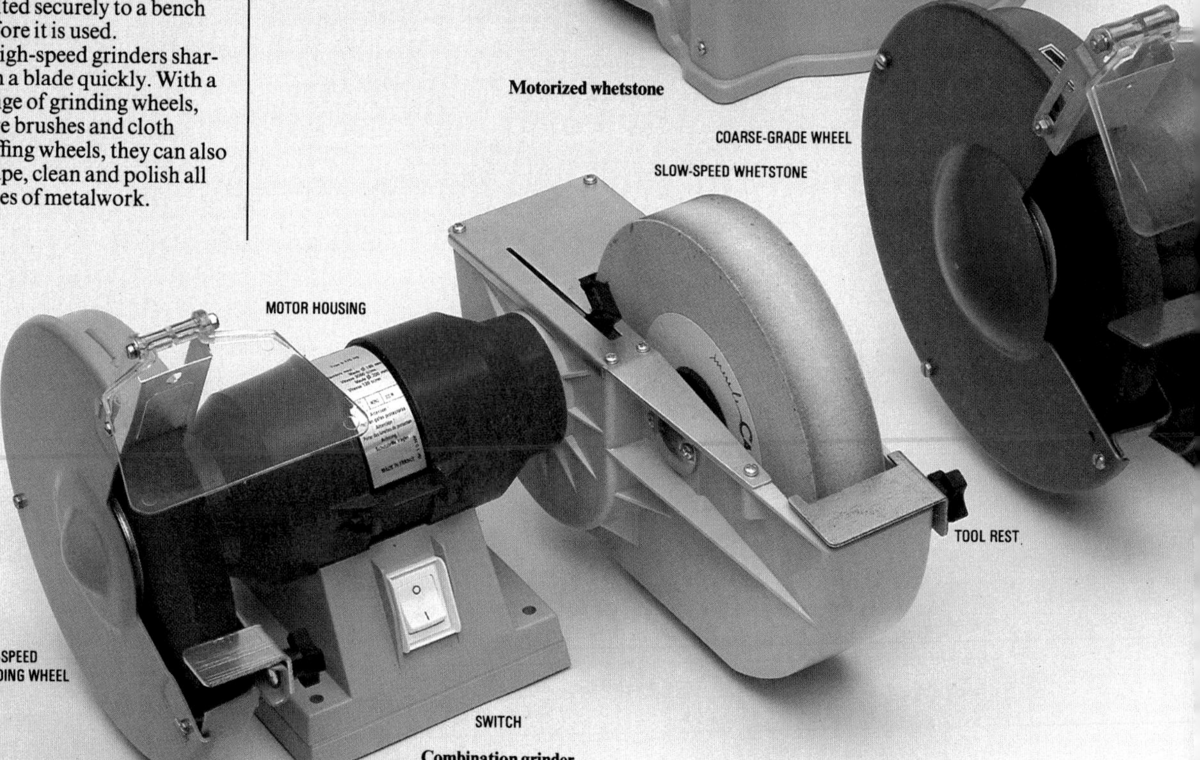

Using a motorized whetstone

COARSE-GRADE WHEEL

SLOW-SPEED WHETSTONE

MOTOR HOUSING

TOOL REST

HIGH-SPEED GRINDING WHEEL

SWITCH

Combination grinder

Motorized whetstone
The common problem of overheating blades is avoided by using a slow-speed motorized whetstone. A stone disc turns at only 500rpm and is lubricated by a continuous stream of water from a reservoir mounted on the machine. A 1000-grit general-purpose stone is fitted as standard, but it is a simple matter to swap this for, say, a 180- or 6000-grit stone. The latter stone is used to hone a fine cutting edge on a blade.

Combination grinders
There are several machines that provide some of the advantages of both high-speed grinding and slow whetstone sharpening. At one end of the machine, for example, is the familiar aluminum-oxide wheel, while at the other end is a clutch-operated whetstone turning in a water bath. Blades are sharpened on the edge of this type of whetstone.

Other machines combine a standard wheel with an abrasive grinding belt. With their larger surface area, belts do not heat quite as quickly as a high-speed stone. If a belt clogs, it is replaced.

High-speed grinder

Star-wheel dressing tool

Grinding wheels

DRESSING A WHEEL

Aluminum-oxide grinding wheels will not cut efficiently when the surface becomes "glazed"–i.e. clogged with metal particles.

A new clean surface is produced by holding a star-wheel dressing tool against the spinning wheel. Alternatively, dress the wheel with a carborundum stick.

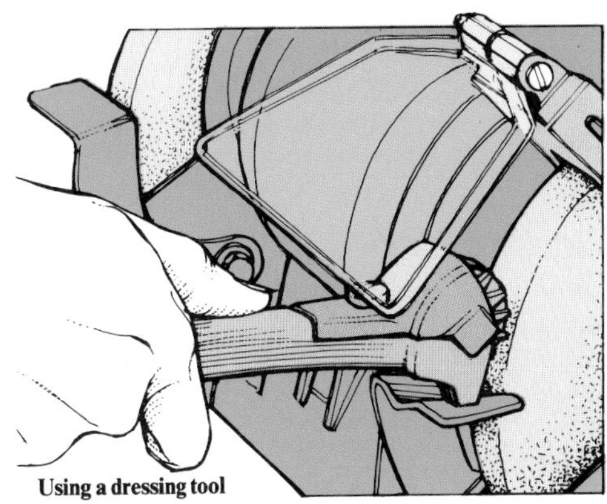
Using a dressing tool

GRINDING A CHISEL OR PLANE IRON

Use a coarse grinding wheel to reshape a badly worn blade, then change to a finer grade.

Before you grind a new bevel on a plane or chisel check the cutting edge with a try square **(1)**. If it has worn unevenly, use a very fine felt-tip pen to mark a line square to the long edges of the blade.

Set the tool rest about ⅛in (3mm) from the grinding wheel, check that the adjusting clamps are all tight, then switch on the machine.

Wearing protective eye wear, dip the blade in water and place it, bevel down, on the tool rest. Gradually feed the cutting edge against the wheel and as soon as it touches, move the blade from side to side, keeping it moving the whole time to stop it from overheating **(2)**. Dip it in water every few seconds.

When you have ground the blade square, switch off and adjust the tool rest to present the blade at an angle of 25 degrees to the wheel.

Switch on and proceed as before, this time grinding an even bevel across the width of the blade **(3)**. Don't press too hard, and keep the blade cool by dipping, or use a fine plant spray while grinding the blade with one hand. If you allow the metal to heat to a temperature at which it turns blue, it will have lost temper and will not hold a sharp cutting edge for very long. The only remedy is to grind the blade beyond the blued area.

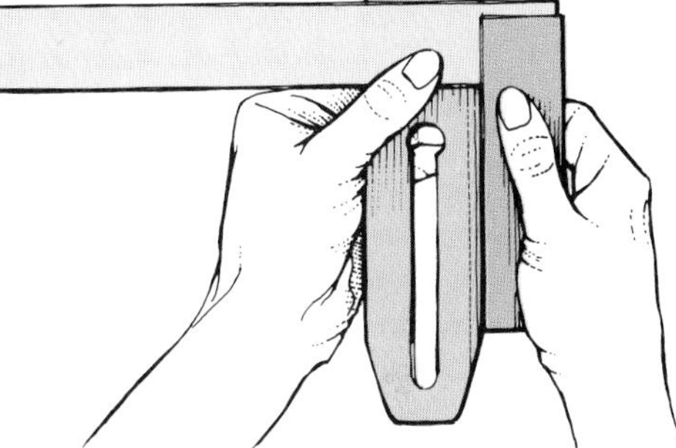
1 Check the edge with a square

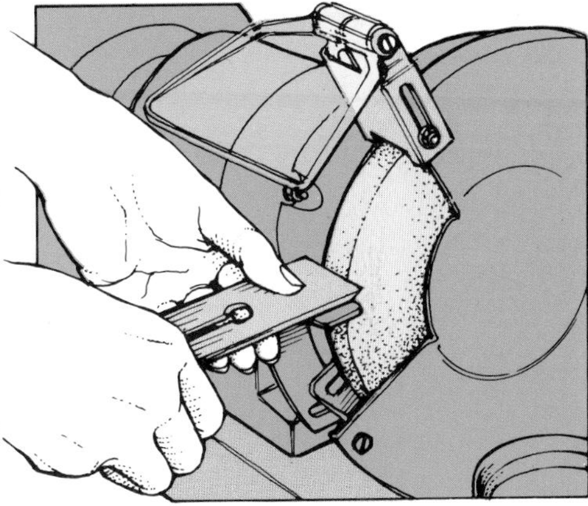
2 Grind the edge square

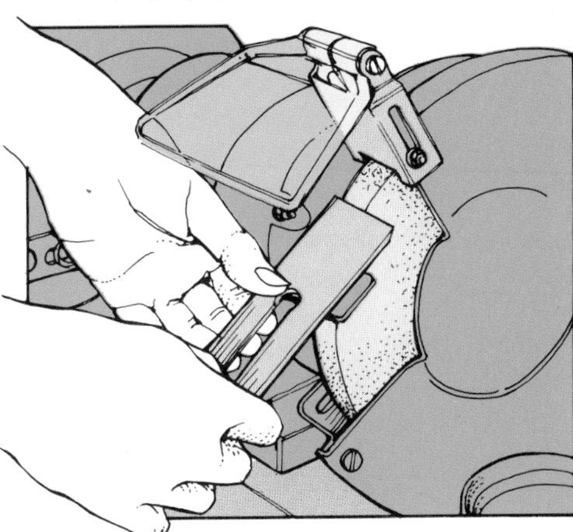
3 Grind a bevel on the blade

SPOKESHAVES

A spokeshave leaves the same finish as a bench plane, but because the sole or "face" of the tool is so narrow it is not as easy to control and a certain knack is required before it will cut smoothly on every stroke. Being designed to smooth curved components, the spokeshave is the only tool for the job in certain situations. But some of the more specialized spokeshaves are not essential, as an ordinary bench or block plane can achieve the same results, if a little slowly.

SEE ALSO

Carved bowls	45
Stick chairs	54
Sharpening stones	102-103
Grinders	106-107
Workbenches	212-213

SPECIALIZED SPOKESHAVES

A craftsman, be he cooper, wheelwright or carpenter, would once have made special-purpose spokeshaves for himself. Tool catalogs still list some spokeshaves that may not be essential to the average woodworker, but can speed up a particular process or make it that much easier to accomplish.

Half-round spokeshave
Having a deep concave face and blade, this is a useful tool for shaping rounded legs and rails. You could do the same job with a bench plane or flat-face spokeshave, but this tool removes more wood per stroke.

Radius spokeshave
This is an excellent tool for scooping out deep hollows like those in a shaped wooden chair seat.

Combination spokeshave
This is a dual-purpose spokeshave, having a half-round spokeshave mounted beside a straight one. It is convenient when shaping work with a frequently changing profile, which otherwise entails swapping one tool for another.

Chamfer spokeshave
This spokeshave has adjustable fences for accurately cutting chamfers up to $1\frac{1}{2}$in (38mm) wide. The tool is held at 45 degrees to the top face of the work.

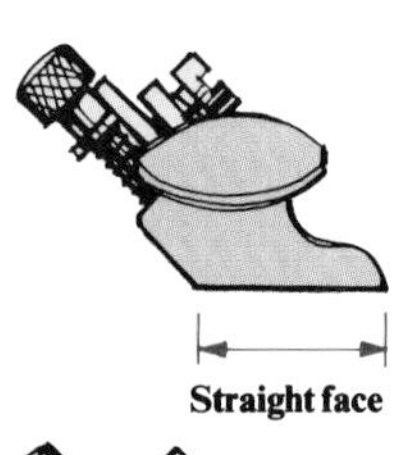

Straight face

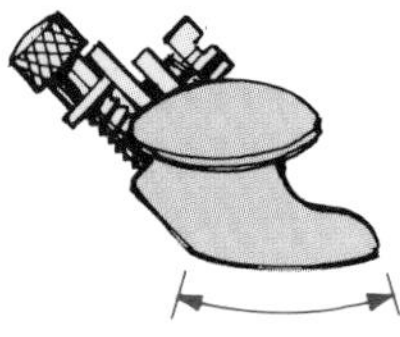

Round face

STANDARD SPOKESHAVES

Round-face spokeshave
This spokeshave has a convex face and is used to smooth a concave-shaped piece of wood. No other tool will do the job as well.

The spokeshave cutter is like a miniature plane blade held in place by a simple cap iron. On basic spokeshaves, blade-depth adjustment is achieved by moving the blade up and down by hand until it looks about right before clamping it with the locking screw on the cap iron. More precise adjustment is possible on spokeshaves having a screw on each top corner of the blade.

Straight-face spokeshave
This spokeshave is identical in every way to the round-face version except for its narrow flat face designed for skimming a convex curve. As always, the work must be positioned in such a way that you can shave the wood in the direction of the grain.

Types of spokeshave

1 Standard spokeshave
2 Combination spokeshave
3 Chamfer spokeshave
4 Half-round spokeshave
5 Radius spokeshave

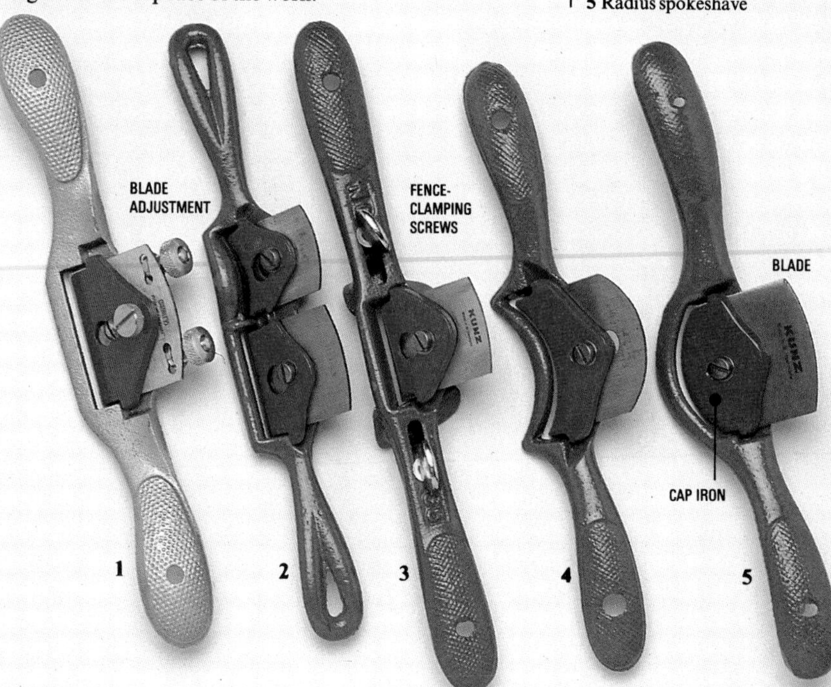

USING & SHARPENING A SPOKESHAVE

Until you develop the right "feel," a spokeshave will either skid across the surface without taking a shaving or try to bury its cutter in the wood. Practice on scrap softwood before working on expensive hardwoods.

Controlling a spokeshave
Spokeshaves cut on the push stroke. To have precise control over the angle of the blade to the work, take the tool in both hands with your thumbs resting on the back edges of the handles. With the tool resting on the work, rock it slightly backward and forward on its face until it is taking a shaving cleanly.

Cut in the direction of the grain only, even if it means turning the work in the vise to shave the curve in two directions.

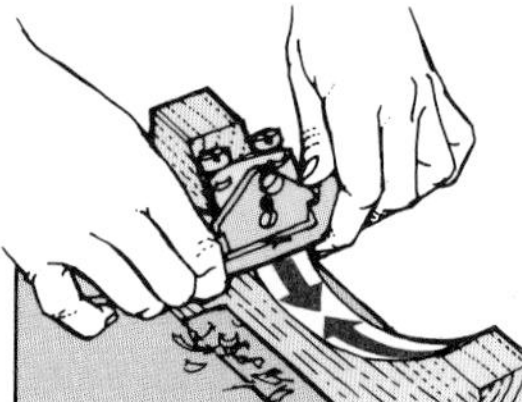

Controlling a spokeshave

Sharpening a spokeshave cutter
A spokeshave cutter is honed on a benchstone like a plane or chisel, but it is difficult to hold such a short blade at a constant angle to the stone. Either clamp it in a honing guide or make a temporary "handle" by cutting a slot in a piece of wood into which you can jam the top edge of the cutter.

Grind a new bevel on a coarse benchstone in the same way or clamp the cutter in locking pliers to hold it firmly for power grinding.

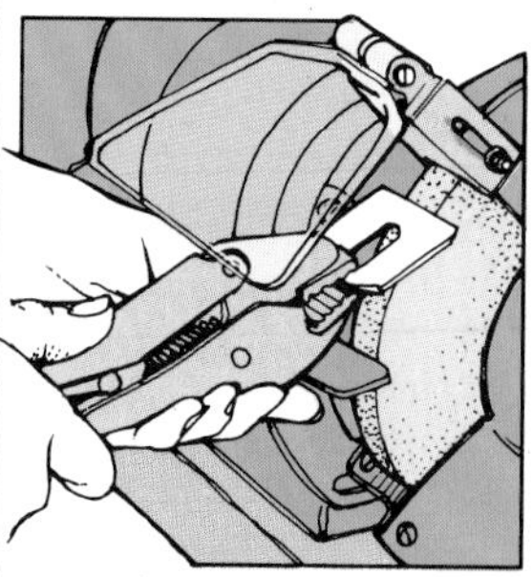

Grinding a spokeshave cutter

DRAWKNIVES

The drawknife ranks with the axe and adze as being one of the earliest-known woodworking tools. It was used by many different craftsmen, from the shipwright to the chairmaker, for quickly shaping components that might then be more finely finished by plane or spokeshave. A drawknife is rarely used today except by those woodworkers who appreciate the speed with which one can reduce a blank to size for carving or turning. It is, however, a versatile tool that, in the hands of a skilled worker, can be used to make curved chairbacks, arms and so on.

Drawknife
Over the centuries, different patterns of drawknife were developed to meet the needs of specialist craftsmen or as a result of local styling. Even today there are several variations on the theme. A basic drawknife might have a straight or curved blade that is beveled on one edge. The metal at each end of the blade is forged into a pointed tang that is bent at right angles and fitted with a turned wooden handle.

CURVED-EDGE BLADE

FORGED TANG

Drawknife (German pattern)

TURNED HANDLE

Swedish push knife

Drawknife (English pattern)

CUTTING EDGE

Inshave

CUTTING EDGE

Scorp

Swedish push knife
A modern derivation of the drawknife, this tool has a short 4 × 1in (100 × 25mm) blade and two straight handles. It is used on both the push and pull stroke.

Inshave
This drawknife is in the shape of a tight curve for working deep hollows. Inshaves are usually beveled on the outside of the curve.

Scorp
A scorp is a one-handed inshave for work such as wooden bowls and spoons.

USING A DRAWKNIFE

When using a drawknife, extend your thumbs along the handles to stop the tool from twisting in your hands and to help you control the angle of the blade to the work. A drawknife cuts on the pull stroke in the direction of the grain. Pulling the blade diagonally across the work produces a slicing action for cutting difficult wood.

- **Sharpening a drawknife** Hold the drawknife upright, resting one handle in a bench vise. Hone with a lubricated sharpening stone, using small circular strokes.

Shaping with a drawknife
If you are working a convex shape, hold the tool bevel upward. Turn the tool over when cutting a concave shape or the bevel will drive the blade deeply into the wood.

Holding the work
When using a drawknife, craftsmen traditionally hold the work in a shaving horse – a long stool with a built-in foot-operated clamp **(1)**.

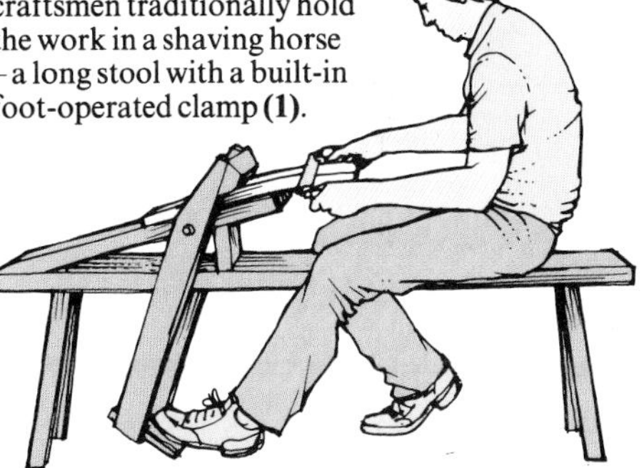

1 Traditional shaving horse

However, it is quite possible to stand at the end of a standard workbench to shave work clamped by one end in a vise **(2)**. Alternatively, use a homemade breast bib – a small board cut from sawn wood and suspended on a piece of string hung around your neck. One end of the work is supported on the edge of a bench, and it is held firmly by pressing against the opposite end with the breast bib **(3)**.

2 Clamp workpiece firmly

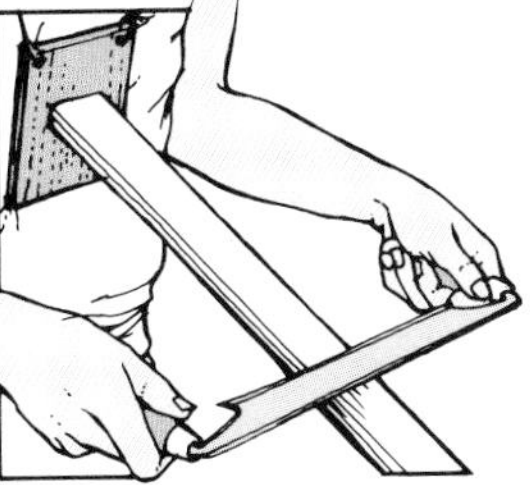

3 Using a breast bib

SCRAPERS

A sharp metal scraper, which removes paper-thin shavings, leaves a finish on a piece of wood that is superior to that left after sanding where the grain is clogged with dust. This is even more true when working "wild" or irregular grain, which would become torn by even the most finely set plane. A scraper is also used to remove patches of hardened glue and other blemishes.

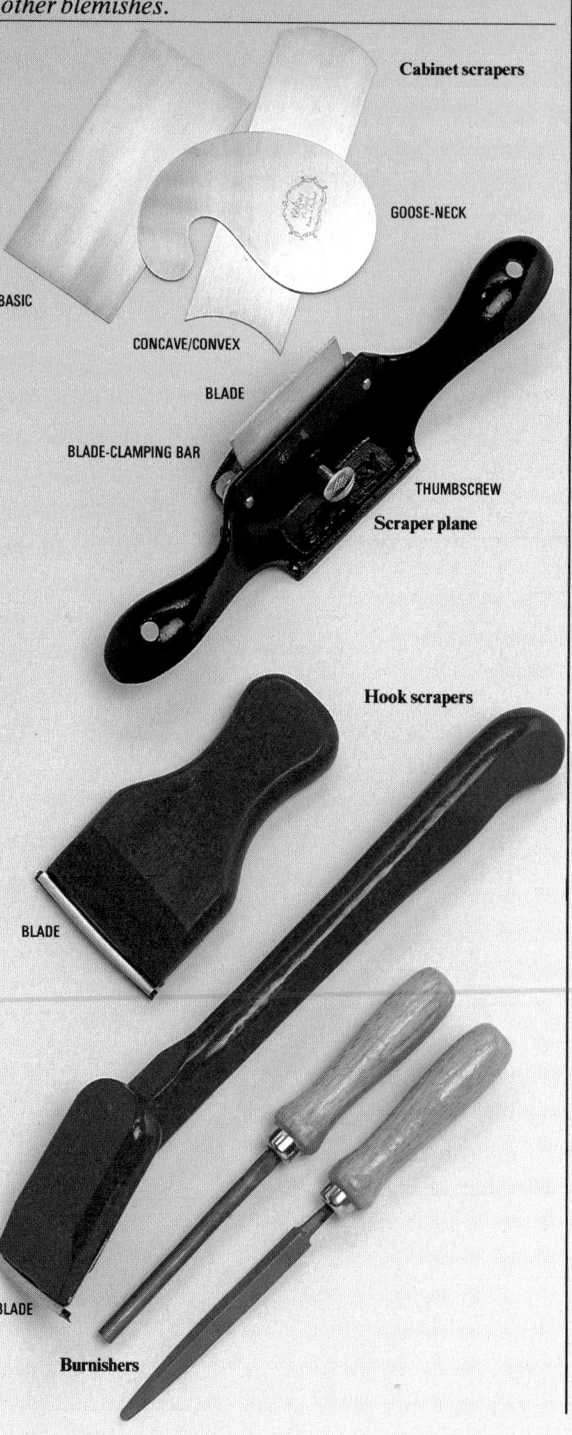

Cabinet scrapers
The basic scraper for working flat surfaces is a simple rectangle of tempered steel. It is supplied as a cropped blank upon which a scraping edge must be raised before it is ready for use.

Goose-neck and concave/convex scrapers are made for finishing moldings and other shaped work.

Hook scrapers
A hook scraper with a wooden handle is easy to use and comfortable to hold. The disposable blades are replaced as soon as they become dull. Long-handle versions of the hook scraper are available for heavy-duty work on wooden floors, boats and so on. When using a hook scraper (which cuts on the pull stroke only), hold it at an angle to the surface.

Scraper plane
A cabinet scraper is hard on the thumbs, especially when it gets hot enough to burn them. A scraper plane is a simple cast-metal jig designed to make the job easier and more comfortable. A scraper blade is clamped to the stock at the optimum angle and is bent into a curve by a centrally placed thumbscrew.

Unlike a standard cabinet scraper, which is cropped with a square edge all around, the scraper-plane cutter is ground at an angle of 45 degrees on two edges. Hone these edges on a stone and raise a scraping burr as for a cabinet scraper.

Clamp the blade in the tool with the bar and retaining screws, then adjust the curve with the thumbscrew until the blade is taking the required shaving – the greater the curve, the coarser the shaving.

Burnishers
Burnishers made from hardened steel with a round, oval or triangular section are used to raise a burr on a scraper.

SHARPENING A SCRAPER

SEE ALSO

Sharpening stones	102-103
Carving	272-281
Preparing wood	284-285
Abrasive papers	285

Any square-cut piece of steel will scrape wood to some extent. It will probably produce dust only, and if it does take a shaving it will be discontinuous and ragged, leaving a poorly finished surface. A cabinet scraper is carefully filed, stoned and burnished until it is left with a tiny burr on its long edges, which acts like a miniature plane iron.

Making a square edge
Clamp a new scraper in a vise and use a smooth metal file to "draw file" its long edges square. Use your fingertips to guide the file and stop it from rocking **(1)** while pulling it along the edge of the scraper.

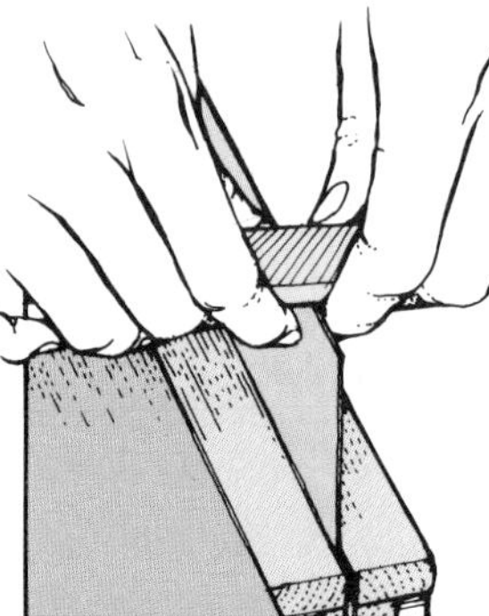
1 Draw-file the edge

Honing with a slipstone
Having filed the edge smooth and shiny, use an oiled slipstone like the file to hone the scraper. Turn the stone frequently to avoid wearing a groove in its surface. Stone each side of the scraper to remove the burr **(2)**.

2 Smooth with stone

Creating a burr
To raise a burr, first hold the scraper on a bench top close to its edge and stroke the face firmly with a burnisher four or five times **(3)**. Then turn the scraper over and repeat the process.

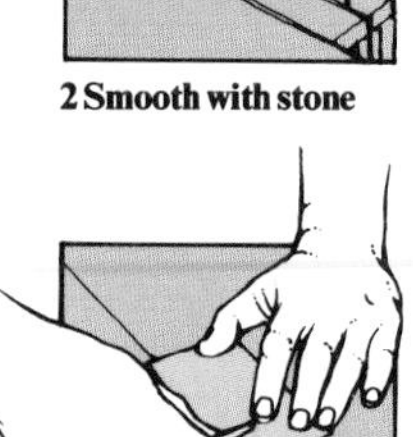
3 Raising a burr

To turn the burr at right angles, hold the scraper on end, and with the burnisher held at about 85 degrees to the face, make two or three firm vertical strokes **(4)**.

When the cutter is not cutting cleanly, raise a new burr. There is no need to square the edge again until it is rounded or damaged.

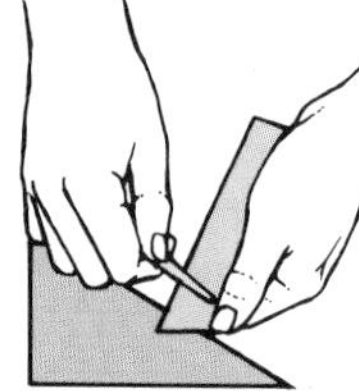
4 Turning the burr

USING A CABINET SCRAPER

Hold a cabinet scraper in both hands, flexing it into a curve by putting pressure on the back face with your thumbs close to the bottom edge.

Scraping technique
Lean the scraper away from you and push the tool to take a shaving **(1)**. Vary both the angle and the curve until the scraper is removing the required amount.

An almost flat scraper skims the surface; a more pronounced curve cuts deeper for removing blemishes.

To scrape a surface flat, cover a wide area by working across it diagonally in both directions with the grain before finishing parallel to the grain. Scrape away from an edge, or alongside an obstruction, by pulling the tool toward you **(2)**.

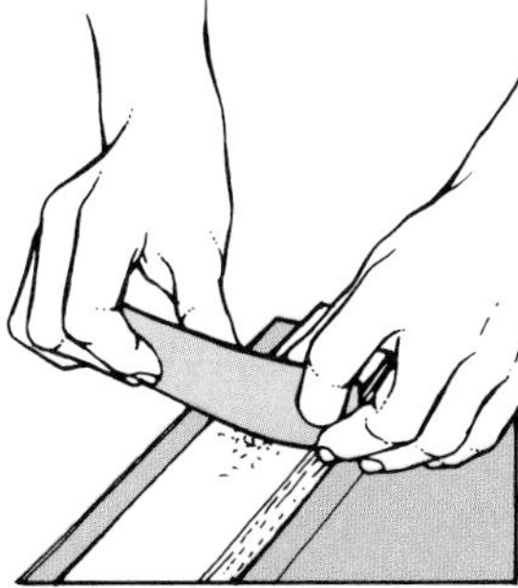

1 Bending a scraper
Bend a scraper with your thumbs to finish a flat surface.

2 Pulling a scraper
Pull the scraper to scrape into a corner.

WOOD RASPS & FILES

Rasps and files are used rarely in the woodwork shop except perhaps by carvers. A rasp, in particular, removes wood very quickly and is frequently used by carvers for preliminary shaping, especially because it is possible to cut both with and against the grain. Rasps leave a rough surface, and files of the same shape are employed to improve the finish.

WIRE BRISTLES
File handle
Half-round rasp
Half-round file
File card
COARSE-FIBER BRUSH
Flat Surform file
Round Surform file
PERFORATED BLADE
Needle files
Rifflers

Rasps
The surface of a rasp is covered with individual teeth that cut on the forward stroke. The size and distribution of teeth determine the degree of coarseness, or cut, of the rasp. There are slight variations in the way the cut is described from one manufacturer to another, but broadly speaking, there are bastard, second-cut and smooth rasps, the bastard cut being the most coarse.

There are flat and round rasps, but the most versatile is the half-round rasp. All versions are made in 8, 10 and 12in (200, 250 and 300mm) lengths, but you will find a 10in rasp a good general-purpose tool.

Wood files
A wood file has rows of closely packed sharp ridges that "plane" off the high points of the roughened wood left by a rasp. File cuts are also described as bastard, second-cut and smooth, but they are all relatively fine, compared with a rasp. For an even finer finish, wrap sandpaper around a file.

Surform tools
Surform tools are a relatively recent development of the rasp. The thin perforated blades are made by punching out regularly spaced teeth with their sharp cutting edges facing forward, leaving holes in the metal through which the wood shavings pass. This enables a Surform tool to cut faster than a regular rasp, without clogging.

There is a range of Surform planes and files, but they are merely variations on the basic principle. The simplest and most generally useful tools are the round hollow file and the flat file.

Rifflers
Rifflers are miniature double-ended files specially designed for working in tight corners and confined spaces. Choose rifflers with rasp heads at one end and file heads at the other.

File cards
When file teeth become clogged with wood debris, the tool can no longer cut. The wire bristles on the back of a file card loosen the packed wood shavings, which are then cleaned out with the coarse brush.

Using a file or rasp
Place your fingertips near the point of the file to steady it. Apply pressure on the forward stroke only.

File handles
Always fit a handle over the pointed tang of a file or rasp. To use an unprotected tool is inviting an accident. If the tool catches and stops suddenly, you could drive the tang through the palm of your hand.

Drive a handle onto the tang by tapping it on a bench **(1)**. Remove an old one by holding the file in one hand and striking the front edge of the handle with a block of wood **(2)**.

1 Tap handle on bench

2 Removing a handle

DRILLS & BRACES

The versatility of the power drill, especially since the introduction of the variable-speed models, has made the hand drill and brace far less commonplace today. And yet these tools still have their place in the workshop. They are uncomplicated, lightweight, quiet and completely independent of a power source.

SEE ALSO

Benchstones	102-103
Power drills	124-127
Drill presses	188-189
Dowel joints	236-237
Wood screws	304-305

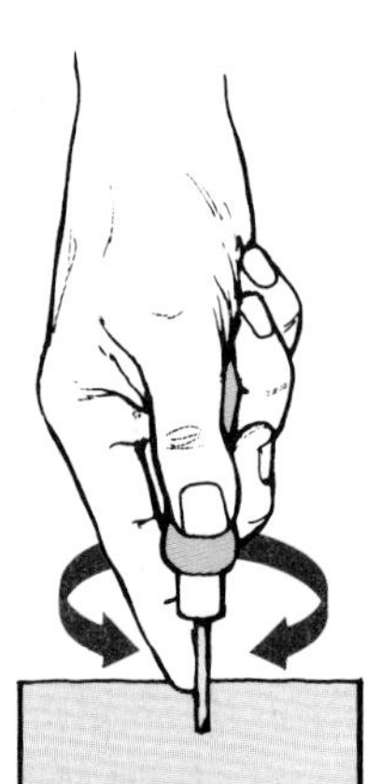

Using a bradawl
To open up a screw-starter hole, twist the tool from side to side as you push it into the wood.

Bradawl
The bradawl is perhaps the simplest hole borer of all. It does not remove wood, like a drill, but merely displaces it by forcing the fibers apart. It is used to make a starter hole for inserting a screw or to hold the point of a drill on its center mark.

By placing it across the grain, the sharp screwdriver-like tip is used to sever the fibers as the awl is pushed into the wood, avoiding the possibility of splitting the grain. Twisting the tool opens up the hole.

Sharpen the tip on the edge of a benchstone.

Gimlet
The gimlet does a job similar to the bradawl, but it is capable of making deeper holes by cutting and removing wood like a drill bit.

Hand drill
Cranking the drive handle of a hand drill rotates the chuck via a system of gear wheels. The chuck contains three self-centering jaws that, depending on the model, clamp twist drills up to $\frac{3}{8}$in (9mm) in diameter. With some hand drills the drive mechanism is kept dust-free by encasing it completely within a cast-metal shell.

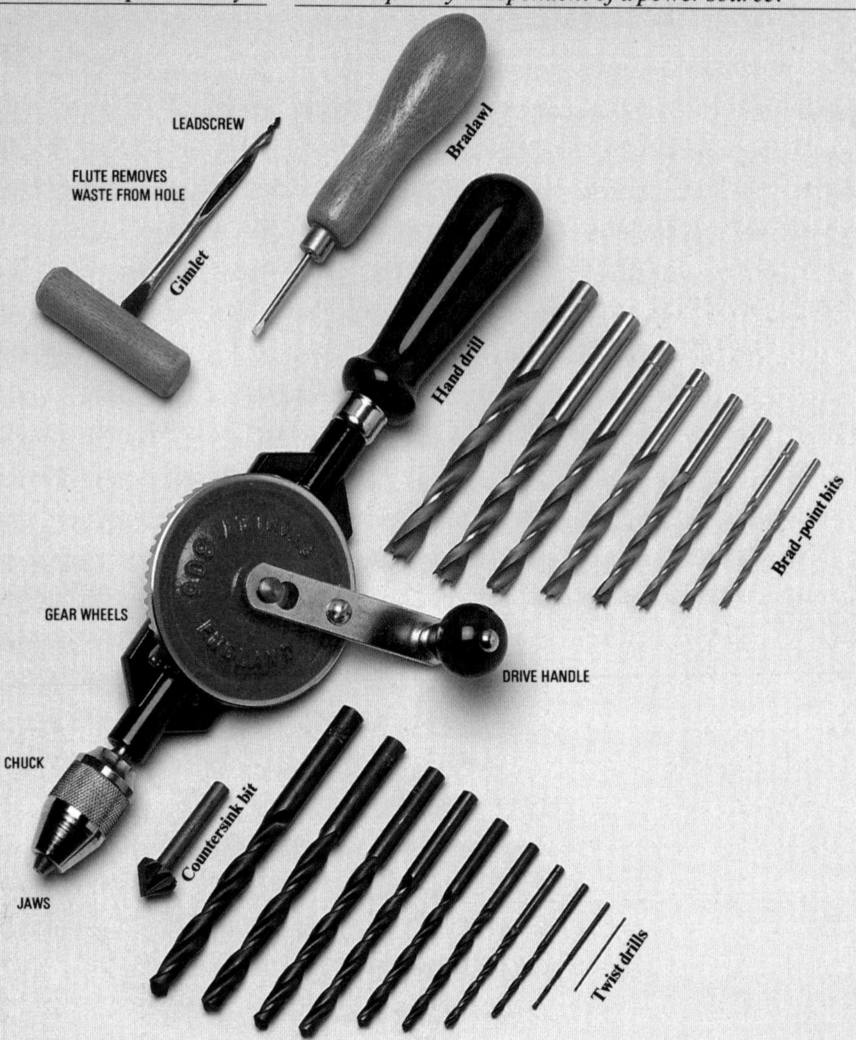

HAND-DRILL BITS

Buy good-quality drill bits only. Cheap drills not only dull quickly, but they are often ground inaccurately.

Twist drills
A twist drill is a simple cylindrical drill bit with two spiral grooves (helical flutes) to clear the waste out of a hole. The flutes culminate in two cutting edges forming a pointed tip. The tips of most drill bits are ground to an angle of 59 degrees for boring into metal. An angle of 45 degrees is recommended for drilling wood, but rather than have two complete sets of drills, most woodworkers are prepared to use high-speed metal drills.

The average set of twist drills comprises a range of sizes from $\frac{1}{16}$ to $\frac{1}{2}$in (1 to 13mm) although a hand-drill chuck will not accept a drill larger than $\frac{3}{8}$in (9mm).

Brad-point bit
This is a twist drill with a central lead point and two spurs to stop the bit from being deflected by wood grain. It will even bore end grain accurately for dowel joints.

Countersink bit
A countersink bit cuts a tapered recess to accept the head of a woodscrew so that it lies flush with the surface of the work. A clearance hole for the screw shank is bored first to automatically center the countersink bit.

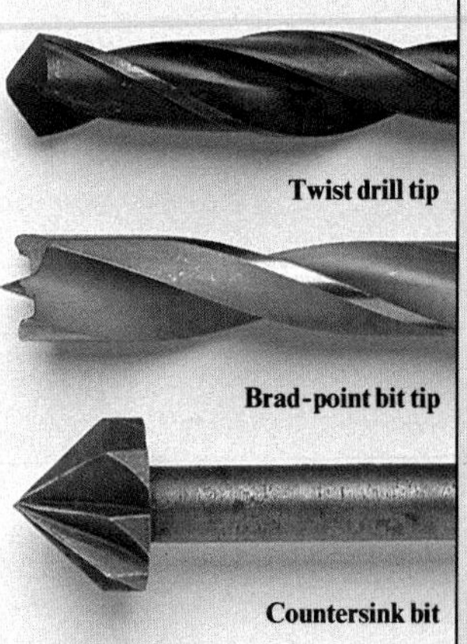

Twist drill tip

Brad-point bit tip

Countersink bit

BRACE BITS

The jaws in a brace chuck are designed to hold special-purpose square-shanked bits. Some braces are made with universal jaws that will also accept round-shanked twist drills.

Center bit
The solid-shank center bit is used for boring shallow holes. The single spur on one side of the bit scores the edge of the hole before the cutting edge on the other side enters the work. This ensures a crisp hole. The leadscrew in the center pulls the bit into the work. Center bits are made in a range of sizes from $\frac{1}{4}$ to 2in (6 to 50mm).

Auger bits
A solid-center auger bit is similar in principle to a center bit, but it has a spiral twist that keeps it on line in a deep hole and brings the waste to the surface. Also, it has two spurs and two cutting edges. A Jennings-pattern auger bit has a double spiral twist.

Solid-center bits are made in sizes from $\frac{1}{4}$ to $1\frac{1}{2}$in (6 to 38mm) in diameter. The range of Jennings-pattern bits is more limited – up to 1in (25mm) only.

Expansion bit
An expansion bit is adjustable to cut a hole of any diameter between limits. The calibrated spurred cutter is held in place by a spring-loaded packing piece or, on some models, a toothed dial. Generally there are two sizes of bit capable of cutting holes from $\frac{1}{2}$ to $1\frac{1}{2}$in (12 to 38mm) and $\frac{7}{8}$ to 3in (22 to 75mm) in diameter.

Countersink bit
Used like the hand-drill countersink bit, this has a square shank to suit the standard brace chuck.

Screwdriver bit
This bit adapts a brace into a heavy-duty screwdriver capable of generating considerable torque for inserting large screws.

Brace
A brace is driven by cranking its frame in a clockwise direction while pressure is applied to the round handle at the rear of the tool. The circle described by moving the frame is known as the sweep, and the size of a brace is given as the diameter of its sweep. Most woodworkers use a 10in (250mm) brace, but they are made with sweeps as small as $5\frac{7}{8}$in (147mm) and as large as 1ft (300mm).

Most braces are made with a ratchet mechanism just behind the chuck so that the tool can be used in places where a complete sweep is impossible. Having driven the bit as far as possible in a clockwise direction, a movement in reverse operates the ratchet, leaving the chuck stationary until the clockwise movement is resumed to drive the bit further. Adjusting a cam ring on the ratchet mechanism reverses its action or locks it solid.

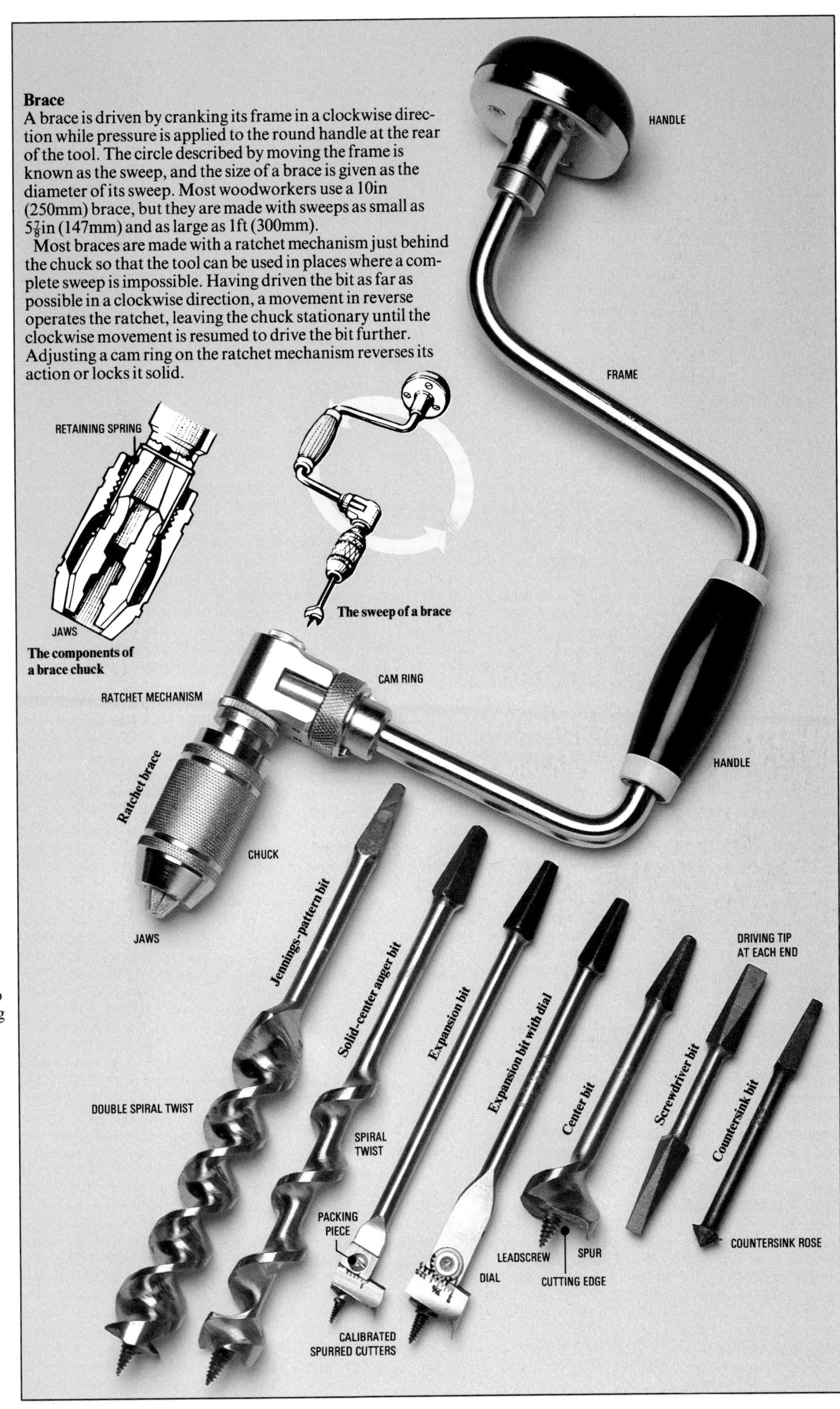

The components of a brace chuck

The sweep of a brace

USING A HAND DRILL AND BRACE

A hand drill is primarily used to bore small holes for fitting wood screws or dowels. Being designed specifically for woodwork, a brace has more uses. With a sharp bit fitted in its chuck, it will bore even large-diameter holes effortlessly.

SEE ALSO

Try square	76-77
Grinders	106-107
Brad-point bits	112
Twist drills	112
Auger bits	113
Center bits	113
Using hammers	116-117
Nails	305

Depth stop
Wrap a strip of tape around a drill as a guide to the depth of a hole.

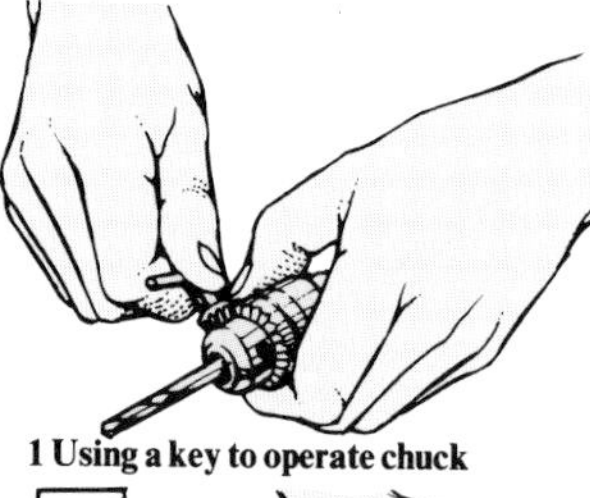

1 Using a key to operate chuck

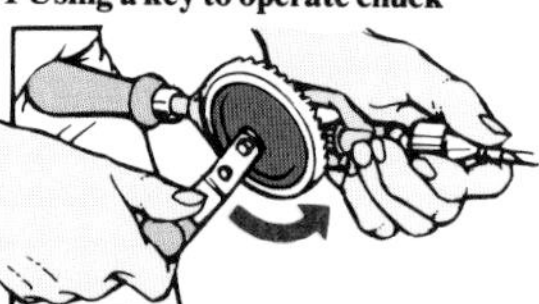

2 Opening a hand-drill chuck

Fitting a bit in a hand drill
Some hand-drill chucks are opened and closed by a key, just like an electric drill **(1)**.

To operate the jaws of an average hand drill, hold the chuck in one hand, then crank the drive handle counterclockwise **(2)**. Load a twist drill into the chuck and tighten the jaws by turning the drive wheel clockwise. Check that the twist drill is centered in the jaws before using the tool.

Using a hand drill
Place the tip of the twist drill accurately on the work, then move the drive handle gently back and forth until the drill enters the wood. Crank the drive handle freely to bore a hole of the required depth.

To avoid breaking small drills, let the weight of the tool drive it into the wood, supporting it in an upright position without applying any force to the handle.

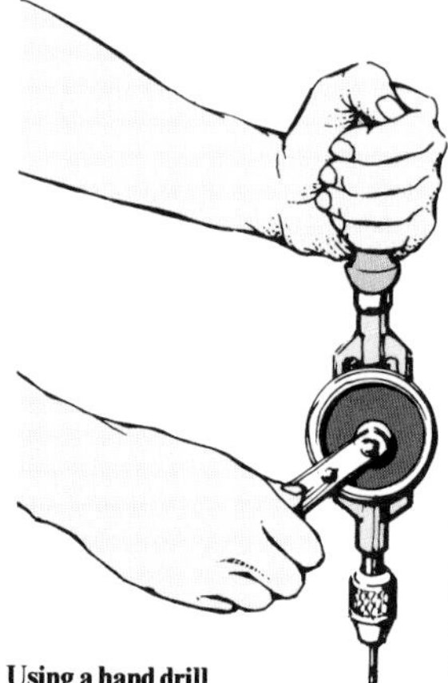

Using a hand drill

Fitting a brace bit
Lock the brace ratchet by centering its cam ring, then hold the chuck firmly while turning the frame clockwise. Drop a square-shanked bit into the open jaws and tighten them by reversing the action of the frame.

Using a brace
Hold the brace upright with one hand while turning the frame with the other **(1)**. To make sure you are drilling vertically, ask an assistant to tell you if the drill leans forward or backward while you concentrate on stopping it from leaning sideways. You can stand a try square on the bench as a guide, but it is difficult to keep your eye on the square and drill at the same time.

You can also use a brace in a horizontal position by steadying the round handle against your body.

The leadscrew of the bit will pull it into the wood. When you have reached the required depth, crank the frame counterclockwise a couple of turns to release the leadscrew, then pull on the tool while moving the frame back and forth to extract the bit and clear the waste from the hole.

If you are drilling right through the wood, either clamp a block of wood on the far side to stop the work from splitting as the bit emerges, or turn the work around as soon as the leadscrew appears and finish the hole from that side, using the small exit hole as a pickup point **(2)**.

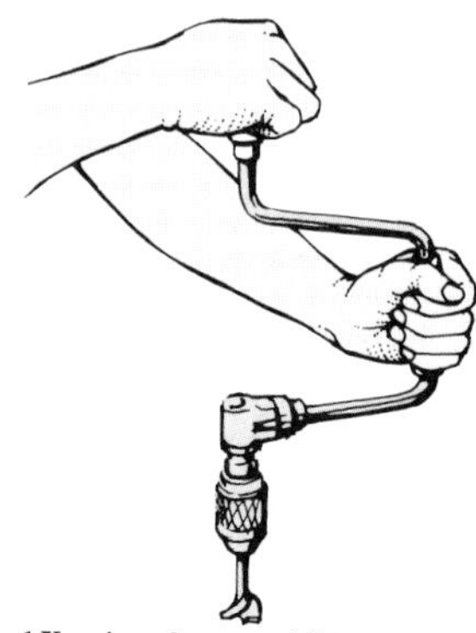

1 Keeping a brace upright

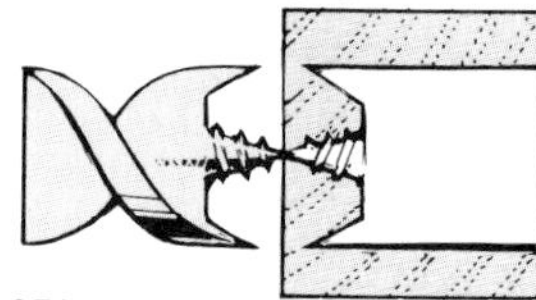

2 Pick up exit hole

SHARPENING DRILL BITS

All drill bits will stay sharp enough to work efficiently for a long time, but if you find you have to apply excessive pressure to bore a hole, sharpen the bit in the appropriate manner.

Brace bits
Sharpen auger and center bits in the same way, using a small flat or triangular file known as a needle file. Put a sharp edge on each spur by stroking its inner face with the file **(1)**. Never file its outer edge. Holding the leadpoint on the bench, sharpen the cutting edges **(2)**.

Sharpen the cutter and spur of an expansion bit with a similar file.

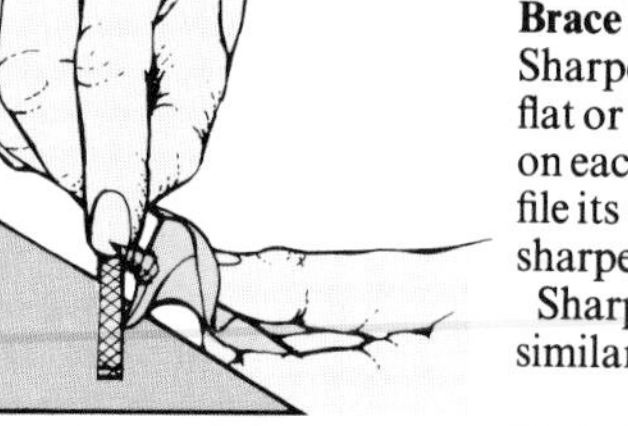

1 Sharpening spurs

2 Sharpening cutting edges

Twist drills
There are several electric drill-sharpening machines that do a perfect job. All you have to do is drop the drill point-first into the machine and switch it on.

Also, there are special jigs for sharpening drills. The drill is clamped at the required angle while the jig is rolled across sandpaper.

Most woodworkers sharpen twist drills by rotating their tips against a bench-grinder wheel **(3)**. Don't press too hard, and concentrate on grinding each side evenly to keep the point in the center of the drill.

Brad-point bit
Touch up the cutting edges and spurs of a brad-point bit with a pointed needle file. Sharpen both sides equally.

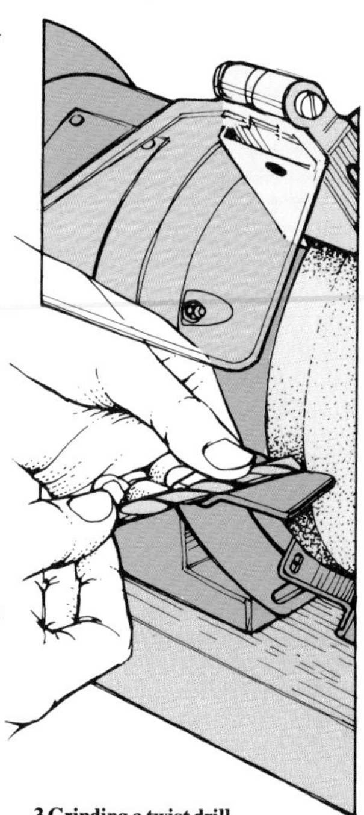

3 Grinding a twist drill

HAMMERS

Although a cabinetmaker uses well-cut glued joints to construct fine pieces of woodwork, every worker needs a selection of hammers to build mock-ups and rough framing. In addition, simple butt, miter and lap joints are secured with nails or brads.

Cross-peen hammer
Most cabinetmakers and carpenters favor a medium-weight – 10 to 12oz (300 to 350g) – cross-peen (or Warrington) hammer for general work. It takes its name from the narrow wedge-shaped part of the head opposite the striking face, and is used for starting nails held between finger and thumb. The head is wedged tightly onto a tough ash or hickory handle.

Pin hammer
A pin hammer is a light-weight $3\frac{1}{2}$oz (100g) cross-peen hammer used to drive small nails, tacks and brads.

Claw hammer
It is worth having at least one 20oz (550g) claw hammer in your tool kit. It is heavy enough to drive large nails with ease and its split peen (claw) is designed to extract bent ones. A curved claw is mostly used, but there is also a straight-claw or ripping hammer for dismantling frames and packing cases.

Pulling nails puts a considerable strain on the handle/head joint. If you think you will be pulling a lot of long nails, choose a hammer with a tubular steel or fiberglass handle permanently fixed to the head to form a one-piece tool. A vinyl or rubber sleeve is molded onto the handle, providing a comfortable nonslip grip.

The traditional adze-eye claw hammer is strong enough for most purposes. A preshrunk hickory handle is forced into the extra-deep socket (eye) where it is spread with hardwood and iron wedges.

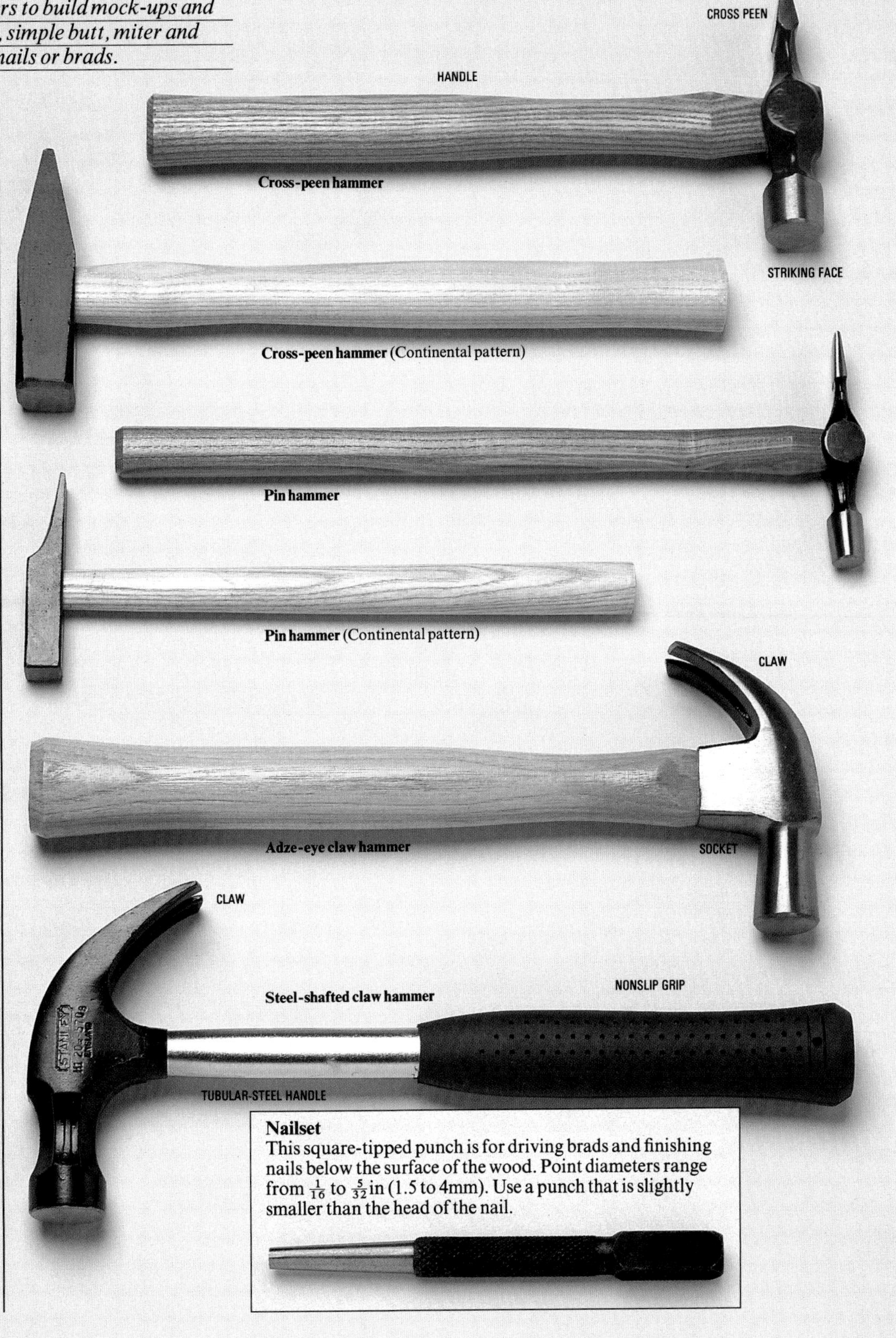

Cross-peen hammer

Cross-peen hammer (Continental pattern)

Pin hammer

Pin hammer (Continental pattern)

Adze-eye claw hammer

Steel-shafted claw hammer

Nailset
This square-tipped punch is for driving brads and finishing nails below the surface of the wood. Point diameters range from $\frac{1}{16}$ to $\frac{5}{32}$in (1.5 to 4mm). Use a punch that is slightly smaller than the head of the nail.

MALLETS

Except for certain plastic-handled chisels, you will need a wooden mallet to drive chisels and gouges. A carpenter's mallet is also used to assemble joints, but a soft-faced mallet is less likely to mark work.

SEE ALSO

Chisels and gouges	98-101
Hammers	115
Abrasive papers	285
Nails	305

Carpenter's mallet
The handle and head of a carpenter's mallet are both cut from solid beech. The head is tapered so that when the tool is swung naturally, one of the striking faces hits the work or end of a chisel squarely. The socket is also tapered to match the flared end of the handle so that the head tightens by centrifugal force with every blow.

Soft mallet
A mallet with a soft rubber head can be used to assemble or dismantle joints without fear of denting the wood.

Carpenter's mallet

Soft mallet

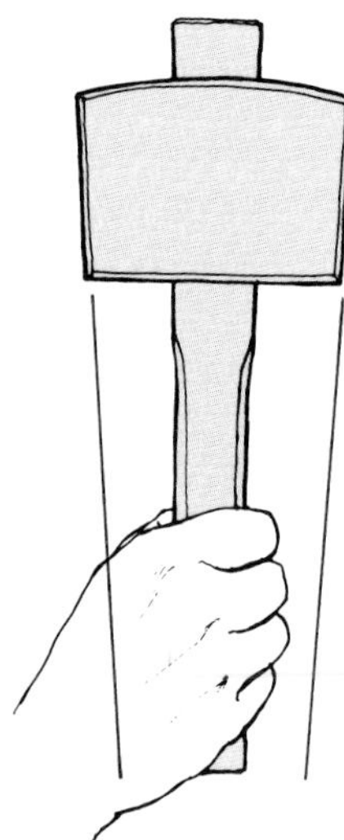
Tapered mallet head
A mallet head tapers toward the handgrip.

USING HAMMERS

There's no real trick to using a hammer, but it takes patience and practice before you can drive a nail quickly and surely without bending it or bruising the wood.

Setting a nail
To start a nail and to make sure it is aimed in the right direction, hold it between finger and thumb and tap it once or twice with a hammer until it stands unsupported with the point in the wood.
  Start small nails or brads with the peen of a hammer **(1)**. If you don't own a cross-peen hammer, push the nail through thin cardboard to set it **(2)**. When the nail sits firmly, tear the cardboard away and drive it home.

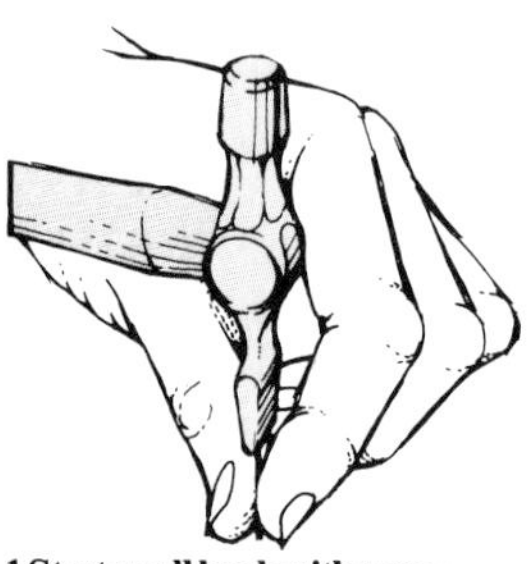
1 Start small brads with a peen

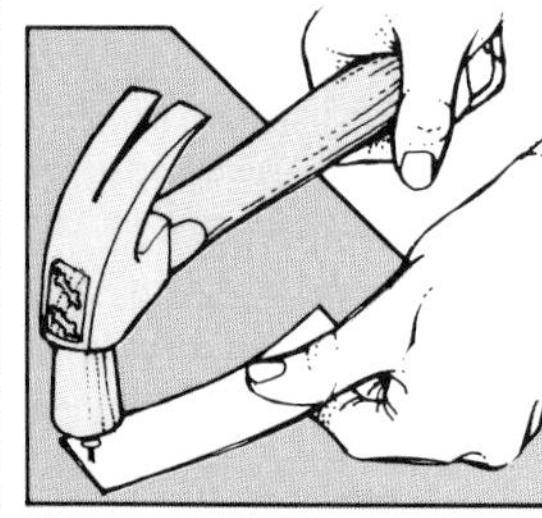
2 Support a nail with cardboard

Driving a nail
You should be able to swing a well-balanced hammer with a minimum of effort. Hold the tool by the end of the handle and swing your arm from the elbow, keeping your wrist fairly firm. If you find you have to slip your hand up the handle toward the head to swing the hammer comfortably, it is too heavy for you. Keep your eye on the nail and strike it firmly with square blows. It should be possible to drive any nail home with only a few strokes. If you are having trouble sinking the nail, either the hammer is too light or the work is flexing and needs backing up with something heavy.

Raising a bruise
If you dent or "bruise" the work with a heavy hammer blow, immediately soak the dent with warm water and let the wood swell, raising the crushed fibers flush with the surface. Let the wood dry and sand it smooth.

Sinking a nail head
Overcome bruising by stopping about $\frac{1}{16}$in (2mm) short of the surface and sink the nail with a nailset. Hold the nailset upright between thumb and fingers, using your ring finger to steady the tip of the tool on the head of the nail. Tap the nailset firmly with a hammer until the nail is flush, or drive it just below for filling and painting.

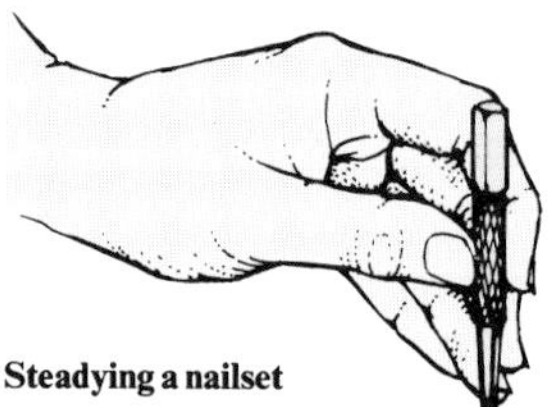
Steadying a nailset

Blind nailing
To disguise a nail in clear-finished wood, lift a sliver of wood with a gouge, then drive a nail below the surface with a nailset and glue the sliver back down with a clamp to cover the sunken head.

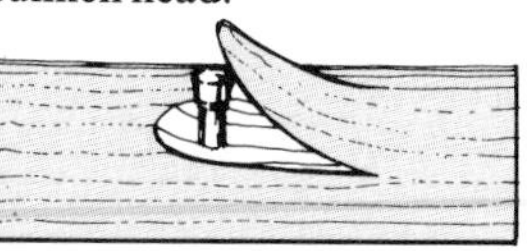
Hide a nail below a sliver

Avoiding a split
Nailing close to the end of a piece of wood will often result in a split along the grain as the nail forces the fibers apart. Blunting the point of the nail with a hammer blow makes it act like a punch, driving a piece of wood ahead of itself instead of splitting it. This simple method works for softwood, but for hardwood, drill a pilot hole just smaller than the nail itself.

CARING FOR HAMMERS

If the face of a hammer gets dirty and greasy it will skid off a nail head, bending the nail and bruising the work. Keep the face clean by rubbing it on a piece of fine emery cloth or sandpaper. Keep a vinyl or rubber handgrip grease-free by scrubbing it with a nail-brush dipped in a solution of mild detergent and warm water.

Fitting a new handle
If you break a wooden handle, drill or knock out the remaining stump, then plane a new handle to make a tight fit in the hammer-head eye.

Make two or three sawcuts (depending on the size of the hammer) across the top of the handle and at a slight angle **(1)**. Saw down about two-thirds the depth of the eye. Fit the head on the handle and tap the other end firmly on the bench to set the head **(2)**. Saw off any part of the handle protruding from the top of the head, then drive iron hammer wedges into each sawcut to spread the handle **(3)**. If the wedges do not lie flush, grind them down on a bench grinder.

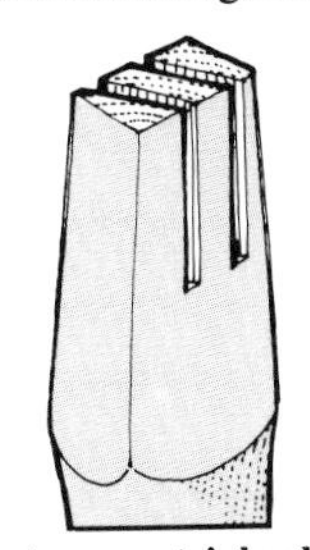

1 Make two sawcuts in handle

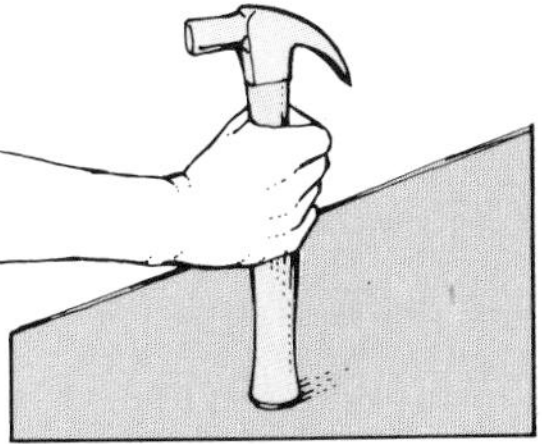

2 Tap handle to set head

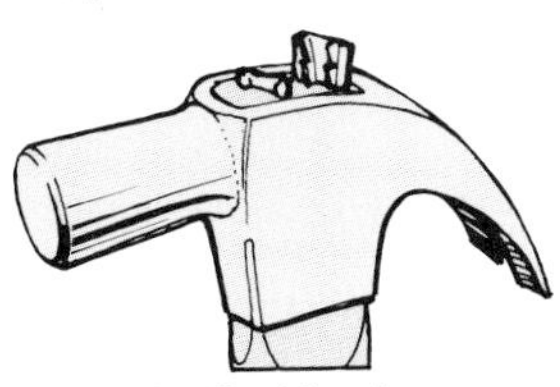

3 Spread handle with wedges

PULLING NAILS

No matter how experienced you become you will inevitably mis-hit the occasional nail and bend it over. Don't try to straighten it in situ because the next blow will almost certainly bend it again and probably drive it sideways into the wood. Extract the bent nail and replace it with a new one.

Pincers
A claw hammer is ideal for pulling large nails with heads, but pincers will enable you to get a better grip on brads and small oval nails.

Lifter
The small curved claw of a lifter is for removing upholstery tacks holding webbing and fabric.

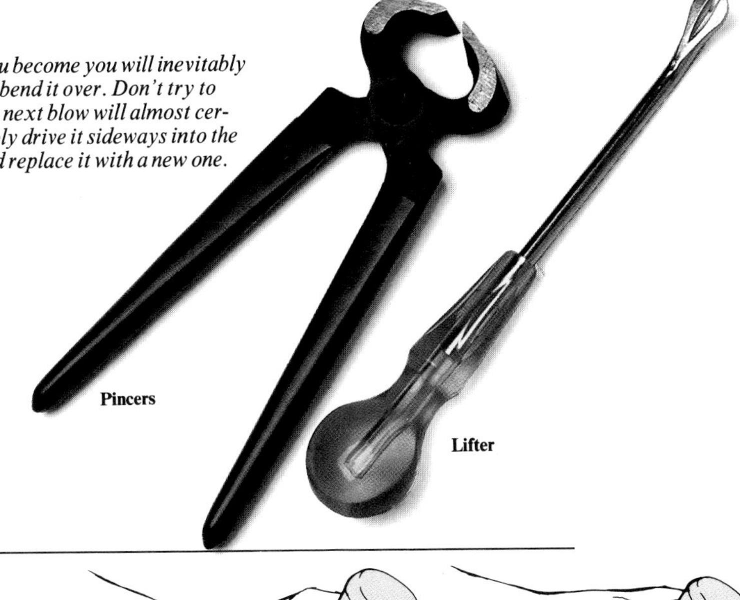

Pincers

Lifter

Using a claw hammer
To pull a partially driven nail, slide the claw under the nail head and lever on the handle. On show wood, protect the surface with thick cardboard **(1)**. If the nail is too long to extract with one pull, raise the hammer on a block of wood **(2)**.

Remove old nails from dismantled framing either by tapping the points to drive the heads clear of the surface or by jamming the claw onto the protruding shaft of a nail so that it bites into the metal, then pulling the nail head right through the wood.

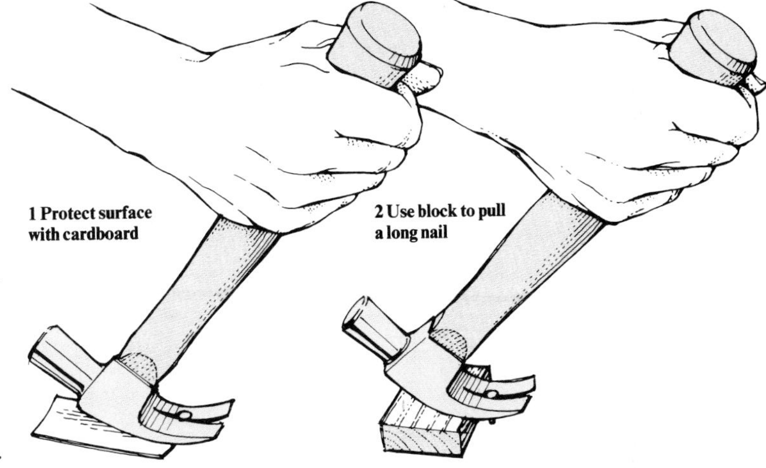

1 Protect surface with cardboard

2 Use block to pull a long nail

Pulling with pincers
Hold the pincers vertically and grip the nail with the jaws resting on the work. Squeeze the handles together and rock the pincers on one of the curved jaws to extract the nail. Pull a long nail in stages or you will bruise the wood by levering the nail sideways.

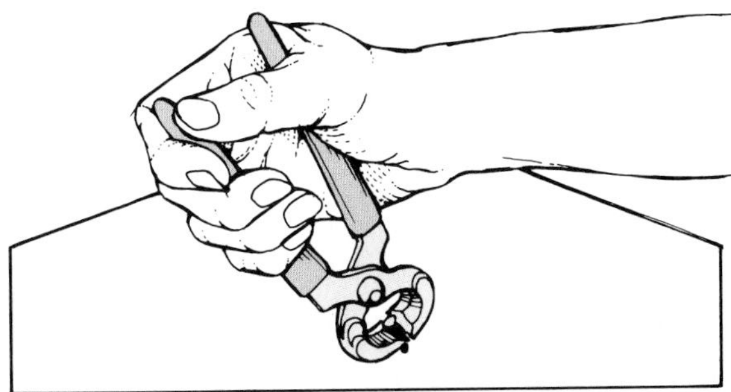

Removing tacks
Work the claw of a lifter under the fabric or webbing beneath the head of a tack, then push on the handle.

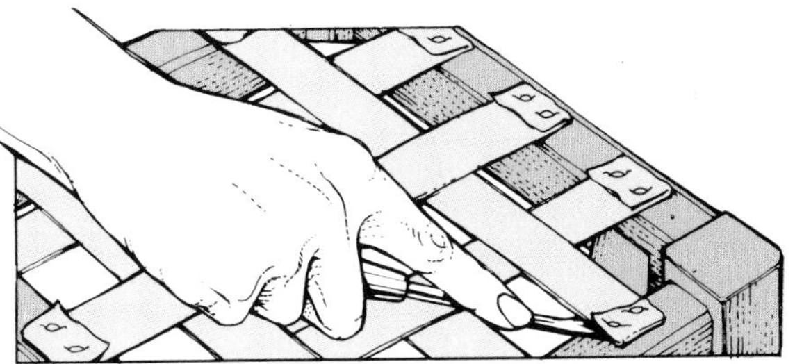

SCREWDRIVERS

The most important point to remember when choosing a screwdriver is that its tip must fit the screw slot – consequently, you will need the same tool in a range of sizes. When it comes to style, select the handle that feels most comfortable, remembering that the smooth bulbous ones will provide the best grip despite the apparently functional appearance of fluted, waisted and faceted handles.

SEE ALSO

Grinders	106-107
Bradawl	112
Countersink bit	112
Drill bits	112
Drills and braces	112-113
Auger bits	113
Screwdriver bits	113,127
Wood screws	304-305

Cabinet screwdriver
The cabinet screwdriver is the customary woodworking tool. Its oval-section hardwood handle fits the human hand to deliver maximum torque at the driving end. Traditionally the blade has a wide, flat heel that fits in a slot in the ferrule.

The design has been modified lately with a cylindrical blade passing straight into a wooden or plastic handle.

The blade of a modern cabinet screwdriver flares at the tip, but this may be ground to traditional shape.

Fluted-handled screwdriver
Some woodworkers prefer the type of driver that was developed for the electrical and automotive industries. The relatively slim handle can be spun with the fingertips and the often-parallel tip will fit the full width of a screw even when it is located at the bottom of a deep hole. The tip will remain the same shape no matter how many times it is reground.

Crosshead screwdrivers
In order to improve the grip between tool and screw, these cylindrical-bladed screwdrivers have pointed tips ground with four flutes to fit the cross-shaped slots in the heads of special screws. There are three common makes – the Phillips-head driver, which fits into a simple cross; the Pozidriv-head, which is designed to fit into a cross incorporating a small square at its center; and the very similar Supadriv, which will hold a screw unsupported on its tip while you locate it in its pilot hole. It is best to match each type of driver to its own brand of screw and always make sure the tip fits snugly or you are sure to damage the slots.

Ergonomic handgrip
Choose a screwdriver with a large handle that fits in the palm of your hand.

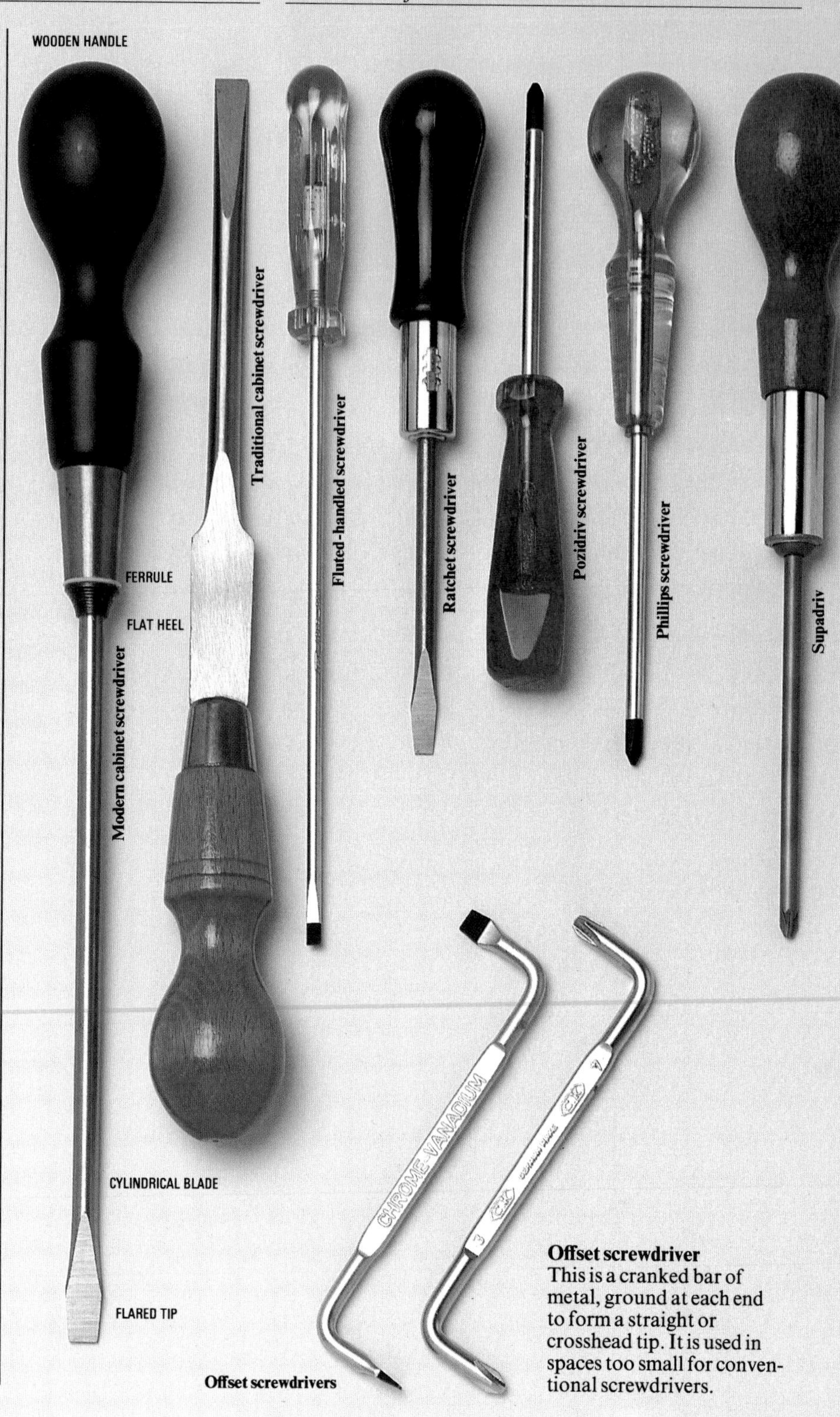

Offset screwdrivers

Offset screwdriver
This is a cranked bar of metal, ground at each end to form a straight or crosshead tip. It is used in spaces too small for conventional screwdrivers.

Stubby screwdriver
This is a screwdriver of any type designed for inserting large screws in restricted spaces. It has a short blade with a wide tip and a full-width handle. Stubby screwdrivers can be improvised by clamping a screwdriver bit in a loose Jacobs chuck.

Jeweler's screwdriver
Use this miniature screwdriver for fine work like screwing small hinges to a box lid. With the index finger applying pressure to the revolving head, the knurled handle of the screwdriver is turned between the thumb and other fingers.

Ratchet screwdriver
A ratchet screwdriver with a straight or crosshead tip allows you to insert or remove a screw without having to change your grip on the tool. A small thumb slide on the ferrule changes the ratchet action for clockwise or counterclockwise movement. Moving the thumb slide to its central position locks the mechanism, and the tool will then act like a conventional screwdriver.

Spiral ratchet screwdriver
This screwdriver is designed for speed. Straight pressure on the handle is converted by spiral grooves along the inner shaft to a rotational movement at the tip. The spring-loaded handle works with a pump action, extending each time pressure is released. The direction of movement is controlled by a ratchet, and a lock-ring fixes the shaft in a retracted position so that the tool can be used like a standard ratchet screwdriver. The chuck takes interchangeable bits with straight or crosshead tips of various sizes.
To load the screwdriver, pull the chuck back, insert a bit and release the chuck.
When using the pump-action mode, always steady the chuck with one hand to prevent the tip from slipping out of the screw slot and being driven into the wood.

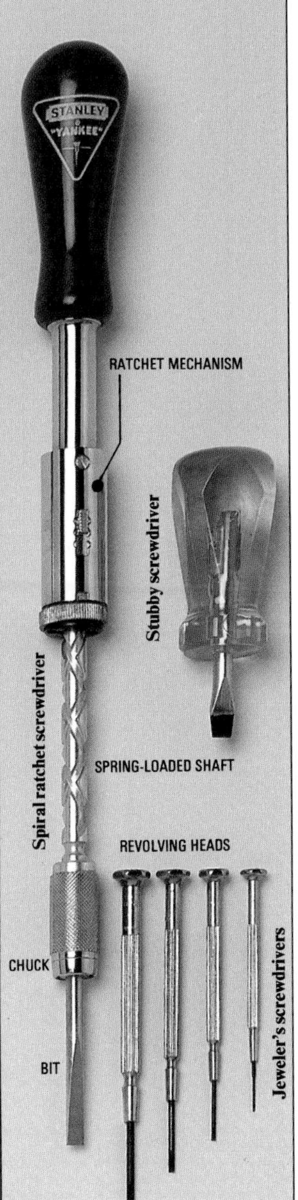

SELECTING A SCREWDRIVER

Select a screwdriver with a tip that fits the screw slot exactly. It will drive the screw with a minimum of effort without damaging either the screw head or the work.

If a screwdriver tip is too wide **(1)**, it will score the surrounding wood as you drive it home. If it is too narrow **(2)**, you won't be able to generate enough torque to turn the screw and it will probably damage the slot.
Test a crosshead screwdriver by placing its tip in the screw head, then twist the very end of the handle with your fingertips. If the driver is too large it will ride out of the slots. If it is too small it will rock back and forth. A driver of the right size will fit snugly in the head without movement.
Don't try to turn crosshead screws with a straight-tip screwdriver. It will almost certainly strip out the center of the cross.

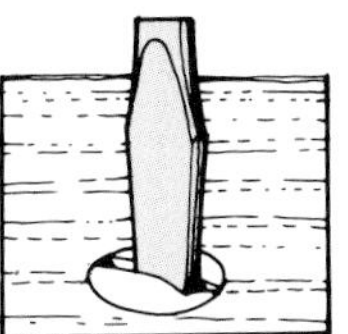
1 Wide tip scores wood

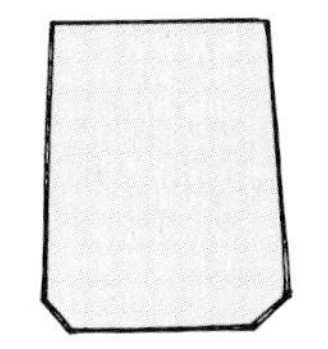
2 Small tip damages slot

INSERTING A WOOD SCREW

It is possible to drive a screw into softwood without any preparation, but there is always the danger of splitting the wood or jamming the screw partway in. It is much better to open up the fibers with a bradawl or, better still, drill pilot and clearance holes to guide the screw and reduce friction. The latter procedure is essential when screwing into hardwood.

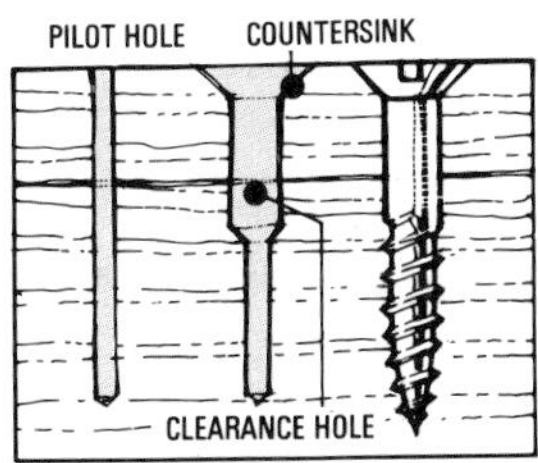

Drilling pilot and clearance holes
For the pilot hole use a drill slightly narrower than the screw's thread, followed partway by a clearance hole the same diameter as the screw shank. If necessary, countersink the top of the clearance hole before inserting the screw. If a screw is too tight, remove it and lightly grease the shank.

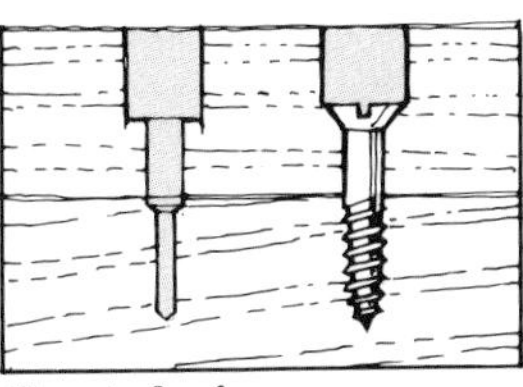

Counterboring a screw
If you have to sink a screw below the surface of the wood – to pass through a deep rail, for example – counterbore it by drilling the large hole first with an auger bit, followed by pilot and clearance holes.

Removing a damaged screw
To remove a damaged screw, choose the largest driver that will fit the slot. Regrind the tool to remove the corners of the tip if that is the only way to make it fit.
Try tapping the end of the screwdriver with a mallet. This sometimes helps to budge a stubborn screw.
Another way is to heat the screw head with a soldering iron. Heat expands the metal, and when it has cooled again you may find the screw has loosened.
If all else fails, use progressively larger drills to bore out the screw. Alternatively, you can use a plug cutter to remove a cylinder of wood that includes the screw, but this technique is only suitable if you intend to remake the workpiece.

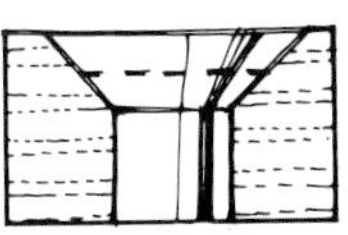
Removing a screw
Grind corners off a large driver tip.

Repairing screwdrivers
A screwdriver with a worn rounded tip is useless. Either sharpen it with a file and benchstone or regrind the tip on a bench grinder. Hollow-grind each side on the wheel **(1)**, then grind the tip square.
It is virtually impossible to regrind crosshead screwdrivers yourself. You can touch up a damaged tip with a small file, but replace a badly worn screwdriver.

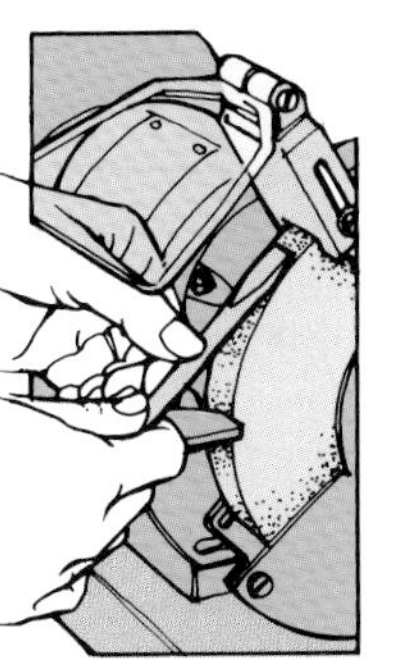
1 Repairing damaged tip
Hollow-grind each side of a screwdriver tip on a bench grinder.

CLAMPS

Every workshop needs a variety of clamps – long bar or pipe clamps for "gluing-up" large constructions; web or miter clamps for mitered picture frames; and several fast-action or C-clamps for gluing small jobs and to provide an "extra hand" when you want to assemble awkward components. Collecting a range of clamps is expensive, but you can acquire them gradually as needed or even rent them.

SEE ALSO

Try square	76-77
Small clamps	122
Miter joints	216-217
Adhesives	302-303

T-section bar clamp
Extra-large clamps are cast with T-section bars for rigidity.

Bar clamp
The bar or sash clamp is an essential piece of woodworking equipment for clamping glue-jointed frames, carcases or solid-wood panels while the adhesive sets. A screw-adjusted jaw is fixed permanently to one end of a rigid steel bar. Another jaw, known as the tail slide, is free to move along the bar to accommodate the size of the workpiece. The tail slide is held in the required position by a tapered steel pin located in one of a series of holes along the bar. Bar clamps sized 18 to 48in (450 to 1200mm) are readily available, but longer clamps can be rented for the exceptionally large job. These longer clamps usually have T-section bars for extra rigidity. Most woodworkers, however, buy a straight extension bar to lengthen a standard bar clamp or bolt two of them end to end.

Fast-action bar clamp
Both the adjustable jaw and the tail slide are free to move on a fast-action bar clamp. As the screw is tightened on the work both jaws rock over and jam on the bar. There are several versions of this type of clamp, but they all work on a similar principle. Fast action clamps can be adjusted in seconds to fit the workpiece.

Clamp heads
Large, custom-made bar clamps can be made using cast-iron clamp heads designed to fit onto a piece of wood 1in (25mm) thick.

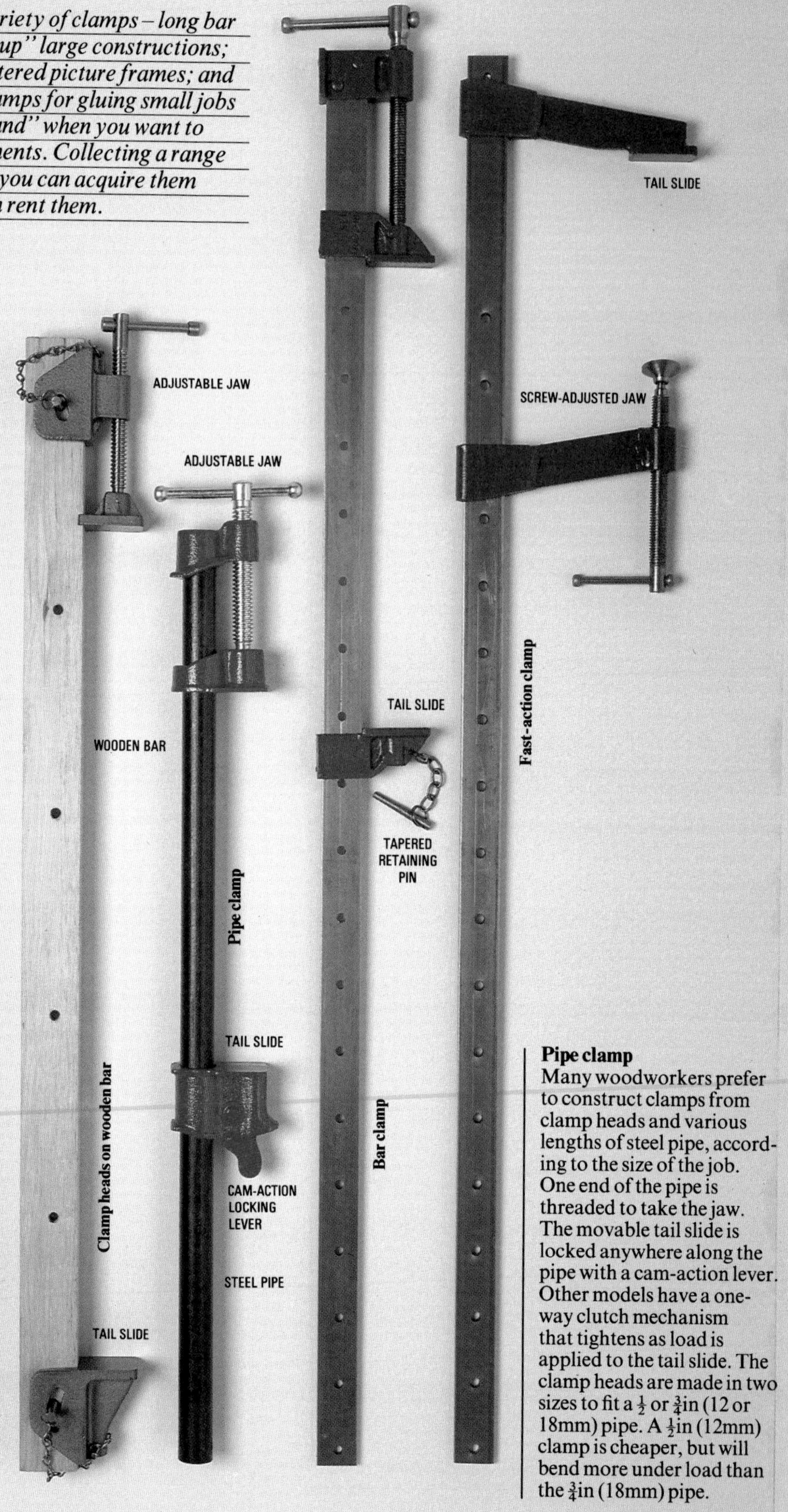

Pipe clamp
Many woodworkers prefer to construct clamps from clamp heads and various lengths of steel pipe, according to the size of the job. One end of the pipe is threaded to take the jaw. The movable tail slide is locked anywhere along the pipe with a cam-action lever. Other models have a one-way clutch mechanism that tightens as load is applied to the tail slide. The clamp heads are made in two sizes to fit a $\frac{1}{2}$ or $\frac{3}{4}$in (12 or 18mm) pipe. A $\frac{1}{2}$in (12mm) clamp is cheaper, but will bend more under load than the $\frac{3}{4}$in (18mm) pipe.

USING BAR CLAMPS

Gluing and clamping a workpiece should be undertaken calmly and with confidence. Consequently, carry out a dry assembly to practice the procedure, to ensure the workpiece assembles accurately and to check that you have all the tools and equipment you need. Try to get an assistant to handle the other end of long clamps. As you run through the sequence, decide who will be responsible for the details of each stage.

Plan your work to make the assembly the last job of the day. The glued work can be left undisturbed overnight, by which time the adhesive has set. However, leave this crucial and irreversible stage until the next morning rather than rushing it or having to leave the glued work in an unheated workshop in freezing conditions.

Clamp up the piece in a series of subassemblies. To construct a table underframe, for example, glue the legs to the end rails first. When the glue has set and you have cleaned up the assembled endframes, join them with the side rails to complete the underframe.

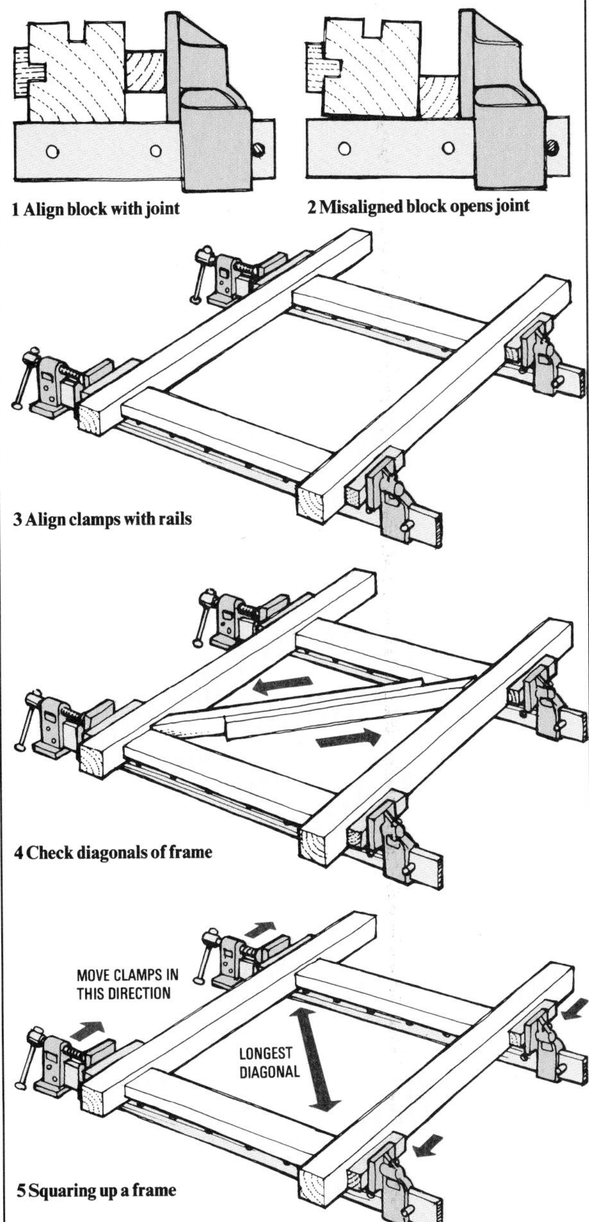

1 Align block with joint

2 Misaligned block opens joint

3 Align clamps with rails

4 Check diagonals of frame

5 Squaring up a frame

Clamping a frame

Adjust a bar clamp for each side of a square or rectangular frame. Cut softwood blocks to protect the work from the metal jaws and to place the force applied by the clamps directly in line with the joints **(1)**. A badly placed block will distort a joint and open the shoulder line **(2)**.

Paint glue thinly and evenly on all mating surfaces of the joints. Applying too much glue is not only wasteful but can hold the joints open or cause the wood to split due to hydraulic pressure.

Assemble the frame, align the clamps with the rails **(3)** and gradually tighten the jaws until the glue is squeezed out of the joints. Wipe excess glue from the surface with a damp cloth.

Checking for wind

Make sure the frame is not "in wind" (twisted) by looking across it to see if the rails align. If not, lift one end of a clamp to correct the distortion, then check for alignment again. If necessary, slacken the clamps slightly and force the frame back in line.

Checking for square

You can use a try square to check that the joints are clamped square. However, it is better to make sure the whole frame is square by gauging the diagonals. Make two pinch rods (slim battens, each planed to a point at one end). Hold the pinch rods side by side and slide them until the points nestle in two opposite corners of the frame **(4)**.

Holding the pinch rods together, lift them out of the frame and fit them into the other diagonal. If the diagonals are not equal, slacken the clamps and set them at a slight angle to squeeze the longest diagonal, bringing the frame back to square **(5)**, and then check the diagonals again.

Web clamp

A length of nylon webbing 1in (25mm) wide is wound around a workpiece and pulled taut by a ratchet mechanism. The web applies equal pressure to the four corners of a mitered frame and can be used to clamp a stool or chair with turned legs – a difficult job with bar clamps. Tighten up the clamp by turning the small ratchet nut with a wrench or screwdriver. Wait until the glue has set, then release the tension by pressing the lever.

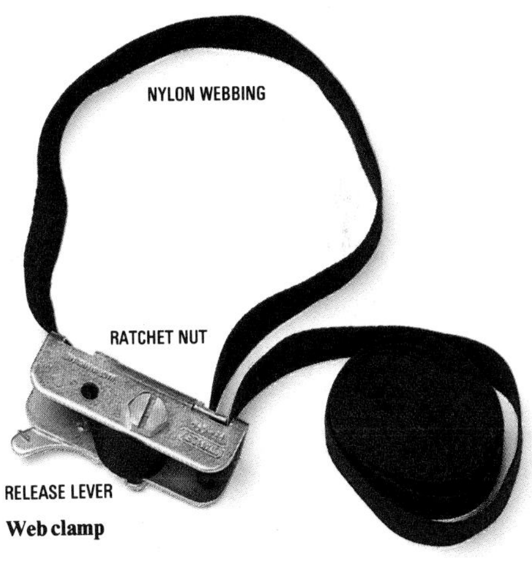

Web clamp

Miter clamp

A miter clamp holds individual mitered joints while glue sets. Insert any reinforcing nails or screws before releasing the clamp. Larger miter clamps have jaw capacities of 4½in (112mm).

Miter clamp

SMALL CLAMPS

C-clamp
A most useful and versatile addition to a workshop, the C-clamp is used for all kinds of gluing procedures and to hold work firmly on the bench. C-clamps are made with jaw capacities ranging from $1\frac{1}{8}$ to 12in (28 to 300mm).

Long-reach C-clamp
This is a C-clamp with a throat depth approximately double that of the standard clamp, for use when work needs to be clamped well in from the edge.

Edge clamp
This special-purpose C-clamp is for clamping lippings onto boards. Edge clamps are especially useful on a curved edge, which is difficult to clamp with a bar clamp. With the edge screw retracted, they can be used as normal C-clamps.

Fast-action clamp
This is a short version of the fast-action bar clamp and performs the same function as a C-clamp, but can be clamped onto the work very quickly – useful when the glue is drying rapidly.

Cam clamp
The cam clamp is a fast-action lightweight clamp with wooden jaws. Having slid the movable jaw up to the work, clamping force is applied by cocking the cam lever. Each jaw is cork-lined to protect the work.

Handscrew
Handscrews are rarely found in workshops these days, despite their unique feature of jaws that can be closed at a variety of angles to clamp tapered or irregularly shaped workpieces.

SEE ALSO

Bar clamps	120
Lippings	248
Adhesives	302-303

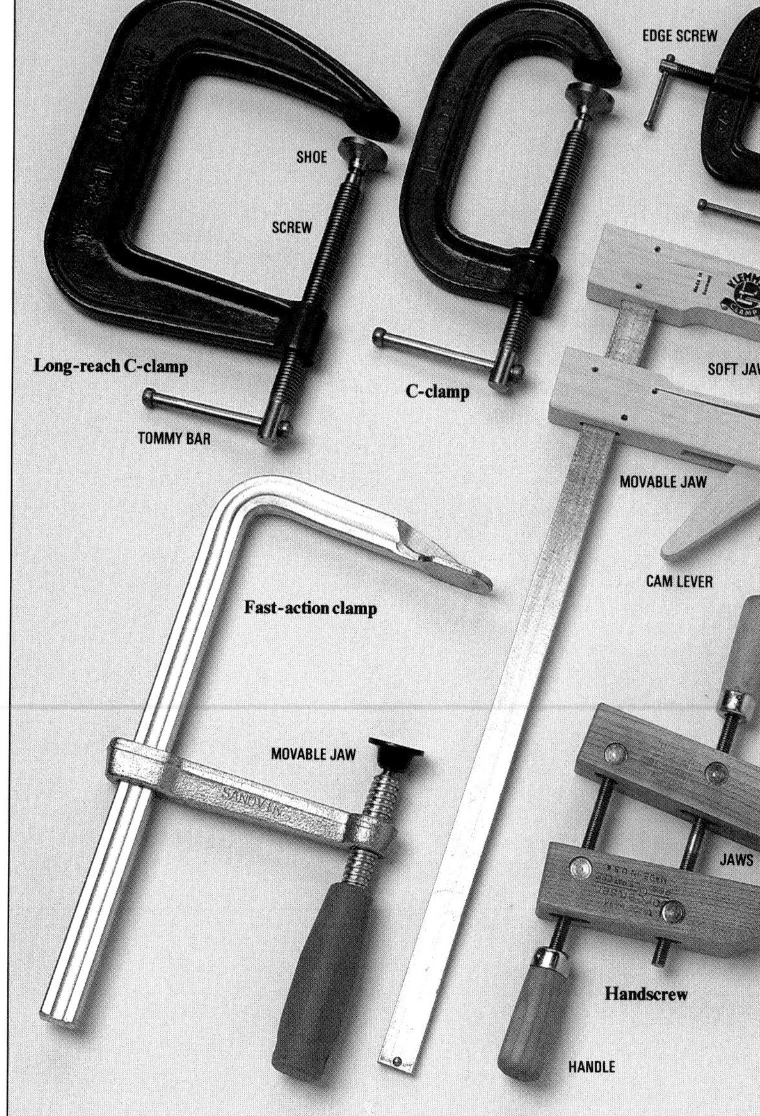

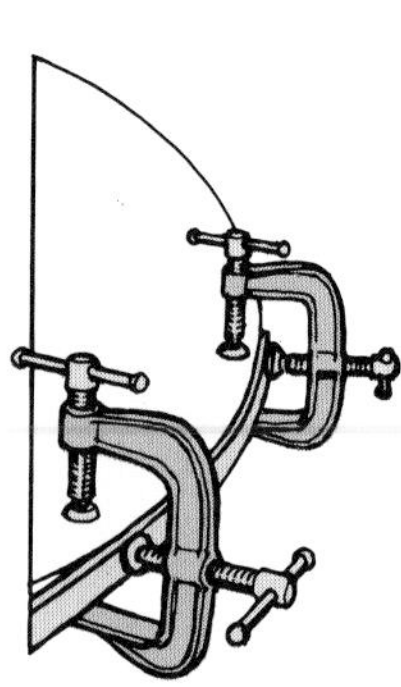
Using edge clamps
Clamp a lipping onto a curved edge with these special-purpose C-clamps.

USING SMALL CLAMPS

Using a C-clamp
Spin the threaded screw between fingers and thumb until the circular "shoe" contacts the work, then apply pressure by screwing up the tommy bar or thumbscrew. As the shoe is attached with a ball joint it automatically adjusts to accommodate angled work. Use a softening block to protect the work as the edge of the shoe dents the wood very easily.

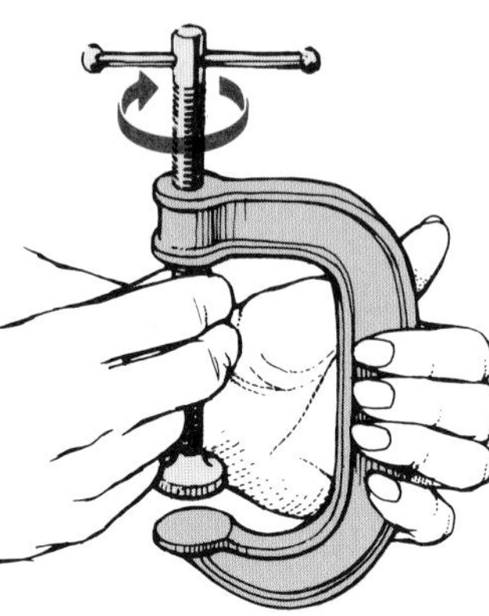
Adjusting a C-clamp
Spin the screw to close the jaws, then tighten with the tommy bar.

Using a handscrew
To adjust the clamp, hold a handle in each hand and rotate the tool to open or close the jaws. Slip the clamp onto the work, then tighten both screws to apply pressure. Being made of wood, the jaws are less likely to bruise the work, but take the precaution of sandwiching paper between them and the wood to make sure that the tool is not accidentally glued in place.

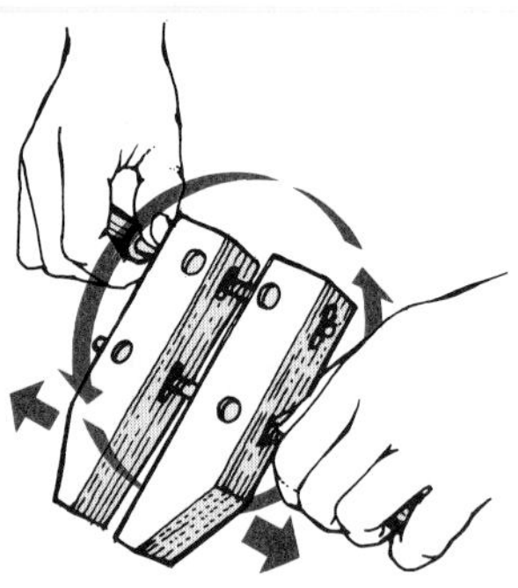
Adjusting a handscrew
Rotate the tool to open or close the jaws.

CHAPTER FOUR

POWER TOOLS

Not many years ago most home workshops were equipped with little more than a single-speed, non-reversing electric drill, a heavy, underpowered circular saw, and perhaps a low-speed, unwieldy, straight-line sander. These tools could be made to work after a fashion, but modern designs now make the early ones seem primitive. Today's power tools are far more advanced in both technology and concept. Modern power tools have lightweight insulated bodies. They are better designed and more powerful than their predecessors, and most of them can be bench-mounted to create what is in effect a serviceable miniature machine shop. Another important development has been the invention of battery-powered cordless tools. As yet the batteries do not store sufficient electricity to drive powerful motors for long periods. But they are adequate for less demanding work, such as drilling and inserting screws, and cordless tools are quiet, efficient and comfortable to use.

POWER DRILLS

The electric power drill is the most widely sold and used power tool on the market. Not only is it an invaluable woodworking tool, it is also found in nearly every home for general household maintenance. Manufacturers try to satisfy the huge demand for power drills by producing an immense range of tools, from cheap "throwaway" drills to more sophisticated and powerful professional models. The woodworker needs a drill that falls somewhere in the middle of the range – a tool that is accurate, with variable speed and the ability to reverse its rotation. Most people buy drills with cords, although quiet cordless drills are popular for small-bore drilling and inserting screws.

SEE ALSO

Drill bits and accessories	126-127
Eye protection	214
Wood screws	304-305

Reverse action
Many power drills have a switch that changes the direction of rotation in order to remove screws.

Trigger lock
A small button on the handle of the drill is pushed in to lock the trigger for continuous running. Squeezing the trigger releases the lock.

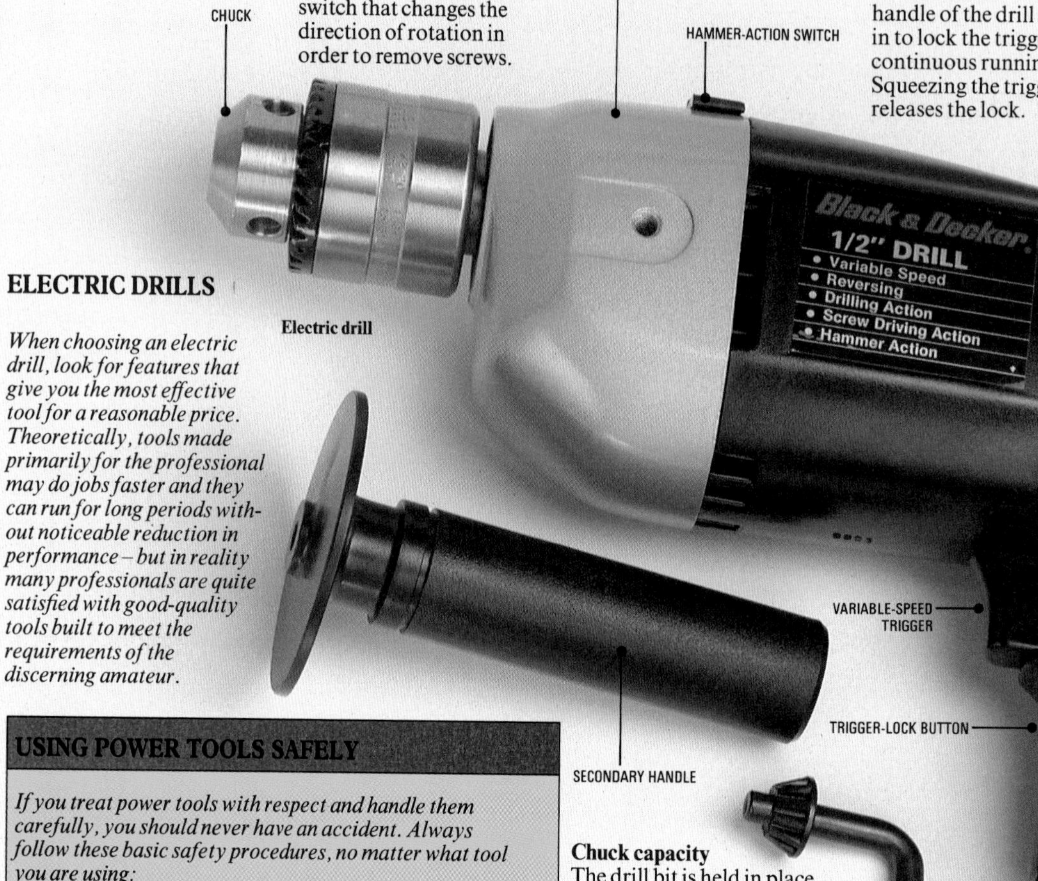

Electric drill

ELECTRIC DRILLS

When choosing an electric drill, look for features that give you the most effective tool for a reasonable price. Theoretically, tools made primarily for the professional may do jobs faster and they can run for long periods without noticeable reduction in performance – but in reality many professionals are quite satisfied with good-quality tools built to meet the requirements of the discerning amateur.

• **Motor size**
Manufacturers normally specify the drill's motor as having a power input of so many watts. A 500 to 600W drill capable of producing about 1200 rpm is suitable for general work.

USING POWER TOOLS SAFELY

If you treat power tools with respect and handle them carefully, you should never have an accident. Always follow these basic safety procedures, no matter what tool you are using:

- Do not wear loose clothing or jewelry that could get caught in the moving parts of a tool. Tie back loose hair.
- Wear protective eye shields whenever you are doing work that could throw up debris.
- Never carry a power tool by its cord or use the cord to pull the plug out of a socket.
- Check the cord and plug regularly for wear or damage.
- Unplug power tools when not in use and before making adjustments or changing accessories and attachments.
- Keep children away from areas where power tools are in use. Lock tools away when you have finished work.
- Always clamp work securely.
- Do not use power tools in the rain or in very damp conditions.
- Keep handles and grips dry and grease-free.
- Don't throw used batteries from cordless tools into water or a fire, as they are likely to explode.

Chuck capacity
The drill bit is held in place by a chuck. Most chucks are operated by a toothed key that opens and closes three self-centering jaws designed to grip the shank of the bit. The "chuck capacity" describes the maximum size of shank the chuck will accept and corresponds to the maximum diameter of the hole the drill is capable of boring in steel. The same drill will bore holes two or three times larger in wood. This is achieved by using large woodworking bits with reduced shanks. Most drills have a chuck capacity between $\frac{1}{4}$ and $\frac{1}{2}$in (6 and 13mm).

Speed selection
You will find that your drill performs a particular function best at a particular speed. There are several systems for controlling and selecting speed. Some basic drills have from two to four fixed speeds selected by means of a switch. Others have a two-speed trigger control – a slow speed being achieved by depressing the trigger partway and full speed by depressing it completely. The trigger can be locked in either position.

More and more drills now have variable-speed trigger control. With this type of control, the speed varies from zero to maximum according to the amount of pressure applied to the trigger. On some drills the movement of the trigger can be limited by selecting an optimum speed with a built-in dial. This is a useful feature for inserting wood screws, which is best done at a slow, controlled speed.

Nowadays very few drills are fitted with gears as a means of controlling the speed – most are controlled electronically. The best electronic speed-control systems maintain the selected speed even when load is applied to the drill bit, and internal torque compensators prevent the motor from being damaged if the bit jams in the work.

Drill manufacturers recommend a range of speeds at which their tools will perform best, but as a general guide, select a slow speed for masonry or metal and a fast speed for wood.

Fast-action chucks
Some top-of-the-line professional drills are fitted with fast-action chucks that need no key. Instead, when the chuck is pulled back it opens automatically and special bits with grooved shanks are inserted; then when the chuck is released, it grips the bit. Bits for this type of drill are made in a range of sizes, all with the same shank size. The chuck takes an adaptor when used with ordinary drill bits.

Hammer action
Although never used for woodworking, it makes sense to buy a drill fitted with a hammer action so that you can bore holes in brick, stone and concrete. Operated by a switch, either before or during drilling, the hammer action delivers several hundred blows per second behind the drill bit to break up masonry as work progresses. It is essential to use special percussion drill bits, and, to make sure they are held firmly in the chuck, each jaw should be tightened individually.

Electrical insulation
The all-plastic body of a power drill protects the user from electric shock should a fault occur within the tool. This is known as "double insulation." When a tool is described as having "full insulation," not only are you protected but the motor is safe from damage even if you inadvertently drill into an electric cable.

Collar size
A drill that has an international-standard 43mm diameter collar directly behind the chuck will fit accessories or attachments made by other manufacturers subscribing to the same system (see drill stand on p. 127). This gives you the option to buy cheaper or better-quality equipment than that made by the drill's manufacturer.

Secondary handle
Most drills can be fitted with an additional handle that either clamps onto the collar or screws into the body. Some secondary handles have an integral stop that comes to rest against the work when the drill bit has reached the required depth and some serve as storage space for spare drill bits.

CORDLESS DRILLS

Within their limits, cordless drills are excellent tools. They are lightweight, silent-running and convenient, doing away with the need for a long extension cord in order to reach a worksite far away from an electrical outlet.

Most cordless drills have a chuck capacity of $\frac{3}{8}$in (10mm) but are not really suitable for drilling holes larger than $\frac{5}{16}$in (8mm) in metal, although they will drill holes up to $\frac{1}{2}$in (12mm) in diameter in wood. They will also drill masonry, provided the bit is sharp and of good quality.

There are both fixed-speed and variable-speed models; all models are fitted with reverse action for use as powered screwdrivers. Because cordless drills generate less torque than 120-volt drills, even the fixed-speed models are easier to control when driving screws.

To ensure that a cordless drill cannot be operated accidentally, especially during transit, many have an on/off safety switch.

Some models are supplied with a wall-hung storage rack incorporating a charging unit. As long as the tool is replaced every evening, it is always fully charged. Other models have removable battery packs that plug into a charger. With this method you can always have a spare pack charged and ready for use.

Whatever system you choose, it normally takes between 3 and 12 hours to fully recharge a cordless drill – unless you buy a rapid charger, which will complete the job in an hour. A drill or battery pack can be recharged several hundred times before it needs replacing.

Long exposure to heat or storing a seldom-used tool in freezing conditions can ruin a cordless drill.

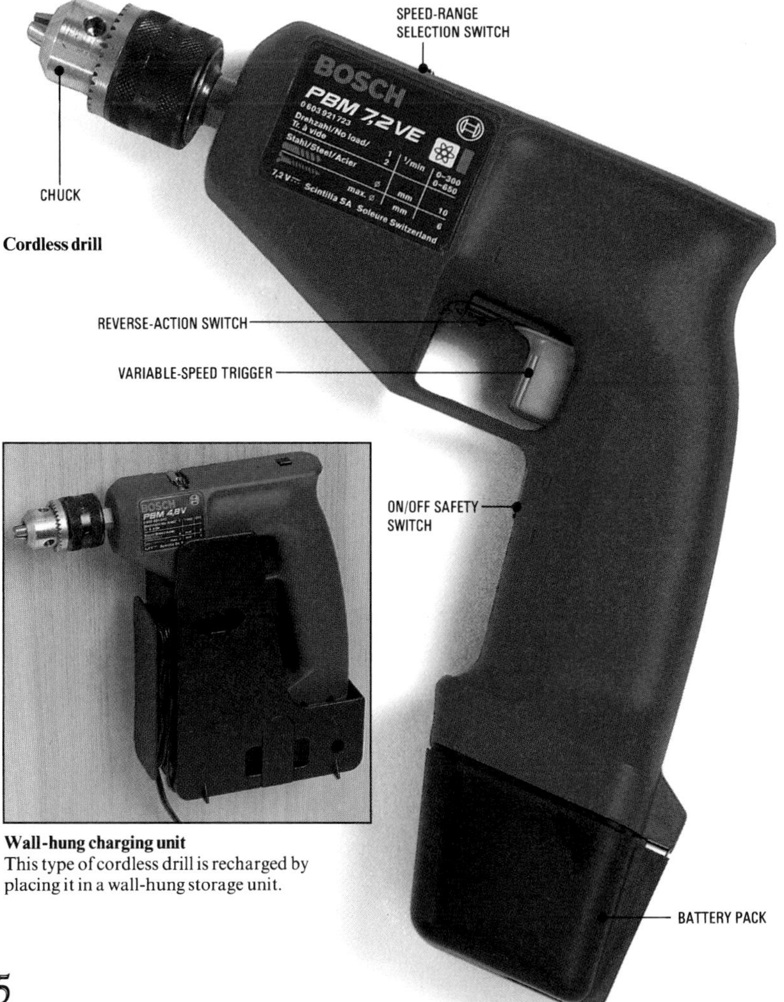

Cordless drill

Wall-hung charging unit
This type of cordless drill is recharged by placing it in a wall-hung storage unit.

DRILL BITS AND ACCESSORIES

As a woodworker you will need a complete set of twist drills up to $\frac{1}{2}$in (13mm) in diameter, but it is probably best to buy reduced-shank and other larger wood-boring bits as the need arises. Accessories merely extend the usefulness of a power drill and are not considered essential workshop equipment. One exception is a vertical drill stand, which – unless you have a drill press – is necessary for drilling accurately and square to the face of the work.

SEE ALSO

Rasps and files	111
Sharpening drill bits	114
Inserting screws	119
Safety tips	124
Power drills	124-125
Drill presses	188-189
Dowel joints	236-237
Wood screws	304-305

Twist drills

Although twist drills are designed for metalwork, they are also good general-purpose wood-boring bits. Carbon-steel bits are perfectly adequate for woodwork, but since you will almost certainly want to drill metal at some time, it is worth investing in the more expensive high-speed-steel bits. Twist drills from $\frac{1}{2}$ to 1in (13 to 25mm) in diameter are made with reduced shanks to fit standard power-drill chucks.

Keep twist drills sharp, and before you use them, pick out any wood dust that has become packed into the flutes.

Twist drills are not easy to center. With hardwoods, it pays to mark the center of the hole first, using a metalworking center punch. To avoid splintering the wood, take the pressure off the drill as the bit emerges from the far side of the work. Alternatively, clamp a piece of scrap wood to the back face.

Brad-point bits

The brad-point bit is a twist drill with a center point to prevent it from wandering off line and two spurs that cut a clean-edged hole.

Spade bits

These are relatively cheap bits for drilling large holes, from $\frac{1}{4}$ to $1\frac{1}{2}$in (6 to 38mm). The long lead point makes for very positive location at the center of the hole, even when drilling at a shallow angle to the face of the work.

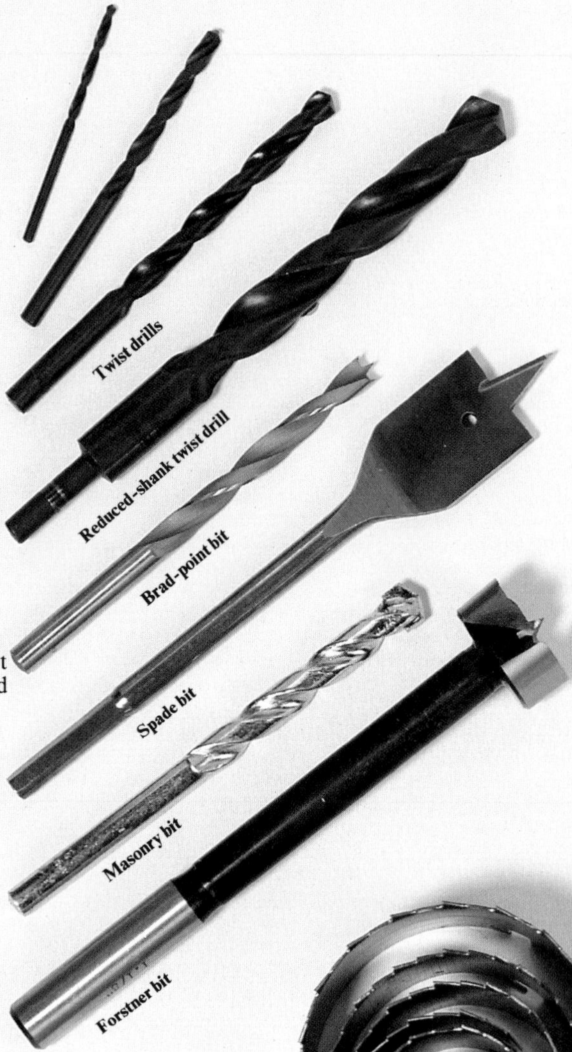

Forstner bits

These are superior-quality drill bits that leave exceptionally clean, flat-bottomed holes. They are available up to 2in (50mm) in diameter. A Forstner bit will not be deflected by knots or wood grain, and will bore overlapping holes and holes that run out to the edge of the work without difficulty.

Countersink bits

A countersink bit makes a tapered recess to accept the countersunk head of a wood screw. Drill the pilot and clearance holes first to center the point of the countersink bit, then run the drill at a fast speed for a clean finish.

Drill-and-countersink bits

This type of bit drills a pilot hole, shank-clearance hole and countersink in one operation. The range of sizes available matches the most common wood screws.

Drill-and-counterbore bits

These perform like drill-and-countersink bits but in addition drill a neat counterbored hole that can be filled with a wooden plug to hide the screw head.

Plug cutters

Driving a plug cutter into the side grain of wood cuts a cylindrical plug of wood to match exactly the hole left by a drill-and-counterbore bit. Cut plugs from wood that closely matches the color and grain pattern of the work.

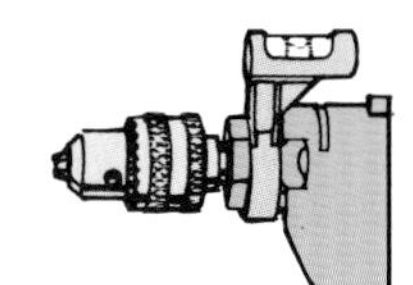

• **Spirit level**
Clamp a small spirit level to the drill collar to help you drill square to the work. For horizontal drilling, keep the bubble centered between the lines; for vertical drilling, center it in the glass end of the spirit level.

Twist drills

Reduced-shank twist drill

Brad-point bit

Spade bit

Masonry bit

Forstner bit

Hole-saw blades

Countersink bit

Drill-and-countersink bit

Drill-and-counterbore bit

Plug cutter

BACKING PLATE

SAWBLADE

DRILL BIT AND RETURN SPRING

Hole saw

Masonry bits
Masonry bits are steel twist drills with brazed tungsten-carbide tips that are designed to bore into brick, stone or concrete.

Percussion bits
These are masonry bits with shatterproof tips designed to withstand the vibration produced by a hammer-action power drill.

Hole saws
A hole saw is a cylindrical-shaped sawblade held in a plastic or metal backing plate that is clamped to a twist drill passing through its center. Hole saws are sold in sets ranging from 1 to $3\frac{1}{2}$in (25 to 89mm) in diameter.

Secure the shank of the bit in the chuck. The sawblade spins much faster than the bit, so select a slower speed than you would normally use for drilling into wood and feed the blade into the work at a steady rate.

Screwdriver bits
Flat tips and all patterns of cross-head tips are available as screwdriver bits for power drills. It is possible to drive screws into wood without having to drill pilot and clearance holes, but it often helps to drill a pilot hole to ensure that the screw does not wander off line and the wood doesn't split.

When inserting or extracting a screw, select the slowest speed and maintain pressure on the drill the whole time to prevent the bit from jumping out of the slot.

Screwdriver bits

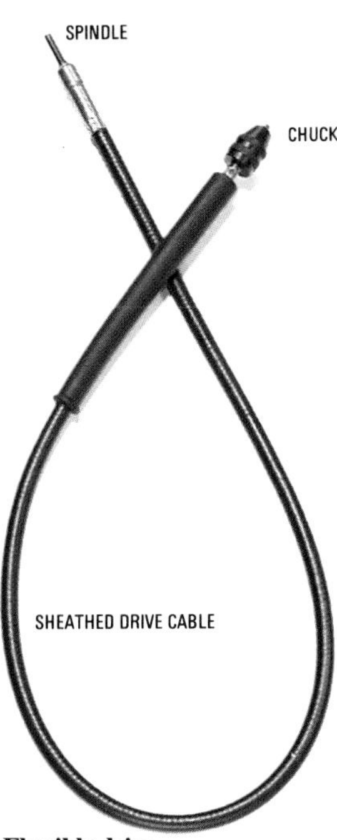

Flexible drive
A flexible drive enables the user to work with drill bits and rotary files or rasps in areas that would be inaccessible with a full-size drill. It consists of a drive cable sheathed in a flexible casing, with a spindle at one end and a small chuck with a short pen-hold grip at the other. The spindle end fits into the chuck of a standard power drill, which ideally should be clamped in a bench stand. Flexible drives have chuck capacities of $\frac{1}{4}$ to $\frac{5}{16}$in (6 to 8mm).

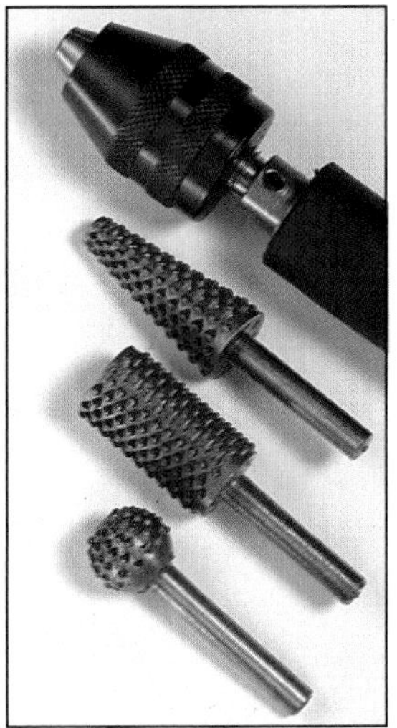
Rotary rasps
Coarse rotary rasps fitted in the flexible-drive chuck are ideal for complicated shaping.

Doweling jig
A doweling jig is a device that guides a drill bit square and true, and provides a means of repeating hole-spacing in the two components of a dowel joint. Choose a jig that is sturdy, well-made and capable of jigging solid-wood rails and wide boards for cabinetmaking. One such jig has a fixed head or fence from which all measurements are taken, joined by two steel rods to a sliding fence that clamps the device to the work. Adjustable drill-bit guides are clamped to the rods to place the dowel holes in the required positions.

Very wide boards can be doweled by using the jig with the end fences removed. Hold the side fences of the drill-bit guides against the work and space holes accurately along the board by locking the first guide over the last-drilled hole with a dowel peg.

Vertical drill stand
A vertical stand converts a portable power drill into a serviceable drill press. Pulling down on the feed lever lowers the drill bit into the work. If the stand is fitted with a return spring, the drill is lifted automatically to its initial position when you release the feed lever.

Make sure the stand you choose has a sturdy, rigid column and a positive clamp to hold the drill itself. It should also have a wide, heavy base that can be bolted to a bench. Slots in the base enable you to attach small vises to it to hold metal components for drilling, but you can also use the slots for bolting a home-made wooden fence to the base, which will help you to position the work directly below the drill bit.

A depth gauge on the stand limits the travel of the drill when you want a stopped hole. When drilling right through the work, place a piece of chipboard or plywood under it to prevent splintering on the underside of the wood.

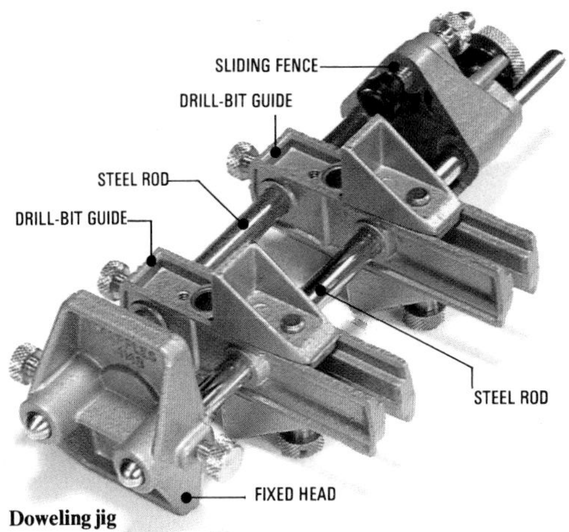

Doweling jig

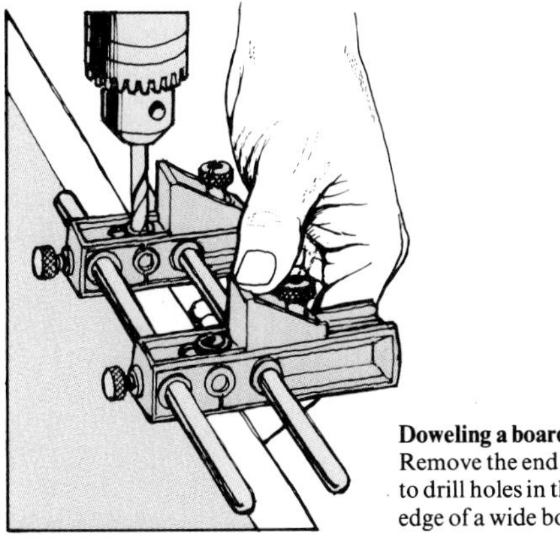
Doweling a board
Remove the end fences to drill holes in the edge of a wide board.

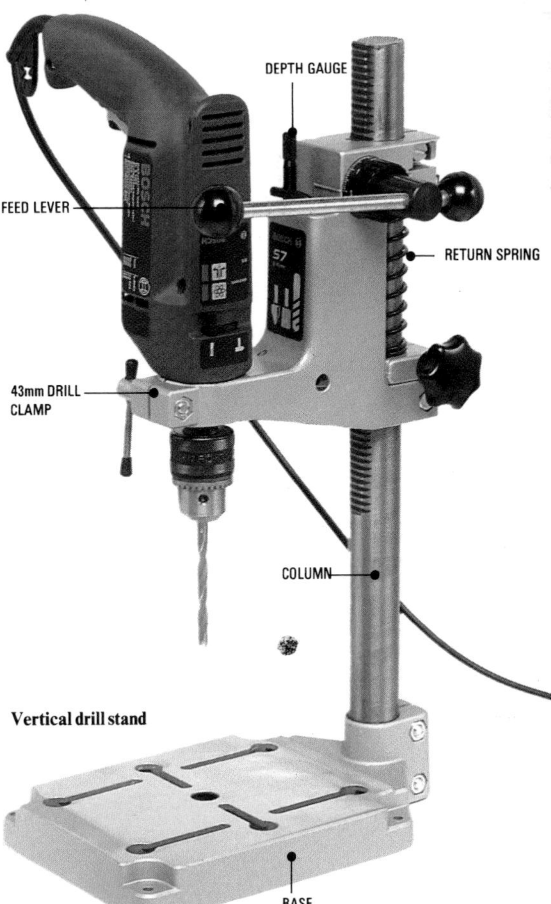

Vertical drill stand

JIGSAWS

Although some manufacturers claim too much for it, the jigsaw, or saber saw, is undoubtedly a versatile tool. It will cut any man-made board and crosscut solid wood reasonably well, but its ability to make curved cuts is its real advantage, especially when working with plywoods and particleboards. The jigsaw is less successful when ripping or curve-cutting thick lumber, because changes in grain direction may deflect the blade off-square. With the appropriate blade, a jigsaw will also cut sheet metal and plastics.

SEE ALSO

Curve-cutting saws	84
Safety tips	124
Jigsaw blades	130,131
Powered scroll saws	178-180
Dust collectors	214

ELECTRIC JIGSAWS

In the past, jigsaws had a poor reputation among serious woodworkers because the narrow blades tended to wander off line and to bend, which made it virtually impossible to make an accurate, square cut. But well-designed jigsaws now have precisely balanced electric motors and plunger mechanisms that produce very little vibration. As long as the blade is sharp, this type of saw is comfortable to use, relatively quiet and a lot easier to control. A basic no-frills jigsaw is perfectly adequate for woodwork, but if you are prepared to pay more, you can have a more versatile machine.

Orbital action
A basic jigsaw moves the blade straight up and down. Saws with orbital action cut faster by advancing the blade into the work on the upstroke, and minimize wear on the sawteeth and clear the kerf at the same time by moving the blade backward on the downstroke. The degree of oscillation is sometimes adjustable to select the best-possible action to suit the material being cut. On maximum advance, the blade cuts easily and quickly through softwoods. Orbital action is gradually reduced for thick sections of softwood and hardwoods, chipboard and soft metals; and finally to zero movement for steel and thin sheet materials.

- **Motor size**
Nearly all electric jigsaws have 350W motors capable of a top speed of about 3000 strokes per minute. The more powerful motors of professional- range saws are designed to cope with cutting thick steel rather than to produce a faster stroke rate.

Electric jigsaw

USING A JIGSAW SAFELY

Follow the basic safety procedures for power tools already described, but take extra care with a jigsaw.

- Check that the intended path of the blade is clear below the work.
- Make sure the cord trails behind the tool, never in front of the blade.
- Use sharp blades only. Dull blades have to be forced through the work.
- Never curl your fingers around the workpiece near the line of cut.
- Relieve the pressure on the saw as you are about to finish a cut – to avoid sudden acceleration as the blade leaves the kerf.
- Switch off the saw and wait until the blade has completely stopped moving before you put it down.

Depth of cut
The average jigsaw will cut softwoods and hardwoods up to 2in (50mm) thick. It will also cut nonferrous metals up to ½in (12mm) and steel up to ⅛in (3mm) thick. Professional-range tools handle only slightly thicker wood, but they are able to cut through ¾in (20mm) aluminum and ⅜in (10mm) steel.

Dust collection
On many jigsaws a jet of air from behind the blade clears the sawdust from the cutting line. This system is sufficient for most woodworking applications; if you are working for prolonged periods or on woods with toxic dust, buy a jigsaw with a dust-collecting facility. This is a flexible hose that plugs into the back of the saw and sucks dust from the cutting area into a domestic vacuum cleaner.

Electrical insulation
Choose a jigsaw with an all-plastic casing that insulates the user from electric shock should a fault occur within the motor.

Speed selection
Single-speed jigsaws operate at high speed the whole time and are primarily woodworking saws, so cannot be expected to cut metal for a prolonged period without overloading the motor.

Some jigsaws are made with dials to select a particular stroke rate, between 500 and 3000 strokes per minute, to suit the material being cut. But on a true variable-speed jigsaw, the stroke rate is controlled by the amount of pressure applied to the operating switch or trigger, although this too can be limited by a dial selector.

Generally, top speed is reserved for cutting wood; the midrange for plastics or soft metals, such as aluminum; and the low speeds for steel and ceramic tiles. But in practice, the sound of the saw and the ease with which it cuts are your best guide to the most suitable stroke rate.

The best saws have built-in electronic feedback to monitor the stroke rate and ensure that a constant speed is maintained within reasonable limits when the tool is cutting.

If you run a jigsaw on its slowest speed for an appreciable length of time, it may overheat – so every now and then let the saw run free at top speed for a couple of minutes so the motor can cool down.

Trigger lock
A button on the handle is depressed to lock the trigger for continuous running. This feature reduces tension and fatigue when making long, complicated cuts.

Scroller jigsaw

SCROLLING

Although, with an appropriately narrow blade, any jigsaw will cut intricately curved shapes, it is necessary to turn the whole saw in the direction of the cut or adjust the position of the work. However, on a scroller jigsaw the blade can be steered independently by a knob mounted on the top of the tool; it can also be locked facing forward, backward or sideways. When scrolling, care must be taken to keep pressure directly behind the cutting edge or the blade will distort and break.

CORDLESS JIGSAWS

Large cordless jigsaws are available for the professional worksite, but very few manufacturers make models designed for the amateur woodworker market. The advantages of a saw without a trailing electrical cord are obvious, but a cordless jigsaw is relatively expensive and is not as powerful as a saw operated on electricity. Its depth-cutting capacity for all materials is about half that of an electric jigsaw; and, when cutting ¾in (18mm) chipboard, it will run efficiently for only 15 minutes before it needs recharging. This is only a minor inconvenience if you keep a spare battery pack fully charged.

Make sure any cordless jigsaw you buy has a safety lock that prevents it from being switched on accidentally.

Splinter control
As the blade cuts on the upstroke, it tends to lift splinters on both sides of the kerf on the upper surface of the work. Consequently, it is important to cut with the "good" surface face down unless your jigsaw supports the wood as it is cut. This is achieved on some models by sliding the shoe or baseplate backward until the blade fits into a narrow slot in the metal. Other models are supplied with a plastic insert that fills the space around the blade.

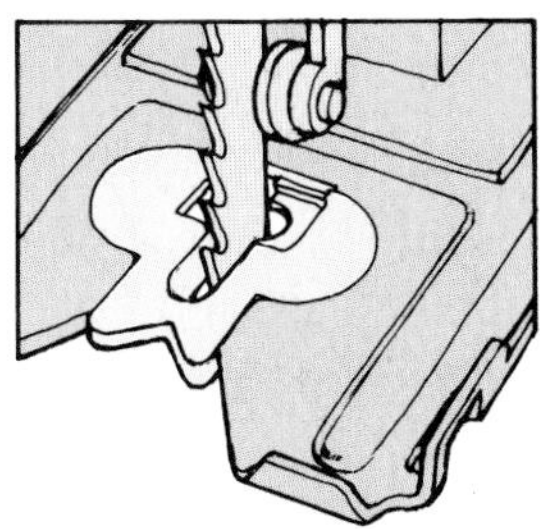
Insert prevents splintering

JIGSAW BLADES

All jigsaws are designed for easy blade replacement, primarily because the blades are never resharpened but are replaced as soon as they become dull or are broken. In addition, different blades are available for cutting a variety of materials, and woodworking blades are made with specific tooth configurations for a finer, faster or cleaner cut.

Although manufacturers describe their blades in different ways, a basic understanding of their construction and specifications will enable you to select the appropriate blade for a particular job.

SEE ALSO

Man-made boards	34-38
Supporting the work	82
Safety tips	124,129
Jigsaws	128-129
Metals	296-297

Blade length
This describes the length of the cutting or toothed section of the blade. It varies from 2 to 4in (50 to 100mm). Since you will usually be using the top half of the blade only, blade length isn't important for most purposes – but when you want to cut thick wood, choose a blade length ⅝ to ¾in (15 to 18mm) longer than the maximum thickness of the wood.

Size of teeth
Some manufacturers specify tooth size by the number of teeth that fit into a 1in length of blade; others use the engineering term "pitch," which describes the gap between two teeth, measured from point to point in millimeters. Thus a blade can be described as having 10 teeth per inch (TPI) or a pitch of 2.5mm.

As a rough guide, the smaller the teeth, the finer the cut; and as tooth size increases, so does the speed at which the blade will cut.

Set of tooth
The slot cut by a sawblade is known as the "kerf." If a blade cut a kerf equal to its own thickness, it would most probably break due to the strain imposed on it by too much friction. Consequently, blades are designed to cut a slightly wider kerf so as to provide a minimum clearance. This is achieved by setting the teeth in one of the following ways.

Saw or side set Alternate teeth are bent sideways to right and left, in the traditional method adopted for handsaws. However, this can be achieved only with relatively large teeth and is reserved for blades designed to cut quickly, leaving a rough-edge kerf.

Ground blades To produce a finer cut, this type of blade is made with teeth that have no set in the true sense; instead, to provide clearance, the blade behind the teeth is ground away to a thinner section. Ground blades cut very clean kerfs in man-made boards as well as solid wood. A blade that has a slight side set in addition to being taper ground will cut a little faster.

Wavy set Blades with extremely small teeth are made to cut a wider kerf by having a serpentine cutting edge. Wavy-set blades are designed for cutting metal but are also useful for making a clean, narrow kerf in plywood and blockboard.

Changing a jigsaw blade
Follow the manufacturer's instructions for changing the blade, and always make sure the roller guide is supporting the blade from behind.

- **Cutting metal**
Cutting sheet metal, even if it is thin, is a slow process, and you should not be tempted to force the saw to increase the speed of cut. Run a thin film of oil or turpentine ahead of the blade as a lubricant. Wear safety glasses and ear protectors.

- **Cutting plastic laminates**
To reduce the chipping of plastic-laminated chipboard, fit a laminate-cutting blade with reversed teeth. Alternatively, use a fine metal-cutting blade – but turn the board over and sandwich it between two sheets of hardboard.

USING A JIGSAW

The reciprocal action of a jigsaw will set up vibration in the work unless it is clamped to a bench or held down firmly on sawhorses. This is especially true of sheets of thin hardboard or plywood, which should be supported on both sides of the line of cut by planks resting on sawhorses.

Freehand sawing
Rest the front of the shoe on the work, with the blade just clear of the edge and aligned with the line of cut. Switch on the saw and advance the blade into the wood just on the waste side of the line. Push the saw through the work at a steady rate, but do not force it. Slow down for the last ½in (12mm) or so, supporting the offcut as it is severed.

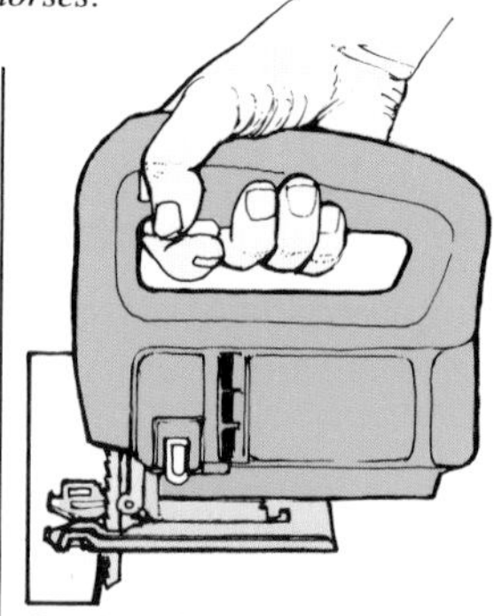
Starting a freehand cut

Cutting parallel to an edge
An adjustable side fence fitted to the shoe guides the sawblade on a path parallel to a straight edge. Make sure the fence clamp is secure and that the fence itself is aligned accurately with the blade. If it isn't, the blade will not cut true and it may burn the work or even break. You can extend a short fence by screwing a longer hardwood strip to it.

Set the fence by measuring from its inner face to the blade; or, with the blade aligned with the line of cut, slide the fence against the edge of the work and tighten the fence clamp. Switch on the saw and advance the blade into the work, pressing the fence against the edge throughout the length of the cut.

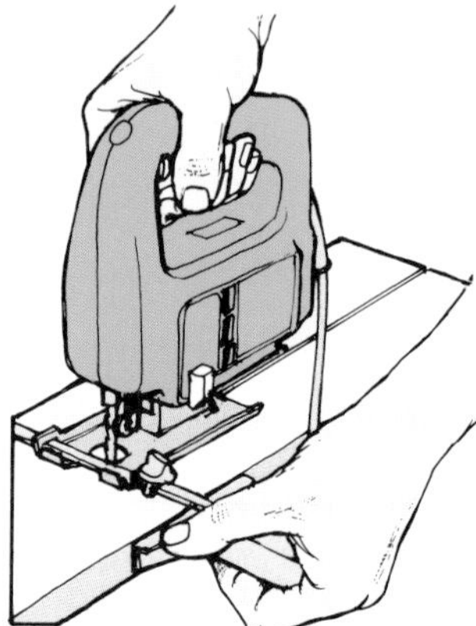
Press fence against the work

Constructing a temporary fence
When the line of cut is too far from an edge to use the side fence, run the side of the shoe against a batten clamped to the work.

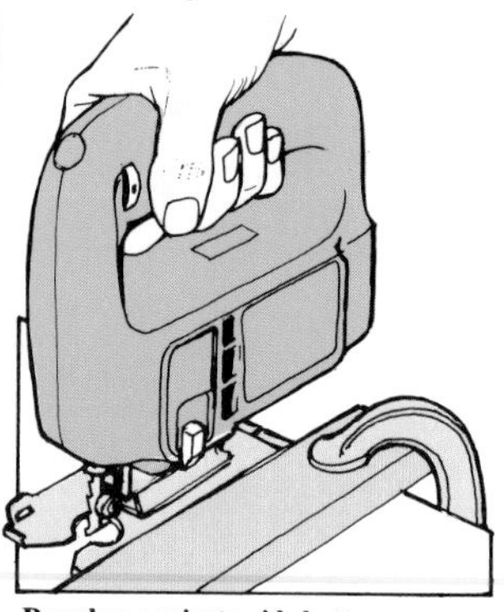
Run shoe against guide batten

Cutting a bevel
The shoe on a jigsaw can be adjusted to any angle up to 45 degrees on either side of the blade. Slightly slacken the shoe-clamping screws, tap the shoe with a screwdriver handle to the required angle indicated on the tilt gauge, then retighten the clamps.

It is difficult to guide an

Cut a bevel using a fence

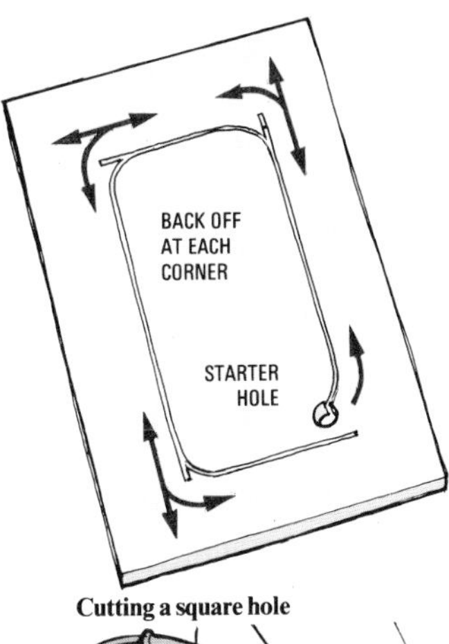

Cutting a square hole

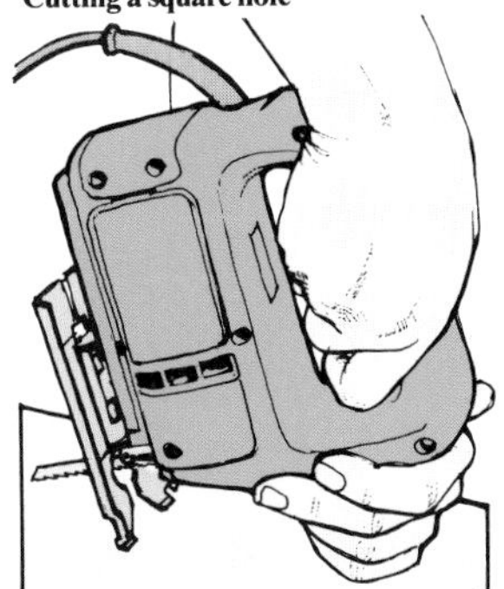
Beginning a plunge cut

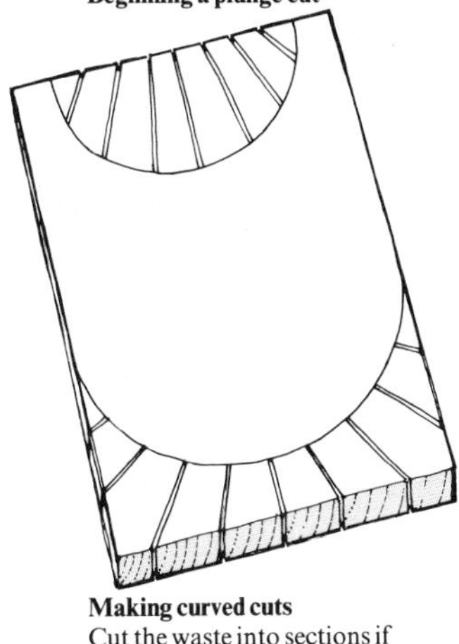
Making curved cuts
Cut the waste into sections if a curve is especially tight.

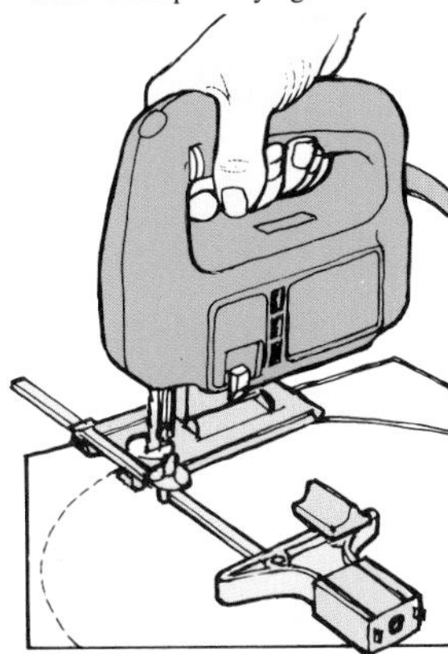
Cutting a circle
Convert the side fence into a compass for cutting a circle.

angled saw freehand, so if possible, use the side fence or clamp a guide batten to the work.

Cutting an aperture
To cut a round aperture in a board, first drill a starter hole for the blade just inside the marked area; then lower the blade into the hole, switch on the saw, and cut the aperture in one pass.

To cut a square hole, follow the same procedure, but cut into each corner and back off about 1in (25mm), then make a curved cut to bring the blade in line with the next side of the hole. Finally, remove the triangular waste left in each corner by sawing back in the opposite direction.

Making a plunge cut
Instead of drilling a starter hole, you can plunge-cut with a jigsaw to begin to cut an aperture. Tip the saw onto the curved front edge of the shoe with the blade clear of the work; then switch on the saw and pivot it on the shoe, gradually lowering the blade into the wood until the tool is upright and the shoe is flat on the work. Always make a plunge cut in the waste, not too close to the line of cut.

Making curved cuts
Very tight bends should be cut with a scrolling blade, but sweeping curves can be cut freehand with virtually any blade in the range. If a blade begins to strain on a tight bend, make straight cuts in the waste up to the line of cut first. This causes the waste to drop out in sections as the cut proceeds, which gives greater clearance for the blade.

To cut a perfectly circular hole or disc, convert the side fence into a compass by attaching to it a "point" supplied as part of the accessory. Press the point into the center of the circle and pivot the running saw around it.

JIGSAW BLADES FOR WOODWORK

EFFECTIVE LENGTH	TOOTH SIZE/ PITCH	SET	USE
3in (75mm) 	8TPI/3mm	Side set	Hard and softwood up to $2\frac{1}{2}$in (60mm) thick. Especially good for ripping with the grain. Rough cut.
3in (75mm) 	6TPI/4mm	Ground & side set	As above, but with a clean cut.
3in (75mm) 	6TPI/4mm	Ground	Hardwood, softwood and man-made boards up to $2\frac{1}{2}$in (60mm) thick. Very clean cut.
2in (50mm) 	12TPI/2mm	Wavy set	Man-made boards up to $1\frac{1}{4}$in (30mm) thick. Very fine cut.
2in (50mm) 	12TPI/2mm	Wavy set	For cutting tight curves in wood and man-made boards up to $\frac{3}{4}$in (20mm) thick.
3in (75mm) 	10TPI/2.5mm	Ground	Reversed teeth to cut on the downstroke. For plastic-laminated boards.
$2\frac{3}{8}$in (60mm) 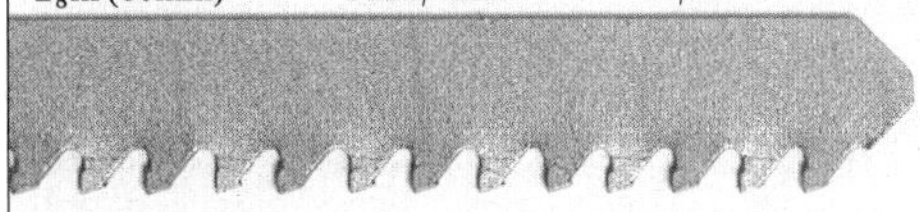	6TPI/4mm	N/A	Tungsten-carbide-tipped teeth, especially good for coping with the high glue content of chipboard.
$2\frac{3}{4}$in (70mm) 	N/A	N/A	Half-round, flat and triangular files. For wood and man-made boards.

METALWORKING BLADES

EFFECTIVE LENGTH	TOOTH SIZE/ PITCH	SET	USE
3in (75mm) 	12TPI/2mm	Ground	Nonferrous metals up to $\frac{3}{8}$in (10mm) thick. Very clean cut.
3in (75mm) 	8TPI/3mm	Side set	High-speed-steel blade, for mild steel up to $\frac{1}{4}$in (6mm) and nonferrous metals up to $\frac{3}{4}$in (20mm) thick.
2in (50mm) 	20TPI/1.2mm	Wavy set	High-speed-steel blade, for mild steel and nonferrous metals up to $\frac{1}{16}$in (1.5mm) thick.

OTHER MATERIALS

EFFECTIVE LENGTH	TOOTH SIZE/ PITCH	SET	USE
$2\frac{1}{8}$in (54mm) 	N/A	N/A	Tungsten-carbide coated for fiberglass and ceramic tiles.
3in (75mm)	N/A	Knife-ground	Soft rubber, cork, cardboard, carpet and plastics.

CIRCULAR SAWS

Even when a woodworker has a fully equipped machine shop with a table saw, you will often find he or she also owns a portable circular saw for the convenience of being able to work on-site or for converting large man-made boards, which can be difficult to handle on a fixed saw unless it has a large table.

- **Motor size**
  As one would expect, the size of the motor increases in proportion to the diameter of the blade – not to produce more speed but to provide more torque to overcome the extra leverage applied to a large blade as it cuts its way through the wood. As a general rule, the larger the motor for a given diameter of blade, the better the performance of the saw.

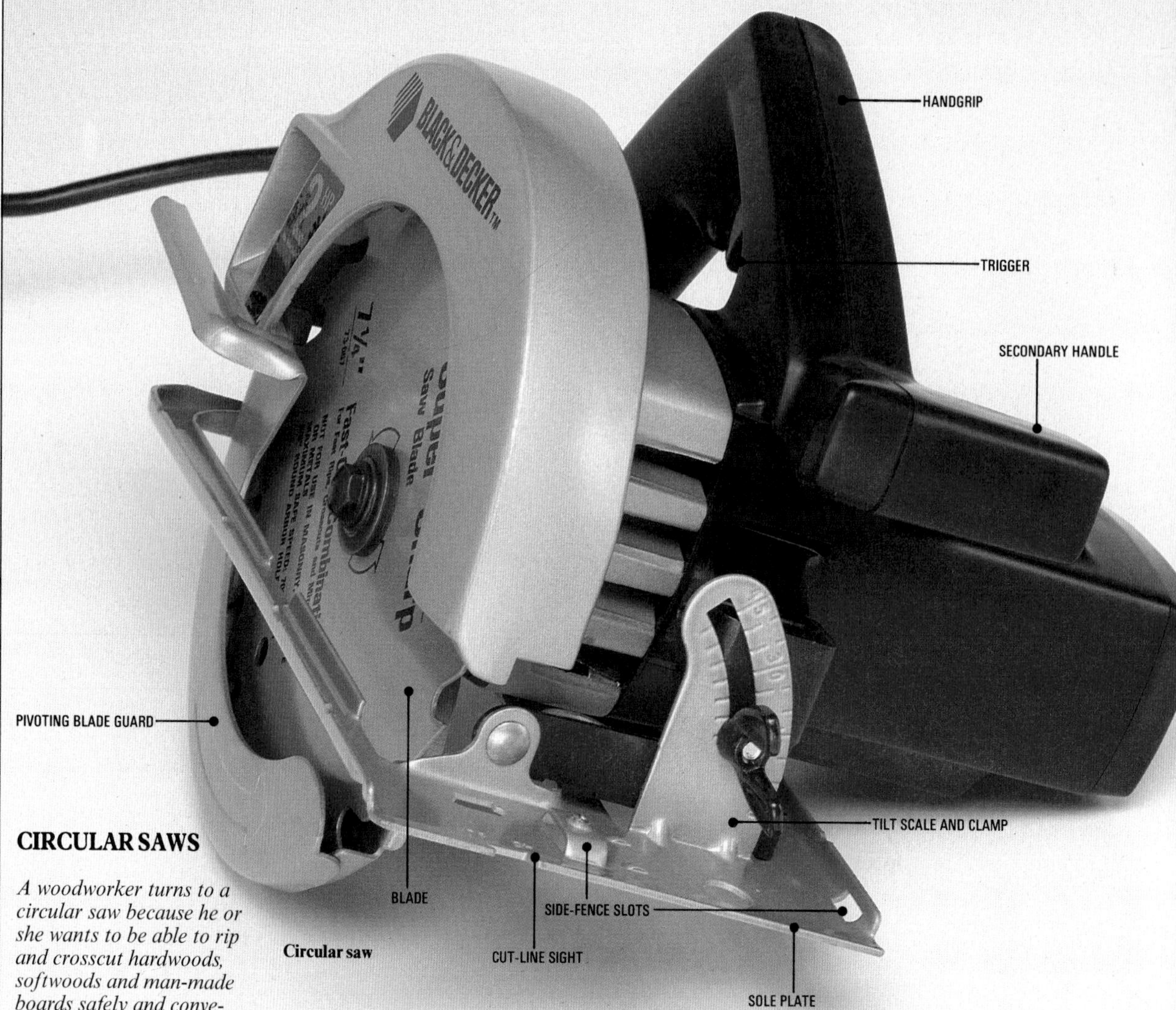

Circular saw

CIRCULAR SAWS

A woodworker turns to a circular saw because he or she wants to be able to rip and crosscut hardwoods, softwoods and man-made boards safely and conveniently. Long a standby of carpenters and construction workers because of its light weight and portability, the circular saw accepts a variety of blade types for fast, rough cutting or for finished work. In addition, a number of toothless abrasive discs are available for cutting sheet metal, stone and ceramics. A circular saw capable of more than your present requirements is a wise investment, especially if there is a chance you will want to convert it into a table saw by bolting it to an appropriate accessory or workcenter (see p. 151).

CUTTING DEPTH OF TYPICAL BLADES

Blade diameter	Cutting depth
4½in (112mm)	1¼in (32mm)
5½in (137mm)	1¾in (44mm)
6½in (162mm)	2⅛in (54mm)
7¼in (181mm)	2⅜in (59mm)
8¼in (206mm)	2⅞in (72mm)
10in (250mm)	3¾in (95mm)

Dust collection
A great deal of sawdust is produced by a powerful circular saw. It makes the workshop floor slippery, it's uncomfortable when it gets caught in your clothing and dust-laden air is unhealthy as well as unpleasant. Saws fitted with an exhaust port in the upper guard throw the sawdust sideways. You can either collect the dust in a bag plugged into the port or insert a nozzle connected to a vacuum cleaner.

Tilting blade
By loosening a clamp, the body and blade of the saw can be tilted to any angle up to 45 degrees. The angle can be read on a quadrant scale, but it is worth measuring the angle on a trial cut if the bevel must be exact. The maximum cutting depth of the saw is reduced when the blade is angled.

Safety lock
To prevent the saw from being switched on accidentally, some are fitted with a safety-lock button, which must be depressed with the thumb before the trigger can be operated. Circular saws are not fitted with trigger-lock buttons for continuous running, but manufacturers of table-saw attachments supply clamps or straps to hold the trigger down.

Guards
The upper part of the blade is enclosed by a fixed guard. As the saw advances into the work, the pivoting lower guard is pushed back by the edge of the wood to reveal the blade. When the blade clears the work, the spring-loaded guard snaps back to enclose it again. Before using a circular saw, make sure the pivoting guard operates smoothly.

Antilocking clutch
Clamping flanges on each side of the blade act as an antilocking clutch. Should the blade jam suddenly, they allow it to slip, protecting the drive mechanism from damage.

Electrical insulation
An all-plastic body enclosing the motor protects the user from electric shock.

Handles
A comfortable ergonomic grip and a secondary handle near the toe of the tool give you positive and safe control over the saw.

Depth of cut
Although a circular saw is often designated by the diameter of its blade, this is not a clear guide to its actual cutting capacity. The table on the facing page gives the cutting depth of a typical range of circular-saw blades. At the very least, most woodworkers need a saw that will cut wood 2in (50mm) thick. At the upper end of the range, the size and weight of the tool become considerations. A 10in (250mm) saw, for example, is heavy and tiring to use for prolonged periods. On the other hand, when it is mounted in a workcenter, its weight is no longer a disadvantage.

Adjusting the depth of cut
You can adjust the depth of cut by raising or lowering the body of the saw in relation to the sole plate. A scale may be provided for reading the depth of cut, but many woodworkers prefer to use the work itself as a guide. With the pivoting guard raised, lay the sole plate on the work with the blade resting against the edge **(1)**. Release the depth-adjusting clamp and raise or lower the blade until it projects about $\frac{1}{8}$in (3mm) below the work, then tighten the clamp.

To cut partially through a piece of wood, mark the depth on the side of the work and adjust the blade to coincide with it **(2)**.

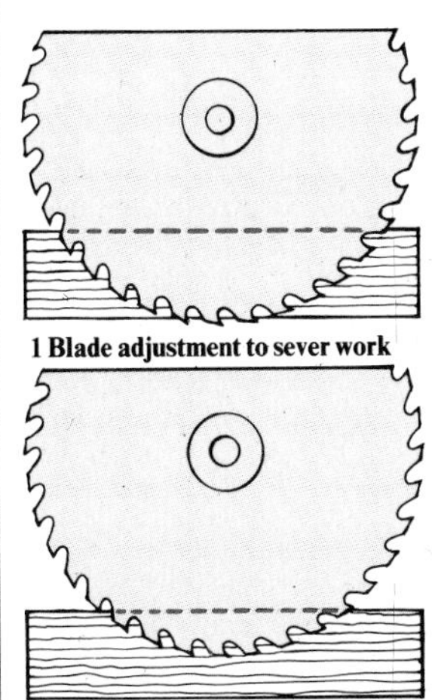

1 Blade adjustment to sever work

2 Adjustment for partial cut

USING A CIRCULAR SAW SAFELY

Even a small circular saw is capable of inflicting serious injury. However, accidents rarely happen if safety procedures are strictly observed. Follow the basic rules that apply to all power tools, but be especially careful with a circular saw and never be tempted to bend the rules.

- Before sawing, check the wood for nails, which will dull or damage the blade, and for loose knots, which could be dislodged and thrown into the air.
- Don't rely on switching off the saw at the socket before changing or adjusting a blade – always unplug the tool first.
- Use only sharp blades and always replace a cracked or bent one.
- Never be tempted to remove the riving knife if one is fitted.
- Never tape or wedge the pivoting guard in the open position, except when it is bolted to a table-saw attachment where another guard is substituted.
- Don't force the blade through the work. If it doesn't feed smoothly, the blade is dull and needs to be replaced.
- Don't attempt to stop a spinning blade by applying side pressure to it.

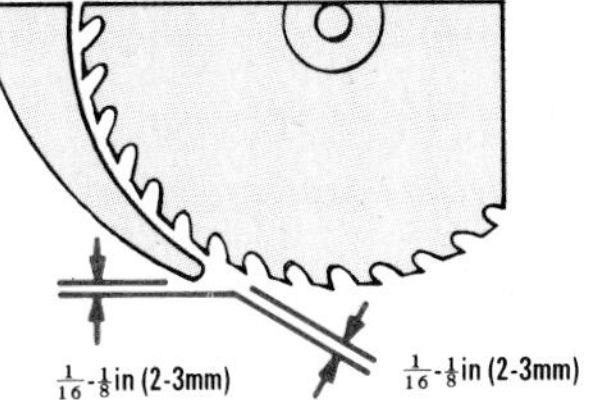

Riving knife or splitter
As solid wood is ripped longitudinally, tensions are released within the grain that can cause the kerf to close behind the blade. On some saws, to prevent the blade from jamming in the kerf, a riving knife is mounted directly behind the blade. The riving knife should be adjusted to within $\frac{1}{16}$ to $\frac{1}{8}$in (2 to 3mm) of the blade. Similarly, the tip of the knife should be $\frac{1}{16}$ to $\frac{1}{8}$in (2 to 3mm) above the lowest sawtooth.

CORDLESS CIRCULAR SAWS

In the past fifteen years, battery technology has developed the cordless drill from an underpowered curiosity to an essential part of many contractors' tool kits.

The circular saw has come a long way, too. Cordless saws are lighter, more powerful and more convenient than ever. A saw's great demands for power mean that a battery-powered saw will not work continuously for long periods—but new quickly recharging spare battery packs are now helping to lessen this problem.

New battery technology means practical power on a jobsite.

CIRCULAR-SAW BLADES

If you want to rip fence posts or crosscut siding, a reasonably cheap sawblade will do the job; if you want a cut straight from the saw that requires very little planing and sanding, you have to use a top-quality blade. A first-class blade is absolutely essential if the saw is to be mounted in a workcenter for accurate joint cutting.

The PTFE coating on a blade reduces friction – thus increasing the life of the blade itself, lessening the wear on the saw drive mechanism and decreasing the risk of burning the work.

Tungsten-carbide-tipped teeth produce a better finish and stay sharp 10 times longer than standard sawteeth.

The blades shown below are typical woodworking blades. Depending on the size and make of your circular saw, you can also buy special blades for cutting metal, plastic and masonry.

SEE ALSO

Safety tips	124,133
Circular saws	132-133
Workcenters	151-153
Dust collectors	214

1 Pointed-tooth blade
2 Fine-tooth blade
3 Rip blade
4 Chisel-tooth blade
5 Carbide-tipped blade

Pointed-tooth blade
A multiple-toothed blade suitable for crosscutting solid wood. It leaves a reasonable finish.

Fine-tooth blade
For a fine cut in chipboard and plastic-laminated boards. It cuts relatively slowly.

Rip blade
A blade with large tungsten-carbide-tipped teeth ideal for ripping softwood; it also cuts hardwoods and man-made boards. Having very few teeth, it does not produce a first-class finish.

Chisel-tooth blade
A medium-priced universal sawblade suited to ripping and crosscutting softwoods, hardwoods and man-made boards.

Carbide-tipped universal blade
A top-quality universal sawblade that leaves an extremely fine finish when crosscutting or ripping solid wood and all man-made boards, including laminate-faced materials.

Changing sawblades
Follow the manufacturer's instructions for changing a sawblade, and make sure you replace it with one having the correct bore diameter (the diameter of the hole in the center). When fitted, ensure the teeth at the bottom of the blade face toward the front of the saw. Always have dull circular-saw blades sharpened by a professional.

USING A CIRCULAR SAW

Since the teeth of a circular saw travel upward when they cut wood, any tearing of the grain will be on the upper surface of the work. A good-quality blade will keep tearout to a minimum, but as a precaution, turn the work "good" side down.

Support the work carefully, either clamped to overhang a bench or, better still, on sawhorses. To avoid having to move sawhorses when making a long through cut, nail battens to the top of them. You can make one continuous pass with the saw without cutting into the sawhorses, but make sure the nails are placed well away from the line of cut.

Cutting freehand
Circular saws are made with a small notch in the sole plate to act as a sight when cutting freehand. Make a few trial cuts to discover the relationship between the sight and the kerf left by the saw. When cutting freehand, keep safely on the waste side of the line. On some saws a second sight is provided to act as a guide when cutting a 45-degree bevel.

Hold the tool in both hands and rest the front section of the sole plate on the work, with the sight aligned with the line of cut. Switch on the saw, and advance it into the work. At the end of the cut, let the guard close, switch off, and let the blade come to rest before laying the saw aside.

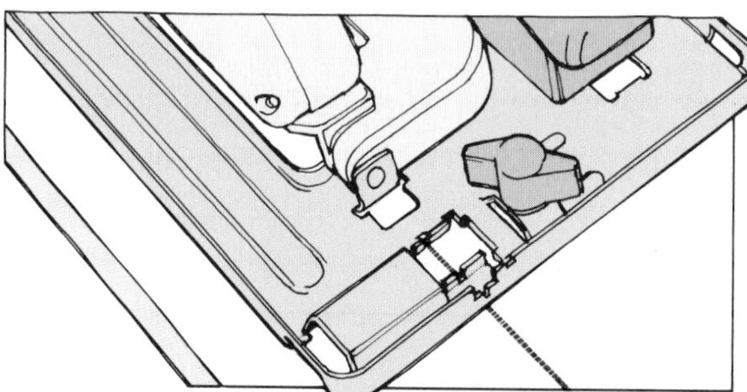
Align the sole-plate sight with a marked line for a freehand cut

Ripping parallel to an edge
All circular saws are supplied with a rip fence that guides the blade to cut a parallel-sided strip from the edge of a piece of wood or board. A well-made fence is sturdy, with a positive mounting and clamp that hold it perfectly parallel to the blade. It can be fitted to either side of the saw, and on a large circular saw, you can screw a hardwood strip to extend the length of the fence.

Use the scale on the fence arm to set the fence, then make a trial cut to check the measurement. When ripping, cut at a steady rate, keeping the fence pressed against the edge of the work throughout.

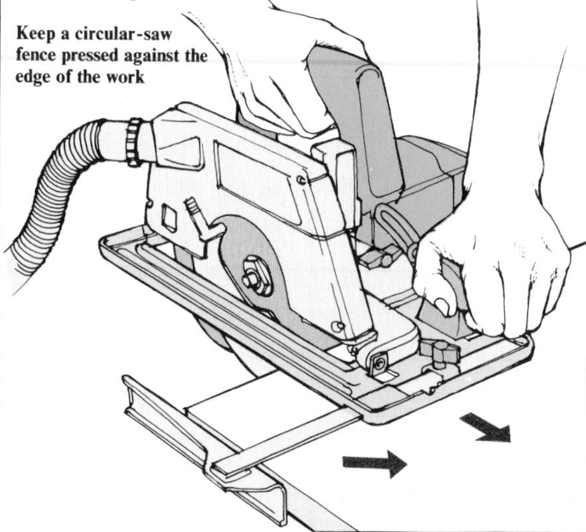
Keep a circular-saw fence pressed against the edge of the work

Ripping with a guide batten

When you need to cut a parallel strip that is too wide for the rip fence, clamp or temporarily nail a straight batten to the work to guide the edge of the sole plate. Keep the plate pressed against the batten during the cut.

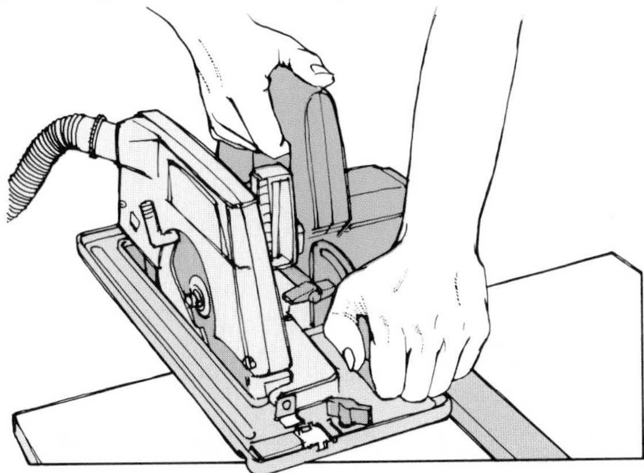

Ripping against a guide batten

Grooving and rabbeting

Cutting a groove or rabbet with a portable saw is a laborious but accurate process. Set the fence to cut the two sides of a groove **(1)** or the inner edge of a rabbet **(2)**. Reset the fence to remove the waste gradually by making successive passes with the saw **(3** and **4)**.

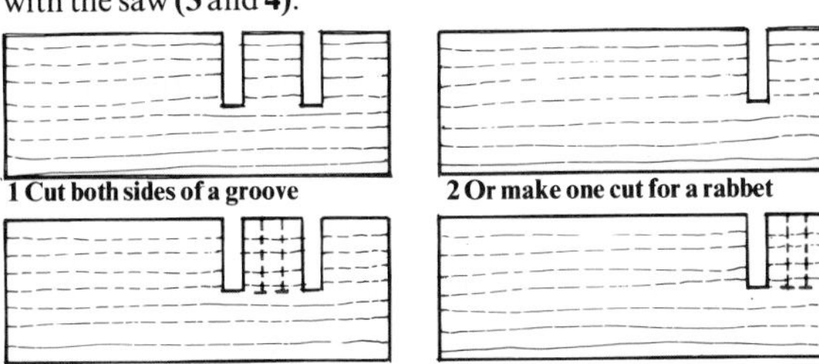

1 Cut both sides of a groove

2 Or make one cut for a rabbet

3 Remove the waste in sections

4 Do the same for a rabbet

Crosscutting

Square and angled crosscuts **(1)** are made by clamping a guide batten to the work.

To cut a number of boards to the same length, nail a stop batten to the bench and butt the squared ends of the boards against it, with their uncut ends overhanging the edge of the bench. Clamp a guide batten across all the boards **(2)** and trim them all with one pass of the saw.

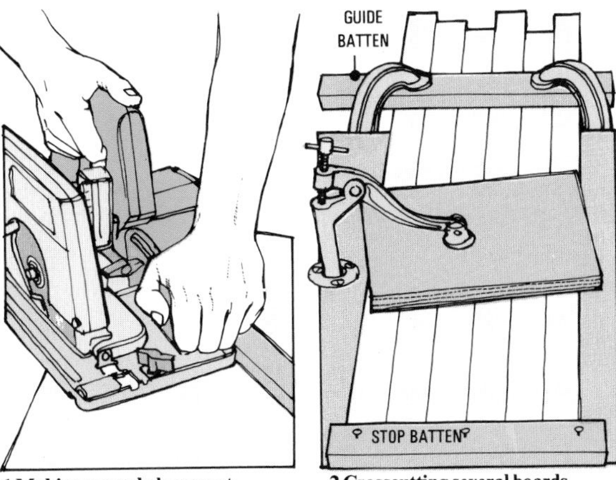

1 Making an angled crosscut

2 Crosscutting several boards

Making a crosscutting T square

You can make a permanent guide for crosscutting by gluing and screwing two sturdy battens together in the form of the letter "T" **(1)**. Hold this T square against a scrap board and run the sole plate of the saw against the crosspiece to trim the end off the "stock" **(2)**. Aligning the trimmed end with a marked line **(3)** automatically sets up the blade to make the cut on the waste side of the line. Stick a strip of coarse sandpaper to the underside of the crosspiece to increase its grip on the work; if you still can't hold the T square steady with one hand, clamp it in place.

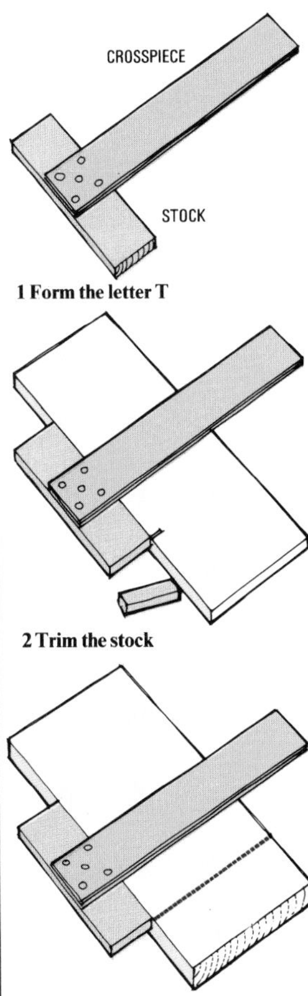

1 Form the letter T

2 Trim the stock

3 Align the stock with the line of cut

TABLE-SAW CONVERSIONS

Most manufacturers supply a bench to convert their portable circular saws into table saws. The saw is bolted upside down to the underside of the bench, with its blade protruding through the table top.

In theory, a table saw has certain advantages. It leaves both hands free to control the work; it should have better guides and fences; and you can use a large, heavy saw safely and without getting tired. Unfortunately, however, most bench conversions are much too small to be practical, and unless they are supplied with extension arms, there is no possibility of passing man-made boards across them. Moreover, the guides and fences are often flimsy or will not slide smoothly, and the guards are sometimes inadequate or so clumsy that the user is tempted to remove them.

Any table saw must have a strong, stable underframe and an accessible on/off switch. Pulling away a saw-trigger clip with a length of string is not an adequate substitute for switching off the saw in an emergency.

A serious woodworker would be better advised to spend a little extra to purchase a good-quality workcenter, which will not only serve as an excellent table-saw base but will also convert to a spindle molder or shaper table by swapping the saw for a router.

Never clamp a circular saw upside down on a bench or fix the handgrip in a bench vise in an attempt to use it as a makeshift table saw. If the blade jams or the user slips while passing a length of wood across the saw, the tool could be wrenched off the bench.

- **Storing blades**
  Preserve non-PTFE-coated blades with a light coating of acid-free grease or oil when in long-term storage, and clean them before using again.

BISCUIT JOINTERS

A biscuit jointer is a specialized miniature plunge saw developed to make a form of tongue and groove joint for cabinet construction. The joint works like a dowel joint, but instead of a round peg in a hole bored in the wood, a flat oval plate or "biscuit" of compressed beech fits into a slot cut by a circular-saw blade. When water-base PVA glue is introduced to the joint, the wooden plate expands to fill the slot and forms an extremely strong bond. Round dowel holes need to be perfectly aligned if the two joint components are to fit snugly. With a biscuit joint, however, slight lateral adjustment is possible by tapping one component sideways.

The biscuit jointer can also be used to cut grooves for drawer bottoms or to trim thin siding, paneling or floorboards.

SEE ALSO

Cabinet joints	63,65
Drawer construction	71
Safety tips	124
Butt joints	216-217
Edge joints	222-223
Adhesives	302

Depth of cut
A biscuit jointer has a variable depth of cut, from 0 to about $\frac{7}{8}$in (22mm). The depth scale should be marked with the dimensions required to accommodate standard-size biscuits. If you are trimming the edge of a piece of wood, adjust the blade depth until the teeth just break through the underside surface.

Plunge action
Depending on the model, a biscuit-jointer blade is lowered into the work by pivoting or pressing down upon the spring-loaded motor housing.

Guide fence
To guide the blade parallel to a straight edge, the biscuit jointer is fitted with an adjustable fence. Some jointers are supplied with an additional bevel fence for cutting a groove in a 45-degree miter joint.

- **No-load speed**
Because the blades are so small, biscuit jointers run at up to 10,000rpm, to drive the sawteeth at a sufficient speed to produce a clean, accurate cut.

Cutting guide
A notch or line cut in the base or fence indicates the center of a plunge-cut slot for jointing.

Dust collection
Sawdust can be collected in a bag or vacuum cleaner via a flexible hose.

Secondary handle
The motor housing acts as the main handgrip, but a biscuit jointer comes with one or sometimes two secondary handles for convenient control of the tool.

On/off switch
The on/off switch will be situated on the motor housing, either underneath for operation by the index finger or on top for the thumb.

BLADES

Biscuit jointers are fitted with miniature 4 to $4\frac{1}{4}$in (100 to 105mm) diameter circular-saw blades with tungsten-carbide-tipped teeth. Jointing and grooving blades cut a $\frac{5}{32}$in (4mm) slot, and slimmer blades are available for trimming wood to length.

BISCUITS

Compressed-beech biscuits come in three common sizes: for board thicknesses of $\frac{3}{8}$ to $\frac{1}{2}$in (10 to 12mm); $\frac{1}{2}$ to $\frac{3}{4}$in (13 to 18mm); and $\frac{3}{4}$in (19mm) and over. Barbed plastic biscuits are available for test assemblies.

Biscuit jointer

Cutting guide in fence indicates center of slot

Compressed-beech biscuits

Wood-trimming blade

Jointing blade

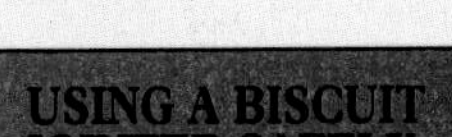

USING A BISCUIT JOINTER SAFELY

Follow the usual safety procedures recommended for power tools. In addition:

- Do not plunge a blade into the wood until the motor is running at full speed.
- Use sharp blades only and discard any that are cracked or bent.
- Do not apply side pressure to a spinning blade in order to slow it down or bring it to a stop.
- Never run the tool with the blade guard removed.
- When cutting a groove, feed the jointer at a steady rate away from you against the rotation of the blade.

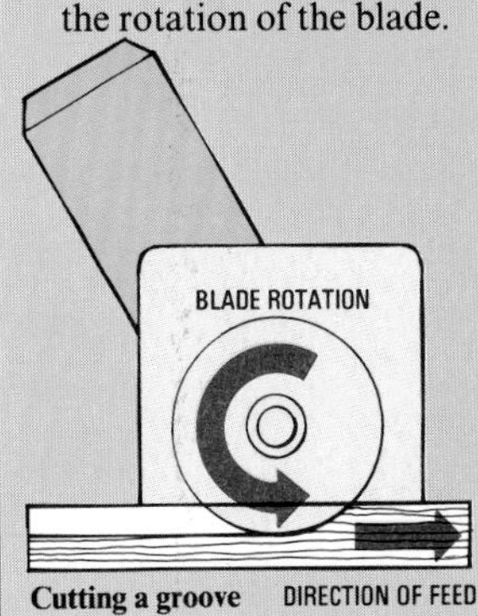

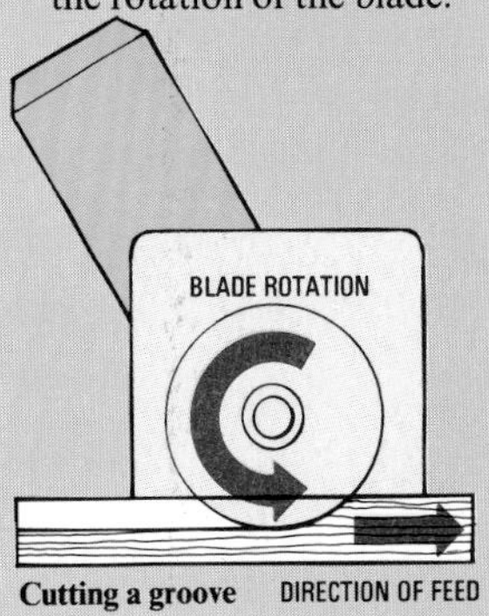

Cutting a groove

CUTTING BISCUIT JOINTS

Biscuit jointing is perfectly suitable for cabinet or frame construction using man-made boards and solid wood with butt, miter or edge-to-edge joints.

Making a butt joint

Having drawn the centerline of the joint on the work, mark along it the central points of the biscuit slots, spaced about 4in (100mm) apart. Set the cutting depth to suit the biscuits you are using and adjust the guide fence to align the blade with the centerline.

Align the cutting guide with the central point of each slot, press the fence against the edge of the work and plunge the blade to make the cut **(1)**.

To cut a slot in the edge of a matching component, place the work on a flat surface and lay the jointer on its side **(2)**. Edge-to-edge joints are cut in the same way.

To cut slots across the central part of a board, hold the matching component on edge and draw a line along one side. Tip the component to that side and align it with the marked line. Use the component as a fence to plunge the slots across the board **(3)**; then, without moving the matching component, cut slots in its edge as described above.

Cutting a miter joint

If the biscuit jointer is supplied with a bevel fence, you can cut slots for a miter joint with the workpiece laid flat on a bench **(1)**.

If the jointer has a right-angle fence only, clamp the work with the joint overhanging a bench and run the fence along the outer edge of the bevel **(2)**.

Cutting a groove

To cut a continuous groove, adjust the jointer as for cutting a butt joint. Place the tool at one end of the work, switch it on, and plunge the saw. Feed the tool to the end of the groove, raise the blade and then switch off the saw.

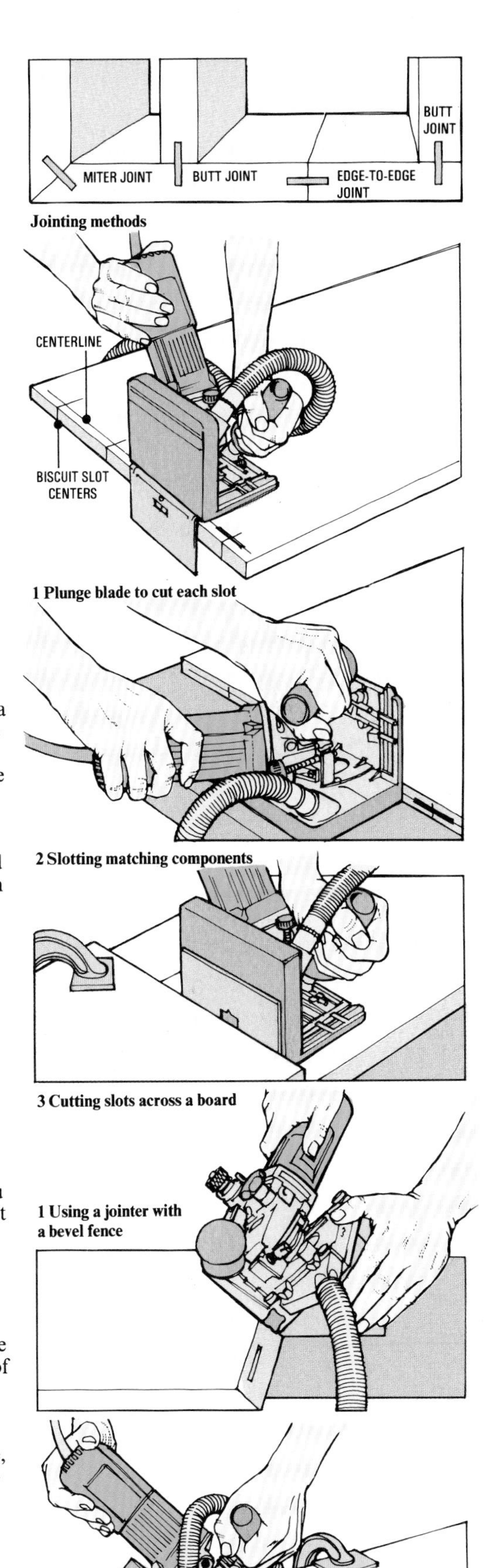

Jointing methods

1 Plunge blade to cut each slot

2 Slotting matching components

3 Cutting slots across a board

1 Using a jointer with a bevel fence

2 Jointing a miter with a standard fence

PORTABLE PLANERS

A portable planer is not the tool for very precise work. However, it is excellent for quickly planing a balk of wood to size ready for skimming with a bench plane. It is also a boon for joinery work, such as relieving the bottom of a door to clear a fitted carpet or planing a beveled rabbet on a windowsill. When mounted in a special-purpose bench stand, it makes a passable surface planer or jointer.

SEE ALSO

Wild grain	15
Safety tips	124
Jointers/planers	180-185
Grain direction	184

Rabbeting depth
A depth gauge attached to the body of the tool determines the maximum depth of a rabbet cut by the planer. The smallest planers will rabbet no deeper than $\frac{5}{16}$in (8mm), but the maximum rabbet depth for most planers is between $\frac{3}{4}$ and 1in (20 and 25mm). A side fence regulates the width of the rabbet.

Portable electric planer

- **Motor size**
  Motor size varies a great deal from planer to planer, but a no-load speed of 12,000 to 14,000rpm is average.

Dust collection
Power planers throw out so many shavings that it is worth attaching a collecting bag or a vacuum-cleaner hose to the exhaust port when the tool is clamped upside down as a jointer.

Cutting depth
Small planers will remove from 0 to $\frac{1}{32}$in (1mm) in one pass, and larger models have a maximum cutting depth of $\frac{1}{16}$in (2mm). Professional-quality planers will plane up to $\frac{1}{8}$in (3mm) deep, but they cost 50 percent more than the average planer, and the extra cutting depth alone is not worth the cost.

Cutting depth is selected by raising or lowering the front or infeed section of the sole. At a zero setting, both sections of the sole are flush. Choose a planer fitted with an adjusting dial or knob that operates smoothly and indicates the depth setting clearly.

Planing width
The width of a planer sole matches the length of the cutters exactly. The majority of planers are $3\frac{1}{4}$in (82mm) wide.

Secondary handle
A secondary handle placed over the toe of a planer helps to control the tool and keep the infeed section of the sole flat on the work.

BEVEL-CUTTING GROOVE

Cutterhead guard
A retractable guard protects the user and the cutterhead.

USING A PLANER SAFELY

Follow the safety advice applicable to all power tools when using a portable planer. In addition:

- Do not use the planer with its guard retracted. The guard should only be retracted when changing the cutters.
- Check the work for nails and screws before planing.
- Do not curl your fingers around the edge of the sole. Keep both hands on the handles.
- Check that the planer switch is not locked before plugging it in.
- Replace dull cutters. They make the user force the planer through the work – increasing the risk that it will be thrown back when the cutters meet tough or irregular grain.

Cutterhead guard
Choose a planer with a guard that completely covers the cutters until it is pushed back by the wood to reveal the revolving cutterhead as the planer is advanced into the work. It protects not only the user but also the cutters from damage should the planer be laid on the bench before the cutterhead stops spinning. The guard can be withdrawn manually for cutter changing by operating a slider on the body of the tool.

Bevel-cutting groove
The "V" groove machined along the center of the infeed sole locates the planer on the 90-degree corner of a piece of wood to guide the tool when planing a bevel. A side fence with a face that adjusts for any angle from 90 to 45 degrees helps to keep the tool at the required angle as the bevel widens.

Electrical insulation
Choose a double-insulated planer with a plastic casing.

Trigger lock
The on/off switch or trigger can be locked for continuous running by depressing a button on the handgrip.

PLANER CUTTERS

The cylindrical cutterhead holds a balanced pair of cutters or blades. There are three types of cutter, all double-sided.

Straight cutter
A general-purpose tungsten-carbide straight-edged cutter.

Straight cutter with rounded corners
For planing a surface wider than the planer. The rounded corners do not leave steps in the wood.

Wavy-edge cutter
Designed to leave a "tooled" surface on "rustic" joinery.

Changing planer cutters
A good planer is designed to make changing the cutters as easy as possible. A cutter should be replaced when both sides are dull. The usual practice is to slide the new cutter into the machined groove in the cutterhead **(1)**, then use a strip of wood to align the end of the cutter with the edge of the sole **(2)**. Tightening two or three screws clamps the blade in the groove.

1 Fit cutter in groove

2 Align cutter with sole

POWER PLANING

Whenever possible, plane in the direction of the grain. If the grain is "wild," adjust the planer to take a finer cut. For the best finish, make two or three passes with a finely set planer rather than remove the same amount of wood in one pass.

Place the infeed sole on the work, with the cutterhead clear of the wood. Press down on the tool with the secondary handle, lining up the planer with the work. Switch on the tool and advance the planer at a steady rate. At the end of the pass, transfer pressure from the secondary handle to the rear of the planer, so that the tool does not "dip" and take a deep scoop out of the end of the work. To correct a mistake of this kind, set the planer for a fine cut and carefully plane the wood below the level of the damage.

Check the work with a try square. Some woodworkers find that the side fence helps them keep the planer square to the work.

To flatten a wide board, plane diagonally across the work in two directions, overlapping the passes each time. Finally, plane parallel to the long edges.

Planing a rabbet
Adjust the side fence and depth gauge to the rabbet dimensions **(1)**. Plane to the required depth, keeping the fence pressed against the work throughout.

To plane a beveled rabbet, proceed as above but set the angle indicator to tilt the planer. It is vital to keep side pressure on the planer when beveling so the tool does not keep on sliding down the slope **(2)**.

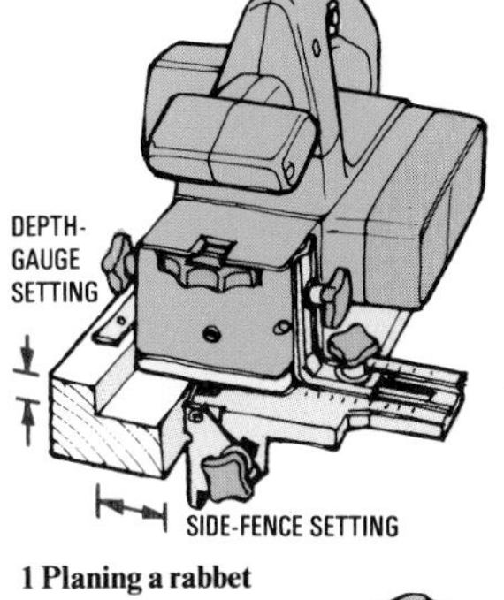

1 Planing a rabbet

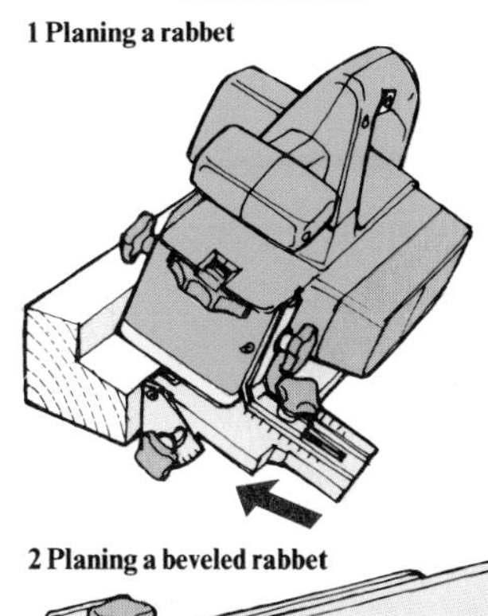

2 Planing a beveled rabbet

Converting to a jointer
When a portable planer is bench-mounted upside down, work can be passed across it using both hands. With the side fence attached, it is possible to plane square shoulders on the work – but portable planers, unlike regular jointers or surface planers, are not usually long enough to guarantee a perfectly straight edge on a long board.

If you buy a portable planer specifically for bench-mounting, examine the way the cutters are guarded before you make your final choice. Ideally, choose a planer already fitted with a retractable guard, so that the cutterhead is covered until the work is pushed across the tool. Also, make sure that when the side fence is adjusted to leave just enough sole to accommodate the width of the work, an unguarded section of cutterhead will never be exposed except to the work itself.

Planers without integral guards are supplied with a spring-loaded guard as part of the bench stand. This guard is pushed aside as the work is passed across the planer. However, check that when the side fence is fitted it does not hold the guard open, partly exposing the cutters.

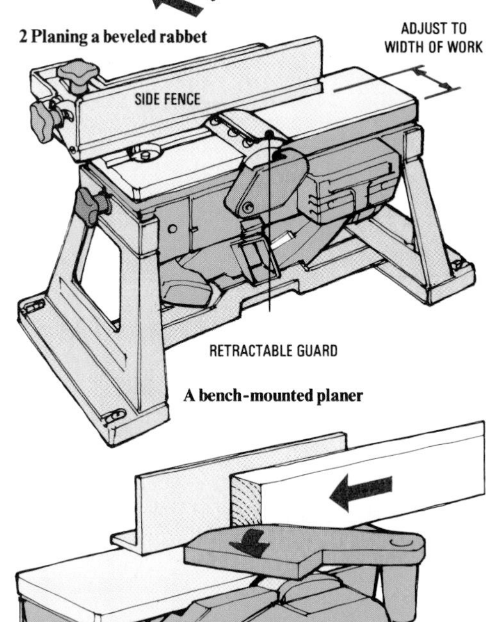

A bench-mounted planer

Some guards are pushed aside by the work

ROUTERS

The electric router has taken the place of a whole family of molding, grooving and rabbeting planes. Unlike many other power tools, it can be fitted with a bit and adjusted to be ready for use in about the same time as it takes to prepare a hand tool for the same kind of job. With a powerful motor driving a bit at high speed, the finished results are precise and professional in appearance. In principle, all routers are constructed similarly. A bit is mounted directly below a motor housing fitted with a handle on each side, and the whole assembly sits on a roughly circular base through which the bit protrudes. The main difference between routers lies in the way the bit is fed into the work to cut a stopped groove or a housing. There are fixed routers, which are suspended above and lowered into the work as one unit. Plunge routers are made with the motor housing mounted above the base on spring-loaded columns. When the base rests on the work, downward pressure on the handles feeds the bit into the wood.

SEE ALSO

Safety tips	124
Router bits	142
Using routers	143-146

Motor size and speed
The great majority of routers have a fixed no-load speed, which can be anywhere between 22,000 and 27,000rpm. Except in special circumstances, a high speed of around 26,000rpm is required to produce a clean finish – especially because the speed drops considerably when a bit encounters hard wood. Motor size varies a great deal from router to router, but the larger ones will maintain a high cutting speed without strain.
A motor with a power input of less than 450W will be hard-pressed to produce a satisfactory finish.

- **Lightweight plastic body**
Modern routers have a lightweight plastic motor housing that insulates against electric shock.

Handgrips
A fixed router has two large ergonomic handles for steering the tool along the intended path. On small plunge routers, one of these handles acts as the plunge lock. A short counter-clockwise turn releases the mechanism; the router is then lowered to the required depth and the handle is tightened to lock the tool. At the end of the operation, the plunge lock is released to allow the router to rise automatically. Larger plunge routers usually lock with a thumb lever.

Electronic feedback
Some top-of-the-line routers are made with an electronic feedback system that prevents the speed from dropping when the tool is under load by feeding more power to the bit. In addition, optimum speed can be selected to suit the size of bit or type of operation. Reducing the speed, for example, increases the life of an expensive large-diameter bit and reduces the risk of burning the wood when doing intricate routing freehand.

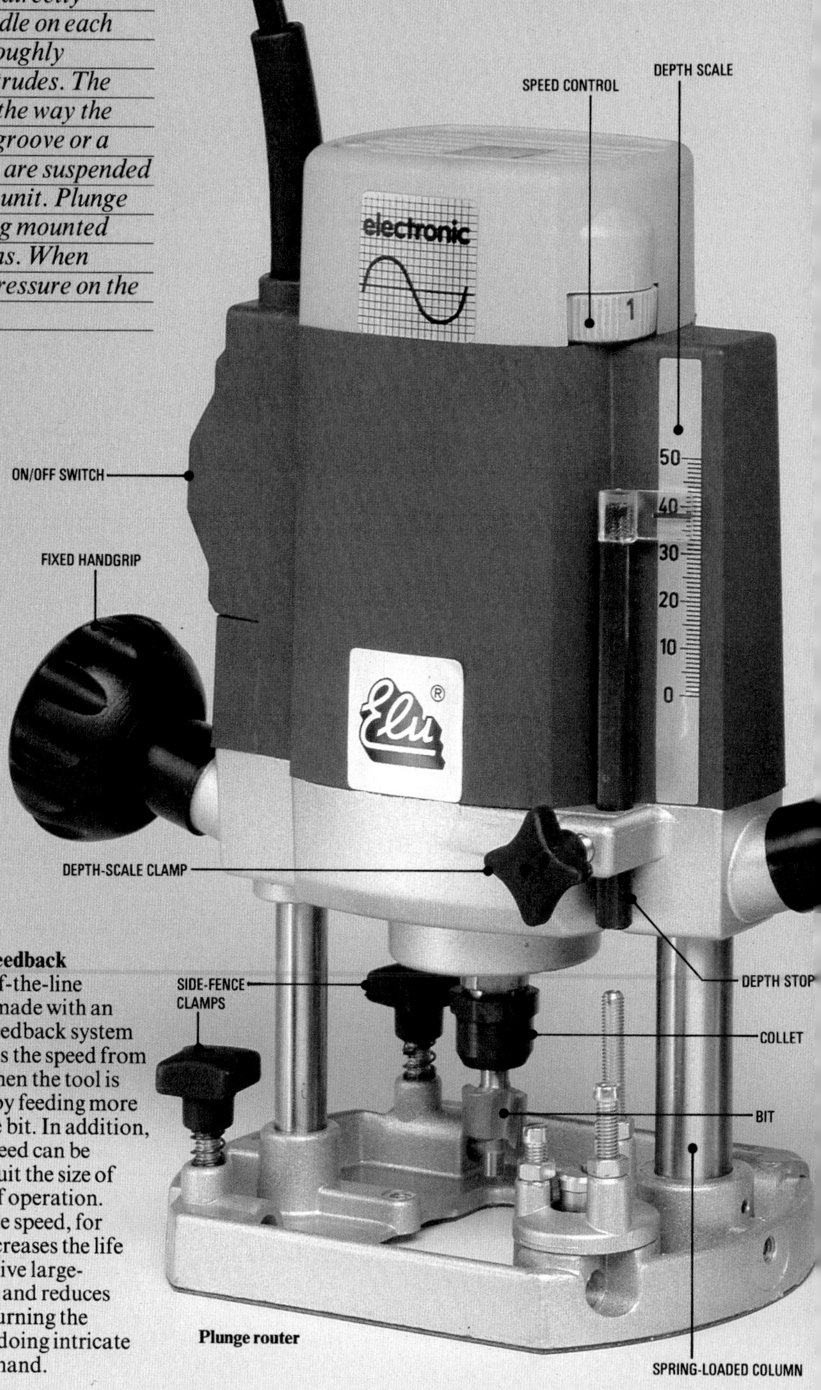

On/off switch
Ideally the on/off switch should be in reach without having to release your grip on the handles.

Base
It is an advantage if the base has a nonstick surface so that the tool slides smoothly across the work.

Plunge router

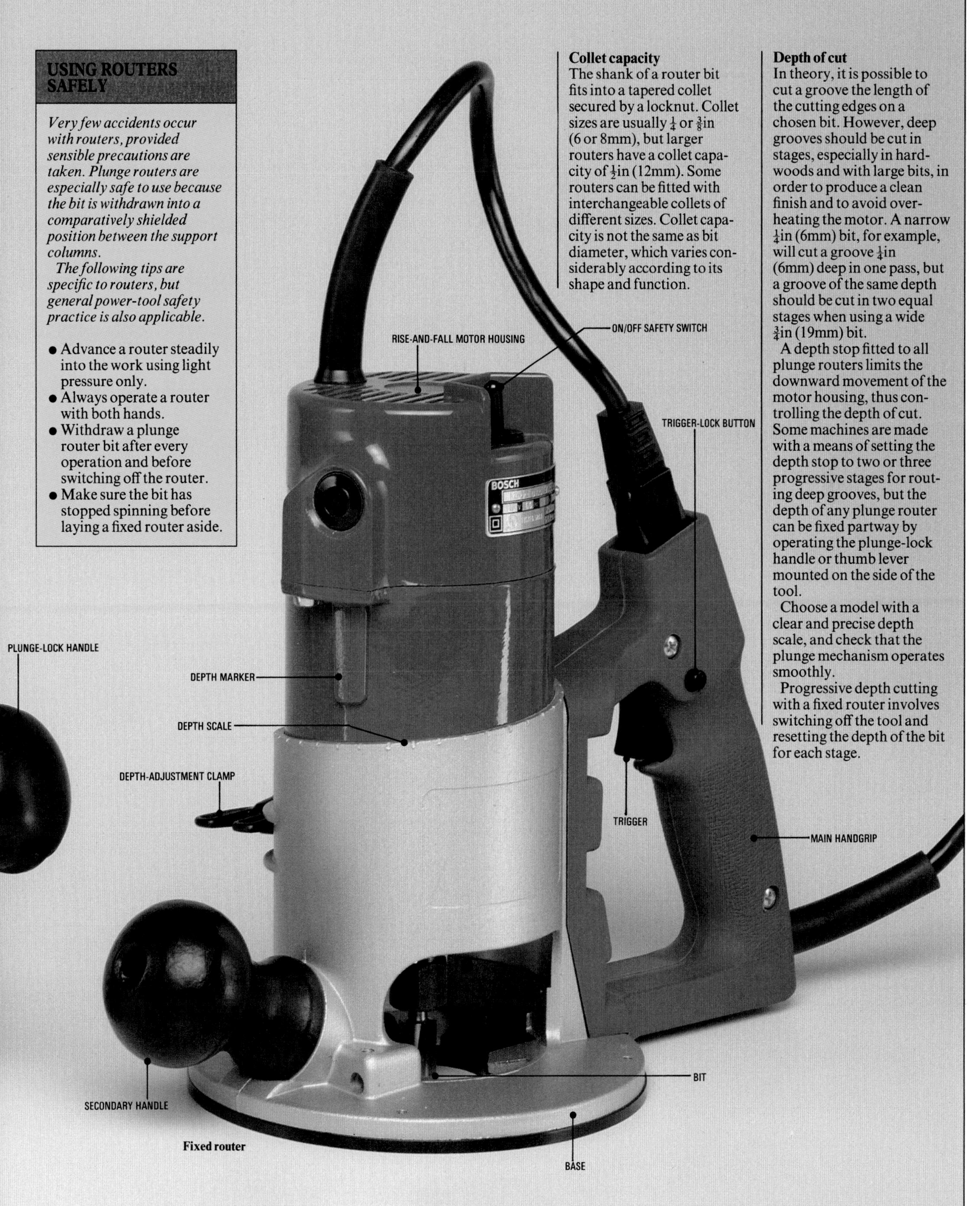

Fixed router

USING ROUTERS SAFELY

Very few accidents occur with routers, provided sensible precautions are taken. Plunge routers are especially safe to use because the bit is withdrawn into a comparatively shielded position between the support columns.

The following tips are specific to routers, but general power-tool safety practice is also applicable.

- Advance a router steadily into the work using light pressure only.
- Always operate a router with both hands.
- Withdraw a plunge router bit after every operation and before switching off the router.
- Make sure the bit has stopped spinning before laying a fixed router aside.

Collet capacity
The shank of a router bit fits into a tapered collet secured by a locknut. Collet sizes are usually $\frac{1}{4}$ or $\frac{3}{8}$in (6 or 8mm), but larger routers have a collet capacity of $\frac{1}{2}$in (12mm). Some routers can be fitted with interchangeable collets of different sizes. Collet capacity is not the same as bit diameter, which varies considerably according to its shape and function.

Depth of cut
In theory, it is possible to cut a groove the length of the cutting edges on a chosen bit. However, deep grooves should be cut in stages, especially in hardwoods and with large bits, in order to produce a clean finish and to avoid overheating the motor. A narrow $\frac{1}{4}$in (6mm) bit, for example, will cut a groove $\frac{1}{4}$in (6mm) deep in one pass, but a groove of the same depth should be cut in two equal stages when using a wide $\frac{3}{4}$in (19mm) bit.

A depth stop fitted to all plunge routers limits the downward movement of the motor housing, thus controlling the depth of cut. Some machines are made with a means of setting the depth stop to two or three progressive stages for routing deep grooves, but the depth of any plunge router can be fixed partway by operating the plunge-lock handle or thumb lever mounted on the side of the tool.

Choose a model with a clear and precise depth scale, and check that the plunge mechanism operates smoothly.

Progressive depth cutting with a fixed router involves switching off the tool and resetting the depth of the bit for each stage.

ROUTER BITS

High-speed-steel router bits are more than adequate for the average woodworker, but tungsten-carbide-tipped bits stay sharp longer, especially when routing chipboard or plastic-laminated materials. You can hone the cutting edges of high-speed-steel bits with an oiled slipstone until they eventually need to be resharpened by a professional. But take care to avoid overheating high-speed-steel bits, which turns them blue so they lose temper and become so soft that they have to be replaced. Tungsten-carbide-tipped bits can be sharpened only by a company with a specialized grinding machine.

There is a range of cheap pressed-steel bits that, although they cannot compare with high-speed-steel bits in quality, will allow you to experiment with different types of bits without having to spend a great deal of money. They are also useful for the amateur woodworker who wants to cut a particular molding only once and does not need a bit that will have to perform for a whole production run.

SEE ALSO

Cabinet construction	62-73
Drawer construction	71
Slipstones	103
Safety tips	124,141
Cutting dadoes	144
Cutting moldings and rabbets	144

High-speed-steel bit

Tungsten-carbide-tipped bit

GROOVE-FORMING BITS

The following basic router bits can make recesses both with and across the grain:

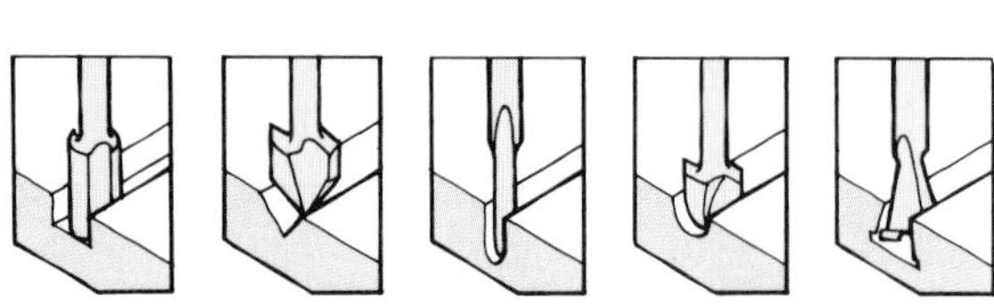

Straight bit
Cuts square-section grooves and housings. You can buy straight bits with either single-fluted or double-fluted cutting edges. The double-fluted variety leaves a better finish.

V-grooving bit
Used mainly for freehand lettering or engraving for signs and wall plaques.

Veining bit
For narrow round-bottom grooves.

Core-box bit
For wider round-bottom grooves.

Dovetail bit
For cutting dovetail joints with the appropriate jig and for dovetail housings.

- **Plunge-cut bits**
If you intend to plunge-cut with a router bit larger than $\frac{3}{8}$in (9mm) in diameter, make sure it has a cutting edge that extends right across its tip.

EDGE-FORMING BITS

Edge-forming bits are made with a pilot tip that rides against the edge of the work, making a guide or fence unnecessary. Fixed pilot tips can burn the wood due to friction, but in normal circumstances, skimming the edge with a finely set plane removes the blemish. However, this can be uneconomical in commercial production and special ball-bearing-tipped bits are made to run against the edge without burning.

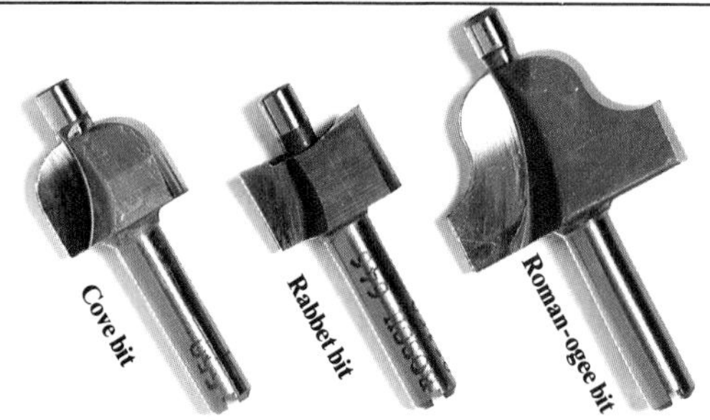

Cove bit
For a decorative scalloped edge, or for cutting a rule joint for the top of a drop-leaf table.

Rabbet bit
Cuts a rabbet without having to use a side fence on the router.

Roman-ogee bit
Produces a specific decorative molding.

Trimmer bit
Bit with ball-bearing pilot for trimming plastic laminates flush with the edge of a board.

Roundover bit
Produces a simple radiused edge. If set lower, cuts an ovolo bead (a radiused edge with a stepped shoulder).

Beading bit
Similar to a roundover bit, but it cuts two shoulders on the beading.

Chamfer bit
Cuts a 45-degree bevel. One bit makes different-size chamfers, depending on its depth setting.

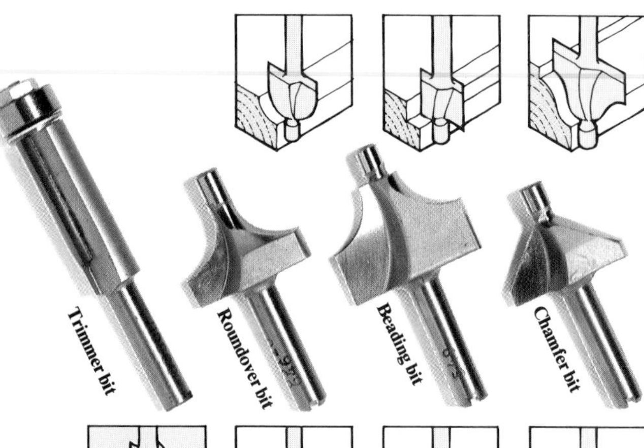

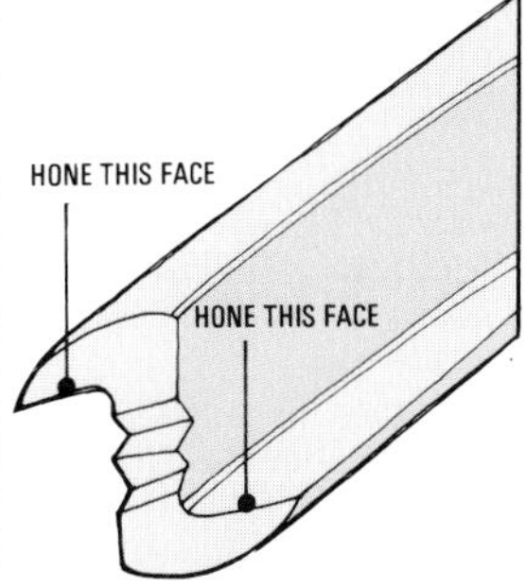

Honing a router bit
To put a sharp edge on a high-speed-steel bit, hone the inner faces only; touching the outer faces will change the bit's diameter.

Fitting a bit
Before using a wrench to loosen the collet locknut, you have to immobilize the spindle connected to the router motor.

On some routers, this is achieved by depressing a spindle-lock button or slide, but with other machines you use either a second wrench or a short metal pin passed through a hole in the spindle **(1)**.

Depending on the design of the router, you may be able to stand the machine upside-down on a bench to change a bit, or it may be easier to remove the motor housing from its base assembly. Whichever method you use, unplug the router first.

If a bit is jammed in the collet, free it by rocking the shaft gently from side to side. Be careful; bits are sharp. Take note that some new "safety collets" require you to break loose the nut twice to remove a bit. Always clean any dust from the collet before inserting another bit.

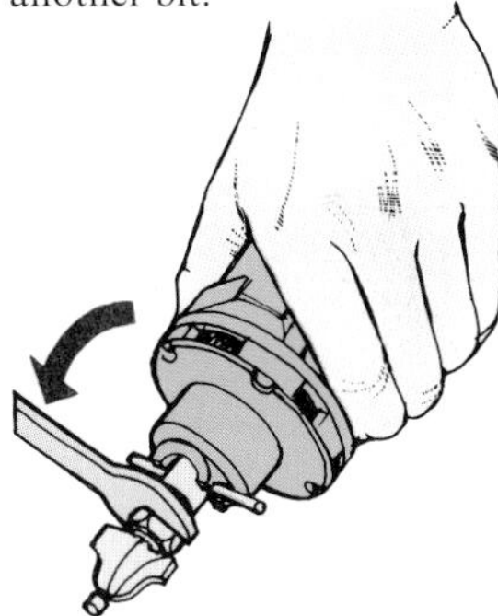

1 Loosening the collet nut
A pin is sometimes used to immobilize the router spindle.

ROUTING GROOVES AND DADOES

A true groove runs in the direction of the grain and is used a great deal in woodwork to hold drawer bottoms, the backs of cabinets, edge-to-edge joints and so on.

A dado is a groove which runs across the grain – for joining fixed shelves to the sides of a bookcase, for example. A groove or housing can run through the work from one edge to another, or it may be stopped at one or both ends.

Although a variety of techniques can be employed to ensure the accuracy of the work, the manipulation of the machine remains more or less the same.

Making a through dado or groove
Lower and lock the tool's plunge mechanism. Rest the router base on the work with the cutter clear of the edge, and then switch on. Feed the router into and through the work at a steady rate until the cutter emerges at the other end. Switch off and let the cutter come to rest before lifting the base off the work.

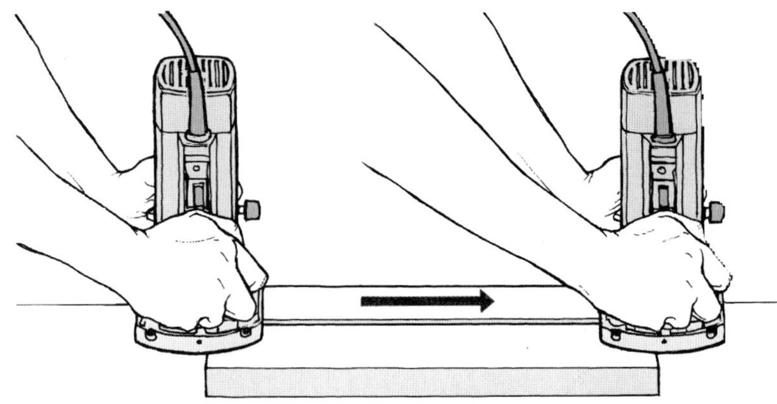

Cutting a through groove

Making a stopped groove or dado
Before switching on a plunge router, lower the cutter to the surface of the work and position it precisely over one end of the groove or dado. Lift the cutter, switch on and slowly plunge the cutter to its maximum depth **(1)**. Advance the tool to the far end, release the plunge mechanism **(2)** and then switch off. Use a chisel to trim the ends of the groove or dado square.

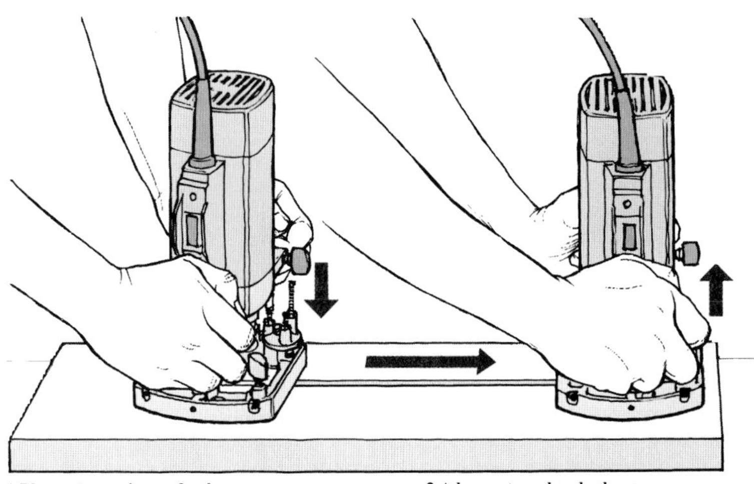

1 Plunge to maximum depth

2 Advance to end and release

Cutting a groove parallel to an edge
Most grooves, be they for drawer runners or a back panel, are usually parallel and quite close to the edge of the work. Manufacturers supply all routers with a bolt-on side fence which can be adjusted to place the cutter the required distance from the edge.

With the tool unplugged, stand the router on the work and align the cutting edge of the cutter with one side of the groove drawn on the surface **(1)**. Adjust the side fence to touch the edge of the work **(2)**, and tighten its clamps. Cut the groove as described above, keeping side pressure on the fence throughout the operation **(3)**.

For greater control, extend a side fence by screwing a strip of hardwood to its face.

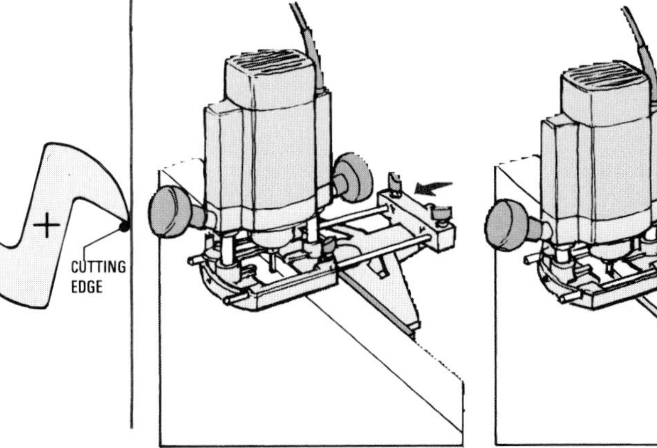

1 Align bit

2 Slide fence up to edge

3 Cut the groove

SEE ALSO
Man-made boards 34-38
Cabinet construction 62-73
Safety tips 124,141
Router bits 142

Cutting a dado using guide battens

Clamp a batten across the work to guide the base when routing a dado across a wide board **(1)**. Choose a batten long enough to extend beyond both edges of the work, and keep the router pressed against it.

To cut a dado wider than the bit, clamp two guide battens to the work parallel to one another and positioned to align the bit first with one side of the dado then with the other. Always make the first pass against the batten on your right-hand side, then move the router over to cut against the left-hand batten **(2)**. This way the rotation of the bit helps to pull the router against the batten.

To cut a barefaced dovetail housing, substitute a dovetail bit for the straight bit after the first pass **(3)**.

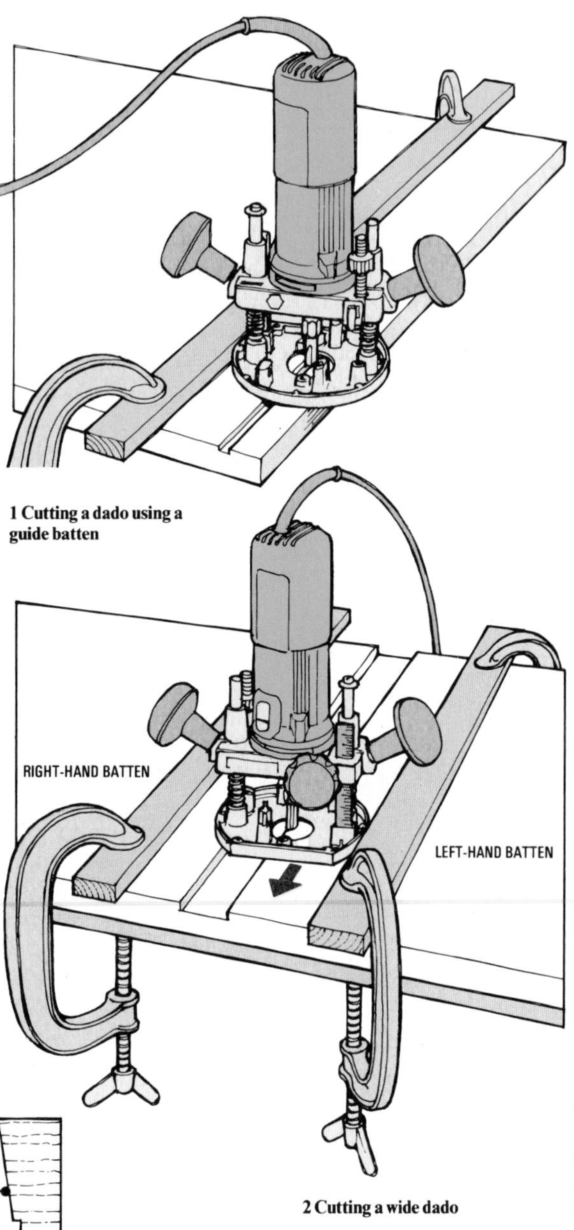

1 Cutting a dado using a guide batten

2 Cutting a wide dado

3 Cutting a barefaced dovetail housing

CUTTING MOLDINGS AND RABBETS

Solid panels and frames are often molded for decorative purposes, to lighten their appearance, or to make a safe rounded edge. Rabbets are more functional – used to recess a panel in a frame, for example.

Rabbeting with a straight bit

It is possible to cut a rabbet with a straight bit by running a guide fence along the opposite edge of the work. The same method can be used to cut a chamfer with a V-grooving bit or a cove with a core-box bit.

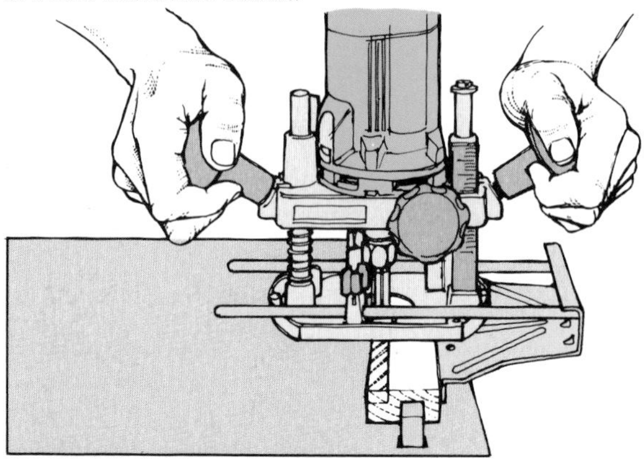

Rabbeting with straight bit and guide fence

Molding with edge-forming bits

Molding or rabbeting the edge of a wide panel is achieved by using an edge-forming bit with a piloted tip. Practice on scrap wood to develop a light touch, which keeps the piloted tip in contact with the work without burning.

Mold the outer edge of a panel in a counterclockwise direction, to ensure the rotation of the bit keeps pulling it into the work **(1)**. If the panel is made of solid wood, mold the end grain first then the side grain **(2)**. This ensures that if the bit tears out the end grain at the far edge of the board, the damage is remedied as the sides of the board are molded. To mold end grain only, clamp a strip of scrap wood to the far edge to support it.

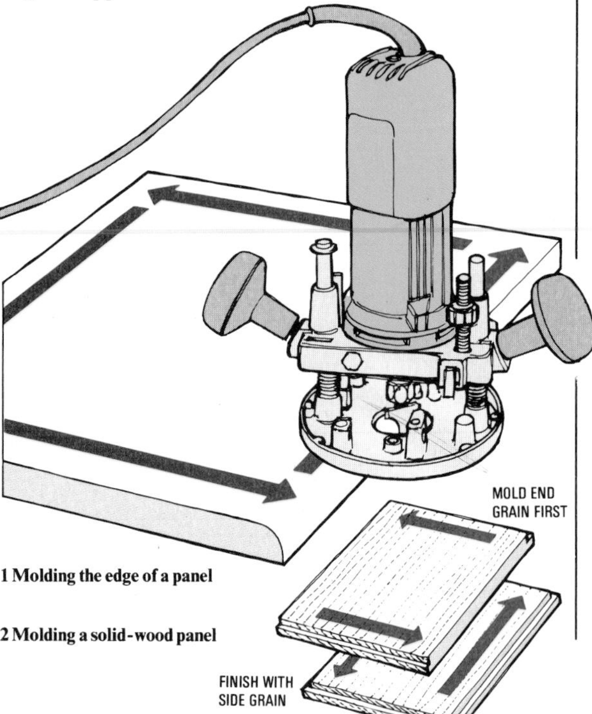

1 Molding the edge of a panel

2 Molding a solid-wood panel

Molding or rabbeting inside a frame
It is sometimes convenient to rabbet or mold a picture or mirror frame after the bare frame has been assembled. The outer edge can be molded as described opposite, and the inner edge rabbeted using an edge-forming rabbet bit or by screwing a 90-degree triangular block of wood to the side fence **(1)**. It is essential that the apex of the triangle be centered on the bit **(2)**.
Move the machine on a clockwise path when routing the inside of a frame. The bit will leave rounded corners – but you can chop them square with a chisel, if you wish.

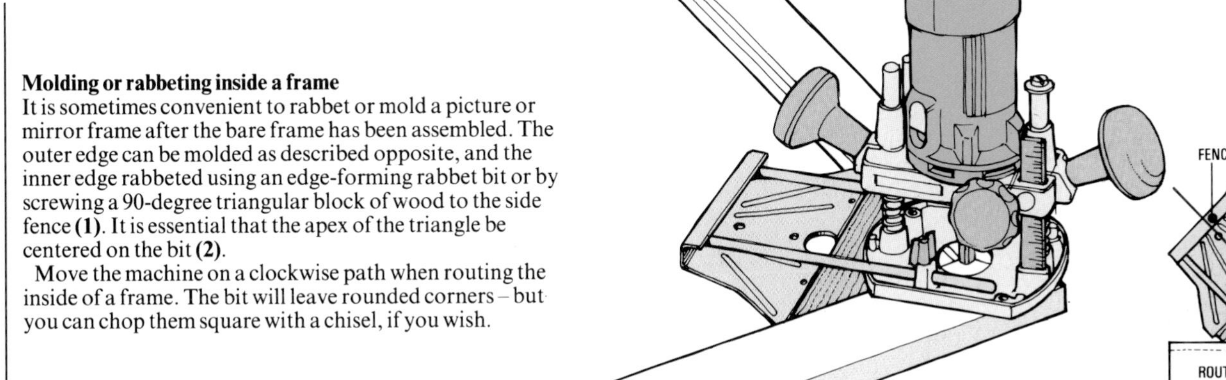

1 Cutting an internal rabbet
Screw a triangular guide block to the router fence.

2 Center the triangle on the bit

ROUTING CIRCLES AND SHAPES

Using commercially made guides or homemade jigs and templates, it is possible to cut intricately shaped work and perfect circles, discs and curves.

Cutting circles
With the addition of a centering pin, the side fence of most routers can be converted into an adjustable trammel for rotating the machine around a central point so you can cut circular grooves or mold the edge of a disc.
The average fence is ideal for detailing small work such as cheese or bread boards. For larger work (for example, to mold the edge of a circular table top) bolt the router to one end of a strip of plywood, cut a hole or slot for the bit and drive a nail through the strip to act as a centering pin.
Use double-faced tape to stick a small patch of plywood to the work, to hold the point of the centering pin and avoid leaving a hole in the wood.

Routing with a template
Routing against a template provides a quick and easy means of making identical components – and once you are satisfied with the accuracy of the template, a perfect result is guaranteed every time.
To assist in the faithful reproduction of the shape of the template, router manufacturers supply template guides for their machines. A template guide, or guide bushing, is simply a cylindrical collar that surrounds the bit and is bolted centrally on the base of the router. The collar runs against the edge of the template so that the bit follows its shape exactly **(1)**. When making a template, you need to allow for the difference between the diameter of the collar and the diameter of the bit itself **(2)**.
Cut a template from a stable sheet material such as plywood, hardboard or MDF. You can either nail it to the wood or attach it with double-faced tape.

Freehand routing
Sign writers and low-relief carvers use a router to engrave lettering or pictures on a flat piece of wood. A V-grooving bit is often used for freehand work because even hardwoods offer very little resistance to its pointed tip. Straight or veining bits are also suitable, but you will need to adjust the router to take a shallow cut only. Since a free-flowing action is essential, choose a style of lettering that allows you to keep the router moving. Regular lettering is best cut with a template.
A plunge router is much better than a fixed machine for freehand work; to be able to lift and replace the bit effortlessly is a considerable advantage.

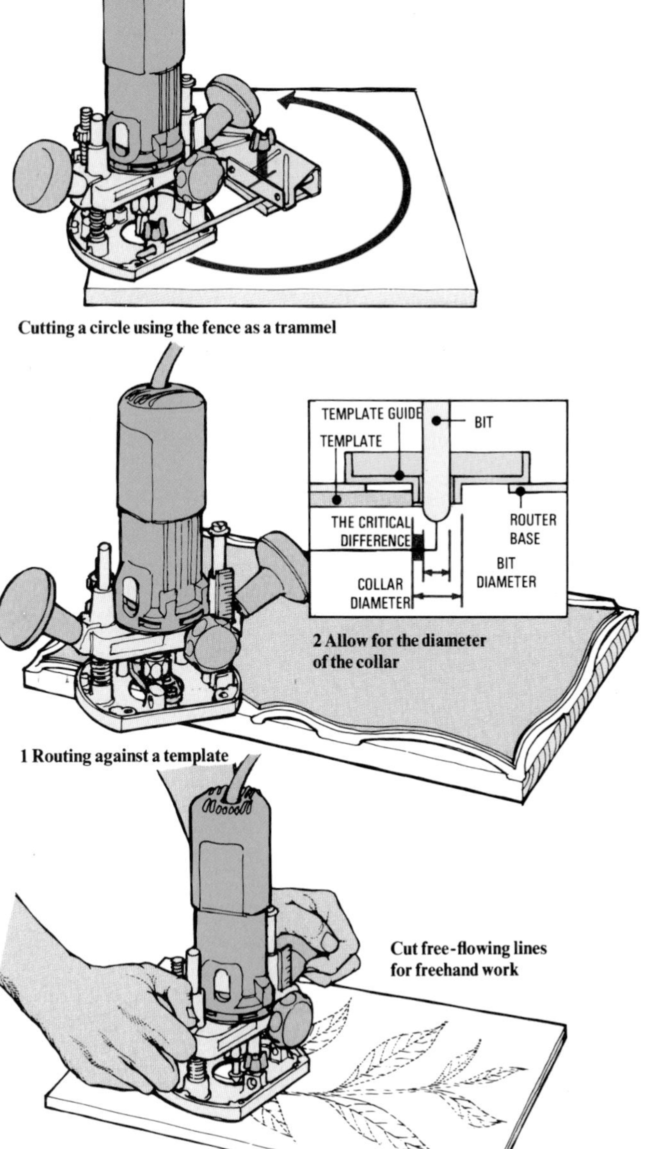

Cutting a circle using the fence as a trammel

2 Allow for the diameter of the collar

1 Routing against a template

Cut free-flowing lines for freehand work

CUTTING JOINTS WITH A ROUTER

Cutting joints is a lot easier if you convert a router into a shaper or spindle molder by bolting it upside down in a workcenter. However, it is possible to cut a number of joints with a hand-held router by using a combination of techniques described in the sections on routing grooves and dadoes and cutting moldings and rabbets.

SEE ALSO

Drop-leaf tables	58-59
Safety tips	124,141
Router bits	142
Sanding-belt grades	148
Workcenters	151,154
Belt sanders	190-191
Dust collectors	214
Face mask	214
Table hinge	307

Rabbeted and grooved joints

Half-blind joints, barefaced housings and half-lapped joints are variations on a basic theme. By clamping several components together on a bench you can cut any of these joints, using a straight bit in a router run against a guide batten.

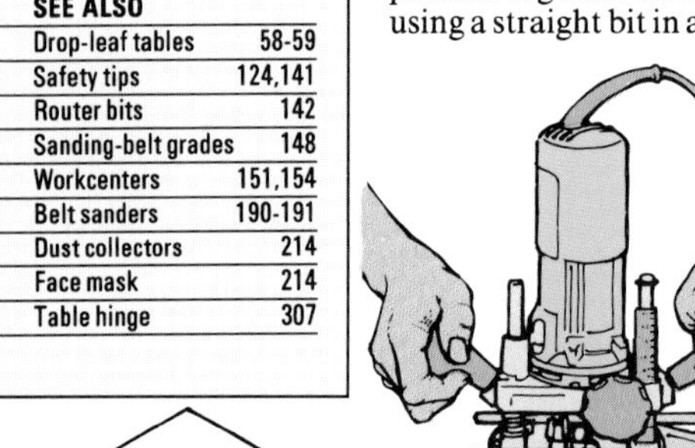

Half-blind joint

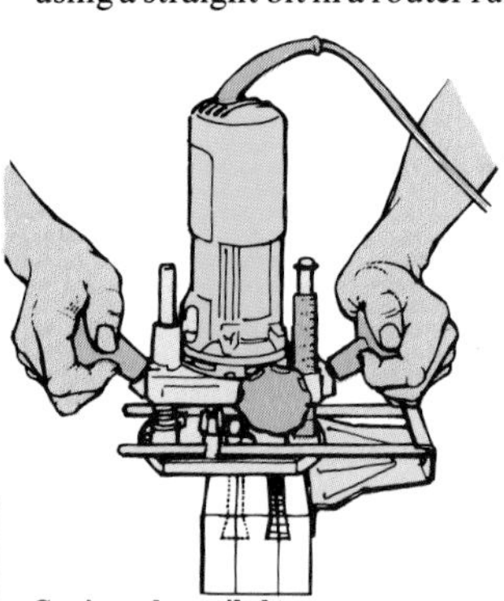

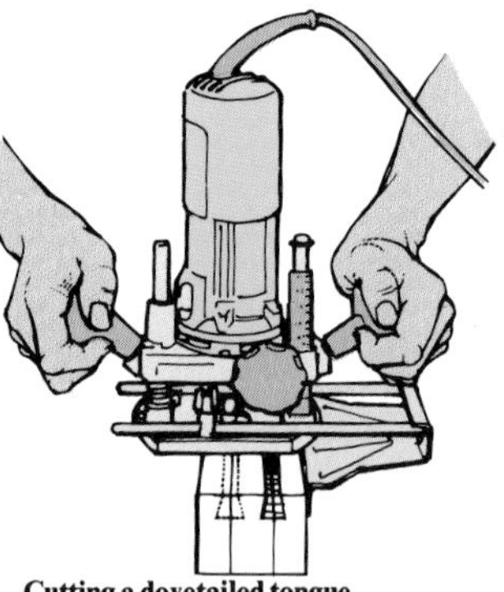

Cutting a dovetailed tongue

Dovetail housing joints

Cutting a dovetail housing joint by hand is a long, difficult process, whereas cutting both components with a router and a dovetail bit is extremely simple.

Cut the housing against a guide batten, then clamp the mating component between two pieces of scrap wood. Use a side fence to guide the bit along both sides of the work to leave a dovetailed tongue that matches the housing exactly.

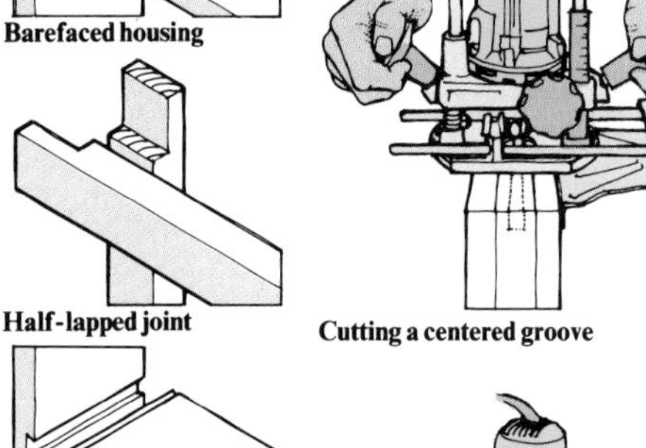

Barefaced housing

Half-lapped joint

Cutting a centered groove

Tongue and groove joints

Use a straight bit to rout a square tongue on the edge of a board, following the method described above for making a dovetailed tongue. Cut a matching groove down the center of the other board, using a wooden strip clamped to both sides to provide a wide flush surface to support the base of the router.

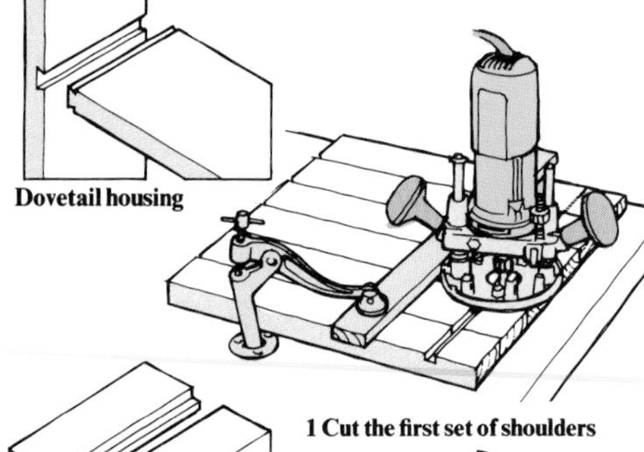

Dovetail housing

1 Cut the first set of shoulders

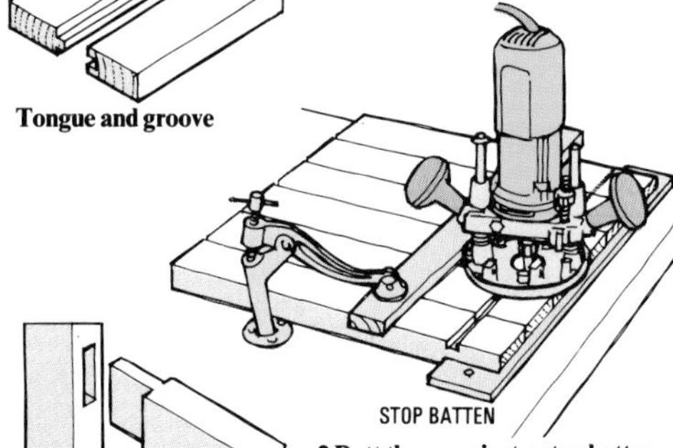

Tongue and groove

2 Butt them against a stop batten

Mortise and tenon

Mortise and tenon joints

A mortise is no more than a short groove and is cut as described above but, being a stopped groove, it is much easier to achieve with a plunge router because the base remains fully supported as the bit enters and leaves the work. Make several passes of increasing depth.

To make matching tenons, lay the components side by side and cut all the shoulders simultaneously, using a clamped batten to guide the router **(1)**. Remove the rest of the waste, working with the router freehand. Rout the ends of the tenons, then work toward the shoulders, so as to leave support for the router base. Turn all the pieces over, butt the newly cut shoulders against a stop batten nailed to the bench **(2)** and repeat the process to complete the tenons.

Rule joints

A rule joint is the traditional way to join the folding flaps to the top of a gate-leg table. It supports the edge of the flap when it is raised, and hides the special table hinges when folded. The knuckles of the hinges must be set directly below the shoulder of the joint. Mold the edges with matching roundover and core-box bits.

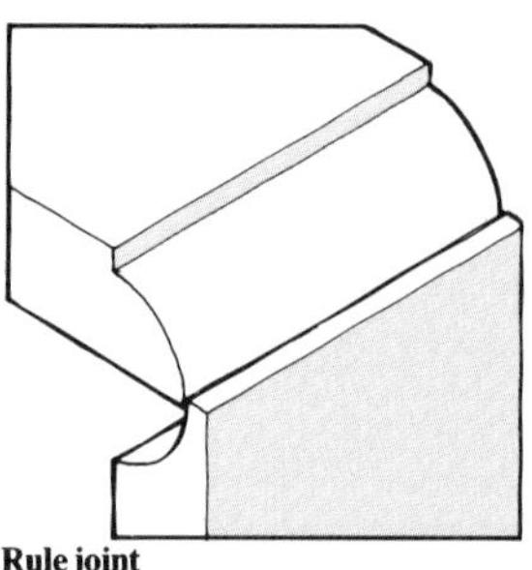

Rule joint

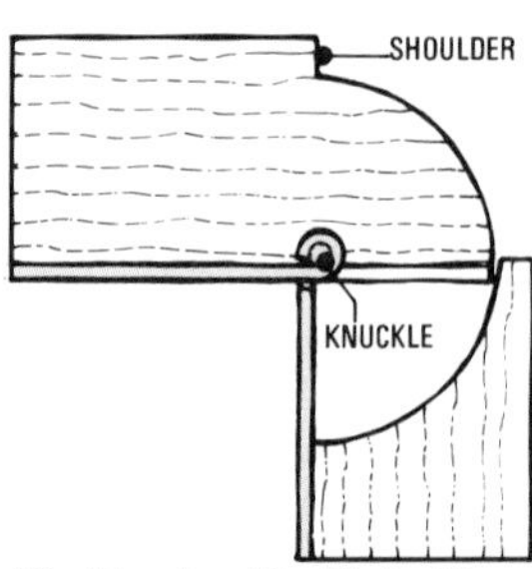

Align hinge knuckle with shoulder

Dovetail joints

Special templates and matching template guides are made for cutting dovetails with hand-held routers. Most of them cut half-blind dovetails only. Although a machine-cut dovetail may not be as attractive as one made by hand, it is just as strong and much faster to make. Detailed instructions for assembling jigs are supplied by the manufacturers, but basically the two matching components are clamped together in the jig, slightly offset and inside out **(1)**. Design the width of the components so that the dovetails and pins are centered on each piece of wood.

Fit a dovetail bit in the router and guide it in and out of the template fingers **(2)**. Remove the components and turn them the right way **(3)** for assembly.

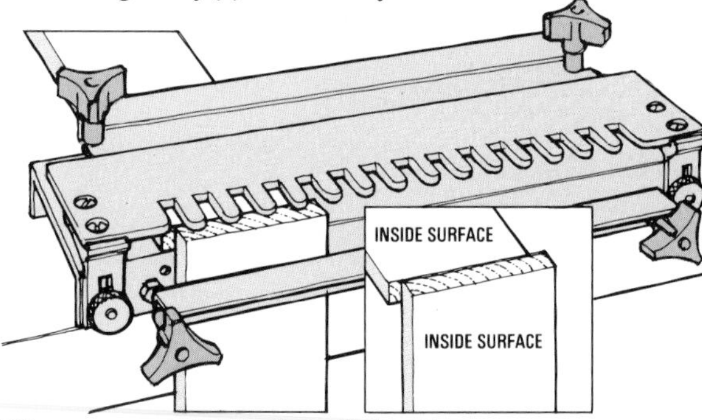

1 Clamp components slightly offset and inside out

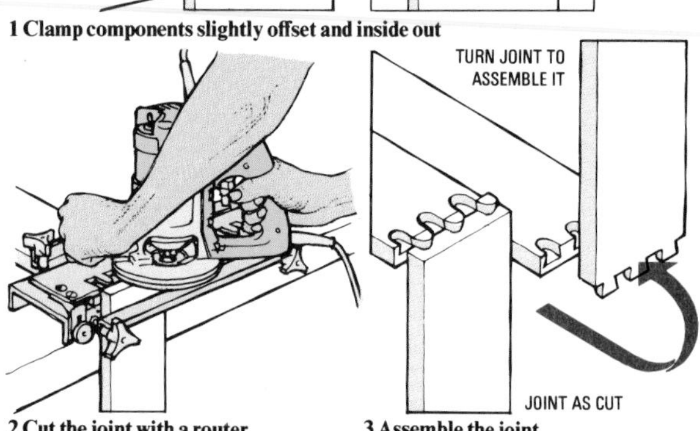

2 Cut the joint with a router

3 Assemble the joint

SANDERS

Electric sanders take most of the effort out of finishing wood, but even the orbital machines – the so-called "finishing sanders" – will not produce a surface that a craftsman would consider ready for polishing or varnishing. A period of hand-sanding is necessary to remove minute scratches left by the machines.

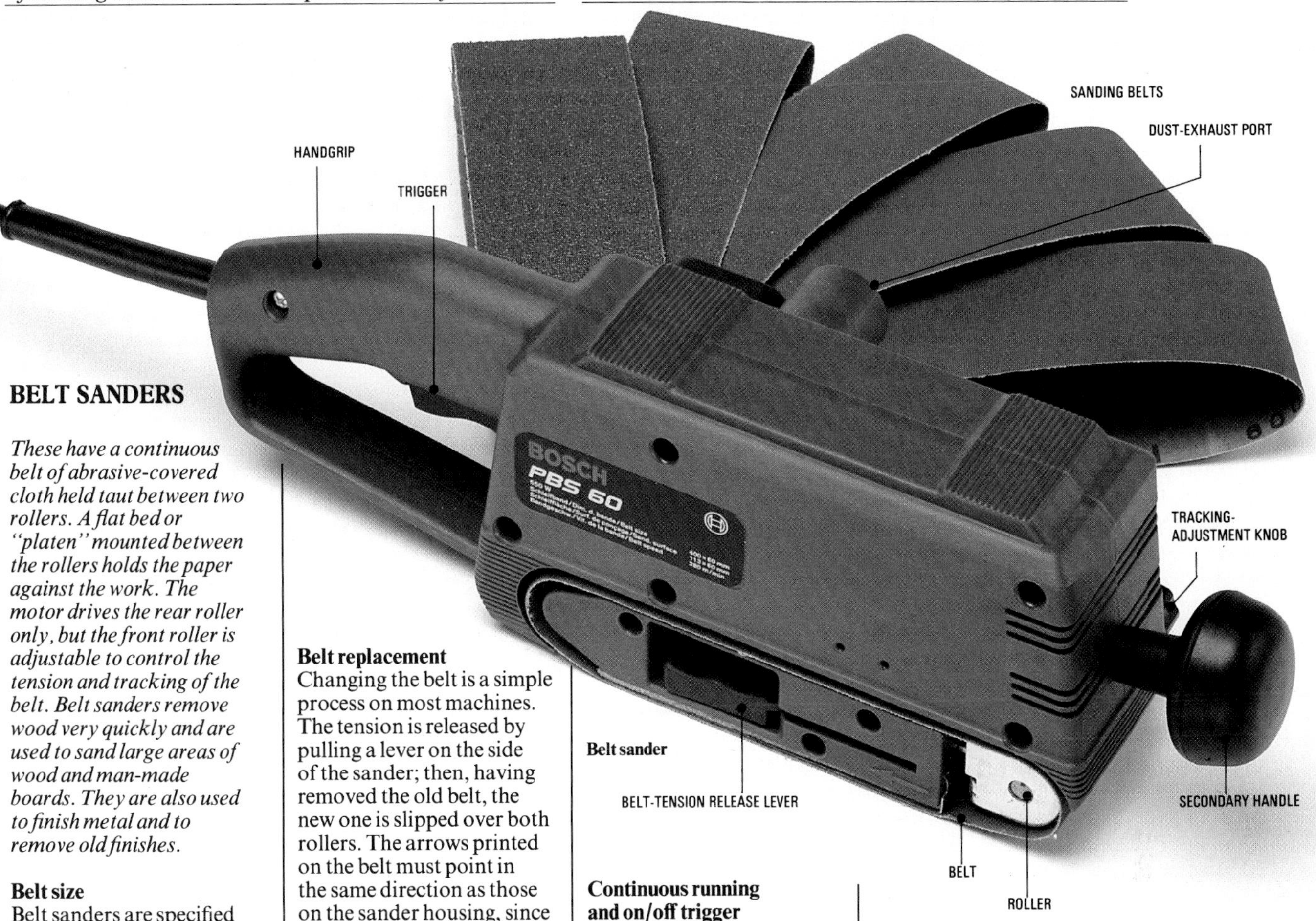

Belt sander

BELT SANDERS

These have a continuous belt of abrasive-covered cloth held taut between two rollers. A flat bed or "platen" mounted between the rollers holds the paper against the work. The motor drives the rear roller only, but the front roller is adjustable to control the tension and tracking of the belt. Belt sanders remove wood very quickly and are used to sand large areas of wood and man-made boards. They are also used to finish metal and to remove old finishes.

Belt size
Belt sanders are specified according to the size of the abrasive belt. A small lightweight machine will have a belt about 2⅜in (60mm) wide and 16in (400mm) long. Larger machines have belt sizes of 3 × 21in (75 × 533mm) and 4 × 24in (100 × 620mm). Large belt sanders are heavy and can be tiring to use for prolonged periods.

Belt speed
Most sanders have a "no-load" speed of between 585 and 1235 sanding feet (180 and 380m) per minute. Variable-speed models can be set as low as 487 SFPM (150m per minute) for heat-sensitive materials, such as paint, and can be adjusted to high speeds for wood and boards.

Belt replacement
Changing the belt is a simple process on most machines. The tension is released by pulling a lever on the side of the sander; then, having removed the old belt, the new one is slipped over both rollers. The arrows printed on the belt must point in the same direction as those on the sander housing, since the joint on the belt will start to open up if it runs the wrong way. The new belt is tensioned by pushing back the lever.

With the sander running, the tracking-adjustment knob is used to move the belt sideways until it is centered on the rollers.

Dust collection
All belt sanders are supplied with a dust-collecting bag. This is an essential safeguard when sanding wood, but the bag must be removed when finishing metal, to avoid the risk of fire caused by sparks.

Electrical insulation
Choose a sander with a plastic body that insulates the user from electric shock.

Continuous running and on/off trigger
The on/off trigger can be locked for continuous running by pressing a button on the handgrip.

Secondary handle
It would be difficult to lower or lift the sander from the wood without the use of a secondary handle on the front of the machine. However, it is convenient if the secondary handle can be removed for sanding up to an obstruction.

Sanding frame
On some machines it is possible to fit an adjustable sanding frame surrounding the belt. This limits the depth of cut, which makes for accurate sanding over a large surface and protects thin veneers.

SAFE SANDING

Sanding machines are not particularly dangerous tools, but a coarse-grade belt running at high speed can cause a very painful wound. Follow the general rules for power-tool safety. In addition:

- Attach a dust bag whenever you are sanding wood – and if the bag cannot cope with the amount of dust being created, wear a face mask.
- Hold the machine in both hands and do not lay the sander aside until the belt has stopped moving.

SANDING BELTS

Use a coarse-grade belt on rough work, following up with a medium-grade and finally a fine-grade belt to remove the scratches left by the previous grade.

A torn, clogged or worn belt will damage the work and should be changed as soon as possible.

SEE ALSO

Safety tips	124,150
Sanding sheets	150
Using orbital sanders	150
Dust collectors	214

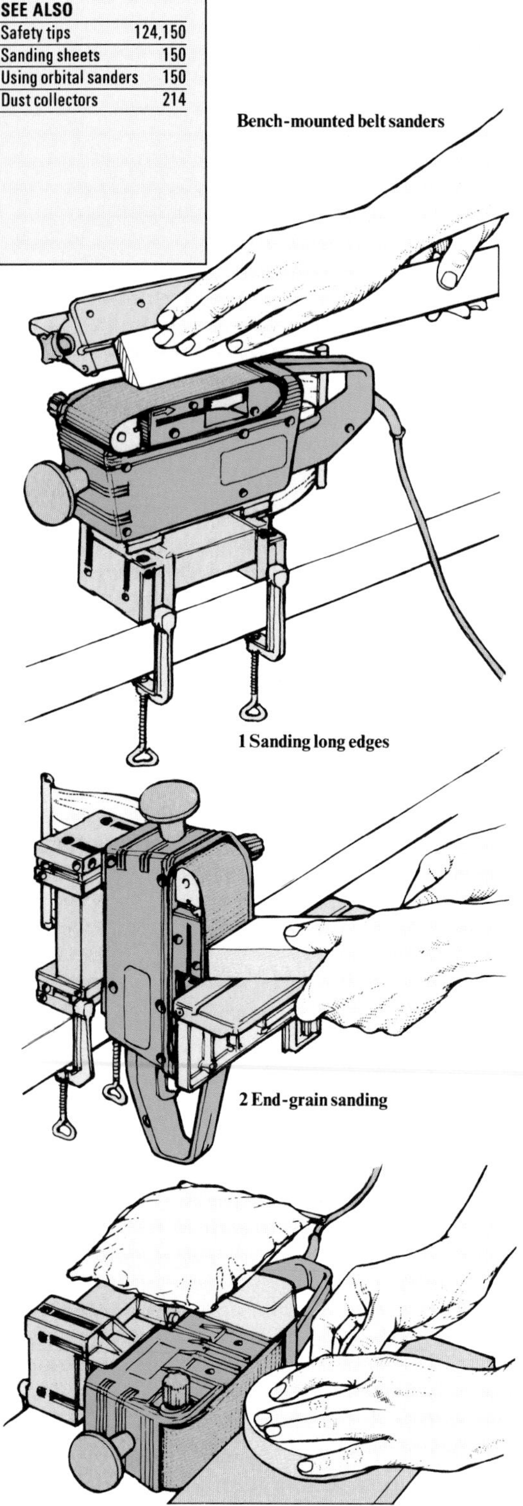

Bench-mounted belt sanders

1 Sanding long edges

2 End-grain sanding

3 Shaping with a belt sander

A typical range of sanding-belt grades	
40 grit	Very coarse
60 grit	Coarse
80 grit	Medium
100 grit	Medium
150 grit	Fine
220 grit	Very fine

Using a belt sander
Switch on the machine and lower it onto the work. As soon as the abrasive touches the surface, move the sander forward; if you hold it in one place, it will leave deep scratches in the wood that may be difficult to remove. Sand with the grain, in parallel overlapping strokes. To remove paint or smooth very rough wood, sand across the grain at 45 degrees in two directions, then finish parallel to the grain.

Take care to keep the machine flat on the work as you sand up to the edges of a board. It is very easy to round over the edges. With veneered board in particular, it is worth pinning narrow softwood battens around the edges, flush with the surface, to make sure you do not sand the edges through to the core.

Lift the machine off the work before you switch it off.

Fixed applications
Belt sanders can be clamped to a bench in various positions. Clamped upside down with an optional fence **(1)**, the tool can be used to sand long square or beveled faces. Stood on end, it can sand end grain **(2)**; and laid on its side, it can be used for shaping work **(3)**.

ORBITAL SANDERS

On an orbital sander, a strip of abrasive paper is stretched across a foam-rubber pad that covers the entire baseplate of the machine. An electric motor drives the plate with a continuous, tight elliptical motion. A few machines are made to switch to a straight reciprocal stroke to remove the swirls of fine scratches left on the surface by this orbital motion. Other sanders are made with a random orbital action that breaks up the regular pattern of scratches, making them less noticeable. Sanding attachments for power drills are clumsy tools that lack many of the features built into more sophisticated machines.

Sanding-sheet size
Although strips of abrasive paper are made specifically to fit sanding machines, they are based on a proportion of the standard-size sheet used for sanding by hand. The larger machines are known as $\frac{1}{2}$ or $\frac{1}{3}$ sheet sanders, with actual sanding areas of 40sq in (260sq cm) and 29sq in (167sq cm) respectively. Small palm-grip models are made as $\frac{1}{4}$ sheet sanders, with a sanding area of 17sq in (110sq cm).

Sanding rate
The sanding rate of an orbital sander is specified in rotations per minute. A fixed rate of about 20,000 to 25,000 rpm is normal, although there are variable-speed sanders that can be adjusted to rates as low as 6000 rpm for working on heat-sensitive plastics and finishes. Sanding rates can be preselected, or varied by the amount of pressure applied to the trigger. If you intend to use a sander for woodwork only, a variable-speed model has limited advantages.

Tool weight
Even $\frac{1}{3}$ sheet sanders are relatively lightweight – and the palm-grip machines designed to be operated with one hand, which weigh about 2lb (1kg) only, are exceptionally easy to use.

1/3 sanding sheets

Straight-line switch
High-speed orbital action produces the most scratch-free surface under general conditions. However, for final smooth sanding with the grain, some sanders may be switched to straight-line action.

Trigger lock
All orbital sanders are made with a trigger lock for continuous running.

Dust collection
The better orbital sanders are made with integral dust-collection systems. Ducts and channels in the base-plate suck dust from around the edge of the machine and deposit it in a dust-collecting bag. Some manufacturers supply a dust shroud that surrounds the base-plate and can be connected to a vacuum cleaner. Other models can be connected to a vacuum cleaner via a hose attachment in place of the dust-collecting bag.

Electrical insulation
Plastic bodies not only make for lightweight sanding machines but also insulate the user from live electrical components.

NEW DESIGNS

Two new orbital sander designs have found wide acceptance among woodworkers since their introduction.

The name "random orbit" these days commonly means a machine with a round sandpaper disc that rotates as it vibrates, in contrast with older square- or rectangular-pad designs. The new machines gain faster cutting action without promoting scratching.

The "detail sander" has a small triangular platten that allows close sanding in restricted areas, such as in corners or around a chair seat's back spindles.

Orbital sander

Palm-grip sander

1/4 sanding sheets

SANDING SHEETS

Sanding sheets, regardless of size, are made in a range of grades, which are used in sequence from coarse to fine.

Change to a finer paper as soon as the scratches left by the previous grade disappear. Coarse grades are suitable for sanding sawn softwood and other rough work. Medium to fine grades produce a good finish ready for a light hand-sanding. On thin veneers, use very fine grades only.

Abrasive grit is packed closely together on "closed-coat" paper for fast general-purpose sanding. "Open-coat" papers have widely spaced grit for sanding resinous softwoods, which would clog other papers very quickly.

Some sheets are already perforated to increase the efficiency of dust collection. Alternatively, special templates are available to punch holes in standard sheets of abrasive paper.

Usually sheets are held by a clamp at each end of the baseplate, but there are also self-adhesive strips that stick onto the baseplate pad.

SEE ALSO

Safety tips	124
Circular saws	132-133
Routers	140-141
Orbital sanders	148-149
Disc sanders	190-191
Health and safety	214

A typical range of sanding-sheet grades

40 grit	Very coarse
50 grit	Very coarse
60 grit	Coarse
80 grit	Coarse
100 grit	Medium
120 grit	Medium
150 grit	Fine
180 grit	Fine
220 grit	Very fine
280 grit	Very fine
320 grit	Very fine
400 grit	Very fine

Using an orbital sander
Keep an orbital sander moving up and down the work in overlapping parallel strokes. When using coarse grades of paper, take care not to round over the edges of the work or sand through veneers. There is no need to apply excessive pressure to the sander – the weight of the tool in itself is usually sufficient to sand the work efficiently.

Finishing with an orbital sander
Sand lightly with overlapping parallel strokes.

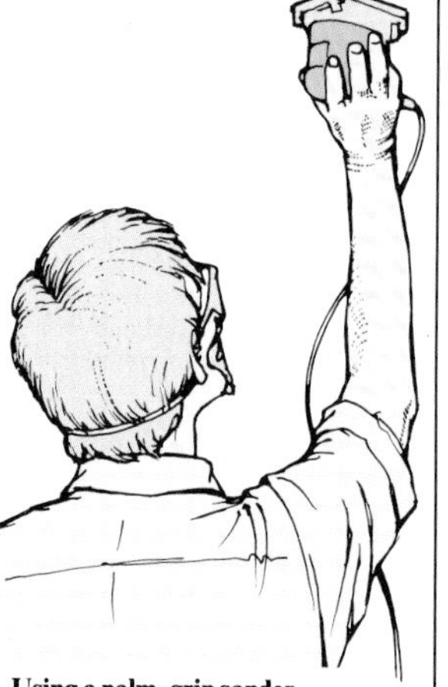

Using a palm-grip sander
This type of sander is light enough to be used overhead.

SAFETY AND SANDING

Provided the user follows the basic safety procedures recommended for power tools, an orbital sander is perfectly safe to operate.

- Wear safety goggles and a lightweight face mask when sanding overhead.
- Always unplug a sander before changing paper.

DISC SANDERS

Flexible-disc sanders made to fit into the chuck of a power drill are often used for sanding floors and old finishes – but they leave deep cross-grain scratches and so are unsuitable for serious woodwork. A bench-mounted rigid-disc sander, on the other hand, is a useful tool in any workshop.

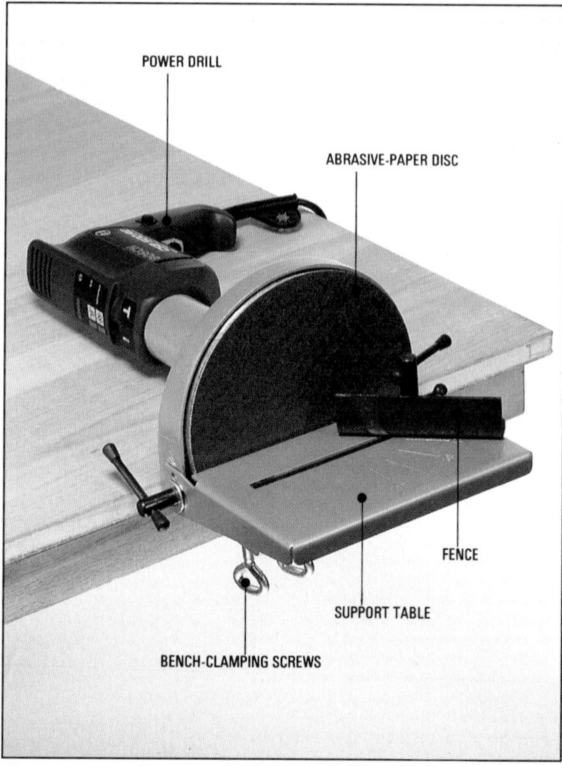

Bench-mounted sanders
A bench-mounted sander is a power-drill accessory used for sanding end grain and for shaping wooden components. It has a rigid metal sanding plate to which you glue abrasive-paper discs. A support table adjustable from horizontal to 45 degrees is bolted across the plate. With the work resting on the table, you can shape work freehand **(1)**. An adjustable fence that slides across the support table is used for accurately sanding square or beveled end grain **(2)**.

Use the "down" side of the disc only – so that the work is driven onto the support table by the rotation of the machine. Keep the work moving and, to avoid burning it, refrain from applying excessive pressure.

1 Freehand sanding
Rotate the work on the table as you lightly press it against the sanding disc.

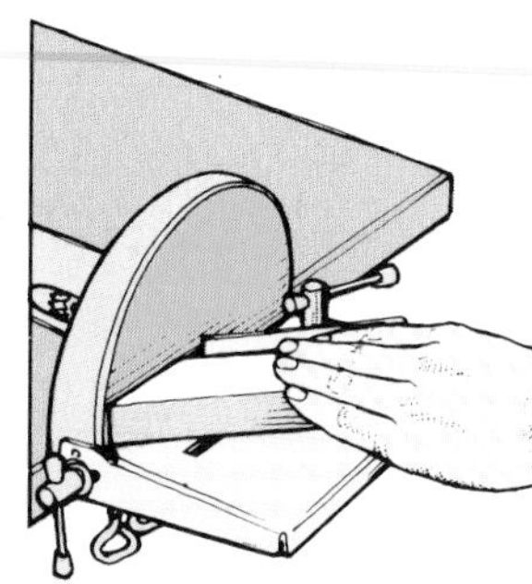

2 Using a fence
Accurately finish square or angled ends with the fence locked at the required angle.

WORKCENTERS

Power-tool manufacturers offer various accessories for converting portable circular saws, routers and jigsaws into bench-mounted tools, but the results rarely live up to the expectations of a serious woodworker. In many cases, the worktable is too small to support man-made boards, and the fences and guides are often short and flimsy. These accessories may be cheap to buy, but they cannot compare with a well-designed workcenter, which provides a generous-size saw-table or spindle-shaper facility, plus the opportunity to use the tools in the more usual overhead mode for crosscutting wide workpieces.

Workcenters are relatively lightweight and portable. They incorporate universal mounting plates, which accommodate any well-known power saw or router – and most woodworkers find it more efficient to have each tool permanently fixed to its own plate for immediate substitution in the workcenter.

ESSENTIAL FEATURES

When you select a workcenter, make certain it has the following features:

- Strong construction, with a rigid underframe supporting the workcenter at a comfortable work height.
- Generous-size table, with an optional extension to handle full-size sheets of chipboard, blockboard, etc.
- Efficient blade and cutter guards, because unless they work well and adjust easily, the user tends to disregard them. A riving knife fixed behind the blade to keep the sawkerf open is an essential safeguard, too.
- Rigid fences that will not move as the work is passed over the cutter or blade.
- A sliding crosscut/miter fence that runs smoothly. It should have a wide face to support the workpiece and should be mounted as close to the blade as possible, so that overhanging work doesn't bend as it is cut.
- Fences with easy-to-read calibrated scales for accurate settings.
- Easy conversion from table to overhead mode and from one tool to another.
- An accessible on/off switch, because having to reach under the workcenter to unplug or turn off a tool may not be fast enough in an emergency.
- An ample crosscutting facility in the overhead mode for wide man-made boards.
- In the overhead mode power tools must be able to slide smoothly without any sideways movement.
- A workcenter that doubles as an assembly bench is useful in a small workshop.
- Options to fit a jigsaw, faceplate sander, planer or drill stand make for a more versatile workcenter – but they are of only minor consideration compared with circular-saw and router performance.

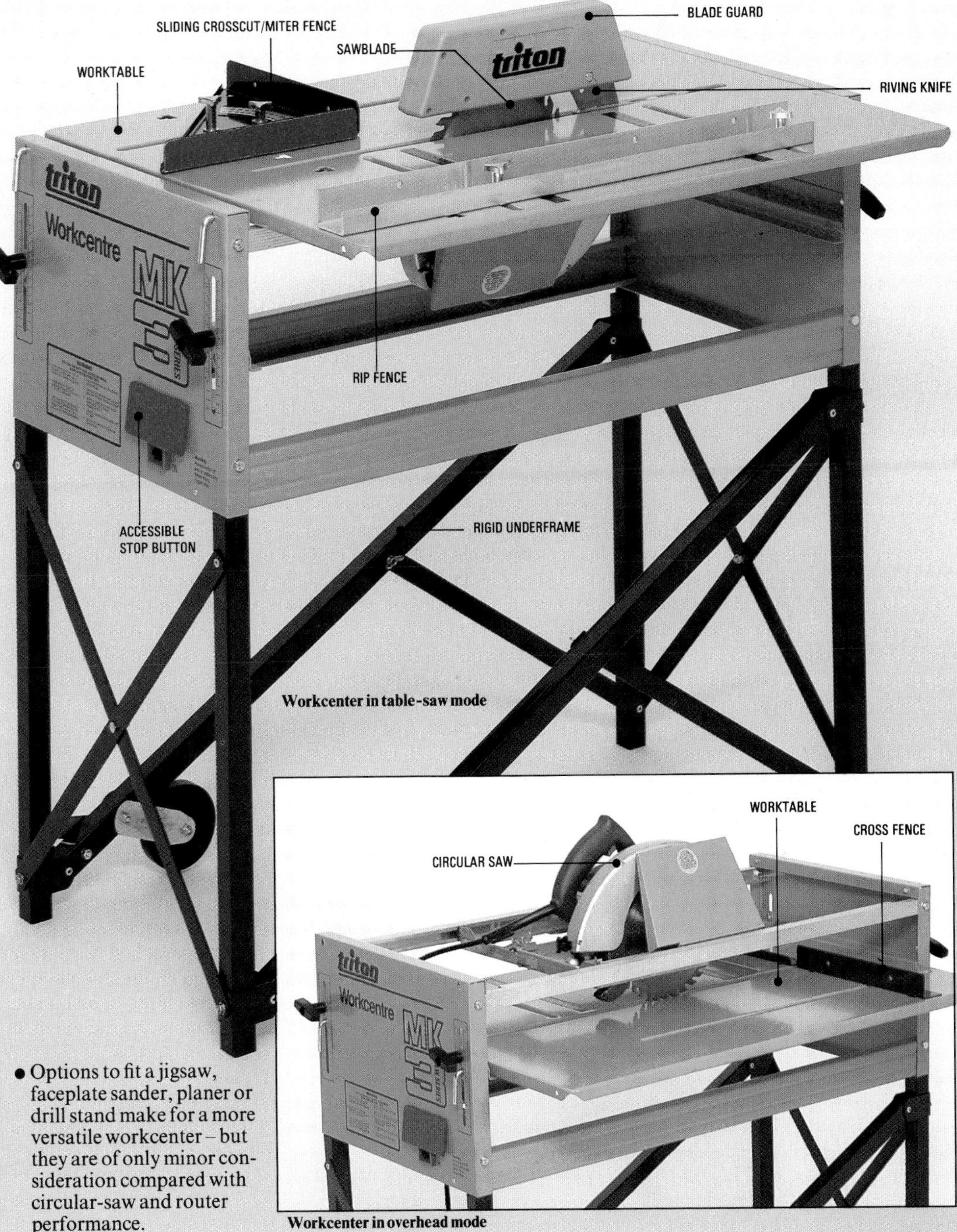

Workcenter in table-saw mode

Workcenter in overhead mode

Although a good workcenter should accept any size circular saw, you will get the best results if you fit a first-class tool with a 9in (230mm) tungsten-carbide-tipped blade. If the saw is to cut true, there must be no arbor float – that is, a tendency for the blade-mounting shaft to move in and out, causing the blade to wander off line.

SEE ALSO	
Circular saws	132-133
Workcenters	151
Adjusting a rip fence	159
Dust collectors	214
Eye protection	214

Ripping
The manufacturer will supply full instructions for assembling a workcenter as a ripsaw. Once assembled, adjust the sawblade depth so that it just breaks through the surface of the wood, and then lower the blade guard to within ¼in (6mm) of the work. Also, make sure the rip fence is set exactly parallel to the blade. If the outfeed end of the fence is set closer to the blade than the infeed end, the work will jam and will be kicked back toward you by the blade.

When ripping a wide board, keep the work pressed against the fence with one hand while supporting the offcut with the other **(1)**. Push steadily but not too fast, trying to keep the work moving throughout the operation. Don't pause, otherwise slight steps in the cut edge may result.

When the cut is completed, push the work clear of the blade. Never pull back the workpiece or offcut while the blade is moving. Have an assistant help you pass a large board over the table.

When ripping a narrow board, use a notched push stick to pass the wood between the blade and fence **(2)**, while holding the work against the fence with a small offcut of man-made board.

1 Ripping a wide board
Keep it pressed against the fence and support the offcut.

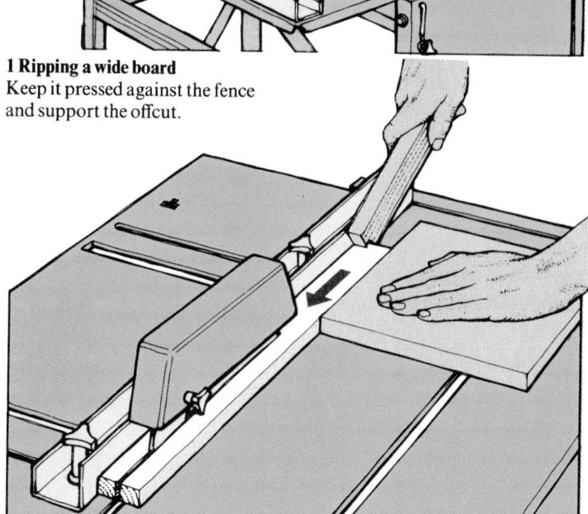

2 Ripping a narrow board
Use a push stick to feed the work.

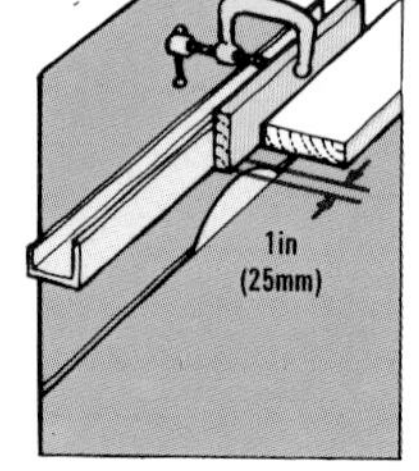

Ripping partially dried wood
Stresses within partially dried wood can be released when it is ripped, causing the kerf to spring open. This can force the work sideways against the blade, which will jam or throw the wood. As a safeguard, provide a clearance by clamping a block of wood to the rip fence at the infeed end.

Crosscutting
Cut work to length by holding it firmly against the face of the sliding fence with one hand, while feeding it smoothly with the other **(1)**. A small offcut could be thrown back by the blade or it could get jammed between the blade and the sides of the slot in the table. If you have to remove ¼in (6mm) of wood or more, do so in two one-blade-width stages. This way the offcut is reduced to sawdust with each cut.

To cut a miter, set the required angle and follow the same procedure **(2)**.

Cutting joints
By lowering the blade to cut partway through the thickness of the work, it is possible to cut tenons, tongues and grooves, rabbets and lap joints. Always cut the shoulders first, then remove the waste one blade-width at a time.

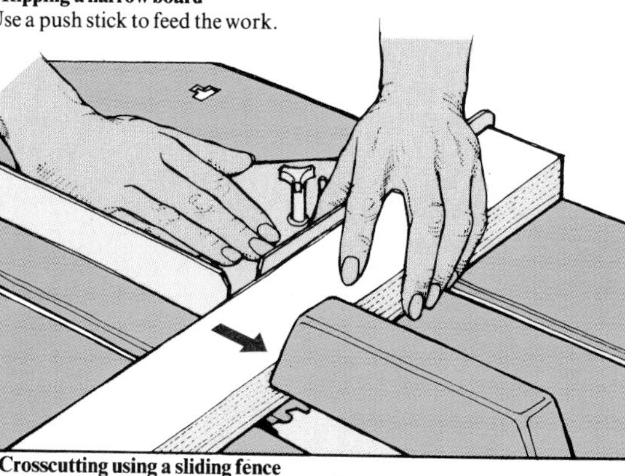

1 Crosscutting using a sliding fence

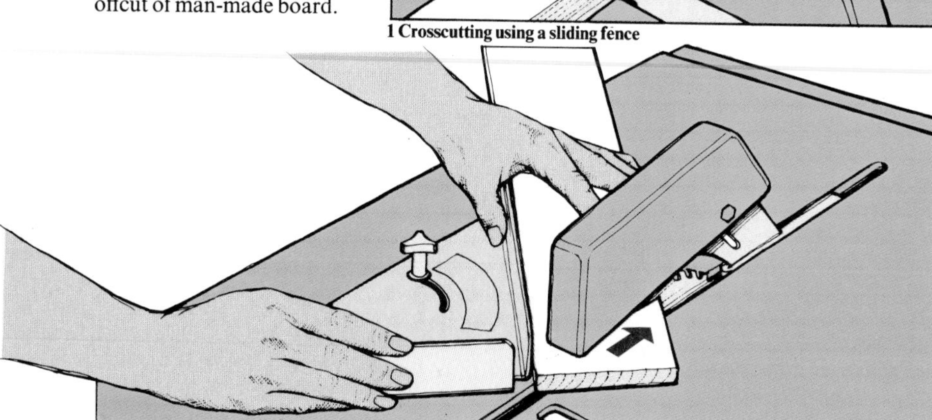

2 Crosscutting one half of a miter joint

TABLE-SAW SAFETY

- Keep fingers clear of the blade and use a push stick whenever necessary.
- Don't lean over a spinning blade to retrieve an offcut or workpiece.
- Make sure both workpiece and offcut are supported throughout the operation.
- Always wear goggles or other eye protection.
- Don't wear loose clothing.
- Remove jewelry, and tie back long hair.
- Work in a tidy, well-lit environment.
- Attach a dust-collecting bag to a table saw whenever possible.
- Unplug the tool after work.
- Always keep unsupervised children away from a workcenter when in use.

THE WORKCENTER AS AN OVERHEAD SAW

With a circular saw fitted to a workcenter in the overhead mode you can make any of the crosscuts and joints that are possible with a hand-held power saw – but in a fraction of the time, since there is no need to set up guide battens. The overhead-saw mode is especially well-suited to crosscutting and beveling wide boards.

Crosscutting wide boards
Having mounted the circular saw and adjusted the blade to the required depth, always slide it the full length of its travel to make sure the blade is unimpeded throughout the operation.

Hold the work firmly against the cross fence and feed the saw smoothly and gently until you have severed the wood. Always switch off the saw and allow the blade to stop spinning before pulling it back.

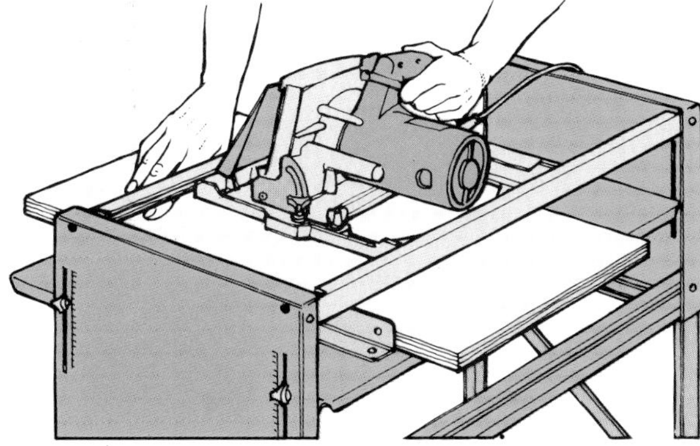

Crosscutting a wide board or panel
Hold the work against the fence and feed the saw smoothly.

Multiple crosscuts
To cut several identical workpieces to the same length, align their square-cut ends, tape them together, then crosscut them as described above.

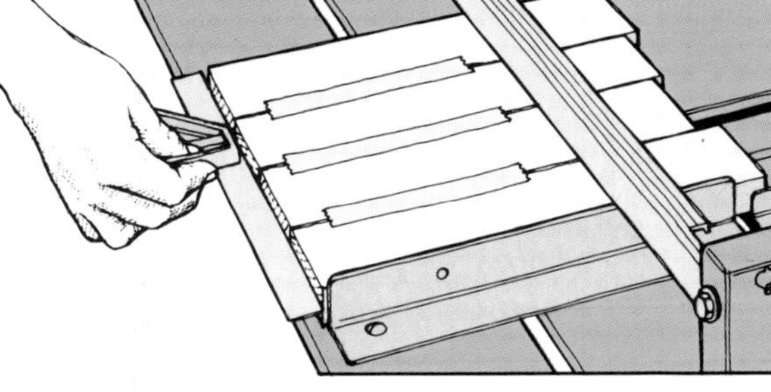

Crosscutting identical pieces
Align their ends and cut them all with one pass of the saw.

Cutting dadoes and rabbets
To cut a dado or rabbet across a board, raise the saw to cut partway through the workpiece, then crosscut each shoulder line before removing the waste one blade-width at a time.

If you need to cut a matching dado or rabbet across several pieces of wood, tape them together beforehand.

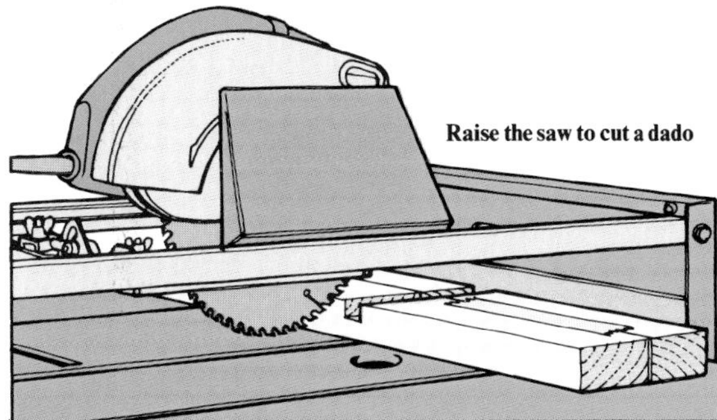

Raise the saw to cut a dado

Cutting bevels
To cut bevels across a workpiece, first place a shim beneath it to raise it from the worktable. Tilt the saw to 45 degrees, then make one pass with it. The slot cut across the packing piece with the tip of the sawblade serves as a guide to positioning the subsequent workpieces.

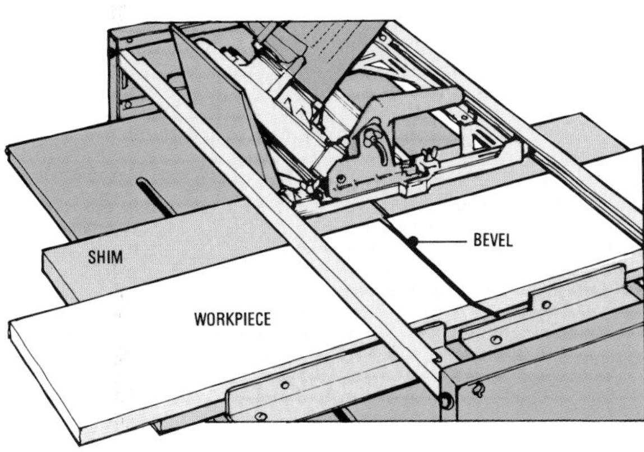

Place a shim beneath a bevel-cut workpiece

Kerfing
Kerfing in order to bend a thick piece of wood is particularly easy with an overhead saw. The sawcuts must be spaced evenly; and you need to cut almost through the work, leaving a strip of wood $\frac{1}{16}$ to $\frac{1}{4}$in (2 to 6mm) thick untouched.

To space the kerfs, first take a batten that is deeper than the workpiece and screw it to the cross fence of the workcenter. Then make a single pass with the saw to cut a notch in the batten, and make a pencil mark on the batten to serve as a guide to the kerfs' spacing **(1)**. After you have made the first kerf in the workpiece, align the cut you have just made with the pencil mark and make the next cut. Repeat this procedure until you have made enough kerfs to bend the wood.

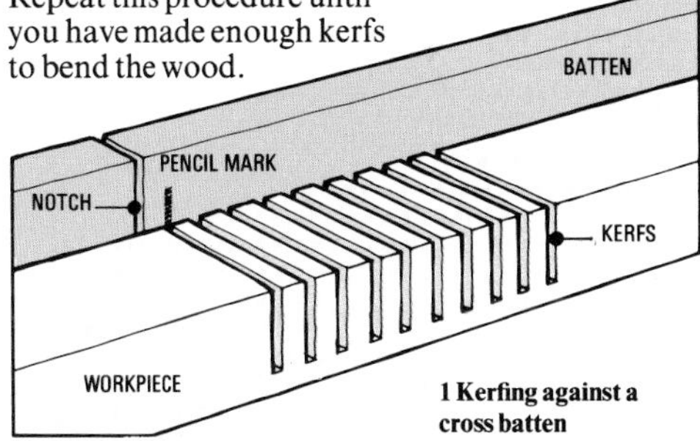

1 Kerfing against a cross batten

SAFETY PROCEDURES

Using a circular saw mounted on a workcenter is usually safer than operating a hand-held one. However, the following safety measures are important:

- Concentrate at all times, and never use a power saw when you are tired.
- Always double-check your settings and run through your planned procedure in your mind before switching on the saw.
- Clamp or hold the work firmly.
- Always wear eye protection when sawing.
- Keep both hands clear of the blade.
- Having cut through a workpiece, switch off the saw before pulling it back, since a small offcut is sometimes thrown by the blade.

ROUTING WITH A WORKCENTER

You can cut dadoes, even in wide boards, quickly and easily by using a router in the overhead mode. For grooves, rabbets and edge moldings, assemble the workcenter as a spindle shaper, following the instructions supplied by the manufacturer.

SEE ALSO

Routers	140-141
Router bits	142
Dust collectors	214
Eye protection	214

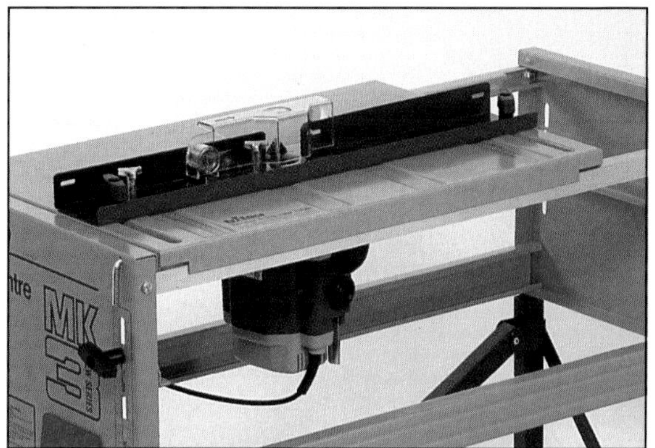

The workcenter in spindle-shaper mode

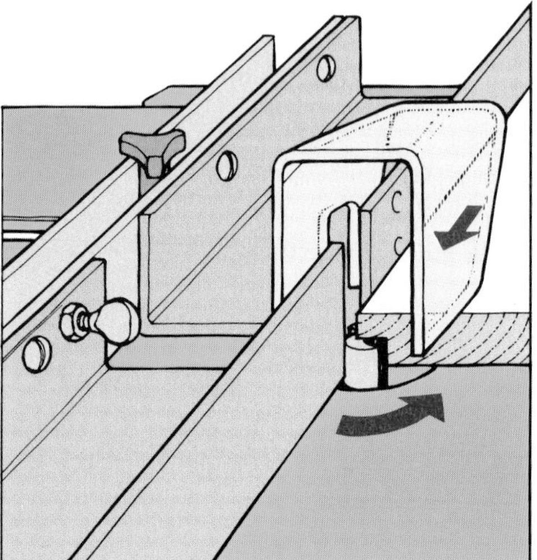

1 Cutting a rabbet
Feed the work against the rotation of the bit.

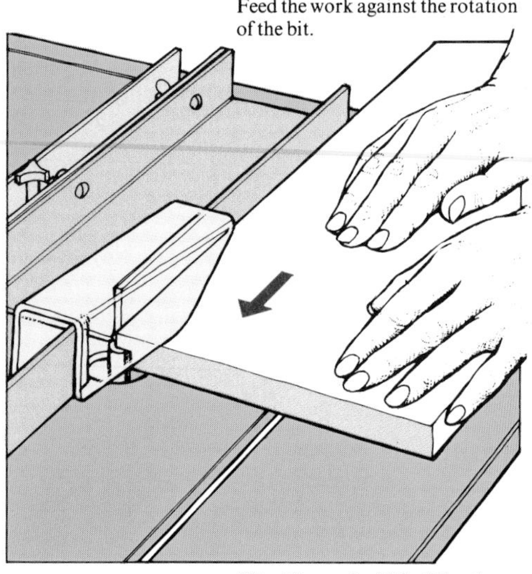

2 Feed the work with both hands

Cutting grooves and rabbets

To cut a longitudinal groove or a rabbet in the edge of a workpiece, set the two guide fences in line and adjust the depth of the router bit as required. When rabbeting, always feed the work against the rotation of the bit **(1)**. Place both hands on top of the workpiece and keep it pressed against the fences while you are feeding it over the bit **(2)**.

SPINDLE-SHAPER SAFETY

- Use the cutter guard whenever possible.
- Never trail your fingers or thumbs behind the work when you are feeding it over a bit.
- When edge-molding or rabbeting, feed against the rotation of the bit; feeding in the same direction as the rotation may result in the work being snatched out of your hands. You can draw an arrow on the worktable to remind you.
- Always keep your router bits sharp.
- Remove large amounts of waste by making two or more passes.
- Always wear some form of eye protection.

Cutting a mortise

To cut a mortise, set up the workcenter for grooving. Hold the work against the fence and lower it onto the spinning bit to start the mortise **(1)**. Feed the work to the end of the mortise, then lift it off the bit **(2)**. To cut a series of identical mortises, clamp a stop block to the fences, one behind and one ahead of the work **(3)**.

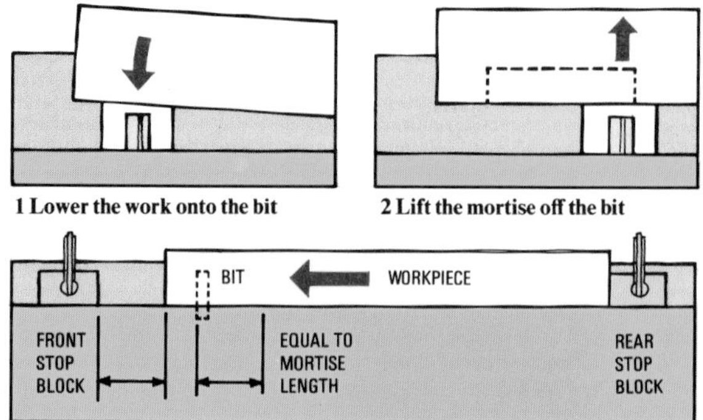

1 Lower the work onto the bit

2 Lift the mortise off the bit

3 Cutting identical mortises

Trimming a square edge

Even a sharp sawblade can leave a chipped edge on a plastic-laminated board. Use a straight router bit to trim the edge perfectly clean and square. Adjust the outfeed fence until it is exactly level with the arc of the cutting edge. The position of the infeed fence determines the depth of cut.

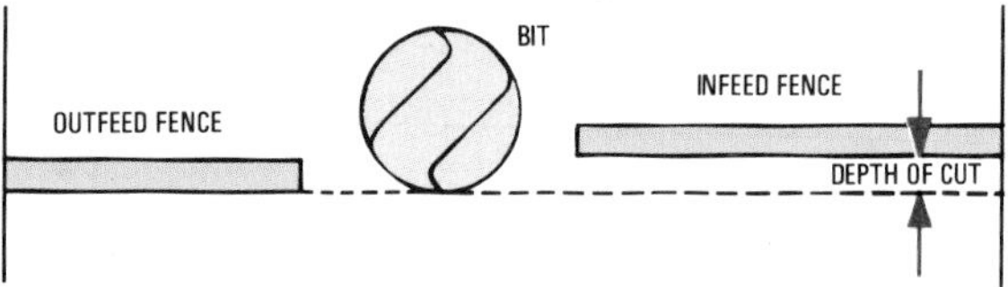

Trimming a laminated board

Molding an edge

When using a pilot bit to edge-mold a workpiece, set the fences close to the bit as a safety measure and use the pilot tip to guide the work in the usual way **(1)**.

If you prefer to feed straight work against the fences, adjust them so the pilot tip is just behind the line of the fences **(2)**.

Whatever method you use, always feed the work against the rotation of the bit.

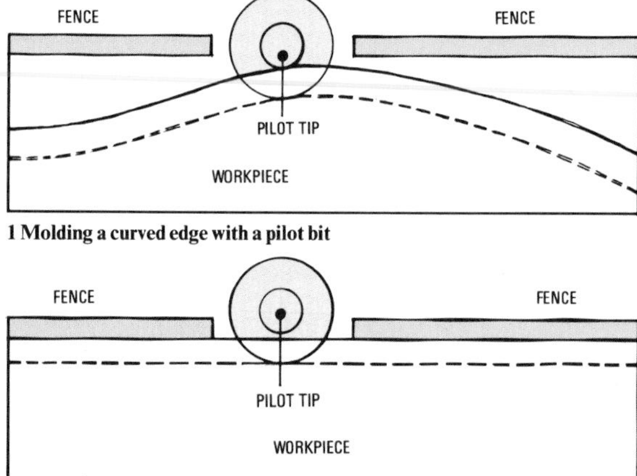

1 Molding a curved edge with a pilot bit

2 Molding a straight edge against a fence

CHAPTER FIVE

MACHINE TOOLS

Many modern woodworking machines offer such a fine degree of accuracy and quality of finish that they provide an incentive to attempt projects that would be difficult or daunting by hand. Powerful machinery also makes light work of ripping, crosscutting and planing heavy balks of wood to size, and most machines are designed to make the cutting of identical components easy and precise. Virtually all woodworking machines are potentially hazardous. It is therefore essential to follow safety procedures to the letter and to fit some form of dust collection to your woodworking machines. You should also never allow your concentration to lapse, nor be tempted to push a machine beyond safe limits. Machine tools are made with either three-phase or single-phase motors. However, to have three-phase wiring run to your workshop is both unnecessary and expensive, whereas single-phase machines can be connected to ordinary household circuits.

TABLE SAWS

In its basic form, a table saw comprises a rotary sawblade protruding through the center of a flat worktable or bench. Fitted with fences and guides, it is primarily used to cut solid wood and man-made boards to size. Despite its seemingly limited function, the table saw is usually the first machine a woodworker buys and it becomes the center of machine-shop activity, since workpieces are returned to the saw again and again as they are squared, shaped, grooved, mitered and joined.

SEE ALSO

Sharpening blades	158
Push sticks	159
Dust collectors	214
Face mask	214
Hearing protectors	214

Sawblade diameter
Table saws for the home workshop are made with blades from 5½in (140mm) up to 12in (300mm) in diameter. The most important factor – maximum depth of cut – is determined by how much of the blade can protrude above the table, and that is only about one-third of its diameter. For serious woodworking, you need to consider buying a saw with a 10in (250mm) or preferably a 12in (300mm) blade.

The blade is usually raised or lowered by means of a handwheel or crank handle. For the cleanest cut and to prolong the life of the blade, adjust its height so that the teeth are about ¼ to ⅜in (6 to 9mm) above the surface of the work.

Sawblade angle
By operating another handwheel or crank, the blade can be tilted to any angle from vertical to 45 degrees to the table. Having adjusted the blade, before switching on the saw always check the position of the guard and fences to make sure they will not retard its movement. Also, read the manufacturer's instructions to determine whether you should remove the table insert or lower the blade before adjustment. Choose a machine with a graduated scale that indicates the angle of the blade clearly.

- **Safety switching**
  All machine tools, including table saws, must be equipped with a latching relay in the power switch. This type of relay will prevent an automatic restart of a machine when electricity is restored after a power failure.

Table insert
A small section of the table immediately surrounding the blade is removable to facilitate the changing of blades. This "table insert" has a slot through which the blade protrudes. Occasionally a poorly made saw is supplied with a table-insert slot that is too wide, so small offcuts become jammed between it and the blade. It may be possible to replace a poorly fitting insert with one made from stable wood or board in which the blade cuts its own slot.

- **Blade-guide design**
  The blade guard on your saw may be designed differently from the one shown opposite and on the following pages. Always follow the saw manufacturer's recommendations for mounting and adjusting the guard.

Riving knife
When wood is seasoned unevenly, it can become "case-hardened" as a result of the moisture content varying throughout its thickness. As soon as case-hardened wood is cut, it begins to move due to the release of stresses created within it. If this movement causes partially sawn wood to close up and pinch a revolving sawblade, the workpiece will be thrown back toward the operator with considerable velocity. For this reason, a curved metal blade known as a riving knife is bolted directly behind the blade to keep the sawkerf open. The riving knife is adjustable to suit blades of different diameters. When adjusted correctly it should be approximately ⅛in (3mm) from the sawteeth at its lowest point, no more than ⅜in (9mm) from the teeth at its tip and a maximum of ⅛in (3mm) below the highest point of the sawblade. Once set, the riving knife cants with the sawblade and automatically follows its vertical movement.

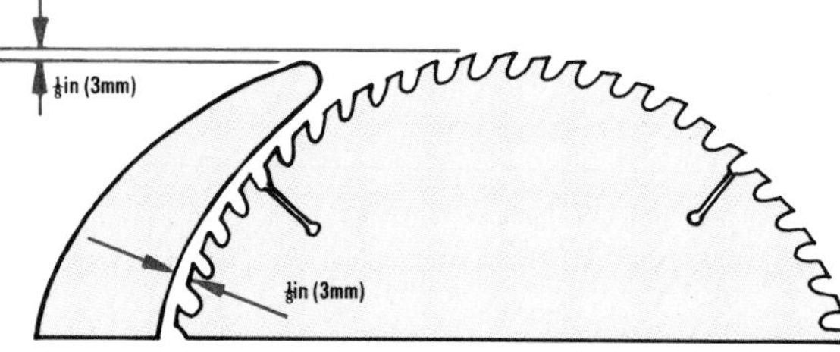

Recommended riving-knife settings

MACHINE-SHOP SAFETY

No matter how experienced you become as a machinist, never deviate from safe working practices in order to save time or money. Most woodworking machines will inflict serious injuries if they are misused.

- Use sound and sharp cutters or blades only. They are safer and produce better work.
- Use proper guards, as recommended by the machine's manufacturer.
- Disconnect a machine from the supply of electricity before changing cutters or blades.
- Do not make any adjustments while cutters or blades are moving.
- Check the work for nails, screws and loose knots.
- Don't operate a machine while wearing loose clothing or jewelry. Tie back long hair.
- Fit some form of dust collection, or wear a face mask.
- Don't operate a machine under the influence of alcohol or drugs, or if you are feeling drowsy.
- Check that wrenches and adjusting keys are removed before switching on the machine.
- Feed the work against the direction of rotation of a blade or cutter.
- Support the work properly when passing it over or through a machine.
- Use a push stick to feed a workpiece rather than risk touching a blade or cutter by approaching it with your fingers.
- Never reach over a blade or cutter to remove waste or offcuts.
- Don't attempt to free a stalled blade or cutter before switching off the machine.
- Do not slow or stop a blade or cutter with a piece of wood. Let both come to rest naturally if the machine is not fitted with a proper brake.
- If you are interrupted when operating a machine, complete the process and switch off before looking up.
- Periodically check that all nuts, bolts and other fastenings are properly tightened.
- Keep the area around the machine clean and free from clutter. Cutting plastic-coated boards leaves especially "slippery" dust on the floor.
- Don't store materials or equipment above a machine in such a way that they could fall onto it.
- After work, disconnect machines and lock your workshop. Keep unsupervised children well away from all machinery, even when not in use.
- Check your machine settings and run through the procedure in your mind before switching it on.

Blade guard
A sturdy metal guard is suspended directly over the blade to prevent the operator from touching it accidentally and also to restrain the workpiece if it is lifted from the table by the motion of the saw. The guard is bolted onto the riving knife or suspended from an adjustable arm. Adjust the guard as close to the work as possible.

Electric motor
Being stationary machines, table saws are equipped with relatively large electric motors more than capable of driving a blade at a speed that will leave a clean-cut edge on the work. However, the larger table-saw motors are less likely to be strained by the cutting of thick, dense hardwood. A 1.5kW (2hp) motor is adequate for a machine fitted with a 10 to 12in (250 to 300mm) blade.

Worktable
The main requisite of a saw table is that it should be rigid and flat. Consequently, the best saws are made with cast-metal or ground fabricated-steel tables. A cheaper folded-metal table is acceptable provided it is rigidly braced. Choose a saw with a generous-size table or one that is equipped with extension pieces to support a full 4 × 8ft (1.22 × 2.44m) board.

Rip fence
A workpiece is run against a rip fence to guide it on a straight path as it is sawn from end to end. It is essential that the fence be sturdy and inflexible. Some fences are held at both the front and back of the saw table, but this is not essential provided the fence is constructed with a well-designed single mounting. The fence should be capable of very fine adjustment from side to side, with a clear graduated scale. Fore and aft adjustment is a useful feature found on few table saws designed for the home workshop.

The rip capacity – the distance between the fence and the blade – varies considerably from saw to saw. Ideally, choose a saw capable of halving a full-size man-made board, but you will find many saws have a smaller capacity.

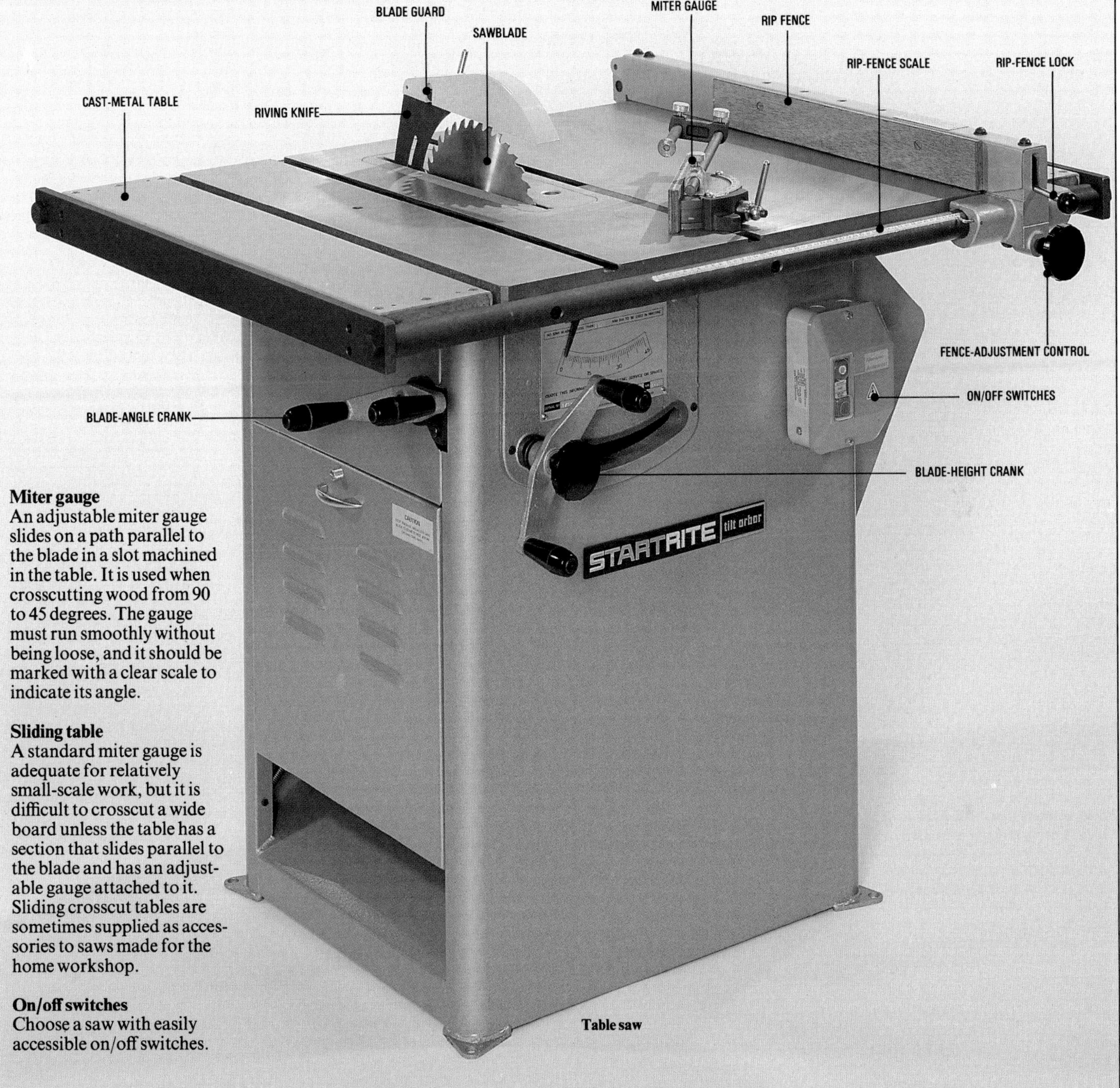

Table saw

Miter gauge
An adjustable miter gauge slides on a path parallel to the blade in a slot machined in the table. It is used when crosscutting wood from 90 to 45 degrees. The gauge must run smoothly without being loose, and it should be marked with a clear scale to indicate its angle.

Sliding table
A standard miter gauge is adequate for relatively small-scale work, but it is difficult to crosscut a wide board unless the table has a section that slides parallel to the blade and has an adjustable gauge attached to it. Sliding crosscut tables are sometimes supplied as accessories to saws made for the home workshop.

On/off switches
Choose a saw with easily accessible on/off switches.

TABLE-SAW BLADES

Special-purpose rip or crosscut blades are used mainly when a machine is set up to perform one function for a period of time. A universal or combination-tooth blade is a better choice for the average home workshop, since the chore of repeatedly changing the blade, perhaps every few minutes, would soon become tedious. Despite its additional cost, a carbide-tipped combination blade is even better. It rips and crosscuts solid wood, leaving a superb finish, and is ideal for cutting chipboard and plywood, which quickly dull ordinary steel blades. Always follow the manufacturer's instructions for changing blades.

1 Rip blade
2 Crosscut blade
3 Combination blade
4 Carbide-tipped universal blade

- **Cleaning a sawblade**
Clean wood resin from a sawblade with a rag soaked in lacquer thinner or mineral spirits. Alternatively, you can use an oven cleaner.

- **Dado head**
Two universal blades are combined with special waste-removal blades to construct a dado head for cutting wide grooves or housings. See radial-arm saws.

Rip blade
A rip blade has large alternately set chisel-like teeth with deep gullets between them for clearing large amounts of waste. It is designed to cut with the grain only.

Crosscut blade
Crosscut teeth are much smaller than those on a rip blade and are shaped to saw across the grain without tearing it out. Hollow-ground blades, which are reduced in thickness toward their centers, are made to produce a top-quality finish and are sometimes known as "planer blades."

Combination blade
Combination blades, which are made to cut both with and across the grain, have groups of crosscut teeth separated by a rip tooth and a deep gullet. A combination blade will not perform quite as well as a special-purpose blade.

Carbide-tipped blade
This type of blade has no "set" in the conventional sense. Instead, a wide tip of tungsten carbide is brazed to each tooth to provide the necessary clearance in the kerf or sawcut. Carbide-tipped blades are often slotted to prevent distortion as the blade expands through heating. To reduce whistling caused by the blade moving through the air at speed, the hole at the root of each slot is sometimes plugged with soft metal.

Sharpening table-saw blades
When a blade becomes dull, you will smell burning and it becomes more difficult to feed the work. A dull blade is also more likely to jam and throw the work back toward the operator. Send a dull blade to a specialist for sharpening or for the replacement of a damaged carbide tip.

WOBBLE WASHERS

A pair of tapered wobble washers causes the edge of the sawblade to move from side to side as it revolves, in order to cut a groove wider than the normal kerf. (Alternatively, you can fit a dado head – see radial-arm saws.) Rotating the washers in opposite directions changes the angle of the blade so as to increase or reduce the width of the groove. It is necessary to remove the riving knife and to substitute a table insert with a wider slot in place of the normal one. If the blade guard is attached to the riving knife, fit a hold-down unit when using wobble washers.

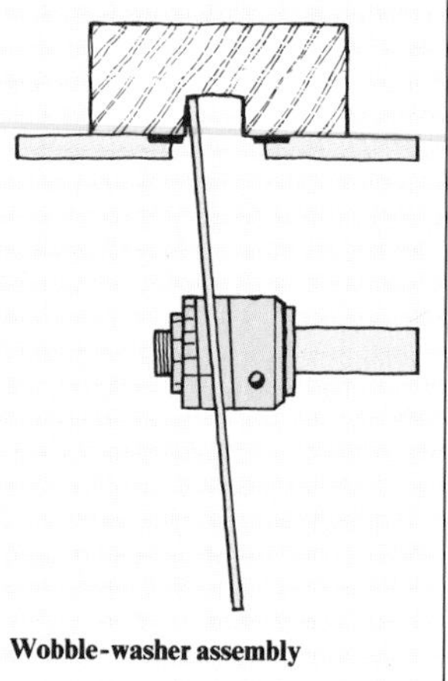
Wobble-washer assembly

RIPPING ON A TABLE SAW

Ripping is used to reduce solid wood to width by cutting more or less parallel to the grain. The work is always run against the rip fence and never cut freehand, in order to avoid the risk of twisting the workpiece and jamming the blade in the kerf. Man-made boards are ripped in the same way. The riving knife and blade guard must be in position when ripping.

Adjusting the rip fence
A rip fence that extends in one piece across the saw table is ideal for cutting stable man-made boards. However, when sawing solid wood there is always the chance that this type of fence will cause an accident. Just as the partially cut kerf in case-hardened wood could close on the blade were it not for the riving knife, similar stresses locked in the wood can make the kerf spring open until pressure against the rip fence forces the workpiece against the side of the blade, causing it to jam and possibly throw the workpiece. If the fence is capable of fore and aft adjustment, it should be withdrawn until its far end is about 1in (25mm) behind the leading edge of the exposed part of the blade **(1)**, providing clearance to the right of the blade. Alternatively, clamp or screw a block of wood to a one-piece fence **(2)** to provide similar clearance. Whatever type of fence is fitted, it must be set parallel to the blade.

Adjust the rip fence to the width of cut according to its graduated scale, then make a test cut in the end of a piece of scrap wood to check the setting. If you cannot trust the scale, use a ruler to measure from the fence to one of the saw-teeth set toward the fence. Before you switch on the saw, check that the fence is securely clamped.

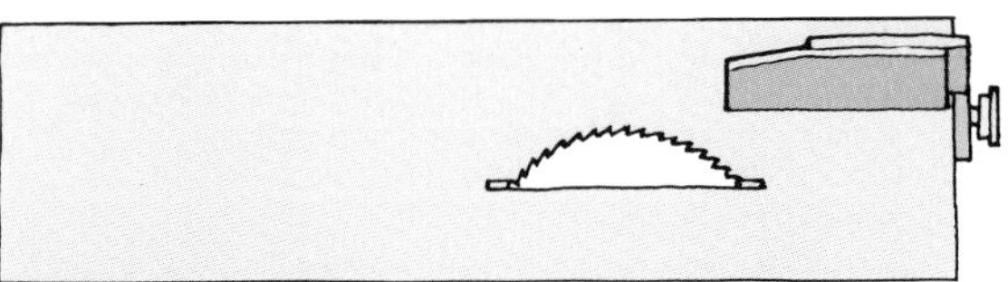
1 Withdraw a two-piece fence

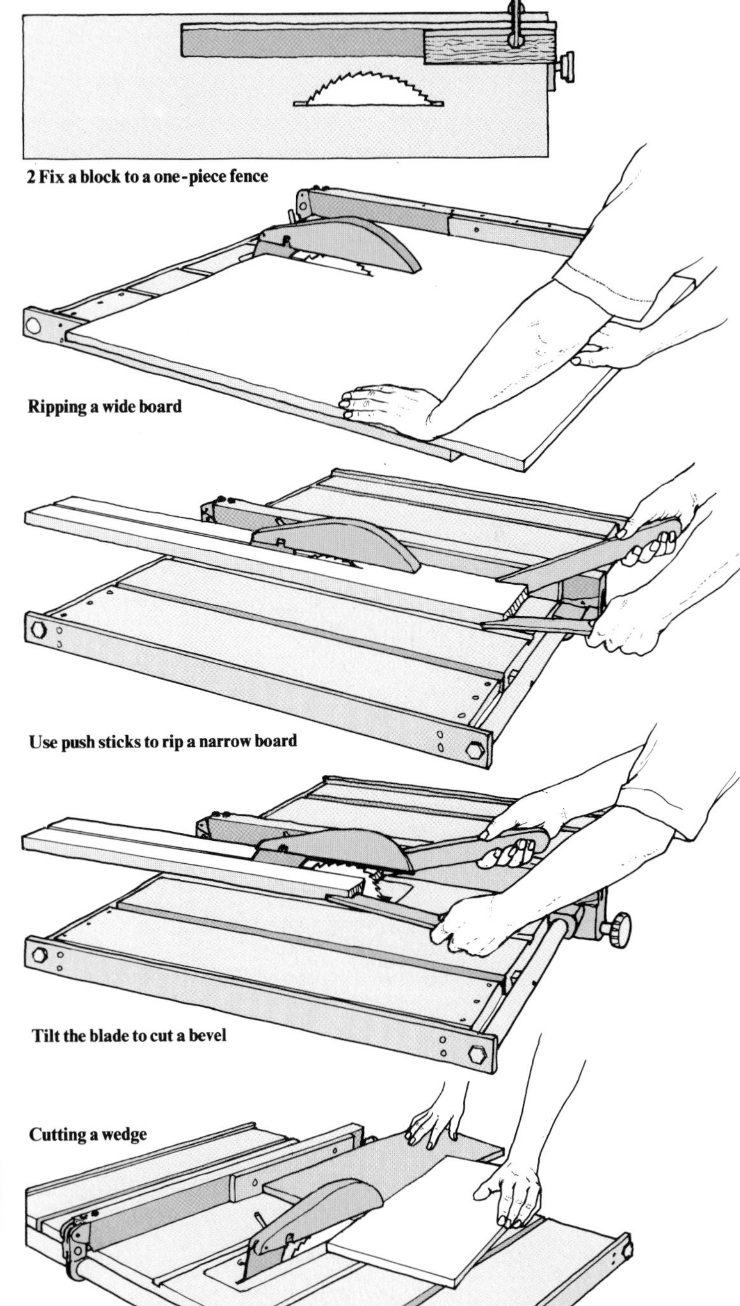
2 Fix a block to a one-piece fence

Ripping a wide board

Use push sticks to rip a narrow board

Tilt the blade to cut a bevel

Cutting a wedge

Ripping a wide board
Use both hands to rip a wide board – applying pressure with one hand directly behind the work but out of line with the blade, while holding the work against the fence and down onto the table with the other. Feed the work at a steady rate, and do not attempt to retrieve the offcut until the blade has stopped moving.

Have an assistant help you support a very wide board when ripping, making it clear that you will guide the workpiece and control the feed rate.

Ripping a narrow board
As you approach the end of a ripcut in a narrow board, feed the work with a push stick – a strip of hardwood notched at one end, with a rounded handgrip at the other – and use a second push stick to apply pressure against the rip fence. Store your push sticks near the table so they are always at hand when needed.

Bevel ripping
To rip a bevel along a workpiece, before you switch the table saw on, tilt the blade to the required angle and check that the blade is not touching the guard or rip fence. Feed the work as for a normal ripcut.

Cutting a tapered workpiece
To saw a tapered workpiece, cut a notch in the side of a plywood or chipboard jig to hold the wood at the required angle to the blade. Keep the jig pressed against the rip fence while feeding it in the normal way.

Ripping a waney-edge board
It is impossible to run a waney edge against the rip fence with any certainty of achieving a straight ripcut. To help keep the cut straight, tack a sheet of thin plywood to the underside of the workpiece so that it projects slightly beyond the waney edge and acts as a guide.

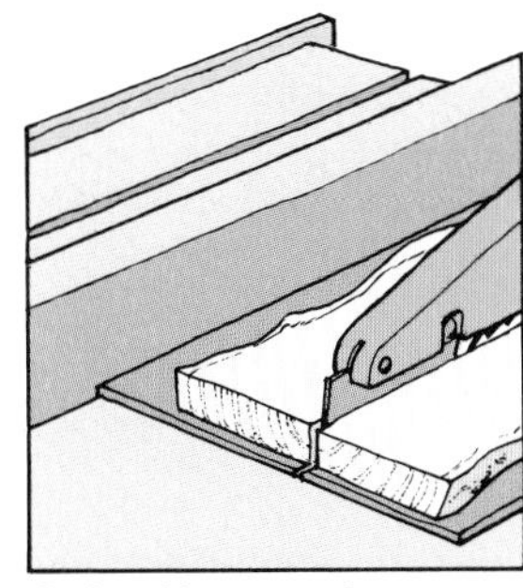
Coping with a waney edge

CROSSCUTTING ON A TABLE SAW

When cutting work to length, use the miter gauge or a sliding crosscut table to guide the wood past the blade. A sharp blade will cut so cleanly that the end grain may need no further finishing. Keep the blade guard and riving knife in position, even though the knife is not essential for crosscutting.

SEE ALSO

Machine-shop safety	156
Riving knife	156
Wobble washers	158
Push sticks	159

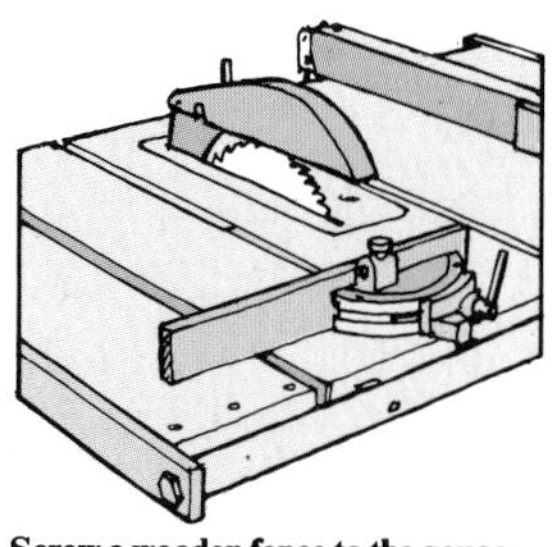
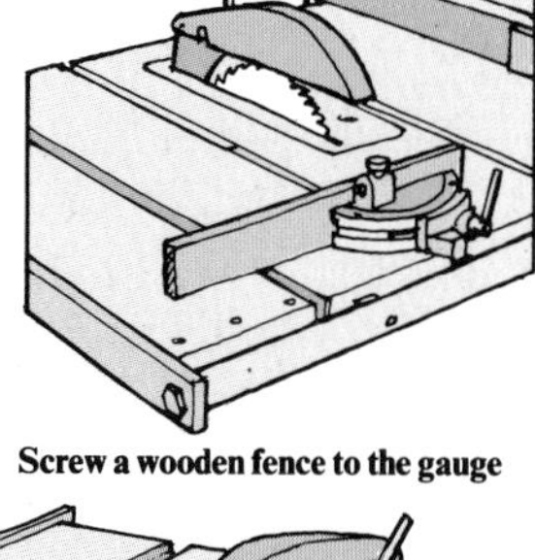

Screw a wooden fence to the gauge

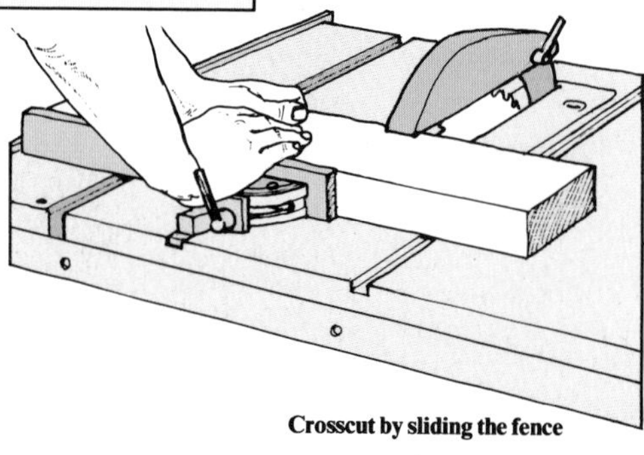

Crosscut by sliding the fence

Crosscutting with a miter gauge

The adjustable miter gauge on the average table saw is relatively short, but it is often drilled so you can screw a longer hardwood fence to its face. Once the wooden fence itself is crosscut on the table saw, it also acts as a backup to the work to prevent the grain from splitting out at the back as it is fed past the blade. Alternatively, as a temporary backup, sandwich a piece of scrap wood between the factory-made miter gauge and the workpiece.

Hold the work firmly against the fence with both hands, and feed it relatively slowly into the blade. If the workpiece is too short to be held with both hands, clamp it to the fence.

Crosscutting on a sliding table

The friction between a large board or a long workpiece and the saw table can make crosscutting with a miter gauge a laborious procedure. A smooth-running, sliding crosscutting action makes for easy and accurate work, regardless of the size or weight of the workpiece. A sliding table is fitted with a longer-than-average crosscut fence that is adjustable to any angle between 90 and 45 degrees to the blade. Most fences are made with an adjustable stop block for use when making identical workpieces.

Cutting a miter

To cut a miter on a table saw, adjust the miter gauge to the required angle, then feed the workpiece past the blade in the normal way **(1)**. Hold the work firmly against the fence, to prevent it from being drawn backward by the blade.

To cut a compound miter (one angled in two planes), first adjust the miter gauge, then tilt the sawblade **(2)**. To cut a miter across the end of a board, tilt the blade to 45 degrees and set the miter gauge at 90 degrees to the blade **(3)**.

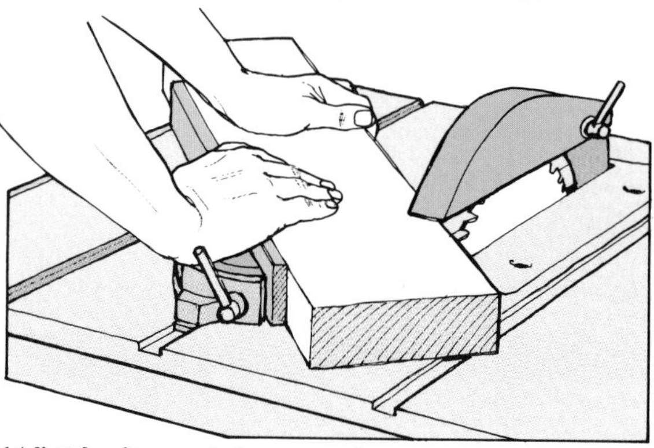

1 Adjust the miter gauge to the proper angle

2 Tilt the blade to cut a compound miter

3 Keep the miter gauge square to miter the end of a board

MAKING MULTIPLE CROSSCUTS

Many woodworking projects require several identical components. Rather than crosscut individually marked workpieces to the line, set up one or two stops to locate the wood accurately in relation to the blade and make repetitive cuts.

Making identical offcuts

It is tempting to butt the end of the work against the rip fence to ensure that offcuts to the right of the blade are of equal length. However, an offcut caught between the fence and a revolving blade can be thrown back into the face of the operator. The correct method is either to withdraw the rip fence clear of the blade or to clamp a spacer block to the fence to act as a stop block for the work, leaving a clearance to the right of the blade **(1)**.

To make the cut, slide the work sideways until it butts against the block and feed it into the blade, then repeat the process to make identical offcuts.

Making identical workpieces

Using the miter gauge, cut each piece of wood square. Clamp a block of wood to the extended miter gauge to act as a stop for the squared end of each workpiece **(2)**.

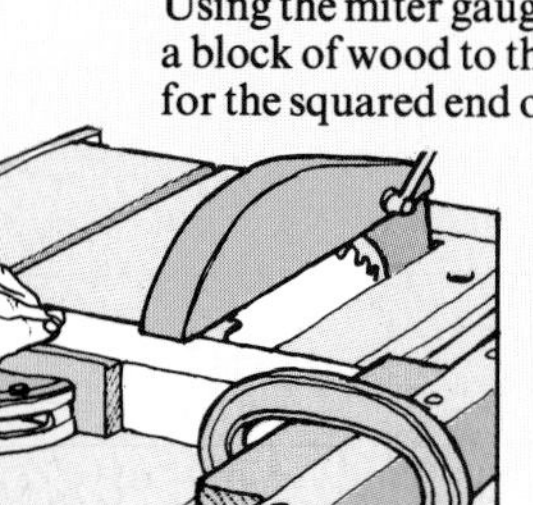
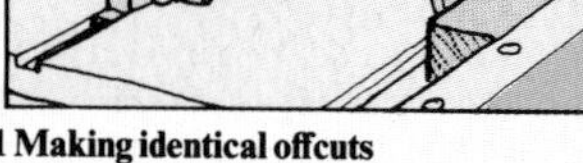

1 Making identical offcuts

2 Cutting identical workpieces

CUTTING RABBETS AND GROOVES ON A TABLE SAW

When cutting a groove or rabbet, on certain table saws it is necessary to remove both the blade guard and the riving knife. As a result, both procedures are more hazardous than standard ripping or crosscutting, so extra concentration and caution are required. Some table saws can be fitted with special vertical/horizontal "hold-down" guards that surround the work in the vicinity of the blade. Alternatively, afford some protection by making a wooden lining for your rip fence incorporating a simple guard to cover the blade.

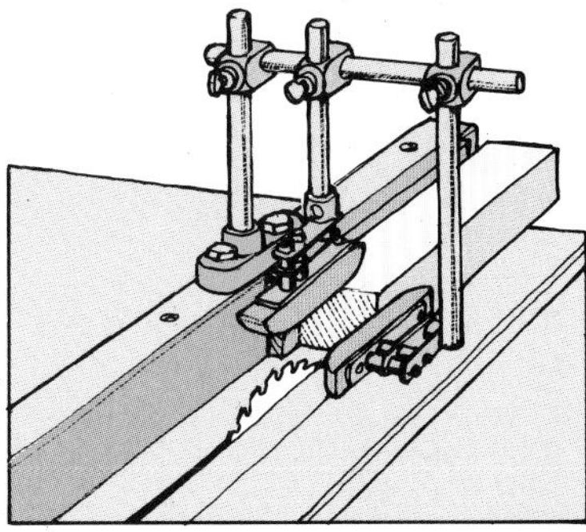
Fit a hold-down guard when grooving or rabbeting

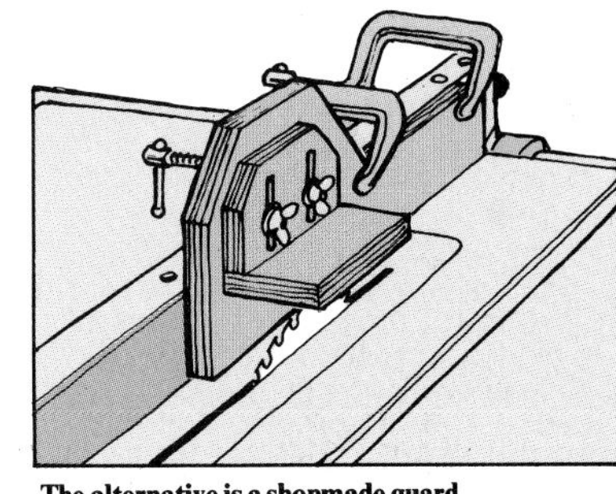
The alternative is a shopmade guard

Cutting a rabbet

Two straightforward ripcuts produce a rabbet on a workpiece. Make the first cut in the narrower face of the workpiece **(1)**, leaving sufficient wood on each side of the kerf to provide adequate support. Reset the rip fence and blade height, then make the second cut to detach the waste from the workpiece **(2)**. Make this second cut with the waste facing away from the fence, since a waste strip trapped between the blade and fence could be thrown back as the last few wood fibers are cut. Stand to one side when feeding work into the blade.

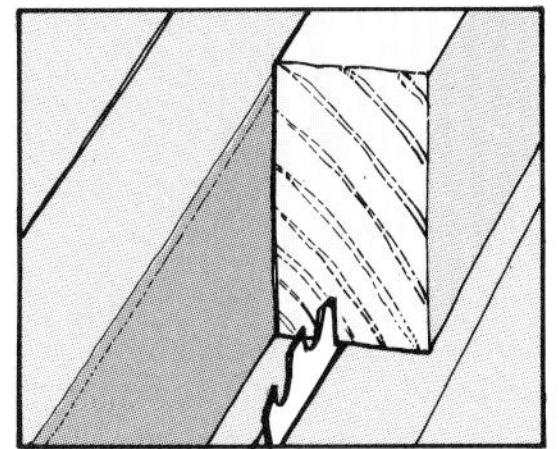
1 Making the first cut

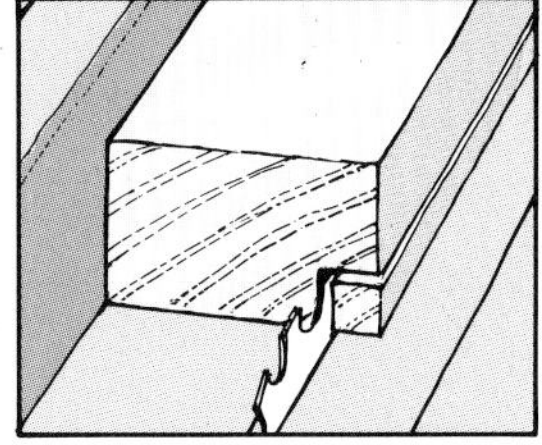
2 Second cut removes the waste

Cutting a groove

A wobble saw allows you to cut a groove in one pass, using a push stick to keep your fingers clear of the blade. Without special equipment, make one sawcut to the required depth on each side of the groove **(1)**, then adjust the rip fence sideways one kerf-width at a time to remove waste in between **(2)**.

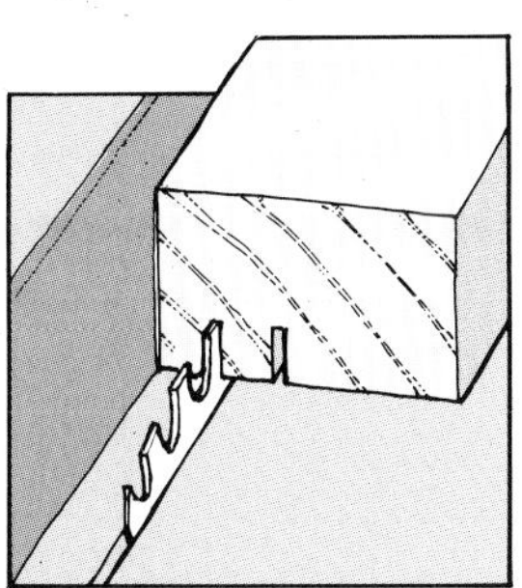
1 Make two sawcuts

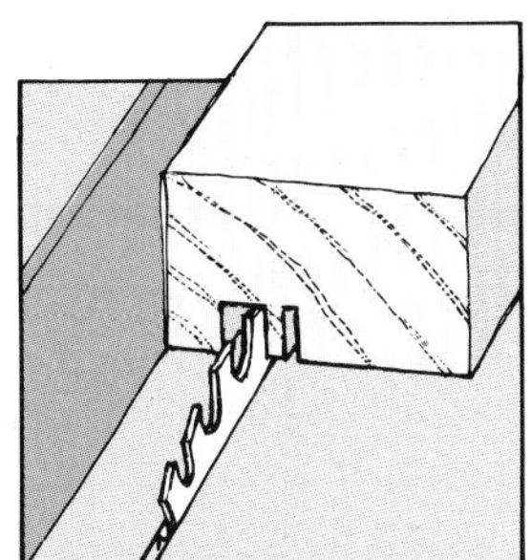
2 Remove waste between them

Cutting a tongue and groove

Leave a centrally placed tongue on the edge of one workpiece by cutting two identical rabbets. Make the first cut in the narrower face, then turn the wood end for end to cut the other side of the tongue **(1)**. Remove the waste from both sides **(2)**.

To saw a matching groove in another workpiece, adjust the fence to cut one side, then turn the work end for end to make the second cut before removing the waste (see left).

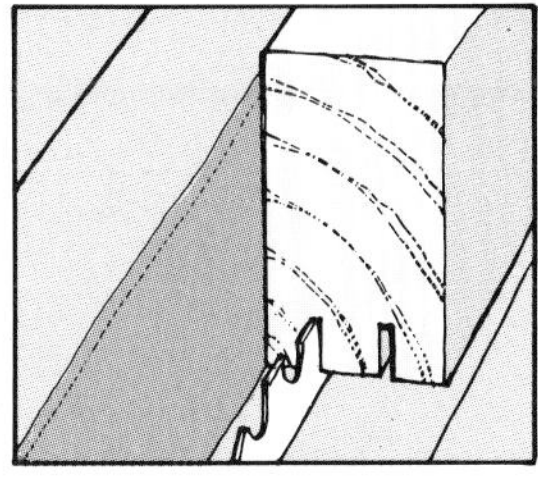
1 Cut each side of a tongue

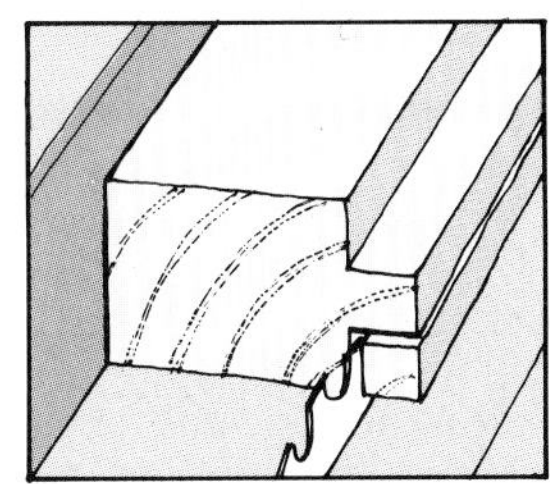
2 Then cut off the waste

KERFING ON A SAW TABLE

If you almost sever a strip of wood with regularly spaced sawcuts, that provides sufficient local flexibility to make a tight bend in a thick workpiece of solid wood. The exact kerf spacing is a matter of experimentation – but as a rough guide, the closer the spacing, the tighter the bend. Adjust the height of the blade to leave an intact strip of wood between $\frac{1}{16}$ to $\frac{1}{4}$in (2 to 6mm) thick, depending on the flexibility of the work. On some saws, no guard can be fitted – in which case, exercise extreme caution.

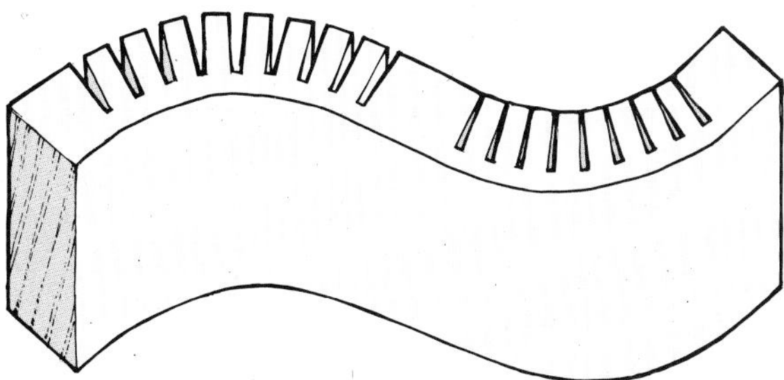
Bend solid wood by kerfing

Accurate spacing is essential if the resulting curve is to be smooth and regular. Screw a temporary auxiliary wooden fence to the saw's miter gauge. Make one cut through the fence, then drive a nail into it to mark the kerf spacing and cut off the head of the nail **(1)**.

Having made one kerf in the workpiece, slot the first kerf onto the nail and cut your second kerf. Slot that kerf over the nail and make your third cut, and so on **(2)**.

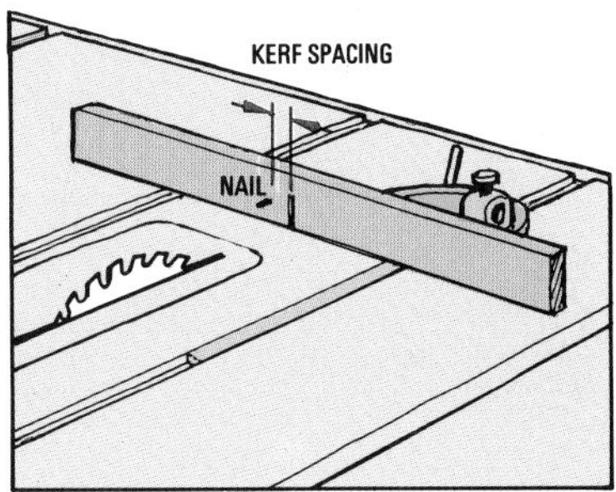

1 Make a jig for accurate kerfing

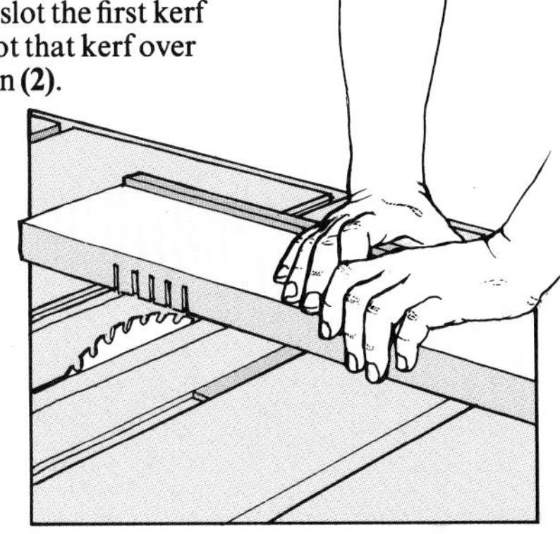
2 Drop each kerf in turn over the nail

CUTTING JOINTS ON A TABLE SAW

A table saw is capable of cutting a variety of woodworking joints with extreme accuracy. As the blade guard and riving knife may have to be removed, proceed with caution when using a table saw for cutting joints.

Lap joints

Both parts of a lap joint are cut in the same way. Clamp a spacer block to the rip fence and use it to align the shoulder of the joint with the blade. Adjust the blade to the required height and make the first cut **(1)**. Then remove the waste one kerf-width at a time, sliding the workpiece to the left against the miter gauge.

A cross-lap joint is cut by a similar method, but use two spacer blocks – clamping one to the rip fence and the other to the miter gauge – to align both shoulders with the blade **(2)**. Having cut both shoulders, remove the waste as above.

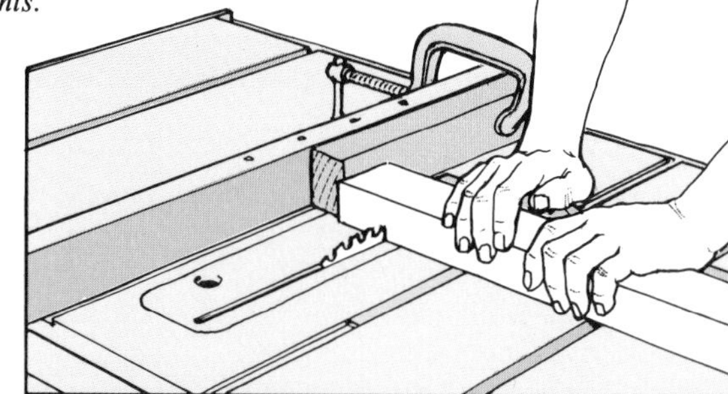
1 Cutting a lap-joint shoulder

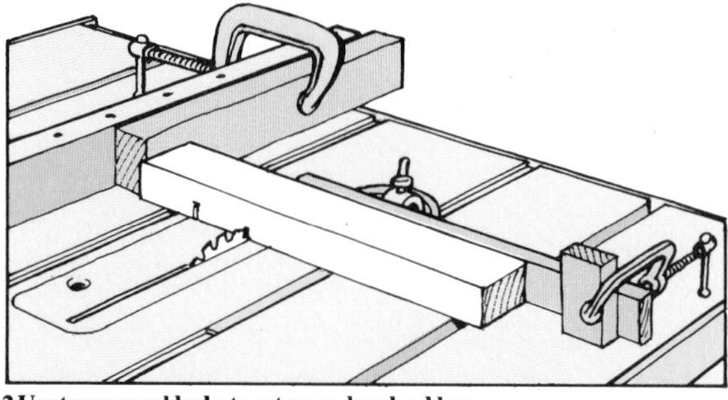
2 Use two spacer blocks to cut cross-lap shoulders

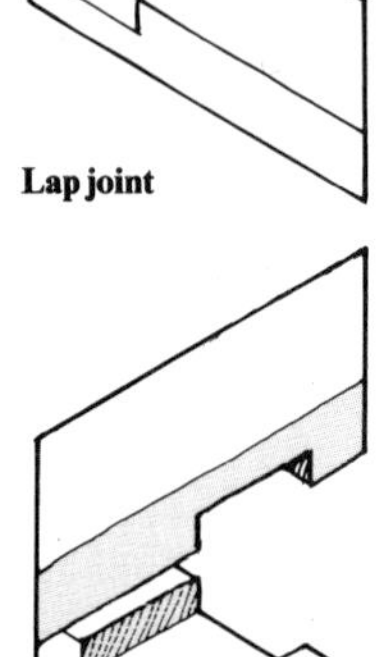
Lap joint

Tenon joints

Having cut the mortises with a router or mortiser, cut the matching tenons on a table saw. Some saw manufacturers supply a tenoning clamp that slides along the machined miter-gauge slot. Alternatively, you can make a wooden jig to support a workpiece while you cut the tenon.

Screw and glue two strips of wood, precisely the same thickness as the work, to a piece of plywood approximately 16 x 8in (400 x 200mm) in size **(1)**. Make sure each strip is square to the long edge of the plywood, and leave enough room to fit a workpiece between one strip and the short edge **(2)**. Restrict screw locations to the top half of the jig, clear of the blade.

Clamp the workpiece to the jig and pass it across the blade to cut one side of the tenon **(3)**. Turn the work around to cut the second side.

Having cut one tenon, remove a short section of waste from each side **(4)** to test its fit in the mortise. If necessary, make adjustments to the fence setting before cutting any remaining workpieces.

Crosscut the shoulder lines **(5)**, clamping a spacer block to the rip fence to align each shoulder line with the blade. If needed, reduce the width of the tenons by cutting the shoulders first, then remove the waste one kerf-width at a time **(6)**.

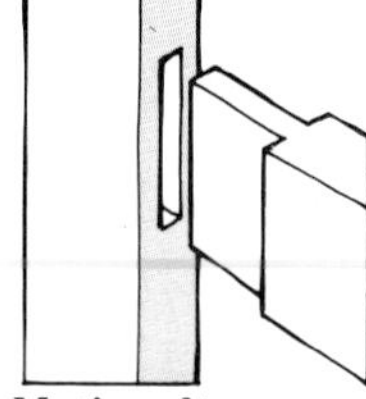
Cross-lap joint

Mortise and tenon

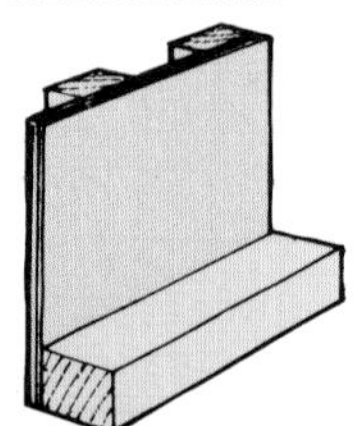
Adding a support
If the saw has a low fence, glue a block to the jig to stop it from rocking.

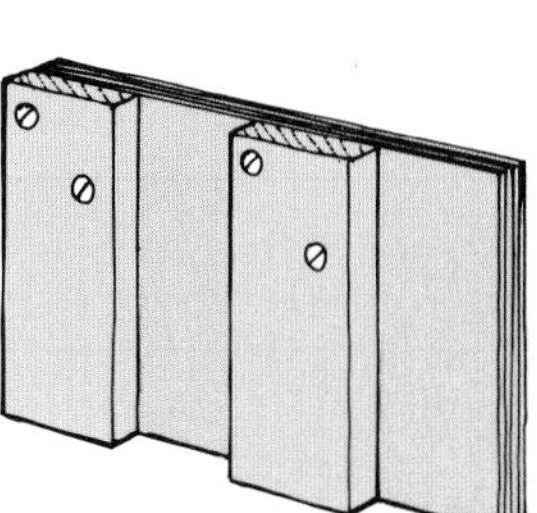
1 Fix wooden strips to plywood

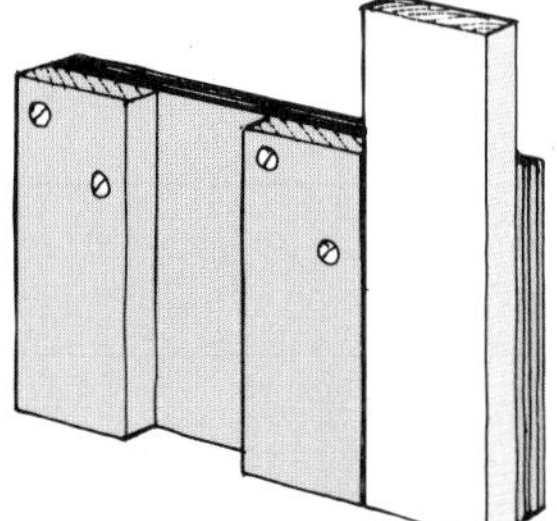
2 Allow space for workpiece

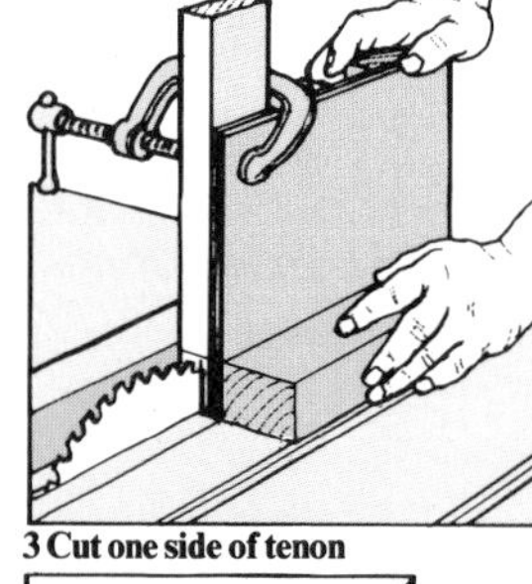
3 Cut one side of tenon

4 Remove a short section of waste from each side of tenon

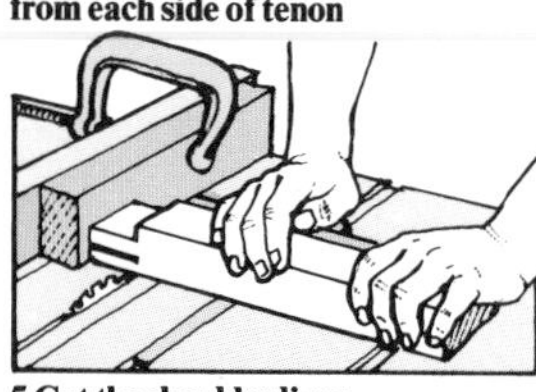
5 Cut the shoulder lines

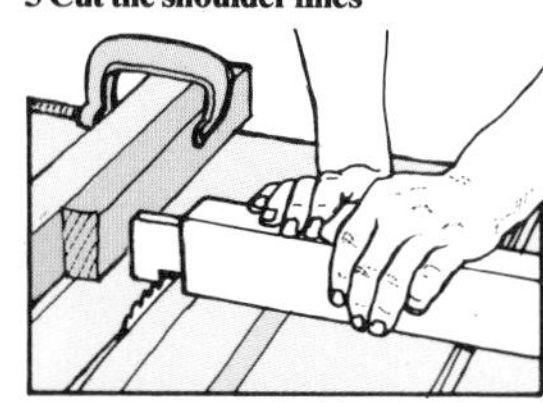
6 Reduce tenon width

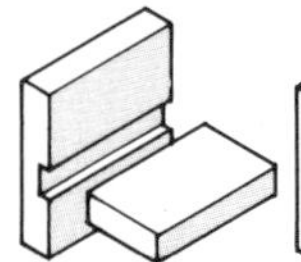
Through dado **Barefaced housing**

Dado joints

Cut a simple through dado or the relatively narrow "groove" of a barefaced housing joint in the same manner as a cross-lap joint, or use a wobble saw to cut them in one pass. Cut the tongue on the other half of a barefaced housing like a lap joint.

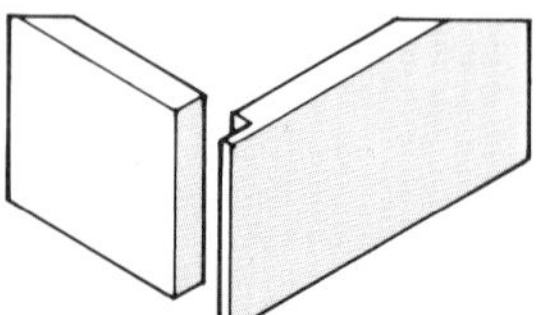

Rabbet joints

Having sawn both of the components square, cut the tongued half of a rabbet joint like a lap joint.

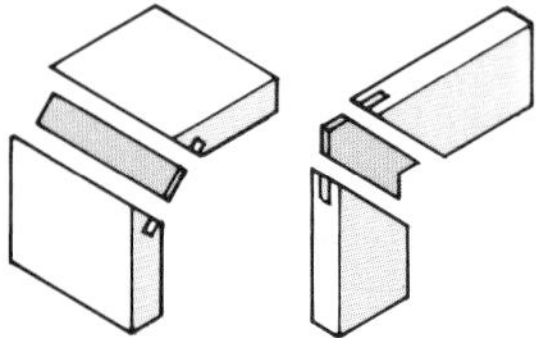

Reinforced miter joints

Having cut miter joints on the table saw, cut slots for plywood splines.

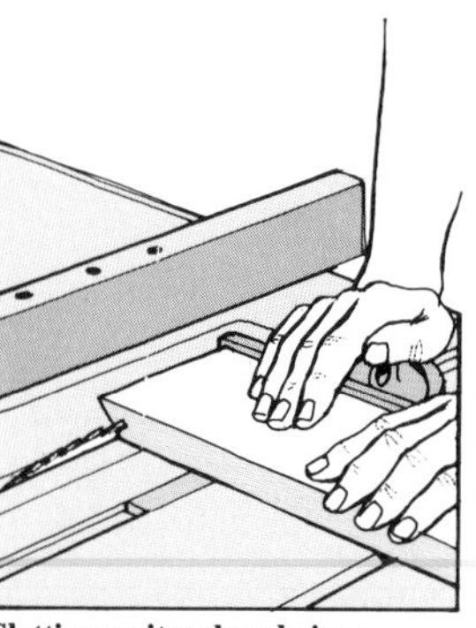
Slotting a mitered workpiece
Tilt the blade to cut a slot for a spline.

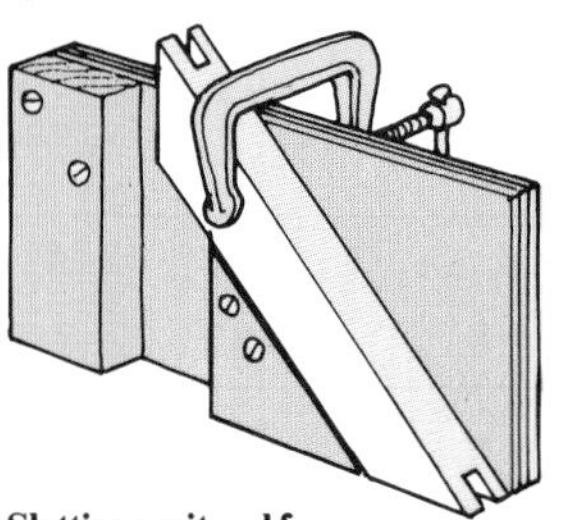
Slotting a mitered frame
Modify the tenon-cutting jig to slot a wide miter.

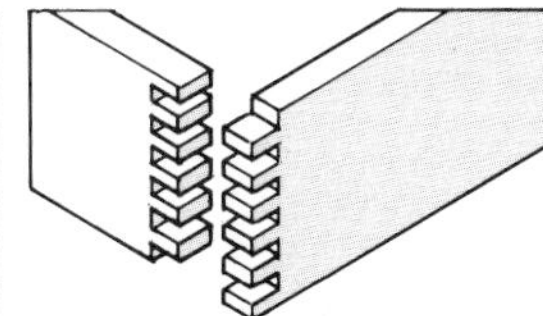

Finger joints

A finger joint is a decorative corner joint often used for box or drawer construction. Cutting it by hand is a laborious process, but with the help of a simple jig you can cut several joints in minutes on a table saw. Use a blade that cuts a wide kerf, or fit wobble washers to cut the spaces between the fingers. Work out the spacing so as to distribute the fingers regularly across each of the workpieces.

To make a jig, clamp a length of wood to the miter gauge and, having adjusted the blade height to just over the thickness of the work, cut a slot through the wood **(1)**. Plane a strip of hardwood to a snug fit in the slot. Cut a piece of wood 2 to 3in (50 to 75mm) long off the strip and glue it into the slot to form a short projecting tongue **(2)**.

Reposition the jig against the miter gauge and place the remainder of the planed strip between the blade and the tongue **(3)**, then screw the wood to the miter gauge and remove the strip.

Stand the first workpiece on end and butt it against the projecting tongue. Clamp the work **(4)**. Feed the work across the saw, then drop the resulting kerf over the projecting tongue and saw another kerf **(5)**. Continue in the same way until you have completed the row of fingers **(6)**.

The fingers on the second workpiece must be offset to fit between the fingers on the first. Place this second piece on end as before, but sandwich the remainder of the wooden strip between it and the tongue **(7)**. Remove the strip and make the first cut, then locate the cut over the tongue and saw the next kerf **(8)**. Repeat the process across the width of the workpiece.

Glue and assemble the joint, then sand the slightly projecting fingers flush once the glue has set.

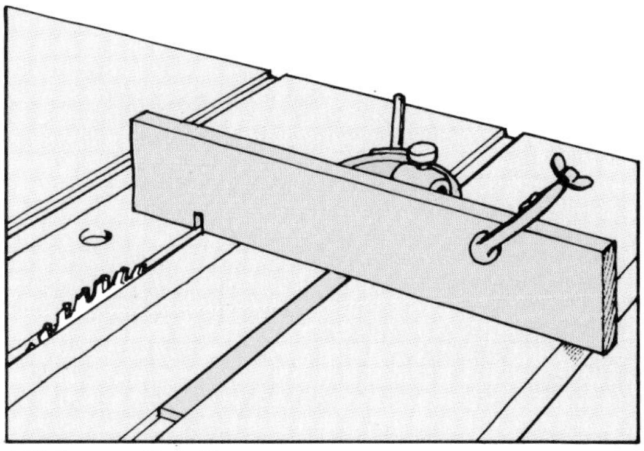

1 Make one cut in the jig

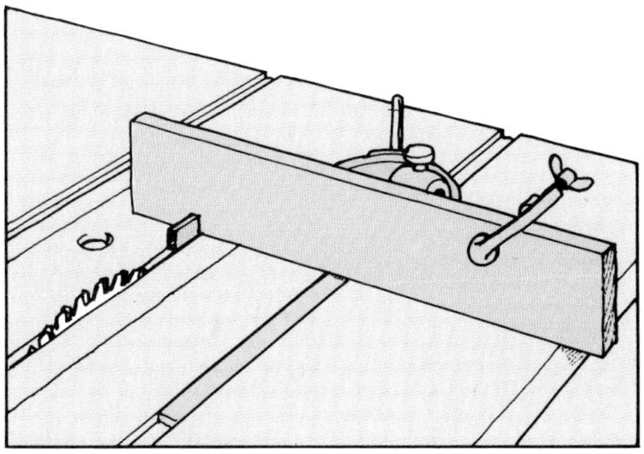

2 Glue a tongue in the slot

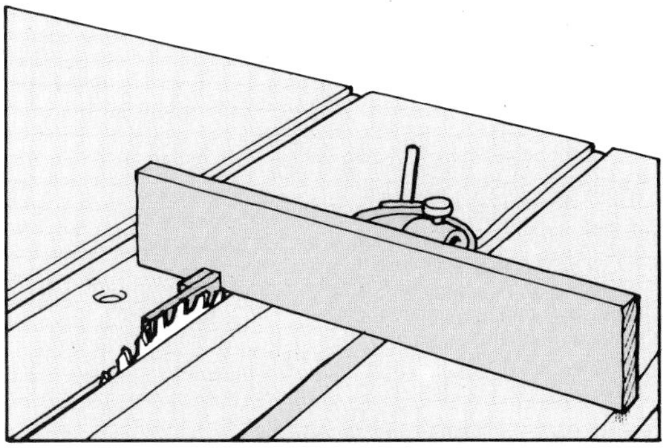

3 Place a strip of wood between the tongue and blade

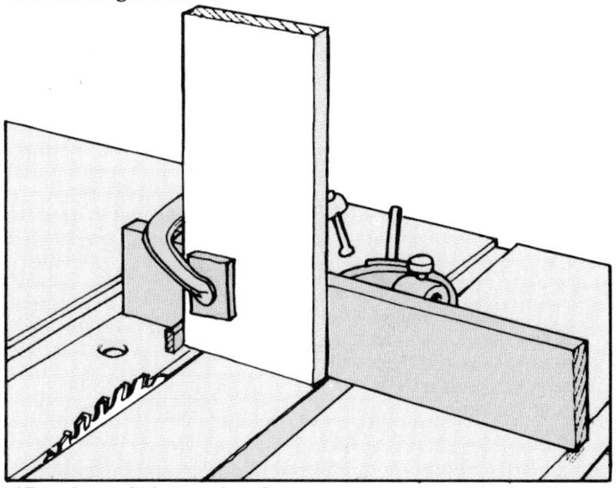

4 Butt the workpiece against the tongue

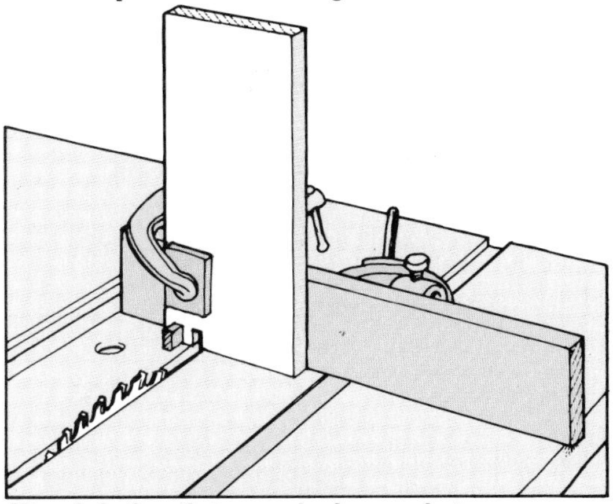

5 Drop the kerf over the tongue and make a second cut

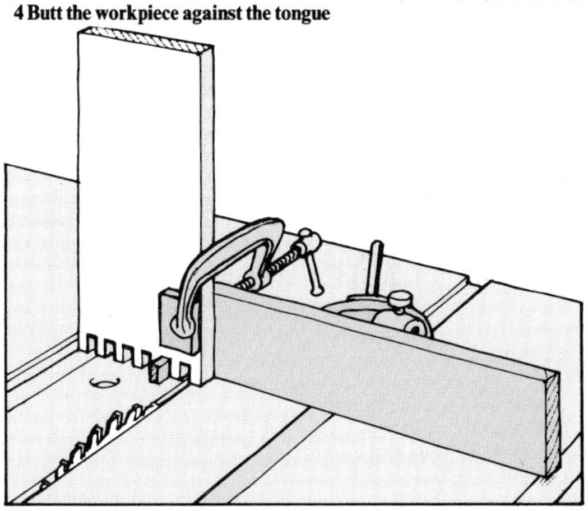

6 Complete the row of fingers

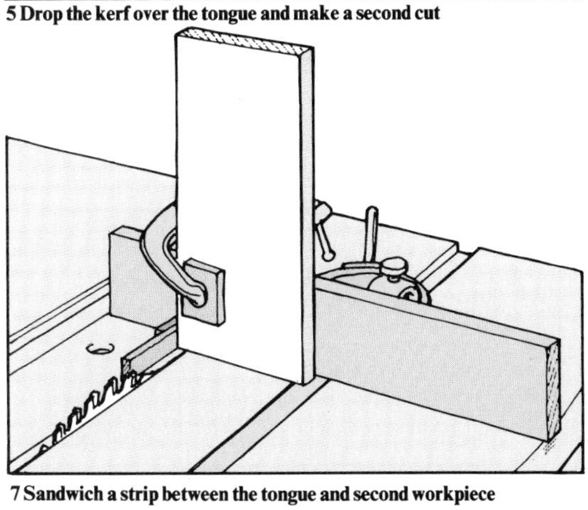

7 Sandwich a strip between the tongue and second workpiece

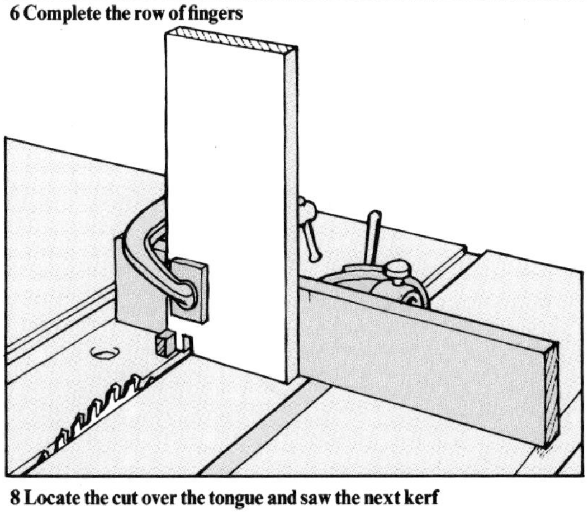

8 Locate the cut over the tongue and saw the next kerf

RADIAL-ARM SAWS

The radial-arm saw is first and foremost a crosscut saw, but it is the machine's versatility that makes it such an attractive proposition for the amateur woodworker. The saw will rip, crosscut, bevel or miter, and with slight modifications the same machine can be converted into a spindle shaper, overhead router, sander or drill. The blade and motor housing on a standard radial-arm saw is suspended below a metal arm mounted on top of a rigid column. The arm swings from side to side to present the blade at an angle to the work for cutting miters. At the same time, the motor housing and blade can be tilted and pivoted to make compound-angle cuts. On one model, the arm is fixed while the table pivots below it. Because the column is mounted to the rear of the worktable, a radial-arm saw can be installed against a wall. Most radial-arm saws stand on a bench or their own open stand, and some can be folded away and hung from wall brackets. Assemble and wire your saw according to the manufacturer's instructions.

SEE ALSO

Machine-shop safety	156
Crosscutting	167
Ripping	168
Saw conversions	170-171
Dust collectors	214
Hearing protectors	214

Electric motor
The average radial-arm saw for the home workshop is fitted with an induction motor rated at about 1.1kW (1½hp). This is powerful enough to generate adequate sawblade speeds of nearly 3000rpm, but is not capable of generating cutter speeds comparable with a spindle shaper unless the motor has a second "arbor," or drive shaft, geared for high-speed work.

Sawblade diameter
Radial-arm saws manufactured for the home workshop are usually supplied with 10in (250mm) blades.

Depth of cut
Most radial-arm saws have a possible maximum depth of cut of about 3in (75mm). The blade, along with the machine's arm, is raised or lowered by operating a crank situated either on top of the column or beneath the worktable.

Arm angle
The arm can be rotated left or right, after releasing the miter clamping lever. A latch positively locates the arm for crosscutting at 90 or 45 degrees. A scale on top of the column indicates the angle of the arm.

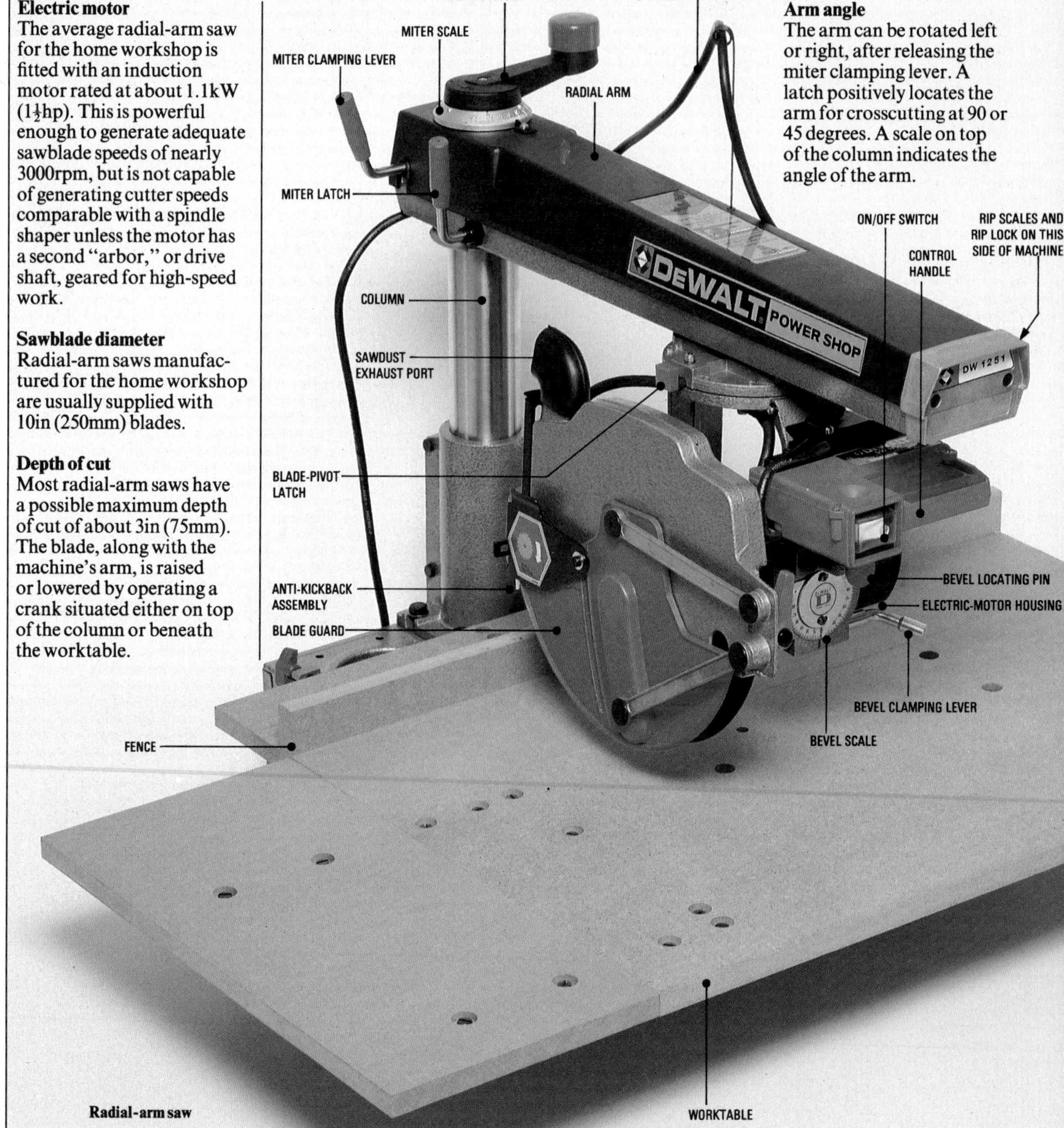

Radial-arm saw

Sawblade angle
You can tilt the sawblade to any angle between vertical and horizontal, having first released the bevel clamping lever and withdrawn a locating pin that engages automatically when the blade is at 90 or 45 degrees. Choose a machine with a scale that indicates the angle of the blade clearly.

Crosscut capacity
The maximum crosscutting width is determined mainly by the length of the arm. The crosscut capacity of home-workshop saws varies from 12 to 18in (300 to 460mm). To make cuts up to 24in (600mm) wide, you need to buy one of the smaller industrial radial-arm saws.

Rip capacity
The width of ripcut – up to a maximum of between 20 and 26in (500 and 650mm) – is selected by sliding the motor housing along the arm and locking it in position with a clamping lever or knob. Scales printed along the arm indicate ripcut width.

Blade guard
The blade on a modern radial-arm saw is enclosed by a "gravity guard" that is raised automatically by the work during sawing, then drops back under its own weight at the completion of the process.

Riving knife
When ripping, to prevent case-hardened wood from closing on the blade, lower the riving knife into position just behind the blade and secure it with the locknut. When crosscutting, the knife is pushed back inside the blade guard.

Anti-kickback assembly
If a blade jams during a ripcut, it can throw the work back toward the operator. To prevent this from happening, an anti-kickback assembly with trailing teeth, or "pawls," is mounted on the saw. The slightest backward movement of the work causes the pointed pawls to pivot downward to restrain the wood. The anti-kickback assembly also acts as a hold-down device to prevent the workpiece from being lifted off the table by the ascending sawteeth.

For ripping, raise or lower the anti-kickback assembly until the points of the pawls hang $\frac{1}{8}$in (3mm) below the surface of the wood. For crosscutting, raise the assembly clear of the work.

Setting the anti-kickback assembly

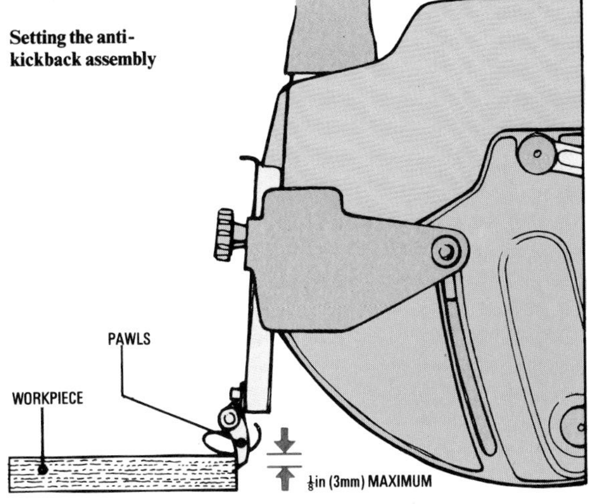

Worktable
A simple worktable of high-density fiberboard or chipboard is fixed to the machine's metal base. Because the blade of a radial-arm saw must cut into the surface of the table, it is worth tacking or spot-gluing a sheet of thin plywood onto the chipboard or fiberboard. Make sure any screws or nails are out of range of the blade's movements.

Fence
A workpiece is crosscut against a fence running across the worktable. The same fence is used to guide the work when ripping.

For crosscutting, the fence is sandwiched between the worktable and a spacer board – the blade being parked behind the fence between cuts. To increase rip capacity, the fence can be placed behind the spacer board.

The fence that comes with the machine is usually made from the same fibrous material as the worktable. However, you can replace it with one made from solid wood – in which case, make it longer than the original since stop blocks for making repetitive crosscuts can be clamped to an extended fence in order to accommodate longer workpieces.

On/off switches
The on/off switches are usually placed either at the end of the radial arm or on the main control handle, where they are within easy reach. Some saws are supplied with removable keys, so they can be rendered inoperable.

Dust collection
Radial-arm saws create a great deal of dust, which is ejected through a rubber exhaust port on the blade guard. Some form of dust collection is required in order to make sure the area surrounding the saw does not become slippery with loose sawdust.

USING A RADIAL-ARM SAW SAFELY

Always follow the general safety recommendations for working in a machine shop and take extra care when operating a radial-arm saw.

- Install the saw sloping backward very slightly, so the blade and motor housing cannot slide toward the operator under their own weight.
- When crosscutting, make sure the hand holding the work is not in line with the blade.
- Always park the blade and motor housing behind the fence between crosscuts.
- Never rip without using the anti-kickback assembly and riving knife.
- Keep anti-kickback pawls sharp. Take care when ripping plastic-laminated board, since it may not provide sufficient grip for the pawls.
- Do not perform an operation freehand. Always use the fence or some other device that will hold the workpiece still and stop it from rotating or twisting.
- Plan a ripcut so that the offcut is free to move sideways away from the blade.
- Do not stand directly in line with the blade when ripping.
- Have an assistant help you to support a long board.
- Don't rip short pieces of wood that will bring your hands close to the blade.
- Keep the blade guard in place and in good working condition.

- **Setting up the machine**
Support a radial-arm saw on a bench at a comfortable working height and allow enough clearance for your knuckles between the column and wall when operating the depth-adjustment crank.

RADIAL-ARM SAWBLADES AND CUTTERS

Blades similar to those used on a table saw are available for radial-arm saws. A general-purpose or universal blade, especially one with tungsten-carbide-tipped teeth, is the best choice for a home workshop. Fitting wobble washers to make the blade move from side to side is one way to cut grooves and housings.

SEE ALSO	
Machine-shop safety	156
Table-saw blades	158
Wobble washers	158
Blade guard	164-165
Anti-kickback assembly	165
Riving knife	165
Safety tips	165
Molding	170-171

Dado head
A dado head fitted to the normal saw arbor provides a means for cutting grooves and housings up to $\frac{7}{8}$in (21mm) wide in one pass. A dado head comprises two universal blades that cut both sides of a groove or dado simultaneously, while "chipper" blades sandwiched between them remove the waste. Paper washers are inserted between the blades to make minute adjustments to the width of cut.

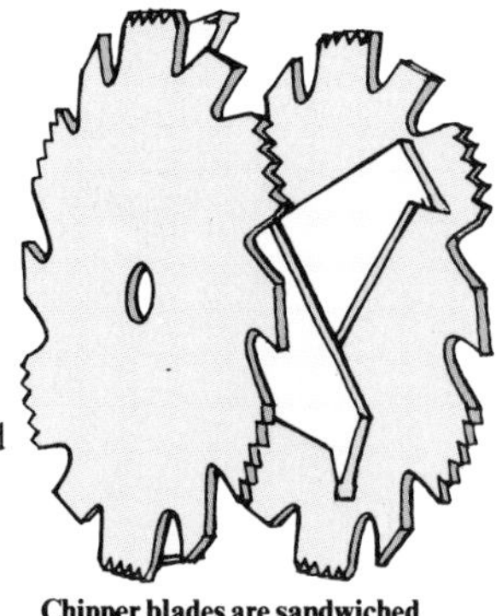
Chipper blades are sandwiched between dado sawblades

Tungsten-carbide-tipped sawblade

Dado head

- **Changing blades and cutters**
Always follow the manufacturer's instructions when fitting blades and molding heads on your radial-arm saw.

MOLDING HEADS

A radial-arm saw is converted to a spindle shaper by replacing the blade with metal molding heads that take two or three shaped cutters. A three-cutter head leaves a much cleaner finish on a workpiece. Each cutter is bolted securely into a slot in the molding head. An extensive range of shaped cutters is available for radial-arm saws.

The machine can be set up with the molding head revolving horizontally, in which case a special guard and fence have to be fitted. On some saws, the molding head can also be mounted vertically, like a sawblade, using the usual guard.

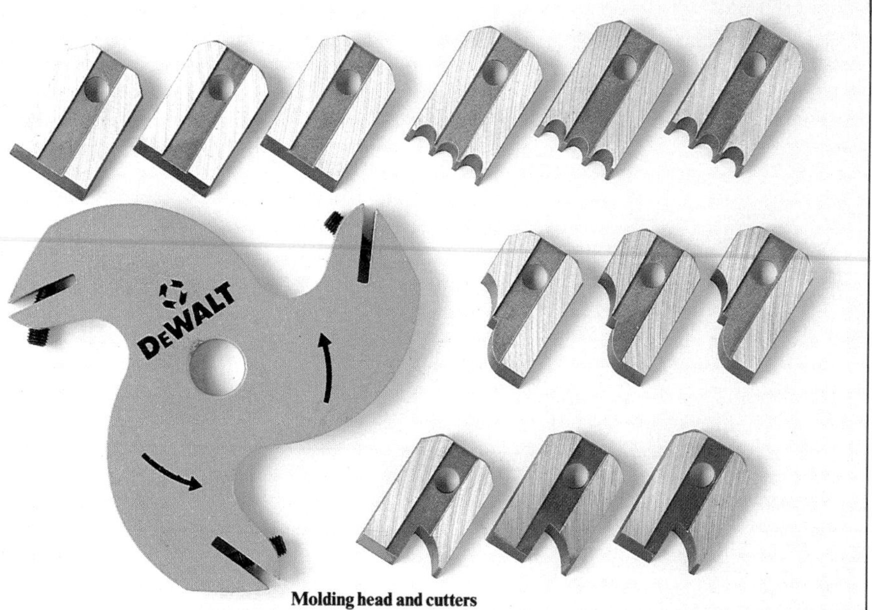

Molding head and cutters

CROSSCUTTING ON A RADIAL-ARM SAW

In order to sever a workpiece completely, the sawblade must cut into the plywood table lining to a depth of about $\frac{1}{16}$in (2mm). This scored line passes across the table and through the fence. The notch cut in the fence makes an ideal guide when you need to line up a marked cut line on a workpiece with the blade. Both the anti-kickback assembly and riving knife must be withdrawn while crosscutting.

Making a square crosscut
With one hand, hold the work face side uppermost against the fence so that the blade will cut on the waste side of the marked line. Make sure all clamping levers are tight, except for the one that allows the blade and motor housing to travel along the arm. Switch on the saw and steadily pull it toward you to just sever the work, then push it back and switch it off.

Crosscutting is a relatively safe procedure, because the action of the blade tends to hold the work against the fence and down onto the table. However, the blade also has a tendency to pull itself toward the operator – a tendency that must be resisted by keeping your forearm in a straight line with the handle of the saw.

Making repetitive crosscuts
If you want to cut several identical workpieces to length, aligning the marked lines with a notch in the fence may not be sufficiently accurate. Instead, clamp a block of wood to the fence to act as a stop block for the workpieces – but never position the stop block so that it restricts the lateral movement of an offcut once it has been severed. Also, always make sure that sawdust does not become trapped between a workpiece and the fence or stop block.

Cutting a wide or thick board
Use a stop block when you want to cut a board that is wider than the saw's crosscut capacity or thicker than its maximum depth of cut.

Cut just over halfway through the work – then turn it over, press it against the stop block and sever the wood with a second cut. This procedure is acceptable only when it is not important to preserve a face side.

Making a bevel crosscut
To make a bevel crosscut, first tilt the blade and clamp it at the required angle, then proceed as if you were making a square crosscut.

Cutting a miter
To cut a miter on the end of a workpiece, keeping the blade vertical, swing the arm to the required angle – usually 45 degrees – and clamp it in place. Holding the work firmly against the fence to make sure it cannot move during the operation, cut the miter by pulling the saw toward the front of the table.

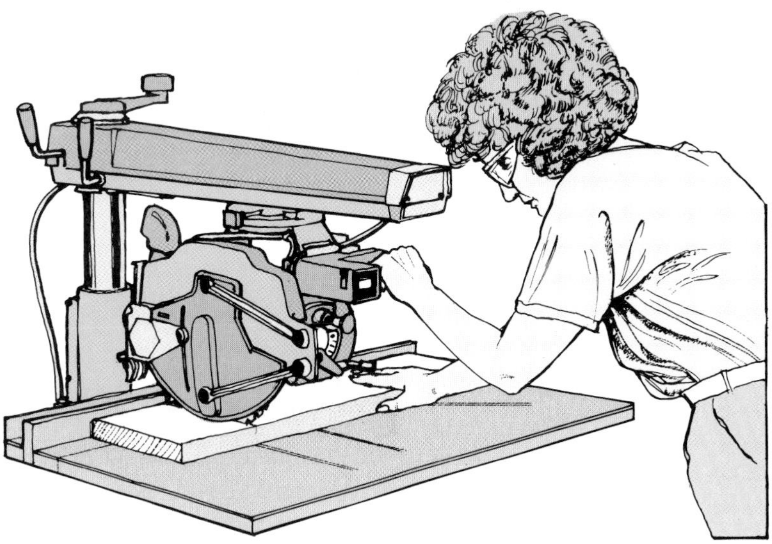

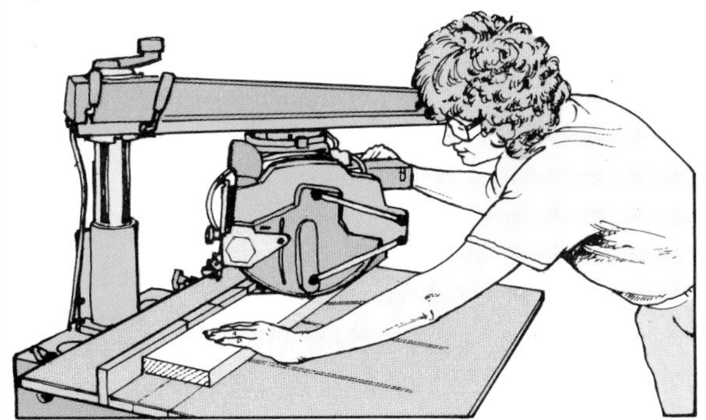

Swing the arm to one side to cut a miter

Hold the work firmly against the fence when making a square crosscut

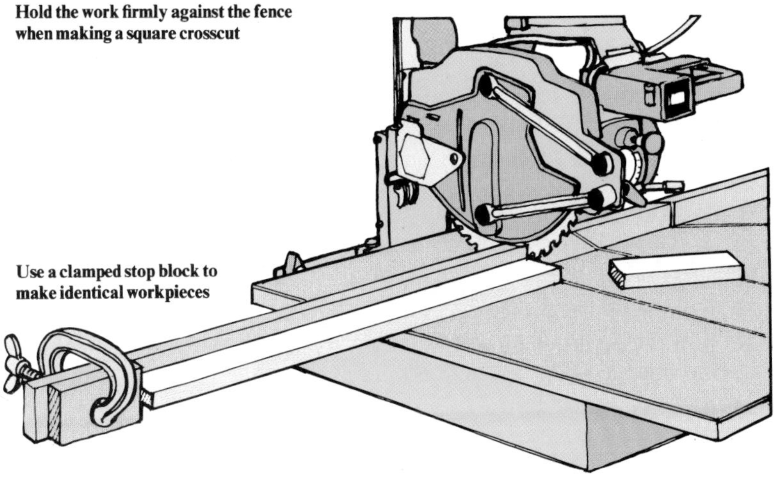

Use a clamped stop block to make identical workpieces

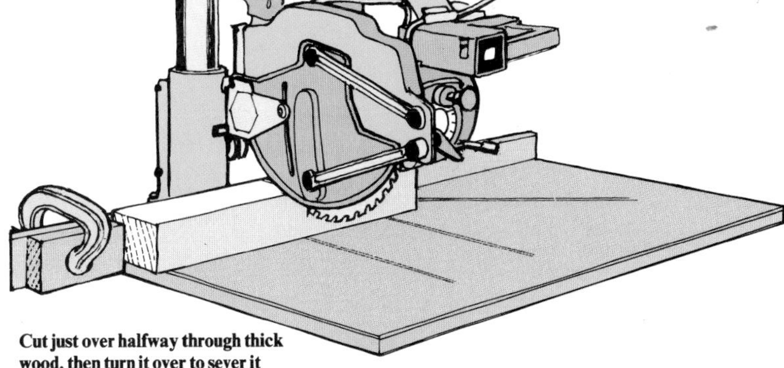

Cut just over halfway through thick wood, then turn it over to sever it

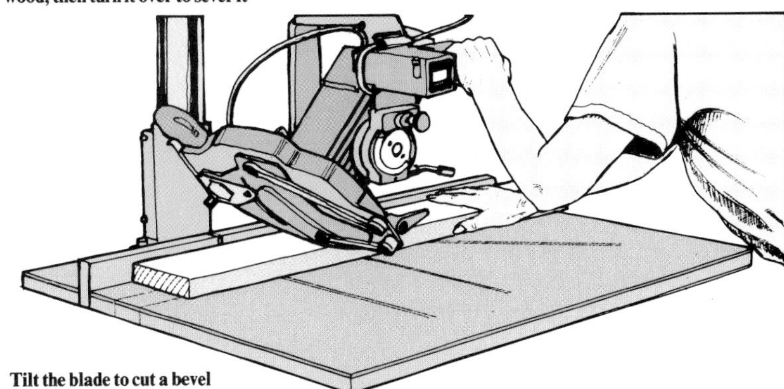

Tilt the blade to cut a bevel

RIPPING ON A RADIAL-ARM SAW

SEE ALSO

Machine-shop safety	156
Wobble washers	158
Anti-kickback assembly	165
Riving knife	165
Safety tips	165
Dado head	166
Crosscutting bevels	167
Cutting mortises	186-187

In order to cut a piece of wood to width, the blade of a radial-arm saw is turned parallel to the fence. For relatively narrow workpieces, the blade faces the saw's column in what is called the "inrip" position. To rip wider boards, the blade is turned to the "outrip" position, facing away from the column.

Feeding the work

A workpiece must be fed into the blade against its direction of rotation. To feed the work in the opposite direction would result in the blade grabbing the work, perhaps pulling the operator's hands toward it. When inripping, the work is fed from one side of the table (usually the right-hand side, but check the manufacturer's instructions); when outripping, it is fed from the other side since the blade is facing in the opposite direction. Both the riving knife and the anti-kickback assembly must be used whenever you are ripping wood.

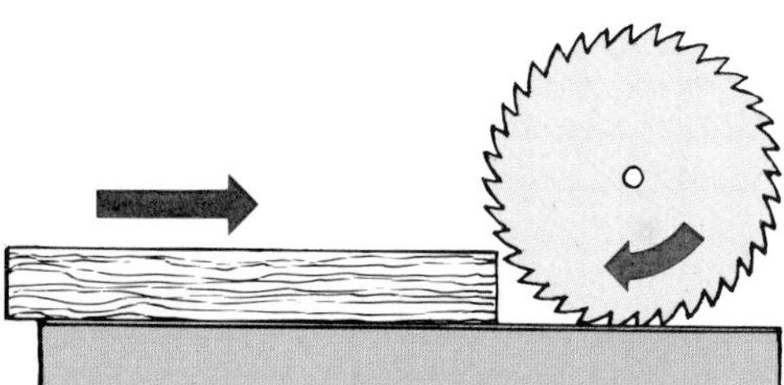

Direction of feed
Always feed wood against the rotation of the blade.

Adjusting the blade

Slide the blade along the arm until the required width of cut is indicated on one of the rip scales. To make sure the setting has not been affected by tightening the clamping lever, make a test cut in the end of a piece of scrap wood. You can increase the rip capacity by placing the fence behind the table's spacer board. To sever a workpiece completely, the blade must be lowered until it cuts into the table lining to a depth of about $\frac{1}{16}$in (2mm).

Ripping a workpiece to width

Check that all clamping levers are tight, then switch on the saw. Keeping the work pressed against the fence, use both hands to feed the work into the blade at a steady rate. Always use a notched push stick to feed a narrow workpiece that would otherwise bring your hands close to the blade. Have an assistant support or withdraw a long workpiece from the opposite side of the worktable.

Bevel ripping

To cut a bevel along one edge of a workpiece, proceed as if you were making a square ripcut, but tilt the blade to the required angle. Follow the manufacturer's instructions for setting the anti-kickback pawls for a tilted blade.

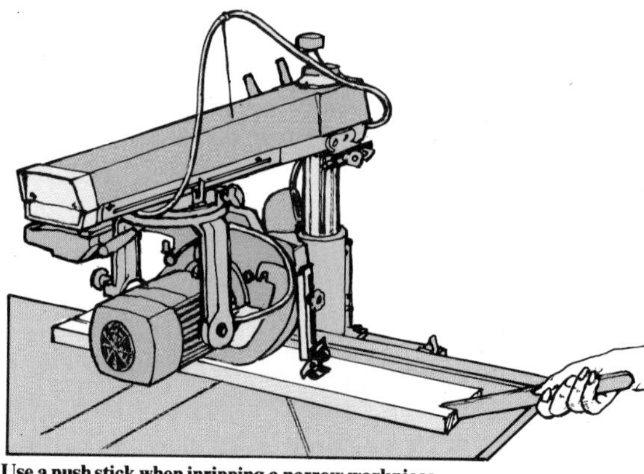

Use a push stick when inripping a narrow workpiece

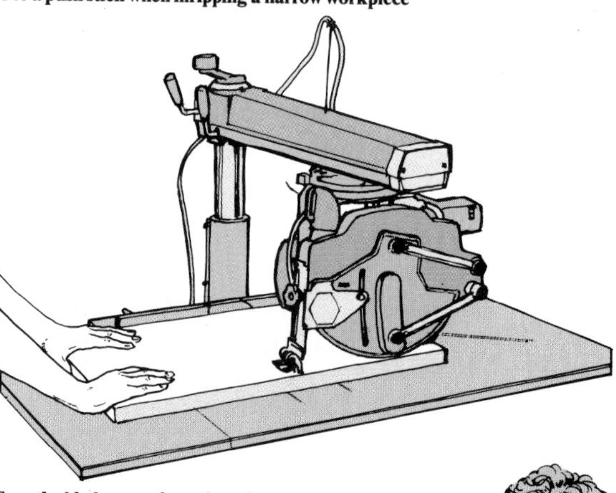

Turn the blade away from the column to outrip a wide board

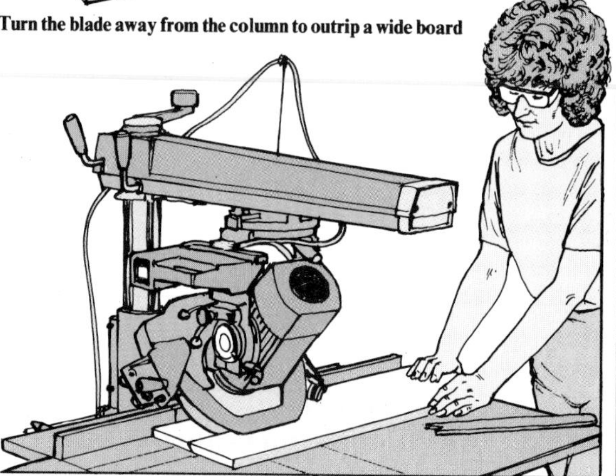

Tilt the blade to cut a bevel

CUTTING DADOES, GROOVES AND RABBETS

It is possible to cut a groove or rabbet parallel to the grain or a dado across a workpiece by using the standard sawblade to cut along both sides, then resetting the saw to remove the waste one blade-width at a time. However, it is easier to cut grooves, dadoes and rabbets with a wobble saw, or better still, a dado head.

Cutting a dado

Cut a dado with a dado head as if you were making a crosscut or miter. Being considerably wider than a single sawblade, a dado head may exaggerate the machine's tendency to pull itself toward the operator, so be prepared to resist it. To repeat a dado on more than one workpiece, clamp a stop block to the fence.

Cutting a groove

Fit a dado-head combination to make up the required width of cut. Remove the riving knife, but keep both the blade guard and anti-kickback assembly in place. Select the inrip or outrip position for the dado head, as appropriate, then proceed as if making a ripcut.

Cutting a rabbet

To cut a rabbet along the edge of a workpiece, use the dado head as if you were cutting a groove.

KERFING

Bending a length of solid wood by kerfing is an easy procedure on a radial-arm saw set up for crosscutting.

You can make a simple jig for accurate kerf spacing by driving a nail into the fence and snipping its head off. Having made one kerf, shift the work sideways, slide the kerf onto the nail and then cut the next kerf. Instead of using a nail, you can make a pencil mark on the fence and align each cut by eye.

Use a stop block to position dadoes accurately

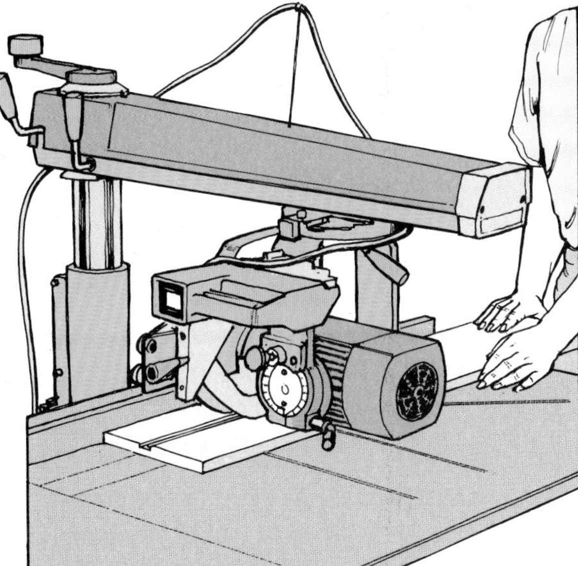

A dado head cuts a wide groove in one pass

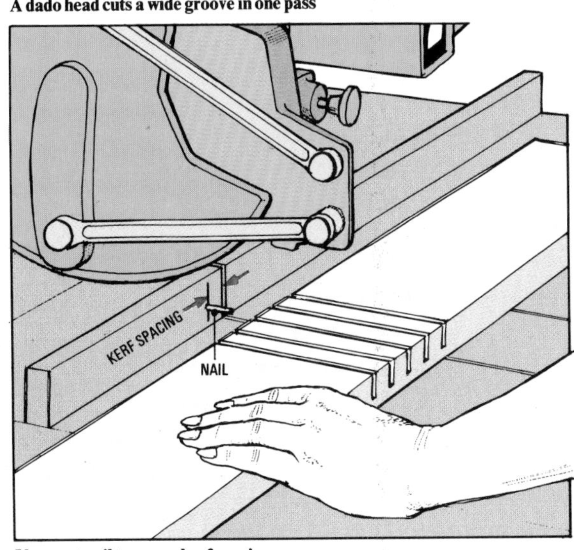

Use a cut nail to gauge kerf spacing

CUTTING JOINTS ON A RADIAL-ARM SAW

Certain simple joints can be cut quickly and accurately on a radial-arm saw. Fit a combination blade, or save time by using a dado head for lap joints, rabbet joints and tenons.

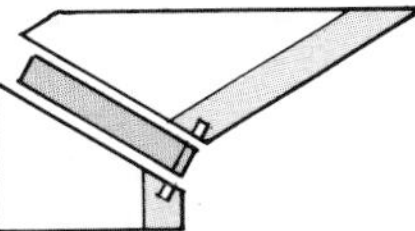

Reinforced miter joint
A plywood spline is often used to reinforce a miter joint. Having made two straightforward bevel crosscuts, adjust the blade depth, then turn the work over and cut a slot for the spline in each bevel. Use a stop block to ensure the slot is identically placed in both halves of the joint.

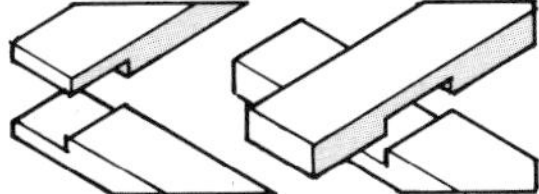

Lap joints
To make a lap or cross-lap joint, first adjust the blade to cut halfway through the work, then make crosscuts on the shoulder lines. Slide the work sideways against the fence, making successive crosscuts to remove the waste little by little.

Use a stop block to repeat shoulder-line cuts accurately. In the case of a cross-lap joint, clamp stop blocks at both ends of the fence – one for each of the shoulder lines.

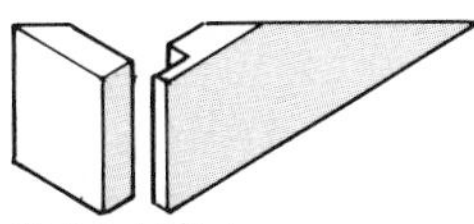

Rabbet joints
Square both halves of the joint with a straightforward crosscut, then adjust the blade height and cut the rabbet in the same manner as a lap joint.

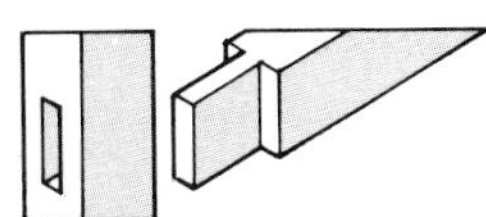

Cutting tenons
With the workpiece butted against a stop block, cut one side of a tenon as you would a lap joint, then turn it over and cut the other side.

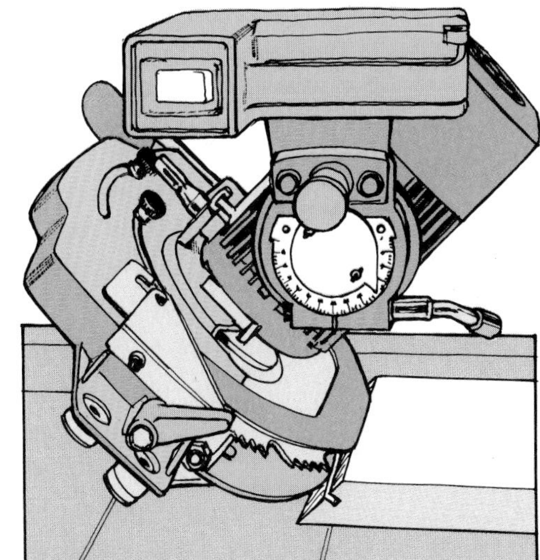

Cut a slot for a miter-reinforcing spline

Cut a lap-joint shoulder first, then remove waste

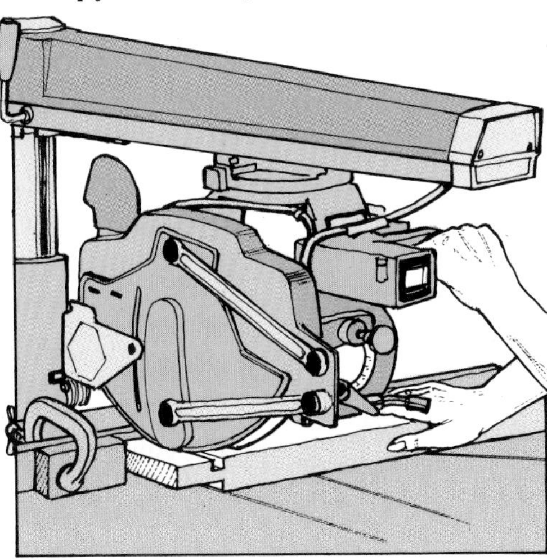

Use a stop block to help cut both sides of a tenon

DRILLING WITH A RADIAL-ARM SAW

You can convert your radial-arm saw into a power drill by fitting a chuck with a capacity of $\frac{3}{8}$in (10mm) to the arbor at the other end of the motor housing from the blade, which must be removed first.

Drilling side grain
To drill into the side of a workpiece, set up the machine so that the drill chuck faces the column. Construct a high fence to serve as a backup, and raise the workpiece on scrap wood. Use a clamped stop block to position the work accurately.
Hold or clamp the workpiece, then switch on the saw and feed the drill into the work by moving the motor housing along the radial arm **(1)**. Drill a series of holes in line to remove the waste from a mortise.

Drilling end grain
To drill into end grain – to insert dowels, for example – turn the motor housing so that the drill bit is parallel to the fence and tighten all clamping levers. Raise the work on a temporarily constructed box or a piece of scrap wood, and feed it against the fence into the drill bit **(2)**. Tack or clamp a block to the fence ahead of the work to act as a depth stop.

1 Feed the drill into side grain

2 Feed end grain toward the drill

ROUTING WITH A RADIAL-ARM SAW

Many radial-arm saws accept mounting brackets to hold popular brands of routers.

Sliding the router back and forth along the radial arm is an excellent method for making stopped housings for bookcase shelves or stair treads.
Cut grooves or rabbets along a workpiece by running it against the fence into a fixed router held in place by the saw's clamping lever. Cutting a stopped groove is less simple, since you have to lower and raise the router during the operation, using the depth-adjusting crank.
When molding or rabbeting an edge, remember to feed the work against the rotation of the router bit.

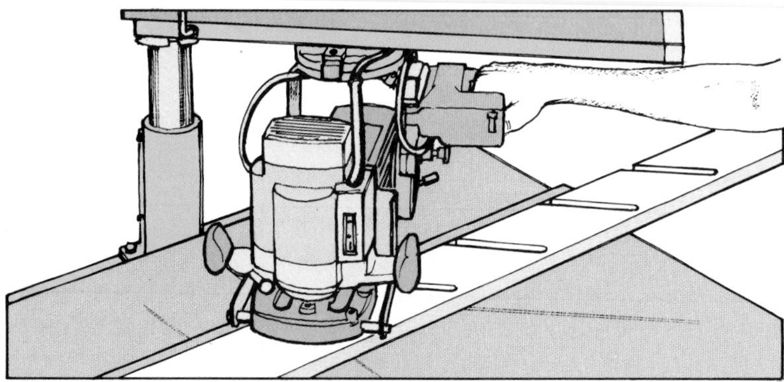

Cut stopped housings with a mobile router

USING THE MOLDING HEAD

If you intend to shape work with a molding head, you must fit a special guard that encircles the cutters. You will also need to make a two-part fence and to take extra care to ensure every procedure is undertaken with safety. Few radial-arm saws are supplied with the vertical/horizontal hold-down guards that are a feature of spindle shapers, so you may have to make a featherboard to hold narrow workpieces firmly against the fence (see opposite).
Always follow the manufacturer's instructions for setting up the machine and for fitting the cutters in the molding head – since a serious accident could occur if a cutter works loose.

Making a fence for shaping
When the molding head is mounted horizontally for shaping the edge of a workpiece, you need a two-part fence through which the cutters protrude. Clamp both halves of the fence between the worktable and the spacer board, adjusting them to provide just enough clearance for the cutters **(1)**. When you are rabbeting or cutting a molding that leaves part of the edge intact, both halves of the fence should be in line **(2)**.
To support a deeply molded edge, the outfeed half of the fence must be set forward **(3)**. The simplest method is to plane two wooden strips to a thickness that exactly matches the amount of wood to be removed. Place one strip in front of the fence, and the other behind the outfeed half **(4)**. Set the strips flush with the worktable.

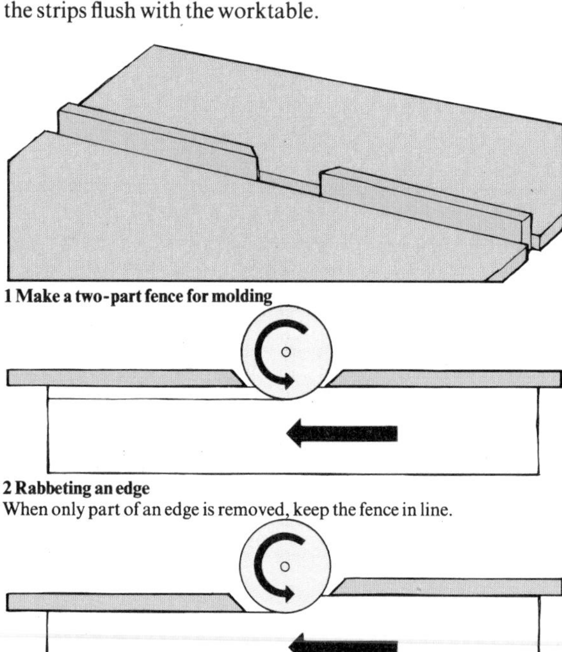

1 Make a two-part fence for molding

2 Rabbeting an edge
When only part of an edge is removed, keep the fence in line.

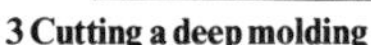

3 Cutting a deep molding
Offset outfeed section of fence to support the molded wood.

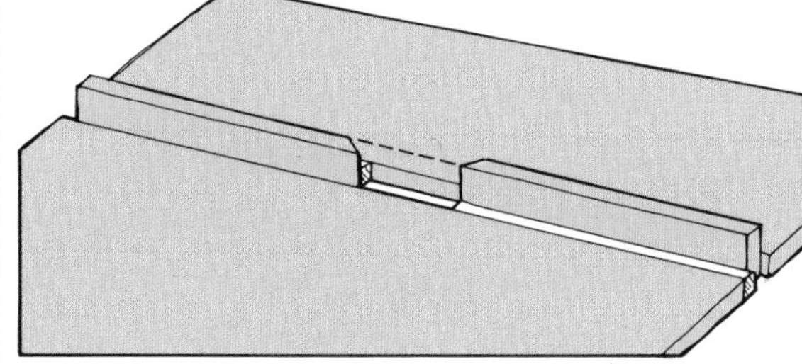

4 Shift the two-part fence out of line with strips of wood

Adjusting the cutter height
Using the saw's controls, you can adjust the height of the cutters to mold a workpiece from above **(1)**. However, molding from underneath **(2)** has two advantages, if the shape of the cutter permits it. First, the work itself protects the operator from the cutters. Second, if a slightly warped workpiece rises on the table, the cutters will not take a deeper bite out of it as they would if the molding head was suspended above it.

Positioning the molding head below the work can be achieved by cutting a hole in the worktable and spacer board, or by laying a board on the table to raise the work.

Molding a wide board
Always feed the work at a steady rate against the rotation of the molding head. Press the work against the fence, keeping both hands flat on the work – never trailing them behind or in line with the cutters. Don't try to remove too much wood in one pass. Shape a deep molding by making two or three shallow cuts and adjusting the molding head between passes.

Molding a narrow board
Don't feed a narrow board past the cutters by hand. With a jigsaw or band saw, make a featherboard by cutting curved fingers along the edge of a piece of wood. Screw the featherboard to the worktable to leave a tight sliding fit for the workpiece between the flexible fingers and the fence. Use a push stick to feed the work past the cutters. Don't try to mold a very narrow strip of wood – instead, shape the edge of a wider board, then saw off a strip the size you want.

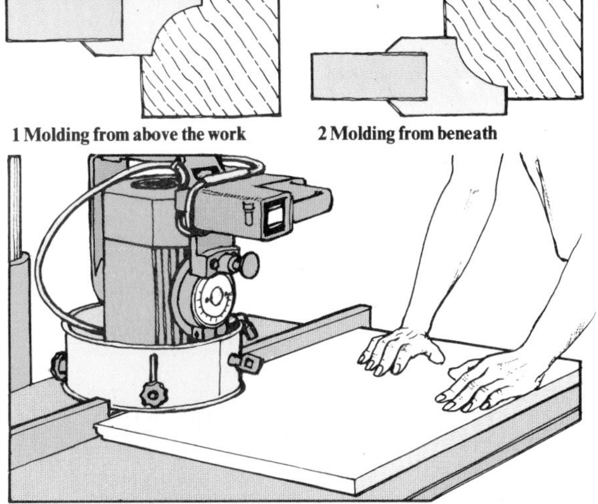

1 Molding from above the work

2 Molding from beneath

Molding a wide board
Feed the work by hand.

Molding a narrow board
Use a featherboard to hold the work against the fence.

USING A RADIAL-ARM SAW AS A SANDER

You can convert a radial-arm saw into a very serviceable sanding machine by adding disc and drum sanders. Both accessories are fitted in place of the standard sawblade.

Drum sanding
The small drum sanders available for radial-arm saws are ideally suited for finishing and shaping the edges of workpieces. With the drum mounted vertically, a contoured workpiece can be fed freehand against the abrasive surface. Separate the table and spacer board with wooden blocks to create a gap through which you can lower the drum level with the worktable surface. Tilt the motor housing to sand a mitered edge.

In order to sand a straight, narrow workpiece with flat surfaces, set the drum horizontally and pass the workpiece under it.

Take care to feed the work against the rotation of the drum, or it will be grabbed from your hands and thrown off the machine.

Disc sanding
To sand end grain, swing the radial arm to one side and lower the motor housing to present the disc alongside a worktable extension. If you do not have room to construct an extension, raise the work by standing it on a temporary box or platform placed on the worktable. Clamp the arm at 90 degrees and adjust the disc so that it will revolve level with the platform.

Work against the "down" side of the disc at all times, so that the work is held down on the table. Sand square or mitered work against a temporarily clamped fence, or use the disc to shape curves freehand.

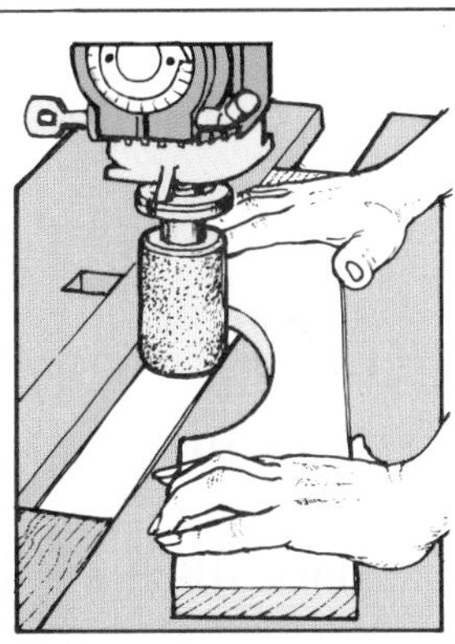

Contour sanding
Mount the drum vertically.

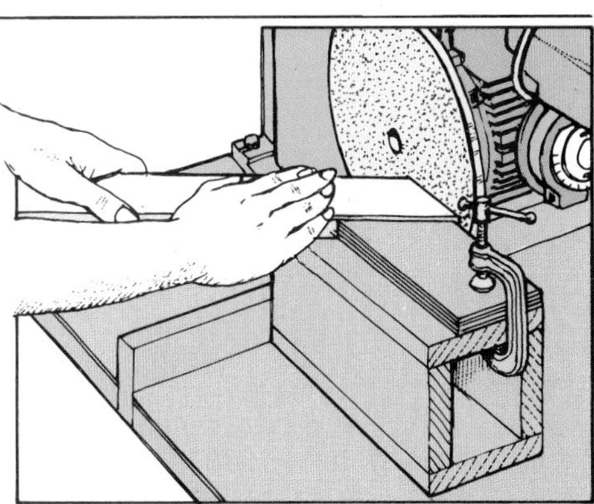

Use a fence for accurate disc sanding

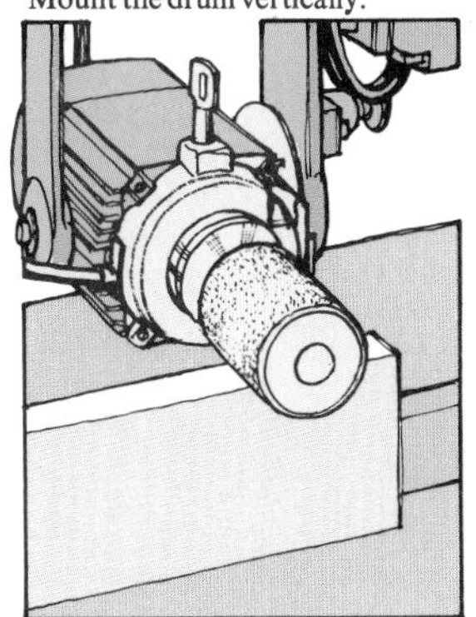

Sanding a straight edge
Set the drum horizontally.

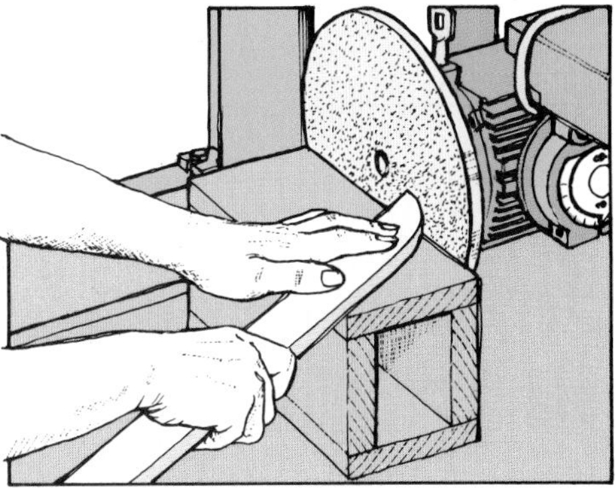

Shape curved work freehand

BAND SAWS

A band-saw blade is a continuous loop of metal driven over two or three large wheels. Because the thrust of the blade is always downward onto the saw table, there is no danger of a kickback throwing the work toward the operator. For this reason, many woodworkers prefer the band saw to a radial-arm saw, even though it neither rips nor crosscuts quite as cleanly or as fast. The band saw has several other advantages. It can be used to cut curved pieces; it will cut thicker wood than the average circular saw will; waste is minimal thanks to the very narrow kerf cut by the blade; and it also costs less than a good table saw. A band saw takes up little floor space, and those designed for the home workshop are light enough to be maneuvered into place without special lifting equipment. A good band saw runs relatively quietly, which is a great advantage if your workshop is situated in your house.

SEE ALSO

Machine-shop safety	156
Replacing blades	175
Making curved cuts	176
Push stick	177
Dust collectors	214

Depth of cut
Many band saws are sold by virtue of the fact that they are capable of cutting thick workpieces. The average home-workshop band saw will cut wood up to 6in (150mm) thick, but the slightly more expensive versions have a maximum capacity of 12in (300mm). This makes a band saw the ideal machine for cutting large timbers into planks or even into veneers.

Width of cut
The band saw's throat – the distance from the blade to the vertical frame member – determines its maximum width of cut. Throat size on most home-workshop band saws is about 12 to 14in (300 to 350mm). If you are likely to cut wider boards, choose one of the smaller industrial band saws.

- **Electric motor**
Band saws for the non-professional market are made with 550 to 750W (¾ to 1hp) electric motors, powerful enough to cope with the demands made on them in a home workshop.

Cutting speed
The cutting speed of a band saw is measured by the number of feet or meters a point on the blade will travel in one minute. Top speed varies considerably from saw to saw, ranging from 720ft (220m) to 4000ft (1220m) per minute. On some band saws, slower speeds can be selected for cutting metals and hard plastics. Others are fitted with variable-speed control between limits. Manufacturers normally recommend the highest speeds for cutting wood, but be prepared to reduce speed if you sense the saw is straining when cutting very thick or dense wood.

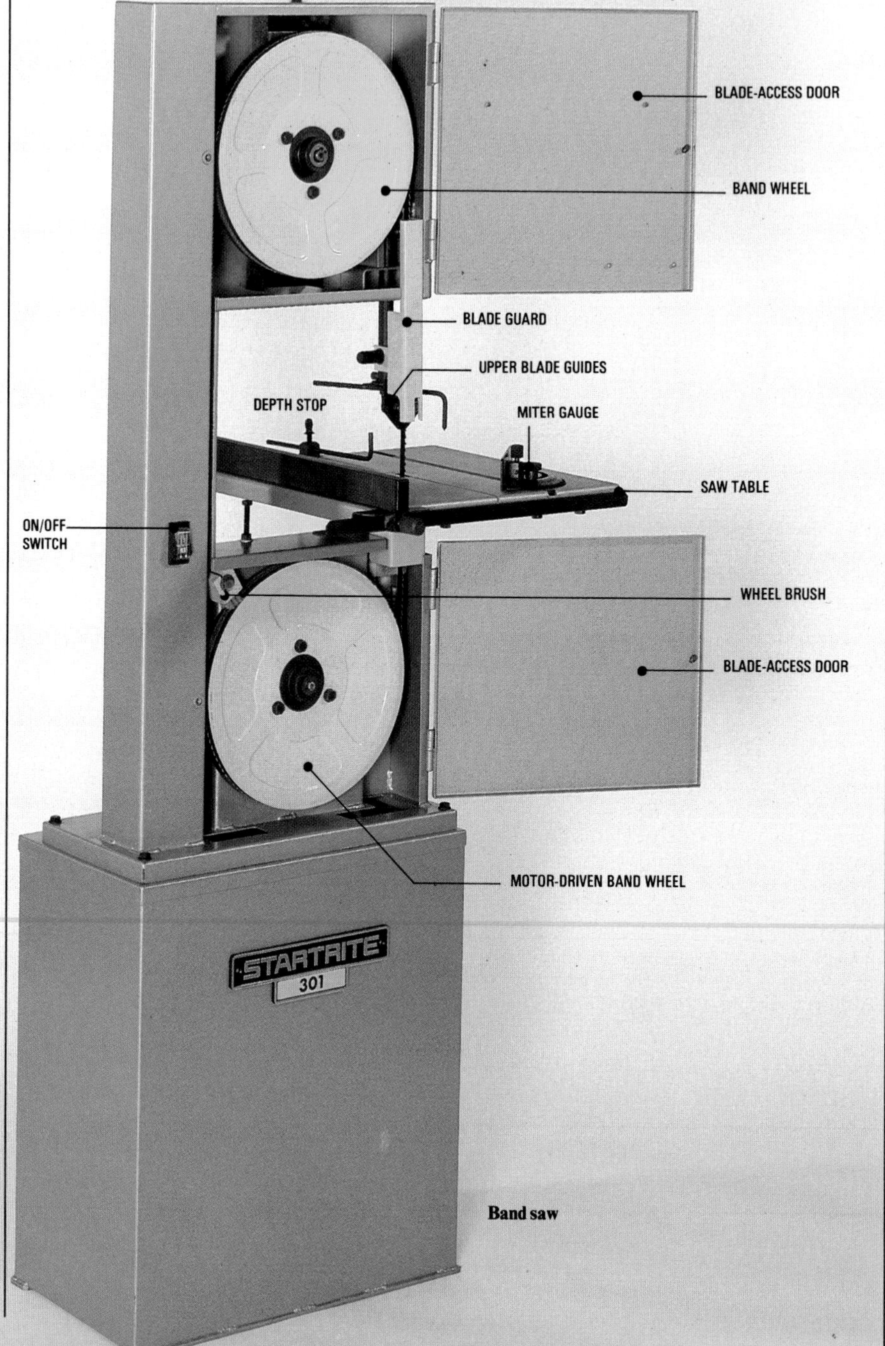

Band saw

Band wheels
All band saws have at least two wheels for the blade, one mounted directly above the other. The lower wheel is driven by the motor. Some saws have a third wheel that has the effect of increasing throat width, since the blade travels to one side before returning to the upper wheel. Three-wheel saws put a greater strain on blades, causing them to break more often. Band wheels are fitted with rubber, cork or PVC tires to preserve the set of the blades.

If possible, choose a saw with a fixed brush that continuously cleans sawdust from the drive-wheel tire while the machine is running, since accumulated sawdust can cause the blade to slip. Also look for band wheels mounted on sealed bearings – they never need lubricating.

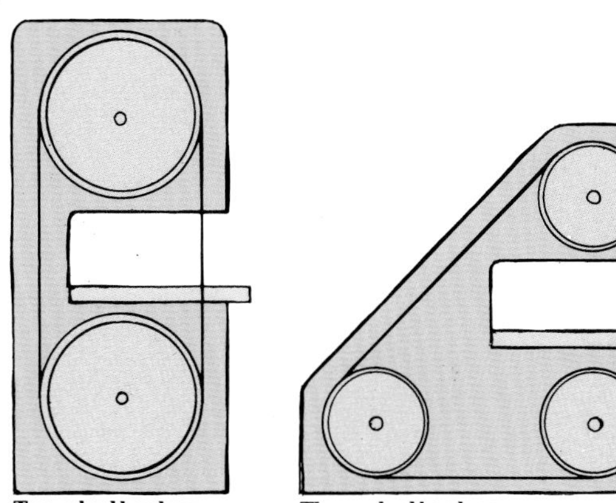

Two-wheel band saw   Three-wheel band saw

Blade guides
Bearings or guide blocks support the blade on both sides and from behind to resist the tendency for it to be twisted and pushed off the band wheels by the action of cutting a workpiece. One set of bearings, mounted above the saw table, is moved up or down to accommodate the thickness of the work; and a fixed set of bearings is usually mounted below the table. Blade guides must be capable of adjustment to very fine tolerances.

Blade tension and tracking
The blade's tension is adjusted by moving the top band wheel up or down. Some saws are made with a scale that indicates the tension for each blade, but usually the correct blade tension has to be ascertained by experimentation and experience. The tracking is adjustable to ensure that the blade runs centrally on the band wheels.

Blade guards
Except for the part exposed to the work, the entire band-saw blade is enclosed by the machine's casing. The exposed section is shielded by a vertically adjustable guard.

Saw frame
The best band saws have a rigid cast-iron or heavy-gauge steel frame to resist the considerable tension applied to the blade. A saw cannot run true if the frame is flexible.

Saw table
The majority of saw tables are made from cast iron, ground fabricated steel or an aluminum alloy. They are machined perfectly flat or have grooves for faster sawdust clearance.

Every band-saw table tilts to 45 degrees for cutting miters and bevels. A scale under the table indicates the angle of tilt. The average table is 16 to 18in (400 to 450mm) square.

Rip fence
Straight ripcuts are made against a short adjustable fence. Very deep or long workpieces may prove unstable when using the rip fence as supplied – in which case, extend the fence by screwing a higher wooden fence onto it. You will find it advantageous if the rip fence can be mounted on either side of the blade, particularly for bevel ripping when gravity will help hold the work against the fence on the tilted table. Some saws are made with a depth stop mounted ahead of the rip fence for cutting tenons and other joints to length.

Miter gauge
A miter gauge slides along a groove machined or cast in the saw table. By adjusting the angle of the gauge, it is possible to make square or mitered crosscuts. Miter gauges are often too short, and should be extended with a wooden facing to support long workpieces.

On/off switches
As a safety feature, on/off switches are sometimes made with a removable key. On some models, opening the blade-access doors automatically immobilizes the machine to ensure that the saw cannot be switched on accidentally when the blade and band wheels are exposed.

Foot brake
Floor-standing band saws are sometimes fitted with a brake to bring the blade to a stop after switching the machine off.

Dust collection
A sawdust exhaust port below the table can be attached to the hose of a portable vacuum.

USING A BAND SAW SAFELY

A band saw is a relatively safe woodworking machine provided you follow general safety recommendations and observe the following rules.

- Always adjust the blade guard and top guides as close as possible to the workpiece.
- Do not feed work with your thumbs directly in line with the blade. Use a push stick to feed a narrow workpiece.
- To avoid pulling the blade off the wheels, never back out of a deep cut without switching off the saw first.
- Should a blade break or slip from the band wheels while you are using the saw, switch it off immediately and stand back. Do not open the blade-access doors until the machine has come to a stop.
- Replace dull or damaged blades before you find you are having to feed the work with excess force.
- Wear gloves when coiling or uncoiling band-saw blades.

TYPES OF BAND SAW

The larger band saws stand on the workshop floor and have a one-piece frame. The smaller models are designed for mounting on a low bench. You can either buy a bench as an accessory or make your own.

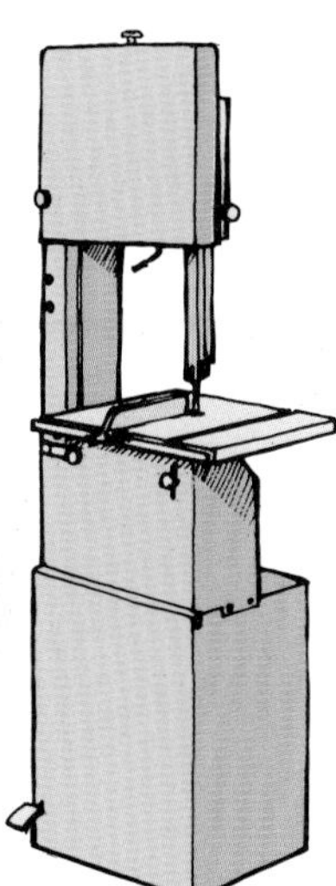

Floor-standing band saw

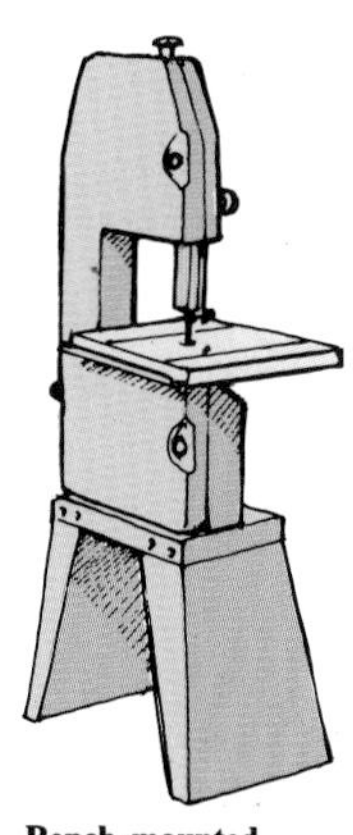

Bench-mounted band saw

BAND-SAW BLADES

When you buy a band saw, it will probably be fitted with one of the wider sawblades available for that particular machine. However, a much wider range of blades is made for every band saw, and even if you decide to continue using one or two blades only, it is worth knowing about the full range in case you want to perform a specific procedure on your saw that your standard blades cannot handle.

SEE ALSO

Machine-shop safety	156
Band-saw components	172
Safety tips	173

Material
Band-saw blades are made from a tough flexible steel with a hard, brittle cutting edge that stays sharp and keeps its set for long periods even when sawing man-made boards. Hard-edged blades cannot be file-sharpened and are thrown away as soon as they become dull.

Although relatively soft nickel-steel blades can be sharpened, reset and even rewelded when broken, the cost of professional repair and maintenance is such that the longer-lasting disposable blades are a better choice.

Tooth size
Sawtooth size is specified by the number of teeth that fit into a 1in length of blade. For a given thickness, hardwood, chipboard and plywood require more teeth per inch (TPI) than resinous softwood. Also, bear in mind that small teeth tend to skid when cutting softwoods.

Generally, the smoothest cut is achieved using relatively fine teeth with a high saw speed and a slow rate of feed. For faster cutting, choose a blade with larger teeth, then increase both the saw speed and feed rate.

Width of blade
Depending on the model of band saw, blades are available from ⅛ to ¾in (3 to 20mm) wide. Wide blades tend to hold a straight line better than narrow ones, and are selected for ripping wood and boards to width.

When you want to cut curves in wood, select the optimum width of blade to suit the minimum radius.

To save time in changing blades, most woodworkers fit a medium-width blade for general-purpose work.

Tooth shape
The shape of the sawtooth is designed either for faster cutting or a clean surface.

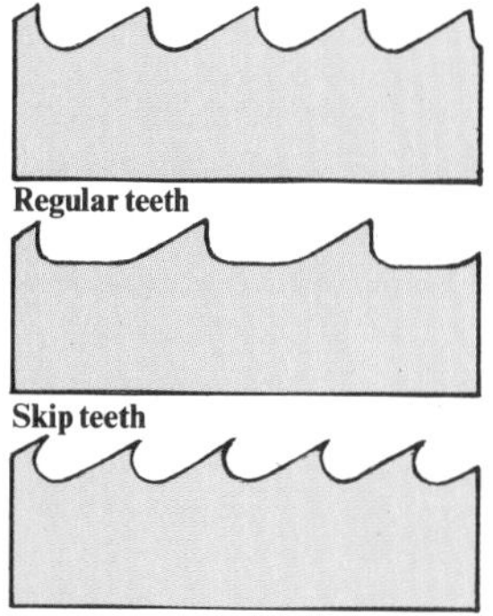

Regular teeth

Skip teeth

Hook teeth

Regular tooth This is the standard type of tooth for most band-saw blades. It will produce an accurate, fine cut on most woods and man-made boards.

Skip tooth The shape of a skip tooth is similar to that of a regular tooth, but each one is separated by a wide gullet for better chip removal. The cut is relatively rough. Skip-tooth blades are particularly suitable for sawing deep workpieces.

Hook tooth This kind of tooth has what is known as a "positive rake" – i.e. the leading edge of each tooth leans at an acute angle. A hook tooth is able to cut hard material quickly.

Tooth set
Band-saw teeth are bent sideways to cut a kerf wider than the body of the blade, thus providing a clearance that reduces friction in a straight cut and also permits the work to be steered on a curved path.

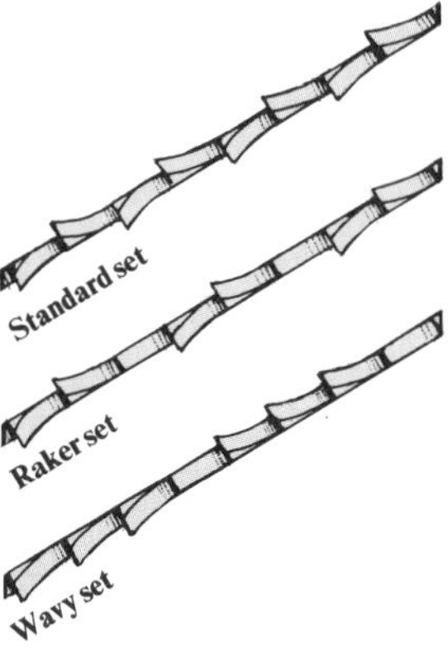

Standard set The teeth are bent alternately to left and right, as on the blades of most woodcutting saws.

Raker set Blades designed primarily for cutting curves have pairs of standard-set teeth separated by a single unset tooth.

Wavy set Groups of teeth set alternately to the left and right form a wavy cutting edge on this type of blade. It is the best sort of blade for cutting thin boards.

Special-purpose bands
Occasionally, you may want to cut materials that require special-purpose bands instead of the usual toothed blades. An abrasive band is fitted like a sawblade, but it is backed up by a rigid plate bolted in place of the blade guides.

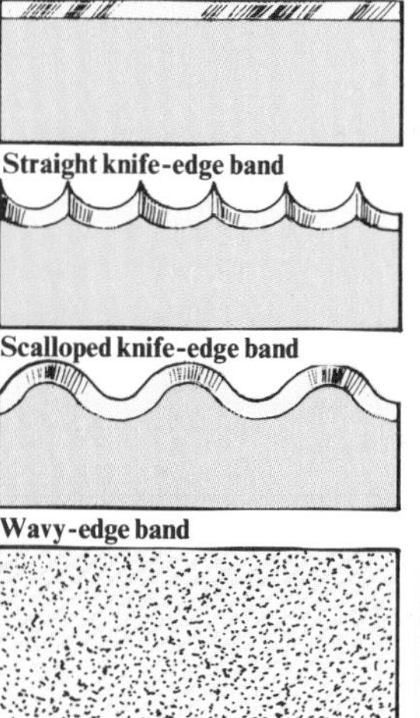

Straight knife-edge band

Scalloped knife-edge band

Wavy-edge band

Abrasive band

Knife-edge bands To cut upholstery foams, fabrics and cork, fit a straight, scalloped or wavy-edge knife band.

Abrasive bands These are narrow flexible bands covered with abrasive material for shaping and sanding straight and curved edges.

BLADE-WIDTH GUIDE

Select the width of blade to suit the minimum radius of a curved cut.

Blade width	in	⅛	¼	⅜	½	⅝	¾
	mm	3	6	10	12	15	20
Minimum radius	in	5/16	1	1½	2½	4	5½
	mm	8	25	38	62	100	136

CHANGING A BAND-SAW BLADE

Whether you need to replace a blade because it has become dull or simply want to swap it for one of a different size or tooth configuration, the procedure is identical.

Replacing the blade

To change a blade, first remove the rip-fence guide rail and blade guard, then retract the blade guides. Lower the upper band wheel by turning the blade-tension adjuster, and lift the blade out of the machine.

Place the new sawblade over the top wheel and work it onto the lower one. The blade teeth should be facing the operator and pointing down toward the saw table.

Tension the blade just enough to take up the slack, then check the tracking by spinning the band wheels by hand. Professional sawyers like to have the blade running close to the front edges of the wheels **(1)**, but it is normally safer to position the blade centrally **(2)**. However, check the manufacturer's recommendations for tracking adjustment. Adjust the tracking device until the blade runs true.

Raise the top wheel until the correct tension is indicated on the appropriate scale or until the unsupported section of the blade can flex no more than about $\frac{1}{4}$in (6mm) to either side. Then check and adjust tracking a final time.

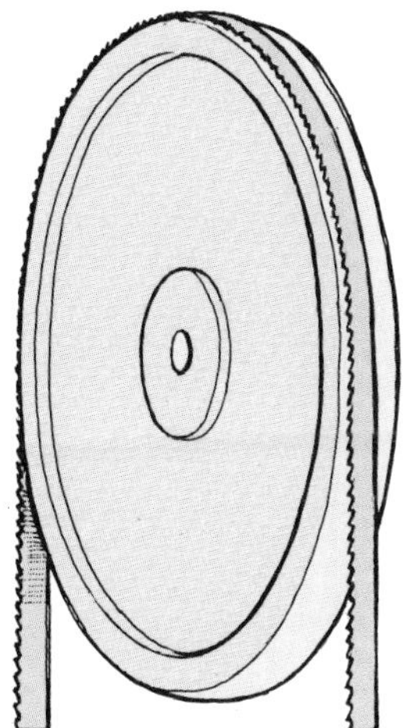

1 Some sawyers track close to the front edges of band wheels

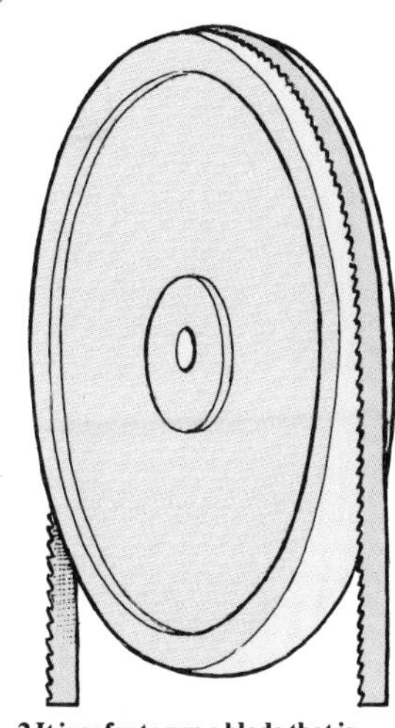

2 It is safer to run a blade that is centered on the wheels

Setting the blade guides

Set both sets of blade guides in the same way. First, adjust the thrust bearing up to the back edge of the blade, leaving the minimum clearance so that contact is made only when pressure is applied to the blade.

Next, adjust the side bearings to leave a paper-thin clearance on each side of the blade **(3)**. Each bearing should be level with the roots of the teeth when the blade is cutting **(4)**. If you advance the bearings too far, they will destroy the set of the blade.

Finally, replace the guard, close the blade-access doors and reassemble the rip fence before switching on the saw.

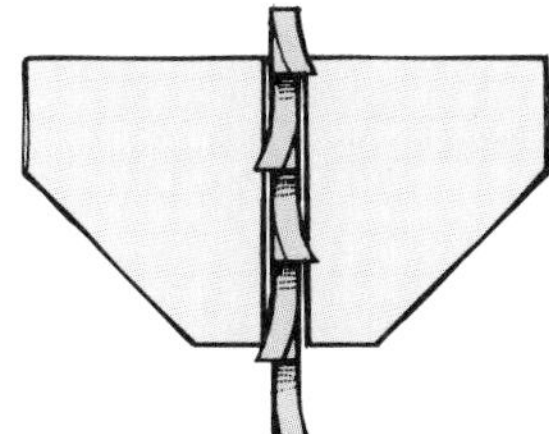

3 Side-bearing adjustment
Leave a tiny gap on each side.

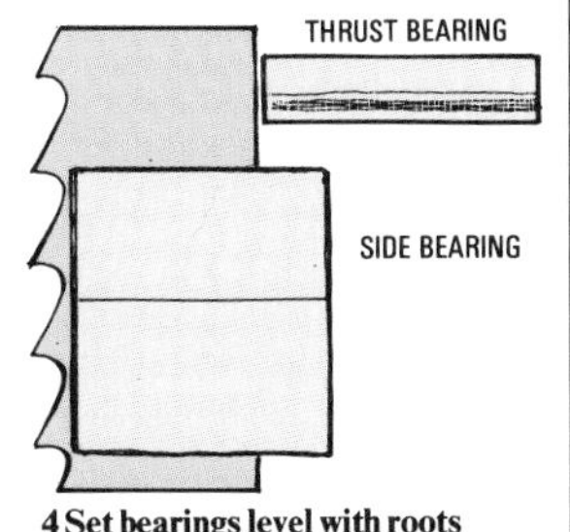

4 Set bearings level with roots

FOLDING A BAND-SAW BLADE

Store band-saw blades by folding them in three coils and hanging them on pegs on the workshop wall. Until you have developed the knack of folding a blade, wear gloves to protect your hands and wrists.

With the teeth facing away from you, hold one side of the loop in each hand; at the same time, hold the blade lightly under one foot **(1)**. Bring your hands together, allowing the top of the loop to bend toward the floor **(2)**. Cross the blade over itself to form three coils **(3)**, then let it fall lightly to the floor.

To unfold a coiled band, hold it securely while you separate the coils slowly and allow the blade to spring open away from you.

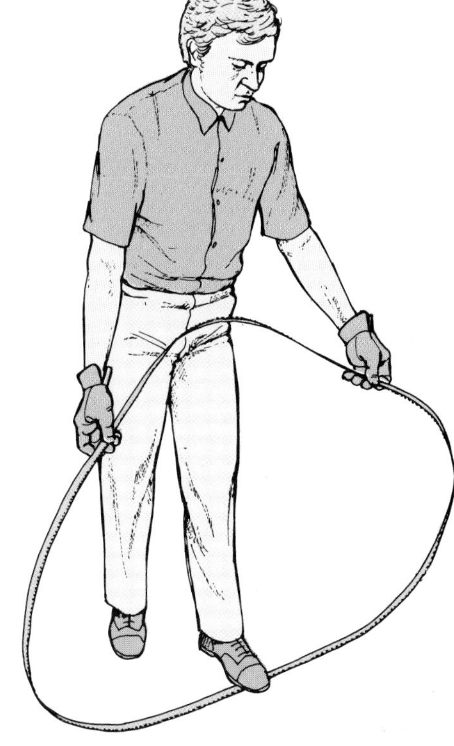

1 Hold the band in both hands and under one foot

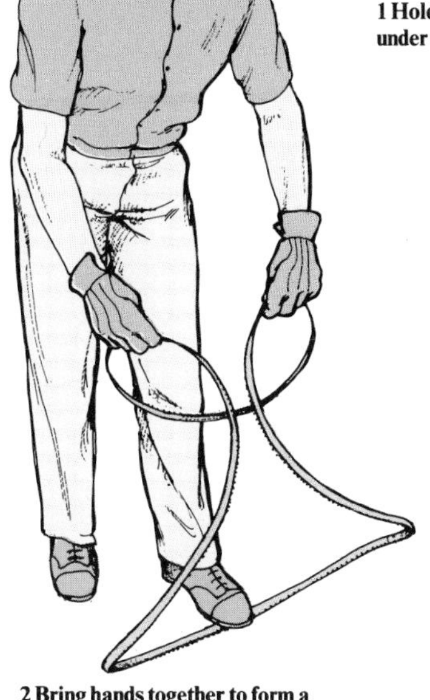

2 Bring hands together to form a loop in the blade

3 Cross the blade over to form three coils, then let it fall

Sawing freehand by following a line marked on a workpiece is not difficult provided the blade is sharp and accurately set. If the blade is dull or damaged, it is much more likely to wander and you will find yourself constantly correcting the line of cut, which inevitably puts a strain on the blade. Select the width of blade to suit the minimum radius you wish to cut, and plan the procedure to ensure that the bulk of the workpiece is able to pass through the throat of the saw.

SEE ALSO

Machine-shop safety	156
Joints	162
Safety tips	173
Blade-width guide	174
Blade guide and tracking	175
Cutting mortises	186-187
Sanding end grain	191
Cabriole leg	311

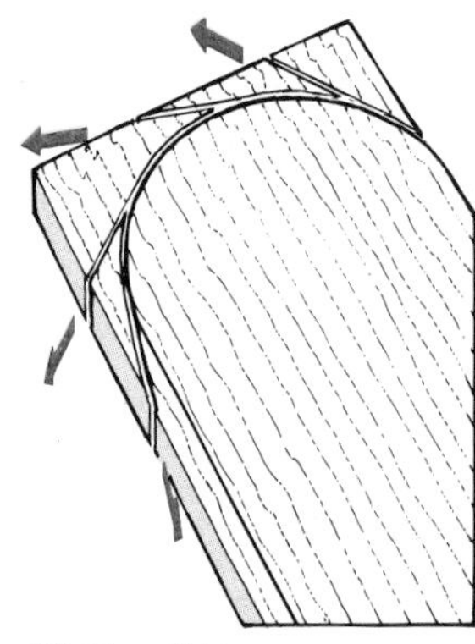

2 Cutting a tight curve
Remove waste in sections.

Following a curve freehand
Feed the work into the blade, cutting at a steady rate on the waste side of the line, and follow the curve without twisting the blade in the kerf. As the blade approaches the end of the cut, keep your hands away from the cutting edge and, if needed, pass one hand behind the blade to guide the work **(1)**.

If the blade begins to bind as you negotiate a tight curve, do not withdraw it. Instead, run it out to the side of the work through the waste and start the cut again. It may be necessary to perform a similar procedure several times to complete a curve **(2)**.

If you suspect in advance that it will be impossible to complete a cut in one flowing movement, make short straight cuts through the waste so it will fall away in sections as the curved cut progresses **(3)**. Alternatively, drill clearance holes at strategic points so that you can turn the blade in another direction **(4)**. If there's no escape route for a binding blade, switch off the saw and slowly back out of the kerf.

1 Freehand cutting
Guide the work with both hands.

3 Cut waste first
Waste falls away as curve is cut.

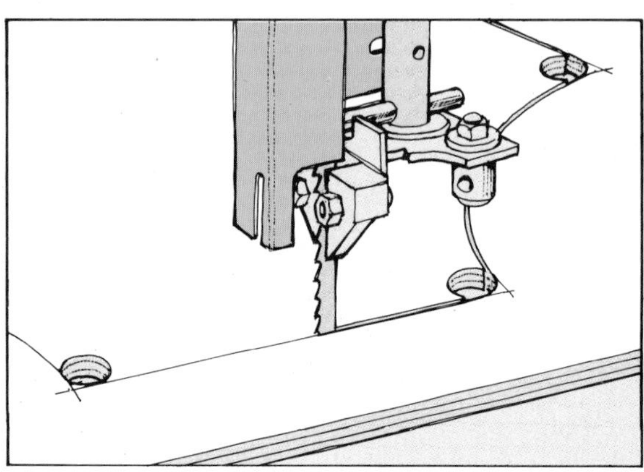

4 Drill holes at strategic points to change direction

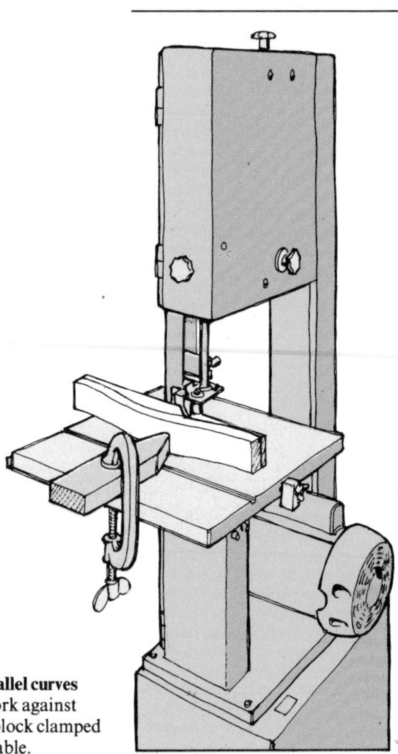

Cutting parallel curves
Feed the work against a rounded block clamped to the saw table.

Cutting parallel curves
Curved components often have parallel sides. To help cut one curve parallel to another, round over the end of a block of wood and clamp it to the saw table, leaving a clearance between it and the blade equal to the width of the finished workpiece. Run one of the curves against the rounded end of the block while following the other marked line with the sawblade.

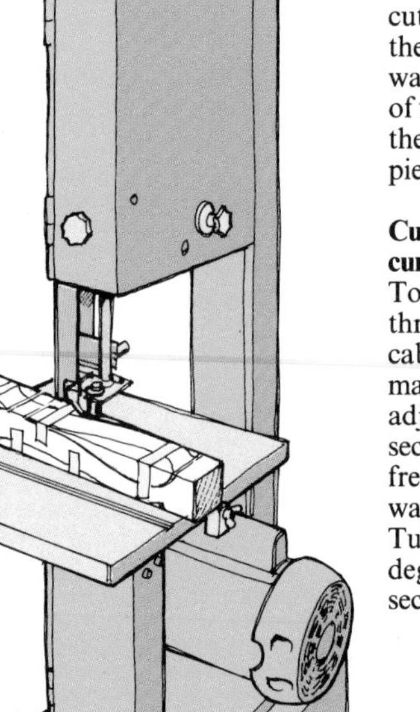

Cutting identical pieces
To make identical pieces, cut several blanks and tack them together through the waste. Following the outline of the workpiece marked on the top blank, cut all the pieces in a single pass.

Cutting three-dimensional curves with a band saw
To cut a shape that has three-dimensional curves (a cabriole leg, for example), mark out its profile on two adjacent sides of a square-section blank. Cut one side freehand, then replace the waste and tape it in position. Turn the workpiece 90 degrees in order to cut the second pair of curves.

Cutting a cabriole leg
Tape waste onto the workpiece before making the second cut.

RIPPING ON A BAND SAW

Making a ripcut parallel to another edge is a straightforward procedure – but unless the blade is sharp and set perfectly, it will tend to drift off line even when you are ripping against a fence. Also, make sure the blade guides are adjusted correctly and the tracking is true.

Ripping against the fence
With the work pressed against it, adjust the rip fence sideways until the blade is just on the waste side of the marked line. Switch on the saw and feed the work at a steady rate, without forcing it. Keep the workpiece pressed against the fence throughout the cut.

Finish cutting a narrow workpiece by feeding it with a push stick, pressing diagonally toward the fence.

Ripping against the fence

Ripping against a block
If a blade persists in wandering when you are using the rip fence, employ a rounded guide block similar to that used for cutting parallel curves. Clamp it to the saw table, leaving the required clearance between blade and block, and make the ripcut freehand so that you can compensate for the sideways drift by slightly changing the direction of feed.

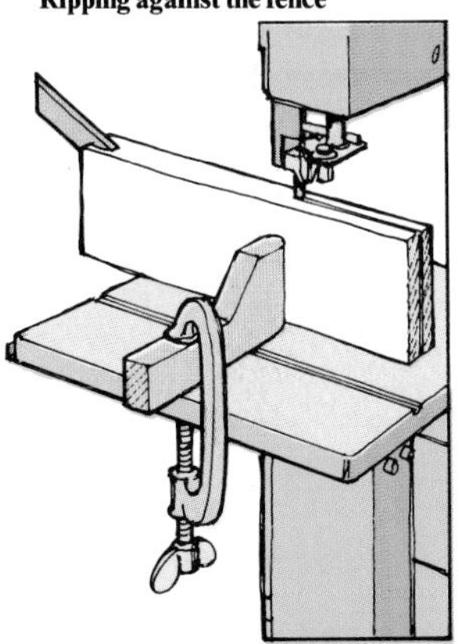

Ripping against a rounded block

Resawing wood
When resawing a piece of wood into thinner planks, fit a wide blade and use either the rip fence or a guide block. Hold the work against the fence with a block of scrap wood and feed it with a push stick.

Bevel ripping
To cut chamfers along a workpiece, tilt the saw table and position the rip fence below the blade. If you cannot fit your fence on the downside of the blade, clamp a temporary wooden fence to the saw table for bevel ripping.

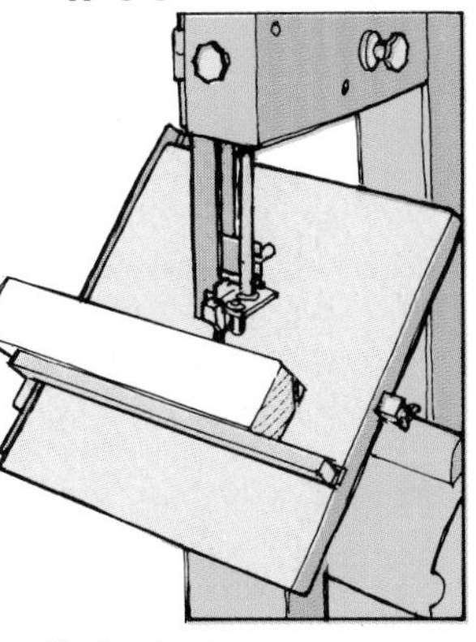

Cutting chamfers
Tilt the table for bevel ripping.

CROSSCUTTING ON A BAND SAW

Reasonably accurate crosscutting is possible on a band saw, but the finish will not be as good as on a table saw. If appearance is important, you will need to plane or sand the end grain.

Hold the work firmly against the miter gauge and feed it past the blade by sliding the gauge along its groove machined in the saw table. Don't force the pace or you will distort the blade.

Clamp a block to the rip fence to serve as a stop block when you want to saw several identical offcuts **(1)**.

To cut a number of workpieces to the same length, extend the saw's miter gauge with a wooden facing and clamp a stop block to it. Butt the squared end of each workpiece against the stop block and cut it to length **(2)**.

Cut a miter by adjusting the angle of the gauge. To make a compound-angle miter, tilt the saw table at the same time.

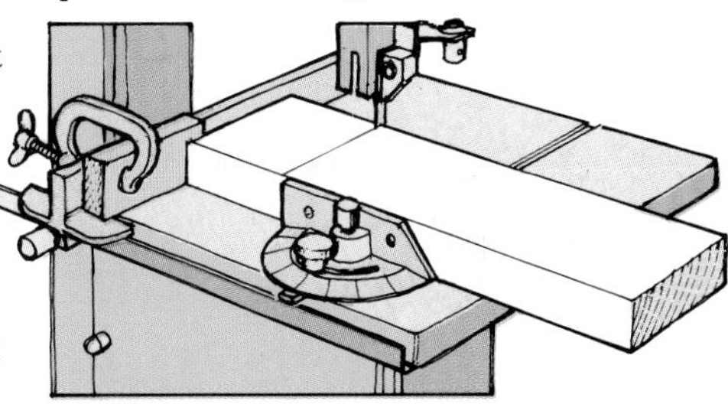

1 Making identical offcuts

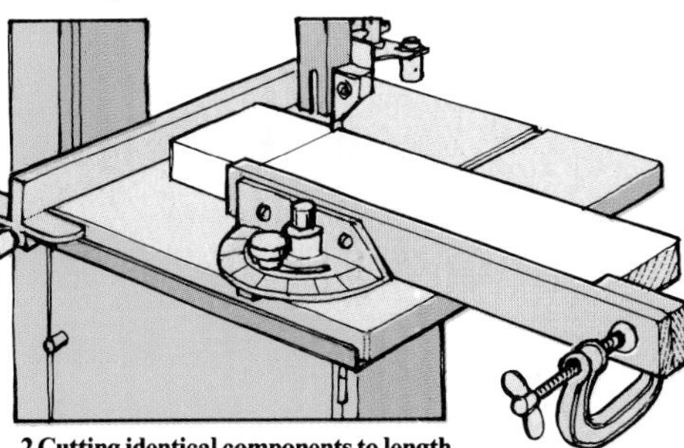

2 Cutting identical components to length

CUTTING JOINTS ON A BAND SAW

Any joint that incorporates a tongue – a tenon, rabbet joint, barefaced housing, corner lap joint and so on – can be cut in a similar way. The procedure for cutting a tenon demonstrates the principle. To avoid having to back out of a deep cut, always saw the shoulders first so that when you cut alongside the tongue, the waste will fall away.

Using a stop block clamped to the rip fence as a guide, crosscut the shoulder lines of the tenon.

Adjust the rip fence to saw alongside the tenon, with the waste facing away from the fence. Set the depth stop to complete the cut on the shoulder line. If your saw is not fitted with a depth stop, clamp a block to the fence ahead of the work.

To ensure that the tenon is centered on the rail, cut one side, then turn the work over and cut the other.

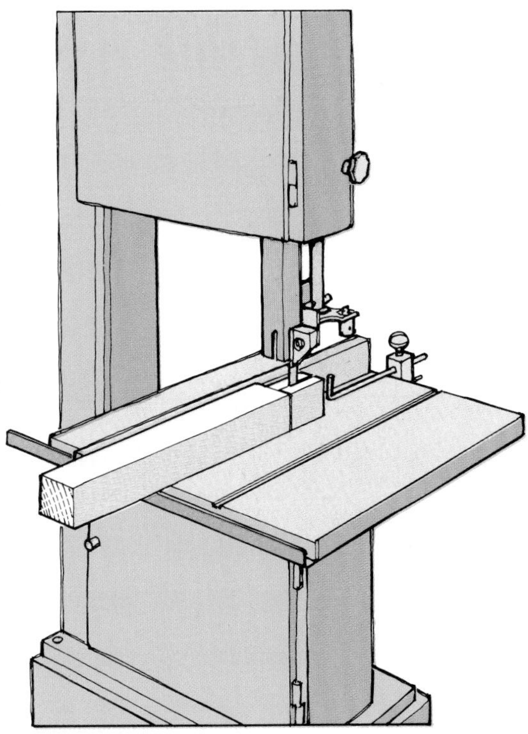

Cutting a tenon
Adjust the saw's depth stop to complete the cut on the tenon's shoulder line.

POWERED SCROLL SAWS

Powered scroll saws are generally associated with model-making and lightweight craftwork, but the better-quality saws will cut relatively thick wood with ease and to a superb finish. The saw's reciprocal action derives from the hand-held scroll saw, but the powered version leaves both hands free to guide the work – enabling you to work accurately and also to cut a very tight curve. To a large extent, the scroll saw's popularity is due to its safety record. Any blade that cuts wood can cut your fingers, but if you operate the saw with care and observe general machine-shop safety procedures, it is practically impossible to have a serious accident. Most powered scroll saws are designed to be bolted to a bench at standing height. Make sure the bench is solidly built, or accuracy will be impaired by excessive vibration.

SEE ALSO

Coping saw	84
Hand-held scroll saw	84
Machine-shop safety	156
Face mask	214

Depth of cut
Even a reasonably small powered scroll saw is capable of cutting 2in (50mm) wood, and the heavy-duty ones can handle wood of twice that thickness.

Saw table
Whether the saw table is made from cast-alloy or pressed metal, it must be flat and rigid. Most tables can be tilted for making bevel cuts, and some can be raised or lowered to utilize another section of the blade as one part becomes worn.

Throat
A scroll saw's throat – the distance between the blade and the column behind the saw table – determines the maximum width of cut possible. A small powered scroll saw has a throat of about 15in (380mm) or less, but you can buy larger saws that will cut boards 24in (600mm) wide. In any case, blades can be turned through 45 or 90 degrees so that a long workpiece can be fed past the column.

Length of stroke
Even though a scroll saw will cut quite thick material, the length of stroke – vertical movement of the blade – is relatively short. As a result, if you cut a lot of thin materials, you will dull a short section of blade just above the table while the rest of the sawteeth remain untouched. To get more use out of the blade, raise the work on a table top made from chipboard or plywood $\frac{3}{4}$in (18mm) thick.

Blade tensioner
Scroll-saw blades are extremely narrow and must therefore be held taut to prevent them from bending when pressure is applied. This is achieved by a strong spring. On some saws, spring tension is adjustable to suit different blade sizes.

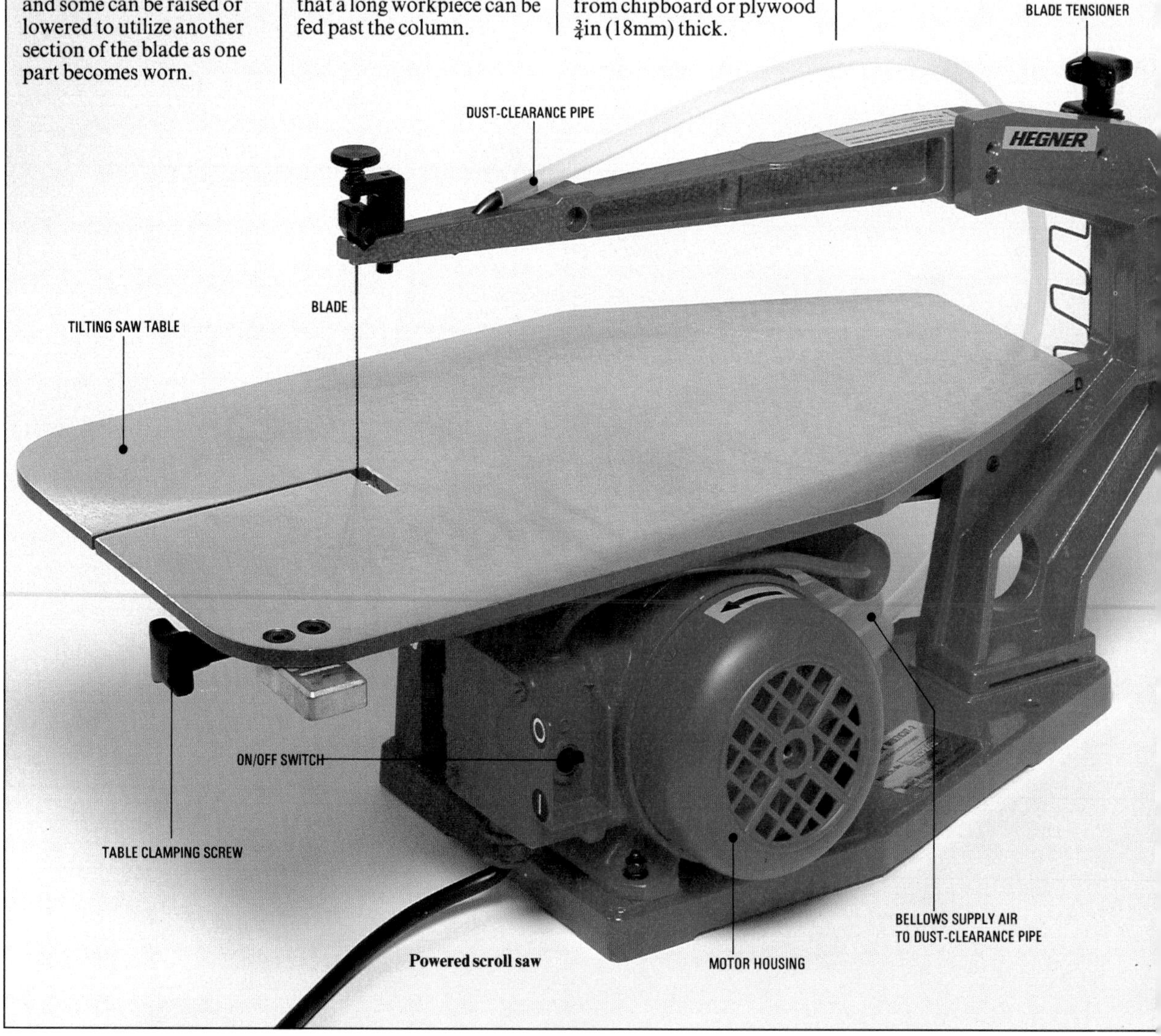

BLADE TENSIONER

DUST-CLEARANCE PIPE

BLADE

TILTING SAW TABLE

ON/OFF SWITCH

TABLE CLAMPING SCREW

BELLOWS SUPPLY AIR TO DUST-CLEARANCE PIPE

MOTOR HOUSING

Powered scroll saw

• **Electric motor**
The tiny 100W induction motor that powers the average machine scroll saw is capable of generating blade speeds of between 2800 and 5750 strokes per minute. Some scroll saws are supplied with variable-speed control.

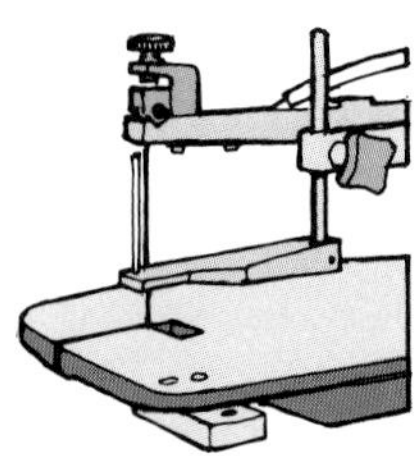

Hold-down
An adjustable hold-down keeps a thin workpiece from vibrating.

SCROLL-SAW BLADES

There are coarse "coping-saw" blades with standard alternate-set teeth for ripping thick wood, but most of the blades made for powered scroll saws have a skip-tooth arrangement – a deep gullet between each tooth – or else pairs of teeth separated by deep gullets. Skip-tooth or double-tooth blades will cut wood and soft metals, and you can also buy jeweler's blades for cutting hard ferrous metals.

Blade guard
A blade guard on a scroll saw is very simple, usually consisting of one or two vertical wire or plastic rods that form part of the hold-down. This type of guard is designed to prevent you from pushing your fingers against the blade. However, if you feed the work correctly, this should never happen. When cutting thick wood, a scroll saw is often operated without a blade guard of any description, especially since with some saws the hold-down, with its integral guard, is offered only as an optional accessory.

Hold-downs
To prevent a thin workpiece from "chattering," or vibrating noisily, scroll saws are supplied with a hold-down to stop the work from being lifted from the table by the action of the blade. A sprung hold-down will lift automatically as thin wood is fed toward the blade, but with thicker wood, it may be necessary to lift the hold-down up onto the workpiece before you can begin to cut. A vertically adjustable hold-down is set to suit the individual workpiece before cutting starts.

Dust collection
Dust-collection systems are not normally supplied for powered scroll saws – but, as the sawdust produced is very fine, if you suffer from respiratory ailments, wear a face mask.

On/off switch
The on/off switch on most scroll saws is of the simple toggle variety.

Dust clearance
A feature of the better-quality scroll saws is a pipe mounted just behind the blade that blows sawdust away from the point of cut before it obscures your view of the marked line.

BLADE-SIZE SELECTION

BLADE SIZE	TPI	MATERIAL THICKNESS
1 2	25 23	Veneers and wood up to ¼in (6mm) Plastics up to ¼in (6mm) Soft metals up to $\frac{1}{16}$in (1.5mm)
3 4	20 18	Hardwoods up to ½in (12mm) Softwoods up to ¾in (18mm) Plastics up to ¼in (6mm) Soft metals up to ⅛in (3mm)
5 6	16½ 15	Hardwood from ¼ to ¾in (6 to 18mm) Softwoods ¼ to 1in (6 to 25mm) Plastics up to ½in (12mm) Soft metals up to ¼in (6mm)
7 8 9	14 14 14	Hardwoods from ¼ to 1in (6 to 25mm) Softwoods ¼ to 2in (6 to 50mm) Plastics up to ½in (12mm) Soft metals up to ½in (12mm)
10 11 12	12½ 12½ 12½	Hardwoods from ¾ to 2in (18 to 50mm) Softwoods ¾ to 2in (18 to 50mm) Plastics up to ¾in (18mm) Soft metals up to ½in (12mm)
		The larger blades may have a similar TPI, but are made to different widths to handle more intricate work.

Selecting the size of blade
Blade size is normally specified by the numbers 1 to 12, although not all manufacturers supply the complete range. Each size of blade is designed to cope with materials of different thicknesses, but the intricacy of cut will also affect your choice. Select a finer blade if the one you are using cannot manage a tight curve.

The chart above is intended as a guide to selecting the appropriate blade size, but the final compromise between smoothness of finish, speed of cut and durability of blade must be a matter of experiment and personal preference.

Fitting a blade
Follow the scroll-saw manufacturer's instructions for fitting and tensioning a blade. The teeth of the blade should always point downward toward the saw table.

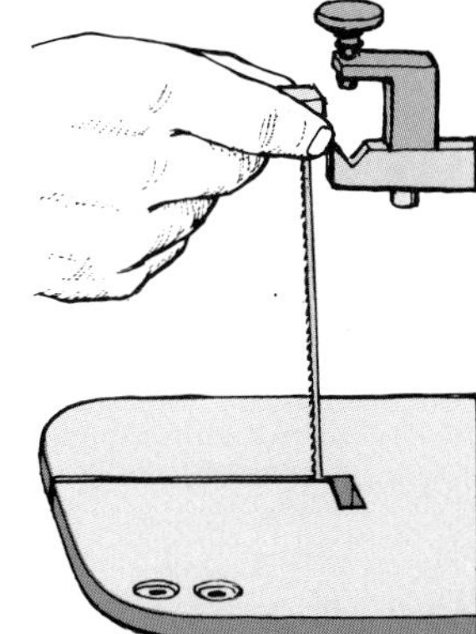

Fitting a scroll-saw blade
Make sure the sawteeth point toward the table.

USING A SCROLL SAW SAFELY

A scroll saw is safe enough to be used by quite young operators, provided they have been trained in general machine-shop safety procedures. Even when a blade breaks, it is unlikely to do you any serious harm.

- When you are feeding a workpiece, keep your fingers out of direct line with the blade – and take care that your thumbs are well out of the way as the blade breaks free at the edge of the work.
- Check that the switch is off before you plug the saw into an electrical outlet.

MAKING CURVED CUTS ON A SCROLL SAW

Cutting a curved workpiece, even one that is quite intricately shaped, is a commonplace task on a powered scroll saw. So long as you are using a blade of the right width, it is easy enough to follow a marked line freehand, always cutting on the waste side of the line to preserve the shape of the finished piece.

SEE ALSO

Sliding bevel	76-77
Try square	76-77
Machine-shop safety	156
Table saws	156-157
Band saws	172-173
Safety tips	179,183
Thickness planer	182-183
Hearing protectors	214

Cutting curves
Feed the work with both hands, holding it flat on the saw table while applying forward pressure into the blade. Keep your hands on either side of the blade, never directly in line with it. Be patient and feed the work slowly, allowing the blade to cut naturally. If you feel you are having to force the cut, change the dull blade for a sharp one.

While concentrating on the point of cut, it is all too easy to distort a narrow blade by unintentional sideways pressure or by twisting the work. To allow the blade to spring back to its natural position, relax fingertip pressure very slightly while continuing to maintain control over the work.

Cutting an aperture

Cutting an aperture
First, drill a small hole in the waste through which you can pass the blade; then, with the saw switched off, connect both ends to the saw. Switch on the saw again and follow your marked line to complete the aperture, then release the blade to remove the workpiece.

Making bevel cuts
To make a bevel cut on a scroll saw, adjust the angle of the saw table, then proceed as if you were cutting a square edge, taking extra care not to distort the blade. To avoid distortion, keep the feed pressure directly in line with the cutting edge.

MAKING STRAIGHT CUTS ON A SCROLL SAW

A powered scroll saw is not especially good for making straight cuts, but you can clamp a temporary wooden fence to the table to guide the work on its intended path.

As most scrollwork consists of a combination of straight and curved shapes, it is usually necessary to follow all marked lines by eye. To make a long, straight cut, following the manufacturer's instructions, turn the blade to an angle that allows you to feed the work past the saw column at the rear of the table.

Cutting with a temporary fence

Combining straight and curved cuts
If the combination of straight and curved lines is such that you will need to change one blade for another, drill access holes at strategic points where the wider blade will have to be swapped for a narrow one and vice versa.

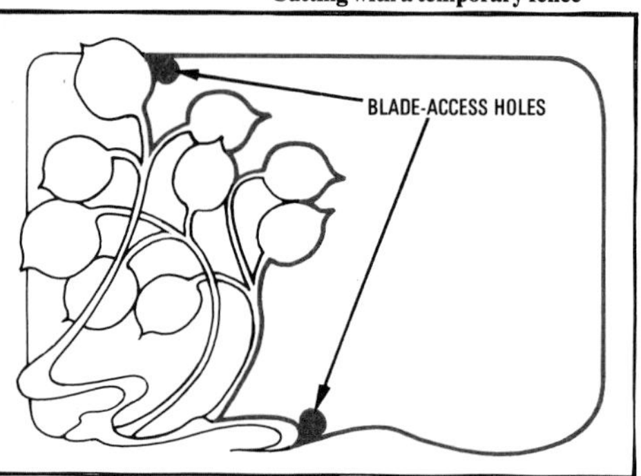

Bore access holes to change blades

PLANERS

Having acquired a table or band saw, most woodworkers begin to think about buying a machine that will plane smooth surfaces on all four sides of a workpiece accurately. A production workshop is often equipped with two separate machines. The first is a surface planer or jointer for dressing the face side and face edge of a workpiece. The same workpiece then passes through a thickness planer that planes the remaining surfaces parallel to the face side and edge. If there is no room or need for two planers, home woodworkers often opt for a jointer/planer that combines both functions in a single machine.

Maximum planing width
Jointers are most often specified according to the widest workpiece you can plane on the machine – which is determined by the length of the cutters, called "knives," that are bolted into the revolving cutterhead. Small special-purpose jointers have short knives – 6in (150mm) or less – but the average home-workshop jointer/planer will have a maximum planing width of about $10\frac{1}{4}$in (260mm).

Cutterhead speed
The cylindrical block with its two or three balanced knives revolves at a very high speed in order to produce a clean, smooth surface. Cutterhead speed is sometimes specified in revolutions per minute, but a more telling figure is the number of cuts produced per minute by the moving cutters. A three-cutter head will produce more cuts per minute than a two-cutter head revolving at the same speed. For a two-cutter head 12,000 cuts per minute is a respectable speed.

Combined length of tables
In order to be able to joint a perfectly straight edge on a workpiece, the overall length of the infeed plus outfeed tables should be as long as possible. The overall length of the average jointer is about 3ft 3in (1m).

Fence
A rigid metal fence is essential for jointing true square or beveled edges on a workpiece. All fences can be tilted to any angle from 90 to 45 degrees to the tables. It is convenient if the fence automatically comes to a stop at both extremes, but check the settings with a try square or sliding bevel.

Maximum depth of cut
The cutterhead is situated between two independently adjustable cast-metal tables. The height of the table to the rear of the cutterhead – the outfeed table – should be adjusted so it is level with the top of the circle described by the revolving cutters. The table in front of the cutterhead – the infeed table – is lowered to produce the required depth of cut, up to a maximum of about $\frac{1}{8}$in (3mm). A very shallow $\frac{1}{32}$in (1mm) cut will produce a superior finish; but for speed, make two or three deeper cuts followed by one or more finishing cuts. Depth of cut is indicated by a scale next to the infeed table.

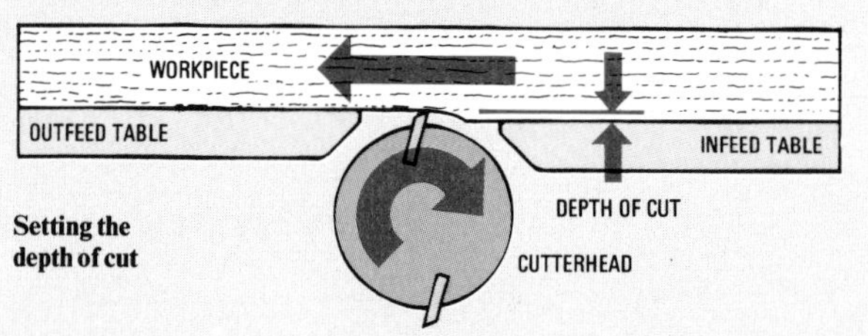

Setting the depth of cut

Cutterhead guard

A jointer's revolving cutters are capable of severing a fingertip in a fraction of a second – so never operate the machine without the appropriate guard.

A bridge guard that is adjustable in height and that can be slid across the entire width of the cutterhead is the ideal form of protection. Some jointers are made with spring-loaded bridge guards that are lifted or pushed aside by the work as it is passed over the cutterhead. This type of guard is superior to the simpler version that merely swings aside to expose the cutters.

In addition, there should be a guard behind the fence that is automatically drawn across the cutterhead as the fence is adjusted sideways.

You should never attempt to rabbet a workpiece without a vertical/horizontal hold-down guard, so your hands need not approach the cutters.

A hold-down guard
Fit this type of guard when planing a rabbet.

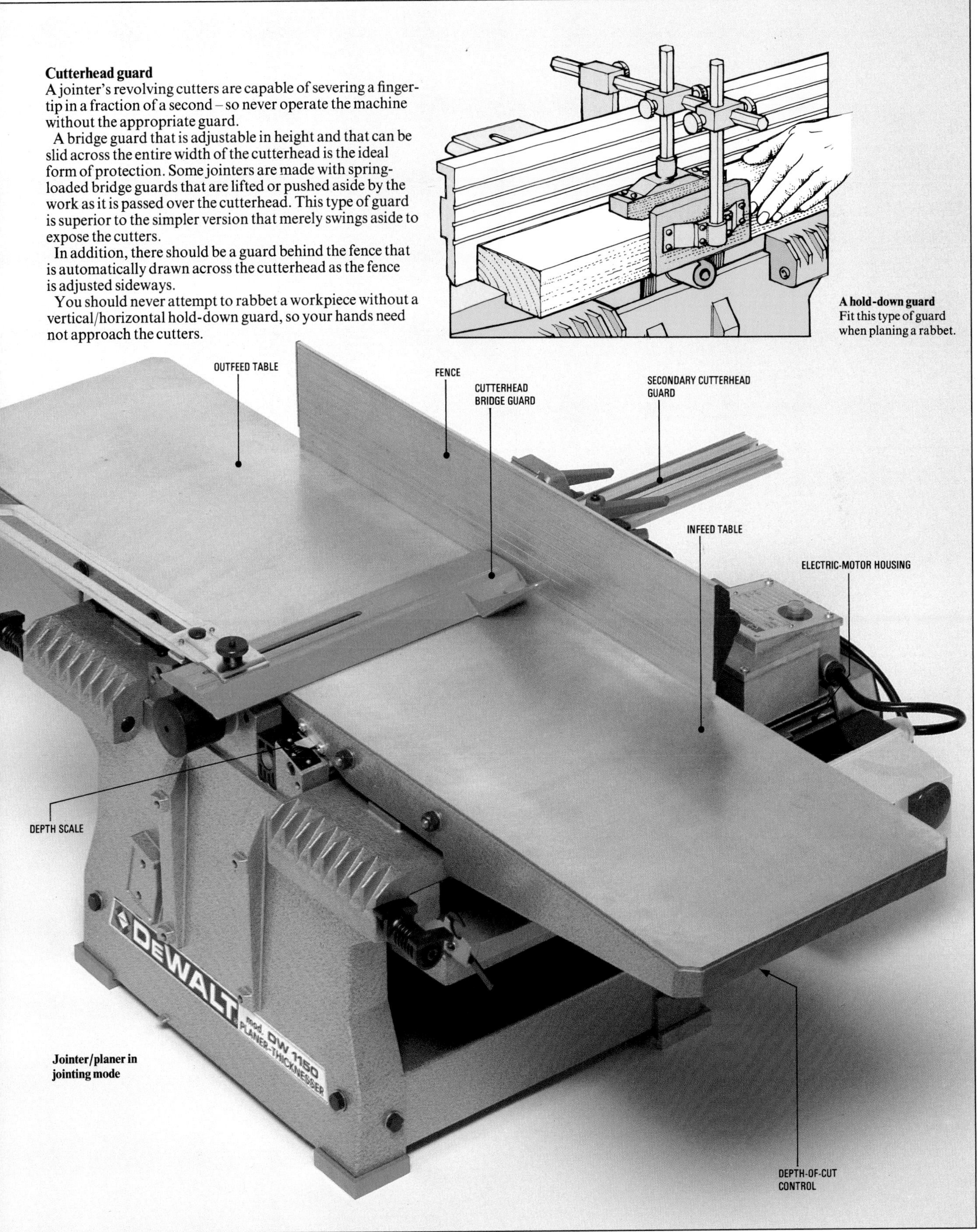

Jointer/planer in jointing mode

SEE ALSO

Machine-shop safety	156
Pawls	165
Direction of feed	180
Surface planer	180-181
Push block	185
Dust collectors	214
Cellulose lacquer	290

On/off switches
On/off switches should be accessible from either end of the machine so you can turn it off quickly in an emergency, no matter whether you happen to be jointing or thicknessing.

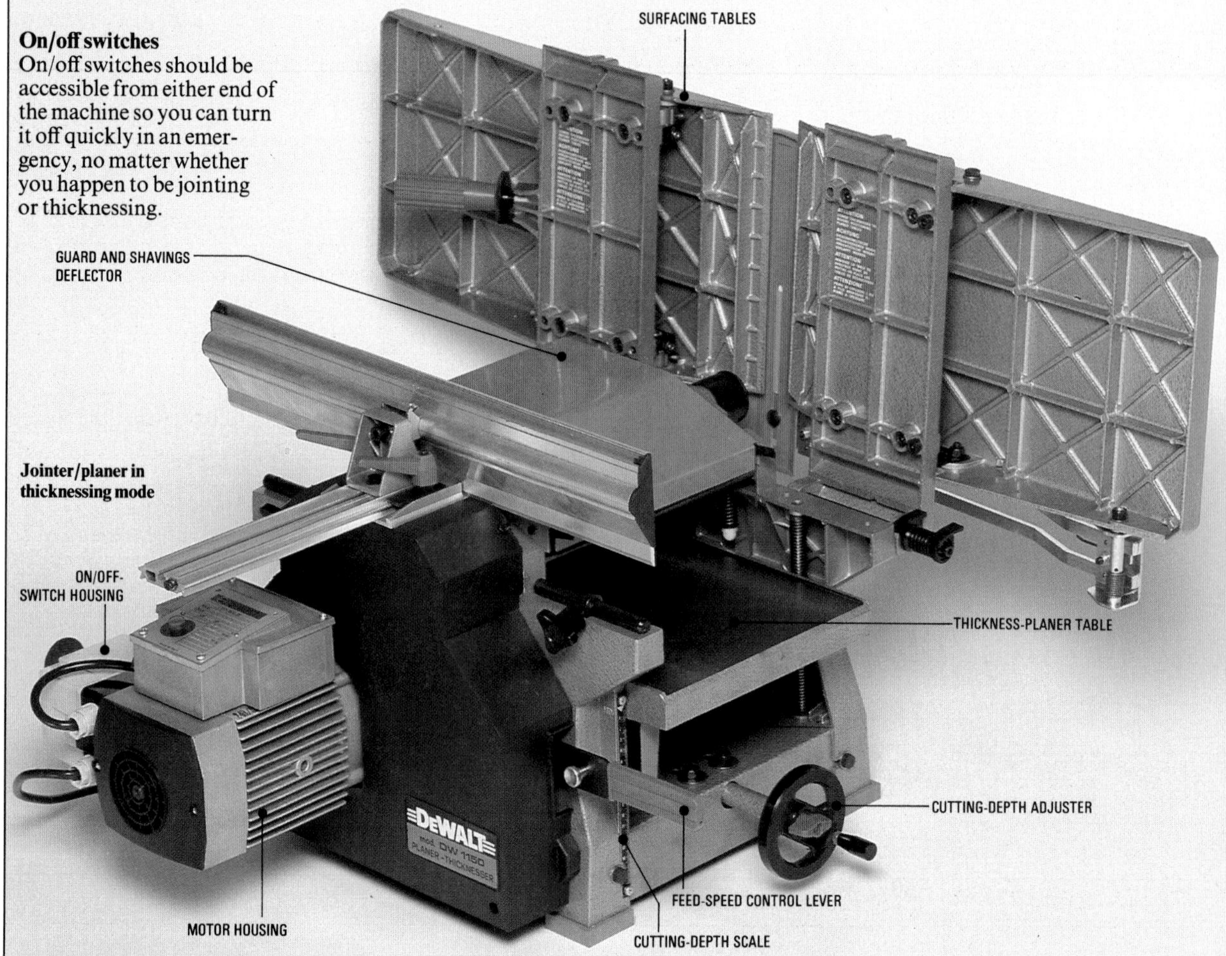

Jointer/planer in thicknessing mode

Width of thickness-planer table
The average thickness-planer table is 10in (250mm) wide. Never attempt to plane a workpiece that is shorter than the width of the table. If a piece of wood is able to turn sideways, it may be splintered by the feed rollers and cutters, and pieces can be thrown out of the planer with considerable force.

Feed rollers
A planer is equipped with two motor-driven spring-loaded feed rollers that pass the workpiece under the revolving cutterhead and out the other end of the machine. The infeed roller, usually a horizontally ribbed steel roller, is situated in front of the cutterhead and provides the main driving force. The outfeed roller, which is situated behind the cutterhead, is smooth – so as not to mark the planed surface – and exerts less pressure on the work. When taking a very shallow cut, the parallel bruising left by a ribbed roller is sometimes detectable on the planed surface. For this reason, some planers are made with rubber-covered drive rollers.

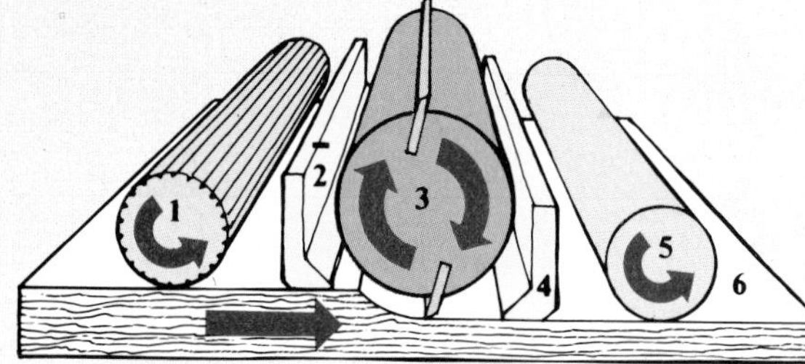

Planer feed rollers
1 Infeed roller
2 Chip breaker
3 Cutterhead
4 Pressure bar
5 Outfeed roller
6 Workpiece

Maximum thicknessing depth
When a workpiece is passed through a planer, it travels on a bed situated beneath the same cutterhead used for jointing. The planer table on the average home-workshop machine can be raised or lowered to accommodate any workpiece up to a maximum thickness of 6 to 7in (160 to 180mm). Even though the planer is power driven, never attempt to take more than $\frac{1}{8}$in (3mm) in one pass.

Electric motors
A small 375W ($\frac{1}{2}$hp) electric motor is powerful enough for a special-purpose jointer. However, on a thickness planer the motor is used to drive the feed rollers and cutterhead simultaneously, so a larger 1.5 to 2.2kW (2 to 3hp) motor is required. On some models, the drive rollers can be disconnected from the motor so that its entire output is available for jointing.

Planer feed rate
Because an amateur woodworker is not primarily concerned with a fast output of work, he or she is more likely to be attracted by a planer that produces a good finish at the expense of speed – since a slow feed rate combined with a high cutterhead speed produces the best finish. Many thickness planers are therefore designed to feed the work at the relatively slow speed of about 16ft (5m) per minute. However, you can buy a planer with a feed rate of 29ft (9m) per minute, which can be increased to 36ft (11m) per minute. As a general rule, feed hardwoods slowly but increase the feed rate for softwoods.

Anti-kickback device
If for some reason the drive rollers lose their grip on a workpiece, it may be thrown out of the machine by the cutterhead and a serious accident can occur if you are feeding the work at the time. To prevent this, a row of pointed metal teeth or "pawls" hang in front of the infeed roller. As the work travels under them, the pawls lift to allow free passage. Should the work begin to travel backward, the pointed pawls catch in the wood surface and restrict its movement.

Dust collection
Without a dust collector, shavings are dumped onto the tables above and below the cutterhead, impairing the efficiency and accuracy of the machine. Consequently, you have to stop the planer regularly to clear the accumulated debris. A hose attachment leading to a portable vacuum solves the problem.

USING A JOINTER/PLANER SAFELY

Always operate a jointer/planer confidently but with extreme caution. An accident can happen so quickly that even the fastest reflexes will not save you from injury. It is therefore essential to cultivate a safe method of working and always observe general machine-shop safety procedures.

- Follow the manufacturer's instructions for installing knives, and always complete the procedure before you leave the machine. If you are distracted and forget to secure a knife, a serious accident could result when you switch on the machine.
- Inspect the machine before you switch it on to make sure nothing is likely to foul the cutterhead.
- Never use a jointer without a properly adjusted guard in position.
- Use a push block to feed a thin workpiece over the cutters. Never attempt to joint a piece of wood less than $\frac{1}{4}$in (6mm) thick.
- Don't attempt to joint a workpiece that is too short to be held firmly in both hands.
- Never trail your fingers or thumb behind a workpiece.
- Always feed work against the direction of rotation of the cutterhead. When jointing, pass the work from infeed to outfeed table. Feed from the opposite end of the machine when thicknessing.
- Feed one workpiece at a time through a thickness planer. The feed-roller pressure may not be consistent across a number of pieces, and one of them could be thrown back by the cutterhead.
- Don't try to force a workpiece through a thickness planer. Let the feed rollers work at their intended rate.
- When planing a workpiece of uneven thickness, set the depth of cut to handle the thickest section first, then gradually raise the planer table between passes until you are cutting the full length of the board.
- Don't feed work that is shorter than the width of the planer table or shorter than the distance between the feed rollers.
- When planing long workpieces, either have an assistant take the weight as they come off the machine or set up a roller stand or sawhorses to support the work.
- Never put your hands into a thickness planer to retrieve a workpiece or clear away shavings. Use a long push stick instead, to extend your reach.

JOINTER AND PLANER KNIVES

A few jointers and planers are made with double-edge disposable cutters similar to those used in portable power jointers. However, the majority of machines are fitted with two or three single-edge cutters or "knives" that need to be honed and sharpened at regular intervals.

Types of cutter
Jointers and planers for the home-workshop market are supplied with high-speed-steel knives that are perfectly adequate unless you expect to plane a lot of chipboard or "gritty" woods like teak. When planing these materials, follow production-workshop practice and fit the more expensive tungsten-carbide knives, which will hold a sharp edge much longer but must, when the time comes, be sent to a professional for sharpening. Even high-speed-steel knives are sent for regrinding, but they can be honed in the meantime by running an oilstone along the cutting edges.

EXPANSION BOLT
COIL SPRING
KNIFE
GIB

A typical cutterhead

Fitting knives
It is important to follow the manufacturer's instructions for fitting knives. However, in principle, each knife fits into a slot in the cylindrical cutterhead. In some cases the knife rests on springs at the bottom of the slot, and height adjustment is simply a matter of holding the knife down against their compression. The knife is normally secured with a wedge-shaped gib held tight by adjusting expansion bolts. Always double-check that the knives are tight before you switch on the machine.

Adjusting knives
Each knife must project from the head by exactly the same amount if it is to do its fair share of the work. If one knife is set higher than another, it will do all the planing and a rougher surface will result. It is possible to buy special equipment for gauging knife setting, but in a home workshop, a straight batten is good enough. Always unplug the machine before making adjustments to the knives.

Adjust all the knives by eye until they appear to project the required amount. Lower the outfeed table slightly, then rest the wooden batten on it overhanging one end of the cutterhead. Mark the edge of the outfeed table on the batten **(1)**. Turn the cutterhead slowly by hand, allowing the knife to lift the batten and carry it forward, then mark the edge of the batten again **(2)**.

Move the batten to the other end of the cutterhead, aligning the first mark with the edge of the table. Turn the cutterhead again. The same knife should move the batten forward by exactly the same amount. If the second mark does not align with the table edge, adjust the height of the knife at that end until it does.

Tighten the gib bolts, then repeat the gauging process at each end to make sure that clamping has not altered the setting. Turn the cutterhead and set each knife in the same way. Finally, raise the outfeed table until each knife just scrapes the underside of the batten.

- **Cleaning the cutterhead**
Before you fit new or reground knives, clean wood resin from the cutterhead slots and gibs with a solvent such as lacquer thinner or mineral spirits.

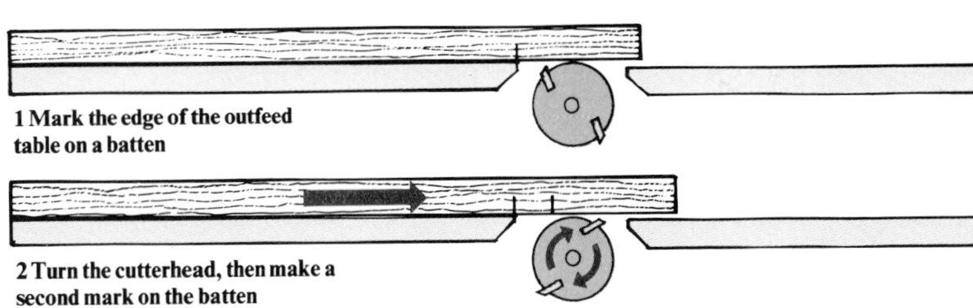

1 Mark the edge of the outfeed table on a batten

2 Turn the cutterhead, then make a second mark on the batten

OPERATING A JOINTER/PLANER

To machine-plane a piece of wood, first prepare the face side and face edge on the jointer, then pass it through the thickness planer to plane the remaining faces.

Inspect the workpiece to select the most suitable faces to plane. If the workpiece is bowed, plane it with the concave face resting on the feed tables – it is virtually impossible to flatten a convex surface on a jointer since the workpiece is sure to rock on the tables as you pass it across the cutters.

To achieve a smooth finish, orientate the wood so that the grain runs at an angle away from the cutters. Occasionally, when the grain runs in different directions, the decision may not be quite so straightforward – in which case, take a fine cut and if the jointer tears the grain, turn the work around and try again.

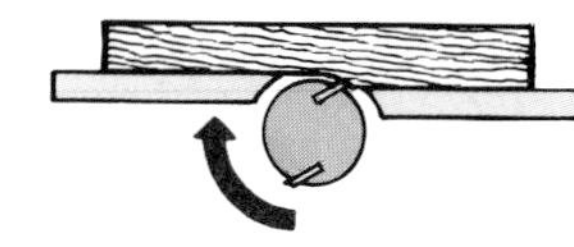

Grain direction
Feed the work with the grain running at an angle away from the knives.

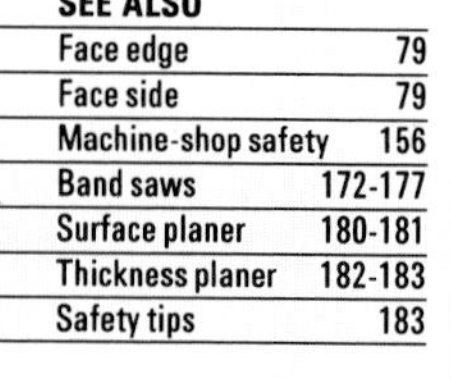

SEE ALSO	
Face edge	79
Face side	79
Machine-shop safety	156
Band saws	172-177
Surface planer	180-181
Thickness planer	182-183
Safety tips	183

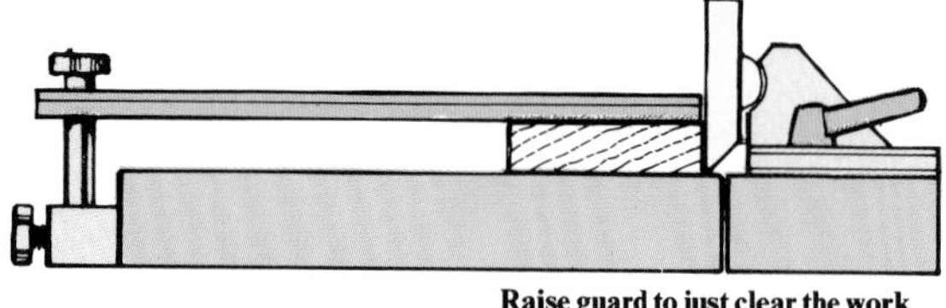

Raise guard to just clear the work

Jointing the face side

Lower the thickness-planer table, then move the fence aside to accommodate the widest face of the workpiece and select the depth of cut by adjusting the infeed table.

Slide the bridge guard to cover the cutterhead and, with the wood resting on the infeed table, raise the guard to just clear the workpiece.

Stand to the side of the infeed table and switch on the jointer. With your right hand flat on the work, feed the wood across the cutters **(1)**. Apply just enough pressure to control the work. If you press a bowed or twisted workpiece flat on the infeed table, the cutters will remove an even layer from the surface – but as soon as you relieve the pressure, the wood will spring back to its distorted condition. Your intention should be to plane just those points in contact with the table, gradually removing wood until the surface is flat.

As soon as the workpiece passes under the guard, shift your body weight to hold the work on the outfeed table with your left hand **(2)**. Continue feeding the work at an even rate, transferring your right hand to the work on the outfeed table **(3)**. Keep the work moving until you have completed the first cut. Return the workpiece to the infeed table and repeat the process until the face side is flat, then switch off the jointer.

1 Feed the work across the cutters

2 Shift your weight to the outfeed table

3 Transfer your right hand to the outfeed table

Adjust guard to joint an edge

Pass work from hand to hand

Jointing the face edge

Brush any shavings away from the fence, and check that it is perfectly upright and tightly clamped.

Lower the guard completely and slide it sideways to allow the work to pass between the guard and the fence with minimum clearance. Check to make sure your fingertips cannot slip between the end of the fence and the workpiece.

Switch on the jointer and, with the face side held firmly against the fence, pass the work from one hand to the other over the cutterhead.

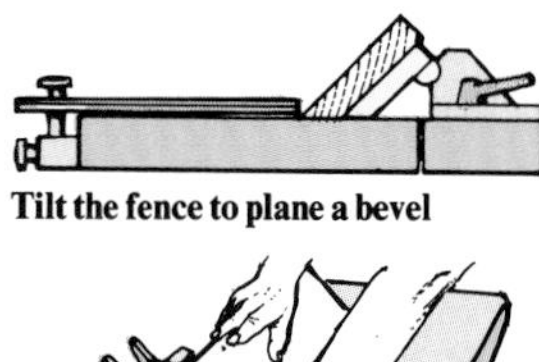

Tilt the fence to plane a bevel

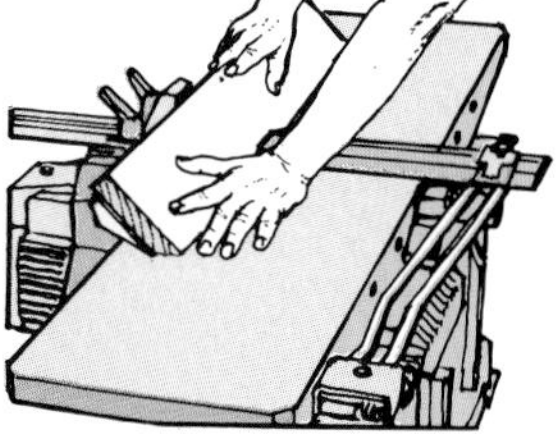

Planing a beveled edge
Support work with your left hand.

Planing a bevel

To plane a bevel edge on a workpiece, tilt the fence to the required angle and slide the bridge guard sideways, allowing the minimum clearance for the work.

To maintain an accurate bevel, you must prevent the bottom edge of the work from sliding away from the fence. Use your left hand as a stationary guide – holding the work against the fence with your index finger and thumb while resting the other three fingers on the outfeed table – and feed the work with your right hand.

Planing a stopped chamfer
A stopped chamfer is often used as a decorative feature in furnituremaking. A jointer is the ideal machine for producing such a detail, but seek professional instruction before attempting the process yourself. It involves lowering both tables by an equal amount, so you can cut the chamfer in one pass. Screw stop blocks to a long board, clamp it to the fence and tilt the fence to 45 degrees. Adjust the guard as if you were planing a normal bevel.

Butt one end of the workpiece firmly against the rearward stop block, while holding the other end above the cutterhead **(1)**. With your fingertips on the very end of the wood, lower the workpiece slowly onto the cutterhead. There will be considerable rearward force on initial contact with the cutters. Feed the work along the fence until it comes to rest against the forward stop block, then carefully lift the wood off the cutters **(2)** and switch off the machine. For safety, plane a stopped chamfer on an overlong piece of wood – then cut it to length at each end after machining.

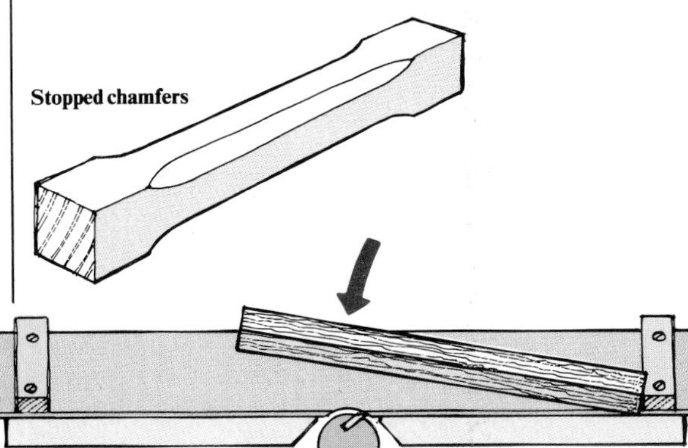

1 Lower the work onto the cutterhead

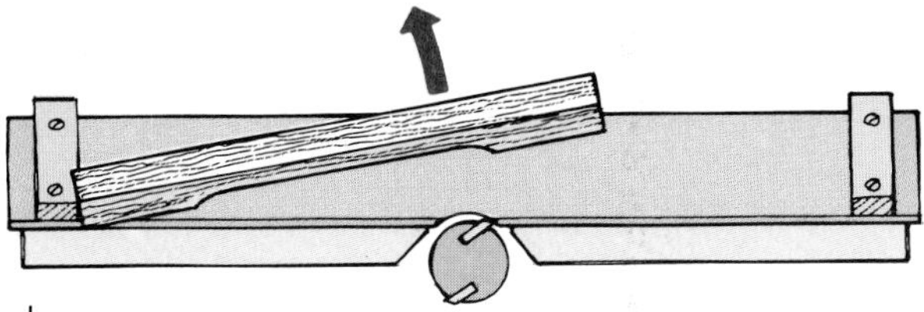
2 When the work touches the stop block, lift it off the cutters

Jointing end grain
To joint end grain, construct a jig similar to the one used for cutting tenons on a table saw. Make the whole jig from softwood – plywood will chip the edges of jointer knives. Clamp the work in the jig before passing it across the cutterhead.

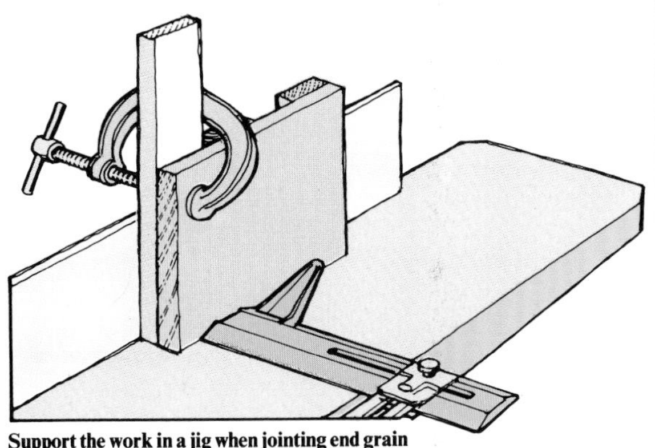
Support the work in a jig when jointing end grain

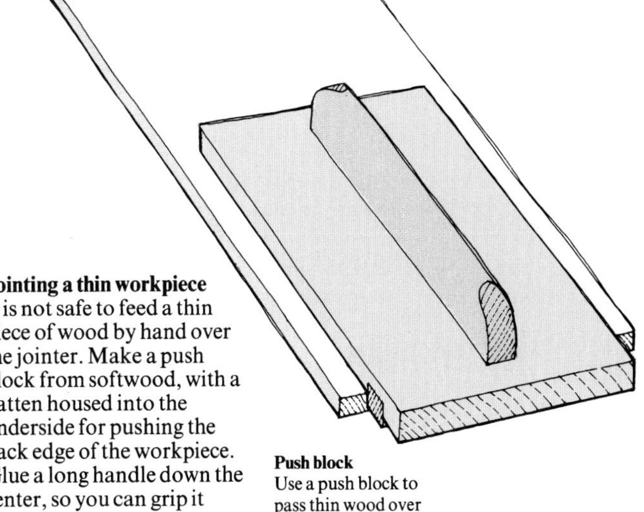

Jointing a thin workpiece
It is not safe to feed a thin piece of wood by hand over the jointer. Make a push block from softwood, with a batten housed into the underside for pushing the back edge of the workpiece. Glue a long handle down the center, so you can grip it with both hands.

Push block
Use a push block to pass thin wood over the jointer.

THICKNESSING

Having jointed a flat face side and face edge, the work is ready for thicknessing, but don't waste time and money by turning more wood than necessary into shavings. Band saw oversize workpieces close to finished width or thickness, then return them to the planer.

Preparing the thickness planer
Remove the fence, then lift and secure one or both surfacing tables, depending on the manufacturer's instructions. Swing the planer's cutterhead guard and shavings deflector into position. Select the depth of cut by adjusting the planer table to the necessary height indicated on its scale.

Feeding the work
Switch on the machine and engage the automatic feed mechanism; then, standing slightly to one side of the machine, pass the end of the workpiece into the thickness planer until the feed rollers draw it under the cutterhead. If the rollers do not take hold of the work, raise the table very slightly.

Move to the other end of the machine and withdraw the work, but don't attempt to accelerate the process by pulling the wood through the thickness planer.

Return to the infeed end of the machine and raise the table to take another cut, then repeat the process.

• **Cleaning the planer**
Clean wood resin from the rollers and table of your thickness planer with a solvent such as mineral spirits or lacquer thinner. Polish the table with a dry cloth, and wax it occasionally to ensure smooth power feeding.

Planing a thin board
To plane a board thinner than the minimum depth of cut on a thickness planer, place it on top of a thicker board already planed to an even thickness and pass both boards through the machine together.

Planing an edge
If a workpiece is thick enough to be stable, you can pass it on edge through a thickness planer – but a thin workpiece can tip over as it is taken by the rollers, crushing the corners. If you suspect there is a possibility of damaging a workpiece, rip it to within $\frac{1}{16}$in (2mm) of its final width on a table saw or band saw. If you are preparing several identical components, rip them all on the same setting. Take one workpiece to the finely set jointer and plane the first 1in (25mm) of the sawn edge. Check the width and, if necessary, adjust the depth of cut and plane the same 1in (25mm) again. When you are satisfied with the width of the workpiece, pass the whole sawn edge over the cutters. Finally, with one pass, plane all the matching components to an identical width.

MORTISING ATTACHMENTS

Industrial workshops where cutting mortise and tenon joints is an integral part of a mass-production program are equipped with heavy-duty mortising machines. These special-purpose machines are prohibitively expensive, but a good-quality mortising attachment that can be powered by another machine, such as a drill press or planer, is a cheaper alternative that many amateur woodworkers find attractive.

SEE ALSO

Machine-shop safety	156
Cutting tenons	162,169,177
Jointer/planer	181
Drill presses	188
Universal machines	204-205

HOLLOW-CHISEL MORTISER

A drill press can be adapted to cut mortises with a hollow-chisel mortising attachment.

The attachment includes a special auger bit in the center of a square, hollow chisel that has four cutting edges. As it is plunged into the wood, the mortiser cuts a perfectly square hole – the auger bit boring out the waste just ahead of the chisel, which slices the corners square. To cut a long, rectangular mortise, slide the workpiece sideways between each plunge of the chisel.

Although larger chisels are used in industrial production, home-workshop attachments are designed to take square chisels $\frac{1}{4}$ to $\frac{3}{4}$in (6 to 18mm) wide.

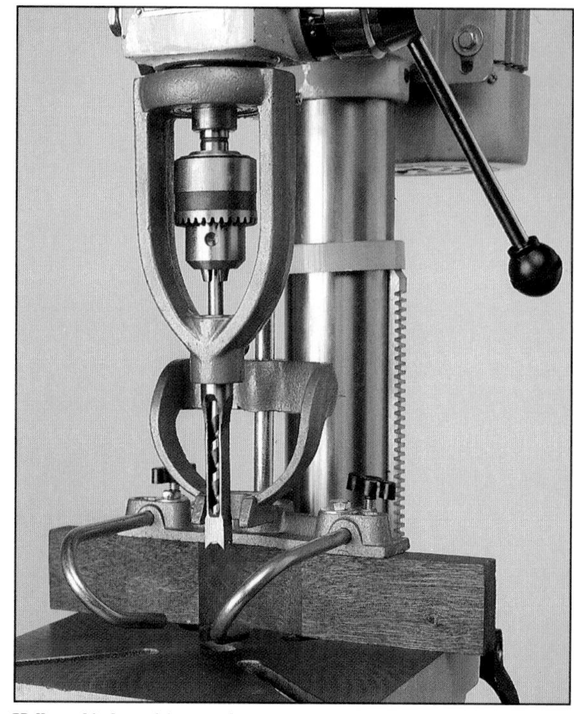

Hollow-chisel mortising attachment

Using a hollow-chisel mortising attachment
Set the drill-press depth stop to determine the depth of the mortise. Plunge the chisel to cut a square hole against one shoulder line of the mortise **(1)**, then slide the workpiece under the chisel and cut the other shoulder line **(2)**. Finally, remove the waste between the holes with several plunges of the chisel **(3)**.

Plunge a chisel at a firm but even rate. Don't force the pace when mortising hardwoods, since small chisels can be split by excessive pressure – but don't labor the process, either, or the chisel will overheat due to friction between it and the auger.

If you are going to cut a through mortise, place a strip of planed wood beneath the work. This will save the chisel from being driven into the metal drill-press table and will also back up the workpiece, preventing the grain from splitting as the chisel breaks through the underside of the wood. Alternatively, you can cut the mortise from both sides, by turning the work over.

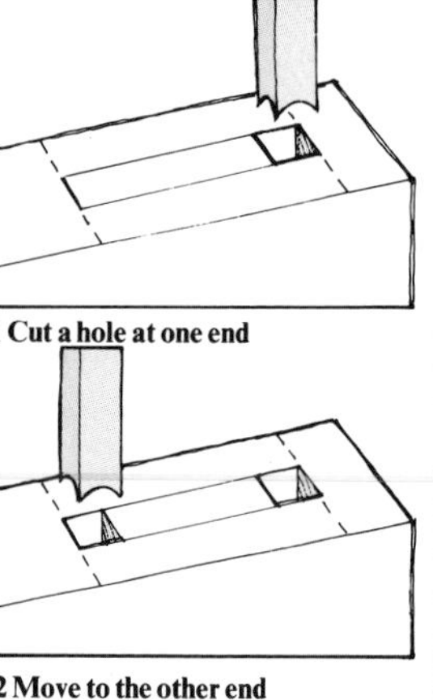

1 Cut a hole at one end

2 Move to the other end

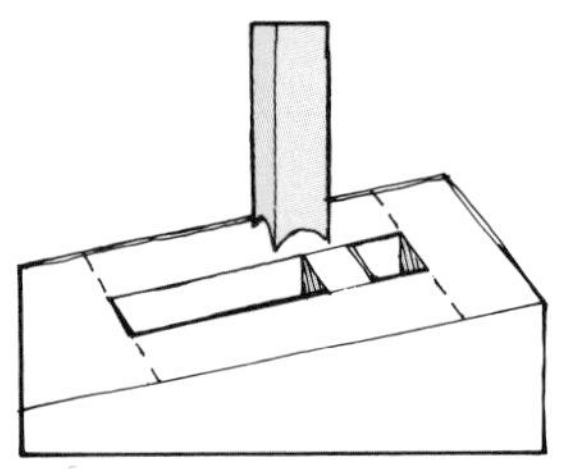

3 Remove the waste between

SHARPENING AN AUGER AND CHISEL

Mortising auger bits, like the ordinary auger bits used in a hand-cranked brace, are sharpened with a small file. The four cutting edges of the square chisel are sharpened simultaneously, using a special tool similar in design to a rose countersink but with a central pilot tip that keeps the tool centered in the chisel. Rotating the tool with a brace hones the chisel. Each chisel has to have its own matching sharpener.

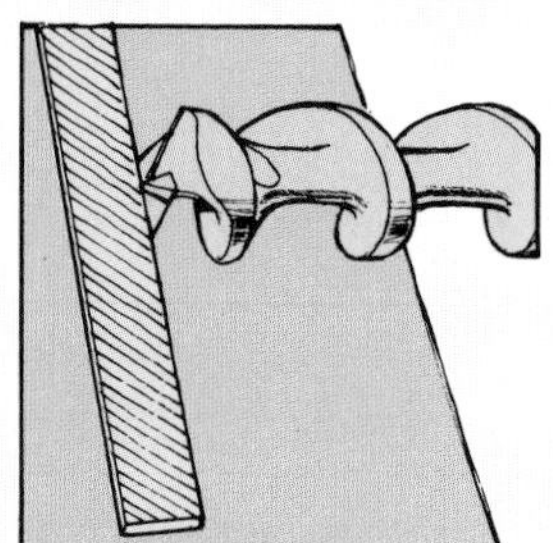

Put a sharp edge on each spur with a small file

Holding the drill tip on a bench, sharpen the cutting edges

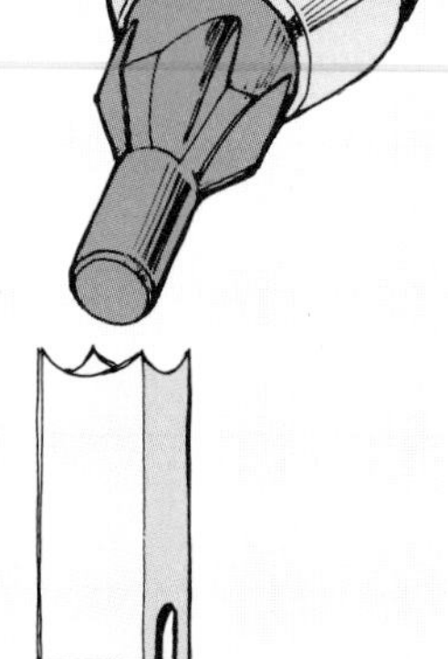

Hone the square chisel with a special tool

SLOT MORTISER

A slot mortiser incorporates a horizontally mounted milling cutter for machining workpieces.

This type of attachment uses the drive mechanism of another machine – typically a jointer/planer or a universal machine – and is fitted to a chuck at the end of the machine's cutterhead. The chuck, similar to one on an electric drill, accommodates $\frac{1}{4}$ to $\frac{5}{8}$in (6 to 16mm) diameter cutters with two cutting edges, one of which may be toothed.

A mortising table, to which the work is clamped, is mounted below the cutter chuck. The table is able to slide sideways, moving the work relative to the stationary chuck, and travels back and forth to adapt to the depth of cut. The table is also adjustable in height and adjustable stops limit its travel, thus regulating the length and depth of the mortise. Lateral movement and fore-and-aft movement are controlled by levers.

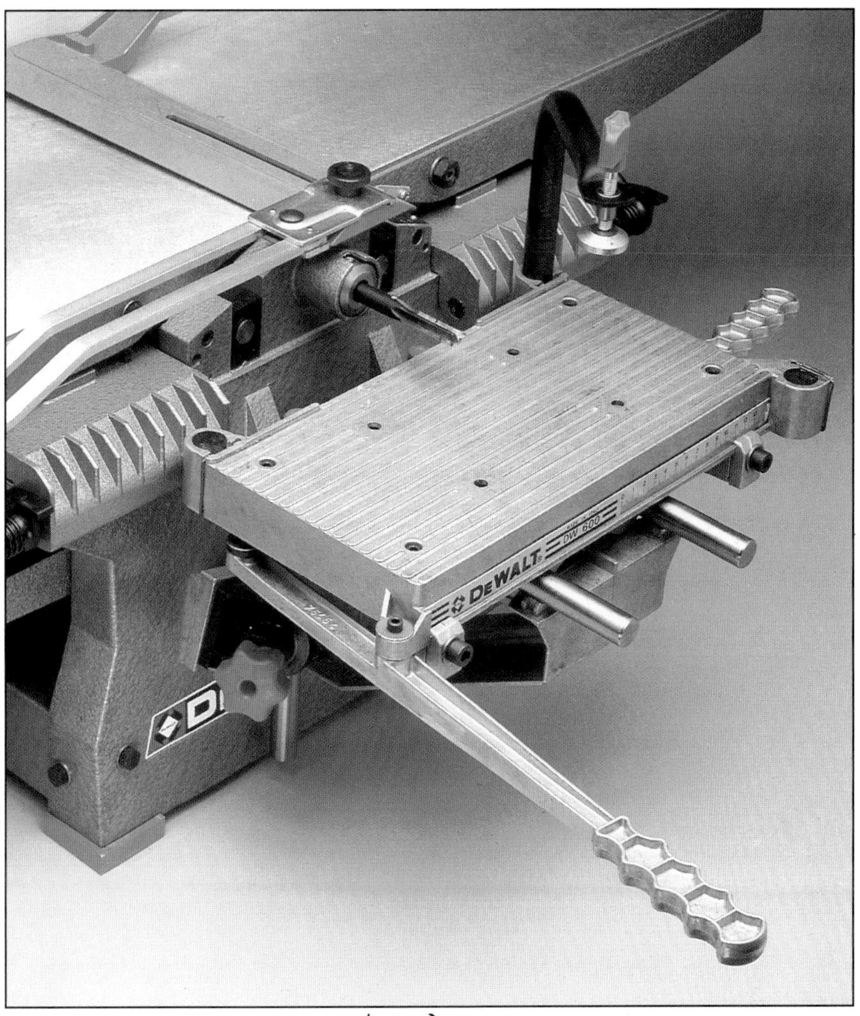

- **Sharpening milling cutters**
  Sharpen a milling cutter by honing the inner faces of the cutting edges on an oiled slipstone. Do not hone the outer surfaces or you will alter the diameter of the cutter. Have cutters reground by an expert when they do not cut efficiently after honing.

Slot mortiser
This particular attachment fits onto a jointer/planer.

USING A SLOT MORTISER SAFELY

Provided you observe general machine-shop safety procedures, using a hollow-chisel mortiser is perfectly safe – but if a jointer/planer is used to power a slot mortiser, you must ensure the machine is guarded to prevent serious accidents.

- Always cover the jointer cutters with a bridge guard before using a mortising attachment.
- The mortising chuck is normally guarded by a built-in casting on the planer bodywork or by a bolt-on guard. However, always remove a milling cutter as soon as you have finished a planned series of mortises.

Using a slot mortiser
Cut a mortise in stages, plunging only as deep as the diameter of the cutter at one pass. To attempt to cut any deeper puts an unacceptable strain on the milling cutter, which may break under side pressure.

Having cut the mortise, you can either cut the shoulders square with a chisel or round over the ends of the matching tenon with a file or machine sander.

Cutting tenons with a mortising attachment
It is possible to remove the waste from both sides of a tenon with a milling cutter – but, since the cutter is not supported on two sides by wood, you must feed the work against its direction of rotation.

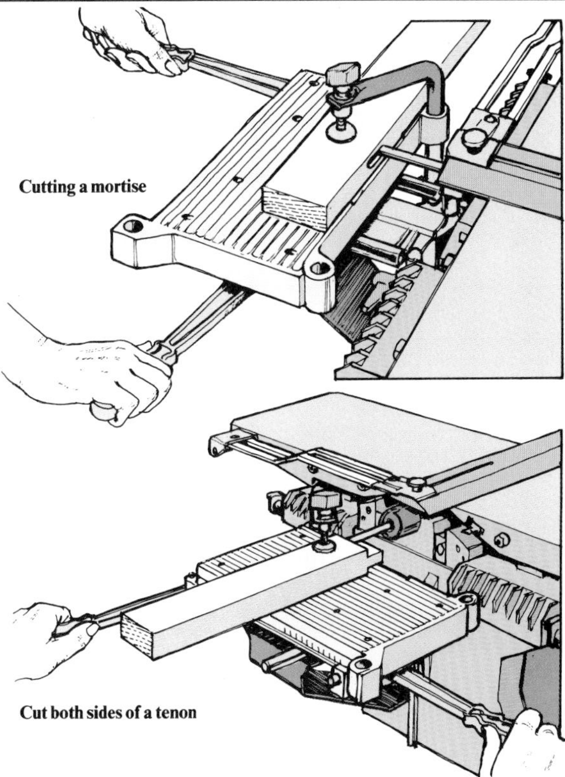

Cutting a mortise

Cut both sides of a tenon

DRILL PRESSES

A drill press is a heavy-duty stationary drilling machine. The drilling head, comprising the chuck for holding the drill bit, drive-belt mechanism and electric motor, is mounted on a rigid metal column. The column is supported by a heavy cast-metal base that is either bolted to a workbench or stands on the floor of the workshop. In the latter case, the column is long enough to raise both the drill and the worktable to a comfortable working height.

SEE ALSO

Bradawl	112
C-clamps	122
Vertical drill stand	127
Machine-shop safety	156
Wood screws	304-305

Chuck
A drill-press chuck has three self-centering jaws operated by a key and is identical in principle to the familiar power-drill chuck. Most drill-press chucks accommodate bits with shanks up to ½in (12mm) in diameter.

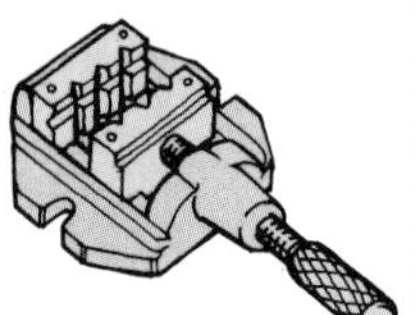

Drill-press vise
This small engineer's vise is for holding metal workpieces on a drill-press table.

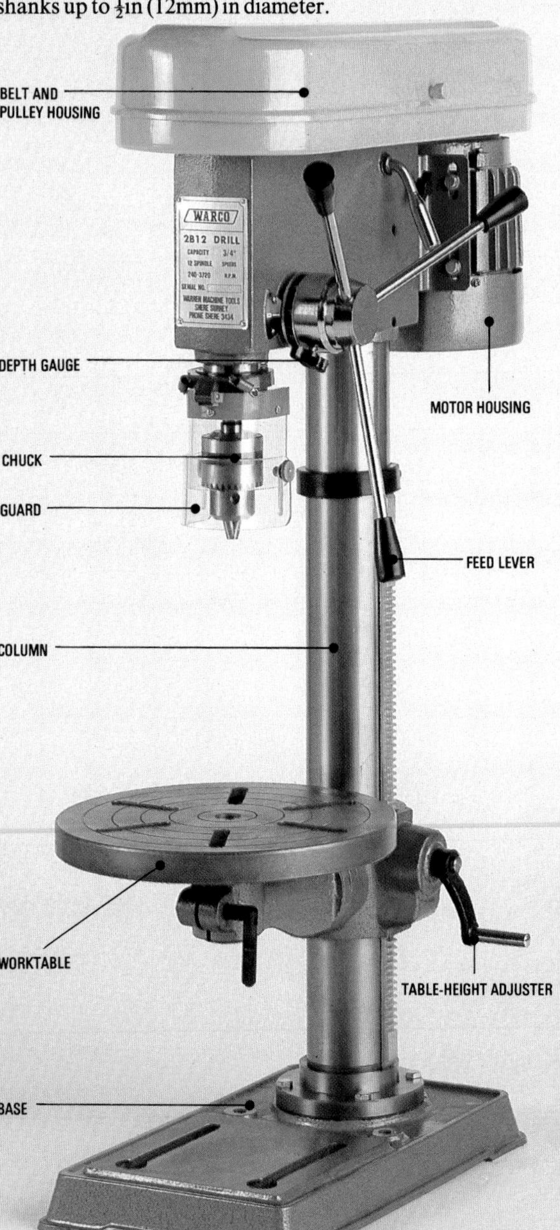

Bench-mounted drill press

Electric motor
Stationary drills are made with induction motors rated between 187 and 750W (¼ and 1hp). This type of motor is very efficient, but even so, it is best to buy a drill with at least a 250W (⅓hp) motor.

The motor's power is transmitted via a V-belt and pulley-wheel system to the spindle and chuck. Moving the rubber V-belt up or down stepped cone pulleys changes the speed in 4 or 5 increments between 450 and 3000 rpm.

The slowest speeds are selected for drilling metal or for boring large holes in hardwood. Increase the speed when working with softwood.

Worktable
A cast-metal worktable is cantilevered from the column. The table on some drills is raised or lowered by hand and clamped to the column in the required position by tightening a pinch bolt. Other drills are made with a rack-and-pinion system, the height of the table being adjusted by means of a crank handle.

Select a machine with a table that can be tilted to 45 degrees and that can be swung to one side by rotating it about the column in order to place a larger-than-average workpiece on the drill-press base.

A hole in the dead center of the rectangular or circular worktable allows the drill bit to pass through a workpiece without damage. Fences, vises or jigs can be bolted to the table, using the slots machined across it.

Drill-press base
For stability, the cast-metal base must be large and heavy. The upper surface is machined perfectly flat and is slotted to serve as a second worktable for large workpieces.

Throat
The throat – the distance from the center of the worktable to the column – should be as large as possible. The throat capacity on home-workshop drill presses can be anywhere from 4 to 8in (100 to 200mm).

Feed lever
The drill bit is plunged into a workpiece by pulling down on the feed lever mounted on one side of the machine. Since it is spring-loaded, the lever returns automatically – but the mechanism can be locked with a clamp lever to run the drill in a lowered position, leaving both hands free for working.

Maximum hole depth
The maximum hole depth that can be bored on a particular drill press is determined by the vertical movement of the chuck. Maximum vertical movement varies from about 2 to 3½in (50 to 90mm) on bench-mounted machines, but you will probably be able to bore deeper holes on a floor-standing drill press.

Depth gauge
Drilling depth is controlled by setting a gauge. Mark the required depth on the side of the workpiece. Lower the chuck until the tip of the drill bit aligns with the mark, then set the depth-gauge stop to limit the vertical travel of the spindle and chuck.

Safety guard
If possible, buy a machine with a safety guard (usually made of transparent plastic) that drops down or swings across to shield the drill-press chuck. The guard prevents hair or loose clothing from becoming caught in the rotating chuck. Closing the guard should also alert you to the presence of a chuck key accidentally left in the machine.

DRILL BITS

You will need a complete set of good-quality twist drills and brad-point bits up to at least $\frac{3}{8}$in (10mm) in diameter. However, as bits larger than that are relatively expensive, it is probably best to acquire them one at a time when the need arises.

Twist drills
Choose high-speed-steel twist drills, since these are equally suitable for wood and metal. Before boring a hole with a twist drill, mark the center with a bradawl – or with a metalworking punch if you are drilling hardwood or metal.

Brad-point bits
Brad-point bits are designed to bore holes in end grain for dowel joints. They are also excellent general-purpose woodboring bits.

Power auger bits
Use power auger bits to drill deep holes in wood. An average set contains augers ranging from $\frac{1}{4}$ to 1in (6 to 25mm) in diameter.

Spade bits
These are relatively cheap bits for drilling holes from $\frac{1}{4}$ to $1\frac{1}{2}$in (6 to 38mm) in diameter. The long lead points make for very positive location at the center of a hole even when the workpiece is clamped to a tilted drill-press table.

Forstner bits
Forstner bits are expensive but they bore exceptionally clean flat-bottomed holes, and they are not deflected by knots or wild grain. Forstner bits are available in a wide range of sizes up to 2in (50mm) in diameter.

Countersink bits
Having drilled a clearance hole for a wood screw, use a countersink bit to cut a tapered recess for the head. Select a high speed for a smooth cut.

Drill-and-countersink bits
Made to match specific wood screws, these bits drill a pilot hole, shank-clearance hole and countersink in a single operation.

Drill-and-counterbore bits
Set wood screws below the surface of a workpiece by using a drill-and-counterbore bit. The neat hole above the screw can be filled with a specially cut wooden plug (see below).

Plug cutters
Drive these cutters into side-grain wood to make plugs for covering counterbored screws. Cut plugs from wood that closely matches the work in color and grain pattern.

Hole saws
Cut a hole up to $3\frac{1}{2}$in (90mm) in diameter by using one of a set of hole saws. Select a slow to medium speed and clamp the work firmly.

USING A DRILL PRESS SAFELY

Provided you follow general machine-shop safety procedures, a drill press is a relatively safe machine. However, you must take certain extra precautions.

- Always remove the chuck key after tightening a bit.
- Lower the safety guard before switching on the drill press.
- Hold the work securely on the drill-press table. If a drill bit catches, it can spin the work with serious consequences. Hold a wooden workpiece against the rigid column or a custom-made fence to resist the turning force, or clamp the work to the table.
- Always clamp a metal workpiece or hold it in a drill-press vise.

USING A DRILL PRESS

Having fitted a drill bit, adjust the worktable to bring the work to within a fraction of an inch or so of its tip. Then set the depth gauge, center the bit and switch on the drill press. Feed the bit into the work steadily – it isn't necessary to apply excessive force to a sharp drill bit. Slowly release the feed lever, allowing it to come to rest in the raised position before switching off the machine.

Holding the work securely
To resist the turning force of the drill press, it is often possible to rest one end of a workpiece against the left-hand side of the column **(1)**. Alternatively, use a C-clamp or small fast-action clamp to fasten the work firmly to the table of the drill press.

A simple wooden fence secured to the worktable with bolts and wing nuts is a useful device for positioning identical workpieces accurately. Butt the end of each workpiece against a stop block clamped to the fence **(2)**. Slide a workpiece along the fence when you want to drill a series of holes in line – to remove waste from a mortise, for example **(3)**.

Cut a V-block on a table saw to serve as a cradle for drilling holes in a cylindrical workpiece **(4)**.

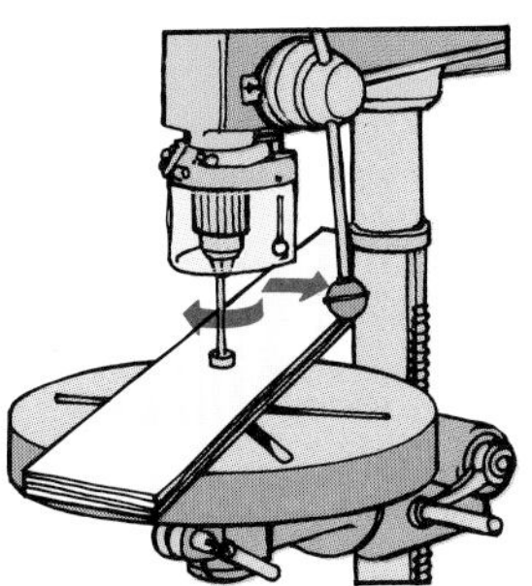
1 Rest the work against the drill-press column

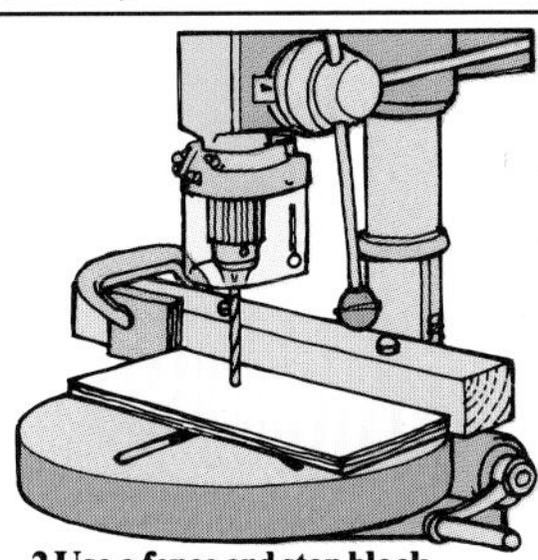
2 Use a fence and stop block to drill identical workpieces

3 Slide the work against the fence to drill holes in line

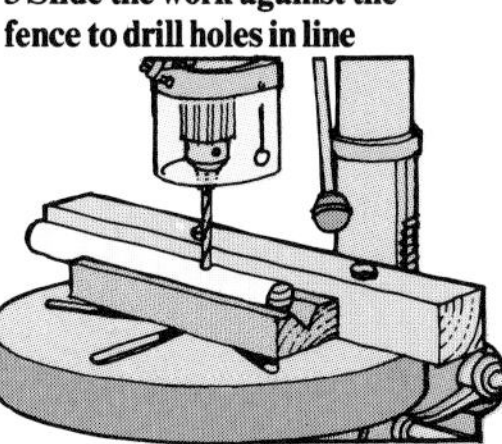
4 Use a V-block to cradle a cylindrical workpiece

- **Drilling a workpiece**
Place a piece of planed wood or man-made board beneath the work when you need to drill a hole right through it.

STATIONARY SANDERS

Most amateur woodworkers find portable orbital and belt sanders perfectly adequate for finishing wide flat panels or boards, but a bench-mounted belt-and-disc combination will provide you with a means for shaping components and sanding end-grain wood, too. It is also ideal for finishing small workpieces.

SEE ALSO
Portable sanders 147-149
Disc sanders 150,171
Machine-shop safety 156
Dust collectors 214

Sanding disc
A vertically mounted metal disc covered with sandpaper is used for sanding square or radiused ends on a workpiece and also for sanding miters.

The maximum width of work that can be sanded on a disc is somewhat less than half its diameter. Much larger discs are available in industry, but a 9in (225mm) disc is a reasonable choice for the home workshop.

Paper-backed abrasives are normally glued to the face of the disc with a special adhesive. When one wears out, simply peel it off and replace it with a fresh paper disc.

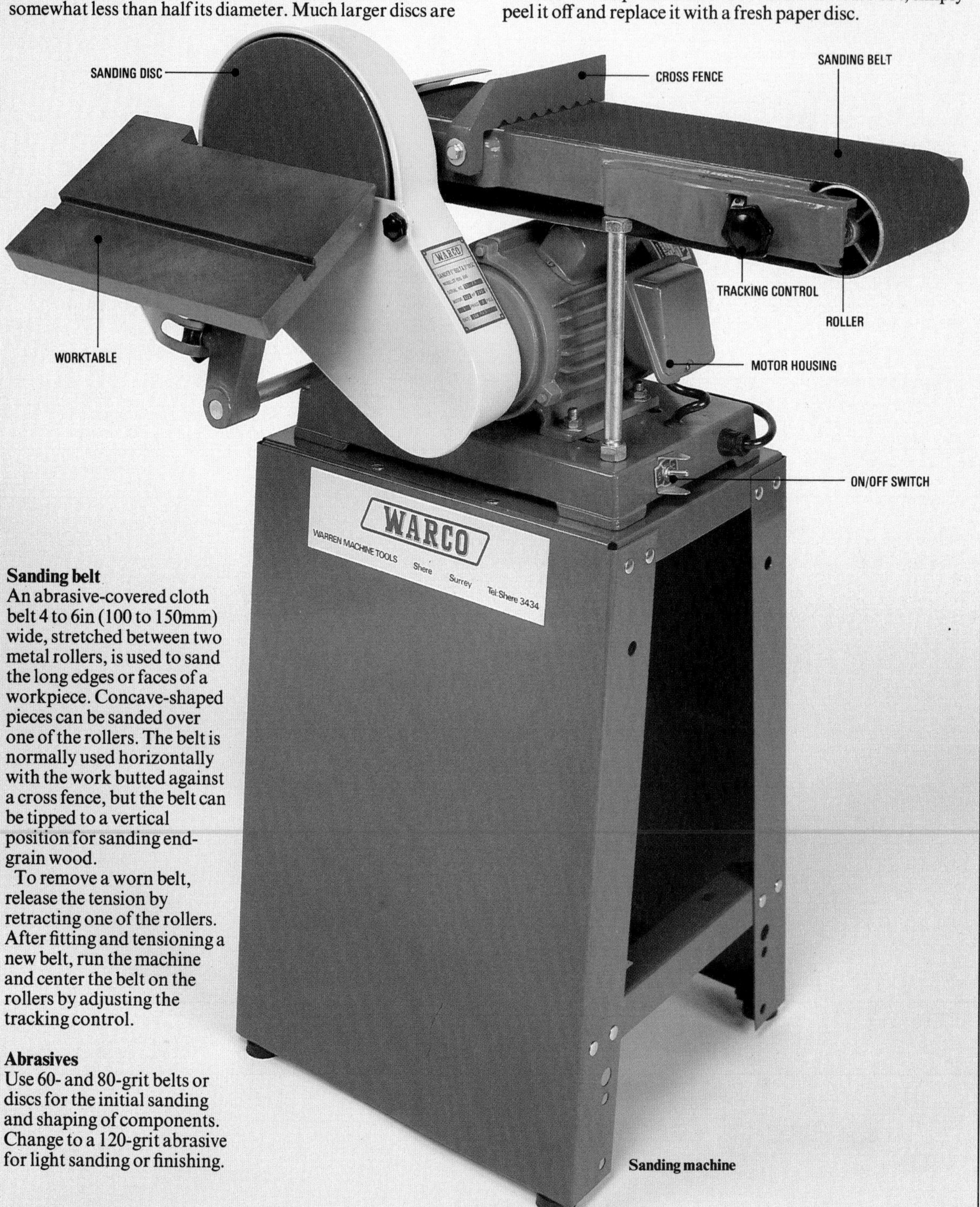

Sanding machine

Sanding belt
An abrasive-covered cloth belt 4 to 6in (100 to 150mm) wide, stretched between two metal rollers, is used to sand the long edges or faces of a workpiece. Concave-shaped pieces can be sanded over one of the rollers. The belt is normally used horizontally with the work butted against a cross fence, but the belt can be tipped to a vertical position for sanding end-grain wood.

To remove a worn belt, release the tension by retracting one of the rollers. After fitting and tensioning a new belt, run the machine and center the belt on the rollers by adjusting the tracking control.

- **Electric motor**
A single 250 to 375W ($\frac{1}{3}$ to $\frac{1}{2}$hp) electric motor drives both the sanding disc and belt.

Abrasives
Use 60- and 80-grit belts or discs for the initial sanding and shaping of components. Change to a 120-grit abrasive for light sanding or finishing.

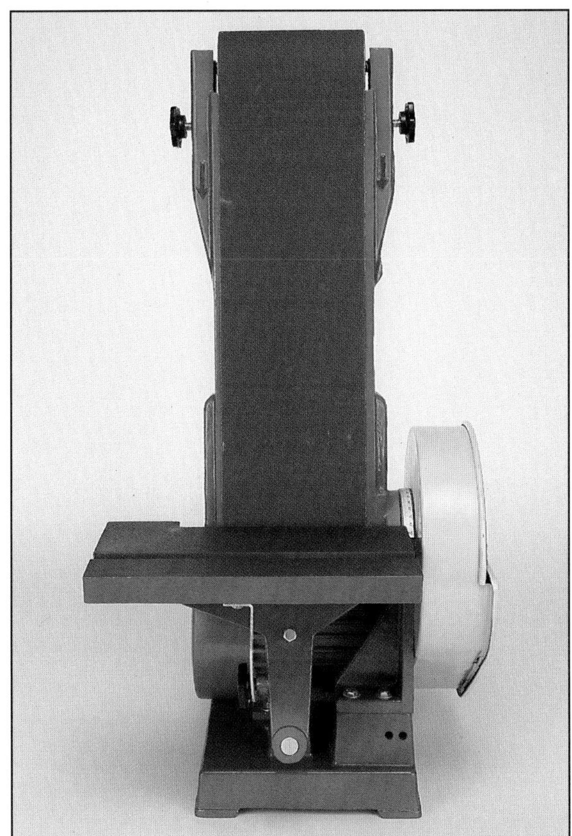

The belt can be set vertically

Worktable
A cast-metal worktable mounted next to the disc sander is fitted with a sliding miter gauge that presents the work to the disc at the required angle.

With the table tilted to any angle up to 45 degrees to the disc, the machine can be used to sand compound miters. The same table can be repositioned to sand a workpiece against a vertically positioned belt.

On/off switches
Some sanders are equipped with individual on/off push buttons. However, many have a simple toggle or rocker switch. Make sure this type of switch is in the off position before plugging the machine into an electrical outlet.

Dust collection
If at all possible, fit a dust collector to a sanding machine. The fine sawdust is detrimental to your health and creates a potentially explosive atmosphere in the workshop.

USING A SANDER SAFELY

Injuries often occur when using a sander because of the operator's failure to anticipate the possibility of an accident on what appears to be an inoffensive machine. So always follow general machine-shop safety procedures, and never take risks when using a sanding machine.

- Do not hold a thin workpiece on a moving belt sander. It may suddenly slip under the cross fence, and the palm of your hand will then be in immediate contact with the abrasive belt.
- To avoid injuring your fingertips, never sand very small components on a belt sander.
- Work against the down side only of a disc sander, to ensure wood is driven onto the table by the machine's rotation.

WORKING WITH A SANDER

Whenever possible, sand in the direction of the grain. Cross-grain sanding with either a disc or belt sander leaves scratches on the work that will be difficult to remove and impossible to disguise with a clear finish.

Using a disc sander
Hold the work firmly against the miter gauge and press the grain against the "down" side of the rotating disc. Keep the work moving back and forth, and don't press too hard or you will burn the end grain.

To shape convex curves on a disc sander, cut away most of the waste with a saw and then remove the miter gauge before sanding down to the marked line, using the table to support the workpiece.

Using a belt sander
To sand the side of a workpiece, butt the end against the cross fence **(1)**. Change the position of the work periodically, in order to maximize the life of the belt, and take care not to round over the edges of the workpiece.

To shape a curved piece, hold it against the roller at the end of the belt **(2)**.

If the size and shape of the workpiece permit, you can tip the belt upright and use its entire width for sanding the work **(3)**.

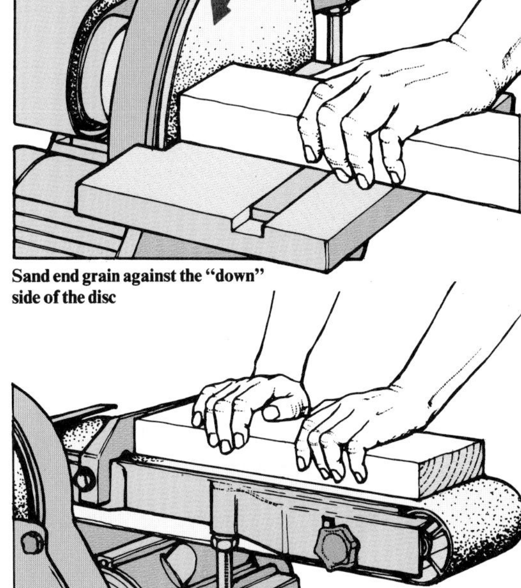

Sand end grain against the "down" side of the disc

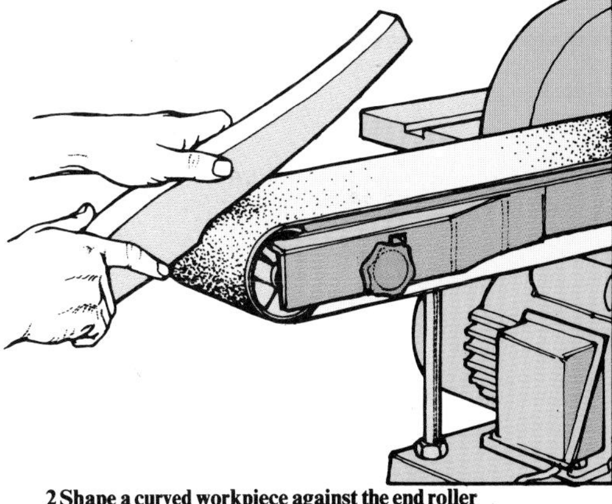

1 Butt a long workpiece against the cross fence

2 Shape a curved workpiece against the end roller

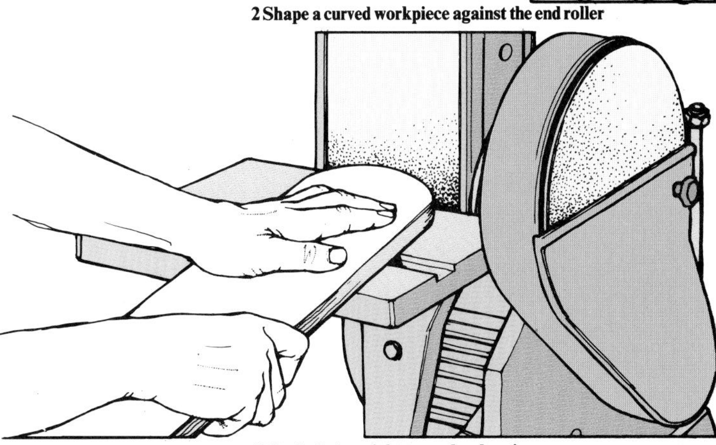

3 Tip the belt upright to sand end grain

LATHES

Woodturning is far more than a simple machining process – at its best it becomes an art form. Successful lathe work requires not only the mastery of very special techniques, but also an appreciation of what constitutes a pleasing shape with flowing lines.

A lathe, unlike other woodworking machines, is rarely used merely to process a workpiece from one stage of its production to the next – complete objects, from a rough blank through to a polished piece, can be created on the one machine.

SEE ALSO

Machine-shop safety	156
Between-center turning	196-200
One-center turning	201
Faceplates	202
Faceplate turning	202-203
Face protectors	214

BENCH-MOUNTED LATHES

Heavy floor-standing lathes may be the norm for industrial turning, but lighter bench-mounted machines are more popular for the home workshop. A rigid bed forms the backbone of the machine, with a drive mechanism housed in a fixed headstock at one end and a sliding tailstock at the other. The workpiece is suspended between the two and is rotated at speed against a hand-held cutting tool. Typically, lathes are designed for two methods of turning: between-center turning for shaping spindles, table legs and other long, thin workpieces, and one-center or faceplate turning for bowls, boxes, egg cups, etc.

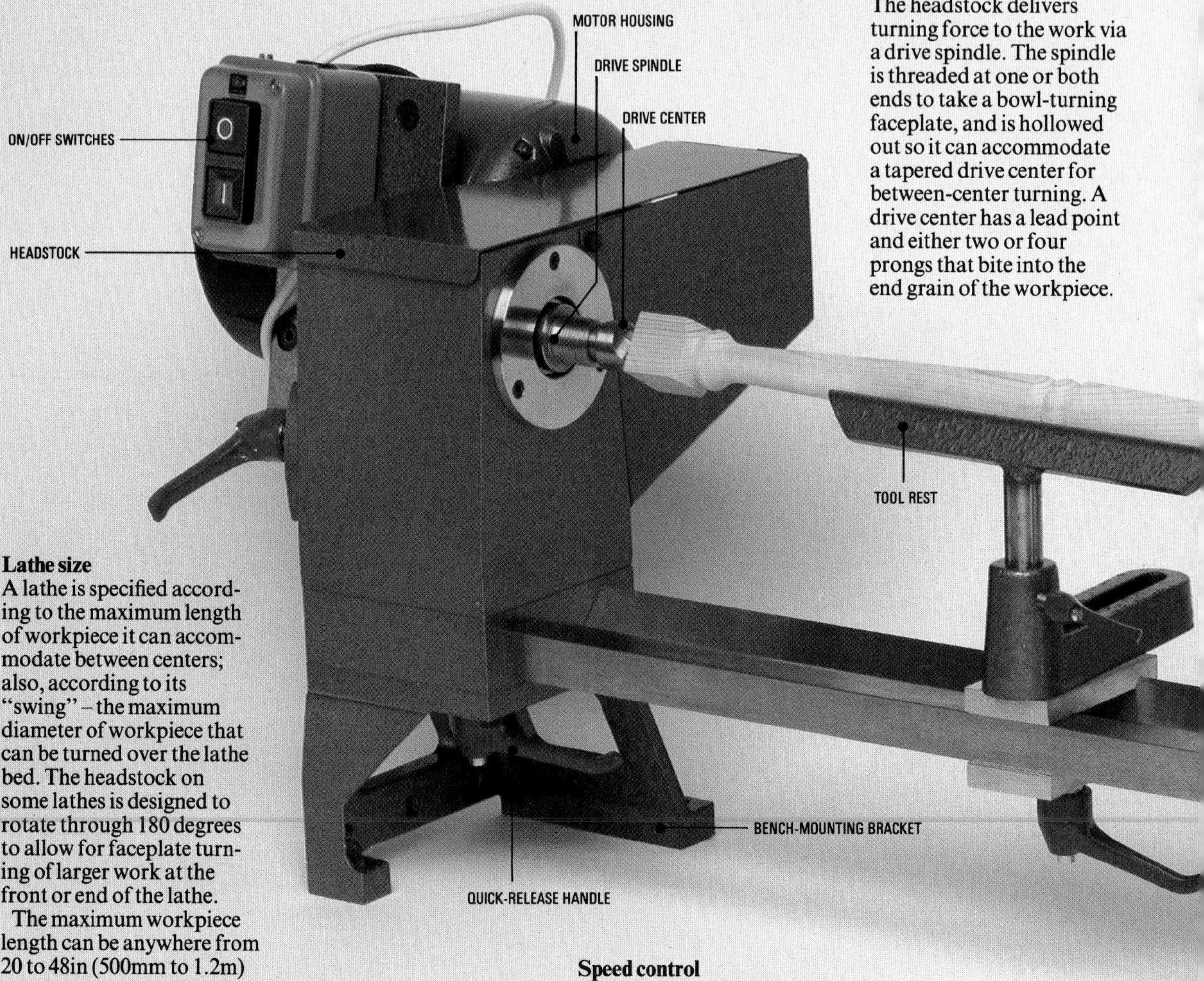

MOTOR HOUSING
DRIVE SPINDLE
DRIVE CENTER
ON/OFF SWITCHES
HEADSTOCK
TOOL REST
BENCH-MOUNTING BRACKET
QUICK-RELEASE HANDLE

Headstock
The headstock delivers turning force to the work via a drive spindle. The spindle is threaded at one or both ends to take a bowl-turning faceplate, and is hollowed out so it can accommodate a tapered drive center for between-center turning. A drive center has a lead point and either two or four prongs that bite into the end grain of the workpiece.

Lathe size
A lathe is specified according to the maximum length of workpiece it can accommodate between centers; also, according to its "swing" – the maximum diameter of workpiece that can be turned over the lathe bed. The headstock on some lathes is designed to rotate through 180 degrees to allow for faceplate turning of larger work at the front or end of the lathe.

The maximum workpiece length can be anywhere from 20 to 48in (500mm to 1.2m) on a bench-mounted lathe. Longer workpieces can be assembled by doweling two or three pieces together. Using the lathe to turn a peg on one end of a piece to fit a hole in another ensures perfect alignment, and a well-placed bead or groove disguises the joint.

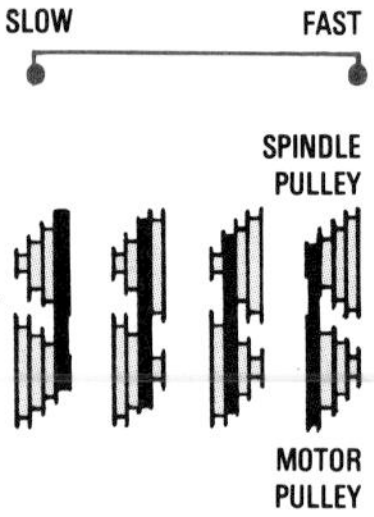

SLOW
FAST
SPINDLE PULLEY
MOTOR PULLEY

Changing lathe speed

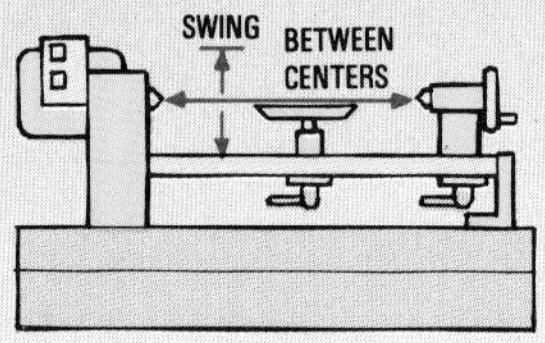

SWING
BETWEEN CENTERS

Dimensions of a lathe

Speed control
Most lathes use a belt drive to transmit power from a 375 to 750W ($\frac{1}{2}$ to 1hp) electric motor to the headstock spindle. Stepped pulleys provide three or four pre-set spindle speeds with a typical range of between 450 and 2000 rpm. Some more expensive lathes use electronic variable-speed control.

Use the lowest speed for rough-cutting workpieces and then move the drive belt up the speed range as work progresses. The size of the work and the type of wood you are turning also affect speed selection. There are no hard and fast rules, but use the chart on the right as a rough guide.

USING A LATHE SAFELY

A lathe is unique among wood-cutting machines in that it does not incorporate a moving cutter or blade. Instead, a hand-held cutting tool is used to shape a spinning workpiece. One reason why the lathe appeals to the amateur woodworker is that it seems a relatively safe machine with little risk of injury to his or her fingers. However, if you neglect to develop safe working practices, a single mistake can cause the work to be hurled across the workshop – so always follow general machine-shop safety procedures and observe the following rules.

- Always work in good light.
- Keep the area around the lathe clear of loose objects and stacks of wood that could fall against a spinning workpiece.
- Select a speed setting suitable for the work.
- Never leave keys or wrenches in a lathe chuck.
- Fit a guard around a three-jaw or four-jaw chuck.
- Before switching on the lathe, check that all clamps and fixings are secure and that the work is free to rotate.
- Switch off the lathe before adjusting the tool rest.
- Make sure a cutting tool is in contact with a tool rest before feeding it into the work.
- Remove the tool rest before sanding a workpiece.
- Never leave a lathe running unattended – it can appear to be stationary.
- Don't wear loose clothing, especially a necktie, when operating a lathe.
- Remove rings and necklaces before you use a lathe, and tie back long hair.
- Wear safety goggles or a full face shield to protect yourself from flying woodchips.
- It is difficult to fit a dust collector to a lathe – so wear a mask, especially if you suffer from respiratory problems.

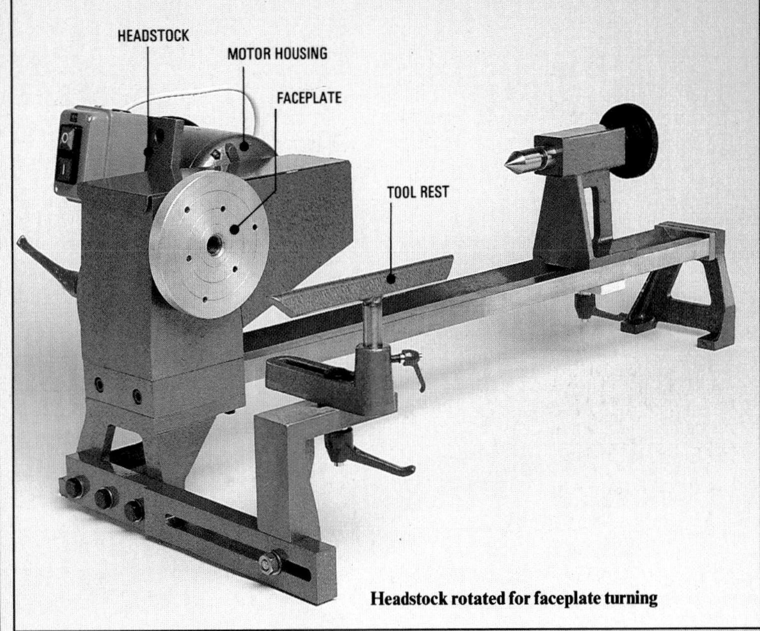

Headstock rotated for faceplate turning

Lathe bed
Bracket-mounted steel bars or tubes support the tailstock, tool rest and other accessories. There must be ample clearance between bed and bench for removing shavings.

Tailstock
The tailstock, which is clamped to the lathe bed with a quick-release lever, supports the end of a workpiece for between-center turning. It is fitted with a sliding hollow spindle, controlled by a handwheel, that takes a tapered tailstock center with a simple central point. If this point is fixed – a "dead" tailstock center – it must be lubricated with wax to prevent it from burning the work. Alternatively, fit a revolving "live" center constructed with ball bearings.

Tool rest
An adjustable tool rest is used to support the blade of a turning tool just in front of a rotating workpiece.

A standard rest – between 8 and 12in (200 and 300mm) long – is slid along the lathe to the most convenient position as work progresses. An extra-long rest that spans the length of the lathe bed is supported by mounting brackets at each end. Curved or cranked tool rests are made for bowl-turning.

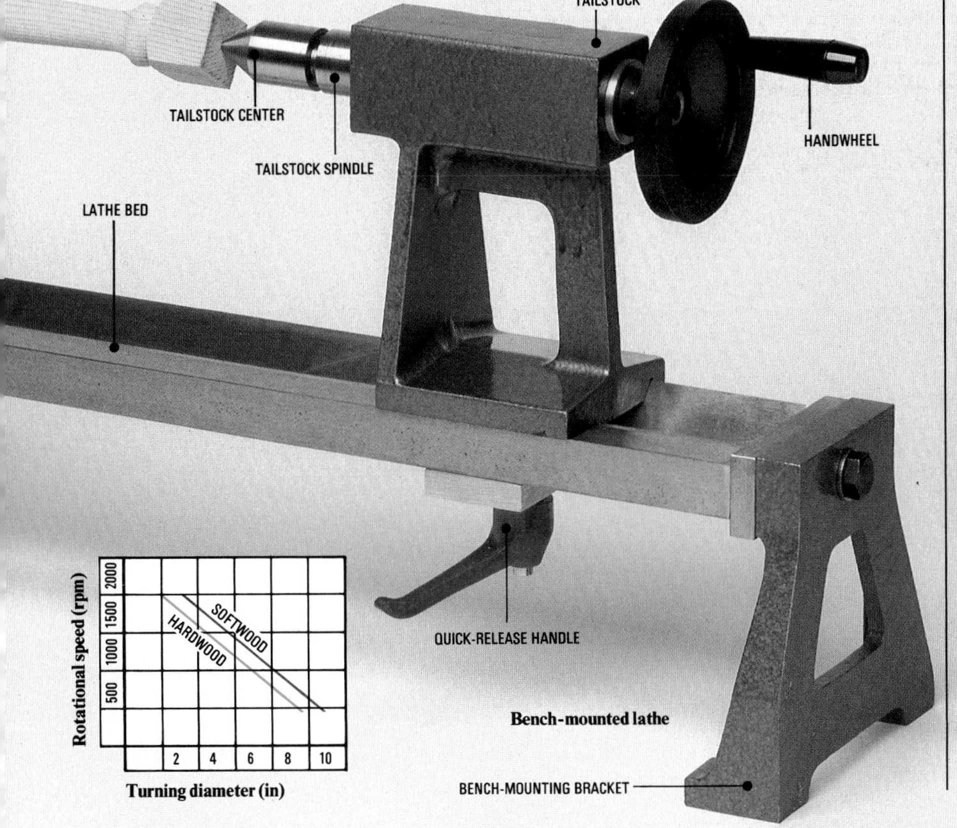

Bench-mounted lathe

TURNING TOOLS

Specially designed cutting tools are used for shaping workpieces on a lathe. The stocky blades are fitted with long, turned handles that provide the leverage required for control of the tools. Carbon-steel blades are relatively inexpensive and are easy to sharpen. As long as you do not turn abrasive woods, such as teak or elm, a carbon-steel blade will hold its edge reasonably well. High-speed-steel tools stay sharp much longer, especially on hard or wet wood, but they cost considerably more.

SEE ALSO

Tape measure	76-77
Rulers	76-77
Machine-shop safety	156
Safety tips	193
Basic tool control	196-197
Using a parting tool	199
One-center turning	201
Turning bowls	203

Basic set of turning tools
There is no need to buy every tool available. Purchase the following to begin with, then add further tools to your basic set as the need arises:

Roughing-out gouge – 1in (25mm)
Spindle gouge – $\frac{1}{2}$in (12mm)
Bowl gouge – $\frac{3}{8}$in (9mm)
Skew chisel – $\frac{3}{4}$in (18mm)
Parting tool – $\frac{1}{8}$in (3mm)
Round-nose scraper – $\frac{1}{2}$in (12mm)

MEASURING AND MARKING TOOLS

In addition to a tape measure and rulers, a woodturner requires special measuring, gauging and marking tools.

Compass
You will need a compass for marking out the diameter of the workpiece. It is not necessary to purchase an expensive compass, but choose one that will maintain its accuracy.

Calipers
These are essential for measuring the diameter of workpieces. Outside calipers are used for gauging the diameter of between-center work; inside calipers for measuring the inside diameter of bowls and other kinds of hollow work.

Sizing tool
A sizing tool is designed to clamp onto the blade of a parting tool. It is used to determine the diameter of a cylindrical workpiece, spigot, or round tenon. Hooked over the workpiece, it guides the tip of the blade to cut the precise diameter that is required.

Roughing-out gouge
Being ground square across the tip, roughing-out gouges are used for turning square or octagonal stock to a cylinder. They are available in widths of $\frac{3}{4}$, 1 and 1$\frac{1}{4}$in (18, 25 and 32mm).

Spindle gouge
This round-nosed gouge takes over from the roughing-out gouge for general between-center turning. Spindle gouges are available in a range of sizes from $\frac{1}{4}$ to 1in (6 to 25mm) wide.

TURNING GOUGES

The blade of a turning gouge has a curved cross section and is ground on the outside only.

Bowl gouge
These deep-fluted gouges allow heavy cuts to be taken when turning hollows. Standard bowl gouges range from $\frac{1}{4}$ to $\frac{3}{4}$in (6 to 18mm). You can buy an extra-long $\frac{3}{4}$in (18mm) gouge for greater control when turning large-diameter bowls.

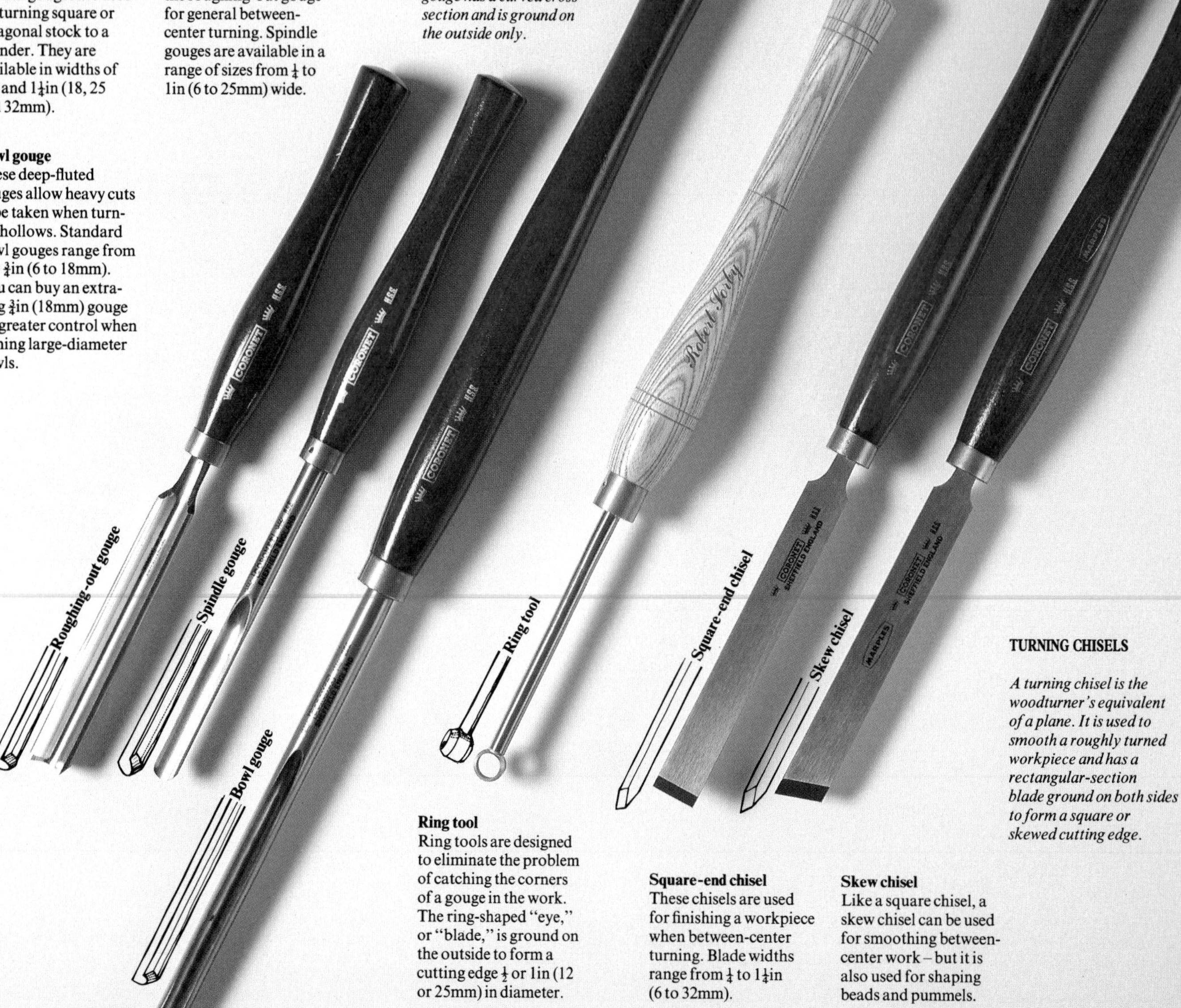

TURNING CHISELS

A turning chisel is the woodturner's equivalent of a plane. It is used to smooth a roughly turned workpiece and has a rectangular-section blade ground on both sides to form a square or skewed cutting edge.

Ring tool
Ring tools are designed to eliminate the problem of catching the corners of a gouge in the work. The ring-shaped "eye," or "blade," is ground on the outside to form a cutting edge $\frac{1}{2}$ or 1in (12 or 25mm) in diameter.

Square-end chisel
These chisels are used for finishing a workpiece when between-center turning. Blade widths range from $\frac{1}{4}$ to 1$\frac{1}{4}$in (6 to 32mm).

Skew chisel
Like a square chisel, a skew chisel can be used for smoothing between-center work – but it is also used for shaping beads and pummels.

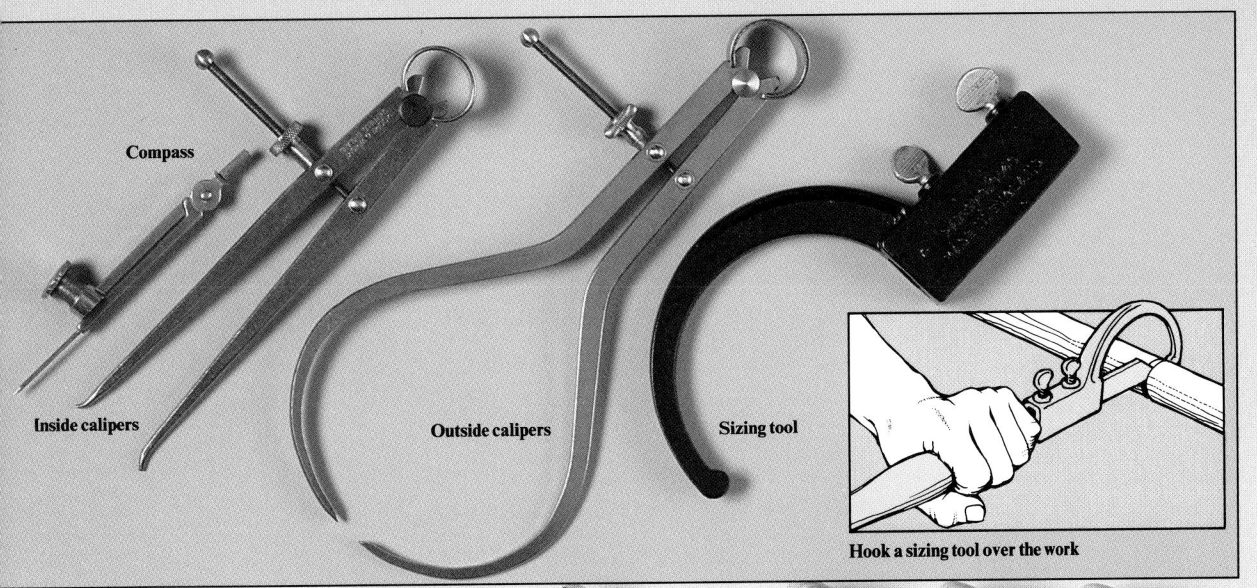

Hook a sizing tool over the work

PARTING TOOLS

These tools are designed primarily for cutting through a workpiece and removing it from the lathe. Consequently, the blade – which usually has a rectangular section but may be faceted or oval-sectioned – is ground to a point that has a cutting edge parallel to its narrrow faces.

Standard parting tool
This type of parting tool is either ⅛ or ¼in (3 or 6mm) wide.

Parting tool

Fluted parting tool

Full-round scraper

Domed scraper

Square-end scraper

Rounded side-cutting scraper

Diamond side-cutting scraper

Diamond-point scraper

Fluted parting tool
This is hollow-ground along one narrow face to form two sharp points that scribe the wood before the tool cuts. This leaves an exceptionally clean finish on end grain when the tool is held flute-down on the lathe rest. A fluted parting tool is usually ⅛in (3mm) wide.

Full-round and domed scrapers
These scrapers are used for working inside bowls and goblets. Blade widths range from ½ to 1in (12 to 25mm).

Square-end scraper
This type of scraper is used mainly on the outside of bowls or the flat bottom of a turned box. Square-end scrapers are made in the same range of sizes as the round and domed varieties.

Side-cutting scrapers
Rounded and diamond side-cutting scrapers are especially useful for working inside all kinds of hollow work. Both types have a blade width of ¾in (18mm).

SCRAPERS

Ground to a shallow cutting angle, scrapers leave a smooth finish on end grain. When you turn a bowl, two areas of end grain are presented to the tool with each revolution of the lathe. For this reason, scrapers are used primarily for cutting bowls and for other deep hollowing operations.

Diamond-point scraper
This kind of scraper is usually ground to a 90-degree pointed tip. It is used for incising V-shaped notches in between-center work and for cleaning up square corners. Blade widths range from ¼ to 1¼in (6 to 32mm).

SHARPENING TURNING TOOLS

Because the work spins so fast on the lathe, a turning tool cuts through a considerable amount of wood in a matter of seconds. As a result, you need to sharpen your tools every few minutes. Many woodturners use a power grinder to sharpen lathe tools; others prefer to hone them frequently on an oilstone. Perhaps the best method is to regrind the cutting bevels for most uses, but hone the ground edge razor-sharp for fine work.

Whichever method you adopt, locate your sharpening bench close to the lathe so you can sharpen your tools frequently. Use a star-wheel dressing tool to renew the grindstone's surface when it becomes clogged with metal particles, and keep a jar of cold water next to the grinder for cooling blades.

New gouges, chisels and scrapers come with their beveled cutting edges ground to the manufacturer's recommended angles. These tools will continue to perform perfectly if you maintain the same angles on a grindstone, but woodturners often regrind their tools to different cutting angles and shapes according to personal preference.

SEE ALSO

Grinders	106-107
Burnisher	110
Machine-shop safety	156
Safety tips	193
Turning tools	194-195

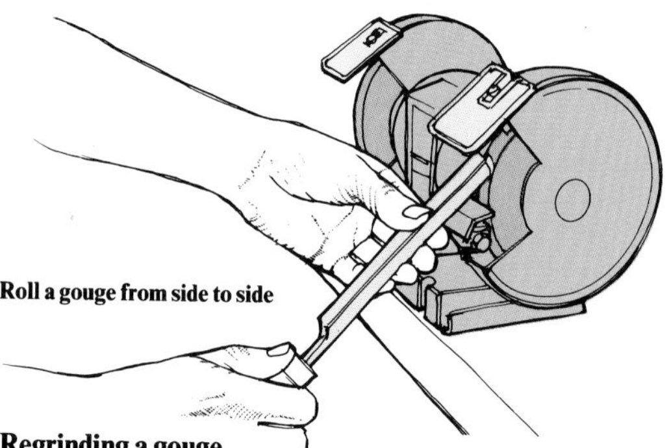

Roll a gouge from side to side

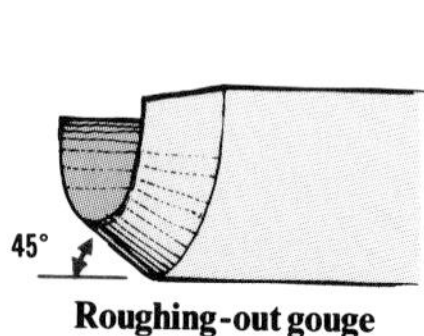

Roughing-out gouge

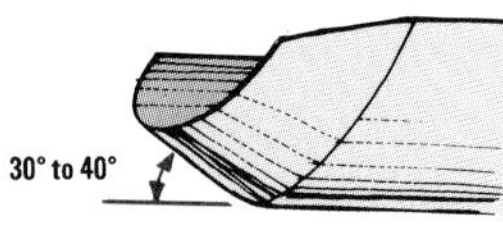

Spindle gouge

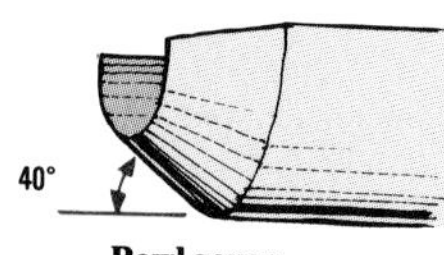

Bowl gouge

Chisel

Parting tool

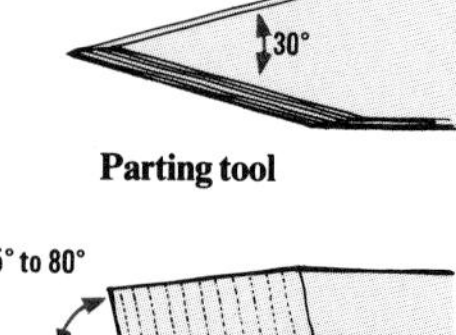

Scraper

Regrinding a gouge

Dip the tip of a gouge in the jar of cool water and lower it bevel downward onto the grindstone. As soon as the bevel touches the stone, roll the tool from side to side to grind the whole bevel evenly. Don't press the blade too hard, and cool the metal frequently in water. Recommended bevel angles are 45 degrees for a roughing-out gouge, 30 to 40 degrees for a spindle gouge and 40 degrees for a bowl gouge.

Regrinding a chisel

Sharpen both sides of a chisel, moving the tool from side to side to grind a straight cutting edge. Apply light pressure only to the tool, taking care not to grind away the points, which would create a curved cutting edge and cool the metal frequently. Grind a chisel to an included angle of 30 degrees, and hone the edge on an oilstone.

Regrinding a parting tool

Regrind a parting tool in the same manner as a chisel, to an included angle of 30 degrees.

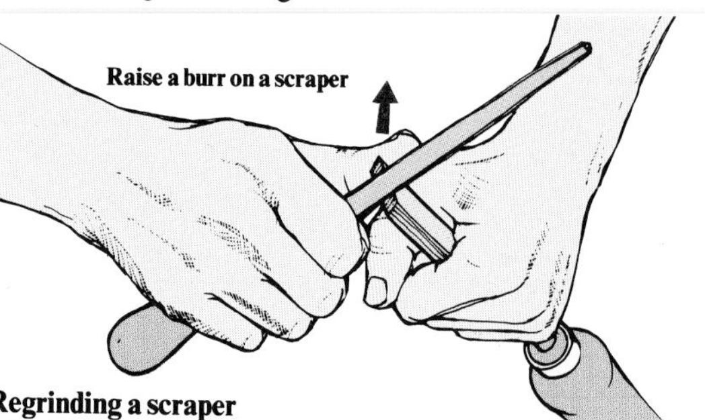

Raise a burr on a scraper

Regrinding a scraper

Most turners use a scraper straight from the grindstone, but a more efficient cutting edge is produced if you hone the bevel afterward, then raise a burr by stroking the edge with a burnisher. Grind a scraper to an angle of 75 to 80 degrees.

BASIC TOOL CONTROL

The way you stand and move your body while woodturning is as important as the way you hold the tool. Even basic tool control demands practice, so begin by turning test pieces in softwood until you get used to the feel of the tools and have developed a sensitive touch.

Working height

Construct a strong bench to support your lathe at a comfortable working height. A height that is perfectly comfortable for one woodturner will not suit another – but as a rough guide, mount your lathe so that the centerline of the workpiece is at elbow height.

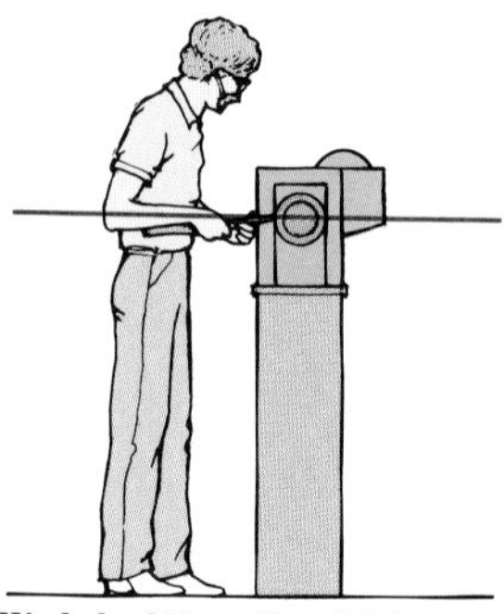

Work should be at elbow height

Correct stance and tool control

When you are turning wood between centers, stand facing the lathe, balanced comfortably with your feet apart. Don't stand so far from the machine that you are forced to lean forward – this soon becomes tiring and you are bound to lose an element of tool control.

Hold the turning tool with its handle more or less in line with your forearm and your elbow tucked into your side.

Control the blade of the tool with your other hand, moving the tool from side to side along the rest. Cup your hand over the blade when rough-cutting **(1)**; for more delicate work, use an underhand grip with your thumb on top of the blade **(2)**. With either grip, tuck your elbow close to your body.

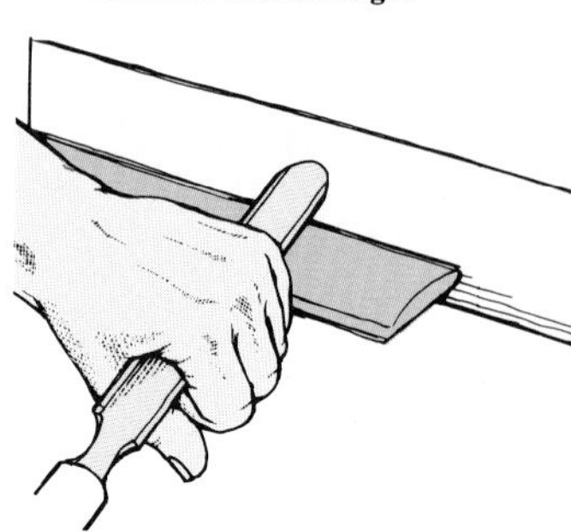

1 Overhand grip for rough-cutting

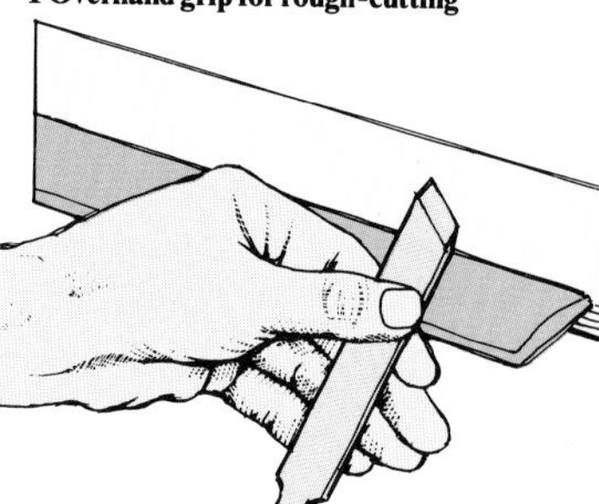

2 Underhand grip for delicate work

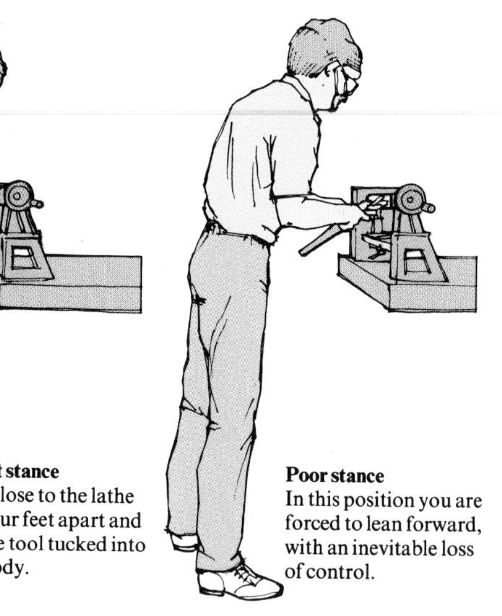

Correct stance
Stand close to the lathe with your feet apart and with the tool tucked into your body.

Poor stance
In this position you are forced to lean forward, with an inevitable loss of control.

Moving with the tool
When you're turning a basic cylinder, you must keep the tool moving on a path that's parallel to the work. If you move your hands and arms only, the tool will tend to swing in an arc. The correct method is to move your whole body in the direction of the cut, in a controlled but fluid manner. Try not to overtense your muscles or grip the tool too firmly.

When working to the left, rotate your shoulders, twisting your body from the waist as you lean into the cut **(1)**. Gradually transfer your weight onto your left leg – bending it to keep your balance as you straighten your right leg **(2)**.

When working to the right, open your stance to enable you to hold the tool at the required cutting angle to the work **(3)**.

If you are left-handed, the reverse stance and body action applies as you move to the right or left.

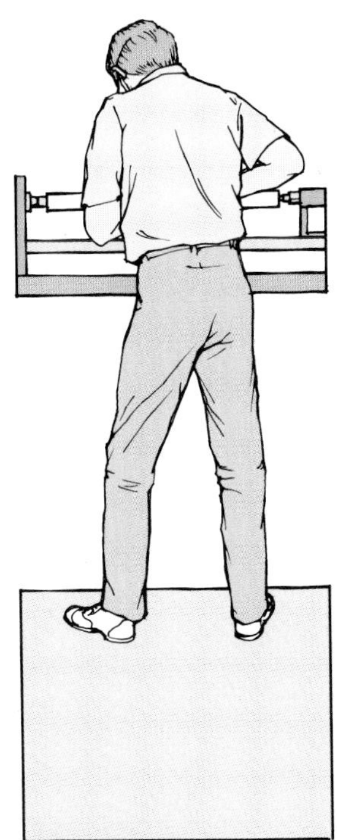

1 Move with the tool
Twist your body from the waist as you lean into the cut.

2 Follow through
As you move, transfer your weight onto your left leg and bend your knee to maintain a balanced stance.

3 Changing direction
When working to the right, re-position your feet for good balance and a comfortable stance.

CUTTING WITH A WOODTURNING TOOL

Present a woodturning scraper square to the work and hold it more or less parallel to the floor. Many beginners use wood-turning gouges and chisels in a similar fashion, scraping the wood rather than cutting it smoothly. Although this is an easy method to learn, it leaves a relatively rough surface that requires more sanding than should be necessary to achieve a satisfactory finish. Experienced woodturners use the tools with a slicing action – a technique that requires more practice, but one that all turners should aspire to.

Adjust the tool rest so that it is within ¼ to ½in (6 to 12mm) of the work and is positioned on its centerline. Turn the workpiece by hand to check work clearance. Switch on the lathe, then place the blade on the rest before any part of the tool comes into contact with the work. If you touch a spinning workpiece with an unsupported tool, the blade will be driven violently against the rest. This will almost certainly damage the work or tool, and may even result in injury.

Hold the tool at an angle, with its bevel resting on the wood **(1)**, then slowly lift the handle to initiate the cut **(2)**. Raising and lowering the handle of the tool gives you precise control over the depth of cut. As you move the tool sideways to the left or right while turning a cylinder, incline the whole tool to induce a slicing action **(3)**. At the same time, roll the blade in the direction of the sideways movement so that the cutting edge does not catch in the work **(4)**. If the tool is cutting correctly, it will produce fine shavings and leave a smooth surface that requires minimum sanding.

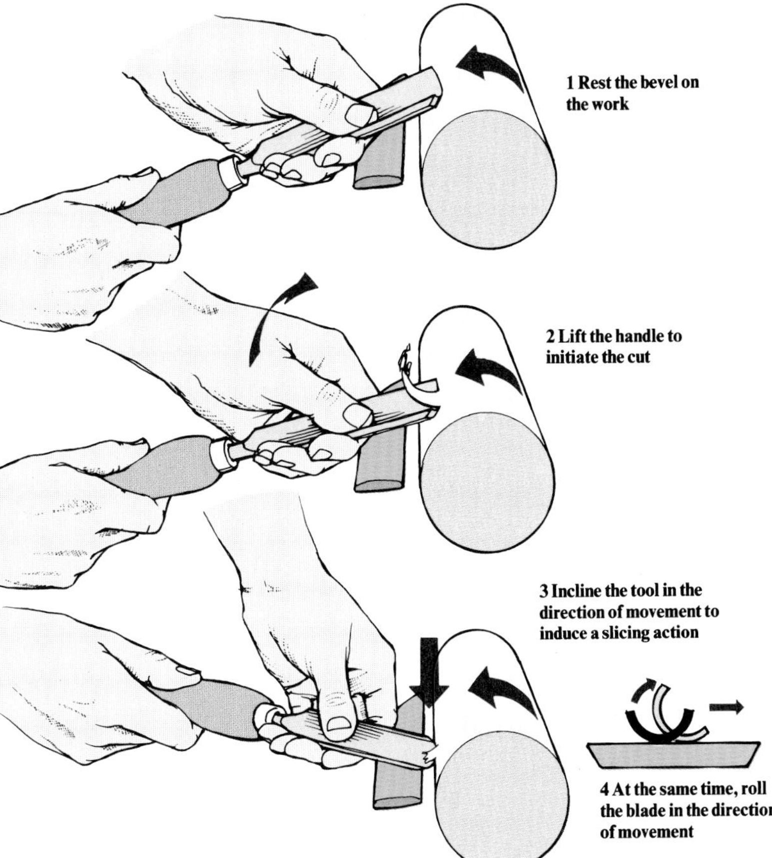

TURNING BETWEEN CENTERS

Between-center turning is used to make cylindrical workpieces – for straightforward chair or table legs, for example. This is a relatively simple procedure, though a woodturner will often want to produce more decorative work incorporating beads and hollows. All between-center projects start in the same manner – by converting the square-section "stock" on the lathe.

SEE ALSO

Machine-shop safety	156
Safety tips	193
Basic tool control	196-197
Decorative turning	200
Face mask	214
Goggles/glasses	214
Abrasive papers	285
Wood finishes	288-294

Preparing and mounting the stock

First prepare an accurately squared workpiece on a jointer/planer, and find its center by drawing diagonals from corner to corner on each end **(1)**. Draw the circumference of the finished workpiece on both ends of the stock with a compass, then mark both centers (where the diagonals cross) with a metalworker's center punch **(2)** or bradawl. Use a tenon saw to cut a shallow kerf along both diagonals on one end to engage the drive-center prongs **(3)**.

An experienced woodturner will mount the stock in the lathe and remove its square corners with a gouge. However, a beginner will find it easier to plane off the corners to make an octagonal workpiece **(4)**. Tap the drive center into the kerfed end of the workpiece **(5)**, then slip the tapered end of the drive center into the headstock.

Slide the tailstock up to the work, locating the point of the tailstock center in the central hole marked in the end grain. Clamp the tailstock to the lathe bed; then, after turning the handwheel to feed the "center" into the work, lock the handwheel.

Adjust the tool rest up to the work, then check clearance by revolving the workpiece by hand. Select a slow speed and check that all adjustments are tight before switching on the lathe. After running the machine for a few minutes, switch it off and put an extra turn on the handwheel to make sure the tailstock center is still secure in the work.

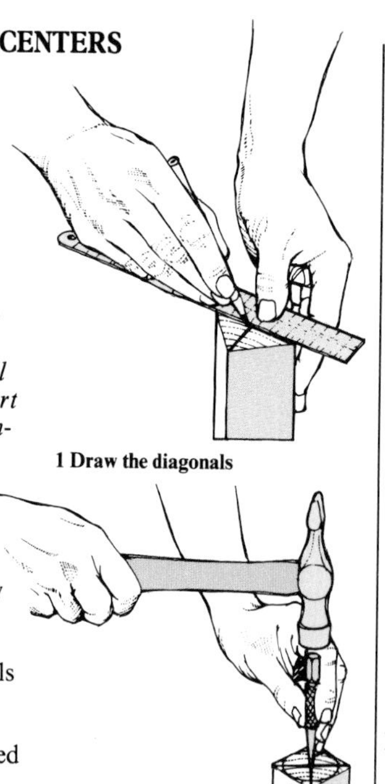

1 Draw the diagonals

2 Mark the centers

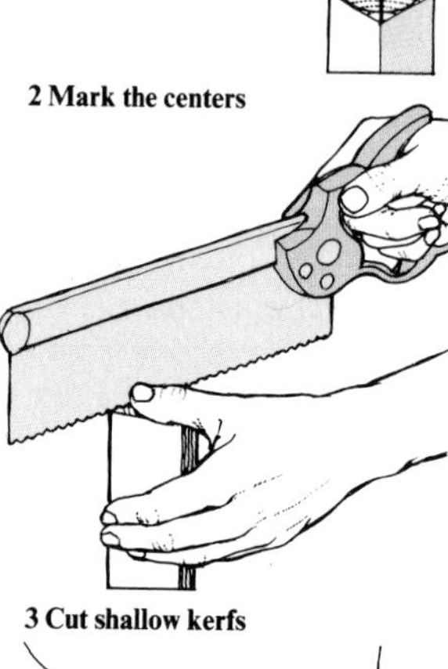

3 Cut shallow kerfs

4 Plane the stock to an octagon

5 Tap drive center into the work

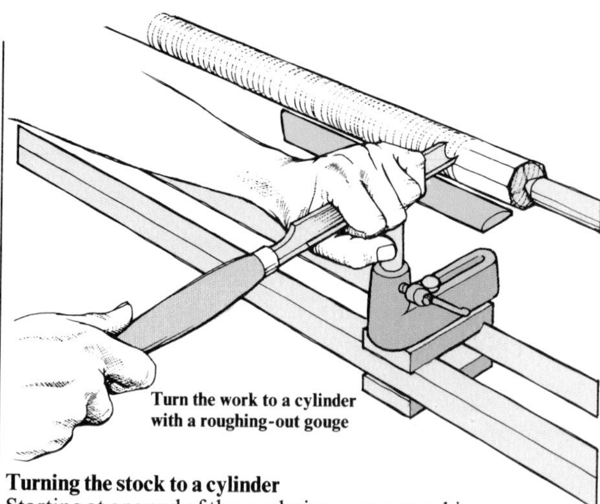

Turn the work to a cylinder with a roughing-out gouge

Turning the stock to a cylinder

Starting at one end of the workpiece, use a roughing-out gouge to remove the corners. Make very light cuts at first, moving the gouge smoothly along the tool rest. If necessary, switch off the lathe, move the rest and reduce the other end of the workpiece to the same diameter. Repeat the process until you have removed all the "flats," leaving a cylindrical workpiece with a uniform diameter from one end to the other.

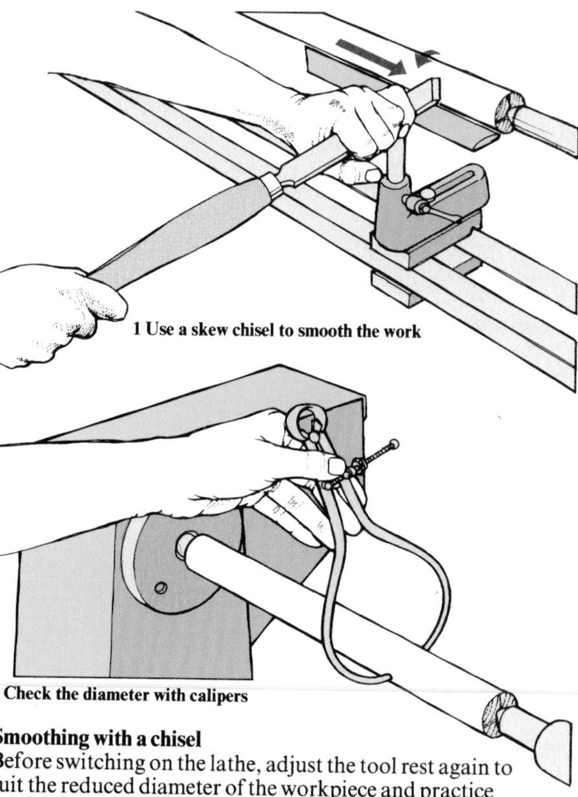

1 Use a skew chisel to smooth the work

2 Check the diameter with calipers

Smoothing with a chisel

Before switching on the lathe, adjust the tool rest again to suit the reduced diameter of the workpiece and practice holding the skew chisel correctly. While resting the cutting bevel on the wood, slightly rock the blade on the rest to lift the "longer" point away from the work and incline the tool toward the direction of cut. Use the middle to bottom part of the cutting edge to make the cut **(1)**.

With the lathe running, start at one end of the work by gently touching the surface of the wood with the chisel until you begin to produce shavings, then smoothly move the tool sideways. Keep the cutting depth constant throughout the pass. A correct cutting action will leave a smooth "planed" surface. At regular intervals, switch off the lathe and check the diameter of the work with calipers **(2)**.

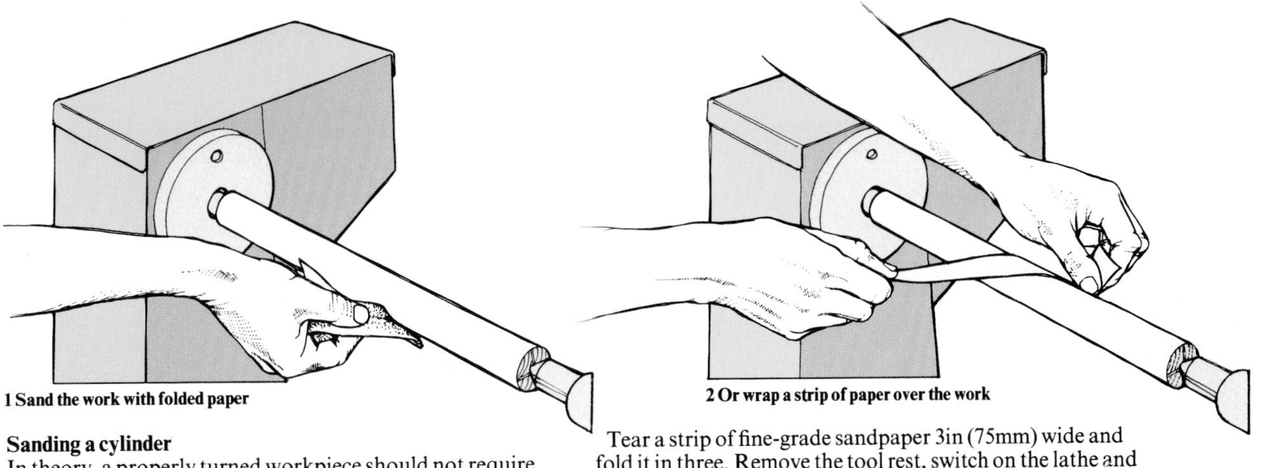

1 Sand the work with folded paper

2 Or wrap a strip of paper over the work

Sanding a cylinder

In theory, a properly turned workpiece should not require sanding – the finish straight from the chisel should be perfect. In practice, most woodturners clean up the surface with a light sanding. Always wear a face mask when sanding on a lathe, since a great deal of fine sawdust is produced.

Tear a strip of fine-grade sandpaper 3in (75mm) wide and fold it in three. Remove the tool rest, switch on the lathe and hold the abrasive pad against the revolving workpiece with your fingertips **(1)**. Keep the paper moving along the work so you don't leave cross-grain scratches. Alternatively, wrap a strip of sandpaper over the work **(2)**.

Cutting the work to length

Replace the tool rest and mark each end of the workpiece by holding the point of a pencil against the spinning cylinder **(1)**. Hold a parting tool square to the work, with its bevel rubbing on the waste side of the marked line. Slowly lift the handle of the tool to cut a deep slot in the wood **(2)**. Leave a small-diameter "neck" at the center of the workpiece at each end **(3)**. Remove the work from the lathe and cut through the waste with a tenon saw **(4)**. Trim the end grain flush, using a sharp firmer chisel.

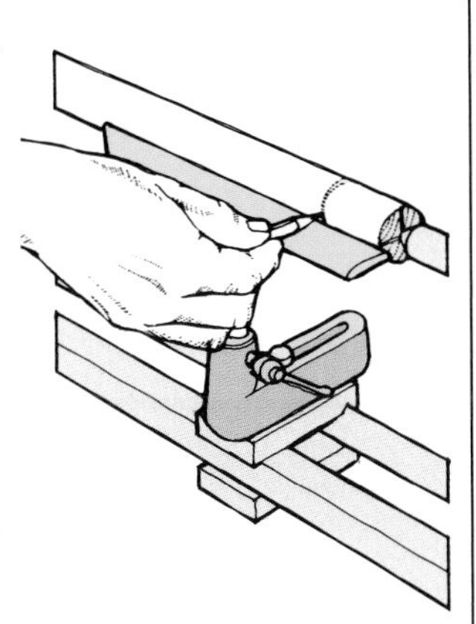

1 Mark the spinning work with the point of a pencil

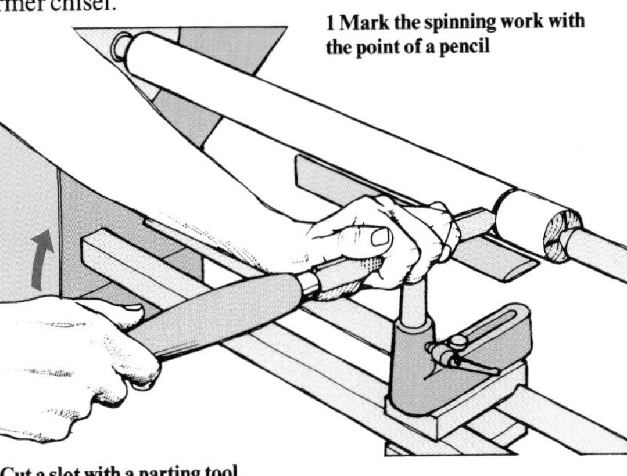

2 Cut a slot with a parting tool

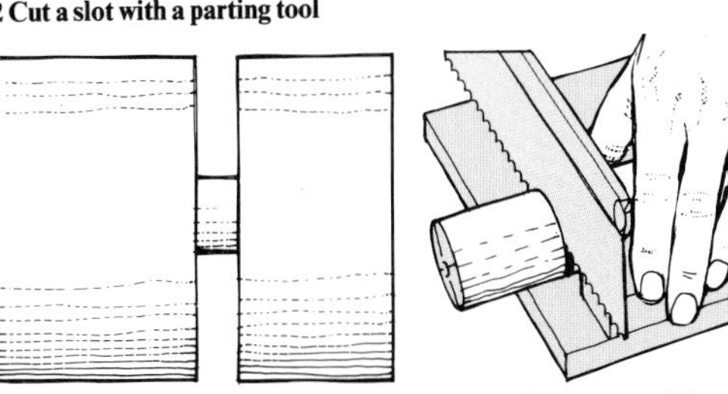

3 Leave a "neck" at the center

4 Cut off the waste with a saw

FINISHING ON A LATHE

You can apply a finish to turned work before taking it from the lathe. French polish is suitable as a sealer for all woods except oily open-grain woods like teak or afrormosia. Choose transparent French polish for pale-colored woods, and button polish or garnet shellac for darker woods. Oils may also be used.

Brush the liquid shellac onto the workpiece **(1)**, then select a slow lathe speed and switch on the machine. Wear goggles or glasses to protect your eyes from polish that might be thrown off as the wood starts moving. Use a bunched-up soft rag to rub the finish into the grain **(2)**. Take special care to keep the cloth away from all moving lathe parts. While the work is still rotating, rub the surface with a stick of hard wax and burnish it with a clean rag.

Apply teak oil to open-grain woods that do not require a gloss finish. Paint it on and burnish it with a rag, like button polish. On salad bowls, use edible vegetable oil or a commercial salad-bowl oil.

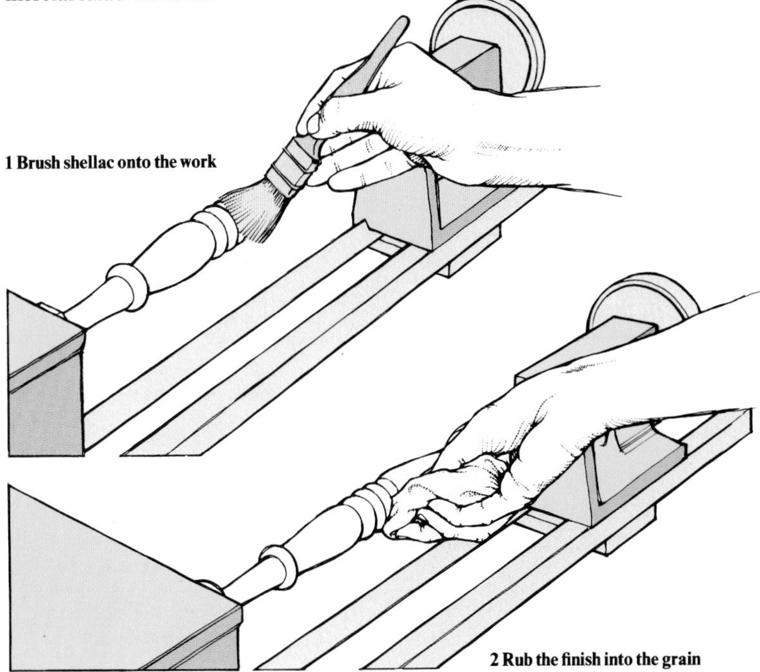

1 Brush shellac onto the work

2 Rub the finish into the grain

DECORATIVE TURNING

If the workpiece is to incorporate beads and hollows as a form of decoration, it is not necessary to smooth or sand the wood accurately before shaping it. Simply turn the rough stock to a cylinder with a gouge, then mark out the beads and hollows.

BEADS, HOLLOWS AND FILLETS

A "bead" is a rounded convex shape used for decorative purposes. Its counterpart, the "hollow" or "cove," is concave. The junction between hollows and beads is often separated by short shoulders known as "fillets."

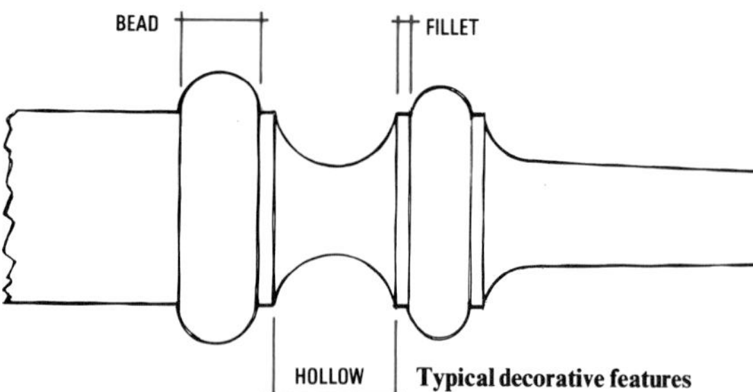

Typical decorative features

Marking out beads and hollows
Use a straight ruler and a pencil to mark out the positions of beads and hollows along the workpiece. When you switch on the lathe, your pencil marks will appear as continuous faint lines. Emphasize the marks by touching them with a pencil point while the lathe is running.

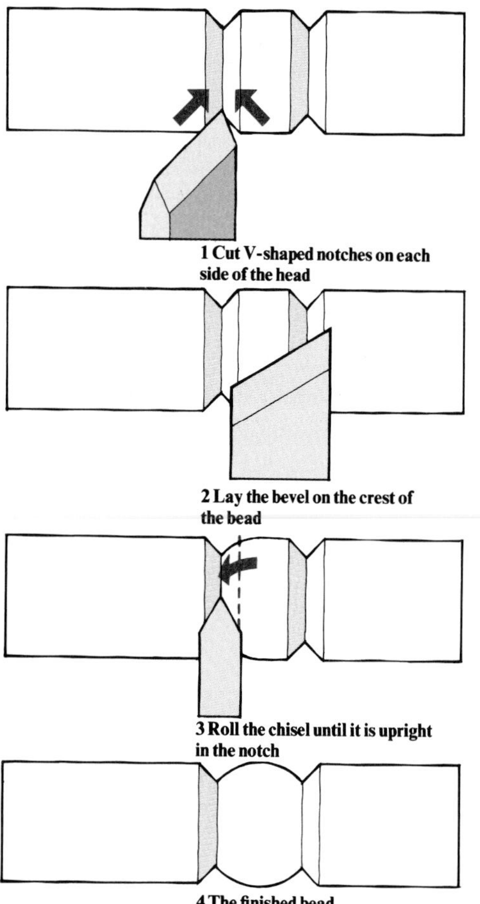
1 Cut V-shaped notches on each side of the head

2 Lay the bevel on the crest of the bead

3 Roll the chisel until it is upright in the notch

4 The finished bead

Cutting beads
Place one narrow edge of a skew chisel on the tool rest, and touch the workpiece with the "longer" point of the chisel to cut an $\frac{1}{8}$in (3mm) groove on each marked line. This is achieved by lifting the tool's handle to lower the point slowly into the workpiece. Rock the chisel to one side then the other to open up the grooves into V-shaped notches **(1)**. Remove about $\frac{1}{8}$in (3mm) of wood on each side of the grooves.

To shape one side of a bead, lay the chisel's cutting bevel on the wood between the V-shaped notches **(2)**, then gradually rotate the tool's handle to bring the blade upright in the center of one of the notches **(3)**. Cut the other side of the bead in a similar way. Repeat the action, taking very shallow cuts to smooth the bead and remove any remaining ridges. Check the "horizon" of the workpiece to see the exact shape of the bead you are cutting **(4)**. Keep the chisel square to the work – if you swing the handle sideways as you rotate it, you may catch the point of the tool in the wood.

Cutting hollows and fillets
To turn hollows, use a $\frac{1}{2}$in (12mm) spindle gouge or a bowl gouge that has its corners ground away to form a cutting tip with a rounded point. Remove some of the waste from between the beads by smoothly sweeping the tip of the gouge from side to side **(1)**.

Use the point of a skew chisel to carefully shape a fillet on each side **(2)**. Shape the hollow, starting on one side with the gouge rolled on the tool rest so that its flute is turned away from the bead. Slide the gouge toward the center of the hollow, while rolling the blade and advancing the tip of the tool into the work **(3)**. Shape the other side of the hollow in the same way.

Repeat the process, taking very shallow cuts with the gouge and always working "downhill" from the outside of the hollow toward the middle. Check the horizon to see the true shape of the hollow. Finally, clean up the fillet on each side with a skew chisel, to leave a neat corner against the bead and a sharp edge to the hollow.

1 Remove some of the waste between beads with a gouge

2 Shape fillets with a chisel

3 Sweep a gouge "downhill" to shape a hollow

TURNING FROM SQUARE TO ROUND

Turned table and chair legs are sometimes left square at one or both ends to receive mortise and tenon or dowel joints for the cross rails. Because this type of leg has to be turned from square-section stock, you need to be an experienced woodturner before attempting this technique.

Cut the joints before you mount the stock on the lathe, and very clearly mark the shoulders of each section that are to be left square **(1)**.

Use the point of a skew chisel to cut a V-shaped notch on the shoulder lines as if you were cutting a bead, then carefully roll the chisel to cut a half "bead" on each side **(2)**. Use a roughing-out gouge to turn the part of the stock between the squared ends to a cylinder, and finish it with a chisel and sandpaper in the usual way.

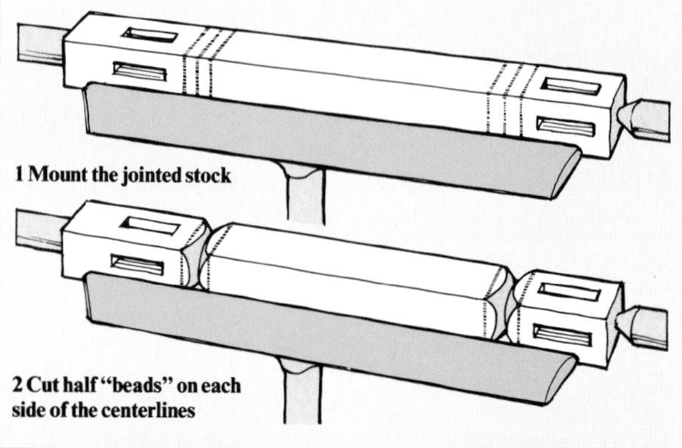
1 Mount the jointed stock

2 Cut half "beads" on each side of the centerlines

TURNING WITH ONE CENTER

When making items such as turned wooden boxes, egg cups and vases that have to be hollowed out, you need to remove the tailstock in order to turn the end grain. Consequently, the workpiece must be held securely at one end by one of several special chucks mounted on the headstock spindle.

Screw chucks
One of the simplest chucks incorporates a threaded screw that is driven into a predrilled hole in the workpiece. The most basic chucks are made with a standard wood screw, but the better-quality versions have a coarse deep-threaded screw that bites securely into end-grain as well as side-grain wood. A wood screw chuck will hold relatively short workpieces only.

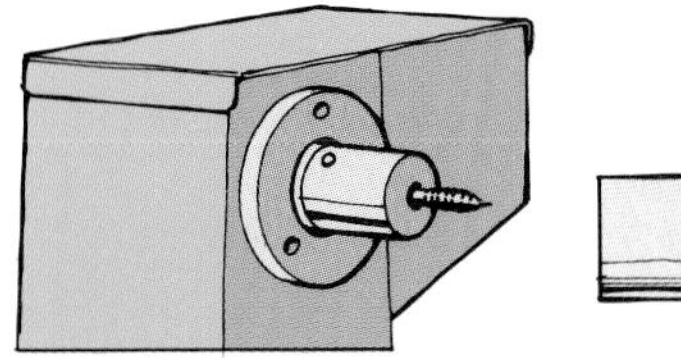
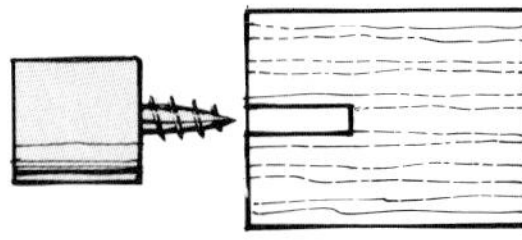
Wood screw chuck

Cup chuck
A cup chuck has a hollow recess that will accommodate a cylindrical spigot turned on one end of a workpiece. Very often a cup chuck is designed to function by means of a good friction fit between it and the work. However, some chucks are made with provision for wood screw fixings for additional security. A cup chuck will support a workpiece that is too long for a wood screw chuck.

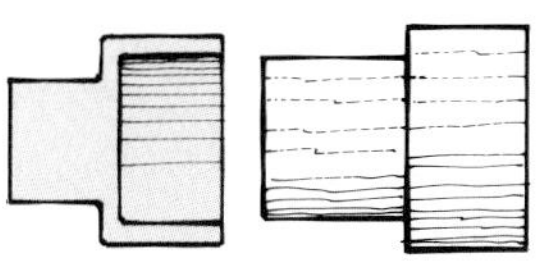
Cup chuck

Pin chuck
A pin chuck is designed to be inserted in a hole drilled in one end of a workpiece. A small-diameter metal pin rests in a shallow depression machined longitudinally in the chuck spigot. When stationary, the spigot, together with the pin, slides effortlessly into the workpiece. Then as soon as the lathe is switched on, centrifugal force causes the pin to climb the sloping face of the depression and grip the wood.

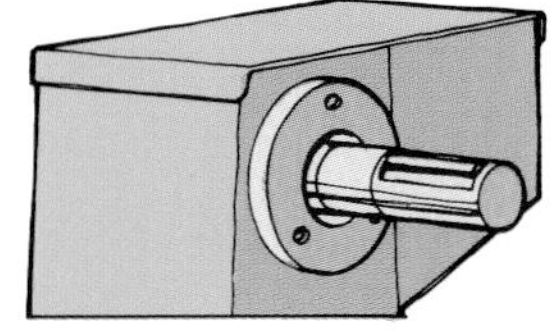
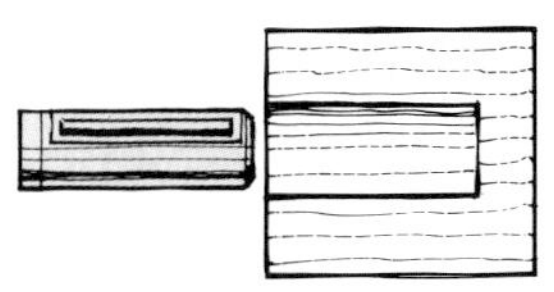
Pin chuck

Three-jaw chuck
This type of chuck has three key-operated self-centering jaws that grip a cylindrical workpiece or spigot, or expand to grip a hollow workpiece. Although it has been used by generations of woodturners, this device is now losing its popularity because of the distinct possibility of injuring one's knuckles on the protruding ends of the jaws while the lathe runs at speed. If you fit a three-jaw chuck to your lathe, protect yourself by mounting the appropriate guard.

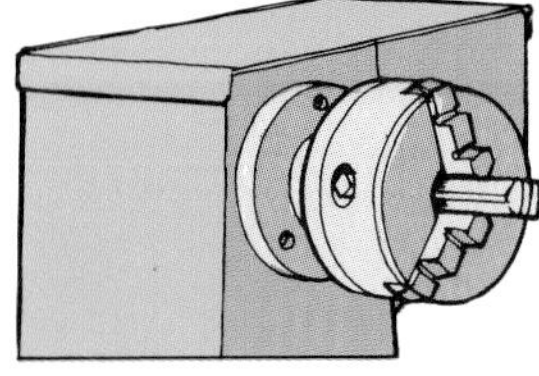
Three-jaw chuck

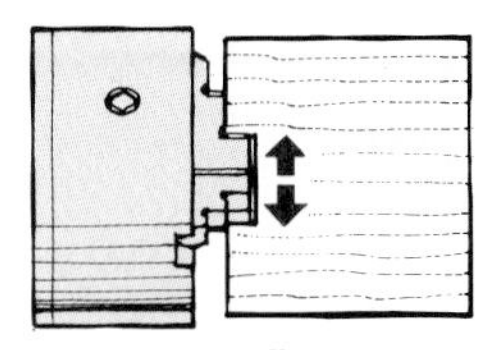
Gripping internally

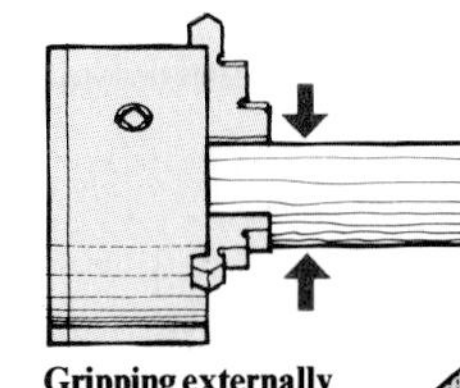
Gripping externally

Combination chucks
Recently, one-center turning has been revolutionized by the development of combination chucks. These ingeniously engineered devices incorporate not only screw-, pin- and cup-chuck facilities but also contracting collets that can grip a cylindrical workpiece or expand to fit a "dovetail" recess turned in the base of a bowl or similar object.

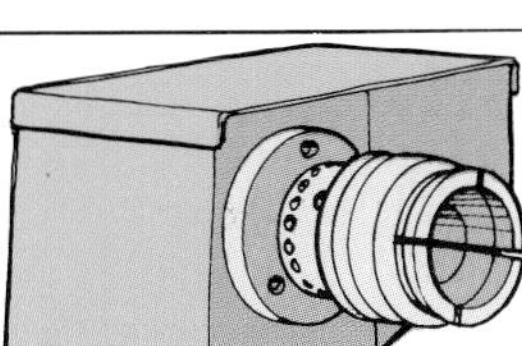
Combination chuck

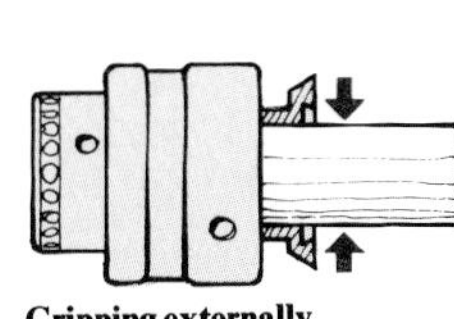
Gripping externally

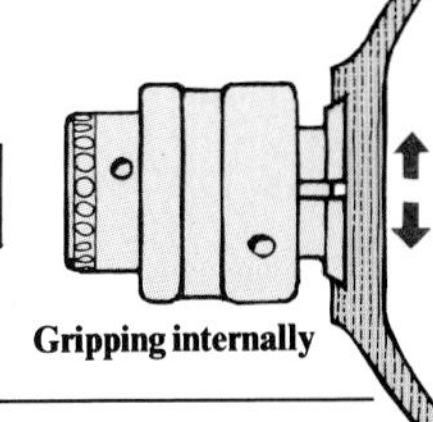
Gripping internally

Turning a hollow workpiece
Rough out the stock between centers and turn the drive-center end to fit whatever type of chuck you plan to use. Remove the tailstock, fit the workpiece to the chuck and skim the wood with a gouge to ensure it is turning centrally. Use a pencil to make alignment marks on the chuck and workpiece for exact replacement should you have to remove the work for any reason. Turn the tool rest across the work to hollow out the inside first, using a bowl gouge or scraper **(1)**. When turning cross-grain wood, work the tool from the outside toward the center; but work in the opposite direction, from the center outward, if you are turning end-grain wood. In either case, use the tool on the down side of the work only – i.e. the half that is moving downward toward the tool rest. You can remove some of the waste beforehand by drilling out the center. Check the internal diameter with inside calipers **(2)**, then turn the outside and detach the workpiece with a parting tool.

1 Hollow the inside first

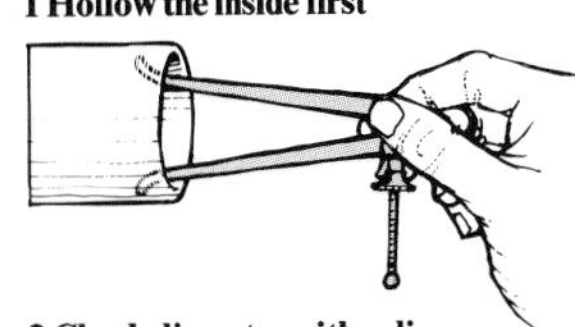
2 Check diameter with calipers

Drilling on a lathe
To bore a hole in the end of a workpiece, fit a drill chuck with a tapered shaft into the tailstock of the lathe. With the work held securely in a one-center chuck, select a slow lathe speed and advance the drill bit by turning the tailstock handwheel. You can use a special sawtooth machine center bit, which cuts end grain cleanly, or an ordinary twist drill, or a spade or Forstner bit.

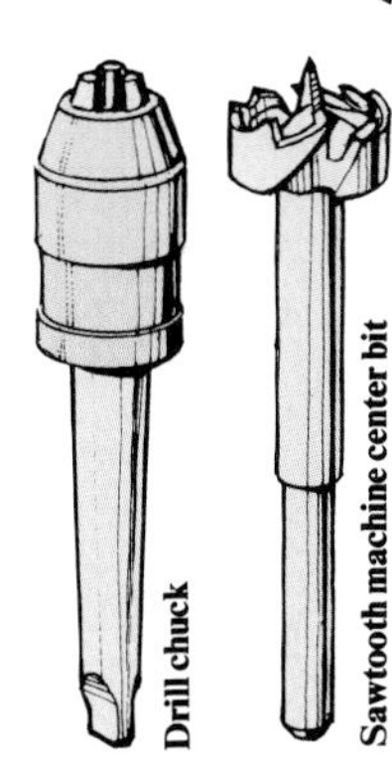

FACEPLATE TURNING

Turning wooden bowls and containers has always been a popular aspect of lathe work – but because the workpiece is usually of a relatively large diameter, bowl-turning demands a high degree of skill, especially when an experienced turner is pushing the craft to its limits to create fine, thin-walled pieces. At that level, one slip of the tool can shatter the workpiece.

The bowl "blank" must be fixed securely to the lathe, since a serious accident is a distinct possibility if a heavy workpiece works loose. A combination chuck provides the most sophisticated and probably the best method of clamping the work, but the traditional faceplate is much cheaper. This is a cast-metal disc, threaded at its center to fit the lathe's drive spindle. The work is attached by passing wood screws through holes in the plate. A 4 to 6in (100 to 150mm) diameter plate is normally supplied with a lathe, but larger ones are available as accessories. Select a plate that is as large as can be comfortably accommodated by the base of the workpiece.

SEE ALSO	
Machine-shop safety	156
Band saws	172-177
Safety tips	193
Gouges	194
Calipers	194-195
Scrapers	195
Wood screws	304-305

Woodturning faceplates

Mounting the faceplate

If the turned piece is designed with a base thick enough to take large wood screws, you can attach the faceplate directly to the bowl blank. However, you will then have to accept screw holes in the base of the finished piece or plug them with wood after turning.

An alternative method is to screw the faceplate to a hardwood disc glued temporarily to the base of the workpiece. First, cut a square workpiece from well-seasoned, knot-free wood and plane one side flat. Draw diagonals from one corner to another to find the center, then use a compass to draw a circle slightly larger than the circumference of the bowl. Draw another circle representing the circumference of its base **(1)**.

Cut a disc from hardwood $\frac{3}{4}$in (18mm) thick, with the same diameter as the bowl's base. Cut another disc the same size from brown paper. This is to serve as a separator sandwiched between the wooden disc and the workpiece so the joint can be split when turning has been completed. Spread glue on both pieces of wood, then stick the paper to the wooden disc and glue both centrally on the workpiece **(2)**. Apply a clamp and leave the glue to set.

Use your compass to draw the circumference of the faceplate on the disc, and attach the plate centrally with three or four # 10 wood screws. The screw threads should penetrate the full thickness of the wooden disc. Cut the waste off the workpiece on a band saw to leave a circular bowl blank **(3)**. Attach the faceplate to the drive spindle – centrifugal force will tighten it on the spindle thread as the lathe starts up.

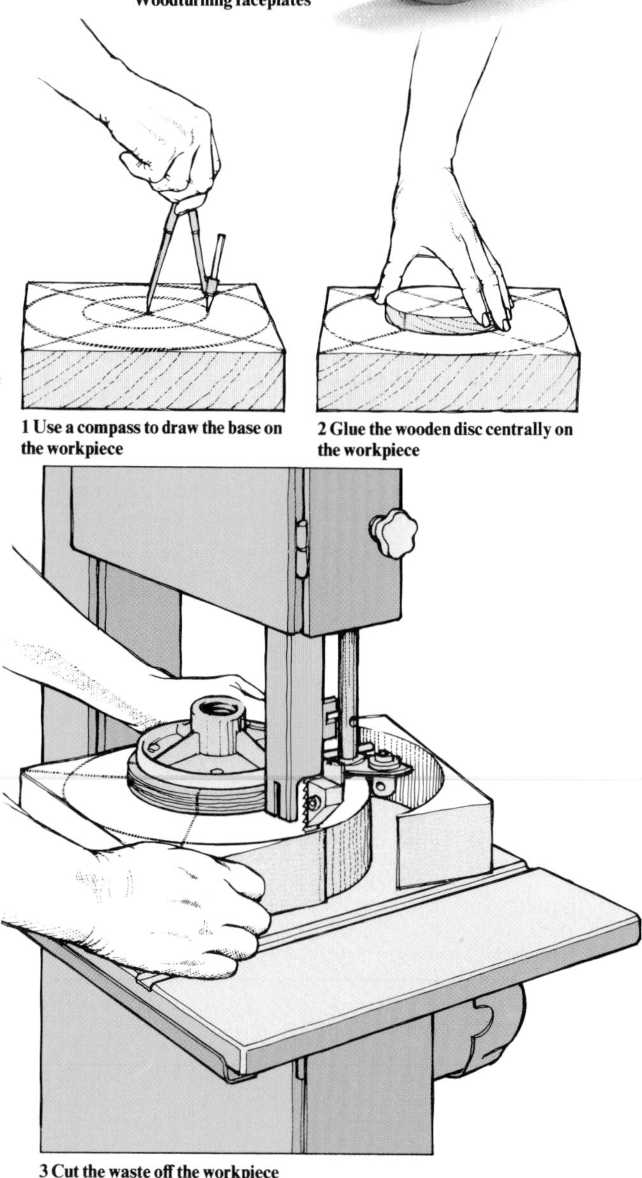

1 Use a compass to draw the base on the workpiece

2 Glue the wooden disc centrally on the workpiece

3 Cut the waste off the workpiece

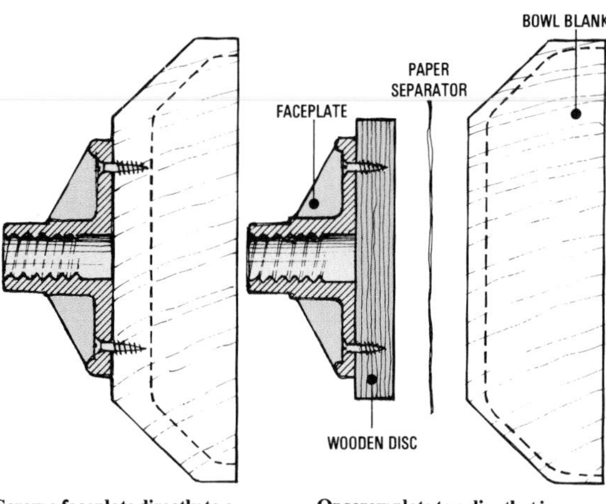

Screw a faceplate directly to a thick base

Or screw plate to a disc that is temporarily glued to workpiece

Turning the outside of a bowl
Center the tool rest on the edge of the bowl blank. Spin the work by hand to check that it is free to rotate, then select a slow speed and switch on the lathe.

True up the circumference of the blank with a roughing-out gouge, then change to a bowl gouge for shaping the outside of the bowl. Never be tempted to take deep cuts – always remove the waste gradually until you obtain the required shape.

Use a round-nose scraper to smooth the work. Lower the tool rest slightly and increase the lathe speed. Hold the chisel more or less square to the work, with its handle raised just above horizontal. Move the tool sideways, taking a light, even cut.

Turning the inside of a bowl
Swing the tool rest around to align with the wide face of the workpiece, and begin to hollow out the bowl with the lathe running at a slow speed. Remember to work on the "down" side only – the half of the workpiece that is moving downward toward the tool rest **(1)**.

Start removing the waste wood with a bowl gouge, cutting back toward the center from a point halfway to the rim of the bowl **(2)**. As you cut deeper, start a little closer to the rim with each pass of the tool and always work toward the center of the bowl.

Once you have removed most of the waste, increase the speed of the lathe. Then, using a scraper, complete the shaping and smooth the inside of the bowl.

Sanding a bowl
Reduce the speed again, remove the tool rest and use a folded strip of sandpaper to sand the surface **(1)**. Use medium to fine paper, and keep the paper moving to avoid leaving scratches. When sanding the inside, trail the paper on the "down" side only **(2)**.

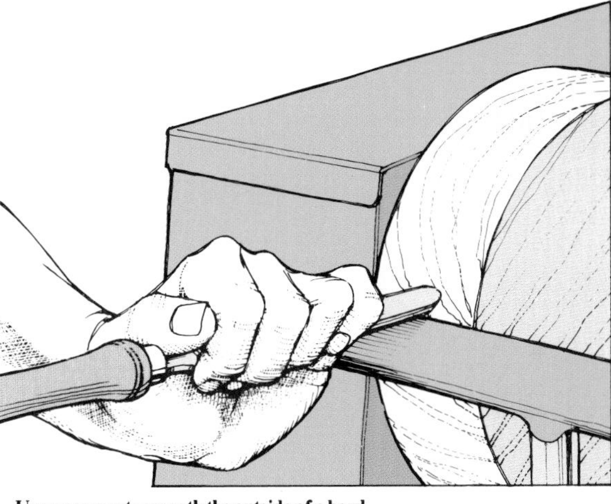
Use a scraper to smooth the outside of a bowl

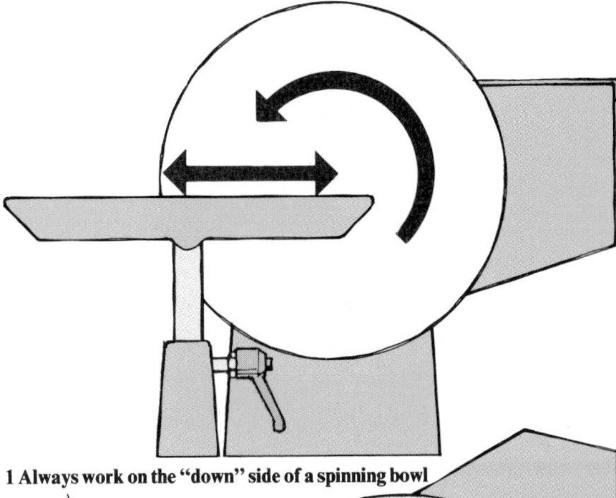
1 Always work on the "down" side of a spinning bowl

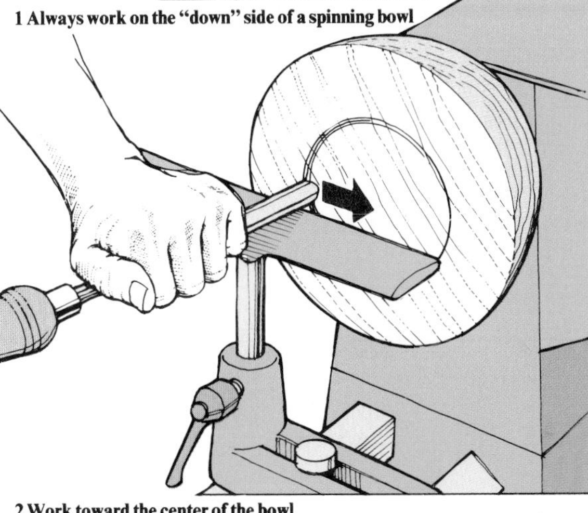
2 Work toward the center of the bowl

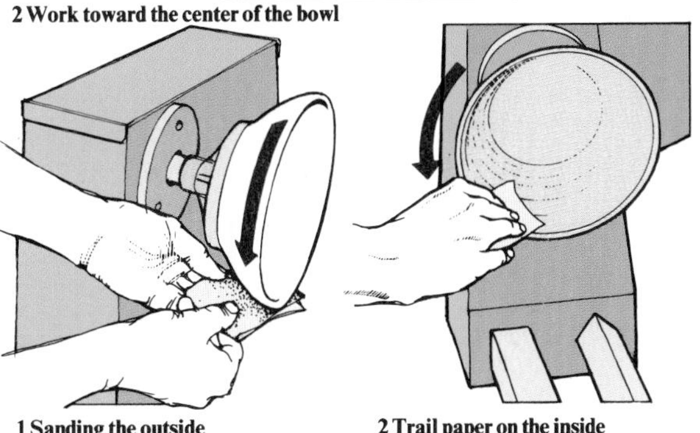
1 Sanding the outside

2 Trail paper on the inside

CHECKING THE SHAPE OF A BOWL

As the work progresses, switch off the lathe from time to time to check the outer shape of the bowl or its depth and rim thickness.

Using a template
Hold a cardboard template against the bowl to check its shape.

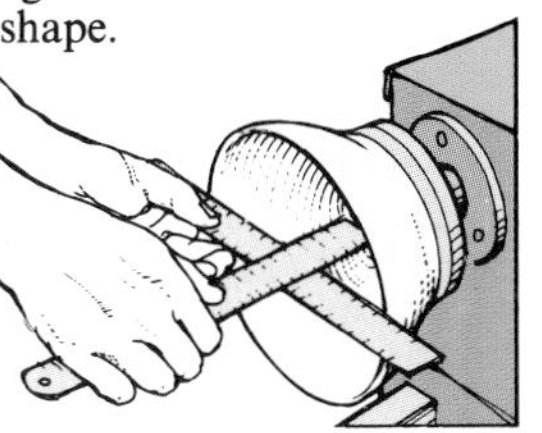

Measuring bowl depth
Hold a straightedge across the rim of the bowl, and use a steel ruler to measure the depth of the bowl.

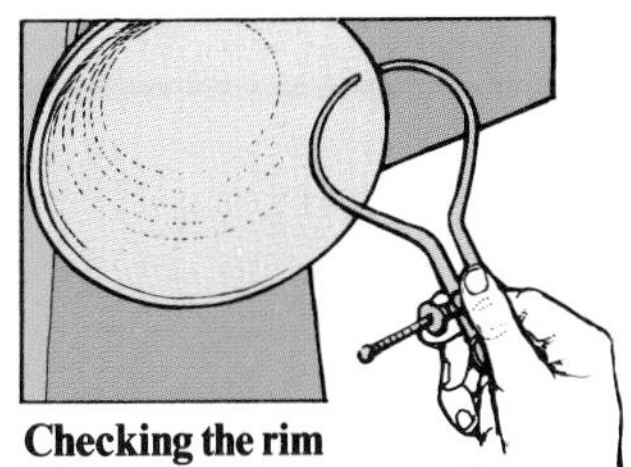

Checking the rim
Use calipers to measure the thickness of the bowl's rim. An experienced turner can reduce a rim to $\frac{1}{8}$in (3mm) or less, but beginners should be less ambitious. A bowl is stronger if the thickness of the sides tapers from the base to the rim.

FINISHING AND DISMANTLING

Apply a polish or oil to the work while it is attached to the lathe, then unscrew the faceplate.

To remove the wooden disc from the base of the bowl, stand it on edge on a bench then place the tip of a sharp chisel on the joint line and tap it gently to split the paper separator. Scrape and finish the bottom by hand.

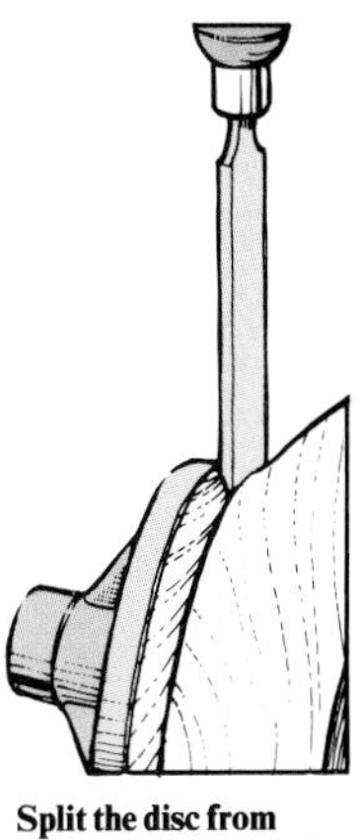
Split the disc from the bowl with a chisel

UNIVERSAL MACHINES

Ideally, a workshop should be equipped with individual woodworking machines adequately spaced apart so that even large workpieces can be passed from one machine to another. However, woodworkers with limited workshop room might consider an alternative occupying the minimum of floor space – a universal machine that combines several functions in one unit. Most universals comprise a table saw, jointer, thickness planer, spindle shaper and horizontal borer/mortiser, built either as separate machines grouped around a single motor or as one machine with shared worktables and, on some models, shared fences. Avoid a cheap underengineered universal – it is best to choose one with specifications that compare favorably with those recommended for special-purpose woodworking machines.

Electric motors

Good-quality universals are fitted with one or more 1.5kW (2hp) electric motors. Clearly, a machine with an individual motor for each main function is preferable, since individual motors are subjected to less wear, and changeover from one function to another can be implemented with a minimum of effort. Not surprisingly, this type of universal machine is relatively expensive.

More commonly, drive belts from a saw, jointer and spindle shaper have to be connected in turn to the pulley of a single motor. Where this can be achieved by the shifting of a lever on the outside of the machine, changeover is practically instantaneous, whereas having to change belts manually is tedious as well as time-consuming.

Changing from function to function

In order to prepare a universal machine for work, it is always necessary to remove certain fences, raise and lower blades or cutters, and to reposition guards – although these changes involve little more effort than setting up a single-purpose woodworking machine. If, however, you have to partly dismantle and reassemble your machine before you can undertake the next process, that will soon prove annoying, and it is especially frustrating if you cannot move effortlessly from saw to planer and vice versa.

Control panels

In addition to the usual side-by-side on/off push buttons, a universal machine is normally fitted with emergency shut-off buttons at strategic points. The main control panel may also include a switch for selecting specific functions. The same selector switch is used to disconnect all motors when the machine is left unattended.

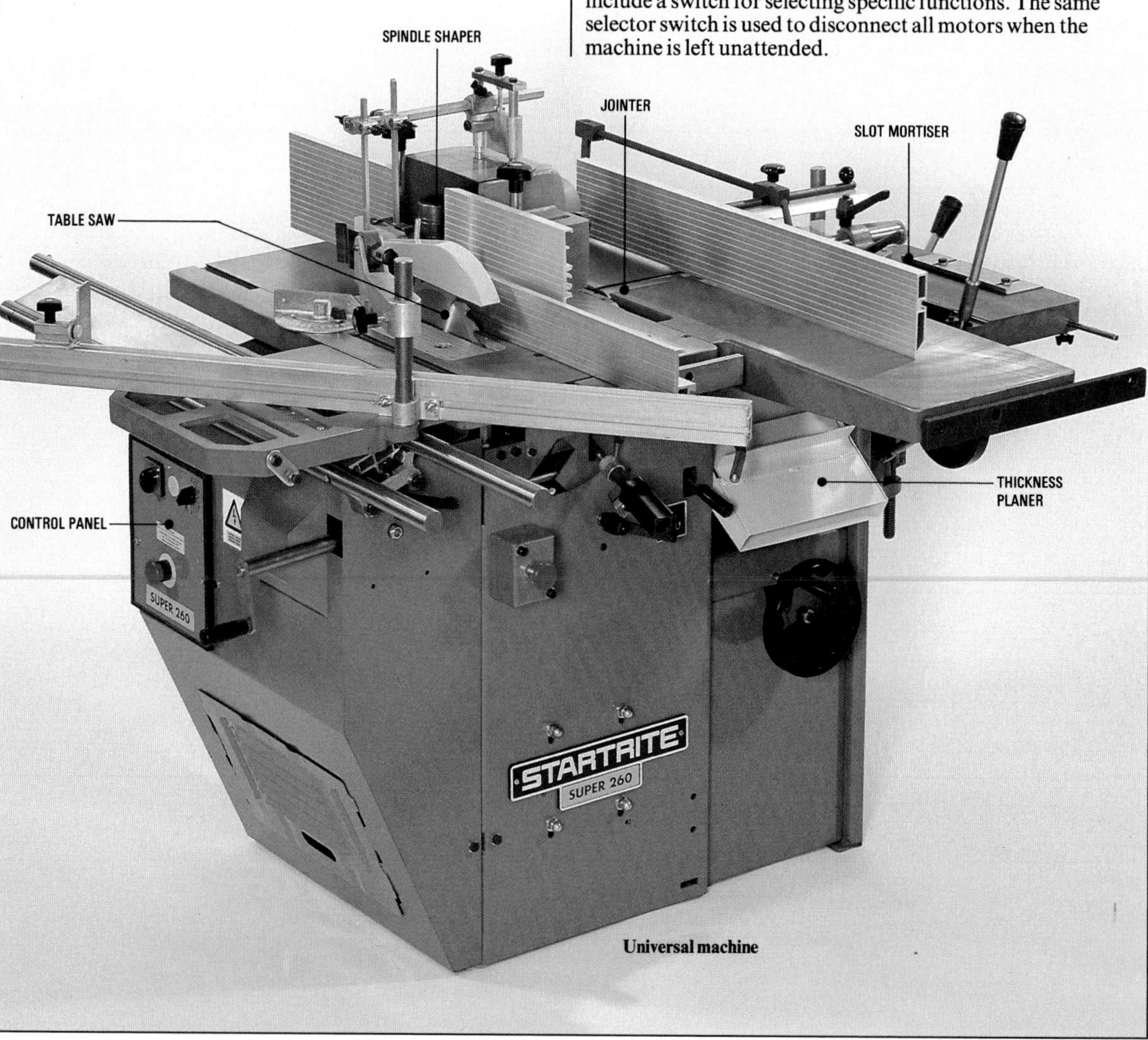

Universal machine

OPERATING A UNIVERSAL MACHINE

There is inevitably an element of compromise in the design of a universal machine – nevertheless, you should be able to operate each element of the machine efficiently, comfortably and, most important of all, safely. Follow the manufacturer's instructions for setting up the machine to perform any of its functions. Operating procedures are identical to those recommended for using the relevant single-purpose machines.

USING A UNIVERSAL MACHINE SAFELY

When using a universal machine, adopt the safe working practices that are recommended for individual table saws, jointers, spindle shapers and mortisers. In addition to general machine-shop safety procedures, observe the following rules:

- Install a universal machine in a position where it can be operated and approached safely from all sides.
- Where possible, connect a dust collector to the machine.
- If drive belts have to be changed manually, tuck away or hang up belts not in use well away from the motor's pulley and other moving parts.
- Support extra-long or very wide workpieces on sawhorses or a roller stand, or have an assistant take the work as it comes off the machine.
- After completion of a procedure, either retract blades and cutters into the machine's casing or enclose them completely with appropriate guards. Always remove a milling cutter as soon as you have finished mortising or boring holes.

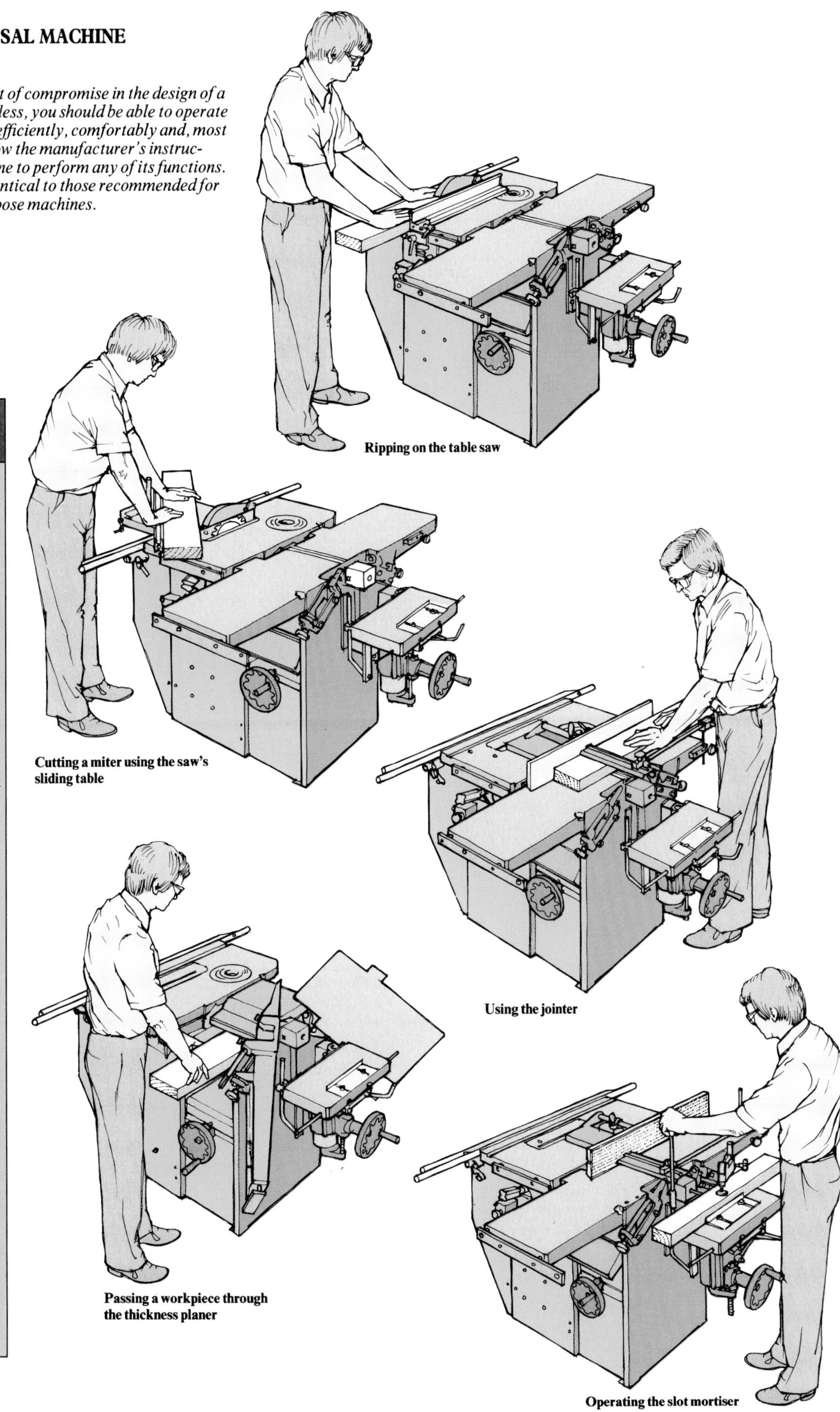

Ripping on the table saw

Cutting a miter using the saw's sliding table

Using the jointer

Passing a workpiece through the thickness planer

Operating the slot mortiser

SHAPING ON A UNIVERSAL MACHINE

Spindle shapers are used primarily for cutting moldings and certain woodworking joints. Shapers may be thought of as the industrial version of the high-speed electric router mounted upside down in a router table that is equipped with adjustable fences, guards and hold-downs. Instead of the router bit, however, shapers are equipped with center-bored cutters that mount on an arbor, or spindle, that projects through the table.

SEE ALSO	
Machine-shop safety	156
Push sticks	159
Safety tips	205
Dust collectors	214

A universal machine set up for spindle shaping

Spindle size

Shapers for home-shop use have belt-driven spindles as small as ½in (12mm), but ¾in (18mm) and 1in (25mm) spindles are less prone to chatter. Universal machines may have the international metric-standard spindle, which is 30mm (1¼in).

Cutters may be bushed down slightly to fit smaller spindles, within reason. In addition, some shapers have interchangeable spindles, including one that accepts standard router bits, which are much less expensive than shaper cutters. When used on the shaper, however, the smaller diameter of router bits makes them less efficient than regular cutters because shaper speeds are normally adjustable only between about 4000 and 10,000rpm. Better shapers can be set to rotate backward, in order to mold profiles on curved work, in which the grain direction reverses.

The method for fitting cutters varies from one model to another, so it is important to follow the manufacturer's instructions. In principle, the spindle is locked from rotating, the cutter is dropped over the shaft and tightened in place with a nut. Various spacers above, below or between pairs of cutters locate their height on the spindle, which itself is adjustable up and down to position the cutters in relation to the work.

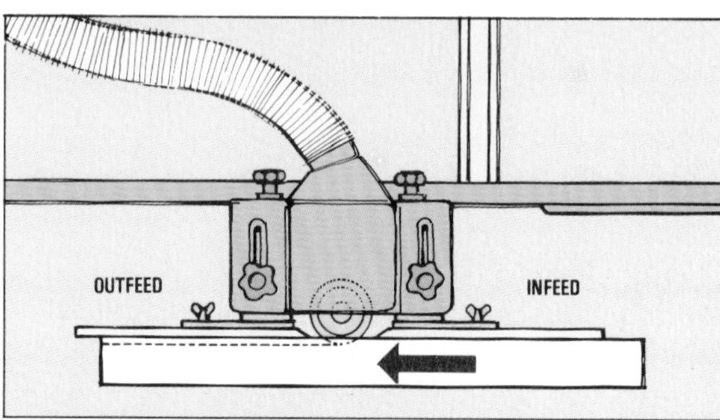

1 When part of the workpiece edge is intact, keep the two-part fence in line

Guards

The spindle and cutter are surrounded by guards and fences except for the parts of the cutters that shape the work. A metal casing encircles the rear of the spindle while adjustable vertical/horizontal hold-down guards hold the work firmly against the fence and worktable.

Guide fence

The guide fence is made in two halves, with a gap in between through which the cutters protrude. Each half is adjustable sideways to give just enough clearance for the cutters.

When cutting a molding that leaves part of the edge of the workpiece intact, both halves of the fence should be in line **(1)**. When removing the edge entirely, the outfeed half of the fence is finely adjusted fore and aft to support the molded edge **(2)**.

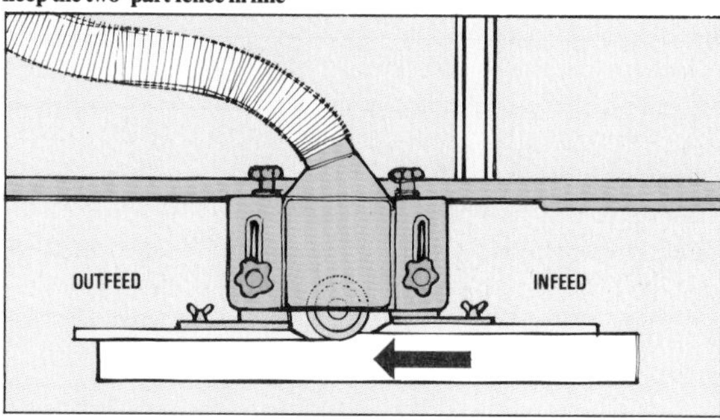

2 Move the outfeed half of the fence forward to support an edge that has been cut away

Spindle shaping
The saw table is also used for shaping.

SETTING UP THE MACHINE FOR SPINDLE SHAPING

It is essential to follow the manufacturer's instructions for converting your particular universal for spindle shaping, but a typical procedure is as follows:

Since the spindle shares a worktable with the circular saw, the saw guard and rip fence have to be dismantled and the blade retracted beneath the table's surface.

Raise the spindle, by operating the appropriate handwheel or crank, and fit the cutter according to the manufacturer's instructions. Having fitted cutter guards and fence, make sure nothing is likely to foul the cutters, then switch on the machine.

USING A SPINDLE SHAPER SAFELY

Even experienced machinists approach a spindle shaper with caution, since it is arguably the most dangerous machine in the workshop. A cutter should never work loose from a well-designed head – but if it does, it is thrown at a lethal velocity. However, an accident is more likely to occur due to the cutters throwing a workpiece back toward the operator, so be on your guard and take precautions to avoid such an eventuality.

If you have never had the experience of operating a spindle shaper, it is advisable to seek instruction from a recommended professional machinist before using one on your own. In addition to general machine-shop safety practices, always observe the following rules:

- Always use approved spindle-shaper guards and hold-downs.
- Only use sharp cutters. Discard cutters and heads when damaged.
- Before switching on the shaper, check your settings and turn the spindle by hand (making sure the power is off) to ensure sufficient clearance all around.
- Always feed the work against the rotation of the cutterhead.
- Use a push stick to feed narrow workpieces.
- Don't attempt to make a deep cut in one pass. Either mold it in stages or remove most of the waste beforehand on a saw or jointer.
- Never attempt to mold across the end grain of a narrow workpiece freehand. Clamp the work to a sliding table or miter fence.

CUTTERHEADS AND CUTTERS

Although these have disappeared from the U.S. market, practically all spindle shapers in Britain and Europe are supplied with a cutterhead designed to take pairs of interchangeable cutters or knives. The head itself is roughly cylindrical, since square heads are now generally considered to be unsafe. Cutters, whether interchangeable or solid-profile, work on the same principles.

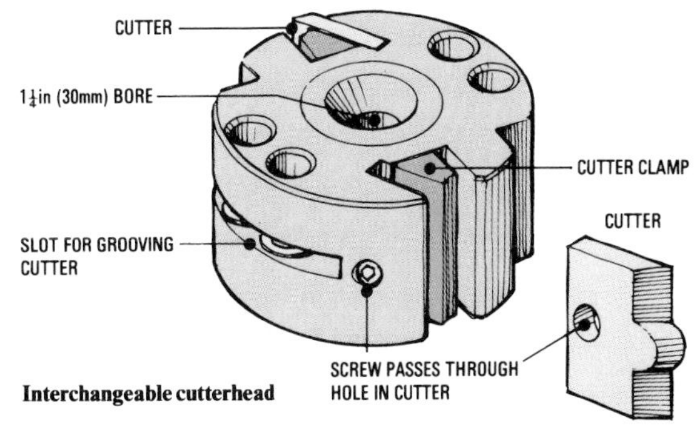

Interchangeable cutterhead

Interchangeable cutterheads

The cylindrical metal head, approximately 4in (100mm) in diameter, is slotted to accommodate two identical cutters. A wedge-shaped clamp, tightened by bolts or machined screws, holds each cutter securely in its slot. A peg or screw passing through a hole in each cutter locates it precisely and provides additional security against it working loose.

The amount a cutter projects from the heads is crucial, so carefully follow any instructions stamped on or supplied with cutters. Cutter projection must be limited to prevent violent kickback of the work, or even cutter failure, as a result of trying to take too deep a cut in one pass. The shape of the cutterhead itself often limits the maximum depth of cut **(1)**. Alternatively, matching pairs of deflectors are mounted just ahead of the cutters **(2)**.

When dull, pairs of cutters should be reground by an expert to ensure they remain perfectly balanced.

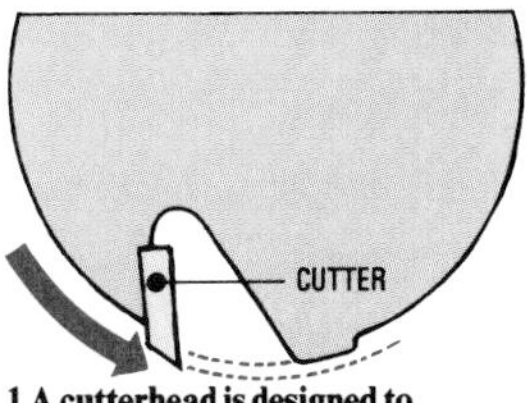

1 A cutterhead is designed to limit cutter projection

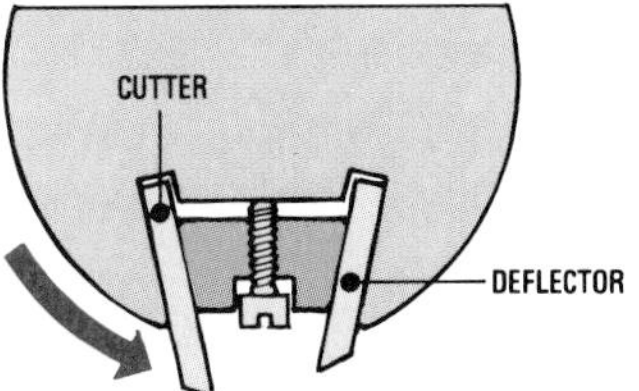

2 Alternatively, deflectors are mounted ahead of the cutters

Wobble saw

Interchangeable cutterhead

Grooving cutters

Molding cutters

Solid-profile cutter

Solid-profile cutters

These cutters are cast in one piece to make industrial-quality, solid-profile cutterheads. This type of cutter has three or four cutting edges that produce a superior-quality finish. Solid-profile heads last longer than conventional interchangeable cutterheads. The best have tungsten-carbide tips and are available in hundreds of standard profiles. Cutters may also be custom-ground in carbide or high-speed steel.

Grooving cutters

Grooving cutters resemble heavy-duty rotary sawblades. Some encircle the spindle and can be adjusted to cut grooves of different widths; others are designed for bolting into the sides of a cylindrical cutterhead.

Wobble saws

You can also buy small-diameter wobble-saw blades for cutting grooves from ⅛ to ⅝in (3 to 16mm) wide.

SHAPING A WORKPIECE

Shaper cutters revolve at such a high speed that they invariably produce a fine finish. Nevertheless, if possible, feed the work so that the machine cuts in the direction of the grain. Disconnect the motor before making cutter adjustments.

SEE ALSO

Machine-shop safety	156
Push stick	159
Safety tips	205,207
Dust collectors	214

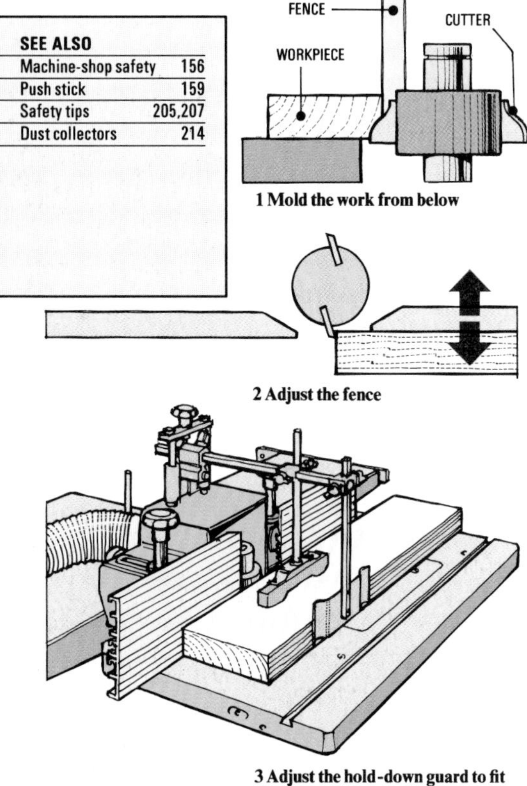

1 Mold the work from below

2 Adjust the fence

3 Adjust the hold-down guard to fit the work

Having mounted the cutter, adjust the spindle to mold the workpiece from underneath **(1)**. In this position the workpiece itself offers extra protection by covering the rotating cutters; also, it is impossible to take a deeper bite out of the wood, even if the workpiece jumps slightly during the molding process.

Holding the end of the work against a stationary cutter, adjust the fence to set the depth of cut **(2)**. (Make a trial cut on scrap wood before you mold the actual workpiece.) Adjust each half of the fence sideways to leave the minimum clearance for the cutters.

Drop the upper hold-down onto the work and clamp it to provide a firm sliding pressure. Adjust the side-pressure plate similarly **(3)**.

Check that the cutter is free to revolve, then switch the shaper on. Press the work against the fence and feed it at a steady rate past the cutter. Keep the work moving and use a push stick to complete the process.

Shaping a short workpiece

It is dangerous to attempt to mold a workpiece that cannot be held comfortably in two hands on either side of the cutter opening in the fence. Instead, feed a longer workpiece through the machine, then cut it to the required length afterward.

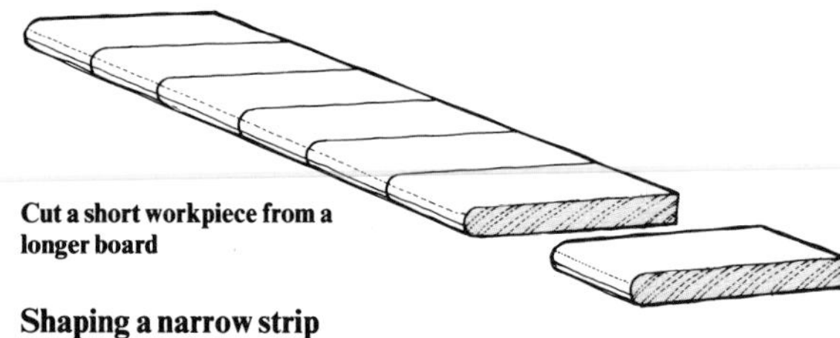

Cut a short workpiece from a longer board

Shaping a narrow strip

Either mold a wide board and rip a narrow strip from its edge **(1)** or mold both sides of a workpiece and rip it down the center **(2)**.

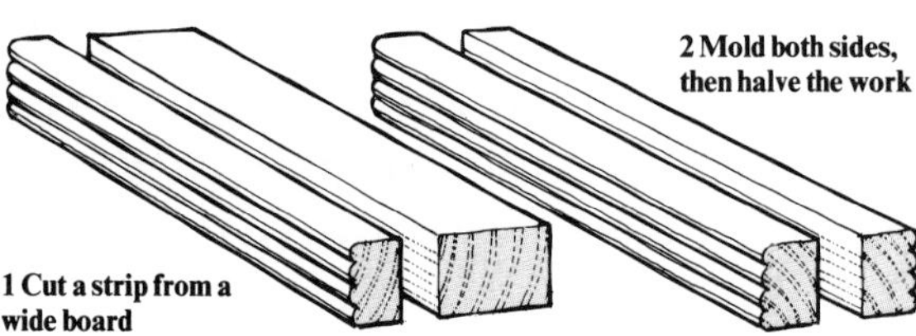

1 Cut a strip from a wide board

2 Mold both sides, then halve the work

SHAPING END GRAIN

To shape a molding across the end grain of a workpiece, set up the machine in the usual way but remove the side-pressure plate. Adjust the hold-down to keep the work pressed against the worktable.

Clamp the work to the universal machine's sliding crosscut table. To prevent the grain from being split from the back edge of the work by the revolving cutters, sandwich a piece of scrap wood between the work and the sliding-table fence. The scrap must extend to the tip of the workpiece. Both pieces of wood are machined together.

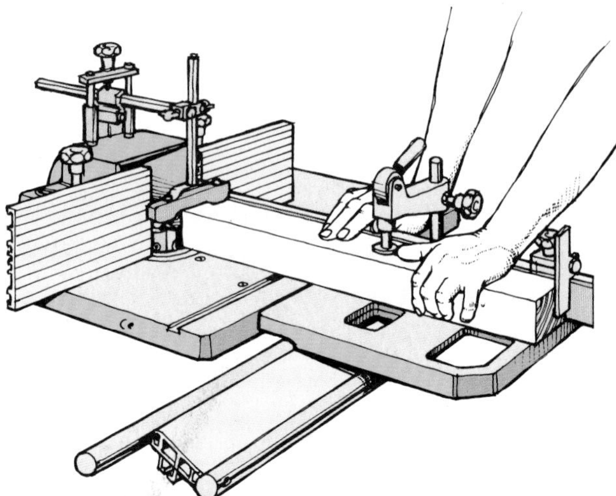

Molding end grain using the machine's sliding table

Cutting joints

With the appropriate cutters, short tenons and finger joints can be cut to perfection on a spindle shaper. However, the special set of cutters and spacers required for finger jointing is expensive and may not be cost-effective, considering the number of times it is likely to be used in a home workshop.

MOLDING A CURVED WORKPIECE

In order to mold a curved workpiece on a spindle shaper, the standard fence and guards have to be replaced by a ring fence and hold-down. The work must be fed freehand into the cutters, which requires some experience if you are to avoid taking a dangerously deep cut that could result in a violent kickback. Unless you are already familiar with this technique, it is a wise precaution to seek professional instruction before attempting it on your own.

A ring fence is required when molding a curve

CHAPTER SIX

HOME WORKSHOPS

Some woodworkers are able to produce surprisingly immaculate work in a chaotic environment, but most woodworkers would agree that a clean, well-planned workshop is conducive to good working practices as well as being a safer and more pleasant place to work in. When planning the layout of your workshop, try to think ahead and make provisions for your future needs. Suppose you have a fairly extensive kit of hand tools and a few portable power tools at the moment; if you can foresee a time when you may want to install woodworking machines, allow space for them or at least make the layout easy to convert at a later date. Most woodworkers hoard odd pieces of wood that may come in handy – but a small workshop soon becomes cluttered if you try to save every offcut and there's no point in hoarding materials if you can never find them when they are wanted. It therefore pays to clear out your workshop ruthlessly every few months, keeping only those items that are really likely to be of use.

HOME WORKSHOPS

Unless you are starting from scratch, it may not be possible to create a perfect working environment, but by careful planning you can convert an existing building, such as a garage, shed or barn, into an effective workshop. Ground-floor accommodation is essential if you plan to install heavy machinery, and it is more convenient for the delivery of materials.

Ideally, a workshop should be located separately from your living quarters in order to reduce noise and to keep dust and fumes away from the house. It's a good idea to install heating, and possibly air conditioning, to keep the workshop at a constant temperature and also to control the humidity.

SEE ALSO

Hand tools	76-122
Machine tools	156-208
Machine-shop safety	156,214
Benches	212-213
Dust collectors	214

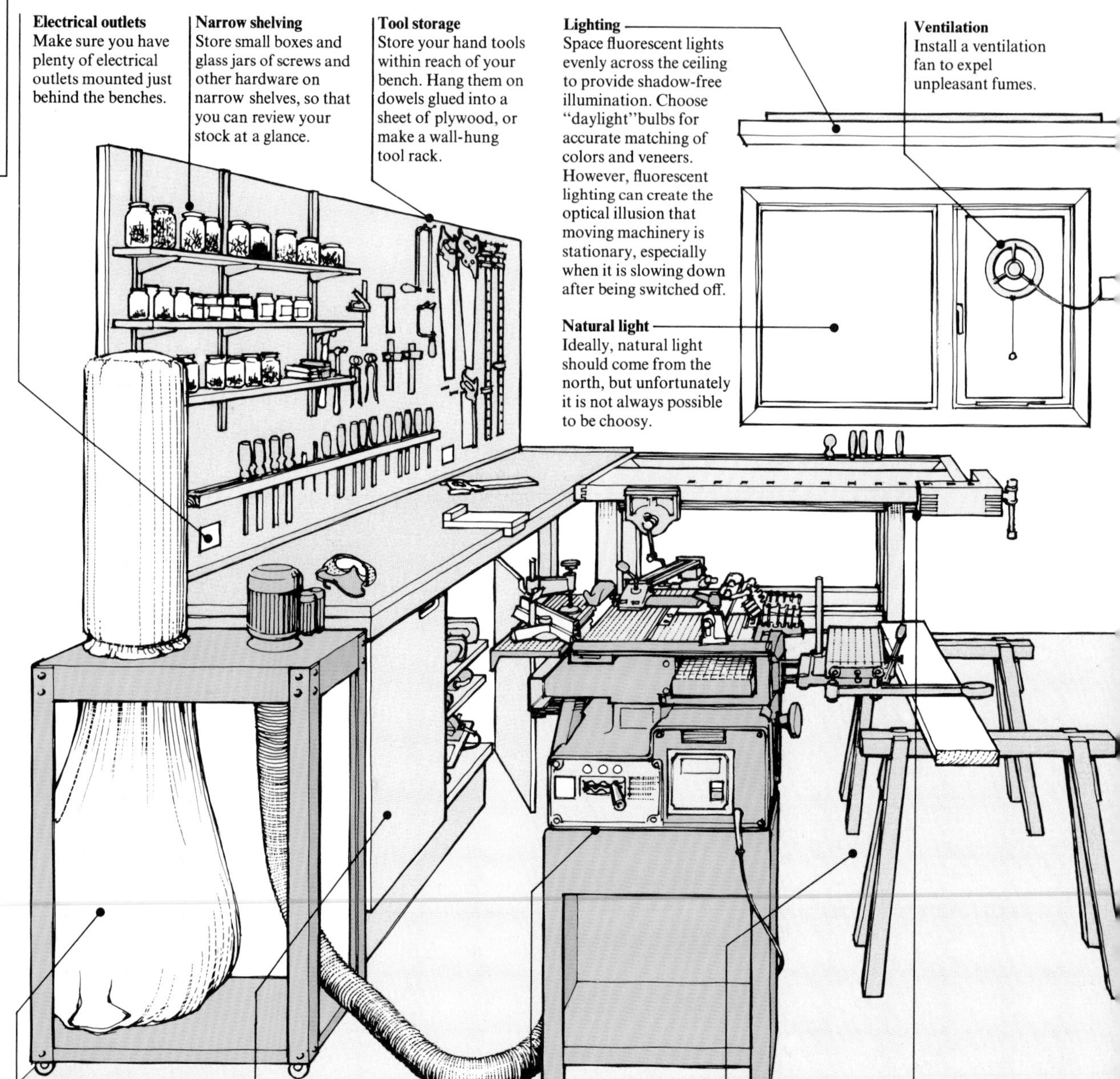

PLANNING A SHOP

The majority of people who do woodwork for pleasure, or even occasional profit, could never afford separate machine and hand workshops even though that would be the ideal arrangement. Consequently, most woodworkers have to find a way to fit a number of machines into a restricted space.

Measure your workshop and plot the ground plan on graph paper, then try various arrangements with scaled paper cutouts of the machines. The object of the exercise is to ensure you will have an unrestricted pathway for workpieces through each machine – and when you consider that you will want to be able to pass a full 4 × 8ft (1.22 × 2.44m) board across a table saw, it becomes obvious how important it is to allow sufficient working space around the machines.

One popular arrangement is to group the machines in the center of the workshop, with their workpiece pathways at right angles to each other (see below). This layout works well, provided you never have to operate all the machines at once, and with a one-person workshop, that should never be necessary. It is clearly also an advantage to be able to run the electrical supply to a common area.

If the workshop is too narrow for this arrangement, it may be possible to arrange the machines in line but stagger them slightly so that a board passing over one machine will be supported by the worktable of a neighboring machine – though you may have to adjust the height of the worktables to create a clear pathway. Alternatively, it may be convenient to position a portable roller stand on the outfeed side of a machine in order to support a long board or feed it over the table of the next machine in line.

To provide extra clearance, you can align a machine with an open door or window, or even with a hole cut into the workshop wall, as long as protruding boards won't endanger passersby. A lathe or drill press can be positioned against a wall, allowing the optimum clearance on both sides of the machines.

Fire prevention
Dispose of dust and shavings regularly, and never store oily rags in your workshop. Always have a good-quality fire extinguisher handy, and install a reliable smoke alarm.

Fire extinguisher

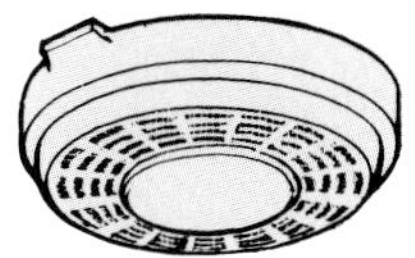

Battery-operated smoke alarm

First-aid kit
Mount a well-stocked first-aid kit in a conspicuous location.

Open shelving
Use open shelving for storing materials and finishes. Keep the bulk of inflammable materials in a separate shed.

Storing wood
Store solid wood and veneers on strong brackets securely bolted to studs.

Security
Fit workshop doors and windows with locks, not only to deter burglars but to keep inquisitive children away from dangerous chemicals and machinery.

Scrap storage
Store short lengths of scrap wood on end in plastic bins.

Storing boards
Store man-made boards on edge between an open-stud partition and a workshop wall, so you can slide boards out without the others falling over. Site the stack in line with an access door.

The small shop
One arrangement for a combined machine and hand workshop is to group the machines in the center. The workpiece pathways cross at right angles.

1 Lathe
2 Bench
3 Dust collector
4 Roller stand
5 Table saw
6 Jointer/planer
7 Drill press
8 Band saw

A woodworker's bench is one of the most important pieces of equipment in the workshop. It is virtually impossible to produce quality work on a bench that is not sturdily constructed and fitted with well-machined vises, so choose your bench carefully. Most workbenches are between 2ft 8in (800mm) and 2ft 10in (850mm) high but you can have higher or lower ones made to order. Some manufacturers offer left-handed benches that are mirror images of the standard format.

SEE ALSO

Sawing planks and boards	82
Backsaws	83
Bench planes	88-91

Woodworker's bench

A good bench will have a hardwood worktop that is at least 2in (50mm) thick. Tough short-grain beech is the most common material for worktop construction, although birch, maple and other hardwoods are also used. Some European benches are made with a worktop partly constructed from plywood. Provided the plywood veneers are thick enough to withstand periodic scraping in order to clean glue and spilled finishes from the surface, a composite construction is not necessarily a disadvantage. You can choose a bench with a plain worktop, but the majority are made with a shallow tool well. This temporary-storage facility enables you to move a large workpiece or frame across the bench without sweeping hand tools onto the floor. Other benches are supplied with a tool tray that can be bolted to the edge of the worktop. A slot or row of holes along the back edge of the bench for storing saws and chisels is yet another option.

One or two models are made with softwood underframes, but most benches are constructed entirely from hardwood. Look for a bench with mortised-and-tenoned end frames that are securely bolted to wide cross rails, and check that the underframe is stable enough not to distort when you apply sideways pressure to the worktop. Most manufacturers offer at least one simple drawer as an optional extra, and some benches are available with the underframe converted to a fully enclosed tool cupboard.

Woodworking vises

Every woodworker needs at least one large vise fixed permanently to the front edge of the worktop as close as possible to one of the legs of the underframe. This leg will prevent any flexing of the worktop caused by working wood clamped in the jaws of the vise. European-style vises are made with wooden jaws to grip the work without marking it. Another common style of vise has cast-metal jaws made to be lined with wood by the woodworker. Both types of vise can be operated by turning a large tommy-bar handle on the front jaw, but some metal vises are also equipped with a quick-release lever that disengages part of the screw mechanism, permitting the jaws to be opened and closed rapidly by a straight pull or push.

End vise

Better-quality benches have a vise built into one end of the worktop. An end vise provides clamping force along the bench to hold a workpiece between metal or wooden stops, called "dogs," dropped into square holes cut into the vise and at regular intervals along one or both sides of the worktop. The workpiece can also be clamped upright in the jaws.

Holdfast

A holdfast is a portable "vise" with a long shaft that fits into a large hole drilled in the worktop, lined with a metal collar. Turning a screw presses a pivoted arm down onto the workpiece, clamping it flat on the worktop. If you fit a second collar in a hole drilled in the bench leg, that will enable you to use the holdfast to provide support for a long workpiece held in a woodworking vise.

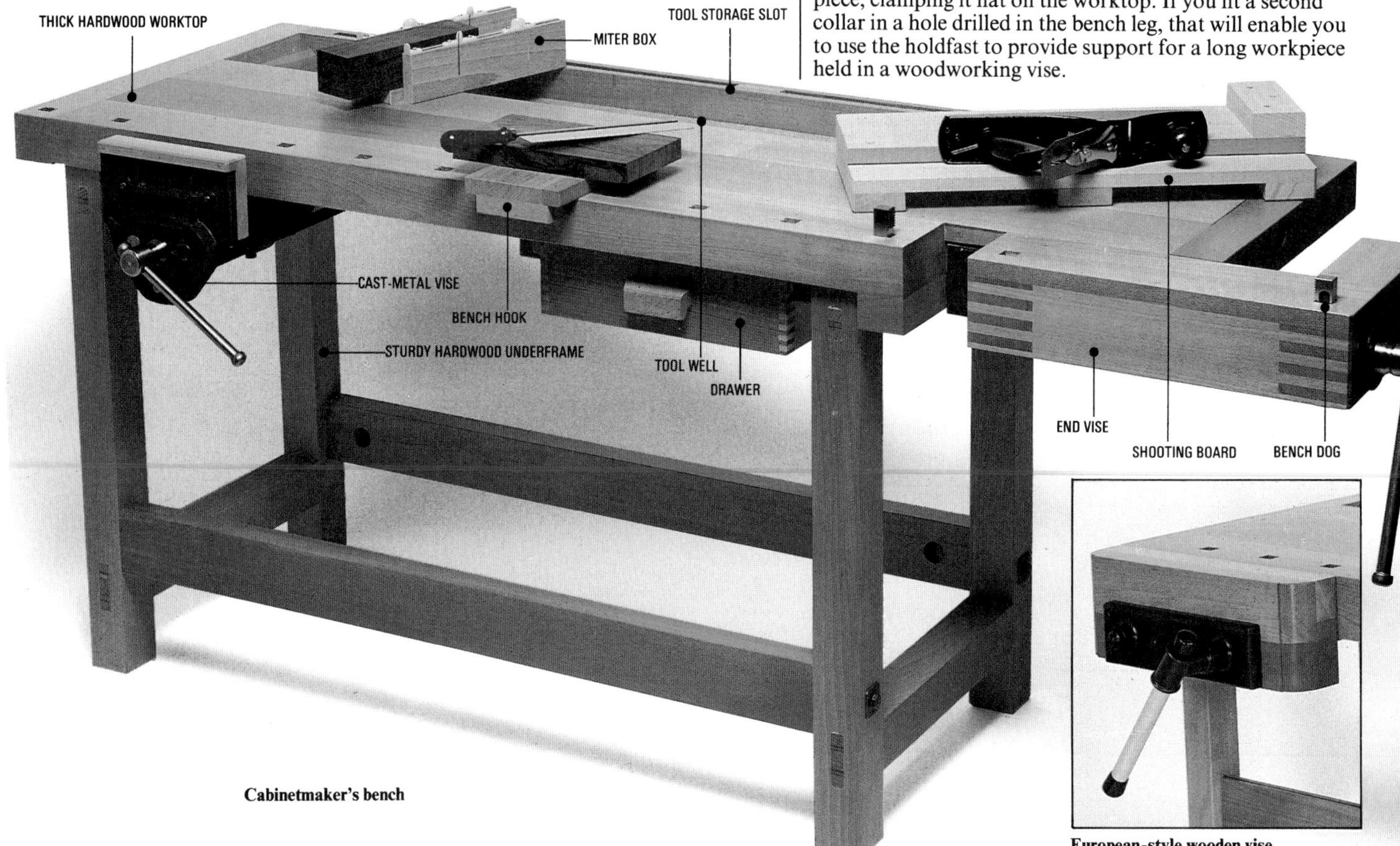

Cabinetmaker's bench

European-style wooden vise

Bench-mounted holdfast

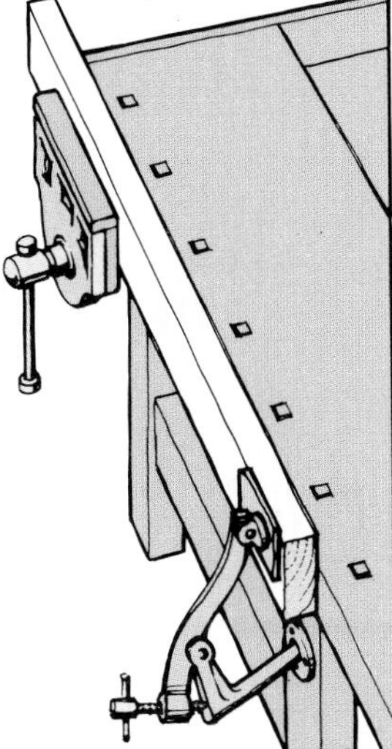

A holdfast supports a long board

Sawhorses

These lightweight trestles are used singly or in pairs to support the work when sawing planks or boards. The legs are splayed and braced to provide a steady platform approximately 2ft (600mm) from the floor.

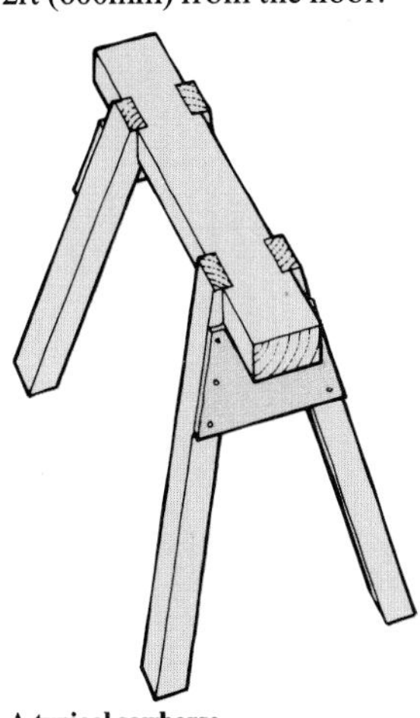

A typical sawhorse

WORKBENCH ACCESSORIES

Cutting wood directly on a bench damages the worktop. Instead, use an appropriate accessory that protects the worktop from sawcuts and chisel marks and also serves as a jig for the work and tool.

Bench hook

A hardwood bench hook is used for crosscutting short lengths of wood with a backsaw. A block fixed to the underside rests against the front edge of the bench and the work is held against a second block, or "stop," fixed to the top. You can buy a ready-made bench hook or you may prefer to make one yourself by doweling two blocks to a flat board.

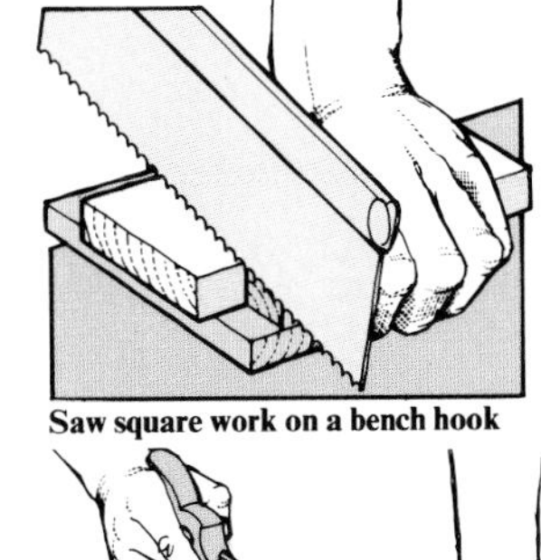

Saw square work on a bench hook

Cut mitered work in a miter box

Miter box

This is a simple wooden jig for cutting miter joints and square ends, using a backsaw. It has two raised sides with slots cut in them to guide the saw. The work is held against the far side of the box. On more expensive miter boxes, the slots are reinforced with adjustable nylon saw guides.

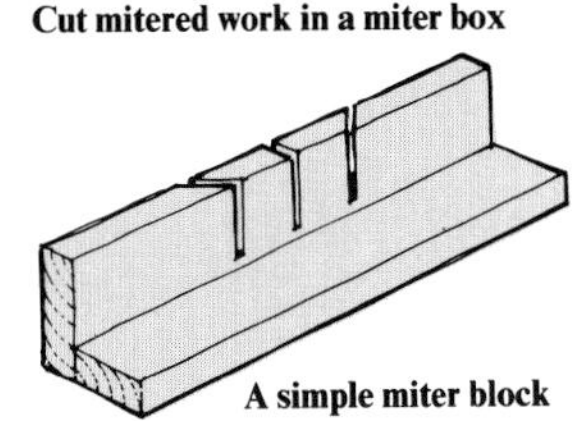

A simple miter block

Miter block

A miter block is a simpler version of the miter box, having only one raised side.

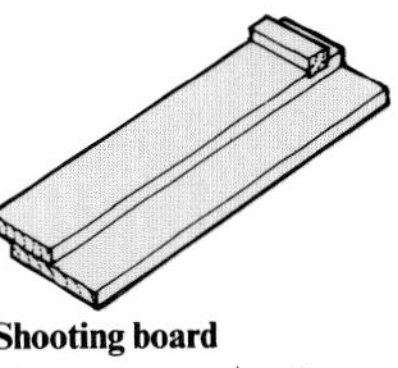

Shooting board

Shooting board

This type of jig is used for planing across end grain. It comprises two boards that are bonded together and staggered so that they form a wide rabbet. The work is held against a wooden stop housed in the upper board while a bench plane is slid along the lower board to take a fine shaving. To trim miter joints, plane them on a miter shooting board, which has angled stops.

Planing on a shooting board

Miter shooting block

A miter shooting block is a jig with a movable clamping jaw designed to hold large mitered or squared workpieces so you can trim them with a sharp, finely set plane. To hold the jig at a comfortable height, clamp the strip fixed to the underside of the shooting block in a vise.

Miter shooting board

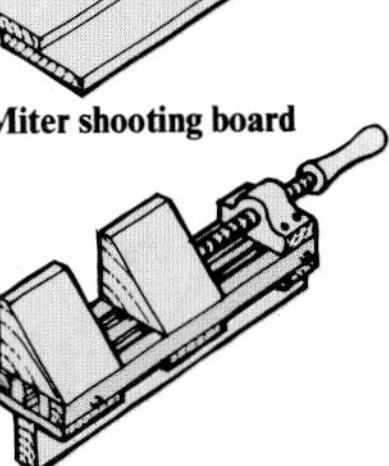

Miter shooting block

FOLDING BENCH

If workshop space is too limited for a permanent bench, use one that folds flat for storage. The worktop comprises two huge vise jaws, one of which can be angled to grip tapered workpieces or straightened up for parallel-sided wood. You can also clamp a workpiece to the top of the bench between plastic pegs. The bench unfolds to standard-bench height for planing, or paring with a chisel, and may be lowered to a convenient height for sawing.

Folding bench

A folding bench can accommodate awkwardly shaped workpieces

HEALTH AND SAFETY IN THE WORKSHOP

Commercial and industrial establishments have to comply with strict regulations and restrictions safeguarding the health and safety of their workers. Although the same rules do not apply to home workshops, it makes sense to protect yourself from harmful fumes or dust, noise, and pieces of wood or metal thrown up by machine or power tools.

SEE ALSO	
Machine-shop safety	156
Power tools	124-154
Machine tools	156-208

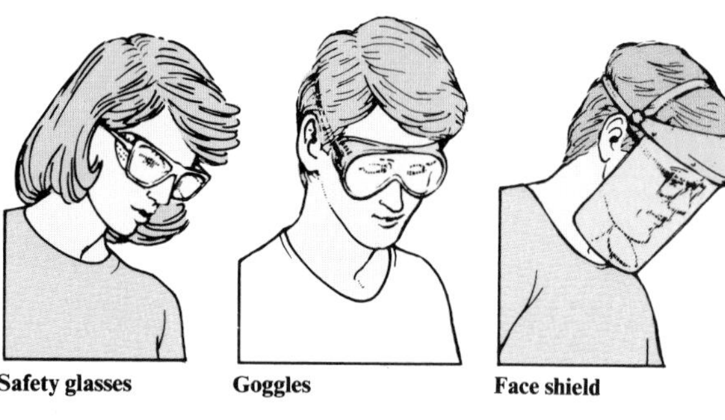

Safety glasses Goggles Face shield

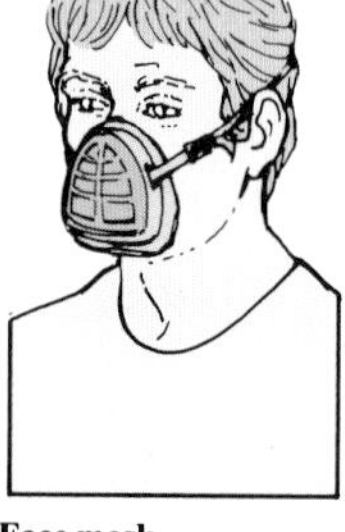

Hearing protectors Face mask Respirator

Safety glasses
The lenses of safety glasses are made from a tough impact-resistant polycarbonate. They not only protect your eyes from projectiles but also shield them from the dust and turbulence created by power tools. Side screens riveted to the frames provide added protection.

Goggles
Being designed to fit tightly against your face, goggles provide all-around eye protection. The lens is usually made from clear semi-rigid plastic and is fitted to a softer vinyl frame perforated to prevent condensation inside the goggles. Some goggles are designed for wearing over ordinary glasses.

Face shield
Total face protection is provided by the hinged plastic visor of a face shield. It is a particularly comfortable form of protection if you wear glasses.

Hearing protectors
Padded earmuffs or earplugs protect your hearing from overexposure to noise that could cause long-term damage. Wear hearing protectors when operating noisy machinery.

Face mask
A simple mask with a replaceable filter protects your lungs from dust and paint or varnish overspray.

Respirator
A professional dual-cartridge respirator provides full protection against the harmful effects of paints, lacquers, adhesives and toxic dust. Interchangeable color-coded cartridges are designed to filter specific materials. This type of respirator can be worn with goggles or safety glasses.

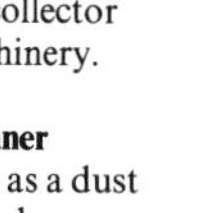

◀ **Large-volume dust collector**
Connect this type of collector to woodworking machinery.

▼ **Industrial vacuum cleaner**
This machine doubles as a dust collector for power tools.

DUST COLLECTION

Sawdust and shavings left to pile up on the workshop floor constitute a serious fire hazard. The risk is increased when very fine dust is allowed to float in the air, contributing to a potentially explosive atmosphere. Moreover, dust makes the floor slippery, is harmful to your lungs and will contaminate freshly lacquered or varnished surfaces. Industrial workshops are equipped with dust-collection systems serving every individual machine. This type of installation is prohibitively expensive for the home woodworker, but simpler portable collectors are available to suit the smaller workshop.

Dust collectors
Mobile large-volume dust collectors are ideal for the small machine shop. Dust sucked through a flexible hose is filtered from the air by a woven-cotton bag mounted on top of the machine and is collected in a plastic sack below. The hose takes a variety of shaped mouthpieces designed to fit different woodworking machines. Some collectors can be equipped with dual hoses to service two machines simultaneously.

Industrial vacuum cleaners
A heavy-duty vacuum cleaner is an essential piece of workshop equipment. It is supplied with the usual range of hoses and nozzles, which you can use for cleaning the floor and your woodworking machinery. When fitted with the appropriate accessories, the same machine can be connected directly to portable power tools, eliminating dust or shavings at source. In this mode, operation is by remote control, being activated by the power-tool switch.

CHAPTER SEVEN

JOINT MAKING

It is hardly surprising that many people regard joinery as a measure of a cabinetmaker's skill, since the ability to cut fine joints takes practice and requires the mastering of a variety of accurate cutting techniques using saws, planes and chisels. However, the choice of joint is no less important than the quality of the making. The design must primarily be functional to provide strength, but it should also be in keeping with the overall style of the project. Most joints are designed to conceal the methods used to hold the parts together, while others, such as decorative dovetails, are made a feature. The following chapter illustrates the most common hand-cut joints and how to make them. Generally, dimensions have not been specified, as different projects require joints of different sizes. Instead, relative proportions are given to enable you to make sound joints to suit your requirements.

BUTT JOINTS

The butt joint is the simplest form of joint where one member meets another with no interlocking elements cut into the parts. It is not a strong joint and is often reinforced in some way. Right-angled joints are used in the construction of light frames and small boxes. The joining ends may be square-cut or mitered.

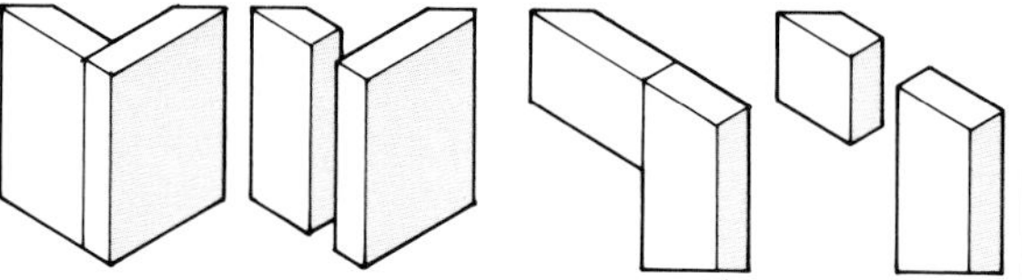

SQUARE-ENDED BUTT JOINT

Butt joints for boxes are made with the end of one member glued to the inside face of the other. For frames, the end is glued to the edge. It is essential for the surfaces to be flat and the ends square.

Cutting the joint

Mark the length of the parts and square a shoulder line all around with a marking knife. Using a bench hook to hold the work, saw off the waste clear of the line **(1)**.

Trim the end grain with a plane to provide the best surface for gluing. Use a shooting board to guide the plane, in order to ensure a square end **(2)**.

Apply glue to the joint and clamp the parts together. Make sure the components are aligned properly, as the joint has no means of locating itself.

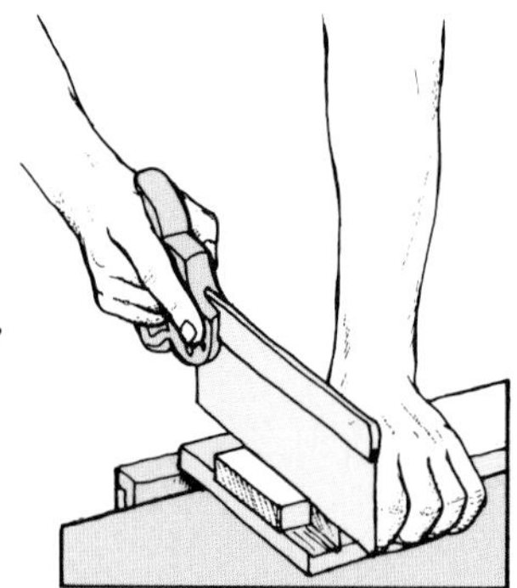

1 Saw off the waste

2 Shoot the ends square

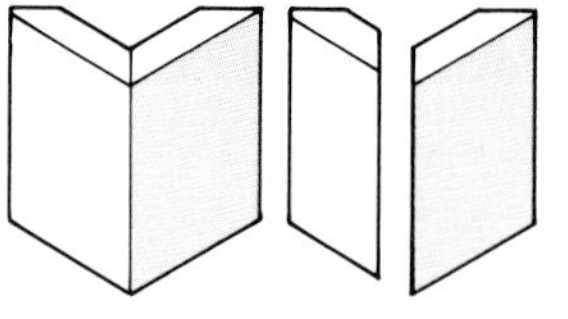

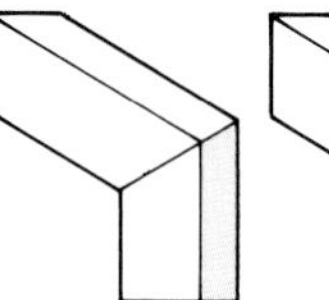

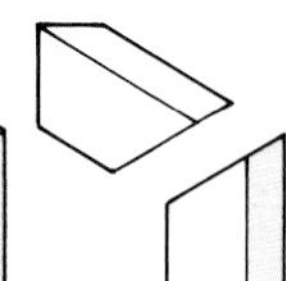

MITERED BUTT JOINT

A miter halves the angle between the parts being joined. In most instances, joints are made at 90 degrees, so the common miter is set at 45 degrees. End grain to end grain does not offer a good gluing surface; but the miter's larger area, compared with the square butt joint, does compensate to some degree. The miter is usually reinforced with nails or tongues.

The importance of accuracy

Miters need to be cut accurately, as gaps will show on the inside or outside if the miter is not exactly half the angle. Use well-seasoned wood, as a gap will open up on the inside of the angle if the wood shrinks after cutting the joint.

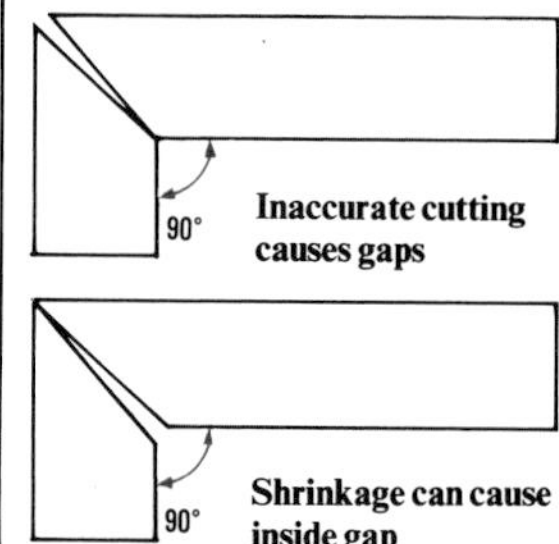

Inaccurate cutting causes gaps

Shrinkage can cause inside gap

Cutting the joint

Mark the cutting lines with a knife and miter square on the face or edge. Square the lines onto the adjacent faces from the miter angle. Cut off the waste with a tenon saw. To guarantee greater accuracy, use a miter box **(1)**, particularly if cutting decorative moldings, which are more difficult to mark with cutting lines.

Trim the cut end with a plane and miter shooting board **(2)**. For wide boards, use a miter shooting block **(3)**. If this is not available, set the work in a vise with a piece of scrap wood at the back edge to prevent break-out **(4)**.

Box joint

Frame joint

Square-ended butt joint

Mitered box joint

Mitered frame joint

Mitered butt joint

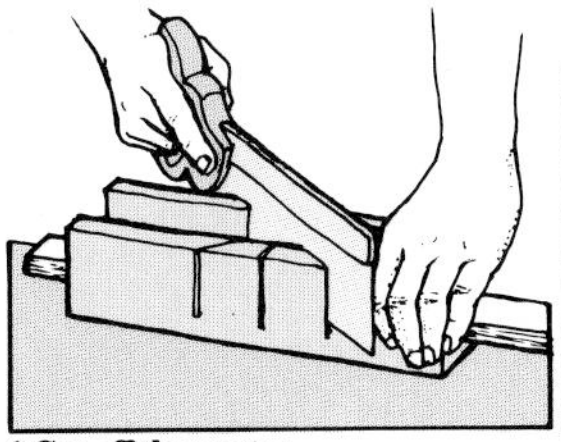

1 Cut off the waste

2 Plane the ends smooth

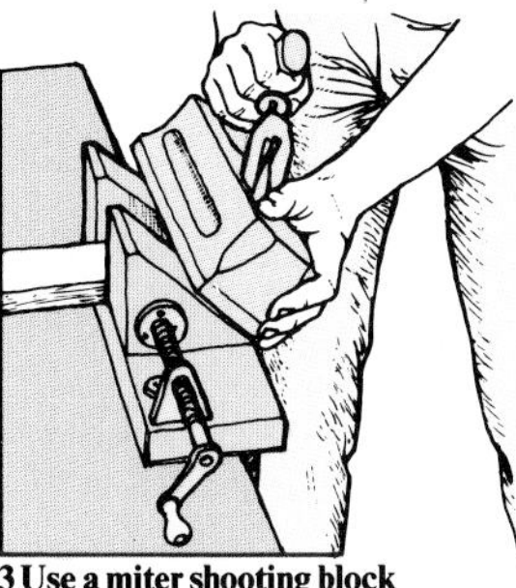

3 Use a miter shooting block

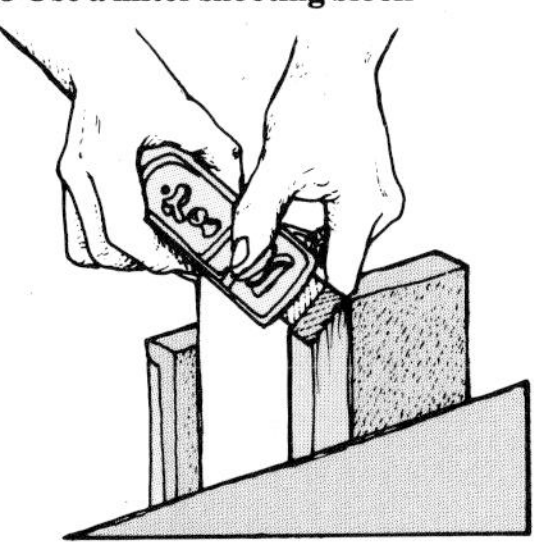

4 Or use scrap-wood backing

Reinforcing a square-ended butt joint
As the end grain does not glue well, additional reinforcement is usually required. You can use fine finishing nails or blocks glued into the angle. Drive the nails into the joint dovetail-fashion to provide additional mechanical strength. In some cases the nails can be used in place of clamps when gluing up. If using glued-block reinforcement, rub-joint them into the angle and leave the glue to set.

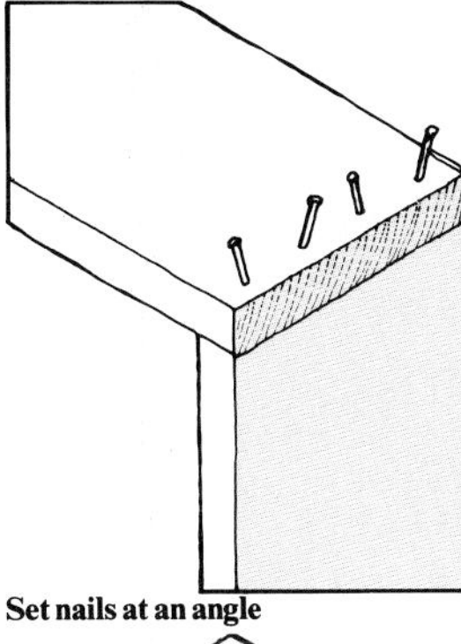

Set nails at an angle

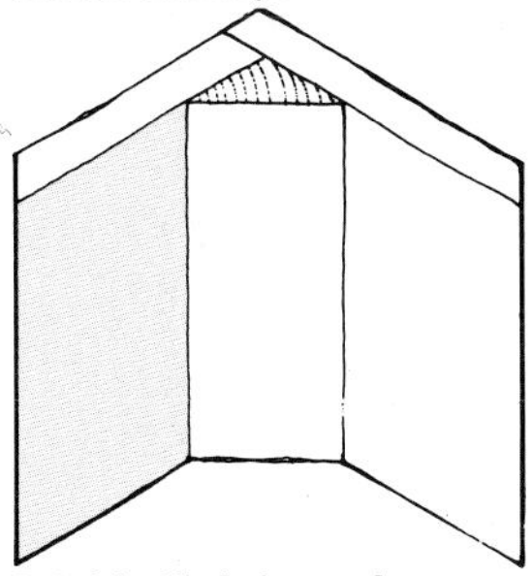

Rub-joint blocks into angle

REINFORCING A MITERED BUTT JOINT

The easiest way to reinforce a mitered joint is to glue it first and add the reinforcement when set. Use a miter clamp or a web clamp for gluing up.

Using nails
For nailing, use brads or fine nails, depending on the size of the joint. Sink the nail heads and disguise the holes, using matching colored filler.

Using splines
For small joints, veneer or plywood splines can be set in sawcuts made across the corner. Make the cuts perpendicular, or angled for additional strength. Glue the splines into the sawcuts and trim them flush when set. Use splines of contrasting wood for a decorative effect.

Using a loose tongue
For larger miters, a loose tongue or key can be fitted. Set a mortise gauge to the thickness of the tongue, which can be solid wood or plywood and about one-third the thickness of the frame material. Mark the gauge lines on the edges and centered on the thickness. Square lines across the end of the gauged lines the same distance from the corner on each edge.

Set the joint in a vise with the shoulder line vertical. Carefully saw down each line and chop out the waste with a chisel, working from both sides toward the middle. Glue the loose tongue and plane it flush when set. If you are using a solid-wood loose tongue, its grain must run across the corner.

Integral reinforcing
A loose tongue is also used to reinforce a miter before the joint is glued together. This type is more easily cut by machine, but can be made by hand.

Make the tongue from $\frac{1}{8}$in (3mm) plywood about $\frac{1}{2}$in (12mm) wide or use solid wood, with the grain running across the width. Cut matching grooves by hand with a saw and chisel or with a plow plane. Center the groove when the tongue runs with the miter **(1)**. When cutting across the miter, set the groove closer to the inside of the angle to avoid leaving weak short grain **(2)**.

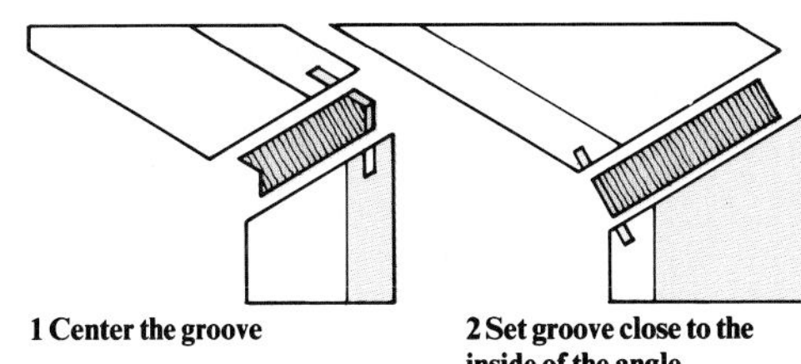

1 Center the groove

2 Set groove close to the inside of the angle

VENEER SPLINES

Splined joint

Loose-tongued joint

LOOSE TONGUE

Loose-tongued joint

LOOSE TONGUE

Loose-tongued joint

LOOSE TONGUE OR KEY

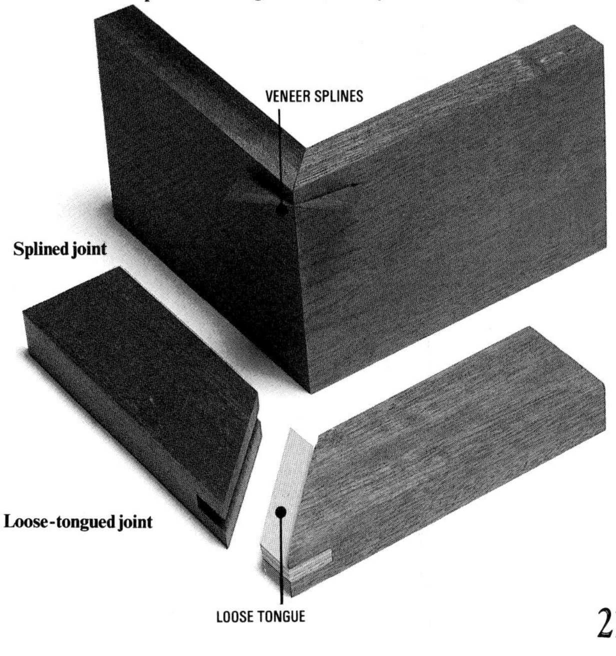

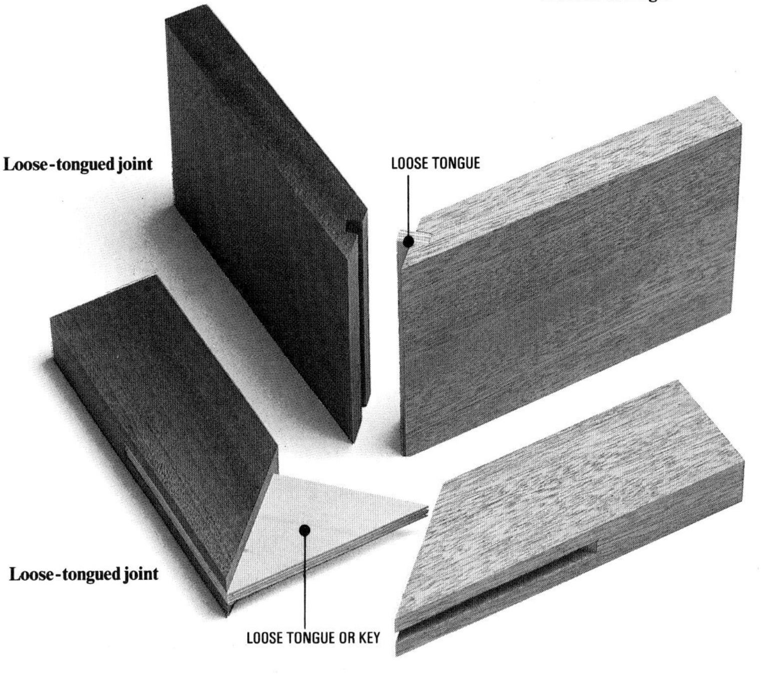

RABBET JOINTS

The rabbet joint is a straightforward corner joint used for simple box and cabinet construction. Also known as a lap joint, the plain end of one part is set in a rabbet cut in the other. It is the remaining wood left by the rabbet that forms the lap and covers the end grain of the other member.

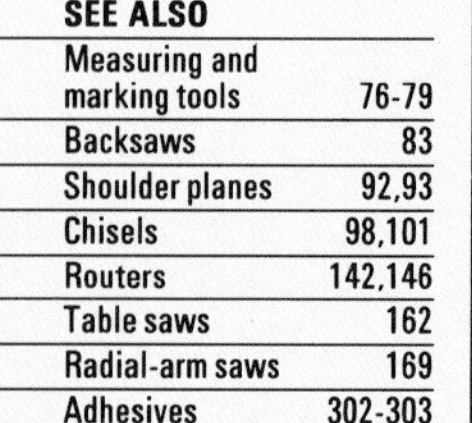

SEE ALSO

Measuring and marking tools	76-79
Backsaws	83
Shoulder planes	92,93
Chisels	98,101
Routers	142,146
Table saws	162
Radial-arm saws	169
Adhesives	302-303

SIMPLE RABBET JOINT

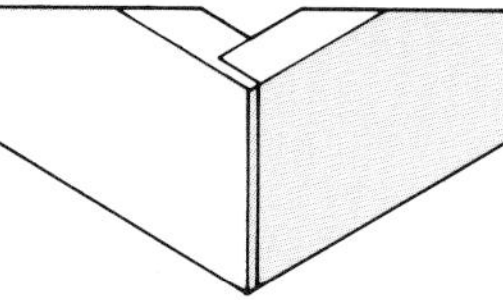

This is not a particularly strong joint and needs pinning, but it is better than a butt joint in strength and appearance.

Cutting the joint

Cut the wood to length. Set a marking gauge to one-quarter or one-third the thickness of the rabbeted member. Scribe a line on the end and over the top and bottom edges, working from the face side **(1)**. Reset the gauge to the thickness of the butting member. Run the gauge against the end of the rabbet member to scribe a line on the back face and edges **(2)**. Mark the waste with a pencil.

Set the rabbet member in the vise. Saw down the lap-gauge line to the shoulder line. Hold the work on a bench hook and cut across the shoulder line to remove the waste **(3)**. Trim the rabbet with a shoulder plane if necessary.

Apply glue to the joining parts, clamp together and secure with pins driven through the side member.

1 Mark the rabbet-gauge line

2 Mark the shoulder line

3 Saw out the waste

- **Scarf joint**
  A form of lap and miter joint in one, this is used to join wood end to end. A long shallow taper in each part gives a large gluing area. Saw or plane the length of the taper to at least four times the thickness of the wood.

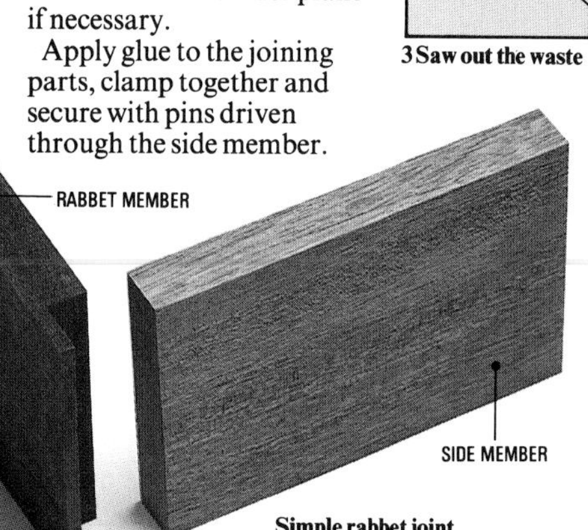

Simple rabbet joint

Scarf joint

MITERED RABBET JOINT

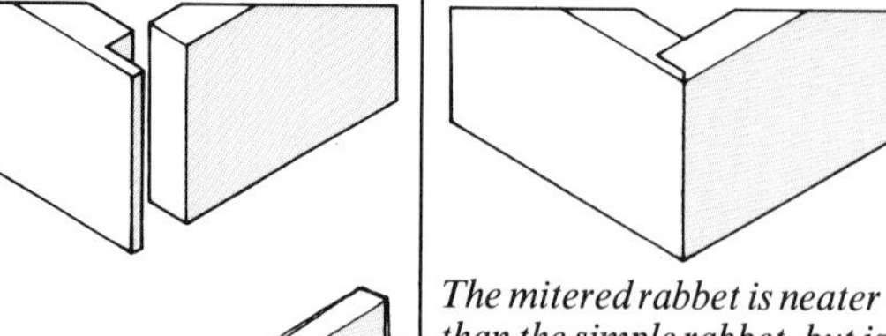

The mitered rabbet is neater than the simple rabbet, but is more difficult to cut.

Cutting the joint

Mark and cut the rabbet as described (see left). Mark a 45-degree miter on the edges of the rabbet **(1)**. Square a line across the inside of the rabbet. Plane off the waste down to the miter line.

Using the marking gauge at the same setting, scribe a shoulder line on the inside and edges of the butting member, working from the end. Then, with the stock against the outside face, scribe a line across the end and over the edges to meet the shoulder line. Mark a miter on each edge from the outside face to the point where the two gauge lines meet each other **(2)**.

Hold the work flat on a bench hook and saw down the shoulder line to the miter. Set it upright in a vise and saw down the gauge line to remove the waste. Reset the work in the vise and, using a shoulder plane, carefully shape the miter **(3)**.

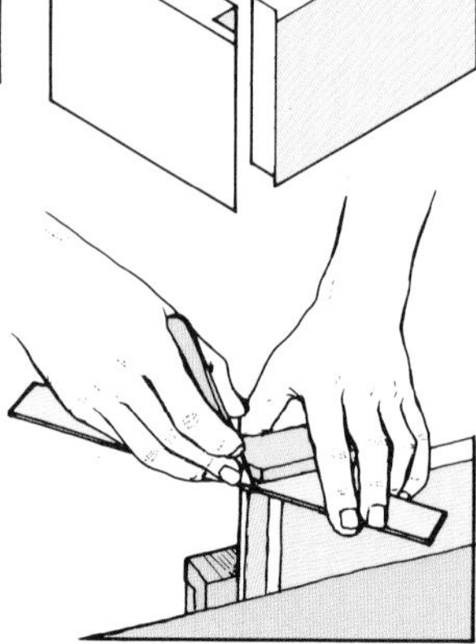

1 Mark the rabbet miter

2 Mark the edge miter

3 Plane the miter

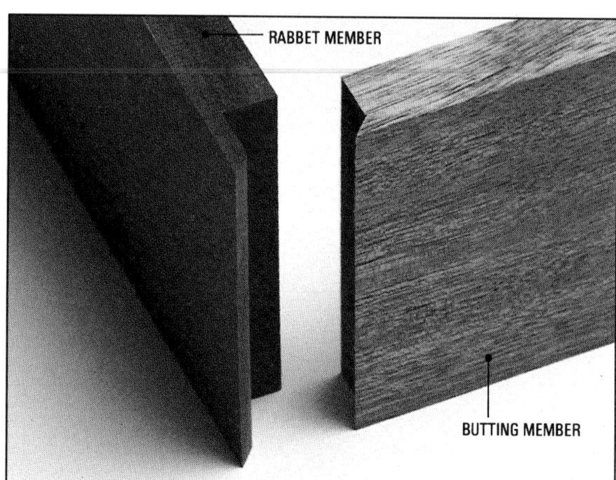

Detail of mitered rabbet joint

LAP JOINTS

Lap joints are usually cut in components of equal thickness and have half the thickness of the wood cut from each piece. They are relatively simple to cut and are used in frame construction where one member must cross or meet another in the same plane. The joint can be cut by hand with a saw and chisel or machine-cut. The methods shown here are for hand-cutting different forms of the basic joint.

CROSS-LAP JOINT

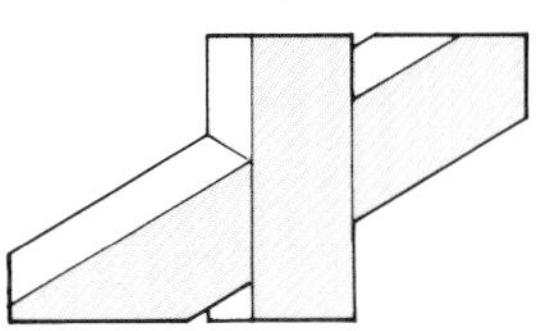

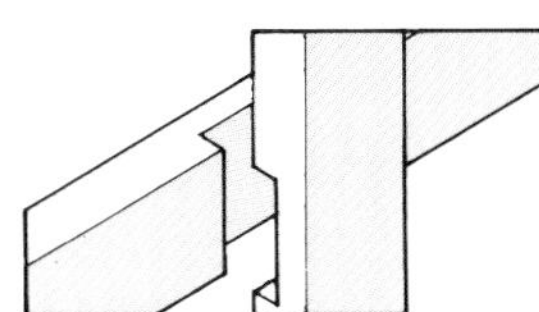

This joint is the best to use when horizontal rails cross vertical members of a frame, such as the divisions in a cabinet front or the glazing bars of a door or window.

Marking out the joint
It is conventional practice for the divider to run through, although the joint is equally strong either way.

Mark the width of the divider on the rail **(1)**. Using a try square and marking knife, square lines across the face of the rail and carry them over and halfway down each edge **(2)**. Turn the wood over and use the same procedure to mark the width of the rail on the back face of the divider.

Set a marking gauge to half the thickness of the wood and scribe a line on the edges between the marked lines, working from the face side of both parts **(3)**. Mark the waste.

Cutting the joint
With the aid of a bench hook, saw along the shoulder line to the depth of the gauged line. Be sure to keep just inside the waste side of the line, as a loose joint is unsightly and weak. Make one or two extra sawcuts evenly spaced across the waste to make chiseling out the waste easier **(4)**.

Set the work in a vise. Using a suitably sized chisel and a mallet, cut away the waste wood. Work toward the middle with the chisel held at a slight upward angle **(5)**. Turn the wood around to cut from the other side. With most of the wood removed, pare away the remaining raised portion in the middle. Use the chisel vertically to sever any wood fibers along the base of the shoulder that were not cut by the saw. Check that the cutout is flat, using the side edge of the chisel.

Cross-lap joint

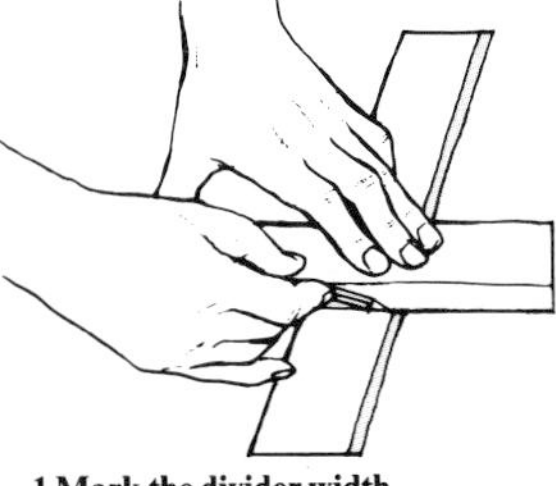
1 Mark the divider width

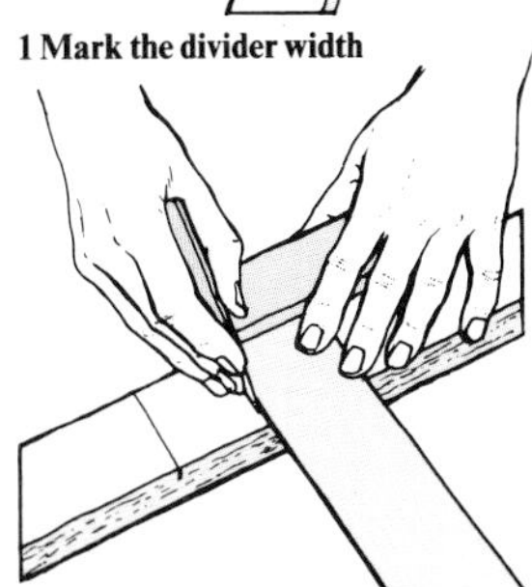

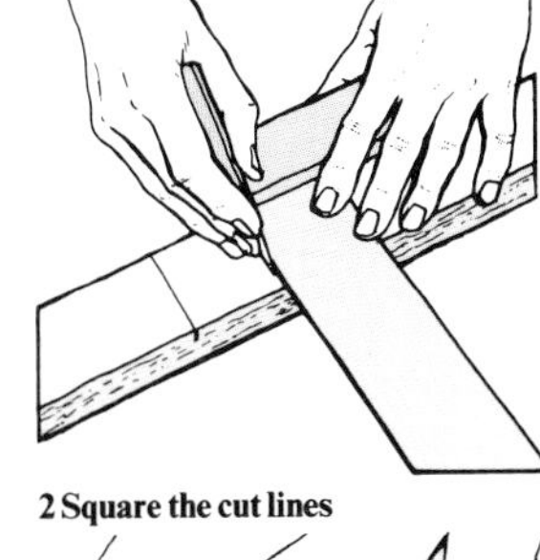
2 Square the cut lines

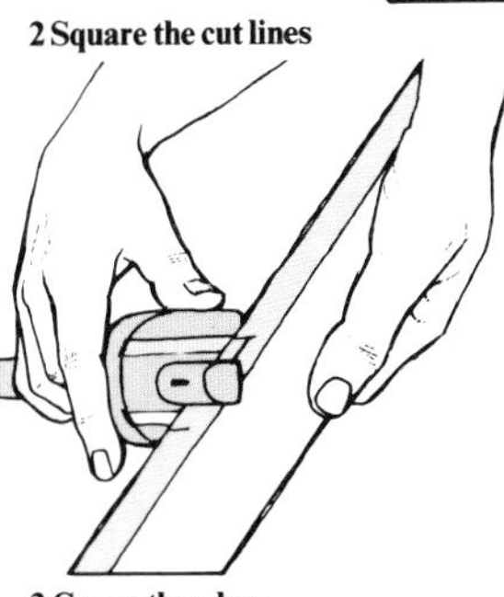
3 Gauge the edges

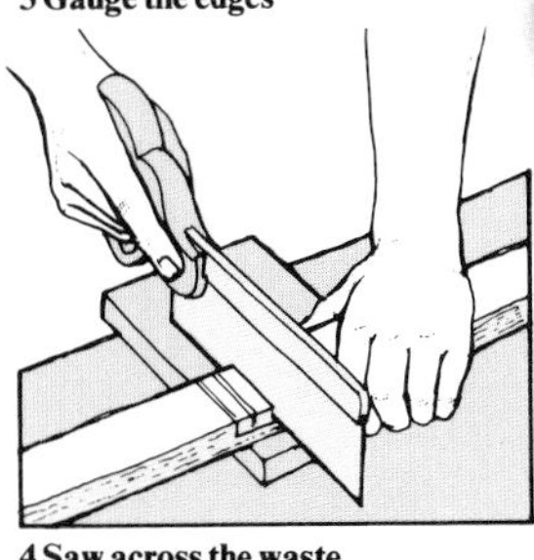

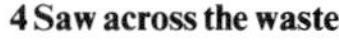
4 Saw across the waste

5 Chisel out the waste

CORNER-LAP JOINTS

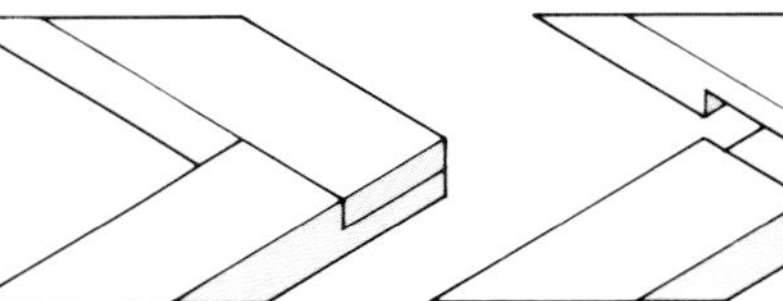

These joints are simple to cut, but rely on the glue for their strength and may require extra support from screws or dowels. The mitered corner lap is a refined version, but is not as strong because of the reduced gluing area.

Corner-lap joint

Mitered corner-lap joint

GLAZING-BAR LAP JOINT

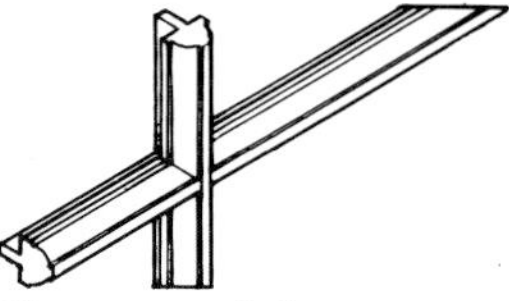

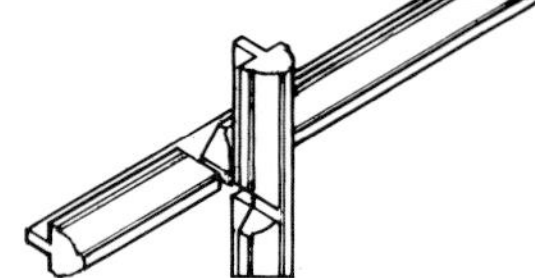

The cutting of a lap joint in a molded glazing bar is basically the same as that used for a cross-lap joint, but there is the added complication of the molded section.

SEE ALSO

Measuring and marking tools	76-79
Backsaws	83
Routers	146
Table saws	162
Radial-arm saws	169
Miter box	213
Dovetail angles	239

Cutting the joint

Cut away the molding on each side of the joint after marking its position. Cut down to the depth of the top face of the molding. The width of the cutout is the same as the top face **(1)**. As it is difficult to mark a line over the contoured surface, use a miter box to make the sawcut **(2)**.

Make a 45-degree miter block for trimming the molding. Clamp the block to the work and pare away the corners of the molding with a chisel **(3)**.

Now cut the lap joint in the remaining section of each part. The depth of the cutout in each should be level with the line of the molding rabbet **(4)**.

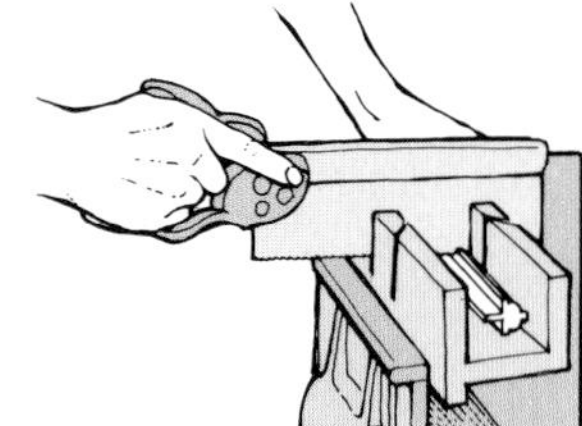

2 Use a miter box

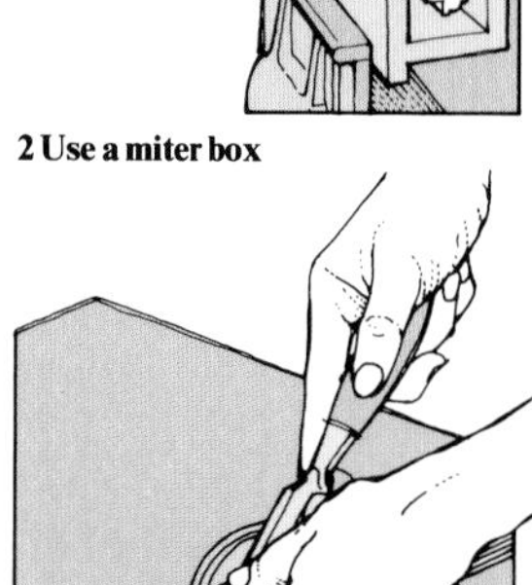

3 Pare away the corners

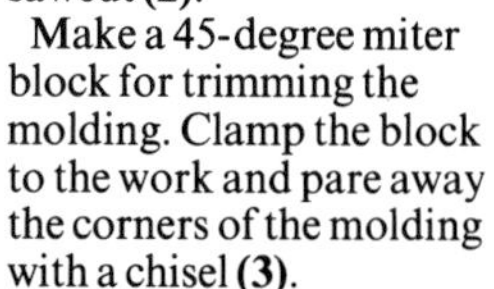

4 Cut the cross lap

1 Width of cutout
Make the cutout the same width as the top face.

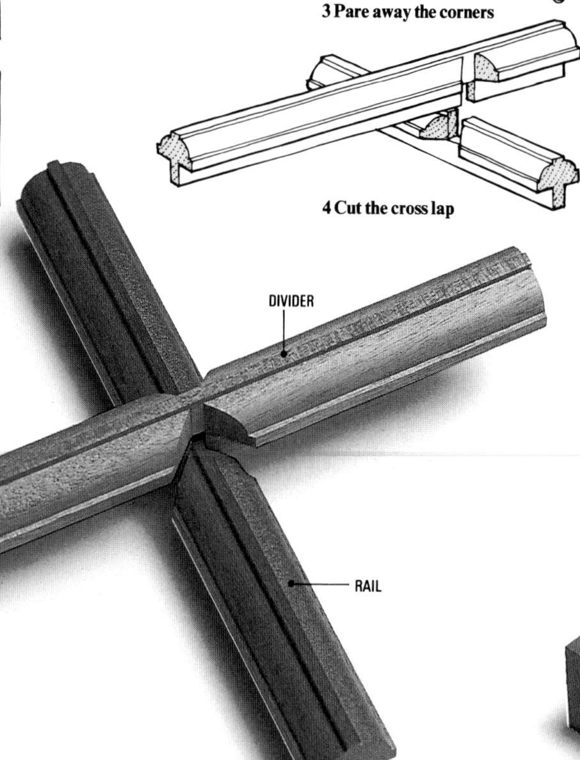

Glazing-bar lap joint

OBLIQUE LAP JOINT

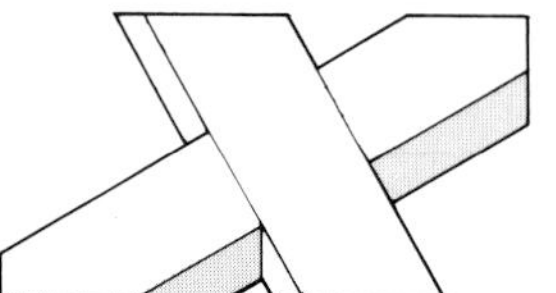

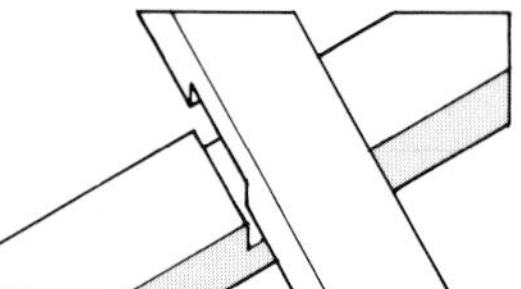

The oblique lap joint is cut in a similar way to the conventional cross-lap joint, but the cutouts are set at an angle. The main difference is the marking out of the shoulder.

Marking out the joint

Making a 45-degree angle is very simple when using a miter square. For any other angle, it is necessary to use a sliding bevel set with the aid of a protractor or by taking the setting from an accurate drawing.

Mark one angled shoulder line on the face side of the bottom member. Place the top member on the line and mark its width **(1)**. Scribe the second shoulder line on the mark. Square the lines halfway down each edge and mark a line between them with a gauge set to half the thickness of the wood.

Place the top member, face side up, in position and mark the width of the bottom piece on both its edges **(2)**. Mark the cutout on the underside with the bevel or square.

Cutting the joint

Saw and chisel out the waste from both parts as for a cross lap, but working at the marked angle.

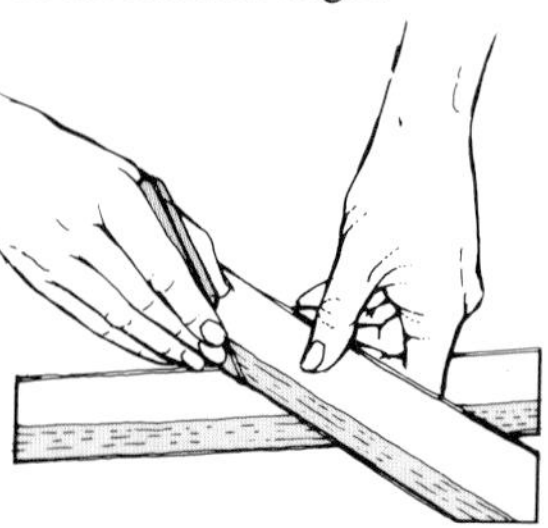

1 Mark top member's width

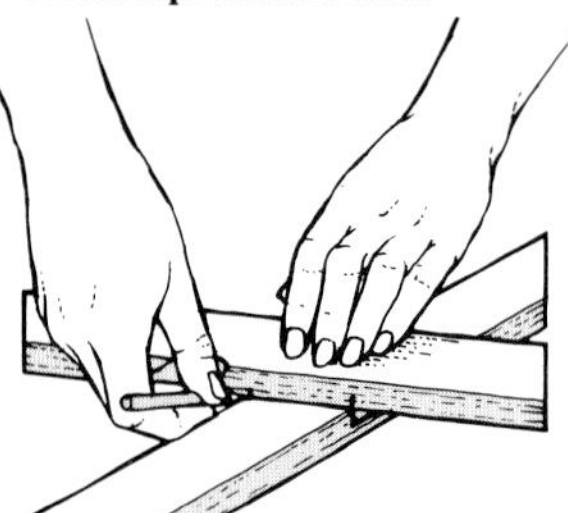

2 Mark bottom member's width

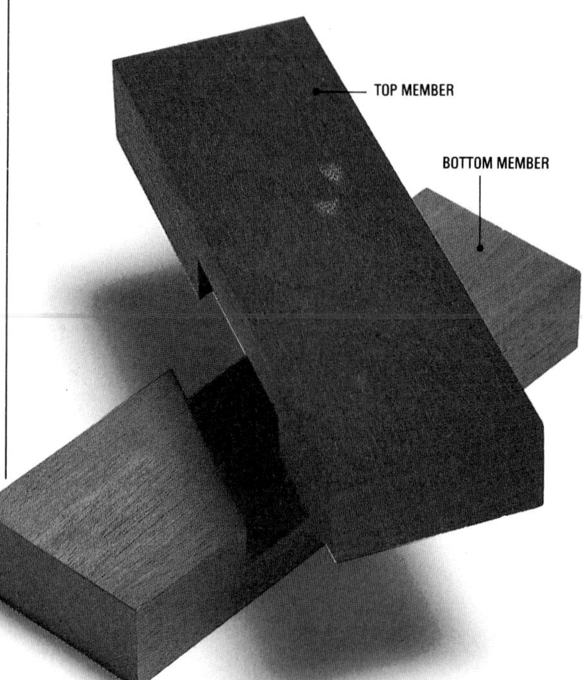

Oblique lap joint

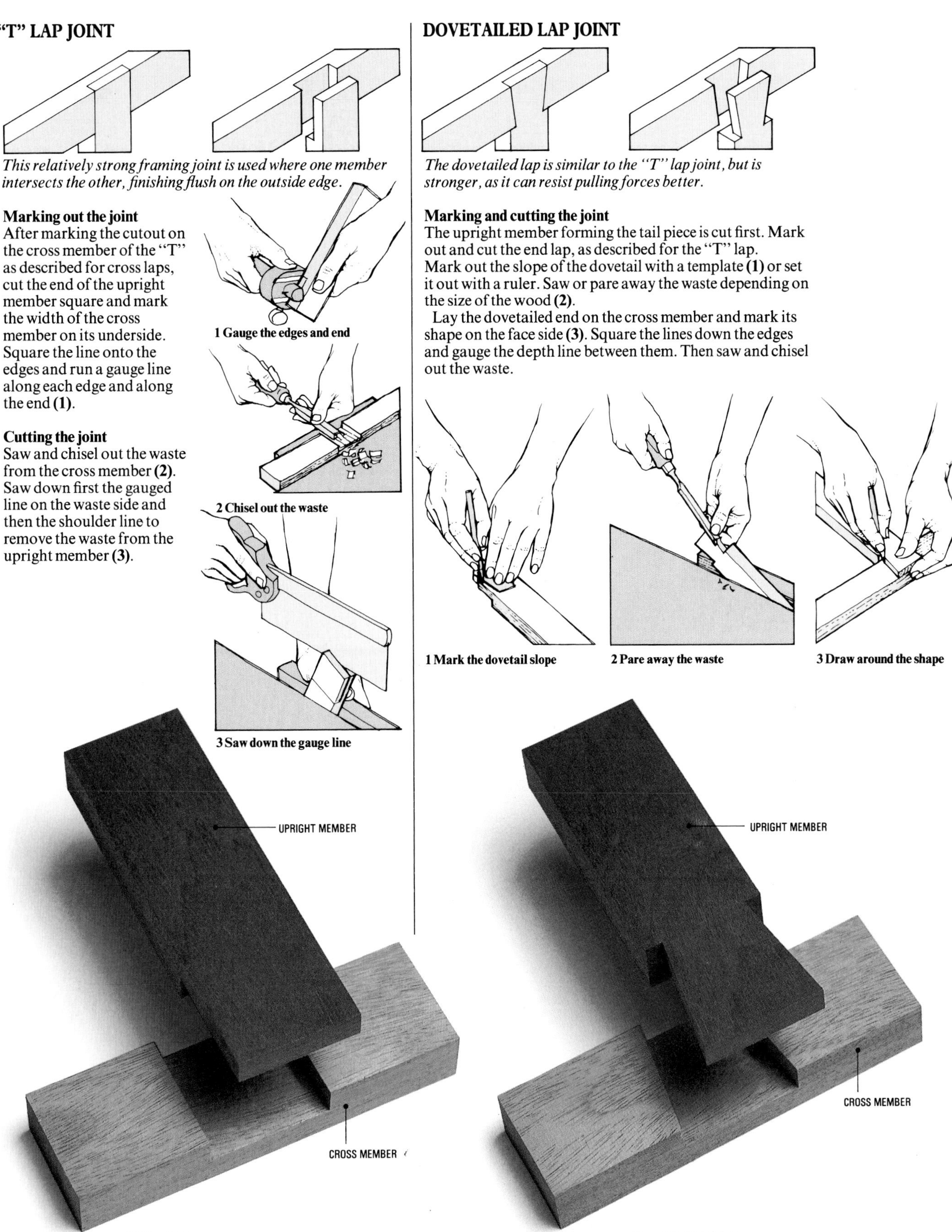

"T" LAP JOINT

This relatively strong framing joint is used where one member intersects the other, finishing flush on the outside edge.

Marking out the joint
After marking the cutout on the cross member of the "T" as described for cross laps, cut the end of the upright member square and mark the width of the cross member on its underside. Square the line onto the edges and run a gauge line along each edge and along the end **(1)**.

Cutting the joint
Saw and chisel out the waste from the cross member **(2)**. Saw down first the gauged line on the waste side and then the shoulder line to remove the waste from the upright member **(3)**.

1 Gauge the edges and end

2 Chisel out the waste

3 Saw down the gauge line

"T" lap joint

DOVETAILED LAP JOINT

The dovetailed lap is similar to the "T" lap joint, but is stronger, as it can resist pulling forces better.

Marking and cutting the joint
The upright member forming the tail piece is cut first. Mark out and cut the end lap, as described for the "T" lap. Mark out the slope of the dovetail with a template **(1)** or set it out with a ruler. Saw or pare away the waste depending on the size of the wood **(2)**.

Lay the dovetailed end on the cross member and mark its shape on the face side **(3)**. Square the lines down the edges and gauge the depth line between them. Then saw and chisel out the waste.

1 Mark the dovetail slope

2 Pare away the waste

3 Draw around the shape

Dovetailed lap joint

EDGE-TO-EDGE JOINTS

Edge joints are used to join relatively narrow boards to make up wider boards or panels for table tops or cabinet work. The edge may be plain or shaped. The shaping of the edge is to increase the gluing area, provide reinforcement and a means of interlocking the edge, which is a help when gluing up. Whichever method is used, they all rely on the strength of the glue joint. Modern glues are very strong and, provided the joining edges are accurately cut, even the plain-edged butt joint will be stronger than the wood itself.

SEE ALSO

Converting wood	12
Measuring and marking tools	76-79
Planes	88-97
Clamps	120-122
Routers	142,146
Table saws	161
Jointing	184
Adhesives	302-303

PREPARING THE WOOD

Start with the boards planed to thickness. Where possible, use quartersawn wood, as this is more stable than wood sawn through and through.

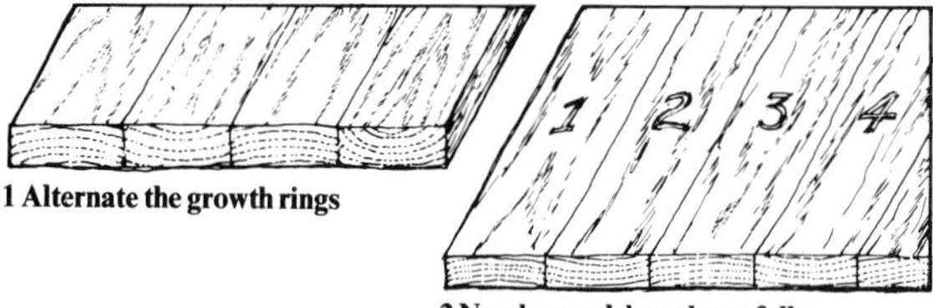

1 Alternate the growth rings

2 Number each board carefully

Selecting and arranging the boards

If you have no choice, or have chosen through and through for its surface figure, select the boards so the direction of the growth rings alternates **(1)**. Also select the boards for color and arrange them so the grain of the wood runs in the same direction; otherwise, final cleaning up of the surface will be more difficult. Number each board on the face side **(2)** and, when working them, keep the numbers facing the same way.

Butt joint

Tongue and groove joint

Loose tongue and groove joint

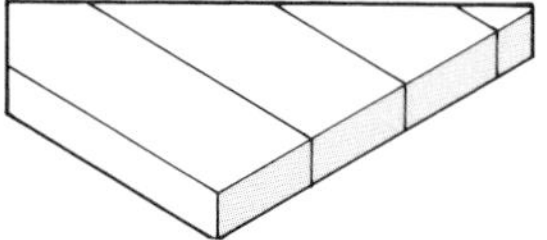

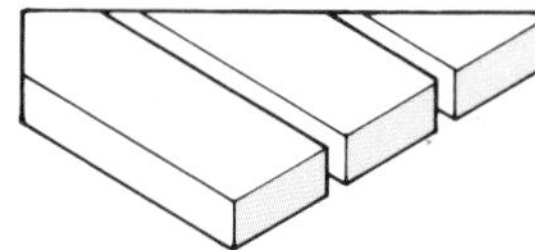

EDGE-TO-EDGE BUTT JOINING

When making a joint between two boards, it is standard practice to plane the meeting edges square to the face side.

Checking for square

Use a try plane or the longest plane available to true each edge **(1)**. Constantly check each edge for square, using a try square. Test that the edge is straight with a metal straightedge **(2)**.

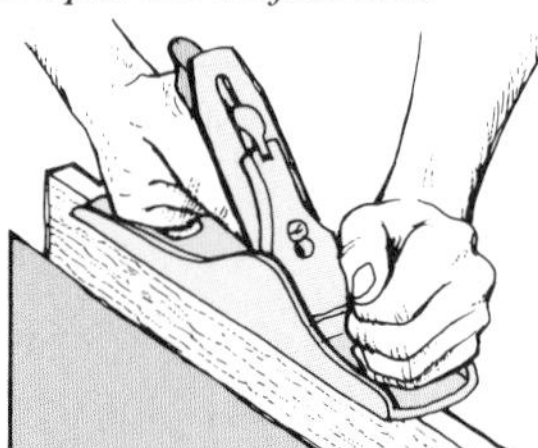

1 Plane the edge true

2 Test that the edge is straight

Irregular boards

A slight hollow is acceptable if the boards are going to be clamped together, but if a rubbed joint is to be used, they must be straight.

Slightly concave edges **(1)** are acceptable for clamping, as the extra pressure at the ends will be released by shrinkage and helps counter end-splitting.

Convex edges **(2)** are unacceptable, as closing the ends with clamps sets up stresses that are likely to cause end splits.

1 Slightly concave edges (exaggerated for clarity) are acceptable

2 Convex edges are unacceptable

CLAMPING EDGE-TO-EDGE JOINTS

Before gluing up, check the boards for fit by setting them in clamps. This will also preset the clamps in readiness for gluing up, which must be done as quickly as possible.

The number of clamps you use will depend on the size of the work, but you should use at least three for most panels. Place "softening," pieces of scrap wood, between the clamp heads and the edge of the boards. Set the boards out on battens laid across the bench.

Gluing up

Apply a thin film of glue to the joining edges. Place a clamp across each end about a quarter of the board's length in from each end **(1)**. Keep the clamps clear of the surface to prevent any reaction with the glue staining the wood. If necessary, tap the joints with a hammer and block to set them flush **(2)**.

Turn the panel over and place a clamp across the middle **(3)**. This clamp not only pulls the joints together, but also counters any tendency for the panel to bow. Wipe away excess glue that is squeezed out from the joints.

Leave the work in the clamps until the glue has cured. If you need to remove the clamped work from the bench, it can be stood against a wall, but make sure it is supported evenly to avoid distortion.

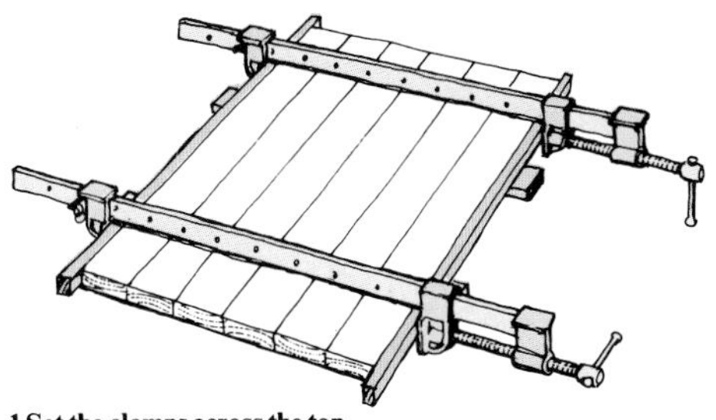

1 Set the clamps across the top

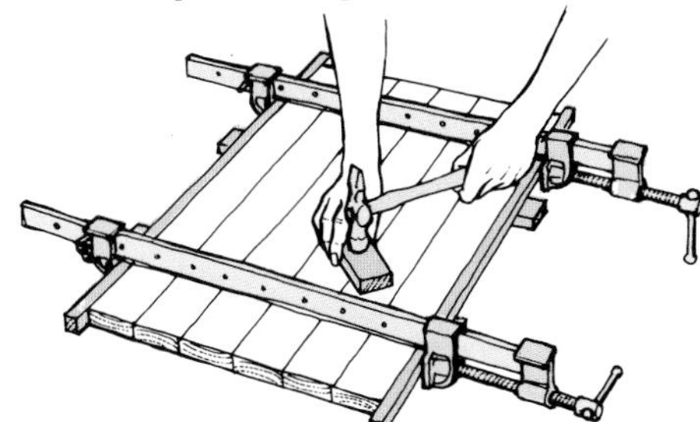

2 Tap the boards flush

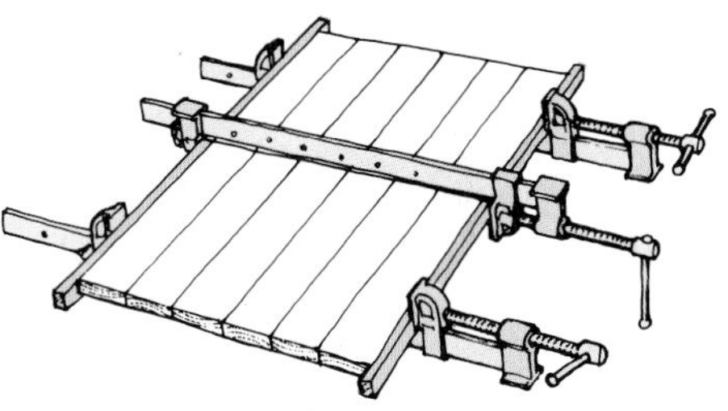

3 Turn and clamp the panel

Planing boards to fit

Planing individual boards straight and square is not easy. A way of making the squareness of the joint less critical is to plane both edges together. Set the two boards level in a vise, back to back with the face sides outward **(3)**. Plane the edges straight. If the edge is not quite square, the boards will still fit together and produce a flat surface **(4)**.

When joining three or more boards edge to edge, the inner boards have both edges planed to fit. Using the back-to-back technique to true the edges, set the first and second board in the vise and plane the edges. Remove the first board, rotate the second and back it up with the third board. Plane the edges of each pair in this way **(5)**.

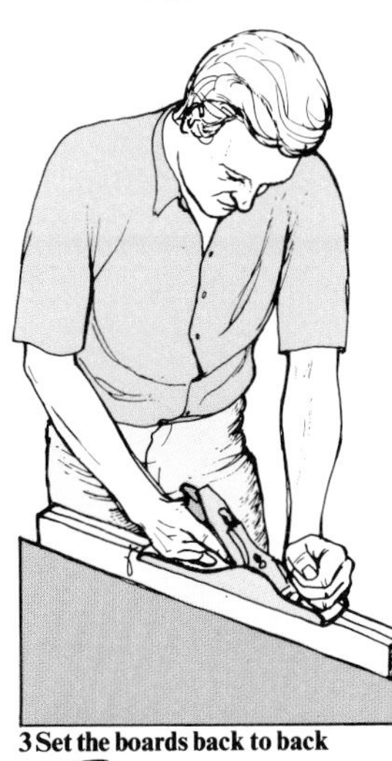

3 Set the boards back to back

4 Out-of-square edges will fit

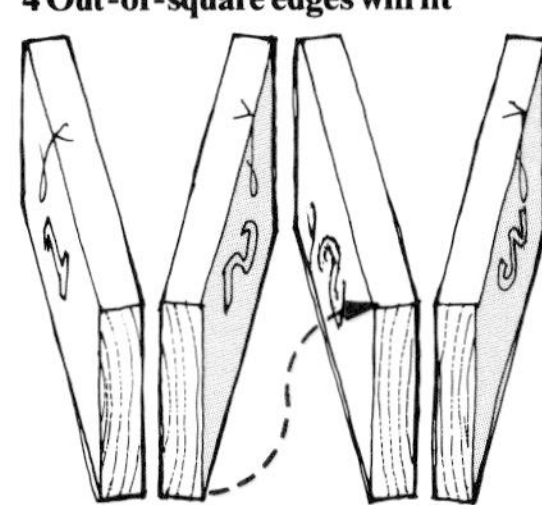

5 Rotate each board in turn

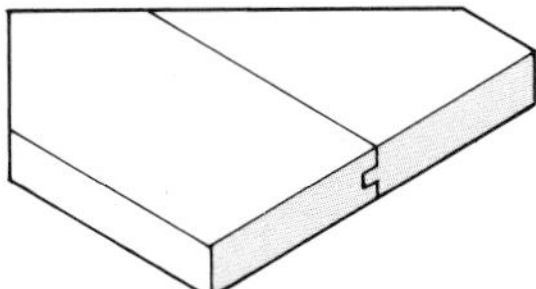

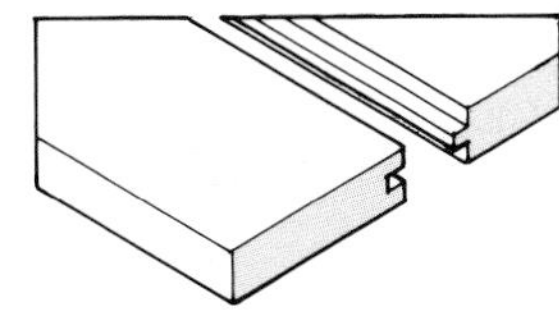

TONGUE AND GROOVE JOINTS

The best tool to use for hand-cutting a tongue and groove joint is a combination plane. Start by cutting the tongue, using a tonguing cutter.

Cutting the tongue

Set the work in the vise with the face side toward you. Adjust the plane's fence to center the tongue on the edge **(1)**. You can check this by making a light indentation, then reversing the plane with the fence against the other face. If the blade aligns with the marks, it is on center. Set the depth stop on the cutter and plane the tongue, starting at the forward end **(2)**.

Cutting the groove

To cut the groove, fit the plowing cutter that matches the width of the tongue into the plane. Sit the cutter on the edge of the tongue and adjust the fence **(3)**. Set the depth stop to produce a groove slightly deeper than the tongue. Place the board in the vise and cut the groove.

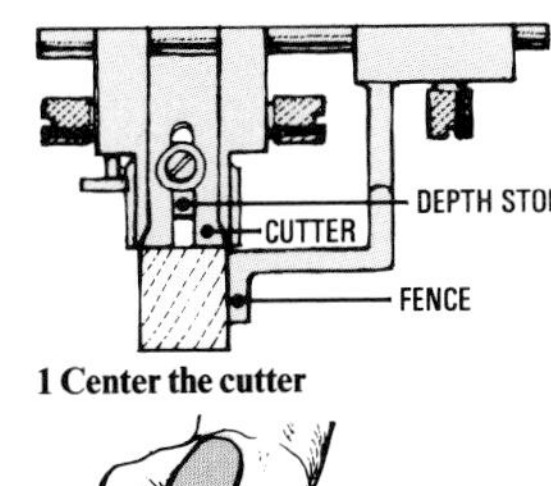

1 Center the cutter

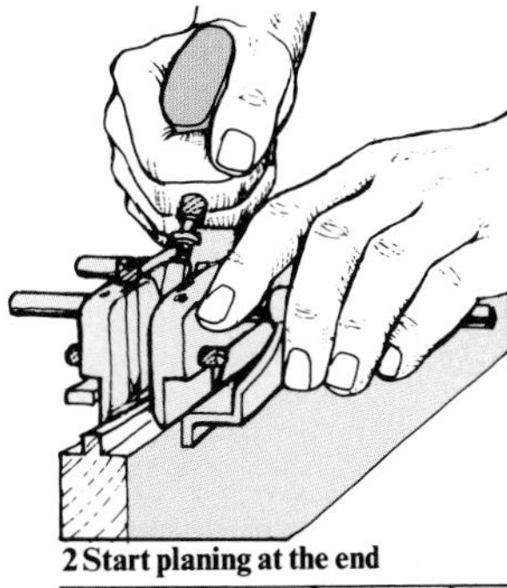

2 Start planing at the end

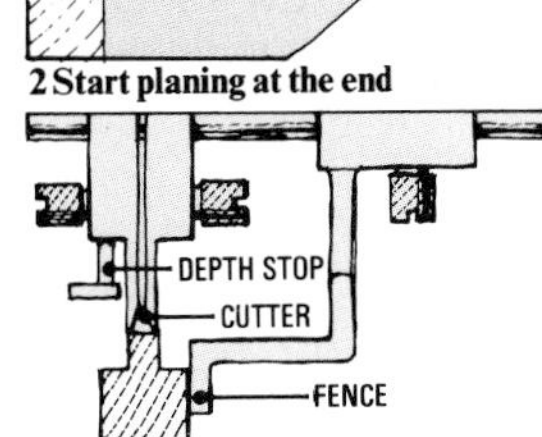

3 Adjust the plane for grooving

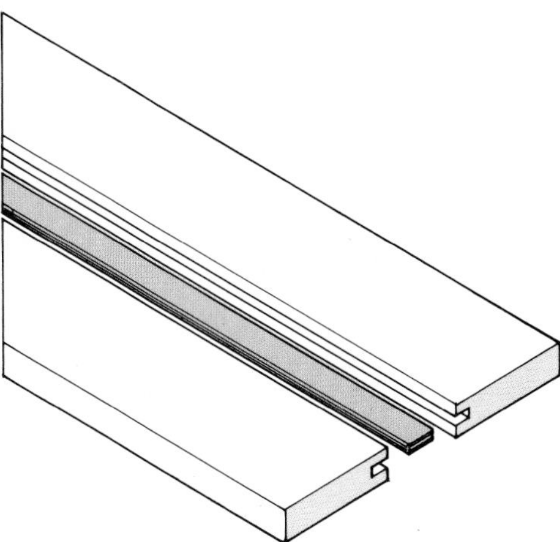

Using a loose tongue

An alternative tongue and groove joint can be made with a loose plywood tongue or spline. This is set in a groove cut in both halves of the joint. The joint can be cut with any of the grooving planes, with a table saw or router.

HOUSING JOINTS

Housings or dadoes are wide, shallow grooves cut across the grain of panels. They are used primarily in the construction of cabinet work to retain fixed shelves or dividers. Various versions of the joint can be made using hand tools or hand-held machine tools. The through housing is the most common and the simplest to make. The best type for strength is the dovetail housing, which uses mechanical strength as well as that provided by glue. Both types can be stopped so the end of the groove does not show on the front edge of the side panel.

SEE ALSO

Measuring and marking tools	76-79
Router planes	95
Forstner bit	126,189
Circular saws	135
Routers	142,146
Table saws	162
Radial-arm saws	168
Board joints	246-248

1 Mark the shelf thickness

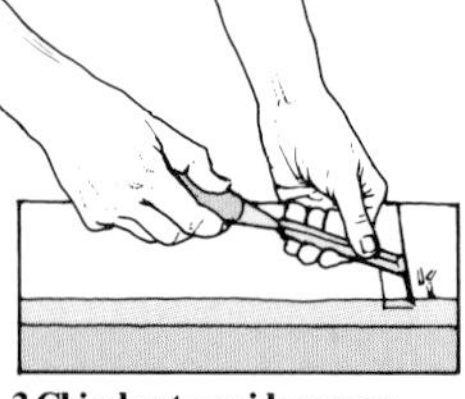

3 Chisel out a guide groove

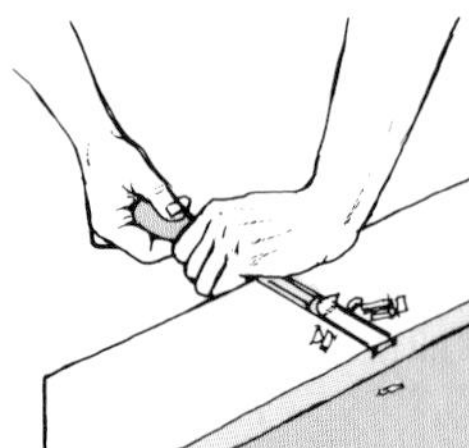

5 Chisel out the waste

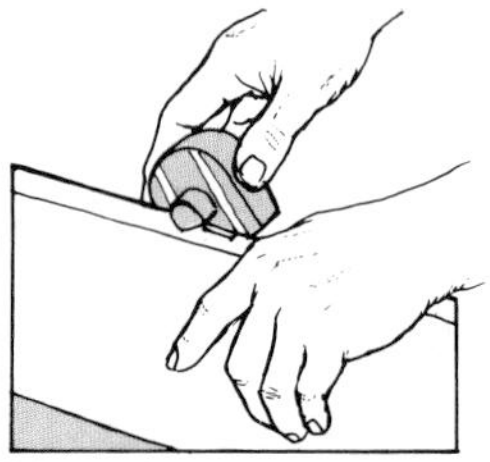

2 Gauge the housing depth

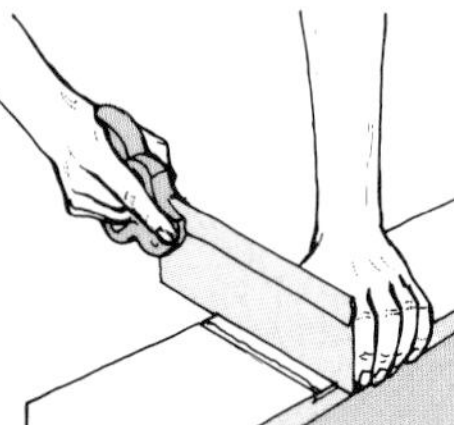

4 Saw along the line

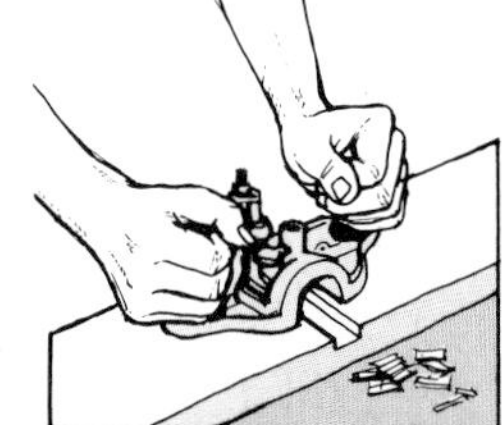

6 Router-plane the groove level

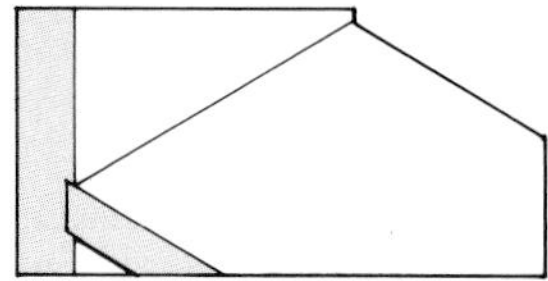

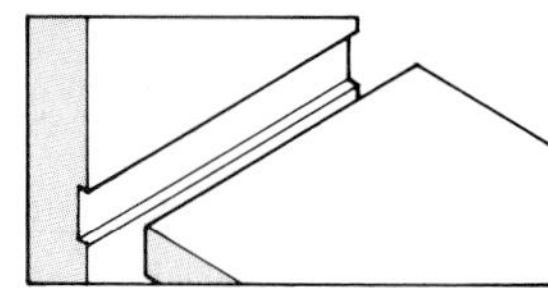

THROUGH DADO JOINT

Dadoes may be cut in manufactured board or in panels made from edge-to-edge joined solid-wood boards. Prepare the surfaces and edges, and select and mark the face side and edge. If manufactured boards are to be veneered, apply lippings and veneers before cutting the joints.

Marking out the joint
Measure and mark the bottom line of the groove to position the joint on the inside face of the side panel. Mark the width of the groove from the thickness of the shelf member **(1)**. Using a marking knife and a large try square, scribe cutting lines across the width of the side panel and square them onto the edges. Make the edge marks not more than one-third of the thickness.

Set a marking gauge to $\frac{3}{16}$ to $\frac{1}{4}$in (5 to 6mm) or not more than one-third the thickness of the panel. Scribe a line between the marks on both edges **(2)**.

Cutting the joint
Using a wide chisel, pare out a shallow wedge-shaped groove from the waste side of the cutting line **(3)**. Use the resulting shoulder to guide a fine-toothed dovetail saw and carefully saw down to the gauged line **(4)**. If you are not confident with a saw, you can clamp a batten along the line to help guide the saw.

Remove most of the waste from a narrow panel with a chisel **(5)** and finish with a hand router plane to level the groove **(6)**. Work from both edges toward the center in order to prevent edge break-out. For wide panels, use the router plane to remove all the waste. Do not try to remove the full depth of the groove in one cut. Make several passes, resetting the cutter until the full depth is reached.

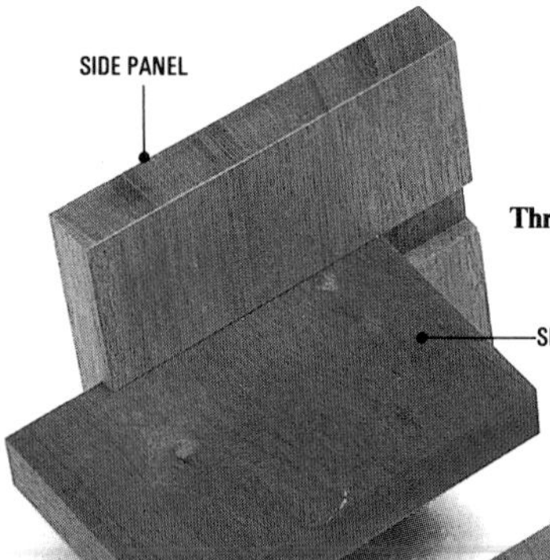

SIDE PANEL

SHELF MEMBER

Through dado joint

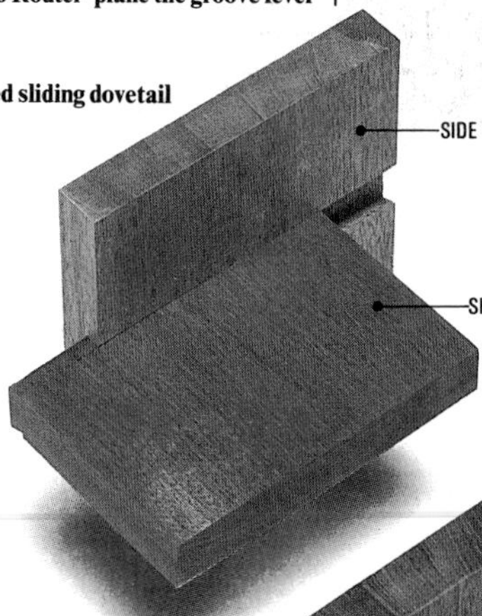

SIDE PANEL

SHELF MEMBER

Single-sided sliding dovetail

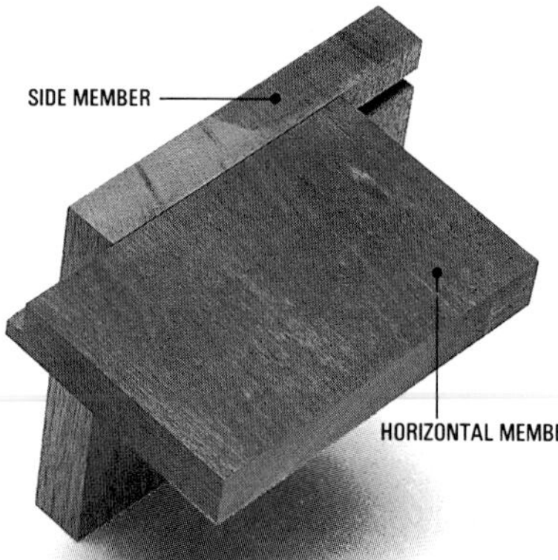

SIDE MEMBER

HORIZONTAL MEMBER

Barefaced housing joint (corner)

SIDE PANEL

SHELF MEMBER

Stopped dado joint

SIDE PANEL

SHELF MEMBER

Stopped dovetail housing

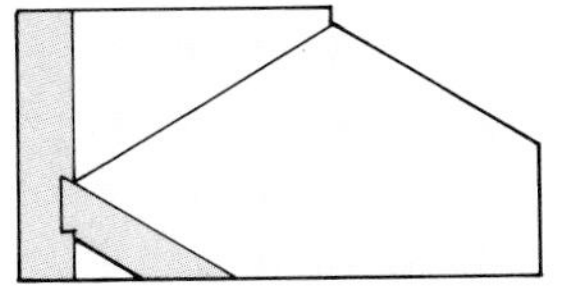

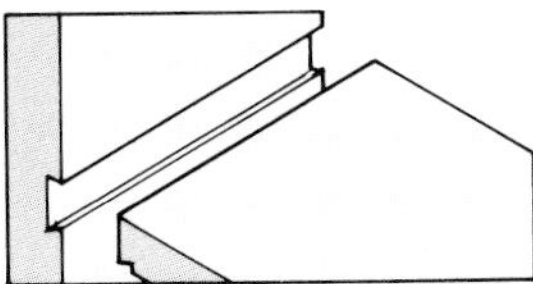

DOVETAIL SLIDING JOINTS

The dovetail housing may be made with one or both sides of the groove cut at an angle. The single-sided version is easier for hand-cutting. The double-sided type lends itself to machine-cutting. It takes accurate cutting, as the tail piece has to slide into the housing from one end.

Single-sided sliding dovetail
Set a marking gauge to one-third of the thickness of the side panel and scribe a shoulder line on the underside of the shelf end **(1)**. Square the line onto the edges. Make a mark on both edges $\frac{1}{8}$in (3mm) in from the underside face. Mark the slope of the dovetail from the end corner to this mark **(2)**. Saw along the shoulder line to the bottom of the slope. Pare out the waste. Use a homemade guide block if you need to cut a number of joints **(3)**.

Mark the width and position of the shelf on the side panel with a pencil. Square the lines onto the edges. Gauge the housing depth on the edges. Mark the dovetail outline on the edge of the side panel, using the shelf as a guide. Saw along the line at the marked angle. Use a guide block if required to help maintain the angle **(4)**. Remove the waste with a bevel-edged chisel and then a router plane.

Stopped dovetail housing
Follow the instructions as outlined for the standard stopped housing, but use the dovetail procedure.

Cut both sides of the housing and shelf end at an angle for a double-sided sliding dovetail.

1 Mark the shelf underside

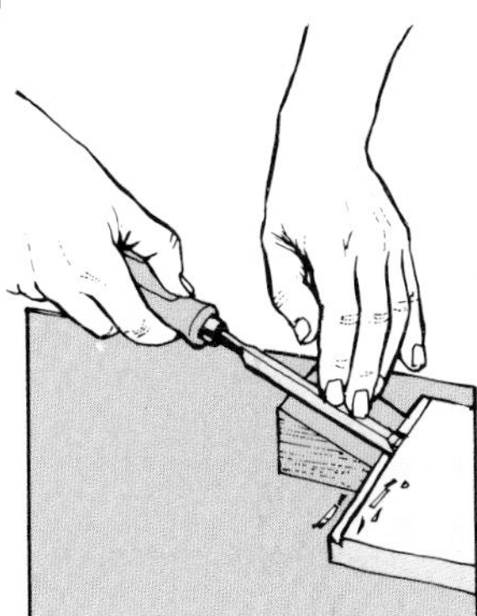

3 Pare the dovetail angle

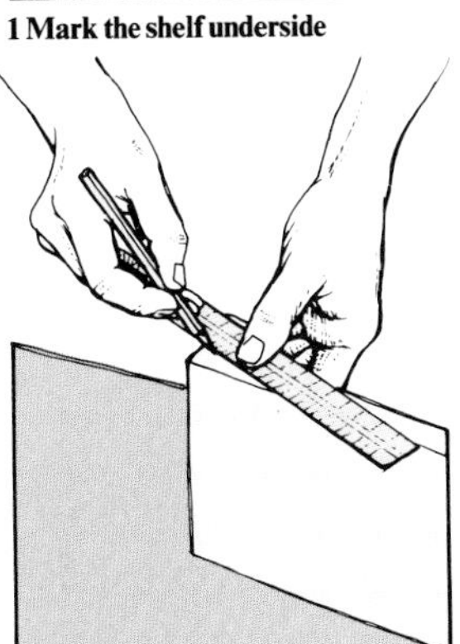

2 Mark the dovetail slope

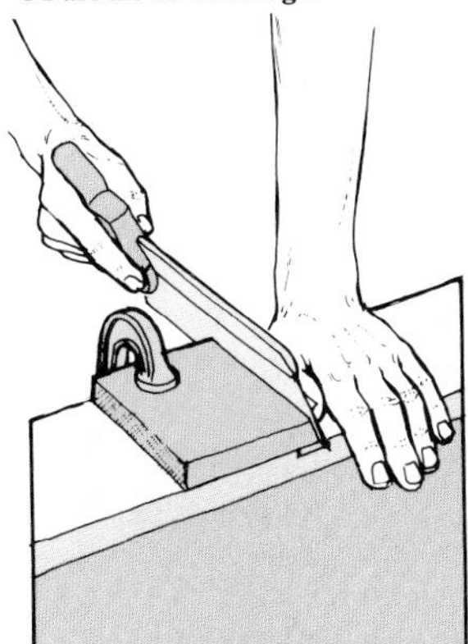

4 Use a guide when sawing

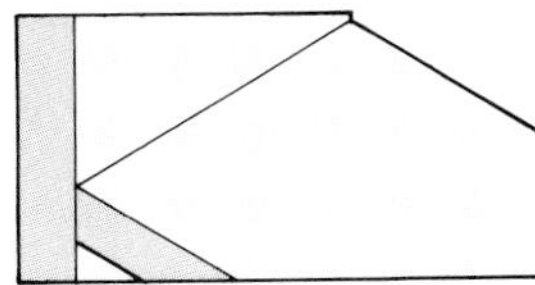

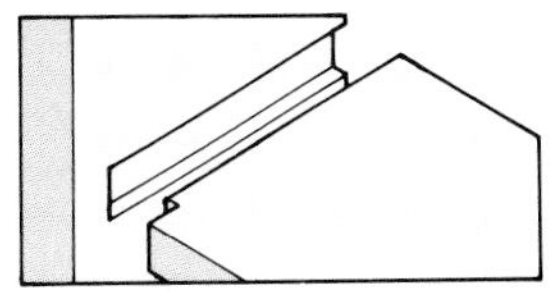

STOPPED DADO JOINT

The housing of a stopped (or blind) dado ends some $\frac{3}{8}$ to $\frac{1}{2}$in (9 to 12mm) short of the shelf width. (The end of the shelf is notched by a corresponding amount.) The front edge of the shelf may finish flush with the front edge of the side panel or be set back from it.

Marking out the joint
Mark the width of the groove, as described for the through dado, to match the depth of the shelf. Set a marking gauge to the depth of the groove and mark the back edge of the side panel. With the same setting, gauge a line around the front edge of the shelf. Cut the notch with a saw **(1)**. Mark the length of the groove from the end of the shelf **(2)**.

Cutting the joint
To cut the groove, first chop a cutout or drill a line of overlapping holes at the stopped end to the required depth. Use a Forstner bit where possible, as it has a short center point. Trim the waste from the holes **(3)**. Saw along the scribed lines toward the cutout and remove the waste with a router plane.

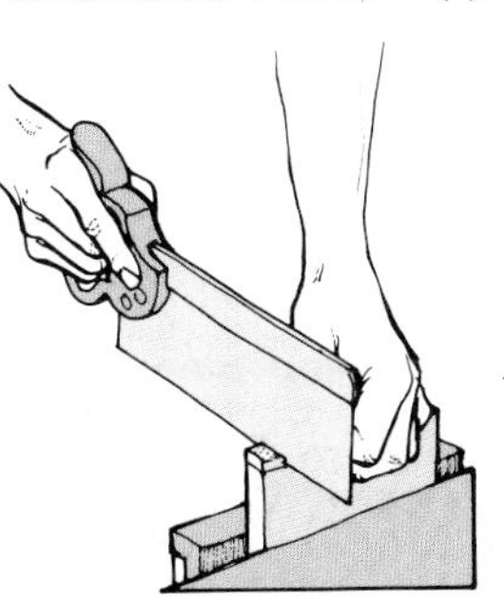

1 Cut the notch

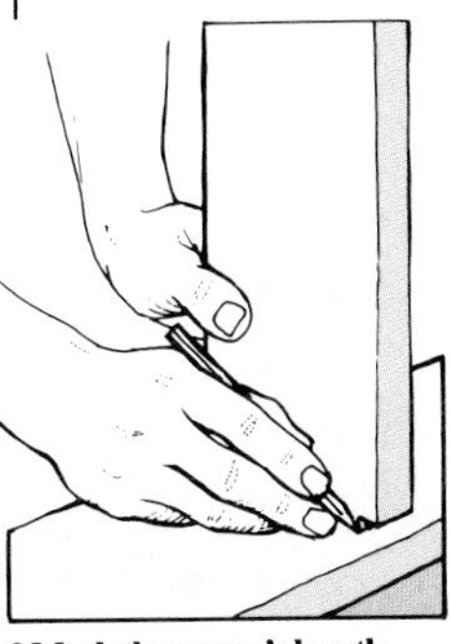

2 Mark the groove's length

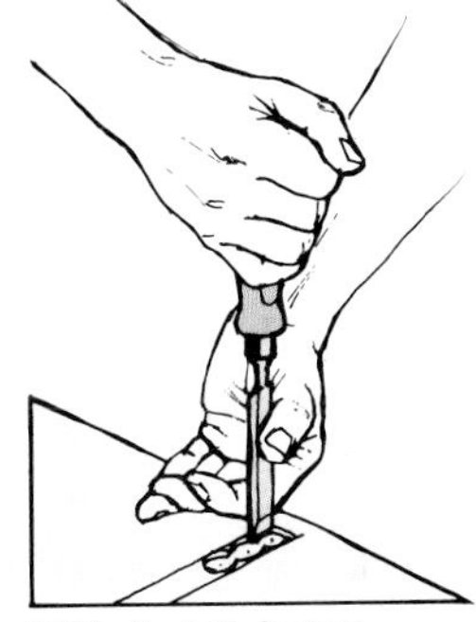

3 Trim the drilled cutout

BAREFACED HOUSING JOINT

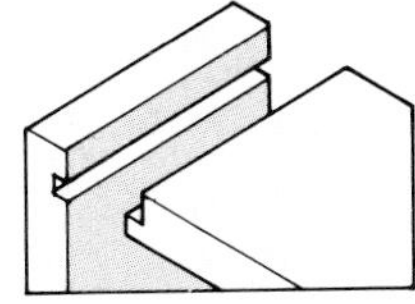

The barefaced housing, often referred to as a rabbet-and-dado joint, is stronger than the standard dado joint and can be used as a corner joint. The shoulder formed by the rabbet on the shelf member means the groove depth is less critical and removal of wood when cleaning up the surfaces does not result in a loose joint.

Marking out the joint
To make a barefaced joint at a corner, first mark the thickness of the horizontal member on the inside face of the side member, then square this line across the face and onto the edges.

Set your marking gauge to not more than one-third of the thickness of the side member. Mark the rabbet shoulder line on the face side and edges of the horizontal member **(1)**. Then gauge the width of the tongue across the end of the horizontal member and onto the edges to meet the first gauge lines, working from the inside face **(2)**. Saw the waste from the rabbet, and use a shoulder plane to clean up if required.

Align the inside face of the horizontal member on the line marked on the side member. Mark the width of the housing from the tongue and square a line across the face and onto the edges. Gauge the depth of the housing on the edges, and then cut the housing as described (see facing page).

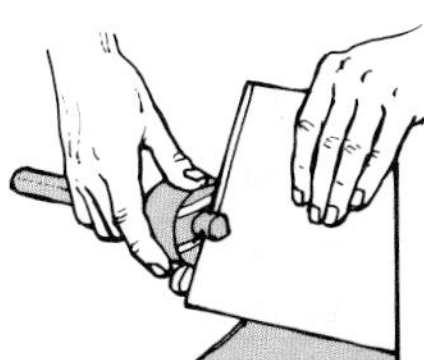

1 Mark the rabbet shoulder

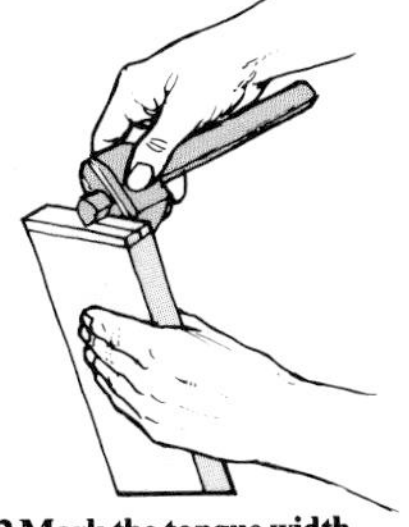

2 Mark the tongue width

MORTISE & TENON JOINTS

The mortise and tenon joint has a long tradition in the construction of wooden frames. One member slots into another to provide a strong mechanical joint that was used to full advantage in traditional timber-framed buildings. It is now rarely used in building construction, where economics dictate a lower specification. The joint has been refined by joiners and furnituremakers over the centuries, and various forms have been developed. The mortise and tenon joint has a large gluing area and is widely used for tables and chairs, where maximum strength is an important consideration.

PROPORTION OF MORTISE TO TENON

The proportion of the mortise and its corresponding tenon is important to the strength of the joint. The form of the joint is largely determined by the section of the tenoned member.

In most instances, the tenoned member is a rectangular-sectioned rail with its width set in the vertical plane. Sometimes the rail is used with its width set in the horizontal plane. In any event, the sides or cheeks of the tenon are cut in the vertical plane to give the maximum long grain for gluing to the mortise sides (below). For rails set horizontally, two or more tenons may be required, as the thickness of the tenon should not exceed its width.

The thickness of a tenon is usually one-third the thickness of the wood where two members of equal thickness are being joined. Its precise thickness is actually taken from the chisel used for cutting the mortise. A thin tenon is relatively weak in "shear," and a wide mortise will produce thin sides that could split out under twisting forces.

Where a tenoned member is joined into a thicker member than itself, the tenon may be as much as half the thickness.

The width of the tenon is usually the full width of the rail. Where this would be excessively wide, as with a rail in a large paneled door, the tenon is divided into two and is known as a double mortise and tenon.

The length of the tenon is mainly determined by the design of the joint. The tenon for a through mortise will match the width of the mortised member. For a stopped (or "stub") mortise and tenon, the length is usually about three-quarters of the width of the mortised member.

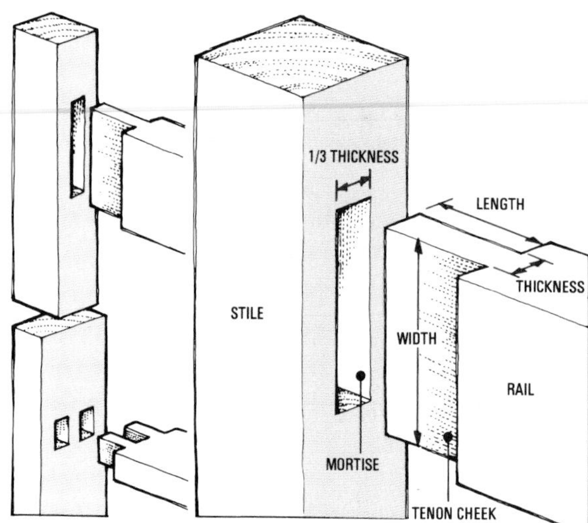

Tenons
Tenons are cut with their sides or cheeks following the grain of the mortised stile or leg.

THROUGH MORTISE AND TENON JOINT

The through mortise and tenon is widely used for frame construction. The end grain of the tenon shows on the edge of the frame stiles. The joint needs accurate cutting for good appearance. Wedges can be used to provide extra strength, and as a decorative detail if made of contrasting wood.

Marking out the joint
Cut the tenon member to length; a little waste can be left to be planed off after gluing up. If the work requires tenons at each end, set out the distance between the shoulders of the tenons precisely. Square the shoulder lines all around with a marking knife **(1)**.

Mark the position of the mortise on the edge of the mortise member; then the width of the mortise, using the tenon member as a guide **(2)**. Square the lines all around using a pencil.

Select a mortise chisel, remembering the mortise should be approximately one-third the thickness of the wood. Set the pins of a mortise gauge to the width of the chisel. Now set the stock of the gauge to center the mortise on the edge of the wood. The gauge should be set and worked from the face side. Scribe the gauge lines between the width marks on both edges **(3)**. Mark the tenon with the gauge at the same setting. Working from the face side, scribe the lines from the shoulder line on one edge, over the end and back down to the shoulder line on the other edge **(4)**. If the tenon member is thinner than the mortise member reset the stock of the gauge only.

Cutting the mortise
Always cut the mortise before the tenon. It is easier to adjust the tenon to the mortise, if required. Clamp the work to the bench. It is a good idea to place a piece of scrap wood under it to protect the bench.

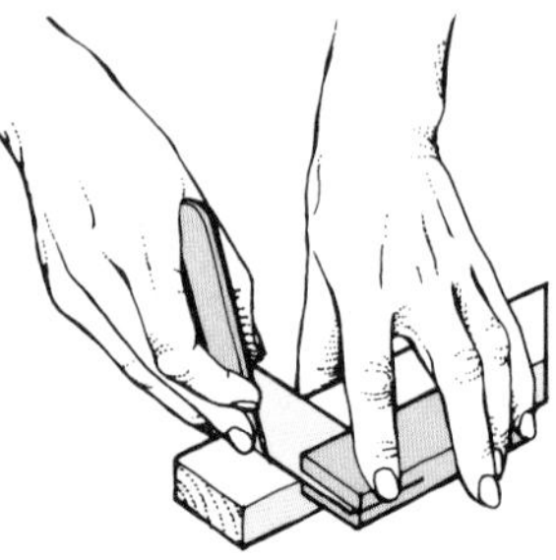

1 Square the shoulder lines

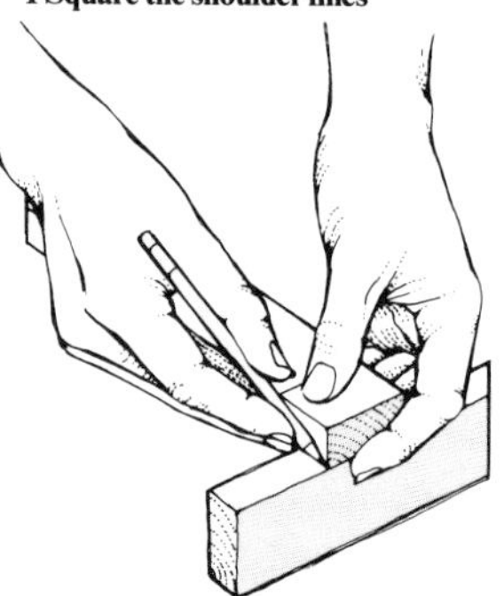

2 Mark the mortise width

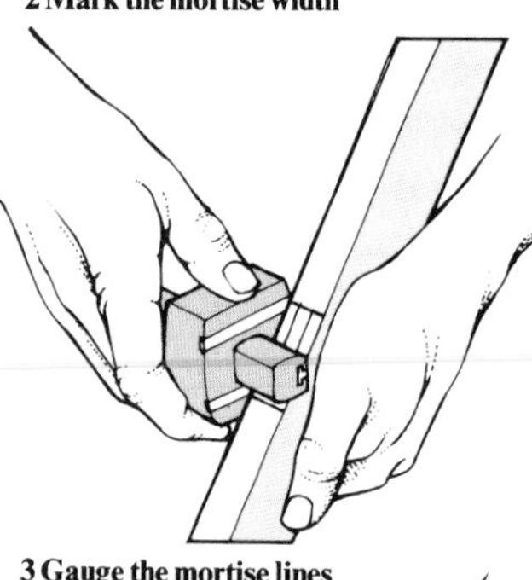

3 Gauge the mortise lines

4 Gauge the tenon lines

Position yourself in line with the work to enable you to check that the mortise chisel is held upright. Start in the middle, with the bevel facing away from you **(5)**. Drive the chisel with a mallet to a depth of about $\frac{1}{8}$in (3mm). Work backward in approximately $\frac{1}{8}$in (3mm) steps and stop $\frac{1}{16}$ to $\frac{1}{8}$in (2 to 3mm) from the end. This is to provide waste for the chisel to lever against when cleaning out the chips. Turn the chisel around and work toward the other end. Remove the chopped waste by levering it from both ends using the chisel bevel-side down **(6)**.

To prevent splitting out the underside, cut halfway through the work only. Cut the remaining waste from the ends with the chisel held vertically, bevel-side in **(7)**. Turn the wood over. Shake out any loose chips and clear the surface before clamping it down, as trapped pieces can bruise the face. Chop out the waste in the same way to meet the first cutout.

Drilling the mortise

As an alternative to chopping out the waste, a mortise can be cut using a drill. The chisel is used to finish the cutout squarely.

Use a drill press or hand power drill in a drill stand. This will give better control and greater accuracy than trying to drill freehand.

Choose a drill bit that matches or is close to the thickness of the mortise. Clamp a fence to the drill-press table, and set it to center the drill on the mortise.

Adjust the depth setting to drill halfway through the wood. Drill a hole at each end of the mortise **(1)**, then drill a series of slightly overlapping holes between them **(2)**. Turn the wood over and, with the same face against the fence, drill through the other side.

Place the work on some scrap wood and clamp it to the bench. Clean out the waste and cut the ends square with a mortise chisel.

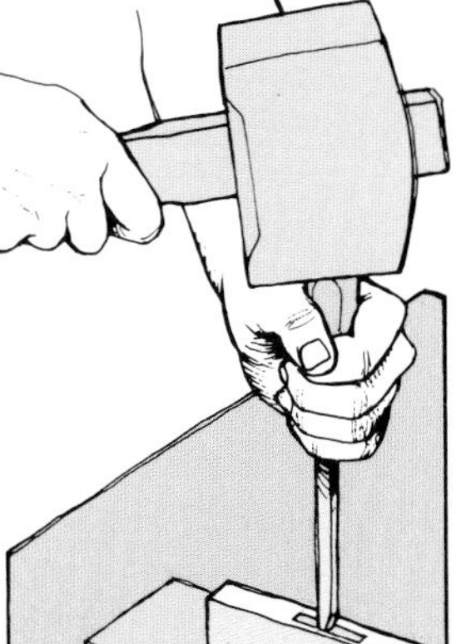

5 Start the cut in the middle

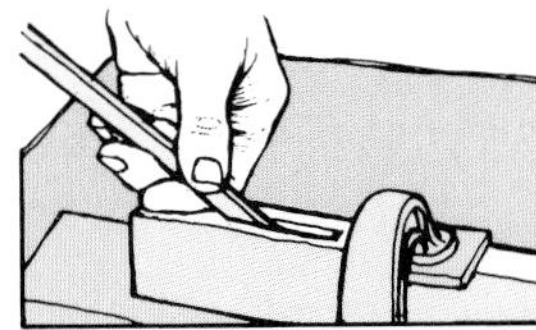

6 Lever out the waste

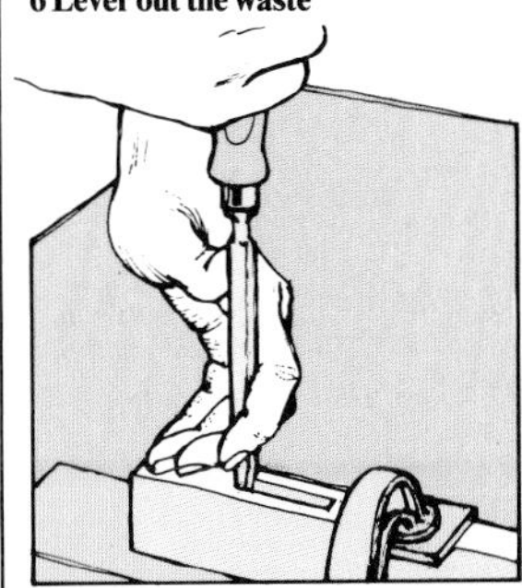

7 Trim the ends square

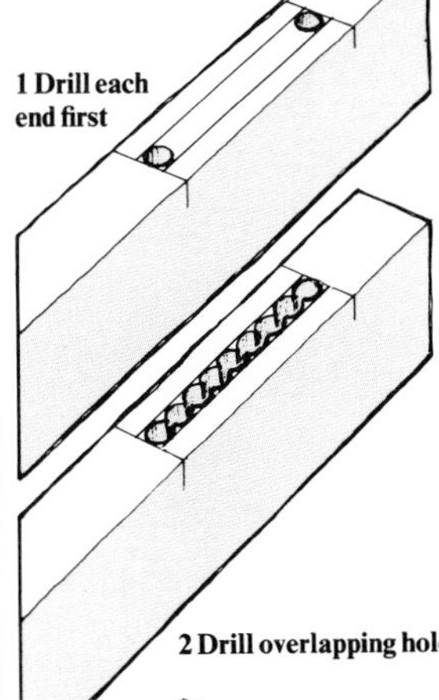

1 Drill each end first

2 Drill overlapping holes

Cutting the tenon

Set the work in a vise at an angle, with the end facing away from you. Using a tenon saw, cut down the waste side of each line, keeping the cutting edge parallel to the bench **(1)**. Stop on the shoulder line, taking care not to overrun.

Reset the work in the vise so it faces you and cut down the other tenon line **(2)**. Then place the work upright in the vise and saw down level with the shoulder **(3)**.

Hold the work on a bench hook and saw along the shoulder line to remove the waste. The tenon should fit the mortise straight from the saw. If it is too tight, pare the cheeks of the tenon with a chisel. Take care to keep the tenon symmetrical.

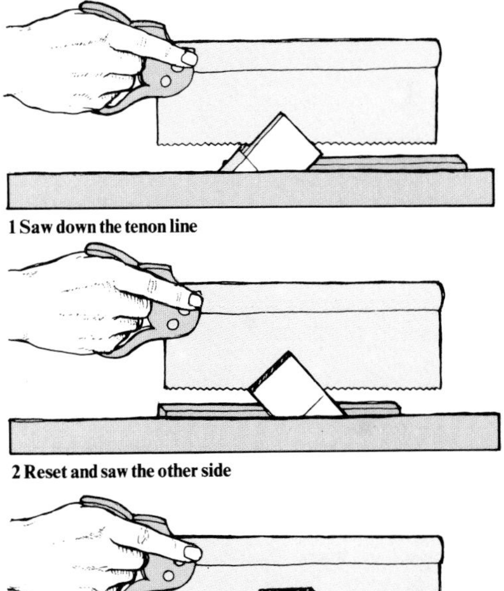

1 Saw down the tenon line

2 Reset and saw the other side

3 Finish level with shoulder

WEDGED THROUGH MORTISE AND TENON JOINT

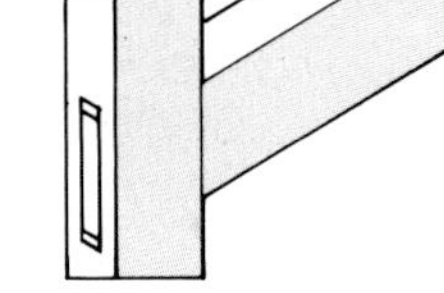

A mortise and tenon joint is strong by virtue of the relatively large gluing area. Mechanical strength can be improved by fitting wedges. A standard through mortise and tenon can be fitted with a pair of wedges in two ways. They can be fitted at the ends or set in sawcuts within the tenon.

Fitting the wedges

Working from the outside edge, cut a shallow taper at each end of the mortise. Cut the wedges from the tenon waste to be slightly steeper than the taper. Make two sawcuts across the tenon about the thickness of the tenon from each edge, if using the inset method. Drill a hole at the end of the sawcut to prevent splitting.

When the joint is glued up, apply glue to the wedges and drive them in alternately to keep them level. Once they have set, trim and plane the ends flush.

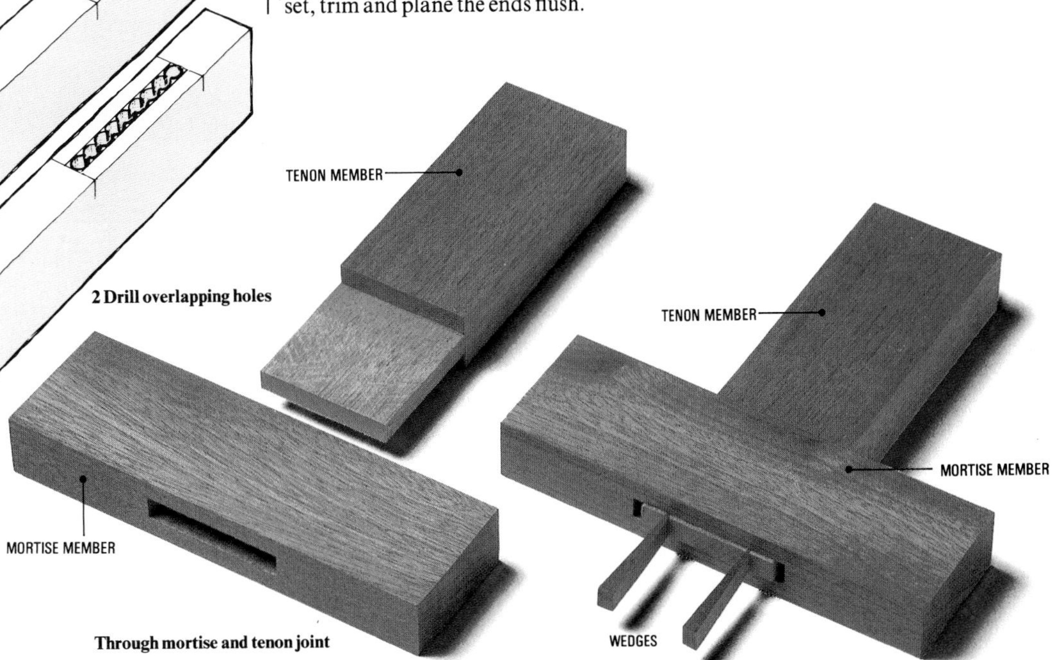

Through mortise and tenon joint

Wedged mortise and tenon joint

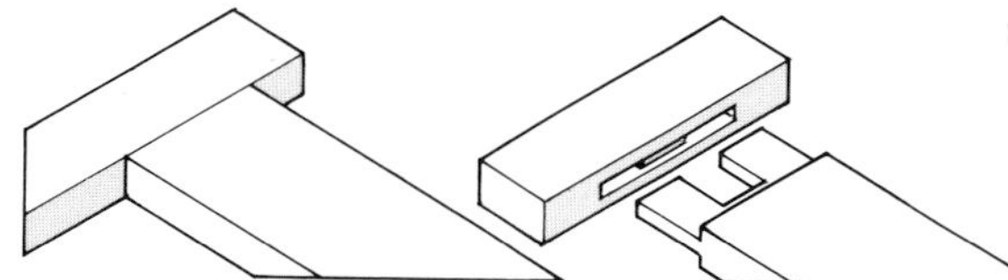

DOUBLE MORTISE AND TENON JOINT

The double mortise and tenon is used for frames that have wide rails where the width of the mortise needed to take a single tenon would weaken the stile. The center rail of a paneled door is usually joined in this way. The joint described here is for a through double mortise and tenon in a square-edged stile and rail.

SEE ALSO	
Chair joints	52
Cabinet construction	64,66,69,70
Measuring and marking tools	76-79
Mortise gauges	78-79
Coping saw	84
Mortise chisels	100,101
Mortisers	186-187

Marking out the joint
Start by measuring and marking the tenon shoulders on the rail. Scribe the lines all around with a marking knife and try square. Lay the rail on the edge of the stile and mark its width and position, then square the marks all around the stile with a pencil.

Set the pins of a mortise gauge to the width of a mortise chisel that is approximately one-third the thickness of the stile. Set the stock of the gauge to center the pins on the edge. Mark the gauge lines between the width marks on both edges of the stile, but use only light pressure on the outside edge, and mark the end of the tenon member with the gauge at the same setting.

The joint has two in-line tenons separated by a gap. In order not to weaken the rail, a haunch is left between them to give support to the tenon shoulder. The width of the tenons and the corresponding mortises will be determined to some degree by the width of the rail. As a guide, make the width of each tenon not less than four times its thickness. If this leaves a gap between them more than one-third the width of the rail, increase the width of the tenons.

Set a marking gauge to the required dimension and, working from each edge in turn, mark the width of the tenons. Run the lines across the end and down both faces to meet the shoulder line.

Mark the length of the haunch, which is equal to the thickness of the tenon, across one edge. Square the line down both faces. Mark the waste as shown **(1)** in order to visualize the shape of the tenons.

Lay the rail in position on the mortise member and mark off the tenons **(2)**. Square the marks all around and mark the mortise waste.

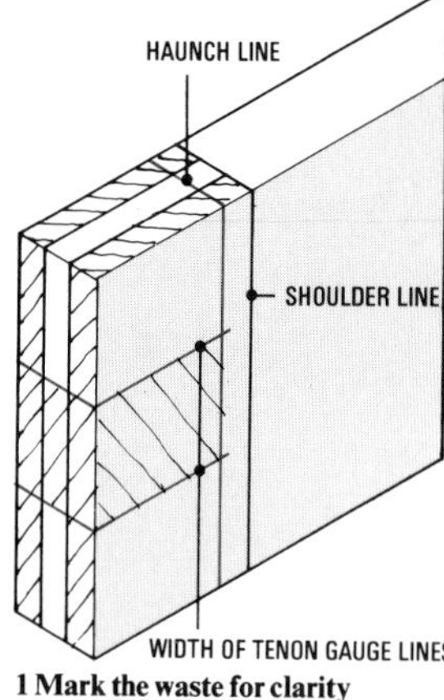

1 Mark the waste for clarity

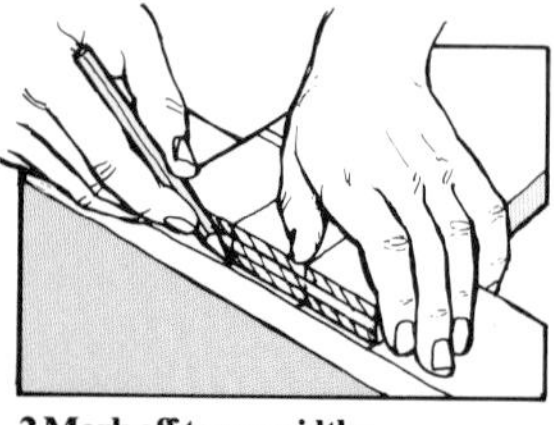

2 Mark off tenon widths

3 Saw haunch waste

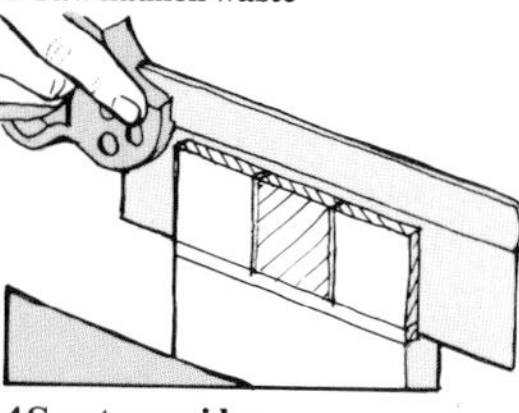

4 Saw tenon sides

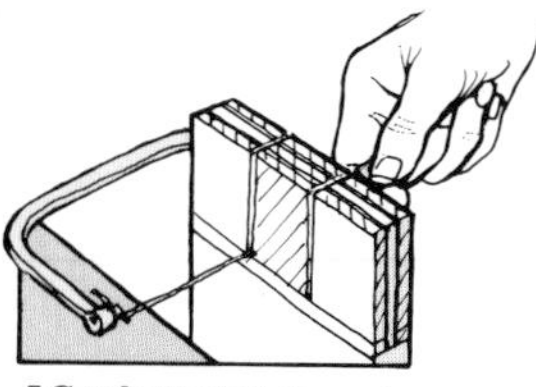

5 Cut the waste between tenons

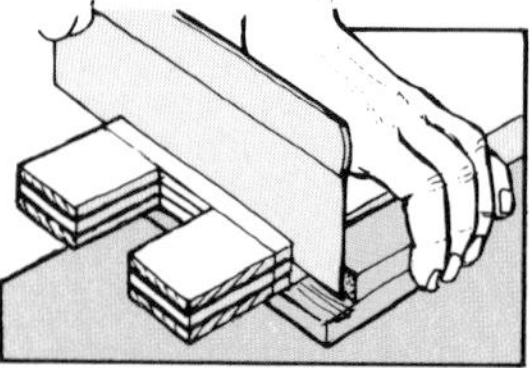

6 Saw along the shoulder line

Cutting the joint
Chop out each mortise as previously described for a through mortise and tenon. If there is sufficient clearance, run a tenon saw down the gauge lines on the inside edge to remove the waste from the haunch cutout **(3)**. Pare out the waste to the depth of the haunch. If sawing first proves difficult, then chop out the waste in the usual way.

Set the tenon member in a vise and cut the tenons by first sawing down the inside edges of each and stop on the haunch line. Next, saw the sides of the tenon, finishing level with the shoulder line **(4)**. Now cut the waste from between the tenons using a coping saw **(5)**. Saw along the shoulder line to remove the remaining waste **(6)**. Glue and wedge the joint as described for a through mortise and tenon joint.

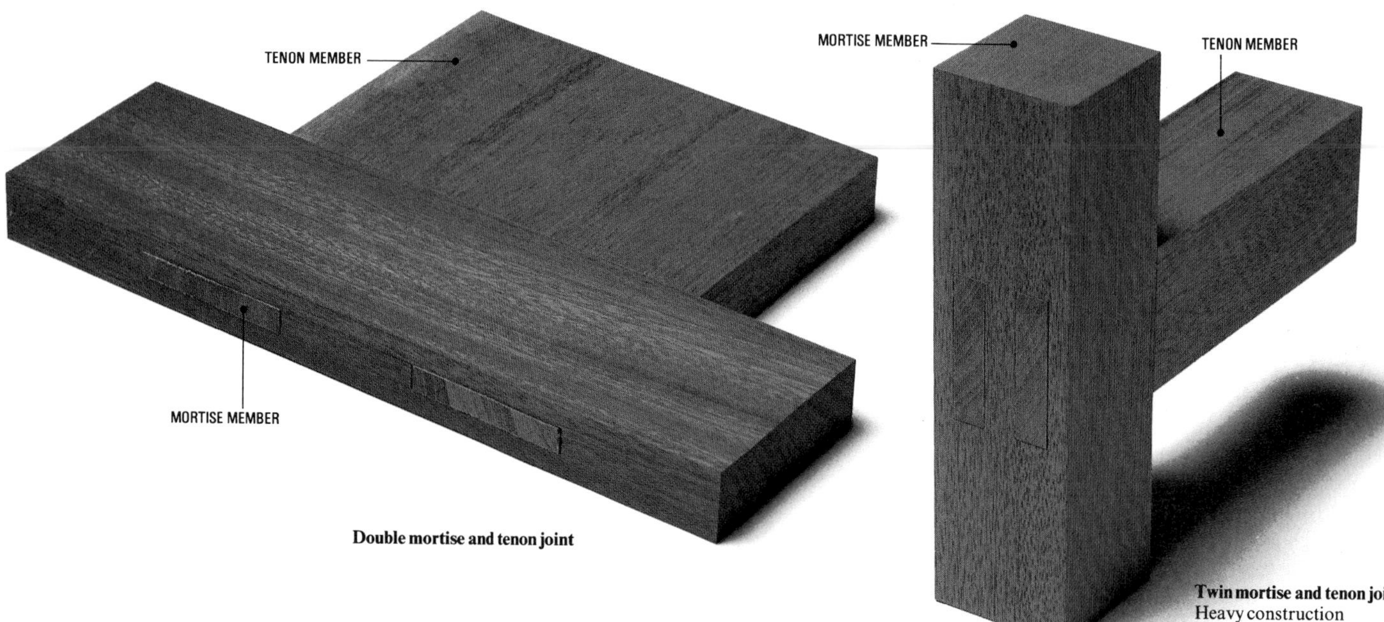

Double mortise and tenon joint

Twin mortise and tenon joint
Heavy construction

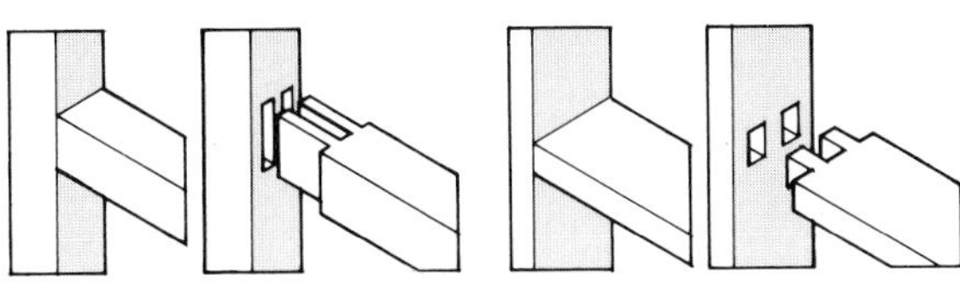

TWIN MORTISE AND TENON JOINT

Twin mortise and tenon joints, like the double version, give maximum strength, but are used where the mortise is cut into the face rather than in the edge of the mortise member. The proportion of the joint will depend on whether it is for a heavy frame or a lighter construction, such as a drawer rail.

Marking out the joint
Measure off and mark the shoulder line all around the end of the tenon member. The thickness of the tenons are marked out across its width. As a guide, make the tenon thickness and the gap between them the same.

Make a mark not less than ¼in (6mm) from each edge. Divide the distance between them into three to give the tenon thickness and provide a gap between **(1)**; in practice, you will have to adjust the tenon thickness to the width of the nearest mortise chisel. Set a mortise gauge to the width of the chisel, and its stock to the required distance from the pins. Mark the tenons, working from both edges of the tenon member **(2)**.

Lay the marked end of the tenon member in position on the mortise member and mark off its width and the tenon lines **(3)**. Square the width lines all around with a pencil. Gauge the mortise lines between them. If the mortise member is wider than the tenon member, reset the gauge stock.

Cutting the joint
Chop out each mortise as previously described for a through mortise and tenon joint. Saw down the sides of each tenon in the usual way. Saw along the shoulder lines to remove the waste from both sides. Cut out the waste between the tenons with a coping saw **(4)** and trim the shoulder square with a chisel. You can also remove the middle waste by first drilling through it at the shoulder and then sawing down the sides of the tenon. You will still need to trim the shoulder with a chisel.

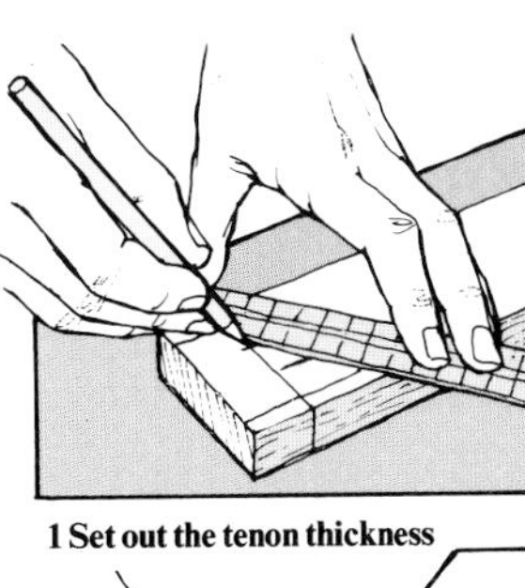

1 Set out the tenon thickness

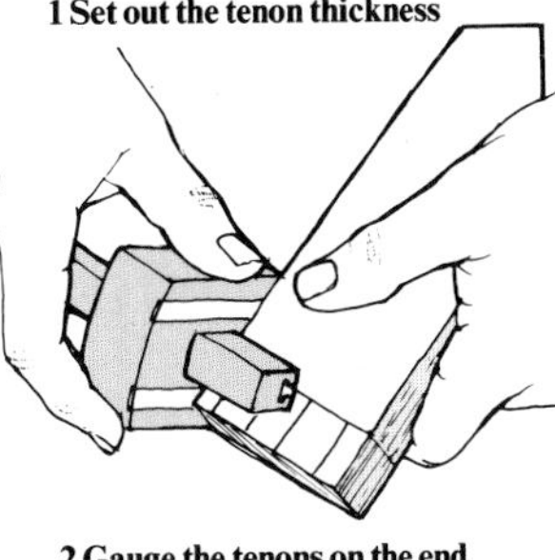

2 Gauge the tenons on the end

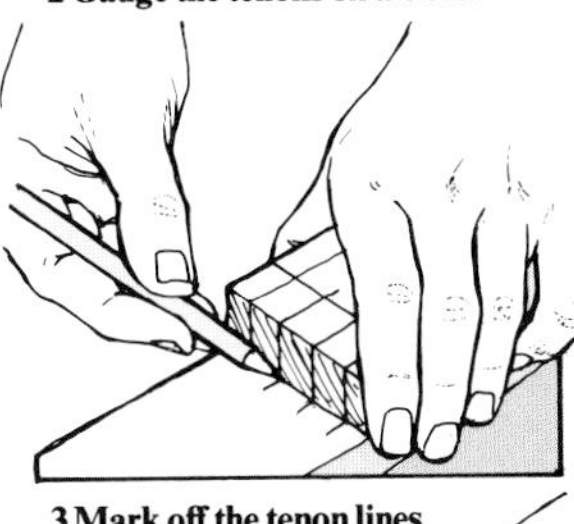

3 Mark off the tenon lines

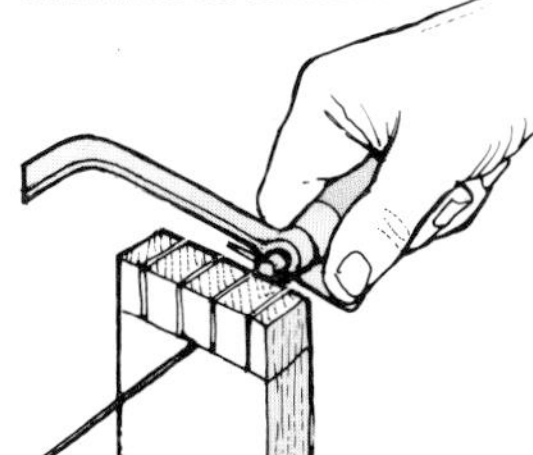

4 Cut out the waste

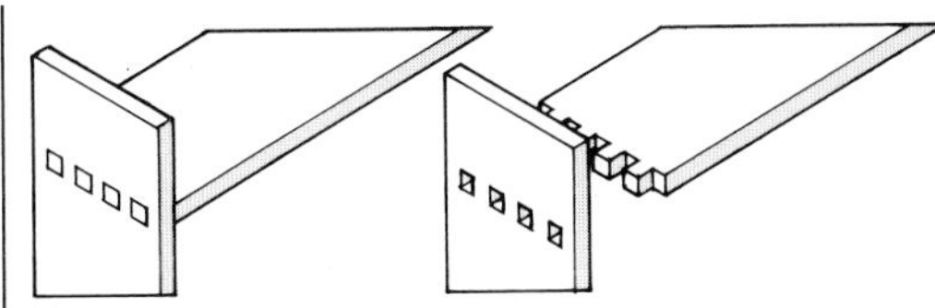

PINNED MORTISE AND TENON JOINT

The pinned mortise and tenon joint is like a multiple version of the twin tenon. It provides a strong carcase joint for vertical partitions or shelves.

Tenon pins
The tenons or pins are usually square in section and evenly spaced. They may be cut through or stopped. Through pins are often wedged with the sawcut made diagonally across the pin **(1)** or square across the grain.

Marking out and cutting the joint
Mark and cut the joint using a similar method to making the twin tenon joint. A stopped housing may also be incorporated for a neater and stronger joint **(2)**.

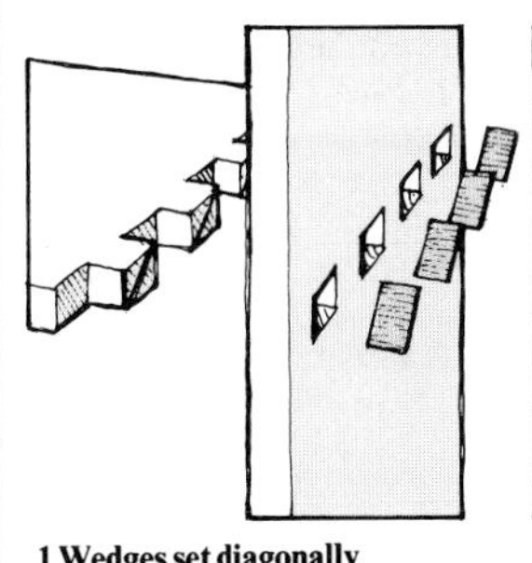

1 Wedges set diagonally

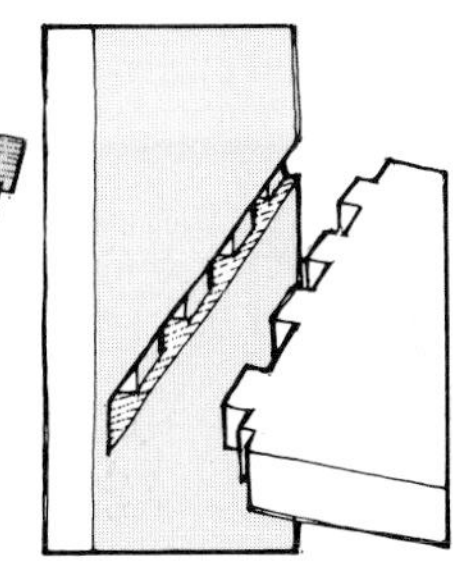

2 Stopped housing type

Twin mortise and tenon joint
Light construction

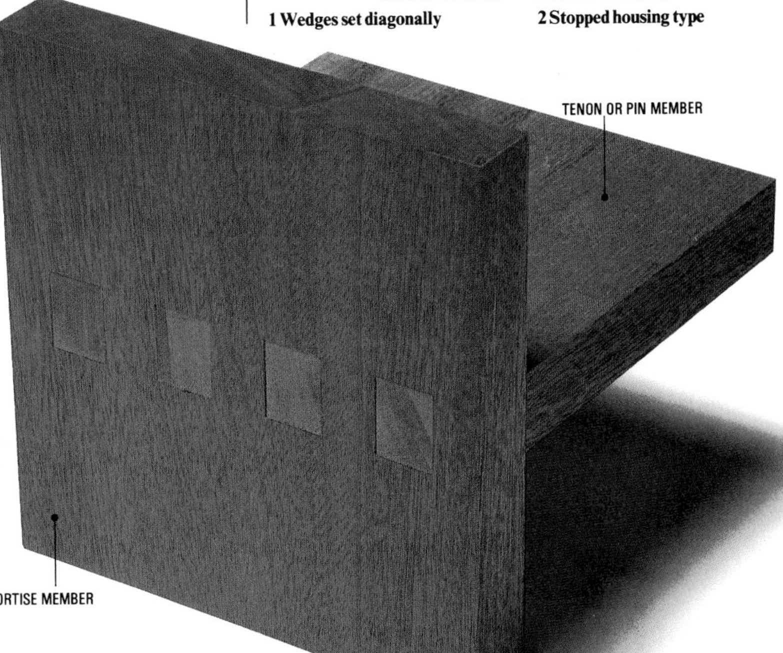

Pinned mortise and tenon joint

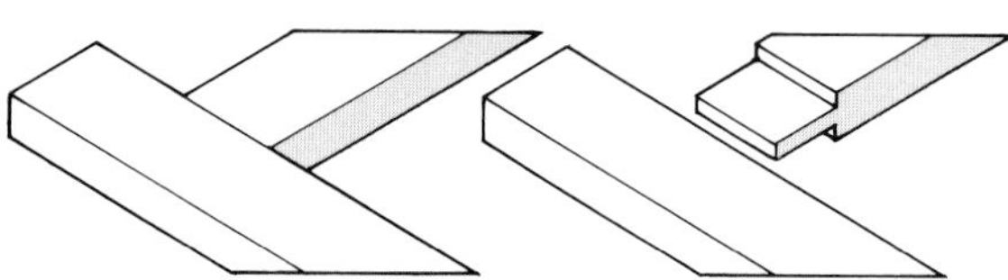

STUB OR STOPPED MORTISE AND TENON JOINT

SEE ALSO	
Chair construction	51-54
Door construction	66
Measuring and marking tools	76-79
Mortise chisels	100,101
Clamps	120,122
Mortisers	186-187
Adhesives	302-303

The stub or stopped mortise and tenon joint is made with a blind mortise so the tenon does not show on the outside face. It is commonly used in furniture construction where a high standard of finish is required. The depth of the mortise needs to be about three-quarters of the width or thickness of the mortise member in order to leave a reasonable amount of wood at the blind end. Skilled Japanese "shoji" (sliding-door) makers, however, take pride in cutting deep mortises, leaving only paper-thin wood at the end. The method described here is the typical Western technique.

Marking out the joint
Measure the width of the mortise member to calculate the depth of the mortise and the length of the tenon. The length of the tenon is about three-quarters of the wood's width **(1)**.

Using a try square and a marking knife, scribe a shoulder line all around the tenon member at the required distance from the end of the wood **(2)**.

Set a mortise gauge to the width of the chisel and adjust the stock to center the pins on the edge of the work. Scribe the tenon lines over the end and mark the waste.

Mark the position and width of the tenon member on the inside edge of the mortise member **(3)** and square the lines across, then scribe the mortise gauge lines between the squared lines.

To establish the depth of cut for the mortise, apply a band of masking tape around the blade of the chisel. Set the tape a little over the length of the tenon from the cutting edge **(4)**.

Cutting the joint
Saw the waste from the tenon as previously described. Chop out the mortise, working from one side only. Stop when the tape guide is level with the surface **(5)**. Ensure that the bottom is level.

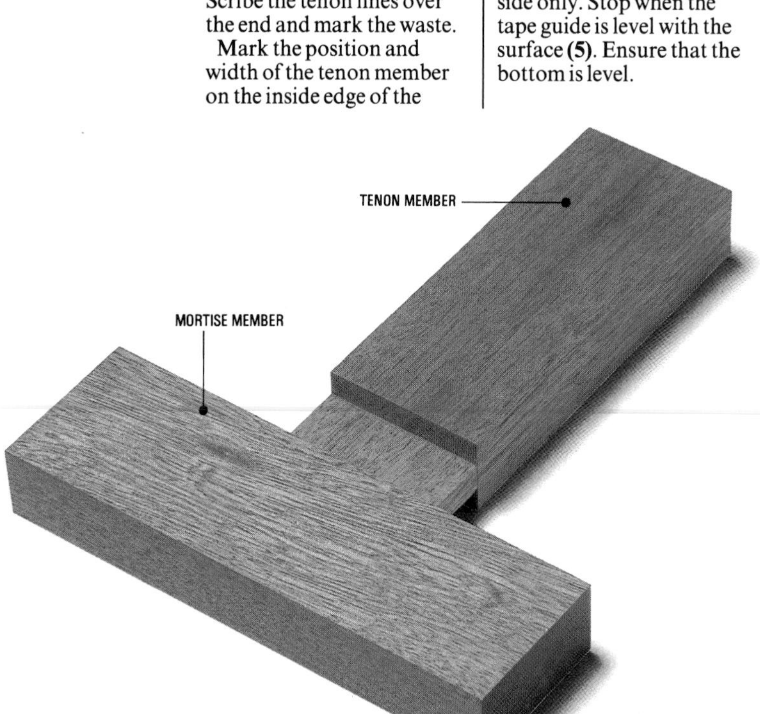

Stub or stopped mortise and tenon joint

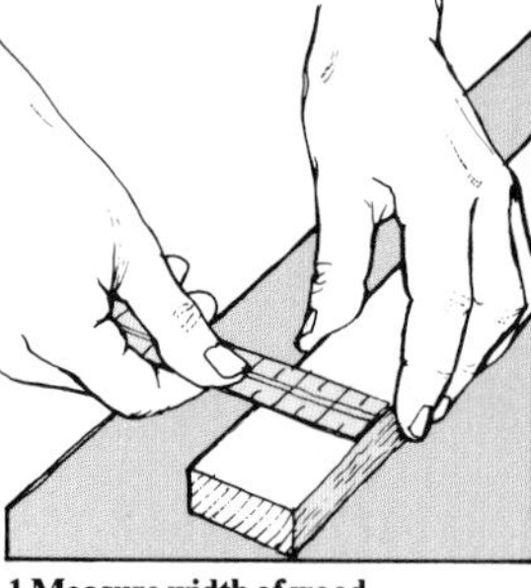
1 Measure width of wood

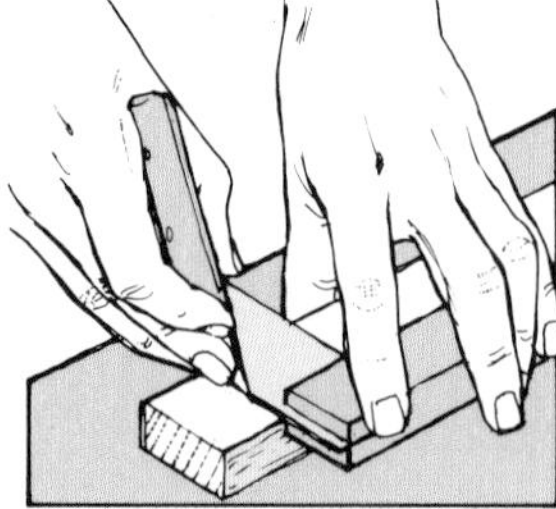
2 Mark the shoulder line

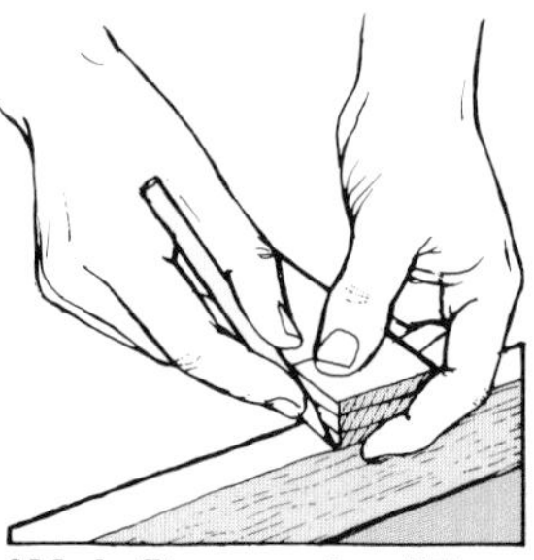
3 Mark off tenon-member width

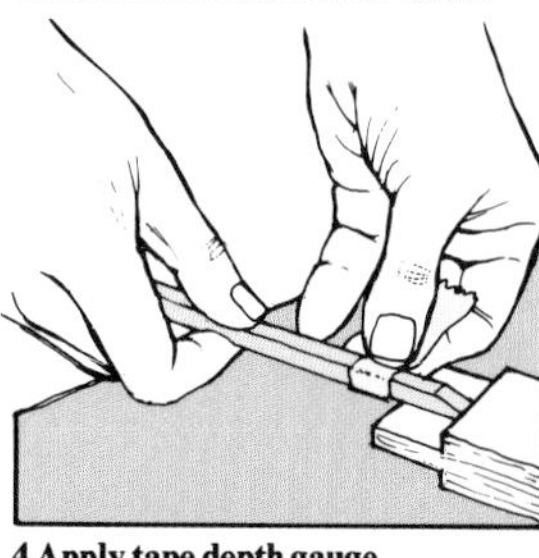
4 Apply tape depth gauge

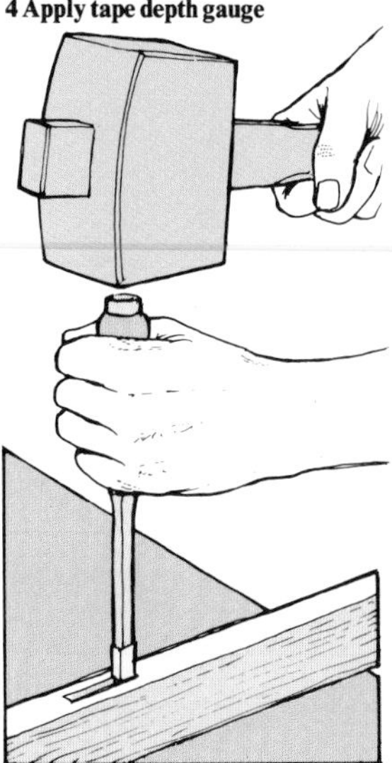
5 Chisel down to the tape

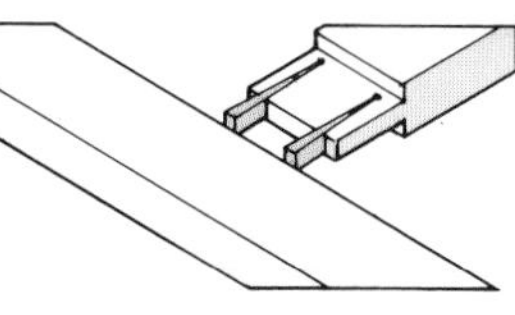

WEDGED STUB OR STOPPED MORTISE AND TENON JOINT

Stub mortise and tenon joints can be fox-wedged for additional strength. The parts must be accurately cut, as once the joint is assembled it cannot be parted for adjustment.

Fitting fox wedges
The ends of the wedges are pressed against the blind end of the mortise, which should not be less than $\frac{3}{8}$in (9mm) thick. Make two sawcuts in the tenon about $\frac{1}{4}$in (6mm) from each edge and drill a small hole at the end.

Make two wedges the same width and length as the tenon and a full $\frac{1}{8}$in (3mm) at the thickest end. Carefully chisel a tapered undercut at each end of the mortise, making the tapers no more than $\frac{1}{8}$in (3mm) at the blind end.

Apply glue to the wedges and the joint itself. Start the wedges in the sawcut and assemble the joint. Press the joint together with a clamp, using scrap-wood blocks under the clamp heads. As the wedges are driven farther into the sawcuts, they spread the tenon so that it fits tightly in the mortise.

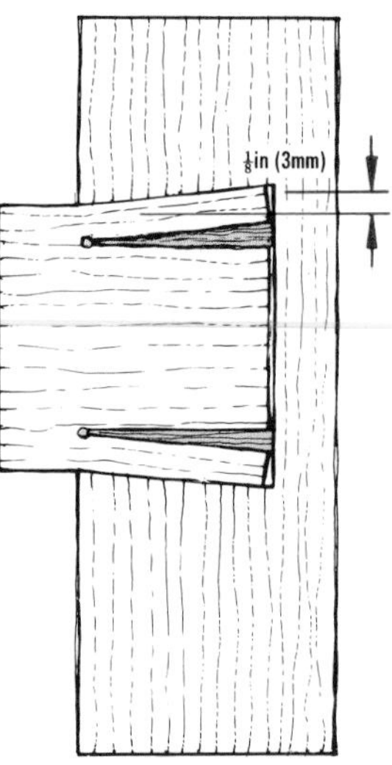

Fox wedging
The hidden wedges spread the tenon inside the mortise, locking it in place.

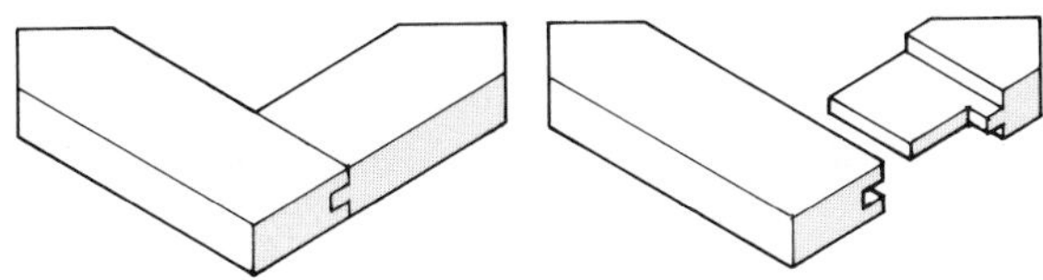

HAUNCHED MORTISE AND TENON JOINT

A mortise and tenon joint at the corner of a typical rectangular frame presents a particular problem if the outside edges are to finish flush. For the rail to be well supported, the tenon should be full width, but this would mean the mortise would be open-ended, like a bridle joint, and relatively weak. The haunch is used to overcome this problem. It allows the width of the tenon to be reduced and the mortise to be set below the end of the mortise member. The haunch can be square or sloping.

The sloping or "secret" haunch is used where appearance is important, such as for the frame of a paneled cabinet door or the joint between the seat rail and front leg of a chair. The haunched mortise and tenon is usually stopped in furniture construction and cut through in joinery work.

Marking out the joint
The proportion of the haunch in relation to the mortise and tenon is important if the joint is to perform satisfactorily. As a general guide, the width of the haunch is not more than one-third the width of the tenon, while the length of the haunch is equal to the thickness of the tenon **(1)**.

The basic method that is described here is for a stub mortise and tenon, using a square haunch between members that are of equal thickness.

First, mark the length of the tenon, normally three-quarters of the mortise member's width, from the end of the tenon member. Square the tenon shoulder line all around with a marking gauge. Set a mortise gauge to the width of your chisel and adjust the stock to center the pins on the edge of the work. Scribe the tenon lines around the end. Mark the width of the tenon with a marking gauge set to two-thirds the width of the tenon member **(2)**. Scribe the line on both faces and the end, working from the inside face edge. Mark the length of the haunch on the top edge. Square a line across the top and down the sides to meet the top line of the tenon **(3)**. Mark the waste by hatching.

Cut the mortise member to rough length, leaving about $\frac{3}{4}$in (18mm) extra wood at the end of it. The "horn," as the extra wood is known, gives support to the end of the wood while the mortise is cut. The horn is sawn off after the joint is glued and set.

Transfer the tenon-width lines to the edge of the mortise member **(4)** and square them across. Scribe the thickness of the mortise on the edge with the mortise gauge, running the lines through to the end and over onto the end grain **(5)**. Set a marking gauge to the length of the haunch and scribe a line on the end between the mortise gauge lines **(6)**. Hatch the waste wood.

Cutting the joint
Remove the waste from the mortise before cutting the haunch. If using a chisel, apply a marker tape to it to gauge the depth of the cut. Set the drill-stand depth stop if drilling out the waste.

Now make the cutout for the haunch. Set the mortise member in a vise and saw along the gauged lines to the depth mark on the end **(7)**. Cut the groove from the end, holding the chisel parallel to the work **(8)**. Take out thin slices rather than chopping out the waste in one piece, thus avoiding cutting too deeply because of uneven grain.

Cut the tenon by first sawing down the gauged sides. Set the work upright in the vise and saw down the top line of the tenon. Reset the work horizontally in the vise and saw away the corner waste following the haunch line. Finally saw along the shoulder lines to remove the remaining waste.

Try the tenon in the mortise. If the shoulder does not seat properly, then deepen the mortise or the haunch groove as appropriate. After gluing, saw off the horn flush with the edge.

Haunched mortise and tenon joint

Sloping haunch
The sloping haunch is marked out and cut in a similar way to the square haunch, but with slight changes. Use the same marking method on the tenon member, but add a line for the slope of the haunch **(1)**. Saw along this line when cutting away the corner waste.

When marking out the gauge lines on the mortise member, there is no need to carry them onto the end grain. Chisel out the slope for the haunch after chopping out the mortise **(2)**.

1 Mark the slope

2 Chisel the slope

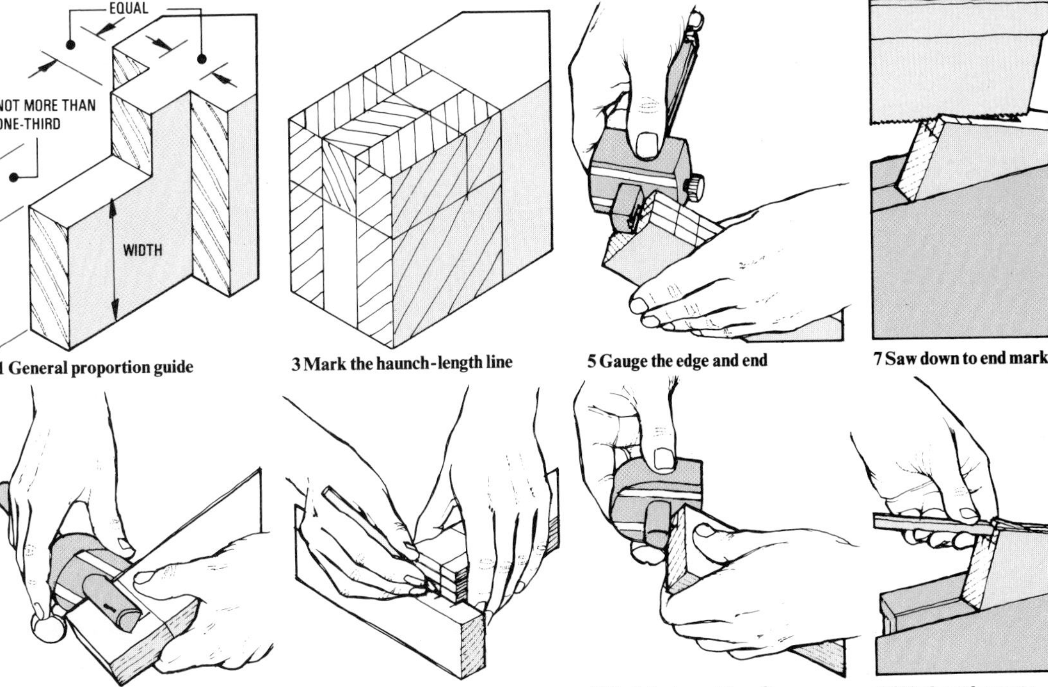

1 General proportion guide

2 Mark the tenon-width line

3 Mark the haunch-length line

4 Transfer the tenon lines

5 Gauge the edge and end

6 Mark the haunch length

7 Saw down to end mark

8 Chisel out the waste

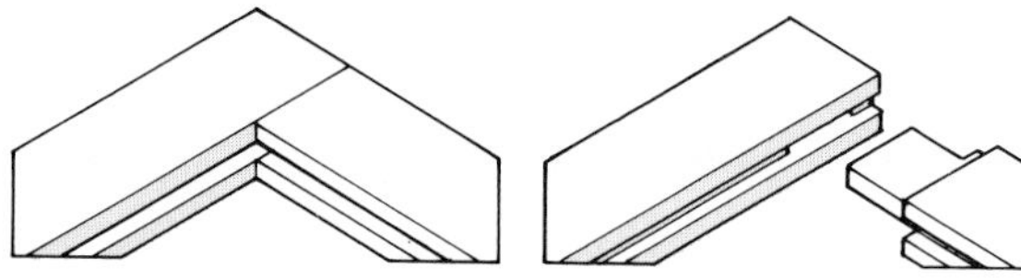

GROOVED-FRAME MORTISE AND TENON JOINT

The frame of a paneled cabinet door is usually grooved to take the panel. The square-haunched mortise and tenon serves to give support to the rail, but also fills the end of the groove in the stile. The thickness of the tenon and the corresponding mortise is made to match the width of the groove. The width of the groove is usually one-third the thickness of the frame members and is centered on the edge following the normal convention for setting out mortise and tenon joints. This may not always be the case, however, and the thickness and position of the joint may vary according to the size and position of the groove. For hand-cutting, the groove may be cut before or after the joint.

SEE ALSO

Chair construction	51
Door construction	66
Measuring and marking tools	76-79
Rabbet planes	92
Plow and combination planes	96-97
Routers	142,146

HAUNCH LINE

GROOVE-DEPTH LINE

1 Mark cutting lines

2 Mark the mortise

Marking out the joint

Set a mortise gauge to the required width of the grooving-plane's cutter and matching mortise chisel. Set the stock and scribe the groove on the inside edges of the rails and stiles. Carry the lines onto the end of the rails and stiles, and follow the procedure for marking the square-haunched mortise and tenon. In addition, set a marking gauge to the length of the haunch and use it to mark the depth of the groove on the end and sides **(1)**. This line represents the bottom edge of the tenon. Alternatively, determine the depth of the groove first and mark the length of the haunch to match. When transferring the tenon dimensions onto the mortise member, remember the width of the mortise is reduced to take the smaller tenon, which is cut down by the depth of the groove **(2)**.

Cutting the joint

Follow the procedure given for the haunched mortise and tenon – but before you cut the shoulders, cut the bottom line of the tenon. It is not necessary to chisel out the waste from the haunch cutout in the stile. This will be removed when the groove is made after cutting the mortise. Plane the groove in the rails and stiles. Try the joints for fit, then cut and fit the infill panel before you glue the joints.

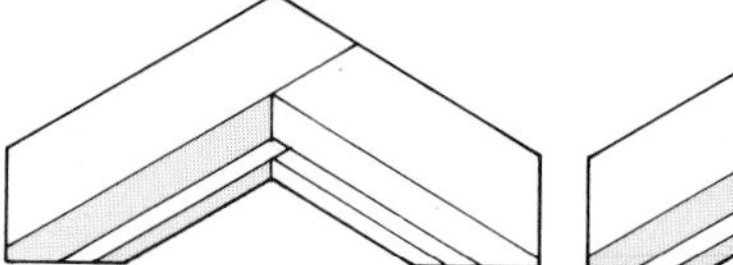

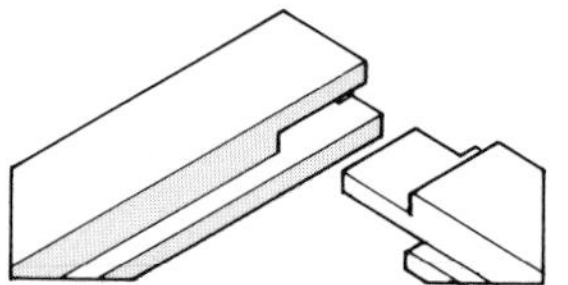

RABBETED-FRAME MORTISE AND TENON JOINT

The frames of glazed cabinet doors are rabbeted rather than grooved to allow fitting and removal of the glass. The glass is held in the rabbet by a bead. A haunched mortise and tenon joint in a rabbeted frame requires the tenon member to have one long and one short shoulder. The short shoulder fills the space left by the rabbet. Like the grooved frame, it is easier to mark out and cut out the joint before cutting the rabbets.

Marking out the joint

Mark the width and depth of the rabbet on the inside edge of the mortise and tenon members with a marking gauge. Set the depth to two-thirds the thickness of the members to correspond with the line of the tenon. Referring to the methods set out for marking the haunched mortise and tenon, measure and mark the long shoulder line on the face of the tenon member. Pencil the line onto the top and bottom edges. Measure the width of the rabbet from this line to mark the short shoulder on the inside face and square it onto the edges. Measure and mark the length and width of the haunch from the short shoulder line, and then use the mortise gauge to mark the thickness of the tenon.

Transfer the tenon-width lines to the mortise member and mark the thickness of the mortise. Extend the gauged lines onto the end and mark the depth of the haunch cutout taken from the long shoulder line on the tenon member. Last of all, mark the waste area.

Cutting the joint

Cut the joint in a similar way to the grooved-frame joint. Plane the rabbet after cutting the joint. Cut the remaining waste from the haunch cutout as described for the haunched mortise and tenon joint.

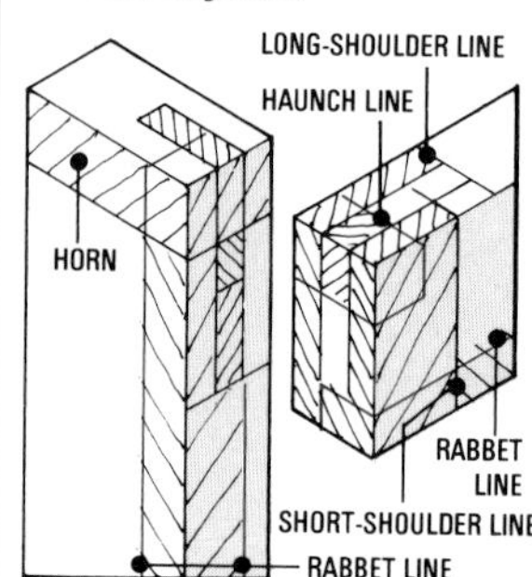

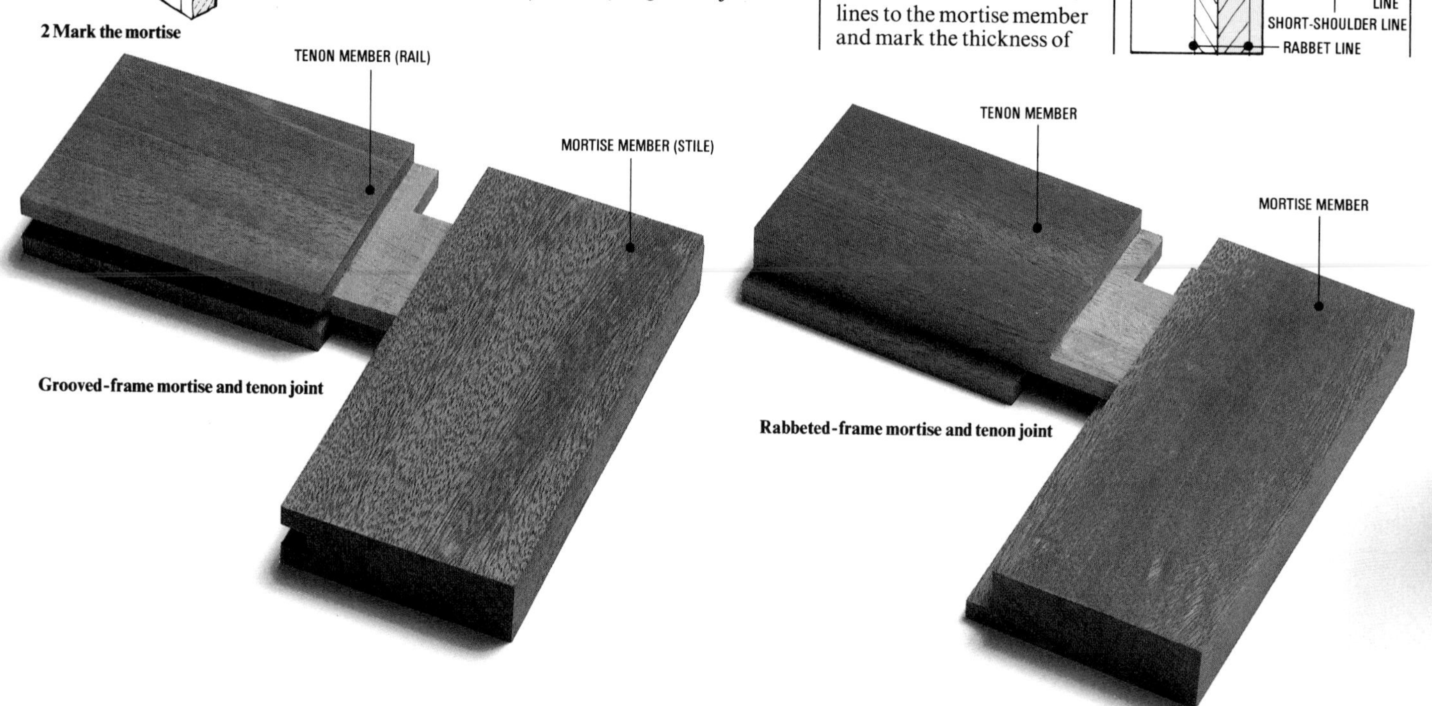

Grooved-frame mortise and tenon joint

Rabbeted-frame mortise and tenon joint

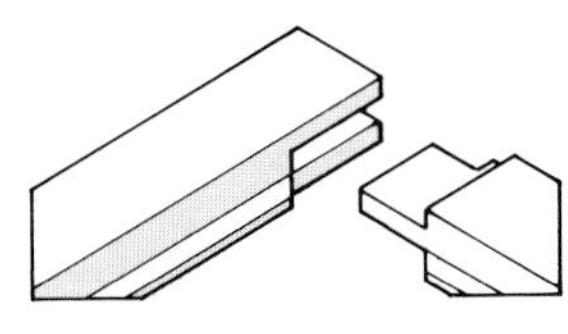

MOLDED-FRAME MORTISE AND TENON JOINT

When making mortise and tenon joints in framing with rabbeted and molded edges, it is necessary to miter or scribe the molding. It is usual for the depth of the rabbet and the molding to coincide, thus allowing the molding to be cut away with a chisel to give a flat shoulder. Trim the stile molding to match the width of the tenon. Miter or scribe the ends of the molding after cutting the joint.

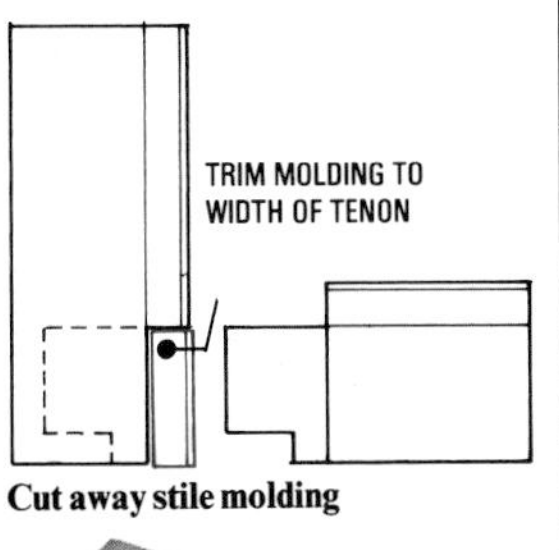

Cut away stile molding

ANGLED MORTISE AND TENON JOINT

Haunched and plain mortise and tenon joints are used in the construction of chair frames. Sometimes a chair design will have the front wider than the back. If the side rails are joined into the front and back legs, the rails must be set at an angle. Various solutions may be used depending on the proportions of the parts. The tenon may be on the same axis as the rail or set at an angle to it. It may also be necessary to offset the tenon to make a barefaced mortise and tenon joint.

Mark out the joint similarly to the conventional square joint, but use an adjustable bevel set to the required angle. Draw a full-size plan of the joint from which to set the bevel.

Angled mortise
For ease of marking out and maximum tenon strength, it is better to have the tenon on the same axis as the rail, so the mortise is cut at an angle. To enable the chisel or drill to be held vertically for easier alignment and control, make a simple jig to hold the mortise member at the required angle. Plane a short board to the same angle as the tenon shoulder and then glue a fence along the edge.

Barefaced tenon
When the face of the rail and leg are required to finish flush, an angled mortise can weaken the side of the leg.

In this case, make a barefaced tenon to set the mortise away from the edge.

Angled tenon
In some instances you may prefer to cut the mortise square and angle the tenon. This sets the tenons on each rail parallel with each other, which makes it easier to fit the assembled back and front frames of the chair when gluing up.

Take care not to make the angle excessive, as short grain will weaken the tenon. Use a set square held against the bevel to mark the tenon, as you will not be able to use the mortise gauge.

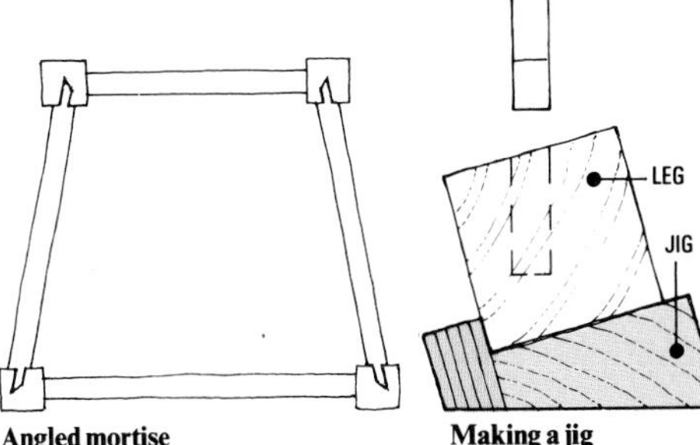

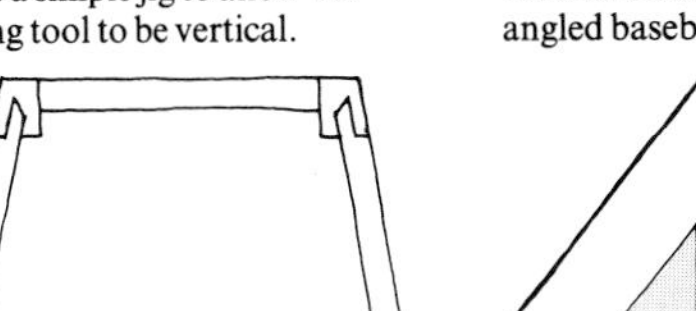

Angled mortise
Make a simple jig to allow the cutting tool to be vertical.

Making a jig
Fix a fence to an angled baseboard.

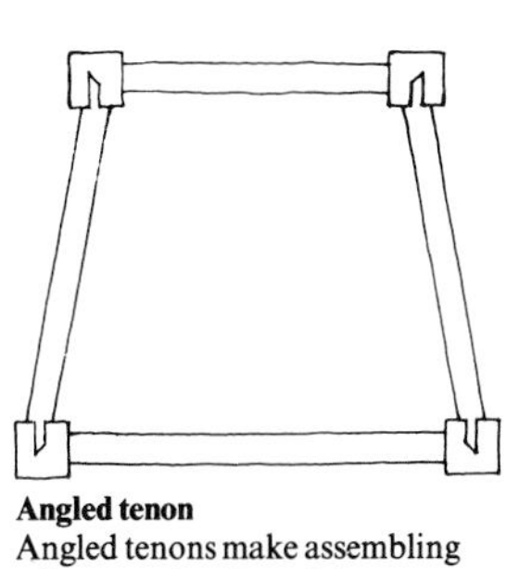

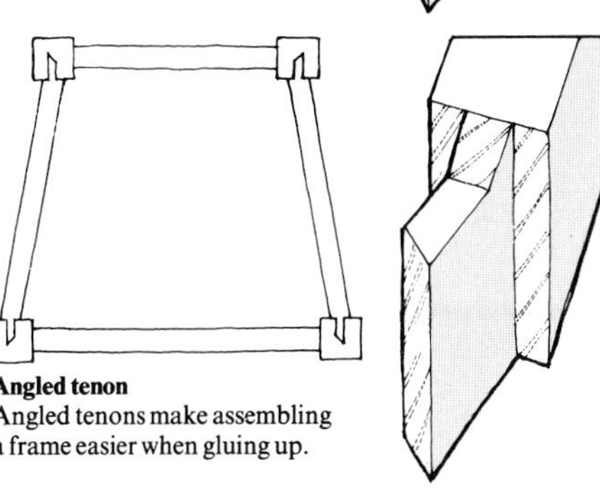

Barefaced tenon
Use a barefaced tenon to avoid the mortise weakening the leg.

Angled tenon
Angled tenons make assembling a frame easier when gluing up.

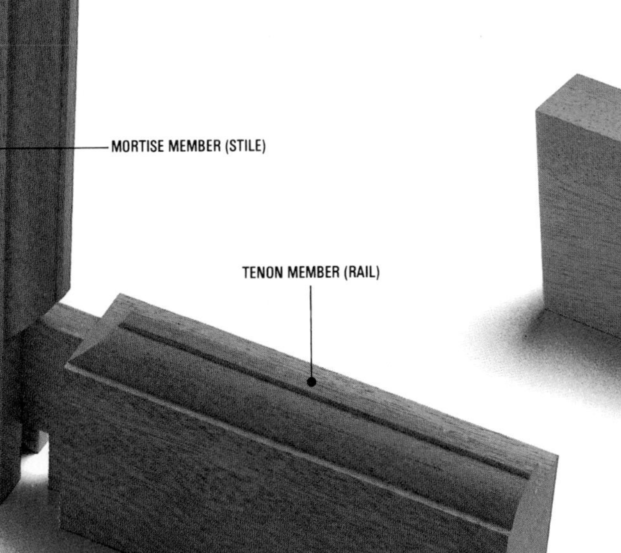

Molded-frame mortise and tenon joint

Barefaced tenon

Angled tenon

CORNER MORTISE AND TENON JOINT

SEE ALSO

Chair construction	50-54
Table construction	55-60
Measuring and marking tools	76-79
Gouge	100
Woodturning	192-200
Machine-cut joints	162,169,177

Mortise and tenon corner joints, as used in the construction of a table or a chair, are marked out and cut in the way described. In the case of the mortise member (the leg), the mortises are marked on adjacent faces. It is usual for the joint to be symmetrical and the mortises to meet. To allow the tenon members (the rails) to fit, it is better to miter the ends of the tenons than to cut them short. The larger gluing area gives a stronger joint.

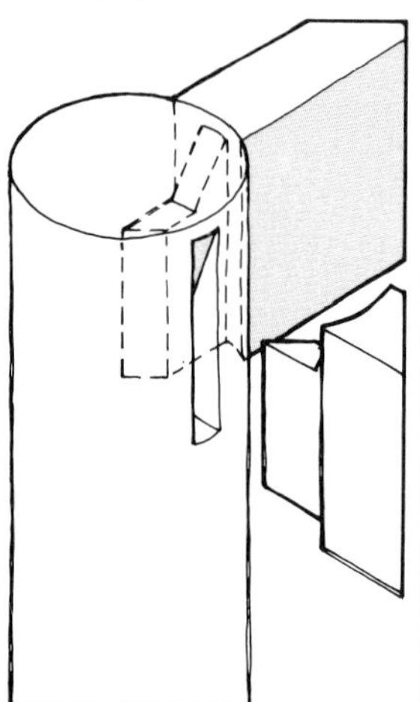

Round-leg corner joint
Set out and cut the mortises before turning the leg. Scribe the tenon shoulders with a gouge to fit the curve.

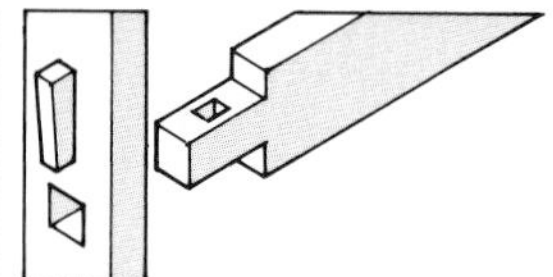

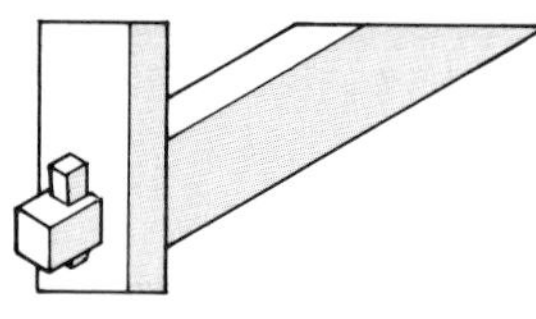

LOOSE-WEDGED MORTISE AND TENON JOINT

The loose-wedged mortise and tenon is demountable and is used in the construction of Tudor-style trestle tables. It is similar to the traditional and stronger tusk tenon used in building construction, but the furniture version does not usually include the tusk element. The proportion of the joint should provide an adequate shoulder on the tenon member and a strong tenon that will resist being split by the wedge. The wedge is usually set vertically, but it can also be fitted horizontally. The following is one method that you can adapt to suit your requirements.

Marking out the joint
The length of the projecting end of the tenon should be at least one and a half times the thickness of the mortise member. Calculate the total length of the tenon and square the shoulder line all around the tenon member **(1)**. Gauge the width of the tenon to be not less than one-third the width of the tenon member **(2)**. Mark the thickness of the mortise member from the shoulder line and square the line all around **(3)**. Mark the waste.
Mark the width and position of the tenon on the mortise member and square the lines all around, then center and gauge the thickness of the tenon between the lines **(4)**.

Cutting the joint
Drill or chop out the mortise, working from both sides. Saw off the waste from the tenon member. Fit the tenon into the mortise; this should be a sliding fit. With the shoulder up tight, mark the thickness of the mortise member on the top of the tenon **(5)**. Take the joint apart and mark the length of the wedge mortise to equal the thickness of the mortise member, but set it about ⅛in (3mm) in from the first line **(6)**. Square the lines all around the tenon. Set a mortise gauge to one-third the thickness of the tenon and mark the thickness of the mortise **(7)**. Make a single sloped wedge to fit, about three times the width of the tenon. Make the slope 1:6. Hold the wedge on the side of the tenon level with the inner mortise line and mark the slope **(8)**. Square the line onto the bottom of the tenon. Chisel out the mortise, taking exta care with the angled face. Assemble the joint and tap in the wedge in order to draw the joint up tight.

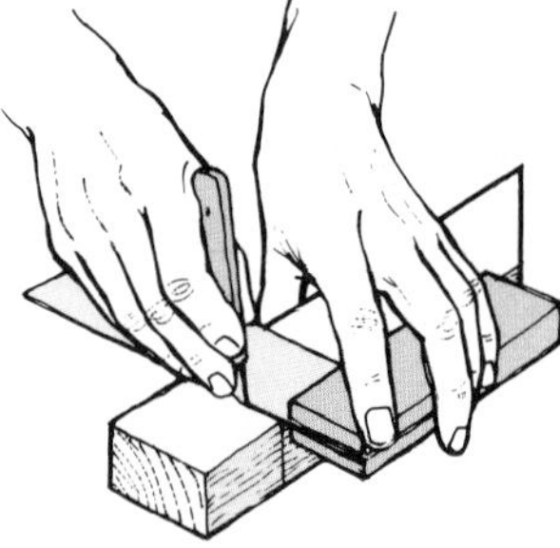

1 Mark the tenon-shoulder line

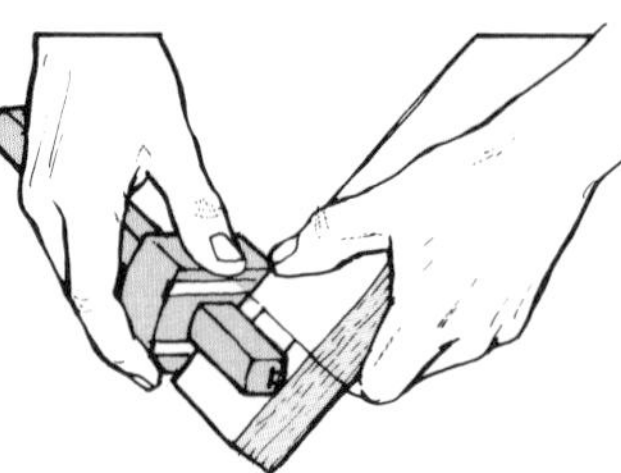

2 Gauge the tenon width

3 Mark mortise-member thickness

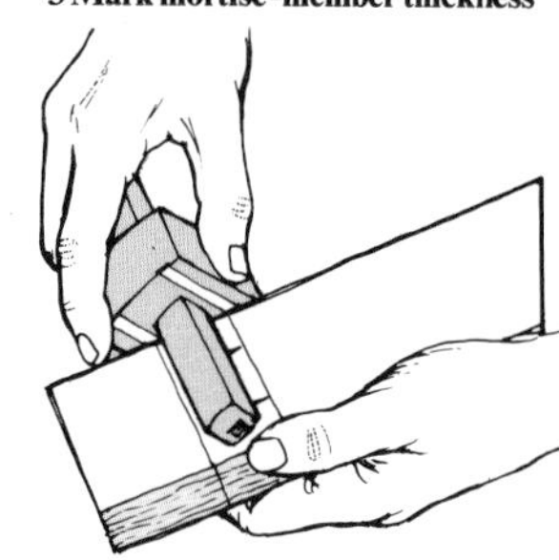

4 Gauge thickness of tenon

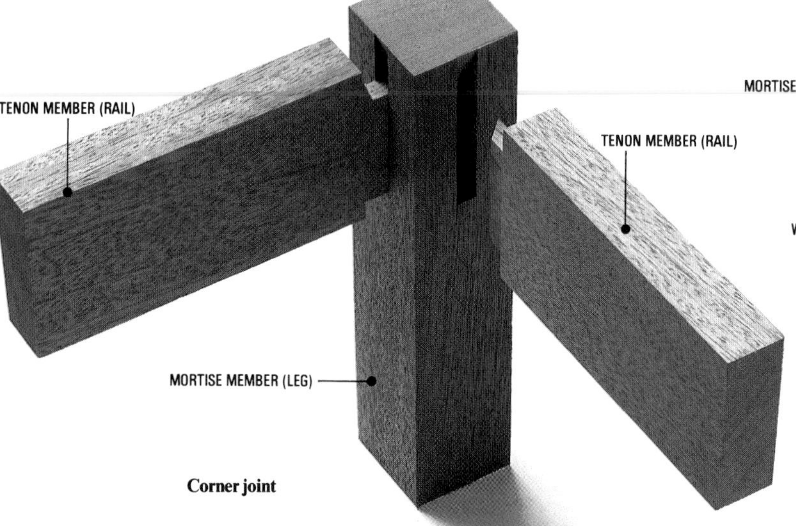

Corner joint

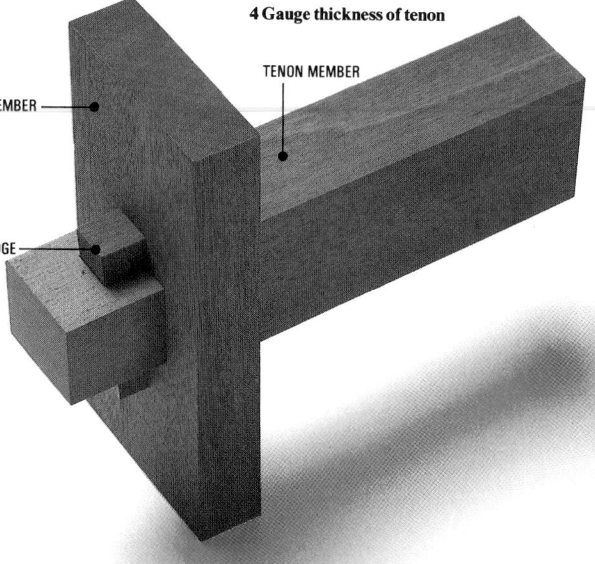

Loose-wedged mortise and tenon joint

BRIDLE JOINTS

The bridle joint is grouped with the mortise and tenon joints by virtue of the methods by which it is marked out. However, the methods used to cut the joint also make it similar to the lap joint. The tenon element of the bridle joint is usually one-third the thickness of the wood, but it can be more where a rail is T-joined into a thicker leg member.

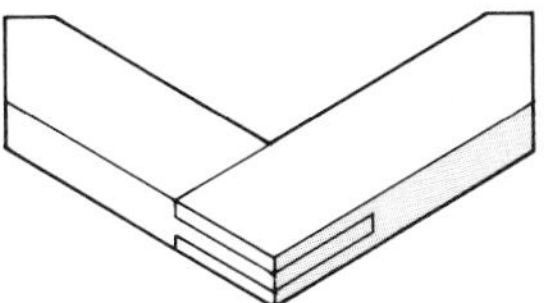

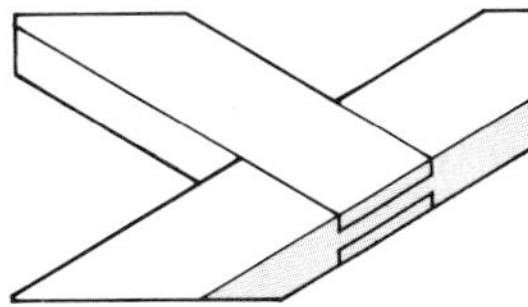

Marking out the joint
To make a corner joint, mark the width of the mortise member on the end of the tenon member. Allow for a little waste to be planed off after gluing up. Square the shoulder lines all around with a marking knife. Use light pressure on the edges.

Mark the width of the tenon member on the mortise member and square the shoulder line using a pencil. Set a mortise gauge to one-third the thickness of the tenon member. It is not necessary to set the gauge to the width of a chisel, as usual for a mortise and tenon, but it can help when cleaning up the shoulder of the mortise cutout.

Set the stock to center the pins and gauge the tenon lines over the end. Mark the mortise-member cutout in the same way, and mark the waste on both parts, as they look identical at this stage **(1)**.

Cutting the joint
Select a drill that is close to the width of the mortise and drill a hole just inside the shoulder line, working from both edges **(2)**. Set the work in the vise and saw down to the hole on the waste side of the gauged lines **(3)**. Pare out the remaining waste level with the shoulder line **(4)**. Alternatively, using a tenon saw, cut down the gauged lines first, then cut out the waste with a coping saw. Cut the tenon as you would for a mortise and tenon.

To mark and cut a "T" bridle joint **(5)**, basically follow the procedure above, but use the lap-joint method to cut the waste from the tenon member.

5 Mark the top of the tenon

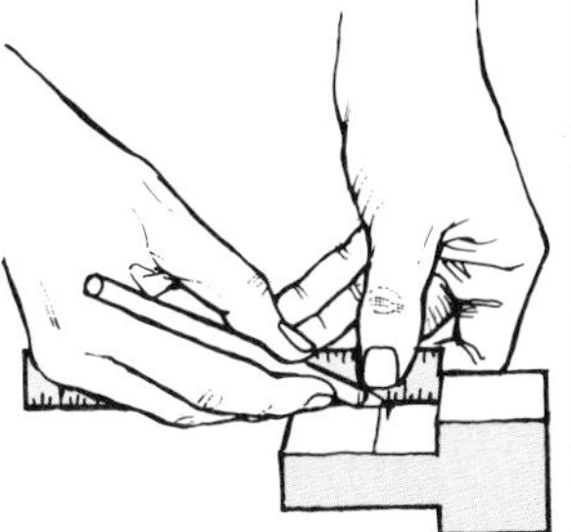

6 Mark $\frac{1}{8}$in (3mm) inside line

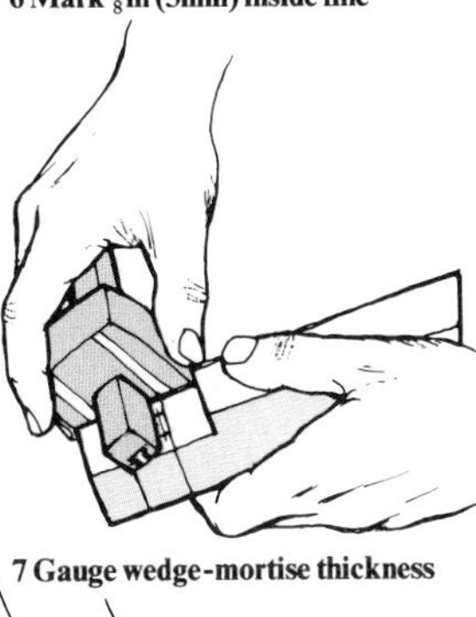

7 Gauge wedge-mortise thickness

8 Mark the slope of the wedge

1 Mark the waste on both parts

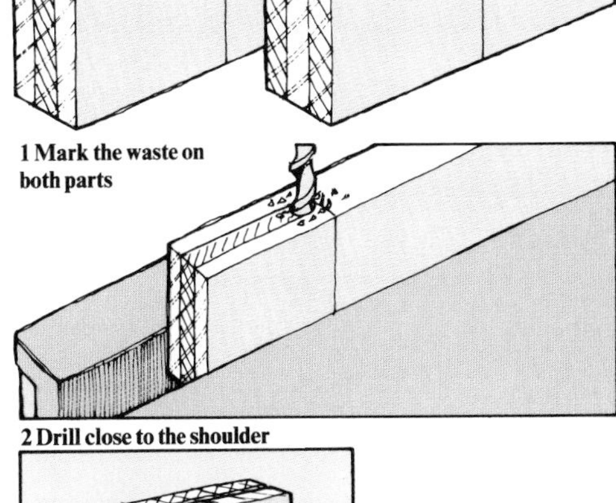

2 Drill close to the shoulder

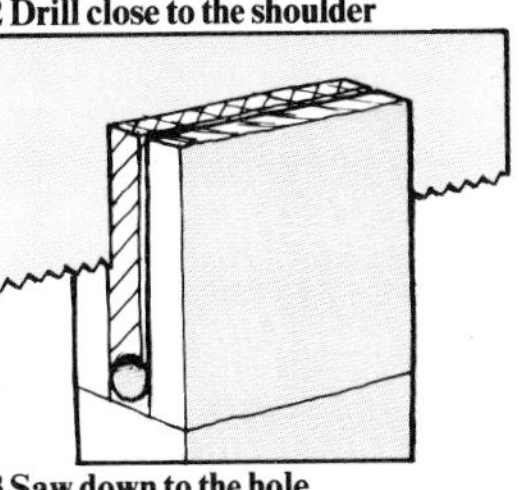

3 Saw down to the hole

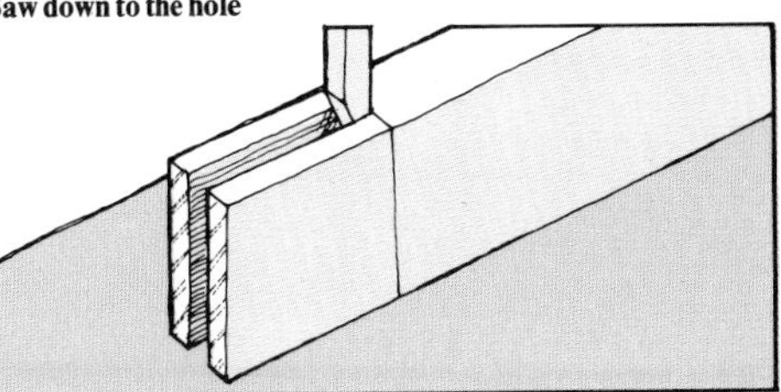

4 Pare out the remaining waste

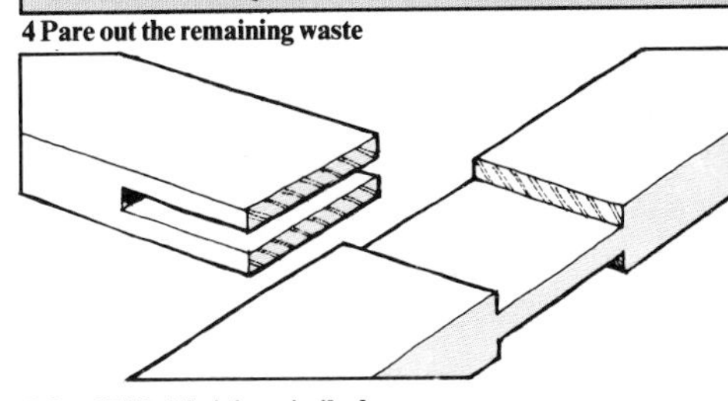

5 Cut "T" bridle joints similarly

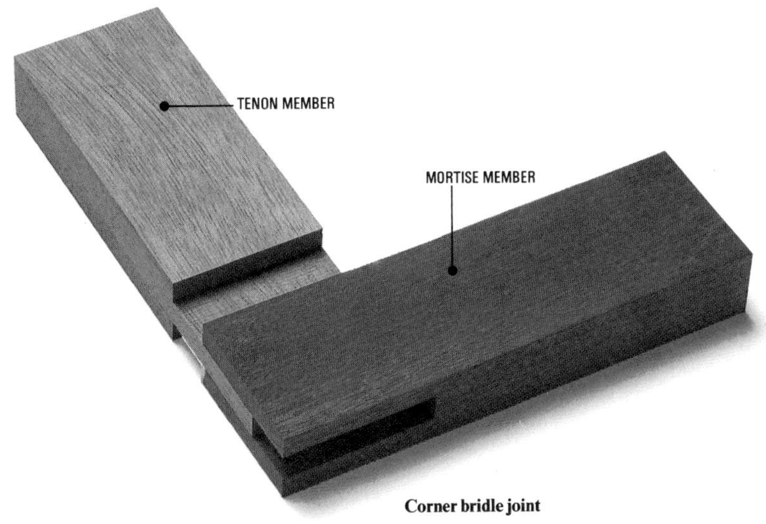

Corner bridle joint

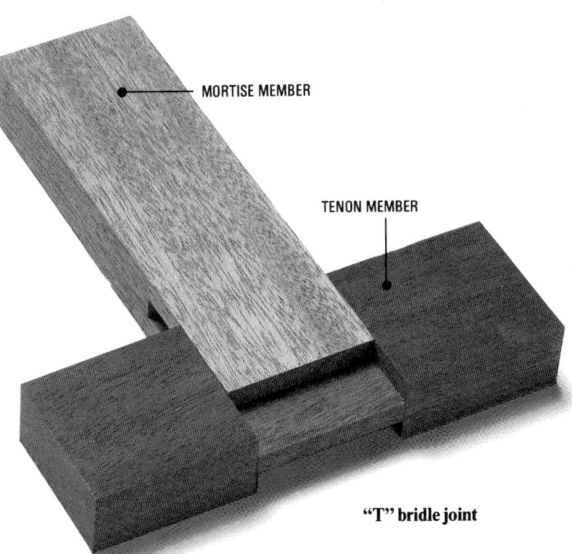

"T" bridle joint

DOWEL JOINTS

The dowel joint is relatively simple and quick to cut. Basically it is a butt joint reinforced with wooden pegs glued into holes drilled in both of the parts being joined. It is used to make a variety of joints for frame and carcase construction. The dowel joint is widely used by furniture manufacturers as a cost-effective substitute for the mortise and tenon. For handwork, the joint does not require complicated marking out and, if using a doweling jig, marking out is minimal.

SEE ALSO

- **Dowel rod**
  Dowel rod is a round-sectioned molding, available in a range of diameters from $\frac{1}{8}$ to $1\frac{7}{8}$in (3 to 47mm). For most work you will only need the $\frac{1}{4}$, $\frac{5}{16}$, $\frac{3}{8}$ and $\frac{1}{2}$in (6, 8, 10 and 12mm) diameters. Check the quality, as it is not always round due to moisture changes or inaccurate machining.

DOWELS

Dowels are made from even-textured hardwoods such as beech, birch, maple or ramin. You can cut your own from commercially produced dowel rod or use ready-made dowels; or, if neither suits your purpose, make them entirely using a dowel plate.

Cutting dowels

Use a fine-toothed saw to cut the dowels to length. Steady the wood with a bench hook or miter box. To avoid break-out of the wood fibers, rotate the dowel as you cut. If making a number of dowels, set up a stop block to gauge the length.

Cut a groove down the length of each cut dowel using the saw. This is to release the hydraulic pressure from the hole as the dowel is glued in. Failure to do this can cause the wood to split. Finally, chamfer the ends to make inserting the dowels easier. You can either use a special dowel-chamfering tool or a sander, or a pencil sharpener for the smaller sizes.

Ready-made dowels are supplied cut to length. They are chamfered and grooved all around with straight or spiraled flutes.

A dowel plate is a thick steel plate with standard-sized dowel holes drilled through it. It is used to produce dowels from lengths of roughly sized wood that are driven through the appropriate holes. You can either make your own plate to produce smooth, round dowels or use a commercial plate that has serrated holes to create relief flutes as the wood is driven through.

The length of the dowel will vary according to the size of the wood into which it is fitted. As a guide, make the length not less than five times the diameter. The longer the dowel, the greater the gluing area will be. The diameter of the dowel can be half the thickness of the wood.

Boring the dowel holes

The strength of the dowel joint is dependent on the fit of the dowel in the hole. The hole must be clean and true and the correct depth. It can be drilled using a brace and auger bit or a brad-point bit in a power drill. If you use a hand-held method, stand so you are looking down the centerline of the holes **(1)**, since it is critical to keep the drill upright in the thickness of the wood.

For greater accuracy, use a commercial doweling jig. Various types are available with a choice of drill-guide bushings, which not only keep the drill upright but accurately position the holes on the individual parts.

The holes must be of consistent depth and only slightly deeper than half the length of the dowel. Use a commercial depth gauge or make your own gauge with a wooden or rubber sleeve that can be cut or positioned as required.

Countersink the holes to aid assembly. If you find you have drilled a hole out of square, fill it with a plug and redrill it.

Marking the joint

Unless you intend to make a number of dowel joints, it is sufficient to mark out the joints using conventional methods.

For edge-to-edge joints, place the boards in a vise with the edges flush and face sides out. Evenly space the positions of the dowels and square the lines across. Set a gauge to half the thickness of the boards and scribe a centerline on each, working from the face sides **(2)**.

The number and spacing of the dowels used in frame joints depend on the width of the rail. Two dowels are usually used. The spacing between the dowels is not critical, but you should inset the dowels not less than $\frac{1}{4}$in (6mm) from the edges.

Prepare and mark the face side and edge of the rail and stile members. Mark their lengths. Plane the ends of the rails square on a shooting board. You can leave the stiles overlength. Set each joint's rail and stile in a vise with the surfaces level and face sides out. Square lines across both members. Set a marking gauge to half the thickness of the rail and mark a centerline on each part, working from the face side **(3)**. Center the drill where the lines cross.

Dowel rod

Prepared dowel

Fluted dowel

Carcase joint

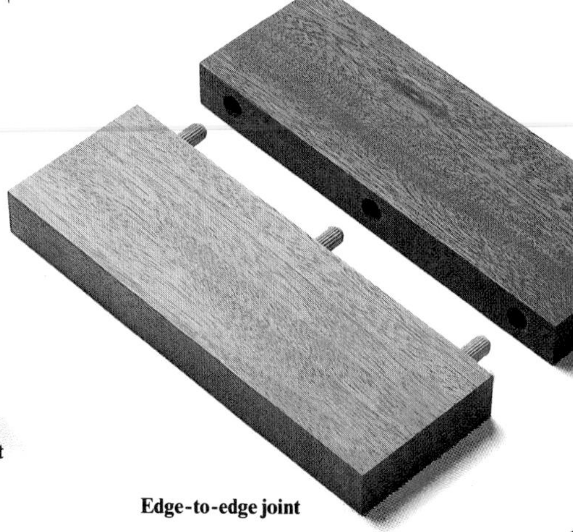

Edge-to-edge joint

Frame joint

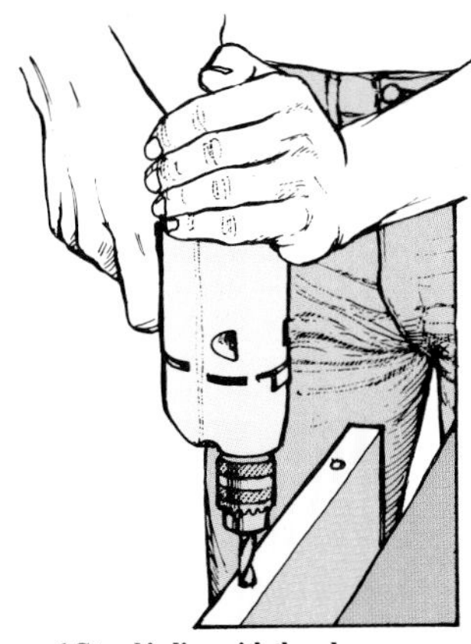
1 Stand in line with the edge

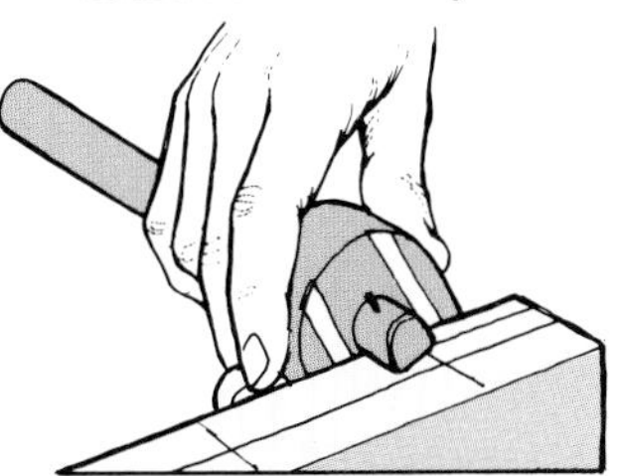
2 Mark the centerlines

3 Mark rail and stile centers

4 Make a right-angled jig

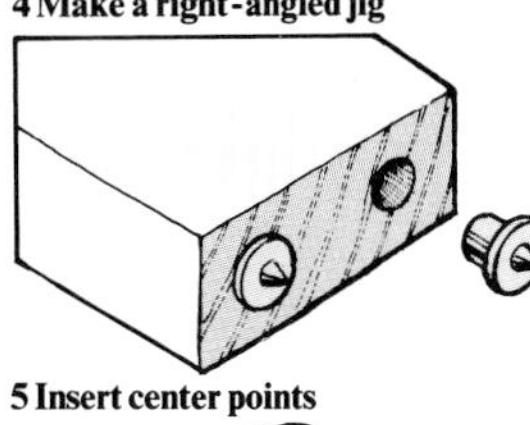
5 Insert center points

6 Mark the stile

Using center points
Another marking method, which is easier to use for awkwardly shaped parts, is to use center points to mark one part from another. You can either make your own or buy commercial dowel center points.

For the brad method, mark the positions on one part. For edge-to-edge joints, use either edge. For the frame-corner joint described here, mark the centers of the dowels on the end of the rail.

Drive the brads into the center marks and snip off the heads. Lay the rail and stile on a flat surface and push them together to impress the nail points into the inside edge of the stile. You can make a simple jig to help keep the parts in line **(4)**.

Using commercial dowel center points, first mark and drill the end of the rail. Then insert the appropriate-sized center point in each hole and press the parts together **(5)**.

Using a template
When making a number of identical dowel joints, a template will speed up marking out. Cut a hardwood fence block to the width of the rail member. Make a sawcut across its center to receive a thin steel plate. Before epoxy-gluing the plate into the slot, mark and drill small guide holes through it at the required setting.

Use a pointed tool to mark the centers through the holes. Always hold the template's fence against the face side. Finally, mark the end of the rail and then invert the template to mark the stile **(6)**.

Using a doweling jig
A doweling jig is designed to clamp onto the work to position and guide the drill accurately. Some are pre-set and have fixed guide holes for $\frac{1}{4}$, $\frac{5}{16}$ and $\frac{3}{8}$in (6, 8 and 10mm) dowels, while others have interchangeable steel guide bushings that can be adjusted to various settings.

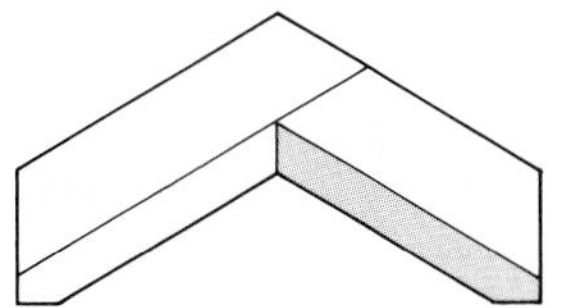

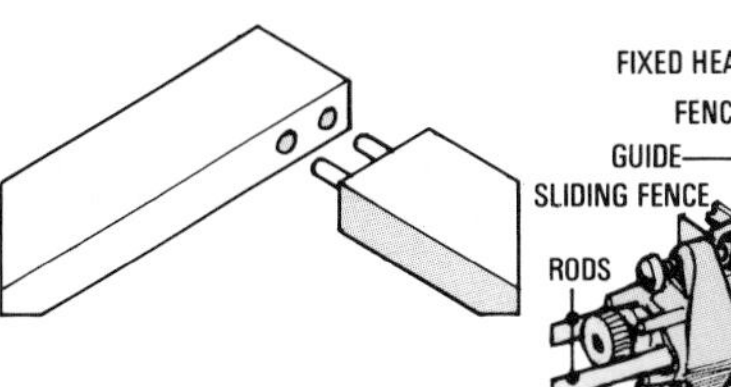

DOWEL FRAME JOINT

Using the adjustable-type jig, set the drill-bit guides on the slide rods to the required spacing to suit the width of the rail. Take the measurements from the jig's fixed head. Set the fences on the drill-bit guides to center the holes on the thickness of the wood. Locate the jig on the end of the rail and clamp it in place with the sliding fence. Make sure the fixed head and fences are set against the face side and face edge. Drill the holes to the required depth **(1)**.

Remove the sliding fence and, without altering the other settings, invert the jig and clamp it to the inside edge of the prepared stile using the clamp provided. Drill the matching holes in readiness for the dowels **(2)**.

1 Drill the rail holes

CLAMP

2 Drill the stile holes

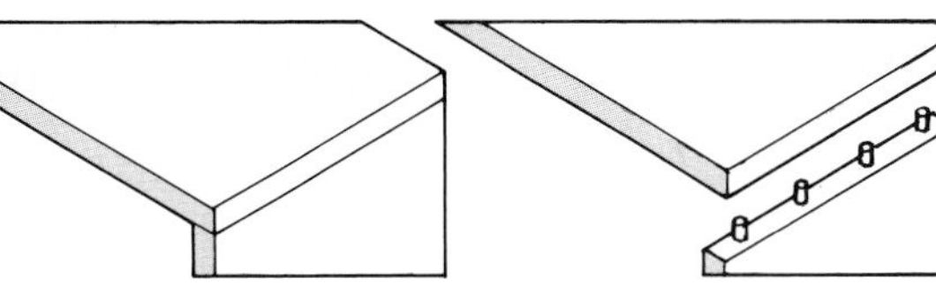

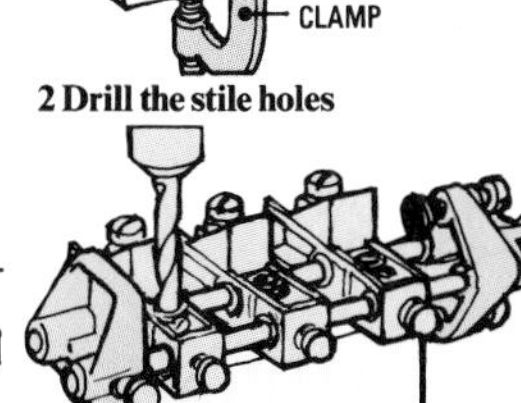
1 Drill end holes

DOWEL CARCASE JOINTS

The jig can be fitted with a range of slide rods, allowing wide boards to be joined. In addition, extra drill-bit guides can be purchased to enable more holes to be drilled without resetting the two guides supplied as standard.

Fit appropriate-sized bushings in the guides to suit the thickness of the board. Set the end bushings about 1in (25mm) from the edges and the others about 3in (75mm) apart.

For a corner joint, set the fences to center the holes on the thickness of the board. Clamp the jig to the end with the sliding fence. Drill the holes **(1)**.

Clamp the end of the other board in the top of the jig. Release the lower clamp screw and invert the board with the jig attached. Drill the stopped holes on the inside face **(2)**.

For a "T" joint, set out and drill the end as before. Remove the fences and clamp the jig across the other board with the bushings centered on a line drawn across for that purpose **(3)**. Always keep the fixed head against the face edge.

2 Drill the stopped holes

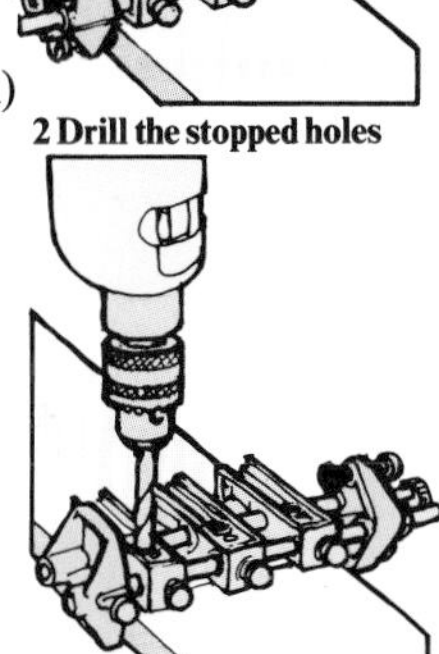
3 Center jig on marked line

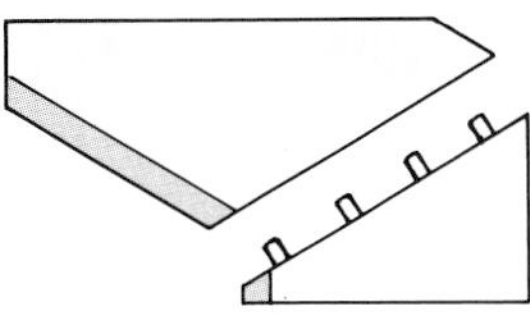

CARCASE MITER JOINT

Miter the ends of the boards. Set the jig in place as described for the corner joint, but following the slope of the miter. Set the fences to place the bushings close to the inside face where the board is thickest. Drill the holes, then transfer the jig to the other board (see above).

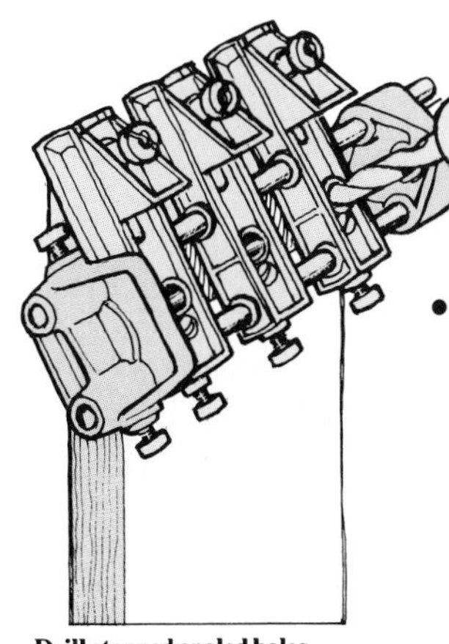
Drill stopped angled holes

- **Gluing the joint**
  Apply a little glue to the joining faces and into each hole with a brush or stick. Dip the ends of the dowels in glue as they are inserted into the holes. Tap them home with a mallet and set the assembly in clamps, as required.

DOVETAIL JOINTS

Dovetail joints, perhaps more than any other type, express what wood joints are all about. In most examples the interlocking wedge-shaped elements of the joint are clearly demonstrated, leaving you with no doubt that the joint would hold together even if it were not glued. Traditional drawer-making is a classic example of the use of the dovetail joint, the inherent strength of the joint's tails and pins being used to resist the pulling forces applied to a drawer front.

Dovetail joints can be made in a number of ways. Some exploit the decorative nature of the repetitive shapes, while others hide them completely. All are a challenge to the maker.

SEE ALSO

Drawer construction	71
Measuring and marking tools	76-79
Dovetail saws	83
Coping saw	84
Routers	146
Shooting board	213

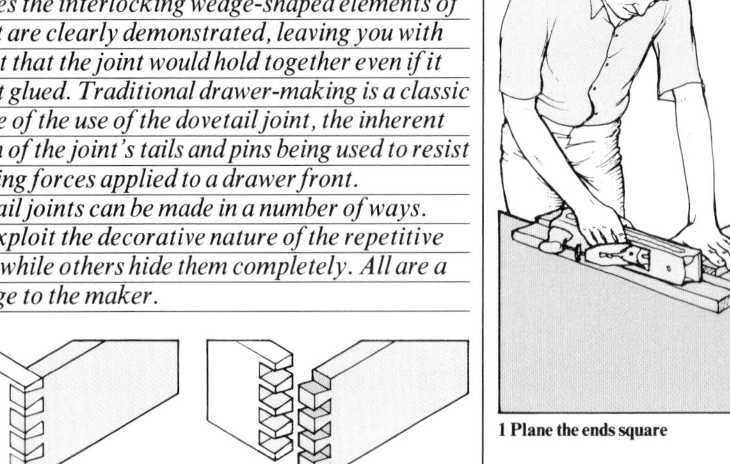

1 Plane the ends square

THROUGH DOVETAIL JOINT

The through dovetail is a traditional joint for joining the ends of solid-wood boards. It is commonly used in the construction of boxes and cabinet work. Through dovetail joints can be cut by hand or machine. A power router and a special jig are used for machining dovetails. Although functional, the even spacing of the machine-cut dovetails is regarded by traditionalists to be less attractive than the well-proportioned hand-cut dovetail joint described here. The through dovetail is the simplest type to make, but it still takes very careful marking out and cutting.

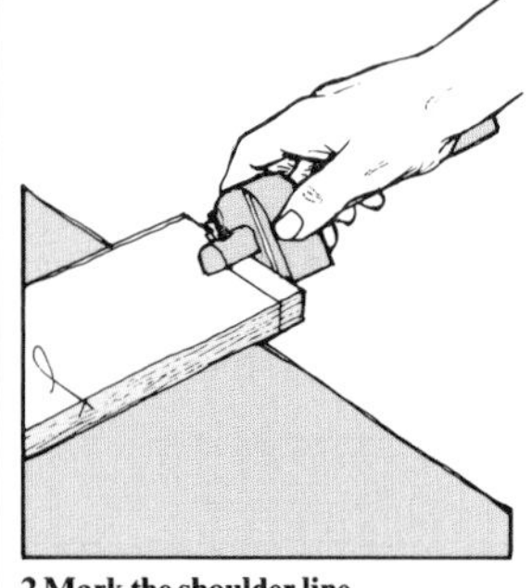

2 Mark the shoulder line

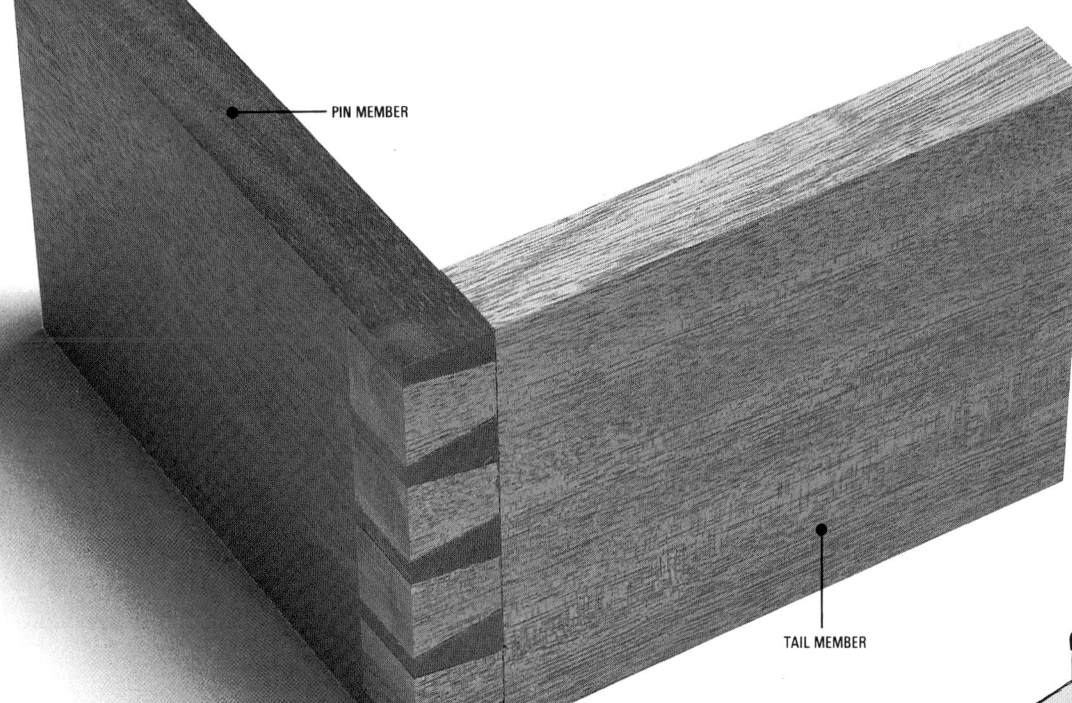

Through dovetail joint

Marking the tails
Mark the face side, face edge and each pair of ends that are to be joined. Accurately cut the components to length and plane the ends smooth and square. The use of a shooting board will make the planing easier **(1)**.

Set a cutting gauge to the thickness of the wood. Mark the shoulder line for the tails all around the end of the tail member **(2)** and on the sides of the pin member. Where the gauge lines could mar the finished work, use a fine pencil line and a try square instead. Next, mark the tails. The size and number can vary according to the width of the boards being joined and the type of wood (softwood needs coarser and fewer tails than hardwood), as well as the appearance of the finished joint. As a general guide, for good appearance the tails should be the same size and equally spaced, but wider than the pins.

Start by squaring a pencil line across the end $\frac{1}{4}$in (6mm) from each edge, then divide the distance between the pencil marks into an even number of equal parts. Measure $\frac{1}{8}$in (3mm) on each side of the marks and square pencil lines across the end **(3)**. Mark the slope of the tails on the face side using an adjustable bevel or a dovetail template. Mark the waste to avoid confusion later.

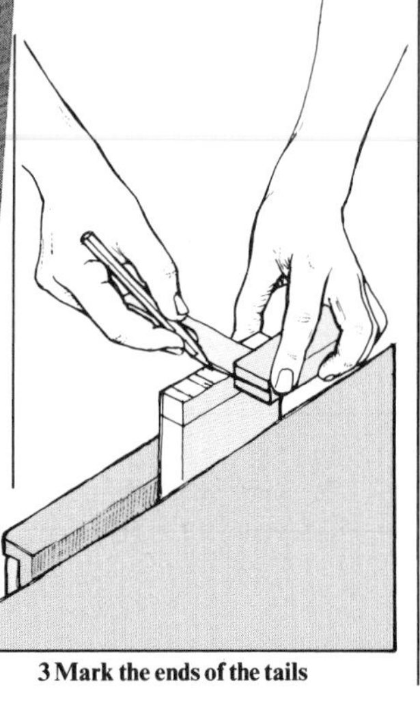

3 Mark the ends of the tails

Cutting the tails

Set each piece of wood in the vise at an angle so that one side of every tail is vertical.

Using a dovetail saw, cut down one side of the tails. Keep close to the line on the waste side **(4)** and take care not to go beyond the shoulder line. After repositioning the work in the vise, cut down the other side of the tails.

Set the work horizontally in the vise and cut away the corner waste, following the shoulder line **(5)**. Remove most of the waste from between the tails with a coping saw **(6)**. Pare out what is left with a bevel-edged chisel, working from both sides toward the middle and finishing level with the shoulder line **(7)**.

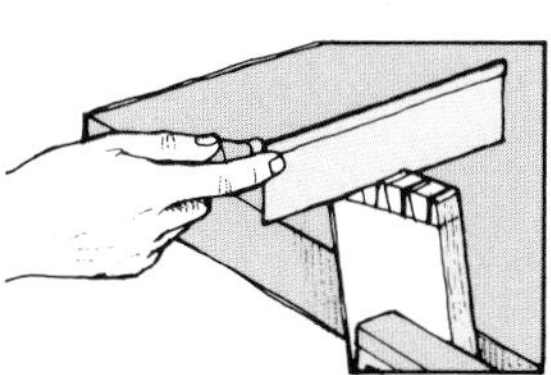

4 Saw the sides of the tails

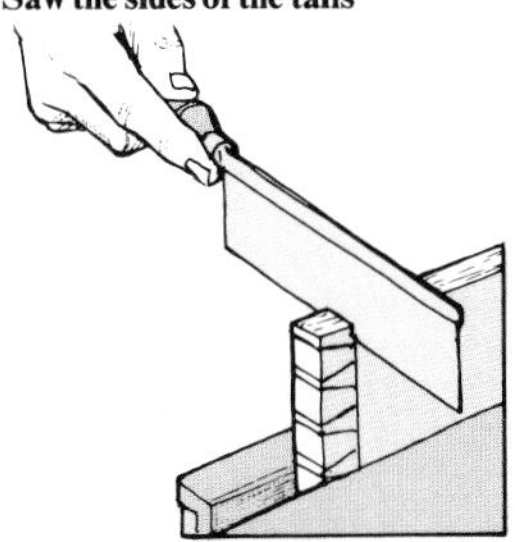

5 Saw off the corner waste

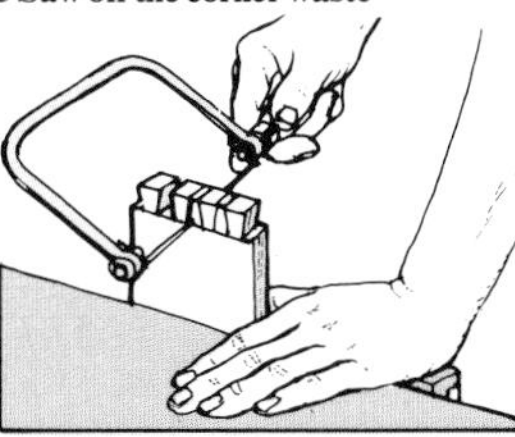

6 Remove the waste between tails

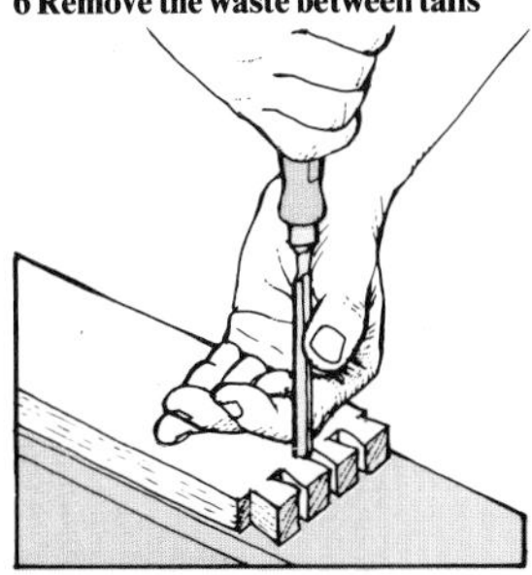

7 Pare out remaining waste

Marking the pins

Rub chalk on the end grain of the prepared wood and set it vertically in the vise. Lay the cut tail member in position, checking that the "face marks" correspond **(8)**. Line up the edges and shoulder line of the tails precisely on the chalked end and mark their shape with a scriber or knife **(9)**, then square the lines down to the shoulders on each face of the wood **(10)**. Mark the waste with a pencil.

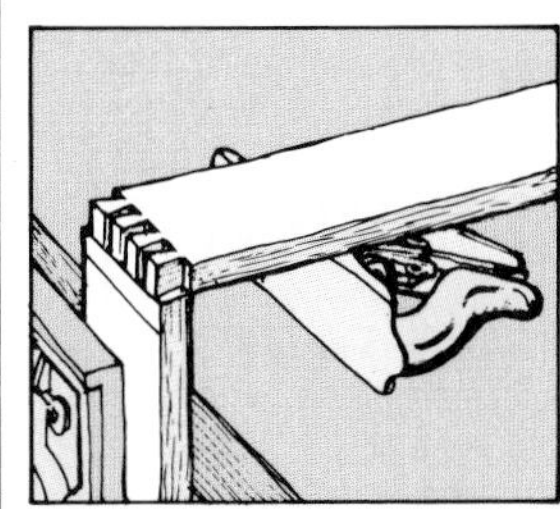

8 Align the tail piece accurately

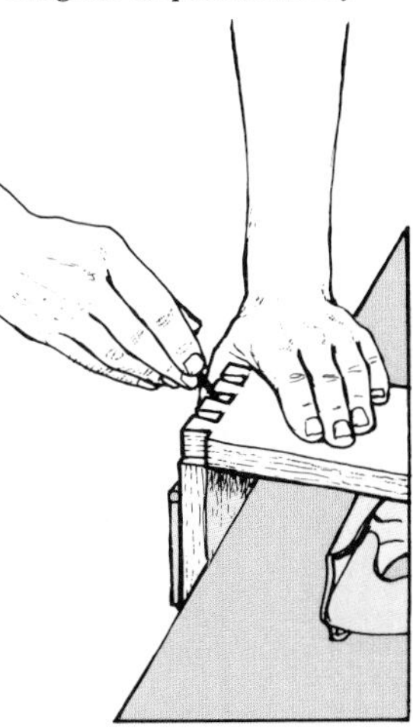

9 Mark around the tails

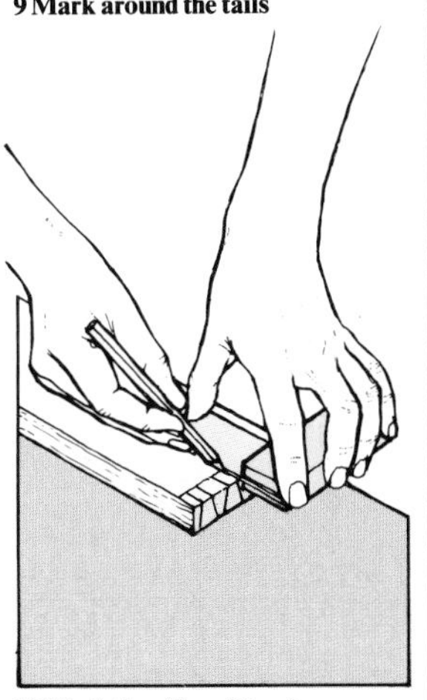

10 Mark the sides of the pins

Cutting the pins

Set each piece vertically in the vise. Saw down to the shoulder line, following the angles marked from the tails **(11)**. Keep the sawcut on the waste side so it just shaves the marked line. Remove most of the waste from between the pins with a coping saw, then trim down to the shoulder line with a bevel-edged chisel. Work from both sides toward the middle. Clean out the corners holding the chisel at the angle of the pins **(12)**.

Assembling the joint

Dovetails are cut to be a close fit and should be fully assembled once only. To check the fit, partly assemble the joint and trim any tight spots. Clean up the inside faces of the parts prior to gluing. Apply glue to both halves and tap the joint together, using a hammer and a piece of scrap wood to protect the surface **(13)**. If you are working on a wide joint, tap across the width as you go in order to keep it level. Wipe away any excess glue before it sets. When the glue has set, clean up the joint with a smoothing plane, working from the edges toward the middle so as to prevent the end grain from breaking out.

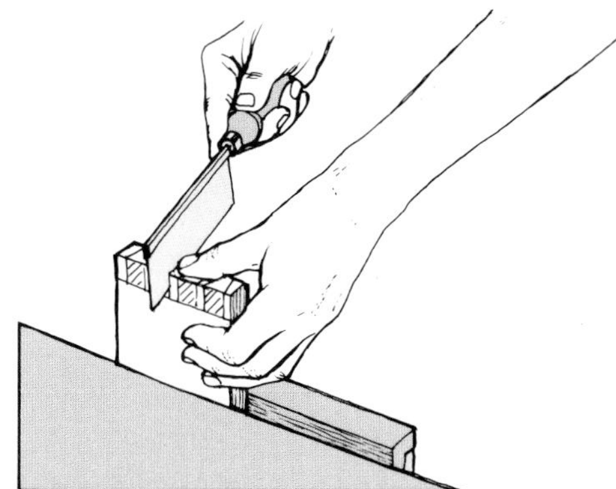

11 Saw the sides of the pins

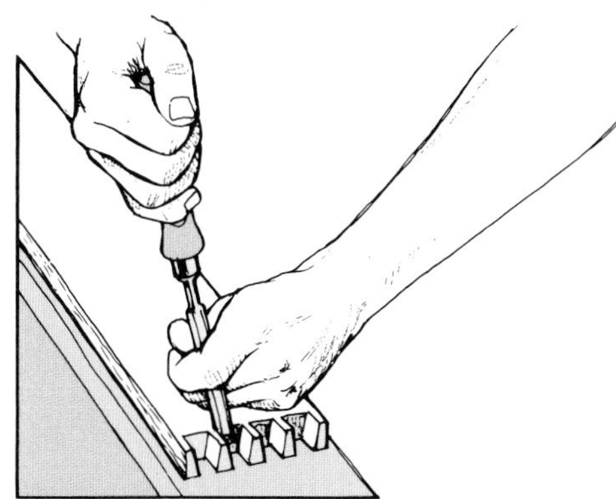

12 Angle chisel to pare corners

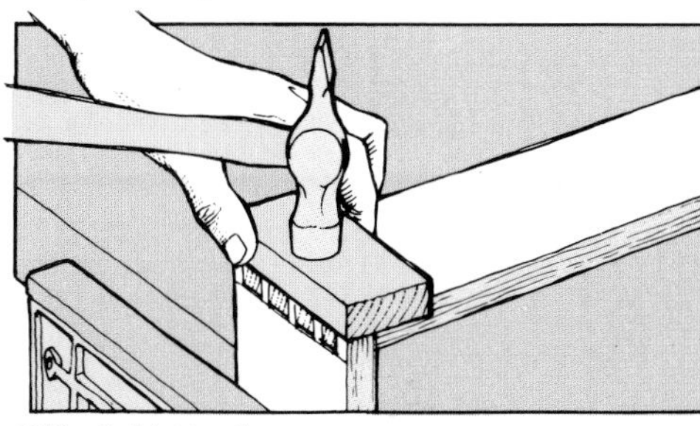

13 Tap the joint together

DOVETAIL ANGLES

The angle of a dovetail should not be too steep or too shallow.

Excessive slope on a dovetail will give weak short grain on the corners **(1)**, while an insufficient slope can reduce the interlocking strength of the joint **(2)**. Mark out the proportions of the slope on a piece of wood and set a sliding bevel to the angle, or use a template. Make the slope 1:8 for hardwoods and 1:6 for softwoods.

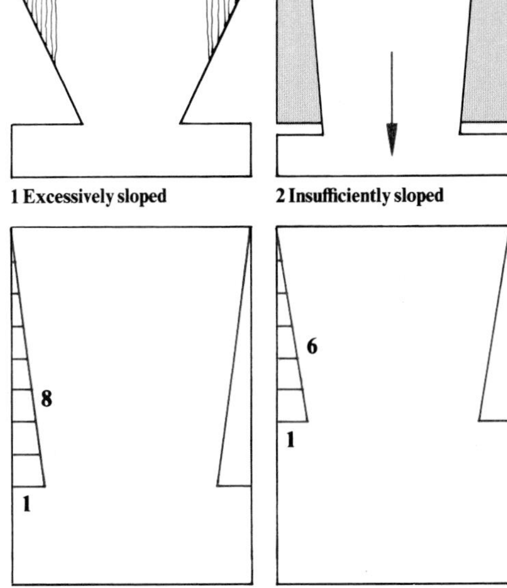

1 Excessively sloped

2 Insufficiently sloped

Hardwood angle

Softwood angle

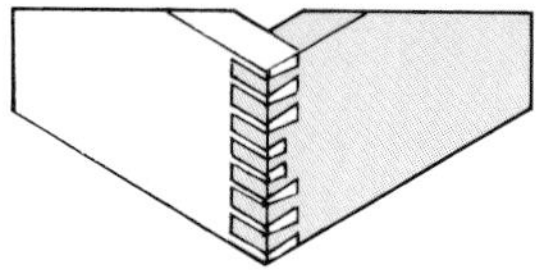

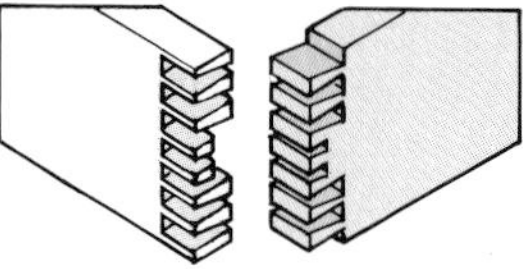

DECORATIVE THROUGH DOVETAIL JOINT

A well-proportioned and accurately cut through dovetail joint makes an attractive feature that is often exploited in the design of a cabinet's construction. Decorative through dovetails are used to enhance this feature and express the skills of the maker. The design of the joint follows basic principles, but the proportion and disposition of the joint's elements is open to interpretation. The example shown here uses fine-cut pins and half-depth dovetails.

SEE ALSO

Measuring and marking tools	76-79
Dovetail saws	83
Coping saw	84
Rabbet planes	92
Routers	144

Marking the tails

Pencil or lightly gauge the shoulder line all around the end of the tail member. Set the try square or the gauge to the thickness of the pin member. Mark the shoulder line of the small dovetails to half the thickness **(1)**. Where the line is to be cut, which is established after marking the tails, enhance the pencil line with a marking knife or deepen the gauge line.

Set out the size and position of the tails and mark the slope with a template **(2)**. The fine pins are created by placing the tails close together. The distance between them needs to be no more than the thickness of the sawkerf. You can measure and mark the tails directly on the wood or work out the design on paper and transfer the dimensions to the tail member. Square the lines onto the end and mark the waste area **(3)**.

Cutting the tails

Cut away the waste in the same manner as a through dovetail, using a dovetail saw and coping saw. Finish the cut along the shoulder line, paring from both sides with a bevel-edged chisel.

Marking the pins

Chalk the end of the pin member. With the cutting gauge set to the length of the small tails, mark the thickness line of the small pins on the end **(4)**. Mark the pins from the tail member using the tip of the saw **(5)** or a scriber. Square the lines down to the shoulder line on each face and mark the waste.

Cutting the pins

Remove most of the waste with a dovetail saw and coping saw, and trim the shoulder line with a chisel. To cut the small pins to size, first clamp the work to the bench on a flat board. Make a cut across the grain close to the shoulder line **(6)**. Carefully pare away the waste, working with the grain **(7)**. Then repeat the operation and finish level with the gauged shoulder and thickness line. Glue and assemble in the same manner as a conventional through dovetail.

1 Mark small dovetail shoulder

2 Set out the tails

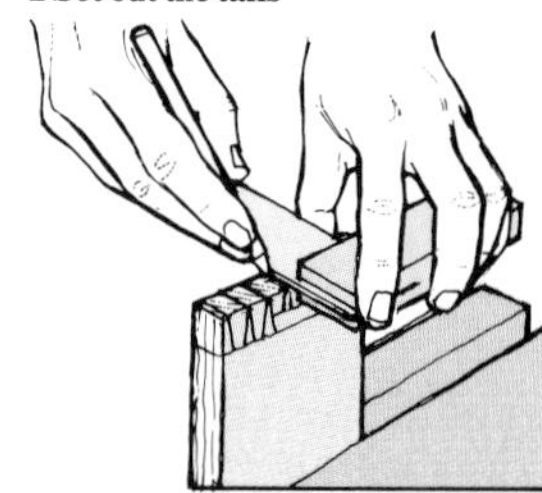

3 Mark the ends of the tails

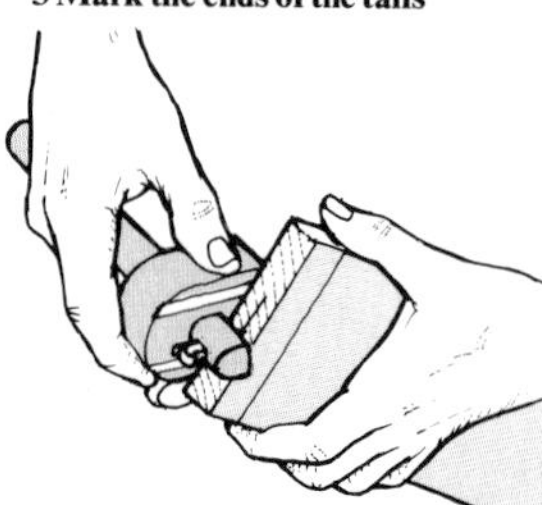

4 Mark thickness of small pins

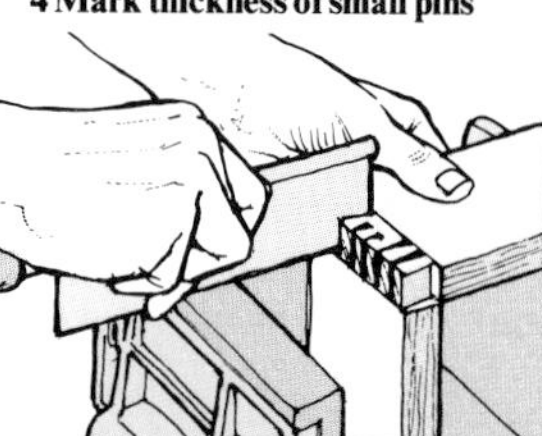

5 Mark the pins with a saw

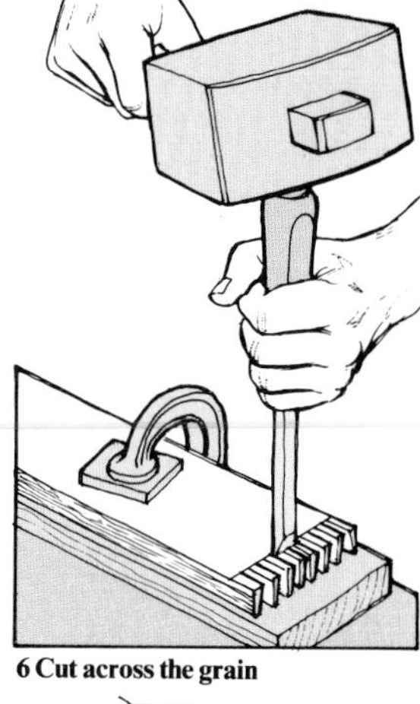

6 Cut across the grain

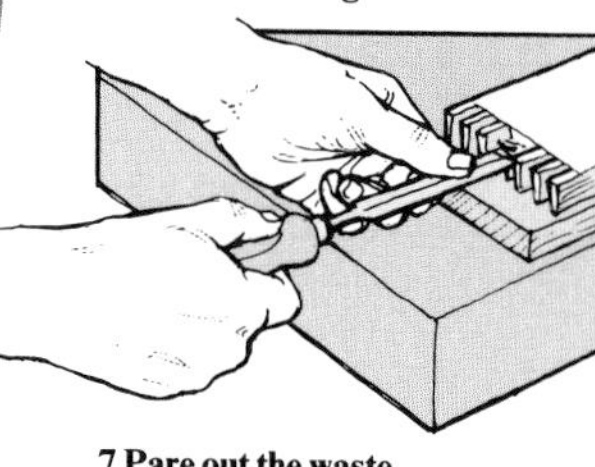

7 Pare out the waste

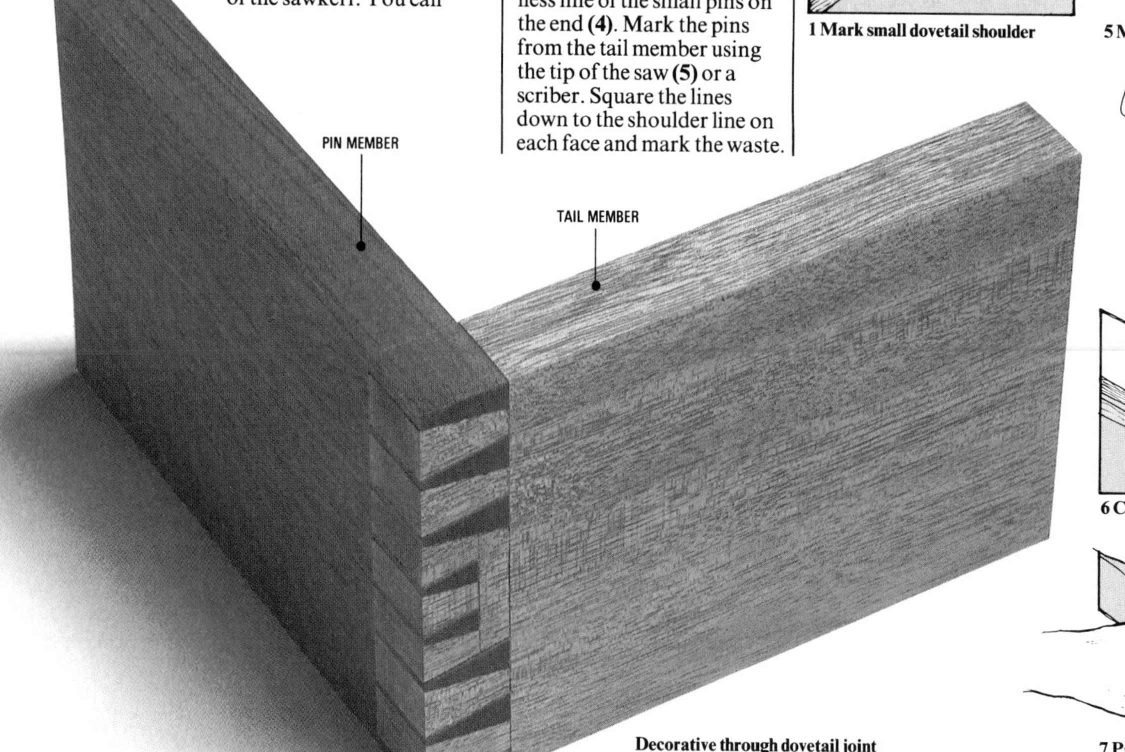

Decorative through dovetail joint

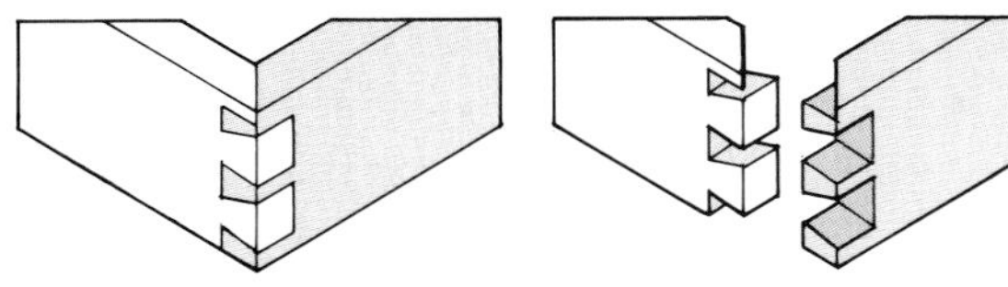

MITERED THROUGH DOVETAIL JOINT

A mitered edge is sometimes incorporated with a through dovetail joint to allow the edge to be molded. The depth of the mitered portion is dependent on the contour of the molding.

Marking the tails
Gauge the shoulder line on the two sides and bottom edge of the tail member. Mark the miter shoulder line on the top edge **(1)**.

Measure down from the top edge the depth required for the molding. Gauge a line at this level across the end and around to the shoulder line **(2)**.

Make a light pencil mark $\frac{1}{4}$in (6mm) below the first mark and also $\frac{1}{4}$in (6mm) up from the bottom edge. Divide the distance between these marks and set out the tails as required. Mark the waste to be cut away.

Cutting the tails
Saw down the sides of the tails and the molding depth line and remove the waste with a coping saw. Trim the shoulders with a bevel-edged chisel. Leave the miter waste at this stage.

Marking the pins
Lightly gauge a shoulder line on both sides of the pin member. Mark the miter shoulder line on the top edge. Chalk the end and mark the pins and miter waste from the tail member.

Square the tail lines down to the shoulder lines on each face and to the miter waste line on the inside face only. Mark the waste.

Cutting the pins
Cut the waste from between the pins. Then cut away the miter waste from the top corner **(3)**. Finally, saw off the miter waste from the tail piece **(4)**. Plane the top edge to the required molding before assembling the joint.

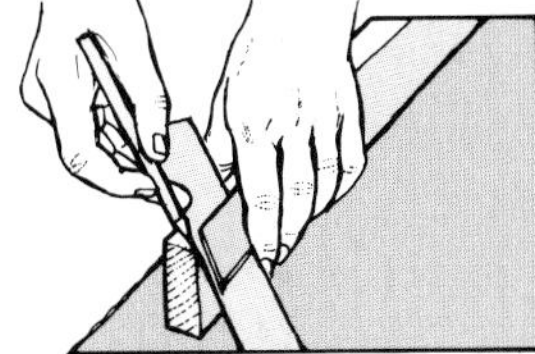

1 Mark the miter line

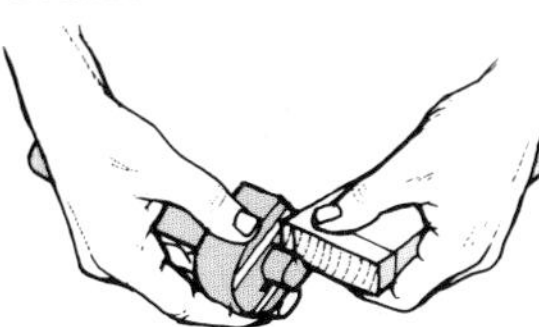

2 Gauge the molding-depth line

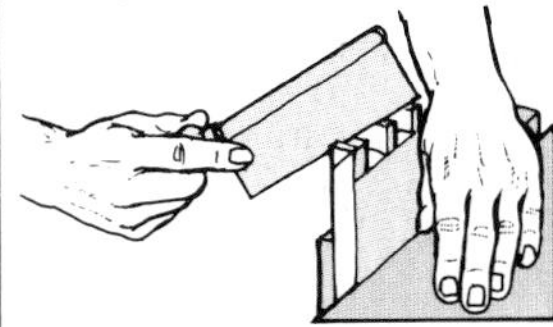

3 Cut away the pin-miter waste

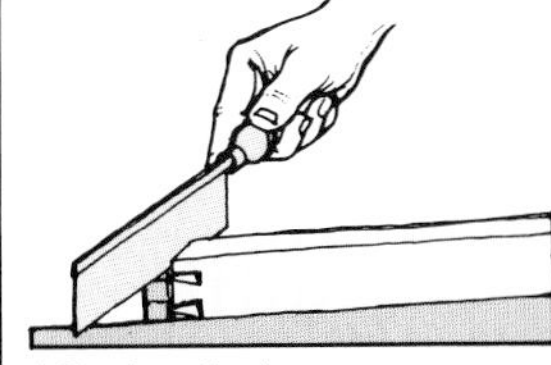

4 Cut the tail-miter waste

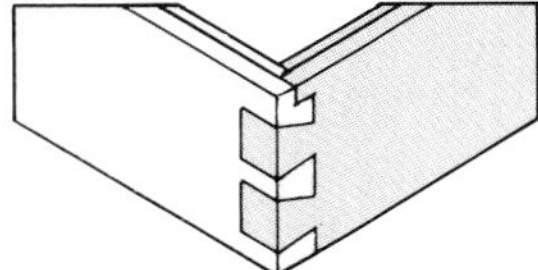

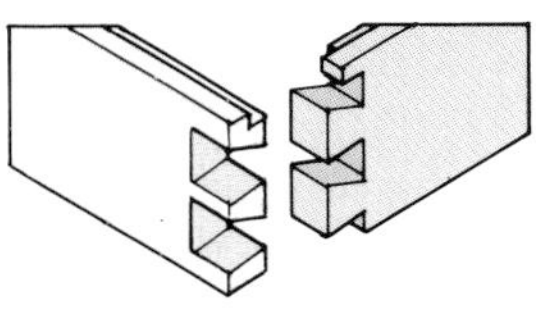

RABBETED THROUGH DOVETAIL JOINT

A box featuring through dovetails and having the bottom panel set in a rabbet requires the joint to be modified if a gap is not to show at the bottom corner. This is done by projecting the shoulder of the tail member to fill the rabbet.

Marking the tails
Gauge the tails' shoulder line on the sides and over the top edge. Gauge the rabbet-depth line along the inside edge, over the end and around to the shoulder line on the face side **(1)**. Also mark the inside face of the pin member at the same setting. Reset the gauge, if necessary, and mark the width of the rabbet on the edge of both parts **(2)**.

Make one pencil mark on the tail member $\frac{1}{4}$in (6mm) below the intended depth of the rabbet and another at $\frac{1}{4}$in (6mm) from the opposite edge. Set out the tails between the marks.

Square a line over the rabbeted edge of the tail member to match the rabbet on the pin member **(3)**, and mark the waste.

Cutting the tails
Saw down the sides of the tails and the rabbet-depth line. Remove the waste with a coping saw and chisel.

Marking the pins
Gauge a shoulder line on both sides of the pin member. Chalk the end and mark the pins from the tail member, using a scriber or sharp pencil. Mark the waste.

Cutting the joints
Cut the sides of the pins and remove the waste with a coping saw and chisel. Plane the rabbet on both pin and tail members. Finally, cut off the waste from the projecting shoulder of the tail member **(4)**.

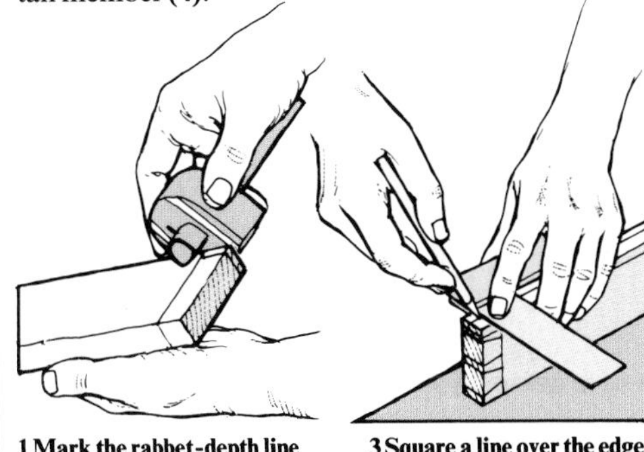

1 Mark the rabbet-depth line

3 Square a line over the edge

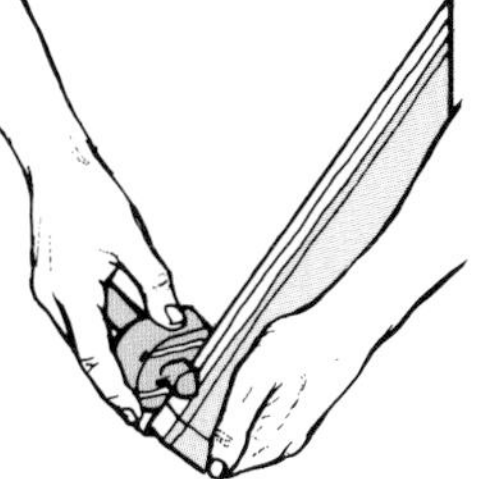

2 Mark the rabbet-width line

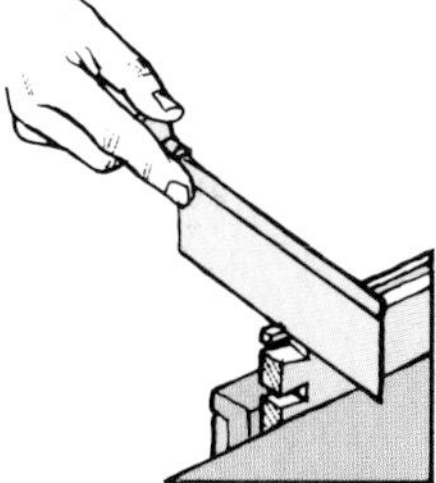

4 Saw off projecting waste

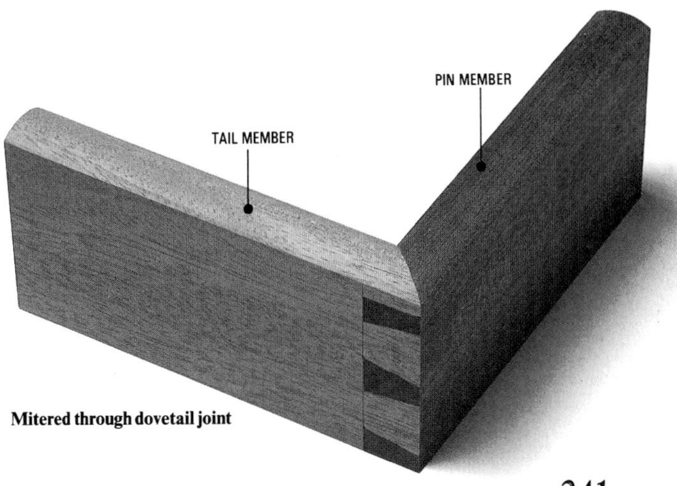

Mitered through dovetail joint

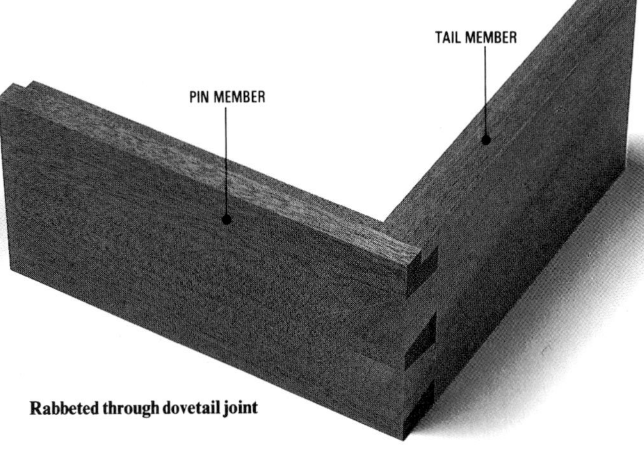

Rabbeted through dovetail joint

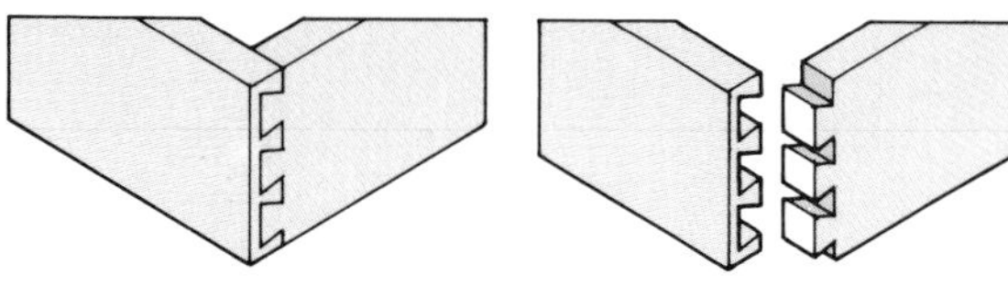

HALF-BLIND DOVETAIL JOINT

The half-blind dovetail joint is used in cabinet construction where the dovetail joint is needed for strength but not to be seen from one side. The joint is typically used for traditional drawer construction. It is similar to the through dovetail to execute except for the marking and cutting of the pins.

SEE ALSO

Cabinet construction	62
Measuring and marking tools	76-79
Dovetail saws	83
Shoulder planes	92,93
Bevel-edged chisels	98,101

Marking the tails
The thickness of the lap must first be determined before the tail member is cut to precise length. As a guide, the lap can be one-third the thickness of the pin member but not less than ⅛in (3mm). Set a cutting gauge to the length of the tails (the thickness of the pin member less the lap) and mark the shoulder all around the prepared end of the tail piece. Then set out the dovetails and mark the waste.

Cutting the tails
Cut away the waste with a dovetail saw and coping saw and trim the shoulders with a bevel-edged chisel.

Marking the pins
With the cutting gauge set to the length of the tails, gauge the lap line on the end of the pin member, working from the inside face.

Reset the gauge to the thickness of the tail member and mark a line across the inside face, working from the end. Chalk the end of the pin member and mark the pins from the tails **(1)**. Square the lines down to the inside shoulder line and mark the waste.

1 Mark the pins from the tails

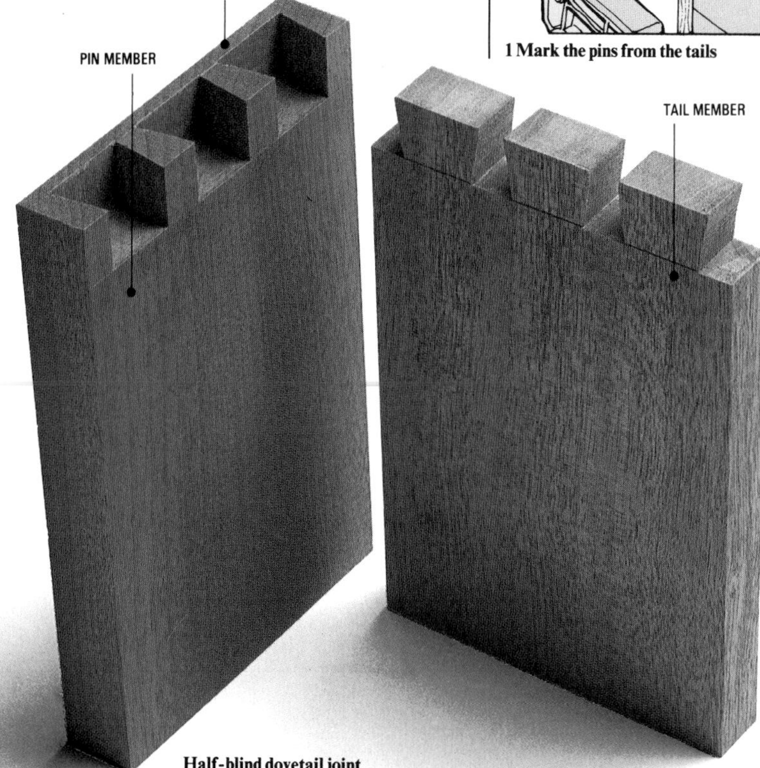

Half-blind dovetail joint

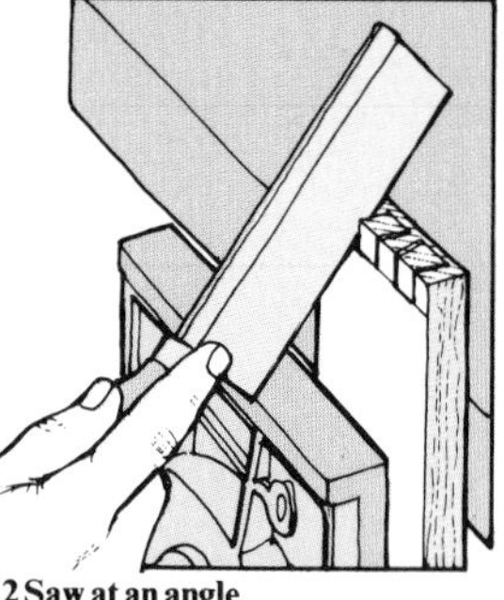

2 Saw at an angle

Cutting the pins
Set the work upright in the vise. Hold the saw at an angle and cut down the waste side of the lines **(2)**. Stop on the lap and shoulder lines. Saw out some of the waste from the corners while you have the wood set up in the vise **(3)**.

Clamp the wood to the bench on a flat board. Chop out the waste with a bevel-edged chisel. Make a series of alternating cuts, first across the grain **(4)**, then with the grain **(5)**. Start the cross-grain cuts away from the shoulder line and work back to it as the waste is removed. Carefully trim away the waste from the corners with a narrow bevel-edged chisel.

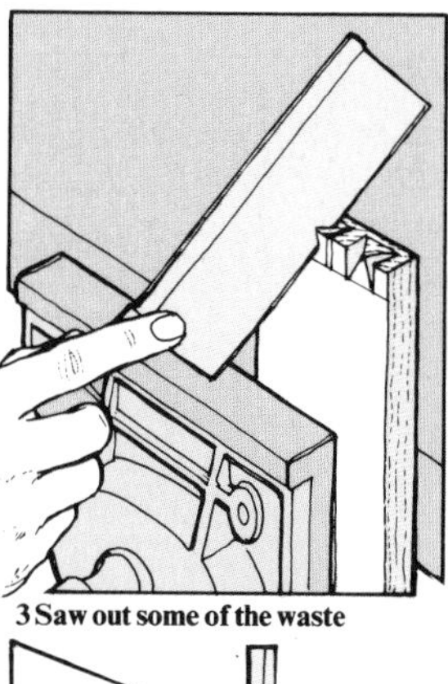

3 Saw out some of the waste

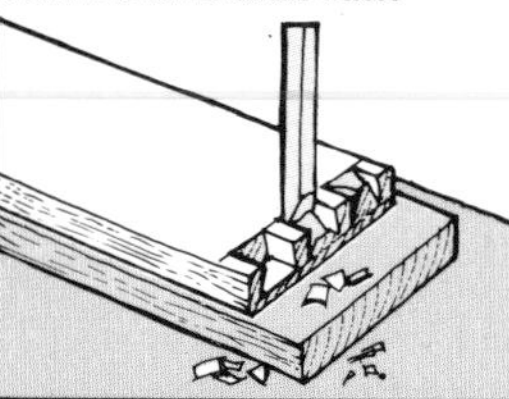

4 Cut across the grain

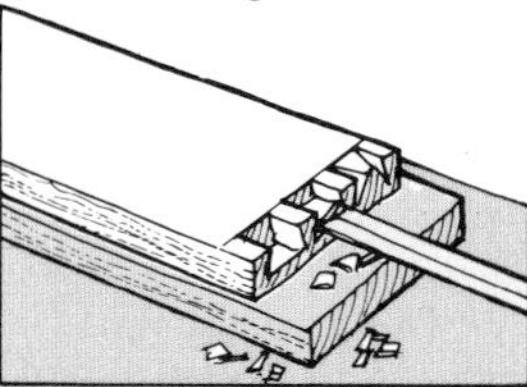

5 Pare out the waste

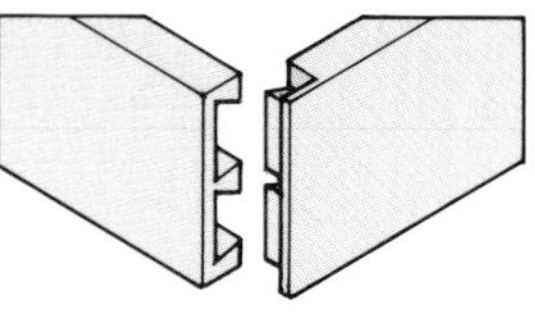

BLIND DOVETAIL JOINT

The blind dovetail is used for cabinet or box construction where the dovetails are required to be hidden. All that is seen of the joint is the end grain of one lap. The lap may be on the tail or pin member. The method you adopt will determine which way around the parts are marked. If the lap is on the pin member, the pins must be cut first and the tails marked from them. The method described here has the lap on the tail piece.

Marking and cutting the tails
Start with the wood cut to length and the ends planed square. Set a cutting gauge to the thickness of the pin member and mark the shoulder line on the inside face and edges of the tail member.

Set the gauge to the width of the lap and mark the end and edges from the outside face. Gauge the rabbet-depth line on the inside and edges at the same setting from the end **(1)**.

You must now cut the rabbet before you can mark the tails. Saw away the rabbet waste, keeping close to the line **(2)**. To help keep the saw on line, chisel a groove on the waste side of the line. Trim the rabbet with a shoulder plane **(3)**.

Set out the width and positions of the tails and mark the slope with a template **(4)**. Square the lines on the end. Mark the waste. Saw and chisel out the waste as for a half-blind dovetail.

Marking and cutting the pins
Gauge the width of the lap on the end of the pin member. Set the gauge to the thickness of the tails and mark a line on the inside face, working from the end. Chalk the end and mark the pins from the tails **(5)**. Square the lines down the inside face. Mark the waste, then saw and chisel it out.

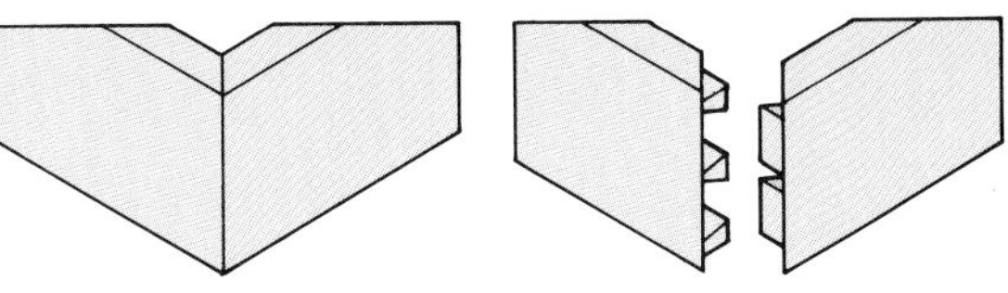

MITERED DOVETAIL JOINT

The construction of this dovetail joint is completely hidden by the mitered laps and is often referred to as a secret mitered dovetail. It is used in fine work and requires careful marking and cutting. The members being joined must be the same thickness and need to be cut to length. The tails can only be marked from the pins, which are cut first.

Marking and cutting the joint
Set a cutting gauge to the thickness of the wood and mark a shoulder line across the inside face, working from the end. Using a marking knife and miter square, mark the miter on each edge between the gauge line and outer corner.

Set the gauge to the width of the lap and mark the rabbet. Mark the end from the outside face and mark the rabbet-depth line from the end **(1)**. Saw out the rabbet waste and trim the surface with a shoulder plane.

Begin marking out the pins by first gauging a line parallel with each edge from the shoulder line to the lap. Set the line not more than ¼in (6mm) from the edge **(2)**.

Set out the width and positions of the pins on the end between the gauged lines. Make a cardboard dovetail template and hold it against the lap face to keep it true. Square the lines down to the shoulder line, then mark the waste.

Saw and chisel out the waste between the pins as for a half-blind dovetail. The saw can cut into the lap slightly **(3)**. Saw off the miter waste. Set the work upright and pare most of the waste from the lap miter with a chisel **(4)**. Finish the miter with a shoulder plane. Back up the edge with a mitered block to help guide the plane.

Marking and cutting the tails
Follow the procedure given for marking out the pin member up to and including cutting the rabbet.

Lay the tail member on the bench, inside face up. Place the pin member on the end with its inside face level with the gauge line. Mark off the shape of the pins with a scriber **(5)**. Square the lines onto the end and mark the waste.

Saw off the miter waste **(6)**. Then saw down the sides of the tails and chop out the waste between the tails and between the end tails and miter shoulder **(7)**. Pare and plane the lap miter in the same way as the pin member to complete the joint. Try the joint for fit before gluing.

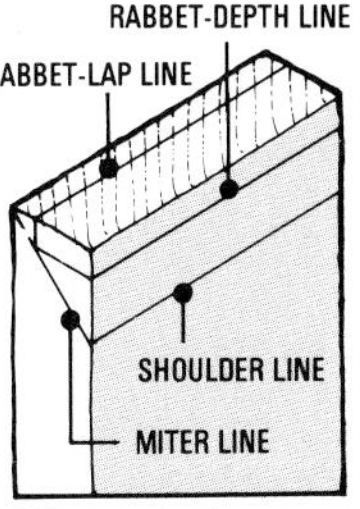

1 Set out the lines

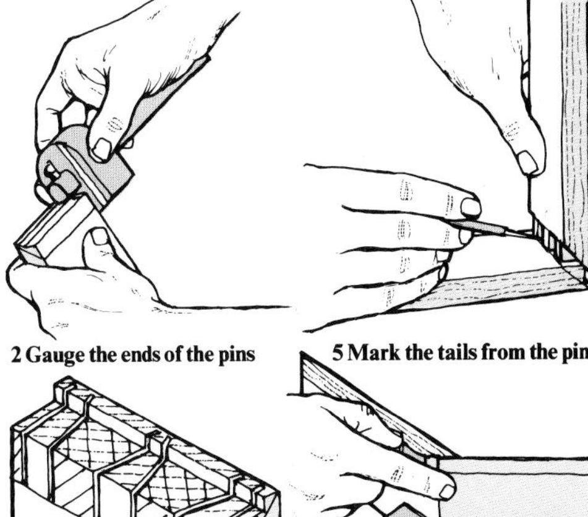

2 Gauge the ends of the pins

5 Mark the tails from the pins

3 Saw the sides of the pins

6 Saw off the miter waste

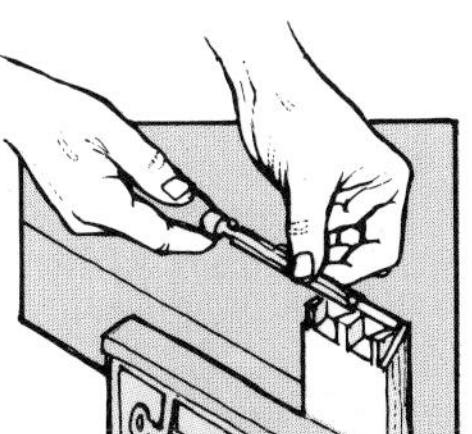

4 Pare the miter waste

7 Chop out the waste

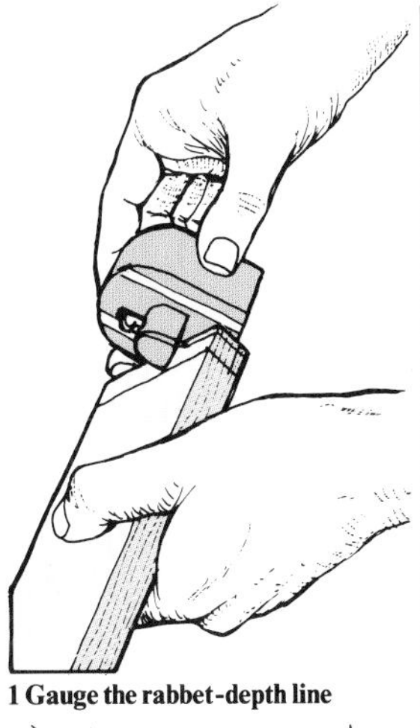

1 Gauge the rabbet-depth line

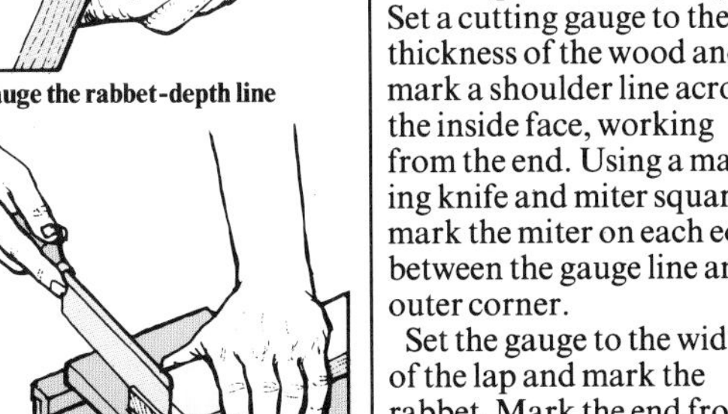

2 Saw away rabbet waste

3 Trim the rabbet

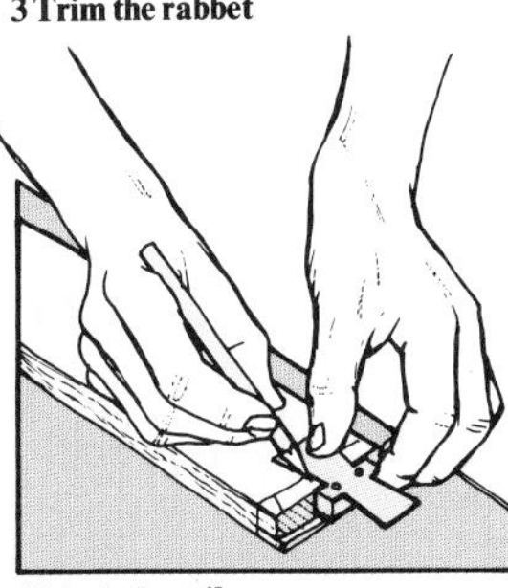

4 Mark the tails

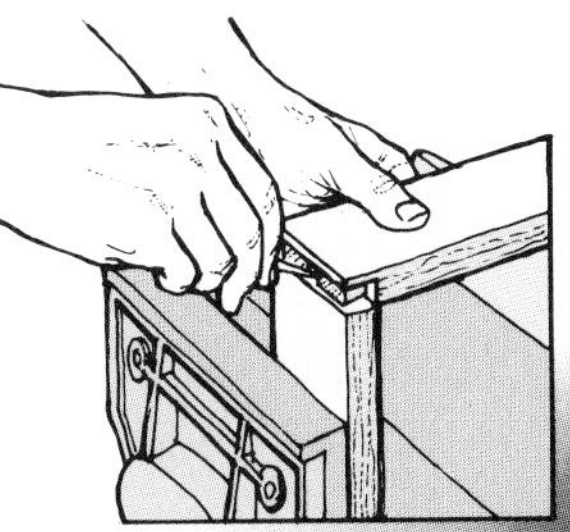

5 Mark the pins from the tails

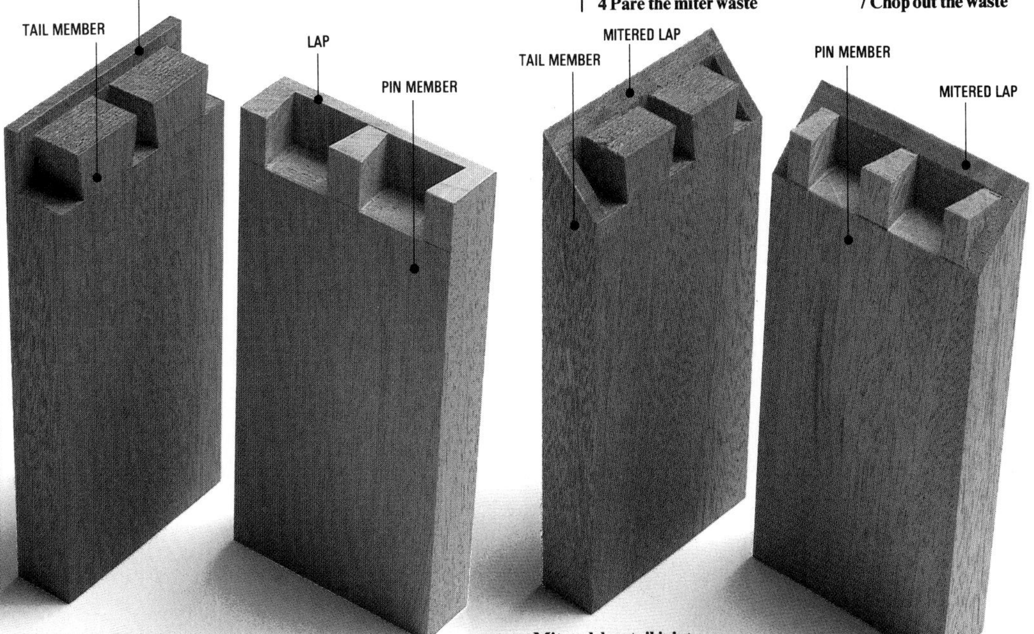

Blind dovetail joint

Mitered dovetail joint

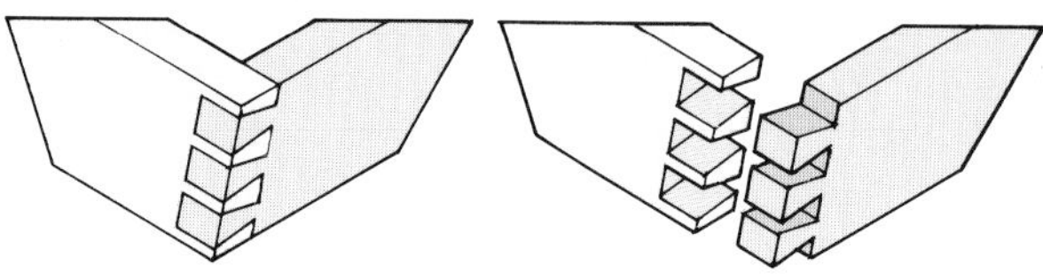

BEVELED DOVETAIL JOINT

The beveled dovetail is used to make a rigid joint in the sloping sides of a frame that meet at a compound angle. It is not an easy joint to make, as it is difficult to visualize, the setting out is complicated and all the edges of the parts are angled, requiring careful cutting. For simplicity, the wood must be the same thickness and has to be cut oversize in length and width. It is necessary to make an elevation drawing from which to calculate the true shape of the parts before the joint can be marked out.

SEE ALSO

Measuring and marking tools	76-79
Sliding bevel	76
Dovetail saws	83
Bevel-edged chisels	98,101
Sash clamp	120
Web clamp	121

Making a drawing

Begin by drawing the side elevation of the frame joint as it would appear when complete. Show the thickness of the wood and add broken lines representing its initial width and length. Draw its plan immediately below the side elevation.

However, neither drawing will give a true view, as the parts seen from these angles are foreshortened. To get the true view, project the side to lie flat **(1)**. Start by setting a pair of compasses on point A. Strike an arc from point A^1 to the baseline at B. Strike a second arc from point A^2. Set the compass point on A^3 and swing an arc to meet a vertical line at C. Draw a line through C parallel to the baseline. Join up points BD and draw a line parallel to it from A, which will give a true section of the side.

Drop a vertical line from A to E on the plan. Drop a line from B to F on a line extended from the outer edge of the plan. Similarly, drop a line from C^1 to G and from D to H. Join G to H with a solid line that represents the inside of the end. Join E to F with a broken line to represent the outside edge. The angle X is the true angle of the end.

To find the true bevel angle, draw a line at right angles to line EF at I. Draw a second line parallel to it and set away from it by the thickness of the wood to point J. Run a line through IJ. The angle Y is the true bevel angle.

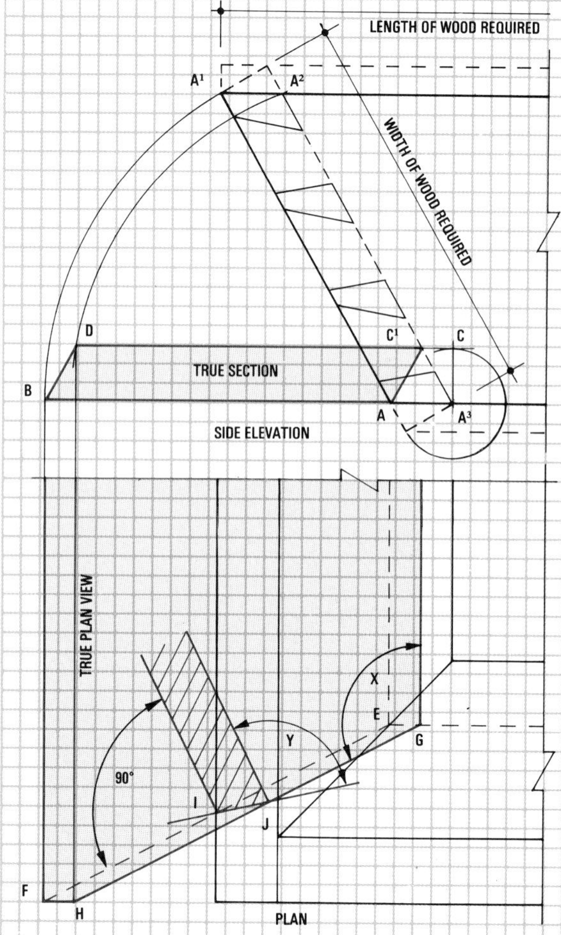

1 Construct an elevation and true-view drawing of the joint

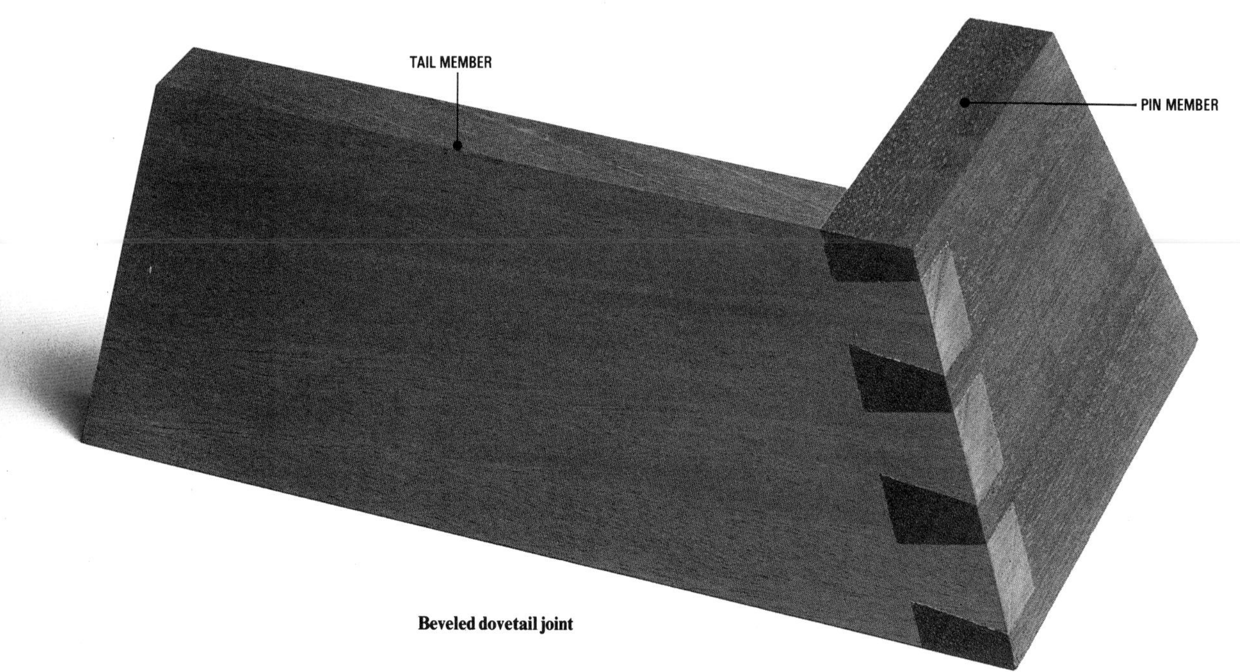

Beveled dovetail joint

Marking and cutting the ends

Cut the parts to length and width as shown by the broken lines on the side elevation. Set an adjustable bevel to the end angle X **(2)**. Mark the angle on the inside face of the wood from the corner **(3)**. Saw the ends to the angle **(4)**. Set a second bevel to the end angle Y. Mark the angle on the edges from the outer face side **(5)**. Join up the edge marks to give a guide line for planing the end bevel. In fact, the bevel should be checked with the adjustable bevel held at right angles to the edge as planing progresses to give the true bevel **(6)**. Set the wood in the vise with the end horizontal and carefully plane the end bevel on each part.

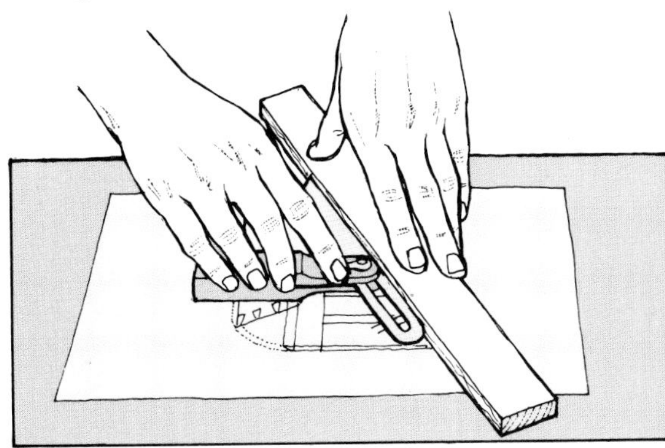

2 Set bevel to the end angle

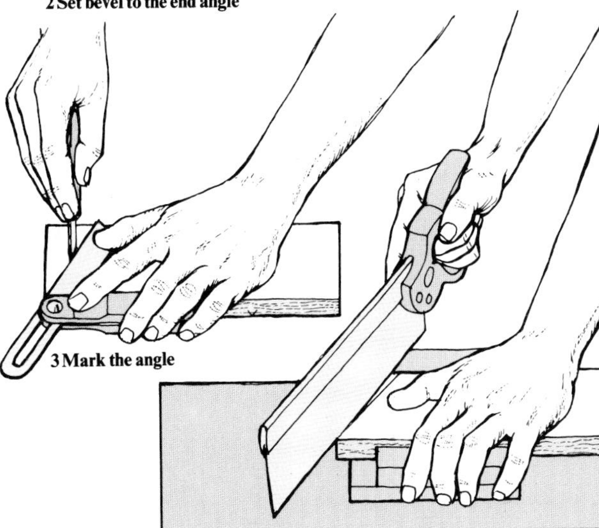

3 Mark the angle

4 Saw the end angle

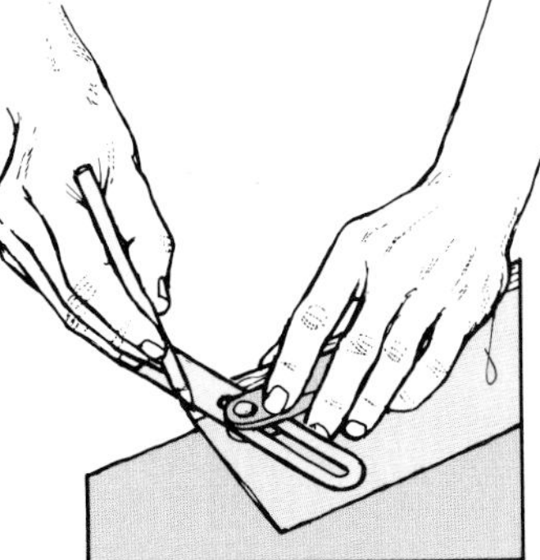

5 Mark angle Y on the edges

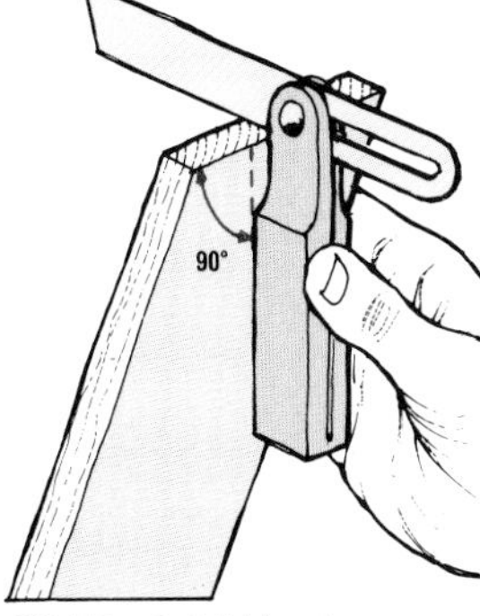

6 Hold bevel at right angles

Marking and cutting the joint

Set out the tails on the face side of the tail member. First mark the thickness of the wood on both faces of both parts, taken from the beveled ends **(7)**. Join the lines on each edge of the tail members.

With the adjustable bevel set to the end angle X, mark a line from the inside bottom corner on the end of the tail member. Make a mark $\frac{1}{4}$in (6mm) down from the top edge and up from the bottom mark. Set out the size and spacing of the tails between these marks. Then set a cardboard dovetail template against a try square and mark out the dovetails on the outside face **(8)**.

Mark the slope of the dovetail ends on the beveled end of the tail member. Use the bevel set to the end angle X. Hold the stock of the bevel square to the end face **(9)**, as it was flat when set from the drawing.

Use the try square and dovetail template to mark the dovetail on the inside face. Mark the waste.

Cut the tails carefully, following the marked angles. Place the work at an angle in the vise to set each cutting line vertical **(10)**.

Mark the cut dovetails on the end of the pin member. Apply chalk to the end to help make clear scriber lines. Lay the tail member on the end with the edges and inner shoulders flush and mark around the tails.

Using the bevel set to the end angle X, mark parallel lines down from each dovetail to the shoulder **(11)**. Mark the waste, then saw and chisel it out carefully, following the angled lines.

You can plane the bevel on the long edges before or after gluing up. Use the bevel set to the end angle X to check the bevel, whichever way you choose. The sloping sides can present problems when gluing up. If you tap the joints home with a hammer, use a block to protect the work.

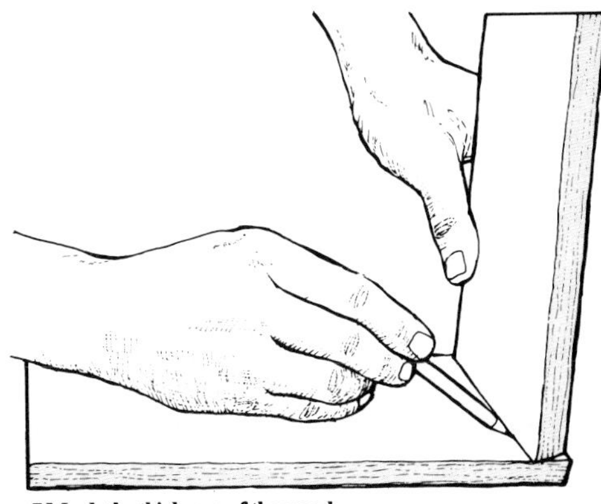

7 Mark the thickness of the wood

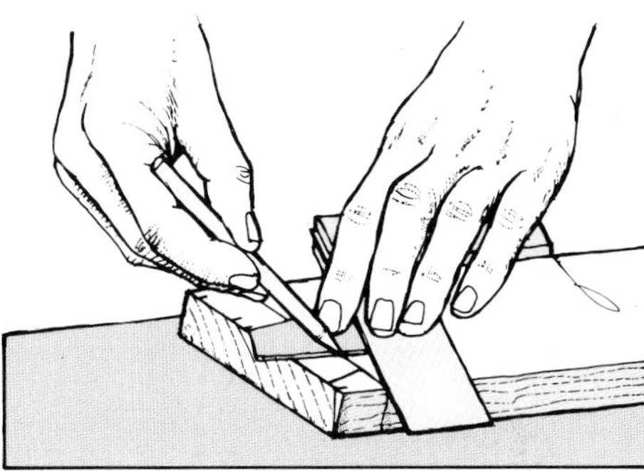

8 Using a cardboard template, mark the tails

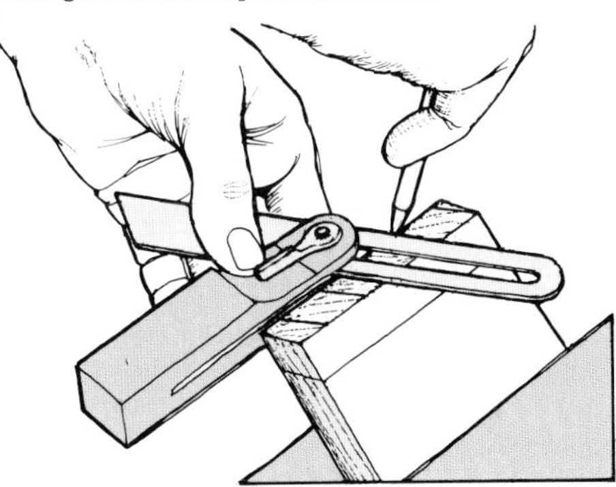

9 Hold the stock square to the end face

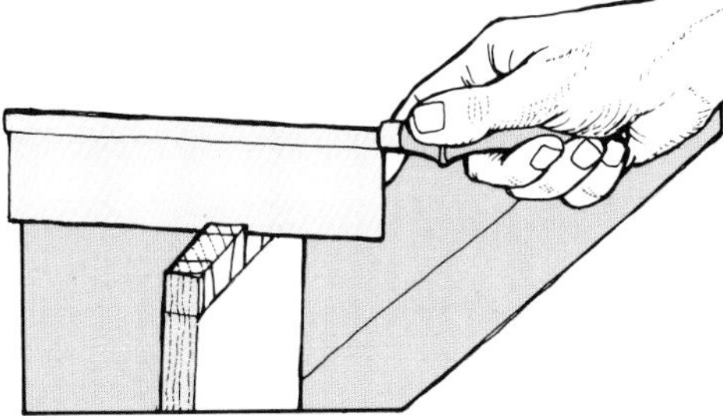

10 Set cutting lines vertical

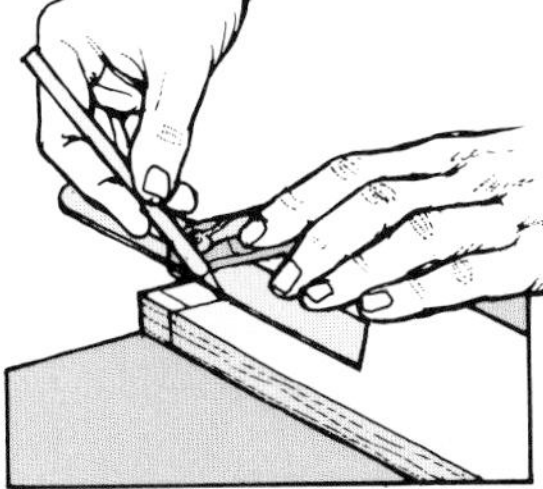

11 Mark pin cutting lines

● **Clamping the joint**
To clamp the joint, use web clamps, or glue wedge-shaped blocks to the surface and use sash clamps. Place thick paper between the block and the surface so you can remove the block without damaging the wood.

BOARD JOINTS

Plywood, blockboard, laminboard, chipboard and medium-density fiberboard (MDF) are all used for carcase construction. Man-made boards are more stable than panels of solid wood, but on the whole they do not have its long-grain strength. The means of joining these boards varies according to their composition. Most joints used for solid-wood carcase construction are suitable. Framing joints, such as mortise and tenon, lap and bridle joints, are unsuitable for joining man-made boards.

SEE ALSO

Man-made boards	34-38
Biscuit joints	136-137
Butt joints	216-217
Rabbet joints	218
Edge joints	222-223
Housing joints	224-225
Dowel joints	236-237
Dovetail joints	238-243

JOINT GUIDE

The chart shows the typical range of man-made boards and the carcase joints suitable for a particular material. The first column indicates the strength of each joint in each material. The second column shows the best ways of making the joints. The third column indicates the relative difficulty in terms of hand-cutting and machine-cutting.

Treat solid-core laminated boards, such as blockboard and laminboard, like solid wood when selecting a joint for a particular application. A dovetail, for example, would be cut in the end grain only, not the side grain.

Dovetails are more difficult to cut in these materials because of the changing grain direction of the board's structure. Make coarse, even-sized tails and pins (machine-cut dovetails are preferable). For dovetail-joined cabinets that are to be veneered, use rabbet joints. The mitered variety is best, as it will not show the joint's construction through the veneer if the wood shrinks or swells.

Man-made boards that are ready-finished with a decorative veneer must be miter-joined if the core material is not to show on the face. The alternative is to use a corner lipping, which makes an attractive decorative feature.

TYPICAL CARCASE JOINTS

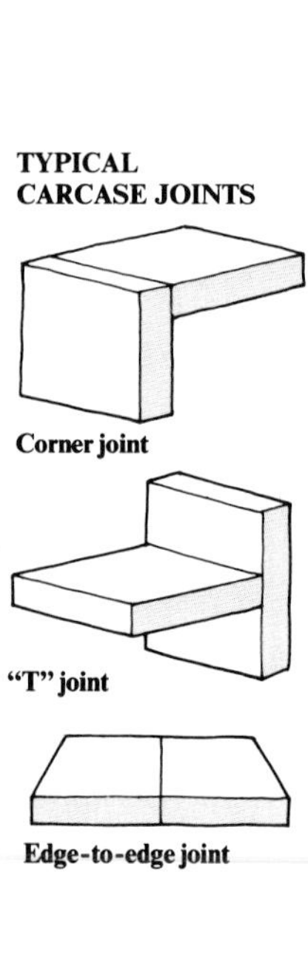

Corner joint

"T" joint

Edge-to-edge joint

CORNER-JOINT OPTIONS	SUITABILITY AND RELATIVE STRENGTH: PLYWOOD	BLOCKBOARD	LAMINBOARD	CHIPBOARD	MDF	SUITABLE METHOD OF MAKING: HAND-CUT	HAND-CUT/JIG	MACHINE-CUT	MACHINE-CUT	RELATIVE DIFFICULTY OF MAKING: HAND-CUT	MACHINE-CUT	COMMENTS
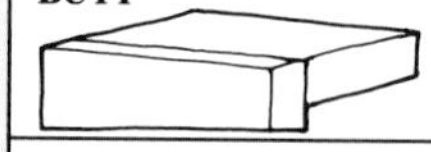 BUTT	▮	▮	▮	▮	▮	△			▲	■	■	Has exposed core. Nail, screw or block reinforcement improves strength.
MITERED BUTT 	▯	▯	▯	▮	▯			△	▲	●	■	Core is hidden. Has similar strength to plain butt. Good for veneering.
SPLINED MITER 	▯	▯	▯	▯	▯			△		●	■	Stronger than plain miter. Can be used as decorative joint.
LOOSE-TONGUED MITER 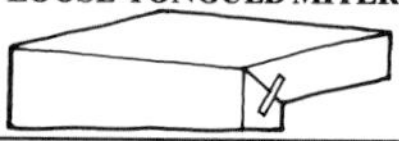	▯	▯	▯	▯	▯				▲	●	■	A strong miter joint. Core is hidden. Good for veneering.
RABBET 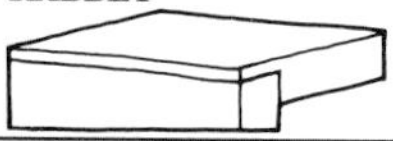	▯	▯	▯	▯	▯	△		△	▲	■	■	Neater and stronger than a plain butt. Shows a little core at corner.
MITERED RABBET 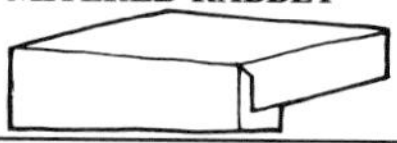	▯	▯	▯	▯	▯	△			▲	●	■	Core is hidden. Better appearance than rabbet but more difficult to cut.
BAREFACED HOUSING 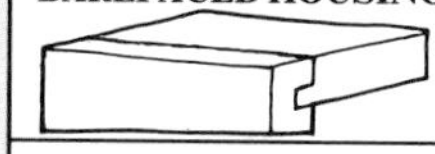	▯	▯	▯	▯	▯	△		△	▲	■	■	Has exposed core. Has greater strength than plain butt.
DOWEL 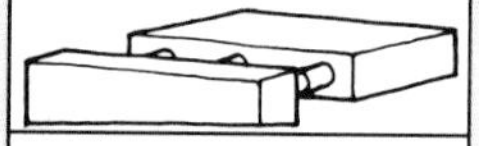	▯	▯	▯	▯	▯	△	▲	△		■	■	Similar in appearance to plain butt joint but is much stronger.
MITERED DOWEL 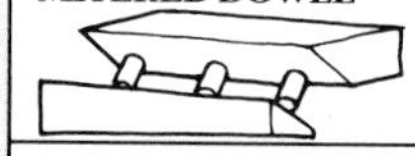	▯	▯	▯	▯	▯		▲	△		●	■	Similar to loose-tongued miter in strength and appearance, cut with jig.
THROUGH DOVETAIL 	▮	▮	▮	▯	▯	△		△		●	■	A strong joint. May show through if covered with veneer.
HALF-BLIND DOVETAIL 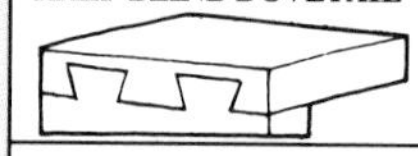	▮	▮	▮	▯	▯	△		△		●	■	Similar in strength to through dovetail with the joint hidden on one face.
BLIND DOVETAIL 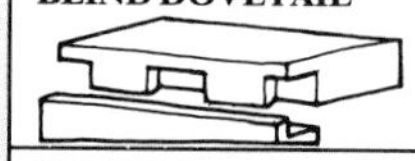	▮	▮	▮	▯	▯	△				●		Similar to the half-blind dovetail but only a thin edge of core exposed.
MITERED DOVETAIL 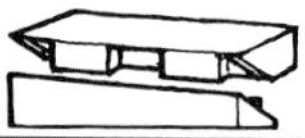	▮	▮	▮	▯	▯	△				●		Strong joint where core is hidden. Best version for veneering.
BISCUIT 	▮	▮	▮	▮	▮			△			■	A strong machine-made joint. Can be butted or mitered.

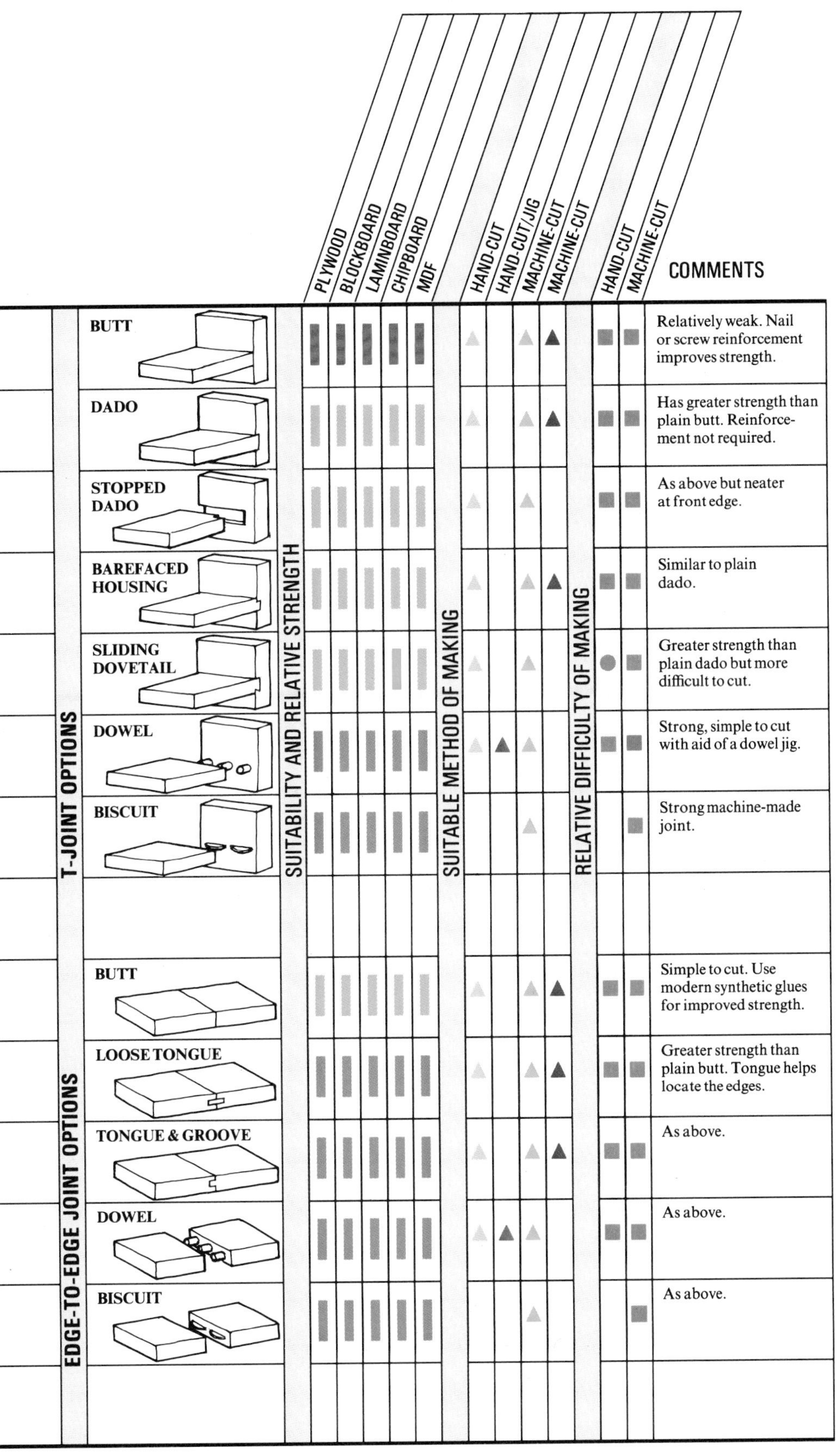

	Joint	Plywood	Blockboard	Laminboard	Chipboard	MDF	Hand-cut	Hand-cut/jig	Machine-cut	Machine-cut	Hand-cut	Machine-cut	Comments
		Suitability and relative strength					Suitable method of making				Relative difficulty of making		
T-JOINT OPTIONS	BUTT	Poor	Poor	Poor	Poor	Poor	▲		▲	▲	■	■	Relatively weak. Nail or screw reinforcement improves strength.
	DADO	Good	Good	Good	Good	Good	▲		▲	▲	■	■	Has greater strength than plain butt. Reinforcement not required.
	STOPPED DADO	Good	Good	Good	Good	Good	▲		▲		■	■	As above but neater at front edge.
	BAREFACED HOUSING	Good	Good	Good	Good	Good	▲		▲	▲	■	■	Similar to plain dado.
	SLIDING DOVETAIL	Good	Good	Good	Good	Good	▲		▲		●	■	Greater strength than plain dado but more difficult to cut.
	DOWEL	Excellent	Excellent	Excellent	Excellent	Excellent	▲	▲	▲		■	■	Strong, simple to cut with aid of a dowel jig.
	BISCUIT	Excellent	Excellent	Excellent	Excellent	Excellent			▲			■	Strong machine-made joint.
EDGE-TO-EDGE JOINT OPTIONS	BUTT	Good	Good	Good	Good	Good	▲		▲	▲	■	■	Simple to cut. Use modern synthetic glues for improved strength.
	LOOSE TONGUE	Excellent	Excellent	Excellent	Excellent	Excellent	▲		▲	▲	■	■	Greater strength than plain butt. Tongue helps locate the edges.
	TONGUE & GROOVE	Excellent	Excellent	Excellent	Excellent	Excellent	▲		▲	▲	■	■	As above.
	DOWEL	Excellent	Excellent	Excellent	Excellent	Excellent	▲	▲	▲		■	■	As above.
	BISCUIT	Excellent	Excellent	Excellent	Excellent	Excellent			▲			■	As above.

KEY TO CHART

Suitability and relative strength

- Excellent
- Good
- Fair
- Poor
- Unsuitable

Suitable method of making

- ▲ Hand-cut (Using hand tools)
- ▲ Hand-cut/jig (Using hand tools with jigs)
- ▲ Machine-cut (Using hand-held power tools)*
- ▲ Machine-cut (Using machine tools)*

**Jigs may also be used*

Relative difficulty of making

- ● Difficult
- ■ Simple

SEE ALSO	
Shelf units	62
Handsaws	80-82
Tongue and groove	96,97
Circular saws	132-135
Molding an edge	142
Trimmer bit	142
Routers	146
Table saws	156-159,161

USING A CORNER LIPPING

For preveneered chipboard, a lipping can be used to make a corner joint that also masks the core. The grain of the lipping is set at right angles to the face veneer of the board and forms a feature. The lipping can be left square or you can shape it. You can also use contrasting wood.

Joints for corner lippings

Butt-join the lipping or, for improved strength, make a tongue and groove joint. Use a loose-tongued joint or cut the groove in the edge of the board and the tongue in the lipping. Whichever way you decide, stop the tongue and the groove so they do not show on the edge **(1)**.

A stronger joint suitable for plinths or carcase construction can be made using a thicker lipping. Cut a barefaced tongue on the board and a matching goove in the lipping. The section can be shaped if required, as indicated by the broken line **(2).**

Shapes for corner lippings

Square

Quarter-round

Chamfered

Beaded

Beveled

Part-round

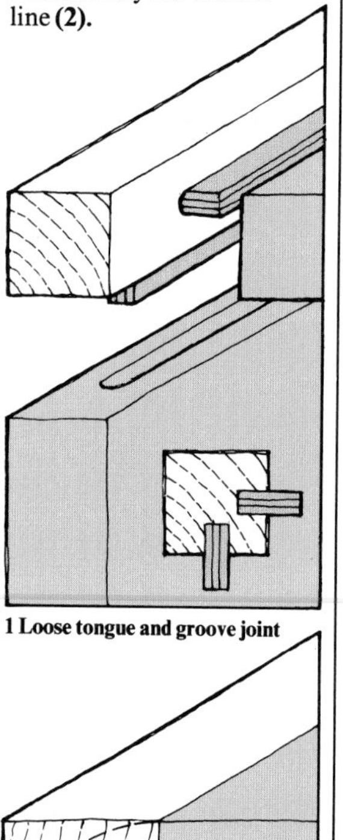

1 Loose tongue and groove joint

2 Shape the lipping if required

TYPES OF LIPPING

The edges of man-made boards must be finished with a lipping to cover the core material. You can use either long-grain or cross-grain veneer or a more substantial solid-wood lipping of matching or contrasting wood. Lippings can be applied before or after surface veneering. In the case of preveneered boards, you have no choice but to lip the edge last.

Applying lippings

The simplest edging to apply is the preglued veneer type that is ironed onto the edge. These edge lippings are primarily sold for finishing veneered chipboard panels and are available in a limited range of matching veneer.

For a more substantial edging, and one that can be shaped, cut thick lippings from matching solid wood. Butt-join the lipping to the edge or tongue and groove it for greater strength.

Miter the corners of thick lippings to improve the finished appearance. This is particularly necessary if the edge is molded.

When gluing up a long lipping, use a stiff batten between the lipping and the clamp heads to help spread the clamping forces over the full length of the work.

When planing glued-on edge lippings to width, take care not to touch the surface veneer, particularly when working across the direction of the grain. Finish the edge with a sanding block.

Deep lippings will substantially stiffen the boards for use as shelves or worktops. Set the full thickness of the board into a rabbet cut in the lipping.

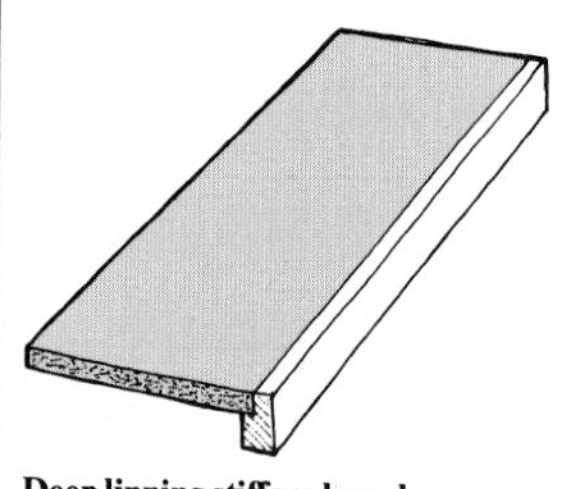

Deep lipping stiffens board

WORKING MAN-MADE BOARDS

Cutting by machine

Man-made boards are best cut to finished dimensions with clean-cutting, high-speed machine tools. Use a circular sawblade with tungsten-carbide-tipped teeth if cutting a lot of board. The teeth of the sawblade should pierce the board from the face side. When using a hand-held power saw, have the panel face down; and for a table saw, face up. Run the board across the saw relatively quickly. If using a band saw, run the saw fast but feed the board slowly. You can also use a hand-held router run against a long fence clamped to the work.

Cutting by hand

For handsawing, use a 10 to 12 PPI panel saw. A tenon saw can also be used for smaller work. To prevent break-out of the surface, make all cutting lines with a knife to sever the fibers or laminate. Also, hold the saw at a shallow angle. Support the board close to the cutting line. Lay it face side up over the bench; or if it is a particularly bulky piece, support it on sawhorses.

If cutting a large board, climb on to it so you can reach the cutting line comfortably. Have an assistant support the offcut if it is unmanageable. Otherwise, set up some means of support so it does not break away before you finish the cut.

Planing the edges

Plane the edges as you would for solid wood, but treat each edge as though it were end grain. You should therefore plane from both ends toward the middle.

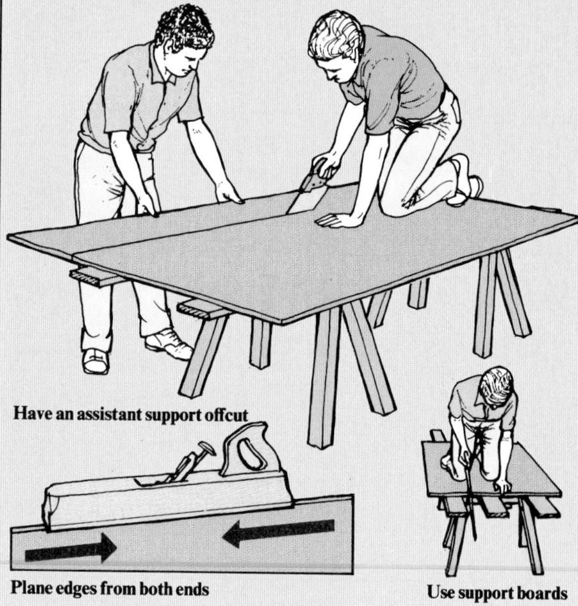

Have an assistant support offcut

Plane edges from both ends

Use support boards

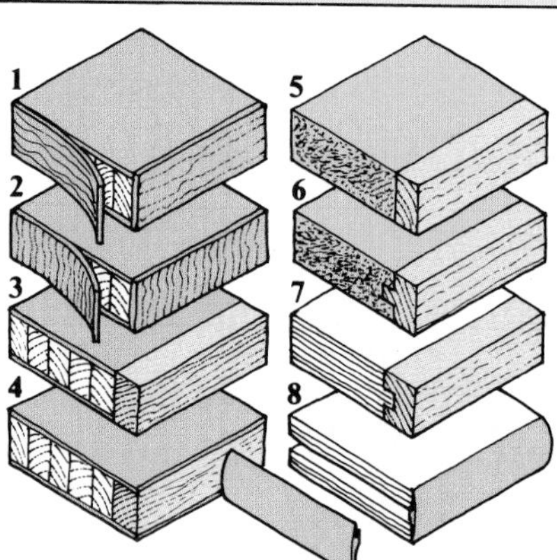

Lippings
1 Long-grain veneer
2 Cross-grain veneer
3 Lipped after veneering
4 Lipped before veneering
5 Butt-joined
6 Tongued lipping
7 Grooved lipping
8 Mitered lipping

CHAPTER EIGHT

BENDING WOOD

Curved furniture frames are difficult to make and extremely curved forms cut from straight sections of wood require complex joinery if weak short grain and costly waste are to be avoided. However, by employing dry or wet bending techniques, you can produce elaborate curvilinear shapes economically and, since the grain runs with the curve rather than across it, the resulting frame will be stronger. Dry bending requires wood cut into thin sections, but thicker sections can be bent if the wood is soaked or steamed. The café and rocking chairs made by Michael Thonet are classic examples of steam-bent furniture; and in the 1930s, laminated furniture became high style, following the development of mass-produced veneers. Both steam bending and laminating can be done in the home workshop, and both techniques are still used commercially for making reproduction furniture and by craftsmen-designers.

KERFING

A stiff section of wood can be dry-bent by kerfing the inside face. Kerfs are the grooves formed by a saw; and if a series of equally spaced sawcuts is made partway through the wood, it can be bent where its thickness is reduced. The technique is mainly used for curved work that shows only one face, such as "bullnose steps" in stairs. It can be used in cabinet-making to make plinths that have radiused corners.

CUTTING THE KERFS

The width of the kerf is determined by the saw used. A fine saw will give a narrow cut; a coarse one, a wide cut. The width of the cuts and their spacing have a direct bearing on the radius of the bend (see facing page). You need more finer-cut kerfs for a given radius than you do coarse kerfs. Closely spaced kerfs give a smoother contour to the bend. However, the face is usually slightly faceted, and it is necessary to sand down the bend to a smooth curve.

Using a power saw

The most efficient way to cut kerfs across a board is to use a radial-arm saw. Circular sawblades are thicker than handsaws and produce a wider kerf. You will therefore need fewer cuts for a given radius. Once set, the radial-arm saw will make square, equal-depth cuts across the board. All you need to concentrate on is the spacing of the cuts. Either do this by eye, using a mark on the back fence to align each cut, or fit a stop tab on which to locate each sawcut.

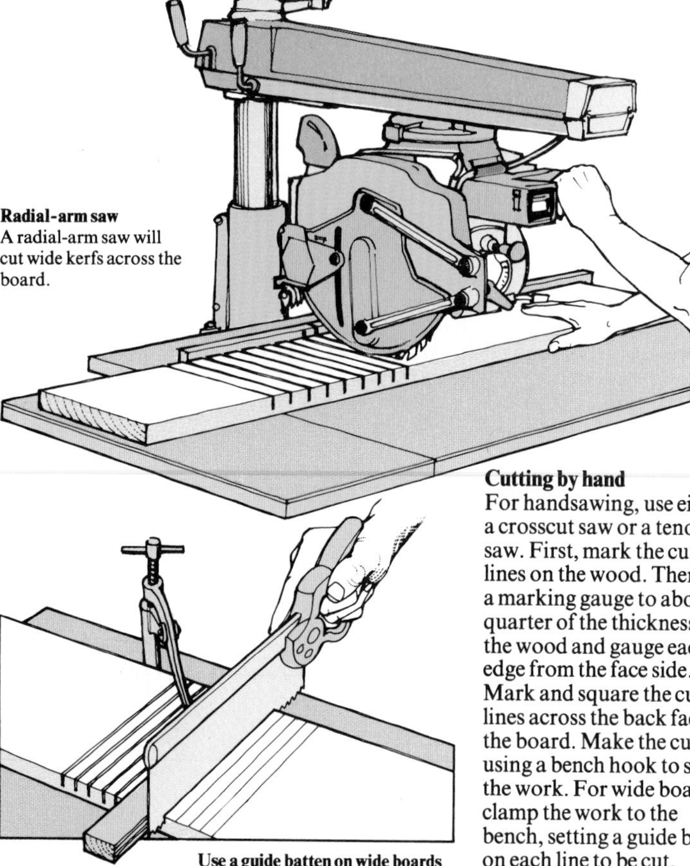

Radial-arm saw
A radial-arm saw will cut wide kerfs across the board.

Use a guide batten on wide boards

Cutting by hand

For handsawing, use either a crosscut saw or a tenon saw. First, mark the cutting lines on the wood. Then set a marking gauge to about a quarter of the thickness of the wood and gauge each edge from the face side. Mark and square the cut lines across the back face of the board. Make the cuts using a bench hook to steady the work. For wide boards, clamp the work to the bench, setting a guide batten on each line to be cut.

MAKING THE BEND

Gluing the bend

Try the bend against your plan elevation. Either hold the curve or pull it into shape using a web clamp. If the curve is satisfactory, open the kerfs, apply glue to each and reclamp. Because only the corners of the saw-cuts meet for gluing, it will not be particularly strong. If the work is likely to be stressed in use, apply reinforcement in the form of glued canvas or veneer around the inside face. Set the grain of the veneer to follow that of the wood and clamp it in the curve with blocks until the glue is set.

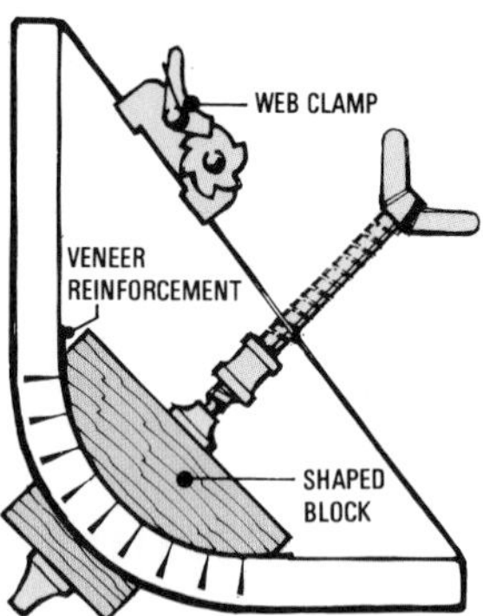

Apply glue and clamp the bend

Adjusting the bend

If the bend is not tight enough, run a triangular file through each sawcut and check again. Remove the same amount from each cut.

If the bend is too tight, insert a piece of paper or cardboard into each cut.

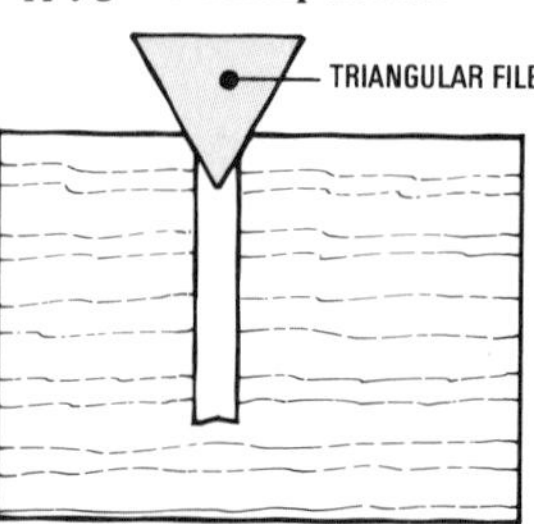

Relieve edges to adjust bend

Dual-faced bends

It is possible to produce kerfed bends with a smooth face on both sides by laminating two kerfed boards back to back. Cut the boards in the normal way, but glue them together using forms where necessary to support the inside curve.

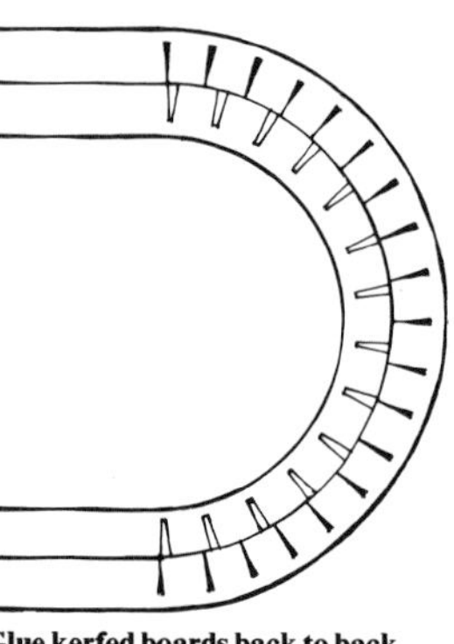

Glue kerfed boards back to back

Laminated kerfed bends

Kerfed bends are usually made with the kerfs cut across the grain. Bends at the end of a section of wood can be made by cutting kerfs with the grain and inserting strips of veneer into them to make a laminated bend.

A sufficient waste allowance must be made at the end to accommodate the shortening of the outside "tongues." Cut a series of equally spaced kerfs on a band saw. The thinner the tongues, the easier they will bend.

Glue oversized strips of veneer into the kerfs. You may have to double them up to increase their thickness to fill the kerfs. Clamp the bend around a form. When set, saw the stepped end square and plane the veneers flush with the sides.

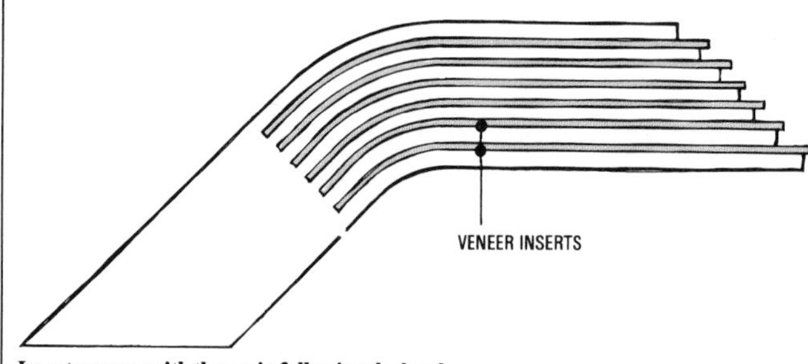

Insert veneers with the grain following the bend

CALCULATING THE KERF SPACING

Draw a full-size plan of the bend to determine its radius and length. Calculate the length mathematically, or measure it directly from the drawing by stepping off or bending a ruler.

When a piece of wood is bent, material on the outside of the bend will tend to stretch while that on the inside is compressed. Somewhere in between will be the neutral line. For greater accuracy, use this line in calculations; as kerfing brings it near the outside face of the member, it is probably sufficient to use this face in calculations.

When kerfing a bend, it is desirable to remove exactly the right amount of wood, as the curve is likely to be more even than if excess material is removed. This is because when the sides of each cut touch, the degree of bending must be the same at each cut **(1)**.

To determine spacing of the kerfs required to produce the bend, saw almost through the thickness of the board at the point from which the bend will spring, leaving at least ⅛in (3mm) of wood. From this cut, measure and mark the length of the radius on the edge. Clamp the end of the board firmly to the bench, then lift the free end of the board until the sawcut closes and bending stops. Wedge the board in this position. At the radius mark, measure the gap between the underside of the board and the bench top. The distance between the two faces gives the spacing of the sawcuts **(2)**.

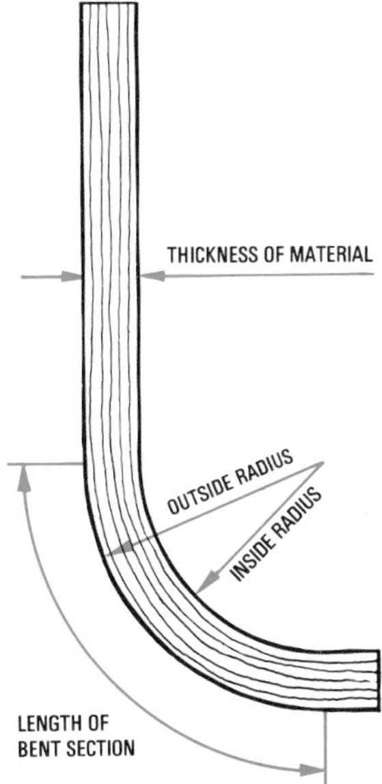

Draw a full-size plan
Use the drawing to determine length of bent section.

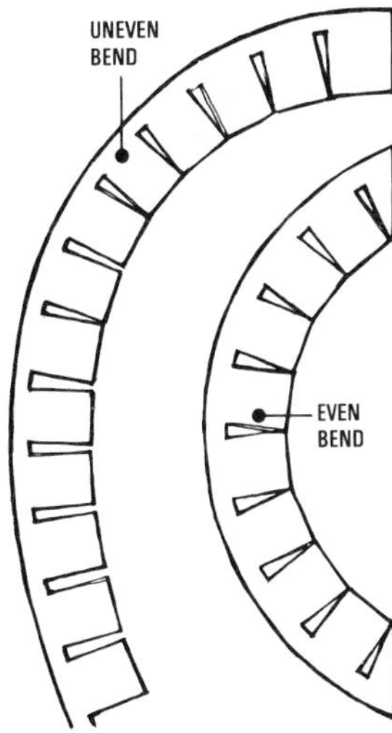

1 The sides of each cut must touch

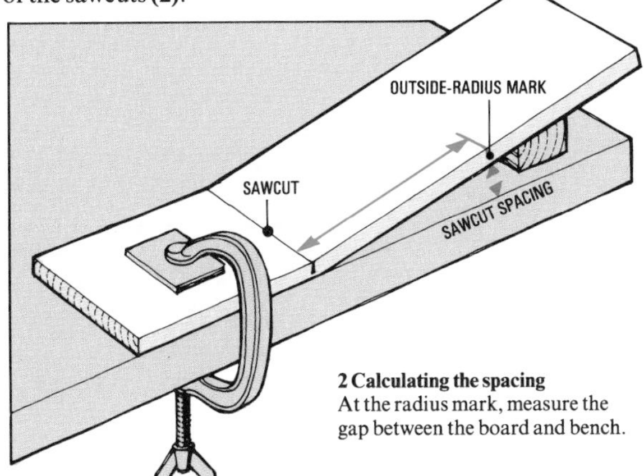

2 Calculating the spacing
At the radius mark, measure the gap between the board and bench.

STEAM BENDING

Steamed wood can be bent into relatively tight curves. The steam softens the wood fibers sufficiently to allow them to bend and compress as the wood is bent around a shaped form. It may take considerable force to bend the wood, but it can be done in a home workshop using basic equipment. You will need to make a form, support strap and steambox. Bending wood is not an exact science. There are many variables, and trial and error is sometimes the only way to achieve satisfactory results.

Bending wood
Thinly cut wood will take a bend without pretreatment. The radius to which it can be bent will depend on the thickness and natural stiffness of the wood. Thin, unrestrained "free-bent" wood will form a ring when both ends are pulled together. For tighter bends, the wood must be steamed and held around a form to "set" the wood to the required shape. When thicker wood is to be bent, it is necessary to restrain the outer fibers of the wood to prevent them from splitting out. The method described here is for bending a relatively thick section of wood.

Preparing the wood
Select straight-grained wood, free of knots and shakes, for bending. Any flaw in the wood is a potential weakness, and you should expect to have some failures. There are dozens of woods that can be steam-bent successfully, many of them hardwoods. You will find a short list of the most suitable ones on the following page.

Well-seasoned wood can be bent, but newly cut green wood is easier. Wood that is air-dried tends to bend better than kiln-dried wood. You can soak the wood for a few hours prior to steaming if it is too dry and proves difficult to work.

Depending on the nature of the work, either prepare the wood to finished size before bending it or reduce it to size with a saw, drawknife or spokeshave after bending. The latter method is often used in making Windsor chairs. Smooth-finished wood is less likely to promote splitting and will make final finishing easier. Prepared green wood will shrink to a greater degree than seasoned wood; and if turned to a round section prior to bending, will tend to become oval when it dries. Whatever the size or shape of the section, cut the wood about 4in (100mm) overlength. Any end splitting or compression damage from the strap can be cut away after the wood has been bent.

To calculate the length, make a full-size drawing of the shape. Measure the outside of the shape to establish the right length to cut. This will ensure that the outer fibers are not stretched, leading to tension fractures. The softened inner fibers will compress sufficiently to take up the smaller inner curve.

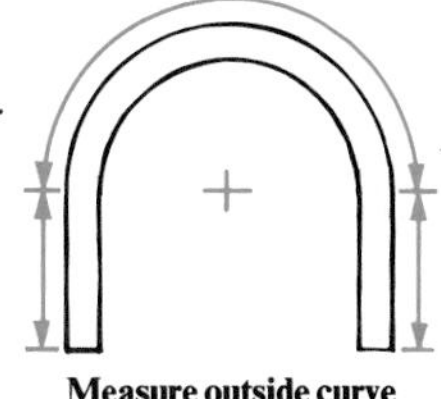

Measure outside curve

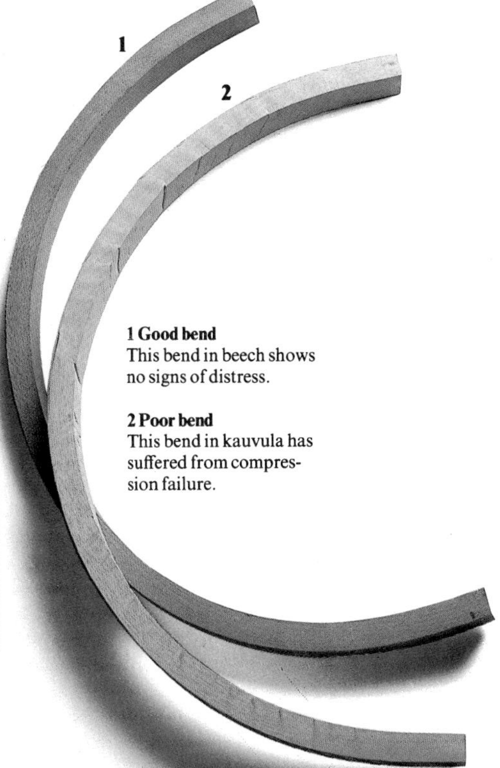

1 Good bend
This bend in beech shows no signs of distress.

2 Poor bend
This bend in kauvula has suffered from compression failure.

Making a strap

The key to bending tight curves successfully is to use a flexible metal backing strap. Make the strap from mild steel $\frac{1}{16}$in (2mm) thick and at least as wide as the wood to be bent. This will suit most work you are likely to tackle. To avoid possible chemical stains, use plated or stainless-steel strapping, or protect the wood with plastic sheeting.

Fit end stops to the strap to restrain the ends of the wood, preventing it from stretching and splitting on the outside of the curve. The end stops must be strong enough to resist the considerable pressure put on them and of sufficient size to support the whole end of the wood. You can make them from thick metal angle or hardwood, though hardwood blocks are usually the easiest to make. To give a good bearing on the strap, make the end blocks about 9in (225mm) long. Drill $\frac{3}{8}$in (9mm) holes about 6in (150mm) apart along the centerline of each block. Mark and drill the strap to take the end-stop bolts. Set the distance between the stops to the length of the work, including the waste. Provide extra leverage by attaching heavy lengths of wood to the back face of the strap, using long end-stop bolts.

SEE ALSO

Man-made boards	34-38
Curve-cutting saws	84-85
Clamps	120-122
Band saws	172-176
Drill presses	188-189

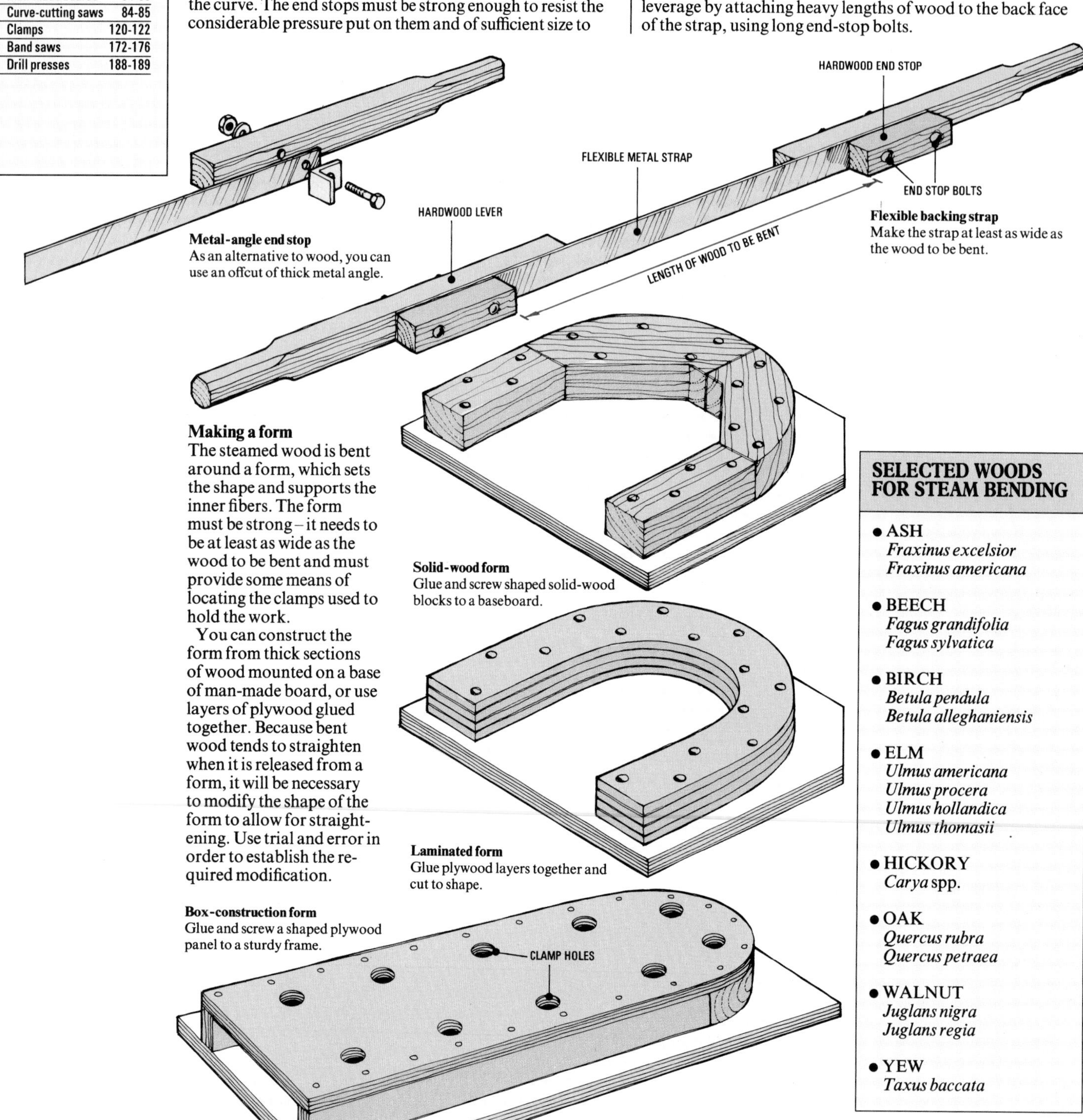

Metal-angle end stop
As an alternative to wood, you can use an offcut of thick metal angle.

Flexible backing strap
Make the strap at least as wide as the wood to be bent.

Solid-wood form
Glue and screw shaped solid-wood blocks to a baseboard.

Laminated form
Glue plywood layers together and cut to shape.

Box-construction form
Glue and screw a shaped plywood panel to a sturdy frame.

Making a form

The steamed wood is bent around a form, which sets the shape and supports the inner fibers. The form must be strong – it needs to be at least as wide as the wood to be bent and must provide some means of locating the clamps used to hold the work.

You can construct the form from thick sections of wood mounted on a base of man-made board, or use layers of plywood glued together. Because bent wood tends to straighten when it is released from a form, it will be necessary to modify the shape of the form to allow for straightening. Use trial and error in order to establish the required modification.

SELECTED WOODS FOR STEAM BENDING

- ASH
  Fraxinus excelsior
  Fraxinus americana
- BEECH
  Fagus grandifolia
  Fagus sylvatica
- BIRCH
  Betula pendula
  Betula alleghaniensis
- ELM
  Ulmus americana
  Ulmus procera
  Ulmus hollandica
  Ulmus thomasii
- HICKORY
  Carya spp.
- OAK
  Quercus rubra
  Quercus petraea
- WALNUT
  Juglans nigra
  Juglans regia
- YEW
  Taxus baccata

Making a steambox

Make a steambox from exterior-grade plywood, or use plastic or metal piping. Plywood allows you to make a simple glued and screwed box to your exact requirements. This type of box is best if you plan to steam batches of wood. A box made from plastic or metal pipe limits your choice to available sizes, but it is adequate for small work.

Cut a length of pipe to suit the size of your work. A 4ft (1.2m) length is a useful size that can contain whole pieces or take longer pieces that only need part of their length to be bent. Make removable push-fit end plugs from exterior-grade plywood. Drill a hole in one end plug for the steam feed pipe and plane the bottom edge of the other flat to provide a vent and a drain hole. Make special open-ended plugs for long pieces to pass through. Fit wooden bridging pieces inside the pipe, to support the wood off the bottom.

Insulate the pipe with thick plastic foam or wooden battens held in place with wire ties. Set the pipe at a slight angle on support brackets so the condensation can run out. Provide a receptacle for the drained water.

You can generate the steam using a small electrically heated boiler, or make your own using a 5 gallon (20 or 25 litre) drum fitted with a removable cap or plug. Fit one end of a short rubber hose to a pipe soldered into the drum, and plug the other end into the end plug of the steambox. Use a portable gas burner or an electric hotplate for heating the water.

Fill the drum halfway and heat the water to 212°F (100°C) to produce a continuous supply of steam. As a rough guide, leave the wood to steam for one hour for every 1in (25mm) of thickness. Prolonged steaming does not necessarily improve pliability and can lead to breakdown of the wood's structure.

Bending the wood

You have only a few minutes to work the wood into a bent shape before it begins to cool and set. Prepare your work area before you begin. Have sufficient clamps on hand and enlist the help of a friend when bending thick material.

Shut down the steam generator. Remove the wood from the steambox and place it in the preset and prewarmed strap. Set the assembly on the form. Clamp the center, placing scrap-wood blocks between the clamp and strap. Pull the wood around the form and fix it securely in place with a series of clamps.

Allow the wood to set for at least 15 minutes before transferring and reclamping it to a similarly shaped drying jig. Alternatively, leave it on the form. Either way, leave it to dry for anywhere from one day to one week.

SAFETY

- Do not overtighten the steam generator's filler cap or plug.
- Vent the steambox.
- Do not let the steam generator run dry.
- Do not stand or reach over the steam generator or box when opening them.
- Wear thick gloves when handling steamed wood and steaming equipment.
- Keep the heat source well away from all flammable materials.

Plywood steambox
Paint all surfaces with exterior-grade varnish.

Basic steambox
Plastic or metal pipe can be used for a small steambox.

Clamp center and pull wood around form

Clamp the wood securely until dry

LAMINATED BENDING

When cut into thin sections, wood is flexible and can be bent dry. In the laminating process used for shaping wood, thin layers of veneer or cut strips are bent around a form and glued together to form a solid shape. Unlike a laminated plywood sheet, which has the grain direction alternating with each veneer, in shaped laminating work, the grain of each laminate follows the same direction. A laminated component can therefore be bent into a tighter curve than a steamed-wood component of comparable dimensions and is more reliable. The layered edges are a strong feature of laminates – however, if the face of a laminated component is cut to a taper, the glue lines can look unsightly.

FREE-FORM BENDING

Free-form compound curves are difficult to visualize and draw, so – instead of making a form first – bend one strip of wood and twist it into the desired shape, then build the form around it to create an interesting and pleasing shape. Experiment with the technique for yourself. The end result will be determined not only by the flexibility of the strip but also by your own skill and imagination.

The basic technique

First, sketch out your idea and cut strips of wood that will suit the size of your design. Next, start to build the form by making a baseboard with a solid post fixed at each end. Clamp the end of the strip to one post, then bend it to shape and clamp the other end to the other post.

Cut and fix triangulated intermediate posts to the baseboard to support the strip at the required angles. Mark the line of the strip on the posts and remove it.

The key to successful free-form bending is to have sufficient clamps to hold the work. A length of bicycle inner tube (with the valve cut away) bound around the work makes a handy and efficient clamp.

Apply resin glue to the strips of laminate and bind them together. Clamp the lamination to the form posts, carefully bending it to follow the marked line.

When set, shape and finish the curved component, using spokeshaves, knives, files, scrapers and abrasives as appropriate.

Free-form bend
Clamp the lamination to the posts.

Preparing the wood

Laminations for frame members such as chair or table legs can be made from strips of thin commercially cut veneer, or you can cut thicker strips from solid wood of the required width. The grain pattern will be more consistent if you cut the laminates yourself from solid wood.

As a general rule, select straight-grained wood that is free of knots and shakes, though a decorative veneer of random grain can be used for face laminates.

Air-dried wood is preferable to kiln-dried wood, as it is not so brittle and will therefore bend more readily. For tight bends or relatively thick laminates, prebend the wood prior to gluing by wetting it and setting it in the form until dry.

Cut veneer strips in the direction of the grain using a knife and straightedge. Choose quartersawn boards from which to cut strips of solid wood. This will ensure that the growth rings run across the width of the strips, which makes them more amenable to bending. Mark the face or the end with a V-shaped reference line to enable you to realign the grain when the strips are glued together **(1)**.

The thinner the veneer or cut strip, the tighter it can be bent. Bends made with thin sections are also less likely to spring back. However, if you are cutting your own strips, it is more economical to make them as thick as possible, as wood is wasted with every saw-cut. Cut a strip and test its bendability.

You can cut the wood on a band saw or table saw. When using a band saw, pass the planed edge of the board through the saw to remove a strip slightly thicker than required. Plane the sawn edge of the board and then cut a second strip. Repeat the process to produce the required number of strips. Run the strips through a thickness planer.

A table saw may be used to cut strips entirely, but it can be hazardous. Make sure there is not a wide gap between the blade and the table insert, if fitted. As the cut strips are flexible, it is helpful to have an assistant receive the cut pieces in order to prevent them from being grabbed and broken or, worse, thrown back at you. If cutting a number of very thin strips, make a guide batten fitted with a stop block to push the workpiece along the fence **(2)**.

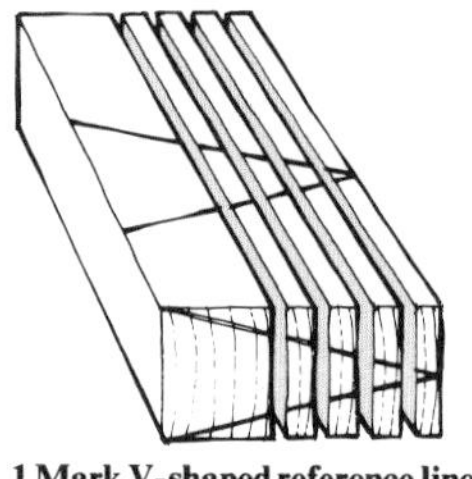

1 Mark V-shaped reference line

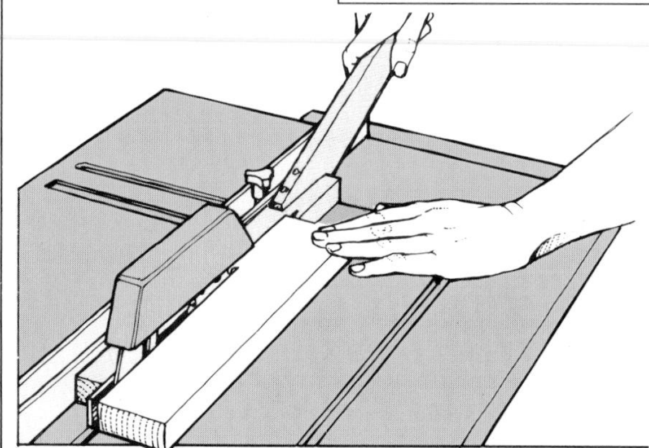

2 Make a guide batten to push the workpiece along the fence

SELECTING WOOD

Virtually any wood can be bent using the laminating process, provided it is thin enough. However, some woods are naturally more pliable than others. A short list of popular woods that bend well would include:

- ASH
  Fraxinus excelsior
  Fraxinus americana
- BEECH
  Fagus grandifolia
  Fagus sylvatica
- BIRCH
  Betula pendula
  Betula alleghaniensis
- ELM
  Ulmus americana
  Ulmus procera
  Ulmus hollandica
  Ulmus thomasii
- HICKORY
  Carya spp.
- OAK
  Quercus rubra
  Quercus petraea
- WALNUT
  Juglans nigra
  Juglans regia

FORMS

A form is used to hold the glued laminates to the desired shape until the glue sets. You can make a single male form or two-part matched male and female forms. The best type to use will depend on the degree of bend and the size and number of pieces.

Making a male form

Male forms are the simplest to make and are suitable for most curved shapes. They are the best type for large bends where the size of two-part forms would be excessive.

Make the form from thick solid wood, or glue up layers of particleboard. The profiled face must be wider and longer than the wood to be bent. Take the shape from a full-size drawing, then mark it out on the face of the block and cut it on a band saw. The clamping force must be applied at right angles to the face of the form, as far as possible. Cut the back of the form to follow the contour of the face, or cut it to the approximate shape **(1)**.

The number of clamps you will need to hold the work will depend on the degree of bend and the pliability of the wood. Use as many as possible to apply even pressure. To help avoid local indentations in the top laminate, cover it with a strip of waxed hardboard or spare laminate. Use softwood blocks under the clamp heads to distribute the load **(2)**.

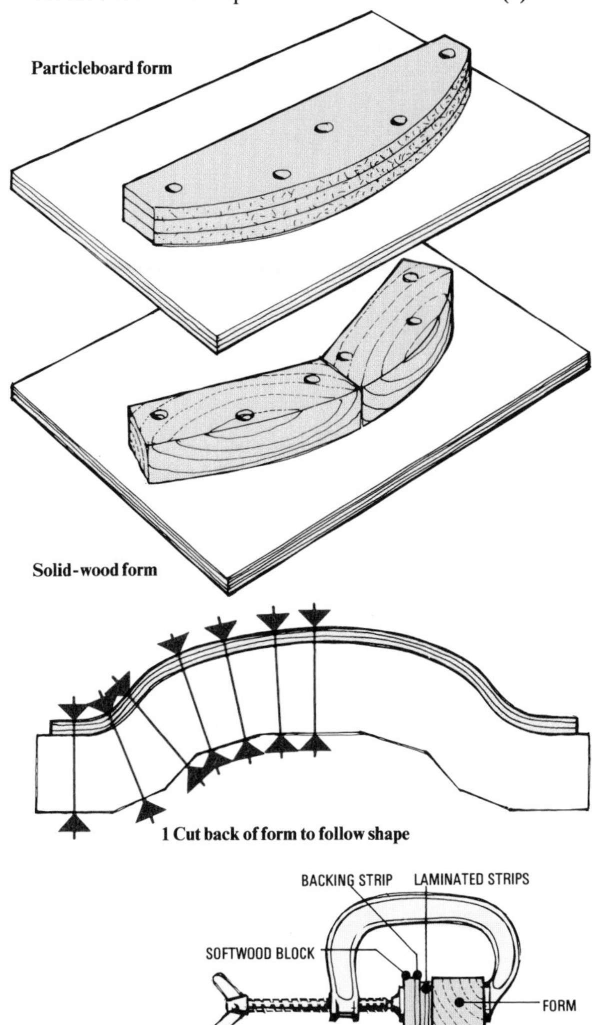

1 Cut back of form to follow shape

2 Use blocks under clamp heads

Male and female forms

The construction of matched two-part forms for making frame members or wide panels is more demanding, since even pressure must be applied along the molding. To apply adequate pressure, use a number of individual clamps or a veneer press, if you have access to one.

If clamps are used, some provision must be made in the design of the male form to accommodate them. Either make the male form from blocks of thick, solid wood, or drill holes in a slab made from man-made board **(1)**. Design the forms to use the minimum amount of material while applying even pressure to the greatest area of the lamination **(2)**. This usually means setting the orientation of the bend at an angle different from the one shown on the drawing **(3)**.

You cannot make two-part forms by simply cutting the material in two with a single contoured cut; two parallel cutting lines are required. Clamp the prepared strips or veneers together and measure the thickness to establish the exact spacing of the cutting lines. For compass-curved bends, simply mark the internal and external radii on the material for the form. For freehand or random bends, mark one contour line and set off the other from it using a compass. Make a series of closely spaced arcs with the radius equal to the thickness of the laminate **(4)**, then draw the second line touching the peak of each arc. Cut each contour line carefully, using a band saw.

In most instances, male and female forms comprise two complete parts. Where the shape to be formed requires the male form to be undercut, it will be necessary to cut the female part into sections to facilitate assembly and removal of the laminates **(5)**.

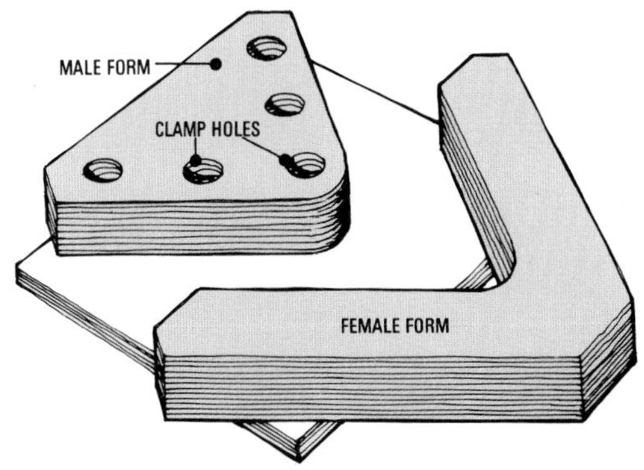

1 Drill holes in male form

2 Design forms to save material and apply even pressure

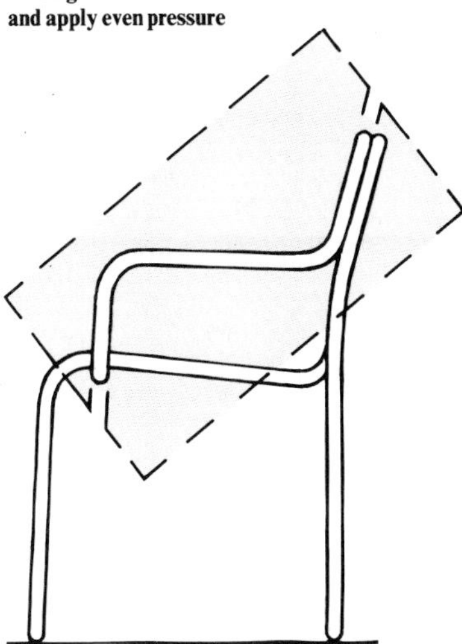

3 Set out shape on drawing

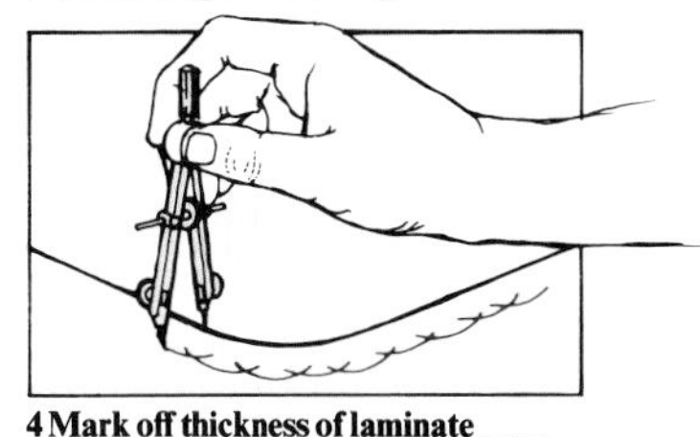

4 Mark off thickness of laminate

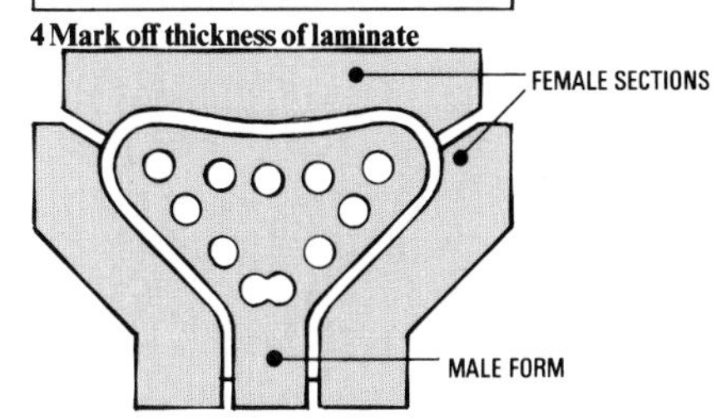

5 Make female form in sections

SEE ALSO

Man-made boards	34-38
Clamps	120-122
Band saws	172-176
Adhesives	302-303

Making wide forms
Wide laminations, such as bowed door panels, would need a considerable amount of material to make solid male and female forms. To save material, make the forms with shaped ribs that are spaced out on a baseboard and faced with thin plywood **(1)**.

First, cut a series of oversized blanks from man-made board. The number you need will be determined by the size of the workpiece and the pressure required to shape it. The higher the pressure, the more ribs you will need to make.

Next, mark out the shape of the bend on the top piece, making an allowance for the thickness of the plywood facing **(2)**. Temporarily pin the blanks together with the edges flush. Cut notches across them to receive spacer rails **(3)**. Band-saw the stack to shape before pulling them apart. Glue the ribs to the spacer rails approximately 2 to 4in (50 to 100mm) apart. Glue and screw each assembly on a baseboard **(4)**. Pin and glue a $\frac{1}{8}$in (3mm) plywood panel to the curved edges of the ribs **(5)**. Seal and wax the surface of the forms to stop the work from sticking, or line them with plastic sheeting. If you do not have a veneer press, clamp the forms between two or more stiff wooden beams **(6)**.

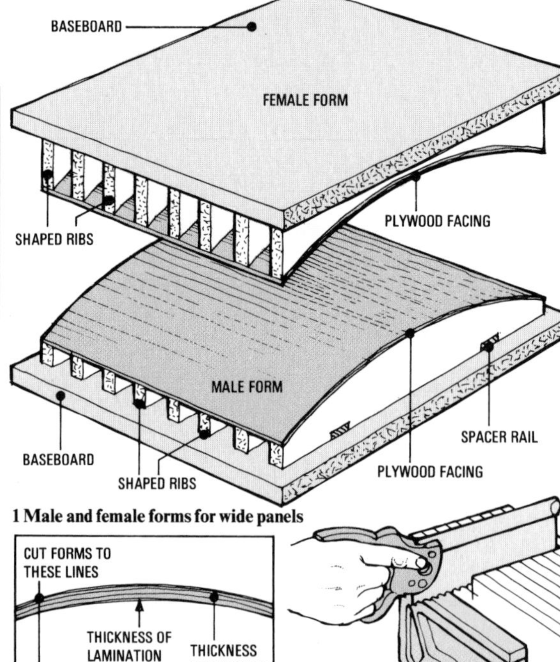

1 Male and female forms for wide panels

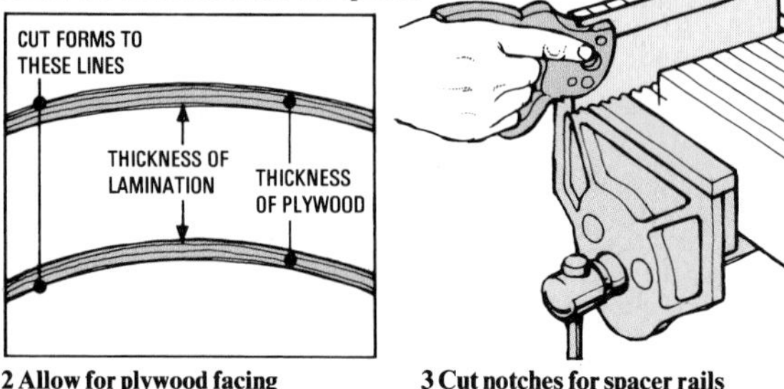

2 Allow for plywood facing

3 Cut notches for spacer rails

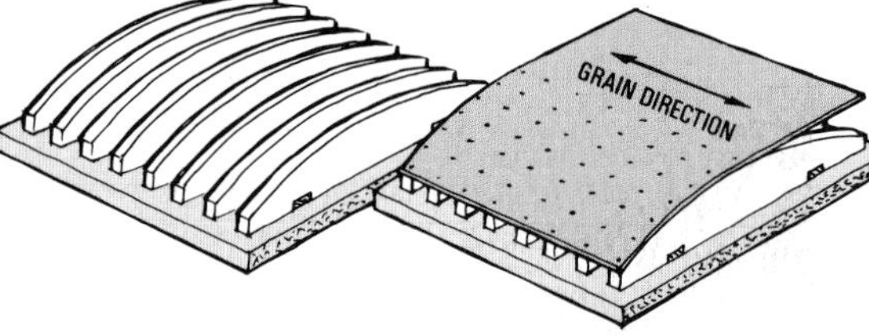

4 Glue assembly to baseboard

5 Fix plywood to curved ribs

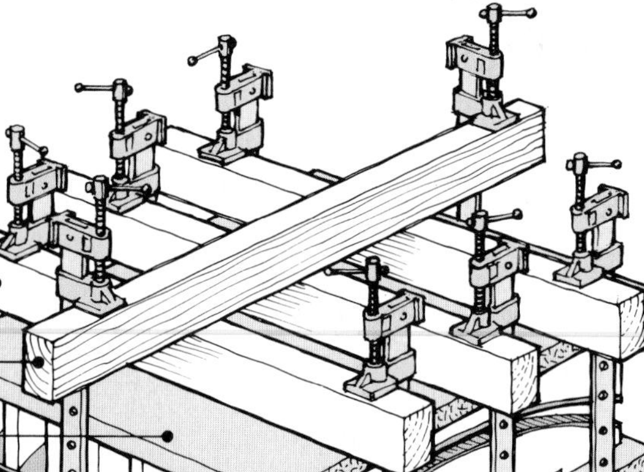

6 Clamping forms
Use clamps and stiff wooden beams to apply pressure if you do not have access to a veneer press.

GLUING AND CUTTING

When gluing laminates, lay them on a flat board covered with plastic sheeting. Use a urea-formaldehyde glue – since it sets slowly, which allows time to assemble the work in the form, and is less likely to creep than PVA glues.

Stack the laminates in the order in which they are to be glued. If decorative face veneers are to be used, place them on the top and bottom.

Apply an even coating of glue with a brush to the meeting faces of each veneer, then restack them in reverse order. Place the stacked laminates on or in the form(s) and clamp them together using even pressure. To exclude air and glue, start from the center and work outward. Strip laminates are liable to slip as the glue is squeezed out. Loosen the clamps slightly and tap the laminates into line, using a block of wood and hammer. When male and female forms are used for shaping wide laminates, bands of masking tape will help keep the laminates together. Leave the work to set for at least 12 hours.

Cutting to size
Before removing a wide lamination from a form, mark the position of the centerline on the edges. Draw a line between the marks to help you mark out the size of the panel. Cut the panel by hand, or use a band saw or table saw. If machine-cutting the work, as you feed the curved panel through the saw keep the point being cut in contact with the table. Finish the edges with a plane.

Mark the length of a narrow piece from reference marks on the form. Trim the edges on a band saw, or plane them flush. Cut the part to length and finish the ends.

If you require a number of narrow pieces with the same curve, make one wide lamination and cut it into identical parts.

CHAPTER NINE

VENEERING & MARQUETRY

A sophisticated process requiring artistic skill as well as manual dexterity, veneering is known to have been practiced by the ancient Egyptians. In Europe, veneered furniture reached its peak of inventiveness and elegance in the eighteenth century and in Victorian times gained popularity as a substitute for solid-wood furniture. Today, veneers are not only made from natural wood but also from plain-colored paper foil or from foil printed to look like wood, which may even have simulated pore indentations. However, the advantages of natural-wood veneer are not always appreciated. Some of the most attractive wood is produced as a result of abnormal or irregular growth, so would be prohibitively expensive in solid form and unsatisfactory because of its lack of stability. But bonded to modern man-made boards with modern adhesives, veneer provides an economic and stable material that stands up well to central heating and offers the aesthetic and tactile qualities of solid wood. In addition, reconstituted wood is now available in a variety of shapes and panels, all of which can be covered with veneer.

TOOLS FOR VENEERING

Veneer laying may require the relatively straightforward application of a single veneer or complicated cutting and fitting of different veneers to make intricate patterns. The woodworker's basic tool kit will contain a number of tools used in veneer work – including measuring and marking tools, a scroll saw, bench, block and shoulder planes, chisels, scrapers and sanding equipment. If you wish to concentrate on veneering, additional specialized tools will be required. Most of the tools you are likely to use are available from good tool stores or from veneer suppliers. You will also need to make some equipment, such as a scratch stock and a shooting board, and a simple cutting jig for parquetry work.

SEE ALSO

Wood stability	13
Veneers	30-33
Plywood construction	34
Man-made boards	34-38
Scratch stock	96
Sharpening stones	102-103
Adhesives	302-303

Sharpening a blade
Usually the point is the only part of a knife blade that becomes dull. To create a new point, hone the back edge only on an oilstone.

Rulers and straightedges
In addition to a steel tape measure, you will find that a graduated metal "safety ruler" 12in (300mm) long is handy since it can double as a straightedge for cutting small work. A safety ruler is designed to grip the work, to prevent slipping when used as a cutting guide, and is wide enough to keep your fingers clear of the knife. For cutting longer veneers, use a steel straightedge.

Cutting mat
Use plywood or other fine-surfaced man-made board for cutting on – or better still, particularly for fine knife-cutting work, use a special cutting mat. This is made of a self-sealing rubber-like compound that allows the point of the knife to penetrate its surface without causing permanent scoring or dulling of the blade.

Veneer saw
A veneer saw can be used, with the aid of a straightedge, to cut veneers of any thickness. It produces a square-edged cut for accurate butt-joining of matched veneers and has a reversible double-edged blade with fine teeth that have no set.

Electric iron
An old household electric iron may be used to soften the hide glue applied to the groundwork and veneer, both for traditional hammer veneering and to activate heat-sensitive glue film.

Knives
Use a surgical scalpel or craft knife fitted with a pointed blade for cutting intricate shapes, and a stiffer curved-edge blade for cutting straight lines (particularly if extra pressure is required).

These blades are ground on both sides, producing a "V" cut. If it is vital that the edge of the veneer is cut square, hold the knife at an angle away from the straightedge.

Veneer punches
Veneer punches are made in eight sizes and used to repair unsightly defects in veneer. Each punch has an irregularly shaped cutter that will make a hole in the defective veneer and will also cut an identical patch from matching veneer. A sprung ejector pushes out the cut patch from the tool.

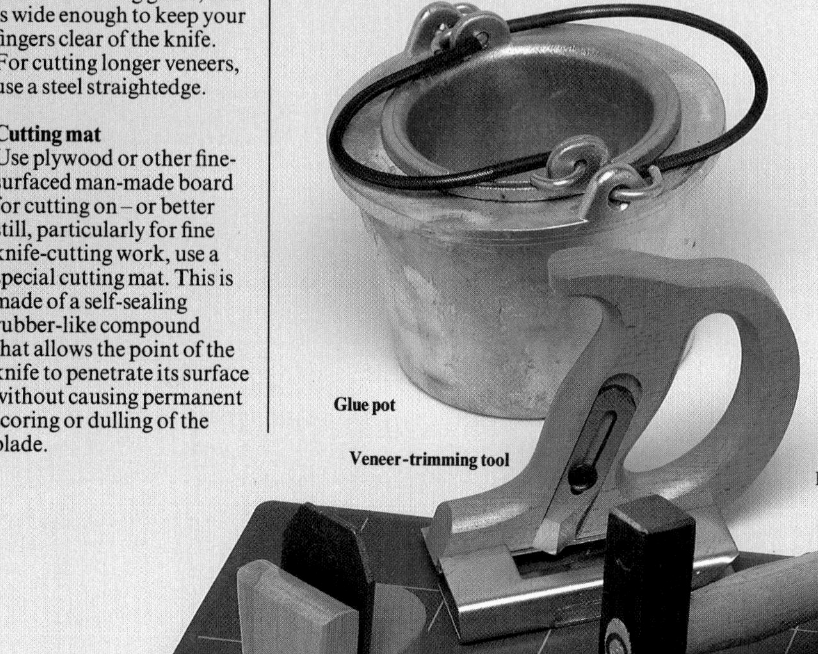

Veneer-trimming tool
A trimming tool is used for removing the surplus veneer around the edges of a panel. One type consists of a short adjustable blade fitted into a wooden handle. The tool is simply run along the edge of the panel and cuts the veneer cleanly both with and across the grain.

Toothing plane
A toothing plane is used to "key" the surface of the groundwork ready for gluing. It differs from a conventional wooden plane in that the blade is set almost vertical. The blade has a finely grooved face with a bevel ground on the back, producing a series of teeth across the blade similar to those of a fine saw. The blade may be sharpened by honing the bevel.

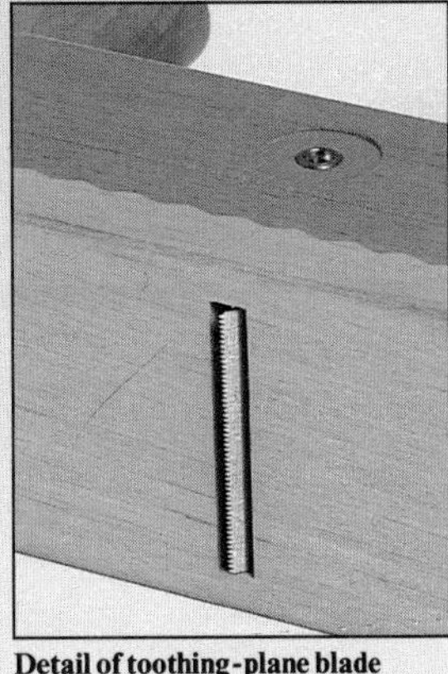

Detail of toothing-plane blade

Glue pot
Traditional veneer laying uses hot hide glue that is prepared in a double or jacketed glue pot. The inner pot holds the glue and the outer pot the water, which is heated to keep the glue at working temperature and to prevent it from burning.

Originally, glue pots were made of cast iron, but modern versions are usually made from aluminum. They are heated by any convenient heat source, such as a gas or electric hot plate.

Thermostatically controlled electric glue pots are also available, but are more expensive.

To prepare pearl hide glue, quarter fill the inner pot with the beads and add an equal quantity of water. Leave the beads to soak, then half fill the outer jacket with water and heat the glue pot in it. Stir the glue to a smooth consistency, adding a little water to it if necessary. Do not let the glue boil or allow the heated water to run dry.

Veneer tape
Gummed paper tape ¾in (18mm) wide is used to hold pieces of veneer together and prevents the joints of newly laid veneer from opening up as a result of shrinkage. The tape is removed, after the glue has set, by wetting and scraping.

Veneer pins
Fine, short pins with large plastic heads are used to hold veneers temporarily while the joints are taped.

Veneer hammers
A veneer hammer is used for hand-laying veneers. The wooden type has a rounded brass-strip blade mounted in the edge of a hardwood head fitted with a handle. The metal type is more like a conventional hammer, but the head is designed for pressing blisters. Work the blade across the panel in a zigzag motion, using firm pressure to press the veneer down and to exclude excess glue and trapped air.

GROUNDWORK

Veneer is always glued to a backing material called the "ground" or "groundwork." The choice and preparation of the groundwork is fundamental to the quality of the work, as the veneer itself will not mask defects. An uneven surface will show, or "telegraph," through the thin veneer and will become plainly obvious when the surface is finished.

Traditionally, solid pine and, for better-quality pieces, mahogany were used for the groundwork of veneered furniture. Today man-made boards are generally used, as they are simpler to prepare and more reliable, though solid wood is still used for flat and curved veneer work.

PREPARING THE GROUNDWORK

Groundwork should provide a smooth, even surface on which to lay the veneer. Solid wood is not ideal since it "moves" with changes in humidity and requires careful preparation, particularly for wide panels. Man-made boards are stable materials and are manufactured in large sheets with flat sanded surfaces. Whichever type of material is used, it must be flat or smoothly shaped and free from dust.

Solid wood
When veneering solid-wood boards, lay the veneer with the grain so that the wood moves together. If only one side of a tangentially cut board is to be veneered, always veneer the heart side. These boards tend to cup – but if laid heart side up, the veneer will help pull them flat as the glue dries.

Where possible, use quartersawn boards, as these are more stable, with only slight shrinkage across the thickness. To maintain an even balance, veneer both sides of the board.

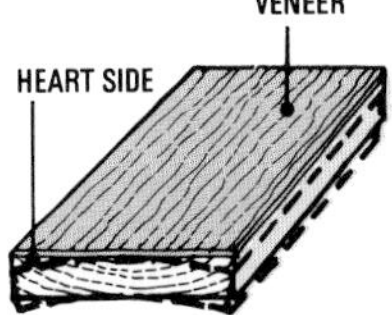

Tangentially cut board
Lay the veneer on the heart side to counter the board's tendency to cup.

Man-made board
Most man-made boards are ready to use, apart from cutting to the required dimensions and (in the case of laminated boards) toothing and sizing the surface. Laminated boards may require the application of a cross-banding veneer if the grain does not run in the opposite direction to the veneer.

Repairing solid-wood defects
Where possible, select defect-free wood. Cut out unavoidable defects such as fine knots to receive diamond or round shaped plugs, which are cut with their grain following that of the wood. Make the plugs slightly thicker than the board, and level them with a plane after gluing.

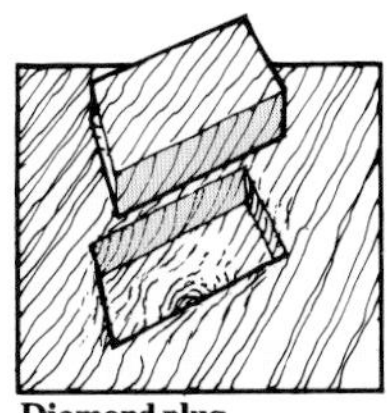

Diamond plug

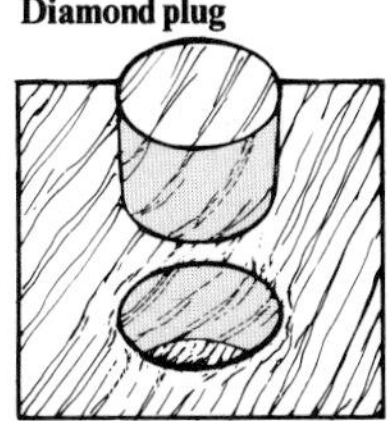

Round plug

Toothing the surface
To improve the adhesion of the glue, "key" the surface of solid-wood or laminated-wood groundwork; either use a toothing plane, working diagonally from opposite sides, or drag a tenon saw across the surface. Blow away loose dust before sizing.

Sizing the surface
Sizing is used to seal the pores and control suction to make gluing easier and improve its performance. The rate of absorption varies, depending on the type of board used.

You can use either hot, diluted hide glue (about one part glue to ten parts water) or cold, synthetic wallpaper paste.

Apply the size evenly to the surfaces and coat the edges liberally. When thoroughly dry, sand the surface lightly to remove any nibs.

SHAPED GROUNDWORK

Since veneer is thin and flexible, it can be laid on curved surfaces and bent with or across its grain. The shaped groundwork can be formed either by laminating thick constructional veneers or by steam-bending solid wood. These techniques are described in the section on bending wood.

SEE ALSO

Veneers	30-33
Plywood construction	34
Compass plane	95
Spokeshaves	108
Bending wood	250-256

Solid wood

Small shallow-curved groundwork can be cut from solid blocks of wood on a band saw. The curved surfaces are planed smooth with a compass plane and spokeshaves, and the surface toothed ready for veneering. The offcuts can be faced with thick felt and used as cauls for laying the veneers.

Brick construction

Cutting curved shapes from solid wood of any reasonable size is wasteful, and short grain can make the component weak. Brick construction is a traditional method of making curved groundwork, such as a bowed drawer front. The wood fibers approximately follow the direction of the curve, thus overcoming the problem of weak grain.

The short "bricks," cut from lengths of wood a little wider than the finished groundwork, are glued end to end to make curved layers or "courses." The joints in each course are staggered or "bonded" as in conventional brickwork, so the joints in one course are reinforced by the bricks in the next.

Coopered construction

This method uses beveled strips of wood glued edge to edge. It is sometimes used for bowed doors. The edges of the strips are planed to the required angle, then glued and clamped together in specially made jigs with shaped saddles to hold the curve. For lighter work, you can use masking tape to bind the glued strips together. When set, the surfaces are smoothed with a compass plane and toothed, ready for cross-banding veneer laid with cauls.

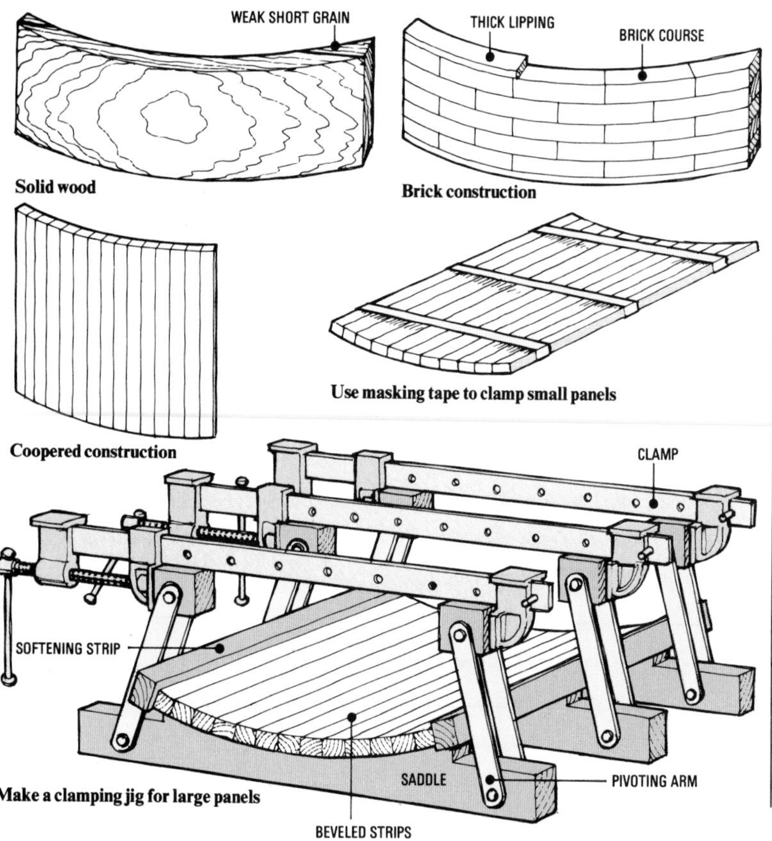

Solid wood

Brick construction

Use masking tape to clamp small panels

Coopered construction

Make a clamping jig for large panels

PREPARING VENEER

One of the joys of veneer is the opportunity it offers to use wood purely for its appearance, without the need to consider its structural properties. The veneer's natural decorative features of figure and color revealed by the cutting process can be used at will, or the leaves can be cut and manipulated to create the pleasing patterns offered by matched veneer.

Handling veneer

Veneer is a fragile material and must be handled with care. Store veneers flat and, for matching purposes, keep them in the order they were supplied. When selecting veneers from a bundle, do not try to pull the lower veneers from the stack, rather lift off the upper veneers to reach them. Long veneers should be handled by two people.

Flattening veneer

You will often find that veneer needs to be flattened before it can be worked. If the veneer is slightly distorted, simply apply moisture by means of steam from a kettle, or light immersion in water or a wipe with a damp sponge, then press it between sheets of chipboard until dry. Use clamps or heavy weights to apply pressure. Flatten veneer just before laying.

Buckled and brittle veneer will respond better if an adhesive is used in the dampening process. You can use wallpaper paste or a weak solution of hot hide glue. Lightly brush on the paste or thinned glue to dampen the veneer, then press it between boards lined with thin plastic sheeting. Leave the veneer in the press for at least 24 hours. You can heat the boards to help speed up the process.

VENEER MATCHING

If your chosen veneer is narrower than the groundwork, you will need to join it. Joining veneer gives the opportunity to create decorative effects by the juxtaposition of the wood's natural features of figure and color.

Slip matching

Slip matching is used to create a wide veneer from narrow ones. Consecutive veneers are slipped sideways and joined together without altering their grain direction.

This method is best used for striped veneers if the joint is not to be obvious. Should the stripes not be parallel to the joining edges, the joint may have a poor match and will require trimming to true up the figure.

Bookmatching

Bookmatching is used for joining two consecutive decorative veneers when the figure is biased to one side of the leaf.

The direction in which the leaves are turned depends on the position of the dominant figure. If it is on the left-hand side, turn the top leaf to the left as if you were opening a book **(1)**. If the figure is on the right-hand side, turn the top leaf to the right **(2)**. The figure must be perfectly aligned to avoid a disjointed match of poor appearance.

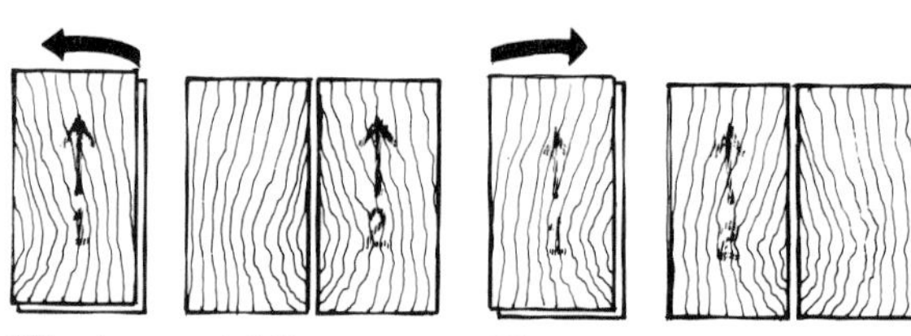

1 Turn top veneer to left

2 Turn top veneer to right

Four-piece matching
This method takes the book-matching technique a stage further. Take four consecutive veneers and select a portion that places the focal point of the figure at the bottom.

Take the first pair of leaves and book-match the vertical edges. To get an accurate match, true the joining edge of one leaf first. Lay the trued edge on the edge of the adjacent leaf and match the pattern, then cut the second leaf to match, and tape the joint **(1)**. Next, cut the horizontal joining edge straight and square.

Book-match the vertical edges of the second pair as for the first, but reverse them along the horizontal edge so they are face down **(2)**.

Now match the horizontal edges by laying the first pair on the second and cutting the veneer at the point where the figure matches. Tape the horizontal joint in readiness for laying.

Diamond matching
For diamond matching, use striped veneers. Lay four consecutive veneers together and true the two long edges. Cut both ends to 45 degrees, making the cuts parallel to each other **(1)**. Open the top two veneers book-match fashion – but turn them along the top diagonal edge to form an inverted "V," then tape the joint **(2)**. Next, make a straight horizontal cut from corner to corner **(3)**. Fit the triangular piece into the "V" at the bottom to form a rectangle **(4)**.

Now repeat the process with the second pair of veneers but first reverse them so they are face down, as for four-piece matching. Finally join the two rectangles along the center **(5)**.

Testing the match
To see how the grain pattern will repeat, hold a mirror perpendicular to the veneer and slide it over the surface. Draw a cutting line along the mirror at the best point, then cut the other veneers to match.

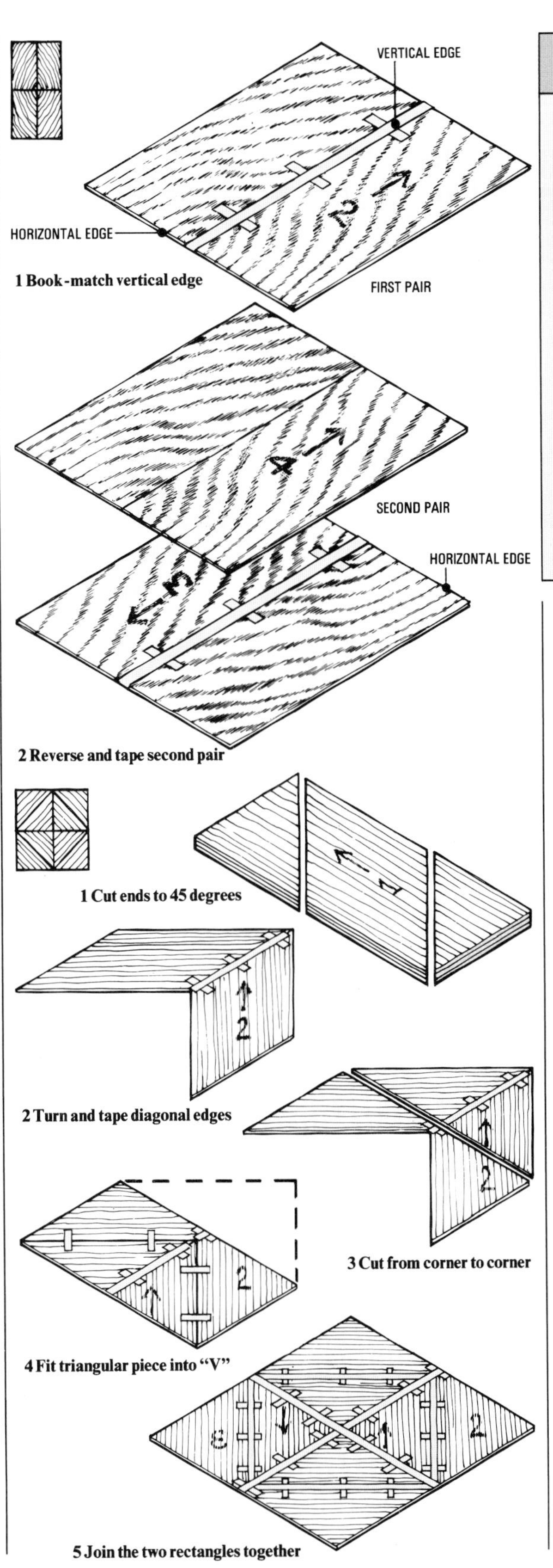

1 Book-match vertical edge

2 Reverse and tape second pair

1 Cut ends to 45 degrees

2 Turn and tape diagonal edges

3 Cut from corner to corner

4 Fit triangular piece into "V"

5 Join the two rectangles together

TONAL VARIATION

Veneers often appear lighter or darker when viewed from a particular direction – so a difference in tone is noticeable if consecutive veneers are laid in opposite directions.

If you chalk numbers and arrows on the top face of the veneers as you take them from the bundle, that will not only make it easier to identify grain direction but will also enable you to tell at a glance which is the better "closed" face and which is the slightly coarser "open" face. Wherever possible, the open face should be laid on the groundwork.

Jointing veneer
The meeting edges of the veneer must be cut straight. When you are matching two veneers, lay them together with the figure accurately aligned. Temporarily pin them to the cutting board and, holding them down with a straightedge set just inside the edge to be cut, cut through both veneers with a knife or veneer saw.

To check the fit, hold the two veneers together against the light. If any gaps show, "shoot" the edges by running a finely set bench plane along the edges of the veneer held between two straight battens.

Taping the joint
Place the two edges together and apply 4in (100mm) lengths of veneer tape across the joint at about 6in (150mm) intervals, then run a length of tape along the joint. The tape will pull the joint together as it shrinks.

Run tape along the joint

CAUL VENEERING

In caul veneering, a press is used to lay the veneer. Cauls are stiff boards, either flat or curved, between which the groundwork and veneer are pressed. Unlike hand-laying techniques, caul veneering requires extra work and materials, both for making the cauls and the press. However, it is the best method for laying veneer made from taped-together pieces or weak veneers, such as burls or curls. It also offers the possibility of veneering both sides of the groundwork simultaneously. With caul veneering, larger curved surfaces are easier to handle as cold-setting glues allow time for "laying up."

SEE ALSO

Veneers	32-33
Man-made boards	34-38
Clamps	120-122
Lippings	248
Male and female forms	256
Coopered construction	260

MAKING A CAUL ASSEMBLY

The complexity of the caul assembly will depend on the size and shape of the work and the extent to which it will be used.

Flat cauls
For small or narrow work, make the cauls from heavy lengths of wood and apply pressure to them with clamps placed along the centerline.

For veneering wide panels, make a simple press with cauls cut from man-made board at least ¾in (18mm) thick and larger than the panel to be veneered.

To provide pressure across the cauls, cut at least three pairs of stiff cross-bearers from 3 × 2in (75 × 50mm) softwood. Plane a shallow convex curve across one narrow edge of each, in order to apply initial pressure at the center of the cauls and force excess glue and trapped air out to the edges. This compensates for the clamping forces, which can only be applied at the ends.

Use clamps to apply the pressure, or bolt the cross-bearers together with threaded rods fitted with nuts and washers.

With resin glues, to accelerate setting time, introduce an aluminum-sheet caul, which can be independently heated. With hide glue, the hot cauls prevent premature gelling during pressing.

You will also need a softening pad of newspaper and a sheet of plastic to overlay each veneer. The pad takes up any unevenness on the surface caused by the tape, and the plastic prevents the work from sticking to it.

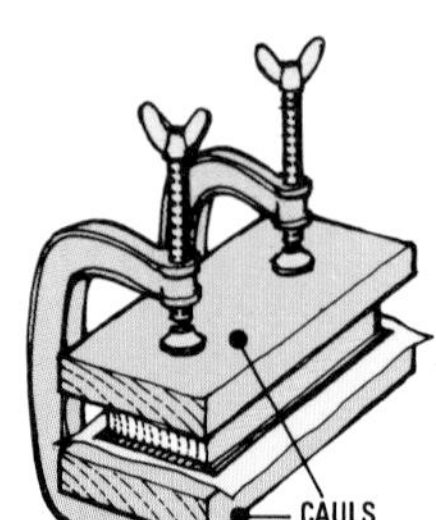

Clamping small work
Use clamps to apply pressure to heavy wooden cauls.

CURVED CAULS

Curved panels can be caul-veneered using male and female forms, as in laminated bending. Or you can make a press similar to the ones used for flat work but with the cauls made from strips of wood and held by shaped cross-bearers.

Make a section drawing to calculate the curves to be cut in the cross-bearers. This should allow for the thickness of the caul material and the groundwork sandwiched between them.

You can make a permanent caul using the coopered groundwork method described earlier, but a flexible caul is more versatile.

Make a flexible caul from strips of wood about ½in (12mm) square and glue them to a sheet of canvas. Cut pairs of top and bottom cross-bearers to the required curvature; make them so they can be spaced about 6in (150mm) apart.

Lay the cauls between the cross-bearers with the canvas side facing upward, and line them with an aluminum or hardboard caul to even out the surface.

Assemble the work in the manner described for flat work. Apply pressure by clamping a pair of stiff bearers along the centerline of the curve, then tighten the cross-bearers.

Using a sandbag
For small curved work, you can press the veneer into place using a hot sandbag.

Make a flat bag and fill it with dry, fine sand. Heat it and press it around or into the shaped work, as appropriate, then clamp it with a caul and clamps.

LAYING THE VENEER

As with any joining process, you should prepare your work area so everything you require is at hand. You can lay the veneer one side at a time or both together. Lay the backing veneer first, if laying them separately.

Using a brush, evenly apply a cold-setting adhesive, such as PVA or urea-formaldehyde glue, to the groundwork only and let it become tacky. Do not apply glue to the veneer.

The sequence illustrated shows how to veneer both sides together. Fit the top cross-bearers, and clamp the cauls applying even pressure. This is best done by two people.

Leave the work to set for up to 12 hours. On release, trim away excess veneer and stand the board on edge to allow even air circulation. Leave it to acclimatize for a few days, then plane and lip the edges to complete the panel.

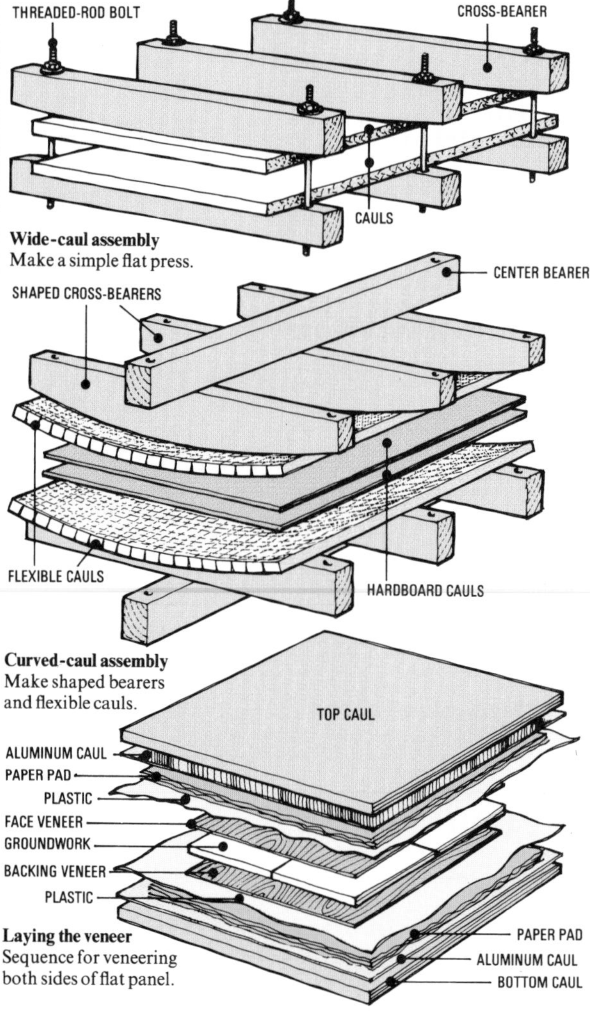

Wide-caul assembly
Make a simple flat press.

Curved-caul assembly
Make shaped bearers and flexible cauls.

Laying the veneer
Sequence for veneering both sides of flat panel.

HAND VENEERING

The centuries-old method of laying veneers by hand with hot hide glue has many advantages. The glue can be softened with heat, even after the veneer has been in place for years, so mistakes can be rectified simply and damaged or blistered veneers easily repaired. However, raw glue must be melted to reduce it to the required consistency, and the laying technique requires practice. Modern glues are cleaner and simpler to use, although they are not quite so versatile. Whatever method you adopt, always prepare and size the groundwork; otherwise too much glue will be absorbed and the bond will be weak. Cut and prepare the veneer and, if necessary, join small leaves together. The methods described here assume the veneer is large enough to cover the groundwork in one piece.

HAMMER VENEERING

The secret of successful hammer veneering lies in keeping the glue at a working temperature. Heat pearl or liquid hide glue in a double or jacketed glue pot until it is about 120°F (49°C). The glue should be of a smooth, lump-free consistency that runs from the brush without separating into droplets. Work in a warm, dust-free atmosphere so that the glue does not cool quickly. Have a bowl of hot water and a sponge at hand, plus a veneer hammer and a household electric iron heated to the setting for silk.

Applying the glue

Brush a thin, even coat of glue onto the groundwork and veneer **(1)**, then lay them aside until the glue is almost dry but still just tacky. Lay the veneer onto the groundwork so it overlaps all around, then smooth it down with the flat of your hand **(2)**.

Pressing the veneer

Dip the sponge in hot water and squeeze it almost dry, then dampen the surface of the veneer **(3)** to close its pores and prevent the iron from sticking to it.

Run the heated iron over the surface **(4)**, in order to melt the glue and draw it into the veneer. Without delay, take the veneer hammer and, starting near the center, press the veneer onto the groundwork using a zigzag stroke toward the outer edges **(5)**.

As air and melted glue are pressed out from beneath the veneer, increase the pressure using two hands on the hammer **(6)**. Take care not to stretch the veneer by applying too much pressure across the grain. Work back toward the other end of the panel – but if the glue cools before you have finished, dampen and iron the veneer again, then repeat the process. Clean off the melted glue with a damp cloth before it sets.

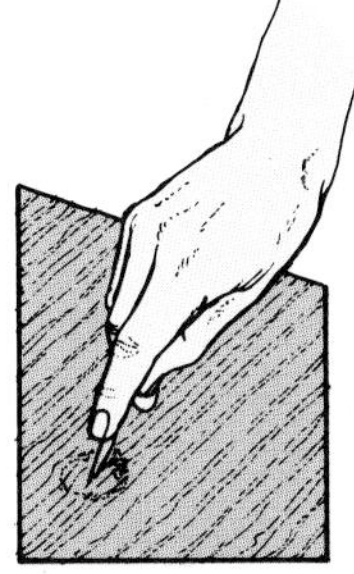

Checking for blisters
Tap the surface with your fingernails to detect air bubbles. Treat any hollow-sounding areas by pressing the veneer again with the hot iron and veneer hammer. If necessary, slit it along the grain with a sharp knife to allow trapped air to escape.

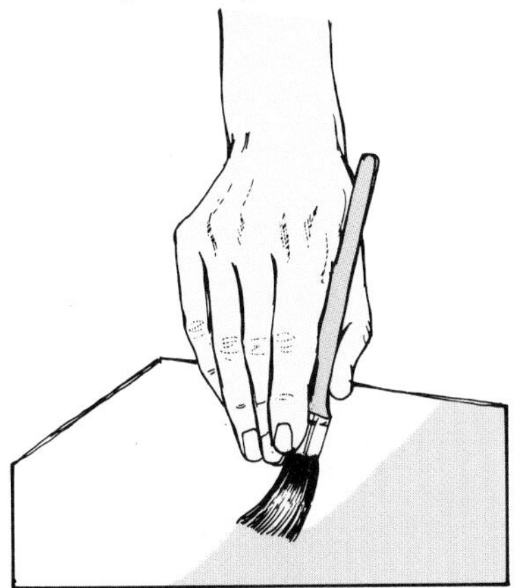

1 Apply glue to groundwork and veneer

3 Dampen the surface of the veneer

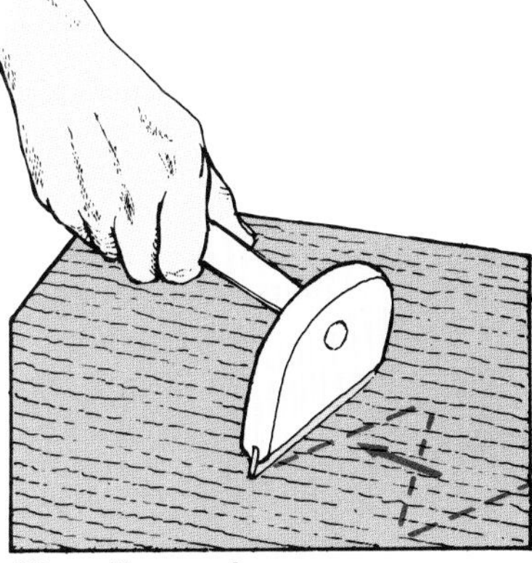

5 Press with a veneer hammer

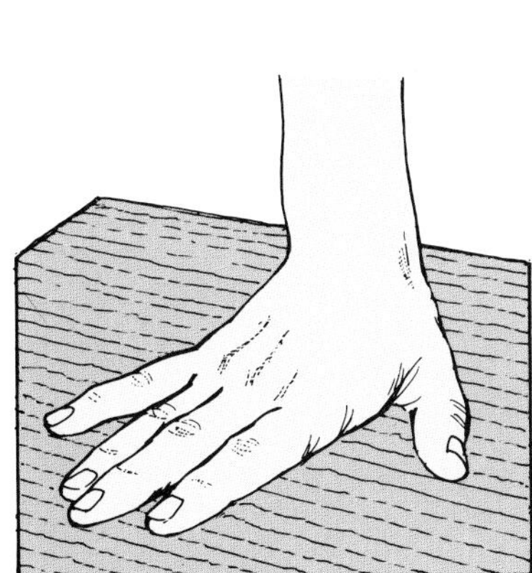

2 Smooth down the veneer

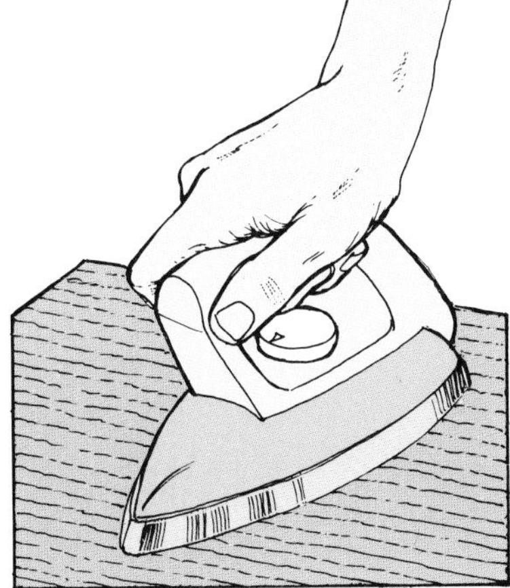

4 Heat glue with an iron

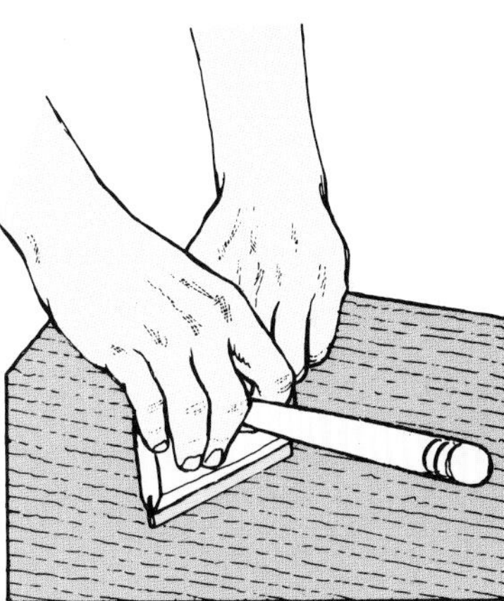

6 Apply more pressure with two hands

USING GLUE FILM

A paper-backed film of glue that becomes liquid only when heated with an iron is the modern equivalent of traditional hide glue. It can be reworked in a similar way, with a further application of heat, comes ready for use and takes less skill to apply. However, experience is required before using glue film to lay difficult veneers such as feathers and burls.

SEE ALSO	
Veneers	32-33
Cutting gauge	78,79
Lippings	248
Adhesives	302-303

Applying the film
Using scissors, cut the glue film slightly larger than the groundwork. Place the film face down on the groundwork and lightly smooth it flat with a domestic iron heated to a medium setting. When the glue has cooled, peel off the backing **(1)**.

Laying the veneer
Lay the veneer on the glued groundwork and place the paper backing on top to protect the veneer. Press with the heated iron, working slowly across the surface from the center outward. Follow behind with a veneer hammer **(2)** or a block of wood to keep the veneer pressed flat as the glue cools. Remove any blisters, as described in the section on hammer veneering, and trim off excess veneer when the glue has set.

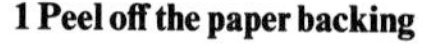

1 Peel off the paper backing

2 Press with iron and hammer

USING CONTACT CEMENT

Special contact cements enable you to veneer flat or curved surfaces without a press or special tools or heat. A solid lipping or other edge protection is recommended, as veneer is more vulnerable to chipping with this type of adhesive. Do not use a contact cement for feather or burl veneers.

Applying the glue
Using a brush or a scrap of thick veneer, apply a thin, even coat of glue to the veneer. Work diagonally from corner to corner, first in one direction then the other, making sure that you cover the surface thoroughly. Apply glue to the groundwork in the same way, then leave it to dry.

Laying the veneer
Lay a sheet of newsprint or brown paper over the groundwork, leaving a 2in (50mm) strip of dried glue exposed at one edge **(1)**. Lay the veneer on top; when it is aligned with the groundwork, press the veneer against the strip not covered by paper. Gradually slide the paper out from between the veneer and groundwork, pressing the two glued surfaces together with a block of wood **(2)**. Finally, rub over with the block to flatten the veneer, then trim off the excess (see left), using a knife or veneer-trimming tool.

Dealing with blisters
Tap across the surface to locate any air pockets under the veneer. Slit along the veneer locally with a sharp knife and work some fresh glue into the blister; roll it down with a hardwood seam-roller, as used for wallpapering. Wipe glue from the surface of the veneer before it can set.

Trimming excess veneer
When the glue has set, trim the edges of the panel, using a trimming tool, or turn it face down on a flat cutting board and use a sharp knife to trim excess veneer flush with the groundwork. Trim cross grain by cutting from the corners toward the center in order to avoid splitting the veneer.

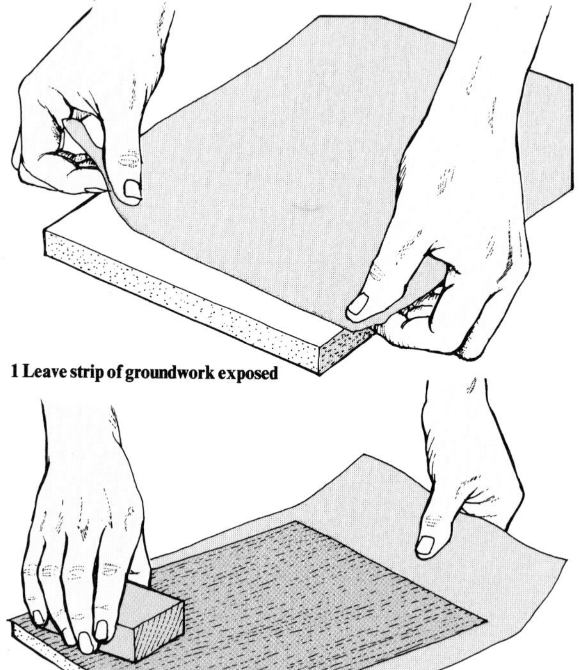

1 Leave strip of groundwork exposed

2 Slide paper from beneath veneer

REMOVING A FOREIGN BODY

If a speck of grit or coarse sawdust gets trapped beneath the veneer, no amount of pressure will remove it. Make a V-shaped incision in the area of the foreign body and peel back the flap of veneer so that you can remove the speck with the point of a knife. With hide glue or glue film, press the flap down using a warm iron and veneer hammer; with contact cement, apply a little fresh glue to the flap and groundwork.

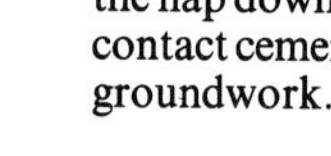

Cut a V-shaped flap to remove foreign body

BANDINGS & INLAYS

Bandings and inlays can transform a plain panel into an attractive piece of decorative woodwork in the traditional manner. Bandings are plain or patterned strips of veneer used to create decorative borders. You can make your own, but commercially produced bandings offer a wide choice and come ready to use.

Inlays are marquetry motifs used as decorative features; they are available in traditional, pictorial or floral patterns. Commercially made inlays are relatively simple to apply either to veneered or solid-wood surfaces. You can hand-lay individual motifs, but use cauls for veneer assemblies.

Veneering a bordered panel
Cut and lay the center-panel veneer so that it stops short of the edges all around. Trim the veneer true to the edges with a cutting gauge set to the planned width of the cross-banding **(1)**. Peel the waste and remove excess glue **(2)**. Soften hide glue with an iron, if necessary.

Cutting cross-bandings
Cut cross-bandings from the ends of consecutive veneers, using a cutting gauge. First, shoot the end of the veneer with a finely set plane; then cut the cross-bandings for the border slightly longer and wider than required. Use a straight-edged board to guide the gauge **(3)**.

1 Trim veneer with cutting gauge

2 Peel the waste

3 Use edge of board as a guide

Hand-laying cross-bandings
The ends of the bandings can either be mitered before laying or cut after they have been glued in place. The latter should guarantee a good fit.

Apply hide glue to the groundwork and both sides of the bandings. Press each in place, using either a veneer hammer or a cross-peen hammer. To cut the miters in place, align a straightedge with the inner and outer corners of the overlapped bandings and cut through both layers carefully **(4)**.

Remove the top waste, then lift the end of the border to remove the bottom piece. Press the mitered ends with the hammer. Cut the waste from the long edges and wipe away the excess glue. Apply veneer tape to the joints and edges.

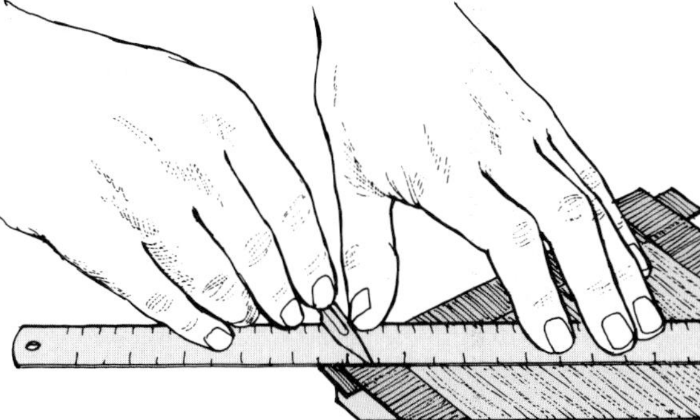

4 Overlap bandings and cut through both layers

Laying stringings and bandings
If you wish to include stringings or decorative bandings between the center panel and the cross-banding, lay them as described above. Then lay the cross-banding the same way.

LINES AND BANDINGS

Commercially produced decorative bandings are made in batches from selected woods. Always buy a sufficient amount when you first order, as you may not be able to obtain an exact match at a later date. Not only will the wood be different, but the size may vary, too.

Stringing lines
Stringings are fine strips of wood used to divide areas of veneer by providing light or dark lines between different types of veneer or where the grain direction changes. Ebony and boxwood were the traditional materials for stringings, but nowadays black dyed wood is used instead of ebony.

Bandings
Decorative bandings are made from side-grain sections of colored woods glued together and sliced to produce strips approximately $\frac{1}{32}$in (1mm) thick. They come ready-edged, with a choice of boxwood or black stringings, and are used to make ornamental borders.

Strips of veneer cut across the grain are known as cross-bandings and are used to make bordered panels. Make cross-bandings yourself, cutting them from the veneer used for the panel.

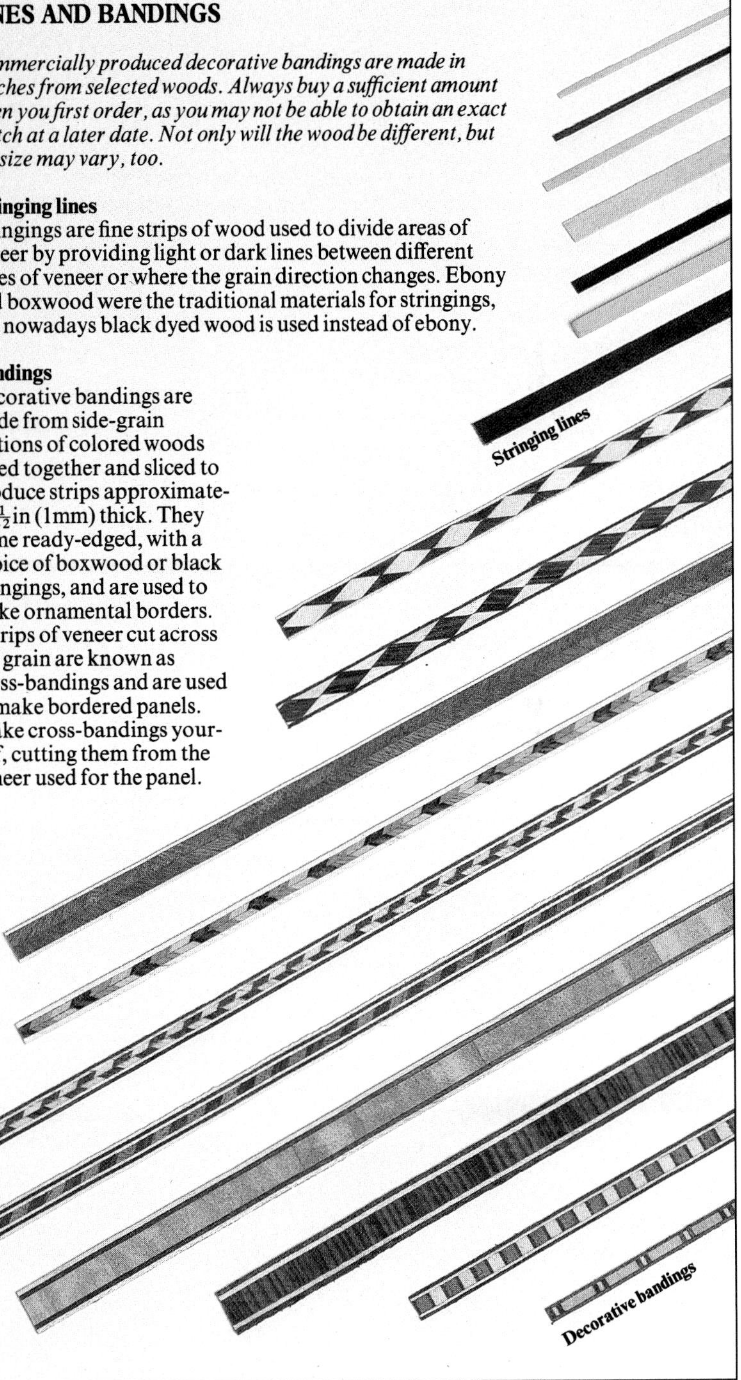

Stringing lines

Decorative bandings

Caul-laying bandings

You can use cauls to lay bandings after the center-panel veneer, or lay them together.

By laying the center panel first and trimming it with a cutting gauge, you can be sure it is centered and that the border will be even all around. You will need to take the veneered panel from the press and trim it before the resin adhesive has cured. Cut and miter the bandings to fit. Apply adhesive to the groundwork border, then tape the veneers in position and return the panel to the press.

Alternatively, cut the center-panel veneer and the banding to size, allowing extra at the border, and tape them together **(1)**. Pencil centerlines across the length and width of the groundwork and the assembled veneer. Apply glue to the groundwork, carefully position the veneer and press it down by hand or with a seam-roller before placing it in the press.

SEE ALSO

Veneers	32-33
Cutting gauge	78
Scroll saw	84,85
Router planes	95
Scratch stock	96
Routers	140-141
Powered scroll saws	178-180
Caul veneering	262
Adhesives	302-303

Inlaying bandings

Bandings can be inlaid into the surface of solid wood, using a cutting gauge and scratch stock to cut the grooves.

Set the gauge to cut the width lines of the groove, working from the edge. Cut the groove with the scratch stock, but use a chisel at the corners. Make the depth of the recess slightly less than the thickness of the banding. Miter the ends of the banding, then apply the glue and press it into place with a cross-peen hammer **(2)**.

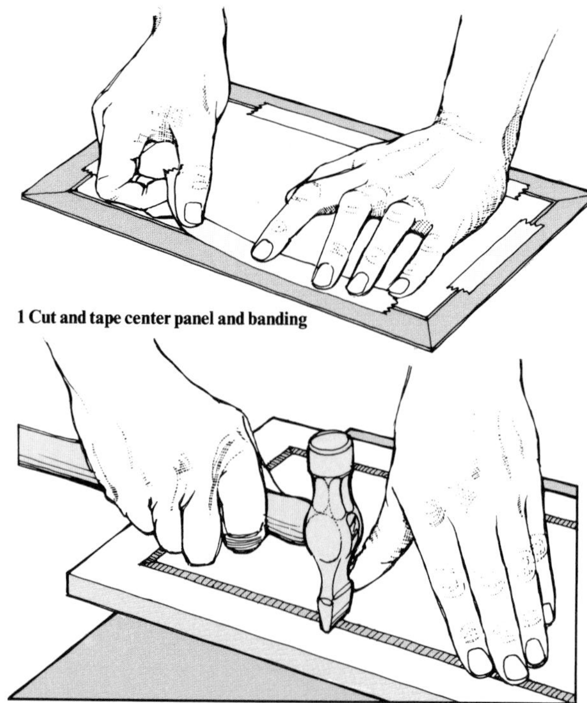

1 Cut and tape center panel and banding

2 Press banding with cross-peen hammer

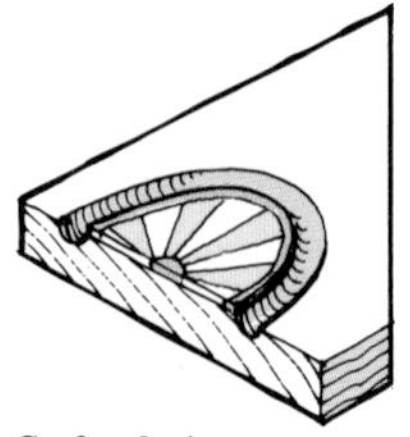

Surface laying
Motifs can be glued directly onto a solid-wood surface without inlaying them. To improve the appearance, gouge a groove around the edge to give a shadow break line.

INLAY MOTIFS

Inlay motifs are supplied with a protective paper backing. They are laid with the paper surface up. Some are made to a finished size and shape, others have spare veneer surrounding the design for cutting to shape.

Insetting an inlay motif

You can inset the inlay into your veneer assembly before caul-veneering. Ideally, the inlay should be the same thickness as the veneer so as to maintain even pressure across the panel.

For a centered motif, mark centerlines on the veneer background and on the motif. Using a patch of double-faced tape, position the motif and carefully trace around it with a knife to cut the shape in the background veneer **(1)**. If the motif has spare material surrounding it, mark the required shape on it and cut both layers together.

Tape the motif in position and then lay the complete assembly with cauls. When set, dampen the paper backing and scrape it off, making it ready for sanding.

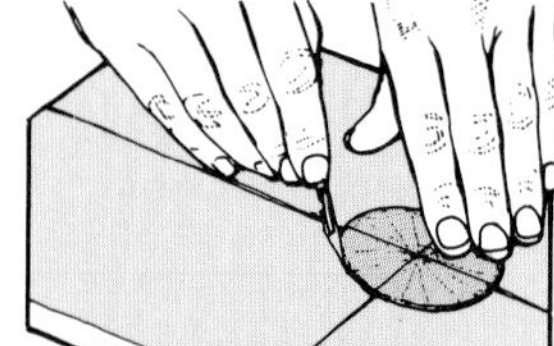

1 Cut the shape in background

Solid-wood inlay

Position the inlay on the surface and cut around it with a knife. Using chisels and gouges, cut the waste from the edges of the recess **(2)**. Remove the remaining waste with a finely set hand router. Alternatively, use a power router first then trim the edges by hand. Make the depth of the recess slightly less than the thickness of the motif.

Glue the inlay into place and clamp it with a block of wood, with a layer of plastic sheeting or waxed paper placed between them.

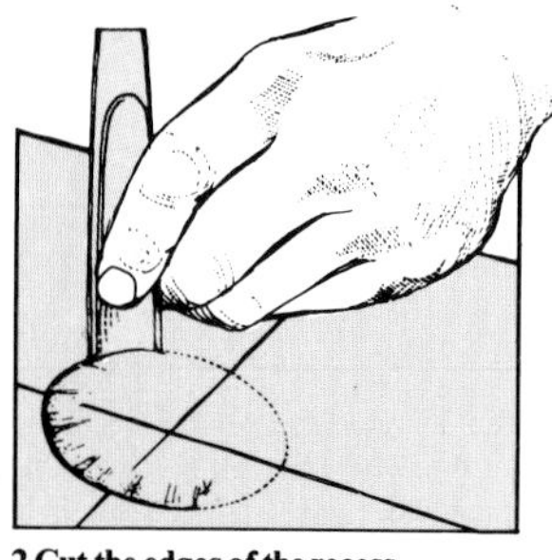

2 Cut the edges of the recess

MARQUETRY

Since recorded history, applied decoration has been used to enhance artifacts beyond their functional needs. Wood veneer has long been used as a decorative medium, and the diversity of natural figure and color has provided craftsmen with a rich "palette" from which to cut and assemble decorative patterns and pictures known as marquetry. Craftsmen of the past keen to express their virtuosity developed marquetry techniques into a fine art and produced elaborate ornamentation based on natural forms. Although it involves skillful handiwork, marquetry is far from being a dying craft – indeed, it is still practiced commercially for applied decoration in the form of inlay motifs and today flourishes in lively fashion in the hands of amateur marquetarians, who often produce work of great beauty as a hobby.

Marquetry work

Marquetry designs can be cut using a scroll saw or a knife. The saw method is generally used for cutting intricate shapes in multiple layers of veneer; the knife method for single layers – when making marquetry pictures, for example.

It takes skill to cut the parts accurately and it is worth practicing on pieces of scrap veneer before tackling a project. You can make your own design or, to begin with, buy a kit containing a pattern and all the material you need.

If you plan to make your own design, collect together a wide selection of veneers. It is not until the veneer is placed in context that you can really see if it has the right effect.

The success of the work lies not just in the skill of cutting and joining the pieces but also in the artistic interpretation of the chosen veneers.

SAW CUTTING

Commercially produced motifs are cut from packs of veneers on a "marquetry donkey" – a specialist's tool on which the operator sits and works a reciprocating scroll saw, while holding the veneer in a foot-operated clamp. Each pack is manipulated in the jaws with the left hand, while the operator works the saw horizontally with the other. The various shaped parts are assembled on a flat table and held together with a layer of gummed paper.

Scroll-saw cutting

For the nonspecialist, an electrically powered scroll saw will make light work of cutting the veneer as well as being generally useful in the workshop.

Alternatively, the traditional hand-held scroll saw and cutting table can be used. Cutting a number of layers accurately with a hand-held scroll saw is difficult, but you can saw a design using two contrasting veneers relatively easily.

Cutting two veneers together

Select your veneers – one for the background and one for the inlay. In fact, this method produces two identical profiles that reverse the colors when assembled. Cut the pieces about ½in (12mm) larger than the proposed design. Tape them together between waste veneers as backing, set with their grain in the opposite direction **(1)**.

Insert the blade through a small starting hole on a line near the center and fix it in the saw. Holding the work firmly on the saw table, cut accurately around the line **(2)**. Turn the work to present the line to the cutting edge, as required.

Assemble the cut pieces together with tape or a sheet of gummed paper. Fill the sawcut with colored wood putty, rubbing it in from the back face, then wipe clean so it'll be ready for laying when dry.

Transposing a design

You can choose a two-dimensional representation of any subject to serve as the basis for your design.

Make a line drawing from your source material. If the scale is not right, reproduce it using a scaled grid or a photocopier that will reduce or enlarge the size. The latter is particularly useful since, apart from altering the scale and producing repeat prints quickly, the design can be offset onto the wood to give a reverse image by hot-ironing the back of the photocopy.

The traditional method for reproducing a number of identical copies and reverse images used a spiked wheel to prick through all the lines of the original. Black bitumen powder was then pounced through the holes and fused to the paper by heating it.

Iron the back of a photocopy

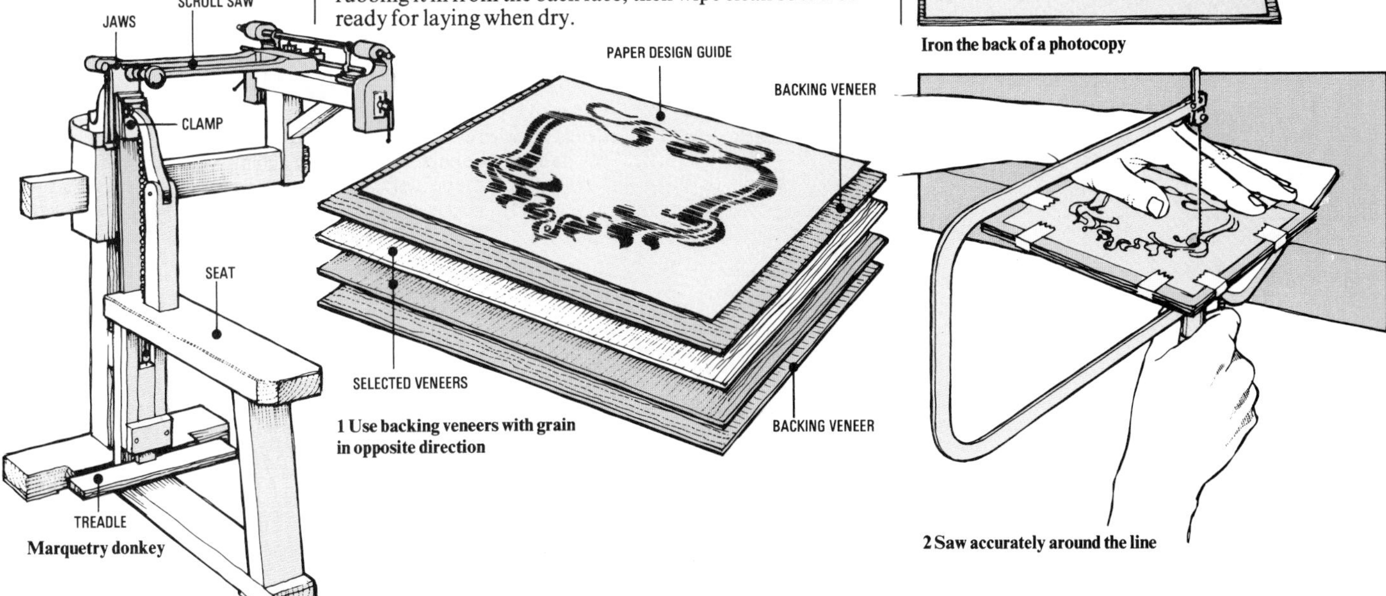

Marquetry donkey

1 Use backing veneers with grain in opposite direction

2 Saw accurately around the line

MAKING A PICTURE

The art of making marquetry pictures is in using the natural features of the veneer to interpret the color, texture, light and shade of the original.

SEE ALSO	
Veneers	32-33
Scrapers	110
Caul veneering	262
Bandings	265
Abrasive papers	285
Adhesives	302-303

Choosing a subject
Any subject – animals, plants, seascapes, landscapes, etc. – can be created by marquetry.

Photographs make a good source of reference from which to trace a design, but choose one with bold areas rather than lots of fine detail.

Photographs show every subtlety of form and must be simplified for a marquetry design. The outline of the features can be simply traced around, but the subtle shading that gives it form has to be interpreted with artistic skill. Shadows will, by the nature of the technique, tend to be hard-edged; but with careful veneer selection and the use of shading techniques, graduated tones can be created to give three-dimensional effects.

Starting marquetry
The beginner is best advised to start with a marquetry kit in which the veneers have been selected and numbered to key in with a printed design guide. However, the chosen veneers will still need to be orientated to provide the right effect for the surfaces they are depicting and will need careful cutting.

The window method
Veneers for picture-making are cut individually and, because they are thin, can be readily cut with a sharp pointed knife.

The "window method" enables the picture to be built up in such a way that the interrelationship of the veneer pieces can be tried before cutting them.

The design is either marked on a background veneer or on a cardboard "waster." One shape is cut out, then the veneer is placed behind the "window aperture" and tested for color and effect. It is then cut to an exact fit, using the window as a template. Successive windows are cut and fitted until the design is completed as a single sheet for caul veneering to the groundwork.

Using the window method
Hinge the design along the top edge of the cardboard waster with tape. Place a sheet of carbon paper under the design sheet (unless the designs are carbon-backed) and mark border lines and centering marks on the three edges **(1)**.

Next, mark the main features of the design, leaving the smaller details until later. Cut out one of the main elements, following its contour precisely but allowing the edges to overlap the border **(2)**.

Place the selected veneer behind the window and position it to give the best grain effect. Lightly tape it in position, then carefully score the veneer with the knife, using the window as a template **(3)**. Remove the veneer and cut it to shape, then retape it into the aperture **(4)**.

Cut the next window and repeat the process; but this time apply PVA glue to the edge that meets the first veneer, then press it flat using a weighted board. Repeat this process until the main picture area is complete.

Turn the hinged design sheet back over the picture; re-mark the border lines and trace the smaller elements onto the veneer now in place. Repeat the window-cutting procedure **(5)** to complete the picture.

Cut the picture from the waster border. Tape overlength decorative border strips around the four edges, and miter the overlapping ends **(6)**. Tape the miters to complete the assembly so it is ready for laying with cauls.

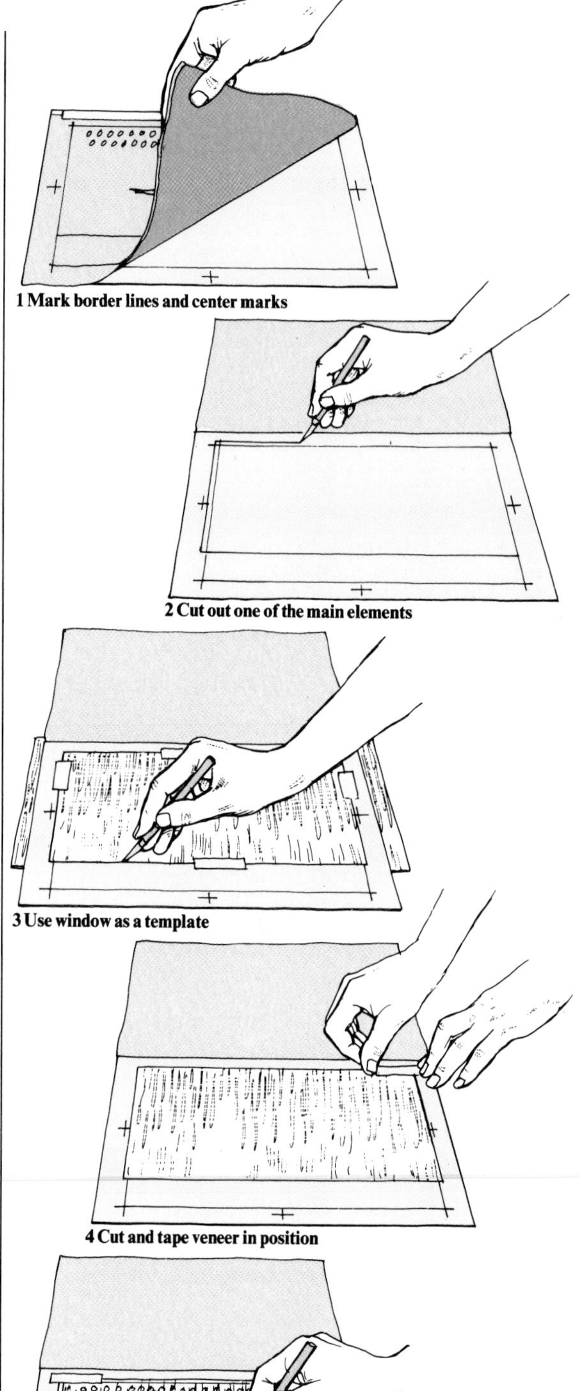

1 Mark border lines and center marks

2 Cut out one of the main elements

3 Use window as a template

4 Cut and tape veneer in position

5 Cut smaller parts using window method

6 Miter ends of decorative border

CLEANING UP MARQUETRY

Before marquetry can be given a finish, the surface must be prepared. Remember that veneer is very thin and must not be overworked.

First, any gummed tape must be removed. Dampen it with a sponge dipped in warm water, do not soak it. Use a wide chisel or scraper to scrape it off, then let the surface dry.

Clean up raised grain or surface unevenness with a scraper. Work with the grain of plain veneer, but for veneer assemblies with varied grain, use the scraper diagonally.

Sand the surface lightly with progressively finer sandpaper. Wrap the paper around a cork block, and sand with the grain as much as possible. Brush away all traces of dust, then wipe the surface with a tacky rag.

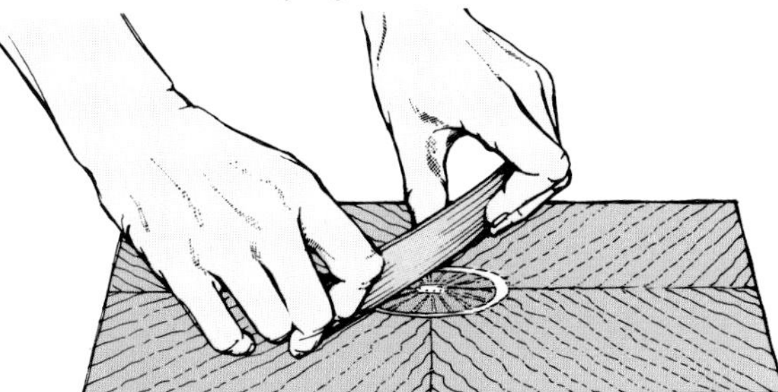

Use scraper diagonally on veneer assemblies

Shading veneer

The traditional method for producing three-dimensional shaded effects for shell, oval and fan inlay motifs is to scorch part of the veneer lightly by inserting it in hot sand. You can use this technique for marquetry pictures. The aim is to produce a subtle, natural-looking gradation of tone to achieve the desired effect. Practice on waste veneer, using trial and error to obtain the best tones.

Heat a bed of fine sand in a baking tray. Maintain an even temperature that will produce the required tonal range in not more than about 10 or 12 seconds. It is better to increase the heat rather than leave the veneer longer, as it will shrink if it is left in the sand too long.

Holding the veneer with tweezers, insert it into the sand. Count the number of seconds, determined by your sampling, and then remove it **(1)**.

You can use oversized pieces of veneer (which will allow you to make some adjustment of effect), using the window-cutting method. Alternatively, cut the pieces to finished shape and size, but be sure to shade them quickly in order to avoid shrinkage and distortion. You can dampen them and press them with a flat board after shading, if necessary.

For shading portions of veneer that are not at the edge, use a spoon to pour the hot sand onto the area that is to be toned down **(2)**.

Mask the veneer with gummed tape to produce "hard-edged" shading, if required.

1 Remove after a few seconds

2 Pour hot sand from spoon

PARQUETRY

Parquetry uses symmetrically shaped pieces of veneer to make geometric patterns or motifs. The shapes are derived from basic geometry. Any number of designs can be created by cutting veneers of different type, color or grain into square, rectangular, triangular, diamond or other polygonal shapes and joining them together.

Working out a design

The permutations of simple geometric forms offer a seemingly endless choice of patterns. You can experiment with pattern-making on graph or isometric-grid paper, using different-colored pens or pencils to fill in the shapes of your design **(1)**.

Designs that form repetitive strips are easier to set out and to cut and assemble accurately. With motifs that have interlocking shapes, such as cubes and stars, you will need to assemble the parts individually.

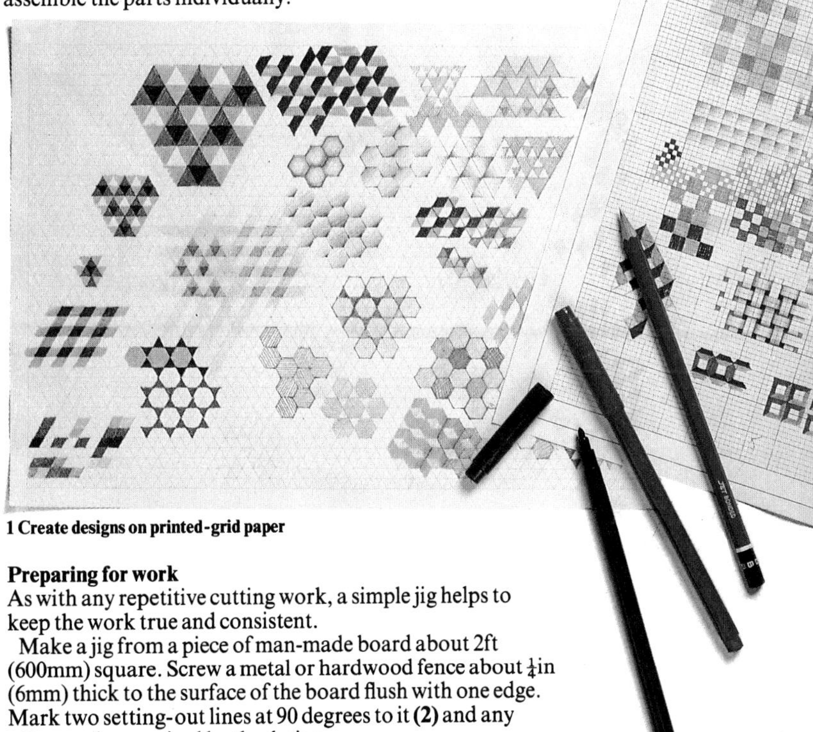

1 Create designs on printed-grid paper

Preparing for work

As with any repetitive cutting work, a simple jig helps to keep the work true and consistent.

Make a jig from a piece of man-made board about 2ft (600mm) square. Screw a metal or hardwood fence about ¼in (6mm) thick to the surface of the board flush with one edge. Mark two setting-out lines at 90 degrees to it **(2)** and any other angles required by the design.

Cutting is done with a knife or veneer saw, always with a straightedge as a guide. To set the straightedge parallel to the fence, cut pairs of thin plywood spacer blocks to the required width. You will also need gummed tape to hold the pieces together.

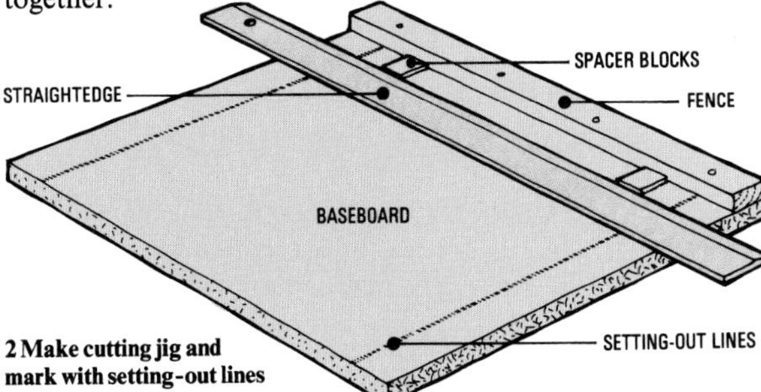

2 Make cutting jig and mark with setting-out lines

MAKING A CHECKERBOARD PATTERN

Perhaps the simplest and most widely known example is the checkerboard pattern of squares of alternating colors. The "color" may be achieved by using contrasting woods or, for subtle effect, the same wood but with contrasting grain direction in alternate squares. Generally, the best effects are produced using straight-grained or plain veneers.

SEE ALSO

Veneers	32-33
Man-made boards	34-38
Caul veneering	262
Bandings	265

Select your contrasting veneers and cut the length of each slightly longer than the proposed baseboard. Cut one edge of each veneer straight. Place this edge against the fence and cut the strips to the required width, using the spacer blocks to position the straightedge **(1)**. Cut four of one color and five of the other, it does not matter which. This is to keep the grain in the same direction when they are assembled. Number them to keep them in the order they were cut.

Carefully butt and tape alternate colored strips together. Place the assembled panel on the cutting board with one side edge on the 90-degree setting-out line. Set the straightedge parallel to the fence, using small spacer blocks, and trim the ends square **(2)**.

Remove the waste and push the cut edge against the fence. Cut the assembled veneer as before, producing strips of alternating squares.

Tape the cut edges together again, but first stagger alternate strips by one square **(3)**. Cut off the projecting squares to leave the checkerboard square.

Complete the assembly by cutting and taping an inlay banding and cross-banding border all around, making it ready for laying with cauls.

1 Cut strips to width

2 Trim ends of strips

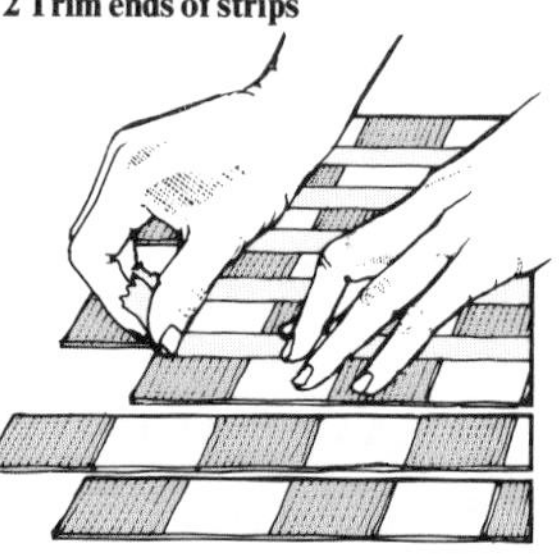

3 Stagger and tape strips

MAKING A CUBE PATTERN

The classic isometric-cube effect is produced by using 60-degree diamonds cut from three shades of wood and set together to form a hexagon.

To make a symmetrical repeat pattern, first cut the diamonds using the strip method but only taping them lightly.

Separate the diamonds and assemble the field of hexagons on a sheet of clear self-adhesive film laid sticky side up over your isometric grid paper.

Cover the assembly with gummed paper and press it between flat boards. When dry, peel off the film, making it ready for laying.

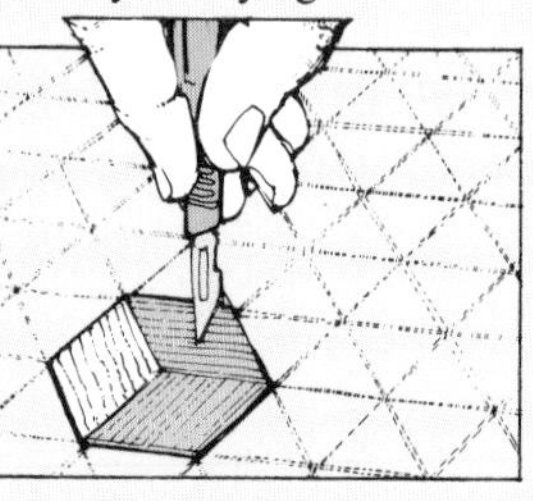

Assemble diamonds over grid

STRIP VARIATIONS

Using the methods described above for the checkerboard design, you can create a variety of patterns. Cutting strips of different widths and offsetting the resulting squares or rectangles by half or whole units will produce alternatives.

If the squares are cut diagonally, strips of right-angle triangles are made that, when half-staggered, produce a zigzag pattern. If alternate strips are reversed and staggered, alternating colored triangles will result.

Diamond patterns are produced by cutting strips at 60 degrees. First, cut parallel strips of contrasting veneer to the required width. Pin the first strip level with a 60-degree setting-out line marked on the board. Then tape the strips together, with the end corners butted against the fence. Trim off the "toothed" ends, using the straightedge and spacer blocks. Remove the pins and push the cut edge against the fence.

Cut the assembly once more into strips, using the same spacer blocks. You will now have strips of 60-degree diamonds that, when staggered by one diamond and taped together, will produce an alternating repeat pattern.

By cutting this arrangement horizontally through the center of the diamonds, strips of equilateral triangles are produced. You can then stagger or reverse these strips to create other patterns.

Make alternative square patterns

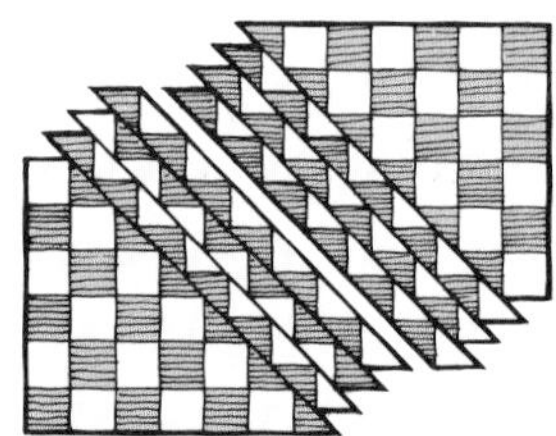

Or cut squares diagonally

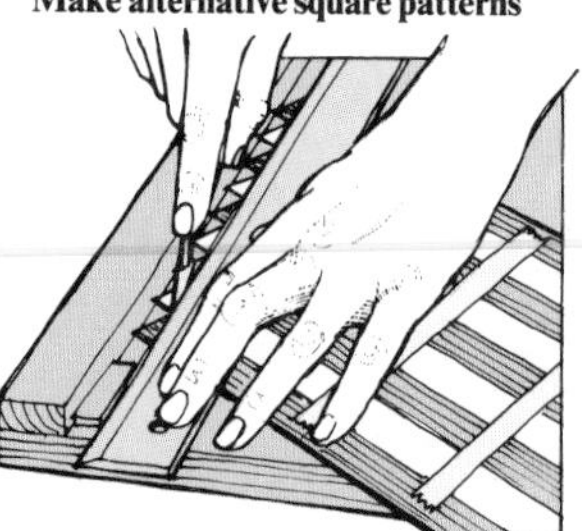

Tape and cut strips to 60 degrees

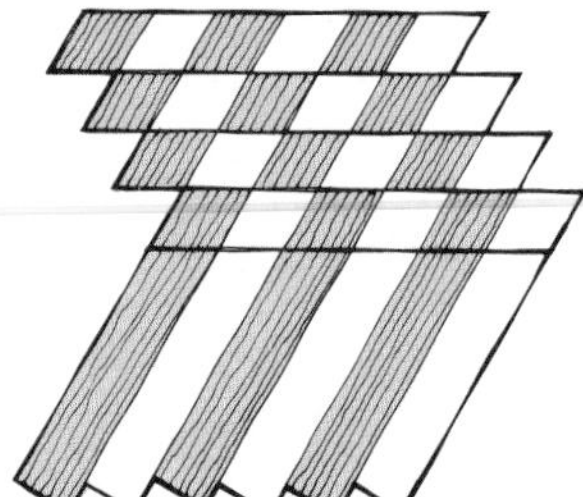

Cut and stagger diamond strips

Cut and stagger or reverse diamonds to create other patterns

CHAPTER TEN

WOOD CARVING

Ever since early man discovered that a sharp instrument could be used to shape a piece of wood, carving has been employed to produce all manner of functional and decorative artifacts ranging from basic utensils to sacred icons. Today, with the development of woodworking machinery and man-made materials, carving has become largely a leisure activity. However, age-old techniques are still used commercially by skilled carvers in restoring buildings and furniture and also for creating new pieces by traditional methods. Woodcarving goes beyond the utilitarian and offers the carver a means of self-expression that raises it to the level of art. In carving perhaps more than in any other kind of woodwork, the ability to execute a fine piece of work only comes with practice, though a natural eye for form is an undoubted advantage. Indeed, the shape and complexity of the work has no limitation other than the imagination of the carver. Specialized chisels, gouges and other hand tools are therefore made to cope with the immense diversity of form.

CARVING CHISELS & GOUGES

A standard range of carving chisels and gouges can include 18 different cutting-edge profiles, with a choice of up to five shapes of blade, and most of them are produced in a range of sizes from $\frac{1}{16}$ in (2mm) up to 2in (50mm). They can be purchased from good tool stores or from specialist mail-order suppliers, some of whom offer a worldwide service. Woodcarving tools are sold with the cutting edges ground but not sharpened. Unlike conventional woodworking chisels and gouges, woodcarving tools are generally beveled on both sides of the cutting edge to facilitate cutting the wood at a variety of angles. The chisels have equal bevels ground on each side, and the gouges and parting tools have a larger bevel on the outside than on the inside. A good-quality sharpening stone and shaped slipstones are essential to maintain a keen edge on these tools. For the beginner, only a few basic tools are necessary.

SEE ALSO

Sharpening stones	102-103
Sharpening	274
Engineer's vise	276
Holding the tools	278

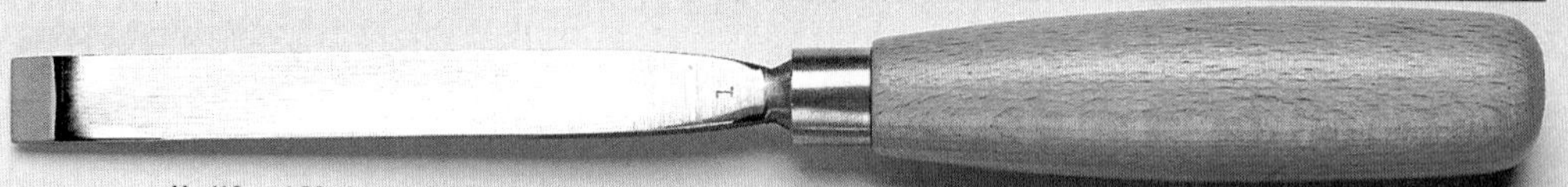

$\frac{1}{2}$in (12mm) No 1 straight chisel
For general shaping, cutting straight lines and finishing.

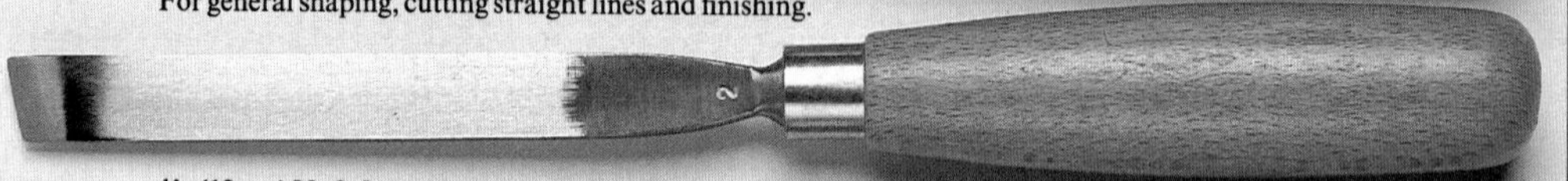

$\frac{1}{2}$in (12mm) No 2 skew chisel
For finishing and undercutting details.

$\frac{1}{8}$in (3mm) No 3 straight gouge
For fine shaping work.

1in (25mm) No 9 straight gouge
For faster cutting or general shaping work.

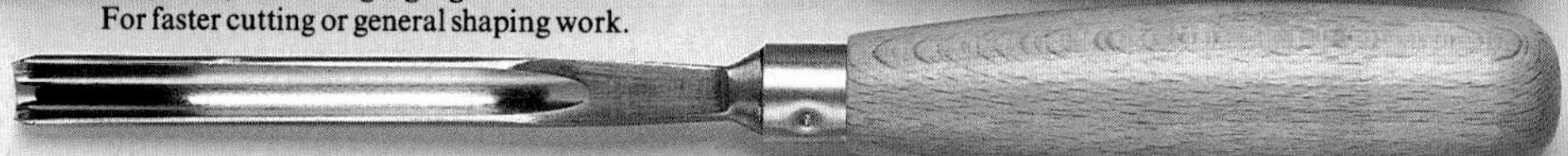

$\frac{5}{16}$in (8mm) No 10 straight gouge
For cutting flutes and general shaping.

$\frac{3}{8}$in (9mm) No 14 curved gouge
For cutting hollows and curved details.

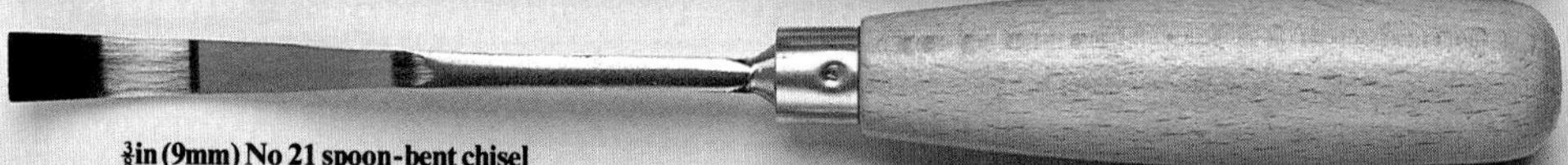

$\frac{3}{8}$in (9mm) No 21 spoon-bent chisel
For cutting and finishing acute recessed curves.

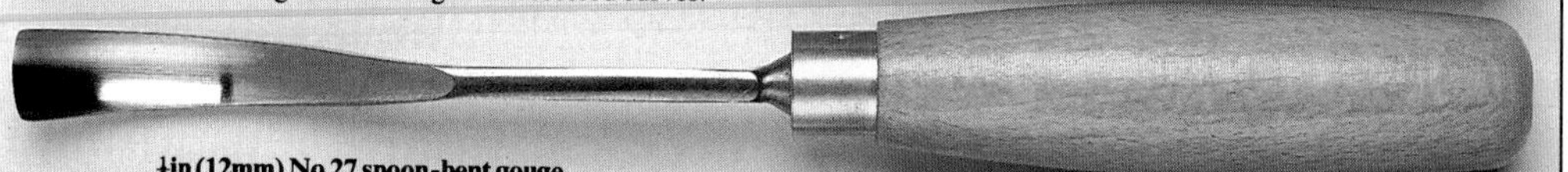

$\frac{1}{2}$in (12mm) No 27 spoon-bent gouge
For shaping tight curves and deeply recessed work.

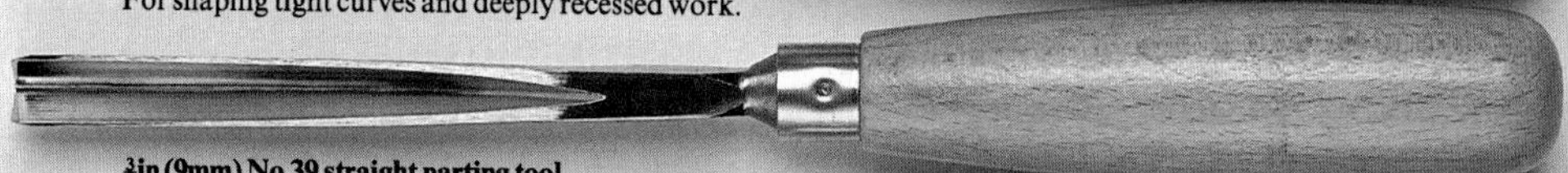

$\frac{3}{8}$in (9mm) No 39 straight parting tool
For outlining separate areas, lettering and detail carving.

Octagonal ash handle

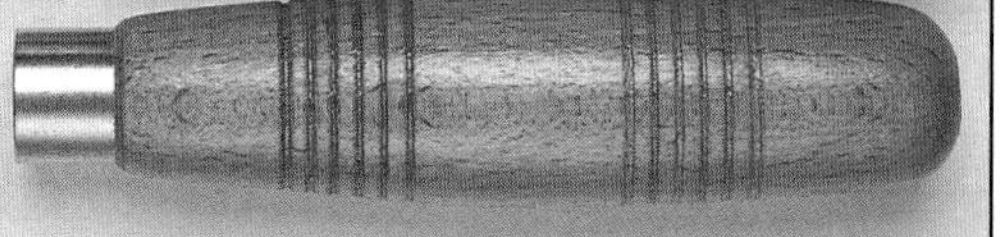

Round beech handle

Carving-tool handles
Hardwoods such as beech, boxwood or ash are used for handles. You can buy round handles with brass ferrules or traditional octagonal handles without ferrules. The flats of octagonal handles prevent small, straight tools from rolling off the bench.

Fitting a handle
Many carving tools are supplied without handles so you can fit a manufactured handle or one of your own. Drill a fine pilot hole down the center of the handle. Set the blade in an engineer's vise fitted with soft jaws. Tap the handle partway onto the tang, then twist it free. Refit the handle and repeat the process until it is about $\frac{1}{4}$in (6mm) from the shoulder of the blade. Check the alignment and tap the handle home.

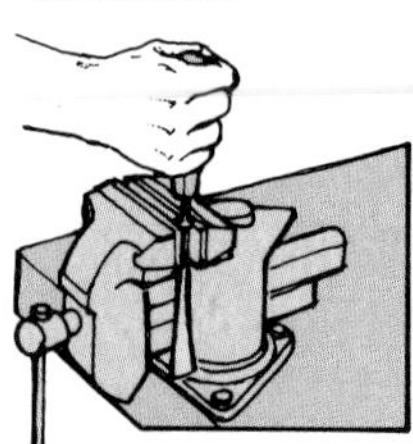

Hold the blade in vise
Support the shoulder of the blade on the jaws.

SHAPES AND SIZES

Carving chisels and gouges are usually referred to by name and number. The names generally describe the shape of the blade and cutting edge – for example, a "straight gouge" or "spoon-bent chisel." However, the profile of the cutting edge can vary too. So, to overcome the need for long descriptions and to make identification easier, a system of numbers was adopted in the nineteenth century, indicating the profile of the cutting edge as well as the shape of the blade.

Chisels and gouges form the majority of carving tools and, although the numbering may vary slightly from one manufacturer to another, it usually starts with the straight-bladed versions of these tools – so No1 is a basic chisel, No2 is a skew chisel, No3 a shallow gouge and so on up to No11, which is a deep gouge. The higher the number, the deeper the curve or "sweep," as it is called, of the gouge's cutting edge. All the sweeps are true radius curves except the "veiner" (No11), which has straighter sides. The next set of numbers (12-20) represents the same sweeps but with a curved blade; the next set (21-32) the same sweeps but with a spoon-bent blade; and so on, each number representing a change in the cross-section shape of the cutting edge combined with the longitudinal shape of the blade. Each number is available in a range of sizes, so the width of the cutting edge should be specified in addition to the identification number when ordering. Manufacturers who do not follow the system (No12, for example, may be a V-parting tool) still usually supply a range of shapes comparable to that shown in the chart at right.

Carving tools
The chart (right) shows the wide range of carving tools available. The red squares refer to the blade shapes illustrated opposite.

CUTTING PROFILES

SPECIALIZED TOOLS

Specialized tools
Special shaped tools are used for intricate or detailed carving whenever a particular tool makes the cut easier or a special shape of cut is required.

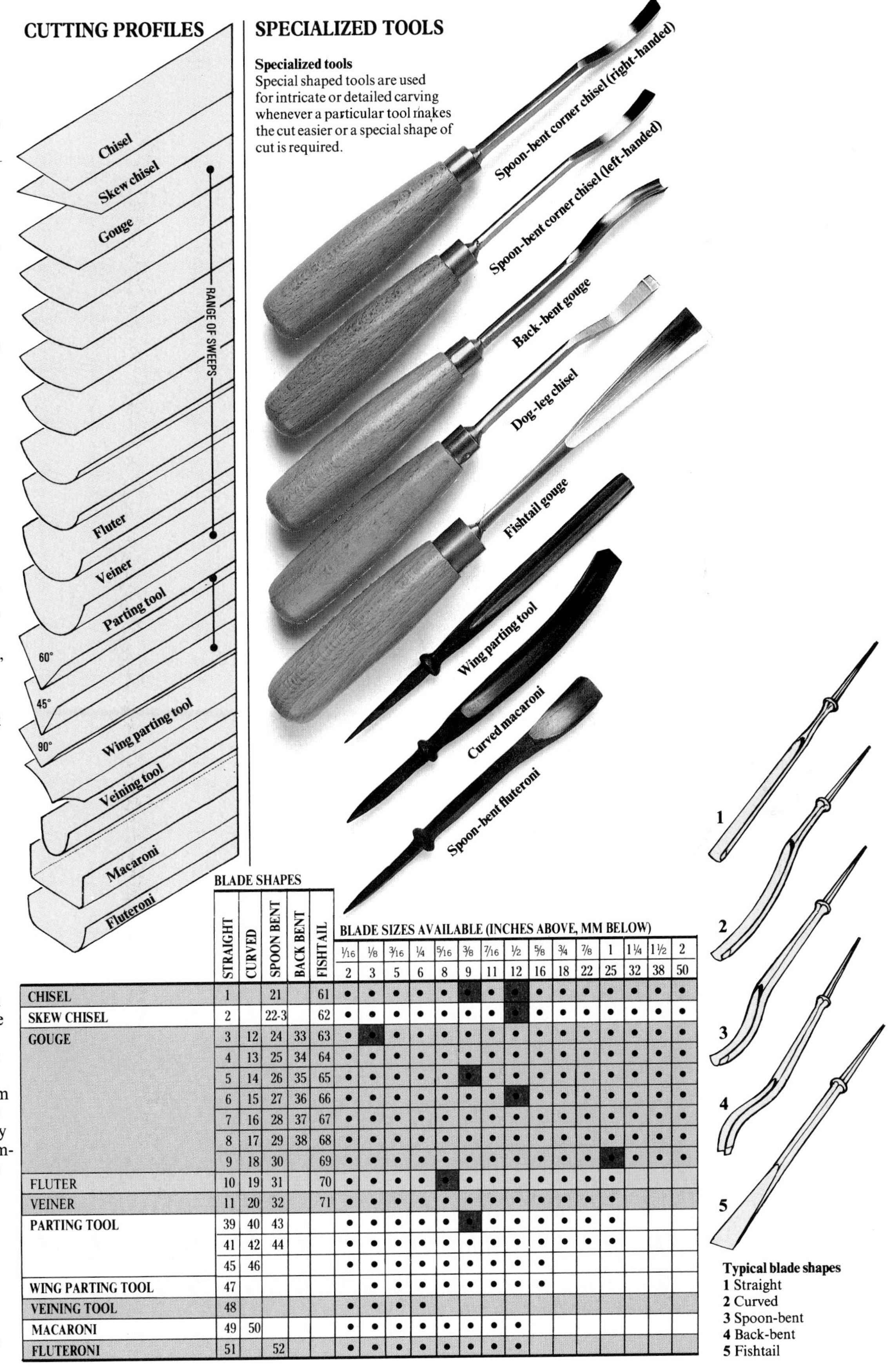

BLADE SHAPES / BLADE SIZES AVAILABLE (INCHES ABOVE, MM BELOW)

	STRAIGHT	CURVED	SPOON BENT	BACK BENT	FISHTAIL	1/16	1/8	3/16	1/4	5/16	3/8	7/16	1/2	5/8	3/4	7/8	1	1 1/4	1 1/2	2
						2	3	5	6	8	9	11	12	16	18	22	25	32	38	50
CHISEL	1		21		61	•	•	•	•	•	•	•	•	•	•	•	•	•	•	•
SKEW CHISEL	2		22-3		62	•	•	•	•	•	•	•	•	•	•	•	•	•	•	•
GOUGE	3	12	24	33	63	•	•	•	•	•	•	•	•	•	•	•	•	•	•	•
	4	13	25	34	64	•	•	•	•	•	•	•	•	•	•	•	•	•	•	•
	5	14	26	35	65	•	•	•	•	•	•	•	•	•	•	•	•	•	•	•
	6	15	27	36	66	•	•	•	•	•	•	•	•	•	•	•	•	•	•	•
	7	16	28	37	67	•	•	•	•	•	•	•	•	•	•	•	•	•	•	•
	8	17	29	38	68	•	•	•	•	•	•	•	•	•	•	•	•	•	•	•
	9	18	30		69	•	•	•	•	•	•	•	•	•	•	•	•	•	•	•
FLUTER	10	19	31		70	•	•	•	•	•	•	•	•	•	•	•	•			
VEINER	11	20	32		71	•	•	•	•	•	•	•	•	•	•	•	•			
PARTING TOOL	39	40	43			•	•	•	•	•	•	•	•	•	•	•	•			
	41	42	44			•	•	•	•	•	•	•	•	•	•	•	•			
	45	46				•	•	•	•	•	•	•	•	•						
WING PARTING TOOL	47						•	•	•	•	•	•	•	•						
VEINING TOOL	48					•	•	•	•											
MACARONI	49	50				•	•	•	•	•	•	•	•							
FLUTERONI	51		52			•	•	•	•	•	•	•	•							

Typical blade shapes
1 Straight
2 Curved
3 Spoon-bent
4 Back-bent
5 Fishtail

CARVER'S MALLETS AND ADZES

In addition to a selection of carver's chisels and gouges, woodcarving uses a number of general woodworking tools, including handsaws, planes, spokeshaves, rasps and files. Machine tools such as a power drill, band saw and chain saw – the latter for roughing out larger work – are used, too. The specialized tools described below also form part of the woodcarver's basic kit.

SEE ALSO

How trees grow	10-11
Drying wood	13
Softwoods	16-19
Hardwoods	20-29
Sharpening stones	102-105
Grinders	106-107

Carver's mallet
A mallet is essential for driving chisels and gouges when cutting across the grain or working hard woods or large pieces.

The carver's mallet has a round head, made from solid or laminated beech or lignum vitae, with a turned ash or beech handle. The round head allows the chisel to be struck from practically any angle.

Carver's mallets are made in a variety of diameters, from 3in (75mm) up to 6in (150mm), and are sometimes specified by weight. A medium size and weight are adequate for most work. A large, heavy mallet is tiring to use for any length of time.

Adzes
Carver's or sculptor's adzes are short single-handed versions of the traditional two-handed carpenter's adze. Both chisel-head and gouge-head types are made. Adzes are designed for the quick removal of waste when roughing out the work. The gouge type is particularly useful for hollowing out wood for bowl carving.

Punches
Carver's punches make indentations in the work and are used to produce crisp carving details or to create a pattern or textured effects. They are made of steel and are available in a wide range of decorative patterns.

SHARPENING WOODCARVING TOOLS

The sight of curling woodshavings and the feel and sound of the cutting edge slicing effortlessly through wood are a joy for any woodcarver. Only razor-sharp woodcarving tools will give the right results, whereas dull tools are hard to use and produce poor results. Resharpen your tools as you work, and at the first sign of a tool catching or tearing the wood, give it a light honing, either by hand or on a buffing wheel, to keep the edge keen.

Sharpening new tools
New carving tools are generally supplied ground but not honed to a razor-sharp edge. Be prepared to spend some time sharpening carving tools, as they are honed on both sides of the cutting edge and need careful handling to maintain the shape. The sharpening stones required are described in the chapter on hand tools.

Sharpening a chisel
The honing angle of a carving chisel, unlike that of an ordinary woodworking chisel, is the same as the bevel. The point where the bevel meets the full thickness of the blade is known as the "heel." This is usually honed down to produce a rounded surface that will not indent the work.

Start with the bevel flat on the lubricated stone and draw the chisel backward, at the same time lowering the handle, then push the tool forward and lift the handle. Repeat this action on both sides until the bevel is smooth and well-rounded and a fine burr is produced on the cutting edge.

Remove the burr and polish the bevel to a razor-sharp edge by stropping the tool on a dressed leather strop (available from carving-tool suppliers).

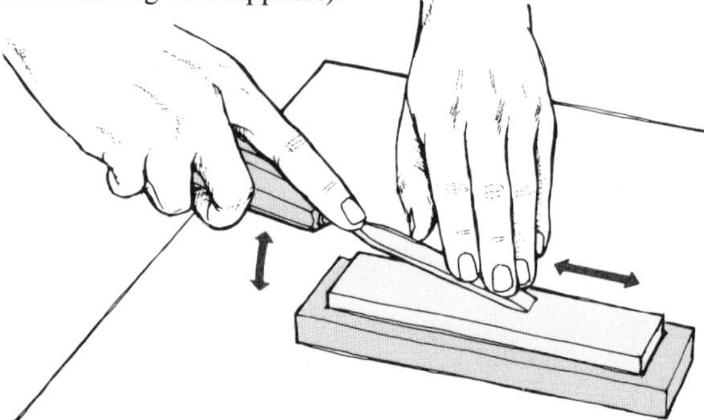

Hone the bevel on both sides

Sharpening a V-tool
When you are sharpening a V-tool, it is important that the point where the two outside bevels meet is first rounded over to follow the inside shape.

Sharpen the bevels on the stone as you would a chisel, but work the "point" as well. This can be done on a benchstone or by working a flat slipstone up and down the corner while rocking the stone from side to side.

Work the inner bevel with a triangular slip, used in a similar way to sharpening a gouge. Strop the inner and outer bevels to produce a razor-sharp edge.

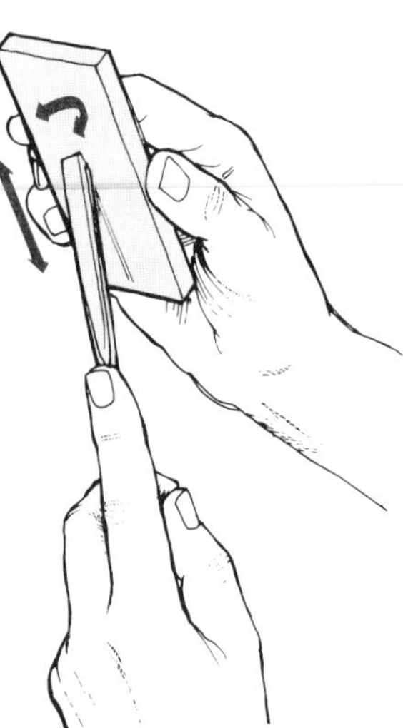

Hone the point with a slipstone

WOODS FOR CARVING

Wood for furnituremaking is converted into regular sections and then joined together to make three-dimensional structures. Carving in the round, on the other hand, starts with an oversized piece of wood that is gradually cut away to reveal the desired form. Virtually any wood can be used for carving, its suitability being largely determined by the size and type of work as well as availability and ease of working. Wood for carving need not be new or "dressed" stock. Old wood reclaimed from buildings, discarded furniture or driftwood found on a beach are all suitable and offer inspiration to the creative carver. Woodcarvers perhaps more than other woodworkers tend to hoard all kinds of pieces of wood – for in their mind's eye, every piece is a special carving waiting to be revealed.

As a general rule, fine-textured straight-grained woods such as basswood and jelutong are easier to work than woods with coarse or interlocked grain. Generally, because of their close grain, hardwoods are chosen for carving in preference to softwoods. This makes them easier to work, both with and across the grain, without splintering. Some softwoods with a distinct difference in hardness between the earlywood and latewood of the growth rings, such as Douglas fir, can be difficult to cut cleanly across the grain.

Both the color and the figure of the wood contribute to the quality of a carving. Choose a wood that is sympathetic to the subject matter. For example, select a light-colored wood such as basswood for a polar bear, and a dark wood such as teak for a brown bear.

The grain of the wood can be used to advantage, but it can also spoil your work. For example, stripy woods with a pronounced figure can look effective on smooth-surfaced forms where the lines emphasize the contoured shape; when used for portrait carving, however, the strong lines can detract from subtle features.

Not all carvings are intended to have a natural finish. If you propose to paint the surface, you can use a cheaper or less attractive wood that is easy to work rather than one that has a fine appearance.

Using dry or wet wood

Newly cut or "green" wood shrinks as it dries, as it contains a high percentage of moisture, and logs or large sections of wood shrink unevenly. As a result, the wood splits. Use well-seasoned wood whenever possible; you can then be sure your work will not be ruined by splitting. However, it is not always easy to find seasoned wood for large carvings.

If you have acquired a log or two from a recently felled tree, to facilitate more even drying, roughly convert it into halves or quarters, depending on its size.

It is possible to use untreated wood in its green state rather than wait years for it to dry, but you run the risk of the finished article splitting as the wood continues to shrink. Thin-sectioned symmetrically shaped carvings are less likely to split. Thick carvings should be hollowed out, leaving a relatively thin wall of wood that will dry out evenly. An alternative is to treat the wood with PEG (see right). To guard against splitting, always work wet wood quickly and keep it covered with a sealed plastic bag while not being worked.

Sharpening a gouge

Hold the gouge at right angles to the side of the stone, with the bevel flat on the surface. Stroke the tool back and forth along the stone while rolling it from edge to edge. Take care not to overrun the edge and round over the corners. If you introduce a rocking motion by lowering and lifting the handle, the heel of the bevel will also be ground into a curve.

Hone the inside bevel with a suitably shaped slipstone, working the stone with a rocking motion to produce a rounded bevel. The inner bevel is about a quarter to one-third the length of the outer bevel.

Strop the outside bevel with a rolling motion, and the inside bevel by pulling the blade along the edge of a folded strop. For wide gouges, hold the strop over a convenient edge to form the appropriate curve.

Roll the gouge from edge to edge

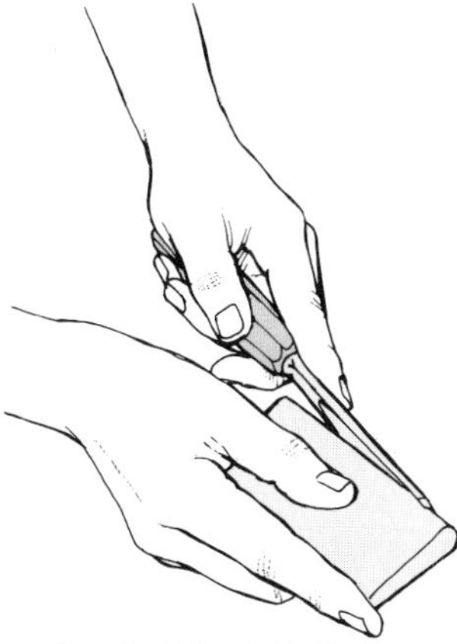

Hone inside bevel with slipstone

Peregrine falcon
The smooth finished plumage is given character by the stripy figure of the wood.

The fool
Lime is a good wood to carve and can be worked to produce fine details and thin sections.

Using PEG

You can confidently carve green wood treated with polyethylene glycol (PEG) stabilizing agent without fear of splitting. PEG 1000 is a water-soluble wax material that diffuses into the wood's structure, rendering it "shrink-proof" in about three to six weeks. It is available in kits from specialist wood suppliers.

HOLDING THE WORK

Woodcarving employs very sharp tools that are either pushed or driven through the wood. It is therefore essential for accurate and safe work that the wood is held firmly. The best method for holding the work depends on the size and shape of the wood being carved. You can use specially manufactured holding devices or standard woodworking clamps, and in some cases you can make your own.

SEE ALSO

Clamps	120-122
Workbenches	212-213
Relief carving	279
Chip carving	281-282
Cabriole leg	311

Engineer's vise
A metalworking vise can be employed for woodcarving, using "soft jaws," since metal jaws will mark the wood unless the work has a waste area that can be gripped in the vise. You will find that a metalworking vise designed to swivel on its base is the most versatile.

Bench holdfast
A bench holdfast is useful for holding flat work securely on the bench. Always use a softening block of scrap wood between the clamp head and the work.

The workbench
You can work carvings on a traditional woodworking bench or a special carver's stand. The choice will depend on the type of carving you propose to do.

The bench or stand must provide a secure and solid surface that is comfortable to work at. For carving in the round, the base of the work should either be about 4in (100mm) below your elbow or level with it.

With some chip-carving techniques, the carving is worked on the seated carver's lap, the carver's hands being the only holding device used. But ultimately, the best way to hold the work is the way that feels most comfortable to you.

Pivoting clamp
It is useful when carving in the round to be able to alter the angle of the work quickly. A special woodcarving clamp allows the work to be set at virtually any angle and securely locked into position. The pivoting head can be fitted with different-sized faceplates to suit the size of the work.

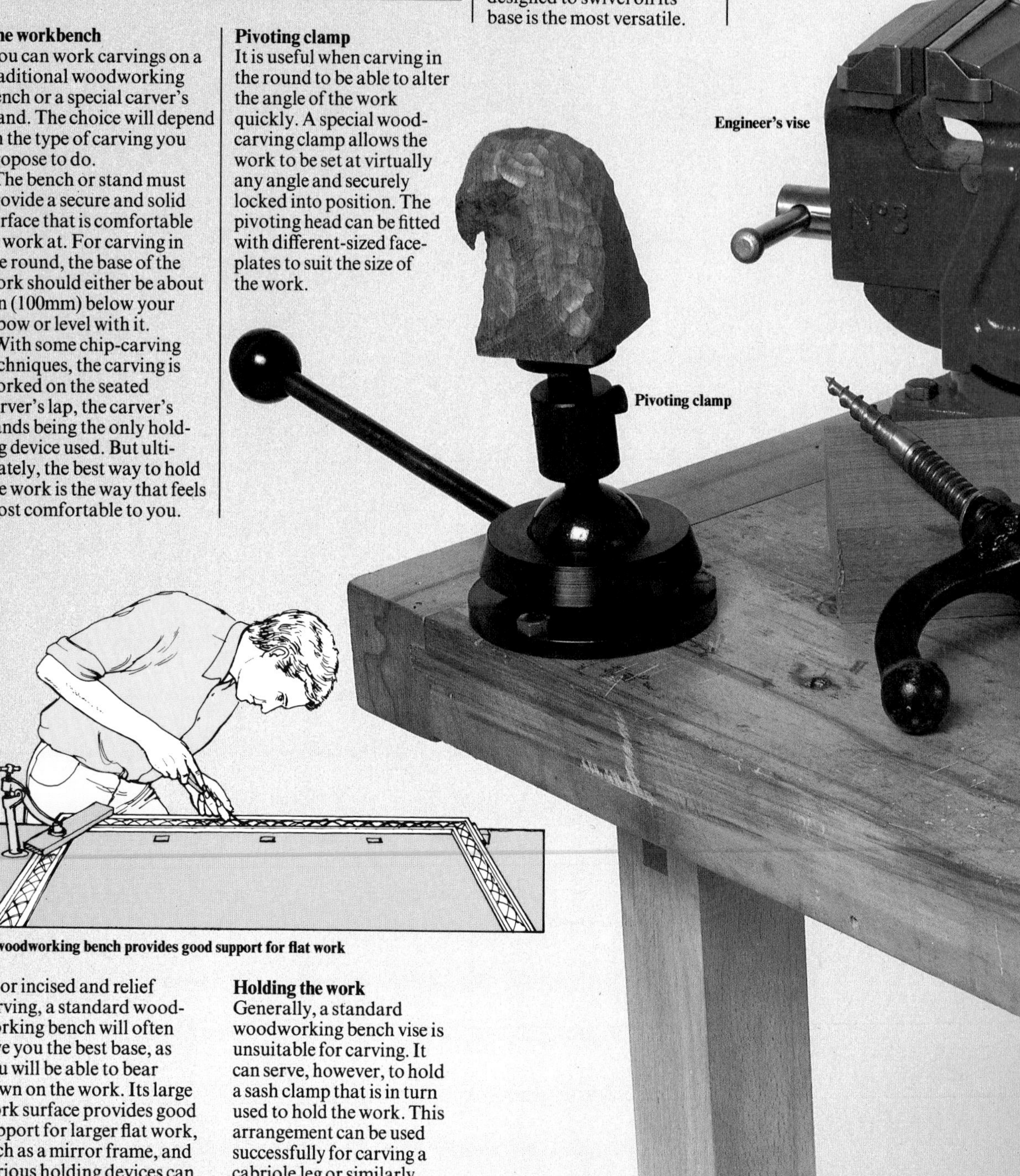

A woodworking bench provides good support for flat work

For incised and relief carving, a standard woodworking bench will often give you the best base, as you will be able to bear down on the work. Its large work surface provides good support for larger flat work, such as a mirror frame, and various holding devices can be fitted to the top.

Holding the work
Generally, a standard woodworking bench vise is unsuitable for carving. It can serve, however, to hold a sash clamp that is in turn used to hold the work. This arrangement can be used successfully for carving a cabriole leg or similarly shaped work.

Bench dogs and stops
These are used to hold flat work on a bench. This is easiest if your bench has an end vise with which to tighten them. If not, apply pressure by using folded wedges between fixed stops. You can screw blocks to the bench on all four sides of a flat panel if it needs to be held more securely.

Carver's vise
A special carver's vise (or "chops") is similar in principle to an engineer's vise but is made of wood. Also, the jaws are deeper and are lined with cork or leather to protect the work. A single bench screw is used to hold the vise on the bench. This allows the vise to be swiveled to any angle. The vise is 9in (225mm) high and when fitted to a standard woodworking bench brings the work up to a comfortable height.

Patternmaker's vise
Often called a gunstock vise, this has large wood-faced jaws that can pivot to hold shaped blocks.

Carver's bench screw
The carver's bench screw is used to hold blocks of wood firmly to a carver's stand or bench. Its threaded point is screwed into the base of the wood, then the shaft is passed through a hole in the bench and clamped with a large wing nut.

Carver's stand
A carver's stand is a specialized bench that is ideal for working carvings in the round, since it allows the work to be carved and viewed from any direction. A traditional wooden stand is constructed with three or four heavy splayed legs that provide a stable base. The thick top is drilled to receive a carver's screw or other holding device, and the bottom shelf or rack can be loaded with weights for additional stability.

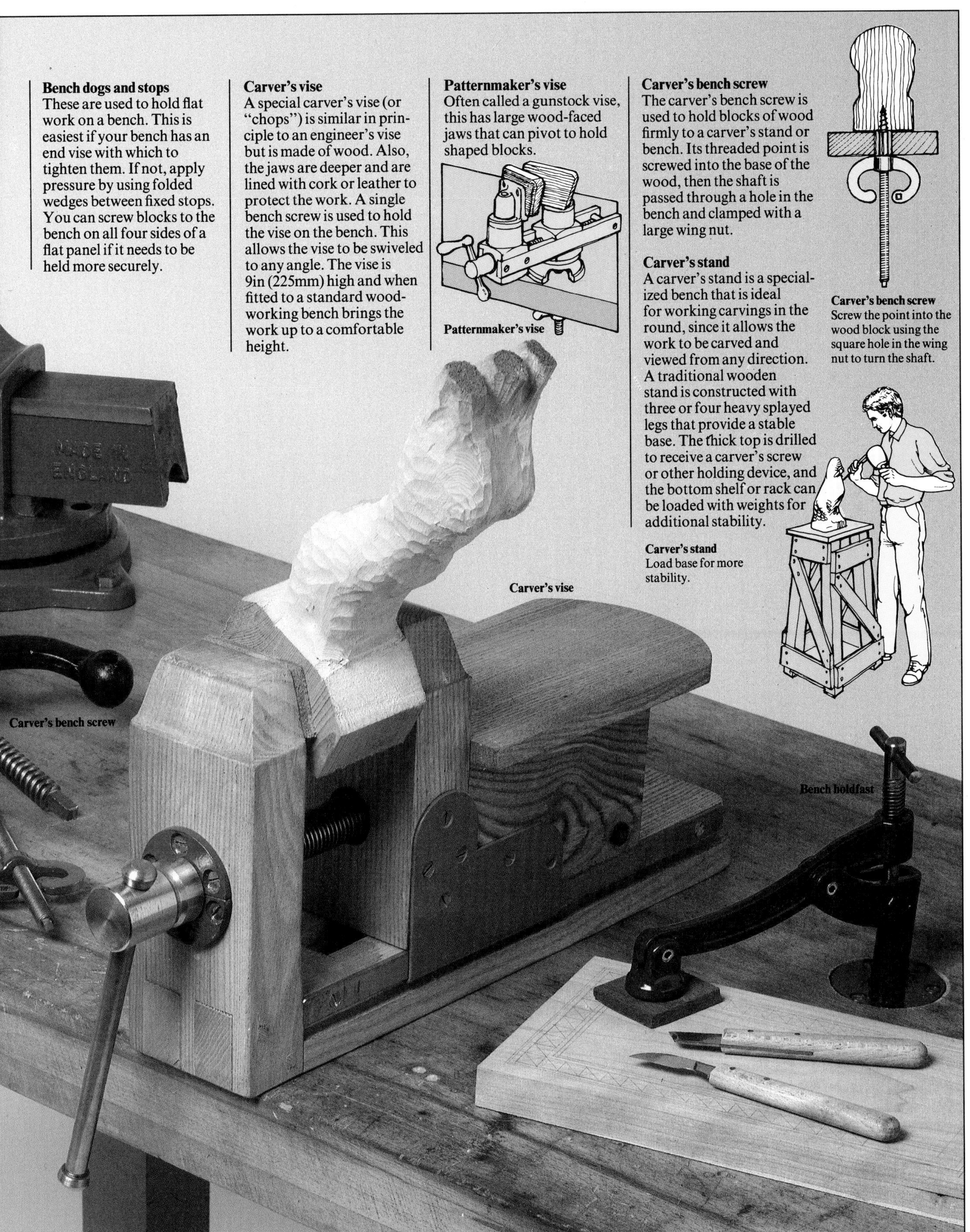

Patternmaker's vise

Carver's bench screw
Screw the point into the wood block using the square hole in the wing nut to turn the shaft.

Carver's stand
Load base for more stability.

Carver's vise

Carver's bench screw

Bench holdfast

MAKING WOOD CARVINGS

The principal forms of woodcarving are relief carving and carving in the round. A relief carving is intended to be viewed from one side and so is nearly always carved from a flat board or relatively thin stock. The thickness of the wood and the degree to which the background is cut away determine whether a piece of work is classified as low-relief or high-relief carving. The technique is used for embellishing furniture and wall panels, and for creating nonfunctional works of art. A carving in the round is fully three-dimensional and is meant to be seen from all sides. It gives the carver complete freedom of expression and is perhaps the most challenging kind of carving since it requires a well-developed or intuitive sense of form.

SEE ALSO

Wood grain	15
Marking gauge	78
Carving tools	272-274

HOLDING THE TOOLS

For both relief carving and carving in the round, the techniques for working the tools are the same. Carving is a craft that draws upon natural skills. Coordination between hand and eye, a sense of proportion, the interpretation of materials and texture and a feel for natural line all contribute to make a fine carving. Holding the tools properly is the first step. The way carving chisels and gouges are handled depends on the type and size of the project, the hardness of the wood and the type of cut being made.

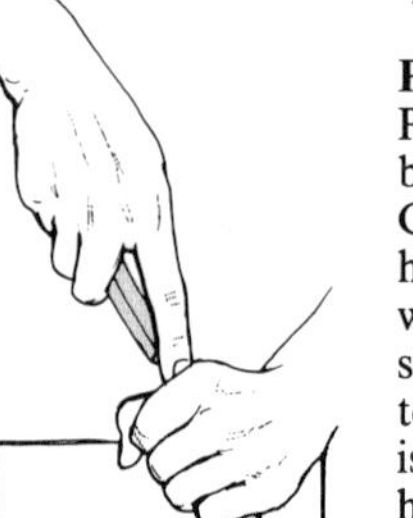

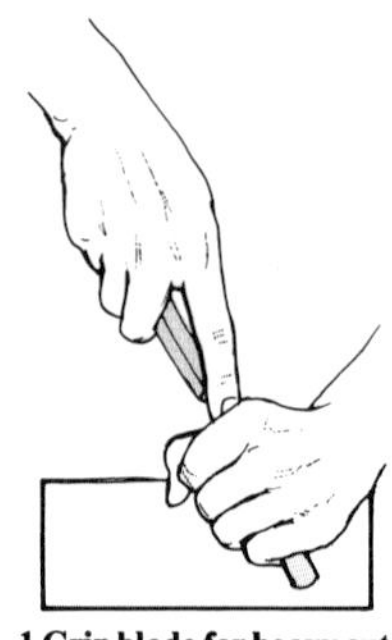

1 Grip blade for heavy cut

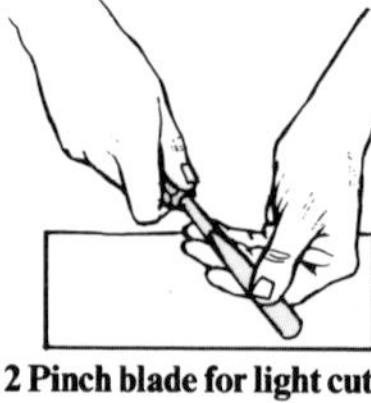

2 Pinch blade for light cut

3 Guide and control blade

Paring cuts

Paring cuts are made with both hands on the tool. Generally, the handle is held in the hand used for writing. However, you should learn to work the tools with either hand, as it is often easier to change hands rather than turn the wood around.

Assuming you are right-handed, hold the handle in your right hand with your forefinger along or in line with the blade. The end of the handle will automatically fall on the center of your palm, giving you good control. The left hand rests on the wood and is used to provide resistance to the thrust from the right hand. It also helps guide the blade. The amount of resistance applied to the blade controls the speed of the cut.

For a heavy cut, place the forefinger of your right hand on top of the blade and grip the blade in the fist of your left hand **(1)**. For lighter cuts, pinch the blade between your left forefinger and thumb, with the hand placed above or below **(2)**.

When making vertical cuts, grip the handle in your fist and place your thumb on the top. Guide and control the blade with the thumb and forefinger of the left hand, the side of which is planted firmly on the surface of the work **(3)**.

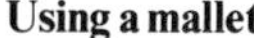

Using a mallet

When carving with a mallet, assuming you are right-handed, the chisel or gouge is held in the left hand and the right hand is used to drive the mallet.

Grip the lower two-thirds of the chisel or gouge handle with the top face of the blade in the same plane as the front of your folded hand **(4)**. In this way, you can change the angle of the cut by rotating your wrist without changing your grip.

Use the mallet to apply short, sharp blows to the tool. With practice, you will sense the correct angle to set the cutting edge and will be able to judge how much force is needed to cut the wood away efficiently.

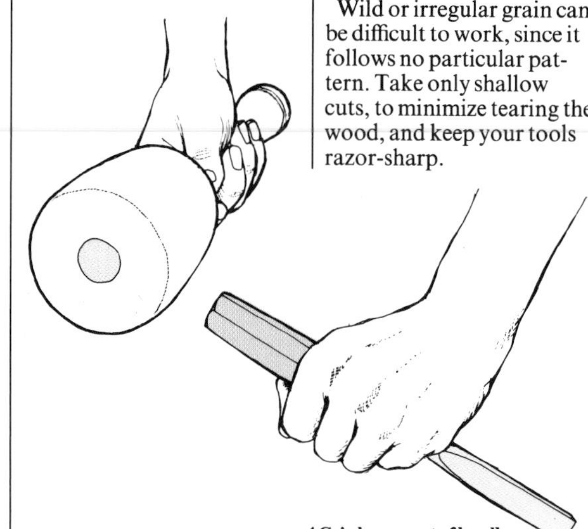

4 Grip lower part of handle

Reading the grain

Woodcarving differs from other methods of cutting wood in that the slicing cuts are generally made across the grain. This is particularly the case when using a gouge for roughing out the shape. Provided the tool is razor-sharp, a controlled, clean cut is possible and the relatively deep cut won't tear into the wood, which can easily happen when working with the grain.

Invariably, the wood is cut from all angles at some point in the work. Study the grain and make the cuts in the direction that is least likely to tear the fibers. The quality of the cut will be your best guide.

A gouged cut made diagonally across the fibers will produce a groove that is clean-cut on one side and a rougher cut on the other, where it runs against the grain **(5)**.

Similarly, where the fibers run at an angle to the surface of the wood, whether a smooth or rough cut will result depends on the direction of the cut **(6)**.

Wild or irregular grain can be difficult to work, since it follows no particular pattern. Take only shallow cuts, to minimize tearing the wood, and keep your tools razor-sharp.

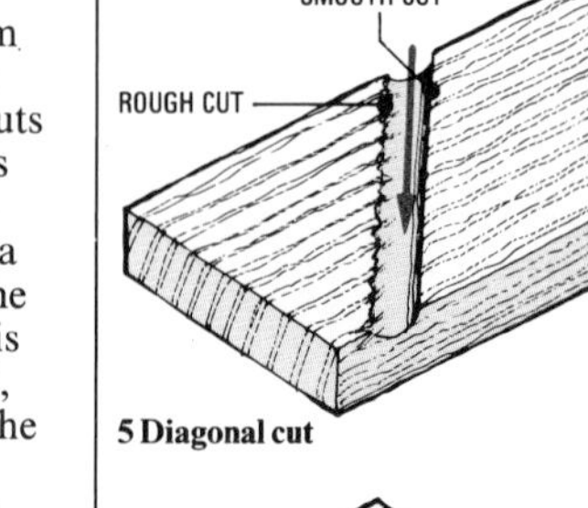

5 Diagonal cut

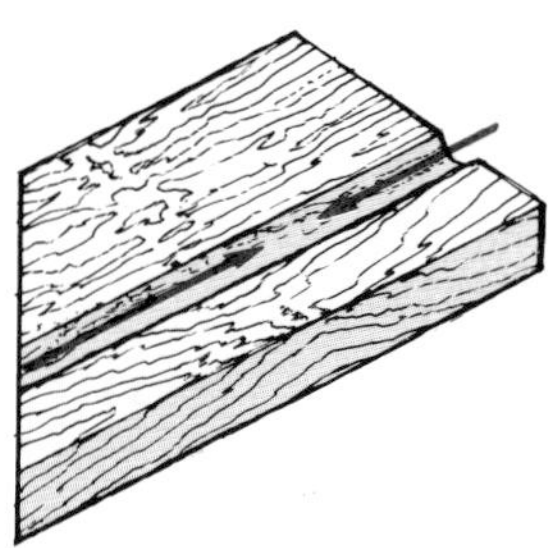

6 Vary cut according to grain

MAKING STUDY DRAWINGS

Most woodcarving work is representational, although often stylized rather than naturalistic. However, if it is to resemble its subject closely, a carving must be well-observed – and a stylized carving must look "right."

To achieve an understanding of the way something looks takes practice and is best achieved by making drawings. These need not be used as subjects in themselves but will help you to see how surfaces, textures and forms relate in the world around.

With this knowledge, you will find it easier to visualize how the shapes should look when you come to make a carving. Also, by making numerous sketches, you will develop the drawing skills that are fundamental to setting out a carving in the first place.

RELIEF CARVING

Relief carving uses the play of light and shade to express form. The greater the degree of relief, the more contrasting and dramatic are the effects. Relief carving makes a good introduction to woodcarving, as it employs most of the carving tools and the work is somewhat easier to visualize. Moreover, it is economic in the use of material and the wood can be worked on a conventional bench without the aid of specialized holding equipment.

Setting out the design
The first step is to make an accurate full-size working drawing of your proposed carving. The example used here is an ornamental letter that includes both geometric and naturalistic forms. It also makes an interesting exercise. If you are working from a reference that is not the right size, scale it up or down using the grid method (see right) or a photocopying machine that can enlarge and reduce. Tape the design to the wood and, using carbon paper, trace it onto the surface. Mark the depth of the relief on the edge of the wood, using a marking gauge set to ¾in (18mm).

Relief carving of ornamental letter

Cutting the background
Start by cutting around the design with a parting tool or deep gouge. Make the cut about ⅛in (3mm) from the line, taking note of the grain direction **(1)**. Next, remove the waste down to about $\frac{1}{16}$in (2mm) from the ground line. Use a No8 or No9 gouge about ¾in (18mm) wide and work across the grain **(2)**.

"Setting in" follows the rough grounding work. Using a chisel, or gouges of appropriate curvature, trim the edges of the design vertically **(3)**. Do not cut too deep or the cuts will show after you have finished the ground area.

Finish the grounding work with a wide shallow gouge, such as a 1in (25mm) No3, then use a spoon-bent gouge for the center of the letter **(4)**. You can either leave the subtle tool marks or level the surface further with a chisel, as you prefer.

Now repeat this procedure to lower the level of the letter's face by ⅜in (9mm), leaving the foliage standing proud.

Using a scaled grid
Draw vertical and horizontal grid lines, say ¼in (6mm) apart, on a tracing of your design reference. Also draw a 1in (24mm) grid on plain paper. Following the lines of your original design carefully, draw in the shape on the larger grid, using the lines of the two grids to help you draw it to scale. This will give you a four-times enlargement, but you can make grids (and therefore the scale) any size suitable for your project.

Draw grid over design

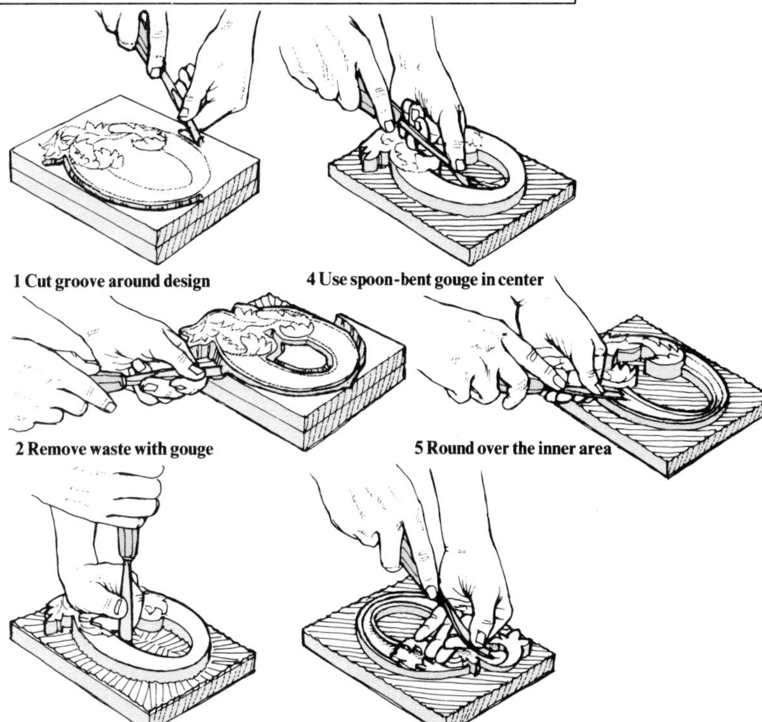
1 Cut groove around design
2 Remove waste with gouge
3 Trim vertical edges of design
4 Use spoon-bent gouge in center
5 Round over the inner area
6 Shape leaves with sweeping cuts

Modeling
The foliage and the letter's face can now be modeled. Draw in the border lines around the edges of the letter. Cut a shallow V-groove around the inside of the borders. Round over the inner area with a chisel **(5)**. You can smooth it with an inverted gouge that fits the curve; otherwise, use sandpaper but only after completing the main carving.

"Roughing out" or roughly cutting the shape of the leaves now follows. Start with a gouge and use a spoon-bent gouge for tight curves.

Set in the tips of the curled leaves. Form and smooth the contoured shapes of the leaves with long sweeping cuts **(6)**, then use a parting tool to detail the veins. Undercut the curled leaf tips to make them appear thin at the edges.

Add the decorative lines on the letter and borders, using a parting tool. Punch or drill the spot detail before cutting the broken decorative lines.

CARVING IN THE ROUND

This type of work represents a challenge to the carver, as it requires an appreciation of aesthetics in addition to well-developed craft skills. The subject matter can be naturalistic or abstract, the concept being dictated by the carver and sometimes by the natural features of the wood. Carvings that are deeply undercut or pierced, leaving thin, weak sections, can be difficult for the beginner. Simple solid shapes are easier to execute successfully while you are developing your techniques.

SEE ALSO

Handsaws	81
Sharpening stones	102-103
Rifflers	111
Rotary rasps	127
Band saws	172-176
Carving tools	272-274
Holding the work	276-277
Finishing wood	284-294
Epoxy-resin glue	303

Setting out the work

For some, carving in the round is a matter of selecting and setting up a block of wood and cutting into it, the shape of the carving evolving as the wood is cut away following an imaginary outline. However, this can be a hit-or-miss process. Until you are an experienced carver, it is better to prepare an accurate drawing and mark guide lines on the block before you start.

A carving of a clenched hand is shown here as a typical example. Hands make an interesting subject for carving in the round. You can study your own as you work and try more complex poses as you progress.

Prepare an actual-size side and front view of your intended carving. A rear view and plan are also helpful. You can base the drawings on your own reference photographs, ideally taken from four sides. Photographs reproduce the effects of perspective, so those parts farthest from the camera will be smaller and you will have to adjust any foreshortening in your drawings. Use the grid method to enlarge the image as required.

Using carbon paper, transfer the side and front views to adjacent sides of a block of prepared wood that will just contain the shape **(1)**. Some extra material on the height is desirable, as it will give you something to hold in a vise.

Initial shaping

The bulk of the waste can be carved away, but it is quicker to use either a handsaw or a machine saw first. With a handsaw, make a series of straight cuts down to the outline, working from each face **(2)**. Chop away the waste with a chisel, leaving a roughly shaped block with square corners. Alternatively, cut around the marked profiles with a band saw. Cut the side view first, then tape or temporarily nail the waste offcuts back in position, using fine nails or brads **(3)**. This keeps the block square and retains the line for cutting the front view. Make sure any nails are driven into waste material only and are kept clear of the sawcut.

Cut around the front-view outline. The roughly shaped block is now ready for carving. If they will be of help, draw in other guide lines that fall within the rough shape.

Rough shaping

With the wood held firmly on your bench, start to rough in the shape by cutting away the square corners, using a gouge and mallet and working across the grain **(4)**.

Using a shallow gouge, shape the planes formed by the folded fingers. Cut into the block where the fingers meet the palm and the hollow of the forefinger and thumb **(5)**. Look at the shape from all sides as you work.

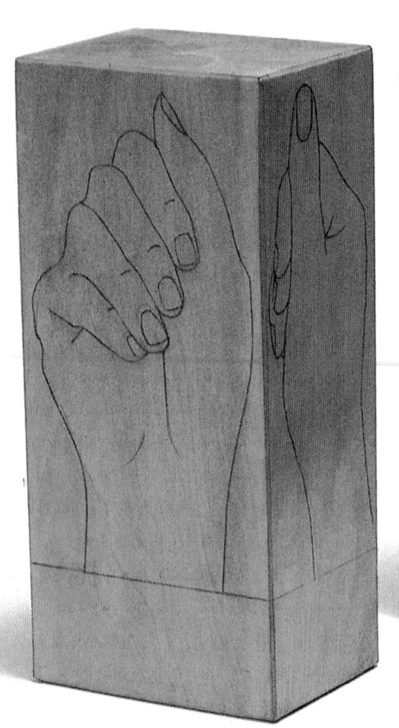

1 Mark out shape on adjacent sides

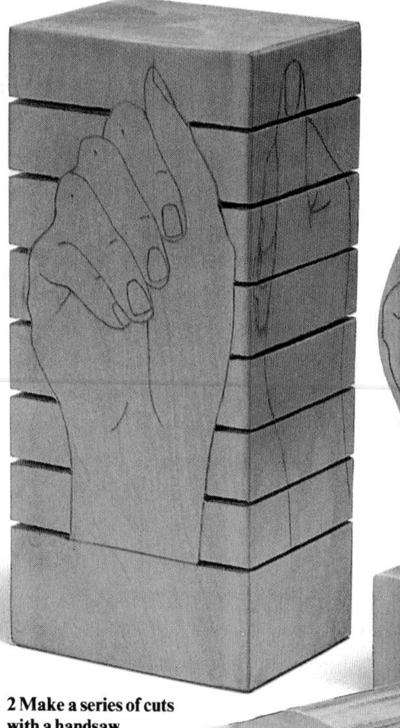

2 Make a series of cuts with a handsaw

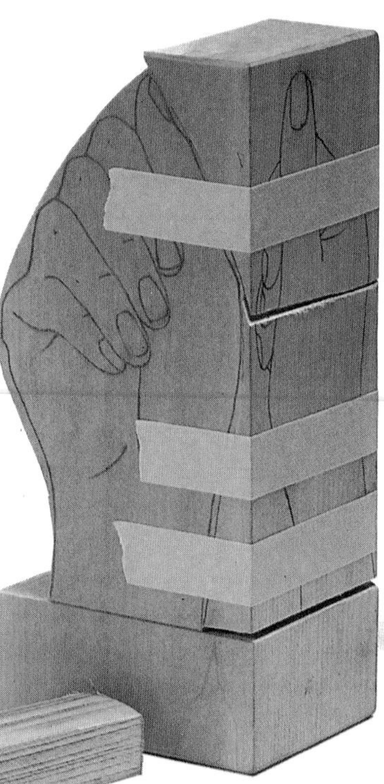

3 Or remove waste with a band saw

4 Start to rough in the shape

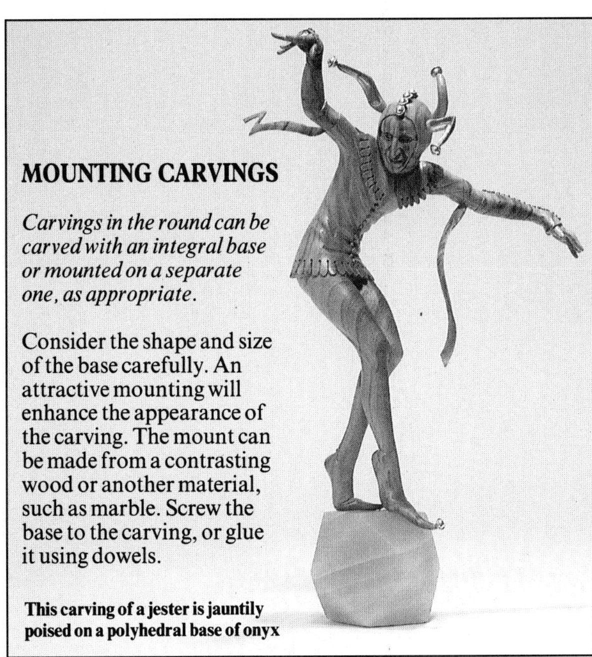

MOUNTING CARVINGS

Carvings in the round can be carved with an integral base or mounted on a separate one, as appropriate.

Consider the shape and size of the base carefully. An attractive mounting will enhance the appearance of the carving. The mount can be made from a contrasting wood or another material, such as marble. Screw the base to the carving, or glue it using dowels.

This carving of a jester is jauntily poised on a polyhedral base of onyx

Modeling
Form the knuckle shapes and rounded fingers by paring the wood with a gouge and chisel. Then refine the shapes of the fingers and thumb, and set in the details of the finger lines, folds of flesh and fingernails **(6)**. Small chisels and gouges will be needed here. The degree to which you smooth the shape is a matter of choice. You can either leave the tool marks or smooth the surface using rifflers and fine sand-paper. Finish the wood with a clear sealer and apply a wax polish.

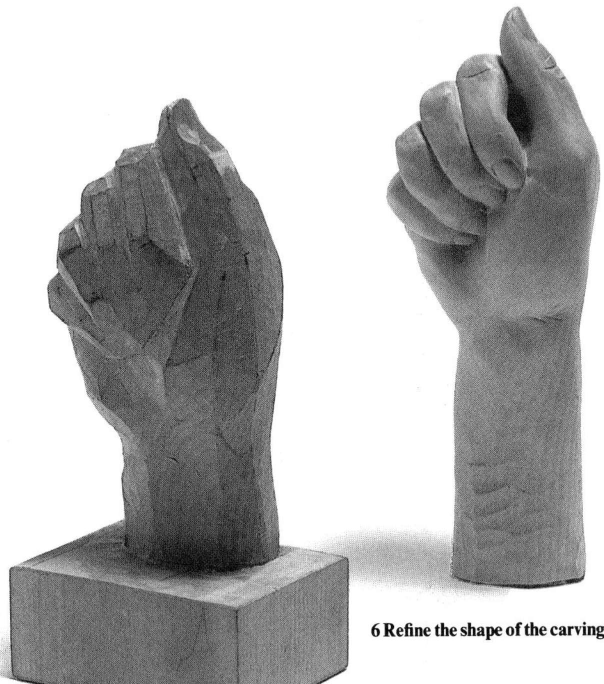

6 Refine the shape of the carving

5 Shape the planes of the hand

CHIP CARVING

Chip carving is an old technique used for decorating furniture, plaques, boxes and other work. A series of simple cuts are combined to produce a variety of incised geometric patterns. The cuts can be made with chisels and gouges, but most chip carvers use knives designed for the purpose.

CHIP-CARVING TOOLS

A good chip-carving knife has a short, stiff blade with a well-shaped handle that fits comfortably in the palm of the hand.

Chip-carving knives are made with various blade shapes. It is not necessary to have a wide range, as you can make most cuts with only two types – the cutting knife and stab knife.

The cutting knife usually has a straight cutting edge and is used for removing wood chips, while the stab knife has a sharpened skewed end that is stabbed into the wood to make short cuts and decorative patterns. The stab knife is not used to remove wood.

Start with these two knives and only try other types if you find your cutting technique is not producing the required clean cuts. In addition to the knives, you will need a ruler, a sharp Grade B pencil, a pair of compasses and a try square for setting out your designs.

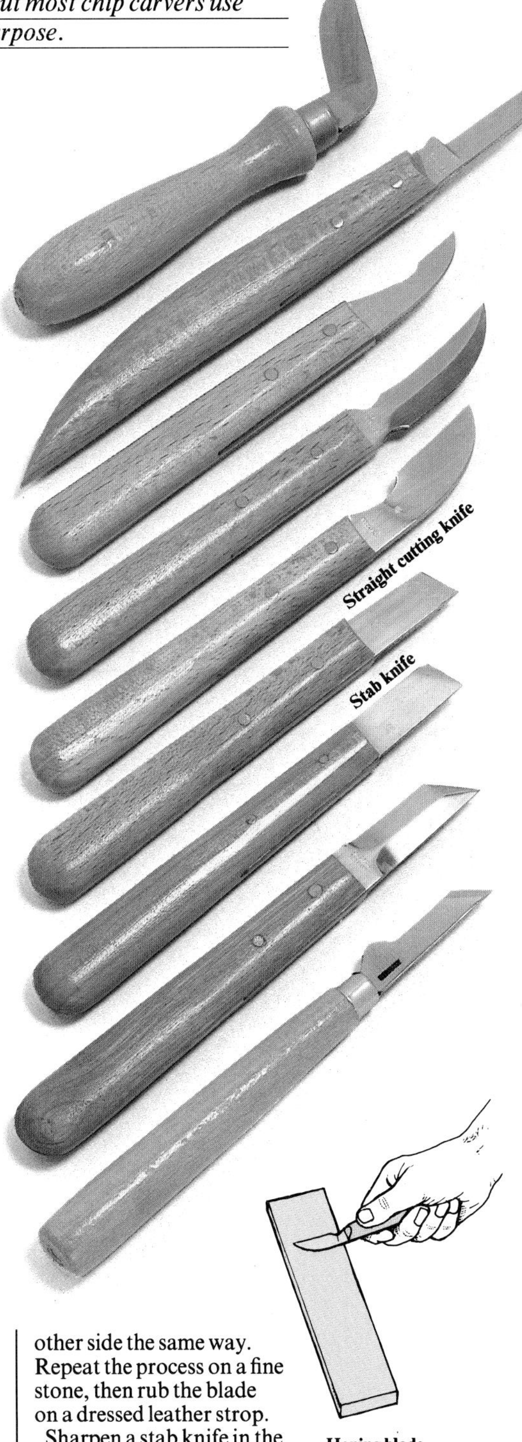

Sharpening knives
Clean, crisply incised shapes are the essence of good chip carving. No matter how well you have set out your design or followed the line, if the cuts are not sharp, the end result is bound to look rough – so keep your knives razor-sharp.

First, hone the cutting knife on a medium-grade stone. Hold the knife blade at right angles to the stone, with the side face at an angle of not more than 10 degrees to the surface.

Rub the blade back and forth, keeping the full length of the cutting edge in contact with the stone. Turn the blade over and treat the other side the same way. Repeat the process on a fine stone, then rub the blade on a dressed leather strop.

Sharpen a stab knife in the same way, but hold it at 30 degrees to the stone.

Honing blade
Hold knife at right angles to the stone.

Marking out
Chip carving is generally based on geometric shapes, although free-form chip carving is also done.

You can set out your design on paper and then transfer it to the surface of the work, or mark it out directly.

Draw accurate, fine guide lines, as many of the lines will remain after the carving is completed. These can be removed with a pencil eraser. If you try to sand them away, you will lose the crisp edge of your carving.

SEE ALSO
Holding the work 276-277
Chip-carving tools 281

Holding the knives
You can use the cutting knife to cut into the work vertically or hold it at an angle to make a sloping cut. A faceted chipcut is made by holding the knife at a constant 45 degree angle.

There are three basic cuts with the cutting knife. The first two are made with a pulling action and the third is pushed away from you. Use your thumb as a guide to steady your hand as a fulcrum when making curved cuts. It also gives you a means of sensing the depth of your cut.

Hold the stab knife vertically and push it into the surface to make short, straight cuts or wedge-shaped indentations.

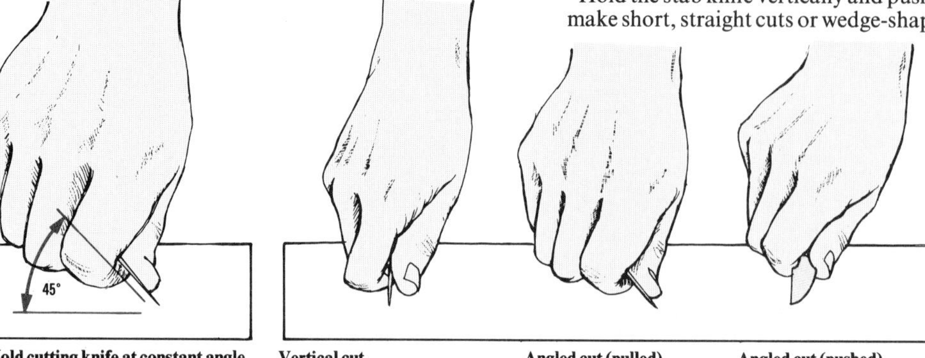

Hold cutting knife at constant angle | Vertical cut | Angled cut (pulled) | Angled cut (pushed) | Stab knife cut

MAKING BORDERS

Borders are a common feature of chip-carved work and are typically based on equilateral or right-angle triangles.

Equilateral-triangle border | Right-angle-triangle border

To make an equilateral-triangle border design, first mark out the guide lines **(1)**. Hold the cutting knife on one side line, with its point on the apex. Press the point straight down into the wood to a depth of about $\frac{1}{8}$in (3mm). Pull the knife toward you so the point rises out to the surface at the marked baseline **(2)**. Repeat the cut on the other side. Slice out the chip with the blade held at a shallow angle and following the baseline **(3)**. Repeat this chipcut to make various border patterns.

To make faceted right-angle-triangle border patterns, first mark a series of squares and draw in the diagonals. Hold the knife at an angle to the surface, with the point on the apex of the triangle. Push the blade into the wood and pull it along the line and out to the surface **(4)**. Repeat this cut on alternate squares. Turn the work around and make the same cut in the adjacent squares, but this time pushing the knife away from you **(5)**.

Now revert back to the first cutting action and cut along the baseline **(6)**, remembering to hold the knife at the same angle so the cuts meet exactly on the center of the chipcut.

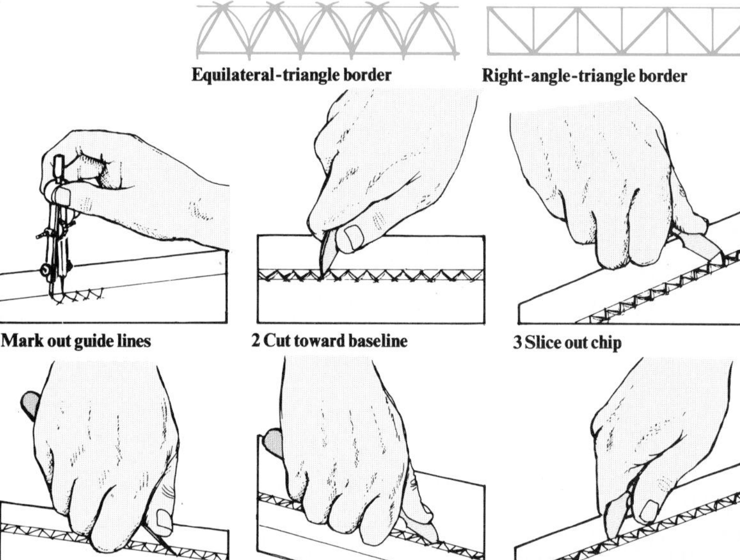

1 Mark out guide lines | 2 Cut toward baseline | 3 Slice out chip
4 Pull blade out to surface | 5 Repeat with a push cut | 6 Finally cut along baseline

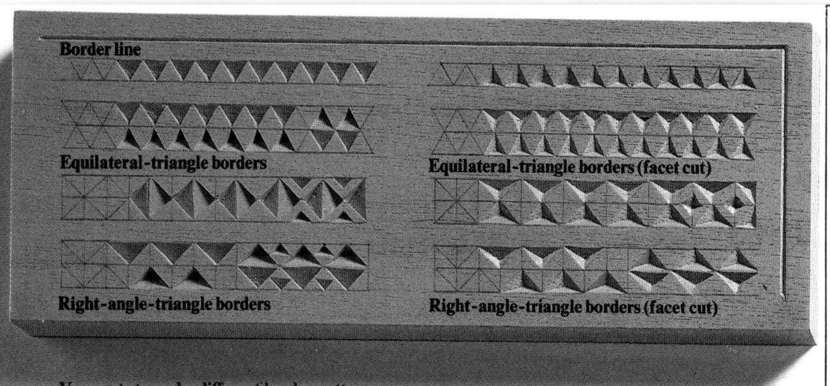

Vary cuts to make different border patterns

CUTTING BORDER LINES

Incised lines are used to define the edges of border patterns. Carve a border line by making two cuts to form a "V."

Your first cut should slope away from the design. Pull the blade through the wood and follow the line accurately by looking just ahead of the blade. Turn the work around and make a similar cut to remove the waste.

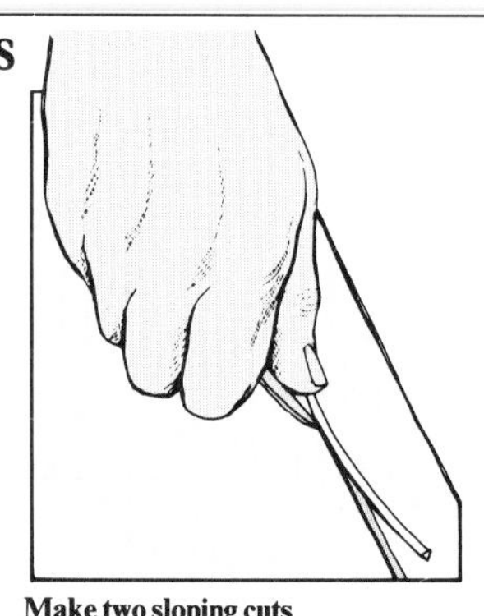

Make two sloping cuts

CHAPTER ELEVEN

FINISHING WOOD

Enhancing the beauty of wood with shellac, lacquer, varnish or oil is one of the most pleasurable aspects of woodworking. Similarly, a great deal of satisfaction can be obtained from staining or coloring wood. Finishing also has a practical purpose – to protect the wood and keep it free from marks. You therefore need to consider how a piece will be used, as well as how it will look, when selecting a finish. If, for example, it is likely to be subjected to hard wear, choose a varnish or lacquer rather than French polish, which is more vulnerable and so better suited to display items where protection is less vital. Another important consideration is the texture of the wood. For smooth-textured hardwoods, such as mahogany and walnut, French polish gives the finest finish. Open-grain woods such as oak, on the other hand, look better with an oil or wax finish that penetrates the grain without forming a thick surface coating. For the best results, whichever finish you choose, always work in a warm, clean and well-lit environment.

PREPARING THE SURFACE

Wood must be smooth, clean and free from blemishes before you apply a surface finish. Paint may cover minor imperfections, but a clear finish will exaggerate every defect, including fine scratches across the grain. Preparing the surface is the first essential stage of finishing wood.

SEE ALSO

Cabinet scrapers	110-111
Sanders	147-150
Fire prevention	211
Face mask/respirator	214
Clear finishes	288,290,294
Opaque paints	290
Primer	290
Spray booth	292

FILLING HOLES AND CRACKS

When selecting wood, you should reject poor-quality materials exhibiting cracks, holes and dead knots, but occasionally it is necessary to accept a less-than-perfect sample, especially when buying wood that is rare or temporarily in short supply. Even when you have chosen carefully, cracks can open up at a later stage and must be dealt with before you apply a finish.

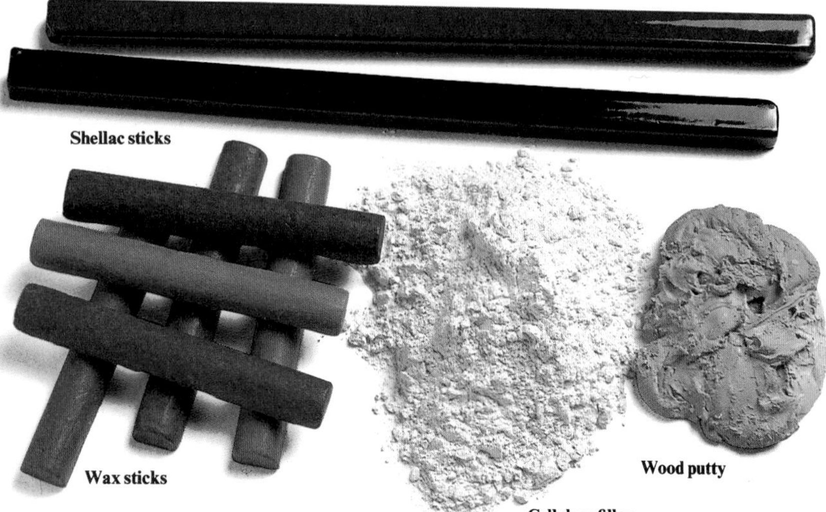

Shellac sticks

Wax sticks

Wood putty

Cellulose filler

Wood putty
A commercial hole filler is a stiff paste made to fill small holes and cracks before applying a clear or opaque finish. Although fillers are made in a range of colors resembling various common species of wood, at best you can only expect a close match and the match will hardly ever be perfect. However, you can adjust the color of the filler with a drop of wood stain – but since hole fillers may be water-, lacquer- or oil-based, make sure you always use a similarly constituted stain.

Cellulose filler
If you are planning to apply an opaque paint finish, you can fill blemishes with ordinary spackle or water putty mixed to a stiff paste.

Shellac sticks
Sticks of solidified shellac are ideal for repairing a crack or small knot holes before applying any type of finish. They are made in dozens of wood-like colors.

Wax sticks
Filling sticks of carnauba wax mixed with resins and coloring pigments are used to disguise small worm holes and hairline cracks in wood. It is advisable to use them only for work that is to be wax-polished, as most finishes will not dry over a wax-filled hole. Special wax crayons are made for retouching scratches in polished surfaces.

- **Removing patches of glue**
  When gluing joints, always wash away excess adhesive from the surface using a cloth dampened with hot water. If you let the glue set, it seals the wood and will show as pale patches after staining or polishing. Use a cabinet scraper to remove any spots of hardened glue before finishing.

- **Sealing knots**
  Resinous knots will "bleed" through paintwork, leaving dark stains on the surface. Before you apply a primer, pick off any hardened resin, then paint the knots with two coats of shellac-based sealer.

Using fillers
Press filler into the blemish with a small flexible blade, such as an artist's palette knife, or even the tip of a chisel. When the filler has set hard, sand it flush with the surface of the wood. If the color match isn't satisfactory, touch in the filler with minute quantities of artist's oil paint, using a fine paintbrush. Let the paint dry thoroughly before applying a surface finish.

Melting a shellac stick
Using the tip of a warm soldering iron, melt the shellac, allowing it to drip onto the blemish. While the shellac is still soft, dip the tip of a chisel in water and use it to press the shellac into the crack or knot. When the shellac is cool and hard, pare it flush with a chisel then sand it with very fine sandpaper.

Melt shellac with a soldering iron

Filling with a wax stick
Sand the surface of the wood and seal it with shellac before filling with wax. Use a warmed knife blade to soften the wax and to press it into cracks or small holes. As the wax hardens, scrape it flush with the knife, then burnish it with the back of a piece of sandpaper.

RAISING A DENT

If you accidentally dent a workpiece, lay a damp cloth over the blemish and apply the tip of a heated soldering iron. The heat generates steam, which causes the wood fibers to swell locally, lifting the dented section flush with the surrounding surface. Allow the wood to dry before sanding.

SAFETY WITH SURFACE FINISHES

When finishing wood, take the following precautions to safeguard health and safety:

- Most of the materials used to finish wood are flammable, so store them in a separate building away from your workshop and your house.
- Keep finishes and thinners locked away from children. If a child should swallow any, do not attempt to make the child vomit but seek medical advice immediately.
- Oily rags are a fire risk. They should be opened flat and allowed to dry outdoors before you throw them away.
- Install a fire extinguisher.
- Don't smoke while applying finishes.
- Inhaling solvent fumes can be very unpleasant, if not actually harmful. Follow manufacturers' instructions with regard to toxicity, and wear a face mask or respirator if you experience any discomfort.
- Provide adequate ventilation and don't spray finishes unless you have proper exhaust facilities.
- Wear protective gloves when applying wood stains.
- Wear barrier cream to protect your hands, and use a skin cleanser to remove paint or other finishes before washing with soap and hot water. Do not use paint thinners to clean your hands.
- If you splash a finish in your eyes, flush them with water and consult the warning label for further action.

Power sanders relieve a woodworker of the chore of smoothing large flat areas – but for best-quality work, give the wood at least one final light sanding by hand.

Abrasive papers
A variety of abrasive materials glued to paper backing sheets are used to smooth wood and hardened surface finishes. All these abrasives are known collectively as sandpaper, though this term was originally used to describe glasspaper only.

Glasspaper is pale yellow in color. It wears quickly and, although not really suitable for fine woodwork, is a cheap option for sanding softwoods. It is also known as flintpaper.

Garnet paper is made from a reddish-brown natural mineral that forms hard particles with sharp cutting edges. Garnet paper is a good-quality abrasive both for softwoods and hardwoods.

Aluminum-oxide paper is even harder than garnet paper. It is produced in standard-size sheets for handwork and is also used widely as an abrasive for power tools. Aluminum-oxide papers are available in different colors. This type of abrasive is especially good for sanding dense hardwoods.

Silicon-carbide paper varies from dark gray to black. It is made from a synthetic material and is used mainly for finishing metals or, with water as a lubricant, for smoothing paintwork between coats. Often referred to as "wet-or-dry paper," it is used without a lubricant for sanding hardwoods. A pale-gray silicon-carbide paper dusted with zinc-oxide powder that acts as a dry lubricant is preferable for rubbing down French polish, which would be spoiled by using water as a lubricant.

Grading sandpaper
Sandpapers are graded according to abrasive-particle size and are roughly classified as having very coarse, coarse, medium, fine or very fine grit. They are also graded by number (typically from 600 to 40 or, using another system, from 9/0 to 1) – the higher the number, the finer the grit. Use progressively finer grits, so that each grade removes the scratches left by the previous paper. As a guide, coarse to fine grades are suitable for general work and very fine grades for cutting back surface finishes.

In addition, there are closed-coat or open-coat types of sandpaper. Closed-coat papers have particles grouped closely together for fast sanding, whereas open-coat abrasives have large gaps between the particles, which clog less readily, and so are better for resinous softwoods.

Sandpaper grades		
Very coarse	40 60	1 ½
Coarse	80 100	0 2/0
Medium	120 150 180	3/0 4/0 5/0
Fine	220 240 280	6/0 7/0 8/0
Very fine	320 360 400 500 600	9/0 — — — —

Sanding by hand
Tear sheets of sandpaper into convenient strips over the edge of a bench. Wrap a strip around a cork sanding block and use it to smooth a flat workpiece, always working with the grain **(1)**. Take care not to round over sharp corners inadvertently when you approach an edge – but if you want to remove the arris (the sharp "line" where two surfaces meet), sand a chamfer deliberately, using the same block **(2)**. Wrap sandpaper around a shaped block when you are sanding moldings **(3)**.

Lay aside sanding blocks and use your fingertips to apply pressure to sandpaper when smoothing curved surfaces or for very light sanding **(4)**. When sandpaper becomes clogged with wood dust, tap it against the workbench to clear the abrasive particles.

When the surface appears to be as smooth as possible, in order to raise the grain, dampen the wood with a wet rag and leave it to dry. A final light sanding will then remove the fine fibers, leaving a perfect finish. Finally, remove the wood dust with a cloth dampened with mineral spirits, or use a commercial "tack rag" (a cloth impregnated with resin).

Sanding end grain
Rub your finger along the surface of end grain before sanding. It will feel rougher in one direction and relatively smooth in another. Sand in the smoother direction for a superior finish.

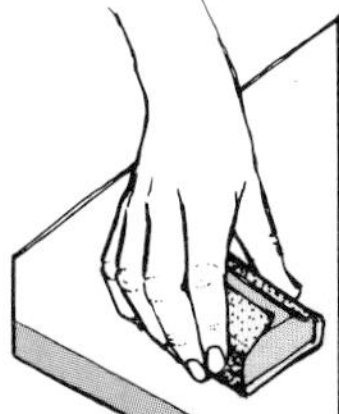
1 Sanding flat work

2 Removing an arris

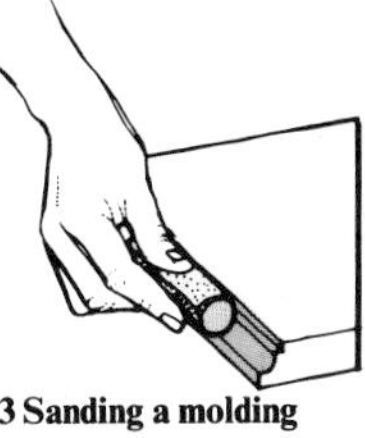
3 Sanding a molding

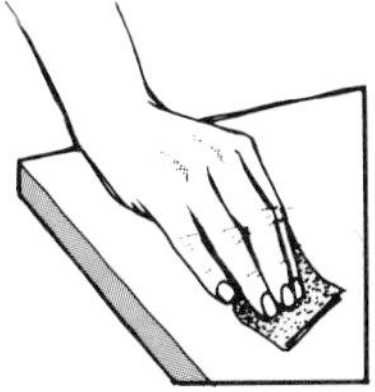
4 Use fingertip pressure for light sanding

- **Storing sandpaper**
  Wrap sheets of sandpaper in plastic to keep them dry while being stored.

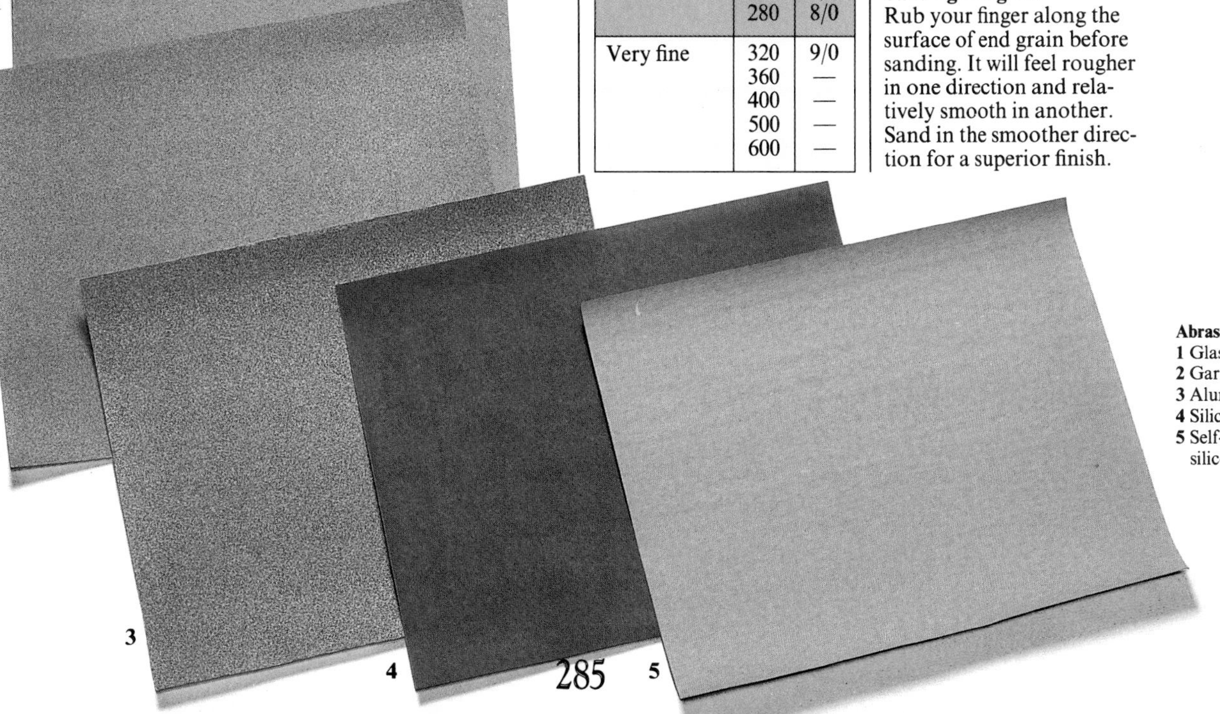

Abrasive papers
1 Glasspaper
2 Garnet paper
3 Aluminum-oxide paper
4 Silicon-carbide paper
5 Self-lubricating silicon-carbide paper

BLEACHING AND STAINING

FILLING THE GRAIN

Always fill the pores of coarse-textured open-grain woods such as mahogany, walnut, oak and ash with a grain filler before applying a glossy finish. If you omit this process, a pitted, uneven finish will result.

The best method is to apply successive coats of varnish, rubbing down in between, until the pores are filled. Color-matching of filler to wood is then not needed. However, this is a laborious process, so most woodworkers prefer to use a commercial grain filler sold as a thin paste colored to match a variety of woods. Choose a filler slightly darker than your wood, since filler dries to a lighter tone and you can always adjust its color by adding a compatible wood stain to the paste.

Rub the filler onto the wood with circular strokes, using a coarse cloth to remove any excess filler, and let it harden overnight before sanding very lightly with a fine-grade paper in the direction of the grain.

Fill the grain of coarse-textured wood

Filling stained wood

If you fill the wood after staining, the dried filler can only be sanded very lightly or you will change its color – and if you stain after filling, uneven absorption may result in patchiness. The safest way is to seal the stained wood with a coat of the intended clear finish, then once it is dry, fill the grain. This way, the sealer coat will protect the color when you sand the filler.

Using sanding sealer

In place of grain filler, use a commercial sanding sealer when preparing fine-textured woods or man-made boards for finishing. Brush the sealer on and sand it when dry with a fine-grade paper. Seal again and rub down the dried surface with 0000 grade (extra-fine) steel wool. Some varnishes may not adhere satisfactorily when applied over sanding sealer.

SEE ALSO

Orbital sanders	148-150
Face mask/respirator	214
Goggles	214
Safety tips	284
Abrasive papers	285

In most cases, a woodworker will apply a clear finish directly to a sanded workpiece, but occasionally it may be necessary to bleach discolored wood before polishing or varnishing. Conversely, you might want to enhance the color of an unusually dull piece of wood with a light coat of stain or use stain to blend poorly matched samples of the same species of wood.

BLEACHING WOOD

Two-part commercial wood bleaches remove the color from wood by chemical action. Having applied the bleach itself, it is necessary to use a neutralizer to arrest the process. Not all woods bleach successfully. Chestnut or rosewood, for example, do not respond favorably to bleach, whereas oak or birch react well. Always test a sample of the wood before attempting to bleach your workpiece. Wood bleach is a potent chemical – so follow the manufacturer's recommendations with care. Wear protective gloves, goggles, old clothes and an apron whenever you handle the chemicals.

Apply an even coat of bleach to the wood, using a clean white rag or an old bristle or nylon brush. Keep checking on the reaction for up to 20 minutes and, as soon as the required tone is achieved, wash the surface with the neutralizer. After about four hours, wash the wood again with clean water, leave it to dry and then sand it smooth.

Bleached utile

Wood stains
1 Colored water-based stain on maple
2 Walnut water-based stain on beech
3 Light-oak alcohol-based stain on beech
4 Red-mahogany oil-based stain on beech

WOOD STAINS

Wood must be perfectly clean, grease-free and sanded smooth in the direction of the grain before you apply wood stain. After using a powered orbital sander, sand by hand to remove the swirls of fine cross-grain scratches left on the wood. Unless you wet the wood first and sand it smooth, a water-based stain will raise the grain, leaving a rough surface after it dries.

TYPES OF STAIN

Ready-mixed wood stains are available in an enormous range of colors from most paint or hardware stores, but dry, powdered pigments that you have to mix for yourself usually have to be bought from a specialist supplier. Ready-mixed stains are very convenient, but many professionals recognize the advantages of being able to mix the exact colors they want using dry pigments.

Water-based stain
Water-based stains flow and penetrate well and, because they are relatively slow to dry, it is easy to get an even distribution of color. You can even shade water stains when they are on the wood, using a damp rag to remove color. Once it is dry, any wood finish may be applied over a water stain. You can buy ready-mixed stain or dry, water-soluble aniline powder. To make your stain, mix about 1oz (30g) of the powder in 1 quart (1 litre) of warm water. Let the stain cool before applying it.

Alcohol-based stain
Alcohol-based stains are not popular with amateur woodworkers because, being dissolved in methylated alcohol, they dry very fast and skillful application is required to avoid overlaps and hard edges showing when the stain dries. For this reason, alcohol-based stains are often sprayed on. This type of stain will not raise the grain of the wood. Buy it ready-mixed or in powder form to be mixed with alcohol, using the same proportions recommended for a water stain. Adding a little shellac (French polish) makes it easier to brush on alcohol stain and helps bind the pigment.

An alcohol-based stain may "bleed" through a subsequent coat of French polish or brushed-on cellulose laçquer, but a sprayed lacquer finish will not be affected in the same way.

Oil-based stain
Oil-based stains evaporate reasonably quickly, but there is usually plenty of time to achieve a satisfactory result. These stains, based on mineral spirits and oil-based solvent naptha, will not raise the grain. Oil-based stains will be redissolved by the solvent content of polyurethane varnish and wax polish. Seal the stained surface with one coat of shellac sanding sealer before applying varnish and two coats before applying wax. Oil stains are only available ready-mixed.

APPLYING WOOD STAIN

You can apply stain to a flat area of wood with a good-quality paintbrush or a paint pad. Spread the stain liberally and evenly; work with the grain and blend wet edges as quickly as possible. As soon as you have applied a coat of water stain, wipe the wet surface with a soft, dry cloth to distribute the color evenly and absorb excess stain.

You may prefer to apply stain with a ball of clean rag – especially if you have to color a vertical panel, since it is easier to control runs. Using a rag is also the only really practical way to stain turned components. Wearing protective gloves, saturate the rag in stain, then squeeze it out to avoid dripping spots of color on the wood. Drips and runs may show through the finished coat of stain unless you can blend them before they begin to dry.

MAKING A TEST STRIP

Each species of wood absorbs stain differently, affecting the color of the stain as it dries. The type of finish you use to overlay the stain also has an effect on its color and tone.

Before you stain a workpiece, make a test strip, using a scrap of the same wood. Paint the test strip with one coat of stain and allow it to dry; then paint the strip with a second coat, but leave a small section of the first application exposed for comparison. Two coats of stain are normally sufficient, but for the purposes of the test make three or even four applications and leave them to dry thoroughly. Paint a band of clear finish along one half of the test strip to see how it affects each coat of stain.

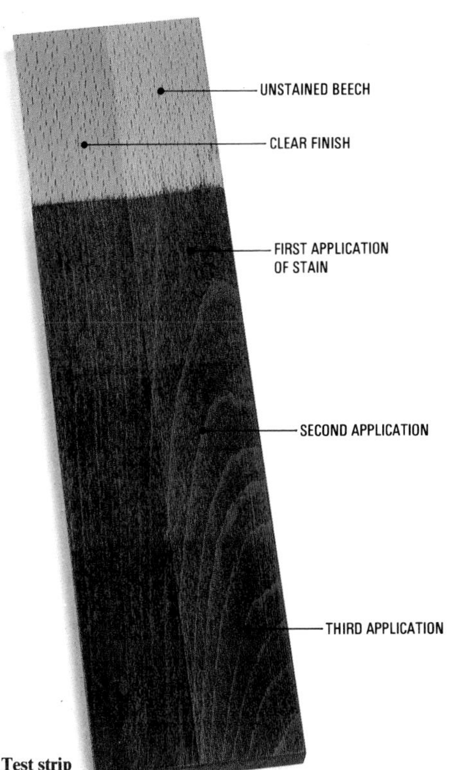

Test strip

FUMING WOOD

Exposure to ammonia fumes chemically colors woods that contain tannic acid. Oak – the most popular wood for fuming – turns a golden honey color to a medium-dark brown, depending on the length of exposure. Mahogany, chestnut and walnut can also be colored with ammonia.

You can obtain a strong ammonia solution (27 to 30 percent) from a retail pharmacy or chemical-supply house. Alternatively, you can use ordinary household ammonia, though expect the process to be slower. Ammonia irritates the eyes, nose and throat – so build a fume cupboard either outside or in a well-ventilated room and wear goggles plus a face mask or respirator when handling the chemical.

Making a fume cupboard
To construct a makeshift fume cupboard, make a scrap-wood framework to enclose the workpiece, then drape the frame with black plastic sheeting to create an airtight tent. Seal all seams and joints with duct tape. Don't use transparent plastic, as daylight can affect the color change.

Place several saucers containing ammonia solution inside the tent along with the workpiece. Do not include metal hardware or exposed screws, since they will stain the wood.

Leave the tent sealed for about 24 hours to obtain a medium-dark color. Check from time to time if you want a lighter tone. Even when you remove the workpiece, the reaction will continue for a while and the wood will darken still further.

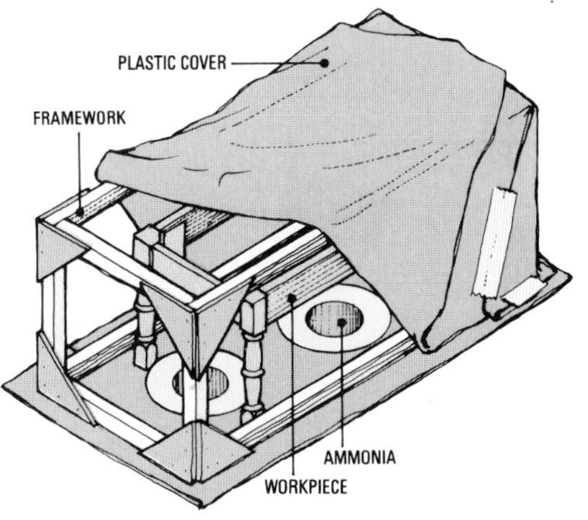

Home-made fume cupboard

FRENCH POLISH

French polish, the most celebrated wood finish of Victorian times, is still very popular today. The polish is made by dissolving shellac, a secretion of the lac insect, in industrial alcohol. It can be burnished to an almost glass-like texture that belies its vulnerability to scratching and its susceptibility to alcohol and water, which etch the surface leaving white stains. Despite these obvious disadvantages, French polish is such an attractive finish that many woodworkers are prepared to put in hours of practice in order to master the technique.

SEE ALSO

Safety tips	284
Abrasive papers	285
Wood stains	286-287
Waxes	294

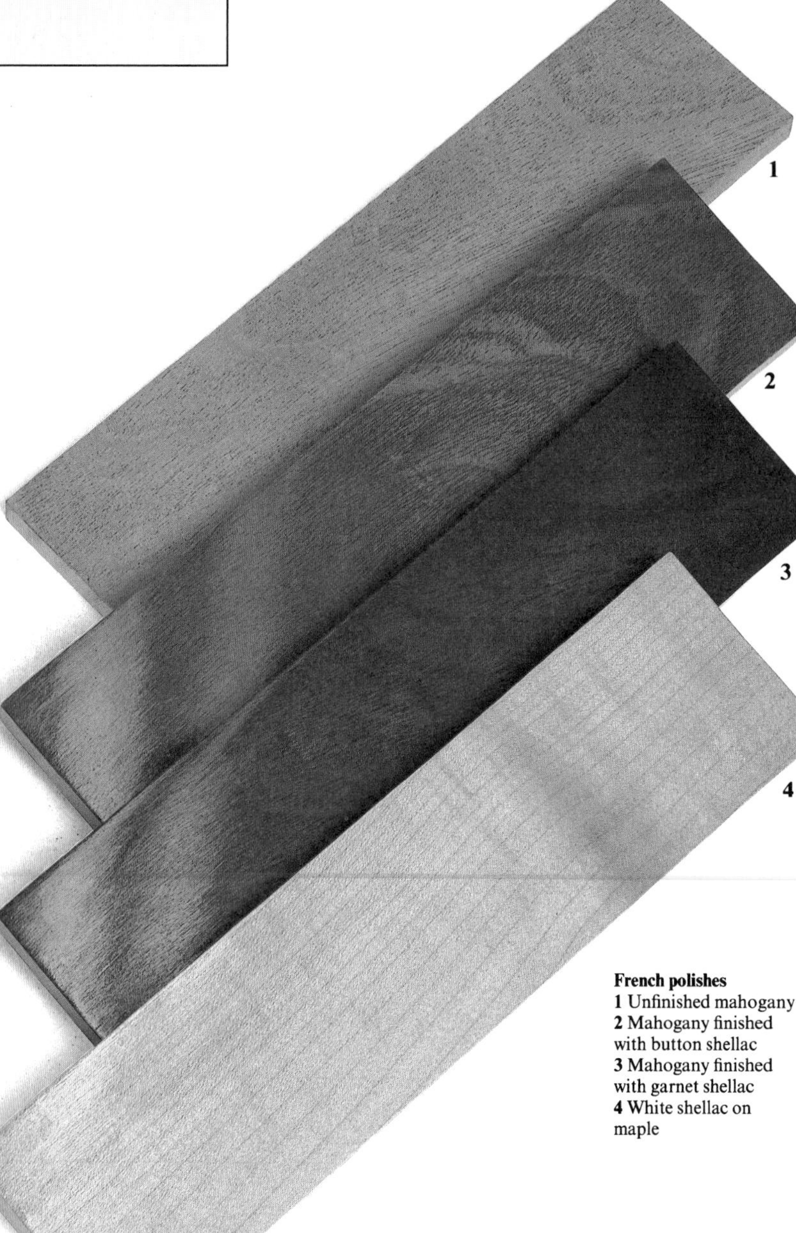

French polishes
1 Unfinished mahogany
2 Mahogany finished with button shellac
3 Mahogany finished with garnet shellac
4 White shellac on maple

TYPES OF SHELLAC

"Orange" and "white" liquid shellacs are widely available commercially, or you can make your own blends by dissolving dry shellac flakes in methylated alcohol. Once mixed, liquid shellac has a limited shelf life, after which it will not dry hard.

Blond shellac
This is the highest grade of shellac flakes, ranging from super-blond, the lightest in color, to various grades known as "lemon."

Button and garnet shellac
Button-lac was once shellac sold in the form of discs or "buttons," but these have not been available for years. Now the term is used to describe a less-refined grade of shellac flake that is darker in color than the blond and lemon varieties. Garnet is a rich red-brown in color.

Orange shellac
Commercial liquid shellac suited to most wood finishing purposes, with a longer shelf life than commercial "white" shellac. It is usually sold in 3lb cut, or three pounds of dry shellac mixed with one gallon of alcohol by the manufacturer. This is a good rough guideline for mixing dry shellacs as well.

White shellac
Bleached "white" shellac has a short shelf life in dry form, and is therefore always sold premixed. Its liquid shelf life is short. It is suitable for use on marquetry or other low-wear applications, especially over light-colored woods.

Dewaxed shellac
Natural shellac contains waxes that very slightly dull the appearance of the film, but also make it more flexible. To achieve finishes of the highest gloss and hardness, manufacturers remove the wax.

Colored shellacs
Shellacs can be tinted with alcohol-soluble dyes. A green color can be used to "tone down" raw-red mahogany; a red-brown will enrich dull-brown wood.

BRUSHING SHELLAC

Traditional French polishing demands skill and practice before you can achieve perfect results. Consequently, many woodworkers prefer to brush slightly thinned shellac onto the wood then rub down between coats rather than apply the polish in the traditional manner.

The technique for brushing shellac is easy to master. Use a soft brush to apply an even coat, then after 15 to 20 minutes, rub down lightly with self-lubricating silicon-carbide paper and apply a second coat. Having applied a third coat in the same way, rub it down with 0000 steel wool dipped in wax polish, then after five minutes, burnish with a soft cloth.

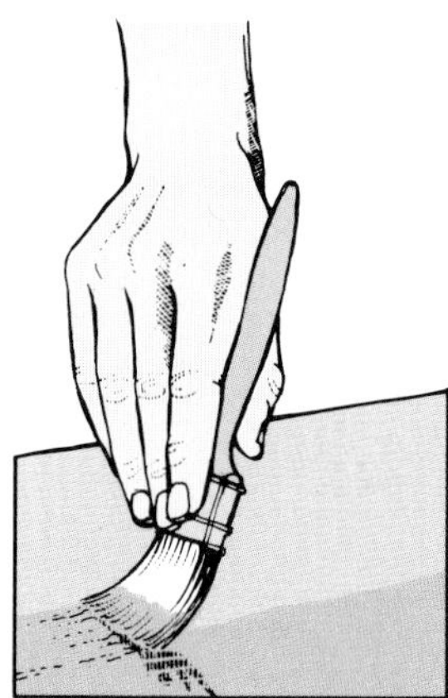

Applying brushing French polish
Use a soft brush to apply an even coat of shellac to the surface.

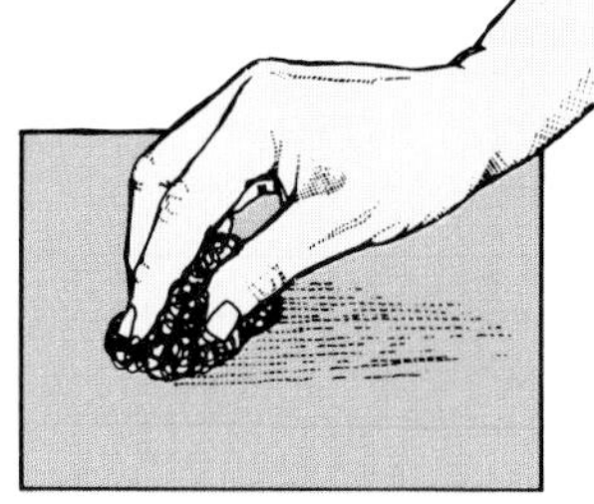

Rubbing down with steel wool
Rub the final coat lightly in the direction of the grain.

TRADITIONAL FRENCH POLISHING

Traditionally, French polish is applied, thin layer upon layer, using a ball of cotton wrapped in a white linen rag to make a soft pad known as a "rubber."

Making a rubber

Upholsterer's skin wadding is the best material for making a rubber, but ordinary cotton will do almost as well. Take a handful of the material, squeeze it roughly egg-shaped and place it in the center of a 9 to 12in (225 to 300mm) square of linen **(1)**. Fold the fabric over the cotton **(2)**, then turn in the edges **(3)**, gathering the loose material in the palm of your hand **(4)**. Smooth out any wrinkles across the sole of the pad.

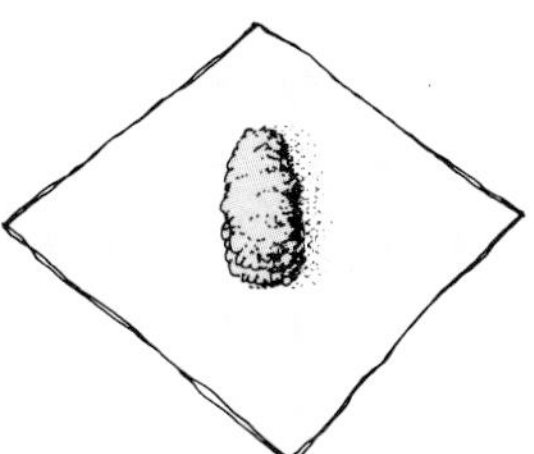

1 Place ball of wadding on a square of linen

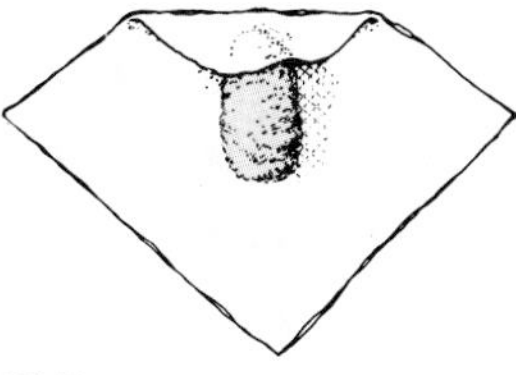

2 Fold one corner

3 Turn in the edges

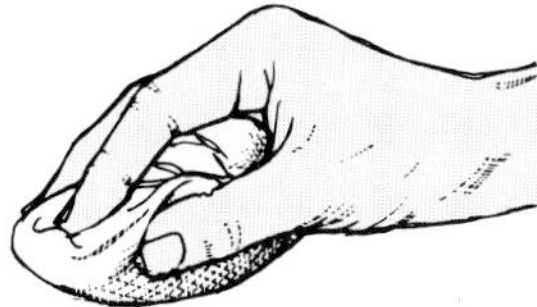

4 Hold in the palm of your hand

Charging a rubber

Unfold the linen square, then, holding the rubber in the palm of your hand, pour shellac polish onto the pad until it is fully charged but not absolutely saturated. Fold the rubber again, as described left, and press it against a scrap board to squeeze out the polish and distribute it evenly across the sole. Use your fingertip to apply a drop of linseed oil to the sole to act as a lubricant.

Applying the polish

To apply French polish to a flat surface, first make overlapping circular strokes with the rubber, gradually covering the whole panel with shellac **(1)**. Then go over the surface again, this time using figure-eight strokes **(2)**. Varying the stroke ensures an even coverage. Finish with straight overlapping strokes parallel to the grain **(3)**.

Very little pressure is required with a freshly charged rubber, but gradually increase the pressure as the work proceeds. Always keep the rubber on the move, sweeping it on and off the surface at the beginning and end of each complete coverage. If you stop with the rubber in contact with the work, it will stick and scar the polish, in which case you must let it harden thoroughly before rubbing it down with very fine self-lubricating silicon-carbide paper. Recharge your rubber with polish as necessary and add another spot of linseed oil when the rubber starts to drag.

Assuming the first application is free from blemishes, leave it to dry for about half an hour, then repeat the process. Build up four or five coats in this way, then leave the shellac to harden overnight. Keep your rubber in a screw-top glass jar while you allow the polish to dry.

The next day, sand out any runs, dust particles or rubber marks with silicon-carbide paper before applying another four to five coats of polish. Judge for yourself when you have built up a protective body of polish with the required depth of color, but 10 to 20 coats will be sufficient.

Polishing moldings and carvings

Panels with large shallow moldings can be polished with a rubber, but use a soft brush to apply slightly thinned shellac to deep moldings or carvings. A squirrel-hair brush from a specialist supplier is ideal, but you can make do with an ordinary good-quality paintbrush. Apply the polish relatively quickly and evenly, but not too quickly or it will run. When the shellac has hardened, spirit off with a rubber as described below, but only burnish lightly or you will remove too much polish from the high points.

Spiriting-off

The linseed-oil lubricant leaves streaks in the surface of the polish. Remove the streaks and burnish the polish to a gloss finish using a rubber practically empty of shellac but with a few drops of methylated alcohol on the sole. Apply the rubber to the polished surface using straight parallel strokes only, gliding on and off the panel at the beginning and end of each stroke. Recharge with more methylated alcohol as soon as the rubber begins to drag. Leave the work for a couple of minutes to see if the streaking disappears. If it doesn't, spirit off again until you have achieved the required finish. After half an hour, burnish the surface with a dry, soft rag, then leave the work for at least a week to harden completely.

Creating a satin finish

If you don't care for a high-gloss finish, matte the fully hardened surface by rubbing it lightly with a ball of 0000 steel wool dipped in soft wax polish. Use straight, parallel, overlapping strokes until the surface is dulled evenly, then burnish it to an attractive satin sheen with a soft cloth, adding a little more wax polish if necessary.

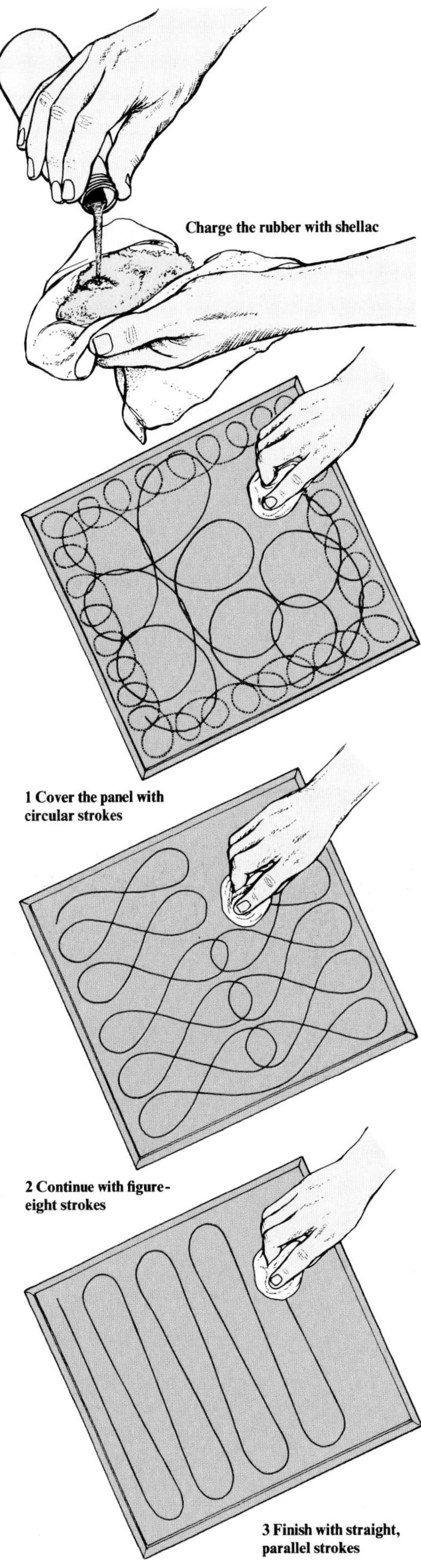

Charge the rubber with shellac

1 Cover the panel with circular strokes

2 Continue with figure-eight strokes

3 Finish with straight, parallel strokes

LACQUER, VARNISH AND PAINT

Lacquer, varnish and paint are grouped together here because these finishes are applied in similar ways, either by brush or spray gun. Consult the label for appropriate solvents, time between coats and precautions for use. Most paints are in effect clear lacquers or varnishes with additional pigments.

SEE ALSO

Safety tips	284
Abrasive papers	285
Applying French polish	289
Spraying finishes	292-293
Waxes	294
Arris	311

Nitrocellulose lacquer
This has been a popular industrial wood finish for decades, primarily because it dries extremely quickly. There are special brushing varieties, but lacquer normally has to be sprayed on to achieve the desired result. Lacquer dries by solvent evaporation, leaving a surface layer that is partly redissolved by the next application – a process that eventually results in one integral coat of lacquer.

Nitrocellulose lacquer is practically water-clear and will hardly change the color of the wood to which it is applied. It forms a hard finish that is resistant to heat and moisture.

Catalyzed lacquers
A catalyzed lacquer cures by chemical action – the lacquer won't set without the introduction of a hardener. With precatalyzed lacquers, the catalyst and lacquer are mixed by the manufacturer, although setting does not occur until the finish is exposed to air. An acid-catalyzed lacquer is supplied as two separate components for the woodworker to mix just before applying it to the work. Catalyzed lacquers are very transparent – they are also exceptionally hard-wearing and stain-resistant. Both gloss and matte lacquers are available, and you can buy opaque black and white acid-catalyzed lacquers as well as the more familiar clear variety. All catalyzed lacquers can be diluted with special thinners for spraying and some are formulated for brushing on. Most are extremely toxic.

Varnishes
Synthetic resins such as polyurethane are used to make modern wood varnishes that are heat-resistant, waterproof and extremely hard-wearing. Although most varnishes can be used straight from the can, some are supplied with a catalyst that is added just before the varnish is applied. These two-part varnishes are so resistant to abrasion that they are used for finishing wooden floors, but they have a relatively short pot life and adhesion between coats is not always satisfactory. They also give off unpleasant fumes.

Exterior-grade varnishes are made to be weather-resistant – and "yacht varnish," which will withstand exposure to salt water, is especially suitable for coastal climates.

There are clear varnishes that dry to a matte, satin or gloss finish, and tinted varnishes are available for coloring wood. As a tinted varnish does not penetrate the wood like a true stain, there is always the possibility of color loss due to localized wear. As a safeguard, apply one or two additional coats of clear varnish to preserve the color. Tinted varnish is useful for adjusting the color of a workpiece that has already been varnished. You can apply varnish with a paintbrush or dilute it with thinner for spraying.

Paint
Solvent-based paints for wood are made from solid pigments suspended in a synthetic resin, such as alkyd, vinyl, acrylic, urea or polyurethane, mixed with oil. Certain additives alter the quality of the paint to make it glossy, matte, satin, fast-drying and so on. Most solvent-based paints have a liquid consistency, but you can also buy thixotropic (nondrip) paints that are jelly-like in the can and flow only when agitated by brushing them onto a surface.

Paints with specific properties are used in sequence to build up a hard-wearing protective coating. A primer is used first, to seal the bare wood and prevent absorption of subsequent coats. It is followed by one or two applications of a heavily pigmented undercoat to obliterate the primer and build up a body of paint. The final top coat provides a wipe-clean surface of the required color and texture.

Opaque paints are intended for finishing cheap hardwood as well as softwood and man-made boards. Resin-based paints can be applied by brush, and all but thixotropic paints can be sprayed. Water-based paints will raise the grain if used to finish wood.

Lacquers, varnishes and paint
1 Cellulose lacquer on maple
2 Clear catalyzed lacquer on pine
3 Black catalyzed lacquer
4 Clear polyurethane varnish on utile
5 Tinted polyurethane varnish on oak
6 Solvent-based paint on pine

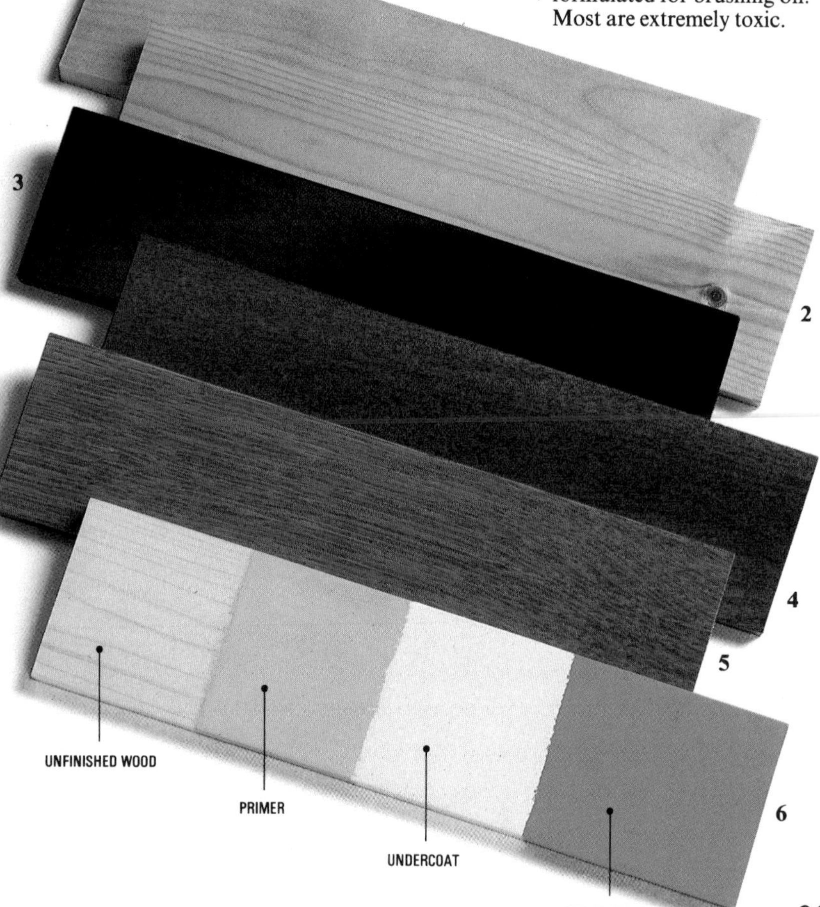

CLEANING PAINTBRUSHES

When you have finished work, brush out excess paint, varnish or lacquer on newspaper in order to clean the bristles. Flex the brush in the finish-maker's recommended thinner (mineral spirits for most paints and varnishes), then wash the dirty thinner from the bristles with hot soapy water and rinse them. Shape the bristles with your fingers while they are still wet. When dry, wrap the bristles in soft paper and slip an elastic band around the ferrule of the brush to secure the wrapping.

Spraying produces the most professional-looking finish, but it is expensive to build and equip a spray booth that complies with health and safety recommendations. Consequently, applying clear finishes and paints with a brush is the only viable option for many amateur woodworkers. However, provided you use well-maintained, good-quality brushes and exercise care and patience, you can achieve more than satisfactory results employing ordinary workshop facilities. Buy a range of brushes – say ½, 1 and 2in (12, 25 and 50mm) wide – for general work, and a 4in (100mm) brush for coating large flat surfaces.

Brushing cellulose lacquer
It requires a certain amount of experience to apply a brushing lacquer without leaving brush marks or ridges that are difficult to rub down. First, using a soft cloth or a brush, apply lacquer thinned by 50 percent to act as a sealer coat. Load a soft brush with full-strength lacquer and, holding the bristles at a shallow angle to the horizontal surface, lay the finish onto the surface with long, straight strokes. Don't attempt to brush it out like varnish, and avoid going back over the same area twice. Quickly pick up wet edges with fresh lacquer and allow the brush marks to flow out by themselves. Build up two or three coats of lacquer, rubbing down with very fine silicon-carbide paper in between. Each coat usually takes about an hour to dry – but check the manufacturer's instructions. If you are unhappy with the appearance of the final coat, flatten it with sandpaper again and apply a commercial rubbing compound with a soft cloth to buff the finish.

Some experienced woodworkers prefer to use a "pull-over solution" made from one part cellulose thinner mixed with three parts mineral spirits to put the final shine on nitrocellulose lacquer. This is not an easy technique to perfect and you must take care to avoid stripping the surface by applying too much solution. Having flattened the lacquer with silicon-carbide paper, moisten a cloth pad with pull-over solution and apply it to the surface, using overlapping circular strokes followed by straight ones in the direction of the grain, as when applying French polish.

Applying acid-catalyzed lacquer
Chemical composition and balance is crucial to the curing of acid-catalyzed lacquer, so it is essential to follow the manufacturer's recommendations for mixing the components and preparing the surface of the wood. Clean the wood well, since the presence of grease or wax, for example, can delay curing for days.

Mix just enough lacquer for your needs, and don't return the residue to the original container or the entire contents will become unusable.

The specific method of application may differ from product to product, but as a rule you can brush a liberal coat of lacquer onto the wood, spreading it with straight, parallel strokes along the grain. There is no need to brush it out like varnish – just leave the film to settle naturally. When you are coating a large area, work relatively quickly to blend wet edges before the lacquer starts to set. This will probably take between 10 and 15 minutes. Apply a second coat about two hours later and, having rubbed it down lightly with very fine silicon-carbide paper to remove dust particles, add a third coat two hours after that. For perfect adhesion between coats, try to apply all three in the same day.

If you want a mirror finish, leave gloss lacquer to harden for 24 hours, then buff it with a polishing compound on a soft cloth. For a satin finish, rub the gloss lacquer with 0000 steel wool dipped in wax polish then buff with a clean, soft rag.

Applying varnish
When finishing bare wood with clear or tinted varnish, first apply a sealer coat thinned by 10 to 20 percent with mineral spirits. Use a soft cloth pad to rub it into the wood in the direction of the grain, or brush on the sealer coat where a pad would be inconvenient. Apply the second coat by brush not less than six hours later – and if more than 24 hours have elapsed between coats, key the surface of gloss varnish with a very fine silicon-carbide paper. Remove the wood dust, using a cloth dampened with mineral spirits, before brushing on the varnish. For a hard-wearing surface, apply a third coat in the same way.

To load a brush with varnish, dip only the first third of the bristles into the finish and touch it off on the inside of the container to remove excess liquid. Do not drag the bristles across the rim of the can, as that promotes bubbles in the varnish – which, if transferred to the work, may end up set in the surface coating.

Paint the varnish onto the wood, brushing it in different directions to spread the finish evenly and blend each new coat with the wet edges of the previous application. Finally, "lay off" with light strokes in the direction of the grain. Don't brush back over a coat of varnish once it has begun to set or you will leave permanent brush marks. If this should happen, leave the finish to harden overnight then rub out the brush marks and any other blemishes with silicon-carbide paper lubricated with water.

If dust particles settle on your final gloss surface, either rub down and varnish again or modify the finish with steel wool and wax. Dip 0000 steel wool in wax polish and burnish the surface in the direction of the grain. Buff the treated surface with a rag to raise an attractive soft sheen free from obvious imperfections.

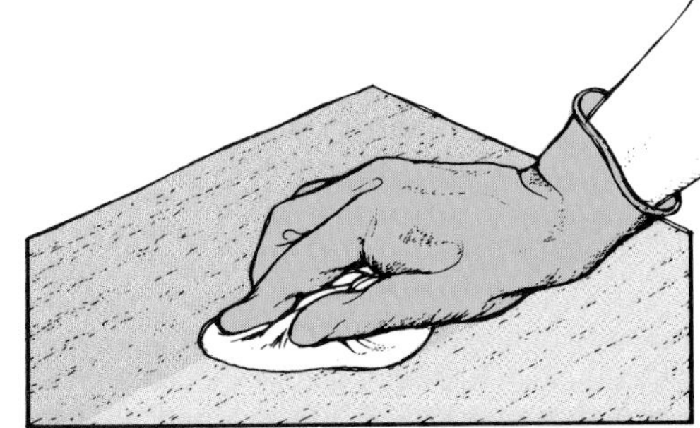
Apply a sealer coat of varnish with a cloth pad

Applying paint
Most solvent-based paints are applied like varnish, brushing them out to provide an even cover, then laying off with parallel strokes of the brush. However, there is no need to brush out thixotropic paints – instead, apply a fairly liberal coat of paint, brushing with virtually parallel strokes only, and leave the brush marks to flow out naturally.

Allow enough time for each coat of paint to dry according to the manufacturer's instructions, then rub down with a very fine silicon-carbide paper and wipe the surface clean with a rag. Leave the final top coat to dry overnight in a dust-free environment before handling the workpiece again.

AVOIDING RUNS IN PAINT OR VARNISH

If you neglect to brush out a liberal coat of normal solvent-based paint or varnish on a vertical surface, it will sag to form a heavy ridge similar in appearance to a draped curtain. Prevent "curtaining" by applying an even coat, then lay off with upward brush strokes **(1)**.

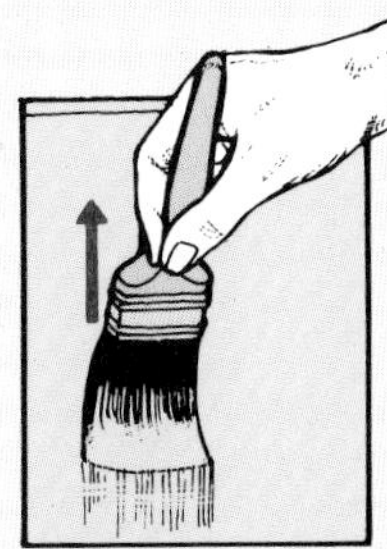
1 Laying off

Teardrop runs are caused by flexing a loaded brush against a molding or the corner of a panel. Always apply paint along moldings – never across them – and pay particular attention to brushing out in both directions from corners where two moldings meet **(2)**.

2 Brush out from corners

When painting up to the edge of a panel, brush outward away from the center **(3)**. If you brush back against the arris, you will scrape paint off the bristles, leaving it to run down.

3 Brush toward edge

SPRAYING WOOD FINISHES

Once you have mastered the basic techniques, you can finish a workpiece with a perfectly even coat of varnish, paint or lacquer, using a spray gun and compressor. When these volatile finishes are distributed as a fine mist in the air, they form a potentially explosive environment and constitute a serious health hazard. You should therefore either spray woodwork outside or build a spray booth equipped with an efficient exhaust system. However, check with your local authorities to see if you are allowed to spray in your locality and to make sure that you will not be violating any fire or safety regulations.

SEE ALSO

Goggles	214
Respirator	214
Safety tips	284
Abrasive papers	285
Lacquer, varnish and paint	290
Waxes	294

SPRAYING EQUIPMENT

Paint-spraying equipment mixes pressurized air with a liquid finish and deposits it in the form of very fine particles on the surface of the work.

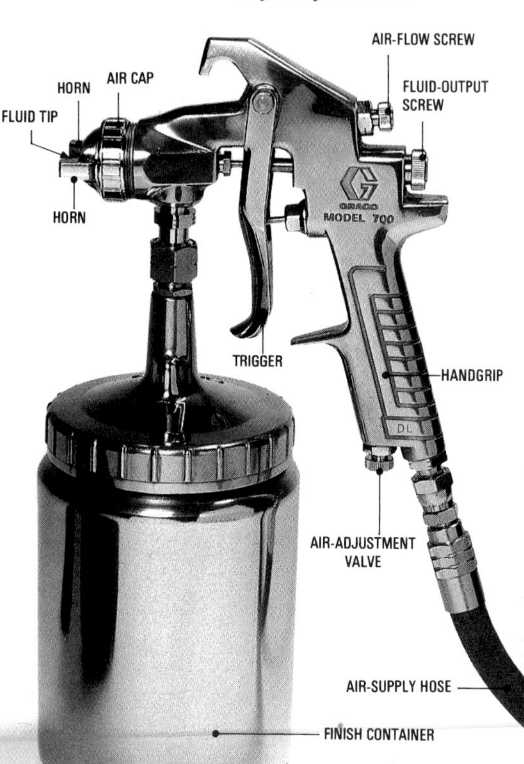

Spray gun

Spray gun and compressor
An electrically powered compressor pressurizes filtered air and delivers it via a flexible hose to a spray gun. Squeezing the gun's trigger opens an air-inlet valve, allowing air to flow through the gun and exit through the fluid tip – a small hole in the center of the air cap – where it is mixed with paint or a clear finish siphoned from a sealed container that is usually mounted below the gun. Some of the pressurized air is diverted to horns on either side of the fluid tip, where it emerges through tiny holes, causing the spray to spread out like a fan. Air flow and fluid output are modified by turning valve screws on the back of the spray gun. Some guns are made with an additional air-adjustment valve at the base of the handgrip for finer tuning.

Use a toothpick to clear a blockage

Cleaning a spray gun
When you have finished spraying, empty the finish container and add clean thinner. Operate the gun until perfectly clear thinner emerges, then release the air pressure, dismantle the air cap and clean the components with a rag dampened in solvent. Use a wooden toothpick to clear a paint blockage in the cap.

Building a spray booth
The only safe way to spray indoors is to construct a fully enclosed booth that will isolate this activity from the rest of the workshop. Install a powerful exhaust fan on an outside wall to remove noxious solvent fumes. However, these fumes create such a flammable atmosphere that even a sparking electric motor can cause them to ignite – so obtain a fan with an explosion-proof motor from a specialist supplier and fit a paint filter in front of the fan to collect the overspray. You will also need explosion-proof lamps that can be switched on or off from outside. Check with your supplier that your compressor is safe to use inside the booth, or install it outside with a connection for the hose fitted to the booth wall. Ideally, include a water trap at this point to prevent moisture in the pressurized air from condensing in the hose and spoiling the work. To hold small workpieces, make a turntable, using a disc of chipboard screwed to an old swivel-chair base, and stand it in front of the filtered fan. Support larger pieces on sawhorses.

SPRAYING SAFELY

Always follow the spray-equipment manufacturer's advice regarding health and safety. In addition:

- Wear goggles and a respirator, even when spraying outside.
- Construct a properly equipped spray booth.
- Never smoke, and extinguish all naked flames when spraying.
- Keep young children away from spraying equipment.
- Never aim a spray gun at anyone.
- Disconnect the equipment and release the pressure in the air hose before trying to clear a blocked spray gun.

THINNING PAINT, VARNISH OR LACQUER

All finishes, most of which are sold in a brushable consistency, must be diluted with the appropriate thinner to render them fluid enough to be sprayed. Check manufacturers' recommendations for the type of thinner to use and the ideal ratio of thinner to finish.

Having measured out and mixed the components, use the following rough rule of thumb to test the consistency of the finish. Stir the finish with a wooden stick, then lift it out and watch how the finish runs from the tip. When the finish runs in a steady, continuous stream, it is about right for spraying. A slow, interrupted stream indicates an over-thick consistency that will not spray efficiently. It is not so easy with this method to tell when a finish is too fluid, but a short burst of diluted finish sprayed onto a vertical practice board will give you a clue – if it runs almost at once, it is too thin.

For a more accurate gauge of consistency, obtain a viscosity cup from the spray-equipment manufacturer. Fill the cup, which is similar to a funnel, with thinned finish and time how long it takes to empty. Adjust the consistency until the time corresponds with the recommended figure.

Use a viscosity cup to test the consistency of a finish

BASIC SPRAYING TECHNIQUES

If you have never sprayed finishes before, it is best to practice on a piece of scrap board before spraying a workpiece.

Spraying a vertical panel
To spray a vertical panel, hold the gun approximately 8in (200mm) away from the surface, with the air horns turned horizontally to create a vertical fan-shaped spray pattern. Point the gun directly at the work and keep it moving on a path parallel to the surface throughout one pass **(1)**. Avoid swinging the gun in an arc **(2)** or the finish will be applied thinly at each end of the pass. Squeeze the trigger just before each pass, and don't release it until the spray pattern is clear of the work at the other end **(3)**. Aim the center of the spray pattern at the edge of the panel. On the return pass, overlap the previous application by about 50 percent **(4)** and continue with overlapping passes until you have covered the panel with finish.

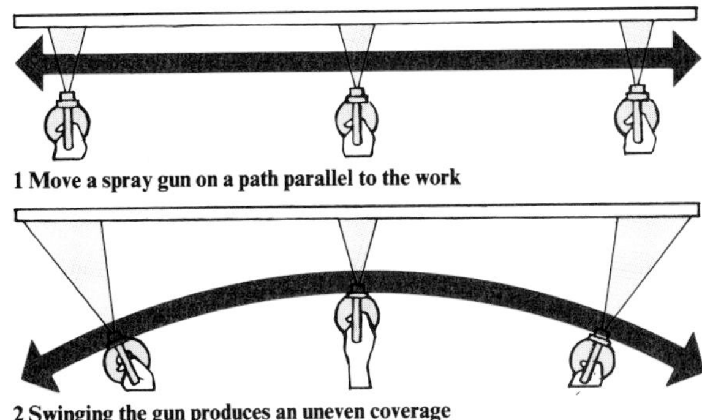

1 Move a spray gun on a path parallel to the work

2 Swinging the gun produces an uneven coverage

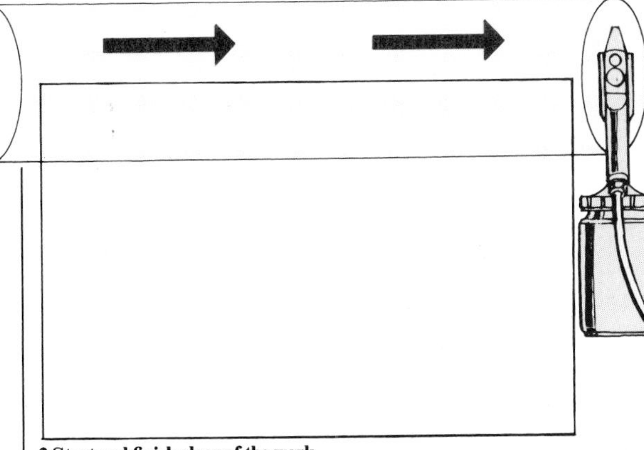

3 Start and finish clear of the work

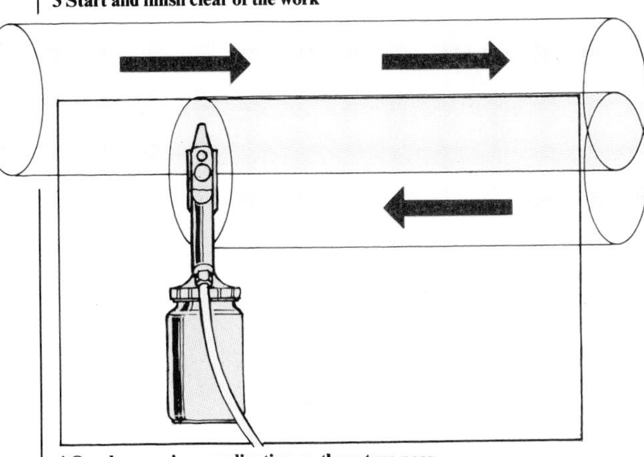

4 Overlap previous application on the return pass

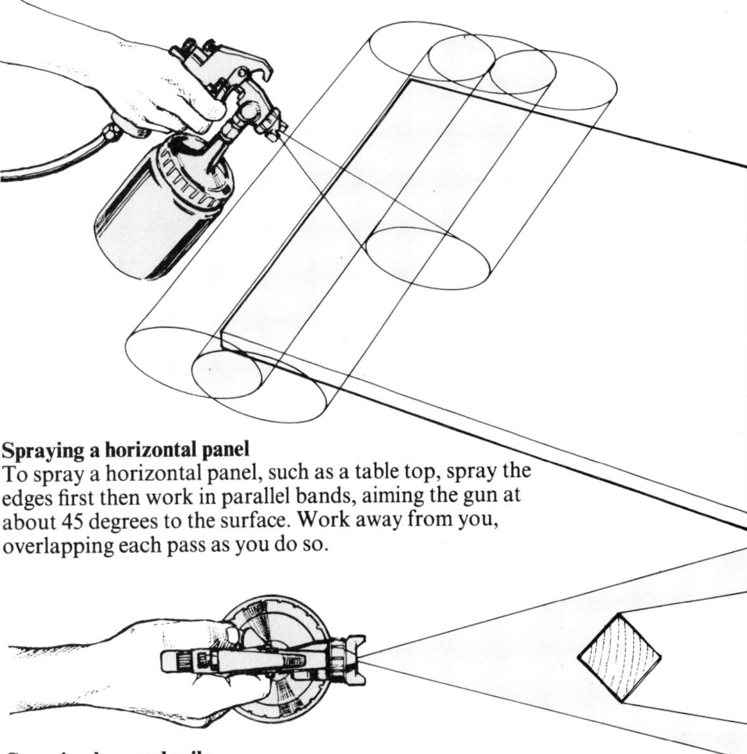

Spraying a horizontal panel
To spray a horizontal panel, such as a table top, spray the edges first then work in parallel bands, aiming the gun at about 45 degrees to the surface. Work away from you, overlapping each pass as you do so.

Spraying legs and rails
Aim the gun at a corner to spray two sides of a leg or rail simultaneously. Spray from the opposite side of the leg to coat the remaining surfaces.

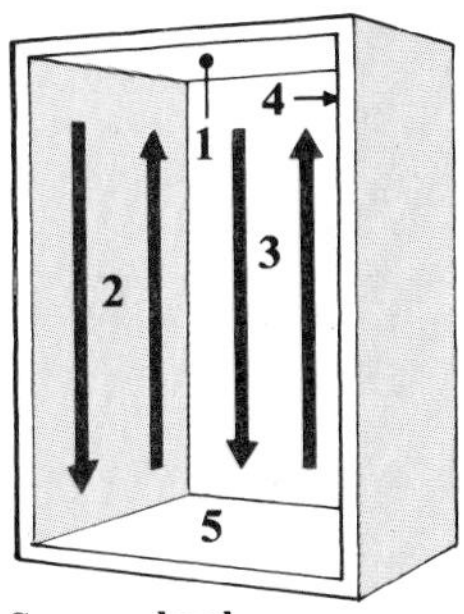

Spray enclosed surfaces in sequence

Spraying inside a cabinet or drawer
When you spray the inside of a cabinet or drawer, be systematic and concentrate on spraying each surface in turn to achieve even coverage. Spray the underside of the top panel first, followed by one side, always using overlapping vertical passes. Continue across the back of the cabinet or drawer in the same way. Then spray the other side, and finally the bottom surface. Spray the outside after finishing the interior.

HVLP TECHNOLOGY

A new approach to spraying – called High Velocity, Low Pressure, or HVLP – is finding its way into the woodshop. Here's why.

Traditional spraying uses a relatively small amount of air under high pressure to atomize the coating and transfer it to the work. The air compressor usually requires a large storage tank to provide a continuous supply of pressurized air.

HVLP takes a different approach. Instead of a compressor, a single or multi-stage turbine delivers a large quantity of air through larger hoses at relatively low pressure. Working with a spray gun designed for this air supply, you will get a better coating of the suface, with less blow-back, overspray and waste.

Costs of the two systems are roughly comparable, and application patterns and gun-handling techniques are very similar.

OIL AND WAX

Oil and wax are among the easiest wood finishes to apply, no experience being necessary in order to achieve first-rate results. Unlike varnishes and lacquers that coat the surface, oil penetrates the wood without leaving a film that holds brush marks or other blemishes – and provided you use a fast-drying variety, it does not form a sticky surface to attract dust particles. Wax is used as a finish in its own right and also as a dressing over varnish and lacquer.

SEE ALSO

Finishing on a lathe	199
Safety tips	284
Abrasive papers	285
Sanding sealer	286
French polish	288

WOOD-FINISHING OILS

Oil is traditionally used to treat naturally oily woods such as teak and afrormosia, which tend to reject the majority of finishes. But it is equally suitable for other hardwoods – and even for softwoods, which it endows with a rich amber color. Oil's water-resistant properties are particularly advantageous for exterior woodwork. Moreover, a subsequent application nourishes oiled wood suffering from the effects of exposure to the sun. However, it is not suitable as a finish for the interior of drawers or cupboards, where it could stain the contents.

- **Restoring an oil finish**
If the surface becomes scratched or stained, you can easily renovate it – simply by applying a dash of fresh oil.

Linseed oil
Raw linseed oil is suitable for small objects only. It can take up to three days to dry, by which time it may be covered with fluff and dust. Boiled linseed oil is marginally better since it dries after 24 hours, but neither oil forms a hard, durable finish.

Tung oil
Pure tung oil, also known as China wood oil, is the most durable oil finish. It shrugs off water and is resistant to heat and alcohol. It takes 24 hours to dry, but careful rubbing down with very fine silicon-carbide paper between coats will produce a superb finish. Apply five or six coats in all.

Danish and teak oils
Tung oil and other vegetable oils usually form the basis of a number of commercially prepared finishes known variously as Danish or teak oils. Driers are incorporated in these oils to shorten the time between applications to about six hours. Heat, alcohol and water may temporarily leave white stains on the surface, but they disappear quickly. More permanent blemishes can be effaced with a wipe of fresh oil.

Salad-bowl oil
Most wood-finishing oils contain toxic materials. However, you can buy non-toxic "salad-bowl oil" for wooden counter tops, chopping blocks and other objects, such as bowls and spoons, that come into contact with food. Or, if you prefer, use olive oil, or other edible oils, instead.

Oil and wax polishes
1 Danish oil on iroko
2 Clear wax on oak
3 Antique wax on oak

WAXES

In the past, woodworkers made paste wax by dissolving a mixture of beeswax and hard carnauba wax in turpentine. These raw materials are still available, but there are so many excellent ready-made preparations on the market that most woodworkers do not find it necessary to make their own.

Wax makes for an attractive mellow finish that seems to improve with age. It is produced in a range of colors, from practically transparent for pale woods to deep brown "antique polishes" that create the impression of an aged patina and will disguise scratches in a finished surface.

Silicones are added to some polishes to make them easier to buff, but if they penetrate the wood, they are difficult to remove and will repel practically any other finish should the workpiece ever have to be restored.

Liquid or cream waxes
Liquid or cream waxes are fluid enough to be brushed onto the wood. Two or three applications are required to build up a protective body of polish.

Paste wax
A paste wax, made to a slightly thicker consistency, is ideal for application with a pad of very fine steel wool or lint-free rag. On hardening, it can be buffed with a clean soft rag to an impressive luster.

Woodturning wax stick
A stick of wax, hard enough to be used as a friction finish, is rubbed against a workpiece spinning on a woodturning lathe.

APPLYING OIL

Apply a generous coat of Danish or teak oil to a clean well-prepared surface with a cloth pad or paintbrush. Leave it to soak into the wood for a few minutes, then wipe over the surface with a clean rag to absorb excess oil. Six hours later, apply a second coat and leave it to dry overnight. The next day apply one more coat, and buff it to create a sheen.

It takes longer to finish a surface with pure tung oil. After the initial coating, applied liberally with a brush and rubbed over as already described, apply several thinner coats to allow the oil to dry between applications. If dust particles adhere to the surface during the 24-hour drying period, rub it down lightly with very fine sandpaper in the direction of the grain.

APPLYING WAX

Although you can apply wax directly to bare wood, it is an advantage to seal the surface first with a varnish or, for superior-quality work or oil-stained wood, with two coats of shellac sanding sealer or white French polish. Sealing prevents the initial coat of wax from being absorbed too deeply into the grain, especially when you are using a liquid wax. It also prevents dirt from sinking through the wax and permeating the wood over a period of time.

Having flattened the sealer coats with very fine silicon-carbide paper, if you are using a liquid wax, apply the first liberal coat with a brush or use a soft cloth pad to rub it into the wood with circular strokes first and then straight ones in line with the grain. One hour later, buff up the wax and apply a thin coat with the pad in the direction of the grain only. Add a third coat, if needed, similarly and buff it as before. Leave the wax to harden for several hours, then burnish the surface vigorously with a clean soft rag.

If you decide to use a paste-wax polish, apply it with a pad of 0000 steel wool, rubbing with the grain only, and bring it to a shine with a soft cloth.

CHAPTER TWELVE

OTHER MATERIALS

From time to time most woodworkers find themselves using materials other than wood, either for practical reasons or to enrich the appearance of a workpiece. Metal parts of shopmade jigs and fixtures can be found in every workshop and metal inlays are used to decorate chair backs, box lids and gunstocks. For pastry-making, nothing compares with a cool marble slab set into a kitchen counter top. Despite improvements in plastics, glass is still the best material for picture-framing and for china cabinets or display cases; and glass or marble table tops are attractive and easy to clean. Leather makes an ideal writing surface for desks and bureaus; it can also be used to line presentation cases or jewelry boxes or as a handsome facing for cabinet or drawer fronts. It is well worth learning the basic skills of cutting, shaping and fitting these materials, or at least enough about them to brief a specialist supplier or craftsman when expert services are needed.

METAL

Metal ornamentation and inlays make a pleasing contrast to the softer and more muted tones of wood. Metalworking skills also enable you to design and make your own fittings such as catches, pulls, escutcheons and other hardware, thus adding a satisfying touch of originality to your work.

SEE ALSO	
Grinders	106-107
Vertical drill stand	127
Routers	140-145
Drill presses	188-189
Face mask	214
Engineer's vise	276
Finishes	290-293
Adhesives	303

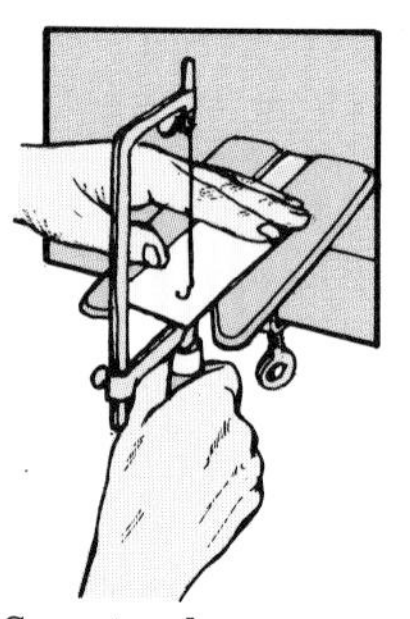

Support work on a notched bird's-mouth

METALWORKING TOOLS

Most metals can be worked by hand with a basic selection of metalworking tools.

For inlays and for inscription plates and other decorative fittings, jeweler's tools are most appropriate.

For heavier work, such as support brackets and frame members, a hacksaw and universal snips are needed plus a range of larger files, both fine-cut and coarse-cut, in flat, half-round and round profiles. For cutting thick metal sections, bars and tubes, use a 1ft (300mm) hacksaw frame with either a medium-tooth or fine-tooth blade. Having hardened teeth fused to a flexible-steel back, bi-metal hacksaw blades last much longer and are less likely to shatter than ordinary carbon-steel blades.

For decorative fretwork, such as keyholes and fancy escutcheons, a jeweler's piercing saw and an assortment of needle files of various shapes is essential. When cutting with a piercing saw, support the work on a bird's-mouth and cut on the downstroke only.

For marking out, you will need a scriber to score the surface of the metal, and dividers for scribing arcs and circles. An engineer's steel square is ideal for checking and marking right angles. Use a steel ruler for setting out and measuring dimensions.

For cutting flat sheets, two smaller pairs of snips are useful – one flat-bladed for cutting straight lines and external curves, and the other with curved blades for cutting internal curves.

A bench-mounted electric grinder is a worthwhile investment. One side of the grinder can be used to drive abrasive grinding and sharpening stones; the other side has a tapered mandrel or spindle so wire brushes and buffing wheels can be interchanged quickly.

Metalworking tools
1 Hacksaw
2 Needle files
3 Piercing saw
4 Metalworking files
5 Engineer's square
6 Dividers
7 Universal snips
8 Straight snips
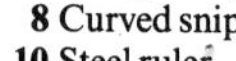
8 Curved snips

10 Steel ruler
11 Scriber

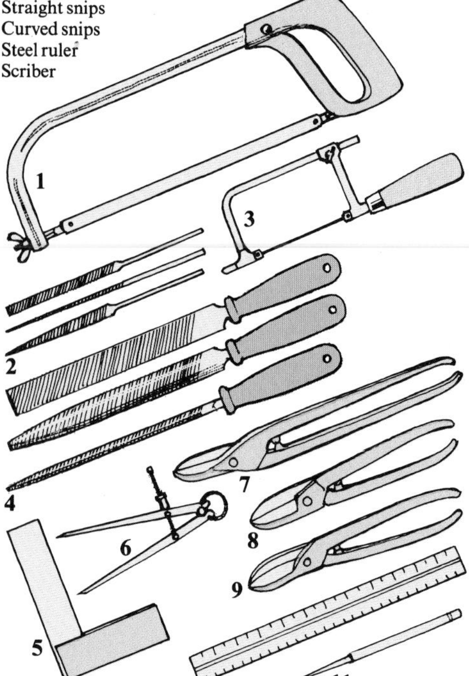

METALWORKING BENCH

If possible, install a separate bench for metalwork. This avoids metal particles straying onto wooden workpieces. It also keeps torches, or other heat sources, and flying sparks away from sawdust and shavings. Ideally, the top of the bench should be covered with galvanized-steel sheeting. As well as the bird's-mouth and electric grinder, bolt a medium-sized engineer's vise rigidly to the bench and a drill press for drilling precise vertical holes. Even if you already have a drill press for woodwork, a vertical power-drill stand for metalwork only will help confine oil and swarf (metal shavings) to a limited area.

JOINING METAL

Metals can be joined either by gluing, soldering, brazing or welding, depending on the strength of joint required.

Gluing

Metals can be bonded to most surfaces (including other metals and glass) using cyanoacrylate, epoxy-resin or rubber-based contact adhesives. Generally, gluing is only used for attaching decorative metals and small fittings, although modern adhesives form an extremely strong bond. Glued metal-to-metal joints are useful for mock-ups and also for temporarily holding items together prior to final fixing. Structural joints should be brazed or welded.

Soldering

Stainless steel, brass and copper can all be joined by soft soldering or by brazing. For soft soldering on brass and copper, you will need one or two 150W electric soldering irons for soldering sheet up to $\frac{1}{16}$in (1.5mm) and one of 40W for thin-gauge sheet, strip or wire. Heavier-gauge sheet can be soft-soldered using a propane torch. (For extra heat use Mapp gas, a mixture of propane and oxygen.) Soft solders, which are alloys of lead and tin, have a low melting point. Do not try to make edge-to-edge joints when soft-soldering, but form overlaps or interlocking seam joints.

Make sure that the surfaces to be joined are perfectly clean and free from grease. In all forms of soldering, a flux is used to keep the surfaces clean during the soldering process and to prevent them from oxidizing.

For most brass and copper fittings, use a paste flux with either bar or wire solder. Avoid the flux-cored type of wire solder, as used for electrical connections, since it tends to be soft and weak. For five times more strength, use low-temperature silver solder (430°F), sold in most hardware stores. High-temperature silver solder (1100° or more F) can even "weld" band saw blades.

Keep the tip of the iron clean and, before using it, tin the tip when hot by fluxing it lightly and running a thin coat of solder over it.

Soldering a joint

To form a joint, wipe flux along the joint lines and bring the heat source close to it. Heat the surface with the tip of the iron or flame. Allow the heat to build up until the solder starts to flow. Do not overheat the surface or burn the flux, otherwise the metal may distort or the solder will not flow properly. Neither will the solder flow if the surfaces are not hot enough, but will remain as small globules along the joint.

To avoid overheating with a torch, apply the flame away from the joint and let the metal conduct the heat to it.

Allow the joint to cool gradually (do not cool it with water or you will weaken it), then clean off any excess flux.

Brazing and welding

Although soft soldering is easily performed in the home workshop, it is generally better to have brazing and welding done professionally. Moreover, service stations and machine shops are often willing to do small brazing or welding jobs.

However, with the availability of small inexpensive metal inert-gas (MIG) welders, which weld aluminum and stainless steels as well as other metals, it is now feasible to make small metal fittings in the home workshop.

METALS

Gold and silver

Traditionally gold and silver have been used as inlays to decorate cabinets, often combined with exotic materials such as tortoiseshell and mother-of-pearl.

Gold alloys, in the form of 9 karat wire or sheets, can be used for inlay work – but because of its cost, gold is more commonly used as thin foil, called "leaf."

Silver is easier to work than gold alloy and is available in a wider range of sheet and wire thicknesses. Since silver is cheaper than gold, thin sheet is often used rather than leaf.

Gold and silver can be purchased from many local jewelry stores or jeweler's supply catalogs.

Brass

Brass is usually available in small quantities from mail-order houses as sheet, rod, tube and strip as well as other sections such as angle and bar. Another good source of supply is hobby shops, which often stock brass (and other metals) in a wide range of profile and sheet thicknesses cut in short lengths and sizes.

Carbon steel

Mild or medium carbon steels (the higher the carbon content, the harder the steel) are available from steel suppliers (listed in the Yellow Pages) in the form of tube, bar and plate (sheet). Most will supply small orders or sell offcuts for making your own frames, brackets and other fittings.

Mild steel is easy to work with hand tools, but difficult to solder. Structural joints are generally brazed or welded, though for concealed work, nuts and bolts or rivets may be used. Carbon steels (other than stainless) rust unless they are painted or plated.

Stainless steel

Stainless steel is available as sheet, tube and angle from metal or boatbuilding-material outlets. Most varieties are easy to work and will retain a good surface finish. Though not easy to join, stainless steel can be glued, soldered, brazed or welded.

Aluminum

Hardware stores and builder's and metal suppliers sell aluminum in a vast variety of sections. It is an easy metal to work, but difficult to solder, and soft varieties clog the teeth of files and hacksaws. To prevent clogging, coat the blade with paint thinner, turpentine or talc. Finished surfaces need to be protected with a clear metal varnish or a professionally applied treatment such as anodizing.

Copper

Copper is available in sheet, tube, rod and strip form from metal suppliers and hobby shops. It is easy to work and join. Polished copper surfaces dull quickly.

LAYING METAL INLAYS

Decorative metal inlays may take the form of strips, bands, circles, ovals, or other regular or irregular shapes.

To recess a metal inlay into the surface of the wood (or "ground"), use a power router guided either by its fence for straight grooves or by a trammel for circles. Other shapes can be cut freehand or with a template. The groundwork must be perfectly flat, particularly when laying thin foil. For most recessing, use a straight, two-flute plunge cutter that has a ¼in (6mm) shank and a diameter of not less than ⅜in (9mm). For intricate figures or thin strips, use a finer cutter.

Square up the corners of the recess by removing the waste with a sharp chisel and check that the inlay lies fractionally below the surface of the wood by laying the edge of a metal ruler or straightedge across it.

Metal inlays are glued to the groundwork with an epoxy-resin adhesive. Apply a thin layer of glue to the metal and press it into the recess. Cover the work with thin plastic sheeting, then – to ensure that the inlay lies flush with the surface – either clamp a flat block over the inlaid area or place the work in a veneer press.

- **Bonding metal to wood**
When gluing metal to wood, seal the wood first with thinned varnish or diluted PVA glue. To allow for shrinkage and expansion, use a flexible contact adhesive when bonding metal to a wide wood surface.

FINISHING METAL

Various skilled techniques can be used to enhance the appearance of metal, including planishing, sandblasting, chasing and embossing.

Scratch-brushing

One technique that does not involve special skills or equipment is scratch-brushing. This produces a satin texture by using a rotating stainless-steel brush (or progressively finer brushes) fitted to the spindle of a bench grinder. The coarseness and speed of the brushes determine the depth of finish.

Polishing

Always wear a face mask when polishing metal, since the fine metal dust raised can be dangerous when inhaled.

If possible, metal inlays and fittings should be polished before fitting, using brushes and buffing wheels fitted to the mandrel of a bench grinder.

Start by removing scratches and marks, using a stiff brush coated with Tripoli (an abrasive polish available from hardware stores and craft-material suppliers).

Next, buff the metal to a high sheen using cloth buffing wheels, first with Tripoli and then with jeweler's rouge or a suitable metal polish.

If you have to polish inlays or fittings *in situ,* use small brushes or wheels held in the chuck of a Dremel or Foredom tool, or in a flexible drive fitted to a bench-mounted drill. Protect the surrounding wood with a thin coat of clear sealer and cover with masking tape to avoid staining.

CUTTING LUBRICANTS

Most metals are easier to cut if you use a lubricant. This prevents the blade or drill from binding, acts as a coolant and prevents swarf from clogging the teeth.

Steels: Machine oil.
Aluminum: Paint thinner, turpentine or talc.
Copper: Light machine oil, paint thinner or talc to stop the teeth from clogging.
Brass: Work dry.

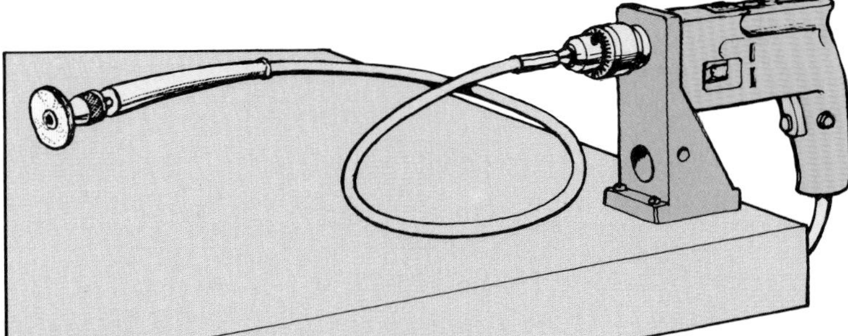

Polishing metal inlays or fittings
A miniature buffing wheel held in a powered flexible drive is ideal for polishing inlays or fittings in place.

Applied finishes

Cellulose-based or polyurethane-based paints and lacquers, used with compatible undercoats and primers, are most suitable for finishing metal. They can be brushed or sprayed on, though spraying generally produces better results more quickly and easily. Aerosols offer an economical method of spraying metal fittings. Small spray guns and compressors also give good results.

When brushing or spraying paint, always work in a dust-free atmosphere – and never spray with a compressor indoors except in a spray booth (see chapter on finishing wood). Make sure that the surface is perfectly clean and grease-free. If better adhesion is needed, score the surface of the metal lightly with steel wool or fine wet-or-dry paper. Allow each coat of paint to dry thoroughly and rub down with wet-or-dry paper between coats.

GLASS

There are three categories of glass: transparent (including polished plate, drawn sheet and float glass), translucent (comprising patterned, frosted and rough-cast glass) and special (for example, tempered, laminated, antique, non-glare and solar-control glass). Other glazing materials include acrylic plastics. Although they scratch easily, they are less liable to break than glass and may be sawn using carbide-tipped blades, or scored with a special tool and snapped.

SEE ALSO

Face mask	214
Eye protection	214
Adhesives	303
Screw covers	305
Knock-down fittings	308-309

- **Safe design**
  Glass shelves should be designed so that the glass is supported over the greatest used area.
- **Retaining glass**
  Where shelves or table tops overhang a support rail or bracket, use clips, screws or other fastenings to retain the glass.

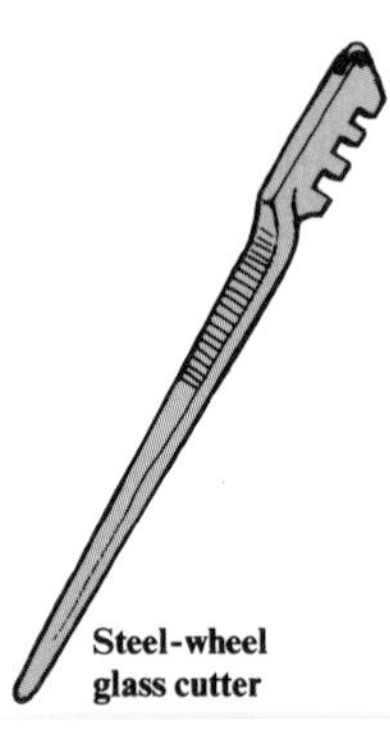
Steel-wheel glass cutter

HANDLING GLASS SAFELY

- Wear leather gloves and take care when handling or disposing of broken glass or glass dust.
- Wear goggles and leather gloves when cutting glass, plus a mask when grinding.

Drawn sheet glass
Virtually obsolete today, but still found in old windows and picture frames. Its wavy surface and irregular thickness cause optical distortion and make cutting somewhat chancy.

Float glass
Float glass is flatter and more uniform than drawn glass. Two thicknesses are universally available: "single strength" is ordinary window glass about $\frac{3}{32}$in (2.5mm) thick; "double strength" is for larger panes, and about $\frac{1}{8}$in (3mm) thick.

Low-grade float glass has defects such as "seeds," bubbles and streaks; medium-grade is ordinary window glass; high-grade is suitable for silvering to make mirrors, and is available in thicknesses up to about 1in (25mm). High-grade float glass is the equivalent of the obsolete "polished plate glass."

Antique glass
Antique glass is still available from specialist sources and is handmade by traditional methods to retain the characteristics of old glass, such as variations in thickness and color, and defects such as flaws and air bubbles.

Opal glass is now generally referred to as antique glass but tends to be more regular in thickness, the color appearing as faintly translucent to opaque.

Non-glare glass
This type of glass is mainly used for framing pictures and bulletin boards. Both sides of the glass are very slightly textured, but when positioned close to an object appear transparent.

In picture frames, the gap between the glass and the picture should not exceed the thickness of the mat. For other purposes, a gap of not more than $\frac{3}{4}$in (18mm) is acceptable.

Heat-treated glass
All float glass is annealed, or heat-treated, to relieve internal stresses. Further treatment produces "heat-strengthened" glass, which cannot be cut by ordinary means. "Tempered" glass is even further treated to induce a deliberate stress pattern, making it four to five times stronger than annealed glass. When broken, tempered glass fractures into myriad small cubes or dice. Because it cannot be cut, tempered glass is manufactured in various standard sizes for use in entry doors and other applications where safety is important. Custom sizes are available but expensive.

Laminated glass
Laminated glass is much stronger than ordinary glass. It is produced by sandwiching a clear plastic film between two sheets of glass. If it is shattered, the film holds the fragments together, possibly saving items standing on it and also reducing risk of injury. As a result, it can be used for load-bearing plinths, bases or shelves.

Where to buy glass
Most types of glass are available from hardware stores and lumberyards. For beveling and mirroring services, check the Yellow Pages.

Drilling glass
Glass can be drilled using a special spearpoint bit running at low speed in a power or hand drill. Mark the center of the hole with the tip of the bit and build a well of putty around the spot filled with paint thinner, turpentine or kerosene to cool the bit.

Cutting glass
Glass over $\frac{5}{32}$in (4mm) thick is best cut or drilled by a professional. But if you prefer to do it yourself, use a diamond-impregnated disc driven by a small cordless angle grinder fitted with a coolant dispenser – which can also be used for grinding edges and trimming corners.

Most flatsheet glass up to $\frac{5}{32}$in (4mm) thick can be cut easily with a steel-wheel or diamond cutter. Lay the glass on a padded surface, such as a piece of blanket or carpet, spread over a flat work surface. Clean all grease from the surface with turpentine or kerosene – a greasy surface will not cut evenly.

Mark each end of the cut line on the edges of the glass with a felt-tip pen and align a T-square or wooden straightedge between them. Holding the cutter firmly between your middle finger and forefinger, with your thumb supporting the back, draw the cutter along the line with a moderate even pressure **(1)**. Take care not to chip the edge of the glass at the end of the cut.

Wearing leather gloves and goggles or safety glasses, lay the glass on a piece of thin board with one of its edges aligned with the cut, leaving one side unsupported. To snap the glass, press down firmly with one hand on each side of the scored line **(2)**.

If any jagged pieces of glass are left along the edge, nibble them off using the correct-width notch on the side of the cutter **(3)** or a pair of pincers. Narrow strips can be broken off the sheet after scoring by holding the glass on each side of the line at one end and snapping along the line **(4)**.

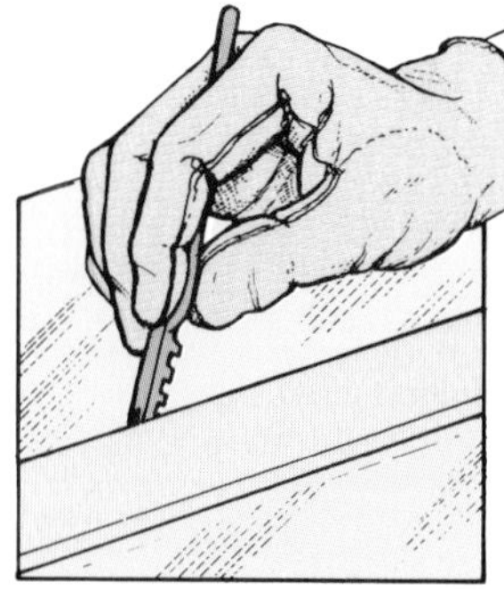
1 Draw a cutter toward you

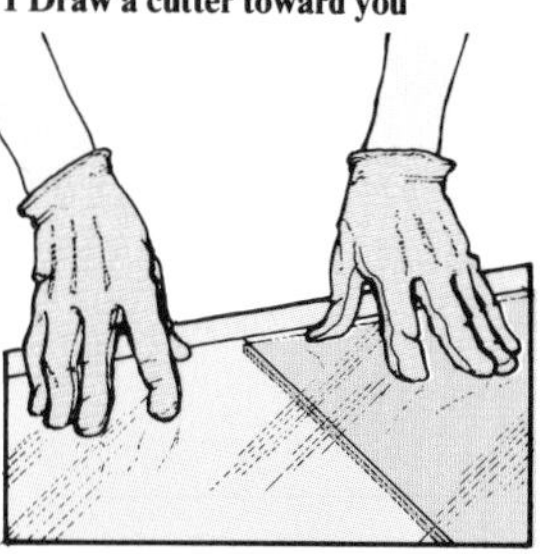
2 Press on each side of line

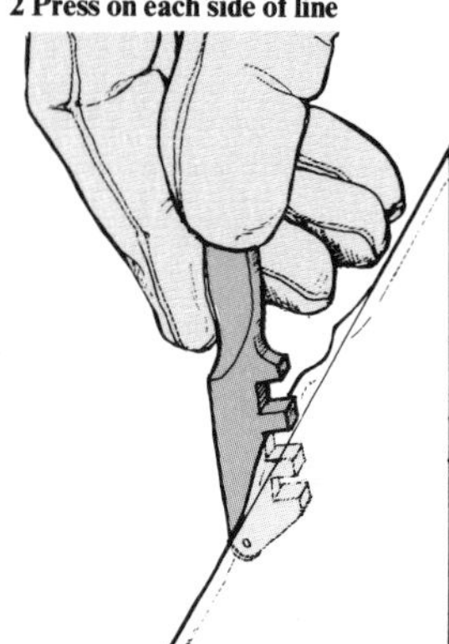
3 Clean up any jagged edges

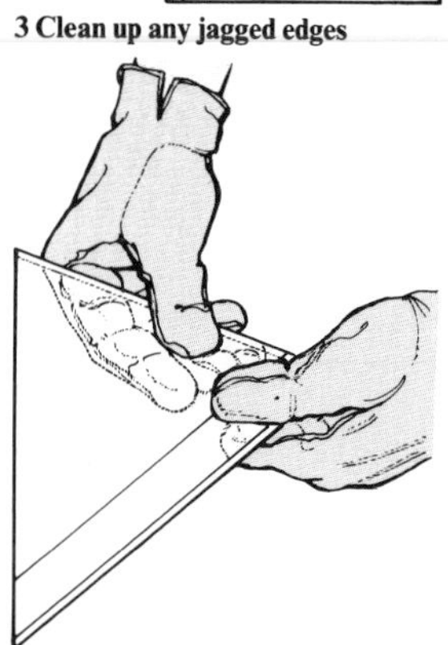
4 Snap a strip off a sheet

Grinding and polishing

On unframed panels, such as table tops and shelves, glass edges must be ground smooth for safety. They can be ground and polished to one of several standard profiles, including flat, beveled, bullnose, mitered, full-round and half-round.

Edge-grinding is best left to the glass supplier, but you can polish the edges yourself using various grades of wet-or-dry paper down to 600 grit, followed by metal polish or a fine rubbing compound as used for repolishing car paintwork.

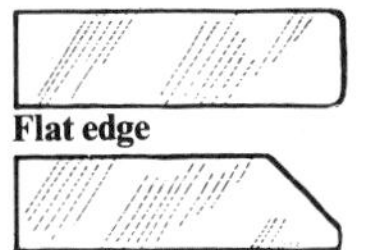

Flat edge

Mitered edge

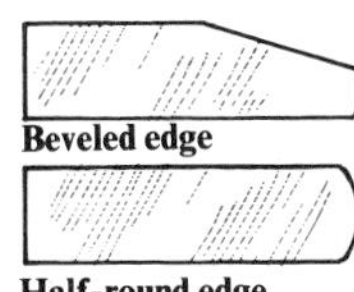

Beveled edge

Half-round edge

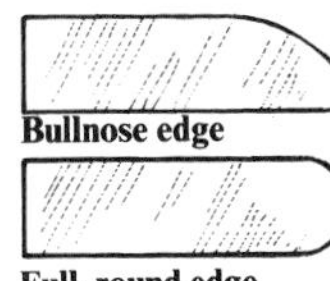

Bullnose edge

Full-round edge

Joining glass

Both butt and lap joints can be formed between glass panels using modern adhesives, such as epoxy resin, silicon sealers or cyanoacrylates. The latter can be used to form virtually invisible joints if the two surfaces are finished so they mate perfectly. Mitered joints are best ground by a glass supplier.

Butt joint

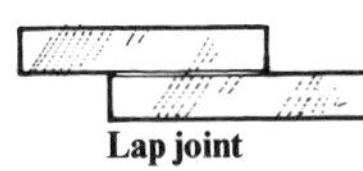

Lap joint

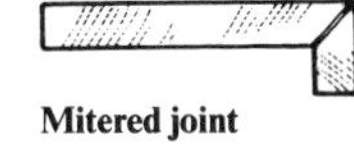

Mitered joint

Selecting glass

For small panes in cabinet doors, picture frames and vertical panels up to 1 × 1ft (300 × 300mm), select single-strength glass.

For cabinet doors and vertical panels up to 2ft 6in × 1ft 3in (750 × 375mm), select double-strength glass.

The safe loading for glass shelves is given in the table below, which is based on the metric formula:

$$\frac{2}{3} \times \frac{\text{width (front to back)}}{\text{span between supports}} \times \text{thickness of glass}^2 = \text{max. load in kilograms.}$$
(measurements in millimeters)

However, the shelf width from front to back should not be less than 6in (150mm) nor greater than a span to width ratio of 7:1. For example, the span of a shelf 6in (150mm) wide should not exceed 3ft (1.05m).

For general storage, design shelves to withstand loads of up to 15 or 20kg. A kilogram is 2.2lb.

Span	Width	$\frac{1}{4}$in	$\frac{3}{8}$in
1ft 8in	6in	15.4lb	44lb
1ft 8in	8in	19.8lb	57.2lb
1ft 8in	12in	30.8lb	88lb
2ft 6in	6in	8.8lb	28.6lb
2ft 6in	8in	13.2lb	37.4lb
2ft 6in	12in	19.8lb	57.2lb
3ft 4in	6in	6.6lb	22lb
3ft 4in	8in	8.8lb	28.6lb
3ft 4in	12in	15.4lb	44lb

Supported table tops

Where the edge of a glass top is fully supported along each edge, the recommended maximum size is:

$\frac{1}{4}$in glass: 1ft 8in × 1ft 8in (500 × 500mm) or 2.78sq ft (0.25sq m).

$\frac{3}{8}$in glass: 2ft 11in × 2ft 11in (875 × 875mm) or 8.50sq ft (0.77sq m).

$\frac{1}{2}$in glass: 3ft 6in × 3ft 6in (1070 × 1070mm) or 12.25sq ft (1.14sq m).

The glass top should be held in the table underframe by a rabbet or with clips.

Overhanging table tops

If the glass overhangs the supporting underframe, it must be held in place by fastenings or by dowels that pass through the glass to prevent it from being pushed off. Metal bolts or dowels should be cushioned with flexible washers.

As a general guide, use $\frac{1}{2}$in (12mm) glass and do not allow the overhang to exceed 1ft 8in (500mm) all around.

MARBLE

Marble is prized for its rich and varied appearance, but it also has its practical uses. As a durable hygienic surface resistant to stains and scratches, it is suitable for use as a cutting or pastry slab inset into a kitchen hutch or a counter top.

Types of marble

Marbles range in coloring from Italian pure whites and creams to the Belgian grays and blacks. Other colors include Green Tinos from Greece; beige and browns from Portugal, Sicily and France; yellow/gold from Iran, Spain and Yugoslavia; and reds to pinks from Italy, Greece, Scandinavia and Portugal.

Some limestones that are not true marbles, such as Travertine (UK), also produce a good natural polish.

Cutting and working marble

Machining marble involves the use of expensive cutters and is best left to a skilled mason. Despite its hardness, marble is worked in a similar way to wood. In fact, standard woodworking machinery is often used (in particular band saws, circular saws and routers) with the blades replaced by diamond-impregnated cutters, bands and discs.

Holes up to $\frac{5}{8}$in (16mm) may be drilled using tipped masonry drills at a cutting speed around 900rpm. Larger holes can be drilled using tipped core drills.

All cutting is performed with water continuously directed onto the tool as a coolant. Steel wool is then used to polish the marble. Steel wool is also used with specially prepared poultices to take out the unsightly surface stains associated with old marble that has been subjected to damp conditions.

Buying marble

The best sources of supply are marble importers or stone suppliers, since both are used to small orders.

When ordering, always give exact measurements, and for shaped work, supply an accurate template with the top face clearly marked. Show also the position and detailing of any decorative machining or carving that you require.

Marble is generally available in thicknesses from $\frac{5}{16}$in (8mm) to 2in (50mm). However, it can be cut to any thickness you want if ordered specially. Most types are supplied in slabs up to 11ft 6in × 5ft 6in (3.5 × 1.7m), although the most common standard size is 2 × 1ft (600 × 300mm).

Hardware and adhesives

Make sure the frame or base is perfectly square, level and rigid to prevent the slab from bending or twisting when fastened down. Successful repairs can be made using an epoxy adhesive.

Table tops are sometimes screwed to the underframe using bolts or screws with decorative screw caps to conceal the heads. For a cleaner look, brass bolts can be set into blind holes drilled in the underside of the slab, using a two-part epoxy glue to secure them. In either case, allow for movement of the wood frame by fastening into buttons **(1)** or into slotted angle brackets **(2)**.

Where the slab is set flush into a worktop or frame, brass edge dowels can be used to locate the slab **(3)**.

Marble can be glued to marble and to most other materials using an epoxy adhesive. However, for gluing to a wood surface, a flexible rubber-based adhesive must be used.

1 Wooden button

2 Metal bracket

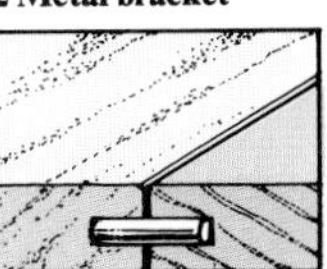

3 Brass edge dowel

LEATHER

Leather is primarily used by furnituremakers in three ways – as a furnishing fabric, as a facing material for writing tables and bureaus, and as a structural material stretched across a frame for various forms of seating.

SEE ALSO

Routers	140-145
Lippings	248
Adhesives	302-303

Buying leather

Traditionally, most leather is sold by the square foot and by thickness. However, some suppliers are now switching to metric units. Alternatively, it may be described by weight – a piece 1ft (300mm) square and $\frac{1}{64}$in (0.4mm) thick, for example, weighs approximately 1oz (25g).

Furniture hide, a specially dressed and softened natural cowhide, is used for upholstery. Usable hide from a full-grown steer covers about 50 to 60sq ft (4.5 to 5.5sq m).

For desk and table tops, skiver leather (sheepskin) is generally preferred. This is thinner and easier to lay than cowhide but is much smaller – the maximum rectangle obtainable being about 2ft 9in × 2ft (840 × 600mm). For larger table tops, it is necessary to join two pieces of hide (they are usually supplied taped together ready for laying).

Small pieces of leather are often available from craft-material shops or suppliers, and it is sometimes possible to buy offcuts from leather-clothing manufacturers. Skivers cut to order for desk tops and other purposes can be obtained from suppliers of materials for cabinet-making and furniture restoring. Skivers are available in several colors and also in "antique" finishes.

Standard cowhide cuts

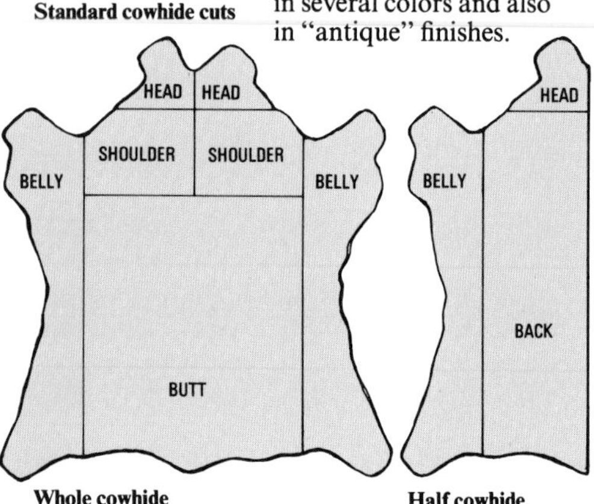

Whole cowhide

Half cowhide

Ordering skivers

When ordering a skiver, it is important to give the exact dimensions of the recess in which it is to be laid. Note all dimensions and angles, and preferably provide an accurate template with the top face clearly marked. A template is essential if you plan to cover a curved or shaped surface, and can be used to indicate the preferred position of any decorative tooling. A professional cutter will allow for a trimming margin and may make slight adjustments to the position of tooling to disguise imperfections or add lines of tooling to hide joins.

TOOLING

Inlaid-leather desk tops are often decorated with gold tooling, the gold being imprinted into an embossed pattern.

You can buy embossing punches and rollers from craft shops. However, for the best results, have leather professionally tooled.

Typical tooling patterns

LAYING A LEATHER SKIVER SURFACE

Skiver leather is often used for writing slopes, desks and bureaus, and as a decorative feature on coffee or wine tables. It is also sometimes used to line cabinets or presentation boxes and as a decorative facing for cabinet or drawer fronts.

Traditionally, leather writing surfaces and panel facings were applied using thin hide glue or a cold-water paste. However, diluted PVA glue (four parts glue to one part water) is now more commonly used.

You can inset the leather into a desk top by creating a recess for it using a router **(1)** or frame it with solid-wood lippings **(2)**. Alternatively, a cushioned effect can be obtained by cutting a radiused V-groove around the perimeter of the writing area **(3)**, pressing and gluing the edge of the leather into the groove.

When fitting a tooled skiver, before trimming make sure that it is accurately aligned within the recess (allowing for equal margins outside the tooling pattern). First trim one long edge using a craft knife and, having covered the surface of the wood with PVA glue, gently press the trimmed edge into the recess **(4)**.

Rub down the skiver with a clean folded felt pad – working along to each end, then across the center to the opposite edge **(5)**, and last of all to the sides and corners. Gently smooth out any wrinkles or bubbles, without stretching the leather, until a taut flat surface is obtained.

The three remaining edges can now be trimmed. Either use a straightedge as a guide or mark the cut lines on the leather by carefully indenting along the edges of the recess with the corner of a wooden ruler **(6)**. Then cut to fit **(7)**, avoiding scraping or cutting into the surrounding wood. While the glue is drying, check periodically for blisters and rub down any that appear.

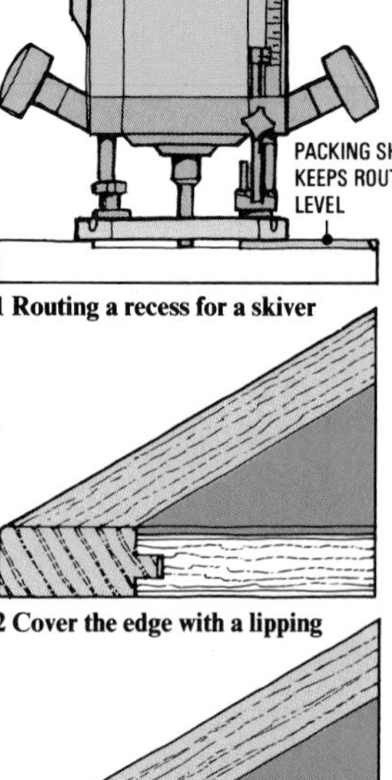

1 Routing a recess for a skiver

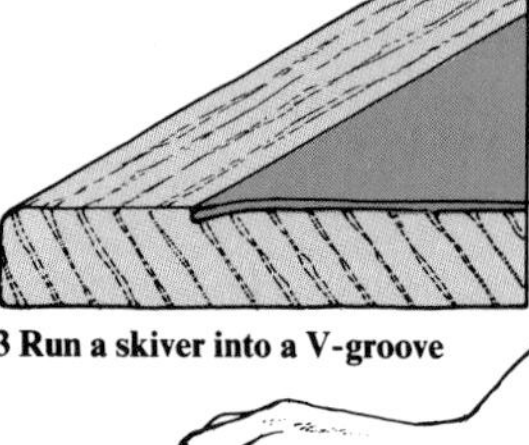

2 Cover the edge with a lipping

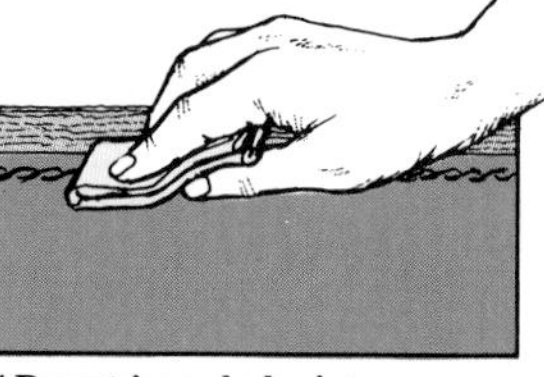

3 Run a skiver into a V-groove

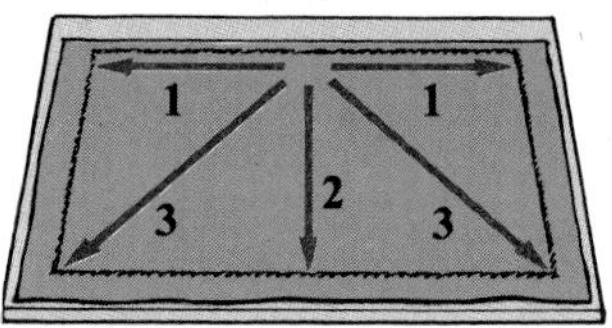

4 Press trimmed edge into recess

5 Rub outward toward edges

6 Mark uncut edges with a ruler

7 Cut edges to fit recess

CHAPTER THIRTEEN

SUPPLIES & FITTINGS

The following pages provide a guide to the supplies and fittings that eventually find their way into just about every home workshop. Screws and nails are needed so regularly, for DIY purposes as well as woodworking projects, that it makes sense to maintain a permanent stock of useful sizes and gauges. Fittings such as handles, locks and good-quality hinges, on the other hand, are often relatively expensive, so it is best to buy them as the need arises. Joining with adhesive is without a doubt the most common method of construction used in woodworking and, given the specialized properties of many modern glues, you will probably find yourself accumulating a range of different types. However, not all glues have a long shelf life. As a result, an almost full can of adhesive that you have had in store for some time may prove to be unusable when you need it again. So, although it may seem cheaper to buy glue in bulk, you may find that bulk buying is not truly economical unless you are planning numerous projects.

WOODWORKING ADHESIVES

For centuries, glue has been used to join wood to wood without the need for mechanical reinforcement. But if you examine old furniture, you will discover that these early glues had distinct disadvantages – notably a tendency to break down due to the presence of moisture, allowing the joints to become loose. Today, woodworkers are able to select from a range of excellent adhesives with different properties, such as resistance to heat or moisture, slow drying, long pot life or fast setting, most of them capable of forming a bond so tough that the glue line is stronger than the surrounding wood fibers.

SEE ALSO

Clamps	120-122
Safety glasses	214
Hand veneering	263
Glue film	264
Using contact cement	264

Hide glues

The traditional woodworker's glue is still made using animal skins and bone to provide the protein that gives this type of glue its adhesive quality. Hide glue was once the staple woodworking adhesive, but today it is rarely used except for hand-laid veneers, where its thermoplastic quality is especially advantageous.

Hide glue is usually supplied in the form of "pearls" or fine granules, ready for dissolving in water in a jacketed glue pot heated either by electricity or on a gas burner. A slower-setting hide glue is also available, which is liquid at room temperature, but this type of glue has a shelf life of little more than one year, after which it will not dry hard.

Hide glues are nontoxic. They form a hard glue line that can be planed and sanded, and they can be resoftened with the application of heat or moisture – a boon for the furniture restorer, though their susceptibility to heat and moisture sometimes leads to structural failure.

Hot-melt glues

Hot-melt glue is sold in the form of cylindrical sticks for application using a special-purpose electrically heated "gun." This type of adhesive is convenient to use and sets within seconds, which makes it ideal for constructing mock-ups and jigs. Different sticks are available for gluing materials other than wood.

Hot-melt glue is also made in thin sheets for veneering. The glue is laid between the veneer and groundwork, then activated by a heated household iron.

Hot-melt-glue gun
Squeezing the trigger melts the glue and drives it out of the nozzle.

Jacketed glue pot

Pearl glue

PVA adhesives

Polyvinyl-acetate (PVA) "white glue" is one of the cheapest and most convenient woodworking adhesives on the market. It is an emulsion of PVA suspended in water that sets when the water evaporates or is absorbed into the wood.

An excellent general-purpose nontoxic wood glue, it has an almost indefinite shelf life, so long as it is kept in reasonably warm conditions. The tough, semi-flexible glue line can creep, though usually only when a joint is subjected to stress over a prolonged period. Standard white glue is not water-resistant, but there is a fully waterproof exterior-grade version.

A slightly thicker, yellow aliphatic-resin PVA glue dries to a less resilient glue line that is resistant to heat and moisture. Unlike white glue, it sands well without clogging sandpaper. You can also buy PVA glues modified to increase gap-filling capacity or to give a slower setting rate for large-scale assemblies.

Urea-formaldehyde adhesives

Urea-formaldehyde glue is an excellent water-resistant gap-filling adhesive that cures by chemical reaction. It can be obtained in a powdered form that, once it has been mixed with water, is applied to both mating surfaces.

Some urea-formaldehyde glues are made to be used in conjunction with a separate liquid catalyst or "hardener." The hardener is applied to one half of the joint and the powdered glue mixed with water is spread onto the other. Clamp the work once the joint is closed.

Wear protective gloves and glasses when handling the uncured materials, and work in a well-ventilated workshop.

Resorcinol-resin glues

Similar in many ways to urea-formaldehyde adhesive, resorcinol-resin glue is completely waterproof and weather-resistant. It is a two-part glue comprising a resin and a separate hardener. Some manufacturers supply both the resin and hardener as liquids; other glues are supplied with one component in powdered form. In each case, the resin and hardener are mixed together before applying the glue to both surfaces of the joint. The cured adhesive forms a reddish-brown glue line that may be noticeable on pale-colored woods. Setting time is accelerated by hot weather and the adhesive may not cure at all at temperatures much below 60°F (15°C). When handling the uncured glue, wear hand and eye protection and ventilate the workshop.

USING ADHESIVE

Contact cements

A contact cement is spread as a thin layer on both mating surfaces. After the glue has set, the two components are brought together and the bond is instant. Modified versions allow the positions of the components to be adjusted until pressure is applied with a block of wood or a roller, causing the glue to bond. This type of adhesive is used extensively for gluing melamine laminates to kitchen counter tops, but soft thixotropic (gel-like) versions are also used for applying wood veneers. Solvent-based glues set quickly, but they are extremely flammable and emit unpleasant fumes. Use them in a well-ventilated workshop only. Water-based contact cements are safer but take longer to dry.

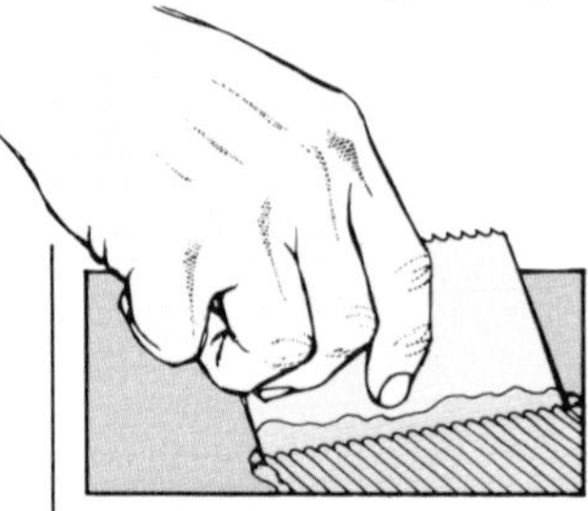

Spread contact cement thinly

Epoxy-resin adhesives

Epoxy adhesive is a synthetic two-part glue consisting of a resin and hardener, normally mixed in equal proportions just before application. The most common form of epoxy glue – sold in tubes – is a general-purpose adhesive for joining diverse materials. As it is relatively thick, it is not really suitable for woodwork except for rub-jointing. However, liquid versions of the adhesive are made for gluing wood. Epoxy glues cure by chemical reaction to form a very strong, insoluble, transparent glue line. Standard epoxy adhesive sets hard in a few hours, but fast-setting glues are also available. Wipe uncured glue from the surface of a workpiece, using a cloth dampened with rubbing alcohol. Epoxy glues may irritate sensitive skin.

A well-prepared joint is essential if glue is to be effective. The joining surfaces must be clean, grease-free, flat and smooth. Roughing them to provide a better "key" is not recommended for wood joints.

Moisture content

The moisture content of the wood can affect the quality of a joint. If it is more than about 20 percent, for example, some glues may never set satisfactorily; and if it is less than 5 percent, the glue may be absorbed too quickly and the bond will be poor.

Applying adhesives

Unless the manufacturer's instructions suggest otherwise, it is best to spread glue evenly but not too thickly onto both surfaces of a joint. This is especially important for joints like a mortise and tenon – where most of the adhesive can be scraped from the tenon as it is inserted, so that the joint is starved of glue.

Some two-part resin-and-hardener glues are applied differently. The resin is spread onto one half of the joint, and the hardener applied to the other. Reaction does not begin until the joint is closed, providing plenty of time to assemble large or complicated workpieces.

Applying glue to a mortise
Unless adhesive is applied to a mortise, the whole joint can be starved of glue.

Clamping glued joints
Most glued joints must be clamped while the adhesive sets.

Clamping joints

Most joints have to be clamped while the glue sets. This brings the joining surfaces in close contact and squeezes excess glue from the joint. Wipe glue from around the assembled joint with a damp cloth before it sets. A few minutes later, return to the assembly to check whether hydraulic pressure within the joint has forced out more glue. If it has, give the clamp screws an extra turn and wipe away the excess glue.

Making a rubbed joint
Rubbing two glued components together achieves a close-fitting butt joint without the use of clamps.

Rub-jointing

A close-fitting butt joint will often bond satisfactorily under atmospheric pressure, without clamping. This is achieved by wetting both surfaces with glue, then rubbing them together to squeeze glue and air out of the joint while aligning the components. This is known as a rubbed joint.

APPLICATORS

Unless an adhesive is sold with a specific applicator, spread glue with a brush, flat stick or roller. When mixing adhesive, always follow the manufacturer's recommendations.

Glue brush
A wire bridle stiffens the bristles of a glue brush. It is removed when the bristles wear down.

Glue syringe
Use a plastic syringe to apply an exact amount of woodworking adhesive when you need to glue inaccessible joints.

WOOD SCREWS

Wood screws are primarily used for joining wood to wood, the clamping force they provide creating an extremely strong joint that is easily dismantled. They are also used for attaching fittings such as hinges, locks and handles. Most screws are made of steel, which is sometimes case-hardened for extra strength. Brass screws are more decorative and stainless-steel screws resist corrosion even outdoors. Both can be used in acidic woods such as oak that are stained by ordinary steel hardware. Steel screws may be zinc coated to prevent corrosion, and chrome plating and black japanning are used as decorative coatings. The common types shown here illustrate the principles. In addition, there are a number of other specialized head profiles and drive shapes, the square-recess Robertson pattern being just one example. The most widely known cross-head screw is Phillips, although there are several others.

SEE ALSO

Screwdriver bits	113,127
Nail punch	115
Hammers	115-117
Pulling nails	117
Screwdrivers	118-119
Inserting wood screws	119
Butt joints	216-217
Miter joints	217
Rabbet joints	218

SCREW SIZES

The specified length of a screw corresponds to the part of it that actually enters the wood as shown in the drawing at left. This measurement can be anywhere from ¼ to 6in (6 to 150mm). Select a screw that is about three times as long as the thickness of the piece of wood or board it is to secure. Even if a screw is not long enough to burst through the back of a workpiece, it will deform the wood fibers, creating a noticeable bulge in the wood, unless you make sure the point stops at least ⅛in (3mm) short of the surface.

Screws are also specified by their nominal diameter or "gauge." This is never described using a precise measurement. Instead, screw gauges are specified by numbers from 0 to 20 – the higher the number, the larger the screw. A No5 screw, for example, is about ⅛in (3mm) in diameter and a No14 screw is about ¼in (6mm). For strength, select the largest possible gauge, though the nominal diameter of the screw should never exceed one tenth of the width of wood into which it is to be inserted. The table of wood-screw sizes below shows the lengths commonly available in the various gauges.

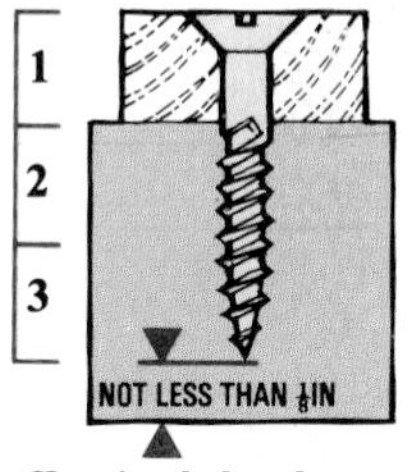

How screws are measured

Conventional wood screws
About 60 percent of the overall length of a conventional wood screw is threaded. The plain cylindrical shank of a wood screw acts like a dowel and is surmounted by a wider head that holds the workpiece or attachment in place.

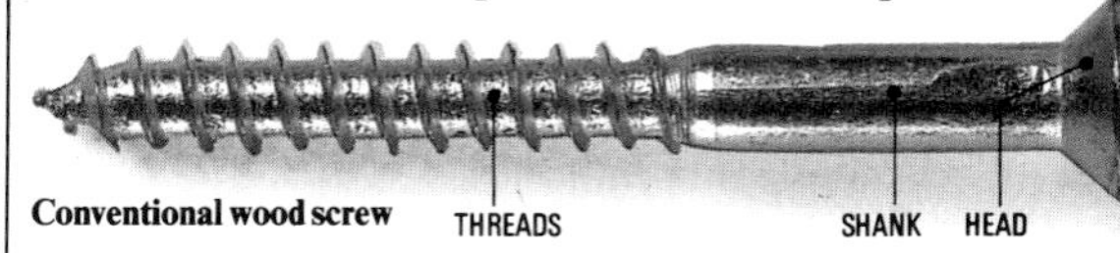

Conventional wood screw

Twin-threaded screws
A newer generation of wood screws is made with coarse twin threads that provide a strong hold even in chipboard or MDF. Compared with a conventional screw, more of the overall length is threaded and the shank is much narrower so there is less risk of splitting the wood. The steep pitch of the threads enables the screw to be driven quickly.

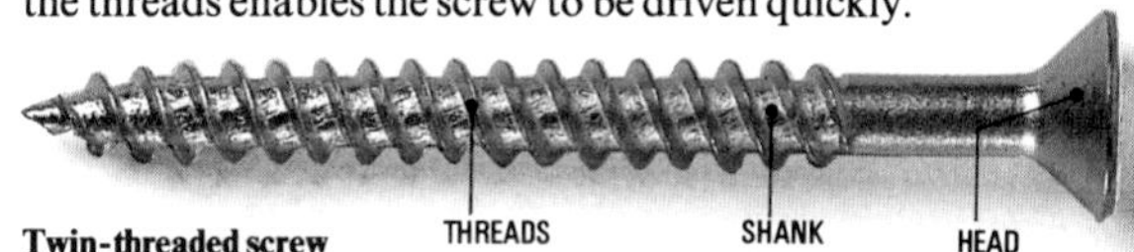

Twin-threaded screw

1
2
3
NOT LESS THAN ⅛IN

Choosing the length of a screw
A screw should be three times as long as the thickness of the wood it is to secure.

Pilot holes
To prevent the wood from splitting, drill a pilot hole in the work to guide a screw. Use a drill bit that is slightly narrower than the width of the screw thread.

WOOD-SCREW SIZES

LENGTH																	
IMPERIAL	METRIC	GAUGE NUMBER															
¼in	6mm	0	1	2	3	4											
⅜in	9mm	0	1	2	3	4	5	6		8							
½in	12mm		1	2	3	4	5	6	7	8							
⅝in	16mm				3	4	5	6	7	8		10					
¾in	18mm				3	4	5	6	7	8	9	10	12				
⅞in	22mm					4		6	7	8							
1in	25mm				3	4	5	6	7	8	9	10	12	14			
1¼in	32mm					4	5	6	7	8	9	10	12	14			
1½in	38mm					4		6	7	8	9	10	12	14	16		
1¾in	44mm							6	7	8	9	10	12	14	16		
2in	50mm							6	7	8	9	10	12	14	16	18	20
2¼in	57mm							6		8		10	12	14			
2½in	63mm							6		8	9	10	12	14	16		
2¾in	70mm									8		10	12	14			
3in	75mm							6		8		10	12	14	16	18	20
3½in	89mm									8		10	12	14	16		
4in	100mm									8		10	12	14	16	18	20
4½in	112mm											10	12	14			20
5in	125mm											10	12	14	16		
6in	150mm												12	14	16		

SCREW SLOTS

Screw slots (the recesses cut in screw heads) are designed to accommodate the tip of a particular type of screwdriver.

Slotted screw
Has a single groove machined across the head for a straight-tipped screwdriver.

Cross-head screw
Has intersecting slots designed to accept the tip of a matching screwdriver.

Clutch-head screw
A 'thief-proof' screw, used for fixing locks or securing valuable objects. Inserted with an ordinary straight-tipped screwdriver, but the tip rides out when the driver is turned counterclockwise.

Slotted screw   Cross-head screw   Clutch-head screw

SCREW HEADS

Most screws are made with a choice of heads. The three most popular are shown below.

Flat head
A flat-topped head, which lies flush with the surface of the work. It fits into a tapered recess.
Oval head
Fits into a similar recess, but has a slightly domed top. Often used if the head will be exposed.
Round head
Normally used to fix flat sheet material to wood. Has an appreciably domed top, but a flat underside.

Flat head   Oval head   Round head

SCREW CUPS AND COVERS

Many woodworkers regard exposed screw heads as unsightly, but there are several types of fitting that conceal screw heads or enhance their appearance.

Recessed screw cup
A durable brass collar for removable countersunk screws. Lies flush with the surface of the wood.
Surface-mounted screw cup
Made from pressed brass. Provides a raised collar for flat-head or oval-head screws. Ideal for softwood, since it increases the bearing area beneath the screw head.
Domed cover
A plastic "dome" that snaps over the rim of a matching screw cup to hide the head of a wood screw.
Cross-head cover
A molded plastic cover with spigots on the underside that provide a tight friction fit in screw slots.
Mirror-screw cover
A chromed brass dome with a threaded spigot that screws into the top of special flat-head screws designed to hold mirror glass.

Screw cups and covers
1 Recessed screw cup
2 Surface-mounted screw cup
3 Domed cover
4 Cross-head cover
5 Mirror-screw cover

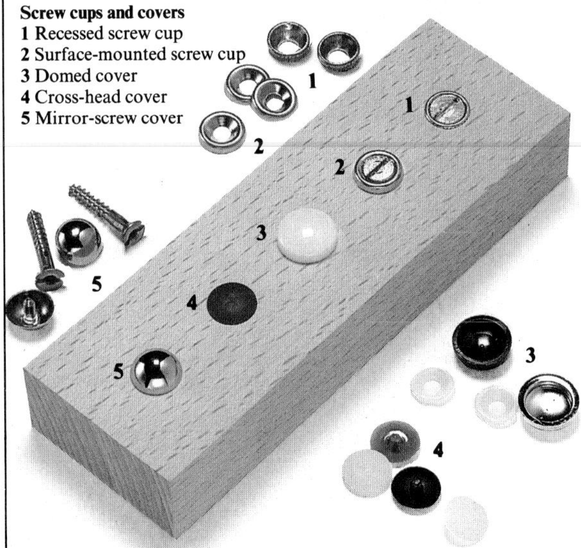

NAILS

A wide variety of nails are made for the building industry, but woodworkers generally use only a limited range, mainly for constructing mock-ups and nailing man-made boards. Specialized tacks and nails are required for attaching upholstery to wooden underframes. The sizes given below are those most commonly available.

Round wire nail
A strong fixing used for rough carpentry and for constructing mock-ups.
Finish: Bright steel or with various coatings and platings.
Size: 1 to 6in (25 to 150mm).

Oval wire nail
Popular in Britain and Europe, a general-purpose nail with an oval-section shank that is designed to reduce the risk of splitting wood. Its head can be punched below the surface.
Finish: Bright steel.
Size: 1 to 6in (25 to 150mm).

Finishing nail
A nail that has a narrow shank. Used in making large butt joints and miters. The head is punched below the surface.
Finish: Bright steel or with various coatings and platings.
Size: 1½ to 4in (40 to 100mm).

Brad
Used for securing thin plywood or hardboard and for securing small joints.
Finish: Bright steel.
Size: ½ to 2in (12 to 50mm).

Corrugated fastener
This device is used when making miters and butt joints for rough framing. Placed across the joint line, the fastener is driven flush with the surface of the wood.
Finish: Bright steel.
Size: ¼ to ⅞in (6 to 22mm) deep.

Wood connector
Spiked metal plate used for securing framework joints. The plate is placed across the joint line and the spikes are driven or pressed into the wood.
Finish: Galvanized steel.
Size: 1 x 5in (25 x 125mm) to 7 x 14in (175 x 350mm).

Cut tack
This nail is designed for attaching fabric to an upholstered underframe. Its sharp point is pushed into the wood, ready for driving. The wide head grips the fabric.
Finish: Blued steel.
Size: ½ to 1¼in (12 to 30mm).

Upholstery nail
With decorative head for upholstery fabric or braid.
Finish: Brass, chrome or bronze.
Size: ½in (12mm).

Gimp pin
These small tacks are for the "invisible" fixing of upholstery braid.
Finish: Various colors to match braid.
Size: ⅜ and ½in (9 and 13mm).

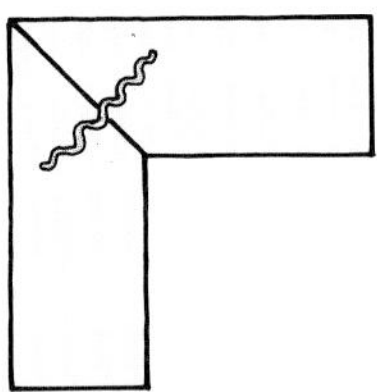

Corrugated fastener
Drive this fastener across a joint

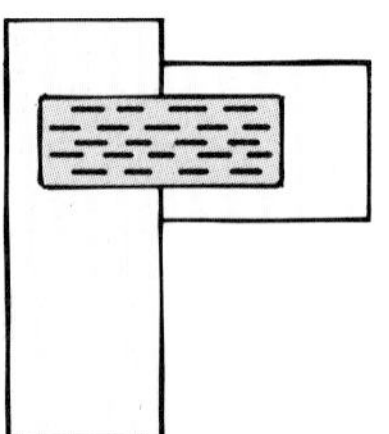

Wood connector
This plate makes a strong butt joint

Nails and fixings
1 Brads
2 Round wire nail
3 Oval wire nail
4 Finishing nail
5 Corrugated fastener
6 Wood connector
7 Cut tacks
8 Upholstery nail
9 Gimp pins

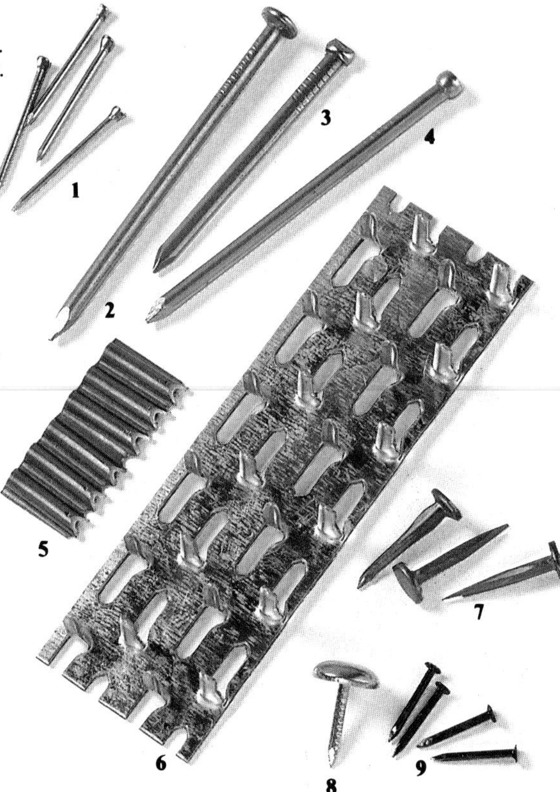

HINGES

Well-made hinges for cabinet doors and fall flaps are relatively expensive, but cheap hardware with loose knuckles, shallow screw recesses and insubstantial leaves can be troublesome and may ruin the appearance of an otherwise handsome piece.

SEE ALSO	
Drop-leaf tables	58-59
Pembroke table	59
Folding-top tables	60
Cupboard doors	66-68
Fall flaps	67
Built-in storage	72-73
Hand tools	76-122
Drill presses	188-189
Wood screws	304-305

Piano hinge
A piano hinge, made in continuous 6ft 6in (2m) lengths, is used where an especially strong fitting is required. The hinge is cut to fit the workpiece.

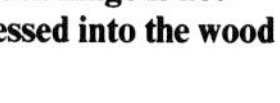

A flush hinge is not recessed into the wood

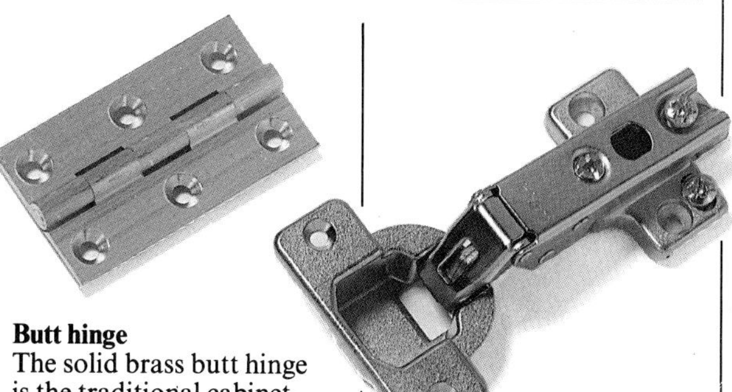

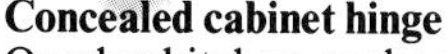

Butt hinge
The solid brass butt hinge is the traditional cabinetmaker's hinge. Broad-suite butt hinges – which have relatively wide leaves – are suitable for wardrobes and large cupboards. Narrow-suite hinges are used for small cabinets and boxes. Butt hinges can be used to hang inset and overlay doors.

Lift-off hinge
Lift-off hinges are used when it is necessary on occasion to be able to remove a hinged component such as a dressing-table side mirror. A good hinge is made of solid brass, usually with a steel pin. Left-hand and right-hand versions are made.

Flush hinge
A flush hinge is used for the same purposes as a butt hinge but for lightweight doors only. This type of hinge is easy to fit, as it does not have to be recessed into the wood.

Concealed cabinet hinge
Overlay kitchen-cupboard doors are usually hung using modern concealed hinges, since these fittings are capable of adjustment so that a row of doors can be aligned accurately. Most concealed hinges have a circular boss, which fits into a hole drilled in the door, and a baseplate that screws to the cabinet. These hinges are designed to allow a door to be opened without colliding with another door butted next to it. Spring-loaded versions keep the door closed.

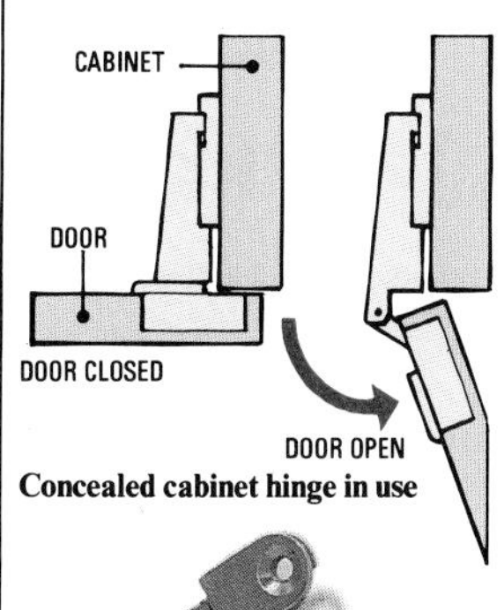

Concealed cabinet hinge in use

Soss invisible hinge
Used in the same situations as a cylinder hinge but for heavier-weight doors.

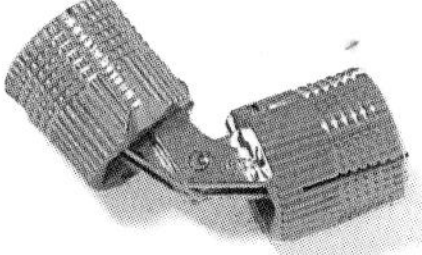

Cylinder hinge
This hinge allows a door to be opened a full 180 degrees, so is especially suitable for bifold or concertina doors. It can also be used for hanging normal inset or overlay doors. Fitted into holes drilled in the wood, cylinder hinges are invisible when the door is closed.

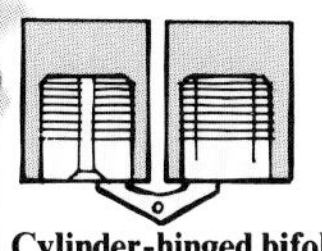

Cylinder-hinged bifold doors

Cranked hinge
The cranked hinge is used for fine cabinetwork with overlay doors. The door can be swung through an arc of 180 degrees.

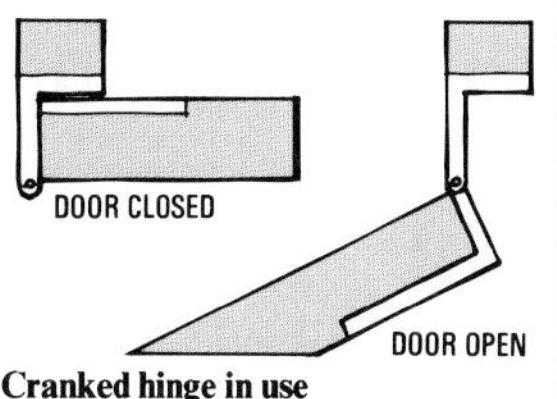

Cranked hinge in use

Flush-fitting flap hinge
This type of adjustable hinge allows an overlay fall flap to lie flush when open.

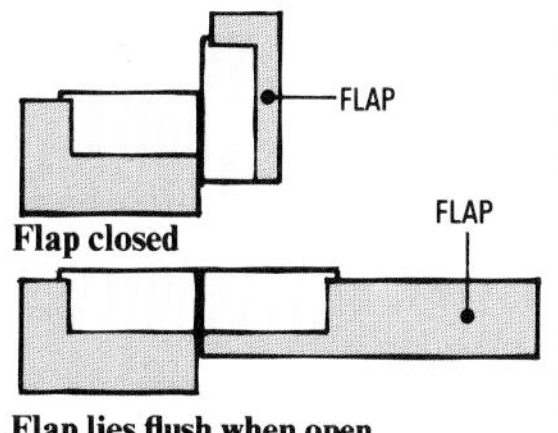

Flap closed

Flap lies flush when open

Backflap hinge
With its wide leaves recessed into the wood, the traditional solid-brass backflap hinge is used for attaching bureau fall flaps.

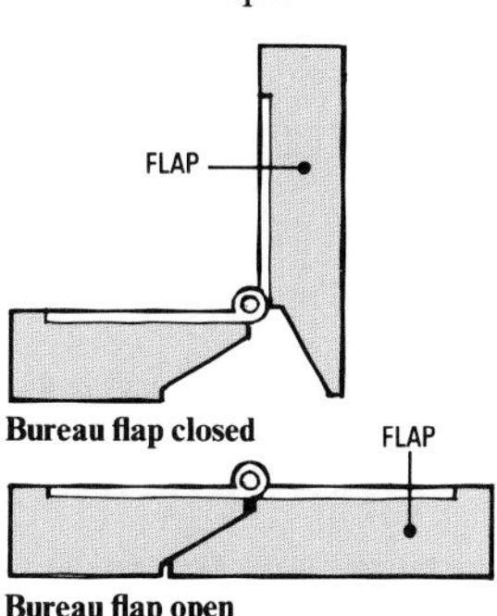

Bureau flap closed

Bureau flap open

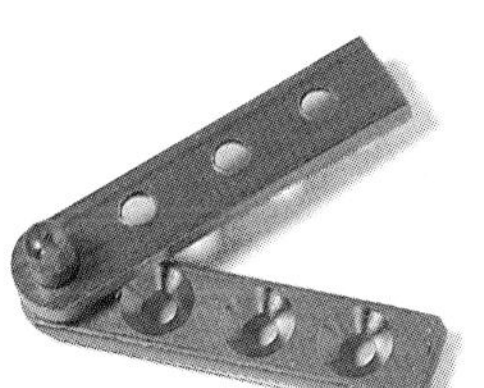

Knife hinge
Recessed into the edge of a door, lid or fall flap, this type of hinge is practically invisible when closed.

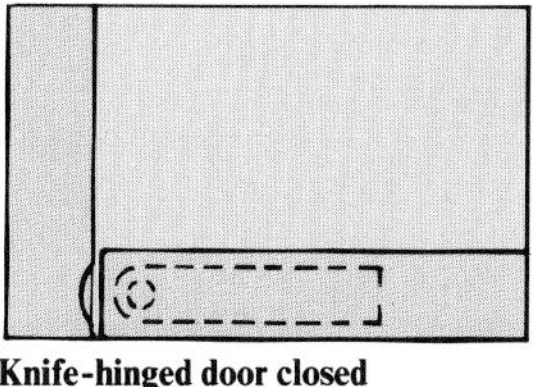

Knife-hinged door closed

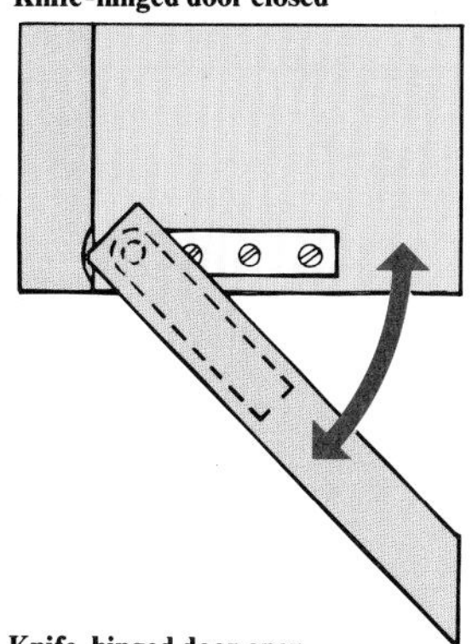

Knife-hinged door open

LOCKS AND CATCHES

Small, finely made locks are fitted to furniture and boxes. However, they do not provide total security – merely some degree of privacy, since most furniture locks can be forced. For everyday storage, a simple catch avoids the inconvenience of having to use a key.

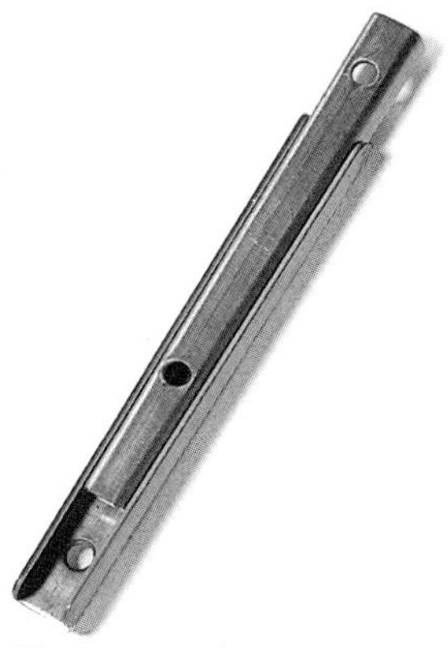

Taper connector
The taper connector is a crude but effective concealed way to hang wall cupboards or large-frame constructions. Since the two parts of the connector are dovetail-shaped as well as tapered, sliding one part into the other locks them securely together.

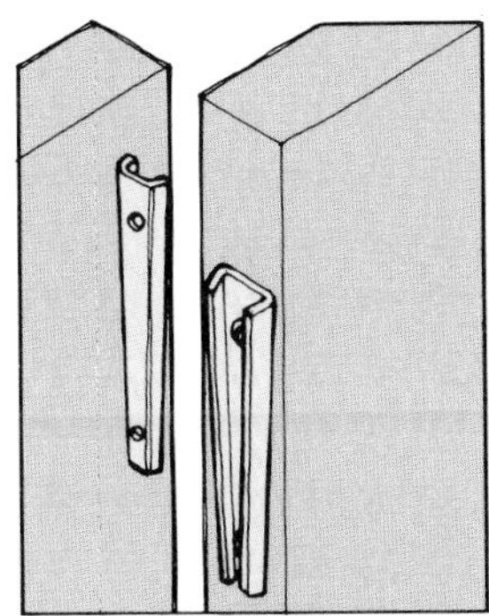

Disassembled taper connector

Bolt and barrel nut
This fixing is so strong and positive that it is used to join table and chair frames. The bolt passes through the upright or leg into the end of the rail, where it meets a threaded hole in the barrel nut. Wooden locating dowels in the end grain keep the rail aligned correctly as the bolt is tightened up with an Allen wrench.

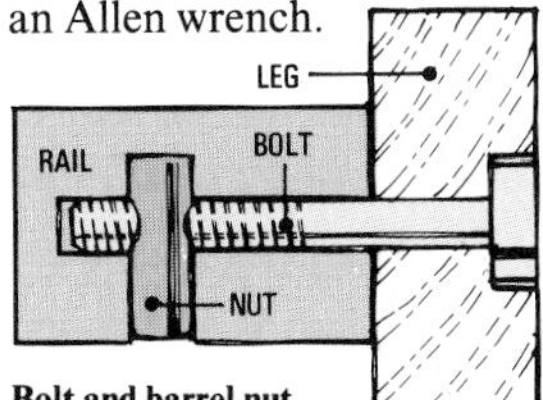

Bolt and barrel nut

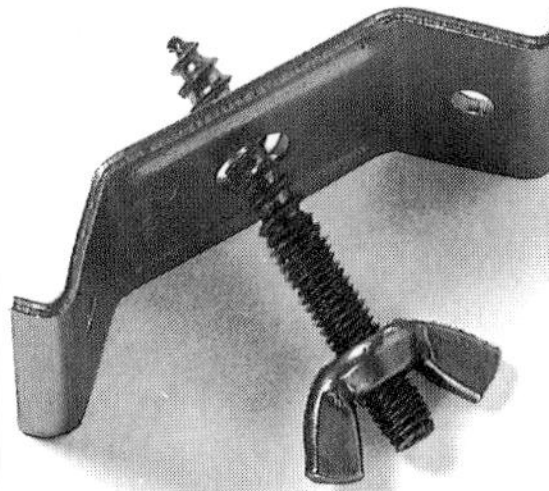

Corner plates
Metal corner plates are used to join table rails at each corner. Flanges on each side of the plate locate in narrow grooves cut into the rails, and wood screws hold the assembly firmly together. A hanger bolt screwed into the chamfered inner corner of the table leg passes through the hole in the plate and is tightened with a wing nut, pulling the leg against the square-cut shoulders of the rails.

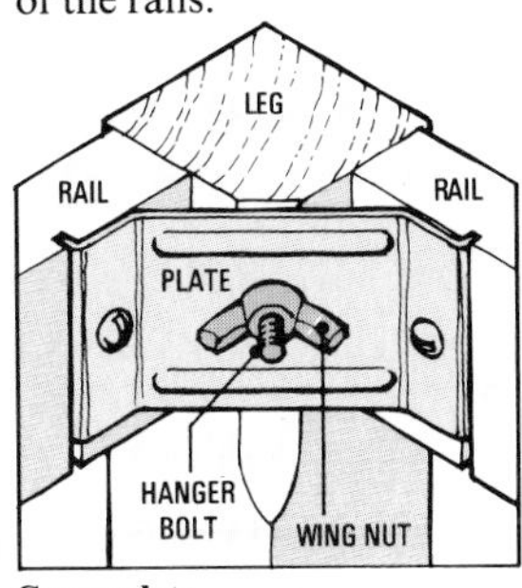

Corner plate

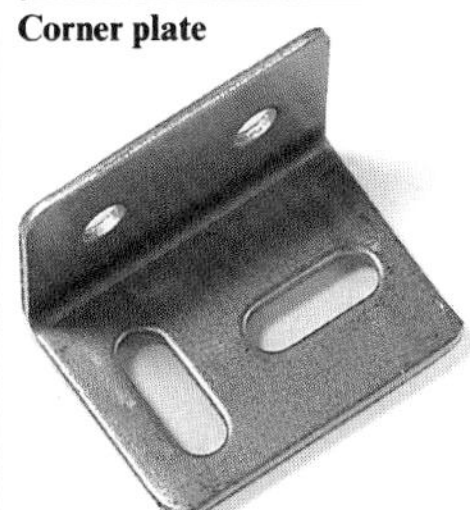

Shrinkage plates
These right-angle plates are designed for attaching a solid-wood table top to its underframe while allowing for the natural shrinkage of the wood. Each plate is screwed to the inside of a rail flush with its top edge. A round-head wood screw is driven into the top through whichever slot in the plate runs across the grain.

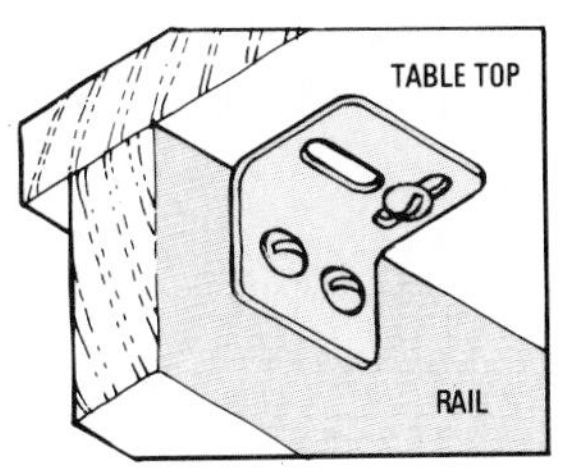

Shrinkage plate

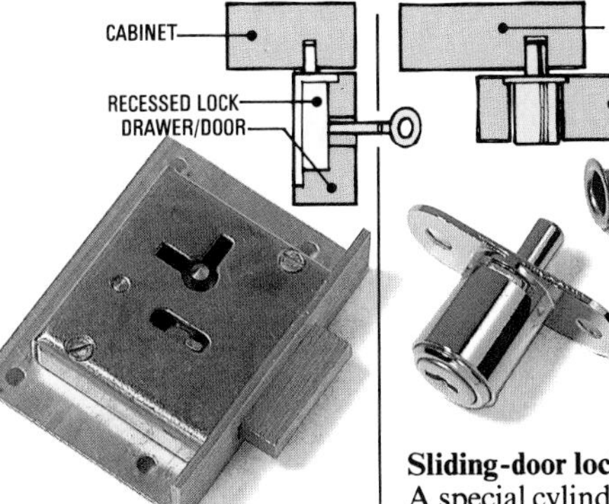

Cabinet lock
The traditional cabinet lock is used to secure drawers and cupboards. A surface-mounted lock is screwed directly to the inside of an overlay door or drawer. When either is inset, it is possible to fit a neater recessed lock that lies flush with the surface of the wood. A similar lock for boxes with lift-up lids has a striker plate with hooked pins that are engaged by the lock mechanism. Cabinet locks are often made with two keyholes at right angles to each other so they can be mounted horizontally or vertically. Left-hand and right-hand versions are available.

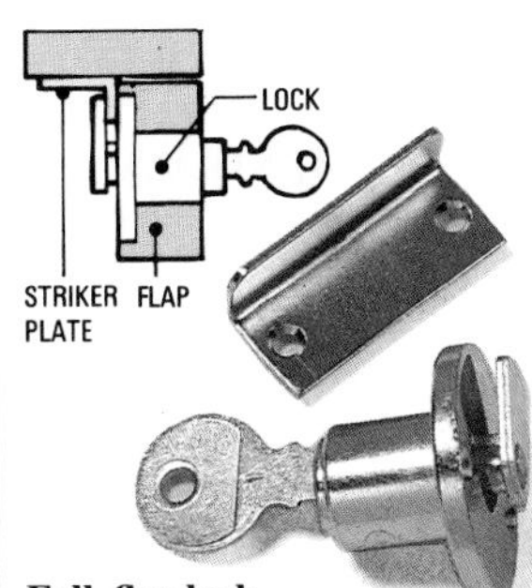

Fall-flap lock
The fall-flap cylinder lock is designed to lie perfectly flush with the inside surface of a fold-down bureau or counter flap. The key, which can only be removed when the flap is closed, is pushed in and turned to operate a spring-loaded bolt.

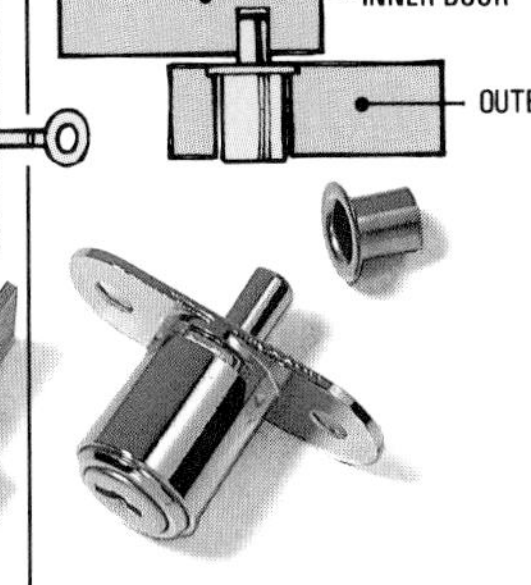

Sliding-door lock
A special cylinder lock is required to secure overlapping sliding doors. The lock, which is fitted to the outer door, is operated by a push button that sends a bolt into a socket recessed in the inner door. A turn of a key withdraws the bolt.

Escutcheons
An escutcheon is a small decorative metal plate used to surround a keyhole cut in wood. Most escutcheons are pinned to the surface, but there are also small unobtrusive recessed versions.

Magnetic catch
Small encased magnets are screwed to the inside of a carcase side panel or located in a hole drilled in its edge. The magnet attracts a flat metal striker plate attached to the cupboard door.

Ball catch
This catch comprises a spring-loaded steel ball trapped in a cylindrical brass case that is inserted in the edge of a cupboard door. When the door is closed, the ball springs into a recess in a metal striker plate screwed to the carcase.

Magnetic touch latch
A cupboard fitted with a touch latch doesn't need a handle. Pressure on the door operates a spring that pushes the door open.

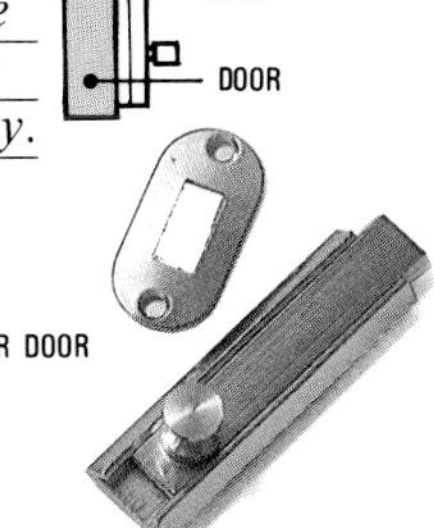

Door bolt
On a twin-door cupboard, one door is often fitted with a pair of neat surface-mounted or flush bolts and the other with a lock or catch.

Magnetic catch

Ball catch

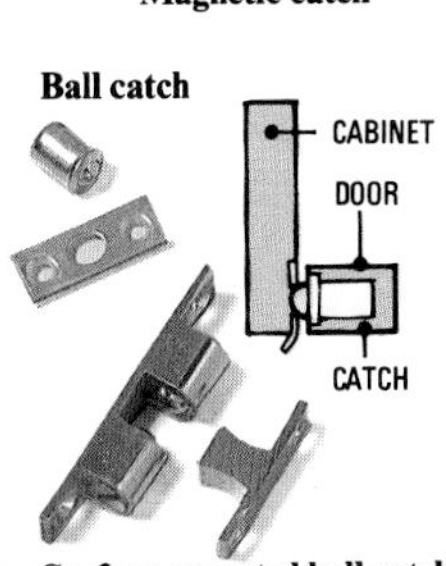

Surface-mounted ball catch

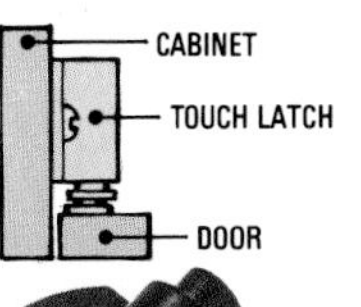

Magnetic touch latch

STAYS AND HANDLES

A stay is a mechanism designed primarily to support a fall flap in a horizontal position, taking the strain off the hinges. However, stays are also used to stop a hinged door from opening more than 90 degrees and to support chest lids or high-level lift-up doors.

Handles are essentially functional pieces of hardware, but they have always been used as decorative features to enhance the appearance of drawers and cabinets. Select an appropriate size and shape to suit the style and scale of your workpiece.

SEE ALSO

Cupboard doors	66-68
Drawers	71
Built-in storage	72-73
Wood screws	304-305

Cabinet handle
The classic cabinet handle is suspended from two pivots, one at each end. It is available in a variety of forms, including the distinctive swan-neck handle and the stronger and even more decorative plate handle.

Drop handle
A single teardrop-shaped or decorative finger grip is suspended from the center of a drop handle. A drop handle is often fitted in the center of a small drawer.

Ring pull
This is similar in construction to a drop handle, but the ring hangs from the top of a backing plate.

Door or drawer knob
Traditional rounded door or drawer knobs are made in wood, metal and ceramic in a variety of sizes to suit furniture ranging from wardrobes to collectors' cabinets. The method of attachment may be a screw projecting from the back of the knob or, alternatively, an ordinary wood screw or a machine screw passed through the cabinet front into the knob.

Flush handle
A pivoted ring or D-shaped handle lies flush with a thick solid-brass backing plate, which is recessed into the drawer front and fixed with countersunk wood screws.

Drawer pull
One-piece cupped drawer pulls were originally used on military chests. They serve as strong screw-fixed handles for cupboards and chests of drawers.

D-handle
These slim metal, plastic or wooden handles suit simple modern-style furniture. They are invariably made with threaded inserts for machine-screw attachment.

Sliding-door handle
Circular or rectangular recessed finger grips are made for gluing into overlapping sliding doors.

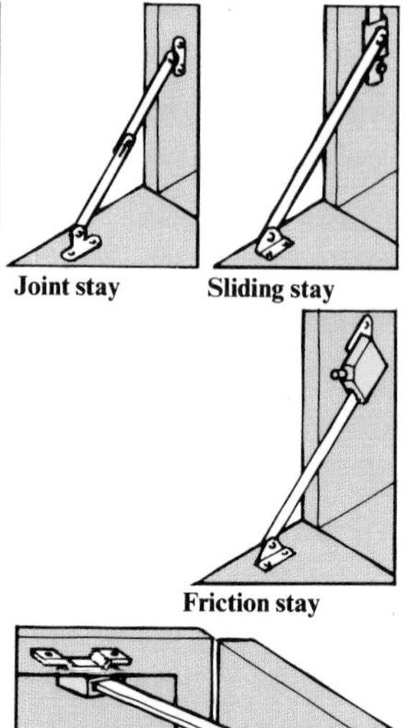

Joint stay

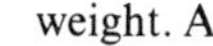

Sliding stay

Friction stay

Door stay

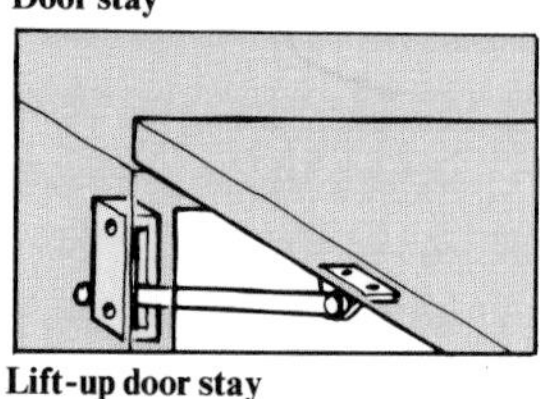

Lift-up door stay

Fall-flap stays
The simplest fall-flap stay is screwed at both ends and has a riveted joint approximately halfway along the arm that breaks to allow the stay to fold back into the cabinet. A better-quality version slides silently on a bar fixed either horizontally or vertically on the inside of the cabinet. A friction stay controls the movement of the flap so that it falls slowly and smoothly under its own weight. A small turnscrew regulates the amount of friction and consequently the rate at which the flap falls.

Door stay
A door stay prevents a cupboard door from being ripped off its hinges or opened too far by restricting its swing to a maximum of 90 degrees. A rigid metal arm, screwed to the door, slides through a pivoting nylon sleeve attached to the cabinet.

Lift-up door stays
Stays for lift-up doors or lids lock automatically when the door or lid is raised, and are released for closure by lifting it slightly before letting it fall. Friction stays that prevent doors or lids from slamming shut are also available.

Handles
1 Swan-neck cabinet handle
2 Plate handle
3 Ring pull
4 Drop handles
5 Drawer pull
6 Knobs
7 Flush handle
8 D-handles
9 Sliding-door handle

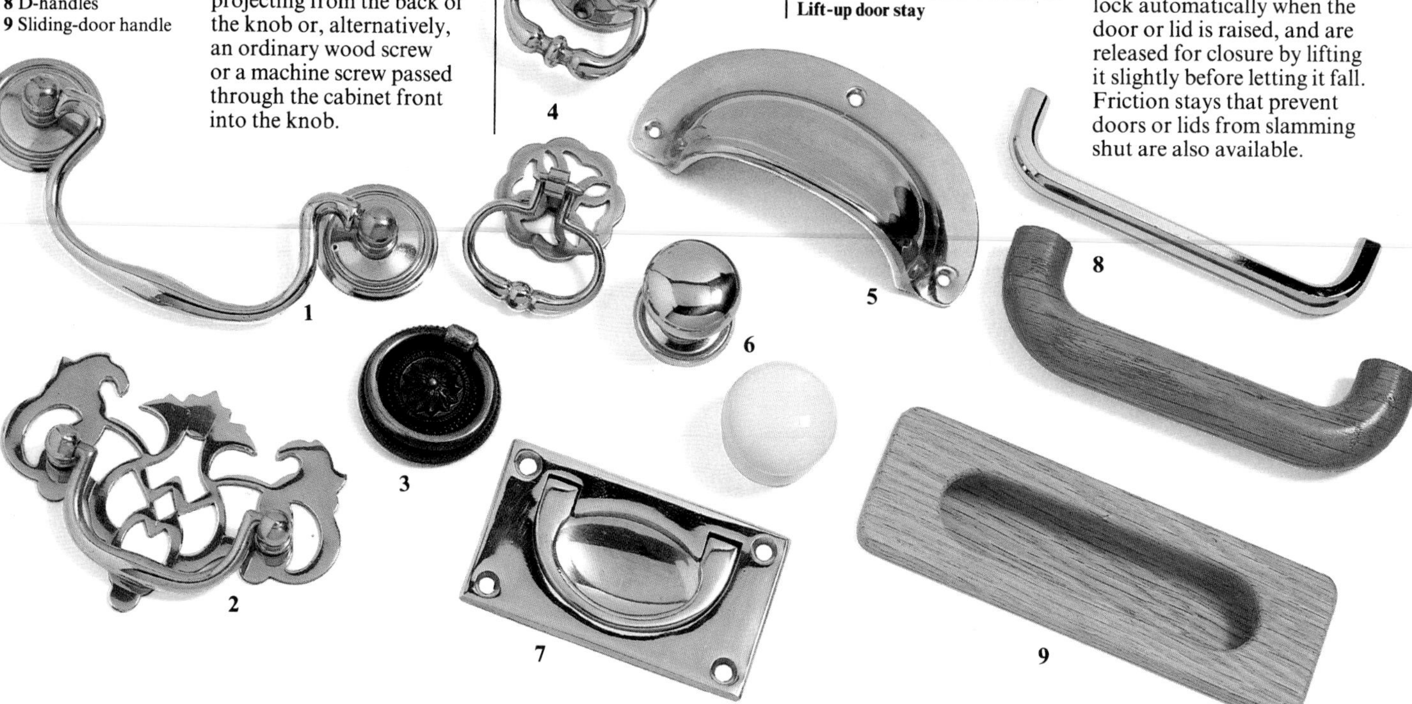

GLOSSARY OF TERMS

A

Air-drying
A method for seasoning wood that permits covered stacks of sawn wood to dry naturally in the open air.
Alloy
A mixture of two or more metals to create a composition with specific properties.
Anthropometry
The comparative study of the dimensions of the human body.
Arc
Part of an unbroken curved line as drawn by a compass.
Arris
The sharp edge where two surfaces meet at an angle.
Axis
The imaginary line about which an object such as a chair rail is symmetrical.

B

Backing grade
The category of cheaper veneers that are glued to the back of a board in order to balance better-quality veneers glued to the front face.
Banding
A plain or patterned strip of veneer used to make decorative borders.
Barefaced
The description of a joint that has one shoulder only.
Batten
A strip of wood.
Bead
A rounded convex shape turned on a lathe. *or* A fine molded strip of wood, also known as beading.
Bench dog
A metal or wooden peg inserted into one of a row of holes.
Bench stop
A flip-up tongue that is permanently inlaid into the bench top.
Bevel
A surface that meets another at an angle other than a right angle. *or* To cut such surfaces. *See also* chamfer.
Bifold door
A type of sliding door made from two hinged panels that fold as the door is slid sideways.
Bird's-mouth
A notched plate of metal or wood that is clamped or screwed to a bench so that the notch overhangs the edge. It is used to support work being cut with a piercing saw or scroll saw.
Blank
A piece of wood roughly cut to size ready for turning on a lathe.
Bleed
A process whereby a substance such as natural wood resin permeates and stains the surface of a subsequent coating.
Blister
A small raised area of veneer resulting from insufficient glue at that point.
Blockboard
A man-made building board with a core of approximately square-section solid-wood strips sandwiched between thin plywood sheets. *See also* laminboard.
Bore
To drill a hole.
Bowed
Twisted.
Bruise
To make a dent in wood by striking it with a hard object such as a hammer.
Burl
A warty growth on the trunk of a tree. When sliced it produces speckled veneer.
Burr
A thin hook of metal left along the cutting edge of a blade after honing or grinding.
Button
A wooden device screwed to the underside of a table top to fix it to an underframe.

C

Cabinetmaker
A manufacturer of good-quality furniture.
Cabriole leg
A furniture leg developed in the 18th century that is made with an upper convex curve that descends, tapering, to a concave curve.
Calibrated
Marked out with one or more scales of measurement.
Carpenter
A woodworker but not necessarily one who specializes in fine work.
Case-hardened
A term used to describe unevenly seasoned wood with residual uneven stresses throughout its thickness.
Catalyst
A substance that stimulates or increases the rate of a chemical reaction.
Cauls
Sheets of wood or metal used to press veneer onto groundwork.
Chamfer
A 45-degree bevel along the edge of a piece of wood or board. *or* To cut such bevels.
Chattering
The noise caused by a workpiece or tool vibrating.
Checks
Splits in wood caused by uneven seasoning. *See also* knife checks.
Chipboard
A mat of small particles of wood and glue compressed into a flat building board.
Claw
A split hammer peen used to grip a nail by its head and lever it out of a piece of wood.
Clear wood
Good-quality wood that is free from defects.
Closed-coat
A term used to describe sandpaper that has abrasive particles packed closely together.
Coarse-textured
See open grain.
Collet
A tapered sleeve made in two or more segments that grips the shaft of a cutter.
Comb-grain
Another term for quartersawn.
Compound miter
A miter that is angled in two planes.
Concave
Curving inwards.
Contact cement
An adhesive that bonds to itself without the aid of clamps when two previously glued surfaces are brought together.
Convex
Curving outwards.
Core
The central layer of plies, particles or wooden strips in a man-made board.
Counterbore
To cut a hole that permits the head of a bolt or screw to lie below the surface of a piece of wood. *or* The hole itself.

GLOSSARY OF TERMS

Cove
A concave molding along the edge of a workpiece. *or* Another term for hollow.

Crest rail
The top rail forming part of the back rest of a chair.

Cross-banding
Strips of veneer cut across the grain and used as decorative borders.

Crosscutting
Sawing across the grain.

Cross grain
Grain that deviates from the main axis of a workpiece or tree.

Crotch figure
Another term for feather figure.

Crown-cut
A term used to describe veneer that has been tangentially sliced from a log, producing oval or curved grain patterns.

Cup
To bend as a result of shrinkage – specifically across the width of a piece of wood.

Cure
To set as a result of chemical reaction.

Curly figure
See curly grain.

Curly grain
Wood grain exhibiting an irregular wavy pattern.

Curtaining
An undulating ridge of sagging paintwork resembling the shape of a draped curtain.

D

Dado
A groove cut across the grain. *or* To cut such a groove.

Dimension lumber
Prepared wood cut to standard sizes.

Double insulated
A power tool with a non-conductive plastic casing that protects the user from electric shock is said to be double insulated.

Dressed lumber
Wood sold with one or more surfaces planed.

Dust panel
A horizontally mounted panel that protects the contents of a drawer from the dust created by the drawer above rubbing on its runners.

E

Earlywood
That part of a tree's annual growth rings that is laid down in the early part of the growing season.

Edge-grain
Another term for quarter-sawn.

End grain
The surface of wood exposed after cutting across the fibers.

Ergonomics
The study of the relationship between the average human body (especially that of a worker or machine operator) and its environment.

Escutcheon
The metal lining of a keyhole or a protective plate that surrounds it.

F

Face edge
The surface planed square to the face side and from which other dimensions and angles are measured.

Face quality
A term used to describe better-quality veneers that are used to cover the visible surfaces of a workpiece.

Face side
The flat planed surface from which all other dimensions and angles are measured.

Feather figure
The grain pattern on wood that has been cut from that part of a tree where a branch joins the main stem or trunk.

Feed
To push a workpiece in a controlled manner toward a moving blade or cutter.

Fence
An adjustable guide to keep the cutting edge of a tool a set distance from the edge of a workpiece.

Ferrule
A metal collar that reinforces the wood where the tang of a chisel or other hand tool enters the handle.

Fiberboards
A range of building boards made from reconstituted wood fibers.

Fielded panel
A solid-wood panel with edges beveled to fit grooves in a frame.

Figure
Another term for grain pattern.

Fillet
A narrow strip of wood.

Flat-grain
Another term for plainsawn.

Flat-sliced
A term used to describe a narrow sheet of veneer that has been cut from part of a log with a knife.

Flatsawn
Another term for plainsawn.

Flitches
Pieces of wood sawn from a log for slicing into veneers. *or* The bundle of sliced veneers.

Flute
A rounded concave groove.

Flux
A substance used to clean the surfaces of metal prior to soldering.

Fox wedging
A joint where wooden wedges are used to spread a tenon in a stopped mortise.

Front elevation
A scale drawing showing the front view of a workpiece.

Grain
The general direction or arrangement of the fibrous materials of wood.

Gravity guard
A blade or cutter guard that is raised by the passage of the work, then drops back under its own weight.

Green wood
Newly cut wood that has not been seasoned.

Groove
A long narrow channel cut in the direction of the grain. *or* To cut such channels.

Groundwork
The backing material to which veneer is glued.

Gullet
The space between sawteeth.

H

Halving joint
A lap joint where each member is relieved halfway through.

Hardwood
Wood cut from broad-leaved, mostly deciduous trees that belong to the botanical group *Angiospermae*.

Haunch
The shortened part of a tenon that prevents it from twisting out of line with the upright member at a corner of a frame.

Heartwood
The mature wood that forms the spine of a tree.

Hide glue
A protein-based wood glue made from animal skins and bone.

Hollow-ground
A term used to describe circular-saw blades that are reduced in thickness toward their centers. Also, a concave bevel on a knife, chisel or other edge tool.

Hollows
Concave shapes turned on a lathe.

Hone
To produce the final cutting edge on a blade or cutter by rubbing it on or with an abrasive stone.

Horn
Excess waste wood left on a workpiece to support the end of a mortise while the joint is being cut. The horn is sawn off after the joint is assembled.

Housing
A dado, either through, blind or half-blind that accepts a shelf, stair tread, dovetail, etc.

I

In-cannel
A term used to describe a gouge with a bevel ground on the inside of the blade.

Infeed
A term used to describe that part of a machine's worktable that is in front of the blade or cutter.

Inlay
To insert pieces of wood or metal into prepared recesses so that the material lies flush with the surrounding surfaces. *or* The piece of material itself.

Isometric drawing
A scale drawing with its main axes equally inclined, but giving an impression of perspective.

GLOSSARY OF TERMS

J

Jig
A device used to hold a workpiece or tool so that an operation can be repeated accurately.
Joiner
A woodworker who specializes in the construction of building components such as windows, doors and stairs.

K

Kerf
The slot cut by a saw.
Kickback
The action of a workpiece being thrown toward a machinist by a moving blade or cutter. *or* The action of a power tool when it jumps backward as a result of its blade or cutter jamming.
Kicker
A strip of wood fixed above a drawer's side to prevent it from tipping upward as the drawer is withdrawn.
Kiln-drying
Methods for seasoning wood that accelerate drying.
Knife checks
Splits along veneer caused by poorly adjusted veneer-slicing equipment.
Knock-down fittings
Mechanical devices for joining components, especially those that may have to be dismantled at a future date.
Knot sealer
A shellac-based sealer used to coat resinous knots that would stain subsequent finishes.
Knuckle
The cylindrical part of a hinge through which the pin passes.

L

Laminate
A component made from thin strips of wood glued together. *or* To glue strips together to form a component.
Laminboard
A man-made building board with a core of narrow strips of wood glued together and sandwiched between thin plywood sheets. *See also* blockboard.
Latewood
That part of a tree's annual growth ring that is laid down in the latter part of the growing season.
Laying off
The action of finishing an application of paint or varnish using upward brush strokes.
Lipping
A protective strip of solid wood applied to the edge of a man-made-board panel or table top.
Long grain
Grain that is aligned with the main axis of a workpiece. *See also* short grain.
Lopers
Draw runners that are pulled from a cabinet in order to support a fall flap.

M

Marquetry
The process of laying relatively small pieces of veneer to make decorative patterns or pictures. *See also* parquetry.
Miter
A joint formed between two pieces of wood by cutting bevels of equal angles (usually 45 degrees) at the ends of both pieces. *or* To cut the joint.
Mock-up
A temporary construction made from scrap materials in order to test a design.
Modesty board
A deep rail fixed between the two end frames of a desk. Its original purpose was to conceal the legs of a seated person.
Mortise
A rectangular recess cut in wood to receive a matching tongue or tenon.
Muntin
The central vertical member of a frame-and-panel door. *or* A grooved strip of wood that divides and supports the two sections of a wide drawer bottom.

O

Offcut
Scrap wood cut from a workpiece.
Open-coat
A term used to describe sandpaper that has widely spaced abrasive particles.
Open grain
A term used to describe ring-porous wood with large pores. Also known as coarse-textured.
Out-cannel
A term used to describe a gouge with a bevel ground on the outside of the blade.
Outfeed
A term used to describe that part of a machine's worktable that is behind the blade or cutter.
Oxidize
To form a layer of metal oxide as in rusting.

P

Pare
To remove fine shavings with a chisel.
Parquetry
A similar process to marquetry but using veneers cut into geometric shapes to make decorative patterns.
Particleboards
Building boards made from small chips or flakes of wood bonded together with glue under pressure.
Patina
The color and texture that a material such as wood or metal acquires as a result of a natural aging process.
Pawls
Pivoted pointed levers designed to grip a workpiece as soon as it is thrown back by a moving blade or cutter.
PEG
Polyethylene glycol – a stabilizing agent used in place of conventional seasoning processes to treat green wood.
Photosynthesis
A natural process that takes place when energy in the form of light is absorbed by chlorophyll, producing the nutrients on which plants live.
Pilaster
A shallow rectangular column of wood attached to the face of a cabinet.
Pilot hole
A small-diameter hole drilled prior to the insertion of a wood screw to act as a guide for its thread.
Plainsawn
A term used to describe a piece of wood with growth rings that meet the faces of the board at angles of less than 45 degrees. *See also* riftsawn.
Plan
A scale drawing showing the top view of a workpiece.
Plan elevation
Another term for plan.
Plywood
A building board made by bonding a number of wood veneers together under pressure.
Pocket screw
To bore a hole at an angle through the inside face of a rail in order to insert a top-fixing screw.
Pumice
A light volcanic rock that is ground to a fine abrasive powder and used to modify the texture of a wood finish.
Pummel
A square section left on a turned workpiece.
Push stick
A notched stick used to feed a workpiece into a blade or cutter.

Q

Quartersawn
A term used to describe a piece of wood with growth rings between 60 and 90 degrees to the faces of the board. *See also* riftsawn.

R

Rabbet
A stepped recess along the edge of a workpiece, usually as part of a joint. *or* To cut such recesses.
Rack
To distort a frame or carcase by applying sideways pressure.
Ratchet
A device that permits motion in one direction only.
Relief carving
A type of carving where the background is cut away, leaving a motif projecting from the surrounding area.
Riftsawn
A term used to describe a piece of wood with growth rings that meet the faces of the board at angles of more than 30 degrees but at less than 60 degrees.
Ripping
Sawing parallel to the grain.
Rotary-cut
A term used to describe a continuous sheet of veneer peeled from a log by turning it against a stationary knife.

GLOSSARY OF TERMS

Rottenstone
An abrasive powder similar to pumice but ground even finer.

Rubber
A cloth pad used to apply polish, stain or varnish.

Runners
Strips of wood that support a drawer and upon which it slides.

S

Sapwood
New wood surrounding the denser heartwood.

Scribe
To mark with a pointed tool. *or* To mark and shape the edge of a workpiece so that it will fit exactly against another surface such as a wall or ceiling.

Seasoning
Reducing the moisture content of wood.

Secret haunch
Another term for sloping haunch.

Section
A scale drawing that shows a view of a workpiece as if it had been cut through.

Set
To bend sawteeth to the right and left of the blade in order to cut a kerf wider than the blade itself.

Setting in
The fine shaping of carved work.

Shank
The cylindrical shaft of a screw or nail. *or* The shaft of a drill or cutter.

Shear force
The force applied to a structure by a transverse load.

Shellac
A secretion of the lac insect used to manufacture French polish.

Shoot
To plane accurately using a finely set plane.

Short grain
A term used to describe where the general direction of wood fibers lies across a narrow section of wood.

Shoulder
The squared end of a workpiece on one or both sides of a tenon or tongue.

Side elevation
A scale drawing showing the side view of a workpiece.

Skiver
Thin leather prepared for gluing to a desk or table top.

Slashsawn
Another term for plainsawn.

Sloping haunch
A tenon haunch cut at an angle so that it is invisible when the joint is assembled.

Softening
Pieces of scrap wood used to protect workpieces from metal vise or clamp jaws.

Softwood
Wood cut from coniferous trees that belong to the botanical group *Gymnospermae*.

Splitting out
When a cutter or drill roughly breaks through the bottom or back of a workpiece.

Springwood
Another term for earlywood.

Stile
A vertical side member of a frame-and-panel door.

Stop
A strip of wood against which a drawer front or door comes to rest when it is closed.

Stopped mortise
A mortise that does not pass right through a piece of wood.

Straight grain
Grain that aligns with the main axis of a workpiece or tree.

Striker plate
The metal plate against which a latch or lock comes to rest.

Stringing
Fine strips of wood used to divide areas of veneer.

Strop
To produce a razor-sharp cutting edge by rubbing it on a strip of leather. *or* The strip of leather itself.

Stub mortise
Another term for stopped mortise.

Stub tenon
A short tenon that does not pass right through a piece of wood.

Summerwood
Another term for latewood.

Sweep
A term used to describe the curved section of a carving gouge.

Swing
The maximum diameter of a workpiece that can be turned over a lathe bed.

T

Tack rag
A cloth impregnated with resin for picking up loose dust. Also known as a tacky rag.

Tang
The pointed end of a chisel or file that is driven into the handle.

Tangentially cut
Another term for plainsawn.

Template
A cut-out pattern to help shape a workpiece accurately.

Tenon
A projecting tongue on the end of a piece of wood that fits in a corresponding mortise.

Thermoplastic
A term used to describe a material that can be resoftened with heat.

Thermosetting
A term used to describe a material that cannot be resoftened with heat once it has set hard.

Thinner
A substance used to reduce the consistency of paint, varnish, shellac or lacquer.

Thixotropic
A property of some paints that have a jelly-like consistency until stirred or applied, at which point they become liquified.

Throat
The clearance between a blade of a machine such as a scroll saw and its frame. *or* The outlet for shavings above the mouth in a plane's sole.

Tongue
The projecting ridge cut along the edge of a board that fits into a corresponding groove in another board. *or* A plywood strip that fits in grooves cut in two boards to be joined.

Tusk tenon
A wedged through tenon used to join floor joists. An additional stub tenon (the tusk) below the through tenon provides extra support. A simplified version is used to allow disassembly of a trestle-table understructure.

V

Veneer
A thin slice of wood used as a surface covering on a less expensive material such as a man-made board.

Vertical grain
Another term for quartersawn.

Viscosity
The extent to which a fluid resists the tendency to flow.

W

Waney edge
The natural wavy edge of a plank. It may still be covered by tree bark.

Wavy grain
A term used to describe the even wave-like grain pattern on wood cut from a tree with an undulating cell structure.

Wild grain
Irregular grain that changes direction, making it difficult to work.

Winding
A warped or twisted board is said to be winding or in wind.

Y

Yacht varnish
An exterior-grade varnish especially suitable for coastal climates.

INDEX

ABC

INDEX

D

E

F

INDEX

INDEX

INDEX

S

T

INDEX